Do you wonder what teaching will be like in the future?

ClassZone

www.mcdougallittell.com

Unlock the world of new ideas through ClassZone

ClassZone, McDougal Littell's companion website, is your classroom's online guide to *¡En español!*

Access the *¡En español!* ClassZone site to find:

- Links correlated to the textbook for relevant Internet exploration
- Online flipcards for vocabulary practice
- Self-scoring quizzes for students to check understanding of concepts
- Internet research tutorial to help students conduct research on the web
- Teacher center for classroom ideas (accessible to teachers only)

Log on to ClassZone at www.mcdougallittell.com

With the purchase of *¡En español!*, you have immediate access to ClassZone.

Teacher Key: MCD2I7CYH6D7J

The teacher key provides access to teacher-specific content.

Student Key: MCDLWPH3AJM1H

The student key provides access for students to build and practice their Spanish as well as explore different Spanish-speaking cultures.

McDougal Littell

A HOUGHTON MIFFLIN COMPANY

www.mcdougallittell.com

1 uno

McDougal Littell

¡En español!

Teacher's Edition

AUTHORS

Estella Gahala

Patricia Hamilton Carlin

Audrey L. Heining-Boynton

Ricardo Otheguy

Barbara J. Rupert

CULTURE CONSULTANT

Jorge A. Capetillo-Ponce

McDougal Littell
A HOUGHTON MIFFLIN COMPANY
Evanston, Illinois • Boston • Dallas

Cover Photography

Center: Large image taken in Mexico City by Martha Granger/EDGE Productions.

Bottom, from left to right: Aztec ceramic, Mexico, Dick Keen/Visuals Unlimited; Windmills in La Mancha, Spain, Michael Busselle/Tony Stone Images, Inc. (also on back cover); Painted wooden sculpture, Guatemala, Private Collection, Tom Holton/Superstock; Calle San Sebastián, Old San Juan, Puerto Rico, Martha Granger/EDGE Productions.

Photography

About the Authors

Estella Gahala holds a Ph.D. in Educational Administration and Curriculum from Northwestern University. A career teacher of Spanish and French, she has worked with a wide range of students at the secondary level. She has also served as foreign language department chair and district director of curriculum and instruction.

Patricia Hamilton Carlin completed her M.A. in Spanish at the University of California, Davis and a Master of Secondary Education with specialization in foreign languages from the University of Arkansas. She currently teaches Spanish and methodology at the University of Central Arkansas.

Audrey L. Heining-Boynton received her Ph.D. in Curriculum and Instruction from Michigan State University. She is a Professor of Education and Romance Languages at The University of North Carolina at Chapel Hill, where she is a second language teacher educator and Professor of Spanish. She has also taught Spanish, French, and ESL at the K–12 level.

Ricardo Otheguy received his Ph.D. in Linguistics from the City University of New York, where he is currently Professor of Linguistics at the Graduate School and University Center. He has written extensively on topics related to Spanish grammar as well as on bilingual education, and the Spanish of the United States.

Barbara J. Rupert has taught Level 1 through A.P. Spanish during her many years of high school teaching. She is a graduate of Western Washington University, and serves as the World Languages Department Chair, District Trainer and Chair of her school's Site Council.

Jorge A. Capetillo-Ponce
Culture Consultant is presently a Ph.D. candidate in Sociology at the New School for Social Research, where he is also Special Consultant to the Dean of The Graduate Faculty. His graduate studies at the New School and El Colegio de México include international relations, socio-political analysis, cultural theory, and sociology.

For further information about the authors see page xxii.

Contributing Writers

Mary Ann Dellinger
University of Phoenix;
Pueblo High School
Tucson, AZ

Jane M. Govoni
Eckerd College; Shorecrest
Preparatory School
St. Petersburg, FL

Willard A. Heller, Jr.
Perry Junior-Senior High School
Perry, NY

Cynthia Prieto
Mount Vernon High School
Fairfax, VA

María Isabel Soto de Marquez
Acton, MA

Morgan Robison
Ohio State University
Columbus, OH

Ann Tollefson
Natrona County School
District
Casper, WY

Jill K. Welch
Ohio State University
Columbus, OH

Consulting Authors

Dan Battisti

Patty Murguía Bohannan

Dr. Teresa Carrera-Hanley

Bill Lionetti

Lorena Richins Layser

Reviewers

Sue Arandjelovic
Dobson High School
Mesa, AZ

Lavonne Berry
Oak Grove High School
North Little Rock, AR

Rebecca Carr
William G. Enloe High School
Raleigh, NC

Kathleen Gliewe
Helena Middle School
Helena, MT

Carol Rechel Espinoza
Boulder High School
Boulder, CO

Sharon Larracochea
South Junior High School
Boise, ID

Maureen Rehusch
Palatine High School
Hoffman Estates, IL

Elena Rivas
Dade County Public Schools
Miami, FL

CONTENTS

¡En español!

1 uno

You're invited...

WHERE: ¡En español!

A new kind of Spanish program

WHAT: A program that...

- Boosts student confidence and retention and motivates language learning.

- Balances teaching for communication and accuracy, offering a balance of proficiency and grammar.

- Adapts to the varied learning styles and ability levels of today's students.

- Integrates technology to immerse students in authentic language and culture.

¡En español!

Building Confidence for Communication

- ### Balances proficiency and grammar

  - Activity sequences lead students through controlled, transitional, and open-ended activities to assure development of communication skills.

  - Grammar is presented with multiple examples, graphics, and visuals to illustrate concepts clearly.

Boosts student confidence and retention

  - Strategies for developing listening, speaking, reading, and writing skills as well as for comparing cultures are included in each *etapa* of the pupil edition.

  - Special student study hints are included in each unit. These hints help students learn how to approach learning a language more effectively.

Adapts to varied learning styles and abilities

- Classroom Community notes in the Teacher's Edition provide guidance for managing pair and group work right at point–of–use.

- Teaching All Students notes in the Teacher's Edition offer extra help and more challenging activities, activities suited to the various intelligences as well as material for the native speaker.

Integrates technology to immerse students in authentic language and culture

- Fully–integrated video provides input for presenting vocabulary and grammar in their cultural context.

- CD-ROM provides levelled practice and review of core vocabulary and grammar in a motivating game format.

- Electronic Teacher Tools with Test Generator offers the flexibility of having all ancillaries on CD-ROM.

- ClassZone, a dynamic Internet connection, is available to all users of *¡En español!*

Program Resources

Extensive resources tailored to the needs of today's students!

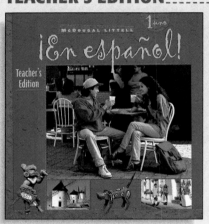

TEACHER'S RESOURCE PACKAGE

- **Unit Resource Books**

Includes resources for each unit:
   Más práctica (cuaderno) TE
   Para hispanohablantes
      (cuaderno) TE
   Information Gap Activities
   Video Activities
   Videoscript
   Audioscript

Assessment Program
   Cooperative Quizzes
   Etapa Exams, Forms A & B
   Para hispanohablantes
      Etapa Exams
   Unit Comprehensive Tests
   Para hispanohablantes
   Unit Comprehensive Tests
   Multiple Choice Test Questions
   Portfolio Assessment

- **Block Scheduling Copymasters**

- **Electronic Teacher Tools/Test Generator CD-ROM**

ADDITIONAL RESOURCES

• **Overhead Transparencies**

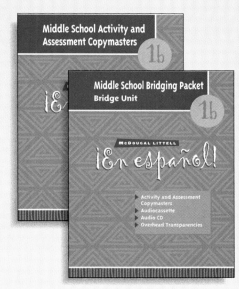

STUDENT WORKBOOKS

• *Más práctica (cuaderno)* **PE**

• *Para hispanohablantes (cuaderno)* **PE**

• **Middle School Bridging Packet**
Activity and Assessment Copymasters
Audiocassette/Audio CD
Overhead Transparencies

INTERNET RESOURCES

Visit the World Languages curriculum area
at **www.mcdougallittell.com** for a wide
range of resources.

TECHNOLOGY

Audio Program
• Completely integrated with
the text and ancillaries.
• Available on cassette and
audio CD.

Canciones
• Audiocassette or
audio CD

Video Program
• Completely integrated
video program provides
comprehensible input
and cultural information
• Available on videocassette
and videodisc

**Intrigas y aventuras
CD-ROM**
• For levels 1 and 2

Easy Articulation

¡En español! addresses the challenges of articulation between levels by providing a unique instructional overlap. All the grammar and vocabulary taught in Units 5 and 6 are covered again in the following level, so teachers can choose how far into the grammatical and functional sequence they wish to go. Students' study of Spanish can continue seamlessly!

GRAMMAR ACROSS LEVELS

LEVEL 2

Unit 1

Etapa 1
- Regular preterite verbs (p. 36)
- Preterite with *-car, -gar,* and *-zar* spelling changes (p. 38)
- Preterite of *ir, ser, hacer, dar, ver* (p. 40)

Etapa 2
- Irregular preterite verbs (p. 61)

Etapa 3
- Demonstrative adjectives and pronouns (p. 82)
- Stem-changing preterite verbs (p. 84)
- Preterite verbs with *i* to *y* spelling change (p. 85)

Unit 2

Etapa 1
- Reflexive pronouns and verbs (p. 110)

Etapa 2
- Progressive tenses (p. 130)
- Ordinal number agreement (p. 132)

Unit 3

Etapa 1
- Pronoun placement (p. 180)

Etapa 2
- Affirmative *tú* commands, regular and irregular (p. 202)
- Negative *tú* commands (p. 204)
- Adverbs ending in *-mente* (p. 206)

LEVEL 1

Unit 5

Etapa 1
- Reflexive verbs (p. 320)
- Irregular affirmative *tú* commands (p. 322)
- Negative *tú* commands (p. 324)
- Pronoun placement with commands (p. 325)

Etapa 2
- Pronoun placement with the present progressive tense (p. 342)
- *deber* (p. 345)
- Adverbs with *-mente* (p. 347)

Etapa 3
- Superlatives (p. 364)
- Regular *-ar* preterite verbs (p. 366)
- *-car, -gar, -zar* preterite verbs (p. 368)

Unit 6

Etapa 1
- Regular *-er, -ir* preterite verbs (p. 392)
- Preterite verbs with *i* to *y* spelling change (p. 394)
- Preterite forms of *ir, hacer, ser* (p. 395)

Etapa 2
- Adverbs of location (p. 414)
- Demonstrative adjectives and pronouns (p. 416)
- Ordinals (p. 418)
- Irregular preterite verbs (p. 419)

Etapa 3
- All review

	Unit 1	Unit 2	Unit 4	Unit 6
LEVEL 3	**Etapa 1** • Preterite/imperfect tenses contrasted (p. 41) • Present/past perfect tenses, regular/irregular, including past participles (p. 44) **Etapa 2** • *Por* vs. *para* (p. 61) • Future tense, regular and irregular (p. 63) • Impersonal *se* (p. 87)	**Etapa 1** • *Nosotros* commands (p. 112) • Conditional tense (p. 115)	**Etapa 1** • Present progressive, regular and irregular (p. 256)	**Etapa 1** • Reported speech (p. 405)

Unit 4	Unit 5	Unit 6
Etapa 2 • Prepositions/adverbs of location (p. 227) **Etapa 3** • Comparisons and superlatives (p. 296) • *deber* (saving and spending money)	**Etapa 1** • Future tense (p. 324) • Using *por* (p. 326) • *Nosotros* commands (p. 328) **Etapa 2** • Irregular future tense (p. 346) • Using *para* (p. 350) **Etapa 3** • *Por* vs. *para* (p. 368) • Conditional tense (p. 370)	**Etapa 1** • Impersonal *se* (p. 399) • Past participles as adjectives (p. 401) **Etapa 2** • Using the preterite and imperfect tenses (p. 418) • Present perfect tense (p. 420) • Irregular verbs in the present perfect tense (p. 423) **Etapa 3** • Reported speech (p. 444)

¡En español!

Level 1 · Scope & Sequence

		COMMUNICATION	GRAMMAR	CULTURE	RECYCLING	STRATEGIES
PRELIMINAR	**Etapa preliminar** p. 1 *¡Hola, bienvenidos!*	• Greet people • Introduce yourself • Say where you are from • Exchange phone numbers • Say which day it is	**Grammar is presented lexically here** • *Me llamo, te llamas* • *Soy, eres, es + de* NOTAS: *encantado / encantada; sí* and *no*	NOTAS CULTURALES • Greetings • Variations on good-bye • Articles before country names		
UNIDAD 1 Mi mundo • Estados Unidos	**Etapa 1** p. 24 **Miami** *¡Bienvenido a Miami!* UNIT OPENER CULTURE NOTES • *Fajitas* • Murals • The Alamo • *Cascarones* • *Sándwich cubano* • Jon Secada	• Greet others • Introduce others • Say where people are from • Express likes	• Familiar and formal greetings • Subject pronouns and *ser* • *Ser + de* • *Gustar* + infinitive: *me, te, le* NOTAS: *le presento a / te presento a; vivo en*	EN VOCES: *Los latinos de Estados Unidos* CONEXIONES: *Los estudios sociales:* compare communities NOTAS CULTURALES • Miami: international city • Architectural influences • Last names	Vocabulary from *Etapa preliminar*	LISTENING: Listen to intonation SPEAKING: Practice; Understand, then speak READING: Preview graphics
	Etapa 2 p. 46 **San Antonio** *Mis buenos amigos*	• Describe others • Give others' likes and dislikes • Describe clothing	• Definite articles • Indefinite articles • Noun–adjective agreement: gender • Noun–adjective agreement: number NOTAS: *¿Qué lleva?; llevo;* shortened forms of adjectives; *como + ser; tiene*	EN COLORES: *El conjunto tejano* (video) CONEXIONES: *La música:* music styles NOTAS CULTURALES • *charros*	**Activity 3:** *gustar* + infinitive **Activity 6:** professions	LISTENING: Listen to stress SPEAKING: Trust your first impulse; Think, plan, then speak CULTURE: Recognize regional music
	Etapa 3 p. 68 **Los Ángeles** *Te presento a mi familia*	• Describe family • Ask and tell ages • Talk about birthdays • Give dates • Express possession	• *Tener* • Possession using *de* • Possessive adjectives • Giving dates NOTAS: *¿De quién es…?, Es de…; ¿Quién es?, ¿Quiénes son?; hay*	EN VOCES: *Las celebraciones del año* EN COLORES: *La quinceañera* TÚ EN LA COMUNIDAD NOTAS CULTURALES • The oldest house in L.A. • Street names • Writing the date	**Activity 4:** physical descriptions **Activity 6:** personal characteristics **Activity 10:** clothing **Activity 13:** clothing **Activity 14:** *ser* **Activity 15:** clothing	LISTENING: Visualize; Get the main idea SPEAKING: Rehearse; Practice speaking smoothly READING: Look for cognates WRITING: Use different kinds of descriptive words CULTURE: Compare rites of passage

		COMMUNICATION	GRAMMAR	CULTURE	RECYCLING	STRATEGIES
UNIDAD 2 Una semana típica • Ciudad de México	**Etapa 1** p. 96 *Un día de clases* UNIT OPENER CULTURE NOTES • *Tortillas* • *Diego Rivera* • *El Palacio de Bellas Artes* • *El Ballet Folklórico* • *El metro* • *Lázaro Cárdenas*	• Describe classes and classroom objects • Say how often you do something • Discuss obligations	• Present tense of regular -*ar* verbs • Adverbs of frequency • *Tener que, hay que* NOTA: Use of articles with titles	EN VOCES: *Una encuesta escolar* CONEXIONES: Las matemáticas: take a survey NOTAS CULTURALES • *Universidad Autónoma de México* • The origin of *pluma*	Activity 3: *hay*, colors Activity 4: *hay*, numbers	LISTENING: Listen for feelings SPEAKING: Develop more than one way of expressing an idea; Expand the conversation READING: Use context clues
	Etapa 2 p. 118 *¡Un horario difícil!*	• Talk about schedules • Ask and tell time • Ask questions • Say where you are going • Request food	• *Ir* • Telling time • *Estar* + location • Interrogative words NOTAS: *¿Quieres comer...?* and *¿Quieres beber...?; al; on"* + days of the week	EN COLORES: *¿Quieres comer una merienda mexicana?* CONEXIONES: La salud: nutrition NOTAS CULTURALES • Mexican school schedules • *torta, bocadillo, pastel* • Olympic Stadium	Activity 3: -*ar* verbs, school terms Activity 7: days of the week	LISTENING: Listen for the main idea SPEAKING: Take risks; Help your partner CULTURE: Compare snack foods
	Etapa 3 p. 140 *Mis actividades*	• Discuss plans • Sequence events • Talk about places and people you know	• *Ir a* + infinitive • Present tense: regular -*er* and -*ir* verbs • Irregular *yo* forms: *hacer, conocer;* personal *a* • *Oír* NOTA: *tener sed, tener hambre*	EN VOCES: *México y sus jóvenes* EN COLORES: *El Zócalo: centro de México* (video) TÚ EN LA COMUNIDAD NOTAS CULTURALES • *Museo Nacional de Antropología* • Mexican mealtimes	Activity 3: *estar* + location, places Activity 6: snack Activity 7: telling time Activity 11: *gustar* + infinitive, *tener que* Activity 13: adverbs of frequency Activity 17: friends and family Activity 19: school terms	LISTENING: Listen and observe SPEAKING: Use all you know; Ask for clarification READING: Skim WRITING: Organize information chronologically and by category CULTURE: Compare places

		COMMUNICATION	GRAMMAR	CULTURE	RECYCLING	STRATEGIES
UNIDAD 3 El fin de semana • San Juan, Puerto Rico	**Etapa 1** p. 168 *¡Me gusta el tiempo libre!* UNIT OPENER CULTURE NOTES • *Gigi Fernández* • *Pasta de guayaba* • *El Morro* • *Luis Muñoz Marín* • *Taínos* • *El loro puertorriqueño*	• Extend invitations • Talk on the phone • Express feelings • Say where you are coming from • Say what just happened	• *Estar* + adjectives • *Acabar de* + infinitive • *Venir* • *Gustar* + infinitive: *nos, os, les* NOTAS: *cuando; del; conmigo, contigo*	EN VOCES: *Bomba y plena* CONEXIONES: La música: songs NOTAS CULTURALES • The name *Puerto Rico* • Ricky Martin	Activity 3: *gustar* + infinitive Activity 4: activities, sequencing Activity 9: activities Activity 13: *ir a* Activity 14: places Activity 17: activities Activity 19: interrogatives	LISTENING: Listen for a purpose SPEAKING: Personalize; Use your tone to convey meaning READING: Scan
	Etapa 2 p. 190 *¡Deportes para todos!*	• Talk about sports • Express preferences • Say what you know • Make comparisons	• *Jugar* • Stem-changing verbs: *e →ie* • *Saber* • Comparatives	EN COLORES: *Béisbol: el pasatiempo nacional* TÚ EN LA COMUNIDAD NOTAS CULTURALES • *La Fortaleza* • Puerto Rico and the U.S. • Roberto Clemente	Activity 12: activities Activity 16: descriptions Activity 19: interrogatives	LISTENING: Listen for "turn-taking" tactics SPEAKING: Monitor yourself; Give reasons for your preferences CULTURE: Reflect on sports traditions
	Etapa 3 p. 212 *El tiempo en El Yunque*	• Describe the weather • Discuss clothing and accessories • State an opinion • Describe how you feel • Say what is happening	• *Tener* expressions • Weather expressions • Direct object pronouns • Present progressive NOTAS: *llevar; creer*	EN VOCES: *El coquí* EN COLORES: *Una excursión por la isla* (video) CONEXIONES: Las ciencias: temperature NOTAS CULTURALES • *El Yunque*	Activity 3: colors, clothing Activity 8: stem-changing verbs: *e →ie* Activity 9: *ir a..., llevar* Activity 11: *tener*, activities Activity 14: sports Activity 19: activities	LISTENING: Sort and categorize details SPEAKING: Say how often; Get specific information READING: Distinguish details WRITING: Appeal to the senses CULTURE: Define travel and tourism

		COMMUNICATION	**GRAMMAR**	**CULTURE**	**RECYCLING**	**STRATEGIES**
UNIDAD 4 ¡De visita! • Oaxaca, México	**Etapa 1** p. 240 ¡A visitar a mi prima! **UNIT OPENER CULTURE NOTES** • Animalitos • Pesos • Mole negro • Rufino Tamayo • Benito Juárez • Monte Albán	• Identify places • Give addresses • Choose transportation • Request directions • Give instructions	• Decir • Prepositions of location • Regular affirmative tú commands **NOTAS:** por; salir; numbers in addresses	**EN VOCES:** ¡Visita Oaxaca! Un paseo a pie **CONEXIONES:** La educación física: Mexican folk dances **NOTAS CULTURALES** • Guelaguetza • The name Oaxaca	**Activity 3:** hay **Activity 5:** seasons **Activity 13:** activities **Activity 14:** direct object pronouns **Activity 15:** sequencing **Activity 16:** direct object pronouns	**LISTENING:** Listen and follow directions **SPEAKING:** Recognize and use set phrases; Use variety to give directions **READING:** Combine strategies
	Etapa 2 p. 262 En el mercado	• Talk about shopping • Make purchases • Talk about giving gifts • Bargain	• Stem-changing verbs: o→ue • Indirect object pronouns • Indirect object pronoun placement **NOTAS:** para; dar	**EN COLORES:** El Mercado Benito Juárez **CONEXIONES:** Las matemáticas: un mercado **NOTAS CULTURALES** • Monte Albán jewelry • Benito Juárez	**Activity 5:** numbers **Activity 7:** places **Activity 8:** time **Activity 9:** places, time **Activity 10:** transportation	**LISTENING:** Observe as you listen **SPEAKING:** Express emotion; Disagree politely **CULTURE:** Compare bargaining customs
	Etapa 3 p. 284 ¿Qué hacer en Oaxaca?	• Order food • Request the check • Talk about food • Express extremes • Say where you went	• Gustar + nouns • Affirmative and negative words • Stem-changing verbs: e→i **NOTAS:** fui/fuiste; ningunos(as); traer; superlatives; poner; desayunar	**EN VOCES:** Andrés, joven aprendiz de alfarero (video) **EN COLORES:** Monte Albán **TÚ EN LA COMUNIDAD NOTAS CULTURALES** • Oaxaca's cuisine • Artesanía • Zapotecas	**Activity 5:** prepositions of location **Activity 6:** stores **Activity 9:** clothing **Activity 19:** direct object pronouns	**LISTENING:** Integrate your skills **SPEAKING:** Vary ways to express preferences; Borrow useful expressions **READING:** Gather and sort information as you read **WRITING:** Tell who, what, where, when, why, and how **CULTURE:** Analyze and recommend
UNIDAD 5 Preparaciones especiales • Barcelona, España	**Etapa 1** p. 312 ¿Cómo es tu rutina? **UNIT OPENER CULTURE NOTES** • Las Ramblas • Joan Miró • Aceitunas • Miguel de Cervantes Saavedra • La Sagrada Familia	• Describe daily routine • Talk about grooming • Tell others to do something • Discuss daily chores	• Reflexive verbs • Irregular affirmative tú commands • Negative tú commands • Pronoun placement with commands	**EN VOCES:** Una exhibición especial de Picasso **CONEXIONES:** El arte: paintings **NOTAS CULTURALES** • Catalán • Rock con raíces • Pablo Picasso	**Activity 3:** time **Activity 16:** restaurant phrases	**LISTENING:** Listen for a mood or a feeling **SPEAKING:** Sequence events; Use gestures **READING:** Scan for crucial details
	Etapa 2 p. 334 ¿Qué debo hacer?	• Say what people are doing • Persuade others • Describe a house • Negotiate responsibilities	• Pronoun placement with present progressive • Deber • Adverbs with -mente **NOTAS:** si; reflexive pronouns	**EN COLORES:** Las tapas: una experiencia muy española **TÚ EN LA COMUNIDAD NOTAS CULTURALES** • Tortilla	**Activity 3:** poner **Activity 8:** reflexive verbs **Activity 13:** irregular affirmative tú commands **Activity 17:** restaurant phrases **Activity 19:** interrogatives	**LISTENING:** Note and compare **SPEAKING:** Negotiate; Detect misunderstandings **CULTURE:** Predict reactions about restaurants
	Etapa 3 p. 356 ¡Qué buena celebración!	• Plan a party • Describe past activities • Express extremes • Purchase food	• Superlatives • Regular -ar preterite verbs • -car, -gar, -zar preterite **NOTA:** ¿A cuánto está(n)…?	**EN VOCES:** Los favoritos de la cocina española **EN COLORES:** Barcelona, joya de arquitectura (video) **CONEXIONES:** La salud: favorite foods **NOTAS CULTURALES:** • Pesetas • Paella • Gothic Quarter	**Activity 7:** furniture **Activity 10:** chores	**LISTENING:** Listen and take notes **SPEAKING:** Say what is the best and worst; Maintain conversational flow **READING:** Reorganize information to check understanding **WRITING:** Engage the reader by addressing him or her personally **CULTURE:** Make a historical time line

		COMMUNICATION	GRAMMAR	CULTURE	RECYCLING	STRATEGIES
UNIDAD 6 La ciudad y el campo • Quito, Ecuador	**Etapa 1** p. 384 *La vida de la ciudad* **UNIT OPENER** **CULTURE NOTES** • *La casa de Sucre* • *Papas* • *La Mitad del Mundo* • *Atahualpa* • *Tapices* • *Rondador*	• Tell what happened • Make suggestions to a group • Describe city buildings • Talk about professions	• Regular -er, -ir preterites • Preterite verbs with $i \to y$ spelling change • Preterite of *ir, hacer, ser* **NOTAS:** *Vamos a* + infinitive *estar de acuerdo; ver*	**EN VOCES:** *Saludos desde Quito* **TÚ EN LA COMUNIDAD** **NOTAS CULTURALES** • *Quito* • *Sucre;* currency • *Colonia/colonial*	**Activity 7:** superlatives **Activity 10:** time	**LISTENING:** Distinguish what is said and not said **SPEAKING:** Exaggerate and react to exaggerations; Relate details **READING:** Recognize place names
	Etapa 2 p. 406 *A conocer el campo*	• Point out specific people and things • Tell where things are located • Talk about the past	• Location words • Demonstrative adjectives and pronouns • Ordinals • Irregular preterite **NOTA:** *darle(s) de comer*	**EN COLORES:** *Los otavaleños* (video) **CONEXIONES:** *Las ciencias:* regional animals **NOTAS CULTURALES** • *Quichua*	**Activity 5:** professions **Activity 7:** prepositions of location **Activity 10:** clothing, sports equipment **Activity 11:** school objects, comparisons **Activity 17:** placs	**LISTENING:** Listen for implied statements **SPEAKING:** Recall what you know; Use words that direct others' attention **CULTURE:** Research cultural groups
	Etapa 3 p. 428 *¡A ganar el concurso!*	• Talk about the present and future • Give instructions to someone • Discuss the past	• Review: present progressive, *ir a…* • Review: affirmative *tú* commands • Review: regular preterite • Review: irregular preterite	**EN VOCES:** *Un paseo por Ecuador* **EN COLORES:** *Cómo las Américas cambiaron la comida europea* **CONEXIONES:** *La salud:* typical food **NOTAS CULTURALES** • *Galápagos* • *Ecuador's diverse regions*	**Activity 3:** vocabualry **Activity 4:** activities **Activity 5:** interrogatives **Activity 6:** professions	**LISTENING:** Listen and take notes **SPEAKING:** Use storytelling techniques; Rely on the basics **READING:** Reflect on journal writing **WRITING:** Support a general statement with informative details **CULTURE:** Identify international foods

¡En español!
Level 2 — Scope & Sequence

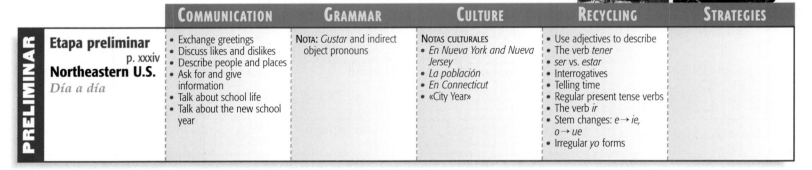

		COMMUNICATION	GRAMMAR	CULTURE	RECYCLING	STRATEGIES
PRELIMINAR	**Etapa preliminar** p. xxxiv **Northeastern U.S.** *Día a día*	• Exchange greetings • Discuss likes and dislikes • Describe people and places • Ask for and give information • Talk about school life • Talk about the new school year	**NOTA:** *Gustar* and indirect object pronouns	**NOTAS CULTURALES** • *En Nueva York and Nueva Jersey* • *La población* • *En Connecticut* • «City Year»	• Use adjectives to describe • The verb *tener* • *ser* vs. *estar* • Interrogatives • Telling time • Regular present tense verbs • The verb *ir* • Stem changes: *e → ie, o → ue* • Irregular *yo* forms	

UNIDAD 1 ¿Qué pasa? • Estados Unidos

	COMMUNICATION	GRAMMAR	CULTURE	RECYCLING	STRATEGIES
Etapa 1 p. 62 **Los Ángeles** *Pasatiempos* UNIT OPENER CULTURE NOTES • *La misión San Fernando rey de España* • *hispaños en Hollywood* • *tostones* • *artistas y la comunidad* • *televisión* • Gloria Estefan • Jorge Ramos & María Elena Salinas	• Talk about where you went and what you did • Discuss leisure time • Comment on airplane travel	**NOTA:** expressions of frequency	**EN VOCES:** *¿Cuánto sabes?* **TÚ EN LA COMUNIDAD** **NOTAS CULTURALES** • *La calle Olvera* • *Los murales*	• Regular preterite • Preterite with *-car, -gar,* and *-zar* spelling changes • Irregular preterite: *ir, ser, hacer, dar, ver* **Ya sabes:** Preterite with *-car, -gar,* and *-zar*	**LISTENING:** Identify key words **SPEAKING:** Encourage others; get more information **READING:** Read, don't translate; use visuals; scan for cognates
Etapa 2 p. 84 **Chicago** *¿Qué prefieres?*	• Comment on food • Talk about the past • Express activity preferences • Discuss fine art	• Irregular preterite verbs	**EN COLORES:** *El arte latino de Chicago:* murals (video) **CONEXIONES:** *El arte:* artists' inspirations **NOTAS CULTURALES** • *Museo de Bellas Artes de Chicago* • *La cena*	• Stem-changing verbs: *e → i, u → ue* **Activity 3:** *¡A viajar!* (travel) **Activity 14:** *¿Cuántas veces?* (expressions of frequency)	**LISTENING:** Identify the main idea **SPEAKING:** Use all you know; give reasons why **CULTURE:** Learn about other cultures; describe the nature of murals
Etapa 3 p. 106 **Miami** *¿Viste las noticias?*	• Discuss ways to communicate • React to news • Ask for and give information • Talk about things and people you know	• Demonstrative adjectives and pronouns • Stem-changing preterite **NOTAS:** *estar bien informado;* adjectives of nationality; *saber* vs. *conocer; hubo; i → y* with preterite	**EN VOCES:** *¿Leíste el periódico hoy?* **EN COLORES:** *Miami: Puerta de las Américas* **CONEXIONES:** *Las matemáticas:* calculate percentages of television viewing **NOTAS CULTURALES** • *A la fiesta* • *Periódicos por computadora*	**Activity 3:** *¡Qué reunión!* (irregular preterite) **Ya sabes:** stem-changing verbs	**LISTENING:** Listen with a purpose **SPEAKING:** Present findings; provide additional information **READING:** Skim for the general idea; scan for specific information **WRITING:** Bring your event to life **CULTURE:** Identify characteristics of neighborhoods

		COMMUNICATION	GRAMMAR	CULTURE	RECYCLING	STRATEGIES
UNIDAD 2 Ayer y hoy • Ciudad de México	**Etapa 1** p. 134 *De pequeño* UNIT OPENER CULTURE NOTES • *Los tamales* • *La piñata* • *Hoy no circula* • *El Popocatépetl* • Christian Castro • Frida Kahlo • *Padre Miguel Hidalgo y Costilla*	• Describe childhood experiences • Express personal reactions • Discuss family relationships	• Possessive adjectives and pronouns • Imperfect tense NOTAS: *dentro y fuera;* uses of *tener (tener hambre, tener sed,* etc.); *habia*	EN VOCES: *El monte de nuestro alimento:* legend CONEXIONES: *Los estudios sociales:* Aztec calendar NOTAS CULTURALES • *Las marionetes* • *El Bosque de Chapultepec*	• Reflexive pronouns and verbs **Activity 3:** *¡Los conozco!* (nationalities)	LISTENING: Listen for related details SPEAKING: Tell when you were always or never (im)perfect; add variety to your conversation READING: Analyze folkloric traditions
	Etapa 2 p. 156 *Había una vez...*	• Narrate in the past • Discuss family celebrations • Talk about activities in progress	• Progressive tenses • Preterite vs. imperfect	EN COLORES: *¡Temblor!:* the earthquake of 1985 CONEXIONES: *El arte: El muralista Diego Rivera* NOTAS CULTURALES • *La piñata* • *El Museo Nacional de Antropología*	**Activity 4:** *Una reunión escolar* (imperfect) **Activity 5:** *Reacciones* (reflexives)	LISTENING: Listen for a series of events SPEAKING: Brainstorm to get ideas; interact by expressing approval, disapproval, or astonishment CULTURE: Observe and generalize
	Etapa 3 p. 178 *Hoy en la ciudad*	• Order in a restaurant • Ask for and pay a restaurant bill • Talk about things to do in the city	• Double object pronouns NOTAS: i.o. pronoun with verbs like *gustar; dar una vuelta*	EN VOCES: *Teotihuacán: Ciudad misteriosa* (video) EN COLORES: *¡Buen provecho! La comida Mexicana* TÚ EN LA COMUNIDAD NOTAS CULTURALES • *El baile folklórico* • *El Palacio de Bellas Artes* • *Las telenovelas*	• Direct object pronouns • Indirect object pronouns **Activity 3:** *¡A divertirse en la ciudad!* (preterite vs. imperfect)	LISTENING: Listen for useful expressions SPEAKING: Personalize responses; resolve misconceptions READING: Identify gaps in knowledge WRITING: Develop your story CULTURE: Compare meals and mealtimes
UNIDAD 3 Sol y sombra • Puerto Rico	**Etapa 1** p. 206 *¿Estás en forma?* UNIT OPENER CULTURE NOTES • *El observatorio de Arecibo* • *Los pasteles* • *Piratas* • *La ceiba de Ponce* • *El Yunque* • Marc Anthony	• Discuss ways to stay fit and healthy • Make suggestions • Talk about daily routine and personal care	• Commands using *usted/ustedes* • Formal *usted/ustedes* commands and pronoun placement	EN VOCES: *Puerto Rico: Lugar maravilloso* CONEXIONES: *La ciencia* NOTAS CULTURALES • *El béisbol* • *El Viejo San Juan*	• Pronoun placement **Activity 4:** *¿Siempre o nunca?* (expressions of frequency, double object pronouns) **Ya sabes:** *las preparaciones*	LISTENING: Listen and sort details SPEAKING: Use gestures to convey meaning; react to daily routines READING: Observe organization of ideas
	Etapa 2 p. 228 *Preparaciones*	• Discuss beach activities • Tell someone what to do • Talk about chores • Say if something has already been done	• Negative *tú* commands NOTA: *acabar de* + infinitive	EN COLORES: *El Yunque Bosque Nacional* (video) TÚ EN LA COMUNIDAD NOTAS CULTURALES • *Después de las clases* • *El manatí*	• Affirmative *tú* commands • Adverbs ending in *-mente* **Activity 3:** *Por la mañana* (daily routine) **Ya sabes:** *los quehaceres*	LISTENING: Listen and categorize information SPEAKING: Improvise; encourage or discourage certain behaviors CULTURE: Recognize unique natural wonders
	Etapa 3 p. 250 *¿Cómo te sientes?*	• Describe time periods • Talk about health and illness • Give advice	• *Hacer* with expressions of time • Subjunctive with impersonal expressions NOTA: *doler* with i.o. pronouns; subjunctive after impersonal expressions	EN VOCES: *El estatus político de Puerto Rico* EN COLORES: *Una voz de la tierra* CONEXIONES: *La historia* NOTAS CULTURALES • *Los huracanes* • *La celebración de carnaval*	**Activity 3:** *Los quehaceres en tu casa* (chores)	LISTENING: listen sympathetically SPEAKING: Give feedback; use language for problem-solving READING: Activate associated knowledge WRITING: Compare and contrast to make strong descriptions CULTURE: Discover many cultures inside one country

		COMMUNICATION	GRAMMAR	CULTURE	RECYCLING	STRATEGIES
UNIDAD 4 Un viaje • Madrid, España	**Etapa 1** p. 278 *En la pensión* UNIT OPENER CULTURE NOTES • *El Prado* • *La guitarra* • *paella* • *El rey y la reina de España* • Antonio Banderas • El Greco	• Talk about travel plans • Persuade others • Describe rooms, furniture, and appliances	• Subjunctive to express hopes and wishes • Irregular subjunctive forms	EN VOCES: *Felices sueños:* hotel descriptions CONEXIONES: *El arte:* Spanish artists NOTAS CULTURALES • *La Plaza de la Cibeles* • *Alojamiento*	**Activity 4:** *Es mejor que…* (subjunctive) **Activity 15:** *El metro de Madrid* (giving directions) **Ya sabes:** expressing hopes and wishes	LISTENING: Listen and check details SPEAKING: Persuade; make and express decisions READING: Compare related details
	Etapa 2 p. 300 *Conoce la ciudad*	• Describe your city or town • Make suggestions • Ask for and give directions	• Subjunctive stem-changes: -ar, -er verbs • Stem-changing -ir verbs in the subjunctive • Subjunctive vs. infinitive NOTAS: *ni;* question words such as *cuando* and *donde* as bridges mid-sentence	EN COLORES: *Vamos a bailar:* Gipsy Kings CONEXIONES: *La tecnología:* creating a webpage NOTAS CULTURALES • *La Plaza Mayor* • *El paseo* • *Los gitanos y flamenco*	**Activity 3:** *Una lección* (giving advice using the subjunctive)	LISTENING: Listen and distinguish SPEAKING: Ask for and give directions; work cooperatively CULTURE: Identify characteristics of successful musical groups
	Etapa 3 p. 322 *Vamos de compras*	• Talk about shopping for clothes • Ask for and give opinions • Make comparisons • Discuss ways to save and spend money	• Subjunctive with expressions of doubt • Subjunctive with expressions of emotion	EN VOCES: *Nos vemos en Madrid:* highlights of the city (video) EN COLORES: *¿En qué te puedo atender?:* shopping TÚ EN LA COMUNIDAD NOTAS CULTURALES • *Miguel de Cervantes* • *¿Qué talla usas?*	• Comparisons and superlatives **Activity 4:** *¿Qué me sugieres?* (making suggestions using the subjunctive) **Ya sabes:** equal/unequal comparisons, expressions of doubt, expressions of emotion	LISTENING: Listen and infer SPEAKING: Interpret the feelings or values of others; observe courtesies and exchange information READING: Categorize details WRITING: Persuade your reader CULTURE: Draw conclusions about shopping as a cultural activity
UNIDAD 5 La naturaleza • Costa Rica	**Etapa 1** p. 350 *En el bosque tropical* UNIT OPENER CULTURE NOTES • Francisco Zúñiga • *Gallo pinto* • *El fútbol* • *La cerámica de nicoya* • *El Parque Nacional Mercedes* • *¿Quién va a ganar?* • José Figueres	• Describe geographical characteristics • Make future plans • Talk about nature and the environment	• Future tense • *Por* • *Nosotros* commands	EN VOCES: *El Parque Nacional de Volcán Poás* CONEXIONES: *La geografía:* tropical forest locations NOTAS CULTURALES • *El 8 de septiembre de 1502* • *Los saludos*	**Activity 3:** *Predicciones* (making predictions)	LISTENING: Organize and summarize environmental information SPEAKING: Share personal plans and feelings; anticipate future plans READING: Confirm or deny hearsay with reliable information
	Etapa 2 p. 372 *Nuestro medio ambiente*	• Discuss outdoor activities • Describe the weather • Make predictions • Talk about ecology	• Irregular future • Weather expressions with *hacer*	EN COLORES: *Costa Rica, ¡la pura vida!* (video) TÚ EN LA COMUNIDAD NOTAS CULTURALES: • *Los parques nacionales* • *Viajar por agua*	**Activity 5:** *¿Qué vas a hacer este verano?* (future tense)	LISTENING: Observe relationships between actions and motives SPEAKING: Define ordinary things; make recommendations READING: to come (TE) CULTURE: Predict appeal to ecotourists
	Etapa 3 p. 394 *¿Cómo será el futuro?*	• Comment on conservation and the environment • Talk about how you would solve problems	• *Por* or *para* • Conditional tense NOTA: *Si estuviera… o Si pudieres…*	EN VOCES: *La cascada de la novia:* legends EN COLORES: *Cumbre ecológica centroamericana: Se reúnen jóvenes en San José* CONEXIONES: *Los estudios sociales:* advertising about the environment NOTAS CULTURALES: • *Los campamentos* • *Las leyendas*	**Activity 5:** *¿Cómo será?* (future tense) **Activity 6:** *¿Por o para?* (por vs. para)	LISTENING: Propose solutions SPEAKING: Identify problems and your commitment to solving them; hypothesize about the future READING: Recognize characteristics of legends WRITING: Present a thorough and balanced review CULTURE: Prioritize

UNIDAD 6 El mundo del trabajo • Quito, Ecuador

		COMMUNICATION	GRAMMAR	CULTURE	RECYCLING	STRATEGIES
Etapa 1	p. 422	• Discuss jobs and professions • Describe people, places, and things • Complete an application	• Impersonal *se* • Past participles used as adjectives	EN VOCES: *Bienvenidos a la isla Santa Cruz:* Galapagos Islands (video) CONEXIONES: *La geografía* NOTAS CULTURALES • *Quito* • *La ocarina*	• Present and present progressive **Activity 5:** *Una cápsula de tiempo* (conditional)	LISTENING: Evaluate a plan SPEAKING: Participate in an interview; check comprehension READING: Use context to find meaning
Se busca: Un trabajo UNIT OPENER CULTURE NOTES • *llapingachos* • *Las Islas Galápagos* • *Andar en bicicleta de montaña* • *Música Andina* • *La toquilla* • Antonio José de Sucre						
Etapa 2	p. 444	• Prepare for an interview • Interview for a job • Evaluate situations and people	• Present perfect • Irregular present perfect	EN COLORES: *Ciberespacio en Quito* CONEXIONES: *La música* NOTAS CULTURALES • *Los grupos indígenas* • *Las empresas del mundo hispano*	• Preterite and imperfect **Activity 3:** *¿Qué está dibujado?* (past participle)	LISTENING: Evaluate behavior SPEAKING: Give advice; refine interview skills CULTURE: Assess use of e-mail
La entrevista						
Etapa 3	p. 466	• Talk on the telephone • Report on past, present, and future events • Describe duties, people, and surroundings	• Reported speech	EN VOCES: Jorge Carrera Andrade- *Pasajero del planeta* EN COLORES: *Música de las montañas:* Andean music TÚ EN LA COMUNIDAD NOTAS CULTURALES • *Guayaquil* • *Los festivales*	• Future tense • Conditional tense **Activity 3:** *¿Nunca?* (frequency, present perfect) **Activity 4:** *¿Quién lo ha hecho?* (present perfect) **Activity 15:** *Una cantita de agradecimiento* (recycles everything learned in the year)	LISTENING: Report what others said SPEAKING: Persuade or convince others; report on events READING: Observe characteristics of poems WRITING: State your message using a positive tone CULTURE: Reflect on origins and changes in music
¡A trabajar!						

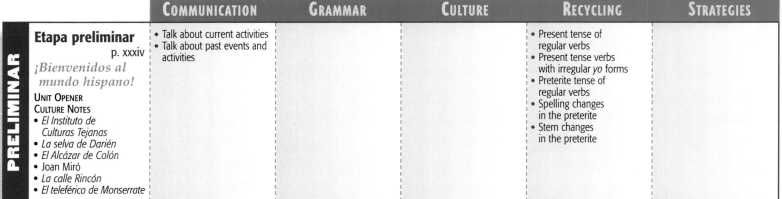

¡En español!

Level 3 — Scope & Sequence

	COMMUNICATION	GRAMMAR	CULTURE	RECYCLING	STRATEGIES
PRELIMINAR **Etapa preliminar** p. xxxiv *¡Bienvenidos al mundo hispano!* UNIT OPENER CULTURE NOTES • *El Instituto de Culturas Tejanas* • *La selva de Darién* • *El Alcázar de Colón* • Joan Miró • *La calle Rincón* • *El teleférico de Monserrate*	• Talk about current activities • Talk about past events and activities			• *Present tense of regular verbs* • *Present tense verbs with irregular yo forms* • *Preterite tense of regular verbs* • *Spelling changes in the preterite* • *Stem changes in the preterite*	
UNIDAD 1 Así somos • Estados Unidos **Etapa 1** p. 30 *¿Cómo soy?* UNIT OPENER CULTURE NOTES • Oscar de la Hoya • la comida mexicana • *Repertorio Español* • Ellen Ochoa • *La Prensa*	• Describe people • Talk about experiences • List accomplishments	• Present and past perfect	EN VOCES: Cristina García-*Soñar en cubano* CONEXIONES: *El arte: un autorretrato* NOTAS CULTURALES • Concept of *barrio* • Nicknames • Spanish-speaking immigrants and identity	• *Ser/estar* • Imperfect tense • Preterite vs. imperfect Ya sabes: *Características*	LISTENING: Give a clear physical description SPEAKING: Add details to descriptions; describe personal characteristics and actions READING: Observe how verb tenses reveal time
Etapa 2 p. 52 *¿Cómo me veo?*	• Describe fashions • Talk about pastimes • Talk about the future • Predict actions	• Future tense • Future of probability	EN COLORES: *Un gran diseñador:* Oscar de la Renta CONEXIONES: *Las matemáticas:* create an annual budget NOTAS CULTURALES • Araceli Segarra, climber of Mt. Everest • Pet sounds and names	• Indirect object pronouns and the verb *gustar* • *Por* and *para* **Activity 4:** *De compras* (clothing) **Activity 15:** *¿Dónde estarán?* (wondering about location) Ya sabes: *¿De qué es?*	LISTENING: Distinguish admiring and critical remarks SPEAKING: Use familiar vocab in a new setting; brainstorm to get lots of ideas CULTURE: Examine the cultural role of fashion
Etapa 3 p. 74 *¡Hay tanto que hacer!*	• Talk about household chores • Say what friends do • Express feelings	• Reflexives used reciprocally NOTA: *saber/conocer*	EN VOCES: Sandra Cisneros-*La casa en Mango Street* EN COLORES: *El legendario rey del mambo:* Tito Puente TÚ EN LA COMUNIDAD NOTAS CULTURALES • *Compadrazgo/padrinos* • Greater Eastside, LA	• Reflexive verbs • Impersonal constructions with *se* **Activity 2:** *¡Hazlo!* (say what you have to do) **Activity 5:** *Un día desastroso* (reflexive verbs) **Activity 9:** *Mi padrino* (imperfect)	LISTENING: Make an argument for and against hiring others to maintain a home SPEAKING: Identify feelings in a friendship READING: Chart contrasts between dreams and reality WRITING: to come CULTURE: Interview, report, and value musical influences

		COMMUNICATION	GRAMMAR	CULTURE	RECYCLING	STRATEGIES
UNIDAD 2 ¡El mundo es nuestro! • México y América Central	**Etapa 1** p. 102 *Pensemos en los demás* UNIT OPENER CULTURE NOTES: • María Izquierdo • *Tejidos Guatemaltecos* • *Ruinas de Copán* • *cebich mixta*	• Say what you want to do • Make requests • Make suggestions	NOTA: pronoun placement with commands	EN VOCES: Elizabeth Burgos-*Me llamo Rigoberta Menchú* TÚ EN LA COMUNIDAD NOTAS CULTURALES • Youth groups in Mexico and C.A. • Young people addressing adults • *Castellano*	• Command forms • *Nosotros* commands • Speculating with the conditional **Activity 2**: *¿Qué vas a hacer?* (say what you are going to do) • **Activity 5**: *La clase de ejercicio (tú, usted o ustedes)* • **Activity 12**: *Costa Rica* (conditional)	LISTENING: Anticipate, compare and contrast SPEAKING: Name social problems then propose solutions; identify the general ideas, then delegate responsibilities READING: Comprehend complex sentences
	Etapa 2 p. 124 *Un planeta en peligro*	• Say what should be done • React to the ecology • React to others' actions	• Present perfect subjunctive NOTA: *-uir* verbs add a *y* in subjunctive form	EN COLORES: *Unidos podemos hacerlo:* literacy in Nicaragua CONEXIONES: *Las ciencias–* recycling NOTAS CULTURALES • Currencies in C.A. and Mexico • *Grupo de los Cien/* international conservation	• Present subjunctives **Activity 2**: *El horario de Ángela* (describe schedules) **Activity 5**: *La ecóloga* (subjunctive) Ya sabes: *Es bueno que…* etc.	LISTENING: Inventory local efforts to save the environment SPEAKING: Consider the effect of words; tone of voice; express support (or lack of). CULTURE: Gather and analyze info about literacy
	Etapa 3 p. 142 *La riqueza natural*	• React to nature • Express doubt • Relate events in time	• Subjunctive with *cuando* and other conjunctions of time NOTA: *-cer* verbs add a *z* in the subjunctive	EN VOCES: Juan José Arreola-*Baby H.P.* EN COLORES: *Un país de encanto:* Costa Rican rainforests CONEXIONES: *Las ciencias–* the products of a rainforest NOTAS CULTURALES • *Isla de Ometepe/Lago Nicaragua* • C.A. and natural reserves	• Subjunctive with expressions of emotion • Subjunctive to express doubt and uncertainty **Activity 3**: *¿Has visto…?* (animals) • **Activity 7**: *El mundo de hoy* (expressing emotion) • **Activity 9**: *No te creo* (expressing doubt) • **Activity 12**: (as soon as) • **Activity 13**: *Los quehaceres* (conjunctions of time) Ya sabes: Expressions of emotion and doubt	LISTENING: Determine your purpose for listening SPEAKING: Gain thinking time before speaking; reassure others READING: Recognize uses of satire, parody, and irony WRITING: to come CULTURE: Analyze advantages and disadvantages of ecotourism
UNIDAD 3 Celebraciones de mi mundo • Caribe	**Etapa 1** p. 174 *¡Al fin la graduación!* UNIT OPENER CULTURE NOTES: • *Los Muñequitos de Matanzas* • *Bakeré* • *frutas tropicales* • *Rosario Ferré* • Juan Luis Guerra • *Parque ceremonial Taíno, Utuado*	• Describe personal celebrations • Say what people want • Link events and ideas	• Subjunctive with conjunctions • Imperfect subjunctive NOTA: *-ger* verbs change *g* to *j* in subjunctive	EN VOCES: Nicolas Guillén-*Ébano Real* TÚ EN LA COMUNIDAD NOTAS CULTURALES • Graduation ceremony in R.D. • *Baile de graduación*	• Subjunctive for expressing wishes **Activity 5**: *Pedro* (subj with impersonal expressions) **Activity 13**: *Los chismes* (expressions of doubt) **Activity 14**: *Permiso* (recreationa) Ya sabes: *otros verbos, conjunciones, el futuro*	LISTENING: Recognize major transitions SPEAKING: Use storytelling techniques; give advice and best wishes READING: Interpret metaphors
	Etapa 2 p. 192 *¡Próspero Año Nuevo!*	• Talk about holidays • Hypothesize • Express doubt and disagree • Describe ideals	• Subjunctive with nonexistent and indefinite • Conditional sentences NOTA: *sembrar, recoger, educar* spelling changes in subjunctive	EN COLORES: *Una tradición de Puerto Rico:* masks CONEXIONES: *El arte: del Caribe* NOTAS CULTURALES • *salsa* • *Chayanne*	• Subjunctive for disagreement & denial **Activity 5**: *En la comunidad* (nonexistent and indefinite) **Activity 14**: *Las profesiones* (subj/profession) Ya sabes: *dar las gracias, dudar que…* etc.	LISTENING: Observe interview techniques SPEAKING: Socialize as host or guest; encourage participation READING: to come (TE) CULTURE: Recognize and describe uses of disguise
	Etapa 3 p. 218 *Celebraciones de patria*	• Describe patriotic events • Make suggestions and wishes • Express emotion and doubt • State cause and effect	• Subjunctive vs. indicative NOTA: *-zer* verbs change *z* to *c* in subjunctive	EN VOCES: José Martí-*de Versos sencillos: I.* EN COLORES: *Una historia única:* celebrations in the R.D. CONEXIONES: *Los estudios sociales–* independence days NOTAS CULTURALES • *El naufragio de la Santa Maria* • *El himno nacional de la R.D.* • *Guantanamera*	• Summary of the subjunctive (parts 1 & 2) **Activity 4**: *Los costumbres* (holidays) **Activity 7**: *¡Santo Domingo!* (subjunctive) **Activity 9**: *La comunidad* (subjunctive) Ya sabes: *dudar/creer* etc.	LISTENING: Listen and take notes SPEAKING: Describe celebrations; express yourself READING: Observe what makes poetry WRITING: to come CULTURE: Analyze national celebrations

		COMMUNICATION	GRAMMAR	CULTURE	RECYCLING	STRATEGIES
UNIDAD 4 Un Futuro brillante • Cono Sur	**Etapa 1** p. 246 *El próximo paso* **UNIT OPENER CULTURE NOTES** • Antonio Berni • *Universidad de Chile* • *El arpa Andina* • *mate* • *La bolsa* • Rafael Guarga	• Describe your studies • Ask questions • Say what you are doing • Say what you were doing	• Progressive with *ir, andar,* and *seguir* • Past progressive	**EN VOCES:** Borges- *"El ciego" y "Últimos instantes"* **TÚ EN LA COMUNIDAD NOTAS CULTURALES** • Hand gestures • First name usage • Professional titles • Borges' blindness	• Interrogatives • Present progressive **Activity 8:** *Las llamadas* (present progressive, reflexives) **Activity 9:** *La limpieza* (present progressive, household chores) **Ya sabes:** question words	**LISTENING:** Listen and summarize **SPEAKING:** Establish closer relationships; extend a conversation **READING:** Analyze the role of identity and fantasy
	Etapa 2 p. 268 *¿Cuál será tu profesión?*	• Talk about careers • Confirm and deny • Express emotions • Hypothesize	• Past perfect subjunctive • Conditional perfect	**EN COLORES:** *Los jóvenes y el futuro:* career choices **CONEXIONES:** *Los estudios sociales:* what professions interest you **NOTAS CULTURALES** • Getting into a university • Popular professions in Spanish-speaking world	• Affirmative and negative expressions **Activity 6:** *Necesitas saber* (affirmative/negative) **Activity 8:** *La celebración* (past perfect subj) **Ya sabes:** negatives/ affirmatives	**LISTENING:** Identify key information for careers **SPEAKING:** Anticipate what others want to know; conduct an interview **CULTURE:** Formulate plans for the future
	Etapa 3 p. 290 *Un mundo de posibilidades*	• Discuss economic information • Avoid redundancy • Express possession • Express past probability	• Future perfect	**EN VOCES:** Isabel Allende- *Paula* **EN COLORES:** *Se hablan... ¡muchos idiomas!:* Spanish language origins **CONEXIONES:** *Los estudios sociales:* ONU / OEA **NOTAS CULTURALES** • Job-hunting process in South America	• Subject and stressed object pronouns • Possessive pronouns **Activity 3:** *Internet* (numbers) **Activity 5:** *¿Quién?* (subject/ stressed object pronouns) **Activity 9:** *¿De Argentina o Chile?* (possessive pronouns) **Ya sabes:** *comparaciones numéricas,* possessive pronouns, subject/object pronouns	**LISTENING:** Locate worldwide production of goods **SPEAKING:** Guess cognates; speculate about the past **READING:** Speculate about the author **WRITING:** to come **CULTURE:** Observe how language reflects culture
UNIDAD 5 Artes en España y las Américas • España	**Etapa 1** p. 318 *Tradiciones españolas* **UNIT OPENER CULTURE NOTES** • Fernando Botero • *chocolate y churros* • *Los cantos gregorianos* • Salvador Dalí • *La reina Isabel* • *Teatro Colón*	• Identify and specify • Request clarification • Express relationships • Discuss art forms	• *¿cuál? vs. ¿qué?* • Relative pronouns	**EN VOCES:** Unamuno and Matute **CONEXIONES:** *Los estudios sociales:* create a timeline of the Spanish Civil War **NOTAS CULTURALES** • *El Museo del Prado*	• Demonstrative adjectives and pronouns **Activity 7:** *Las respuestas* (*¿qué? vs. ¿cuál?*) **Activity 14:** *Los artistas* (relative pronouns, literature) **Ya sabes:** *La pintura, La literatura*	**LISTENING:** Use advanced knowledge of the topic **SPEAKING:** Discuss a painting; organize ideas for research **READING:** Compare famous authors
	Etapa 2 p. 340 *El Nuevo Mundo*	• Refer to people and objects • Express relationships • Make generalizations • Describe arts and crafts	• Relative pronouns • *Lo que*	**EN COLORES:** *Un arquitecto y sus obras:* Mexican architect **CONEXIONES:** *Las matemáticas:* Mayan numerals **NOTAS CULTURALES** • Regional dances • *El inca Garcilaso de la Vega*	• Direct object pronouns • Indirect object pronouns **Activity 4:** *¿Lo conoces?* (direct object pronouns) **Activity 7:** *Después de la entrevista* (indirect object pronouns, work) **Activity 8:** *El viaje* (indirect object pronouns)	**LISTENING:** Improve your auditory memory **SPEAKING:** Maintain a discussion; discuss Latin American dance **CULTURE:** Use architecture as a cultural text
	Etapa 3 p. 362 *Lo mejor de dos mundos*	• Talk about literature • Talk about film • Avoid redundancy	• Nominalization [box 1] • Nominalization [box 2]	**EN VOCES:** Lorca- *La casa de Bernarda Alba* **EN COLORES:** *Tres directores:* Spanish-speaking film directors **TÚ EN LA COMUNIDAD NOTAS CULTURALES** • Movie titles in Spanish and English • Boom in Latin American fiction	• Double object pronouns **Activity 5:** *El(La) presidente(a)* (double object pronouns) **Activity 12:** *Clarificaciones* (nominalization)	**LISTENING:** Evaluate discussions **SPEAKING:** discuss a novel; critique a film **READING:** Interpret a drama **CULTURE:** Reflect on the international appeal of movies

UNIDAD 6 ¡Ya llegó el futuro! • Venezuela, Ecuador, Colombia, Bolivia, Perú

	COMMUNICATION	GRAMMAR	CULTURE	RECYCLING	STRATEGIES
Etapa 1 p. 390 *¿Qué quieres ver?* **UNIT OPENER** **CULTURE NOTES** • *Parque de Ciencia y Tecnología Maloka* • Cuzco • *El teléfono celular* • Simón Bolívar • Reverón • hallacas	• Narrate in the past • Express doubt and certainty • Report what others say • Talk about television	• Sequence of tenses	**EN VOCES:** *Brillo afuera, oscuridad en casa:* Spanish language soap operas **TÚ EN LA COMUNIDAD** **NOTAS CULTURALES** • Invitation implies inviter pays • Mexican soap operas and their success throughout L.A.	• Preterite vs. imperfect • Indicative vs. subjunctive • Reported speech **Activity 1:** *¿Por qué no…?* (movies) **Activity 9:** *¡Es dudoso!* (subjunctive with doubt) **Activity 14:** *Abuelo* (reported speech)	**LISTENING:** Keep up with what is said and agreed **SPEAKING:** Negotiate; retell memories **READING:** Distinguish facts and interpretation
Etapa 2 p. 412 *Aquí tienes mi número…*	• Talk about technology • State locations • Make contrasts • Describe unplanned events	• *Pero* vs. *sino* • *Se* for unplanned occurrences	**EN COLORES:** *¿Un aparato democrático?:* cell phones in Latin America **CONEXIONES:** *El arte:* make an ad for electronics **NOTAS CULTURALES** • Game shows in Spanish	• Conjunctions • Prepositions and adverbs of location **Activity 2:** *¡Voy a ElectroMundo!* (electronics) **Ya sabes:** *De compras,* prepositions/adverbs of location	**LISTENING:** Analyze the appeal in radio ads **SPEAKING:** Make excuses; consider the factors for and against an electronic purchase **CULTURE:** Survey technology in daily life
Etapa 3 p. 434 *¡Un viajo al ciberespacio!*	• Compare and evaluate • Express precise relationships • Navigate cyberspace	• Summary of prepositions • Verbs with prepositions	**EN VOCES:** Gabriel García Marquez **EN COLORES:** *Bolivia en la red:* Brazilian web page **CONEXIONES:** *La tecnología:* evaluate computer configurations for your classroom **NOTAS CULTURALES** • Spread of computer technology in Latin America • Searching for Spanish websites	• Comparatives and superlatives **Activity 4:** *Comparaciones* (comparatives) **Activity 5:** *Marcos* (comparatives, computers) **Ya sabes:** verbs with prepositions	**LISTENING:** Identify important computer vocabulary **SPEAKING:** Compare and evaluate films; compare and evaluate computer configurations **READING:** Monitor comprehension **CULTURE:** Evaluate Internet as means for cultural knowledge

Setting the Stage for Communication

BOOST · CONFIDENCE

Each unit is set in a different Spanish-speaking country to excite students about the new places and new things they're going to learn.

● **Unit Objectives** preview for the students what they will be able to do at the end of the unit.

UNIDAD 3

SAN JUAN
PUERTO RICO
EL FIN DE SEMANA

ETAPA 1 OBJECTIVES

¡Me gusta el tiempo libre!
- Extend invitations
- Talk on the phone
- Express feelings
- Say where you are coming from
- Say what just happened

ETAPA 2

¡Deportes para todos!
- Talk about sports
- Express preferences
- Say what you know
- Make comparisons

ETAPA 3

El tiempo en El Yunque
- Describe the weather
- Discuss clothing and accessories
- State an opinion
- Describe how you feel
- Say what is happening

ALMANAQUE

Población: 3.522.000
Altura: 0 metros (el nivel del mar)
Clima: 27° C (80° F)
Comida típica: pasta de guayaba, tostones, pernil
Gente famosa de Puerto Rico: Gigi Fernández (tenista), Luis Muñoz Marín (político), Luis Rafael Sánchez (escritor), Chayanne (cantante)

¿Vas a Puerto Rico? No necesitas pasaporte. Puerto Rico es una parte de Estados Unidos.

For more information about Puerto Rico, access www.mcdougallittell.com

EL MORRO is a fortress that the Spanish began in 1539 and finished in 1787. How could such a fortress protect the city of San Juan?

ARECIBO

SAN JUAN

PUERTO RICO

EL YUNQUE

HUMACAO

VIEQUES

MAYAGÜEZ

GIGI FERNÁNDEZ won the gold medal in women's tennis (doubles) in the 1992 and 1996 Summer Olympics. What other Latin American athletes do you know?

PONCE

LUIS MUÑOZ MARÍN (1898–1980) became the island's first elected governor in 1948. In 1952 he signed an agreement making Puerto Rico a Commonwealth of the U.S. What other U.S. territories do you know that aren't states?

TAÍNOS were natives on the island when Columbus arrived in 1493. They left these glyphs. Their language survived in words like **huracán** (hurricane). What other Native American cultures can you name?

EL CARIBE

Estados Unidos
Islas Bahamas
Cuba
Jamaica Haití
República Dominicana
Puerto Rico
Antillas Menores

PASTA DE GUAYABA is a popular dessert. This sweet, thick paste made from the guava fruit is usually eaten with white cheese. What tropical fruits have you eaten?

EL LORO PUERTORRIQUEÑO became an endangered species in 1971, when only twenty of these parrots were left. Their numbers have now increased. You might see one in El Yunque, the tropical rain forest. What other animals have been saved from extinction?

166

167

● **Unit Openers** highlight the people, places, food and music of the new culture so students learn Spanish in its authentic context.

Etapa Openers remind students of the communicative objectives.

"Everything ties nicely together. The unit has a good introductory theme so that students can take vocabulary and structures and apply them to talk about themselves."

Elizabeth Torosian
Doherty Middle School
Andover, MA

UNIDAD 3

El tiempo en El Yunque

- Describe the weather
- Discuss clothing and accessories
- State an opinion
- Describe how you feel
- Say what is happening

¿Qué ves?

Mira la foto de El Yunque, el bosque tropical.

1. ¿Hay muchas plantas verdes?
2. ¿Ignacio está ocupado o no?
3. ¿Diana y Roberto están alegres o preocupados?
4. ¿Cómo se llama el lugar?

212

213

VEREDA
↑ EL YUNQUE
EL YUNQUE TRAIL
BOSQUE NACIONAL
DEL CARIBE

¿Qué ves? reviews language for application in the new cultural context.

MOTIVATE TO COMMUNICATE
¡En español!

Strengthen proficiency through meaningful communicative contexts

IMPROVE · COMPREHENSION

Two stages of vocabulary introduction better prepare students for recognition and comprehension.

- **En contexto** visually preteaches active vocabulary in a relevant context.

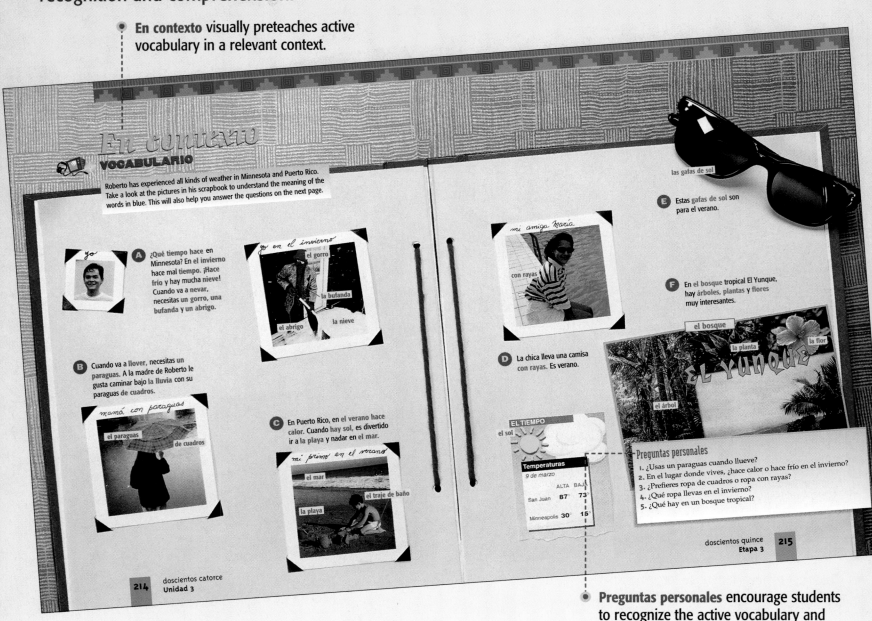

En contexto
VOCABULARIO

Roberto has experienced all kinds of weather in Minnesota and Puerto Rico. Take a look at the pictures in his scrapbook to understand the meaning of the words in blue. This will also help you answer the questions on the next page.

A ¿Qué tiempo hace en Minnesota? En el invierno hace mal tiempo. ¡Hace frío y hay mucha nieve! Cuando va a nevar, necesitas un gorro, una bufanda y un abrigo.

yo
yo en el invierno
el gorro
la bufanda
el abrigo
la nieve

B Cuando va a llover, necesitas un paraguas. A la madre de Roberto le gusta caminar bajo la lluvia con su paraguas de cuadros.

mamá con paraguas
el paraguas
de cuadros

C En Puerto Rico, en el verano hace calor. Cuando hay sol, es divertido ir a la playa y nadar en el mar.

mi primo en el verano
el mar
la playa
el traje de baño

D La chica lleva una camisa con rayas. Es verano.

mi amiga María
con rayas

E Estas gafas de sol son para el verano.

las gafas de sol

F En el bosque tropical El Yunque, hay árboles, plantas y flores muy interesantes.

el bosque
la planta
la flor
EL YUNQUE
el árbol

EL TIEMPO
el sol

Temperaturas 9 de marzo	ALTA	BAJA
San Juan	87°	73°
Minneapolis	30°	15°

Preguntas personales
1. ¿Usas un paraguas cuando llueve?
2. En el lugar donde vives, ¿hace calor o hace frío en el invierno?
3. ¿Prefieres ropa de cuadros o ropa con rayas?
4. ¿Qué ropa llevas en el invierno?
5. ¿Qué hay en un bosque tropical?

doscientos catorce
Unidad 3
214

doscientos quince
215
Etapa 3

- **Preguntas personales** encourage students to recognize the active vocabulary and make it meaningful to them.

• **Listening strategies** provide a starting point and focus for the dialog to help comprehension.

"I think your dialogs are terrific. They move along quickly, with humor, a touch of conflict, and with the embedded vocabulary and grammar points well contextualized for elaboration in the etapas."

Marco García
Lincoln Park High School
Chicago, IL

En vivo
DIÁLOGO

Diana Roberto Ignacio

PARA ESCUCHAR • STRATEGY: LISTENING

Sort and categorize details Minneapolis and San Juan are a world apart, yet in at least one way they are similar. How? What does Roberto say? What differences are mentioned? Use a Venn diagram to sort these details.

MINNEAPOLIS   SAN JUAN
hay nieve   no hay nieve

¡Qué tiempo!

1 ► Diana: ¡Qué mona tu bufanda! Me gusta tu gorro. ¿Hace mucho frío en Minneapolis?

2 ► Roberto: En el invierno, sí, ¡hace mucho frío! ¡Brrr! Tengo frío cuando pienso en los inviernos de Minneapolis.

3 ► Diana: ¿Nieva mucho?
Roberto: Bueno, en el invierno, nieva casi todas las semanas. Pero en verano, es como aquí. Hace mucho calor.

4 ► Ignacio: ¿Qué vas a hacer con toda esta ropa de invierno? Aquí nadie la necesita.
Roberto: Tienes razón. Voy a necesitar shorts, trajes de baño y gafas de sol.

5 ► Diana: ¡Ay! Pues, ya tienes ropa de verano.
Roberto: Claro que la tengo. ¡En Minneapolis no es invierno todo el año!

6 ► Roberto: ¡Qué día bonito! Hace muy buen tiempo. Tengo ganas de ir a El Yunque.
Diana: Perfecto, porque el proyecto de Ignacio para el concurso es sobre el bosque tropical. Y está preparando el proyecto este mes.

7 ► Ignacio: Sí, y necesito sacar fotos del bosque. Y las quiero sacar hoy mismo.
Roberto: Tengo suerte, ¿no lo creen?
Diana: Creo que tienes mucha suerte.
Ignacio: Tengo prisa. Es buena hora para sacar fotos porque hay sol.

8 ► Ignacio: ¡Qué bonito! Los árboles, las flores…
Roberto: Sí, muy bonita.
Ignacio: No es como Minneapolis, ¿verdad, Roberto?
Roberto: Tienes razón, Ignacio.

9 ► Ignacio: Mi proyecto va a estar bien chévere, ¿no creen?… ¿No creen?…
…Sí, Ignacio, creo que tu proyecto va a ser muy impresionante.

10 ► Ignacio: ¡Está lloviendo! ¡Y no tengo paraguas!
Roberto: Te estamos esperando, hombre.

216 doscientos dieciséis
Unidad 3

doscientos diecisiete **217**
Etapa 3

• **Motivating dialogs** with embedded vocabulary and structures depict real-life situations.

MOTIVATE TO COMMUNICATE
¡En español!

Build vocabulary for success from recognition to production

The carefully-crafted vocabulary supports the students' learning to insure confidence and success.

Objectives remind students again what they're learning and why.

También se dice features regionalisms to show that there is usually more than one way to say what you mean.

En acción
VOCABULARIO Y GRAMÁTICA

OBJECTIVES
- Describe the weather
- Discuss clothing and accessories
- State an opinion
- Describe how you feel
- Say what is happening

ACTIVIDAD 1

¿Qué lugar?

Escuchar ¿Qué lugar describe cada oración, Puerto Rico o Minnesota? ¡Ojo! Algunas oraciones describen los dos lugares. *(Hint: Which place is described?)*

1. En el invierno, hace mucho frío.
2. La gente no necesita ropa de invierno.
3. Nieva casi todas las semanas en el invierno.
4. En el verano, hace calor.
5. Necesitas shorts, traje de baño y gafas de sol.
6. Hay un bosque tropical.

ACTIVIDAD 2

Oraciones revueltas

Escuchar Completa las siguientes oraciones según el diálogo, combinando frases de las dos columnas. *(Hint: Complete the sentences by matching.)*

1. El proyecto de Ignacio para el concurso es sobre _____.
2. Tengo frío cuando pienso en _____.
3. ¿Qué vas a hacer con _____?
4. Es buena hora para _____.

a. sacar fotos
b. toda esta ropa de invierno
c. el bosque tropical
d. los inviernos de Minneapolis

ACTIVIDAD 3

♻ ¿Qué hay en la maleta?

Hablar/Escribir Describe lo que hay en la maleta de Roberto. *(Hint: Describe what's in Roberto's suitcase.)*

modelo

Hay un abrigo marrón.

TAMBIÉN SE DICE

There are different ways to say *cute*.
- **bonito**: Mexico and other countries
- **mono(a)**: Puerto Rico, Spain
- **lindo(a)**: many countries

218 doscientos dieciocho
Unidad 3

"I find it very cohesive. I could follow the progression without difficulty. The unit theme is well represented throughout."

Jim Rudy
Glen Este High School
Cincinnati, OH

pressions
ssions
t

gressive

ACTIVIDAD
4

¡Todos van de vacaciones!

Hablar/Escribir Todas las personas van de vacaciones. Explica adónde van, usando elementos de cada columna. ¿Qué van a llevar y qué van a hacer? *(Hint: Explain where people are vacationing, what they're taking with them, and what they'll be doing.)*

modelo

Yo voy a la playa en el verano.

Voy a llevar un traje de baño, gafas de sol y bronceador para tomar el sol.

Ignacio y Diana Roberto	la playa	
tú	las montañas	primavera
yo	el desierto	verano
mi amigo(a)	el lago	otoño
mis amigos	el bosque tropical	invierno
mi familia y yo	¿otro lugar?	

la bufanda	tomar el sol
el traje de baño	andar en bicicleta
el paraguas	nadar
las gafas de sol	jugar a (¿qué deporte?)
el abrigo	esquiar
el bronceador	patinar sobre hielo
los shorts	descansar
el gorro	ver las plantas y las flores
el impermeable	sacar fotos
	¿?

rio

nes

rano   el otoño

tomar el sol   el viento   la montaña

dor   los shorts   el río

invierno   la primavera

la tormenta

cero grados   el impermeable

actividad te gusta hacer en cada estación?

doscientos diecinueve **219**
Etapa 3

Activities begin with basic recognition of new vocabulary and progress to production.

MOTIVATE TO COMMUNICATE
¡En español!

Present grammar concepts visually to improve comprehension & retention

Illustrated grammar makes it easier for students to understand, remember, and apply new concepts.

• **Visual grammar concepts** help students see how the language works.

ACTIVIDAD 13

Yo tengo...

Hablar Dile a otro(a) estudiante cómo te sientes en cada situación. Usa estas palabras: **calor, frío, miedo, prisa, razón, suerte.** Cambien de papel. *(Hint: Say how you feel.)*

modelo

no comer por muchas horas

Tú: *¿Cómo estás cuando no comes por muchas horas?*

Otro(a) estudiante: *¡Tengo hambre!*

1. correr a la escuela
2. jugar al tenis en el sol
3. ver una película de horror
4. caminar en la nieve
5. saber hacer un examen
6. ganar mucho

■ MÁS COMUNICACIÓN p. R9

NOTA CULTURAL

El Yunque is a rain forest. All rain forests have four zones. They are (from lowest to highest) the floor, the understory, the canopy, and the emergent layer. Some zones are more humid than others; some get more sunlight. Each is a habitat for different kinds of animals and plants.

GRAMÁTICA

Direct Object Pronouns

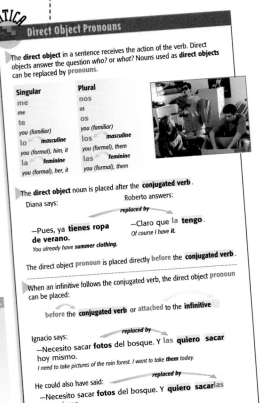

The **direct object** in a sentence receives the action of the verb. Direct objects answer the question *who?* or *what?* Nouns used as **direct objects** can be replaced by **pronouns**.

Singular		Plural	
me	me	nos	us
te	you (familiar)	os	you (familiar)
lo	**masculine** you (formal), him, it	los	**masculine** you (formal), them
la	**feminine** you (formal), her, it	las	**feminine** you (formal), them

The **direct object noun** is placed after the **conjugated verb**.

Diana says:

Roberto answers:

replaced by

—Pues, ya **tienes ropa de verano.**
You already have summer clothing.

—Claro que **la tengo**.
Of course I have it.

The **direct object pronoun** is placed directly **before** the **conjugated verb**.

When an infinitive follows the conjugated verb, the direct object **pronoun** can be placed:

before the **conjugated verb** or **attached to** the **infinitive**

Ignacio says:

replaced by

—Necesito sacar **fotos** del bosque. Y **las quiero sacar** hoy mismo.
I need to take pictures of the rain forest. I want to take them today.

He could also have said:

replaced by

—Necesito sacar **fotos** del bosque. Y **quiero sacarlas** hoy mismo.

ACTIVIDAD 14 Gramática

♻ ¿Qué compran?

Hablar Habla con otro(a) estudiante para explicar qué compran. *(Hint: Say what they buy.)*

modelo

Roberto: el guante de béisbol

Tú: *¿Roberto compra el guante de béisbol?*

Otro(a) estudiante: *Sí, lo compra.*

1. Diana: los patines
2. Ignacio: la raqueta
3. Roberto: las pelotas
4. Diana: las pesas
5. Roberto: el casco
6. Roberto: los bates
7. Diana: la patineta
8. Diana: el traje de baño

ACTIVIDAD 15 Gramática

La fiesta

Leer Diana y su amiga se escriben por Internet. Completa su conversación con el pronombre apropiado. *(Hint: Complete their conversation.)*

Diana: Sara, ¿Juan _____ invita a ti a su fiesta?

Sara: Sí, _____ invita. ¿A ustedes _____ invita?

Diana: Sí, _____ invita.

Sara: ¿Invita a Tina y a Graciela?

Diana: No, no _____ conoce.

Sara: ¿Y a Roberto?

Diana: Sí, _____ invita.

Sara: ¿Invita a Julio y a Fernando?

Diana: Sí, _____ invita. Son sus mejores amigos.

Sara: ¿Y a Mónica?

Diana: No, no _____ invita. Ella es su hermana.

■ MÁS PRÁCTICA *cuaderno* p. 79
■ PARA HISPANOHABLANTES *cuaderno* p. 77

ACTIVIDAD 16

Una visita

Hablar Tú y un(a) amigo(a) van a San Juan. Pregúntense qué van a llevar en el viaje. *(Hint: Tell your friend what you are taking on the trip.)*

modelo

tu traje de baño

Tú amigo(a): *¿Vas a llevar tu traje de baño?*

Tú: *Sí, voy a llevarlo.* o
Sí, lo voy a llevar.

Nota

You learned that **llevar** means *to wear*. In this example, **llevar** means *to take along*.

1. tus gafas de sol
2. tu abrigo
3. tu bufanda
4. tus shorts
5. tu gorro
6. tu impermeable
7. tu raqueta de tenis
8. tus camisetas
9. tus libros de español
10. ¿?

ACTIVIDAD 17

¿Qué pasa?

Escuchar Escucha la conversación. Luego, decide si las oraciones son ciertas o falsas. Corrige las falsas. *(Hint: True or false?)*

1. Cuando llueve, Raúl ve la televisión.
2. Raúl lee revistas. Las lee cuando llueve.
3. María lleva paraguas. Lo lleva cuando llueve.
4. Raúl necesita gafas de sol para ir a la playa.
5. María tiene bronceador. Va a llevarlo a la playa.

• **The activity sequence**, from controlled to open-ended activities, guides students through a solid progression that builds vocabulary and grammar skills.

"I love it!! It is very practical and students are able to learn the material because of the variety of activities."

Lucy García
Pueblo East High School
Pueblo, CO

● **Clear models** make it easier for students to understand what they are supposed to do.

ACTIVIDAD 18

Creo que...

Hablar Tienes que pensar en el tiempo. ¿Qué necesitas llevar? Cambien de papel. *(Hint: Say if you think so.)*

modelo

calor (chaqueta)

Tú: Hace **calor**.

Tu amigo(a): ¿Necesito **chaqueta**?

Tú: Creo que no. No la necesitas.

Nota

Creer *(to think, to believe)* can be used to state an opinion.

Creo que sí.   Creo que no.

1. sol (gafas de sol)
2. llover (bronceador)
3. sol (¿?)
4. llover (¿?)

Juego

¿Qué describe la oración?

Hace buen tiempo.

a.

b.

GRAMÁTICA

Saying What Is Happening: Present Progressive

▶ When you want to say that an action is happening now, use the *present progressive.*

estoy **esperando**	estamos **esperando**
estás **esperando**	estáis **esperando**
está **esperando**	están **esperando**

Ignacio says: —¡Está **lloviendo**!
  It's raining!

Roberto replies: —Te estamos **esperando**...
  We're waiting for you...

▶ To form this tense, use:

the present tense of estar + **present participle**

▶ To form the present participle of a verb, drop the **ending** of the infinitive and add **-ando** or **-iendo**.

-ar verbs	esperar *ar*	**ando**	esperando
-er verbs	comer *er*	**iendo**	comiendo
-ir verbs	escribir *ir*	**iendo**	escribiendo

▶ When the **stem** of an **-er** or **-ir** verb ends in a vowel, change the **-iendo** to **-yendo**.

leer	→	le**y**endo
oír	→	o**y**endo
creer	→	cre**y**endo

MOTIVATE TO COMMUNICATE
¡En español!

Help students communicate with confidence

Since one of students' biggest fears is being embarrassed in front of their peers, the pronunciation strand and study hints help take away their fears and make it fun.

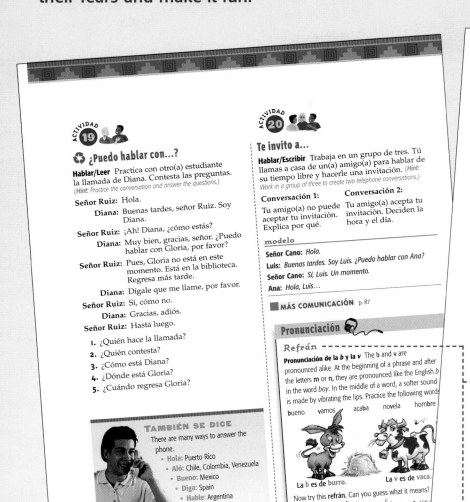

ACTIVIDAD 19

¿Puedo hablar con...?

Hablar/Leer Practica con otro(a) estudiante la llamada de Diana. Contesta las preguntas. *(Hint: Practice the conversation and answer the questions.)*

Señor Ruiz: Hola.

Diana: Buenas tardes, señor Ruiz. Soy Diana.

Señor Ruiz: ¡Ah! Diana, ¿cómo estás?

Diana: Muy bien, gracias, señor. ¿Puedo hablar con Gloria, por favor?

Señor Ruiz: Pues, Gloria no está en este momento. Está en la biblioteca. Regresa más tarde.

Diana: Dígale que me llame, por favor.

Señor Ruiz: Sí, cómo no.

Diana: Gracias, adiós.

Señor Ruiz: Hasta luego.

1. ¿Quién hace la llamada?
2. ¿Quién contesta?
3. ¿Cómo está Diana?
4. ¿Dónde está Gloria?
5. ¿Cuándo regresa Gloria?

TAMBIÉN SE DICE
There are many ways to answer the phone.
- Hola: Puerto Rico
- Aló: Chile, Colombia, Venezuela
- Bueno: Mexico
- Diga: Spain
- Hable: Argentina
- Oigo: Uruguay

ACTIVIDAD 20

Te invito a...

Hablar/Escribir Trabaja en un grupo de tres. Tú llamas a casa de un(a) amigo(a) para hablar de su tiempo libre y hacerle una invitación. *(Hint: Work in a group of three to create two telephone conversations.)*

Conversación 1:
Tu amigo(a) no puede aceptar tu invitación. Explica por qué.

Conversación 2:
Tu amigo(a) acepta tu invitación. Deciden la hora y el día.

modelo

Señor Cano: Hola.

Luis: Buenas tardes. Soy Luis. ¿Puedo hablar con Ana?

Señor Cano: Sí, Luis. Un momento.

Ana: Hola, Luis…

■ **MÁS COMUNICACIÓN** p. R7

Pronunciación

Refrán

Pronunciación de la b y la v The b and v are pronounced alike. At the beginning of a phrase and after the letters m or n, they are pronounced like the English b in the word *boy*. In the middle of a word, a softer sound is made by vibrating the lips. Practice the following words.

bueno   vamos   acaba   novela   hombre

La **b** es de **burro**.   La **v** es de **vaca**.

Now try this *refrán*. Can you guess what it means?

No hay mal que por bien no ve...

ciento ochenta y tres **183**
Etapa 1

ACTIVIDAD 18

¡Lógicamente!

Escuchar Todos hablan de los deportes. Escucha lo que dicen. Luego, indica la respuesta más lógica. *(Hint: Listen and indicate the most logical response.)*

1. a. ¡Qué bien! Tenemos más de cinco minutos.
   b. ¡Ay! Tenemos menos de cinco minutos.
2. a. ¿Tienes tu raqueta?
   b. ¿Tienes tu tarea?
3. a. Sí, me gusta nadar.
   b. ¡Claro que sí! Me gusta patinar.
4. a. No necesita un guante.
   b. ¿Va a la tienda de deportes?
5. a. Prefiere nadar.
   b. Prefiere levantar pesas.

ACTIVIDAD 19

¿Cuál es tu deporte favorito?

Hablar/Escribir Habla con otros estudiantes sobre los deportes. Escribe sus respuestas. Prepara un resumen para la clase. *(Hint: Ask classmates about sports. Record responses and report them.)*

La encuesta	Estudiante 1	Estudiante 2
1. ¿A qué deportes sabes jugar?		
2. ¿A qué deportes juegas mucho?		
3. ¿A qué deporte prefieres jugar?		
4. ¿Cómo es?		
5. ¿Qué deporte prefieres ver?		
6. Compara el deporte que prefieres ver con el deporte que prefieres jugar.		
7. ¿Cuál es tu equipo favorito?		
8. ¿Cómo es?		
9. ¿Pierde mucho?		

■ **MÁS COMUNICACIÓN** p. R8

Pronunciación

Trabalenguas

Pronunciación de la ñ The letter ñ does not exist in English, but the sound does. It is the sound made by the combination of the letters *ny* in the English word *canyon*. To practice the sound, pronounce the following tongue twister.

ñ

La ñ es la n con bigote.

¡La araña se baña mañana!

doscientos cinco **205**
Etapa 2

● **Pronunciation** is taught through **Trabalenguas** and **Refranes** to make it both memorable and fun!

ACTIVIDAD 17

¿Qué piensas tú?

Hablar Trabaja con otro(a) estudiante para comparar los deportes. Cambien de papel. *(Hint: Compare sports with a classmate.)*

modelo

interesante

Estudiante A: *Para ti, ¿qué deporte es más **interesante**, el tenis o el béisbol?*
Estudiante B: *Para mí, el tenis es más interesante que el béisbol.*
Estudiante A: *Para mí, el tenis es tan interesante como el béisbol.*

Estudiante A PREGUNTAS

1.
2.
divertido | peligroso
3.
4.
difícil | malo
5.
6.
bueno | interesante

Estudiante B RESPUESTAS

Para mí, ... es más... que...
Para mí, ... es menos... que...
Para mí, ... es tan... como...

APOYO PARA ESTUDIAR

Comparatives

When comparing, picture these visual cues:
(+) más que   (−) menos que
                  (=) tan como
Think about extremes that would illustrate **más** and **menos**, such as **UN ELEFANTE** [(+) **más grande**] and **un ratón** [(−) **menos grande**]. Now think of two very different athletes or performers about whom you have an opinion. How would you compare them?

Study hints direct students with strategies for production and retention.

ACTIVIDAD 19 Gramática

♻ ¡Están ocupados!

Hablar Todos están haciendo sus actividades favoritas. ¿Qué están haciendo? *(Hint: Say what everyone is doing.)*

1. Diana: comprar ropa
2. Roberto y su hermano: hablar
3. Luis: abrir un libro
4. Paco y yo: pasar un rato con los amigos
5. tú: bailar con tus amigos
6. nosotros: leer una novela
7. yo: ver la televisión
8. sus amigos: oír música
9. Carlos: escribir una carta
10. la familia: comer

MÁS PRÁCTICA *cuaderno* p. 80
PARA HISPANOHABLANTES *cuaderno* p. 78

ACTIVIDAD 20

¿Qué están haciendo?

Hablar Es sábado por la tarde. ¿Qué están haciendo estas personas? *(Hint: Say what everyone's doing.)*

1. tus padres
2. tú y tus amigos
3. tu hermano(a)
4. tu amigo(a)
5. tú

ACTIVIDAD 21

¡Qué buenas vacaciones!

Escribir Elena y su familia están de vacaciones en la playa. Describe lo que está pasando. Usa las preguntas como guía. *(Hint: Describe what is happening. Use the questions as a guide.)*

 la señora Álvarez
Pablo
el señor Álvarez
Ana
Marta
Elena

- ¿Qué tiempo hace?
- ¿Qué están haciendo las personas?
- ¿Cómo están? ¿Tienen frío? ¿Tienen hambre?

MÁS COMUNICACIÓN p. R9

Pronunciación

Trabalenguas

Pronunciación de la _j_ y la _g_ The letter **j** is pronounced somewhat like the _h_ in the English word _hope_, but a bit stronger. Before the letters **e** and **i**, the Spanish **g** is pronounced just like the **j**. Listen to this tongue twister, then try it yourself to practice.

"Ji, ji, ji" **ríen Javier y Jorge cuando miran a Jazmín la jirafa ingerir jarabe.**

MOTIVATE TO COMMUNICATE
¡En español!

Improve students' reading skills with a variety of high-interest selections

Engaging reading selections, that are read and summarized on audio, provide students a tremendous advantage to increase their literacy in Spanish.

- **Reading strategies** develop students' skills by emphasizing different ways to approach a variety of readings and genres.

En voces
LECTURA

PARA LEER
STRATEGY: READING
Scan Reading very quickly to get a specific piece of information, like a football score or a movie time, is called scanning. Scan this poster and decide whether Ignacio and Roberto can attend the festival. (Remember their plans for Saturday.)

¡TODOS A BAILAR!
Concierto espectacular de
BOMBA y PLENA
¡Músicos sensacionales!

Claudio de Mata: maracas

Rubén López: cuatro

Lucio Escobar: tamborín

¡Y la actuación especial de los bailarines

Lilián y Alberto!

Sábado 16 de octubre
a las 5 de la tarde
en el Instituto de Cultura

Bomba y plena

La bomba y la plena son danzas típicas de Puerto Rico. Tienen sus orígenes en la música africana. Los instrumentos originales para tocar esta música alegre son los tambores[1], las panderetas[2], las maracas y el cuatro. El cuatro es un tipo de guitarra española pequeña, originalmente con cuatro cuerdas[3]. Las personas que bailan estas danzas llevan ropa de muchos colores. La música tiene mucho ritmo[4] y las personas ¡mueven todo el cuerpo[5]!

[1] drums	[4] rhythm
[2] type of tambourine	[5] body
[3] strings	

¿Comprendiste?
1. ¿Cuándo es el concierto?
2. ¿En qué tienen sus orígenes la bomba y la plena?
3. ¿Es una música triste o alegre?
4. ¿Qué es el cuatro?
5. ¿Qué otros instrumentos hay?
6. ¿Qué ropa llevan las personas que bailan?

¿Qué piensas?
1. Hoy hay un concierto de bomba y plena en tu ciudad. ¿Qué ropa llevas y por qué?
2. ¿Un concierto de bomba y plena es divertido? ¿Por qué sí o por qué no?

- **¿Comprendiste?** checks students' basic understanding of what they've read.

- **¿Qué piensas?** asks students to think critically about the reading selection.

"The strategy boxes will be useful. I'm a true believer in the metacognitive focus of teaching strategies."

Bill Heller
Perry Jr./Sr. High School
Perry, NY

En voces
LECTURA

PARA LEER · STRATEGY: READING
Distinguish details Find out what **coquíes** are. What features do they have? Use the word web to describe a **coquí** and name its identifying characteristics.

COQUÍ

VEREDA NATURAL
BAÑO GRANDE
NATURE TRAIL

Si visitas Puerto Rico, vas a ver imágenes del coquí en muchos lugares —en nombres de tiendas, artículos de promoción y libros. La tradición puertorriqueña es que si ves un coquí vas a tener mucha suerte. Y si quieres tener un bonito recuerdo⁹ de Puerto Rico es posible comprar un coquí verde de juguete¹⁰, símbolo de la isla.

---
⁹souvenir   ¹⁰toy

Coquí
ARTEL
Puerto Rico
En su tamaño y color natural

El coquí

No muy lejos de¹ San Juan está el Bosque Nacional del Caribe. En este bosque tropical, El Yunque, hay animales y plantas que no ves en ninguna otra parte² del mundo. El coquí, el animal más conocido de todo Puerto Rico, vive protegido³ en El Yunque.

---
¹Not far from   ²any other part   ³protected

El coquí es una rana⁴ de tamaño⁵ pequeño que vive en los árboles. Los coquíes son de diferentes colores. Hay coquíes grises⁶, marrones, amarillos y verdes. Reciben su nombre por su canto⁷ característico. Hay 16 especies de coquíes en Puerto Rico, pero sólo dos producen el canto típico «coquí». Dos están en peligro⁸ de extinción. Casi todos los coquíes empiezan a cantar cuando llega la noche.

---
⁴frog   ⁶grey   ⁸danger
⁵size   ⁷song

¿Comprendiste?
1. ¿Dónde vive el coquí?
2. ¿Qué es el coquí? ¿Por qué se llama coquí?
3. ¿Cómo es el coquí?
4. ¿Cuándo canta el coquí?
5. ¿Por qué es bueno ver un coquí?

¿Qué piensas?
¿Por qué piensas que dos especies de coquí están en peligro de extinción?

Hazlo tú
Estudia más sobre el coquí y dibuja o describe las plantas típicas que hay donde vive.

228 doscientos veintiocho
Unidad 3

doscientos veintinueve **229**
Etapa 3

● **Hazlo tú** expands upon the information in the reading for students for application.

MOTIVATE TO COMMUNICATE
¡En español!

Encourage students to experience different cultures

EXPAND · VIEWPOINTS

Focused cultural strategies improve students ability to understand and appreciate the target culture.

● **Cultural strategies** help students understand their own culture and other cultures to broaden their worldview.

En colores
CULTURA Y COMPARACIONES

PARA CONOCERNOS
STRATEGY: CONNECTING CULTURES

Reflect on sports traditions Can you think of any sports in the U.S. that have players from other countries? What sports are they? Are some countries associated with certain sports more than others? Why do you think that might be true? Use this chart to organize your answers.

Deporte	País 1	País 2	País 3
el béisbol	Cuba	Japón	
el hockey	Canadá	Rusia	

Do you associate other countries with areas such as science, music, or art? If so, which ones? Why?

Béisbol
El pasatiempo nacional

En Puerto Rico el béisbol es muy popular. La temporada[1] de béisbol es de octubre a marzo. Los equipos que juegan forman la liga de invierno[2] y hay un partido casi todos los días.

Cada ciudad principal tiene un equipo. Unos jugadores[3] de las ligas mayores y menores[4] de Estados Unidos participan junto con los jugadores puertorriqueños.

[1] season   [2] winter league   [3] players   [4] major and minor leagues

Roberto Clemente (1934–1972), jugador de los Piratas de Pittsburgh, es el puertorriqueño más famoso del béisbol. El primer latino elegido[5] para el Salón de la Fama[6] en 1973, Clemente empezó[7] su carrera con el equipo de Santurce, Puerto Rico. Hoy, en la ciudad de San Juan, el estadio principal de béisbol se llama Coliseo Roberto Clemente.

En el resto del Caribe el béisbol es tan importante como en Puerto Rico. Muchos jugadores importantes vienen de esta región. Juan Marichal de la República Dominicana está en el Salón de la Fama. Andrés Galarraga de Venezuela, Edgar Rentería de Colombia, Liván Hernández de Cuba y Fernando Valenzuela de México son otras figuras latinoamericanas importantes de las ligas mayores de béisbol de Estados Unidos.

[5] elected
[6] Hall of Fame
[7] began

Sandy Alomar, Jr. e Iván Rodríguez son dos jugadores de Puerto Rico.

NOTA CULTURAL

On December 31, 1972, Roberto Clemente was about to deliver supplies to earthquake survivors in Nicaragua when his plane crashed. He is remembered not only as a great baseball player, but also as an outstanding humanitarian.

¿Comprendiste?

1. ¿En qué meses juegan los equipos de la liga de invierno?
2. ¿De dónde vienen los jugadores de la liga de invierno?
3. ¿Quién es el primer latino elegido para el Salón de la Fama?
4. ¿Qué países latinos tienen jugadores en las ligas mayores?

¿Qué piensas?

1. ¿Por qué juegan en Puerto Rico los jugadores de las ligas mayores y menores de Estados Unidos?
2. ¿Por qué vienen a Estados Unidos los jugadores de otros países?

● **¿Comprendiste?** asks students to recall the information in the selection.

"Teaching culture is a real challenge but so important. You have done more with culture than any other series that I have seen."

Deborah Hagen
Ionia High School
Ionia, MI

En colores
CULTURA Y COMPARACIONES

PARA CONOCERNOS
STRATEGY: CONNECTING CULTURES
Define travel and tourism Look at a travel brochure. (Get one from a travel agency or hotel.) What does it contain? What does it *not* contain? Do you think there is a difference between being a *traveler* and being a *tourist*? List the interests of each. Explain your ideas.

Viajero	Turista

Una excursión por la isla

Roberto tiene ganas de pasear por Puerto Rico otra vez. Diana e Ignacio lo llevan de excursión por la isla. En la Oficina de Turismo ven este folleto[1].

―――――
[1] brochure

230   doscientos treinta
Unidad 3

Descubra la isla de Puerto Rico
¡La hija del mar y del sol!

El mar y Puerto Rico tienen una unión fuerte. Las primeras personas de la isla, los taínos, llegan en canoas. Cristóbal Colón también llega a la isla por el mar. Y por el mar Puerto Rico sufre[2] ataques por muchos años. Los españoles construyen[3] El Morro en el siglo XV[4] como protección contra los ingleses, los holandeses y los piratas. Hoy una excursión por San Juan siempre incluye[5] una visita a esta gran fortaleza.

[2] suffers
[3] build
[4] 15th century
[5] includes
[6] waves
[7] national anthem
[8] indigenous, native
[9] land

Tanto para el turista como para el puertorriqueño, el mar ofrece muchas actividades. En las playas es posible practicar muchos deportes: nadar, practicar el surfing o esquiar. El surfing es muy popular. En Puerto Rico hay playas que tienen olas[6] grandes, donde hay competiciones internacionales.

Es Borin...
la hija del mar y el sol...

¿Comprendiste?
1. ¿Cuál es el grupo que llega primero a Puerto Rico?
2. ¿De quiénes vienen los ataques contra los españoles de Puerto Rico?
3. ¿Cuáles son unos deportes populares en las playas de Puerto Rico?
4. ¿De qué deporte hacen competiciones internacionales?
5. En el himno nacional de Puerto Rico, ¿qué es Borinquen?

¿Qué piensas?
1. Si algún día vas a Puerto Rico, ¿qué vas a hacer? ¿Te gustaría visitar lugares históricos o pasar toda tu visita en la playa? ¿Por qué?
2. ¿Cómo imaginas tu vacación perfecta? ¿Adónde vas? ¿Qué tiempo hace?

Hazlo tú
¿Cuáles son los deportes más populares en tu comunidad? Trabaja con otro(a) estudiante para preparar un folleto sobre las atracciones de tu estado.

doscientos treinta y uno
Etapa 3   231

● **Hazlo tú** sometimes offers a pair activity for students to try out the new cultural concepts.

● **¿Qué piensas?** helps students to think critically about the target culture as well as their own culture.

MOTIVATE TO COMMUNICATE
¡En español!

Follow up with diagnostic review

The comprehensive review, correlated to the etapa objectives, thoroughly reviews and prepares the students to be successful for assessment.

● **The side column learning channel** helps students self-diagnose and review what they can do and where they can go to get help.

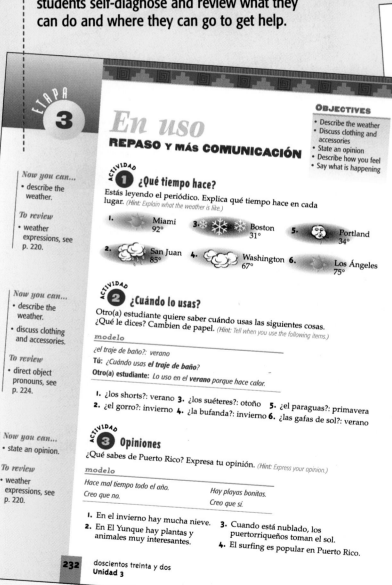

ETAPA 3

Now you can...
- describe the weather.

To review
- weather expressions, see p. 220.

Now you can...
- describe the weather.
- discuss clothing and accessories.

To review
- direct object pronouns, see p. 224.

Now you can...
- state an opinion.

To review
- weather expressions, see p. 220.

En uso
REPASO Y MÁS COMUNICACIÓN

OBJECTIVES
- Describe the weather
- Discuss clothing and accessories
- State an opinion
- Describe how you feel
- Say what is happening

ACTIVIDAD 1 ¿Qué tiempo hace?

Estás leyendo el periódico. Explica qué tiempo hace en cada lugar. *(Hint: Explain what the weather is like.)*

1. Miami 92°
2. San Juan 85°
3. Boston 31°
4. Washington 67°
5. Portland 34°
6. Los Ángeles 75°

ACTIVIDAD 2 ¿Cuándo lo usas?

Otro(a) estudiante quiere saber cuándo usas las siguientes cosas. ¿Qué le dices? Cambien de papel. *(Hint: Tell when you use the following items.)*

modelo

¿el traje de baño?: verano
Tú: ¿Cuándo usas **el traje de baño**?
Otro(a) estudiante: Lo uso en el **verano** porque hace calor.

1. ¿los shorts?: verano
2. ¿el gorro?: invierno
3. ¿los suéteres?: otoño
4. ¿la bufanda?: invierno
5. ¿el paraguas?: primavera
6. ¿las gafas de sol?: verano

ACTIVIDAD 3 Opiniones

¿Qué sabes de Puerto Rico? Expresa tu opinión. *(Hint: Express your opinion.)*

modelo

Hace mal tiempo todo el año.
Creo que no.

Hay playas bonitas.
Creo que sí.

1. En el invierno hay mucha nieve.
2. En El Yunque hay plantas y animales muy interesantes.
3. Cuando está nublado, los puertorriqueños toman el sol.
4. El surfing es popular en Puerto Rico.

232 doscientos treinta y dos
Unidad 3

ACTIVIDAD 5 ¿Qué opinas tú?

PARA CONVERSAR
STRATEGY: SPEAKING
Give reasons for your preferences Support your choices in different ways. Compare (1) how you feel about the sports, (2) what you know or don't know about them, or (3) basic similarities and differences among them. Think of different ways of explaining your choices.

Habla con otro(a) estudiante sobre los deportes. Explícale cuáles son tus preferencias y por qué. *(Hint: Talk about sports.)*

modelo

Tú: ¿Prefieres levantar pesas o jugar al voleibol?
Otro(a) estudiante: Prefiero jugar al voleibol. El voleibol es más interesante que levantar pesas.
Tú: Para mí, levantar pesas es más divertido.

ACTIVIDAD 6 Un paseo por el club

Imagínate que trabajas en un nuevo club de deportes. Muéstrales el club a tus amigos, describiendo las actividades. *(Hint: Show your friends the new sports club where you work.)*

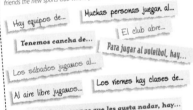

Hay equipos de...
Muchas personas juegan al...
El club abre...
Tenemos cancha de...
Para jugar al voleibol, hay...
Los sábados jugamos al...
Al aire libre jugamos...
Los viernes hay clases de...
Para las personas que les gusta nadar, hay...

ACTIVIDAD 7 En tu propia voz

ESCRITURA Imagínate que tienes que preparar un folleto para promover el club nuevo de la Actividad 6. Incluye información sobre las actividades y el horario del club. *(Hint: Write a brochure promoting the new sports club.)*

TÚ EN LA COMUNIDAD

Sarah is a Florida student who uses Spanish at her job as a restaurant hostess and sends e-mails in Spanish. She also used her Spanish when she went to Venezuela as a volunteer with a medical mission group. Sarah spoke Spanish to the patients and translated doctors' questions and instructions. Do you use Spanish to help others?

210 doscientos diez
Unidad 3

● **Tú en la comunidad,** which occurs once in every unit, features real students using their Spanish in their own community.

- **Speaking strategies** help students become better communicators by expanding their repertoire of expressions through tone of voice, personalization, gestures, etc.

  - **En tu propria voz** prompts students with a short writing assignment to sharpen their language skills.

"I like the fact that there seems to be a good balance between activities that practice new structures and then progress to activities that require more creative uses of language in communicative situations."

Vickie Mike
Horseheads High School
Horseheads, NY

ACTIVIDAD 6 — ¿Adónde voy?

PARA CONVERSAR
— STRATEGY: SPEAKING

Get specific information To find out someone's vacation plans ask questions about all the specifics. Ask about weather (**el tiempo**), clothing (**la ropa**), or activities (**actividades y deportes**) at their destination. The model shows you how.

Imagínate que vas a uno de estos lugares. Los otros estudiantes tienen que adivinar adónde vas. Contesta sus preguntas. *(Hint: Answer your classmates' questions as they try to guess where you are going.)*

el desierto
el bosque tropical
la playa en verano
las montañas en invierno
el lago en otoño

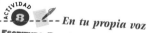
modelo

Otro(a): ¿Va a nevar?
Tú: No, no va a nevar.
Otro(a): ¿Vas a llevar el traje de baño?
Tú: Sí, voy a llevarlo.
Otro(a): ¿Vas a practicar el surfing?
Tú: Sí, voy a practicarlo.
Otro(a): ¿Vas a la playa?
Tú: Sí, voy a la playa.

ACTIVIDAD 7 — Por teléfono

Estás de vacaciones. Hablas con tu amigo(a) por teléfono. Describe el tiempo que hace, cómo estás y lo que está haciendo tu familia en ese momento. *(Hint: Describe the weather, how you feel, and what your family is doing on your vacation.)*

ACTIVIDAD 8 — En tu propria voz

ESCRITURA Tu amigo(a) puertorriqueño(a) viene a vivir con tu familia por un año. Escríbele una carta describiendo qué tiempo hace durante cada estación del año, la ropa que necesita llevar y las actividades que él o ella puede hacer en cada estación. *(Hint: Write your Puerto Rican friend a letter describing the weather and items he or she should bring when visiting.)*

En la primavera hace...

Para el frío, necesitas llevar...

En el verano hace...

Llueve mucho en...

CONEXIONES

Las ciencias The Fahrenheit temperature scale is used in Puerto Rico. However, most Spanish-speaking countries use the Celsius scale. On this scale, water freezes at 0° and boils at 100°. To convert, use these formulas.

$100°C \times 9/5 + 32 = 212°F$ $212°F - 32 \times 5/9 = 100°C$

Convert the temperatures in the chart and write what seasons they might represent. Explain the other weather conditions. Choose a location in the Spanish-speaking world. Find out its average temperature and weather conditions in each season.

C	F	Estación	Tiempo
0°			
10°			
	68°		
25°			
30°			
	95°		

234 doscientos treinta y cuatro
Unidad 3

En resumen
REPASO DE VOCABULARIO

DESCRIBING THE WEATHER

¿Qué tiempo hace?	What is the weather like?
Está nublado.	It is cloudy.
Hace...	It is...
buen tiempo	nice outside
calor	hot
fresco	cool
frío	cold
mal tiempo	bad outside
sol	sunny
viento	windy
Hay...	It's...
sol	sunny
viento	windy
el grado	degree
llover	to rain
la lluvia	rain
nevar	to snow
la nieve	snow
el sol	sun
la temperatura	temperature
el tiempo	weather
la tormenta	storm
el viento	wind

Seasons

las estaciones	seasons
el invierno	winter
el otoño	fall
la primavera	spring
el verano	summer

DESCRIBING HOW YOU FEEL

tener...	to be...
calor	hot
cuidado	careful
frío	cold
miedo	afraid
prisa	in a hurry
razón	right
sueño	sleepy
suerte	lucky
tener ganas de...	to feel like...

STATING AN OPINION

creer	to think, to believe
Creo que sí/no.	I think so. / I don't think so.

CLOTHING AND ACCESSORIES

Clothing

el abrigo	coat
la bufanda	scarf
el gorro	cap
el impermeable	raincoat
los shorts	shorts
el traje de baño	bathing suit

Styles

con rayas	striped
de cuadros	plaid, checked

Accessories

el bronceador	suntan lotion
las gafas de sol	sunglasses
el paraguas	umbrella

OTHER WORDS AND PHRASES

sacar fotos	to take pictures
tomar el sol	to sunbathe

Places

el bosque	forest
el desierto	desert
el lago	lake
el mar	sea
la montaña	mountain
la playa	beach
el río	river

Vegetation

el árbol	tree
la flor	flower
la planta	plant

Juego

Es julio. Hace frío y nieva mucho. Mucha gente esquía en las montañas. ¿En qué país están?

a. **México**
b. **Estados Unidos**
c. **Chile**

doscientos treinta y cinco **235**
Etapa 3

- **Conexiones** thematically links and expands the language cultural concepts to other subject areas for better long-term retention.

MOTIVATE TO COMMUNICATE
¡En español!

Cultivate better writers through the writing process

The writing process, at the end of each unit, works as a tutor-in-the-book to teach students how to improve their writing step by step.

- **Writing strategies** offer a variety of prewriting strategies to improve students' writing skills.

- **Student models** show students what to watch out for, and how the assignment is supposed to look.

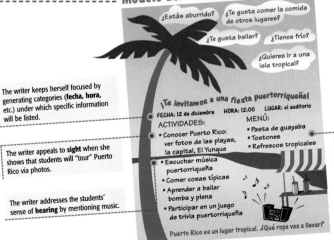

UNIDAD 3

EL MORRO
SAN JUAN

En tu propia voz
ESCRITURA

Una fiesta puertorriqueña

The Spanish classes at your school are sponsoring an all-school celebration of Puerto Rican culture. It is your job to design the posters. Use the student model as your guide.

Purpose: Invite others to an all-school party
Audience: Students and faculty
Subject: Puerto Rico
Structure: Poster-sized invitation

PARA ESCRIBIR · STRATEGY: WRITING

Appeal to the senses A well-constructed poster will entice people to attend the party. One way to do so is to include details that appeal to the senses: sight (**la vista**), hearing (**el oído**), touch (**el tacto**), taste (**el gusto**), and smell (**el ofato**).

Modelo del estudiante

¿Estás aburrido?   ¿Te gusta comer la comida de otros lugares?

¿Te gusta bailar?   ¿Tienes frío?

¿Quieres ir a una isla tropical?

The writer keeps herself focused by generating categories (**fecha, hora,** etc.) under which specific information will be listed.

¡Te invitamos a una fiesta puertorriqueña!
FECHA: 12 de diciembre   HORA: 12:00   LUGAR: el auditorio
ACTIVIDADES: MENÚ:
• Conocer Puerto Rico: • Pasta de guayaba
  ver fotos de las playas,   • Tostones
  la capital, El Yunque   • Refrescos tropicales
• Escuchar música
  puertorriqueña
• Comer cosas típicas
• Aprender a bailar
  bomba y plena
• Participar en un juego
  de trivia puertorriqueña

Puerto Rico es un lugar tropical. ¿Qué ropa vas a llevar?

The writer appeals to **sight** when she shows that students will "tour" Puerto Rico via photos.

The writer addresses the students' sense of **hearing** by mentioning music.

The invitation appeals to **taste** and **smell** by mentioning various Puerto Rican foods.

236

"All the pieces are there for a good text that will bring us to the 21st century."

Janet Wohlers
Weston Middle School
Weston, MA

egias para escribir

de escribir...

nother student, discuss what
ve learned about Puerto Rico.
observation chart to help
ze your thoughts. Short on
Review this unit, or use the
or Internet to find more
nation. Then bring the details
er to make an exciting poster
party). Be sure to include: date,
and place of the party; activities;
and drink; suggested dress; decorations.

Una fiesta puertorriqueña

la vista	el oído	el tacto	el gusto	el olfato
el sol	música bomba y plena	la playa	tostones	las flores
				la comida
el Viejo San Juan	el mar			

siones

e you have a draft, share it with a partner. Then ask:

Can you tell where/when the party takes place?
Does the poster appeal to the senses?
Does it make you want to go to the party?
Does it communicate the island theme?

versión final

fore you create the final draft of your invitation, look
er your work with the following questions in mind:

• *Did I use gustar correctly?*

y this: Underline each use of **gustar**. Check to make
re that it is used with an infinitive and the correct
onoun: **me, te, le, nos, os,** or **les.**

• *Are adjectives used correctly?*

ry this: Circle every noun/adjective combination.
Check to make sure that each adjective matches the
gender and number of the noun it modifies.

¡FIESTA PUERTORRIQUEÑO! A

¡Me gusta ir a la playa!

¡Me gusta ver la ciudad vieja!

¿Te gusta escuchar música?

¡Vamos todos a la fiesta puertorriqueña!

Share your writing on
www.mcdougallittell.com

237

● **The Internet connection** will offer more writing
support. The best written submissions will be
posted on the McDougal Littell website.

MOTIVATE
TO COMMUNICATE
¡En español!

Implement ideas and lesson plans easily and effectively

The Ampliación and Etapa Overview in the teacher's edition offer outstanding support to make teaching Spanish adaptable to every situation.

● **Ampliación** features multi-modal activities that spark students' excitement with new ways to learn language and culture.

Ampliación

These activities may be used at various points in the Unit 3 sequence.

■ For Block Schedule, you may find that these projects will provide a welcome change of pace while reviewing and reinforcing the material presented in the unit. See the **Block Scheduling Copymasters.**

PROJECTS

Plan a seasonal vacation Divide the class into four groups: **el verano, el otoño, el invierno, la primavera.** Each group is responsible for researching a great vacation spot (in Puerto Rico or another Spanish-speaking country) for their season. They should prepare:
• a map showing where the place is
• a poster depicting what the area looks like (buildings, plants, animals, etc.)
• a catalog of pictures of appropriate clothing to bring
• a poster depicting what activities are available
Display the projects in four corners of the room. Have students travel to each season and vote on which vacation spot they prefer.
    PACING SUGGESTION: Have students begin research at the beginning of the unit. Final projects are completed at the end of Unit 3.

Record a telephone answering machine message Have students write and record an appropriate phone machine message, using the Ortiz family's message as a model if needed. They may want to accompany it with a background of Latin music.
    PACING SUGGESTION: Upon completion of Etapa 1.

STORYTELLING

Poemas After reviewing the vocabulary for all three Etapas, model the following rhyme (using objects or pictures). Tell students that it is used in Puerto Rican schools to teach English to the students.

    Pollito, chicken. Gallina, hen. Lápiz, pencil. Y pluma, pen.
    Ventana, window. Puerta, door. Maestra, teacher. Y piso, floor.

Pause as the rhyme is being told, giving students a chance to fill in words or act out gestures. Students then write and read aloud a rhyme of their own, using vocabulary from this unit. They should continue supplying a Spanish word first, then the English translation.

Más poemas Now have students reverse the order of the words. They should give an English word first, and then try to rhyme the Spanish translations.
    PACING SUGGESTION: Upon completion of Etapa 3.

BULLETIN BOARD/POSTERS

Bulletin Board Have students create a "Puerto Rico: Isla del encanto" bulletin board. They should decorate it with brochures from travel agencies, hand-drawn visuals, articles from magazines and newspapers, etc.

Posters Have students create •**Travel** posters for Puerto Rico •**Topographical maps** of Puerto Rico •**Musical instrument** posters •**Ads** for CDs of Puerto Rican music artists •**Lyrics poster** of the words to "La Borinqueña," the Puerto Rican national anthem (For more information, go to www.mcdougallittell.com)

GAMES

Pantomimas
Divide the class into two teams, A and B, and then into pairs. After reviewing the vocabulary from all 3 **Etapas,** have each pair write an original sentence on a slip of paper. Collect the sentences and put them in a separate box for each team. A player from Team A picks a sentence from Team B's box and vice versa. That player must pantomime each word in the sentence until someone on the team guesses it. Place a 3-minute time limit and let students know that using English disqualifies the team for that round. The team with the most correct sentences is the winner.
    PACING SUGGESTION: Upon completion of Etapa 3.

MUSIC

Teach your students the simple folk song **El coquí.** (For more information, go to www.mcdougallittell.com) Discuss if there is an animal that represents or typifies your area or state. Are there others that are associated with different areas of the U.S. or the world? More music samples are available on your *Canciones* Cassette or CD.

HANDS-ON CRAFTS

• Have students create cardstock dominoes with vocabulary words and pictures from the unit. Pairs of students can play as a review activity.
• Have students create their own **coquí** mascots using papier-mâché, paints, pipe cleaners, and small beads (if available). Work with the art department to make the papier-mâché ahead. Using the **coquí** shown above or the one on p. 228 as a model, form the body and head. Let dry and then paint as desired. Glue beads for eyes and add pipe cleaners for feet.

RECIPE

Piraguas **Piraguas** are sold by **piragüeros** in the parks and on the streets of Puerto Rico. These refreshing treats are similar to snow cones, but with tropical fruit flavors. You can make them right in your classroom with only a blender for equipment.

Encourage students to try the juices of fruits they have not eaten before.

Dominós

Domino games are a common sight in the parks and plazas throughout Puerto Rico. Obtain several sets of dominoes and have students learn how to play. On a specified day, hold a double or triple elimination tournament (so that everyone gets to play at least two or three matches). If your class periods are too short to complete the tournament in one day, keep track of the results on a grid and continue play on another day.
    PACING SUGGESTION: For use at any point in the unit.

Receta

Piraguas
1 bolsa de hielo
3 o más latas de jugo concentrado congelado de
    sabores tropicales (piña, mango, papaya, etc.)
vasos de cartón pequeños
cucharitas de plástico

En un jarrón, diluir cada lata de jugo concentrado a 1/3 de lo que indican las instrucciones (usualmente una lata de agua en vez de tres). Triturar hielo en la licuadora y ponerlo en pequeños vasos de cartón. Verter el almíbar sobre el hielo y servir con una cucharita.

● **Easy-to-prepare recipes** give students a delicious opportunity to experience new cultural cuisines.

● **At-a-glance overview** outlines the objectives, strategies and program resources for time-saving support.

"WOW! ¡En español! has it all. I'd love to teach from this book."

Kathleen Gliewe
Helena Middle School
Helena, MT

UNIDAD 3 ETAPA **3** EL TIEMPO EN EL YUNQUE
pages 212–237

Planning Guide CLASSROOM MANAGEMENT

OBJECTIVES

Communication
• Describe the weather pp. 214–215, 216–217
• Discuss clothing and accessories pp. 214–215
• Describe the geography of a place, its plants and animals pp. 216–217, 228–229, 230–231

Grammar
• Use weather expressions pp. 220–222
• Use **tener** expressions pp. 223–224
• Use direct object pronouns pp. 224–226
• Use present progressive pp. 226–227

Pronunciation
• j and g p. 227
• Dictation TE p. 227

Culture
• El Yunque p. 224
• El coquí p. 228–229
• Tourism in Puerto Rico pp. 230–231

Recycling
• Hay
• Preferir
• Ir a
• Tener
• Sports vocabulary
• Estar

STRATEGIES

Listening Strategies
• Sort and categorize details p. 216

Speaking Strategies
• Say how often p. 222
• Get specific information p. 234

Reading Strategies
• Distinguish details p. 228
• Look at graphics p. 230

Writing Strategies
• Brainstorm and organize information by category p. 234
• Appeal to the senses pp. 236–237

Connecting Cultures Strategies
• Recognize variations in vocabulary pp. 218, 222
• Learn about rain forests pp. 224, 228–229
• Connect and compare what you know about travel and tourism in your community to help you learn about travel and tourism in a new community pp. 230–231

PROGRAM RESOURCES

Print
• *Más práctica* Workbook PE, pp. 73–80
• Block Scheduling Copymasters, pp. 73–80
• Unit 3 Resource Book
  Más práctica Workbook TE, pp. 103–110
  Para hispanohablantes Workbook TE, pp. 111–118

Information Gap Activities pp. 119–122
Family Involvement pp. 123–124
Video Activities pp. 125–127
Videoscript pp. 128–130
Audioscript pp. 131–134
Assessment Program, Unit 3 Etapa 3 pp. 135–186
Answer Keys pp. 187–202

Audiovisual
• Audio Program Cassettes 9A, 9B / CD 9
• Canciones Cassette / CD
• Video Program Videotape 3 / Videodisc 2A
• Overhead Transparencies M1–M5; GO1–GO5; 72, 93–102

Technology
• Electronic Teacher Tools/Test Generator
• Intrigas y aventuras CD-ROM, Disc 1
• www.mcdougallittell.com

Assessment Program Options
• Cooperative Quizzes (Unit 3 Resource Book)
• Etapa Exam Forms A and B (Unit 3 Resource Book)
• *Para hispanohablantes* Etapa Exam (Unit 3 Resource Book)
• Portfolio Assessment (Unit 3 Resource Book)
• Unit 3 Comprehensive Test (Unit 3 Resource Book)
• *Para hispanohablantes* Unit 3 Comprehensive Test (Unit 3 Resource Book)
• Midterm Test (Unit 3 Resource Book)
• Multiple Choice Test Questions (Unit 3 Resource Book)
• Audio Program Testing Cassette T1 / CD T1
• Electronic Teacher Tools/Test Generator

Native Speakers
• *Para hispanohablantes* Workbook PE, pp. 73–80
• *Para hispanohablantes* Workbook TE (Unit 3 Resource Book)
• *Para hispanohablantes* Etapa Exam (Unit 3 Resource Book)
• *Para hispanohablantes* Unit 3 Comprehensive Test (Unit 3 Resource Book)
• Audio *Para hispanohablantes* Cassettes 9A, 9B, T1 / CD 9, T1
• Audioscript *Para hispanohablantes* (Unit 3 Resource Book)

Student Text Listening Activity Scripts

Diana   Roberto   Ignacio

Videoscript: Diálogo pages 216–217
• Videotape 3 • Videodisc 2A

Search Chapter 7, Play to 8
U3E3 • En vivo (Dialog)

• Use the videoscript with **Actividades 1, 2** page 218

Diana: ¡Qué mona tu bufanda! Me gusta tu gorro. ¿Hace mucho frío en Minneapolis?

Roberto: En el invierno, sí, ¡hace mucho frío! ¡Brrr! Tengo frío cuando pienso en los inviernos de Minneapolis. Los detesto.

Diana: ¿Nieva mucho?

Ignacio: Diana, ¡qué pregunta! Claro que nieva mucho en Minnesota.

Diana: Pues, yo no sé.

Roberto: Bueno, en el invierno, nieva casi todas las semanas. Pero en verano, es como aquí. Hace mucho calor.

Ignacio: ¿Y qué vas a hacer con este abrigo? ¿Y con toda esta ropa de invierno? Aquí nadie la necesita.

Roberto: Tienes razón. Voy a necesitar shorts, trajes de baño y gafas de sol.

Diana: ¡Ay! Pues ya tienes ropa de verano.

Roberto: Claro que la tengo. ¡En Minneapolis no es invierno todo el año! ¡Qué día bonito! Hace muy buen tiempo. ¿Sabes qué, Ignacio? Tengo muchas ganas de ir a El Yunque.

Ignacio: ¡Perfecto!

Roberto: ¿Por qué perfecto?

Diana: Perfecto porque el proyecto de Ignacio para el concurso es sobre el bosque tropical. Y está preparando el proyecto este mes.

Ignacio: Sí, y necesito sacar fotos del bosque. Y las quiero sacar hoy mismo.

Roberto: ¡Qué chévere! Tengo suerte, ¿no lo creen? ¡Yo los acompaño con mucho gusto! ¡Vamos a El Yunque!

Diana: Creo que sí. Creo que tienes mucha suerte.

Ignacio: Tengo prisa. Es buena hora para sacar fotos porque hay sol. ¡Tenemos que ir ahora mismo a El Yunque! ¡Avancen! ¡Qué bonito! Los árboles, las flores...

Roberto: Sí, muy bonita.

Ignacio: No es como Minneapolis, ¿verdad, Roberto?

Roberto: Tienes razón, Ignacio. No es para nada como Minneapolis.

Ignacio: Mi proyecto va a estar bien chévere, ¿no creen? ¿No creen? ¿Dónde está el paraguas? Lo necesito. ...Sí, Ignacio, creo que tu proyecto va a ser muy impresionante. ¡Está lloviendo! ¡Y no tengo paraguas!

Roberto: Te estamos esperando, hombre.

El tiempo page 221

1. Hace fresco. Llueve mucho. Las flores son bonitas.
2. Hace mucho frío. Nieva. Quiero patinar sobre hielo.
3. Hace frío y hay mucho viento. Quiero ir a un partido de fútbol americano.
4. Hace calor. La temperatura es de noventa grados. Voy a la piscina.

¿Qué pasa? page 225

María: ¡Hola, Raúl! Llueve mucho, ¿verdad?

Raúl: Sí. Yo veo la televisión cuando llueve.

María: Yo también la veo, pero no es mi actividad favorita. Prefiero leer unas revistas.

Raúl: A mí me gusta leer las revistas. A veces las leo cuando llueve.

María: Me gusta caminar en la lluvia.

Raúl: ¿Llevas paraguas?

María: No, no lo llevo.

Raúl: ¡Ay! Cuando quiero nadar, ¡voy a la playa!

María: ¡Buena idea! ¿Va a llover mañana?

Raúl: Creo que no.

María: Entonces, ¿vamos a la playa? Tengo muchas ganas de nadar.

Raúl: Sí. Pero tengo que comprar gafas de sol. Las necesito para ir a la playa.

María: ¿Necesito llevar bronceador?

Raúl: No. Yo lo tengo.

Quick Start Review Answers

p. 214 Adjectives of feeling
Answers will vary.
Answers could include:
1. tengo un partido de béisbol muy importante más tarde
2. saco buenas notas en matemáticas
3. va a un concierto
4. tienen un examen de español
5. no tenemos mucha tarea

p. 218 Dialog review
1. Ahora Roberto vive en Puerto Rico.
2. En Minnesota en el invierno hace mucho frío.
3. En Minnesota y Puerto Rico en el verano hace calor.
4. Roberto tiene ganas de ir a El Yunque.

p. 220 Seasons/sports
Answers will vary.
Answers could include:
1. el béisbol, el tenis, el surfing
2. el fútbol, el fútbol americano
3. el hockey, esquiar
4. el baloncesto, el voleibol

p. 223 Tener
1. tiene   3. tenemos   5. tiene
2. tienes   4. tengo

p. 224 Gender
1. el   3. el   5. el   7. los
2. los   4. las   6. la   8. el

p. 226 Direct object pronouns
1. las revistas / Sí, las tengo.
2. la camisa con rayas / Sí, la lleva.
3. las pelotas / Sí, las compra.
4. los bates /Sí, los buscan.
5. el libro / Sí, lo lee.
6. el bronceador / Sí, lo necesito.

p. 235 Seasons/weather/clothing
Answers will vary.
Answers could include:
otoño
• Hace fresco y hace viento.
• un suéter
• el fútbol americano
• tengo ganas de bailar

● **Listening scripts** in the Teacher's Edition provide practical information needed for easier lesson preparation.

MOTIVATE TO COMMUNICATE
¡En español!

Suggests practical teaching ideas for lesson planning

The comprehensive Teacher's Edition and resource materials provide the support you need to introduce, explain, and expand your lessons.

- **Time-saving lessons** present sequenced teaching suggestions and ideas.

UNIDAD 3 ETAPA 3 Pacing Guide

Sample Lesson Plan - 50 Minute Schedule

DAY 1

Etapa Opener
- Quick Start Review (TE, p. 212) 5 MIN.
- Anticipate/Activate prior knowledge: Have students look at the *Etapa* Opener and answer the questions. 5 MIN.

En contexto: Vocabulario
- Quick Start Review (TE, p. 214) 5 MIN.
- Have students use context and pictures to learn *Etapa* vocabulary. In pairs, have students answer the questions, p. 215. Use the Situational OHTs for additional practice. 10 MIN.

En vivo: Diálogo
- Quick Start Review (TE, p. 216) 5 MIN.
- Review the Listening Strategy, p. 216. Play audio or show video for the dialog, pp. 216–217. 10 MIN.
- Replay twice. Read aloud, having students note similarities and differences between Minneapolis and San Juan. 10 MIN.

Homework Option:
- Video Activities, Unit 3 Resource Book, pp. 125–127.

DAY 2

En acción: Vocabulario y gramática
- Check homework. 5 MIN.
- Quick Start Review (TE, p. 218) 5 MIN.
- Have students open to *En contexto*, pp. 214–215, for reference. Use OHT 93 and 94 to review vocabulary by asking yes/no questions (*¿Es un[a]...?*). 5 MIN.
- Play the audio; have students do *Actividades* 1 and 2 orally. 10 MIN.
- Students complete *Actividad* 3 in writing. Go over answers orally. Have volunteers write out answers on the board. 10 MIN.
- Present *Vocabulario*, p. 219. Model pronunciation. 5 MIN.
- Have students do *Actividad* 4 orally. 5 MIN.
- Have students complete *Actividad* 5 in writing, then exchange papers for peer correction. 10 MIN.

Homework Option:
- Have students complete *Actividad* 4 in writing.

DAY 3

En acción (cont.)
- Check homework. 5 MIN.
- Quick Start Review (TE, p. 220) 5 MIN.
- Present *Gramática:* Describing the Weather, p. 220. 10 MIN.
- Play the audio; have students do *Actividad* 6. 5 MIN.
- Do *Actividad* 7 orally. 5 MIN.
- In pairs, have students do *Actividad* 8. They should take turns asking and answering the questions. Call on several pairs to present their answers. 10 MIN.
- Present the Speaking Strategy, p. 222. Have students do *Actividad* 9 in pairs. 5 MIN.
- Have students complete *Actividad* 10. Choose one or two groups to present their work to the class. 10 MIN.

Homework Option:
- Have students complete *Actividad* 7 in writing. *Más práctica* Workbook, p. 77. *Para hispanohablantes* Workbook, p. 75.

DAY 4

En acción (cont.)
- Check homework. 5 MIN.
- Quick Start Review (TE, p. 223) 5 MIN.
- Present *Gramática:* Special Expressions Using *tener*, p. 223. 5 MIN.
- Have students complete *Actividad* 11 in writing, then go over the answers orally. 5 MIN.
- Do *Actividad* 12 orally. 5 MIN.
- Have students complete *Actividad* 13 in pairs. Expand using Information Gap Activities, Unit 3 Resource Book, p. 119; *Más comunicación*, p. R9. 10 MIN.
- Quick Start Review (TE, p. 224) 5 MIN.
- Present *Gramática:* Direct Object Pronouns, p. 224. 5 MIN.
- Have students work in pairs to complete *Actividad* 14. 5 MIN.
- Have students read and complete *Actividad* 15. 5 MIN.

Homework Option:
- *Más práctica* Workbook, pp. 78–79. *Para hispanohablantes* Workbook, pp. 76–77.

DAY 5

En acción (cont.)
- Check homework. 5 MIN.
- Do *Actividad* 16 in pairs. 5 MIN.
- Play the audio; have students do *Actividad* 17. 5 MIN.
- Do *Actividad* 18 in pairs. 5 MIN.
- Quick Start Review (TE, p. 226) 5 MIN.
- Present *Gramática:* Present Progressive, p. 226. 10 MIN.
- Do *Actividades* 19 and 20 orally. 5 MIN.
- Do *Actividad* 21 in writing. Expand using Information Gap Activities, Unit 3 Resource Book, pp. 120–121; *Más comunicación*, p. R9. 10 MIN.

Pronunciación
- Play the audio and have students practice the *Trabalenguas.* 5 MIN.

Homework Option:
- *Más práctica* Workbook, p. 80. *Para hispanohablantes* Workbook, p. 78.

DAY 6

En voces: Lectura
- Check homework. 5 MIN.
- Quick Start Review (TE, p. 228) 5 MIN.
- Present the Reading Strategy, p. 228. 5 MIN.
- Have volunteers read the selection aloud and answer the questions, p. 229. 10 MIN.

En colores: Cultura y comparaciones
- Quick Start Review (TE, p. 230) 5 MIN.
- Discuss the Connecting Cultures Strategy, p. 230. 5 MIN.
- Have volunteers read the selection aloud and answer the questions, p. 231. 10 MIN.
- Review *En uso* for *Etapa* 3 Exam. 10 MIN.

Homework Option:
- Prepare *En uso Actividades* 1–5. Review for *Etapa* 3 Exam.

DAY 7

En uso: Repaso y más comunicación
- Check homework. 5 MIN.
- Quick Start Review (TE, p. 232) 5 MIN.
- Review *Actividades* 1–5 orally. 5 MIN.
- Present the Speaking Strategy, p. 234. Do *Actividad* 6 in groups and *Actividad* 7 in pairs. 10 MIN.

En resumen: Repaso de vocabulario
- Complete *Etapa* 3 Exam. 20 MIN.

En tu propia voz: Escritura
- Do *Actividad* 8 in writing. 5 MIN.

Conexiones
- Present *Las ciencias*, p. 234. 5 MIN.

Homework Option:
- Review for Unit 3 Comprehensive Test.

DAY 8

En resumen: Repaso de vocabulario
- Quick Start Review (TE, p. 235) 5 MIN.

En tu propia voz: Escritura
- Do the writing activity, pp. 236–237. 10 MIN.

Unit 3 Comprehensive Test
- Review grammar questions, etc. as necessary. 5 MIN.
- Complete Unit 3 Comprehensive Test. 30 MIN.

Ampliación
- Optional: Use a suggested project, game, or activity. (TE, pp. 167A–167B) 15 MIN.

Homework Option:
- Preview *Unidad* 4 Opener: Have students read and study pp. 238–239.

211C Pacing Guide • UNIDAD 3 Etapa 3

- **Block Scheduling Lesson Plans** offer options for pacing and variety.

> "There is a step-by-step sequence. The whole unit is structured around a topic and each etapa contributes meaningful elements to the whole."
>
> M. Mercedes Stephenson
> Hazelwood Central High School
> Florissant, MO

...ple Lesson Plan - Block Schedule (90 minutes)

DAY 1

...pener
...t Review (TE, p. 212)

.../Activate prior
...e: Have students
...e *Etapa* Opener and
...e questions. 5 MIN.
...k Scheduling
...sters. 5 MIN.

...texto:
...ulario
...art Review (TE, p. 214)

...udents use context and
...s to learn *Etapa*
...ulary. In pairs, have
...ts answer the questions,
... Use the Situational OHTs
...ditional practice. 10 MIN.

...vo: Diálogo
...: Start Review (TE, p. 216)
...

...w the Listening Strategy,
...6. Play audio or show the
...o for the dialog, pp. 216–217.
...MIN.
...ay twice. Read aloud, having
...ents note similarities and
...erences between Minneapolis
...d San Juan. 10 MIN.

...acción: Vocabulario
...ramática
...uick Start Review (TE, p. 218)
...
...ay the audio; have students
...o *Actividades* 1 and 2. 10 MIN.
...ave students do *Actividad* 3 in
...riting, and go over answers
...rally. 5 MIN.
...resent *Vocabulario*, p. 219. 5 MIN.
...Have students do *Actividad* 4
...orally and *Actividad* 5 in writing.
...10 MIN.

...Homework Option:
... Video Activities, Unit 3 Resource
Book, pp. 125–127. Have
students complete *Actividad* 4
in writing.

DAY 2

En acción (cont.)
- Check homework. 5 MIN.
- Quick Start Review (TE, p. 220) 5 MIN.
- Present *Gramática:* Describing the Weather, p. 220. 10 MIN.
- Replay dialog to demonstrate usage. 5 MIN.
- Play the audio; have students do *Actividad* 6. 5 MIN.
- Have students do *Actividad* 7 orally. 5 MIN.
- In pairs, have students do *Actividad* 8. They should take turns asking and answering the questions. Call on several pairs to present their answers. 10 MIN.
- Present the Speaking Strategy, p. 222. Have students do *Actividad* 9 in pairs. 5 MIN.
- Have students complete *Actividad* 10. Choose one or two groups to present their work to the class. 5 MIN.
- Quick Start Review (TE, p. 223) 5 MIN.
- Present *Gramática:* Special Expressions Using *tener*, p. 223. 10 MIN.
- Have students complete *Actividad* 11 in writing, then go over the answers orally. 5 MIN.
- Do *Actividad* 12 orally. 5 MIN.
- Have students complete *Actividad* 13 in pairs. Expand using Information Gap Activities, Unit 3 Resource Book, p. 119; *Más comunicación*, p. R9. 10 MIN.

Homework Option:
- Have students write 10 original sentences using weather/season vocabulary. *Más práctica* Workbook, pp. 77–78. *Para hispanohablantes* Workbook, pp. 75–76.

DAY 3

En acción (cont.)
- Check homework. 5 MIN.
- Quick Start Review (TE, p. 224) 5 MIN.
- Present *Gramática:* Direct Object Pronouns, p. 224. 10 MIN.
- Have students work in pairs to complete *Actividad* 14. 5 MIN.
- Have students read and complete *Actividad* 15. Go over answers orally. 10 MIN.
- Do *Actividad* 16 in pairs. 5 MIN.
- Play the audio; have students do *Actividad* 17. 10 MIN.
- Have students do *Actividad* 18 in pairs. Call on a few pairs to present their answers. 10 MIN.
- Quick Start Review (TE, p. 226) 5 MIN.
- Present *Gramática:* Saying What Is Happening: Present Progressive, p. 226. 10 MIN.
- Do *Actividades* 19 and 20 orally. 5 MIN
- Do *Actividad* 21 in writing. Expand using Information Gap Activities, Unit 3 Resource Book, pp. 120–121; *Más comunicación*, p. R9. 10 MIN.

Pronunciación
- Play the audio and have students practice the *Trabalenguas*. 5 MIN.

Homework Option:
- *Más práctica* Workbook, pp. 79–80. *Para hispanohablantes* Workbook, pp. 77–78.

DAY 4

En voces: Lectura
- Check homework. 5 MIN.
- Quick Start Review (TE, p. 228) 5 MIN.
- Present the Reading Strategy, p. 228. 5 MIN.
- Have volunteers read the selection aloud and answer the questions, p. 229. 10 MIN.

En colores: Cultura y comparaciones
- Quick Start Review (TE, p. 230) 5 MIN.
- Present the Connecting Cultures Strategy, p. 230. 5 MIN.
- Have volunteers read the selection aloud and answer the questions, p. 231. 15 MIN.

En uso: Repaso y más comunicación
- Quick Start Review (TE, p. 232) 5 MIN.
- Do *Actividades* 1–5 orally. 15 MIN.
- Present the Speaking Strategy, p. 234. Do *Actividad* 6 in groups and *Actividad* 7 in pairs. 10 MIN.
- Do *Actividad* 8 in writing. 10 MIN.

Homework Option:
- Review for *Etapa* 3 Exam.

DAY 5

En resumen: Repaso de vocabulario
- Quick Start Review (TE, p. 235) 5 MIN.
- Review grammar questions, etc. as necessary. 5 MIN.
- Complete *Etapa* 3 Exam. 20 MIN.

Conexiones
- Read and discuss *Las ciencias*, p. 234. 10 MIN.

Unit 3 Comprehensive Test
- Review grammar questions, etc. as necessary. 5 MIN.
- Complete Unit 3 Comprehensive Test. 30 MIN.

En tu propia voz: Escritura
- Do the writing activity, pp. 236–237. 15 MIN.

Ampliación
- Optional: Use a suggested project, game, or activity. (TE, pp. 167A–167B) 15 MIN.

Homework Option:
- Preview *Unidad* 4 Opener: Have students read and study pp. 238–239.

▼ Ignacio, Diana y Roberto en El Yunque.

MOTIVATE
TO COMMUNICATE
¡En español!

Support students' varied learning styles & ability levels

The Teacher's Edition and ancillaries offer strategies that address the multiple intelligences, different ability levels, and native-speaker needs.

- **Classroom Community** provides paired, group, and cooperative learning activities to help build your classroom community of Spanish speakers.

UNIDAD 3 Etapa 3
Vocabulary/Grammar

Teaching Resource Options

Print
Más práctica Workbook PE, p. 78
Para hispanohablantes Workbook PE, p. 76
Block Scheduling Copymasters
Unit 3 Resource Book
  Más práctica Workbook TE, p. 108
  Para hispanohablantes Workbook TE, p. 114

Audiovisual
OHT M5; 93, 94, 100 (Quick Start)

Technology
Intrigas y aventuras CD-ROM, Disc 1

Teaching Suggestions
Reinforcing vocabulary
- Before assigning **Actividad 9** for pair work, use OHT 93 and 94 to review clothing vocabulary.
- Display a world map or OHT M5 in the classroom. After students read **Actividad 10**, have them locate each of the cities listed.

Actividad 9 Objective: Open-ended practice Describing weather and clothing in conversation

Answers will vary.

Alternate: You may wish to introduce the following expressions:
  —¿Cómo te vas a **vestir** hoy?
  —¿Qué te vas a **poner**?

Actividad 10 Objective: Open-ended practice Describing weather in conversation

Answers will vary.

Culture Highlights

- **PUERTO RICO** Due to its beautiful scenery and tropical climate, Puerto Rico is also known as **Isla del encanto.** Each year thousands of tourists visit Puerto Rico, bringing in $1.4 billion annually.

ACTIVIDAD 9

¿Qué vas a llevar?

PARA CONVERSAR

STRATEGY: SPEAKING
Say how often Generalize by saying how often you wear an item in this weather. (**Siempre / A veces) llevo shorts cuando hace calor.**

Hablar La ropa que llevas depende mucho del tiempo. Trabaja con otro(a) estudiante para explicar qué vas a llevar según el tiempo. *(Hint: Explain what you'll be wearing.)*

modelo

hace calor

Estudiante A: *Hace calor. ¿Qué vas a llevar hoy?*

Estudiante B: *Voy a llevar una camiseta y shorts. Siempre llevo shorts cuando hace calor.*

1. hace mucho frío
2. hace fresco
3. hace mucho calor
4. hay sol
5. llueve
6. ¿?

ACTIVIDAD 10

El tiempo hoy

Hablar/Leer Tienes un periódico de San Juan. Tus amigos quieren saber qué tiempo hace en varias ciudades. Trabaja en un grupo de tres para hacer y contestar las preguntas sobre el tiempo. *(Hint: Say what the weather is in various places)*

¿Qué tiempo hace en…?
¿Cuál es la temperatura en…?
¿Hace buen/mal tiempo en…?
¿Dónde hace/hay…?

EL TIEMPO 4 de enero	Tiempo	Temperatura mínima	Temperatura máxima
San Juan		70°	82°
Buenos Aires		75°	90°
Los Ángeles		50°	64°
Madrid		37°	46°
México		48°	61°
Miami		59°	70°
Nueva York		28°	32°
Quito		50°	59°
San Antonio		39°	51°

Clave: sol ☀ lluvia 🌧 nieve ❄ nublado ☁ viento 🌬

TAMBIÉN SE DICE There are different ways to say the following:

sunglasses	*T-shirt*	*shorts*
• gafas de sol: Puerto Rico, Spain, Ecuador	• camiseta: Puerto Rico and many countries	• shorts: Puerto Rico
• lentes de sol: many countries	• playera: Mexico	• pantalones cortos: many countries
	• polera: Chile	• pantalonetas: Colombia, Ecuador
	• remera: Argentina	

Classroom Community

Storytelling Each student will state a sentence in order to form a short story entitled **Vamos de vacaciones.** The first student starts with one sentence about the things they need to pack for their vacation; each student adds one sentence. Alternate: **Vamos de vacaciones y vamos a llevar…** [article of clothing]. Each student must remember all previous articles and add a new one. This activity may also be done in groups.

Portfolio Have students write the date, the season, the weather, and what they are wearing. They might also write what they are going to do and wear after school.

Group Activity Divide the class into groups of 4. Have each group write an explanation for the difference between **tener** and **tener ganas de,** including two or three model sentences. Ask several groups to present their explanations to the class.

"This incorporates many positive features: relevant context, much exposure to culture, strategy development, recycling, and meaningful practice."

Pam Urdal Silva
East Lake High School
Tarpon Springs, FL

Expressions Using tener

...GAS? p. 148 You learned to ...omeone is hungry or thirsty ...verb tener. You also learned ...ll age using tener.

tener	**hambre**
tener	**sed**
tener...	**años**

...e verb tener in many expressions.

tener ganas de...
to feel like...

bailar	*dancing*
cantar	*singing*

Roberto says:
—Tengo **suerte.**
I'm lucky.

Ignacio says:
—Tengo **prisa.**
I'm in a hurry.

...tica

...s de...

...Qué tienen ganas de hacer estas personas?
...el like doing?)

...de ir a la playa.

...aminar
...la televisión
...ticar deportes

4. tú: patinar
5. yo: ¿?

...ICA *cuaderno* p. 78
...ANOHABLANTES *cuaderno* p. 76

ACTIVIDAD 12 ¿Qué pasa aquí?

Hablar ¿Cómo se sienten estas personas? Describe cada dibujo, usando una expresión con **tener.** *(Hint: Describe each picture with a tener expression.)*

1. la amiga de Roberto

2. su prima

3. su hermana

4. su vecino

5. su amigo

doscientos veintitrés
Etapa 3 · **223**

Quick Start Review

♻ **Tener**

Use OHT 100 or write on the board: Complete the sentences with the correct form of **tener.**

1. Ud. ____ dos hermanas.
2. Tú ____ mucha tarea.
3. Mis amigos y yo ____ sed.
4. Yo ____ hambre.
5. Elena ____ 14 años.

Answers *See p. 211B.*

Teaching Suggestions
Presenting Special Expressions Using tener

• Refer back to the **Diálogo,** pp. 216–217. Have students identify the **tener** expressions.
• Make up a short scenario using several of the expressions with **tener.** When students hear one of these expressions, they should raise their hands or write down the expression.

ACTIVIDAD 11 Objective: Controlled practice
Using **tener ganas de...**

♻ **Tener**

Answers
1. Nosotras tenemos ganas de caminar.
2. Usted tiene ganas de ver la televisión.
3. Ellos tienen ganas de practicar deportes.
4. Tú tienes ganas de patinar.
5. Yo tengo ganas de [tomar el sol].

ACTIVIDAD 12 Objective: Transitional practice
Expressions using **tener**

Answers
1. La amiga de Roberto tiene sueño.
2. Su prima tiene frío.
3. Su hermana tiene calor.
4. Su vecino tiene prisa.
5. Su amigo tiene razón.

▪ Block Schedule

Change of Pace Have students work in pairs to plan the perfect vacation for their partner. They should (1) develop a "client" profile by asking questions, (2) research tourist guides/books/videos, and (3) present the plan to their partner. (For additional activities, see **Block Scheduling Copymasters.**)

Vocabulary/Grammar • UNIDAD 3 Etapa 3   **223**

...ing All Students

...elp Provide various scenarios (with visuals, ...le), and have students write responses using ...or example: **Hace calor./La temperatura es** **Yo... (tengo calor) / Hace fresco. Ud... / Hay** ...rmenta. Ellos... / Es la verdad. Tú...

...e Speakers Discuss how students spend their ...rs. Work, summer school, camps, or visits to ...me country may be described.

Multiple Intelligences

Kinesthetic In groups, have students act out the various expressions with **tener.** The other students will offer various items to them and say why. For example: **Necesitas una bufanda porque tienes frío.**

Musical/Rhythmic Have students develop a short rap or chant to practice the expressions with **tener.**

• **Quick Start Reviews** set up short student-directed activities that review and reinforce previously learned vocabulary and grammar concepts.

• **Teaching All Students** features numerous creative ideas to address different types of students.

• **Block Scheduling Suggestions** at point-of-use help teachers vary and streamline their lessons.

MOTIVATE TO COMMUNICATE
¡En español!

Cultural References

Note: *Page numbers in bold type refer to the Teacher's Edition.*

CULTURAL REFERENCES

¡En español!

INSERVICE WORKSHOPS

This section of your Teacher's Edition contains professional development materials for reference throughout the school year. You may also access www.mcdougallittell.com for additional information.

Making Block Work for You

Audrey L. Heining-Boynton
University of North Carolina
Chapel Hill, NC

Block scheduling provides simultaneous rewards and challenges for the foreign language educator. Whether using the 4×4 model, or the alternating days model, second language teachers are afforded the opportunity to bring to the forefront their creative spirits, and provide their students with activities that engage them in meaningful communication.

The Key to Successful Teaching

The key to any successful teaching is, as all teachers recognize, good planning. Well-planned, age-appropriate lessons that acknowledge and reinforce what the students already know about life and the world around them will captivate and motivate the students to acquire another language.

Other essential ingredients to a successful foreign language class include the incorporation of a balance between the skills of listening, speaking, reading and writing, and the American Council on the Teaching of Foreign Languages (ACTFL) five Cs of foreign language education: **communication, cultures, connections, comparisons,** and **communities.** (See pages T54–T55 for further information on Standards.)

Add to this mixture the final important element: a student-centered classroom where a variety of learning styles and multiple intelligences are utilized. Also, the research conclusively states that students learn best from other students. Hence, paired and cooperative learning activities, the backbone of a student-centered classroom, can abound. The role of teacher goes from that of center-stage actor (in a teacher-centered class) to that of award-winning director (in the student-centered class). The students reap the benefits by participating in meaningful activities in which they are able to put their new language knowledge to use.

Components and Strategies for Block Scheduling

So how do these components and strategies differ for block scheduling? They don't! The only difference is that concentrated time now exists for the teacher to bring together all of the curricular elements of the language "weave" into one longer class period. Also, block scheduling allows teachers to plan a consistent incorporation of critical thinking skills, interdisciplinary connections, communication and learning strategies, and technology along with listening, speaking, reading, writing, and culture.

A concern with block scheduling is that some teachers perceive that drastic changes must be made in the delivery of their classes, when in fact, if they already provide student-centered instruction, few modifications need to be made. The notion of a fast-paced class with a wide variety of activities still holds true. The "ten minute rule," that is, that few activities should go on for more than ten minutes, must continue to drive lesson planning. *¡En español!* gives special Block Schedule hints and activities on every page of the Teacher's Edition, as well as a set of expanded Block Scheduling Copymasters and sample Block Schedule Lesson Plans for every Etapa.

Another important issue for block scheduling is that students should spend the majority of their foreign language classes actively engaged in language-producing activities. Since the vast majority of students will have the opportunity to use the second language in a speaking context upon graduating from high school, practicing speaking should be the priority of the block scheduled language class. The more the teacher can create an immersion setting for speaking the language, the more orally proficient the students have the potential to become.

Block Schedule

Change of Pace Have students sign up for the day when they will be the weather forecaster. Each day a different student will start class with the day, date, season, temperature, and weather report.

Block Schedule

Variety Divide the class into small groups. Give each group a season. Groups must devise a visual (collage, poster, mural, diorama, brochure, etc.) to represent their season.

Block Schedule

Peer Teaching Have pairs of students work together to compile a list of the key words used in the reading. Then have them make flashcards of the words and quiz each other. In addition, they could work together to write original sentences using the words.

Incremental Spiraling in the Block

Perhaps one of the biggest advantages of block scheduling is that it allows teachers to move more naturally from controlled to transitional to open-ended communicative exercises, and to incorporate higher-order thinking skills more readily. Block scheduling allows teachers in one class period to see the incremental spiraling of their students' ability to function in the language. The *¡En español!* Teacher's Edition helps teachers identify activity objectives and track the incremental development and practice of skills.

When planning lessons for block scheduling, the checklist below can be used to record the components included in your lessons. Do you have a balance?

✔ BLOCK SCHEDULING COMPONENT CHECKLIST	
☐ **Language system**	☐ **Communication**
☐ listening	☐ **Cultures**
☐ speaking	☐ **Connections**
☐ reading	
☐ writing	☐ **Comparisons**
☐ culture	☐ **Communities**
☐ **Cultural knowledge**	Other lesson planning
☐ **Communication strategies**	components to take into consideration are:
☐ **Critical thinking skills**	☐ **Student-centered class**
☐ **Learning strategies**	☐ **Peer teaching**
☐ **Other subject areas**	☐ **The ten minute "rule"**
☐ **Technology**	

Block scheduling offers students extended practice in meaningful contexts that encourages the acquisition of Spanish. The *¡En español!* program gives teachers the added support that develops a smooth adaptation to Block Schedule and continued success and enjoyment as it "makes the Block work for *you*."

Addressing the Standards in Your Teaching

Ann Tollefson
Natrona County Schools
Caspar, WY

UNIDAD 3
Cultural Opener

Unit Theme
Living in and visiting Puerto Rico, discussing weather, and participating in leisure activities

Communication
- Expressing feelings and emotions
- Discussing what just happened
- Talking on the telephone
- Discussing sports
- Talking about clothes and accessories
- Describing the weather
- Stating preferences and opinions

Cultures
- Learning about regional vocabulary
- Learning about leisure activities in Puerto Rico
- Learning about the history, geography, and wildlife of Puerto Rico
- Learning about some important people from Puerto Rico

Connections
- Connecting to Music: Music and dance in Puerto Rico and in the U.S.
- Connecting to Science: Using the Celsius scale in Spanish-speaking countries and learning the conversion formula

Comparisons
- Comparing music and dance in Puerto Rico and in the U.S.
- Comparing sports traditions in Puerto Rico with sports traditions in the U.S.
- Comparing tourist attractions in Puerto Rico and in the U.S.

Communities
- Using Spanish for personal interest
- Using Spanish to help others

¡En español!, the Spanish program you have selected for your classroom and students, will help you integrate the national Standards for Foreign Language Learning into your Spanish program. It reflects what we know about best practices and has been reviewed by classroom teachers across the country. Like you, they are excited, and a little nervous, about the times in which the profession finds itself, times rife with changes, challenges and opportunities!

The Standards: Essential Knowledge and Skills

Consider the national Standards. For the first time in the history of the profession, we have reached general consensus on the essential knowledge and skills that students progressing through our programs should be able to demonstrate.

The Standards suggest best practices and new pedagogical approaches that will help our students reach higher degrees of facility and competence in a language, but in no way do they imply that classroom teachers should discard everything they have done in the past. Rather, they encourage us to examine what we do in light of the skills and knowledge we have agreed our students should demonstrate, to weave together the best of the new with the best of what we already know. Without implying that we must begin all over again, they suggest to us proven approaches that may improve the opportunities and experiences we offer our students.

Empowering Teachers

In essence we have empowered ourselves as language teachers. With the Standards, we have together established a measure against which we as individual teachers can measure our own programs and students.

With that common vision we have achieved three major milestones in the profession: 1) we are better able to build programs that we know will allow our students to compare favorably with their counterparts across the nation; 2) students going from one program to another will be more likely to succeed because we as a profession can more realistically expect to be working toward similar measures of achievement; 3) we have some consensus to help us as we design and implement extended sequences of study. Now that we know what the destination is, we are better able to design programs to help our students to get there!

Successful Learning Contexts

In addition, the Standards have defined the contexts within which successful language learning occurs. Language teachers have always known that learning another language is far more than mastering a body of words and the rules that tell us how to combine them in a meaningful manner. But describing and communicating the "more" is something with which we have struggled.

In addressing this issue, the Standards have enabled us to come to agreement on the goals and context that give life to those words and rules. The five goals of Communication, Culture, Connections, Comparisons, and Communities have given us a common framework within which to design significant, challenging language experiences for our students.

Consensus: Goals and Products

Teachers now have a number of tools that have never before been available. With both the Standards for Learning Spanish and the generic national Standards we have achieved an important objective: Spanish teachers are no longer faced with the task of deciding independently what the goals and products of each program should be. They are now free to tailor and adapt what we have agreed upon as a profession to what they know about their own schools and students. The new Standards for Heritage Language Speakers go a step further, providing teachers a tool to help them adapt classroom instruction to the needs and abilities of students for whom the Spanish language is part of their cultural heritage.

Teaching Today

Where do we find ourselves as language teachers in the profession today? What is happening to make our jobs easier, to free us to be more creative, to help us become more effective teachers?

With the publication of the national Standards, we have established together what we want for our students: "Knowing how, when and why to say what to who" in the languages we teach. We have agreed upon what our students should know and be able to do at several steps in their sequence of language study.

We are learning together as a profession, working together to build new and ever more effective programs like ¡En español!

Further, with the ACTFL Proficiency Guidelines for K-12 Learners we have defined how well our students should be able to achieve those standards. Currently, an anthology of assessments for the Standards is being field-tested nationally.

Classroom teachers now have standard guidelines for how well students should be able to meet them, and sample measurements to see whether or not they have indeed done so. Yet nowhere is there any suggestion that there is only one instructional approach. How we adapt the Standards and assessments to our own classrooms and students is rightly left to us as professionals.

¡En español! and the Standards

¡En español! was designed to help your students meet the national Standards while offering you the same freedom to choose among and to tailor any number of instructional approaches. Each Unit Opener in your Teacher's Edition shows you how the instructional material was written directly to the Standards, leaving you the choice of individualizing to meet your own students' needs.

What might we consider as we revisit and enliven teaching and learning in our programs? Surely, we may want to consider redesigning assessments as we redesign instruction, developing more holistic assessments that reflect changing practices and expectations for students. *¡En español!* presents a wide variety of assessment options, as well as point-of-use assessment rubrics in your Teacher's Edition.

The Standards movement is a process: there is no one expert to tell us how to transform our classrooms into magical places where all students will effortlessly master the Spanish language. In fact, we are the experts, the professionals best equipped to design instruction for our own classrooms and for our own students. The Standards challenge us to continually revisit and refine the experiences and opportunities we offer our students.

What Exciting Times!

We are learning together as a profession, working together to build new and ever more effective programs like *¡En español!,* yet providing individual teachers the tools and freedom to tailor best practices to their own classrooms. Stay tuned—it is only going to get better!

Integrating Technology in the Language Classroom: A Common-Sense Approach

Willard A. Heller, Jr.
Perry Junior High School
Perry, NY

Language teachers have always been pioneers in using the latest technology to enhance the effectiveness of instruction. The language labs of the sixties were the first large scale integration of a subject curriculum and the latest available technology. Time is the most valuable resource for the language teacher. Language teachers continue to recognize the value of using instructional technology to maximize the effective use of class time.

Teaching Resource Options

Audiovisual

OHT 93, 94, 95, 95A, 96, 96A, 99 (Quick Start)
Audio Program Cassette 9A / CD 9
Audio *Para hispanohablantes* Cassette 9A / CD 9
Video Program Videotape 3 / Videodisc 2A

Search Chapter 6, Play to 7
U3E3 • En contexto (Vocabulary)

Technology

Intrigas y aventuras
CD-ROM, Disc 1

Why Use A Variety of Instructional Technologies?

There are many compelling reasons to motivate the classroom teacher to use a wide variety of technologies. Aside from making most efficient use of class time, judiciously selected computer and multimedia technology can help the language teacher:

- Address multiple learning styles, intelligences and preferences
- Provide variety and interest to the language learning experience
- Encourage multiple repetitions of content in different contexts
- Obtain current cultural information
- Facilitate communication by language learners with classmates and peers

Audiovisual Technology

For many years, language teachers have successfully and skillfully incorporated audiovisual technology into lessons to enrich the learning experience. These "older" technologies still can serve the learning goals of the language classroom.

Overhead Projector Overhead transparencies can be used to introduce vocabulary, practice listening comprehension, and prompt speaking and writing tasks. Students can use overhead transparencies to narrate stories or to summarize readings from the text. The *¡En español!* Overhead Transparencies also contain situational transparencies, maps, fine art, and even graphic organizers.

Audio Program Cassettes/CDs Audio can offer students a sampling of the wide variety of accents and dialects among native speakers in many authentic contexts. Student presentations and dialogues can be taped for diagnosis, instruction, assessment, and portfolios. The *¡En español!* Audio Program contains activities, dialogs, and recorded readings as well as an additional native speaker component.

Videotapes/Videodiscs Video can enhance the listening experience by offering visual cues to the listener and by supplying a culturally authentic setting and context for the language. See the *¡En español!* Videotapes, Videodiscs, and Video Activities.

Video Cameras Student pair and group activities can be recorded. Playing back student work gives a chance to develop listening comprehension and can be used to provide feedback on fluency, accuracy, pronunciation, and accent. These video presentations are also perfect for Parents' Night!

Language Labs Technological advances have transformed the hard-wired language laboratory of the sixties into a flexible solution for meeting the varied needs of learners. In addition to supplying listening practice, language labs allow teachers to monitor and record individual responses to recorded cues. Many modern language labs allow the teacher to pair or group students for participation in dialogs.

Computer Technology

Computers are becoming more commonly available in the classroom and in laboratory settings. They are valuable in giving the type of individualized repetition and feedback necessary to build confidence in language learners. As availability increases, language teachers will be able to more easily integrate this technology into lessons. The most useful applications include:

CD-ROM Programs Compact discs can hold the quantity of programming necessary to be able to provide interactive multimedia practice for listening, reading, speaking and writing, as well as grammar and vocabulary drill and practice. The *¡En español! Intrigas y aventuras* CD-ROM program offers lesson-specific practice in an engaging, student-friendly format.

Integrated Software Word processing, spreadsheet, and page layout software can be used as a tool for students to share writing, research results, and cultural information with classmates.

Presentation Software Students can create their own multimedia presentations in the target language, incorporating text, graphics, sound, and video.

The Internet offers abundant opportunity to take language learning beyond the walls of the classroom and the borders of the community.

Program-specific Software Test Generators and Electronic Teacher Tools, such as those in the *¡En español!* program, allow teachers to individualize assessment and ancillaries to suit the needs of their own classrooms.

Internet Resources

The Internet offers abundant opportunity to take language learning beyond the walls of the classroom and the borders of the community. There are several significant uses of the Internet.

E-mail and "Key Pals" Instant worldwide communication encourages frequent exchanges between Internet pen pals, commonly called "key pals." Many websites and resources are available to connect students with Spanish-speaking pen pals.

World Wide Web The World Wide Web provides a vast source of reading material containing the most up-to-the-minute cultural information and authentic documents in the target language. Newspapers, national and regional tourist offices, and museums have rich websites and provide a good starting place for Internet exploration.

The *¡En español!* website offers program participants a forum for exchanging ideas and additional support and information on a wide variety of topics. (See page T64 for more information.)

 www.mcdougallittell.com

Technology and Professional Enrichment

Technology can also be a valuable tool for individual teachers to continue to develop as scholars of the target language and culture and as classroom practitioners. Particularly through the vast resources of the World Wide Web, teachers can stay current with cultural and linguistic developments in the target culture. Newspapers on the Internet can help the language teacher keep up with current events in target culture countries. In addition, reading popular resources can provide insights into current vocabulary and usage.

Participation in e-mail Mailing Lists (called LISTSERVs) allow the language teacher to contribute to and learn from a worldwide community of L2 educators. One such moderated listserv is FLTEACH. (FLTEACH@LISTSERV.ACSU.BUFFALO.EDU) E-mail messages posted to the list are distributed to each member of the list. Members of the list represent all levels of L2 instruction all over the country and all over the world. Through active participation in the list, participants can discuss current pedagogical issues and share information on all aspects of language instruction. [For more information about this listserv, contact the moderators of the list at FLTEACH@SNYCORVA.CORTLAND.EDU or see page T64.]

Classroom Delivery

The manner in which technology is available is as varied as the technology itself. Teacher-directed lessons can be enriched through incorporation of audiovisual and computer technology to prompt or reinforce vocabulary development or grammar skills, to promote skill building in speaking, listening, reading, and writing, or to deepen cross-cultural understanding. Any phase of a lesson can be enhanced with the use of carefully selected instructional media. When using instructional technology, always (1) give a purpose and strategy for each listening or viewing and (2) provide a way for students to respond to content. The response can be providing non-verbal cues, answering questions, or giving a summary.

Learning Stations can be set up to exploit limited technological resources. Small groups of students can rotate through various activities over the course of one or more classes. Activities can include:

Listening Station Tapes, headsets, and response sheets are available to complete directed listening or music activities.

Computer Station Even one computer in a classroom can be used by a small group to use a CD-ROM, to produce a graph of survey results, to create a newsletter or advertisement integrating text and graphics, or to compose a story.

Games Station Students can play commercial or teacher-made games to reinforce Etapa vocabulary or grammar patterns.

Realia Station Guided reading of posters, city plans, tour brochures or other authentic documents related to the Etapa theme can be done.

Speaking Station Group speaking tasks or prepared dialogs can be recorded for feedback and evaluation.

Puzzle Station Crossword puzzles, word finds, scavenger hunts, and other creative practice activities can be completed.

Cooperative Learning Group activities, projects or productions can incorporate technology by using presentation or page layout software; videotaping, audio taping with sound effects; overhead transparencies or visual aids to liven presentations in the target language.

Language or Computer Lab The entire class can engage in projects using Internet resources, presentation software, word processing and page layout software. Within the lab setting, it is still possible to offer considerable creativity, flexibility, and individualization of student responses.

Planning for the widest possible variety of carefully selected technology resources can maximize the use of scarce class time, increase active involvement of students, address individual needs, and motivate curiosity about the target culture. The *¡En español!* program resources (see pages T8–T9) help both students and teachers easily integrate technology into the learning experience and successfully adapt to varied learning styles and ability levels.

Strategies for Foreign Language Learning

Estella Gahala
Albuquerque, NM

As foreign language educators have reached out to increase numbers of foreign language students, there has been recognition of the need to expand effective instruction. Learners have many different ways of learning. Our well-crafted instruction is a net in which we hope to catch them all, but capable students can sometimes elude our best efforts. How shall we teach different types of students?

One Source of Success

A series of research studies has direct bearing on the question: What distinguishes successful learners of another language from unsuccessful ones? Success is measured by performance in the five skills. Findings include:

- Differences among students are less evident at low-levels of proficiency. As competence increases, more differences emerge. A major difference is in their personal strategies for learning.

- Successful students have a larger repertory of strategies. They start with "top-down" strategies ("What is the gist?") and resort to "bottom-up" strategies ("What does the word mean?") when completely stymied.

- Unsuccessful students have a smaller repertory of strategies. They start with "bottom-up" strategies and give up more quickly.

Feedback revealed an impressive array of student-initiated strategies, including memory strategies, cognitive strategies, compensation strategies, metacognitive strategies, affective strategies, and social strategies. Students are inventive in how they learn, including incorporating personal experience and learning from other students.

Definition of Strategies

A strategy is a plan, step, or series of actions toward achievement of a goal. Rebecca Oxford's[1] comprehensive work on language learning strategies

---

PARA LEER
STRATEGY: READING
Scan Reading very quickly to get a specific piece of information, like a football score or a movie time, is called scanning. Scan this poster and decide whether Ignacio and Roberto c...

PARA CONVERSAR
STRATEGY: SPEAKING
Use your tone to convey meaning Words alone do not reveal meaning. Your tone of voice makes a difference. In both your invitations and answers, express different feelings (happy, nervous, ... etc.).

PARA CONOCERNOS
STRATEGY: CONNECTING CULTURES
Reflect on sports traditions Can you think of any sports in the U.S. that have players from other countries? What sports are they? Are some countries associated with certain sports more than others? Why do you think that might be true? Use this chart to organize your answers.

Deporte	País 1	País 2	País 3
el béisbol	Cuba	Japón	
el hockey	Canadá	Rusia	

...A ESCUCHAR • STRATEGY: LISTENING
...for a purpose Listening for specific information is like ...ning when reading. Practice listening for one idea. What ...e exact day and time of an ...ortant event for Ignacio? ...y is it important?

El evento	El día	La hora

PARA ESCRIBIR • STRATEGY: WRITING
Appeal to the senses A well-constructed poster will entice people to attend the party. One way to do so is to include details that appeal to the senses: sight (la vista), hearing (el oído), touch (el tacto), taste (el gusto), and smell (el ofato).

explains how strategies help the classroom teacher become more collaborative with students in the teaching/learning process. Strategies are learner centered. They provide the means to acquire, store, retrieve, and use information. But they also have an emotional connection to learning, making it easier, faster, more enjoyable, more self-directed, more effective, and more transferable to new situations. Otherwise stated, strategies are a significant component of brain-compatible learning.

¡En español!: A Strategic Approach to Learning

¡En español! students encounter strategies as they begin the task of comprehending, communicating, and developing cultural knowledge and awareness. Strategies are not *the* way, but rather *a* way of going about the task. As learners progress, they gain exposure to a full repertory of strategies. Teachers encourage students to reflect on what helps and what doesn't and to exchange ideas on what works best. Such metacognition empowers the teacher to be strategic in the selection of activities and validates successful learning efforts. The teacher can thus select appropriate steps to increase student learning based on a new understanding of student needs.

Strategies for Receiving and Comprehending Language

Listening and reading have in common these characteristics: (a) prior knowledge improves comprehension, (b) the general idea is often sufficient for comprehension, (c) different purposes permit different strategies, (d) authentic input through listening and reading is essential in developing communicative competence.

A major difference is that one can reread a text and extract knowledge through contextual guessing and cognates; whereas opportunities to re-listen may be outside students' control, and recognition of cognates is less likely in listening than in reading.

Listening Listening strategies initially focus on *oral features:* intonation indicating a question or a command, or sounds and short words meaning "Now it's my turn to speak." Throughout Levels 1 and 2, listeners deal with *content:* get the gist, identify related details, sequence events, sort

information. Occasionally they are asked to borrow language relating to useful expressions and social formulas. Gradually they use graphic organizers in *higher order thinking* to organize details, compare two situations, make inferences. Level 3 listening strategies focus on real-world tasks like listening to a music awards show, debates on environmental issues, or job interviews. The strategy activates listener knowledge, focuses on key aspects of the text, then prompts reflection upon their opinions. Periodically, across levels, students *recombine strategies* for a familiar task such as listening to a vacation guide or a lecture in science class.

Reading Reading strategies contain many parallels. Learners *anticipate and predict content* by examining graphics, visuals, or titles. They use skimming and scanning techniques. Attention is directed to the *organization* of the reading text: main ideas, related details, sequence, various narrative devices. They also *recombine strategies.* Graphic organizers guide them in managing larger amounts of text. A major thrust of Level 3 strategies is to build toward reading literature: coping with complicated time sequences, complex sentence structure, and metaphoric texts.

Strategies for Producing and Communicating with Language

Listening gives models of oral language for speaking; reading gives models for writing. Students write what they can say, but since more class time is often spent on writing activities, sometimes their writing may be more polished than their speech.

Speaking A well-known survey of adults reveals that many are extremely afraid of public speaking. We have all had students who seemed to reflect comparable feelings. Before deciding what to say and constructing it with vocabulary, grammar, and pronunciation, they have emotional and social hurdles to leap. So those are the first strategies. *Attitudinal or emotional strategies* urge them not to be afraid of making mistakes, to think positively, take risks, take time, improvise. *Social strategies* show them how to work with others, encourage others, negotiate, brainstorm. With the right mind-set, they can comfortably use the *functional strategies* to express preferences, agree, disagree, encourage, persuade,

describe, give advice, borrow and use set expressions, summarize, circumlocute, and use story-telling techniques. Examples or models guide them.

Writing Because novice and intermediate learners write the way they speak, they can apply functional speaking strategies to informal writing activities in *En tu propia voz*. The linguistic elements are the same: spelling is added, and they have more time for reflection, organization, and correction of their postcards, posters, and personal communication.

¡En español! has a carefully sequenced and developmentally appropriate process writing strand that gives students step-by-step instruction in producing a polished finished product. Writing strategies help students to approach their writing tasks in a creative and intelligent fashion, encouraging both individual and group work.

Study Hints *Apoyos para estudiar* focus on difficulties that arise in contrasts between English and Spanish. Students are unaccustomed to thinking about the structure of language and using terms like gender, verb conjugations, and interrogatives. The novice learner gets useful tips about how to practice, to learn, and to remember. In addition, *apoyos* help all learners connect new structures to familiar concepts. *Apoyos* provide a bridge of support between study-friendly grammar explanations and language use in learning activities.

Interrelationships among the linguistic strategies influence each learner's journey toward communicative competence. Yet why learn another language if not to communicate with its speakers and appreciate the richness of their culture? This interrelationship of language and culture is an important aspect of the *¡En español!* program.

Culture Culture is interwoven and embedded throughout *¡En español!* The section *En colores* brings learners into direct contact with practices, products, and perspectives of Spanish-speaking cultures. Our students are scarcely aware that they themselves live in a culture; they perceive their culture as the norm and all else as "weird." As beginners develop intercultural sensitivities, they first recognize the cultural topic in their own milieu, reflect upon it, then explore it in the target culture. Emphasis is on similarities before observing differences. Observe ourselves and then observe "other." In the light of "other," we reexamine self.

Food is one of the most powerful purveyors of cultural experience. One reading is about *tapas* in Spain.

The strategy reminds students that fast food chains are a US invention being exported to other countries. They are to think of their favorite one and make personal responses to questions about the foods that are served, reasons for going there, and with whom they go. After reading about *tapas,* they are asked to compare the two eating experiences and then speculate on how the two young Spaniards in the story might feel on a first trip to our student's favorite fast food restaurant. In a post-reading activity, they bring language and culture together in a role-play set in a restaurant where they order *tapas.* The strategy is the first step in opening students to a new experience and developing sensitivity about it. Students begin to understand and appreciate the new culture from an "insider" rather than an "outsider" perspective.

Benefits of Strategic Learning

Student strategies for learning are introspective and not easily observed. By making students aware of different approaches to learning, they become more self-directed and more successful. Because strategies involve social, emotional, reflective, and cognitive dimensions of learning, the whole person is involved and supported in the learning process. Direct teaching of strategies provides the teacher with more diagnostic tools to use in problem solving with students. This problem-solving approach reflects and respects individuality. Everyone benefits by sharing insights and experiences, by building a repertory of learning and strategies, and by building confidence.

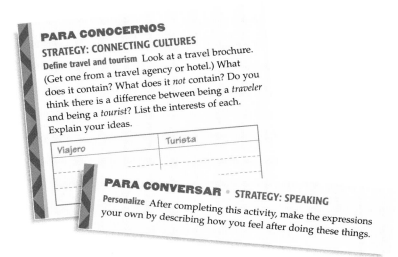

PARA CONOCERNOS
STRATEGY: CONNECTING CULTURES
Define travel and tourism Look at a travel brochure. (Get one from a travel agency or hotel.) What does it contain? What does it *not* contain? Do you think there is a difference between being a *traveler* and being a *tourist*? List the interests of each. Explain your ideas.

Viajero	Turista

PARA CONVERSAR · STRATEGY: SPEAKING
Personalize After completing this activity, make the expressions your own by describing how you feel after doing these things.

[1] Oxford, Rebecca. (1990). *Language Learning Strategies: What Every Teacher Should Know.* New York, NY: Newbury House.

Professional Bibliography and Additional Resources

Audrey L. Heining-Boynton
University of North Carolina
Chapel Hill, NC

Part of being a dedicated teacher is committing to life-long learning, keeping abreast of the latest trends and issues. What follows is a synthesis of a variety of texts and articles that will provide you with a starting point to explore pertinent issues and "hot topics," such as: *At-risk Students, Assessment, Culture and Multiculturalism, Foreign Language Standards, Second Language Acquisition, Classroom Management, Multiple Intelligences, and Block Scheduling.*

At-risk Students

• *Readings from Educational Leadership: Students At Risk.* Edited by Ronald S. Brandt (1990). Alexandria, VA: Association for Supervision and Curriculum Development.

For anyone who wants a thorough overview of the problem of at-risk students, this collection of readings is the place to begin. *Educational Leadership,* one of the finest journals for all K-12 teachers, compiles books that are collections of articles from previous editions, and this edition combines over forty articles on this topic.

• Heining-Boynton, A. (1994). "The At-Risk Student in the Foreign Language Classroom." In *Meeting New Challenges in the Foreign Language Classroom.* Edited by Gale K. Crouse. Lincolnwood, IL: National Textbook Company.

This article provides a review of the literature regarding at-risk students, and then provides teaching techniques on how best to meet the needs of these special students.

Assessment

• Herman, J.L., Aschbacher, P.R. and Winters, L. (1992). *A Practical Guide to Alternative Assessment.* Alexandria, VA: Association for Supervision and Curriculum Development.

This text provides teachers with ways to determine the purpose of assessment, select the tasks and set the criteria, ensure reliable scoring, and incorporate interdisciplinary factors in the equation.

• Marzano, R.J., Pickering, D. and McTighe, J. (1993). *Assessing Student Outcomes: Performance Assessment Using the Dimensions of Learning Model.* Alexandria, VA: Association for Supervision and Curriculum Development.

Beginning with a definition of how assessment standards are linked to the five dimensions of learning, the text offers suggestions on how teachers can assess and keep track of student performance.

• Moeller, A. (1994). "Portfolio Assessment: A Showcase for Growth and Learning in the Foreign Language Classroom." In *Meeting New Challenges in the Foreign Language Classroom.* Edited by Gale K. Crouse. Lincolnwood, IL: National Textbook Company.

This article offers a rationale for the process of portfolio assessment and provides a step-by-step method for foreign language teachers to include this as a holistic component to their instruction and assessment.

• *Teaching, Testing, and Assessment: Making the Connection.* (1994). Northeast Conference Reports. Editor, Charles Hancock. Lincolnwood, IL: National Textbook Company.

Besides an overview of conceptualization that connects teaching, testing, and assessment, the chapters offer ideas for assessing all language skills in a variety of ways.

Culture and Multiculturalism

• Noble, J. and Lacasa, J. (1995). *The Hispanic Way.* Lincolnwood, IL: Passport Books.

This small books provides cultural/sociological information on a variety of topics that encompass the attitudes, behavior, and customs of the Spanish-speaking world.

• Richard-Amato, P. and Snow, M. (1992). *The Multicultural Classroom.* White Plains, NY: Longman.

An overview of why we teach culture.

• *Newsweek en español, People en español, etc.*

A number of weekly and monthly publications exist to help Spanish teachers maintain a current knowledge of what is happening throughout the Spanish-speaking world. Publications like *Newsweek en español, People en español,* and daily newspapers from the countries that can be accessed on the WWW are with news from Spanish-speaking countries. Another excellent resource is *National Geographic.*

• *Teaching Tolerance*

This free quarterly publication available from the Southern Poverty Law Center is an outstanding resource for teachers. Write to: Teaching Tolerance, 400 Washington Ave., Montgomery, AL 36014.

Foreign Language Standards

* *National Standards: A Catalyst for Reform.* Edited by Robert C. Lafayette. (1996). Lincolnwood, IL: National Textbook Company.

  This compendium looks at the foreign language standards and how they impact all aspects of foreign language teaching.

* *Standards for Foreign Language Learning: Preparing for the 21st Century.* (1996). American Council on the Teaching of Foreign Languages, 6 Executive Plaza, Yonkers, NY.

  Foreign language teaching and learning is now organized by five principles known as the five C's of foreign language education: communication, cultures, connections, comparisons, and communities.

General Educational Issues

Block Scheduling

* Canady, R.L. & Rettig, M.D. (1995). *Block Scheduling: A catalyst for change in high schools.* Larchmont, NY: Eye on Education.
* Canady, R.L. & Rettig, M.D. (1996). *Teaching in the Block: Strategies for engaging active learners.* Larchmont, NY: Eye on Education.
* Cunningham, R. David. Jr. & Nogle, Sue Ann. (December 1996). "Six keys to block scheduling." *The High School Magazine*, 29-32.
* Elkins, G. (Spring 1996). "Making longer better: Staff development for block scheduling." Arlington, VA: ASCD Professional Development Newsletter.
* Gerking, Janet L. (April 1995). "Building block schedules: A firsthand assessment of restructuring the school day." *The Science Teacher*, 23–27.
* Hottenstein, D.S. (Winter 1996). "Supporting block scheduling: A response to critics." *Alliance* 1(2), 11. Reston, VA: The National Alliance of High Schools, a division of the National Association of Secondary School Principals.
* Wisconsin Association of Foreign Language Teachers. (1995). *Redesigning high school schedules: A report of the Task Force on Block Scheduling by the Wisconsin Association of Foreign Language Teachers.* Madison, WI: WAFLT (can be found on ERIC on the Internet).

Classroom Management

* Johnson, D. and Johnson, R. (1995). *Reducing School Violence Through Conflict Resolution.* Alexandria VA: Association for Supervision and Curriculum Development.

  This text discusses how to teach conflict resolution.

* Jones, F. (1987). *Positive Classroom Discipline.* New York, NY: McGraw Hill.

  Jones has foolproof ways to have the discipline and classroom management we all want and deserve.

* Kohn, A. (1996). *Beyond Discipline: From Compliance to Community.* Alexandria, VA: Association for Supervision and Curriculum Development.

  This text takes a new approach to classroom management/ discipline.

Multiple Intelligences

* Armstrong, Thomas. (1991). *Awakening Your Child's Natural Genius.* Los Angeles: Jeremy P. Tarcher, Inc.
* Armstrong, Thomas. (1987). *Discovering and Encouraging Your Child's Personal Learning Style.* Los Angeles: Jeremy P. Tarcher, Inc., Distributed by St. Martin's Press.
* Armstrong, Thomas. (1994). *Multiple Intelligences in the Classroom.* Alexandria, VA: Association for Supervision and Curriculum Development.
* Gardner, Howard. (1983). *Frames of Mind: The Theory of Multiple Intelligences.* New York, NY: Basic Books.
* Kline, Peter. (1988). *The Everyday Genius: Restoring Children's Natural Joy of Learing, and Your Too.* Arlington, VA: Great Ocean Puublishers.
* Lazear, David. *Seven Pathways of Learning: Teaching Students and Parents about Multiple Intelligences.* Zephyr Press, Tucson, Arizona, 1994.

Second Language Acquisition

* Krashen, S.D. and Terrell, T.D. (1983) *The Natural Approach: Language Acquisition in the Classroom.* Englewood Cliffs, NJ: Prentice-Hall.

  This text provides the philosophy and approach to teaching second language based on research in linguistics, psychology, and psycholinguistics. Its major concepts are the Input Hypothesis and the Affective Filter Hypothesis.

* Larsen-Freeman, D. and Long, M.H. (1992). *An Introduction to Second Language Acquisition Research.* New York, NY: Longman.

  A complete overview of second language theories, this is a sophisticated text that provides a lengthy bibliography and set of references for further investigation.

* *Research in language Learning: Principles, Processes and Prospects.* (1993) Editor, Alice Omaggio Hadley. Lincolnwood, IL: National Textbook Company.

  One of the series of ACTFL Foreign Language Education Series, this text is dedicated to research in language learning, and offers a variety of perspectives on language acquisition research and how it applies to the classroom.

* *TESOL Quarterly*

  This journal provides research articles on second language acquisition.

* Omaggio Hadley, A. (1993) *Teaching Language in Context.* Boston, MA: Heinle and Heinle.

  Omaggio Hadley's text sets the standard for a thorough exploration of the teaching of the four skills and references which are a good place to begin for anyone who wishes additional information on a given topic.

Additional Resources

There are many organizations that can provide a wealth of additional information and support for Spanish teachers. The list below will help you to expand your classroom resources and contact other teachers. Remember, however, that addresses and telephone numbers often change; it is advisable to verify them before sending inquiries.

Professional Organizations

The American Council on
  the Teaching of Foreign
  Languages (ACTFL)
6 Executive Plaza
Yonkers, NY 10701
(914) 963-8830
http://www.actfl.org/

American Association of
  Teachers of Spanish
  and Portuguese (AATSP)
Gunter Hall, Room 106
University of Northern Colorado
Greely, CO 80639
(303) 351-1090
http://www.aatsp.org/home.html/

Cultural Offices/Embassies/Consulates/Tourist Offices

Consult the telephone listings in most major cities for a listing of the embassies and consulates of Spanish-speaking countries closest to you.

Tourist Office of Spain
665 Fifth Avenue
New York, NY 10022
(212) 759-8822
http://www.okspain.org/

Mexican Government Tourist Office
2707 N. Loop West, Suite 450
Houston, TX 77008
(713) 880-5153
http://www.mexico-travel.com

Penpal Exchanges

Student Letter Exchange
  (League of Friendship)
630 Third Avenue
New York, NY 10017
(212) 557-3312

World Pen Pals
1694 Como Avenue
St. Paul, MN 55108
(612) 647-0191

Travel/Cultural Exchange

CIEE Student Travel Services
205 East 42nd St.
New York, NY 10017
(212) 661-1414
http://www.counciltravel.com/

American Field Service
220 East 42nd St., 3rd Floor
New York, NY 10017
(212) 949-4242
http://www.afs.org/usa/

Periodicals/Films

Subscriptions may be purchased for the school through the companies listed below, or through others in your local area:

EBSCO Subscription Services
P.O. Box 1943
Birmingham, AL 35201-1943

Gessler Publishing Company
55 West 13th St.
New York, NY 10011
(212) 627-0099

Continental Book Company
8000 Cooper Avenue Bldg. 29
Glendale, NY 11385
(718) 326-0572

The International Film Bureau
332 South Michigan Avenue
Chicago, IL 60604-4382
(312) 427-4545

Online Contacts

Many organizations now maintain websites. Since, again, these are subject to change, it is advisable to check before contacting. We encourage you to visit the McDougal Littell website for materials specific to the *¡En español!* program. In addition, FLTEACH provides an additional discussion forum for teacher exchange of ideas and information:

www.mcdougallittell.com

FLTEACH
To subscribe or obtain information:
  LISTSERV@listserv.acsu.buffalo.edu

In your message, put the following:
  SUBSCRIBE FLTEACH, first name, last name
  (to unsubscribe, send UNSUB FLTEACH,
  first name, last name)

To send messages to all FLTEACH subscribers:
  FLTEACH@listserv.acsu.buffalo.edu

1 *uno*

MCDOUGAL LITTELL

¡En español!

AUTHORS

Estella Gahala

Patricia Hamilton Carlin

Audrey L. Heining-Boynton

Ricardo Otheguy

Barbara J. Rupert

CULTURE CONSULTANT

Jorge A. Capetillo-Ponce

McDougal Littell
A HOUGHTON MIFFLIN COMPANY
Evanston, Illinois • Boston • Dallas

i

Cover Photography

Center: Large image taken in Mexico City by Martha Granger/EDGE Productions.

Bottom, from left to right: Aztec ceramic, Mexico, Dick Keen/Visuals Unlimited; Windmills in La Mancha, Spain, Michael Busselle/Tony Stone Images, Inc. (also on back cover); Painted wooden sculpture, Guatemala, Private Collection, Tom Holton/Superstock; Calle San Sebastián, Old San Juan, Puerto Rico, Martha Granger/EDGE Productions.

ISBN: 0-395-91081-1   1 2 3 4 5 6 7 8 9 - VJM - 05 04 03 02 01 99

Internet: www.mcdougallittell.com

CONTENIDO

OBJECTIVES

- Greet people
- Introduce yourself
- Say where you are from
- Exchange phone numbers
- Say which day it is

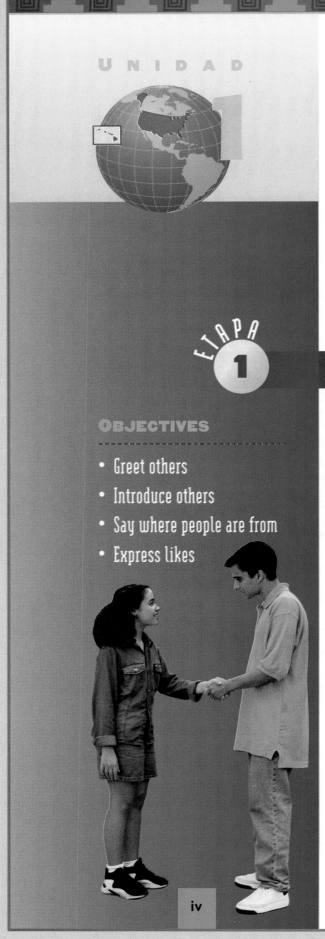

ESTADOS UNIDOS

MI MUNDO

Visit Miami, San Antonio, and Los Angeles with Francisco and his friend Alma.

ETAPA 1

OBJECTIVES

- Greet others
- Introduce others
- Say where people are from
- Express likes

ETAPA
2

OBJECTIVES

- Describe others
- Give others´ likes and dislikes
- Describe clothing

UNIDAD 1

ETAPA 3

OBJECTIVES

- Describe family
- Ask and tell ages
- Talk about birthdays
- Give dates
- Express possession

UNIDAD 2

ETAPA 1

OBJECTIVES

- Describe classes and classroom objects
- Say how often you do something
- Discuss obligations

CIUDAD DE MÉXICO
MÉXICO

UNA SEMANA TÍPICA

Explore exciting Mexico City with Isabel and Ricardo, two Mexican teenagers.

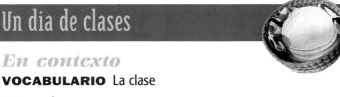

UNIDAD 2

ETAPA 2

¡Un horario difícil!　118

ETAPA 3

Mis actividades 140

OBJECTIVES

- Discuss plans
- Sequence events
- Talk about places and people you know

UNIDAD

SAN JUAN
PUERTO RICO
EL FIN DE SEMANA

Enjoy the weather and the landscape of Puerto Rico with three friends.

ETAPA **1**

OBJECTIVES

- Extend invitations
- Talk on the phone
- Express feelings
- Say where you are coming from
- Say what just happened

UNIDAD 3

ETAPA 2

OBJECTIVES

- Talk about sports
- Express preferences
- Say what you know
- Make comparisons

¡Deportes para todos! 190

¡Los deportes!
El baloncesto El voleibol
El fútbol americano El fútbol

xi

ETAPA
3

El tiempo en El Yunque   212

Puerto Rico
En su tamaño y color natural

OBJECTIVES

- Describe the weather
- Discuss clothing and accessories
- State an opinion
- Describe how you feel
- Say what is happening

OAXACA
MÉXICO

¡DE VISITA!

Enjoy regional handicrafts and food with Rosa, Carlos, and Sofía.

ETAPA
1

OBJECTIVES

- Identify places
- Give addresses
- Choose transportation
- Request directions
- Give instructions

ETAPA
2

OBJECTIVES

- Talk about shopping
- Make purchases
- Talk about giving gifts
- Bargain

UNIDAD 4

ETAPA 3

OBJECTIVES

- Order food
- Request the check
- Talk about food
- Express extremes
- Say where you went

¿Qué hacer en Oaxaca? 284

UNIDAD

5

BARCELONA
ESPAÑA

PREPARACIONES ESPECIALES

Have fun organizing a surprise birthday party for Luis.

ETAPA

1

OBJECTIVES

- Describe daily routine
- Talk about grooming
- Tell others to do something
- Discuss daily chores

OBJECTIVES

- Say what people are doing
- Persuade others
- Describe a house
- Negotiate responsibilities

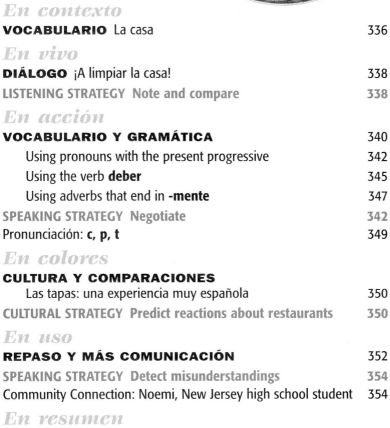

ETAPA
3

¡Qué buena celebración! 356

OBJECTIVES

- Plan a party
- Describe past activities
- Express extremes
- Purchase food

QUITO
ECUADOR

LA CIUDAD Y EL CAMPO

Compare life in the city to life in the countryside with Patricia, Miguel, and his family.

ETAPA
1

OBJECTIVES

- Tell what happened
- Make suggestions to a group
- Describe city buildings
- Talk about professions

UNIDAD 6

ETAPA 2

OBJECTIVES

* Point out specific people and things
* Tell where things are located
* Talk about the past

A conocer el campo 406

About the Authors

Estella Gahala holds a Ph.D. in Educational Administration and Curriculum from Northwestern University. A career teacher of Spanish and French, she has worked with a wide range of students at the secondary level. She has also served as foreign language department chair and district director of curriculum and instruction. Her workshops at national, regional, and state conferences as well as numerous published articles draw upon the current research in language learning, learning strategies, articulation of foreign language sequences, and implications of the national Standards for Foreign Language Learning upon curriculum, instruction, and assessment. She has coauthored six basal textbooks.

Patricia Hamilton Carlin completed her M.A. in Spanish at the University of California, Davis, where she also taught as a lecturer. She also holds a Master of Secondary Education with specialization in foreign languages from the University of Arkansas. She has taught preschool through college, and her secondary programs in Arkansas have received national recognition. A coauthor of the *¡DIME! UNO* and *¡DIME! DOS* secondary textbooks, she currently teaches Spanish and methodology at the University of Central Arkansas, where she also supervises student teachers. She is a frequent presenter at local, regional, and national foreign language conferences.

Audrey L. Heining-Boynton received her Ph.D. in Curriculum and Instruction from Michigan State University. She is a Professor of Education and Romance Languages at The University of North Carolina at Chapel Hill, where she is a second language teacher educator and Professor of Spanish. She has also taught Spanish, French, and ESL at the K–12 level. Dr. Heining-Boynton was the president of the National Network for Early Language Learning, has been on the Executive Council of ACTFL, and involved with AATSP, Phi Delta Kappa, and state foreign language associations. She has presented both nationally and internationally, and has published over forty books, articles, and curricula.

Ricardo Otheguy received his Ph.D. in Linguistics from the City University of New York, where he is currently Professor of Linguistics at the Graduate School and University Center. He has written extensively on topics related to Spanish grammar as well as on bilingual education, and the Spanish of the United States. He is coauthor of *Tu mundo: Curso para hispanohablantes,* a Spanish high school textbook for Spanish speakers, and of *Prueba de ubicación para hispanohablantes,* a high school Spanish placement test.

Barbara J. Rupert has taught Level 1 through A.P. Spanish during her many years of high school teaching. She is a graduate of Western Washington University, and has broadened her knowledge and skills base with numerous graduate level courses emphasizing language acquisition, authentic assessment, and educational leadership and reform. She serves as the World Languages Department Chair, District Trainer and Chair of her school's Site Council. Barbara is the author of CD-ROM activities for the *¡Bravo!* series and presents at a variety of foreign language conferences. In 1996, Barbara received the Christa McAuliffe Award for Excellence in Education.

Culture Consultant

Jorge A. Capetillo-Ponce is presently a Ph.D. candidate in Sociology at the New School for Social Research, where he is also Special Consultant to the Dean of The Graduate Faculty. His graduate studies at the New School and El Colegio de México include a diversity of fields such as international relations, sociopolitical analysis, cultural theory, and sociology. He has published a wide range of essays on art, politics, religion, international relations, and society in Latin America, the United States, and the Middle East; as well as being an advisor to a number of politicians and public figures, a researcher and editor, and a college professor and television producer in Mexico, Nicaragua, and the United States.

Consulting Authors

Dan Battisti
Patty Murguía Bohannan
Dr. Teresa Carrera-Hanley
Bill Lionetti
Lorena Richins Layser

Regional Language Reviewers

Dolores Acosta (Mexico)
Jaime M. Fatás Cabeza (Spain)
Grisel Lozano-Garcini (Puerto Rico)
Isabel Picado (Costa Rica)
Juan Pablo Rovayo (Ecuador)

Contributing Writers

Ronni L. Gordon
Christa Harris
Debra Lowry
Sylvia Madrigal Velasco
Sandra Rosenstiel
David M. Stillman
Jill K. Welch

Ad hoc Representatives

Vicki Armstrong
Jane Asano
Kathy Cavers
Dan Griffith
Rita McGuire
Gretchen Toole

Senior Reviewers

O. Lynn Bolton
Dr. Jane Govoni
Elías G. Rodríguez
Ann Tollefson

Teacher Reviewers

Susan Arbuckle
Mahomet-Seymour High School
Mahomet, IL

Silvia Armstrong
Mills High School
Little Rock, AR

Sandra Martín Arnold
Palisades Charter High School
Pacific Palisades, CA

Warren Bender
Duluth East High School
Duluth, MN

Adrienne Chamberlain-Parris
Mariner High School
Everett, WA

Norma Coto
Bishop Moore High School
Orlando, FL

Roberto del Valle
Shorecrest High School
Shoreline, WA

Rubén D. Elías
Roosevelt High School
Fresno, CA

José Esparza
Curie Metropolitan High School
Chicago, IL

Lorraine A. Estrada
Cabarrus County Schools
Concord, NC

Alberto Ferreiro
Harrisburg High School
Harrisburg, PA

Judith C. Floyd
Henry Foss High School
Tacoma, WA

Lucy H. García
Pueblo East High School
Pueblo, CO

Marco García
Lincoln Park High School
Chicago, IL

Raquel R. González
Odessa High School
Odessa, TX

Linda Grau
Shorecrest Preparatory School
St. Petersburg, FL

Deborah Hagen
Ionia High School
Ionia, MI

Sandra Hammond
St. Petersburg High School
St. Petersburg, FL

Bill Heller
Perry Junior/Senior High School
Perry, NY

Jody Klopp
Oklahoma State Department
of Education
Edmond, OK

Richard Ladd
Ipswich High School
Ipswich, MA

Carol Leach
Francis Scott Key High School
Union Bridge, MD

Laura McCormick
East Seneca Senior High School
West Seneca, NY

Rafaela McLeod
Southeast Raleigh High School
Raleigh, NC

Kathleen L. Michaels
Palm Harbor University
High School
Palm Harbor, FL

Vickie A. Mike
Horseheads High School
Horseheads, NY

Terri Nies
Mannford High School
Mannford, OK

María Emma Nunn
John Tyler High School
Tyler, TX

Lewis Olvera
Hiram Johnson West Campus
High School
Sacramento, CA

Anne-Marie Quihuis
Paradise Valley High School
Phoenix, AZ

Rita Risco
Palm Harbor University
High School
Palm Harbor, FL

James J. Rudy, Jr.
Glen Este High School
Cincinnati, OH

Pamela Urdal Silva
East Lake High School
Tarpon Springs, FL

Kathleen Solórzano
Homestead High School
Mequon, WI

Sarah Spiesman
Whitmer High School
Toledo, OH

M. Mercedes Stephenson
Hazelwood Central High School
Florissant, MO

Carol Thorp
East Mecklenburg High School
Charlotte, NC

Elizabeth Torosian
Doherty Middle School
Andover, MA

Wendy Villanueva
Lakeville High School
Lakeville, MN

Helen Webb
Arkadelphia High School
Arkadelphia, AR

Jena Williams
Jonesboro High School
Jonesboro, AR

Janet Wohlers
Weston Middle School
Weston, MA

Teacher Panel

Linda Amour
Highland High School
Bakersfield, CA

Dena Bachman
Lafayette Senior High School
St. Joseph, MO

Sharon Barnes
J. C. Harmon High School
Kansas City, KS

Ben Barrientos
Calvin Simmons
Junior High School
Oakland, CA

Paula Biggar
Sumner Academy of
Arts & Science
Kansas City, KS

Edda Cardenas
Blue Valley North High School
Leawood, KS

Joyce Chow
Crespi Junior High School
Richmond, CA

Mike Cooperider
Truman High School
Independence, MO

Judy Dozier
Shawnee Mission South
High School
Shawnee Mission, KS

Maggie Elliott
Bell Junior High School
San Diego, CA

Dana Galloway-Grey
Ontario High School
Ontario, CA

Nieves Gerber
Chatsworth Senior High School
Chatsworth, CA

Susanne Kissane
Shawnee Mission Northwest
High School
Shawnee Mission, KS

Ann Lopez
Pala Middle School
San Jose, CA

Beatrice Marino
Palos Verdes Peninsula
   High School
Rolling Hills Estates, CA

Barbara Mortanian
Tenaya Middle School
Fresno, CA

Vickie Musni
Pioneer High School
San Jose, CA

Rodolfo Orihuela
C. K. McClatchy High School
Sacramento, CA

Terrie Rynard
Olathe South High School
Olathe, KS

Beth Slinkard
Lee's Summit High School
Lee's Summit, MO

Rosa Stein
Park Hill High School
Kansas City, MO

Urban Panel

Rebecca Carr
William G. Enloe High School
Raleigh, NC

Norha Franco
East Side High School
Newark, NJ

Kathryn Gardner
Riverside University High School
Milwaukee, WI

Eula Glenn
Remtec Center
Detroit, MI

Jeana Harper
Detroit Fine Arts High School
Detroit, MI

Guillermina Jauregui
Los Angeles Senior High School
Los Angeles, CA

Lula Lewis
Hyde Park Career Academy
   High School
Chicago, IL

Florence Meyers
Overbrook High School
Philadelphia, PA

Vivian Selenikas
Long Island City High School
Long Island City, NY

Sadia White
Spingarn Stay Senior High School
Washington, DC

Block Scheduling Panel

Barbara Baker
Wichita Northwest High School
Wichita, KS

Patty Banker
Lexington High School
Lexington, NC

Beverly Blackburn
Reynoldsburg Senior High School
Reynoldsburg, OH

Henry Foust
Northwood High School
Pittsboro, NC

Gloria Hawks
A. L. Brown High School
Kannapolis, NC

Lois Hillman
North Kitsap High School
Poulsbo, WA

Nick Patterson
Central High School
Davenport, IA

Sharyn Petkus
Grafton Memorial High School
Grafton, MA

Cynthia Prieto
Mount Vernon High School
Alexandria, VA

Julie Sanchez
Western High School
Fort Lauderdale, FL

Marilyn Settlemyer
Freedom High School
Morganton, NC

Student Review Board

Andrea Avila
Fannin Middle School
Amarillo, TX

Maya Beynishes
Edward R. Murrow High School
Brooklyn, NY

James Dock
Guilford High School
Rockford, IL

Richard Elkins
Nevin Platt Middle School
Boulder, CO

Kathryn Finn
Charles S. Pierce Middle School
Milton, MA

Robert Foulis
Stratford High School
Houston, TX

Lorrain Garcia
Luther Burbank High School
Sacramento, CA

Katie Hagen
Ionia High School
Ionia, MI

Steven Hailey
Davis Drive School
Apex, NC

Eli Harel
Thomas Edison
   Intermediate School
Westfield, NJ

Cheryl Kim
Dr. Leo Cigarroa High School
Laredo, TX

Jennifer Kim
Kellogg Middle School
Seattle, WA

Jordan Leitner
Scripps Ranch High School
San Diego, CA

Courtney McPherson
Miramar High School
Miramar, FL

Zachary Nelson
Warsaw Community High School
Warsaw, IN

Diana Parrish
Oak Crest Junior High School
Encinitas, CA

Kimberly Robinson
Perryville Senior High School
Perryville, AR

John Roland
Mountain Pointe High School
Phoenix, AZ

Nichole Ryan
Bermudian Springs High School
York Springs, PA

Ryan Shore
West Miami Middle School
Miami, FL

Tiffany Stadler
Titusville High School
Titusville, FL

Michael Szymanski
West Seneca East High School
West Seneca, NY

Anela Talic
Soldan International Studies
   High School
St. Louis, MO

Gary Thompson
Fort Dorchester High School
Charleston, SC

Bethany Traynor
Glen Este High School
Cincinnati, OH

Gerard White
Paramount High School
Paramount, CA

Nichols Wilson
Waubonsie Valley High School
Aurora, IL

Amy Wyron
Robert Frost Intermediate School
Rockville, MD

Karina Zepeda
West Mecklenburg High School
Charlotte, NC

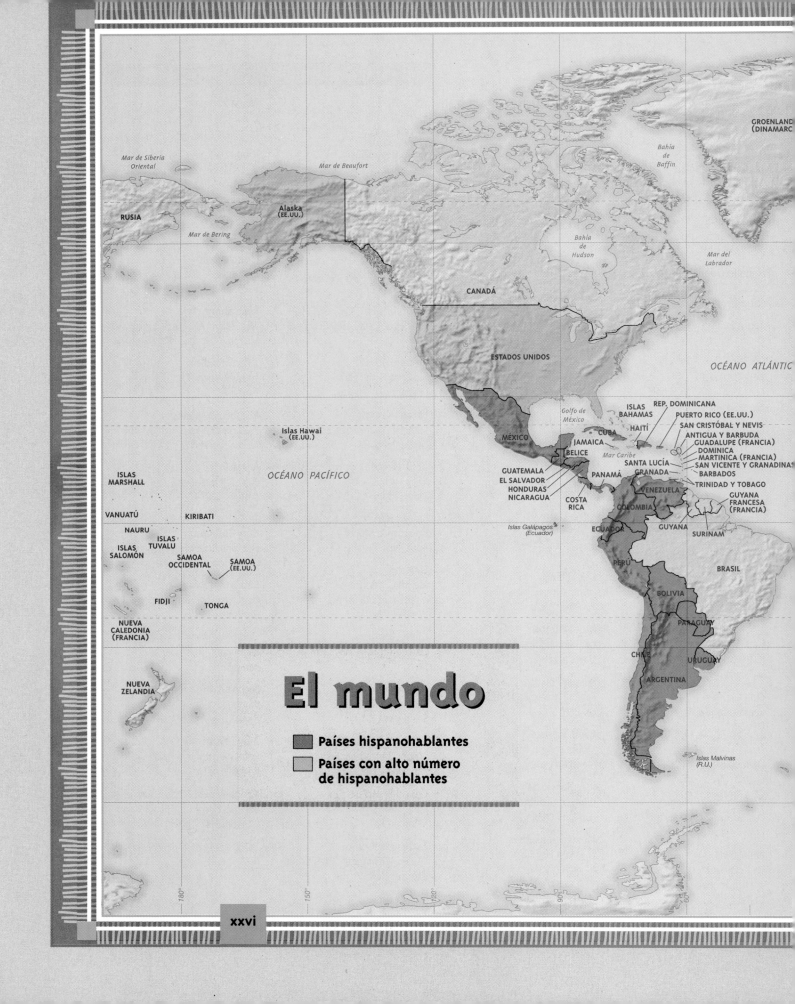

El mundo

- ⬛ Países hispanohablantes
- ⬜ Países con alto número de hispanohablantes

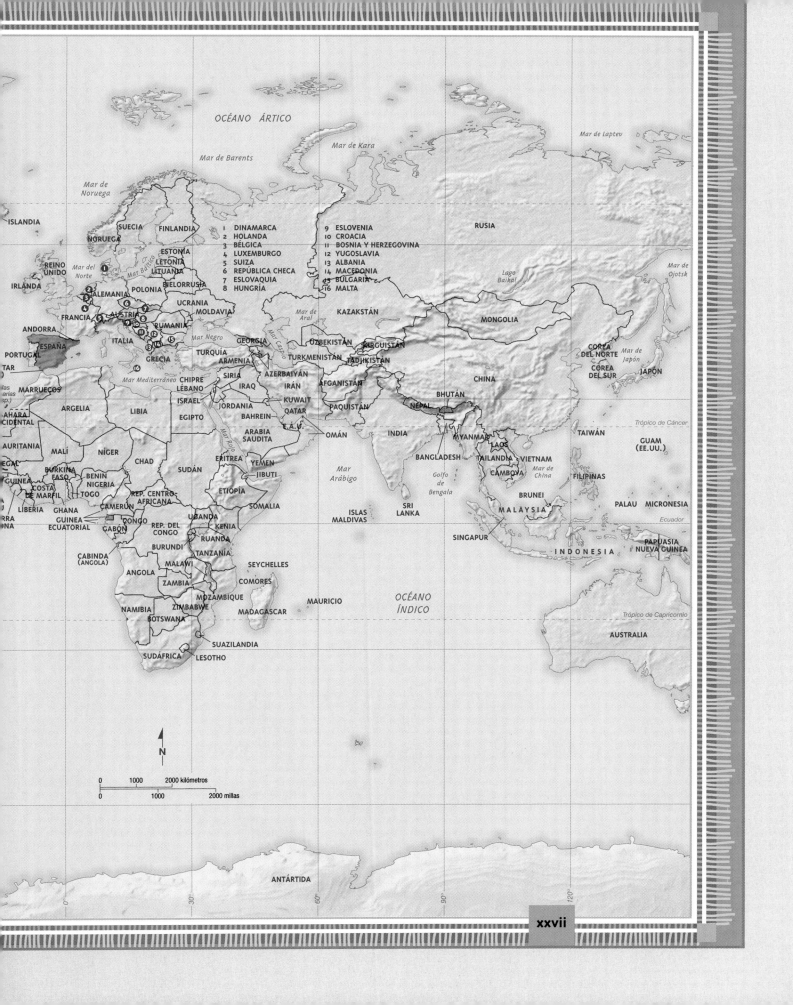

OCÉANO ÁRTICO

Mar de Laptev

Mar de Kara

Mar de Barents

Mar de
Noruega

ISLANDIA

RUSIA

Mar de
Ojotsk

SUECIA
FINLANDIA

1	DINAMARCA	9	ESLOVENIA
2	HOLANDA	10	CROACIA
3	BÉLGICA	11	BOSNIA Y HERZEGOVINA
4	LUXEMBURGO	12	YUGOSLAVIA
5	SUIZA	13	ALBANIA
6	REPÚBLICA CHECA	14	MACEDONIA
7	ESLOVAQUIA	15	BÚLGARIA
8	HUNGRÍA	16	MALTA

NORUEGA

REINO
UNIDO

Mar del
Norte

ESTONIA
LETONIA
LITUANIA

Mar Báltico

Lago
Baikal

MONGOLIA

KAZAKSTÁN

IRLANDA

ALEMANIA

POLONIA

BIELORRUSIA

COREA
DEL NORTE

Mar de
Japón

JAPÓN

FRANCIA

UCRANIA
MOLDAVIA

AUSTRIA

RUMANIA

Mar de
Aral

Mar Caspio

UZBEKISTÁN

KIRGUISTÁN

COREA
DEL SUR

ANDORRA

Mar Negro

ITALIA

GEORGIA

TURKMENISTÁN

TADJIKISTÁN

CHINA

ESPAÑA

GRECIA

TURQUÍA

ARMENIA

AZERBAIYÁN

AFGANISTÁN

PORTUGAL

Mar Mediterráneo

CHIPRE
LÉBANO

SIRIA

IRAQ

IRÁN

BHUTÁN

TAR

las
arias
sp.)

MARRUECOS

ISRAEL

JORDANIA

KUWAIT

QATAR

PAQUISTÁN

NEPAL

Trópico de Cáncer

ARGELIA

LIBIA

EGIPTO

BAHREIN

E.A.U.

OMÁN

INDIA

TAIWÁN

GUAM
(EE.UU.)

AHARA
CIDENTAL

ARABIA
SAUDITA

MYANMAR

AURITANIA

MALÍ

NÍGER

CHAD

ERITREA

YEMEN

Mar
Arábigo

BANGLADESH

LAOS

TAILANDIA

VIETNAM

Mar de
China

FILIPINAS

EGAL

SUDÁN

JIBUTI

Golfo
de
Bengala

CAMBOYA

BURKINA
FASO

GUINEA

BENIN
NIGERIA

REP. CENTRO-
AFRICANA

ETIOPÍA

BRUNEI

COSTA
DE MARFIL

TOGO

SRI
LANKA

MALAYSIA

PALAU

MICRONESIA

LIBERIA

GHANA

CAMERÚN

SOMALIA

ISLAS
MALDIVAS

rra

GUINEA
ECUATORIAL

CONGO

UGANDA

GABÓN

na

REP. DEL
CONGO

KENIA

Ecuador

SINGAPUR

INDONESIA

PAPUASIA
NUEVA GUINEA

BURUNDI

RUANDA

CABINDA
(ANGOLA)

TANZANIA

ANGOLA

MALAWI

ZAMBIA

SEYCHELLES

COMORES

MOZAMBIQUE

MAURICIO

OCÉANO
ÍNDICO

NAMIBIA

ZIMBABWE

BOTSWANA

MADAGASCAR

Trópico de Capricornio

AUSTRALIA

SUAZILANDIA

SUDÁFRICA

LESOTHO

N

0	1000	2000 kilómetros
0	1000	2000 millas

ANTÁRTIDA

30°

60°

90°

120°

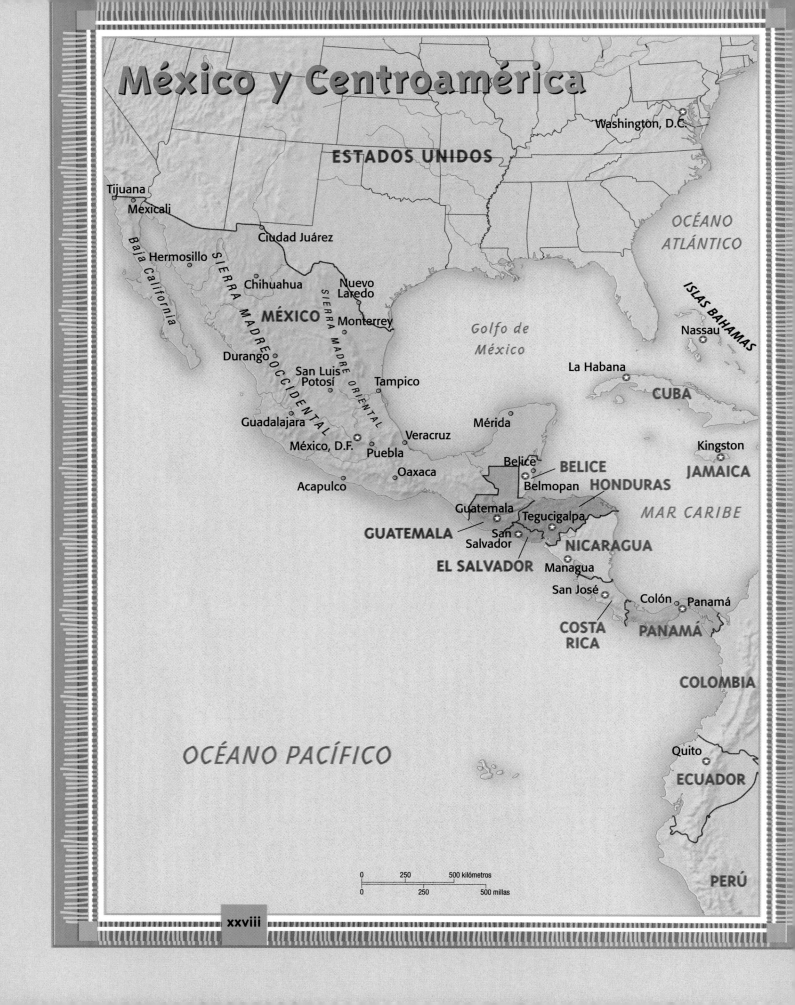

México y Centroamérica

ESTADOS UNIDOS

Washington, D.C.

OCÉANO ATLÁNTICO

Tijuana
Mexicali
Ciudad Juárez
Hermosillo
Chihuahua
Nuevo Laredo
Baja California
SIERRA MADRE OCCIDENTAL
SIERRA MADRE ORIENTAL
MÉXICO
Monterrey
Durango
San Luis Potosí
Tampico
Guadalajara
México, D.F.
Veracruz
Puebla
Oaxaca
Acapulco

Golfo de México

ISLAS BAHAMAS
Nassau

La Habana
CUBA

Mérida

Belice
BELICE
Belmopan
HONDURAS

Kingston
JAMAICA

MAR CARIBE

Guatemala
GUATEMALA
San Salvador
Tegucigalpa
EL SALVADOR
Managua
NICARAGUA

San José
COSTA RICA
Colón
Panamá
PANAMÁ

COLOMBIA

OCÉANO PACÍFICO

Quito
ECUADOR

PERÚ

0   250   500 kilómetros
0   250   500 millas

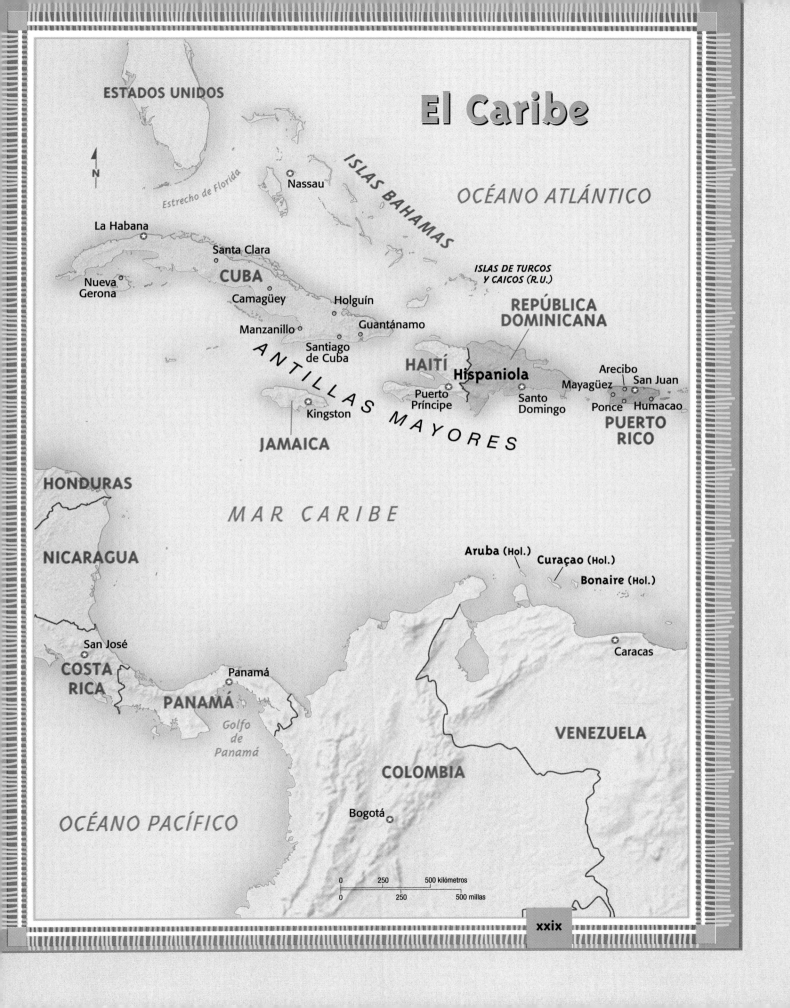

El Caribe

ESTADOS UNIDOS

Estrecho de Florida

Nassau

ISLAS BAHAMAS

OCÉANO ATLÁNTICO

La Habana

Santa Clara

Nueva Gerona

CUBA

Camagüey

Holguín

Manzanillo

Guantánamo

Santiago de Cuba

ISLAS DE TURCOS Y CAICOS (R.U.)

REPÚBLICA DOMINICANA

HAITÍ

Hispaniola

Arecibo

San Juan

Mayagüez

ANTILLAS MAYORES

Puerto Príncipe

Santo Domingo

Ponce

Humacao

PUERTO RICO

Kingston

JAMAICA

HONDURAS

MAR CARIBE

NICARAGUA

Aruba (Hol.)

Curaçao (Hol.)

Bonaire (Hol.)

San José

Caracas

COSTA RICA

Panamá

PANAMÁ

Golfo de Panamá

VENEZUELA

COLOMBIA

Bogotá

OCÉANO PACÍFICO

| 0 | 250 | 500 kilómetros |
| 0 | 250 | 500 millas |

Sudamérica

MAR CARIBE

OCÉANO ATLÁNTICO

Barranquilla
Cartagena
Maracaibo
Caracas
TRINIDAD Y TOBAGO
Puerto España
Lago Maracaibo

VENEZUELA

Georgetown
Paramaribo
GUYANA
Cayena
SURINAM
GUYANA FRANCESA (FRANCIA)

N

Medellín
Manizales
Bogotá

COLOMBIA

Cali

Otavalo
Quito
ECUADOR
Guayaquil
Cuenca

Ecuador

Río Negro
Río Amazonas

PERÚ

Río Madeira
Río Tapajóz
Río Xingú
Río Tocantins

Trujillo

C
O
R
D
I
L
L
E
R
A

Lima
Callao

BRASIL

Río São Francisco

Lago Titicaca

BOLIVIA
La Paz
Cochabamba
Santa Cruz
Sucre

Brasilia

Islas Galápagos
(Ecuador)

Bogotá
COLOMBIA

Quito
ECUADOR

PERÚ

OCÉANO PACÍFICO

0   250 kilómetros
0   250 millas

GRAN CHACO

PARAGUAY
Asunción

Trópico de Capricornio

Salta
San Miguel
de Tucumán
Resistencia

CHILE

A
N
D
E
S

Córdoba

Valparaíso
Santiago

Mendoza
Rosario
URUGUAY

Buenos Aires
La Plata
Montevideo

ARGENTINA

OCÉANO PACÍFICO

Concepción

Temuco

PAMPAS

Bahía
Blanca
Mar del Plata

P
A
T
A
G
O
N
I
A

OCÉANO ATLÁNTICO

0   250   500 kilómetros
0   250   500 millas

Estrecho de
Magallanes
Tierra del
Fuego

Islas Malvinas
(R.U.)

Cabo de Hornos

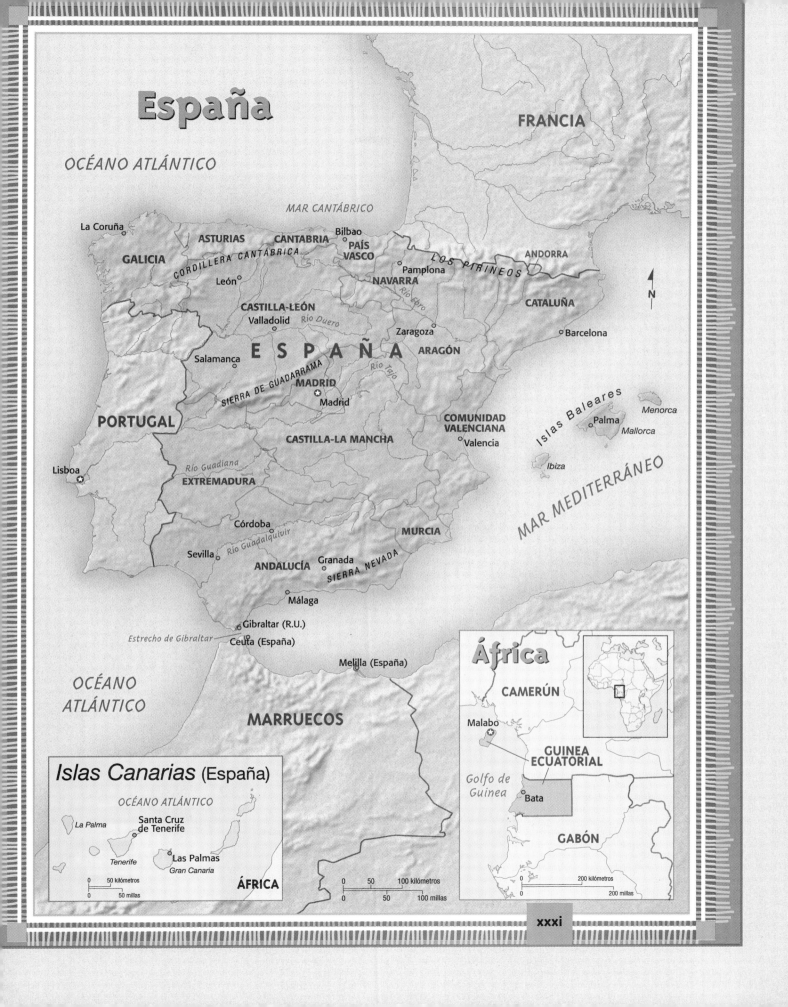

España

FRANCIA

OCÉANO ATLÁNTICO

MAR CANTÁBRICO

La Coruña

ASTURIAS   CANTABRIA   Bilbao
                            PAÍS
GALICIA   VASCO   ANDORRA
      CORDILLERA CANTÁBRICA   LOS PIRINEOS
León   NAVARRA
                            Pamplona
                            Río Ebro   CATALUÑA
CASTILLA-LEÓN
Valladolid   Río Duero
                            Zaragoza   Barcelona
             E S P A Ñ A   ARAGÓN
Salamanca
                   Río Tajo
      SIERRA DE GUADARRAMA
                   MADRID   Islas Baleares   Menorca
                   Madrid   Palma
PORTUGAL   COMUNIDAD   Mallorca
                            VALENCIANA
              CASTILLA-LA MANCHA   Valencia
                                              Ibiza
      Río Guadiana
Lisboa
      EXTREMADURA   MAR MEDITERRÁNEO

                   Córdoba
      Río Guadalquivir   MURCIA
Sevilla   Granada
             ANDALUCÍA   SIERRA NEVADA

             Málaga

OCÉANO   Gibraltar (R.U.)
ATLÁNTICO   Estrecho de Gibraltar
                   Ceuta (España)   **África**

                   Melilla (España)

                                              CAMERÚN
MARRUECOS

                                              Malabo
                                                   GUINEA
                                                   ECUATORIAL
Islas Canarias (España)   Golfo de
                                              Guinea   Bata
OCÉANO ATLÁNTICO
                                              GABÓN
La Palma   Santa Cruz
            de Tenerife
      Tenerife   Las Palmas
                      Gran Canaria
      0 50 kilómetros   ÁFRICA
      0 50 millas

0 50 100 kilómetros
0 50 100 millas

0 200 kilómetros
0 200 millas

Why Learn Spanish?

To Appreciate the Importance of Spanish in the U.S.

The influence of Spanish is everywhere. Spanish words like **plaza** and **tornado** have become part of the English language. Just think of U.S. place names that come from Spanish: **Colorado, Florida, Nevada, Los Angeles, San Antonio, La Villita,** etc. You can see Spanish on signs. There are Spanish radio and television stations. Singers such as Jon Secada perform in Spanish as well as English.

To Connect

Spanish will help you **communicate** with other people. Spanish is the second most common language in the U.S. and the third most common in the world. You will be able do things like **ask someone for directions, bargain at a market,** and **order in a restaurant** in Spanish.

To Have Fun

Taking Spanish is a new experience that will expose you to the **food,** the **music,** the **celebrations,** and other aspects of Spanish-speaking cultures. It will make travel to other countries as well as to different places in the United States much more enjoyable and more meaningful.

To Be Challenged

Studying Spanish is a challenge. There is a lot to learn, but it's not just vocabulary and grammar in a textbook. In the future you **will be able to read** Spanish-language **newspapers, magazines,** and **books.** Imagine reading *Don Quijote de la Mancha* by Miguel de Cervantes in the original Spanish someday!

To Help You in the Future

Taking a foreign language like Spanish is an accomplishment to be emphasized on college and job applications. It can also help you fulfill college language requirements. Spanish can be **useful in many careers,** from doctor, bank teller, and social worker to teacher, tour guide, and translator.

How to Study Spanish

Use Strategies

Listening strategies provide a starting point to help you understand.

Speaking strategies will help you express yourself in Spanish.

Reading strategies will show you different ways to approach reading.

Writing strategies help you out with your writing skills.

Cultural strategies help you compare Spanish-speaking cultures of the world to your own culture.

> **PARA LEER** • **STRATEGY: READING**
>
> **Look for cognates** These are words that look alike and have similar meanings in both English and Spanish, such as **europeo** and **artificiales**. What other cognates can you find in **"Las celebraciones del año"**?

Use Study Hints

The **Apoyo para estudiar** feature provides study hints that will help you learn Spanish.

APOYO PARA ESTUDIAR

Gender

Knowing the gender of nouns that refer to people is easy. But how do you learn the gender of things? When learning a new word, such as **camiseta,** say it with the definite article: **la camiseta.** Say it to yourself and say it aloud several times.

Build Your Confidence

Everyone learns differently, and there are different ways to achieve a goal. Find out what works for you. Grammar boxes are set up with an explanation, a visual representation, and examples from real-life contexts. Use this combination of words and graphics to help you learn Spanish. Focus on whatever helps you most.

GRAMÁTICA

Expressing Feelings with **estar** and Adjectives

 ¿RECUERDAS? *p. 130* You learned that the verb **estar** is used to say where someone or something is located.

▶ **Estar** is also used with **adjectives** to describe how someone feels at a given moment.

estoy	estamos
estás	estáis
está	están

agrees

Diana **está preocupada** por Ignacio.
*Diana **is worried** about Ignacio.*

agrees

Ignacio **está preocupado** por Roberto.
*Ignacio **is worried** about Roberto.*

> Remember that **adjectives** must **agree** in gender and number with the nouns they describe.

Have Fun

Taking a foreign language does not have to be all serious work. The dialogs in this book present the Spanish language in **entertaining, real-life contexts.**

- Pair and group activities give you a chance to **interact with your classmates.**
- Vocabulary and grammar puzzles will test your knowledge, but will also be **fun to do.**

Listen to Spanish
Inside and Outside of Class

Hearing Spanish will help you understand it. Pay attention to the **dialogs** and the **listening activities** in class.

Take advantage of opportunities to **hear Spanish outside of class** as well.

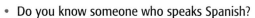

- Do you know someone who speaks Spanish?
- Are there any Spanish-language radio and/or television stations in your area?
- Does your video store have any Spanish-language movies?

Take Risks

The goal of studying a foreign language like Spanish is to **communicate.**

Don't be afraid to **speak.**

Everyone makes mistakes, so don't worry if you make a few. When you do make a mistake, **pause and then try again.**

Planning Guide CLASSROOM MANAGEMENT

OBJECTIVES

Communication
- Greet people *pp. 2–3*
- Introduce yourself *pp. 4–5, 10–11*
- Say where you are from *pp. 6–9*
- Exchange phone numbers *pp. 12–13*
- Say which day it is *p. 13*
- Recognize classroom and text instructions *pp. 14–15*

Grammar
- Introduction to the concept of gender *p. 4*

Pronunciation
- How to say the name of each letter of the Spanish alphabet *p. 11*

Culture
- Greeting customs in Spanish-speaking countries *p. 2*
- Expressions used to say good-bye in Spanish *p. 3*
- Saying country names in Spanish *pp. 6–7*

¡Gran concurso!

"¿QUÉ SIGNIFICA SER LATINO DE CORAZÓN?"

¡Lee más información en la revista!

PROGRAM RESOURCES

Print

- *Más práctica* Workbook PE, *pp. 1–8*
- Block Scheduling Copymasters, *pp. 1–8*
- Preliminary/Unit 1 Resource Book
  Más práctica Workbook TE, *pp. 3–10*
  Para hispanohablantes Workbook TE, *pp. 11–18*
- Information Gap Activities *pp. 19–22*
- Family Involvement *pp. 23–24*
- Audioscript *pp. 25–28*
- Assessment Program, Etapa preliminar *pp. 29–49, 230–232*
- Answer Keys *pp. 233–237*

Audiovisual

- **Audio Program** Cassettes 1A, 1B / CD 1
- *Canciones* Cassette / CD
- **Video Program** Videotape 1 / Videodisc 1A
- **Overhead Transparencies** M1–M5; P1–P5

Technology

- **Electronic Teacher Tools/Test Generator**
- *Intrigas y aventuras* CD-ROM, Disc 1
- www.mcdougallittell.com

Assessment Program Options

- **Cooperative Quizzes** (Preliminary/Unit 1 Resource Book)
- **Etapa Exam** Forms A and B (Preliminary/Unit 1 Resource Book)
- *Para hispanohablantes* **Etapa Exam** (Preliminary/Unit 1 Resource Book)
- **Portfolio Assessment** (Preliminary/Unit 1 Resource Book)
- **Multiple Choice Test Questions** (Preliminary/Unit 1 Resource Book)
- **Audio Program** Testing Cassette T1 / CD T1
- **Electronic Teacher Tools/Test Generator**

Native Speakers

- *Para hispanohablantes* Workbook PE, *pp. 1–8*
- *Para hispanohablantes* Workbook TE (Preliminary/Unit 1 Resource Book)
- *Para hispanohablantes* Etapa Exam (Preliminary/Unit 1 Resource Book)
- Audio *Para hispanohablantes* Cassettes 1A, 1B, T1 / CD 1, T1
- Audioscript *Para hispanohablantes* (Preliminary/Unit 1 Resource Book)

Francisco | **Isabel** | **Ignacio** | **Carlos** | **Mercedes** | **Patricia**

Student Text
Listening Activity Scripts

 Videoscript: Onda Internacional *pages 16–17*

• Videotape 1 • Videodisc 1A

Search Chapter 1, Play to 2
Prologue

¡Hola! Tengo aquí el nuevo número de la revista *Onda Internacional.* Hay muchos artículos diferentes. Hay artículos sobre países hispanohablantes, deportes, moda, comida, escuela, pasatiempos y mucho más. ¡Y mira! Hay un concurso. Escribe un artículo o prepara un reportaje fotográfico sobre lo que significa ser latino de corazón. Los dos ganadores van a viajar por el mundo hispano y trabajar para la revista. ¡Qué suerte! Bueno, ¡saquen las cámaras, los lápices, el papel y las ideas, y participen en el concurso!

*Hi! I've got the new edition of **Onda Internacional** magazine. It has many different articles. There are articles about Spanish-speaking countries, sports, fashion, food, school, leisure activities, and much more. And look! There's a contest. Write an article or prepare a photo essay about what it means to you to be **latino** or **latina**. The two winners will travel to parts of the Spanish-speaking world and work for the magazine. How lucky! Well, get out your cameras, pencils, paper, and ideas, and take part in the contest!*

The following presentations are recorded in the Audio Program:

 **¡Hola! / Adiós** *pages 2–3*

 **¿Cómo te llamas?** *pages 4–5*

 **¿De dónde es?** *pages 6–7*

 **Soy de...** *page 8*

 **Los números de cero a diez / ¿Qué día es hoy?**
pages 12–13

Frases útiles *pages 14–15*

ACTIVIDAD 3 **¿Saludo o despedida?** *page 3*

Modelo: *You hear:* Buenas noches.
You say: saludo

1. Hasta luego.
2. Buenos días.
3. Adiós.
4. Nos vemos.
5. Buenas tardes.
6. Hola.
7. Hasta mañana.
8. Buenas noches.

ACTIVIDAD 10 **Nuevos amigos** *page 9*

Modelo: *You hear:* Hola. Me llamo Álvaro. Soy de Colombia.
You write: Álvaro es de Colombia.

1. Mi nombre es Alma. Mucho gusto. Soy de Costa Rica.
2. Me llamo Guillermo. ¿De dónde soy? Soy de Estados Unidos.
3. Buenos días. Me llamo Carmen. Soy de Uruguay.
4. Hola. Me llamo Eduardo. Soy de México.
5. Encantada. Me llamo Yolanda. Soy de Guatemala.
6. Me llamo Adán. Es un placer. Soy de Argentina.

ACTIVIDAD 12  **Información** *page 11*

1. Hola. Mi nombre es Micaela, M-I-C-A-E-L-A. Mi apellido es Salazar, S-A-L-A-Z-A-R. Mucho gusto.
2. Buenas tardes. Mi nombre es Alejandro, A-L-E-J-A-N-D-R-O. Mi apellido es Mesquita, M-E-S-Q-U-I-T-A. Es un placer.

 Pronunciación *page 11*

a, avión	h, huevo	ñ, ñu	t, tijeras
b, bota	i, imán	o, oso	u, unicornio
c, cerdo	j, jarra	p, paraguas	v, video
d, dinero	k, kiwi	q, queso	w, wafle
e, escalera	l, lápiz	r, reloj	x, xilófono
f, flor	m, maleta	rr, guitarra	y, yogur
g, gafas	n, nieve	s, sombrero	z, zanahoria

Sample Lesson Plan - 50 Minute Schedule

DAY 1

- Greet students/take care of school business. **15 MIN.**
- Have students explore books as you check out texts. **10 MIN.**

Etapa Opener
- Have students look at the photo and respond to the *¿Qué ves?* questions on p. xxxvi. **10 MIN.**

Vocabulary/Activities
- Quick Start (TE, p. 2) **5 MIN.**
- Present *¡Hola! / Adiós* on pp. 2–3. Have students repeat these greeting/good-bye expressions after you and with each other. **10 MIN.**

Homework Option:
- Have each student choose his/her favorite greeting/good-bye expression and make a flashcard on construction paper. Each greeting should be written in Spanish on the front (with an illustration/magazine cut-out that demonstrates the chosen expression) and the English translation on the back.

DAY 2

Vocabulary/Activities (cont.)
- Check homework. **5 MIN.**
- Review the greeting/good-bye expressions on pp. 2–3. Show selected flashcards to the class. **10 MIN.**
- In pairs, have students practice greeting each other and saying good-bye. Direct them to vary their choice of greetings and good-byes. **5 MIN.**
- Have students do *Actividades* 1 and 2 on p. 3 orally. **10 MIN.**
- Play the audio for *Actividad* 3. If necessary, repeat. Ask students to record their answers, *saludo* or *despedida,* in their notebooks. Go over responses. **15 MIN.**
- In pairs, have students complete *Actividad* 4 on p. 3 in pairs. Ask for volunteers to act out their greetings/good-byes. **10 MIN.**

Homework Option:
- *Más práctica* Workbook, p. 1. *Para hispanohablantes* Workbook, p. 1.

DAY 3

Vocabulary/Activities (cont.)
- Check homework. **5 MIN.**
- Quick Start Review (TE, p. 4) **5 MIN.**
- Have students look at the photos on pp. 4–5 and describe what they see. Ask them what they think *¿Cómo te llamas?* and *Me llamo...* mean. **5 MIN.**
- Read aloud the list of Spanish names on p. 4. Have students repeat each name after you. Ask students if they can think of English equivalents for any of the names on the list. **10 MIN.**
- Have students pick Spanish names, then introduce themselves to the class with their new Spanish names. **10 MIN.**
- Read aloud the conversations on pp. 4–5. Have students repeat each sentence after you. **10 MIN.**
- Have pairs of students act out the conversations. **10 MIN.**

Homework Option:
- *Más práctica* Workbook, p. 2. *Para hispanohablantes* Workbook, p. 2.

DAY 4

Vocabulary/Activities (cont.)
- Check homework. **5 MIN.**
- Calling on different students, do *Actividad* 5 on p. 5 orally. **5 MIN.**
- Have students circulate to complete *Actividad* 6 on p. 5. **5 MIN.**
- Have students work in groups of 3 or 4 to complete *Actividad* 7 on p. 5. **5 MIN.**
- Quick Start Review (TE, p. 6) **5 MIN.**
- Present *¿De dónde es?* on pp. 6–7. Read country names aloud, while pointing to the appropriate country on the map. Have students repeat after you. **10 MIN.**
- Teach the *Es de...* construction. **5 MIN.**
- Brainstorm a list of Spanish-speaking celebrities, athletes, and historical figures and their countries of origin. Have students make sentences using the *Es de...* construction. **15 MIN.**

Homework Option:
- *Más práctica* Workbook, p. 3. *Para hispanohablantes* Workbook, p. 3.

DAY 5

Vocabulary/Activities (cont.)
- Check homework. **5 MIN.**
- Quick Start Review (TE, p. 8) **5 MIN.**
- Present the *Soy de...* construction and the conversations on p. 8. **5 MIN.**
- In pairs, have students do *Actividades* 8 and 9 on p. 9. **10 MIN.**
- Play the audio for *Actividad* 10 on p. 9. Have students record their answers in notebooks. Go over answers. **5 MIN.**
- In groups, do *Actividad* 11 on p. 9. **5 MIN.**
- Quick Start Review (TE, p. 10) **5 MIN.**
- Present *El abecedario (El alfabeto)* on pp. 10–11. **10 MIN.**
- Play the audio and have students practice the *Pronunciación* on p. 11. **5 MIN.**

Homework Option:
- *Más práctica* Workbook, p. 4. *Para hispanohablantes* Workbook, p. 4.

DAY 6

Vocabulary/Activities (cont.)
- Check homework. **5 MIN.**
- Play the audio and do *Actividad* 12 on p. 11. Go over answers. **5 MIN.**
- Have students do *Actividad* 13 on p. 11 in groups. **5 MIN.**
- Quick Start Review (TE, p. 12) **5 MIN.**
- Present *Los números de cero a diez* on p. 12. **5 MIN.**
- Have students complete *Actividad* 14 on p. 13 in groups. **5 MIN.**
- Present *¿Qué día es hoy?* on p. 13 and do *Actividad* 15 orally. **5 MIN.**
- Do *Actividad* 16 on p. 13 in pairs. **5 MIN.**
- Quick Start Review (TE, p. 14) **5 MIN.**
- Present *Frases útiles* on pp. 14–15 and do *Actividad* 17. **10 MIN.**

Homework Option:
- *Más práctica* Workbook, pp. 5–6. *Para hispanohablantes* Workbook, pp. 5–6.

DAY 7

Vocabulary/Activities (cont.)
- Check homework. **5 MIN.**
- Do *Actividad* 18 on p. 15 orally. **5 MIN.**
- In groups, have students do *Actividades* 19 and 20 on p. 15. **10 MIN.**

Video: Onda Internacional
- Quick Start Review (TE, p. 16) **5 MIN.**
- Have students look at the photos on pp. 16–17. Play the Video Prologue. Have students answer the questions on p. 17. **10 MIN.**

En uso: Repaso y más comunicación
- Quick Start Review (TE, p. 18) **5 MIN.**
- Do *Actividades* 1–4 orally, *Actividad* 5 in pairs, and *Actividad* 6 in groups. **15 MIN.**

Homework Option:
- *Más práctica* Workbook, pp. 7–8. *Para hispanohablantes* Workbook, pp. 7–8. Review for *Etapa preliminar* Exam.

DAY 8

En uso: Repaso y más comunicación (cont.)
- Check homework. **5 MIN.**
- Have students work individually on *Actividad* 7. As students are writing their pen pal letters, circulate around the classroom answering questions and offering suggestions. **20 MIN.**

En resumen: Repaso de vocabulario
- Quick Start Review (TE, p. 21) **5 MIN.**
- Review *Etapa* content and questions as necessary. **5 MIN.**
- Administer *Etapa preliminar* Exam. **20 MIN.**

Homework Option:
- Students should prepare final drafts for their pen pal letters.
Preview *Unidad* 1 Opener: Have students jot down their observations.

Sample Lesson Plan - Block Schedule (90 minutes)

DAY 1

- Greet students/take care of school business. 10 MIN.
- Have students explore books as you check out texts. 10 MIN.

Etapa Opener

- Have students look at the photo and respond to the ¿Qué ves? questions on p. xxxvi. 10 MIN.
- Use Block Scheduling Copymasters. 5 MIN.

Vocabulary/Activities

- Quick Start (TE, p. 2) 5 MIN.
- Present ¡Hola! / Adiós on pp. 2–3. Have students repeat these greeting/good-bye expressions after you and with each other. 10 MIN.
- In pairs, have students practice greeting each other and saying good-bye. Direct them to vary their choice of greetings and good-byes. 10 MIN.
- Have students do Actividades 1 and 2 on p. 3 orally. 10 MIN.
- Play the audio for Actividad 3. If necessary, repeat. Ask students to record their answers, saludo or despedida, in their notebooks. Go over responses. 10 MIN.
- In pairs, have students complete Actividad 4 on p. 3 in pairs. Ask for volunteers to act out their greetings/good-byes. 10 MIN.

Homework Option:

- Have each student choose his/her favorite greeting/good-bye expression and make a flashcard on construction paper. Each greeting should be written in Spanish on the front (with an illustration/magazine cut-out that demonstrates the chosen expression) and the English translation on the back. Más práctica Workbook, p. 1. Para hispanohablantes Workbook, p. 1.

DAY 2

Vocabulary/Activities (cont.)

- Check homework. 5 MIN.
- Quick Start Review (TE, p. 4) 5 MIN.
- Have students look at the photos on pp. 4–5 and describe what they see. Ask them what they think ¿Cómo te llamas? and Me llamo... mean. 5 MIN.
- Read aloud the list of Spanish names on p. 4. Have students repeat each name after you. Ask students if they can think of English equivalents for any of the names on the list. 5 MIN.
- Have students pick Spanish names, then introduce themselves to the class. 5 MIN.
- Read aloud the conversations on pp. 4–5. Have students repeat each sentence after you. 5 MIN.
- Have pairs of students act out the conversations. 5 MIN.
- Calling on different students, do Actividad 5 on p. 5 orally. 5 MIN.
- Have students circulate to complete Actividad 6 on p. 5. 10 MIN.
- Have students work in groups of 3 or 4 to complete Actividad 7 on p. 5. 10 MIN.
- Quick Start Review (TE, p. 6) 5 MIN.
- Present ¿De dónde es? on pp. 6–7. Read country names aloud, while pointing to the appropriate country on the map. Have students repeat after you. 5 MIN.
- Teach the Es de... construction. 5 MIN.
- Brainstorm a list of Spanish-speaking celebrities, athletes, and historical figures and their countries of origin. Have students make sentences using the Es de... construction. 15 MIN.

Homework Option:

- Más práctica Workbook, pp. 2–3. Para hispanohablantes Workbook, pp. 2–3.

DAY 3

Vocabulary/Activities (cont.)

- Check homework. 5 MIN.
- Quick Start Review (TE, p. 8) 5 MIN.
- Present the Soy de... construction and the conversations on p. 8. 5 MIN.
- In pairs, have students do Actividades 8 and 9 on p. 9. 10 MIN.
- Play the audio for Actividad 10 on p. 9. Have students record their answers in notebooks. Go over answers. 5 MIN.
- In groups, do Actividad 11 on p. 9. 5 MIN.
- Quick Start Review (TE, p. 10) 5 MIN.
- Present El abecedario (El alfabeto) on pp. 10–11. 5 MIN.
- Play the audio and have students practice the Pronunciación on p. 11. 5 MIN.
- Play the audio and do Actividad 12 on p. 11. Go over answers. 5 MIN.
- Have students do Actividad 13 on p. 11 in groups. 5 MIN.
- Quick Start Review (TE, p. 12) 5 MIN.
- Present Los números de cero a diez on p. 12. 5 MIN.
- Have students complete Actividad 14 on p. 13 in groups. 5 MIN.
- Present ¿Qué día es hoy? on p. 13 and do Actividad 15 orally. 10 MIN.
- Have students do Actividad 16 on p. 13 in pairs. 5 MIN.

Homework Option:

- Más práctica Workbook, pp. 4–6. Para hispanohablantes Workbook, pp. 4–6.

DAY 4

Vocabulary/Activities (cont.)

- Check homework. 5 MIN.
- Quick Start Review (TE, p. 14) 5 MIN.
- Present Frases útiles on pp. 14–15 and do Actividad 17. 10 MIN.
- Do Actividad 18 on p. 15 orally. 5 MIN.
- In groups, have students do Actividades 19 and 20 on p. 15. 10 MIN.
- Play a quick game of charades, using the vocabulary and expressions from "In the Classroom" and "In the Text" instructions on pp. 14–15. 10 MIN.

Video: Onda Internacional

- Quick Start Review (TE, p. 16) 5 MIN.
- Have students look at the photos on pp. 16–17. Play the Video Prologue. Have students answer the questions on p. 17. 10 MIN.

En uso: Repaso y más comunicación

- Quick Start Review (TE, p. 18) 5 MIN.
- Do Actividades 1–4 orally. 15 MIN.
- Have students complete Actividad 5 in pairs. Have volunteer pairs present their dialogs to the class. 10 MIN.

Homework Option:

- Más práctica Workbook, pp. 7–8. Para hispanohablantes Workbook, pp. 7–8 Review for Etapa preliminar Exam.

DAY 5

En uso: Repaso y más comunicación (cont.)

- Check homework. 5 MIN.
- Have students complete Actividad 6 in groups. 10 MIN.
- Have students work individually on Actividad 7. As students are writing their pen pal letters, circulate around the classroom answering questions and offering suggestions. 20 MIN.

En resumen: Repaso de vocabulario

- Quick Start Review (TE, p. 21) 5 MIN.
- Review Etapa content and questions as necessary. 10 MIN.
- Administer Etapa preliminar Exam. 20 MIN.
- Have a few students who enjoy drawing go up to the board and illustrate objects from pp. 10–11. With books closed, have the other students try to say the appropriate noun in Spanish. 20 MIN.

Homework Option:

- Students should prepare final drafts for their pen pal letters. Preview Unidad 1 Opener: Have students jot down their observations.

Etapa Theme
Learning about greetings and introductions
Exchanging personal information

Objectives
- Expressions for hello and good-bye
- Saying your name
- Saying where you are from
- The days of the week
- The Spanish alphabet
- Numbers 0–10
- Classroom expressions

Teaching Resource Options
Print
Block Scheduling Copymasters

Audiovisual
OHT M1–M5; P4 (Quick Start)

🔔 Quick Start
♻ **What do you already know?**
Use OHT P4 or write on board:
List at least 3 items in each of the
following categories:

- Spanish-speaking countries
- Spanish-speaking people
- Words you know in Spanish

Answers will vary.

Teaching Suggestions
Previewing the Etapa
- Ask students to talk about how they
  greet the following people: a friend, a
  neighbor, a teacher, and a parent of
  one of their friends. Have students
  look at the photo on pp. xxxvi–1.
- Ask them to point out any similarities
  and differences they notice between
  greeting styles in Spanish-speaking
  cultures and those in English-
  speaking cultures.
- Use the ¿Qué ves? questions to focus
  discussion.

ETAPA PRELIMINAR

¡Hola, bienvenidos!

- Greet people
- Introduce yourself
- Say where you are from
- Exchange phone numbers
- Say which day it is

¿Qué ves?
Look at the photo of the
first day of school.
1. How might the students
   be greeting one another?
2. What are they carrying?
3. Where should new
   students go? At what
   time?

¡Bienvenidos
estudiantes nuevos!
Reunión: 8:30
Auditorio Colón

Classroom Management

Planning Ahead Prepare large posters of Spanish
names (p. 4), the alphabet (p. 10), numbers (p. 12),
and **Frases útiles** (pp. 14–15) to post in the classroom
for quick reference during the first few days of school.

Bulletin Board Use the posters prepared for the
alphabet, etc. (see above) as the basis for a bulletin
board display. Add maps, travel brochures, or posters
from various countries. Have students make attractive,
colorful versions of the Spanish words they list (see
Quick Start) and add them to the board.

Organizing Paired/Group Work Assign students
to pairs/groups and arrange classroom locations for group
work early in the year. Post this information to facilitate
students' work. Monitor pairs/groups to encourage on-
task interactions and good habits. See p. T56 in the
Teacher's Edition for further information.

Cross Cultural Connections

Have students brainstorm and demonstrate greeting and farewell gestures in the U.S. Also brainstorm other greetings and farewells they might know from other cultures, such as bowing.

Culture Highlights

● **ACÉRCATE** Point out that personal space in Spanish-speaking cultures is generally smaller than in U.S. culture. The typical distance between two people talking is 6–12 inches.

Teaching Note

You may wish to establish some easily recognizable signals for getting attention and changing or ending activities by putting the following phrases (or others you may choose) on a poster:

- **Pónganse a pensar.**   Heads together
- **En voz baja.**   Quiet voices
- **Concéntrense.**   Stay on task
- **Túrnense.**   Take turns
- **Anímense a los otros.** Encourage others.

Block Schedule

Change of Pace Have students brainstorm and compile a list of the names of foods, geographic names, and well-known Spanish-speaking public figures (politicians, film stars, singers, authors, etc.). Post the list and add to it during the first few weeks of school. (For additional activities, see **Block Scheduling Copymasters**.)

Teaching All Students

Extra Help Ask students to guess the meaning of the **Etapa** title. Point out the list of objectives and have students use them as headings on note cards or in their notebooks. Tell students that as they learn new words and phrases they should list them under the appropriate heading.

Native Speakers Have native speakers demonstrate typical greetings and farewells with gestures.

Multiple Intelligences

Verbal Model introducing yourself in Spanish, then have students follow your model: **Buenos días./¡Hola! Me llamo... Soy de...** (point to an appropriate point on a map or map OHT). If students seem to grasp the concept, ask volunteers to model introducing themselves.

Teaching Resource Options

Print 📖

Más práctica Workbook PE, p. 1
Para hispanohablantes Workbook
 PE, p. 1
Block Scheduling Copymasters
Preliminary/Unit 1 Resource Book
 Más práctica Workbook TE, p. 3
 Para hispanohablantes Workbook
  TE, p. 11
 Audioscript, p. 25
 Audioscript *Para hispanohablantes*,
  p. 25

Audiovisual 🎧

Audio Program Cassettes 1A, 1B / CD 1
Audio *Para hispanohablantes*
 Cassette 1A / CD 1
OHT P4 (Quick Start)

Technology 💻

Intrigas y aventuras CD-ROM, Disc 1

🔔 Quick Start

♻️ Greeting people and saying
  good-bye

Use OHT P4 or write on board:
Look at pp. 2–3 in your text (1 min.).
Then close your books and match the
times in column A with the appropriate
expression in column B:

1. ___ 10:00 A.M. a. **Buenas noches.**
2. ___ 1:00 P.M. b. **Buenos días.**
3. ___ 8:00 P.M. c. **Buenas tardes.**

Answers
1. b
2. c
3. a

Teaching Suggestions

• Ask students to look at the photos on
 pp. 2–3 and say what they notice.
• Use Audio Program Cassette 1A /
 CD 1 to present the vocabulary.
• Use the TPR suggestion to reinforce
 the concepts.

¡Hola!

Hola.

NOTA CULTURAL

When greeting, it is customary to shake hands. Many people also exchange a kiss on the cheek or a hug. The greeting changes with the time of day. **Hola** can be used anytime. **Buenos días** is used in the morning, **Buenas tardes** in the afternoon and early evening, and **Buenas noches** at night.

Buenos días.

Buenas tardes.

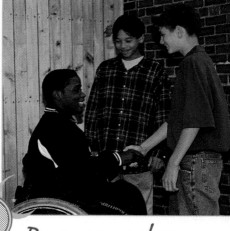

Buenas noches.

2 dos
Etapa preliminar

Classroom Community

TPR Divide the class into 2 circles, 1 inside the other. Have students greet each other, then "turn" the circle and say good-bye to the next person. Continue revolving the circles until all students have greeted and said good-bye to each other.

Group Activity Divide the class into groups of 4 or 5. Each group lists 5–6 places and times where they usually meet other people (at school, at a mall). Have 2 groups work together to take turns giving a place. The other group states an appropriate greeting and farewell.

Adiós

NOTA CULTURAL

These expressions are all used to say good-bye. **Adiós** means *Good-bye*. **Hasta mañana** literally means *Until tomorrow*. You can say **Hasta luego** or **Nos vemos** if you expect to see the person later that day or in the near future.

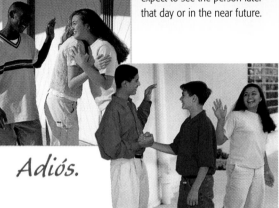

Adiós.

Hasta luego.

Hasta mañana.

Nos vemos.

 1 Buenos días

How would you greet a friend at these times?

modelo

5:00 P.M.	*Buenas tardes.*

1. 8:00 P.M.   3. 2:00 P.M.   5. anytime
2. 10:45 A.M.   4. 8:30 A.M.   6. 9:00 P.M.

 2 Hasta mañana

Use different expressions to say good-bye to these people.

1. Ana
2. Señor Ruiz
3. Señora Díaz
4. Alfredo

 3 ¿Saludo o despedida?

Imagine that you are in a Spanish-speaking community. Identify what you hear as a greeting (**saludo**) or a farewell (**despedida**).

 4 Nos vemos

Greet and say good-bye to your partner, according to these situations.

1. Greet in the afternoon. You will see each other tomorrow.
2. Greet in the evening. You don't expect to see each other anytime soon.
3. Greet in the morning. You will see each other later today.

tres
Etapa preliminar | 3

Gestures

In Spanish-speaking countries it is common for 2 women or a woman and a man to kiss on the cheeks when they greet each other. In Spain, 2 kisses, one on each cheek, are used. In Latin America only 1 kiss is used.

 1 **Objective:** Controlled practice
Greetings

Answers
1. Buenas noches.   4. Buenos días.
2. Buenos días.   5. Hola.
3. Buenas tardes.   6. Buenas noches.

2 **Objective:** Transitional practice
Farewells

Answers
Answers will vary. Any of these expressions:
Adiós.   Hasta mañana.
Hasta luego.   Nos vemos.

3 **Objective:** Transitional practice
Listening comprehension/greetings and farewells

Answers (See script, p. xxxvB.)
1. despedida   5. saludo
2. saludo   6. saludo
3. despedida   7. despedida
4. despedida   8. saludo

 4 **Objective:** Transitional practice
Greetings and farewells

Answers
Answers will vary. Answers could include:
1. Buenas tardes. Hasta mañana.
2. Buenas noches. Adiós.
3. Buenos días. Hasta luego. (Nos vemos.)

Quick Wrap-up

Have students say good-bye to you in Spanish as they leave class, using **Adiós** and another expression. Tell students to prepare to greet you in Spanish at the beginning of the next class.

Block Schedule

Variety Ask students to draw 4 situations/cartoons and label the drawings with appropriate greetings or farewells on the back. Divide the class into pairs and have students take turns showing their drawings and giving the correct greeting/farewell. (For additional activities, see **Block Scheduling Copymasters**.)

Teaching All Students

Extra Help Ask students to look at pages 2–3. Point to the icon for morning (sunrise). Ask: ¿Qué dices? (Buenos días.). Then point to the icon for afternoon (full sun), etc., and repeat to elicit all new vocabulary.

Challenge Write on the board: **Tú dices....** (You say). Write different hours of the day on the board and have students give the correct greeting: ¿Qué dices? Tú dices, ¡Buenos días!

Native Speakers Ask native speakers to expand the new vocabulary with additional simple greetings. Have all students record them in a Supplementary Vocabulary List for challenge and extra credit activities.

Teaching Resource Options

Print

Más práctica Workbook PE, p. 2
Para hispanohablantes Workbook PE,
  p. 2
Block Scheduling Copymasters
Preliminary/Unit 1 Resource Book
  Más práctica Workbook TE, p. 4
  Para hispanohablantes Workbook
    TE, p. 12
  Audioscript, p. 25
  Audioscript *Para hispanohablantes,*
    p. 25

Audiovisual

Audio Program Cassettes 1A, 1B / CD 1
Audio *Para hispanohablantes*
  Cassette 1A / CD 1
OHT P4 (Quick Start)

Technology

Intrigas y aventuras CD-ROM, Disc 1

Quick Start Review

♻ **Greetings**

Use OHT P4 or write on board:
Complete the following expressions:

1. Buenas t _ _ _ _ _ .
2. B _ _ _ _ _ n _ _ _ _ _ .
3. B _ _ _ _ _ d _ _ _ .
4. Nos _ _ _ _ _ _ .
5. H _ _ _ _ l _ _ _ _ .

Answers

1. Buenas tardes.   4. Nos vemos.
2. Buenas noches.   5. Hasta luego.
3. Buenos días.

Teaching Suggestions

- Have students scan pages 4–5 (1 min.).
- Use Audio Program Cassette 1A / CD 1
  to present the vocabulary and dialogs.
- Have students choose a Spanish
  name and write it on a name tag.
- Use the TPR activity to reinforce the
  new vocabulary and dialogs.
- Ask yes/no questions: ¿Me llamo Sr./
  Sra. ___? (Sí) ¿Me llamo Superman?
  (No) (Pointing to a student) ¿Se
  llamo ___? ¿Te llamas ___?

¿Cómo te llamas?

Me llamo Tomás.

Chicos

Adán	Fernando	Marcos
Alejandro	Francisco	Mateo
Álvaro	Gerardo	Miguel
Andrés	Gilberto	Nicolás
Arturo	Gregorio	Pablo
Benjamín	Guillermo	Patricio
Carlos	Ignacio	Pedro
Cristóbal	Iván	Rafael
Daniel	Jaime	Ramón
David	Javier	Raúl
Diego	Jorge	Ricardo
Eduardo	José	Roberto
Enrique	Juan	Teodoro
Esteban	Julio	Timoteo
Federico	Leonardo	Tomás
Felipe	Luis	Vicente

Me llamo Alma.

Chicas

Alejandra	Elena	Mercedes
Alicia	Emilia	Micaela
Alma	Estefanía	Mónica
Ana	Estela	Natalia
Andrea	Eva	Patricia
Anita	Francisca	Raquel
Bárbara	Graciela	Rosa
Beatriz	Isabel	Rosalinda
Carlota	Juana	Rosana
Carmen	Julia	Sofía
Carolina	Luisa	Susana
Claudia	Margarita	Teresa
Consuelo	María	Verónica
Cristina	Mariana	Victoria
Diana	Marta	Yolanda

APOYO PARA
ESTUDIAR

Chico, chica

In Spanish, all nouns have either a
masculine or feminine gender.
Masculine nouns usually end in **-o**
and feminine nouns usually end in **-a.**

Francisco: Hola. ¿Cómo te llamas?

Alma: Me llamo Alma.

Francisco: Encantado, Alma.
Me llamo Francisco.

Alma: Es un placer, Francisco.

el apellido   el nombre

4   cuatro
Etapa preliminar

Classroom Community

TPR Ask students to stand up and mingle as if they
were at a party, practicing ¡Hola! Buenas tardes./
Buenas noches. ¿Cómo te llamas? Me llamo _____.
Allow 3 minutes for practice, then have volunteers
present the dialog to the whole group.

Paired Activity Have students begin a role-play by
using the dialogs on pp. 4–5. Then have students
create their own dialogs using the Spanish names on
their name tags.

Raquel: Hola.
Me llamo Raquel.

Susana: Me llamo
Susana. Encantada.

Raquel: Igualmente.

Susana: ¿Cómo se
llama el chico?

Raquel: Se llama Jorge.

Jorge: ¿Cómo se
llama la chica?

Enrique: Se llama
Ana.

Rosa: Buenos días. Me llamo Rosa. ¿Cómo te llamas?

Carlos: Mucho gusto, Rosa. Me llamo Carlos.

Rosa: El gusto es mío.

ACTIVIDAD 5 — Me llamo...

How do these people introduce themselves?

modelo

Marcos García   *Me llamo **Marcos García.***

1. Marta Blanco
2. Raúl Morales
3. Rosa Vivas
4. Felipe Estrada
5. Ana Martínez
6. Ricardo Herrera
7. Arturo Cruz
8. Sofía Ponce

ACTIVIDAD 6 — ¿Cómo te llamas en español?

Find out the Spanish names of five classmates and list them.

modelo

You: *¿Cómo te llamas?*   **Classmate:** *Me llamo Ana.*

ACTIVIDAD 7 — ¿Cómo se llama?

- Greet and introduce yourself to a classmate.
- Point to other students and find out their names.
- Say good-bye.

modelo

You: *Buenos días. Me llamo… ¿Cómo te llamas?*

Classmate: *Me llamo Mónica. Encantada.*

You: *Es un placer. ¿Cómo se llama la chica?*

Classmate: *Se llama Mariana.*

You: *Adiós. Hasta luego.*

Classmate: *Nos vemos.*

Nota

If you are a boy, say **encantado.** If you are a girl, say **encantada.**

Language Note

Point out that **nombre** refers to a person's first name and **apellido** to a person's last name, or surname.

Culture Highlights

● **LOS NOMBRES** Some Spanish names have common nicknames, just like English. Here is a list of some names and their nicknames.

Adolfo: Fito	Guillermo: Guille
Alberto: Beto	José: Pepe
Antonio: Nito	Josefa: Pepa
Concepción: Conchita	Marcela: Chela
Cristina: Tina	Óscar: Cacho
Dolores: Lola	Roberto: Beto
Francisco: Paco, Pancho	Rodolfo: Fito, Rolo
	Teresa: Tere
Gonzalo: Gonzo	Yolanda: Yoli

ACTIVIDAD 5 — Objective: Controlled practice
Introductions

Answers
1. Me llamo Marta Blanco.
2. Me llamo Raúl Morales.
3. Me llamo Rosa Vivas.
4. Me llamo Felipe Estrada.
5. Me llamo Ana Martínez.
6. Me llamo Ricardo Herrera.
7. Me llamo Arturo Cruz.
8. Me llamo Sofía Ponce.

ACTIVIDAD 6 — Objective: Transitional practice
Introductions

Answers will vary.

ACTIVIDAD 7 — Objective: Open-ended practice
Greeting and introducing people

Answers will vary.

Teaching All Students

Extra Help Have students write each line of the dialogs on a separate piece of paper or file card and scramble the pieces. Students must then unscramble them to create complete correct dialogs.

Native Speakers Have students work in pairs to create slightly longer dialogs/variations and record or video them as models for additional practice activities for the class. For example, in Colombia the expression ¿Qué hubo? ("¿Quiubo?") is sometimes used for ¿Qué tal?

Multiple Intelligences

Visual Ask students to cut out photos from magazines or make drawings to create amusing introduction situations (animals, famous people, historical figures).

Block Schedule

Retention Have students prepare flashcards for the new phrases they have learned. These cards can be used for review at various points in the instructional sequence. (For additional activities, see **Block Scheduling Copymasters.**)

Teaching Resource Options

Print

Más práctica Workbook PE, p. 3
Para hispanohablantes Workbook
 PE, p. 3
Block Scheduling Copymasters
Preliminary/Unit 1 Resource Book
 Más práctica Workbook TE, p. 5
 Para hispanohablantes Workbook
 TE, p. 13
 Audioscript, p. 26
 Audioscript *Para hispanohablantes,*
 p. 26

Audiovisual

Canciones Audiocassette/CD
Audio Program Cassette 1A / CD 1
Audio *Para hispanohablantes*
 Cassette 1A / CD 1
OHT M1; P4 (Quick Start)

Technology

Intrigas y aventuras CD-ROM, Disc 1

Quick Start Review

🔔 **Introductions**

Use OHT P4 or write on board:
Complete the following sentences:
1. Me llam _ Pablo Ramos. ¿Cómo
 t _ ll _ _ _ _ ?
2. La chica, ¿cómo _ _ _ _ _ _ _ ?
3. Mucho gusto. M _ ll _ _ _ Luis.

Answers
1. Me llamo Pablo Ramos. ¿Cómo te llamas?
2. La chica, ¿cómo se llama?
3. Mucho gusto. Me llamo Luis.

Teaching Suggestions

• Have students look at the map and
 photos on pp. 6–7 (1 min.) and say
 what they notice.
• Have students read the **Nota cultural.**
 Then point out the form **Es de...**
 under each photo, asking **¿Es de
 México el chico? (Sí/No)** and
 indicating location on the map.
• Use Audio Program Cassette 1A / CD
 1 to model correct pronunciation of
 country names.
• Use the TPR activity to increase
 retention.

¿De dónde es?

Es de México.

**Es de Estados
Unidos.**

NOTA CULTURAL

Spanish speakers sometimes use
the articles **el, la, las,** or **los**
before these country names.
Their use is optional.

(la) **Argentina**
(el) **Ecuador**
(los) **Estados Unidos**
(las) **Filipinas**
(el) **Paraguay**
(el) **Perú**
(la) **República Dominicana**
(el) **Uruguay**

Es de Ecuador.

Es de Perú.

6 seis
Etapa preliminar

Classroom Community

TPR Use OHT M1 and have students stand in 2
parallel lines. Pairs will then say in turn, pointing to the
student in the other line, **Es de** + *country* and point to
the correct country on the map. Continue until all
students have had a turn.

Cooperative Learning Prepare ahead: blank
maps of the Spanish-speaking world. Divide the class
into groups of 3. Student 1 is the researcher, student 2
is the recorder, and student 3 is the spellchecker. Each
group has 15 minutes to fill in the names of as many of
the Spanish-speaking countries as possible. The groups
then present their maps to the class.

Es de España.

Es de Puerto Rico.

Es de Costa Rica.

Es de Argentina.

LOS PAÍSES DEL MUNDO HISPANOHABLANTE

Argentina 21
Belice 4
Bolivia 17
Chile 18
Colombia 14
Costa Rica 8
Cuba 10
Ecuador 15
El Salvador 5
España 22
Estados Unidos 1
Filipinas 24
Guam 25
Guatemala 3
Guinea Ecuatorial 23
Honduras 6
México 2
Nicaragua 7
Panamá 9
Paraguay 19
Perú 16
Puerto Rico 12
República Dominicana 11
Uruguay 20
Venezuela 13

Color Key

Spanish is the official language.

Much Spanish is spoken.

Cross Cultural Connections

Prepare ahead: books, magazines, newspapers, brochures, and maps from various Spanish-speaking countries. Create a classroom Reference Table and rotate groups of students at 10-minute intervals to investigate similarities between U.S. culture and those of the other countries. Each group must list 3 similarities. Compile as lists on the board.

Culture Highlights

● **EL MUNDO HISPANOHABLANTE**

• Puerto Rico and Guam are territories of the U.S.
• Some countries in the Caribbean and South America that are *not* Spanish-speaking include: Brazil (Portuguese), Guyana (English), Suriname (Dutch, English), Haiti (Creole, French), etc.

More Practice

Have student complete the conversations, choosing the correct words:

– Hola. Me (nombre/llamo) Jaime. ¿Cómo te (llamas/llama)?
– Encantado, Jaime. Mi (llama/nombre) es Carlos.
– Es un (igualmente/placer), Carlos. ¿Cómo (se/te) llama la chica?
– Se (llamo/llama) Eva.
– Hola, Eva. (Me/Te) llamo Jaime.
– Mucho (nombre/gusto), Jaime.

Dictation

Read each sentence twice.

– Buenos días. Me llamo Ana. ¿Cómo te llamas?
– Mucho gusto, Ana. Me llamo Roberto.

Teaching All Students

Extra Help Be sure that students can correctly identify the area of the U.S. they are from on the map on pp. 6–7 before beginning. Then, using the map and illustrations, have students point to each photo as you ask, ¿Es de... ? Students respond with **Sí/No** at first. Once students are comfortable, encourage a complete response by modeling, **Sí, es de...**

Multiple Intelligences

Musical/Rhythmic Use the **Canciones** Audiocassette/CD to introduce students to the variety of musical styles in the Spanish-speaking world. Point to the country of origin as the songs are presented.

Kinesthetic In groups, have students cut out big colored-paper countries of Latin America and label the countries. Then have them put the puzzles together.

Block Schedule

Process Time Give students 5 minutes to look at the map and write down 1 thing that surprised them when they saw the map. Share the responses with the class. (For additional activities, see **Block Scheduling Copymasters**.)

Teaching Resource Options

Print 📖

Más práctica Workbook PE, p. 4
Para hispanohablantes Workbook PE, p. 4
Block Scheduling Copymasters
Preliminary/Unit 1 Resource Book
  Más práctica Workbook TE, p. 6
  Para hispanohablantes Workbook TE, p. 14
  Audioscript, p. 26
  Audioscript *Para hispanohablantes*, p. 26

Audiovisual 🎧

Audio Program Cassettes 1A, 1B / CD 1
Audio *Para hispanohablantes*
  Cassette 1A / CD 1
OHT P4 (Quick Start)

Technology 💻

Intrigas y aventuras CD-ROM, Disc 1

🔔 Quick Start Review

♻️ Spanish-speaking countries/**Es de...**
Use OHT P4 or write on board:
1. Write the names of 3 Spanish-speaking countries.
2. Write sentences saying where these people are from:
   Ana: México
   Roberto: Puerto Rico
   Diana: Panamá

Answers
1. *Answers will vary.*
2. Ana es de México. / Roberto es de Puerto Rico. / Diana es de Panamá.

Teaching Suggestions

• Have students skim the dialogs on p. 8. Then use Audio Program Cassette 1A / CD 1 to model them.
• Ask students yes/no, either/or, and simple comprehension questions.
• Use the TPR activity to encourage conversational exchanges.

Supplementary Vocabulary

el país	country
la ciudad	city
el pueblo	town

Soy de...

Raquel: ¿De dónde es?
Susana: Es de Uruguay.

Ricardo: ¿De dónde eres?
Manuel: Soy de Guatemala.

8

Classroom Community

TPR Divide the class into groups. Have each group develop a series of gestures to indicate the meaning of the dialog sentences (e.g., pointing at partner, then toward map while asking, ¿De dónde eres?).

Game Have students work in small groups to create chain stories. The first student says hello, the next introduces himself/herself and a Spanish-speaking friend. The next student says where he/she is from,

until the chain is complete. The most creative story wins.

Portfolio Students create short informational profiles for a pen pal with at least 4 sentences about themselves.

Rubric A = 13–15 pts. B = 10–12 pts. C = 7–9 pts. D = 4–6 pts. F = < 4 pts.

Writing criteria	Scale
Logical sentence order	1 2 3 4 5
Accuracy	1 2 3 4 5
Creativity	1 2 3 4 5

ACTIVIDAD 8 ¿De dónde es?

You and your partner have made some new friends. Tell where they are from. Change roles.

modelo

Tomás: España

You: *¿De dónde es **Tomás**?*

Partner: *Es de **España**.*

1. Estefanía: Panamá
2. Graciela: Cuba
3. Vicente: Costa Rica
4. Ignacio: Honduras
5. Mercedes: México
6. Alejandro: Nicaragua
7. Iván: Puerto Rico
8. Claudia: El Salvador

ACTIVIDAD 9 ¿De dónde eres?

You meet several South Americans. Role-play the situation with your partner.

modelo

1

You: *¿De dónde eres?* **Partner:** *Soy de Ecuador.*

ACTIVIDAD 10 Nuevos amigos

Listen as several people introduce themselves to you. Identify their country of origin.

modelo

Álvaro: ¿Cuba o Colombia?

***Álvaro** es de Colombia.*

1. Alma: ¿Puerto Rico o Costa Rica?
2. Guillermo: ¿Honduras o Estados Unidos?
3. Carmen: ¿Uruguay o Paraguay?
4. Eduardo: ¿México o España?
5. Yolanda: ¿Venezuela o Guatemala?
6. Adán: ¿Argentina o Nicaragua?

ACTIVIDAD 11 ¿Eres de...?

Imagine that everyone in your class is from different Spanish-speaking countries. Ask questions to find out which country each person is from.

modelo

Student 1: *¿Eres de Honduras?*

You: *No.*

Student 2: *¿Eres de Guatemala?*

You: *Sí, soy de Guatemala.*

Nota

To say yes, use **sí. No** is the same as in English.

Teaching All Students

Extra Help First, point to yourself, saying **Yo soy de...** Next, point to a photo on pp. 6–8 and ask a student about the person pictured: **¿Es de México?** (Sí). Then ask, **¿De dónde es?** (Es de México). Finally, ask the student while pointing to the student himself/herself, **¿De dónde eres? ¿Eres de...?** (Sí). Repeat until at least 1 student is able to use the question forms to help other students continue to practice.

Native Speakers Have students prepare short presentations on the countries they or their families have come from, indicating on a map for the class where the countries are located.

Multiple Intelligences

Naturalist Have students research 2–3 Spanish-speaking countries for interesting geographical facts or information about animal life to share with the class.

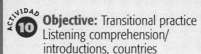

ACTIVIDAD 8 Objective: Controlled practice
¿De dónde?/Es de...

Answers
1. ¿De dónde es Estefanía? / Es de Panamá.
2. ¿De dónde es Graciela? / Es de Cuba.
3. ¿De dónde es Vicente? / Es de Costa Rica.
4. ¿De dónde es Ignacio? / Es de Honduras.
5. ¿De dónde es Mercedes? / Es de México.
6. ¿De dónde es Alejandro? / Es de Nicaragua.
7. ¿De dónde es Iván? / Es de Puerto Rico.
8. ¿De dónde es Claudia? / Es de El Salvador.

ACTIVIDAD 9 Objective: Controlled practice
Saying where you are from

Answers
1. ¿De dónde eres? / Soy de Ecuador.
2. ¿De dónde eres? / Soy de Argentina.
3. ¿De dónde eres? / Soy de Venezuela.
4. ¿De dónde eres? / Soy de Perú.
5. ¿De dónde eres? / Soy de Paraguay.
6. ¿De dónde eres? / Soy de Bolivia.
7. ¿De dónde eres? / Soy de Chile.
8. ¿De dónde eres? / Soy de Colombia.
9. ¿De dónde eres? / Soy de Uruguay.

ACTIVIDAD 10 Objective: Transitional practice
Listening comprehension/
introductions, countries

Answers (See page xxxvB for script.)
1. Alma es de Costa Rica.
2. Guillermo es de (los) Estados Unidos.
3. Carmen es de Uruguay.
4. Eduardo es de México.
5. Yolanda es de Guatemala.
6. Adán es de Argentina.

ACTIVIDAD 11 Objective: Open-ended practice
Introducing people and saying where they are from

Answers will vary.

Critical Thinking

Ask students to look at the map on pp. 6–7 and count the number of countries where Spanish is spoken. (They may research population figures also.) Have them discuss why it is important to learn Spanish.

Block Schedule

Expansion Expand on **Actividad 10** by having students associate famous names, products, cultural items with various countries. For example: **el mariachi: ¿México o Chile?; el tango: ¿Argentina o Puerto Rico?** (For additional activities, see **Block Scheduling Copymasters.**)

Teaching Resource Options

Print 📖

Más práctica Workbook PE, p. 5
Para hispanohablantes Workbook PE, p. 5
Block Scheduling Copymasters
Preliminary/Unit 1 Resource Book
  Más práctica Workbook TE, p. 7
  Para hispanohablantes Workbook
  TE, p. 15
  Audioscript, p. 27
  Audioscript *Para hispanohablantes*, p. 27

Audiovisual 📽️

Audio Program Cassettes 1A, 1B / CD 1
Audio *Para hispanohablantes*
  Cassette 1A / CD 1
OHT P1, P4 (Quick Start)

Technology 💻

Intrigas y aventuras CD-ROM, Disc 1

🔔 Quick Start Review

♻️ Spanish-speaking countries
Use OHT P4 or write on board:
Find the names of 7 Spanish-speaking
countries—horizontally and vertically:

```
J É G O X M L
C U B A L É M
H P R E C X O
I L C S L I P
L Ñ G P E C E
E C U A D O R
L C A Ñ P T Ú
B S M A A M O
```

Answers
Horizontally: Cuba, Ecuador
Vertically: Chile, Guam, España, México, Perú

Teaching Suggestions

• Use OHT P1 and Audio Program
  Cassette 1A / CD 1 to present the
  alphabet on pp. 10–11.
• Have students practice pronunciation.
• If students have not noticed the **ñ**,
  point it out and reinforce the difference
  between the pronunciation of **n/ñ**.
• Have each student write his/her name
  on a sheet of paper in large letters
  and practice spelling it aloud in Spanish.

El abecedario
(El alfabeto)

 A — **avión**

 B — **bota**

 C — **cerdo**

 D — **dinero**

 E — **escalera**

 F — **flor**

 G — **gafas**

 H — **huevo**

 I — **imán**

 J — **jarra**

 K — **kiwi**

 L — **lápiz**

 M — **maleta**

 N — **nieve**

 Ñ — **ñu**

 O — **oso**

 P — **paraguas**

 Q — **queso**

📖 **APOYO PARA ESTUDIAR**

Dictionary
Dictionaries published before 1994 include **ch**
and **ll** as separate letters in the Spanish alphabet.

Classroom Community

Paired Activity Prepare ahead: randomized
alphabet charts on posterboard. Divide the class into
pairs and give each pair an "eye chart." Students take
turns calling out the letters in Spanish.

Learning Scenario Divide the class into groups.
Give each group 5 minutes to prepare a short scenario
in which spelling a person's name in Spanish solves a
problem. For example: You are a telephone operator.

Someone calls for assistance in finding a friend's
number, but they don't speak English. You ask, **¿Cómo
se llama? ¿De dónde es?** To confirm the name, you
spell it: **¿Juan Díaz? J-U-A-N D-Í-A-Z.**

Game Prepare ahead: alphabet bingo cards, single
alphabet letters. Hand out cards and call letters until
one student has 5 in a row.

reloj

guitarra

sombrero

tijeras

unicornio

video

wafle

xilófono

yogur

zanahoria

ACTIVIDAD 12 🎧 **Información**

Listen to two people introduce themselves. Complete the information, writing down their first and last names as they are spelled.

1. a. nombre
   b. apellido

2. a. nombre
   b. apellido

ACTIVIDAD 13 **¿Cómo te llamas?**

Find out the Spanish names of five classmates. Write the names down as they spell them.

modelo

You: ¿Cómo te llamas?

Classmate: Me llamo Esteban, E - S - T - E - B - A - N.

(e, ese, te, e, be, a, ene)

Pronunciación 🎧

Here is how to say the name of each letter of the Spanish alphabet.

a = a	k = ka	rr = erre
b = be, be larga	l = ele	s = ese
c = ce	m = eme	t = te
d = de	n = ene	u = u
e = e	ñ = eñe	v = ve, uve, ve corta
f = efe	o = o	w = doble ve, doble uve
g = ge	p = pe	x = equis
h = hache	q = cu	y = i griega, ye
i = i	r = ere	z = zeta
j = jota		

once
Etapa preliminar 11

Culture Highlights

● **EL ABECEDARIO** Many young children learning the Spanish alphabet begin with an illustrated book of letters called an **abecedario**. Ask students if they can explain the connection between the word and its function.

ACTIVIDAD 12 Objective: Transitional practice Listening comprehension/spelling

Answers (See script, p. xxxvB.)
1. a. Micaela
   b. Salazar
2. a. Alejandro
   b. Mesquita

ACTIVIDAD 13 Objective: Open-ended practice Spelling

Answers will vary.

Dictation

Read a randomized alphabet list and ask students to write down the correct letter.

Block Schedule

FunBreak Put all student name sheets (see Teaching Suggestions, TE p. 10) in a pile. One student chooses a name and spells it; everyone who recognizes the name raises his/her hand. The student then chooses one person to give the correct answer. (If the student whose name was spelled did NOT raise a hand, he/she is out of the game!) Continue until all names have been spelled. (For additional activities, see **Block Scheduling Copymasters**.)

Teaching All Students

Extra Help Have students identify letters they are having trouble pronouncing and give them extra modeling and practice by making a list of additional words/phrases.

Native Speakers Ask native speakers to help in modeling correct pronunciation in small groups or one-on-one. If students know some easy **trabalenguas**, they may teach them to the class or small groups.

Multiple Intelligences

Musical/Rhythmic Use the tune for the alphabet song in English to practice the Spanish alphabet.

Visual Have students illustrate their own examples of alphabet letters and display them in the classroom.

Verbal Hold a class Spelling Bee.

Teaching Resource Options

Print 📖

Más práctica Workbook PE, p. 6
Para hispanohablantes Workbook PE, p. 6
Block Scheduling Copymasters
Preliminary/Unit 1 Resource Book
  Más práctica Workbook TE, p. 8
  Para hispanohablantes Workbook TE, p. 16
  Audioscript, p. 27
  Audioscript *Para hispanohablantes*, p. 27

Audiovisual 🎧

Audio Program Cassette 1A / CD 1
Audio *Para hispanohablantes*
  Cassette 1A / CD 1
OHT P2, P5 (Quick Start)

Technology 💻

Intrigas y aventuras CD-ROM, Disc 1

🔔 Quick Start Review

♻️ Greetings/Introductions

Use OHT P5 or write on board:
Unscramble the following words to create correct sentences:

1. Raúl / de / Estados Unidos / es
2. nombre / Susana / es / Mi
3. llamas? / te / ¿Cómo
4. un / Ricardo / placer / Es

Answers
1. Raúl es de Estados Unidos.
2. Mi nombre es Susana.
3. ¿Cómo te llamas?
4. Es un placer, Ricardo.

Teaching Suggestions

• Use OHT P2 and Audio Program Cassette 1A / CD 1 to present and practice the numbers and the dialog on p. 13.
• Use the TPR activity to reinforce acquisition of the numbers.

Culture Highlights

● **LOS NÚMEROS** In many Spanish-speaking countries the numbers 1 and 7 are written in a special way. 1 7

Los números de cero a diez

cero	uno	dos	tres	cuatro
 0	1	2	3	 4

cinco	seis	siete	ocho	nueve
5	 6	 7	 8	 9

diez

 10

Roberto: ¿Cuál es tu teléfono?
Ignacio: 8–9–7–3–1–4–2.

12 doce
Etapa preliminar

Classroom Community

Group Activities Numbers: Divide the class into groups of 10. Have students write the numbers 1–10 on separate pieces of paper or note cards. Then scramble the numbers upside down and have students choose a card, say the number, and line up in correct order.
Days of the Week: Divide the class into groups of seven. Using the number cards 1–7 from the **Numbers** activity, have students write the days of the week on each card (1–**lunes**, 2–**martes**, etc.), then scramble, choose and line up, saying the days of the week in order.

TPR Have students hold up the correct number of fingers as you count. Then ask individual students to say the number in Spanish while they hold up the correct number of classroom objects (one book, two pencils, etc.).

¿Qué día es hoy?

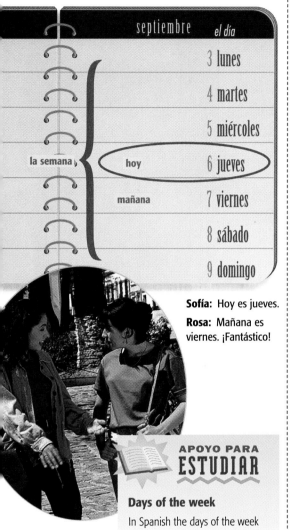

septiembre	el día
	3 lunes
	4 martes
	5 miércoles
la semana hoy	6 jueves
mañana	7 viernes
	8 sábado
	9 domingo

Sofía: Hoy es jueves.

Rosa: Mañana es viernes. ¡Fantástico!

APOYO PARA ESTUDIAR

Days of the week

In Spanish the days of the week are not capitalized.

 ACTIVIDAD 14 ¿Cuál es tu teléfono?

Ask for and write down the telephone numbers of five classmates.

modelo

You: *Carolina, ¿cuál es tu teléfono?*

Classmate: *Seis - seis - tres - seis - nueve - cinco - siete.*

ACTIVIDAD 15 El día

Tell what day it is today and tomorrow.

modelo

jueves 　　*Hoy es **jueves**. Mañana es viernes.*

1. lunes	4. martes
2. sábado	5. domingo
3. miércoles	6. viernes

 ACTIVIDAD 16 ¿Qué día?

You often forget what day it is. Ask your partner for help. Change roles.

modelo

lunes

You: *¿Qué día es hoy?*

Partner: *Hoy es **lunes**.*

You: *¡Sí! Mañana es martes.*

1. sábado	4. domingo
2. miércoles	5. jueves
3. viernes	6. martes

Teaching Suggestions

- Use OHT P2 and Audio Program Cassette 1A / CD 1 to present and practice the days of the week and the dialog on p. 13.
- Use the TPR activity to help students retain the new vocabulary.

Culture Highlights

● **EL CALENDARIO** In Spanish-speaking countries, the calendar week begins with Monday and ends with Sunday.

ACTIVIDAD 14 **Objective:** Open-ended practice
Numbers

Answers will vary.

ACTIVIDAD 15 **Objective:** Controlled practice
Days of the week

Answers

1. Hoy es lunes. Mañana es martes.
2. Hoy es sábado. Mañana es domingo.
3. Hoy es miércoles. Mañana es jueves.
4. Hoy es martes. Mañana es miércoles.
5. Hoy es domingo. Mañana es lunes.
6. Hoy es viernes. Mañana es sábado.

ACTIVIDAD 16 **Objective:** Transitional practice
Days of the week

Answers

1. ¿Qué día es hoy? / Hoy es sábado. / ¡Sí! Mañana es domingo.
2. ¿Qué día es hoy? / Hoy es miércoles. / ¡Sí! Mañana es jueves.
3. ¿Qué día es hoy? / Hoy es viernes. / ¡Sí! Mañana es sábado.
4. ¿Qué día es hoy? / Hoy es domingo. / ¡Sí! Mañana es lunes.
5. ¿Qué día es hoy? / Hoy es jueves. / ¡Sí! Mañana es viernes.
6. ¿Qué día es hoy? / Hoy es martes. / ¡Sí! Mañana es miércoles.

Block Schedule

Change of Pace Assign each student a number from 0–10. Play music and have students walk around the class, then stop when you call a number. The students whose number is called must sit down. Continue until all are sitting. (For additional activities, see **Block Scheduling Copymasters**.)

Teaching All Students

Extra Help **Numbers:** In pairs, have students take turns, one thinking of a number and writing it down in Spanish, the other guessing it. Use objects (marbles, etc.) to enhance retention. **Days of the Week:** In pairs, have students take turns saying the days of the week in order as they point to the correct day in the illustration on p. 13.

Multiple Intelligences

Logical/Mathematical Teach students: **más** = plus, **menos** = minus, **es igual a** = makes, equals; **Dos más dos es igual a cuatro.** Then have students make up simple arithmetic problems on flashcards and exchange them.

Intrapersonal Have each student begin a personal log with the days of the week written in Spanish, leaving a space for the date. (Explain that the dates will be added later.) Continue to use the log throughout the year.

Teaching Resource Options

Print

Más práctica Workbook PE, p. 7
Para hispanohablantes Workbook
   PE, p. 7
Block Scheduling Copymasters
Preliminary/Unit 1 Resource Book
   Más práctica Workbook TE, p. 9
   Para hispanohablantes Workbook
   Audioscript, p. 28
   Audioscript *Para hispanohablantes*,
   p. 28

Audiovisual

Audio Program Cassette 1A / CD 1
Audio *Para hispanohablantes*
   Cassette 1A / CD 1
OHT P3, P5 (Quick Start)

Technology

Intrigas y aventuras CD-ROM, Disc 1

Quick Start Review

♻ **Days of the week/Numbers**
Use OHT P5 or write on board:
Complete the following sentences:

1. ¿Qué día es hoy? Hoy es _____.
2. ¿Qué día es mañana? Mañana es _____.
3. ¿Cuál es tu teléfono? (Write the numbers in Spanish.)

Answers will vary.

Teaching Suggestions

• Use OHT P3 to present **Frases útiles**.
• Model pronunciation of "In the Classroom" on p. 14, or use Audio Program Cassette 1A / CD 1, while demonstrating the meaning.
• Remind students that this material is to help them understand recurring Spanish phrases used in class.
• Point out that the phrases listed under "Helpful Spanish Phrases" will be very useful. Review these phrases often and post them in the classroom until students are comfortable using them.
• Model pronunciation of "In the Text" on p. 15, or use Audio Program Cassette 1A / CD 1. Practice them with sample situations.

Frases útiles

In the Classroom

Abran los libros.	Open your books.
Cierren los libros.	Close your books.
Escriban…	Write…
Escuchen…	Listen (to)…
Lean…	Read…
Levanten la mano.	Raise your hand.
Miren el pizarrón.	Look at the chalkboard.
la foto.	the photo.
Pásenme la tarea.	Pass in the homework.
Repitan.	Repeat.
Saquen un lápiz.	Take out a pencil.
Siéntense.	Sit down.

Skills

Escuchar   Hablar

Leer   Escribir

Helpful Spanish Phrases

¿Cómo se dice…?	How do you say…?
Más despacio, por favor.	More slowly, please.
No sé.	I don't know.
¿Qué quiere decir…?	What does… mean?
Repita, por favor.	Repeat, please.

14 catorce
Etapa preliminar

Classroom Management

Time Saver Review several **Frases útiles** at the beginning and end of each class early in the year to facilitate the use of Spanish in the classroom. A quick game of **Simón dice** also provides good review and a change of pace. In addition, you may want to put the phrases on posters with visuals to be used all year.

Planning Ahead If you wish to use additional classroom vocabulary, a poster listing the new words may be useful. Add additional phrases as needed:

   Miren el video.
   Escuchen el casete.
   Miren la transparencia.
   ¿Cómo se dice (X) en español?

In the Text

Cambien de papel.
Change roles.

Completa la conversación.
Complete the conversation.

Contesta las preguntas.
Answer the questions.

Di quién habla.
Say who is speaking.

¿Es cierto o falso?
True or false?

Escoge la respuesta correcta.
Choose the correct response.

la palabra
word
la frase
phrase
la oración
sentence

Escucha…
Listen to…

Explica…
Explain…

Lee…
Read…

Pregúntale a otro(a) estudiante…
Ask another student…

Trabaja con otro(a) estudiante…
Work with another student…

Trabaja en un grupo de…
Work in a group of…

---

17 Instrucciones

Repond to your teacher's classroom instructions.

18 En la clase

What is the teacher telling the students? Match the picture with the instructions below.

a. Abran los libros.   c. Miren el pizarrón.
b. Pásenme la tarea.   d. Levanten la mano.

19 ¡Atención, clase!

Take turns giving classroom instructions to your partners, who will respond with appropriate gestures.

20 ¡Abran los libros!

Working in groups, look through your textbook to find examples of the different instructions you have learned. Write down the page number where you find each one.

quince
Etapa preliminar   15

17 Objective: Controlled practice
Classroom commands

Answers will vary according to teacher choice.

18 Objective: Transitional practice
Classroom commands

Answers
1. c. Miren el pizarrón.
2. b. Pásenme la tarea.
3. d. Levanten la mano.
4. a. Abran los libros.

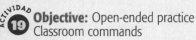

19 Objective: Open-ended practice
Classroom commands

Answers will vary.

20 Objective: Open-ended practice
Text instructions

Answers will vary.

Extra Practice

Divide the class into pairs. Ask students to go through the lists and note the items that each has difficulty remembering. Partners then devise a way to help each other remember (flashcard, drawing, rhyme, etc.) according to their preferred learning style.

Quick Wrap-up

Play **Simón dice** to review classroom vocabulary (3 min.).

Teaching All Students

Extra Help Prepare ahead: drawings of classroom commands; audiocassette/CD of commands. Some students will need to listen to the classroom commands frequently in order to retain them. Prepare a Review Corner with pictures and audio that can be used as needed.

Native Speakers Ask native speakers to help in expanding the list of classroom vocabulary as students ask for new words during the year by preparing and updating a **Frases útiles** Dictionary for classroom reference.

Multiple Intelligences

Kinesthetic Have students mime the classroom vocabulary and prepare a videotape for classroom reference.

Block Schedule

Variety Ask each student to create one "scrambled command" for others to correct. Humor should be encouraged. For example: **Miren la mano. Escuchen el pizarrón.** (For additional activities, see **Block Scheduling Copymasters**.)

♻ Quick Start Review

♻ Numbers/Days of the week

Use OHT P5 or write on board:
Complete the following patterns:

1. uno, tres, cinco, ____
2. seis, cinco, ____
3. siete, ocho, ____
4. martes, miércoles, ____
5. lunes, miércoles, ____
6. martes, lunes, ____

Answers
1. siete
2. cuatro
3. nueve
4. jueves
5. viernes
6. domingo

Teaching Suggestions

- Use Videotape 1 / Videodisc 1A to present the Video Program Prologue.
- Explain to students that *Onda Internacional* and its contest are a part of the ongoing storyline of the textbook and its fictitious characters.
- Bring in some Spanish-language magazines to class. Many popular U.S. magazines, such as *Discover,* are also published in Spanish. If you have concurrent issues of one magazine in English and Spanish, have students compare them.

Onda Internacional

El concurso

In this book you will get to know teens from different parts of the Spanish-speaking world. Many of these young people are interested in a contest sponsored by a Spanish magazine for young people called *Onda Internacional.* Why are they interested? Read on!

Hi! I've got the new edition of Onda Internacional magazine. It has many different articles. There are articles about Spanish-speaking countries, sports, fashion, food, school, leisure activities, and much more. And look! There's a contest. Write an article or prepare a photo essay about what it means to you to be latino or latina. The two winners will travel to parts of the Spanish-speaking world and work for the magazine. Well, get out your cameras, pencils, paper, and ideas, and take part in the contest!

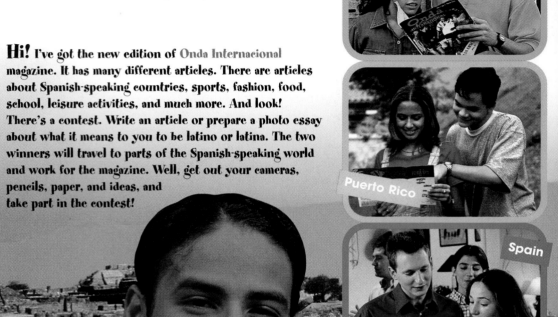

16 **Etapa preliminar**

Classroom Community

Group Activity Have small groups of students research the names of Spanish-language magazines at a bookstore, library, or on the Internet. Have them compile a list, indicating the audience and focus of each title. Also have them give a comparable magazine in English.

Portfolio Have students look through a Spanish-language magazine or newspaper and write a list of words they can recognize/guess, as well as a short list of words they would like to know. Refer to the lists during the year, filling in meanings as new words are learned.

APOYO PARA ESTUDIAR

Reading a poster

When you read a poster, look at the size of lettering, kinds of words, colors, visuals, and any other items it contains. Based on what you already know about *Onda Internacional* and what you see on this poster, why might someone use a poster? Give as many reasons as you can.

¡Gran concurso!

"¿QUÉ SIGNIFICA SER LATINO DE CORAZÓN?"

¡Lee más información en la revista!

Año 2. No. 1 Precio $2.95

Onda INTERNACIONAL

¡GRAN CONCURSO! pág. 31

¿Comprendiste?

1. Although you may know little Spanish, are there words whose meaning you can guess? Which ones? What do you think they mean? What helps you guess their meaning?
2. What do you notice different about punctuation? What does that tell you about the meaning of the phrases?

¿Qué piensas?

What about this poster catches your attention or stimulates your interest?

Etapa preliminar **17**

Cross Cultural Connections

List several cultures on the board (e.g., Hispanic, Native American, Middle Eastern, etc.). Have students brainstorm words each might use to describe what it means to be of each cultural heritage.

Critical Thinking

Ask students why they think *Onda Internacional* might be having this contest. Have they ever seen similar contests in any of their favorite magazines? Have they ever heard about contests on the radio? What is their purpose?

Teaching Note

Many Internet sites list titles of Spanish-language magazines and their contents. Look especially at foreign language teaching resource sites and online bookstores. Local bookstores often have lists as well.

¿Comprendiste?

Answers will vary. Answers could include:
1. **gran** = grand; **significa** = signifies, means; **latino** = Latin; **corazón** = heart; **lee** = read; **información** = information; **revista** = review, magazine
2. The exclamation point and question mark are inverted at the beginning of a phrase/sentence.

Teaching All Students

Native Speakers Have students bring in and share Spanish-language magazines they might have. They should point out what they like in the magazines.

Multiple Intelligences

Verbal Photocopy pages from Spanish-language magazines. Have students circle or highlight words or cognates they recognize. Have them use these and visual cues to guess the topic of the article(s) on their pages.

 **Block Schedule**

Personalizing Have students write a brief explanation about what it means to be of their cultural background.

Etapa preliminar
Review

Teaching Resource Options

Print

Más práctica Workbook PE, p. 8
Para hispanohablantes Workbook PE, p. 8
Block Scheduling Copymasters
Preliminary/Unit 1 Resource Book
  Más práctica Workbook TE, p. 10
  Para hispanohablantes Workbook TE, p. 18
  Information Gap Activities, pp. 19–20
  Family Involvement, pp. 23–24
  Multiple Choice Test Questions, pp. 45–47

Audiovisual

OHT P5 (Quick Start)
Audio Program Testing Cassette T1 / CD T1

Technology

Electronic Teacher Tools/Test Generator
Intrigas y aventuras CD-ROM, Disc 1

Quick Start Review

♻ **Numbers/Days of the week**
Use OHT P5 or write on the board:
Write the days of the week, then write out the numbers in Spanish that indicate their correct order.

lunes	uno
m _ _ _ _ _	_ _ _ _
m _ _ _ _ _ _ _ _	_ _ _ _
j _ _ _ _ _	_ _ _ _
v _ _ _ _ _ _	_ _ _ _
s _ _ _ _ _	_ _ _ _
d _ _ _ _ _ _	_ _ _ _

Answers
martes, dos; miércoles, tres; jueves, cuatro; viernes, cinco; sábado, seis; domingo, siete

✔ Teaching Suggestions
What Have Students Learned?

• Have students look at the "Now you can…" notes and give examples of each category. Have them spend extra time reviewing categories they feel they are weak in by consulting the "To review" notes.
• Divide the class into groups to complete the activities.

Now you can…
• greet people.
• introduce yourself.

To review
• greetings and introductions, see pp. 2–5.

Now you can…
• say where you are from.

To review
• saying where you are from, see pp. 6–8.

En uso
REPASO Y MÁS COMUNICACIÓN

OBJECTIVES
• Greet people
• Introduce yourself
• Say where you are from
• Exchange phone numbers
• Say which day it is

ACTIVIDAD 1 En la clase

Marta speaks with two people. Complete the conversations with the words given.

adiós · hasta · llamo · se · placer · llama · encantada · llamas · mañana · tardes · hola · mucho · me · vemos · mío

Marta: ¡__1__! Me llamo Marta. ¿Cómo te __2__?
Andrea: __3__ llamo Andrea. __4__.
Marta: Igualmente. ¿Cómo se __5__ el chico?
Andrea: __6__ llama Mateo.
Marta: Es un __7__, Andrea. Nos __8__.
Andrea: __9__, Marta. __10__ luego.
Marta: Buenas __11__, Mateo. Me __12__ Marta.
Mateo: __13__ gusto, Marta.
Marta: El gusto es __14__. Hasta __15__.

ACTIVIDAD 2 ¿De dónde eres?

You are talking to some international students. Where is each one from?

modelo

Luisa (Chile) / Jorge (Puerto Rico)
*Me llamo **Luisa**. Soy de **Chile**. **Jorge** es de **Puerto Rico**.*

1. Julio (Panamá) / Mónica (Bolivia)
2. Diana (Estados Unidos) / Rafael (Uruguay)
3. Patricio (España) / Alejandra (Guatemala)
4. Natalia (Argentina) / Benjamín (México)
5. Gregorio (Cuba) / Verónica (El Salvador)

Classroom Community

Learning Scenario Divide the class into groups. Have each group create a dialog to present to the class that solves the following problem: You are at the airport trying to find your pen pal, who has just arrived and doesn't speak English. You locate a group of Spanish-speaking students. Verify your identity and that of your pen pal.

Portfolio Record/video the learning scenario dialogs to retain in a Progress Portfolio for parents.

Rubric

Criteria	Scale	
Vocabulary	1 2 3 4 5	A = 17–20 pts.
Pronunciation	1 2 3 4 5	B = 13–16 pts.
Fluency	1 2 3 4 5	C = 9–12 pts.
Variety	1 2 3 4 5	D = 5–8 pts.
		F = < 5 pts.

ACTIVIDAD **3** Teléfonos

You need some phone numbers. Write the conversations as you ask for friends' numbers.

modelo

Rosana: 530-4401

You: *Rosana, ¿cuál es tu teléfono?*

Rosana: *Cinco - tres - cero - cuatro - cuatro - cero - uno.*

Rosana
530-4401

1. Timoteo: 927-2296
2. Mariana: 820-3981
3. Cristóbal: 450-5649

4. Emilia: 392-4100
5. Leonardo: 758-3141

ACTIVIDAD **4** ¿Qué día es hoy?

Tell what day it is today, based on what tomorrow is.

modelo

Mañana es viernes.

Hoy es jueves.

1. Mañana es domingo.
2. Mañana es miércoles.
3. Mañana es lunes.
4. Mañana es jueves.
5. Mañana es martes.
6. Mañana es sábado.

diecinueve
Etapa preliminar 19

Now you can...
• exchange phone numbers.

To review
• numbers, see p. 12.

Now you can...
• say which day it is.

To review
• days of the week, see p. 13.

ACTIVIDAD **1** Answers

1. ¡Hola!
2. llamas
3. Me
4. Encantada
5. llama
6. Se
7. placer
8. vemos
9. Adiós
10. Hasta
11. tardes
12. llamo
13. Mucho
14. mío
15. mañana

ACTIVIDAD **2** Answers

1. Me llamo Julio. Soy de Panamá. Mónica es de Bolivia.
2. Me llamo Diana. Soy de Estados Unidos. Rafael es de Uruguay.
3. Me llamo Patricio. Soy de España. Alejandra es de Guatemala.
4. Me llamo Natalia. Soy de Argentina. Benjamín es de México.
5. Me llamo Gregorio. Soy de Cuba. Verónica es de El Salvador.

ACTIVIDAD **3** Answers

1. Timoteo, ¿cuál es tu teléfono?
   Nueve-dos-siete-dos-dos-nueve-seis.
2. Mariana, ¿cuál es tu teléfono?
   Ocho-dos-cero-tres-nueve-ocho-uno.
3. Cristóbal, ¿cuál es tu teléfono?
   Cuatro-cinco-cero-cinco-seis-cuatro-nueve.
4. Emilia, ¿cuál es tu teléfono?
   Tres-nueve-dos-cuatro-uno-cero-cero.
5. Leonardo, ¿cuál es tu teléfono?
   Siete-cinco-ocho-tres-uno-cuatro-uno.

ACTIVIDAD **4** Answers

1. Hoy es sábado.
2. Hoy es martes.
3. Hoy es domingo.
4. Hoy es miércoles.
5. Hoy es lunes.
6. Hoy es viernes.

Quick Wrap-up

Ask short review questions (¿Cómo te llamas? ¿Cuál es tu teléfono? ¿De dónde eres? ¿Qué día es hoy/ mañana?). Then have students write down their phone numbers in Spanish.

Teaching All Students

Extra Help Have students find and write down 2 sample sentences containing material they have learned corresponding to each objective.

Native Speakers If students need additional practice in correct writing skills, have them complete the activities in writing. If not, allow students to read magazines, newspapers, or stories in Spanish and write a short synopsis of what they have read.

Multiple Intelligences

Visual Have students draw or cut out photos and create short dialogs between 2 people greeting and introducing themselves, saying where they are from, and exchanging phone numbers. A locator map can also be drawn.

Block Schedule

Peer Teaching Divide the class into groups of 3 and have students practice the completed dialog from **Actividad 1**. (For additional activities, see **Block Scheduling Copymasters**.)

Teaching Resource Options

Print

Preliminary/Unit 1 Resource Book
Information Gap Activities, pp. 21–22
Cooperative Quizzes, pp. 31–32
Etapa Exam, Forms A and B,
   pp. 33–42
Para hispanohablantes Etapa Exam,
   pp. 43–47
Portfolio Assessment, pp. 48–49
Multiple Choice Test Questions,
   pp. 230–232

Audiovisual

OHT P5 (Quick Start)
Audio Program Testing Cassette T1 /
CD T1

Technology

Electronic Teacher Tools/Test
Generator
www.mcdougallittell.com

ACTIVIDAD 5

Rubric: Speaking

Criteria	Scale	
Sentence structure	1 2 3	A = 8–9 pts.
Vocabulary use	1 2 3	B = 6–7 pts.
Fluency	1 2 3	C = 4–5 pts.
		D = 3 pts.
		F = < 3 pts.

ACTIVIDAD 6 *Answers will vary.*

ACTIVIDAD 7 **En tu propia voz**

Rubric: Writing

Criteria	Scale	
Vocabulary use	1 2 3 4 5	A = 14–15 pts.
Accuracy	1 2 3 4 5	B = 12–13 pts.
Creativity, appearance	1 2 3 4 5	C = 10–11 pts.
		D = 8–9 pts.
		F = < 8 pts.

Supplementary Vocabulary

Querido(a)... Dear…
Tu amigo(a) Your friend…

ACTIVIDAD 5  **Hola**

Greet a partner and introduce yourself. Talk about which day it is today and tomorrow. Say good-bye.

modelo

You: *Hola. Me llamo…
¿Cómo te llamas?*

Partner: *Mucho gusto. Me llamo…*

You: *¿Qué día es…?*

ACTIVIDAD 6  **Mucha información**

Imagine that everyone has a new identity. Ask three classmates for the information needed to complete the chart.

modelo

You: *Hola. Me llamo… ¿Cómo te llamas?*

Student 1: *Es un placer. Me llamo Carolina. Soy de Perú. ¿De dónde eres?*

You: *Soy de Honduras. ¿Cuál es tu teléfono?*

Student 1: *Siete - tres - cero - siete - seis - seis - dos. ¿Cuál es tu…?*

Nombre	País	Teléfono
1. Carolina	Perú	730-7662
2.		
3.		

ACTIVIDAD 7 **En tu propia voz**

ESCRITURA Write to your new pen pal. Include the following information.

- Write a greeting.
- Introduce yourself.
- Say where you are from.
- Write three questions for your new pen pal to answer.

Classroom Community

Paired Activity For **Actividad 7**, have students check each other's writing for errors and suggest improvements.

Portfolio Use the corrected writing sample from **Actividad 7: En tu propia voz** to save as the first writing of the year. Use the Writing Rubric for grading.

Game Prepare ahead: bingo cards and numbers. You may want to have students create the cards. Pass out the cards and have students mark off the numbers as they are called until there is a winner. Variation: Make cards using other vocabulary from the **Etapa,** such as days, countries, etc.

En resumen

REPASO DE VOCABULARIO

GREETINGS

Greeting People

Buenos días.	Good morning.
Buenas tardes.	Good afternoon.
Buenas noches.	Good evening.
Hola.	Hello.

Responding

El gusto es mío.	The pleasure is mine.
Encantado(a).	Delighted/Pleased to meet you.
Es un placer.	It's a pleasure.
Igualmente.	Same here.
Mucho gusto.	Nice to meet you.

Saying Good-bye

Adiós.	Good-bye.
Hasta luego.	See you later.
Hasta mañana.	See you tomorrow.
Nos vemos.	See you later.

INTRODUCING YOURSELF

el apellido	last name, surname
¿Cómo te llamas?	What is your name?
¿Cómo se llama?	What is his/her name?
Me llamo…	My name is…
Se llama…	His/Her name is…
el nombre	name, first name

SAYING WHERE YOU ARE FROM

¿De dónde eres?	Where are you from?
¿De dónde es?	Where is he/she from?
Soy de…	I am from…
Es de…	He/She is from…

EXCHANGING PHONE NUMBERS

¿Cuál es tu teléfono?	What is your phone number?

Numbers from Zero to Ten

cero	zero
uno	one
dos	two
tres	three
cuatro	four
cinco	five
seis	six
siete	seven
ocho	eight
nueve	nine
diez	ten

SAYING WHICH DAY IT IS

¿Qué día es hoy?	What day is today?
Hoy es…	Today is…
Mañana es…	Tomorrow is…
el día	day
hoy	today
mañana	tomorrow
la semana	week

Days of the Week

lunes	Monday
martes	Tuesday
miércoles	Wednesday
jueves	Thursday
viernes	Friday
sábado	Saturday
domingo	Sunday

OTHER WORDS AND PHRASES

no	no
sí	yes

Skills

escribir	to write
escuchar	to listen
hablar	to talk
leer	to read

SPANISH IS THE OFFICIAL LANGUAGE OF THESE COUNTRIES:

Argentina	Argentina
Bolivia	Bolivia
Chile	Chile
Colombia	Colombia
Costa Rica	Costa Rica
Cuba	Cuba
Ecuador	Ecuador
El Salvador	El Salvador
España	Spain
Guatemala	Guatemala
Guinea Ecuatorial	Equatorial Guinea
Honduras	Honduras
México	Mexico
Nicaragua	Nicaragua
Panamá	Panama
Paraguay	Paraguay
Perú	Peru
Puerto Rico	Puerto Rico
República Dominicana	Dominican Republic
Uruguay	Uruguay
Venezuela	Venezuela

veintiuno **21**
Etapa preliminar

Teaching Suggestions
Vocabulary Review
• Have students study the **Repaso de vocabulario** on p. 21.
• Ask students to review conversational exchanges by role-playing in pairs.
• Have students make lists with Spanish words in one column and English in the other. Students fold and review, looking at the English column and recalling the Spanish side.

Community Connections
Have students look in the TV guide to see what channels in your area broadcast Spanish-language programs. Have students choose one program to watch and see if they can describe the gist of the show.

Interdisciplinary Connection
Social Studies Work with the Social Studies teacher to come up with a list of several well-known historical and contemporary Spanish speakers and what they are known for.

Block Schedule
Change of Pace Play selections from the **Canciones** Cassette/CD while students study their vocabulary lists or flashcards. (For additional activities, see **Block Scheduling Copymasters**.)

Teaching All Students

Extra Help Have a Spelling Bee to practice both the alphabet and new vocabulary.

Native Speakers Have students create crossword puzzles with the new vocabulary to help the class review.

Multiple Intelligences
Kinesthetic Have groups choose 10 words or phrases to act out for the rest of the class to identify.

Verbal Have groups develop a short dialog using the new vocabulary. Remind students that they should try to re-combine the material in new and interesting ways. The most creative dialog wins 5 extra points on the **Etapa** Exam score.

Unit Theme
Exchanging greetings in Spanish-speaking communities (United States), talking about friends, and introducing family.

Communication
- Greeting and introducing others
- Saying where people live and are from
- Expressing likes and dislikes
- Describing people and their clothing
- Identifying family members, their ages, and their birthdays
- Expressing possession

Cultures
- Learning about the influence of Spanish speakers in the United States
- Learning about Tejano music
- Learning about a traditional birthday celebration
- Learning about traditional holidays

Connections
- Connecting to Social Studies: Hispanic traditions and events and those of other communities in the U.S.
- Connecting to Social Studies: Hispanic celebrations and those of other communities in the U.S.

Comparisons
- Comparing unique music forms
- Comparing events marking transition from childhood to adulthood
- Comparing important holidays

Communities
- Using Spanish in Spanish-speaking communities for personal enjoyment
- Using Spanish in the workplace

Teaching Resource Options

Print
Block Scheduling Copymasters, pp. 9–10

Audiovisual
OHT M1, M2; 1, 2
Canciones Audiocassette/CD
Video Program Videotape 1 / Videodisc 1A

Search Chapter 2, Play to 3
U1 Cultural Introduction

UNIDAD 1

ESTADOS UNIDOS

MI MUNDO

OBJECTIVES

ETAPA 1
¡Bienvenido a Miami!
- Greet others
- Introduce others
- Say where people are from
- Express likes

ETAPA 2
Mis buenos amigos
- Describe others
- Give others' likes and dislikes
- Describe clothing

ETAPA 3
Te presento a mi familia
- Describe family
- Ask and tell ages
- Talk about birthdays
- Give dates
- Express possession

22

MURALS are popular art sometimes found on the sides of buildings in L.A. Often their artists are Chicano, or Mexican American. What street art have you seen?

• SAN JOSÉ

FAJITAS reflect the Mexican influence on Los Angeles cuisine. What Mexican dishes have you tried?

LOS ÁNGELES
•
SAN DIEGO
•

ISLAS HAWAI

ALASKA

Classroom Community

Paired Activity Divide the class into pairs. Give students 5 minutes to discuss and write down as many things they can think of that have Spanish names. Use **San Francisco** and **llama** as examples.

Group Activity Working in small groups, have students look at the maps on pp. 22–23 to find states that share a border with Mexico. Then have them locate Cuba and the Dominican Republic.

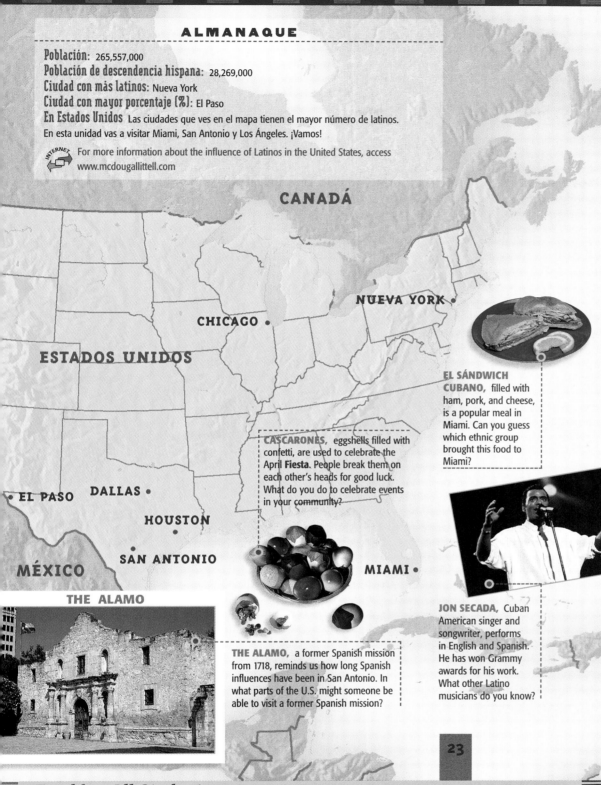

ALMANAQUE

Población: 265,557,000
Población de descendencia hispana: 28,269,000
Ciudad con más latinos: Nueva York
Ciudad con mayor porcentaje (%): El Paso
En Estados Unidos Las ciudades que ves en el mapa tienen el mayor número de latinos. En esta unidad vas a visitar Miami, San Antonio y Los Ángeles. ¡Vamos!

For more information about the influence of Latinos in the United States, access www.mcdougallittell.com

CANADÁ

NUEVA YORK

CHICAGO

ESTADOS UNIDOS

EL PASO   DALLAS

HOUSTON

MÉXICO   SAN ANTONIO

THE ALAMO

MIAMI

EL SÁNDWICH CUBANO, filled with ham, pork, and cheese, is a popular meal in Miami. Can you guess which ethnic group brought this food to Miami?

CASCARONES, eggshells filled with confetti, are used to celebrate the April **Fiesta**. People break them on each other's heads for good luck. What do you do to celebrate events in your community?

JON SECADA, Cuban American singer and songwriter, performs in English and Spanish. He has won Grammy awards for his work. What other Latino musicians do you know?

THE ALAMO, a former Spanish mission from 1718, reminds us how long Spanish influences have been in San Antonio. In what parts of the U.S. might someone be able to visit a former Spanish mission?

23

Teaching All Students

Extra Help Have students pronounce the city and country names that appear on the map. Explain to them why certain letters have accents.

Native Speakers Ask students if they use commas or periods to separate millions, thousands, and hundreds in Spanish. (Although Spanish usually uses periods, the numbers are given with commas in the **Almanaque** because this unit's focus is the U.S.)

Multiple Intelligences

Logical/Mathematical Ask students to research the Hispanic population of other major U.S. cities. Have them calculate what percentage that figure is of each city's total population.

Musical/Rhythmic Play the *Canciones* Cassette/CD. Ask students what they like about each selection and guess what country's heritage each selection represents.

Teaching Suggestion
Previewing the Unit

Tell students this unit centers on Miami, San Antonio, and Los Angeles. Ask students to scan these two pages for 15 seconds, then close their books. Then ask them to tell you what they remember. You may wish to use the introduction to the video to preview the unit.

Culture Highlights

● **MURALES** In the 20th century, Diego Rivera, José Clemente Orozco, and David Alfaro Siqueiros, three Mexican artists, painted works of art on the walls of public places. The main themes of these murals are the liberation of the masses, the Mexican revolution, and Mexico's past culture.

● **FAJITAS** This "Tex-Mex" dish usually consists of vegetables, meat, or chicken wrapped in flour tortillas.

● **EL ÁLAMO** This Franciscan mission was converted into a fortress in 1793. In 1836, during the Texan Revolution against Mexican rule, a group of Texans, including Davy Crockett, retreated to the Alamo. They remained under siege for 12 days. Eventually all Texans inside were killed.

● **CASCARONES** Cascarón makers often use these brightly colored eggs as heads of figurines. **Cascarones** are also often collected as pieces of folk art.

● **EL SÁNDWICH CUBANO** Some other traditional Cuban dishes are **arroz con pollo** (rice with chicken), **moros y cristianos** (rice with beans), and **yuca con mojo** (cassava root with marinated sauce.)

● **JON SECADA** Jon Secada's album **Otro día más sin verte** won a Grammy for Best Latin Pop Album; his album **Amor** won a Grammy for Latin Pop Performance.

Block Schedule

Reference Lists Have students compile lists of famous Spanish speakers, foods from Spanish-speaking countries, and U.S. city/place names that are Spanish. Use these for projects and discussions. (For additional activities, see **Block Scheduling Copymasters**, pp. 9–10.)

Ampliación

These activities may be used at various points in the Unit 1 sequence.

📖 For Block Schedule, you may find that these projects will provide a welcome change of pace while reviewing and reinforcing the material presented in the unit. See the **Block Scheduling Copymasters.**

● PROJECTS

Create travel brochures for Miami, San Antonio, and Los Angeles. Divide the class into groups, assigning each group one of the three cities. Students should focus on the main tourist attractions and cultural events.

Each group is responsible for writing and illustrating its brochure. The completed projects may be duplicated and published for display, or shared with other Spanish classes or family members.

> **PACING SUGGESTION:** Have students begin research at the beginning of the unit. Final projects are completed at the end of Unit 1.

Film or record an audiovisual fashion show Working in pairs, students should "design" unusual outfits to present in a fashion show. One student will model the outfits while the other narrates the descriptions. They might also play Hispanic music in the background.

> **PACING SUGGESTION:** Upon completion of Etapa 2.

LOS ÁNGELES

ESTADOS UNIDOS

● STORYTELLING

Descripciones/Presentaciones After reviewing the vocabulary for describing and introducing people, model a mini-story (using puppets, student actors, or pictures from the text) that students will retell and revise:

DALLAS

HOUSTON

> Diana y Jaime están en la escuela. Jaime dice, "¿Cómo se llama esa muchacha?" Diana dice, "¿Quién?" Jaime responde, "La muchacha que lleva el vestido rojo y el sombrero". Diana dice, "Es mi amiga Amalia." Jaime dice, "¿Me la presentas?" Diana dice, "¡Cómo no!"

Pause as the story is being told, giving students a chance to fill in words or act out gestures. Students then write, narrate, and read aloud a longer main story. This new version should include vocabulary from the previous story.

SAN ANTONIO

Otros amigos y amigas Ask students to create their own describing/introducing stories. They may imagine getting to know someone at school, at a party, or at a mall. Suggest that students use the text dialogs as a model and personalize/expand.

> **PACING SUGGESTION:** Upon completion of Etapa 2.

MÉXICO

● BULLETIN BOARD/POSTERS

Bulletin Board   Plan ahead: Collect newspapers and magazines that show Hispanic current events—cinema, theater, sports, festivals, restaurants, music, etc. Have students cut out the ads and create a collage, highlighting and decorating the events.

Posters   Have students create •**Travel** posters for Miami, San Antonio, and Los Angeles •**Maps** showing areas in the U.S. where Spanish speakers have settled, including population figures. •**Music** posters for Tejano singers and albums.

CANADÁ

• GAMES

Espalda a espalda

Select a student to be "it." Have him/her sit on a chair at the front of the class blindfolded. Have another student also sit on a chair at the front the class. One-by-one, the rest of the class provides clues describing the second student to the blindfolded student. The blind-folded student gets one guess after each clue. When correct, the student who provided the last clue is the next one to be "it." Play continues until a pre-determined time limit is reached. To keep hesitations to a minimum, keep a reference vocabulary list available for students.

PACING SUGGESTION: Upon completion of Etapa 2.

Escucha y dibuja

For homework, students write a description of a friend or family member, being sure to include physical characteristics and clothing. They bring the assignment to class, along with a small box of crayons or colored markers and plain sheets of paper. One person reads his/her description to the class twice, while the other students draw who is being described. The person who read the description then looks at the pictures and decides who has come closest to the description. The winner is the next one to read his/her description.

PACING SUGGESTION: Upon completion of Etapa 3.

• MUSIC

Hispanic music is enjoyed today by both Spanish and English speakers in the U.S. Some popular singers are Gloria Estefan, Linda Ronstadt, and Jon Secada. Have students go to a music store and find out the names of other Hispanic singers and groups. Play some of the music they research. Discuss what music they like and why. More music samples are available on your *Canciones* Cassette or CD.

• HANDS-ON CRAFTS

Work with the art department to make **cascarones.** With a thick wool needle, poke a hole at each end of a raw egg. Twist the needle to break the yoke, then gently blow out the insides of the egg. Remind students to wash their hands. Rinse and dry the shells. Pour confetti into them and tape over the holes. Paint the eggs in acrylic paint and decorate. When dry, spray with varnish. Eggs may be displayed in class or in the school display case.

MIAMI

RECIPE •

Guacamole is the second most popular dip in the southwestern U.S. (after **salsa**). It is generally served with fried corn chips, **tostadas,** but can also be served with flour tortillas cut into strips. With your students, try this quick-and-easy recipe for **Olé Guacamole.**

WARNING: After handling the **jalapeños,** students should avoid contact with their eyes and should wash hands thoroughly.

Receta

Olé Guacamole
4 aguacates bien maduros
1 tomate: pelado, despepitado y en trozos pequeños
1/4 taza de cebolla bien picada
1/4 taza de hojas de cilantro picadas
1-2 pimientos jalapeños: despepitados y picados
2 cdas. de jugo fresco de limón verde
sal a gusto

Cortar los aguacates por la mitad, quitar el hueso y sacar la pulpa. Majar la pulpa con un tenedor; añadir el tomate, la cebolla, el cilantro, los jalapeños, el jugo de limón verde y la sal a gusto. Refrigerar cubierto con papel de plástico por 1/2 hora. Servir con tortillas. (Sirve a 6–8.)

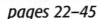
Planning Guide CLASSROOM MANAGEMENT

OBJECTIVES

Communication
- Greet others *pp. 26–27*
- Introduce others *pp. 28–29*
- Say where people live and are from *pp. 40–41*
- Express likes *pp. 28–29*

Grammar
- Use familiar and formal greetings *pp. 32–33*
- Use subject pronouns and the verb **ser** *pp. 33–35*
- Use **ser de** to express origin *pp. 35–36*
- Use verbs to talk about what you like to do *pp. 37–38*

Pronunciation
- Pronouncing vowels *p. 39*
- Dictation, *TE p. 39*

Culture
- Distinguishing between familiar and formal greetings *pp. 28–29*
- Spanish-speaking communities in the U.S. *pp. 22–23, 26–27; 35; 36; 40–41*

♻ Recycling
- Saying hello and good-bye
- Introductions
- Spelling your name
- Numbers 0–10
- Days of the week

STRATEGIES

Listening Strategies
- Listen to intonation *pp. 28–29*

Speaking Strategies
- Practice *p. 33*
- Understand, then speak *p. 44*

Reading Strategies
- Preview graphics *pp. 40–41*

Writing Strategies
- Brainstorm possible vocabulary before writing *p. 44*

Connecting Cultures Strategies
- Think about your relationship to a person before using **tú** or **usted** *pp. 28–29*
- Connect and compare what you know about your own community to help you learn about a new community *pp. 22–23; 26–27; 35; 36; 44*

PROGRAM RESOURCES

 Print
- *Más práctica* Workbook PE, *pp. 9–16*
- Block Scheduling Copymasters, *pp. 9–16*
- Unit 1 Resource Book
  Más práctica Workbook TE, *pp. 52–59*
  Para hispanohablantes Workbook TE, *pp. 60–67*

- Information Gap Activities *pp. 68–71*
- Family Involvement *pp. 72–73*
- Video Activities *pp. 74–76*
- Videoscript *pp. 77–79*
- Audioscript *pp. 80–83*
- Assessment Program, Unit 1 Etapa 1 *pp. 86–102; 232–241*
- Answer Keys *pp. 242–261*

 Audiovisual
- **Audio Program** Cassettes 1A, 1B / CD 1
- *Canciones* Cassette / CD
- **Video Program** Videotape 1 / Videodisc 1A
- **Overhead Transparencies** M1–M5; 1–14

 Technology
- Electronic Teacher Tools/Test Generator
- *Intrigas y aventuras* CD-ROM, Disc 1
- www.mcdougallittell.com

 Assessment Program Options
- **Cooperative Quizzes** (Unit 1 Resource Book)
- **Etapa Exam** Forms A and B (Unit 1 Resource Book)
- *Para hispanohablantes* **Etapa Exam** (Unit 1 Resource Book)
- **Portfolio Assessment** (Unit 1 Resource Book)
- **Multiple Choice Test Questions** (Unit 1 Resource Book)
- **Audio Program** Testing Cassette T1 / CD T1
- **Electronic Teacher Tools/Test Generator**

Native Speakers
- *Para hispanohablantes* Workbook PE, *pp. 9–16*
- *Para hispanohablantes* Workbook TE (Unit 1 Resource Book)
- *Para hispanohablantes* Etapa Exam (Unit 1 Resource Book)
- Audio *Para hispanohablantes* Cassettes 1A, 1B, T1 / CD 1, T1
- Audioscript *Para hispanohablantes* (Unit 1 Resource Book)

Student Text
Listening Activity Scripts

 Videoscript: Diálogo *pages 28–29*

• Videotape 1 • Videodisc 1A

Search Chapter 4, Play to 5
U1E1 • En vivo (Dialog)

• Use the videoscript with **Actividades 1, 2** *page 30*

Alma:	¡Hola! *(louder)* ¡Hola!
Francisco:	¡Hola!
Alma:	Me llamo Alma Cifuentes. Soy tu vecina. Ésa es mi casa.
Francisco:	Mucho gusto, Alma, ¿mi vecina?
Alma:	Y tú, ¿cómo te llamas?
Francisco:	¿Yo? Yo me llamo Francisco García Flores.
Alma:	Encantada, Francisco García Flores.
Francisco:	Papá, te presento a Alma Cifuentes. Alma, mi papá.
Sr. García:	Es un placer, Alma.
Alma:	Mucho gusto, señor García.
Sr. García:	Permiso.
Francisco:	Mamá, Alma Cifuentes. Alma, mi mamá.
Sra. García:	Mucho gusto, Alma.
Alma:	El gusto es mío, señora.
David:	Y yo, ¿qué?
Francisco:	¡Ay, David! Alma, te presento a David. David es el monstruo de Miami.
David:	¡No soy monstruo! ¡Y no soy de Miami!
Alma:	Es un placer, señor David García.
Alma:	Pues, si no son de Miami, ¿de dónde son ustedes?
Francisco:	Es difícil explicar. Nosotros somos de muchos lugares. Mamá es de Puerto Rico. Papá es de México. Yo soy de Puerto Rico y David… David es de San Antonio.
Alma:	Entonces, Francisco García, ¡bienvenido a Miami y bienvenido a mi comunidad!

Francisco:	Muchas gracias, Alma.
Arturo:	¡Alma, chica! ¿Qué tal?
Alma:	Muy bien, gracias, Arturo. Arturo, te presento a Francisco García. Él es mi vecino.
Arturo:	Francisco, es un placer.
Francisco:	Igualmente, Arturo.
Alma:	A Arturo le gusta mucho correr. A mí me gusta también. ¿Te gusta correr, Francisco?
Francisco:	No, no me gusta mucho correr.
Arturo:	¡Muy bien! ¡Hasta luego!
Francisco/Alma:	¡Hasta luego! / ¡Adiós!
Francisco:	Mira, Alma, ¡qué interesante!
Sr. Estrada:	¡Buenas tardes, Alma! ¿Cómo estás hoy?
Alma:	Muy bien, gracias, señor Estrada, ¿y usted?
Sr. Estrada:	Hoy es lunes, ¿no? Si es lunes, estoy terrible.
Alma:	¡Ay, señor Estrada!, es un día fenomenal. Señor Estrada, le presento a mi amigo Francisco García Flores.
Francisco:	Es un placer, señor Estrada.
Sr. Estrada:	El gusto es mío, Francisco.
Alma:	¿Vamos?
Francisco:	Vamos.
Alma:	Hasta luego, señor.
Francisco:	Este concurso es muy interesante, muy interesante.

ACTIVIDAD 10 🎧 **¡Escucha! ¿Quién es?** *page 34*

1. El chico se llama Francisco.
2. Los hombres son policías.
3. A Arturo le gusta correr.
4. María no está bien hoy.
5. Las muchachas son estudiantes.

ACTIVIDAD 20 🎧 **¡Un nuevo amigo!** *page 39*

¡Hola! Me llamo Enrique. Soy de Los Ángeles. Estoy muy bien hoy. Y tú, ¿cómo estás? Me gusta bailar y patinar. Pero no me gusta trabajar. ¿Qué te gusta?

Quick Start Review Answers

p. 28 People
Foto 3:
Francisco	chico, amigo
Sr. García	hombre, papá
Sra. García	mujer, mamá
Alma	chica, amiga

Foto 9:
Sr. Estrada	hombre
Alma	chica, amiga
Francisco	chico, amigo

p. 32 Vocabulary
chaval(a): Spain; chavo(a): Mexico; chico(a): many countries; niño(a): many countries; joven: many countries; muchacho(a): many countries; pibe(a): Argentina

p. 33 Familiar and formal greetings
¿Qué tal?: informal; How are you?
¿Cómo está usted?: formal; How are you?
¿Cómo estás?: informal; How are you?

p. 35 Subject pronouns
1. Ellas/Ustedes   4. Nosotras
2. Él/Usted   5. Yo
3. Tú

p. 40 Introducing oneself
Answers will vary.
Answers could include:
1. Me llamo…
2. Soy de…
3. Sí, me gusta nadar./No, no me gusta nadar.
4. Me gusta…

Pacing Guide

Sample Lesson Plan - 50 Minute Schedule

DAY 1

Unit Opener
- Anticipate/Activate prior knowledge: Present the *Almanaque* and the cultural notes. Use Map OHTs as needed. **10 MIN.**

Etapa Opener
- Quick Start Review (TE, p. 24) **5 MIN.**
- Have students look at the *Etapa* Opener and answer the questions. **5 MIN.**

En contexto: Vocabulario
- Quick Start Review (TE, p. 26) **5 MIN.**
- Have students use context and pictures to learn *Etapa* vocabulary, then answer the questions, p. 27. Use the Situational OHTs for additional practice. **10 MIN.**

En vivo: Diálogo
- Quick Start Review (TE, p. 28) **5 MIN.**
- Review the Listening Strategy, p. 28. Play audio or show video for the dialog, pp. 28–29. Replay and have students take the roles of the characters. **10 MIN.**

Homework Option:
- Video Activities, Unit 1 Resource Book, pp. 74–75.

DAY 2

En acción: Vocabulario y gramática
- Check homework. **5 MIN.**
- Quick Start Review (TE, p. 30) **5 MIN.**
- Have students open to *En contexto*, pp. 26–27, for reference. Use OHT 5 and 6 to review vocabulary. **5 MIN.**
- Play the video/audio; have students do *Actividades* 1 and 2 orally. **5 MIN.**
- Have students do *Actividad* 3 orally, then read and complete *Actividad* 4. **10 MIN.**
- Have students complete *Actividad* 5 in writing, then exchange papers for peer correction. **5 MIN.**
- Quick Start Review (TE, p. 32) **5 MIN.**
- Present *Gramática:* Familiar and Formal Greetings, p. 32. **5 MIN.**
- Have students do *Actividad* 6 in pairs and *Actividad* 7 orally. **5 MIN.**
- Present the Speaking Strategy, p. 33. Do *Actividad* 8 in pairs. **5 MIN.**

Homework Option:
- *Más práctica* Workbook, p. 13. *Para hispanohablantes* Workbook, p. 11.

DAY 3

En acción (cont.)
- Check homework. **5 MIN.**
- Quick Start Review (TE, p. 33) **3 MIN.**
- Present *Gramática:* Describing People: Subject Pronouns and the Verb *ser,* p. 33. **10 MIN.**
- Have students do *Actividad* 9. **5 MIN.**
- Play the audio; do *Actividad* 10. **5 MIN.**
- Do *Actividad* 11 orally. **5 MIN.**
- Have students complete *Actividad* 12 in writing. Have volunteers go to the board and write out answers. Expand using Information Gap Activities, Unit 1 Resource Book, p. 68; *Más comunicación,* p. R1. **5 MIN.**
- Quick Start Review (TE, p. 35) **5 MIN.**
- Present *Gramática:* Using *ser de* to Express Origin, p. 35. **2 MIN.**
- Do *Actividad* 13 orally, *Actividad* 14 in pairs, and *Actividad* 15 in groups. **10 MIN.**

Homework Option:
- *Más práctica* Workbook, pp. 14–15. *Para hispanohablantes* Workbook, pp. 12–13.

DAY 4

En acción (cont.)
- Check homework. **5 MIN.**
- Quick Start Review (TE, p. 37) **5 MIN.**
- Present *Gramática:* Using Verbs to Talk About What You Like to Do, p. 37. **10 MIN.**
- Present the *Vocabulario:* Verb Infinitives, p. 37. Have students act out the verbs. **10 MIN.**
- Have students do *Actividad* 16 orally and *Actividad* 17 in pairs. **10 MIN.**
- Do *Actividad* 18 orally and *Actividad* 19 in groups. **10 MIN.**

Pronunciación
- Play the audio and have students practice the *Refrán.* **5 MIN.**

Homework Option:
- Have students complete *Actividad* 16 or 18 in writing. *Más práctica* Workbook, p. 16. *Para hispanohablantes* Workbook, p. 14.

DAY 5

En acción (cont.)
- Check homework. **5 MIN.**
- Play the audio; do *Actividad* 20. **10 MIN.**
- Have students complete *Actividad* 21 in writing. Expand using Information Gap Activities, Unit 1 Resource Book, pp. 69–70; *Más comunicación,* p. R1. **10 MIN.**

En voces: Lectura
- Quick Start Review (TE, p. 40) **5 MIN.**
- Review the Reading Strategy, p. 40. **5 MIN.**
- Have students read the *Lectura* silently. Then have various students read the *Lectura* aloud. **10 MIN.**
- Call on volunteers to answer the questions, p. 41. **10 MIN.**

Homework Option:
- Have students write answers to the *¿Comprendiste?* questions, p. 41. Review in preparation for *En uso.*

DAY 6

En uso: Repaso y más comunicación
- Check homework. **5 MIN.**
- Quick Start Review (TE, p. 42) **5 MIN.**
- Present the *Repaso y más comunicación* using the Teaching Suggestions (TE, p. 42) **5 MIN.**
- Have students write *Actividades* 1 and 2, then check answers with the whole class. **15 MIN.**
- Have students do *Actividades* 3 and 4 orally. **10 MIN.**
- Use the suggested activities, TE, pp. 42–43. **15 MIN.**

Homework Option:
- Have students complete *En uso Actividades* 3 and 4 in writing.

DAY 7

En uso: Repaso y más comunicación (cont.)
- Check homework. **5 MIN.**
- Present the Speaking Strategy, p. 44, and have students do *Actividad* 5 in pairs. **10 MIN.**
- Have students do *Actividad* 6 in groups. Have volunteers perform their dialogs for the class. **10 MIN.**

En tu propia voz: Escritura
- Do *Actividad* 7 in writing. Ask volunteers to present their letters to the class. **10 MIN.**

Conexiones
- Read and discuss *Los estudios sociales,* p. 44. Have students complete their own diagrams. **20 MIN.**

Homework Option:
- Review for *Etapa* 1 Exam.

DAY 8

En resumen: Repaso de vocabulario
- Quick Start Review (TE, p. 45) **5 MIN.**
- Review grammar questions, etc., as necessary. **10 MIN.**
- Complete *Etapa* 1 Exam. **20 MIN.**

Ampliación
- Use a suggested project, game, or activity. (TE, pp. 23A–23B) **15 MIN.**

Homework Option:
- Preview *Etapa* 2 Opener.

Sample Lesson Plan - Block Schedule (90 minutes)

DAY 1

Unit Opener
- Anticipate/Activate prior knowledge: Present the *Almanaque* and the cultural notes. Use Map OHTs as needed. 10 MIN.

Etapa Opener
- Quick Start Review (TE, p. 24) 5 MIN.
- Have students look at the *Etapa* Opener and answer the questions. 5 MIN.
- Use Block Scheduling Copymasters. 5 MIN.

En contexto: Vocabulario
- Quick Start Review (TE, p. 26) 5 MIN.
- Have students use context and pictures to learn *Etapa* vocabulary, then answer the questions, p. 27. Use the Situational OHTs for additional practice. 10 MIN.

En vivo: Diálogo
- Quick Start Review (TE, p. 28) 5 MIN.
- Review the Listening Strategy, p. 28. Play audio or show video for the dialog, pp. 28–29. Replay and have students take the roles of the characters. 10 MIN.

En acción: Vocabulario y gramática
- Quick Start Review (TE, p. 30) 5 MIN.
- Have students open to *En contexto*, pp. 26–27. Use OHT 5 and 6 to review vocabulary. 5 MIN.
- Play the video/audio; do *Actividades* 1 and 2 orally. 10 MIN.
- Do *Actividades* 3 and 4 orally and *Actividad* 5 in writing. 15 MIN.

Homework Option:
- Video Activities, Unit 1 Resource Book, pp. 74–75. Have students complete *Actividades* 3 and 4 in writing.

DAY 2

En acción (cont.)
- Check homework. 10 MIN.
- Quick Start Review (TE, p. 32) 5 MIN.
- Present *Gramática:* Familiar and Formal Greetings, p. 32. 10 MIN.
- Have students do *Actividad* 6 in pairs and *Actividad* 7 orally. 5 MIN.
- Present the Speaking Strategy, p. 33. Do *Actividad* 8 in pairs. 5 MIN.
- Quick Start Review (TE, p. 33) 5 MIN.
- Present *Gramática:* Describing People: Subject Pronouns and the Verb *ser,* p. 33. 10 MIN.
- Have students do *Actividad* 9. 5 MIN.
- Play the audio; have students do *Actividad* 10. 5 MIN.
- Do *Actividad* 11 orally. 5 MIN.
- Have students complete *Actividad* 12 in writing. Have students exchange papers for peer correction. Expand using Information Gap Activities, Unit 1 Resource Book, p. 68; *Más comunicación,* p. R1. 5 MIN.
- Quick Start Review (TE, p. 35) 5 MIN.
- Present *Gramática:* Using *ser de* to Express Origin, p. 35. 5 MIN.
- Have students do *Actividad* 13 orally, *Actividad* 14 in pairs, and *Actividad* 15 in groups. Use Block Scheduling Copymasters for a change of pace as needed. 10 MIN.

Homework Option:
- Have students complete *Actividades* 7, 11, and 13 in writing. *Más práctica* Workbook, pp. 13–15. *Para hispanohablantes* Workbook, pp. 11–13.

DAY 3

En acción (cont.)
- Check homework. 10 MIN.
- Quick Start Review (TE, p. 37) 5 MIN.
- Present *Gramática:* Using Verbs to Talk About What You Like to Do, p. 37. 10 MIN.
- Present the *Vocabulario:* Verb Infinitives. Have students act out the verbs. 10 MIN.
- Have students do *Actividad* 16 orally. 5 MIN.
- Have students complete *Actividad* 17 in pairs. 5 MIN.
- Do *Actividad* 18 orally and *Actividad* 19 in groups. 10 MIN.
- Play the audio; have students do *Actividad* 20. 5 MIN.
- Have students complete *Actividad* 21 in writing. Expand using Information Gap Activities, Unit 1 Resource Book, pp. 69–70; *Más comunicación,* p. R1. 10 MIN.
- Use Block Scheduling Copymasters for a change of pace as needed.

Pronunciación
- Play the audio and have students practice the *Refrán.* 10 MIN.

Ampliación
- Use a suggested project, game, or activity. (TE, pp. 23A–23B) 10 MIN.

Homework Option:
- Have students complete *Actividades* 16 and 18 in writing. *Más práctica* Workbook, p. 16. *Para hispanohablantes* Workbook, p. 14.

DAY 4

En voces: Lectura
- Check homework. 10 MIN.
- Quick Start Review (TE, p. 40) 5 MIN.
- Review the Reading Strategy, p. 40. 5 MIN.
- Have students read the *Lectura* silently. Then have various students read the *Lectura* aloud. 15 MIN.
- Call on volunteers to answer the *¿Comprendiste?* and *¿Qué piensas?* questions. 5 MIN.

En uso: Repaso y más comunicación
- Quick Start Review (TE, p. 42) 5 MIN.
- Have students write *Actividades* 1 and 2, then check answers with the whole class. 15 MIN.
- Have students do *Actividades* 3 and 4 orally. 10 MIN.
- Present the Speaking Strategy, p. 44, and have students do *Actividad* 5 in pairs. 10 MIN.
- Have students do *Actividad* 6 in groups. Have volunteers perform their dialogs for the class. 10 MIN.

Homework Option:
- Review for *Etapa* 1 Exam.

DAY 5

En tu propia voz: Escritura
- Do *Actividad* 7 in writing. Ask volunteers to present their letters to the class. 15 MIN.

Conexiones
- Read and discuss *Los estudios sociales,* p. 44. Have students complete their own diagrams. 20 MIN.

En resumen: Repaso de vocabulario
- Quick Start Review (TE, p. 45) 5 MIN.
- Review grammar questions, etc., as necessary. 10 MIN.
- Complete *Etapa* 1 Exam. 20 MIN.

Ampliación
- Use another suggested project, game, or activity. (TE, pp. 23A–23B) 20 MIN.

Homework Option:
- Preview *Etapa* 2 Opener

▼ Francisco, Alma y el señor Estrada en Miami.

Etapa Theme
Getting to know people and learning about the Hispanic community in the U.S.

Grammar Objectives
- Familiar and formal greetings
- Describing people: subject pronouns and the verb **ser**
- Using **ser de** to express origin
- Using verbs to talk about what you like to do

Teaching Resource Options

Print

Block Scheduling Copymasters, pp. 9–10

Audiovisual

OHT 2, 11 (Quick Start)

Quick Start Review
♻ Hispanic communities in the U.S.

Use OHT 11 or write on board:
With your books closed, write a list of as many Hispanic communities in the U.S. as you can remember. Remember the accents!

Answers
Answers will vary. Answers could include:
San José, Los Ángeles, San Diego, El Paso, Dallas, Houston, San Antonio, Miami, Chicago, Nueva York

Teaching Suggestion
Previewing the Etapa
- Ask students to study the picture on pp. 24–25 (1 min.).
- Close books; ask students to share at least 3 things that they noticed.
- Reopen books and look at the picture again (1 min.); close books and share 3 more details.
- Use the **¿Qué ves?** questions to focus the discussion.

UNIDAD 1

ETAPA 1

¡Bienvenido a Miami!

- Greet others
- Introduce others
- Say where people are from
- Express likes

¿Qué ves?

Look at the photo of Máximo Gómez Park in Miami.

1. Which people do you think are the main characters in this **Etapa**?
2. Look at their gestures. What are they doing?
3. What do the photos tell you about the community?

24

CITY OF MIAMI
MAXIMO GOMEZ PARK
DOMINO CLUB   OPEN DAILY 9A.M. TO 8P.M.

Classroom Management

Planning Ahead Review words/expressions of greeting and introducing from the **Etapa preliminar**. In pairs, have students greet, introduce themselves, and say where they are from.

Time Saver If time is short, begin discussion of the **¿Qué ves?** questions in class and have students finish them as homework.

Cross Cultural Connections

Ask students if they recognize what game the two men seated at the table are playing. Find out if dominoes is a popular game with students. Can they think of other games that may vary in popularity depending on the culture?

✦ Culture Highlights

● **DOMINÓS** Dominós is frequently played all over Latin America. It is generally played with 28 small, flat, rectangular tiles (**fichas**) that are made of bone (**hueso**), plastic (**plástico**) or wood (**madera**). The face of each tile is divided into halves, each half being blank or marked by one to six dots (**puntos**) resembling those on dice. It can be played by two or more people. Perhaps someone in the photo is about to shout ¡**Gané!**–I won!

● **MÁXIMO GÓMEZ** General Máximo Gómez (1836–1905) was a prominent leader in the Ten Years War (1868–1878), the important struggle for Cuban independence from Spain. He also served as General-in-Chief in the final war for independence. This photograph was taken at the Dominó Club in Máximo Gómez Park, Little Havana, in Miami.

▉ Block Schedule

Process Time Allow students time to look at the photos and read the questions in the **¿Qué ves?** box to themselves before discussing the **Etapa** Opener. (For additional activities, see **Block Scheduling Copymasters,** pp. 9–10.)

Teaching All Students

Extra Help Students may find it helpful to look at the Objectives on p. 24 and think about some of the Spanish words and phrases they already know: ¡**Hola!, Buenos días, Soy (de)..., Es (de)...,** etc.

Native Speakers Ask students to list 3 things they like to do and 3 things they don't like to do, using the expressions **Me gusta** and **No me gusta.** Add any new vocabulary words generated to an on-going supplementary vocabulary list.

Multiple Intelligences

Naturalist Have students look at the photo and list elements that indicate what kind of physical environment is shown (plants, temperature indicated by clothing, etc.). Have students list at least 2 similarities or differences between the area shown and the students' local area.

Teaching Resource Options

Print

Unit 1 Resource Book
  Video Activities, pp. 74–75
  Videoscript, p. 77
  Audioscript, p. 80
  Audioscript *Para hispanohablantes,*
    p. 80

Audiovisual

OHT 5, 6, 7, 7A, 8, 8A, 11 (Quick Start)
Audio Program Cassette 1A / CD 1
Audio *Para hispanohablantes*
  Cassette 1A / CD 1
Video Program Videotape 1 / Videodisc
  1A

Search Chapter 3, Play to 4
U1E1 • En contexto (Vocabulary)

Technology

Intrigas y aventuras CD-ROM, Disc 1

Quick Start Review

♻ **Miami**

Use OHT 11 or write on board:
List at least 3 things you know about
Miami.

Answers will vary.

Teaching Suggestions
Introducing Vocabulary

• Have students look at pages 26–27.
  Use OHT 5 and 6 and Audio Cassette
  1A / CD 1 to present the vocabulary.
• Ask the Comprehension Questions in
  order of yes/no (questions 1–3),
  either/or (questions 4–6), and simple
  word or phrase (questions 7–10).
  Expand by adding similar questions.
• Use the TPR activity to reinforce the
  meaning of individual words.
• Use the video vocabulary presentation
  for review and reinforcement.

En contexto

🖥🎧 VOCABULARIO

Francisco García Flores has just moved into his new community
in Miami. He is getting to know the people there. Look at the
illustrations. They will help you understand the meanings of the
words in blue and answer the questions on the next page.

Ⓐ La chica es Alma Cifuentes. **El chico**
es Francisco García. **Son amigos.**

Alma: ¿Qué tal?
Francisco: Estoy bien, ¿y tú?
Alma: Regular.

un policía

**Ⓑ El policía vive en
el apartamento.**

un apartamento

un chico

una chica

una mujer

Ⓒ Mujer: Gracias.
Francisco: De nada.

26   veintiséis
   Unidad 1

Classroom Community

TPR Divide the class into 4 groups: 1. un(a)
estudiante; 2. un(a) maestro; 3. un(a) policía; 4. un(a)
doctor(a). Name famous or familiar people from each
category. When the group hears someone from their
category, they should all raise their hands. Then one
person from the group should give the appropriate
form (for example, either **un estudiante** or **una
estudiante**).

Paired Activity Have students work in pairs and
practice dialogs A, D, and F.

Group Activity **Prepare ahead:** copies of the Video
dialog (URB 1 Videoscript, p. 77). Divide the class into
groups, assigning each group a different section of the
dialog. Then have students cut the dialog into strips,
and exchange with another group. Students should then
form complete conversations to share with the class.

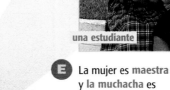

una familia
un señor
una señora
una señorita
un muchacho

una maestra
una estudiante

D La familia García vive en una casa. La señora García es doctora.

Francisco: Alma, **te presento** a mi familia.
Señor García: Mucho gusto. ¿Cómo estás?
Alma: Bien, gracias. ¿Cómo está usted?
Señor García: No muy bien hoy.

E La mujer es **maestra** y la muchacha es estudiante.

una casa

TENEMOS TAMALES HOJA

un hombre

F El hombre es el señor Estrada. Alma es una amiga.

Alma: Le presento a mi amigo, Francisco.
Señor Estrada: Encantado. ¿Cómo estás?
Francisco: Muy bien, gracias, ¿y usted?
Señor Estrada: Si es lunes, estoy terrible.

Preguntas personales

1. ¿Tienes amigos?
2. ¿Eres maestro(a) o estudiante?
3. ¿Vives en un apartamento o en una casa?
4. ¿Cómo se llaman las personas de tu familia?
5. ¿Cómo estás hoy?

veintisiete
Etapa 1 **27**

Comprehension Questions

1. ¿Son amigos Alma y Francisco? (Sí.)
2. ¿Vive el policía en una casa? (No.)
3. ¿Es doctora la señora García? (Sí.)
4. ¿Quién vive en una casa, el policía o la familia García? (la familia García)
5. ¿Quién está terrible, Francisco o el señor Estrada? (el señor Estrada)
6. ¿Cómo está el señor García hoy, bien o no muy bien? (no muy bien)
7. ¿Cómo se llama el amigo de Alma? (Francisco)
8. ¿Cuál es el apellido de Alma? (Cifuentes)
9. ¿Quién vive en un apartamento? (el policía)
10. ¿Cómo está Alma hoy? (regular, bien)

Culture Highlights

● **MIAMI** A large percentage of the population of Miami is of Spanish-speaking origin, especially Cuban, Caribbean, and Central American. The metropolitan area's southwestern quadrant includes Miami's Little Havana, a predominately Cuban neighborhood where the video and photographs were taken. Miami is an important resort and cruise ship center.

Block Schedule

FunBreak Have students form groups of 4 or 5. Each student in the group chooses a number from 1 to 6. Depending on what number was chosen, the student now has to write that number of words (in English) of things (buildings, people, etc.) they would expect to find in a typical neighborhood. (For example, a student who chose number 5 needs to come up with 5 words.) Once this is complete, students consult their glossaries/dictionaries to find the Spanish equivalent of these words. Each group then designs a map of a created neighborhood, labeling the map with the Spanish words that they found. Display the maps on the bulletin board.

Teaching All Students

Extra Help Randomly call out the nouns in the new vocabulary. Have students point to what you are saying in the pictures.

Native Speakers Ask students to share other words commonly used for the vocabulary presented here. For example: **de nada / no hay de qué; el hombre / el caballero; la mujer / la dama; el apartamento / el piso; el (la) amigo(a) / el (la) compañero(a).**

Challenge Have pairs of students create and present dialogs based on the **Preguntas personales.**

Multiple Intelligences

Verbal State the nouns for each photo. Ask student volunteers to form a sentence with each noun; for example, **un policía—Un policía vive en un apartamento.** Use the "magic" overhead transparencies to encourage participation.

Teaching Resource Options

Print 📖

Más práctica Workbook PE, pp. 9–12
Para hispanohablantes Workbook PE, pp. 9–10
Block Scheduling Copymasters, p. 13
Unit 1 Resource Book
  Más práctica Workbook TE, pp. 52–55
  Para hispanohablantes Workbook TE, pp. 60–61
  Video Activities, pp. 74–75
  Videoscript, p. 78
  Audioscript, p. 80
  Audioscript *Para hispanohablantes*, p. 80

Audiovisual

OHT 9, 10, 11 (Quick Start)
Audio Program Cassette 1A / CD 1
Audio *Para hispanohablantes* Cassette 1A / CD 1
Video Program Videotape 1 / Videodisc 1A

Search Chapter 4, Play to 5
U1E1 • En vivo (Dialog)

Technology 💻

Intrigas y aventuras CD-ROM, Disc 1

🔔 Quick Start Review

  ♻ **People**

Use OHT 11 or write on board:
Complete the chart.

	NOMBRES	DESCRIPCIONES
FOTO 1	Alma	chica, amiga
	Francisco	chico, amigo
FOTO 3		
FOTO 9		

Answers *See p. 23D.*

Gestures

Ask students if they noticed how Alma and Francisco greeted each other. Point out that shaking hands when greeting is common in many Spanish-speaking cultures.

Language Note

In Photo 1 of the dialog, the word **vecina(o)** is presented passively; students are not expected to produce it.

En vivo

🎧💿 DIÁLOGO

¡Bienvenido!

| Alma | Francisco | David | Arturo | Sr. Estrada |

PARA ESCUCHAR • STRATEGY: LISTENING

Listen to intonation A rising or falling voice (intonation) helps a listener understand meaning as much as individual words do. The voice rises at the end of a question and falls at the end of a statement. Listen carefully. Can you tell which sentences are questions? Being a good listener will help you become a good speaker. When you speak, try to imitate the intonation.

1 ▶ Alma: Hola, me llamo Alma Cifuentes. Soy tu vecina. Ésa es mi casa.
Francisco: Mucho gusto, Alma.

5 ▶ Francisco: ¡Ay, David! Alma, te presento a David. David es el monstruo de Miami.
David: ¡No soy monstruo! ¡Y no soy de Miami!
Alma: Es un placer, señor David.

6 ▶ Alma: Pues, ¿de dónde son ustedes?
Francisco: Nosotros somos de muchos lugares. Mamá es de Puerto Rico. Papá es de México. Yo soy de Puerto Rico y David es de San Antonio.
Alma: Entonces, ¡bienvenido a Miami!

7 ▶ Arturo: ¡Alma, chica! ¿Qué tal?
Alma: Muy bien, gracias, Arturo. Arturo, te presento a Francisco García. Él es mi vecino.
Arturo: Francisco, es un placer.
Francisco: Igualmente, Arturo.

28   veintiocho
      Unidad 1

Classroom Community

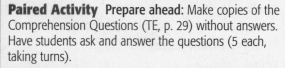

Paired Activity **Prepare ahead:** Make copies of the Comprehension Questions (TE, p. 29) without answers. Have students ask and answer the questions (5 each, taking turns).

TPR Divide the class into groups. Half the group sits down, the other half stands. As the dialog is played or read, students shake hands at each introduction, reversing the stand up/sit down positions each time.

Group Activity Divide the class into groups of 3. Student A turns to student B and says **Hola, me llamo (Pablo).** Student B responds with **Mucho gusto,** then turns to student C and says **Hola, me llamo (Sylvia).** Continue until each student has responded and introduced him/herself.

2 ▶ Alma: Y tú, ¿cómo te llamas?
Francisco: ¿Yo? Yo me llamo Francisco García Flores.
Alma: Encantada, Francisco.

3 ▶ Francisco: Papá, te presento a Alma Cifuentes. Alma, mi papá.
Sr. García: Es un placer, Alma.
Alma: Mucho gusto, señor García.

4 ▶ Francisco: Mamá, Alma Cifuentes. Alma, mi mamá.
Sra. García: Mucho gusto, Alma.
Alma: El gusto es mío, señora.

8 ▶ Alma: A Arturo le gusta mucho correr. A mí me gusta también. ¿Te gusta correr, Francisco?
Francisco: No, no me gusta mucho correr.

9 ▶ Sr. Estrada: ¡Alma! ¿Cómo estás hoy?
Alma: Muy bien, señor Estrada, ¿y usted?
Sr. Estrada: Hoy es lunes, ¿no? Si es lunes, estoy terrible.
Alma: Le presento a mi amigo Francisco.
Francisco: Es un placer, señor Estrada.

10 ▶ Francisco: Este concurso es muy interesante.

veintinueve
Etapa 1
29

Teaching All Students

Extra Help Have students draw a simple family tree of the García family. The drawing should also show where each person is from.

Native Speakers Ask students to share the customs for greeting in their community. Include gestures such as handshaking, kissing, and hugging. If they have come from another country, ask them to talk about their experience learning how to greet people in the U.S.

Multiple Intelligences
Kinesthetic Have one student role play one of the lines from the dialog, while the others guess his/her identity. Continue with several student actors.

Dialog • UNIDAD 1 Etapa 1   29

Teaching Suggestions
Presenting the Dialog

• Prepare students for listening by focusing on the dialog context using yes/no or either/or questions. Reintroduce the characters' names and the setting. **¿La muchacha se llama Alma? ¿Cómo se llama el chico, Felipe o Francisco? ¿Es el padre de Francisco el señor García? Y el hombre, ¿es el señor López o el señor Estrada?**

• Use the video, audio cassette, or CD to present the dialog. The expanded dialog on video offers additional listening practice opportunities.

Video Synopsis

• Alma Cifuentes introduces herself to Francisco García. She then introduces him to other neighbors. For a complete transcript of the video dialog, see p. 23D

Comprehension Questions

1. ¿La chica se llama Alma? (Sí.)
2. ¿Francisco es de Miami? (No.)
3. ¿A Alma le gusta correr? (Sí.)
4. ¿Hoy es lunes? (Sí.)
5. ¿David es de Miami o de San Antonio? (de San Antonio)
6. ¿El Sr. Estrada está bien o terrible? (terrible)
7. ¿Le gusta correr a Arturo o a Francisco? (a Arturo)
8. ¿El Sr. García es de San Antonio o de México? (de México)
9. ¿De dónde es Francisco? (de Puerto Rico)
10. Y Alma, ¿cómo está hoy? (Está muy bien.)

Block Schedule

Process Time After students have heard the audio and watched the video for **En vivo**, have them sit quietly and read the dialog. Allow time for questions at the end of the Process Time. (For additional activities, see **Block Scheduling Copymasters**, p. 13.)

Teaching Resource Options

Print
Unit 1 Resource Book
Video Activities, p. 76
Videoscript, p. 79
Audioscript, p. 80
Audioscript *Para hispanohablantes,*
p. 80

Audiovisual
OHT 12 (Quick Start)
Audio Program Cassette 1A / CD 1
Audio *Para hispanohablantes*
Cassette 1A / CD 1
Video Program Videotape 1 / Videodisc
1A

Quick Start Review
New neighbors

Use OHT 12 or write on the board:
Complete the following:
1. Alma vive en una ___ .
2. David es de ___ .
3. Francisco es de ___ .
4. Arturo es el ___ de Alma.
5. La señora García es ___ .

Answers
1. casa   2. San Antonio   3. Puerto Rico
4. amigo/vecino   5. doctora

Teaching Suggestions
Comprehension Check
With books closed, ask students to
name the people from the dialog and
give words associated with them.

Objective: Transitional practice
Listening comprehension/vocabulary
Answers (See script, p. 23D.)
1. Alma   4. Sr. Estrada
2. Francisco   5. Francisco
3. Alma

Objective: Transitional practice
Listening comprehension/vocabulary
Answers (See script, p. 23D.)
1. Falso. Alma es de Miami.
2. Falso. Francisco es el vecino de Alma.
3. Cierto.
4. Falso. Francisco dice: No, no me gusta mucho
correr.
5. Cierto.
6. Falso. Está terrible.

En acción
VOCABULARIO Y GRAMÁTICA

ACTIVIDAD 1

¿Quién?
Escuchar ¿Quién habla, Alma, Francisco o el
señor Estrada? *(Hint: Say who speaks.)*

Sr. Estrada   Alma   Francisco

1. «Soy tu vecina. Ésa es mi casa.»
2. «Nosotros somos de muchos lugares.»
3. «A Arturo le gusta mucho correr.»
4. «Si es lunes, estoy terrible.»
5. «Este concurso es muy interesante.»

ACTIVIDAD 2

¿Cierto o falso?
Escuchar ¿Es cierto o falso? Si es falso, di lo que
es cierto. *(Hint: True or false? If it is false, say what is true.)*

1. Alma es de San Antonio.
2. Francisco es el vecino de Arturo.
3. David no es de Miami.
4. Francisco dice: «Me gusta correr.»
5. Francisco dice que el concurso es
interesante.
6. El señor Estrada está muy bien.

ACTIVIDAD 3

¿Quién es?
Hablar Describe a las personas de la comunidad:
una chica, un chico, un muchacho, un hombre o
una mujer. *(Hint: Describe the people from the community.)*

modelo

Es **un hombre.**

1.   2.   3.

4.   5.

TAMBIÉN SE DICE
There are different ways to say *boy* and *girl* in Spanish.
• **chaval(a):** Spain
• **chavo(a):** Mexico
• **chico(a):** many countries
• **joven:** many countries
• **muchacho(a):** many countries
• **niño(a):** many countries
• **pibe(a):** Argentina

30   treinta
Unidad 1

Classroom Management

Peer Review Using **Actividad 3** as a model, have
pairs of students write how they would refer to three
family members and/or friends. For example: **Mi padre
es un hombre.** Have pairs exchange papers and
correct.

Time Saver Prepare copies of the answers to
Actividades 1–5 to allow students to correct their own
work.

- *Use familiar and formal greetings*
- *Use subject pronouns and the verb **ser***
- *Use **ser de** to express origin*
- *Use verbs to talk about what you like to do*

ACTIVIDAD 4

¿Qué son?

Leer ¿Qué es cada persona de la comunidad de Alma: **estudiante, señora, maestra, mujer, doctora, policía** o **chica**? *(Hint: Say who each person from Alma's community is.)*

modelo

La __mujer__ es doctora.

1. La mujer es la _____ Durán.
2. La _____ es una vecina.
3. La señorita Galdós es _____ .
4. El señor Durán es _____ .
5. La muchacha es _____ .
6. La mujer es _____ .

ACTIVIDAD 5

¿Quiénes son?

Escribir Escribe quién es y dónde vive. *(Hint: Write who each one is and where he or she lives.)*

modelo

la señorita Álvarez:

La señorita Álvarez es maestra. Vive en **un apartamento.**

1. el señor Gómez:
2. Alma: 🏠
3. la señora García: 🏠

treinta y uno
Etapa 1
31

Answers
1. Es una mujer.
2. Es un hombre (un muchacho).
3. Es un chico (un muchacho).
4. Es una chica (una muchacha).
5. Es un chico (un muchacho).

ACTIVIDAD 4 Objective: Transitional practice Vocabulary

Answers
1. señora
2. chica
3. maestra
4. policía
5. estudiante
6. doctora

ACTIVIDAD 5 Objective: Open-ended practice Vocabulary

Answers
1. El señor Gómez es policía. Vive en un apartamento.
2. Alma es estudiante. Vive en una casa.
3. La señora García es doctora. Vive en una casa.

🔔 Quick Wrap-up

Have students write 5 true/false statements about the people in the dialog (pp. 28–29), then exchange papers and correct. Give extra credit for 5 correct responses.

Teaching All Students

Extra Help Have students make flashcards with a subject pronoun on one side and the correct form of the verb **ser** on the other side. Display the pronoun side of the card and prompt students to give the correct form of the verb. (Alternate: Show the side with the conjugated verb and have students give the correct pronoun.)

Multiple Intelligences
Visual Send artistic volunteers to the board to draw cartoons of the people in the dialog (pp. 28–29). Have another group of students go to the board and write the names under each drawing. Have a third group go to the board and write one thing about each person.

▣ Block Schedule

Variety Working in pairs, have students interview their partners and then introduce them to the class. They should include: name, gender, origin, etc.

Teaching Resource Options

Print 📖

Más práctica Workbook PE, p. 13
Para hispanohablantes Workbook PE, p. 11
Block Scheduling Copymasters, pp. 11, 13
Unit 1 Resource Book
 Más práctica Workbook TE, p. 56
 Para hispanohablantes Workbook TE, p. 62

Audiovisual 🎧

OHT 12 (Quick Start)

Technology 💻

Intrigas y aventuras CD-ROM, Disc 1

🔔 Quick Start Review

♻ Vocabulary

Use OHT 12 or write on the board: Identify either the specific country where each word is used or whether it is used in many countries.

chaval(a)	niño(a)	muchacho(a)
chavo(a)	joven	pibe(a)
chico(a)		

Answers *See p. 23D.*

Teaching Suggestions
Reinforcing Familiar and Formal Greetings

After explaining greetings, have students walk around the class greeting each other (and you), as if at a party.

Objective: Controlled practice Familiar and formal greetings

Answers
1. b   2. a   3. d   4. c

Objective: Transitional practice Familiar and formal greetings

Answers
1. ¿Cómo estás/Qué tal, Antonio?
2. ¿Cómo está usted, señorita Díaz?
3. ¿Cómo estás/Qué tal, Felipe?
4. ¿Cómo está usted, señor Castro?
5. ¿Cómo estás/Qué tal, Luisa?
6. ¿Cómo está usted, señora Ramos?
7. ¿Cómo estás/Qué tal, Paquita?
8. ¿Cómo está usted, doctora Flores?

GRAMÁTICA

Familiar and Formal Greetings

There are different ways to say *How are you?* in Spanish.

Familiar:

Mr. Estrada greets Alma by saying:

—¡Alma!
¿Cómo estás hoy?
Alma! ***How are you*** *today?*

¿Cómo estás? is a familiar greeting.

Use with: • a friend
• a family member
• someone younger

Another familiar greeting: **¿Qué tal?**

Tú is a familiar way to say *you.*

Formal:

If Alma had spoken first, she might have said:

—¡Señor Estrada!
¿Cómo está usted?
Mr. Estrada! ***How are you?***

¿Cómo está usted? is a formal greeting.

Use with: • a person you don't know
• someone older
• someone for whom you want to show respect

Usted is a formal way to say *you.*

ACTIVIDAD 6 · Gramática

¿Quién dice qué?

Hablar ¿Quién habla? Trabaja con otro(a) estudiante para practicar las conversaciones.
(Hint: Who is speaking? Work with another student to practice the conversations.)

1. Francisco y Arturo
2. Alma y el señor Estrada
3. David y el señor García
4. el señor Estrada y la señora García

a. —¿Cómo está usted?
   —Muy bien, ¿y tú?
b. —¿Qué tal?
   —Regular. ¿Y tú?
c. —¿Cómo está usted?
   —Bien, ¿y usted?
d. —¿Cómo estás, papá?
   —Muy bien, ¿y tú?

■ **MÁS PRÁCTICA** *cuaderno* p. 13
■ **PARA HISPANOHABLANTES** *cuaderno* p. 11

ACTIVIDAD 7

¿Cómo estás? o ¿Cómo está usted?

Hablar/Escribir Pregúntale a cada persona cómo está. *(Hint: Ask each person how he or she is.)*

modelo

Juan

*¿Cómo estás, **Juan**?*

1. Antonio	5. Luisa
2. señorita Díaz	6. señora Ramos
3. Felipe	7. Paquita
4. señor Castro	8. doctora Flores

---

32 treinta y dos
Unidad 1

Classroom Community

Paired Activity Using information learned in both **Gramática** presentations, pairs of students should have short conversations. Each person should give at least three statements or questions.

Portfolio Have students write a paragraph containing as much information about themselves as they now know how to say (name, where they are from, that they are a student, how they feel today, etc.).

Rubric A = 13–15 pts. B = 10–12 pts. C = 7–9 pts. D = 4–6 pts. F = < 4 pts.

Writing criteria	Scale
Vocabulary use	1 2 3 4 5
Logical sentence order	1 2 3 4 5
Grammar/spelling accuracy	1 2 3 4 5

ACTIVIDAD 8

¿Tú o usted?

Hablar Practica los saludos con otro(a) estudiante. Cambien de papel. *(Hint: Practice the greetings with another student. Change roles.)*

modelo

Juan–señor Álvarez

Juan: *¿Cómo está usted, señor Álvarez?*

Sr. Álvarez: *Bien, gracias, ¿y tú, Juan?*

Juan: *Regular.*

1. Pablo–Felipe
2. señora Ruiz–señor Muñoz
3. Francisco–señor Fernández
4. Juan–Julia
5. señora Campos–Susana

PARA CONVERSAR
STRATEGY: SPEAKING

Practice To become a good speaker, practice aloud—to yourself and with a partner. When talking with a partner, make it sound like a real conversation. Soon you'll be a good speaker of Spanish.

GRAMÁTICA

◆ Describing People: Subject Pronouns and the Verb ser

▶ To discuss people in Spanish, you will often use **subject pronouns**. When you want to describe a person or explain who he or she is, use the verb ser.

When Alma introduces Francisco to Arturo, she uses a **subject pronoun** with ser.

—**Él es** mi vecino.
He is my neighbor.

Francisco uses other examples.

—**Nosotros somos** de muchos lugares.
We are from many places.

—**Yo soy** de Puerto Rico.
I am from Puerto Rico.

Singular		Plural	
yo soy		**nosotros(as)** somos	
I am		*we are*	
tú eres	*familiar*	**vosotros(as)** sois	
you are		*you are*	
usted es	*formal*	**ustedes** son	
you are		*you are*	
él, ella es		**ellos(as)** son	
he, she is		*they are*	

▶ If Alma were to say that someone is a neighbor, she would say:

—**Él es un** vecino.

However, if she were to say that someone is a policeman, she would say:

—**Él es** policía.

> The word **un** or **una** does not appear before a profession.

treinta y tres
Etapa 1 **33**

Teaching All Students

Extra Help Provide common and proper nouns. Students state how they would greet that person; for example, **el presidente, la reina Isabel, una amiga, un policía, el doctor (Sánchez),** etc.

Native Speakers Have students talk about the use of **tú** and **usted** by young people, their parents, and other adults in their community.

Multiple Intelligences

Visual Have students make a personal **ser** verb chart, using color-coding on a small piece of posterboard.

Kinesthetic In small groups, have students prepare 9 index cards: 3 subject pronoun cards, 3 corresponding forms of **ser** cards, and 3 profession cards: ELLA ES DOCTORA. Exchanging cards, each group forms correct sentences and shows them to the class.

ACTIVIDAD 8

Objective: Open-ended practice
Greeting others

Answers will vary.

Rubric: Speaking

Criteria	Scale	
Vocabulary use	1 2 3	A = 10–12 pts.
Fluency, intonation	1 2 3	B = 8–9 pts.
Pronunciation	1 2 3	C = 6–7 pts.
Accuracy	1 2 3	D = 4–5 pts.
		F = < 4 pts.

🔔 Quick Start Review

♻ **Familiar and formal greetings**
Use OHT 12 or write on the board: First, indicate whether the following greetings are formal or informal. Then, write the meaning of each expression.

¿Qué tal?
¿Cómo está usted?
¿Cómo estás?

Answers *See p. 23D.*

Teaching Suggestions
Teaching Subject Pronouns and the Verb ser

• Point out that when the context is clear, subject pronouns are often omitted in Spanish. When necessary, they are used to clarify (**Él** [not <u>ella</u>] **es de Miami.**) and to emphasize (**Ella es mi vecina.** <u>She</u> is my neighbor.)

• After presenting pronouns and the verb **ser,** have students work in pairs. One student gives a pronoun and the other gives the corresponding verb, and vice versa. They should then reverse roles.

▪ Block Schedule

Streamlining Have students create a blank verb chart on a large index card. It should contain subject pronouns, and should be decorated. Laminate the cards. Students can use the charts for each new verb. They should write on them with felt tip pens. (For additional activities, see **Block Scheduling Copymasters,** p. 11.)

Teaching Resource Options

Print

Más práctica Workbook PE, p. 14
Para hispanohablantes Workbook PE, p. 12
Block Scheduling Copymasters

Unit 1 Resource Book
 Más práctica Workbook TE, p. 56
 Para hispanohablantes Workbook TE, p. 61
 Information Gap Activities, p. 68
 Audioscript, pp. 80–81
 Audioscript *Para hispanohablantes*, p. 80

Audiovisual

OHT 13 (Quick Start)
Audio Program Cassettes 1A, 1B / CD 1
Audio *Para hispanohablantes*
 Cassettes 1A, 1B / CD 1

Technology

Intrigas y aventuras **CD-ROM**, Disc 1

9 **Objective:** Controlled practice Pronouns and **ser**

Answers
1. b. Tú
2. g. Nosotras
3. c. Usted / d. Él
4. h. Ustedes / j. Ellas
5. f. Nosotros / g. Nosotras
6. h. Ustedes / i. Ellos
7. c. Usted / e. Ella
8. a. Yo
9. h. Ustedes / i. Ellos
10. c. Usted / d. Él / e. Ella

10 **Objective:** Controlled practice Listening comprehension/pronouns and **ser**

Answers (See script, p. 23D.)
1. b   3. a   5. b
2. b   4. a

11 **Objective:** Transitional practice Pronouns and **ser**

Answers
1. Ellos son Francisco y Alma. Son amigos.
2. Ella es la señora García. Es doctora.
3. Él es el señor Gómez. Es policía.
4. Él es Arturo. Es un amigo.
5. Ella es Alma. Es estudiante.
6. Ellas son la señora Díaz y la señora Castro. Son maestras.

ACTIVIDAD 9 · Gramática

¡Descríbelos!

Leer Explica quién es cada persona de la comunidad. Usa cada pronombre sólo una vez. *(Hint: Explain who each person from the community is. Use each pronoun only once.)*

1. _____ eres doctora.
2. _____ somos amigas.
3. _____ es doctor.
4. _____ son amigas.
5. _____ somos estudiantes.
6. _____ son amigos.
7. _____ es maestra.
8. _____ soy estudiante.
9. _____ son maestros.
10. _____ es policía.

a. yo
b. tú
c. usted
d. él
e. ella
f. nosotros
g. nosotras
h. ustedes
i. ellos
j. ellas

ACTIVIDAD 10 · Gramática

¡Escucha! ¿Quién es?

Escuchar Escoge la oración correcta para indicar quién es la persona. *(Hint: Choose the correct sentence to indicate who the person is.)*

1. a. Ella se llama Francisca.
   b. Él se llama Francisco.

2. a. Ellas son policías.
   b. Ellos son policías.

3. a. A él le gusta correr.
   b. A ella le gusta correr.

4. a. Ella no está bien.
   b. Él no está bien.

5. a. Ellos son estudiantes.
   b. Ellas son estudiantes.

■ **MÁS PRÁCTICA** *cuaderno* p. 14
■ **PARA HISPANOHABLANTES** *cuaderno* p. 12

ACTIVIDAD 11

¿Quién es Francisco?

Hablar/Escribir Explica quiénes son las personas. *(Hint: Explain who the people are.)*

modelo

Francisco: estudiante

Él es **Francisco**. *Es* **estudiante**.

1. Francisco y Alma: amigos
2. la señora García: doctora
3. el señor Gómez: policía
4. Arturo: un amigo
5. Alma: estudiante
6. la señora Díaz y la señora Castro: maestras

34 treinta y cuatro
Unidad 1

Classroom Community

Paired Activity Working in pairs, students take on the roles of the people in **Actividad 11**. They should introduce themselves, state who they are, and say where they are from. For example: **Yo soy Francisco. Soy estudiante. Soy de Puerto Rico.**

Game Write a list of Spanish-speaking countries on the board. Each student will pretend he/she is from one of these countries. The first students says, **Me llamo __. Soy de __.** The next student points to the first student and says, **Se llama __. Es de __.** That student then adds his/her own information: **Me llamo ___**... Play continues in this fashion.

ACTIVIDAD 12

Yo soy...

Escribir Decide la profesión de las personas de tu comunidad. Escribe cinco oraciones.

(Hint: Decide the profession of the people in your community. Write five sentences.)

modelo

Ella es doctora.

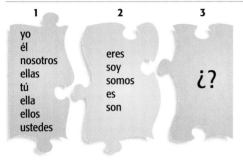

1	2	3
yo		
él	eres	
nosotros	soy	
ellas	somos	¿?
tú	es	
ella	son	
ellos		
ustedes		

■ **MÁS COMUNICACIÓN** p. R1

NOTA CULTURAL

Spanish is the native language of about half the residents of Miami. Cubans are the majority group within Spanish-speaking Miami, but there are people from all over the Spanish-speaking world here. When in Miami, you can use your Spanish to make new friends from all over the world without leaving the United States!

GRAMÁTICA

Using **ser de** to Express Origin

To say where a person is from use: **ser + de + place**

—David **es de** San Antonio.

—Papá **es de** México.

Francisco says:
—Nosotros **somos de muchos lugares**.
*We **are from** many places.*

—Mamá **es de** Puerto Rico.
—Yo **soy de** Puerto Rico.

San Antonio, Texas

MÉXICO

PUERTO RICO

treinta y cinco **35**
Etapa 1

Teaching All Students

Extra Help Rewrite **Actividad 9,** this time giving the subject pronouns and omitting the verbs. Have students fill in the correct pronouns.

Native Speakers Ask students to point out their family's place of origin on a map of the world.

Multiple Intelligences

Musical/Rhythmic Bring in music from various Spanish-speaking countries or the *Canciones* Cassette/CD. Play each selection and have students point out each country on a map of the world.

ACTIVIDAD 12

Objective: Open-ended practice
Introducing others

Answers will vary.

Critical Thinking

After discussing the **Nota cultural,** have students discuss where the major areas of Spanish speakers in the U.S. are located. Assign groups to research population figures and report back to the whole class.

🔔 Quick Start Review

♻ Subject pronouns
Use OHT 13 or write on the board:
Complete each sentence with the correct subject pronoun(s).

1. ____ son doctoras.
2. ____ es maestro.
3. ____ eres policía.
4. ____ somos amigas.
5. ____ soy estudiante.

Answers *See p. 23D.*

Teaching Suggestions
Reinforcing Using ser de to Express Origin

Tell students to imagine they are from a Spanish-speaking country. Have them choose a country (see pp. 6–7 of the **Etapa preliminar**) and write this country in large letters on a piece of paper (you should do this also). Beginning with yourself, hold up your paper, point to yourself, and say **Soy de ___.** Choose a student, have him/her stand up with his/her paper visible. Point to the student and say **(Él) Es de ___.** Continue, using different pronouns to practice all forms.

▮ Block Schedule

Change of Pace Have students research athletes from different Spanish-speaking countries. They should give each person's name and country of origin. (For additional activities, see **Block Scheduling Copymasters.**)

Teaching Resource Options

Print

Más práctica Workbook PE, pp. 15–16
Para hispanohablantes Workbook PE, pp. 13–14
Block Scheduling Copymasters, p. 15
Unit 1 Resource Book
  Más práctica Workbook TE, pp. 58–59
  Para hispanohablantes Workbook TE, pp. 63–64

Audiovisual

OHT 13 (Quick Start)

Technology

Intrigas y aventuras CD-ROM, Disc 1

---

13 **Objective:** Controlled practice
Using **ser de** to express origin

Answers
1. Carlos es de España.
2. Tú eres de Panamá.
3. Luisa es de Colombia.
4. Nosotros somos de México.
5. Ana y Felipe son de Bolivia.
6. Rita es de Argentina.
7. Ellos son de Chile.
8. Carmen y yo somos de Costa Rica.
9. Ella es de Miami.
10. Él es de Los Ángeles.

14 **Objective:** Controlled practice
Using **ser de** to express origin

Answers
1. A: ¿De dónde son los muchachos?
   B: Ellos son de Bolivia.
2. A: ¿De dónde es la muchacha?
   B: Ella es de Perú.
3. A: ¿De dónde es Elena?
   B: Ella es de Los Ángeles.
4. A: ¿De dónde es Luisa?
   B: Ella es de Ecuador.
5. A: ¿De dónde es Ramón?
   B: Él es de los Estados Unidos.
6. A: ¿De dónde son las mujeres?
   B: Ellas son de Panamá.
7. A: ¿De dónde es Paco?
   B: Él es de Bolivia.
8. A: ¿De dónde son las estudiantes?
   B: Ellas son de San Antonio.
9. A: ¿De dónde es Inés?
   B: Ella es de Colombia.
10. A: ¿De dónde son los hombres?
    B: Ellos hombres son de Argentina.

15 **Objective:** Transitional practice
Saying where people are from

Answers will vary.

ACTIVIDAD 13 Gramática

¿De dónde son?

Hablar/Escribir ¿De dónde son los estudiantes de intercambio? *(Hint: Where are the exchange students from?)*

modelo

Elena / Argentina
***Elena** es de **Argentina**.*

1. Carlos / España
2. tú / Panamá
3. Luisa / Colombia
4. nosotros / México
5. Ana y Felipe / Bolivia
6. Rita / Argentina
7. ellos / Chile
8. Carmen y yo / Costa Rica
9. ella / Miami
10. él / Los Ángeles

NOTA CULTURAL

Spanish influences are seen in Miami's architecture. The tower of this hotel was modeled after La Giralda, part of the cathedral in Sevilla, Spain.

ACTIVIDAD 14 Gramática

¡Son de muchos lugares!

Hablar Estás en una comunidad nueva. Pregúntale a otro(a) estudiante de dónde son las personas. Cambien de papel. *(Hint: You are in a new community. Ask another student where the people are from. Change roles.)*

modelo

Ana: México
Estudiante A: *¿De dónde es **Ana**?*
Estudiante B: *Ella es de **México**.*

el policía: Chile
Estudiante B: *¿De dónde es **el policía**?*
Estudiante A: *Él es de **Chile**.*

1. los muchachos: Bolivia
2. la muchacha: Perú
3. Elena: Los Ángeles
4. Luisa: Ecuador
5. Ramón: Estados Unidos
6. las mujeres: Panamá
7. Paco: Bolivia
8. las estudiantes: San Antonio
9. Inés: Colombia
10. los hombres: Argentina

■ **MÁS PRÁCTICA** *cuaderno* p. 15
■ **PARA HISPANOHABLANTES** *cuaderno* p. 13

ACTIVIDAD 15

¡Somos de lugares diferentes!

Hablar/Escribir Imagínate que eres de otro lugar. Pregúntales a otros estudiantes de dónde son. Escribe una lista. *(Hint: Imagine you are from another place. Ask other students where they are from. Write a list.)*

modelo

Tú: *¿De dónde eres, Juan?*
Juan: *Soy de San Francisco.*

Nombre	Es de...
1. Juan	San Francisco
2.	
3.	
4.	
5.	

Classroom Community

TPR Have various students act out the verb infinitives. Other students state what the person is doing and then say whether they like the activity or not.
A: (Acting out **correr**)
B: **A Arturo le gusta correr. (No) me gusta correr.**

Portfolio Have students add on to the paragraph they wrote earlier about themselves (see TE, p. 32).

They should write two things they like to do and two things they do not like to do.

Rubric: Writing

Criteria	Scale	
Correct sentence structure	1 2 3	A = 11–12 pts.
Vocabulary use	1 2 3	B = 8–10 pts.
Creativity	1 2 3	C = 6–7 pts.
Logical organization	1 2 3	D = 4–5 pts.
		F = < 4 pts.

GRAMÁTICA

Using Verbs to Talk About What You Like to Do

When you want to talk about what you like to do, use the phrase:

Me gusta + *infinitive*

The ***infinitive*** is the basic form of a verb.

Other helpful phrases to talk about what people like:

Te gusta correr.	*You like to run.*
Le gusta correr.	*He/She likes to run.*
¿Te gusta correr?	*Do you like to run?*
¿Le gusta correr?	*Does he/she like to run?*

Arturo would say: —**Me gusta correr.**
I like to run.

To say someone doesn't like something, say **no** before the phrase.

—**No** me gusta **correr.**
I don't like to run.

16 Gramática

Le gusta...

Hablar/Escribir Explica lo que le gusta o no le gusta hacer a cada persona. *(Hint: Explain what each person likes or doesn't like to do.)*

modelo

Marisol: correr (sí)   tú: trabajar (no)
Le gusta **correr.**   **No** te gusta **trabajar.**

1. Mario: comer (sí)
2. tú: escribir (no)
3. Susana: patinar (no)
4. yo: cantar (sí)
5. él: nadar (sí)
6. Elena: bailar (no)
7. tú: leer (sí)
8. yo: trabajar (sí)

■ MÁS PRÁCTICA *cuaderno* p. 16
■ PARA HISPANOHABLANTES *cuaderno* p. 14

Vocabulario

Verb Infinitives

bailar

leer

cantar

nadar

comer

patinar

escribir

trabajar

¿Qué te gusta?

treinta y siete
Etapa 1   **37**

🔔 **Quick Start Review**

♻ **Ser**

Use OHT 13 or write on the board: Complete these sentences with the correct forms of the verb **ser.**

1. Yo ____ de Puerto Rico.
2. Nosotros ____ de Nicaragua.
3. Marta ____ de España.
4. Teresa y Gregorio ____ de Ecuador.
5. Tú ____ de Guatemala.

Answers
1. soy   4. son
2. somos   5. eres
3. es

Teaching Suggestions
Presenting Verb Infinitives
Personalize each verb by asking students if they like to do the things pictured.

16 Objective: Controlled practice
Using verb infinitives

Answers
1. Le gusta comer.
2. No te gusta escribir.
3. No le gusta patinar.
4. Me gusta cantar.
5. Le gusta nadar.
6. No le gusta bailar.
7. Te gusta leer.
8. Me gusta trabajar.

Block Schedule

Change of Pace Have students count off by 2s in Spanish. The **uno** students stand and form a circle facing outward. The **dos** students stand in an outer circle, facing one of the **uno** students. The **uno** students ask the **dos** students ¿Te gusta [correr]? (infinitive of their choice). The **dos** students respond either affirmatively or negatively (Sí, me gusta correr./No, no me gusta correr.) After 10 seconds, tell students to move two places to the right and repeat the exercise. (For additional activities, see **Block Scheduling Copymasters,** p. 15.)

Teaching All Students

Extra Help Name a person (a friend or a public figure) who is well-known for each of the verb infinitives. Students say what that person likes to do.

Native Speakers Ask students to expand on each of the verb infinitives, according to their cultural community. For example: **Me gusta comer churrasco. Me gusta bailar la cumbia. Me gusta nadar en el Caribe.**

Multiple Intelligences

Logical/Mathematical Write each infinitive on a large piece of paper and post them around the classroom. Ask students to line up in front of the activity they like best. Have students count how many are in each group and graph the results. If space is limited, have students put their names on a list under their favorite activity.

Teaching Resource Options

Print

Block Scheduling Copymasters
Unit 1 Resource Book
  Information Gap Activities,
    pp. 69–70
  Audioscript, pp. 80–81
  Audioscript *Para hispanohablantes*,
    pp. 80–81

Audiovisual

Audio Program Cassettes 1A, 1B / CD 1
Audio *Para hispanohablantes*
  Cassette 1A / CD 1

Technology

Intrigas y aventuras CD-ROM, Disc 1

 Objective: Transitional practice
Using verbs to talk about what you
like to do

Answers

1. A: ¿Te gusta correr?
2. A: ¿Te gusta leer?
3. A: ¿Te gusta bailar?
4. A: ¿Te gusta nadar?
5. A: ¿Te gusta escribir?
6. A: ¿Te gusta comer?

 Objective: Open-ended practice
Using verbs to talk about what you
like to do

Answers

1. (No) Me gusta cantar.
2. (No) Me gusta trabajar.
3. (No) Me gusta patinar.
4. (No) Me gusta comer.
5. (No) Me gusta nadar.
6. (No) Me gusta correr.
7. (No) Me gusta bailar.
8. (No) Me gusta leer.

Preferencias

Hablar Pregúntale a otro(a) estudiante qué le gusta hacer. Cambien de papel. *(Hint: Ask another student what he or she likes to do. Change roles.)*

modelo

Estudiante A: *¿Te gusta patinar?*
Estudiante B: *Sí, me gusta patinar.*

Estudiante A
PREGUNTAS

¿Te gusta...?

1.

2.

3.

4.

5.

6.

Estudiante B
RESPUESTAS

Sí, me gusta...   No, no me gusta...

Me gusta

Hablar/Escribir Explica lo que te gusta y lo que no te gusta hacer. *(Hint: Explain what you like and don't like to do.)*

modelo

escribir

Me gusta escribir.

1. cantar	5. nadar
2. trabajar	6. correr
3. patinar	7. bailar
4. comer	8. leer

APOYO PARA
ESTUDIAR

Cracking the language code

Spanish is not translated English. Spanish has its own way of expressing ideas. Grammar is the rules for putting words together in order to make sense. How many expressions can you find where Spanish and English express the same idea differently? Think about these when practicing so you prepare yourself for real communication. Read Spanish examples carefully. Read English equivalents when you need help.

Classroom Community

TPR Have students act out the various infinitives. The facial expression on the student acting out the activity should indicate whether or not he/she likes the activity. The other students need to guess the activity and form a sentence that says whether or not the person likes that activity. (For example: The "acting" student simulates skating with a smile on his/her face. The "answering" student should say, **Le gusta patinar.**)

Cooperative Learning Have students form groups of 3 or 4. Each group should come up with a 5 question **pruebita** that tests information from this **Etapa.** Groups then exchange their **pruebitas,** respond, and do peer corrections.

Presentaciones

Hablar Trabaja en un grupo de tres. Tus amigos no se conocen. Preséntalos. *(Hint: Work in a group of three. Your friends don't know each other. Introduce them.)*

modelo

señor Estrada–David

Tú: *Señor Estrada, le presento a mi amigo, David.*

Señor Estrada: *Mucho gusto, David.*

David: *Igualmente, señor Estrada.*

Nota

To make a formal introduction, use **Le presento a…** To make a familiar introduction, use **Te presento a…**

I. Alma–Jorge
2. señor Gómez–Carlos
3. Arturo–David
4. señorita Álvarez–Manuel
5. señora Delgado–Emilio

Pronunciación

Refrán

Pronunciación de las vocales The vowels a, e, i, o, u are always pronounced the same way. One word in Spanish that uses all the vowels is the word for the animal known as a bat. It is **murciélago**. Try to pronounce it.

Here is a popular nonsense rhyme that children use when playing games. It is the Spanish version of "Eeny, meeny, miney, moe." Use it to practice vowels.

Tin, marín

de dos Pingüés

cúcara, mácara

títere, fue.

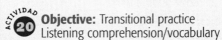

SOY UN MURCIÉLAGO.

¡Un nuevo amigo!

Escuchar Escucha lo que dice tu nuevo amigo. Contesta las preguntas. *(Hint: Listen to what your new friend says. Answer the questions.)*

I. ¿Cómo se llama el chico?
   a. Ángel
   b. Enrique

2. ¿De dónde es?
   a. Los Ángeles
   b. Miami

3. ¿Cómo está hoy?
   a. Muy bien.
   b. Bien.

4. ¿Qué le gusta hacer?
   a. bailar y patinar
   b. bailar y cantar

5. ¿Le gusta trabajar?
   a. sí
   b. no

¿Quién eres tú?

Hablar/Escribir Escribe algo de ti. *(Hint: Write about yourself.)*

modelo

¡Hola! Me llamo Elena. Yo soy de Miami. Vivo en un apartamento. Me gusta leer, bailar y cantar.

Nota

To say what kind of home you live in, use the phrase **Vivo en…**

■ MÁS COMUNICACIÓN p. R1

---

19 Objective: Transitional practice Introductions in conversation

Answers
1. A: Alma, te presento a mi amigo, Jorge.
   B: Mucho gusto, Jorge.
   C: Igualmente, Alma.
2. A: Señor Gómez, le presento a mi amigo, Carlos.
   B: Mucho gusto, Carlos.
   C: Igualmente, señor Gómez.
3. A: Arturo, te presento a mi amigo, David.
   B: Mucho gusto, David.
   C: Igualmente, Arturo.
4. A: Señorita Álvarez, le presento a mi amigo, Manuel.
   B: Mucho gusto, Manuel.
   C: Igualmente, señorita Álvarez.
5. A: Señora Delgado, le presento a mi amigo, Emilio.
   B: Mucho gusto, Emilio.
   C: Igualmente, señora Delgado.

Note: To extend the activity, have students ask what the other person likes to do:

(Ex. 1:   B: ¿Te gusta nadar?
         C: No, no me gusta nadar.)

20 Objective: Transitional practice Listening comprehension/vocabulary

Answers (See script, p. 23D.)
1. b   2. a   3. a   4. a   5. b

21 Objective: Open-ended practice Introducing oneself and expressing likes

Answers will vary.

Dictation

After students have read the rhyme in the **Pronunciación,** have them close their books. Dictate the rhyme in segments while students write it.

■ Block Schedule

Peer Teaching Have each student write a "tip" of how he/she remembers a concept/vocabulary word/verb conjugation from this **Etapa.** Compile the suggestions and make a study sheet to be passed out to the class. (For additional activities, see **Block Scheduling Copymasters.**)

Teaching All Students

Extra Help Ask students to draw cartoons of 5 activities on the board. Ask students to name the activity, spell it, and state if they like to do it.

Native Speakers Ask students if they know any additional **refranes** that would help the class practice vowel sounds.

Multiple Intelligences

Interpersonal Have all students close their eyes. Select one student to read his/her description for **Actividad 21,** leaving out the name and trying to disguise his/her voice. The other students try to guess who it is.

Teaching Resource Options

Print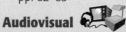
Unit 1 Resource Book
  Audioscript, pp. 82–83
  Audioscript *Para hispanohablantes*,
    pp. 82–83

Audiovisual
Audio Program Cassette 1A / CD 1
Audio *Para hispanohablantes*
  Cassette 1A / CD 1
OHT M1, 13 (Quick Start)
Canciones Cassette / CD

Quick Start Review

♻ Introducing oneself
Use OHT 13 or write on the board:
Answer the following questions; then
exchange papers for peer correction.

1. ¿Cómo te llamas?
2. ¿De dónde eres?
3. ¿Te gusta nadar?
4. ¿Qué te gusta hacer?

Answers *See p. 23D.*

Teaching Suggestions

- **Prereading** Ask students to identify
  the cognate words in **lectura**
  (lecture, lectern).

- **Strategy: Preview graphics** Have
  students look at the pictures on
  pp. 40–41 and quickly scan the
  reading. Have them write down a
  guess as to what the reading will be
  about.

- **Reading** Before asking students to
  read the text on their own, have
  them follow along in their textbooks
  as you read the information aloud to
  them.

- **Post-reading** Ask students to pick a
  person from the text whom they
  would like to meet. Why did they
  choose this person? What questions
  would they ask this person?

En voces
LECTURA

PARA LEER • STRATEGY: READING
Preview graphics Think about how you
read English. Do you check photos or
other graphics before reading an article?
View these graphics, then predict what
this reading is about. After reading it,
decide whether your prediction was on
target or needs adjustment.

Los latinos de Estados Unidos

En Estados Unidos hay personas de
muchos países de Latinoamérica.

Francisco: ¿Qué tal?
Me llamo Francisco
García Flores. Soy de
Puerto Rico, pero vivo
en Miami. El hombre
de México es mi papá.
La mujer es mi mamá.

PUERTO RICO

Sra. García: Me
llamo Anita
García. También
soy de Puerto
Rico pero trabajo
como doctora en
Miami.

MÉXICO

Sr. García:
Buenos días. Yo
me llamo Juan
García. Soy de
México. Vivo en
Miami con mi
familia.

40 cuarenta
Unidad 1

Classroom Community

Learning Scenario Have students select one of the
areas where the characters are from: Colombia, Cuba,
the Dominican Republic, Mexico, or Puerto Rico. They
should research at least 5 facts about this area. As a
class, compile all the facts about each area. If there is
access to the Internet, students may wish to use the
computer as a research tool.

Portfolio Have students develop a detailed
Almanaque about one of the areas in the reading.

Rubric: Writing

Criteria	Scale
Accuracy of information	1 2 3
Logical organization	1 2 3
Vocabulary use	1 2 3

A = 9 pts.
B = 7–8 pts.
C = 5–6 pts.
D = 3–4 pts.
F = < 3 pts.

CUBA

Sr. Estrada: Hola. Me llamo Felipe Estrada. Yo soy de Cuba, pero vivo en Miami.

CENTRO Y SUDAMÉRICA

Alma: Mi nombre es Alma. Soy de Colombia, pero también vivo en Miami.

NOTA CULTURAL

Francisco introduces himself as **Francisco García Flores**. **García** is his father's last name, and **Flores** is his mother's. In Spanish-speaking cultures most people use both last names. Some women add their husband's name after the word **de**. So Francisco's mother's name might be **Anita Flores de García** in many countries. In the U.S. some Spanish-speaking women use just their husband's name, as **Anita García** does here.

REPÚBLICA DOMINICANA

Arturo: Hola. Me llamo Arturo. Soy estudiante en Miami, pero soy de la República Dominicana.

¿De dónde son los latinos de Estados Unidos?

Pie chart:
- México 64.2%
- Centro y Sudamérica 14.3%
- Otros 7.2%
- Puerto Rico 10.7%
- Cuba 3.6%

¿Comprendiste?

1. ¿De dónde es la doctora? ¿Cómo se llama?
2. ¿De dónde es el señor García?
3. ¿Cómo se llama el señor de Cuba?
4. ¿De dónde es la chica?
5. ¿Cómo se llama el estudiante? ¿De dónde es?

¿Qué piensas?

¿De dónde son los latinos de Estados Unidos? ¿De dónde son las personas de tu comunidad? Compara tu comunidad con la comunidad de Francisco.

Culture Highlights

● **LA AMÉRICA LATINA** The countries of North America, South America, and the Caribbean that were settled by Spain, Portugal, and France make up what is known as Latin America. The name Latin America is used because the languages of the three European countries—Spanish, Portuguese, and French—are derived from Latin.

● **LOS LATINOS** In many cities in the U.S., Hispanics play an important role in the civic and cultural life of the area. In Miami, FL, for example, Hispanics now make up 62.5% of the city's population. In San Antonio, TX, 55.6% of the population is Hispanic.

Cross Cultural Connections

Strategy A Venn diagram may help students answer the ¿Qué piensas? questions, comparing and contrasting members of the communities.

Interdisciplinary Connection

History Have students research and create a timeline showing major population influx from various parts of the world into the U.S. during the last 150 years.

¿Comprendiste?

Answers
1. La doctora es de Puerto Rico. Se llama Anita García.
2. El señor García es de México.
3. El señor de Cuba se llama Felipe Estrada.
4. La chica es de Colombia.
5. El estudiante se llama Arturo. Es de la República Dominicana.

Quick Wrap-up

Ask students to write a short (3-sentence) description of themselves, modeling it after the mini-biographies from **En voces**. Ask volunteers to read their descriptions to the class.

Block Schedule

Time Saver Assign the reading as homework so that students can get a head start on comprehension.

Teaching All Students

Extra Help Remind students that there are several slightly different ways to express "My name is" in Spanish. Have them locate the 3 ways that are used in the biographies from **En voces** (Me llamo... , Yo me llamo... , Mi nombre es...).

Multiple Intelligences

Logical/Mathematical Using OHT M1 or a map of North America and the Caribbean, mark where each character lives and where he/she came from. Using a piece of string, have students measure the distance between the two places. Then using the map's key, have students calculate the actual distance.

Teaching Resource Options

Print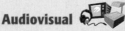

Para hispanohablantes Workbook PE, pp. 15–16
Unit 1 Resource Book
  Para hispanohablantes Workbook TE, pp. 66–67
  Information Gap Activities, p. 71
  Family Involvement, pp. 72–73
  Multiple Choice Test Questions, pp. 232–241

Audiovisual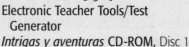

OHT 14 (Quick Start)
Audio Program Testing Cassette T1 / CD T1

Technology

Electronic Teacher Tools/Test Generator
Intrigas y aventuras CD-ROM, Disc 1

🔔 Quick Start Review

♻ **Ser de** to express origin

Use OHT 14 or write on the board: Make a list of as many "people" nouns and as many Spanish-speaking countries that you can remember. Use your list to write 3 sentences that indicate where each person is from.

Answers
Answers will vary. Answers could include:
People nouns: **el chico, la muchacha, el policía, el hombre, la familia, los amigos**

Spanish-speaking countries: **Nicaragua, Puerto Rico, España, Chile, México, Cuba**

La muchacha es de Chile.
La familia es de Nicaragua.
Los amigos son de Cuba.

✔ Teaching Suggestions
What Have Students Learned?

Have students look at the "Now you can…" notes listed in the left margin of pages 42–43. Point out that if they need to review material before doing the activities or taking the test, they should consult the "To review" notes.

Now you can...
• greet others.

To review
• vocabulary for greetings, see p. 26.
• familiar and formal greetings, see p. 32.

Now you can...
• introduce others.

To review
• making introductions, see p. 27 and p. 39.

En uso
REPASO Y MÁS COMUNICACIÓN

OBJECTIVES
• Greet others
• Introduce others
• Say where people are from
• Express likes

ACTIVIDAD 1   ¡Hola!

Escuchas esta conversación en tu comunidad. Completa la conversación con las palabras apropiadas. *(Hint: You hear this conversation in your community. Complete the conversation with the appropriate words.)*

> bien   **gusto**   está   usted   **estás**   cómo   tal   tú   **gracias**   presento

   Carlos: Hola, Sara. ¿Qué __1__?
     Sara: Muy bien, gracias, ¿y __2__?
   Carlos: No muy __3__. Hoy es lunes.
     Sara: Carlos, te __4__ a mi maestro de español, el señor Sánchez.
Sr. Sánchez: Mucho __5__, Carlos. ¿__6__ estás?
   Carlos: Estoy terrible. ¿Y __7__? ¿Cómo __8__ hoy?
Sr. Sánchez: Regular. ¿Cómo __9__ tú, Sara?
     Sara: Estoy muy bien, __10__.

ACTIVIDAD 2   Te presento a...

Presenta a las siguientes personas.
(Hint: Introduce the following people.)

modelo
_____
Daniela–Antonio
Daniela, *te presento a* **Antonio.**

  1. doctora Cruz–Miguel
  2. Jorge–Gabriel
  3. señora Ramos–Eva
  4. señor Orozco–Víctor
  5. Celia–Yolanda
  6. Pablo–Juan
  7. señorita Quintana–Ana
  8. Mónica–Octavio

42   cuarenta y dos
Unidad 1

Classroom Community

Group Activity Have students get in groups of 3 and complete **Actividad 1**. After the correct answers have been placed in the blanks, have them each select a role (**Carlos, Sara, Sr. Sánchez**) and act out the conversation. Ask for a volunteer group to present their skit to the class. Remind students to use appropriate body language/facial expressions according to what is being said.

Learning Scenario Have students form groups of 3. Student 1 pretends to be a new Spanish-speaking exchange student. Student 2 has already met this student and needs to introduce him/her to Student 3. Have the groups prepare a conversation in which everybody greets each other, and the introduction is made.

ACTIVIDAD 3 ¿Quiénes son?

Hay una fiesta. ¿Quiénes son y de dónde son estas personas?
(Hint: Who are these people at a party and where are they from?)

modelo

la señora Moreno: policía (Bolivia)

*Ella es **policía**. Es de **Bolivia**.*

1. el señor Ortiz: maestro (Venezuela)
2. Julia: mi amiga (Paraguay)
3. tú: estudiante (Miami)
4. María y Rosa: amigas (Colombia)
5. Roberto y yo: vecinos (Chile)
6. usted: doctor (Puerto Rico)
7. la señora Romero: mi vecina (Los Ángeles)
8. José y yo: amigos (Guatemala)
9. yo: estudiante (Estados Unidos)
10. las mujeres: doctoras (Costa Rica)

ACTIVIDAD 4 Preferencias

¿Qué le gusta o no le gusta hacer? *(Hint: What does the person like or not like to do?)*

modelo
Marta: sí
Le gusta correr.

tú: no
No te gusta patinar.

1. Adriana: sí

2. la maestra: sí

3. tú: sí

4. ella: no

5. Raúl: no

6. yo: sí

7. yo: no

8. tú: sí

Now you can...
- say where people are from.

To review
- subject pronouns and the verb **ser**, see p. 33.
- **ser de** to express origin, see p. 35.

Now you can...
- express likes.

To review
- verbs to talk about what you like to do, see p. 37.

ACTIVIDAD 1 Answers

1. tal
2. tú
3. bien
4. presento
5. gusto
6. Cómo
7. usted
8. está
9. estás
10. gracias

ACTIVIDAD 2 Answers

1. Doctora Cruz, le presento a Miguel.
2. Jorge, te presento a Gabriel.
3. Señora Ramos, le presento a Eva.
4. Señor Orozco, le presento a Víctor.
5. Celia, te presento a Yolanda.
6. Pablo, te presento a Juan.
7. Señorita Quintana, le presento a Ana.
8. Mónica, te presento a Octavio.

ACTIVIDAD 3 Answers

1. Él es maestro. Es de Venezuela.
2. Ella es mi amiga. Es de Paraguay.
3. Tú eres estudiante. Eres de Miami.
4. Ellas son amigas. Son de Colombia.
5. Nosotros somos vecinos. Somos de Chile.
6. Usted es doctor. Es de Puerto Rico.
7. Ella es mi vecina. Es de Los Ángeles.
8. Nosotros somos amigos. Somos de Guatemala.
9. Yo soy estudiante. Soy de los Estados Unidos.
10. Ellas son doctoras. Son de Costa Rica.

ACTIVIDAD 4 Answers

1. Le gusta nadar.
2. Le gusta leer.
3. Te gusta bailar.
4. No le gusta escribir.
5. No le gusta trabajar.
6. Me gusta comer.
7. No me gusta patinar.
8. Te gusta cantar.

Block Schedule

Retention Now that you are nearly at the end of **Etapa 1**, have students compose a short test that covers the different grammatical points they have learned. Pairs/trios of students could write the test material for a single section. Suggest that each section contain between 4–5 questions. Administer the compiled test to the class.

Teaching All Students

Extra Help Have a short conversation with each student. For example, ask the student **¿Te gusta nadar?** and have him/her respond. Then say something about yourself, such as **Me gusta correr**. Ask the student **¿Me gusta correr?** and have the student answer. Use third-person questions also. Continue until the student has a firm grasp of the grammar point.

Multiple Intelligences

Interpersonal Have students form groups of 4 or 5. Each person in the group should choose a Spanish-speaking country. Have each student put a sticker on his/her shirt with the name of the country and his/her Spanish name. Each group takes a turn in front of the class pretending they are at a party. Students introduce themselves and each other.

Teaching Resource Options

Print

Unit 1 Resource Book
Cooperative Quizzes, pp. 84–85
Etapa Exam, Forms A and B,
  pp. 86–95
Para hispanohablantes Etapa Exam,
  pp. 96–100
Portfolio Assessment, pp. 101–102
Multiple Choice Test Questions,
  pp. 232–241

Audiovisual

OHT 14 (Quick Start)
Audio Program Testing Cassette T1 /
  CD T1

Technology

Electronic Teacher Tools/Test
  Generator
www.mcdougallittell.com

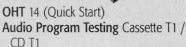

ACTIVIDAD 5

Rubric: Speaking

Criteria	Scale	
Sentence structure	1 2 3	A = 11–12 pts.
Vocabulary use	1 2 3	B = 9–10 pts.
Originality	1 2 3	C = 7–8 pts.
Fluency	1 2 3	D = 4–6 pts.
		F = < 4 pts.

ACTIVIDAD 6 *Answers will vary.*

ACTIVIDAD 7
En tu propia voz

Rubric: Writing

Criteria	Scale	
Vocabulary use	1 2 3 4 5	A = 14–15 pts.
Accuracy	1 2 3 4 5	B = 12–13 pts.
Creativity, appearance	1 2 3 4 5	C = 10–11 pts.
		D = 8–9 pts.
		F = < 8 pts.

Language Note

The word **conexiones**, related to the verb **conexionar**, refers to a community of ideas or interests. It is sometimes confused with **conección**, which is primarily a mechanical connection.

ACTIVIDAD 5 **Nuevos amigos**

PARA CONVERSAR
STRATEGY: SPEAKING
Understand, then speak Make sure you understand what your partner says. If you don't, say **Repite, por favor** (Please repeat). Once you understand, speaking clearly helps make you understood.

Imagínate que eres un(a) nuevo(a) estudiante. Contesta las preguntas de otro(a) estudiante. Cambien de papel. *(Hint: Imagine you are a new student. Answer the questions of another student. Change roles.)*

1. ¿Cómo te llamas?
2. ¿Cómo estás hoy?
3. ¿De dónde eres?
4. ¿Te gusta…?

ACTIVIDAD 6  **¡Mucho gusto!**

Usando la información de la Actividad 5, preséntale tu nuevo(a) amigo(a) a otro(a) estudiante o a tu maestro(a). *(Hint: Using the information from Activity 5, introduce your new friend to another student or to your teacher.)*

ACTIVIDAD 7 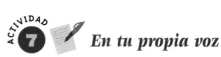 *En tu propia voz*

ESCRITURA Le escribes a un(a) amigo(a). Explícale quiénes son y de dónde son las personas de tu comunidad. ¡Usa la imaginación! *(Hint: Explain who the people in your community are and where they are from. Use your imagination!)*

¿Quién?

¿Qué le gusta?   ¿De dónde es?

CONEXIONES

Los estudios sociales Compare Francisco's community with your own. Draw two intersecting circles. In one circle, write about the people in Francisco's new community. For example, Arturo is a student. Who are the people in your community? What do they do and where are they from originally? If they were all born in the U.S., do you know what country their families were originally from? Write about them in the second circle. What things does your circle have in common with Francisco's? List them where the two circles overlap.

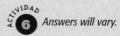

LA COMUNIDAD DE FRANCISCO   MI COMUNIDAD

Arturo Francisco | estudiante vive en una casa | mi amiga yo

Venn diagram

44 cuarenta y cuatro
Unidad 1

Classroom Community

TPR Have a student describe a well-known person in the community to the class. Students should raise their hands when they think they know the person being described. That student then describes another well-known person. Students may use the person they wrote about in **Actividad 7.**

Cooperative Learning Have students do research on Puerto Rico (where Francisco is from). Divide the class into 4 groups and have each research an aspect of Puerto Rico. Group 1: location/population/language, etc.; Group 2: cuisine; Group 3: traditions and holidays; Group 4: leisure activities. Each group can illustrate and label a poster in Spanish of its findings. Any native speaker from Puerto Rico can enhance the research with first-hand experience. Prepare a class bulletin board of the posters.

En resumen
REPASO DE VOCABULARIO

SAYING WHERE PEOPLE ARE FROM

¿De dónde + ser...?	Where is… from?
ser de...	to be from…

People

el (la) amigo(a)	friend
la chica	girl
el chico	boy
la familia	family
el hombre	man
la muchacha	girl
el muchacho	boy
la mujer	woman
el señor	Mr.
la señora	Mrs.
la señorita	Miss

Professions

el (la) doctor(a)	doctor
el (la) estudiante	student
el (la) maestro(a)	teacher
el (la) policía	police officer

Subject Pronouns

yo	I
tú	you (familiar singular)
él	he
ella	she
usted	you (formal singular)
ustedes	you (plural)
nosotros(as)	we
vosotros(as)	you (familiar plural)
ellos(as)	they

Places

la comunidad	community
el mundo	world
el país	country

GREETING OTHERS

¿Cómo está usted?	How are you? (formal)
¿Cómo estás?	How are you? (familiar)
¿Qué tal?	How is it going?
Estoy...	I am…
(No muy) Bien, ¿y tú/usted?	(Not very) Well, and you (familiar/formal)?
Regular.	So-so.
Terrible.	Terrible./Awful.
Gracias.	Thank you.
De nada.	You're welcome.

INTRODUCING OTHERS

Te/Le presento a...	Let me introduce you (familiar/formal) to…

SAYING WHERE YOU LIVE

Vivo en...	I live in…
Vive en...	He/She lives in…
el apartamento	apartment
la casa	house

EXPRESSING LIKES

¿Te gusta...?	Do you like…?
¿Le gusta...?	Does he/she like…?
Me gusta...	I like…
Te gusta...	You like…
Le gusta...	He/She likes…

Activities

bailar	to dance
cantar	to sing
comer	to eat
correr	to run
escribir	to write
leer	to read
nadar	to swim
patinar	to skate
trabajar	to work

OTHER WORDS AND PHRASES

bienvenido(a)	welcome
el concurso	contest
el lugar	place
mucho(a)	much, many
no	not
o	or
pero	but
también	also, too
y	and

Juego

Le gusta bailar pero no le gusta correr. Le gusta leer pero no le gusta cantar. Le gusta nadar pero no le gusta comer mucho. ¿Qué actividades no le gusta hacer a Marisol?

Marisol

correr

cantar

comer

Teaching All Students

Extra Help Using the video and videoscript, have students listen for vocabulary words used and circle them on the script.

Native Speakers Have students slowly read aloud each word of the vocabulary list, articulating each syllable. They should then pronounce the word as in everyday conversation. Start at the beginning of the list and switch to a new student at appropriate intervals.

Challenge Have students study the list of words for 2 minutes. Close books. Allow each student 2 minutes to list all the words he/she can remember. Then they exchange papers with another person and cross out words that are misspelled or incorrect. Next they exchange papers with a third person and return papers to the original student for final checking.

Interdisciplinary Connection

Social Studies After assigning the **Conexiones**, ask students to complete a similar diagram using another Spanish speaker they know or know about.

Quick Start Review

♻ Etapa vocabulary

Use OHT 14 or write on the board. Make flashcards of the **Repaso de vocabulario** words that are difficult for you to remember (p. 45).

Answers will vary.

Teaching Suggestions
Vocabulary Review

Using the flashcards from the Quick Start, put students in groups of 3. Deal 5 cards per group. In 3 minutes, see how many sentences students can make using one card per sentence.

Juego

Answer: A Marisol no le gusta hacer las actividades con la letra *c*.

Block Schedule

Variety Using all the new vocabulary (in addition to the vocabulary in the **Etapa preliminar**), have students write a short profile of a fictitious person. They can give the person a name, a profession, tell where he/she lives and where he/she is from, how he/she is feeling, what he/she likes/dislikes to do, etc. Allow students 5–10 minutes to compose their profile. Each student can than present "himself/herself" to the class. Students can also be encouraged to look up new words in the dictionary to make their profile more interesting!

Planning Guide CLASSROOM MANAGEMENT

OBJECTIVES

Communication
- Describe others *pp. 48–49*
- Give others' likes and dislikes *pp. 50–51*
- Describe clothing *pp. 50–51*
- Discuss music *pp. 62–63*

Grammar
- Use definite articles *pp. 54–55*
- Use indefinite articles *pp. 55–56*
- Use adjectives with gender agreement *pp. 57–58*
- Use adjectives with number agreement *pp. 58–60*

Pronunciation
- Pronunciation of **f, s,** and **ch** *p. 61*
- Dictation *TE p. 61*

Culture
- A Mexican-style rodeo *p. 58*
- Tejano music groups *pp. 62–63*

♻ Recycling
- **Gustar** *p. 52*
- People vocabulary *p. 55*

STRATEGIES

Listening Strategies
- Listen to stress *pp. 50–51*

Speaking Strategies
- Trust your first impulse *p. 61*
- Think, plan, then speak *p. 66*

Reading Strategies
- Look for cognates *pp. 62–63*
- Skim *pp. 62–63*

Writing Strategies
- When writing a description, visualize what you are describing *p. 61*

Connecting Cultures Strategies
- Learn about a regional competition *p. 58*
- Recognize regional music *pp. 62–63*
- Connect and compare what you know about music in your community to help you learn about music in a new community *pp. 62–63, 66*

PROGRAM RESOURCES

 Print
- *Más práctica* Workbook PE, *pp. 17–24*
- Block Scheduling Copymasters, *pp. 17–24*
- Unit 1 Resource Book
  Más práctica Workbook TE, *pp. 103–110*
  Para hispanohablantes Workbook TE, *pp. 111–118*

- Information Gap Activities *pp. 119–122*
- Family Involvement *pp. 123–124*
- Video Activities *pp. 125–127*
- Videoscript *pp. 128–130*
- Audioscript *pp. 131–134*
- Assessment Program, Unit 1 Etapa 2 *pp. 135–153; 232–241*
- Answer Keys *pp. 242–258*

 Audiovisual
- Audio Program Cassettes 2A, 2B / CD 2
- *Canciones* Cassette / CD
- Video Program Videotape 1 / Videodisc 1A
- Overhead Transparencies M1–M5; 3, 15–24

 Technology
- Electronic Teacher Tools/Test Generator
- *Intrigas y aventuras* CD-ROM, Disc 1
- www.mcdougallittell.com

✓ Assessment Program Options
- Cooperative Quizzes (Unit 1 Resource Book)
- Etapa Exam Forms A and B (Unit 1 Resource Book)
- *Para hispanohablantes* Etapa Exam (Unit 1 Resource Book)
- Portfolio Assessment (Unit 1 Resource Book)
- Multiple Choice Test Questions (Unit 1 Resource Book)
- Audio Program Testing Cassette T1 / CD T1
- Electronic Teacher Tools/Test Generator

Native Speakers
- *Para hispanohablantes* Workbook PE, *pp. 17–24*
- *Para hispanohablantes* Workbook TE (Unit 1 Resource Book)
- *Para hispanohablantes* Etapa Exam (Unit 1 Resource Book)
- Audio *Para hispanohablantes* Cassettes 2A, 2B, T1 / CD 2, T1
- Audioscript *Para hispanohablantes* (Unit 1 Resource Book)

Raúl   Rosalinda   Graciela   Guillermo

Student Text
Listening Activity Scripts

 Videoscript: Diálogo *pages 50–51*

• Videotape 1 • Videodisc 1A

Search Chapter 6, Play to 7
U1E2 • En vivo (Dialog)

• Use the videoscript with **Actividades 1, 2** *page 52*

Francisco:	¡Hola, Alma!
Alma:	¡Paco! ¡Cuántas fotos!
Francisco:	Son fotos de mis amigos y de mi familia. Son para el concurso.
Alma:	¿Ah, sí?
Francisco:	Voy a escribir algo para el concurso, y usar estas fotos de mi familia y de mis amigos como ilustraciones.
Alma:	¿Son tus amigos?
Francisco:	Sí, son mis amigos de San Antonio. Tengo un video de mis amigos. ¿Te interesa?
Alma:	¡Claro que sí, cómo no!
Francisco:	Son mis amigos Raúl, Rosalinda, Bill—pero en la clase de español se llama Guillermo—y Graciela.
Alma:	¡Qué divertidos son!
Francisco:	Es verdad. Raúl es muy cómico.
Alma:	¿Raúl?
Francisco:	Raúl lleva jeans y una camiseta roja. A Raúl le gusta ser cómico.
Raúl:	¡Oye, Paco! ¿Te gusta mi camiseta?
Alma:	Raúl es muy guapo.
Francisco:	¡Por favor! ¡No digas eso! Es muy egoísta.
Alma:	Y la chica que lleva la blusa morada, ¿cómo se llama?
Francisco:	Ella es mi amiga Rosalinda.
Alma:	¡Tiene el pelo largo!
Rosalinda:	¡Francisco! ¡Basta ya!
Alma:	Es muy bonita.
Francisco:	Es verdad, Rosalinda es muy bonita. También es muy inteligente. En el colegio, es seria y trabajadora. Le gusta mucho estudiar.
Alma:	Y tu amiga pelirroja, ¿cómo se llama?
Francisco:	Es Graciela. Graciela es muy simpática. Es mi mejor amiga.
Graciela:	¡Ay, Paco! ¡No me abandones con estos locos! ¡Por favor!
Raúl:	¡Ay, Graciela! La loca es ella.
Alma:	El chico rubio es Guillermo, ¿no?
Francisco:	Uh-huh, Guillermo es rubio. Y su perro Bud, ¡es gordo! A Guillermo le gusta caminar con el perro. ¡Guillermo es fuerte! Pero es un poco perezoso.
Todos:	¡Adiós, Francisco!
Alma:	¡Qué buen amigo eres! ¡Y qué buenos amigos tienes!
Francisco:	Sí. Son buenos amigos.
Alma:	Pues, ahora tienes una nueva amiga.
Francisco:	¡Sí! ¡A los nuevos amigos!

13 🎧 **¡Muchos colores!** *page 59*

Raúl es un chico muy cómico. Le gusta llevar ropa interesante. ¡Hoy lleva unos pantalones amarillos y una camisa roja! ¡Lleva una chaqueta anaranjada y unos calcetines morados! ¡Y sus zapatos son blancos!

19 🎧 **¿Cómo es Teresa?** *page 61*

Teresa es una chica simpática y bonita. Es alta y rubia. Tiene los ojos azules y el pelo muy largo. En el colegio, es seria y trabajadora. Es una chica muy inteligente. Le gusta leer. Pero también le gusta bailar y patinar.

Quick Start Review Answers

p. 50 People vocabulary
Answers will vary.
Answers could include:
Alma: morena, guapa, simpática
Francisco: moreno, guapo, simpático
Raúl: cómico, castaño, alto, guapo, egoísta
Rosalinda: bonita, inteligente, morena, baja, seria, trabajadora
Graciela: guapa, pelirroja, simpática
Guillermo: simpático, rubio, delgado, fuerte, perezoso

p. 52 Ser

1. soy	4. es
2. son	5. somos
3. es	6. eres

p. 55 Definite articles

1. el	6. la
2. la	7. el
3. el	8. los
4. los	9. el
5. la	10. los

p. 57 Gender of adjectives
1. Luisa es rubia.
2. Luisa es interesante.
3. Luisa es guapa.
4. Luisa no es morena.
5. Luisa es seria.

p. 58 Gender of adjectives
1. b, c, d
2. a, d
3. a, d
4. b, c, d

Sample Lesson Plan - 50 Minute Schedule

DAY 1

Etapa Opener
- Quick Start Review (TE, p. 46) **5 MIN.**
- Anticipate/Activate prior knowledge: Have students look at the *Etapa* Opener and answer the questions. **5 MIN.**

En contexto: Vocabulario
- Quick Start Review (TE, p. 48) **5 MIN.**
- Have students use context and pictures to learn *Etapa* vocabulary. In pairs, have students answer the questions, p. 49. Use the Situational OHTs for additional practice. **10 MIN.**

En vivo: Diálogo
- Quick Start Review (TE, p. 50) **5 MIN.**
- Review the Listening Strategy, p. 50. Play audio or show video for the dialog, pp. 50–51. **10 MIN.**
- Replay twice. Read aloud, having students take the roles of characters. **10 MIN.**

Homework Option:
- Video Activities, Unit 1 Resource Book, pp. 125–126.

DAY 2

En acción: Vocabulario y gramática
- Check homework. **5 MIN.**
- Quick Start Review (TE, p. 52) **5 MIN.**
- Use OHT 15 and 16 to review *En contexto* vocabulary. Ask students for a summary of the dialog to check recall. **5 MIN.**
- Play the video/audio; have students do *Actividades* 1 and 2. **10 MIN.**
- Have students complete *Actividad* 3 in groups. **5 MIN.**
- Have students complete *Actividad* 4 orally and *Actividad* 5 in pairs. **5 MIN.**
- Quick Start Review (TE, p. 54) **5 MIN.**
- Present *Gramática:* Using Definite Articles with Specific Things, p. 54. **10 MIN.**
- Present the *Vocabulario,* p. 54. Have students find these articles of clothing elsewhere in the textbook. **5 MIN.**

Homework Option:
- Have students complete *Actividades* 4 and 5 in writing.

DAY 3

En acción (cont.)
- Check homework. **5 MIN.**
- Have students read and complete *Actividad* 6 and do *Actividad* 7 orally. **10 MIN.**
- Quick Start Review (TE, p. 55) **5 MIN.**
- Present *Gramática:* Using Indefinite Articles with Unspecified Things, p. 55. **5 MIN.**
- Have students complete *Actividad* 8 in pairs and *Actividad* 9 orally. **10 MIN.**
- Quick Start Review (TE, p. 57) **5 MIN.**
- Present *Gramática:* Using Adjectives to Describe: Gender and *Vocabulario,* p. 57. Mime the words as appropriate. **10 MIN.**
- Have students read and complete *Actividad* 10 and do *Actividad* 11 in pairs. Expand using Information Gap Activities, Unit 1 Resource Book, p. 119; *Más comunicación,* p. R2. **5 MIN.**

Homework Option:
- *Más práctica* Workbook, pp. 21–23. *Para hispanohablantes* Workbook, pp. 19–21.

DAY 4

En acción (cont.)
- Check homework. **5 MIN.**
- Quick Start Review (TE, p. 58) **5 MIN.**
- Present *Gramática:* Using Adjectives to Describe: Number, p. 58. **5 MIN.**
- Present the *Vocabulario: Los colores,* p. 58. Point to items in the classroom to show different colors. **5 MIN.**
- Have students do *Actividad* 12 in pairs. **5 MIN.**
- Play the audio; do *Actividad* 13. **5 MIN.**
- Have students do *Actividades* 14 and 15 orally. **10 MIN.**
- Have students do *Actividad* 16 in groups and *Actividad* 17 in pairs. **5 MIN.**
- Present the Speaking Strategy, p. 61, and have students do *Actividad* 18 in pairs. **10 MIN.**

Homework Option:
- Have students complete *Actividad* 14 or 15 in writing. *Más práctica* Workbook, p. 24. *Para hispanohablantes* Workbook, p. 22.

DAY 5

En acción (cont.)
- Check homework. **5 MIN.**
- Play the audio; do *Actividad* 19. **5 MIN.**
- Have students complete *Actividad* 20. Expand using Information Gap Activities, Unit 1 Resource Book, p. 120; *Más comunicación,* p. R2. **10 MIN.**

Pronunciación
- Play the audio and have students practice the *Trabalenguas.* **10 MIN.**

En colores: Cultura y comparaciones
- Quick Start Review (TE, p. 62) **5 MIN.**
- Review the Connecting Cultures Strategy, p. 62. Have volunteers read the selection aloud and answer the questions, p. 63. Show video culture presentation for expansion. **20 MIN.**

Homework Option:
- Have students complete the *¿Comprendiste?/¿Qué piensas?* questions in writing.

DAY 6

En uso: Repaso y más comunicación
- Check homework. **5 MIN.**
- Quick Start Review (TE, p. 64) **5 MIN.**
- Have students write *Actividades* 1 and 2. Have students exchange papers for peer correction. **15 MIN.**
- Have students do *Actividades* 3 and 4 orally. **10 MIN.**

Ampliación
- Use a suggested project, game, or activity. (TE, pp. 23A–23B) **20 MIN.**

Homework Option:
- Have students complete *Actividades* 3 and 4 in writing.

DAY 7

En uso: Repaso y más comunicación (cont.)
- Check homework. **5 MIN.**
- Present the Speaking Strategy, p. 66, and have students do *Actividad* 5 in pairs. **10 MIN.**
- Have students prepare *Actividad* 6 in groups. Then have them present their descriptions to the class. **15 MIN.**

En tu propia voz: Escritura
- Do *Actividad* 7 in writing. Ask volunteers to present their descriptions to the class. **15 MIN.**

Conexiones
- Present *La música,* p. 66. **10 MIN.**

Homework Option:
- Research music as presented in *Conexiones.* Review for *Etapa* 2 Exam.

DAY 8

En resumen: Repaso de vocabulario
- Check homework. **5 MIN.**
- Quick Start Review (TE, p. 67) **5 MIN.**
- Review grammar questions, etc. as necessary. **10 MIN.**
- Complete *Etapa* 2 Exam. **20 MIN.**

Ampliación
- Use another suggested project, game, or activity. (TE, pp. 23A–23B) **15 MIN.**

Homework Option:
- Preview *Etapa* 3 Opener.

Sample Lesson Plan - Block Schedule (90 minutes)

DAY 1

Etapa Opener
- Quick Start Review (TE, p. 46) **5 MIN.**
- Anticipate/Activate prior knowledge: Have students look at the *Etapa* Opener and answer the questions. **10 MIN.**
- Use Block Scheduling Copymasters, pp. 17–18. **5 MIN.**

En contexto: Vocabulario
- Quick Start Review (TE, p. 48) **5 MIN.**
- Have students use context and pictures to learn *Etapa* vocabulary. In pairs, have students answer the questions, p. 49. Use the Situational OHTs for additional practice. **10 MIN.**

En vivo: Diálogo
- Quick Start Review (TE, p. 50) **5 MIN.**
- Review the Listening Strategy, p. 50. Play audio or show video for the dialog, pp. 50–51. **10 MIN.**
- Replay twice. Read aloud, having students take the roles of characters. **5 MIN.**

En acción: Vocabulario y gramática
- Quick Start Review (TE, p. 52) **5 MIN.**
- Use OHT 15 and 16 to review *En contexto* vocabulary. Ask students for a summary of the dialog to check recall. **5 MIN.**
- Play the video/audio; have students do *Actividades* 1 and 2 orally. **10 MIN.**
- Do *Actividad* 3 in groups. **5 MIN.**
- Have students complete *Actividad* 4 orally and *Actividad* 5 in pairs. **10 MIN.**

Homework Option:
- Video Activities, Unit 1 Resource Book, pp. 125–126. Have students complete *Actividades* 4 and 5 in writing.

DAY 2

En acción (cont.)
- Check homework. **10 MIN.**
- Quick Start Review (TE, p. 54) **5 MIN.**
- Present *Gramática:* Using Definite Articles with Specific Things, p. 54. **10 MIN.**
- Present the *Vocabulario,* p. 54. Have students find these articles of clothing elsewhere in the textbook. **10 MIN.**
- Have students read and complete *Actividad* 6 and do *Actividad* 7 orally. **10 MIN.**
- Quick Start Review (TE, p. 55) **5 MIN.**
- Present *Gramática:* Using Indefinite Articles with Unspecified Things, p. 55. **10 MIN.**
- Have students complete *Actividad* 8 in pairs and *Actividad* 9 orally. **10 MIN.**
- Quick Start Review (TE, p. 57) **5 MIN.**
- Present *Gramática:* Using Adjectives to Describe: Gender and *Vocabulario,* p. 57. Mime the words as appropriate. **10 MIN.**
- Have students read and complete *Actividad* 10 and do *Actividad* 11 in pairs. Expand using Information Gap Activities, Unit 1 Resource Book, pp. 119 *Más comunicación,* p. R2. **5 MIN.**

Homework Option:
- Have students complete *Actividad* 7 or 9 in writing. *Más práctica* Workbook, pp. 21–23. *Para hispanohablantes* Workbook, pp. 19–21.

DAY 3

En acción (cont.)
- Check homework. **10 MIN.**
- Quick Start Review (TE, p. 58) **5 MIN.**
- Present *Gramática:* Using Adjectives to Describe: Number, p. 58. **10 MIN.**
- Present the *Vocabulario: Los colores,* p. 58.. Point to items in the classroom to show different colors. **5 MIN.**
- Have students do *Actividad* 12 in pairs. **5 MIN.**
- Play the audio; have students do *Actividad* 13. **5 MIN.**
- Have students do *Actividades* 14 and 15 orally. **10 MIN.**
- Have students do *Actividad* 16 in groups and *Actividad* 17 in pairs. **10 MIN.**
- Present the Speaking Strategy, p. 61, and have students do *Actividad* 18 in pairs. **5 MIN.**
- Play the audio; do *Actividad* 19. **5 MIN.**
- Have students complete *Actividad* 20 in writing, then orally in pairs. Expand using Information Gap Activities, Unit 1 Resource Book, p. 120; *Más comunicación,* p. R1. Use Block Scheduling Copymasters, p. 23 for a change of pace as needed. **10 MIN.**

Pronunciación
- Play the audio and have students practice the *Trabalenguas.* **10 MIN.**

Homework Option:
- Have students complete *Actividades* 14 and 15 in writing. *Más práctica* Workbook, p. 24. *Para hispanohablantes* Workbook, p. 22.

DAY 4

En colores: Cultura y comparaciones
- Check homework. **10 MIN.**
- Quick Start Review (TE, p. 62) **5 MIN.**
- Review the Connecting Cultures Strategy, p. 62. Have volunteers read the selection aloud and answer the questions, p. 63. Show video culture presentation for expansion. **25 MIN.**

En uso: Repaso y más comunicación
- Quick Start Review (TE, p. 64) **5 MIN.**
- Have students write *Actividades* 1 and 2. Have them exchange papers for peer correction. **15 MIN.**
- Do *Actividades* 3 and 4 orally. Have volunteers go to the board and write out answers. **10 MIN.**
- Present the Speaking Strategy, p. 66, and have students do *Actividad* 5 in pairs. **10 MIN.**

Conexiones
- Present *La música,* p. 66. **10 MIN.**

Homework Option:
- Research music as presented in *Conexiones.* Review for *Etapa* 2 Exam.

DAY 5

En uso: Repaso y más comunicación (cont.)
- Check homework. **10 MIN.**
- Have students prepare *Actividad* 6 in groups. Then have them present their descriptions to the class. **10 MIN.**

En tu propia voz: Escritura
- Do *Actividad* 7 in writing. Ask volunteers to present their descriptions to the class. **15 MIN.**

En resumen: Repaso de vocabulario
- Quick Start Review (TE, p. 67) **5 MIN.**
- Review grammar questions, etc. as necessary. **10 MIN.**
- Complete *Etapa* 2 Exam. **20 MIN.**

Ampliación
- Use a suggested project, game, or activity. (TE, pp. 23A–23B) **20 MIN.**

Homework Option:
- Preview *Etapa* 3 Opener.

▼ Raúl, Rosalinda, Guillermo y Graciela en el Álamo, San Antonio.

Etapa Theme
Describing others and discussing their likes and dislikes

Grammar Objectives
- Using definite articles with specific things
- Using indefinite articles with unspecified things
- Using adjectives to describe: gender
- Using adjectives to describe: number

Teaching Resource Options

Print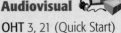
Block Scheduling Copymasters

Audiovisual
OHT 3, 21 (Quick Start)

Quick Start Review
♻ Numbers and verbs

Use OHT 21 or write on board:
Look at page 47 and answer the following questions:

1. ¿Cuántas personas hay?
2. ¿Cuántos son chicos?
3. ¿Cuántas son chicas?
4. ¿Estos amigos hablan o escriben?

Answers
1. Hay cuatro personas.
2. Dos son chicos.
3. Dos son chicas.
4. Estos amigos hablan.

Teaching Suggestions
Previewing the Etapa
- Ask students to study the picture on pp. 46–47 (1 min.).
- Ask students to identify the city and tell what they know about it.
- Have them talk about their initial impressions of the city—the weather, cultural influences, activities, etc.
- Use the ¿Qué ves? questions to focus the discussion.

UNIDAD 1
ETAPA 2

Mis buenos amigos

- Describe others
- Give others' likes and dislikes
- Describe clothing

¿Qué ves?
Look at the photo of the River Walk in San Antonio.
1. What do the teenagers look like?
2. What have they been buying?
3. What handicrafts do you see in the photo?
4. Which street name do you think comes from Spanish?

46

PASEO DEL RÍO, SAN ANTONIO

TRAVIS
COLLEGE
COMMERCE
MARKET
PASEO DE LA VILLITA

El Álamo
Plaza del Álamo
Paseo del Río
Parque HemisFeria
La Villita

Classroom Management

Planning Ahead Set the stage by preparing students to observe and talk about clothing: ask them if they are wearing any traditional clothing or clothing made in other countries. Talk about fashion trends and their personal likes and dislikes in clothing. Show them photos of a variety of fashions. Have them say **Sí, me gusta** or **No, no me gusta.**

Time Saver In case students have questions about **El Álamo,** have information ready to pass around the class. You may want to ask students ahead of time if anyone has already visited **El Álamo.** If anyone has, ask that person to bring in any souvenirs, photographs or postcards they may have to share with classmates.

Cross Cultural Connections

Ask students if the architecture of the building seen here is similar to buildings in their neighborhood. If it is not, ask them if they have ever visited any area that had similar constructions. Do they like this type of building? Why or why not?

Culture Highlights

● **SAN ANTONIO** San Antonio is located on the San Antonio River and San Pedro Creek in south-central Texas. The site of the city was long inhabited by Native Americans of the Coalhuiltec and Papaya tribes. The first permanent European settlement was established in 1718 by the Spanish. San Antonio was incorporated as a city in 1809.

● **PASEO DEL RÍO** The **Paseo del Río** in San Antonio is a walkway that borders the San Antonio River. This popular tourist attraction is made up of shops, restaurants, and an open-air amphitheater.

Interdisciplinary Connection

Social Studies With a history/geography class, do a report on the founding of San Antonio. What sort of influences did the Native American tribes of Coalhuiltec and Papaya have on this city?

Teaching All Students

Extra Help Have students study the picture for 1 minute. Then give them a list that contains five items that are found in the picture and five that are not. Have them check the items that are in the picture.

Multiple Intelligences

Verbal Have students discuss the advantages and disadvantages to visiting a place for the first time. They may also discuss the advantages and disadvantages to acting as a tour guide for someone visiting their town or city for the first time.

Block Schedule

Variety Have tourist information regarding the **Paseo del Río** (brochures, fliers, etc.) available for the class. Ask students to explain what is interesting to them and why. (For additional activities, see **Block Scheduling Copymasters**.)

Teaching Resource Options

Print 📖

Unit 1 Resource Book
  Video Activities, pp. 125–126
  Videoscript, p. 128
  Audioscript, p. 131
  Audioscript *Para hispanohablantes*,
    p. 131

Audiovisual 📽️

OHT 15, 16, 17, 17A, 18, 18A, 21 (Quick
  Start)
Audio Program Cassette 2A / CD 2
Audio *Para hispanohablantes*
  Cassette 2A / CD 2
Video Program Videotape 1 / Videodisc
  1A

Search Chapter 5, Play to 6
U1E2 • En contexto (Vocabulary)

Technology 💻 CD-ROM
Intrigas y aventuras CD-ROM, Disc 1

🔔 Quick Start Review

♻️ **Ser**

Use OHT 21 or write on board:
Complete with the correct forms of the
verb **ser**:

yo ____	nosotros(as) ____
tú ____	vosotros(as) ____
usted ____	ustedes ____
él/ella ____	ellos/ellas ____

Answers

yo **soy**	nosotros(as) **somos**
tú **eres**	vosotros(as) **sois**
usted **es**	ustedes **son**
él/ella **es**	ellos/ellas **son**

✴️ Culture Highlights

● **MARIACHIS** The **mariachis** are
strolling bands that consist of a standard
group of instruments: two violins, two
five-string guitars, a **guitarrón** (large bass
guitar), and usually two trumpets.

En contexto

🎧💿 **VOCABULARIO**

Francisco's friends back in San Antonio are waiting to go
to a Tejano music concert. Look at the illustrations. They
will help you understand the meanings of the words in
blue and answer the questions on the next page.

A Raúl, Rosalinda, Bill y Graciela son
los amigos de Francisco.

castaño
el pelo
alto
morena
rubio
el pelo corto
el pelo largo
delgado
pelirroja
la blusa blanca
la falda morada
baja
el perro
gordo
la bolsa

Raúl es **cómico**.

Rosalinda es **bonita**
y muy **inteligente**.

Bill (o Guillermo en español) es muy **simpático**.
Tiene **un perro** que se llama Bud. Bud es **gordo**.

Graciela es
guapa.

Classroom Community

Paired Activity The **Preguntas personales** can be
done as a paired activity. Encourage students to
communicate with each other by responding accurately.

TPR Ask questions such as: ¿Quién tiene el pelo
rubio?, ¿Quién tiene un perro?, ¿Quién es alto?, etc.
After each question, have appropriate students stand
and direct the same question to a student at his/her

seat. For example: **Raúl, ¿quién tiene el pelo rubio?**
Raúl: **Susana tiene el pelo rubio.**

Storytelling Divide the class into groups of 5. Each
student takes on the role of one character and restates
the description using **yo**. (For example, the student
acting as Raúl would say, **Yo soy cómico.**) Students
should also add: where they are from, something they
like/dislike, and the name of a friend.

B Los mariachis llevan chaquetas y pantalones negros. Los sombreros son grandes.

los zapatos   los pantalones

trabajador

los ojos
la camiseta

C El hombre trabaja en el bote. Es muy trabajador. No es perezoso.

el gato

D El sombrero es grande. Los cascarones son pequeños. ¡Hay cascarones azules y verdes!

verde

azul

Preguntas personales

1. ¿Eres alto(a)?
2. ¿Tu pelo es largo o corto?
3. ¿Eres trabajador(a) o perezoso(a)?
4. ¿Eres rubio(a), moreno(a), castaño(a) opelirrojo(a)?
5. ¿Cómo eres tú?

La chica es paciente y seria. El gato es feo.

cuarenta y nueve
Etapa 2   **49**

Teaching Suggestions
Introducing Vocabulary

• Have students look at pages 48–49. Use OHT 15 and 16 and Audio Cassette 2A / CD 2 to present the vocabulary.
• Ask the Comprehension Questions in order of yes/no (questions 1–3), either/or (questions 4–6), and simple word or phrase (questions 7–10). Expand by adding similar questions.
• Use the TPR activity to reinforce the meaning of individual words.
• Use the video vocabulary presentation for review and reinforcement.

Comprehension Questions

1. ¿Es gordo el perro? (Sí.)
2. ¿Es Graciela pelirroja? (Sí.)
3. ¿El perro se llama Bill? (No.)
4. ¿Quiénes llevan sombreros grandes— los mariachis o los amigos? (los mariachis)
5. ¿El hombre que trabaja en el bote es perezoso o trabajador? (Es trabajador.)
6. ¿Es Rosalinda guapa o fea? (Es guapa.)
7. ¿Cómo se llama el chico alto? (Raúl)
8. ¿Cómo es la chica con la camiseta? (paciente y seria)
9. ¿Qué llevan los mariachis? (chaquetas, pantalones, sombreros, zapatos)
10. ¿Cómo son los cascarones? (pequeños, azules y verdes)

Language Note

The word **mariachi** perhaps comes from the French word "mariage" *(marriage)*. **Mariachi** music may be so-called because it originated at weddings in Jalisco, Mexico, where there was a French settlement.

▌Block Schedule

Change of Pace Either have the following supplies on hand or ask students to bring them in: old magazines, scissors, markers, plain paper. Using the **En contexto** photos as a model, students come up with at least 2 new people labeled with descriptions. Display on the bulletin board.

Teaching All Students

Extra Help Describe the characters from this section one at a time, ask ¿**Quién es?**, and have students respond.

Native Speakers Ask students to give synonyms used in their community for the descriptive adjectives included in this section.

Multiple Intelligences

Verbal Describe students in the class and have them guess whom you are describing.

Visual Display several pictures of people taken from magazines. Describe each picture and have students guess which person you are describing.

Teaching Resource Options

Print

Más práctica Workbook PE, pp. 17–20
Para hispanohablantes Workbook PE, pp. 19–20
Block Scheduling Copymasters
Unit 1 Resource Book
  Más práctica Workbook TE, pp. 103–106
  Para hispanohablantes Workbook TE, pp. 111–112
  Video Activities, p. 127
  Videoscript, pp. 129–130
  Audioscript, p. 131
  Audioscript *Para hispanohablantes*, p. 131

Audiovisual

OHT 19, 20, 21 (Quick Start)
Audio Program Cassette 2A / CD 2
Audio *Para hispanohablantes* Cassette 2A / CD 2
Video Program Videotape 1 / Videodisc 1A

Search Chapter 6, Play to 7
U1E2 • En vivo (Dialog)

Technology

Intrigas y aventuras CD-ROM, Disc 1

Quick Start Review

♻ People vocabulary

Use OHT 21 or write on board: List descriptive adjectives related to **Alma, Francisco, Raúl, Rosalinda, Graciela,** and **Guillermo.**

Answers *See p. 45B.*

Teaching Notes

• Close and easily recognizable cognates (ex: **foto**) are sometimes used in the dialogs to increase naturalness of language.
• Students may be interested to know that photos 3–6 show **El Álamo,** photo 7 shows **El mercado,** and photo 8 shows **La Villita.** All are located in San Antonio.

En vivo

 DIÁLOGO

| Raúl | Rosalinda | Graciela | Guillermo |

PARA ESCUCHAR • STRATEGY: LISTENING

Listen to stress Voice emphasis (stress) helps you understand sentences with extra emotion. Listen for greater emphasis on the first word of the sentence and rising voice at the end. Can you hear that emphasis? When these stressed sentences are written, they have exclamation points. Don't look at the written words. Can you guess which sentences are being written with exclamation points as you listen?

Con los amigos...

1 ▶ Alma: ¡Paco! ¡Cuántas fotos!
Francisco: Son fotos de mis amigos y de mi familia. Son para el concurso.

5 ▶ Alma: Y la chica que lleva la blusa morada, ¿cómo se llama?
Francisco: Ella es mi amiga Rosalinda.
Alma: ¡Tiene el pelo largo!

6 ▶ Alma: Es muy bonita.
Francisco: También es muy inteligente. En el colegio, es seria y trabajadora. Le gusta mucho estudiar.

7 ▶ Alma: Y tu amiga pelirroja, ¿cómo se llama?
Francisco: Es Graciela. Graciela es muy simpática. Es mi mejor amiga.

50 cincuenta
Unidad 1

Classroom Community

Paired Activity Have students bring in photos of sports teams, family members, or groups of friends. Each student should say who is in the picture and describe some of the people.

Learning Scenario Students imagine that there is a good friend of Francisco who is not in the video he shows Alma. Students need to come up with a name and description of that friend, as if he/she were being introduced in the video. Ask volunteers to share the descriptions of these new **amigos** with the class.

Game Have one student think of a famous person. He/she then describes that person, while the class tries to guess the identity. Whoever guesses correctly gets to give the next description.

2 ▶ Francisco: Tengo un video de mis amigos. ¿Te interesa?
Alma: ¡Claro que sí, cómo no!

3 ▶ Alma: ¡Qué divertidos son!
Francisco: Es verdad. Raúl es muy cómico. Raúl lleva jeans y una camiseta roja.

4 ▶ Raúl: Paco, ¿te gusta mi camiseta?
Alma: Raúl es guapo.
Francisco: ¡Por favor! ¡No digas eso! Es muy egoísta.

8 ▶ Francisco: Guillermo es rubio. Y su perro Bud, ¡es gordo! A Guillermo le gusta caminar con el perro.

9 ▶ Francisco: ¡Guillermo es fuerte! Pero es un poco perezoso.

10 ▶ Alma: ¡Qué buen amigo eres! ¡Y qué buenos amigos tienes! Pues, ahora tienes una nueva amiga…
Francisco: ¡Sí! ¡A los nuevos amigos!

cincuenta y uno
Etapa 2 **51**

Teaching Suggestions
Presenting the Dialog

• Prepare students for listening by focusing on the dialog context using yes/no or either/or questions. Use the "magic" OHTs if you wish. Reintroduce Alma and her friends: **¿Habla Francisco con Alma? ¿Hay tres amigos en la foto número 3? En la foto número 7, ¿es Rosalinda o Graciela? En la foto número 9, ¿está Bill con un gato o con un perro?**

• Use the video, audiocassette, or CD to present the dialog. The expanded dialog on video offers additional listening practice opportunities.

• You may want to remind students that **concurso** means "contest."

Video Synopsis

• Alma visits Francisco and watches a video of his friends from San Antonio. For a complete transcript of the video dialog, see p. 45B.

Comprehension Questions

1. ¿Son las fotos de Francisco para el concurso? (Sí.)
2. ¿Tiene Francisco un video de sus amigos? (Sí.)
3. ¿Lleva Raúl una camiseta azul? (No.)
4. ¿Es gordo Bud? (Sí.)
5. ¿Son Guillermo y Raúl nuevos amigos? (No.)
6. ¿Es Alma de Miami o de San Antonio? (de Miami)
7. ¿Es Rosalinda guapa o fea? (guapa)
8. ¿Quién es muy inteligente? (Rosalinda)
9. ¿Quién es fuerte pero perezoso? (Guillermo)
10. ¿Quién es la mejor amiga de Francisco? (Graciela)

Teaching All Students

Extra Help Divide the class into groups of 6. Have each group role play the scenes of the **Diálogo,** adding their own creative touches.

Multiple Intelligences

Interpersonal Choose 6 students to play the roles of the characters in the **Diálogo.** Have them walk around the room, introducing themselves. The other students will greet them, adding other appropriate phrases they have learned.

Intrapersonal Students write a description of themselves in their notebooks. Remind them to refer to the descriptions from **En vivo** as a model.

Block Schedule

Retention Have students read the **Diálogo** before coming to class, making note of new vocabulary in this **Etapa.** (For additional activities, see **Block Scheduling Copymasters.**)

Teaching Resource Options

Print 📖

Unit 1 Resource Book
  Videoscript, pp. 129–130
  Audioscript, p. 131
  Audioscript *Para hispanohablantes,*
    p. 131

Audiovisual 📼

OHT 22 (Quick Start)
Audio Program Cassette 2A / CD 2
Audio *Para hispanohablantes*
  Cassette 2A / CD 2
Video Program Videotape 1 / Videodisc
  1A

🔔 Quick Start Review

♻ **Ser**

Use OHT 22 or write on the board:
Complete the following with **ser**:

1. Yo ____ inteligente.
2. Francisco y Alma ____ amigos.
3. Bud ____ un perro gordo.
4. Raúl ____ cómico.
5. Nosotros ____ serios.
6. ¡Tú ____ muy fuerte!

Answers *See p. 45B.*

Teaching Suggestions
Comprehension Check

Use **Actividades 1** and **2** to assess retention after the dialog. Have students close their books. Read the phrases and see if students can comprehend and answer correctly.

Objective: Transitional practice
Listening comprehension/vocabulary

Answers (See script, p. 45B.)
1. Cierto.
2. Falso. Son de San Antonio.
3. Falso. Raúl es muy cómico.
4. Cierto.
5. Cierto.

Objective: Transitional practice
Listening comprehension/vocabulary

Answers (See script, p. 45B.)
1. Raúl
2. Rosalinda
3. Graciela
4. Guillermo

En acción
VOCABULARIO Y GRAMÁTICA

ACTIVIDAD 1

¿Cierto o falso?

Escuchar ¿Es cierto o falso? Si es falso, di lo que es cierto. *(Hint: True or false? If it is false, say what is true.)*

1. Francisco tiene un video de sus amigos.
2. Los amigos de Francisco son de Miami.
3. Raúl no es cómico.
4. Alma dice: «Ahora tienes una nueva amiga.»
5. Para Francisco, los nuevos amigos son importantes.

TAMBIÉN SE DICE
Did you notice that Alma calls Francisco **Paco**? **Paco** is a nickname for **Francisco,** just like *Frank* is a nickname for *Francis* or *Franklin.*

ACTIVIDAD 2

¿Quién es?

Escuchar ¿Quién es: Rosalinda, Graciela, Guillermo o Raúl? *(Hint: Who is it?)*

Rosalinda   Graciela   Guillermo   Raúl

1. Es cómico y guapo.
2. Es seria y trabajadora.
3. Es pelirroja y simpática.
4. Es fuerte pero un poco perezoso.

ACTIVIDAD 3

♻ ¿Te gusta?

Hablar/Escribir Habla con cinco estudiantes. ¿Qué le gusta hacer a cada uno? Completa un cuadro. *(Hint: Talk with five students. What does each one like to do? Complete a chart.)*

modelo

Tú: *Rosa, ¿te gusta **leer**?*

Rosa: *Sí, me gusta **leer**.*

Persona	patinar	leer	correr	nadar	cantar	bailar
Rosa	sí	sí	no	sí	sí	sí

52 cincuenta y dos
Unidad 1

Classroom Management

Streamlining Convert **Actividad 2** to ¿Cierto o falso?, adding a name to each description. Then combine this with **Actividad 1** for use as a quick quiz. Have students check their own answers.

Time Saver **Prepare ahead:** Prepare an overhead or have photocopied answers ready for **Actividades 1, 2,** and **4.** Once students have completed these activities, display or hand out the answers. Have students exchange papers and do peer corrections.

- Use definite articles
- Use indefinite articles
- Use adjectives with correct gender
- Use adjectives with correct number

ACTIVIDAD 4

¿Cómo es?

Hablar Describe a cada persona o animal, usando la palabra correcta. (*Hint: Describe each person or animal, using the correct word.*)

modelo

El gato es _feo_ . (bonito, feo)

1. Ella tiene el pelo _____. (largo, corto)
2. El perro es _____. (grande, pequeño)
3. Él es _____. (gordo, delgado)
4. Ella es _____. (rubia, pelirroja)
5. El perro es _____. (trabajador, perezoso)
6. Él es _____. (alto, bajo)

ACTIVIDAD 5

La verdad es...

Hablar Tu amigo(a) no dice la verdad. Explica cómo es cada uno en realidad. Cambien de papel. (*Hint: Your friend doesn't tell the truth. Explain what each one is really like. Change roles.*)

modelo

Bud / delgado

Estudiante A: *Bud es delgado.*

Estudiante B: *No es delgado. Es gordo.*

1. Raúl / rubio
2. Guillermo / moreno
3. Bud / trabajador
4. Rosalinda / alta
5. Graciela / rubia
6. Raúl / serio
7. el gato / guapo
8. Guillermo / castaño
9. Rosalinda / pelirroja
10. Graciela / fea
11. Raúl / bajo
12. Guillermo / gordo

ACTIVIDAD 3
Objective: Transitional practice
Expressing likes/dislikes
♻ **Me/te gusta** + infinitive
Answers will vary.

ACTIVIDAD 4
Objective: Transitional practice
Vocabulary

Answers
1. largo   4. pelirroja
2. grande   5. perezoso
3. delgado   6. alto

ACTIVIDAD 5
Objective: Open-ended practice
Describing others

Answers
1. A: Raúl es rubio.
   B: No es rubio. Es moreno.
2. A: Guillermo es moreno.
   B: No es moreno. Es rubio.
3. A: Bud es trabajador.
   B: No es trabajador. Es perezoso.
4. A: Rosalinda es alta.
   B: No es alta. Es baja.
5. A: Graciela es rubia.
   B: No es rubia. Es morena.
6. A: Raúl es serio.
   B: No es serio. Es cómico.
7. A: El gato es guapo.
   B: No es guapo. Es feo.
8. A: Guillermo es castaño.
   B: No es castaño. Es rubio.
9. A: Rosalinda es pelirroja.
   B: No es pelirroja. Es morena.
10. A: Graciela es fea.
    B: No es fea. Es guapa.
11. A: Raúl es bajo.
    B: No es bajo. Es alto.
12. A: Guillermo es gordo.
    B: No es gordo. Es delgado.

▪ Block Schedule

Variety You will need magazine pictures that have a variety of people with different physical traits. Tape the pictures on the board. Have the class give names to each one, and write the names next to each picture. *[You (pointing to a picture of a girl with long blonde hair):* **Es una chica. ¿Cómo se llama?** *Student:* **Se llama Anita.**] After all photos have been "named," a student stands and describes one of the people without mentioning his/her name. The other students guess who it is. *[Student questioning:* **Es una chica. Es rubia. Tiene el pelo largo. ¿Quién es?** *Student answering:* **Es Anita.**]

Teaching All Students

Extra Help Ask students to cut out pictures of people and animals from magazines. Then have them describe each one, using a list of adjectives that you provide.

Native Speakers Have students share popular names and nicknames in their language community; for example, **Guadalupe/Lupita, Macarena/Maca.**

Multiple Intelligences

Kinesthetic Ask students to note their favorite activity from the chart in **Actividad 3.** Then have them form 6 "Favorite Activity" groups. They should greet all the students within their group, describe themselves, and give their likes and dislikes.

Teaching Resource Options

Print 📖

Más práctica Workbook PE, p. 21
Para hispanohablantes Workbook PE, p. 19
Block Scheduling Copymasters
Unit 1 Resource Book
  Más práctica Workbook TE, p. 107
  Para hispanohablantes Workbook TE, p. 113

Audiovisual 🎧

OHT 22 (Quick Start)

Technology 💻

Intrigas y aventuras CD-ROM, Disc 1

🔔 Quick Start Review

♻ Adjectives

Use OHT 22 or write on board:
Give the opposite of each of the following adjectives:

1. bajo
2. trabajador
3. gordo
4. rubio
5. guapo
6. serio

Answers

1. alto
2. perezoso
3. delgado
4. moreno
5. feo
6. cómico

Teaching Suggestions
Presenting Definite Articles with Specific Things

- Tell students that *masculine* and *feminine* are just terms used to describe nouns in some languages, and that they do not mean *male* and *female.*
- Give students a list of nouns ending in -o, -os, -a, -as. Have students underline the last vowel or vowel + s. Then have them write el, los, la, las before each noun.

GRAMÁTICA
Using Definite Articles with Specific Things

▶ Nouns name people, animals, places, or things.

  ¥ All Spanish nouns have masculine or feminine gender.

  el chico   la chica

  ¥ When nouns identify one item, they are **singular**.

  el amigo   la amiga

  ¥ When they identify more than one item, they are **plural**.

  los amigos

▶ In Spanish, the **definite article** that accompanies a noun will match its gender and number.

		Definite Article	Noun
Masculine	Singular	el *the*	chico *boy*
Masculine	Plural	los *the*	chicos *boys*
Feminine	Singular	la *the*	chica *girl*
Feminine	Plural	las *the*	chicas *girls*

matches gender
matches number

Alma says: *matches*

—¡Tiene **el** pelo largo!
She has long hair!

Francisco says: *matches*

—¡A **los** nuevos amigos!
To new friends!

▶ The gender of a noun must be learned. Usually

  ¥ nouns ending with -o are masculine.

  ¥ nouns ending with -a are feminine.

To help you learn the gender of a noun, each **noun** is given with its definite article.

APOYO PARA ESTUDIAR

Gender

Knowing the gender of nouns that refer to people is easy. But how do you learn the gender of things? When learning a new word, such as **camiseta**, say it with the definite article: **la camiseta.** Say it to yourself and say it aloud several times. That will help you remember its gender.

Vocabulario

La ropa

los calcetines   el sombrero

la camisa   el suéter

la chaqueta   el vestido

los jeans

¿Cuál es tu ropa favorita?

---

54 cincuenta y cuatro
Unidad 1

Classroom Community

Learning Scenario Ask students to bring in articles of clothing that they have learned the names for in Spanish. Have students arrange the clothing on tables in preparation for a **Mercado estudiantil**. Students will look at and discuss the clothing, using **gustar**, clothing vocabulary, and definite and indefinite articles.

Cooperative Learning Divide the class into groups of 4. Student 1 writes a noun with its definite article (**el perro**); student 2 writes the correct form of **ser** (**es**); student 3 adds an adjective that agrees with the noun and is logically associated with it (**grande**); student 4 reads the sentence aloud and says if it is correct or not. The group works together to fix incorrect sentences.

 ACTIVIDAD 6 Gramática

 Los vecinos de Raúl

Leer Raúl describe a sus vecinos. Completa sus oraciones con **el, la, los** o **las**. *(Hint: Raúl is describing his neighbors. Complete his sentences with the correct article.)*

1. _____ chicas son Ana y Luisa.
2. _____ señorita Madrigal es maestra.
3. _____ muchacho es Juan.
4. _____ hombres son doctores.
5. _____ muchachos son estudiantes.
6. _____ mujer es la señora Ramos.
7. _____ muchacha es estudiante.
8. _____ señoras son doctoras.
9. _____ señor Robles es policía.
10. _____ señores Suárez son maestros.

▨ **MÁS PRÁCTICA** *cuaderno* p. 21
▨ **PARA HISPANOHABLANTES** *cuaderno* p. 19

ACTIVIDAD 7

¿Qué llevan?

Hablar/Escribir Explica lo que llevan Graciela y Rosalinda en su viaje. *(Hint: Explain what Graciela and Rosalinda are taking on their trip.)*

modelo

1. *el vestido* 2. *las blusas*

Graciela

Rosalinda

 GRAMÁTICA

Using Indefinite Articles with Unspecified Things

A noun may sometimes appear with an indefinite article. The **indefinite article** that accompanies a noun will also match its gender and number.

		Indefinite Article	Noun
		matches gender	
Masculine	Singular	un / *a*	chico / *boy*
		matches number	
	Plural	unos / *some*	chicos / *boys*
Feminine	Singular	una / *a*	chica / *girl*
	Plural	unas / *some*	chicas / *girls*

Francisco says: *matches gender*

—Raúl lleva **una** camiseta...
Raúl wears a T-shirt...

cincuenta y cinco
Etapa 2 **55**

Teaching All Students

Extra Help Have students refer back to the **En contexto**, pp. 48–49, and describe what each person is wearing.

Native Speakers Have students talk about the way teenagers dress in their cultural community. Have them discuss how people dress for school, for social gatherings, and for special occasions.

Multiple Intelligences

Visual Bring in a suitcase or doll's trunk packed with various articles of clothing. Name and describe each item as you unpack them. Then have students name and describe the items as you repack them. After closing the suitcase, have students list all the clothing items they remember.

ACTIVIDAD 6 **Objective:** Controlled practice
Definite articles
♻ People vocabulary

Answers
1. Las 3. El 5. Los 7. La 9. El
2. La 4. Los 6. La 8. Las 10. Los

ACTIVIDAD 7 **Objective:** Transitional practice
Definite articles/vocabulary

Answers
1. el vestido 7. los calcetines
2. las blusas 8. la camisa
3. la falda 9. los pantalones
4. el suéter 10. los zapatos
5. los jeans 11. la chaqueta
6. las camisetas

Quick Start Review
♻ Definite articles

Use OHT 22 or write on the board: Give the appropriate definite article for the following:

1. ___ sombrero 6. ___ camisa
2. ___ chica 7. ___ pelo
3. ___ suéter 8. ___ chicos
4. ___ calcetines 9. ___ vestido
5. ___ chaqueta 10. ___ jeans

Answers *See p. 45B.*

Teaching Suggestions
Presenting Indefinite Articles with Unspecified Things

• Point out that *indefinite* articles refer to items in general, not specific ones. Compare these sentences: *I need a pencil; any pencil will do.* / *I need the pencil on your desk. Yes, that one.*

• Give students the same list of nouns ending in **-o, -os, -a, -as** (see Teaching Suggestions, TE p. 54). Have students underline the last vowel or vowel + **s**. This time, have them write **un, unos, una, unas** before each noun.

Block Schedule

Variety Provide students with a list of all items of clothing they have learned. Have them design **Lotería** (Bingo) cards with an item of clothing on each square. Photocopy the cards. Using the list and the cards, play **Lotería**. (For additional activities, see **Block Scheduling Copymasters**.)

Teaching Resource Options

Print

Más práctica Workbook PE, pp. 22–23
Para hispanohablantes Workbook PE, pp. 20–21
Block Scheduling Copymasters
Unit 1 Resource Book
 Más práctica Workbook TE, pp. 108–109
 Para hispanohablantes Workbook TE, pp. 114–115

Audiovisual

OHT 23 (Quick Start)

Technology

Intrigas y aventuras CD-ROM, Disc 1

 Objective: Controlled practice
Indefinite article in conversation

Answers

1. A: ¿Qué lleva Guillermo?
   B: Guillermo lleva unos pantalones y una camisa.
2. A: ¿Qué lleva Rosalinda?
   B: Rosalinda lleva un vestido y un suéter.
3. A: ¿Qué lleva el chico?
   B: Él lleva unos jeans, una camisa y una camiseta.
4. A: ¿Qué lleva Graciela?
   B: Graciela lleva una blusa y una falda.

 Objective: Open-ended practice
Describing clothing

Answers will vary.

ACTIVIDAD 8 — Gramática

¿Qué lleva?

Hablar Pregúntale a otro(a) estudiante qué lleva cada persona. Cambien de papel. *(Hint: Ask another student what each person is wearing. Change roles.)*

modelo

la chica

Estudiante A: ¿Qué lleva **la chica**?
Estudiante B: *Ella lleva unos jeans y una camiseta.*

Nota

To ask what a person is wearing, say **¿Qué lleva?** To answer, use **lleva.**

1. Guillermo   **2.** Rosalinda

3. el chico   **4.** Graciela

 **MÁS PRÁCTICA** *cuaderno* p. 22
 **PARA HISPANOHABLANTES** *cuaderno* p. 20

ACTIVIDAD 9

¿Qué llevas tú?

Hablar/Escribir Explica lo que llevas para ir a cada lugar. *(Hint: Explain what you wear to each place.)*

modelo

Llevo unos jeans y un suéter.

Nota

To say what you wear, use **llevo.**

1.   **2.**

3.   **4.**

TAMBIÉN SE DICE

Different Spanish words can be used to talk about jeans. Sometimes the word **jeans** is used, just as in English. This is called a loan word. Other words are:
bluyines: many countries
mahones: Caribbean countries
mezclillas: Mexico
vaqueros: Argentina, Spain
tejanos: Spain

Classroom Community

Paired Activity Working in pairs, have students describe their friends, using **Actividad 8** as a model. One student asks about a particular person and the other student gives a description.

TPR Props: Blue and red index cards. Give each student a blue and a red card. On the board, draw a stick figure of a boy (**Antonio [Toni]**) and a girl (**Antonia [Toni]**).

[point to the boy figure] **Es Toni. Es un amigo.**
[point to the girl figure] **Es Toni. Es una amiga.**
Hold a blue card next to **Toni (Antonio)** and a red card next to **Toni (Antonia).**
[point to the boy figure] **La carta azul es para Toni.**
[point to the girl figure] **La carta roja es para Toni.**
Read descriptions using new vocabulary and have students hold up the right card.
Toni es alto. *[blue card]* **Toni es seria.** *[red card]*

GRAMÁTICA

Using Adjectives to Describe: Gender

Adjectives describe nouns. Like articles, they match the gender of the nouns they describe. In Spanish, adjectives usually follow the noun.

Masculine adjectives often end in **-o**.

agrees

el chico **guapo**
the good-looking boy

Feminine adjectives often end in **-a**.

agrees

la chica **guapa**
the good-looking girl

Most adjectives that end with **-e** match both genders.

el chico **paciente** ◄ *same word* ► la chica **paciente**

Many adjectives that end with a **consonant** match both genders.

el chico **fenomenal** ◄ *same word* ► la chica **fenomenal**

Some add **-a** to become feminine. These adjectives must be learned.

becomes

el chico **trabajador**
the hard-working boy

la chica **trabajadora**
the hard-working girl

ACTIVIDAD 10 · Gramática

Los amigos de Francisco

Leer Tu amigo(a) es curioso(a). Descríbele a los amigos de Francisco. (*Hint: Your friend is curious. Describe Francisco's friends to him or her.*)

1. Graciela es una amiga _____ [simpático(a)].
2. Mónica es _____ [malo(a)].
3. Javier no es un chico muy _____ [interesante].
4. Rosalinda es una chica _____ [bonito(a)].
5. Felipe es un amigo _____ [aburrido(a)].
6. ¡Qué _____ [cómico(a)] es Raúl!
7. Linda es _____ [divertido(a)].
8. Es un perro muy _____ [inteligente].
9. ¡Qué _____ [fuerte] es Guillermo!
10. Alma es _____ [bueno(a)].

■ **MÁS PRÁCTICA** *cuaderno* p. 23
■ **PARA HISPANOHABLANTES** *cuaderno* p. 21

Vocabulario

Adjectives

aburrido(a) *boring*	**fuerte** *strong*
bueno(a) *good*	**interesante** *interesting*
divertido(a) *enjoyable*	**malo(a)** *bad*
¿Cómo eres?	

---

cincuenta y siete
Etapa 2 **57**

Teaching All Students

Extra Help Have students say what they wear to different places and events. **A la fiesta, yo llevo...** Additional cues: **Al concierto/Al trabajo/A la escuela/A un baile formal/En casa**. If students are still having difficulty, give them a list of clothing and a list of places/events and have them match the two lists appropriately.

Multiple Intelligences

Intrapersonal Have students list the characteristics of the ideal student and prioritize their importance. (**El/la estudiante ideal es...**)

Musical/Rhythmic Have students write a song/rap that contains both the masculine and feminine forms of at least 3 adjectives learned in this **Etapa**.

Quick Start Review
♻ Gender of adjectives

Use OHT 23 or write on the board: Luis and Luisa are twins who are exactly alike. Read the descriptions for Luis and write the same sentence for Luisa, making any necessary changes.

Modelo: **Luis es alto.**
You write: **Luisa es alta.**

1. Luis es rubio.
2. Luis es interesante.
3. Luis es guapo.
4. Luis no es moreno.
5. Luis es serio.

Answers *See p. 45B.*

Teaching Suggestions
Reinforcing Using Adjectives to Describe: Gender

After presenting the **Gramática**, write **Masculino** and **Femenino** on the board, using two colors of chalk (or use a whiteboard with markers). Hand the two pieces of chalk to two students. Each writes an appropriate adjective in his/her column. If the adjective can go in either column, they must write it in both columns with the appropriate color. They pass off the chalk to two more students, who each add an appropriate adjective, and so on.

ACTIVIDAD 10 · **Objective:** Controlled practice
Gender of adjectives

Answers

1. simpática	6. cómico
2. mala	7. divertida
3. interesante	8. inteligente
4. bonita	9. fuerte
5. aburrido	10. buena

Block Schedule

Process Time Allow students 5 minutes to read the **Gramática** to themselves before you present the information. Then ask them to try to do #1–5 in **Actividad 10** by themselves. They will complete this exercise after you have thoroughly gone over the **Gramática** with them. (For additional activities, see **Block Scheduling Copymasters**.)

Teaching Resource Options

Print

Más práctica Workbook PE, p. 24
Para hispanohablantes Workbook PE,
  p. 22
Block Scheduling Copymasters
Unit 1 Resource Book
  Más práctica Workbook TE, p. 110
  Para hispanohablantes Workbook
    TE, p. 116
  Information Gap Activities, p. 119
  Audioscript, pp. 131–132
  Audioscript *Para hispanohablantes*,
    pp. 131–132

Audiovisual

OHT 23 (Quick Start)
Audio Program Cassettes 2A, 2B / CD 2
Audio *Para hispanohablantes*
  Cassette 2A / CD 2

Technology

Intrigas y aventuras CD-ROM, Disc 1

ACTIVIDAD 11 **Objective:** Transitional practice
Gender of adjectives in conversation

Answers

1. A: ¿Cómo es Graciela?
   B: Ella es interesante y divertida.
2. A: ¿Cómo es Guillermo?
   B: Él es fuerte y trabajador.
3. A: ¿Cómo es Raúl?
   B: Él es delgado y simpático.
4. A: ¿Cómo es Rosalinda?
   B: Ella es morena y bonita.
5. A: ¿Cómo es tu amigo?
   B: Él es [divertido y paciente].
6. A: ¿Cómo es tu amiga?
   B: Ella es [trabajadora e interesante].
7. A: ¿Cómo es tu vecina?
   B: Ella es [guapa e inteligente].
8. A: ¿Cómo es el (la) maestro(a)?
   B: Él (Ella) es [interesante y fenomenal].

Quick Start Review

 Gender of adjectives

Use OHT 23 or write on the board:
Match the nouns with all possible
adjectives:

1. ___ una vecina   a. trabajador
2. ___ un perro   b. seria
3. ___ un chico   c. guapa
4. ___ una maestra   d. fenomenal

Answers See p. 45B.

N O T A CULTURAL

During **Fiesta** week in San
Antonio, there is a **charreada**, or
Mexican- style rodeo. The
contestants, **los charros**, compete
in activities that display equestrian
skills developed from ranch work.

ACTIVIDAD 11

¡Todos son diferentes!

Hablar Tu amigo(a) no conoce a estas personas. Explícale cómo
son. *(Hint: Your friend doesn't know these people. Explain what they're like.)*

modelo

Ana: interesante y guapo(a)

Estudiante A: ¿Cómo es *Ana*?

Estudiante B: *Ella es **interesante** y **guapa**.*

Nota

To ask what someone is like, use:
¿Cómo + ser + noun?

¿Cómo es Guillermo?

What is Guillermo **like?**

■ **MÁS COMUNICACIÓN** p. R2

1. Graciela: interesante y
   divertido(a)
2. Guillermo: fuerte y
   trabajador(a)
3. Raúl: delgado(a) y
   simpático(a)
4. Rosalinda: moreno(a)
   y bonito(a)
5. tu amigo: ¿?
6. tu amiga: ¿?
7. tu vecina: ¿?
8. el (la) maestro(a): ¿?

GRAMÁTICA

Using Adjectives to Describe: Number

Adjectives must also match the number of the nouns they describe.
To make an adjective plural, add **-s** if it ends with a vowel, **-es** if it ends
with a consonant.

los chicos**:**
  guapos y **divertidos**
  fenomenales

las chicas**:**
  guapas y **divertidas**
  fenomenales

When an adjective describes a group with both genders, the **masculine**
form of the adjective is used.

  El chico y la chica son **guapos**.

Vocabulario

Los colores

Colors are adjectives too.

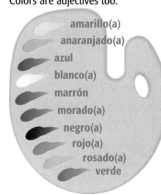

  amarillo(a)
  anaranjado(a)
  azul
  blanco(a)
  marrón
  morado(a)
  negro(a)
  rojo(a)
  rosado(a)
  verde

The plural form of **marrón** is
marrones. Other words for *brown*
are **café** and **pardo(a)**.

¿Cuál es tu color favorito?

58 cincuenta y ocho
Unidad 1

Classroom Community

Group Activity First find out each student's favorite
color. Then divide the class into groups by these colors
(there may be more than one group for a particular
color). Then have students compile a list of items in
Spanish that are typically that color. Students can use
the text and a dictionary to help compile their lists.

Portfolio Ask students to choose three of the
characters from this **Etapa**. Have them write complete

descriptions of each person, including clothing and
adjectives of description.

Rubric: Writing

Criteria	Scale	
Correct sentence structure	1 2 3	A = 11–12 pts.
Vocabulary use	1 2 3	B = 8–10 pts.
Creativity	1 2 3	C = 6–7 pts.
Logical organization	1 2 3	D = 3–5 pts.
		F = < 3 pts.

ACTIVIDAD 12 Gramática

¿De qué color es?

Hablar Tu amigo(a) está en una fiesta y tú estás en casa. Hablan por teléfono de la ropa que llevan las personas. Tu amigo(a) dice qué ropa llevan y de qué color es. Cambien de papel. *(Hint: Your friend at a party tells you over the phone about the clothing people are wearing. Work with a partner to say what the item is and its color. Change roles.)*

Roberto

> **modelo**
>
> **Estudiante A:** *Roberto* lleva *una camisa* interesante.
>
> **Estudiante B:** *¿De qué color es la camisa?*
>
> **Estudiante A:** *Es roja.*

1. Rosalinda   **2.** Francisco   **3.** Raúl   **4.** Alma

5. David   **6.** Ana   **7.** Graciela   **8.** Guillermo

ACTIVIDAD 13 Gramática

¡Muchos colores!

Escuchar Raúl lleva ropa de muchos colores. Escucha y escribe los colores de la ropa. *(Hint: Raúl wears colorful clothing. Listen and write the color of the clothing.)*

1. los pantalones   **3.** la chaqueta   **5.** los zapatos

2. la camisa   **4.** los calcetines

■ **MÁS PRÁCTICA** *cuaderno* p. 24

■ **PARA HISPANOHABLANTES** *cuaderno* p. 22

ACTIVIDAD 14

Los ojos y el pelo

Hablar/Escribir Descríbele a un(a) amigo(a) los ojos y el pelo de Francisco y de sus amigos. *(Hint: Describe for a friend the eyes and hair of Francisco and his friends.)*

> **modelo**
>
> *Tiene los ojos marrones y el pelo corto. Es moreno.*

Nota

Tener means *to have*. Use **tiene** to talk about the features a person has.

1.   2.

3.   4.

Teaching All Students

Extra Help Have students describe the eye and hair color of students next to them.

Native Speakers The **charreada** is a Mexican-American tradition. Similar to the American rodeo, it involves a number of competitions derived from ranching. However, the **charreada** involves more symbolism and pageantry. Teamwork and skill are more highly regarded than speed. Ask students if they have ever been to a **charreada** (Mexican-style rodeo) and, if so, to share their impressions with their classmates.

Multiple Intelligences

Visual Give each student a blank sheet of paper and a black crayon or marker. Tell students to think of a color and draw a large object often associated with that color (**amarillo** → sun). Call on students at random to show their drawings as other students identify the color.

Teaching Suggestions
Presenting Using Adjectives to Describe: Number
Point out the repeated marking of plurals in every word of this sentence: **Los gatos negros son bonitos.** Remind students that **son** is a verb, and therefore does not end in **-s**.

ACTIVIDAD 12 Objective: Controlled practice
Number of adjectives/vocabulary

Answers
1. A: Rosalinda lleva unos zapatos interesantes.
   B: ¿De qué color son los zapatos?
   A: Son rojos.
2. A: Francisco lleva una camiseta interesante.
   B: ¿De qué color es la camiseta?
   A: Es verde.
3. A: Raúl lleva una chaqueta interesante.
   B: ¿De qué color es la chaqueta?
   A: Es blanca.
4. A: Alma lleva un vestido interesante.
   B: ¿De qué color es el vestido?
   A: Es amarillo.
5. A: David lleva un suéter interesante.
   B: ¿De qué color es el suéter?
   A: Es anaranjado.
6. A: Ana lleva una blusa interesante.
   B: ¿De qué color es la blusa?
   A: Es marrón.
7. A: Graciela lleva una falda interesante.
   B: ¿De qué color es la falda?
   A: Es morada.
8. A: Guillermo lleva una camisa interesante.
   B: ¿De qué color es la camisa?
   A: Es negra.

ACTIVIDAD 13 Objective: Controlled practice
Listening comprehension/vocabulary

Answers (See script, p. 45B.)
1. amarillos   3. anaranjada   5. blancos
2. roja   4. morados

ACTIVIDAD 14 Objective: Transitional practice
Number of adjectives/vocabulary

Answers
1. Tiene los ojos verdes y el pelo largo. Es pelirroja.
2. Tiene los ojos azules y el pelo corto. Es rubio.
3. Tiene los ojos marrones y el pelo largo. Es moreno.
4. Tiene los ojos marrones y el pelo corto. Es castaño.

■ **Block Schedule**

Peer Teaching Ask students to choose two colors that have not appeared in the **Etapa**. He/she will be responsible for finding the Spanish words for these colors. Students should present their color names on cards of those colors. (For additional activities, see **Block Scheduling Copymasters**.)

Teaching Resource Options

Print
Block Scheduling Copymasters
Unit 1 Resource Book
  Information Gap Activities, p. 120
  Audioscript, p. 131
  Audioscript *Para hispanohablantes,*
    p. 131

Audiovisual
Audio Program Cassette 2A / CD 2
Audio *Para hispanohablantes*
  Cassette 2A / CD 2

Technology
Intrigas y aventuras CD-ROM, Disc 1

 Objective: Transitional practice
Adjectives/clothing and color vocabulary

Answers
1. Alma lleva un vestido azul y blanco, una blusa blanca y zapatos negros. Le gusta correr.
2. La Sra. García lleva una chaqueta blanca, una blusa azul, una falda negra y zapatos negros. Le gusta trabajar.
3. Guillermo lleva una camisa roja, unos pantalones negros y zapatos blancos. Le gusta leer.
4. Raúl lleva unos jeans, una chaqueta azul, una camiseta amarilla y zapatos negros. Le gusta nadar.
5. Rosalinda lleva un suéter azul, un vestido amarillo, unos calcetines amarillos y unos zapatos blancos. Le gusta cantar.

Objective: Open-ended practice
Describing clothing

Answers will vary.

Objective: Open-ended practice
Describing others

Answers will vary.

ACTIVIDAD 15

¿Qué lleva y qué le gusta?

Hablar/Escribir Estás con un(a) amigo(a). Él (Ella) quiere saber algo de estas personas. Describe qué lleva cada persona y qué le gusta hacer. *(Hint: You are with a friend. He/She wants to know something about these people. Describe what each person is wearing and what he or she likes to do.)*

modelo

Graciela: escribir

Graciela *lleva una blusa blanca, una falda morada y zapatos negros. Le gusta* **escribir.**

1. Alma: correr   **2.** la Sra. García: trabajar

3. Guillermo: leer   **4.** Raúl: nadar   **5.** Rosalinda: cantar

ACTIVIDAD 16

¿Qué lleva hoy?

Hablar/Escribir Descríbele a la clase la ropa que llevan cinco estudiantes. *(Hint: Describe for the class the clothing that five students have on.)*

Nombre	Lleva...
1. Juana	una falda marrón, una camisa blanca, unos zapatos marrones
2.	

ACTIVIDAD 17

Es...

Hablar Describe a una persona de la clase. Otro(a) estudiante tiene que adivinar quién es. *(Hint: Describe a person from your class. Another student must guess who it is.)*

modelo

Estudiante A: *Tiene el pelo corto y castaño. Tiene los ojos azules. Lleva una falda marrón, una camisa blanca y unos zapatos marrones.*

Estudiante B: *Es Juana.*

Classroom Community

Group Activity Have students cut out magazine pictures of people and glue them individually to pieces of cardboard. Each student chooses one picture, but does not show it to the other group members. Students then take turns describing their pictures while the others try to draw the person. When all descriptions are complete, students decide which drawing comes closest to the original.

Portfolio Have students write 3–4 sentences describing what they are wearing today: **Hoy, yo llevo...**

Rubric: Writing

Criteria	Scale	
Grammar	1 2 3	A = 8–9 pts.
Spelling	1 2 3	B = 6–7 pts.
Originality	1 2 3	C = 4–5 pts.
		D = 2–3 pts.
		F = < 2 pts.

ACTIVIDAD 18 ¿Cómo son?

PARA CONVERSAR

STRATEGY: SPEAKING

Trust your first impulse When speaking, your first impulse will usually be right. Go ahead and engage in this conversation. Making mistakes is natural, and you will make more when speaking than when writing. When you make a mistake, pause and correct yourself. We all make mistakes, so don't worry if you make a few!

Hablar Da tu opinión de cada persona. Cambien de papel. *(Hint: Give your opinion of each person. Change roles.)*

modelo

el señor Álvarez: el maestro / bueno

Estudiante A: ¿Cómo es **el señor Álvarez?**

Estudiante B: No es un **buen maestro.**
      o: Es un **buen maestro.**

Nota

Sometimes an adjective may precede a noun. When **bueno** or **malo** precedes a masculine singular noun, they are shortened to **buen** and **mal**. When **grande** precedes any singular noun, it becomes **gran** and its meaning changes to *great*.

1. Francisco: el estudiante / malo
2. la señorita Álvarez: la maestra / grande
3. Raúl: el amigo / grande
4. el señor Gómez: el policía / bueno
5. Alma: la vecina / malo
6. Rosalinda: la estudiante / bueno

ACTIVIDAD 19 ¿Cómo es Teresa?

Escuchar Escucha el párrafo. ¿Son las oraciones ciertas o falsas? Si una oración es falsa, di lo que es cierto. *(Hint: Listen to the paragraph. Are the sentences true or false? If a sentence is false, say what is true.)*

1. Teresa es baja y rubia.
2. Ella tiene los ojos azules y el pelo largo.
3. En el colegio, es cómica y divertida.
4. Es una chica muy inteligente.
5. Le gusta bailar, pero no le gusta patinar.

ACTIVIDAD 20 ¿Cómo es tu amigo(a)?

Escribir Describe a un(a) amigo(a). Otro(a) estudiante va a dibujar según tu descripción. *(Hint: Describe a friend. Another student will draw your description.)*

modelo

Mi amiga Marta es baja y rubia. Tiene el pelo corto y los ojos azules. Ella es trabajadora y paciente. Le gusta leer y bailar. Es una buena estudiante.

■ **MÁS COMUNICACIÓN** p. R2

Pronunciación

Trabalenguas

Pronunciación de f, s y ch The letters **f** and **s**, and the combination **ch**, are pronounced the same in Spanish as they are in English. To practice the sounds, repeat these tongue twisters.

—¡Qué falda fantástica! —dice Sara Sánchez.

¿Con cuántas planchas plancha Pancha?

Teaching All Students

Extra Help Have students make flashcards of **Etapa 2** vocabulary and grammar. They should draw pictures for words whenever possible. Have them test each other.

Multiple Intelligences

Verbal Working in pairs, have students interview each other. They should use vocabulary from **Etapas 1** and **2**. Have students present their partner to the class.

Interpersonal Working in pairs, have students interview each other. Have them ask questions such as their name, where they're from, what they like/dislike, what they like to wear, etc. Have them be as imaginative as possible. They should use vocabulary from **Etapas 1** and **2**. Have several students present their partner to the class.

ACTIVIDAD 18 Objective: Controlled practice
Giving opinions in conversation

Answers
1. A: ¿Cómo es Francisco?
   B: (No) Es un mal estudiante.
2. A: ¿Cómo es la señorita Álvarez?
   B: (No) Es una gran maestra.
3. A: ¿Cómo es Raúl?
   B: (No) Es un gran amigo.
4. A: ¿Cómo es el señor Gómez?
   B: (No) Es un buen policía.
5. A: ¿Cómo es Alma?
   B: (No) Es una mala vecina.
6. A: ¿Cómo es Rosalinda?
   B: (No) Es una buena estudiante.

ACTIVIDAD 19 Objective: Transitional practice
Listening comprehension/vocabulary

Answers (See script, p. 45B.)
1. Falso. Es alta y rubia.
2. Cierto.
3. Falso. Es seria y trabajadora.
4. Cierto.
5. Falso. Le gusta bailar y patinar.

ACTIVIDAD 20 Objective: Open-ended practice
Describing others/giving others' likes and dislikes

Answers will vary.

Quick Wrap-up

Show pictures of various outfits to the class. Ask students if they like them; for example, **¿Te gusta la camiseta roja?**

Dictation

After students have read the tongue twisters in the **Pronunciación,** have them close their books. Dictate the tongue twisters in segments while students write them.

Block Schedule

FunBreak Tape two large pieces of paper to the board with a drawing of a stick figure on each. Place two sets of crayons or markers on your desk. Divide the class in half. Describe one thing about the stick figure. Have students raise hands. Choose one student from each side to go up and draw what you just described. Continue to call on different students for each description. Compare drawings for accuracy when completed. Start over if time permits. (For additional activities, see **Block Scheduling Copymasters,** p. 23.)

Teaching Resource Options

Print

Unit 1 Resource Book
  Audioscript, pp. 133–134
  Audioscript *Para hispanohablantes,*
    pp. 133–134

Audiovisual

Audio Program Cassette 2A / CD 2
Audio *Para hispanohablantes*
  Cassette 2A / CD 2
OHT 23 (Quick Start)
Canciones Cassette / CD
Video Program Videotape 1 / Videodisc
  1A

Search Chapter 7, Play to 8
U1E2 • En colores (Culture)

Quick Start Review

♻ **Descriptions**

Use OHT 23 or write on the board:
Using vocabulary from **Etapas 1** and
2, write a description of two of the
musicians on pp. 62–63.

Answers will vary.

Teaching Suggestions
Presenting Cultura y comparaciones

• Have students look at the pictures on
  pp. 62–63 and make observations.
  How do the musicians compare with
  their favorite musicians?
• Play some samples of Tejano music.
  How does it compare with students'
  favorite music? Have them identify
  the instruments used.

Reading Strategies

Tell students to always remember to look
for cognates, familiar words, phrases, or
items in the illustrations before beginning
to read. Skimming the **¿Comprendiste?**
questions will also help them focus on the
important points in the reading.

En colores
CULTURA Y
COMPARACIONES

EL CONJUNTO

PARA CONOCERNOS
STRATEGY: CONNECTING CULTURES

When learning about another language, you
also learn about the people who speak it—
their way of life, traditions, and contributions
to the world. In addition, you learn to think
about your own culture.

Recognize regional music Is there a kind of music
unique to your area or that you like a lot?
What people or events influenced its
development? What instruments are used?
See p. R20 for the names of instruments
in Spanish. Compare this music to Tejano
music, using a Venn diagram.

JAZZ   TEJANO

saxofón (guitarra) acordeón

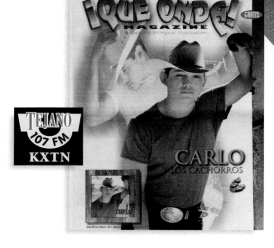

**Un instrumento
típico es el bajo
sexto. Es una
guitarra española
grande. Tiene
doce cuerdas[3].**

[3] twelve strings

**Hay mucha música
tejana en las estaciones
de radio de San Antonio.
También hay información
en revistas[1] y periódicos[2].**

[1] magazines   [2] newspapers

62 sesenta y dos
Unidad 1

Classroom Community

Paired Activity Have one student name a musical
group and the other give comments; for example, **Me
gusta escuchar la música tejana. Es excelente.**

Portfolio Have students write a brief description in
Spanish of their favorite musical group. They should
talk about the music, the way the musicians dress, and
the instruments they use. Students may want to include
photos from magazines.

Learning Scenario Have students reread **El
conjunto tejano.** Divide the class in half. Explain that
the right side of the class knows nothing about **La
música tejana,** while the left side is fairly familiar with
it. The right side must ask questions of the left side in
order to find out about this type of music. If necessary,
allow the left side to refer back to the reading to
answer the questions posed by the right side.

Selena: una artista famosa de la música tejana

TEJANO

Los músicos de la foto llevan camisas negras, chaquetas y sombreros.

En San Antonio hay muchos grupos de música tejana. Un grupo de música tejana se llama «un conjunto tejano».

La música tejana tiene influencias de la música de Europa y de México. También tiene influencias de la música de Estados Unidos.

Otro instrumento típico es el acordeón. Tiene teclas⁴ blancas y negras y un sonido⁵ divertido.

⁴keys   ⁵sound

¿Comprendiste?

1. ¿Cómo se llama un grupo de música tejana?
2. ¿De dónde tiene influencias la música tejana?
3. ¿Cuáles son los instrumentos típicos?
4. ¿Qué es un bajo sexto?

¿Qué piensas?

1. ¿Cuál es tu música favorita?
2. ¿Cómo se llama tu grupo favorito? Compara el grupo con un conjunto tejano.

sesenta y tres
Etapa 2 **63**

Culture Highlights

● **MÚSICA TEJANA** Tejano music reflects the combination of Mexican and U.S. lifestyles. The music and the lyrics incorporate characteristics of each cultural group. Tejano music combines the accordion with a blend of rock 'n' roll, country, rhythm and blues, and jazz.

¿Comprendiste?

Answers
1. Se llama «un conjunto tejano».
2. La música tejana tiene influencias de música de Europa, de México y de Estados Unidos.
3. Los instrumentos típicos son el acordeón y el bajo sexto.
4. Un bajo sexto es una guitarra española grande. Tiene doce cuerdas.

Quick Wrap-up

Have students list or say as many things as they know of **La música tejana** (influences, instruments, artists, clothing, etc.) as possible.

Teaching All Students

Extra Help Have students look in newspapers or magazines for ads for Hispanic musicians, albums, or concerts. Have them talk about the ads, then display them on the bulletin board.

Challenge Have students research an Hispanic musical artist. Explain that they can use the Internet or music magazines.

Native Speakers Ask students to bring in their favorite music from their community.

Multiple Intelligences

Musical/Rhythmic Working with a music teacher or musically talented students, teach the class a Hispanic song. Also play the music samples provided on the *Canciones* Cassette/CD.

Block Schedule

Variety Have students reread **El conjunto tejano,** then write a similar description about the music popular in your area.

Teaching Resource Options

Print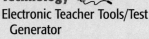

Para hispanohablantes Workbook PE, pp. 23–24

Block Scheduling Copymasters

Unit 1 Resource Book
Para hispanohablantes Workbook TE, pp. 117–118
Information Gap Activities, pp. 121–122
Family Involvement, pp. 123–124
Multiple Choice Test Questions, pp. 232–241

Audiovisual

OHT 24 (Quick Start)
Audio Program Testing Cassette T1 / CD T1

Technology

Electronic Teacher Tools/Test Generator
Intrigas y aventuras CD-ROM, Disc 1

Quick Start Review

 Clothing

Use OHT 24 or write on the board: Write a description of what you are wearing today.

Answers.
Answers will vary. Answers could include:
Hoy llevo una camiseta roja, un suéter azul, unos jeans, unos calcetines blancos y unos zapatos blancos.

Teaching Suggestions
What Have Students Learned?

- Have students look at the "Now you can…" notes listed on the left side of pages 64–65. Point out that if they feel they need to review material before doing the activities, they should consult the "To review" notes.
- Use the video to review vocabulary and structures.

ETAPA 2

Now you can…
- describe others.

To review
- definite and indefinite articles, see p. 54 and p. 55.
- adjectives, see p. 57 and p. 58.

Now you can…
- give others' likes and dislikes.

To review
- verbs to talk about what others like to do, see p. 52.

En uso
REPASO Y MÁS COMUNICACIÓN

OBJECTIVES
- Describe others
- Give others' likes and dislikes
- Describe clothing

ACTIVIDAD 1 La comunidad

Describe a las personas de la comunidad. *(Hint: Describe the people of the community.)*

modelo

ella: bueno(a) / amigo(a)	muchachos: estudiante / inteligente / trabajador(a)
Ella es una **buena amiga.**	Los **muchachos** son **estudiantes inteligentes** y **trabajadores.**

1. señora: maestro(a) / paciente / cómico(a)
2. muchacho: bueno(a) / amigo(a)
3. señores: policía / fuerte / simpático(a)
4. yo: estudiante / trabajador(a)
5. él: grande / maestro(a)
6. nosotros: estudiante / interesante / serio(a)
7. chico: malo(a) / estudiante
8. señoras: vecino(a) / aburrido(a) / perezoso(a)
9. tú: estudiante / inteligente
10. señor: bueno(a) / doctor(a)

ACTIVIDAD 2 ¡Muy diferentes!

El señor García y la señora García son muy diferentes. Lee lo que al señor le gusta hacer y di lo que a la señora le gusta hacer. *(Hint: Mr. and Mrs. García are very different. Read what he likes to do and then tell what she likes to do.)*

modelo

Le gusta leer. (cantar)
No le gusta leer. Le gusta cantar.

1. Le gusta trabajar. (escuchar música)
2. Le gusta correr. (nadar)
3. Le gusta patinar. (bailar)
4. Le gusta llevar jeans. (llevar pantalones)
5. Le gusta comer pizza. (comer un sándwich)
6. Le gusta hablar. (escuchar)
7. Le gusta leer. (escribir)
8. Le gusta llevar una camiseta. (llevar una blusa)

Classroom Community

Cooperative Learning Divide the class into 4 groups. Assign each group a "Now you can…" / "To review" section. Each group should review the concepts and present a short overview with examples to the class.

TPR Have students review **Actividad 2.** Have flashcards with a single activity used in **Actividad 2** on each one. Say **Al señor García le gusta/no le gusta…** *or* **A la señora García le gusta/no le gusta…** and then show one of the activity flashcards. Call on the first student who raises his/her hand. Have students respond with complete sentences according to the answers in **Actividad 2.**

Now you can...
- describe clothing.

To review
- vocabulary for clothing, see p. 54.
- definite and indefinite articles, see p. 54 and p. 55.
- colors, see p. 58.

ACTIVIDAD 3 ¿Qué llevan?

¿Qué llevan estas personas hoy? *(Hint: Tell what they are wearing today.)*

modelo

chico

El **chico** lleva **una camiseta amarilla** y **unos pantalones blancos.**

1. mujer   **2.** hombre   **3.** muchacho

4. chica   **5.** señorita   **6.** señor

Now you can...
- describe others.
- describe clothing.

To review
- vocabulary for clothing, see p. 54.
- adjectives, see p. 57 and p. 58.
- colors, see p. 58.

ACTIVIDAD 4 Mis amigos

Alma habla de sus amigos.
¿A quién describe?
(Hint: Tell which friend Alma describes.)

Nico   Anita   Horacio   Conchita   Gustavo

1. Es alto y tiene el pelo corto y negro.

2. Es bajo, feo y anaranjado.

3. Lleva una blusa blanca, una falda anaranjada y calcetines blancos.

4. Es pelirrojo y tiene una camisa blanca.

5. Tiene el pelo largo y rubio.

6. Lleva una chaqueta azul y pantalones negros.

7. Lleva una camiseta roja, jeans y zapatos blancos.

8. Es gordo y perezoso.

9. Lleva un suéter morado, pantalones amarillos y zapatos marrones.

10. Es alta, rubia y bonita.

sesenta y cinco
Etapa 2
65

ACTIVIDAD 1 Answers

1. La señora es una maestra paciente y cómica.
2. El muchacho es un buen amigo.
3. Los señores son policías fuertes y simpáticos.
4. Yo soy un(a) estudiante trabajador(a).
5. Él es un gran maestro.
6. Nosotros somos estudiantes interesantes y serios.
7. El chico es un mal estudiante.
8. Las señoras son vecinas aburridas y perezosas.
9. Tú eres un(a) estudiante inteligente.
10. El señor es un buen doctor.

ACTIVIDAD 2 Answers

1. No le gusta trabajar. Le gusta escuchar música.
2. No le gusta correr. Le gusta nadar.
3. No le gusta patinar. Le gusta bailar.
4. No le gusta llevar jeans. Le gusta llevar pantalones.
5. No le gusta comer pizza. Le gusta comer un sándwich.
6. No le gusta hablar. Le gusta escuchar.
7. No le gusta gusta leer. Le gusta escribir.
8. No le gusta llevar una camiseta. Le gusta llevar una blusa.

ACTIVIDAD 3 Answers

1. La mujer lleva un vestido morado y un suéter blanco.
2. El hombre lleva una chaqueta roja y unos pantalones marrones.
3. El muchacho lleva una camiseta verde y unos jeans (azules).
4. La chica lleva unos calcetines azules y unos zapatos negros.
5. La señorita lleva una blusa amarilla y una falda morada.
6. El señor lleva una camisa blanca y un suéter azul.

ACTIVIDAD 4 Answers

1. Horacio	5. Anita	9. Conchita
2. Nico	6. Gustavo	10. Anita
3. Anita	7. Horacio	
4. Gustavo	8. Nico	

Teaching Resource Options

Print

Unit 1 Resource Book
Cooperative Quizzes, pp. 135–136
Etapa Exam, Forms A and B,
  pp. 137–146
Para hispanohablantes Etapa Exam,
  pp. 147–151
Portfolio Assessment, pp. 152–153
Multiple Choice Test Questions,
  pp. 232–241

Audiovisual

OHT 24 (Quick Start)
Audio Program Testing Cassette T1 /
  CD T1

Technology

Electronic Teacher Tools/Test
  Generator
www.mcdougallittell.com

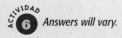

Rubric: Speaking

Criteria	Scale	
Sentence structure	1 2 3	A = 11–12 pts.
Vocabulary use	1 2 3	B = 9–10 pts.
Originality	1 2 3	C = 7–8 pts.
Fluency	1 2 3	D = 4–6 pts.
		F = < 4 pts.

6 *Answers will vary.*

7 En tu propia voz

Rubric: Writing

Criteria	Scale	
Vocabulary use	1 2 3 4 5	A = 14–15 pts.
Accuracy	1 2 3 4 5	B = 12–13 pts.
Creativity, appearance	1 2 3 4 5	C = 10–11 pts.
		D = 8–9 pts.
		F = < 8 pts.

Interdisciplinary Connection

Music Visit your school's music department. Find a musician who can play a song you found from the Spanish-speaking country that you researched for **Conexiones.** Arrange for this student to come to your class and perform this song.

---

5 **Amigos**

PARA CONVERSAR

STRATEGY: SPEAKING
Think, plan, then speak
Think about what you want to say. Rely on what you have practiced and memorized. Plan, then speak, using what you know.

Describe a uno de los amigos de Francisco. Incluye características y ropa. Otro(a) estudiante tiene que adivinar quién es. *(Hint: Describe one of Francisco's friends, including characteristics and clothing. Another student will guess who it is.)*

Raúl   Arturo   Guillermo
  Alma   Rosalinda   Graciela

6 **Los estudiantes de la clase**

Describe a un(a) estudiante de la clase. Incluye características y ropa. Di lo que le gusta. La clase tiene que adivinar quién es. *(Hint: Describe a student in the class, including characteristics and clothing. Say what he or she likes. The class will guess who it is.)*

7 *En tu propia voz*

ESCRITURA Escribe una descripción de una persona famosa o popular. Incluye sus características, la ropa que lleva y las actividades que le gusta o no le gusta hacer. Lee la descripción mientras los otros estudiantes la dibujan y adivinan quién es. *(Hint: Write a description of a famous or popular person. Include characteristics, clothing, and what he or she likes to do. Read your description while other students draw it and guess who the person is.)*

modelo

Es gordo. Lleva una chaqueta roja y unos pantalones rojos. Tiene el pelo blanco. Es un hombre simpático. Le gusta comer.

Es Santa Claus.

CONEXIONES

La música Research music of the Spanish-speaking country of your choice. Report to the class. Your presentation may use writing, drawing, and/or music recordings. To learn the names of common instruments, see p. R20. Use **ser** and **tiene** to describe the music. For example, **Es música interesante y divertida.** As you hear your classmates' reports, write down the characteristics of the different types of music. Which ones are similar?

	Tejana
Influencias	Europa, México, Estados Unidos
¿Cómo es?	alegre
Los músicos llevan...	jeans
Instrumentos	acordeón, bajo sexto

66 sesenta y seis
Unidad 1

Classroom Community

Peer Review Ask students to review the **Repaso de vocabulario** and write down the words that are the most difficult to recall. Compile a list and have pairs of students use it as a review.

Games ¿Quién soy yo? Have students describe an item from the vocabulary list while others try to guess who/what it is.

En resumen
REPASO DE VOCABULARIO

DESCRIBING OTHERS

¿Cómo es? — *What is he/she like?*

Appearance

alto(a)	*tall*
bajo(a)	*short (height)*
bonito(a)	*pretty*
castaño(a)	*brown hair*
corto(a)	*short (length)*
delgado(a)	*thin*
feo(a)	*ugly*
fuerte	*strong*
gordo(a)	*fat*
grande	*big, large*
guapo(a)	*good-looking*
largo(a)	*long*
moreno(a)	*dark hair and skin*
pelirrojo(a)	*redhead*
pequeño(a)	*small*
rubio(a)	*blond*

Features

Tiene...	*He/She has...*
los ojos (verdes, azules)	*(green, blue) eyes*
el pelo (rubio, castaño)	*(blond, brown) hair*

Personality

aburrido(a)	*boring*
bueno(a)	*good*
cómico(a)	*funny, comical*
divertido(a)	*enjoyable, fun*
inteligente	*intelligent*
interesante	*interesting*
malo(a)	*bad*
paciente	*patient*
perezoso(a)	*lazy*
serio(a)	*serious*
simpático(a)	*nice*
trabajador(a)	*hard-working*

DESCRIBING CLOTHING

What one is wearing

¿De qué color...?	*What color...?*
Llevo.../Lleva...	*I wear...He/She wears...*
¿Qué lleva?	*What is he/she wearing?*

Clothing

la blusa	*blouse*
el calcetín	*sock*
la camisa	*shirt*
la camiseta	*T-shirt*
la chaqueta	*jacket*
la falda	*skirt*
los jeans	*jeans*
los pantalones	*pants*
la ropa	*clothing*
el sombrero	*hat*
el suéter	*sweater*
el vestido	*dress*
el zapato	*shoe*

Colors

amarillo(a)	*yellow*
anaranjado(a)	*orange*
azul	*blue*
blanco(a)	*white*
marrón	*brown*
morado(a)	*purple*
negro(a)	*black*
rojo(a)	*red*
rosado(a)	*pink*
verde	*green*

OTHER WORDS AND PHRASES

la bolsa	*bag*
el (la) gato(a)	*cat*
el (la) perro(a)	*dog*
nuevo(a)	*new*
otro(a)	*other, another*
pues	*well*
¡No digas eso!	*Don't say that!*
¡Qué (divertido)!	*How (fun)!*
Es verdad.	*It's true.*

Juego

La mujer alta tiene el pelo corto y negro. Lleva una chaqueta azul y una falda larga. ¿Quién es?

a.

b.

c.

Quick Start Review

♻ Etapa vocabulary

Use OHT24 or write on the board. Have students make flashcards of the **Repaso de vocabulario** on p. 67. These can be used later as vocabulary review.

Answers will vary.

Teaching Suggestions
Vocabulary Review

Using the flashcards from the Quick Start, put students in groups of 3. Deal 5 cards per group. In 3 minutes, see how many sentences they can make using one card per sentence. The team with the most grammatically correct sentences wins.

Juego

Answer: b.

Block Schedule

Variety In small groups, have students write a short dialog or conversation that incorporates 7–10 vocabulary words.

Teaching All Students

Extra Help Using the video and videoscript, have students listen for the vocabulary words and circle them on the script.

Native Speakers Have students describe a family member or pet using as many vocabulary words as possible. They should also use words learned in the **Etapa preliminar** and **Etapa 1**.

Challenge Have students study the first word list of the **Repaso de vocabulario** for 1 minute. Close books. Allow each student 2 minutes to list all the words he/she can remember. Exchange papers with another person. Cross out words that are misspelled or incorrect. Exchange papers with a third person and make corrections. Return papers to the original student for final checking. Continue with the other lists.

Planning Guide CLASSROOM MANAGEMENT

OBJECTIVES

Communication
- Describe family *pp. 70–71*
- Ask and tell ages *pp. 72–73*
- Talk about birthdays *pp. 86–87*
- Give dates *pp. 82–83*
- Express possession *pp. 70–71, 72–73*

Grammar
- Use the verb **tener** *pp. 76–77*
- Express possession using **de** *pp. 78–79*
- Use possessive adjectives *pp. 80–81*
- Use dates and months *pp. 82–83*

Pronunciation
- Pronunciation of **m** and **n** *p. 83*
- Dictation *TE p. 83*

Culture
- **La quinceañera** *pp. 70–71, 86–87*
- Hispanic influences in Los Angeles *pp. 76, 78*
- Traditional celebrations *pp. 84–85*

♻ Recycling
- Adjectives: gender/number agreement *pp. 75, 76*
- Clothing vocabulary *pp. 78, 81*
- **Ser** *p. 81*
- Definite article *p. 81*

STRATEGIES

Listening Strategies
- Visualize *pp. 72–73*
- Get the main idea *pp. 72–73*

Speaking Strategies
- Rehearse *p. 79*
- Practice speaking smoothly *p. 90*

Reading Strategies
- Look for cognates *pp. 84–85*

Writing Strategies
- Use a graphic organizer to organize your writing *p. 90*
- Use different kinds of descriptive words *pp. 92–93*

Connecting Cultures Strategies
- Recognize Hispanic influences in your community *pp. 76, 78, 90*
- Connect and compare what you know about rites of passage in your community to help you learn about rites of passage in a new community *pp. 86–87*

PROGRAM RESOURCES

 Print
- *Más práctica* Workbook PE, *pp. 25–32*
- Block Scheduling Copymasters, *pp. 25–32*
- Unit 1 Resource Book
  Más práctica Workbook TE, *pp. 154–161*
  Para hispanohablantes Workbook TE, *pp. 162–169*
- Information Gap Activities *pp. 170–173*
- Family Involvement *pp. 174–175*
- Video Activities *pp. 176–178*
- Videoscript *pp. 179–181*
- Audioscript *pp. 182–185*
- Assessment Program, Unit 1 Etapa 3 *pp. 186–220; 232–241*
- Answer Keys *pp. 242–258*

 Audiovisual
- **Audio Program** Cassettes 3A, 3B / CD 3
- *Canciones* Cassette / CD
- **Video Program** Videotape 1 / Videodisc 1A
- **Overhead Transparencies** M1–M5; GO1–GO5; 4, 25–34

 Technology
- **Electronic Teacher Tools/Test Generator**
- *Intrigas y aventuras* CD-ROM, Disc 1
- www.mcdougallittell.com

 Assessment Program Options
- **Cooperative Quizzes** (Unit 1 Resource Book)
- **Etapa Exam** Forms A and B (Unit 1 Resource Book)
- *Para hispanohablantes* **Etapa Exam** (Unit 1 Resource Book)
- **Portfolio Assessment** (Unit 1 Resource Book)
- **Unit 1 Comprehensive Test** (Unit 1 Resource Book)
- *Para hispanohablantes* **Unit 1 Comprehensive Test** (Unit 1 Resource Book)
- **Multiple Choice Test Questions** (Unit 1 Resource Book)
- **Audio Program** Testing Cassette T1 / CD T1
- **Electronic Teacher Tools/Test Generator**

Native Speakers
- *Para hispanohablantes* Workbook PE, *pp. 25–32*
- *Para hispanohablantes* Workbook TE (Unit 1 Resource Book)
- *Para hispanohablantes* Etapa Exam (Unit 1 Resource Book)
- *Para hispanohablantes* Unit 1 Comprehensive Test (Unit 1 Resource Book)
- Audio *Para hispanohablantes* Cassettes 3A, 3B, T1 / CD 3, T1
- Audioscript *Para hispanohablantes* (Unit 1 Resource Book)

Javier   Verónica   Yolanda   Andrés

Student Text
Listening Activity Scripts

 Videoscript: Diálogo *pages 72–73*

• Videotape 1 • Videodisc 1A

Search Chapter 9, Play to 10
U1E3 • En vivo (Dialog)

• Use the videoscript with **Actividades 1, 2** *page 74*

Alma:	¿Y quién es este señor?
Francisco:	Es mi tío Javier. La foto es de su cumpleaños. Tiene ahora 39 años.
Alma:	Ah, tu tío Javier. ¿Él es el hermano de tu madre o de tu padre?
Francisco:	Mi tío Javier es el hermano menor de mi papá.
Alma:	¿Cómo es él?
Francisco:	Mi tío Javier es muy creativo. Es artista.
Alma:	¿Qué le gusta pintar?
Francisco:	Le gusta pintar murales en la comunidad. Hay muchos murales en la ciudad de Los Ángeles.
Alma:	¡Ay! ¡Qué chévere! Y esta chica, ¿quién es?
Francisco:	¡Oh!, ¿esa chica? Esa chica es mi prima Verónica. Verónica es muy divertida.
Alma:	¿Qué edad tiene Verónica?
Francisco:	Pues, su cumpleaños es en octubre. Así que ahora tiene quince años. Verónica es muy atlética.
Alma:	Y esta familia, ¿quién es?
Francisco:	Bueno, éstos son mis abuelos. En esta foto están en el observatorio.
Alma:	¡Qué simpáticos son tus abuelos!
Francisco:	Son muy activos. Mi abuelo siempre dice: «Soy viejo por fuera pero soy joven por dentro.»
Alma:	Y tu abuela, ¿cómo es?
Francisco:	Mi abuela es muy paciente, especialmente con sus queridos nietos. Ella adora a sus nietos.
Alma:	¿Quién es la mujer que está con tu tío Javier?
Francisco:	¿Ella? Ella es su esposa. Es mi tía Yolanda. Ellos son los hijos de mi tío Javier y mi tía Yolanda.
Alma:	¡Ah, sí!, ésa es Verónica, tu prima.
Francisco:	Sí, y él es Andrés, mi primo. Andrés es un niño muy activo.
Alma:	¿Cuántos años tiene Andrés?
Francisco:	Andrés tiene siete años.
Alma:	Tu familia es muy fotogénica. ¡Tu proyecto va a ser espectacular!
Francisco:	Gracias, Alma. Oye, ¿cúal es la fecha de hoy?
Alma:	Hoy es el once de noviembre. ¿Por qué?
Francisco:	¡Ay! Sólo tengo diez días más.

 **La familia de Antonio** *page 77*

En mi familia somos siete personas. Andrés es mi hermano menor. Él tiene ocho años y es muy activo. Luisa es mi hermana mayor. Ella tiene diecisiete años y es muy inteligente. Yo soy Antonio. Tengo quince años y ¡soy muy guapo! Nuestros abuelos se llaman Rosa y Alberto. Ellos tienen sesenta años. Son viejos, pero son muy divertidos. Nuestros padres se llaman Marta y Rafael. Ellos son jóvenes. Tienen sólo cuarenta años y son muy divertidos también.

¿Cuál es la respuesta? *page 83*

1. Él es mi abuelo.
2. Juana tiene quince años y tiene dos hermanas menores.
3. Yo tengo quince años.
4. Hoy es el cuatro de julio.

Quick Start Review Answers

p. 72 Family vocabulary
Answers will vary.
Answers could include:

Hombres/Chicos	Mujeres/Chicas
abuelo	abuela
tío	tía
primo	prima
padre	madre
hijo	hija
hermano	hermana

p. 74 Dialog review
1. Mi tío Javier tiene 39 años.
2. Verónica es muy divertida.
3. Tu familia es muy fotogénica.
4. Mi abuela es muy paciente.
5. Es artista y le gusta pintar murales.

p. 76 Adjective agreement
1. alto
2. simpático
3. delgada / morena
4. simpáticos
5. guapa

p. 80 Plurals
1. unas blusas
2. unos vestidos
3. unos zapatos
4. unas camisetas
5. unas chaquetas
6. unos suéteres
7. unos calcetines
8. unas camisas
9. unos sombreros
10. unas bolsas

p. 82 Numbers
1. veinte
2. quince
3. veintiocho
4. cinco
5. setenta
6. diecisiete
7. sesenta y cinco
8. treinta y seis
9. cincuenta
10. cuarenta y nueve

p. 84 Dates
Answers will vary.
Answers could include:
1. Hoy es [lunes].
2. Hoy es [el doce de mayo].
3. Mañana es [el trece de mayo].
4. Mi cumpleaños es [el primero de junio].
5. Mi día favorito de la semana es [viernes].
6. Mi día favorito del año es [el cuatro de julio].

p. 88 Tener
1. Nosotros tenemos 16 años.
2. Yo tengo una hermana bonita.
3. Francisco tiene 15 años.
4. Raúl y Rosa tienen un perro.
5. Tú tienes dos primos activos.

Sample Lesson Plan - 50 Minute Schedule

DAY 1

Etapa Opener
- Quick Start Review (TE, p. 68) 5 MIN.
- Anticipate/Activate prior knowledge: Have students look at the *Etapa* Opener and answer the questions. 5 MIN.

En contexto: Vocabulario
- Quick Start Review (TE, p. 70) 5 MIN.
- Have students use context and pictures to learn *Etapa* vocabulary. In pairs, have students answer the questions, p. 71. Use the Situational OHTs for additional practice. 10 MIN.

En vivo: Diálogo
- Quick Start Review (TE, p. 72) 5 MIN.
- Review the Listening Strategies, p. 72. Play audio or show video for the dialog, pp. 72–73. 10 MIN.
- Replay twice. Read aloud, having students take the roles of characters. 10 MIN.

Homework Option:
- Video Activities, Unit 1 Resource Book, p. 176.

DAY 2

En acción: Vocabulario y gramática
- Check homework. 5 MIN.
- Quick Start Review (TE, p. 74) 5 MIN.
- Ask students for a summary of the dialog to check recall. 5 MIN.
- Play the video/audio; have students do *Actividades* 1 and 2 orally. 10 MIN.
- Have students read and complete *Actividad* 3 in writing. Have them exchange papers for peer correction. 5 MIN.
- Have students complete *Actividades* 4 and 5. 10 MIN.
- Quick Start Review (TE, p. 76) 5 MIN.
- Present *Gramática:* Saying What You Have: The Verb *tener,* p. 76. 5 MIN.
- Have students complete *Actividad* 6 orally. 5 MIN.

Homework Option:
- Have students complete *Actividad* 4 in writing. *Más práctica* Workbook, p. 29. *Para hispanohablantes* Workbook, p. 27.

DAY 3

En acción (cont.)
- Check homework. 5 MIN.
- Present the *Vocabulario,* p. 77. 10 MIN.
- Have students do *Actividad* 7 in writing. Have students exchange papers for peer correction. 10 MIN.
- Play the audio; do *Actividad* 8. 5 MIN.
- Have students do *Actividad* 9 in pairs. Expand using Information Gap Activities, Unit 1 Resource Book, p. 170; *Más comunicación,* p. R3. 5 MIN.
- Quick Start Review (TE, p. 78) 5 MIN.
- Present *Gramática:* Expressing Possession Using *de,* p. 78. 5 MIN.
- Have students complete *Actividades* 10 and 11 orally. 10 MIN.

Homework Option:
- Have students complete *Actividad* 11 in writing. *Más práctica* Workbook, p. 30. *Para hispanohablantes* Workbook, p. 28.

DAY 4

En acción (cont.)
- Check homework. 5 MIN.
- Present the Speaking Strategy, p. 79, and have students do *Actividad* 12 in pairs. 10 MIN.
- Quick Start Review (TE, p. 80) 5 MIN.
- Present *Gramática:* Expressing Possession: Possessive Adjectives, p. 80. 15 MIN.
- Have students do *Actividades* 13–15 in pairs. 15 MIN.
- Have students do *Actividad* 16 orally. 5 MIN.

Homework Option:
- Have students complete *Actividad* 16 in writing. *Más práctica* Workbook, p. 31. *Para hispanohablantes* Workbook, p. 29.

DAY 5

En acción (cont.)
- Check homework. 5 MIN.
- Quick Start Review (TE, p. 82) 5 MIN.
- Present *Gramática:* Giving Dates: Day and Month and the *Vocabulario: Los meses del año,* p. 82. 15 MIN.
- Do *Actividades* 17 and 18. 10 MIN.
- Play the audio; do *Actividad* 19. 5 MIN.
- Do *Actividad* 20 in writing. Expand using Information Gap Activities, Unit 1 Resource Book, pp. 171–172; *Más comunicación,* p. R3. 10 MIN.

Pronunciación
- Play the audio and have students practice the *Trabalenguas.* 5 MIN.

Homework Option:
- *Más práctica* Workbook, p. 32. *Para hispanohablantes* Workbook, p. 30. Preview the *Lectura,* pp. 84–85.

DAY 6

En voces: Lectura
- Check homework. 5 MIN.
- Quick Start Review (TE, p. 84) 5 MIN.
- Present the Reading Strategy, p. 84. 5 MIN.
- Have volunteers read the selection aloud and answer the questions, p. 85. 10 MIN.

En colores: Cultura y comparaciones
- Quick Start Review (TE, p. 86) 5 MIN.
- Discuss the Connecting Cultures Strategy, p. 86. 5 MIN.
- Have volunteers read the selection aloud and answer the questions, p. 87. 10 MIN.
- Review *En uso* for *Etapa* 3 Exam. 10 MIN.

Homework Option:
- Have students complete *En uso Actividades* 1–5 in writing. Review for *Etapa* 3 Exam.

DAY 7

En uso: Repaso y más comunicación
- Check homework. 5 MIN.
- Quick Start Review (TE, p. 88) 5 MIN.
- Review *Actividades* 1–5 orally. 5 MIN.
- Present the Speaking Strategy, p. 90. Do *Actividades* 6 and 7 in groups. 10 MIN.

En resumen: Repaso de vocabulario
- Complete *Etapa* 3 Exam. 20 MIN.

En tu propia voz: Escritura
- Do *Actividad* 8 in writing. 5 MIN.

Tú en la comunidad
- Present *Tú en la comunidad,* p. 90. 5 MIN.

Homework Option:
- Review for Unit 3 Comprehensive Test.

DAY 8

En resumen: Repaso de vocabulario
- Quick Start Review (TE, p. 91) 5 MIN.

En tu propia voz: Escritura
- Present the Writing Strategy, p. 92. Do the writing activity, pp. 92–93. 10 MIN.

Unit 3 Comprehensive Test
- Review grammar questions, etc. as necessary. 5 MIN.
- Complete Unit 3 Comprehensive Test. 30 MIN.

Ampliación
- Optional: Use a suggested project, game, or activity. (TE, pp. 23A–23B) 15 MIN.

Homework Option:
- Preview *Unidad 2* Opener: Have students read and study pp. 94–95.

Sample Lesson Plan - Block Schedule (90 minutes)

DAY 1

Etapa Opener
- Quick Start Review (TE, p. 68) 5 MIN.
- Anticipate/Activate prior knowledge: Have students look at the *Etapa* Opener and answer the questions. 5 MIN.
- Use Block Scheduling Copymasters. 5 MIN.

En contexto: Vocabulario
- Quick Start Review (TE, p. 70) 5 MIN.
- Have students use context and pictures to learn *Etapa* vocabulary. In pairs, have students answer the questions, p. 71. Use the Situational OHTs for additional practice. 10 MIN.

En vivo: Diálogo
- Quick Start Review (TE, p. 72) 5 MIN.
- Review the Listening Strategies, p. 72. Play audio or show video for the dialog, pp. 72–73. 10 MIN.
- Replay twice. Read aloud, having students take the roles of characters. 10 MIN.

En acción: Vocabulario y gramática
- Quick Start Review (TE, p. 74) 5 MIN.
- Ask students for a summary of the dialog to check recall. 5 MIN.
- Play the video/audio; do *Actividades* 1 and 2 orally. 10 MIN.
- Have students read and complete *Actividad* 3 in writing. Have them exchange papers for peer correction. 5 MIN.
- Have students complete *Actividades* 4 and 5. 10 MIN.

Homework Option:
- Video Activities, Unit 1 Resource Book, p. 176. Have students complete *Actividad* 4 in writing.

DAY 2

En acción (cont.)
- Check homework. 10 MIN.
- Quick Start Review (TE, p. 76) 5 MIN.
- Present *Gramática:* Saying What You Have: The Verb *tener*, p. 76. 5 MIN.
- Have students complete *Actividad* 6 orally. 5 MIN.
- Present the *Vocabulario*, p. 77. 10 MIN.
- Have students do *Actividad* 7 in writing. Have students exchange papers for peer correction. 10 MIN.
- Play the audio; do *Actividad* 8. 5 MIN.
- Have students do *Actividad* 9 in pairs. Expand using Information Gap Activities, Unit 1 Resource Book, p. 170; *Más comunicación*, p. R3. 5 MIN.
- Quick Start Review (TE, p. 78) 5 MIN.
- Present *Gramática:* Expressing Possession Using *de*, p. 78. 10 MIN.
- Have students do *Actividades* 10 and 11 orally. 10 MIN.
- Present the Speaking Strategy, p. 79, and have students do *Actividad* 12 in pairs. Use Block Scheduling Copymasters for a change of pace as needed. 10 MIN.

Homework Option:
- Have students complete *Actividad* 11 in writing. *Más práctica* Workbook, pp. 29–30. *Para hispanohablantes* Workbook, pp. 27–28.

DAY 3

En acción (cont.)
- Check homework. 10 MIN.
- Quick Start Review (TE, p. 80) 5 MIN.
- Present *Gramática:* Expressing Possession: Possessive Adjectives, p. 80. 10 MIN.
- Have students do *Actividades* 13–15 in pairs. 15 MIN.
- Have students do *Actividad* 16 orally. 5 MIN.
- Quick Start Review (TE, p. 82) 5 MIN.
- Present *Gramática:* Giving Dates: Day and Month and the *Vocabulario: Los meses del año,* p. 82. 10 MIN.
- Have students do *Actividad* 17 in writing. Have volunteers write anwers on the board. 10 MIN.
- Have students do *Actividad* 18 in groups. 5 MIN.
- Play the audio; do *Actividad* 19. 5 MIN.
- Do *Actividad* 20 in writing. Expand using Information Gap Activities, Unit 1 Resource Book, pp. 171–172; *Más comunicación*, p. R3. 10 MIN.

Ampliación
- Optional: Use a suggested project, game, or activity. (TE, pp. 23A–23B) 15 MIN.

Homework Option:
- Have students complete *Actividad* 16 in writing. *Más práctica* Workbook, pp. 31–32. *Para hispanohablantes* Workbook, pp. 29–30.

DAY 4

Pronunciación
- Check homework. 10 MIN.
- Play the audio and have students practice the *Trabalenguas*. 5 MIN.

En voces: Lectura
- Quick Start Review (TE, p. 84) 5 MIN.
- Present the Reading Strategy, p. 84. 5 MIN.
- Have volunteers read the *Lectura* aloud and answer the questions, p. 85. 10 MIN.

En colores: Cultura y comparaciones
- Quick Start Review (TE, p. 86) 5 MIN.
- Discuss the Connecting Cultures Strategy, p. 86. 5 MIN.
- Call on volunteers to read the selection aloud and to answer the questions, p. 87. 10 MIN.

En uso: Repaso y más comunicación
- Quick Start Review (TE, p. 88) 5 MIN.
- Do *Actividades* 1–5 orally. 10 MIN.
- Present the Speaking Strategy, p. 90. Do *Actividades* 6 and 7 in groups. 15 MIN.
- Do *Actividad* 8 in writing. 5 MIN.

Homework Option:
- Review for *Etapa* 3 Exam.

DAY 5

En resumen: Repaso de vocabulario
- Quick Start Review (TE, p. 91) 5 MIN.
- Review grammar questions, etc. as necessary. 5 MIN.
- Complete *Etapa* 3 Exam. 20 MIN.

Tú en la comunidad
- Present *Tú en la comunidad*, p. 90. 10 MIN.

Unit 3 Comprehensive Test
- Review grammar questions, etc. as necessary. 5 MIN.
- Complete Unit 3 Comprehensive Test. 30 MIN.

En tu propia voz: Escritura
- Present the Writing Strategy, p. 92. Do the writing activity, pp. 92–93. 15 MIN.

Homework Option:
- Preview *Unidad 2* Opener: Have students read and study pp. 94–95.

▼ La familia García en casa, Los Ángeles.

Etapa Theme
Discussing family and talking about possessions

Grammar Objectives
- Using the verb **tener**
- Expressing possession using **de**
- Using possessive adjectives
- Using dates and months

Teaching Resource Options

Print
Block Scheduling Copymasters

Audiovisual
OHT 4, 31 (Quick Start)

Quick Start Review
♻ People, adjectives, clothing

Use OHT 31 or write on board:
Draw a sketch/cartoon of a friend and write a description. Include the following:
- name
- clothing
- personality
- what he/she likes/doesn't like to do

Answers
Answers will vary. Answers could include:
Se llama Mike. Lleva unos jeans y una camiseta blanca. Es simpático y cómico. Le gusta nadar.

Teaching Suggestions
Previewing the Etapa
- Ask students to study the picture on pp. 68–69 (1 min.).
- Close books; ask students to share at least 3 things they remember.
- Reopen books and have students describe the people and the setting.
- Use the **¿Qué ves?** questions to focus the discussion.

UNIDAD 1

ETAPA 3

Te presento a mi familia

- **Describe family**
- **Ask and tell ages**
- **Talk about birthdays**
- **Give dates**
- **Express possession**

¿Qué ves?

Look at the photo of a home in Los Angeles.
1. Describe who you see.
2. What do you think their relationships are?
3. What is each person doing?
4. Where in the United States might you see houses like this one?

LOS ÁNGELES

OLVERA STREET

68

Classroom Management

Planning Ahead Prepare to introduce the theme of the family by having students bring in photos of their own families or pictures of families from magazines. You may also wish to bring in photos of your own family to share with students.

Time Saver To facilitate organization, it is important to post agendas and assignments with instructions and deadlines. This way classroom procedures become routine.

Cross Cultural Connections

Have students discuss different types of housing and family spaces. Ask them to think about the impact of the weather on housing and family activities. Have them compare their homes and family activities with regions they have studied.

Culture Highlights

● **LA FAMILIA** In Spanish-speaking countries, grandparents frequently live with their sons, daughters, and grandchildren. The whole family, including aunts, uncles, and cousins, gathers to celebrate holidays and participate in family activities.

● **ARQUITECTURA MEXICANA** There are many examples of Mexican architecture in the U.S., especially in California and Texas. One typical feature of this architecture is a courtyard in the interior of the house. Another feature is a patio. In areas of warm, dry weather, the courtyard and patio allow the family to eat meals, study, read, or relax outdoors.

● **CALLE OLVERA** Named after the first County judge of Los Angeles, Agustin Olvera, in 1877, the street where this photograph was taken is situated in the heart of historic Los Angeles. It was converted to a colorful Mexican marketplace in 1930. La Golondrina Cafe, the first restaurant to serve authentic Mexican food, moved there the same year. Several of the merchants are descendants of the original vendors. It often serves as a setting for holiday celebrations with Mexican dancing and music.

Teaching All Students

Extra Help Have one student describe a person in the picture. The other students identify that person.

Challenge Have students make up a simple scenario to go with the photo. They can give the people names and personalities and make up a short story about them.

Multiple Intelligences

Logical/Mathematical Have students sketch a drawing of a house/apartment and show the relative size of the area the family would relax in. They can also sketch the ideal room in the ideal house/apartment. The drawings should be done to scale. If computer time is available, this activity can be done with the "draw" tools.

Block Schedule

Process Time Have students spend 3 minutes on their own looking at the photo and noting one personal observation to share with the class. (For additional activities, see **Block Scheduling Copymasters**.)

Teaching Resource Options

Print

Unit 1 Resource Book
  Video Activities, p. 176
  Videoscript, p. 179
  Audioscript, p. 182
  Audioscript *Para hispanohablantes*,
    p. 182

Audiovisual

OHT 25, 26, 27, 27A, 28, 28A,
31 (Quick Start)
Audio Program Cassette 3A / CD 3
Audio *Para hispanohablantes*
  Cassette 3A / CD 3
Video Program Videotape 1 / Videodisc
1A

Search Chapter 8, Play to 9
U1E3 • En contexto (Vocabulary)

Technology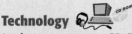

Intrigas y aventuras CD-ROM, Disc 1

Quick Start Review

 Greetings

Use OHT 31 or write on board:
Copy these sentences in logical order
to create a conversation.

¿De dónde eres?
¡Hola! Me llamo Maricarmen.
Soy de Miami. ¿Y tú?
Mucho gusto.
¡Hola! Me llamo Gloria. ¿Y tú?
El gusto es mío.
Soy de Puerto Rico.

Answers
¡Hola! Me llamo Gloria. ¿Y tú?
¡Hola! Me llamo Maricarmen.
Mucho gusto.
El gusto es mío.
¿De dónde eres?
Soy de Miami. ¿Y tú?
Soy de Puerto Rico.

En contexto

VOCABULARIO

Francisco's cousin Verónica is having a party for her
fifteenth birthday. Look at the illustrations. They will help
you understand the meanings of the words in blue and
answer the questions on the next page.

¡FELICIDADES!

el abuelo   la abuela

A Hoy es **una fecha** muy especial. Es **el
cumpleaños** de Verónica. Ella está
feliz. **¿Cuántos años tiene** ella? Tiene
quince años de **edad**. ¡Tiene una
fiesta quinceañera!

B Los señores García son los más
viejos de la familia. Son **los
abuelos** de Verónica. Javier y Juan
García son **los hijos** de ellos.

Feliz Quince Años

70 setenta
Unidad 1

Classroom Community

Paired Activity The **Preguntas personales** can be
done as a paired oral activity or paired written activity,
where one student asks the questions and the other
writes the answers. (Students should take turns.)

TPR Divide students into "family groups." Have each
student choose a role and identify him/herself while
gesturing to explain the relationship: **Soy Andrés. Soy
el hermano de Verónica.** etc.

Group Activity Have students take on the roles of
the characters in the dialog. They should interview the
other students in the group to find out who they are
and then greet them. They should also introduce one
person to another person in the group.

C Los padres de Verónica tienen una familia simpática. Verónica y Andrés son **hermanos**. Andrés es **joven**. Es el **hermano menor** de Verónica. Verónica es **la hija** y Andrés es **el hijo** de Javier y Yolanda. Verónica es la hija **mayor**.

Javier García

el padre

la madre

la hermana   el hermano

Yolanda

Verónica   Andrés

Juan García   Anita

el tío   la tía   el primo

el primo

David   Francisco

D Los padres de Francisco son **los tíos** de Verónica. Verónica es **la prima** de Francisco y de David.

Otras palabras para hablar de la familia:

el (la) esposo(a) husband (wife)
el (la) hermanastro(a) stepbrother (stepsister)
la madrastra stepmother
el (la) medio(a) hermano(a) half-brother (half-sister)
el (la) nieto(a) grandson (granddaughter)
el padrastro stepfather

Preguntas personales

1. ¿Tienes primos? ¿Tíos? ¿Abuelos?
2. ¿Tu familia es grande o pequeña?
3. ¿Tienes hermanos mayores o menores?
4. ¿Cuántos hermanos tienes?
5. ¿Cómo se llaman tus padres? ¿Tus hermanos?

setenta y uno
Etapa 3   **71**

Teaching Suggestions
Introducing Vocabulary

- Have students look at pages 70–71. Use OHT 25 and 26 and Audio Cassette 3A / CD 3 to present the vocabulary.
- Ask the Comprehension Questions below in order of yes/no (questions 1–3), either/or (questions 4–6), and simple word or phrase (questions 7–10). Expand by adding similar questions.
- Use the TPR activity to reinforce the meaning of individual words.
- Use the video vocabulary presentation for review and reinforcement.

Comprehension Questions

1. ¿Es hoy el cumpleaños de Verónica? (Sí.)
2. ¿Tiene ella quince años? (Sí.)
3. ¿Son los señores García los más jóvenes de la familia? (No.)
4. ¿Quién es el hermano menor de Verónica, Andrés o David? (Andrés)
5. ¿Es Francisco un amigo o un primo de Verónica? (un primo)
6. ¿Quién es la madre de Francisco, Anita o Yolanda? (Anita)
7. ¿Cómo se llama la fiesta de hoy? (la quinceañera)
8. ¿Quién es el padre de Francisco? (Juan)
9. ¿Cuál es el apellido de los primos? (García)
10. ¿Cómo está Verónica hoy? (feliz)

Culture Highlights

● **LA QUINCEAÑERA** The tradition of the **quinceañera** was first established during the years of Spanish colonization in Latin America. When a girl reached the age of fifteen, a party was celebrated where she was "presented to society." In some present-day celebrations, the girl dances a waltz with her father and other male members of her family. (See also pp. 86–87.)

Block Schedule

Change of Pace Have students prepare a research project on the **quinceañera,** as well as other similar celebrations (Sweet 16 Party, Debutante Ball). They should compare and contrast the events.

Teaching All Students

Extra Help Review descriptions of people by having students complete a chart of **Características físicas** and **Personalidades.** Have them list all possible vocabulary under each heading. Then have them describe the García family members using the lists.

Native Speakers Ask students to bring in photos of family gatherings or **quinceañeras** with labels for names and relationships to post in class.

Multiple Intelligences

Visual Have students make up and label a simple family tree for a television family, a famous family, or a family from literature.

Naturalist Have students research and give a short explanation of Mendel's Law, drawing a chart to explain inheritance characteristics in plants. Students may wish to work with the Science Department.

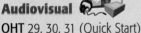
Quick Start Review

♻ Family vocabulary

Use OHT 31 or write on board:
List as many family members as
possible in each column.

Hombres/Chicos	Mujeres/Chicas
abuelo	*tía*

Answers *See p. 67B.*

Teaching Note

The untitled mural shown in photo 2
was painted by the Sunset Junction
Neighborhood Alliance; photo 3 is near
the beach in Santa Monica; photo 6 shows
the Griffith Park Observatory; photos 8
and 9 show another area in Griffith Park.

En vivo

 **DIÁLOGO**

Con la familia...

Javier Verónica Yolanda Andrés

PARA ESCUCHAR • STRATEGIES: LISTENING

Visualize As you listen, point to the images that you hear named.
Link the image and the name. This helps you learn and
remember.

Get the main idea In order to understand, listen first to try to get
the general idea of what is happening. What is the general topic
of conversation between Francisco and Alma here?

1 ▶ Alma: ¿Y quién es este señor?
Francisco: Es mi tío Javier. La foto
es de su cumpleaños. Tiene ahora
39 años. Es el hermano menor de
mi papá.

 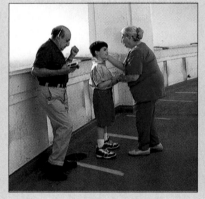 

5 ▶ Alma: Y esta familia, ¿quién es?
Francisco: Bueno, éstos son mis
abuelos.

6 ▶ Alma: ¡Qué simpáticos son tus abuelos!
Francisco: Son muy activos. Mi abuelo
siempre dice: «Soy viejo por fuera pero soy
joven por dentro.»

7 ▶ Alma: Y tu abuela, ¿cómo es?
Francisco: Mi abuela es muy
paciente, especialmente con sus
queridos nietos. Ella adora a sus
nietos.

72 setenta y dos
Unidad 1

Classroom Community

Paired Activity Ask a student volunteer to make
copies of the Comprehension Questions (TE, p. 73)
without the answers. Then give pairs of students a copy
of the Comprehension Questions and have them
collaborate on the answers. For questions 1–3, they
should supply the correct information if the answer is
no.

Game Have students work in groups of 3. Each
student takes on the identity of a character in Unit 1.
Two students prepare a true statement about their new
identity. The other prepares a false statement. The
groups stand in front of the class, introduce themselves,
and give their statements. The rest of the class tries to
determine who is not telling the truth.

2 ▶ **Francisco:** Es artista. Le gusta pintar murales. Hay muchos murales en la ciudad de Los Ángeles.
Alma: ¡Ay! ¡Qué chévere!

3 ▶ **Alma:** Y esta chica, ¿quién es?
Francisco: ¡Oh!, ¿esa chica? Esa chica es mi prima Verónica. Verónica es muy divertida.

4 ▶ **Alma:** ¿Qué edad tiene Verónica?
Francisco: Pues, su cumpleaños es en octubre. Así que ahora tiene quince años. Verónica es muy atlética.

8 ▶ **Alma:** ¿Quién es la mujer que está con tu tío Javier?
Francisco: Ella es su esposa. Es mi tía Yolanda.

9 ▶ **Francisco:** Ellos son los hijos de mi tío Javier y mi tía Yolanda.
Alma: ¡Ah, sí!, ésa es tu prima.
Francisco: Sí, y él es Andrés, mi primo.
Alma: ¿Cuántos años tiene Andrés?
Francisco: Andrés tiene siete años.

10 ▶ **Alma:** Tu familia es muy fotogénica.
Francisco: Gracias, Alma. Oye, ¿cuál es la fecha de hoy?
Alma: El once de noviembre. ¿Por qué?
Francisco: ¡Ay! Sólo tengo diez días más para el concurso.

setenta y tres
Etapa 3 | 73

Teaching All Students

Extra Help Have students make a list of the family members' names, their family relationship, and their ages (if possible).

Challenge Have students write short descriptions of one picture in the dialog. Collect the descriptions, read several aloud, and have students guess which scene is being described.

Multiple Intelligences

Verbal Have students cover the words under scenes 1–4. Read the words under one of the scenes. Students give the number of the scene. Continue for the other scenes. Then do the same for scenes 5–7 and 8–10.

Teaching Resource Options

Print

Unit 1 Resource Book
  Video Activities, p. 178
  Videoscript, p. 181
  Audioscript, p. 182
  Audioscript *Para hispanohablantes,*
    p. 182

Audiovisual

OHT 32 (Quick Start)
Audio Program Cassette 3A / CD 3
Audio *Para hispanohablantes*
  Cassette 3A / CD 3
Video Program Videotape 1 / Videodisc
  1A

Quick Start Review

♻ Dialog review
Use OHT 32 or write on the board:
Unscramble the words to make
sentences from the dialog.

1. tío / tiene / Javier / Mi / años / 39
2. muy / es / Verónica / divertida
3. fotogénica / familia / es / Tu / muy
4. paciente / Mi / es / muy / abuela
5. pintar / le / murales / artista / y /
   Es / gusta

Answers *See p. 67B.*

Teaching Suggestions
Comprehension Check

Use **Actividades 1** and **2** to assess
retention after the dialog. Have
students close their books. Read the
phrases and see if students can
comprehend and answer correctly.

 Objective: Transitional practice
Listening comprehension/vocabulary

Answers (See script p. 67B.)
1. Javier
2. Verónica
3. Andrés
4. Yolanda
5. Verónica

En acción
VOCABULARIO Y GRAMÁTICA

OBJECTIVES
• Describe family
• Ask and tell ages
• Talk about birthdays
• Give dates
• Express possession

ACTIVIDAD 1

¿Quién es?

Escuchar ¿Quién es cada persona? *(Hint: Who is each person?)*

1. Le gusta pintar murales.
2. Es muy atlética.
3. Tiene siete años.
4. Es la tía de Francisco.
5. Tiene quince años.

TAMBIÉN SE DICE

Alma says **¡Qué chévere!** in the dialog. There are many
ways to say *How awesome!* in Spanish.

• **¡Qué bárbaro!:** Argentina
• **¡Qué buena nota!:** Ecuador
• **¡Qué guay!:** Spain
• **¡Qué padre!:** Mexico

ACTIVIDAD 2

¿Cierto o falso?

Escuchar ¿Es cierto o falso? Si es falso, di lo que
es cierto. *(Hint: True or false? If it is false, say what is true.)*

1. Javier es el tío de Andrés.
2. Verónica es la prima de Francisco.
3. Andrés es el hermano mayor de Verónica.
4. Yolanda es la abuela de Javier.
5. Verónica y Andrés son los hijos de Javier y
   Yolanda.

ACTIVIDAD 3

La familia

Leer Explica quiénes son los miembros de la
familia de Francisco, usando la palabra correcta:
**abuelos, primo, prima, hermano, tía, tío, tíos,
madre, padre, padres.** *(Hint: Explain who the members of
Francisco's family are.)*

1. Verónica es la _____ de Francisco.
2. Yolanda y Javier son los _____ de él.
3. David es su _____.
4. Andrés es su _____.
5. Juan y Anita son sus _____.
6. Los señores García mayores son sus _____.
7. Anita es su _____.
8. Yolanda es su _____.
9. Javier es su _____.
10. Juan es su _____.

Classroom Management

Time Saver Focus on a quick whole-class review of
the dialog. Begin by saying: **El tío de Francisco se
llama Javier.** Start the next sentence and have the class
complete it. Students then continue to add information
about Francisco's family members.

Peer Review Divide the class into several groups.
Ask each group to complete one item from **Actividad
4.** Check the group descriptions first. If students make
errors in a description, have group members make
appropriate corrections. Then have them present the
descriptions to the class.

- Use the verb **tener**
- Express possession using **de**
- Use possessive adjectives
- Use dates and months

ACTIVIDAD 4

♻ **¿Cómo son?**

Hablar/Escribir Describe a las personas de Los Ángeles. (Hint: Describe the people from Los Angeles.)

modelo

Francisco
Francisco es alto, delgado y moreno. Es joven y simpático. Tiene el pelo corto.

1. Andrés   **2.** Verónica   **3.** Rafael

4. el abuelo   **5.** la abuela   **6.** Yolanda   **7.** Javier

ACTIVIDAD 5

¡**Una familia simpática!**

Leer Describe a la familia de Verónica, usando **los padres, el cumpleaños, la hermana, los hijos, el hermano, la familia, mayor, quince, los abuelos** o **menor**. (Hint: Describe Veronica's family.)

1. _____ García es pequeña.

2. Los señores García son _____ de Verónica.

3. Verónica es _____ de Andrés.

4. Ella es la hermana _____ .

5. Yolanda y Javier son _____ de Andrés.

6. Andrés es _____ de Verónica.

7. Él es el hermano _____ de ella.

8. Verónica y Andrés son _____ de Yolanda y Javier.

9. Hoy es _____ de Verónica.

10. Ella tiene _____ años.

setenta y cinco   **75**
Etapa 3

Vocabulary/Grammar • UNIDAD 1 Etapa 3   **75**

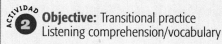
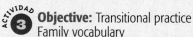

ACTIVIDAD 2 **Objective:** Transitional practice
Listening comprehension/vocabulary

Answers (See script p. 67B.)
1. Falso. Javier es el tío de Francisco.
2. Cierto.
3. Falso. Andrés es el hermano menor de Verónica.
4. Falso. Yolanda es la esposa de Javier.
5. Cierto.

ACTIVIDAD 3 **Objective:** Transitional practice
Family vocabulary

Answers
1. prima	6. abuelos
2. tíos	7. madre
3. hermano	8. tía
4. primo	9. tío
5. padres	10. padre

ACTIVIDAD 4 **Objective:** Transitional practice
Vocabulary

♻ Adjectives: gender/number agreement

Answers
1. Andrés es bajo, delgado y moreno. Es joven y simpático. Tiene el pelo corto.
2. Verónica es...
3. Rafael es...
4. El abuelo es...
5. La abuela es...
6. Yolanda es...
7. Javier es...

ACTIVIDAD 5 **Objective:** Transitional practice
Vocabulary/negatives in conversation

Answers
1. La familia
2. los abuelos
3. la hermana
4. mayor
5. los padres
6. el hermano
7. menor
8. los hijos
9. el cumpleaños
10. quince

Block Schedule
Peer Teaching Prepare Ahead: Answer Key Sheets for **Actividades 1, 2, 3, 5,** pp. 74–75. Divide the class into groups and have them exchange papers and correct these activities.

Teaching All Students

Extra Help Based on **Actividad 1,** have students share 3 facts about each character.

Native Speakers Ask students if they use any of the expressions given in **También se dice.** Have them give any other expressions they might use.

Multiple Intelligences

Verbal In pairs, have students play a guessing game called **¿Quién?** Students take turn asking and answering questions. For example: **¿Quién tiene siete años? ¿Quién es la tía de Francisco? ¿Quién es muy paciente?**

Teaching Resource Options

Print 📖

Más práctica Workbook PE, p. 29
Para hispanohablantes Workbook PE, p. 27
Block Scheduling Copymasters
Unit 1 Resource Book
  Más práctica Workbook TE, p. 158
  Para hispanohablantes Workbook TE, p. 164
  Information Gap Activities, p. 170
  Audioscript, pp. 182–183
  Audioscript *Para hispanohablantes*, pp. 182–183

Audiovisual 📽️

OHT 32 (Quick Start)
Audio Program Cassette 3B / CD 3
Audio *Para hispanohablantes* Cassette 3A / CD 3

Technology 💻

Intrigas y aventuras CD-ROM, Disc 1

🔔 Quick Start Review

♻️ Adjective agreement

Use OHT 32 or write on the board: Describe the following people by completing the sentences.

1. Francisco es a _ _ _.
2. Raúl es s _ _ _ _ _ _ _ _.
3. Estela es d _ _ _ _ _ _ y m _ _ _ _ _.
4. Los primos de Juan son s _ _ _ _ _ _ _ _ _.
5. Eva es muy g _ _ _ _.

Answers *See p. 67B.*

Teaching Suggestions
Presenting the verb tener / Los números de 11 a 100

• Point out that **tener** has special spellings. Have students look carefully to notice any pattern.
• Point out that the numbers from 16–29 have written accents if they end in the letter -s: **dieciséis, veintidós, veintitrés,** and **veintiséis.** If you wish, you may also mention the older, optional spelling of some numbers: **diez y seis, veinte y dos.**

GRAMÁTICA

Saying What You Have: The Verb tener

When you want to talk about what you have, use the verb **tener.**

yo	tengo	nosotros(as)	tenemos
tú	tienes	vosotros(as)	tenéis
usted, él, ella	tiene	ustedes, ellos(as)	tienen

Francisco says:
—¡Sólo **tengo** diez días más!
I have only ten more days!

Tener is also used to talk about how old a person is.

—¿**Cuántos años** tiene Verónica?
How old is Verónica?

—**Tiene** quince **años.**
She is fifteen years old.

ACTIVIDAD 6 Gramática

♻️ ¡Unas familias interesantes!

Hablar Explica cómo son los miembros de las familias de estas personas. *(Hint: Explain what the family members of these people are like.)*

modelo

ella: *hermana / inteligente*   ***Ella** tiene una **hermana inteligente.***

1. Paco: prima / cómico(a)
2. Alma: hermana / trabajador(a)
3. Verónica: tía / bonito(a)
4. los señores García: hijo / activo(a)
5. Verónica y Andrés: primos / aburrido(a)
6. nosotros: padres / ¿?
7. yo: tío / ¿?
8. mi familia y yo: abuelos / ¿?
9. tú: hermano(a) / ¿?
10. yo: familia / ¿?

■ **MÁS PRÁCTICA** *cuaderno* p. 29
■ **PARA HISPANOHABLANTES** *cuaderno* p. 27

76 setenta y seis
Unidad 1

Classroom Community

Game Advance organizer: Have students prepare their personal "biographies" on index cards. Use this information when giving clues. Have all students stand up. Secretly select one student and give clues, from general to specific, to reveal the student's identity. For example: **Esta persona tiene trece años.** All students who do not fit the category must sit down. Continue with clues until one student is left standing.

Portfolio Write a description of each member of your immediate family or of an imaginary family: name, relationship, personality characteristics, and age.

Rubric: Writing

Criteria	Scale
Accuracy	1 2 3 4 5
Vocabulary use	1 2 3 4 5
Creativity, appearance	1 2 3 4 5

A = 14–15 pts.
B = 13 pts.
C = 11–12 pts.
D = 9–10 pts.
F = < 9 pts.

ACTIVIDAD 7

¿Qué edad?

Escribir Explica cuántos años tiene cada persona.
(Hint: Explain how old each person is.)

modelo

la abuela: 70   **La abuela** tiene **setenta** años.

I. Andrés: 7   **4.** yo: ¿?

2. Verónica: 15   **5.** mis padres: ¿?

3. Javier: 39   **6.** mi amigo(a): ¿?

Vocabulario

Los números de 11 a 100

11	once	25	veinticinco
12	doce	26	veintiséis
13	trece	27	veintisiete
14	catorce	28	veintiocho
15	quince	29	veintinueve
16	dieciséis	30	treinta
17	diecisiete	31	treinta y uno
18	dieciocho	40	cuarenta
19	diecinueve	50	cincuenta
20	veinte	60	sesenta
21	veintiuno	70	setenta
22	veintidós	80	ochenta
23	veintitrés	90	noventa
24	veinticuatro	100	cien

For 21, 31, and so on, use **veintiún, treinta y un,** and so on before a masculine noun and **veintiuna, treinta y una,** and so on before a feminine noun.

Tengo **veintiún** años. Tienes **treinta y una** camisetas.

¿Cuántos años tienes?

ACTIVIDAD 8

La familia de Antonio

Escuchar Lee las preguntas. Luego, escucha lo que dice Antonio de su familia. Escoge la respuesta correcta. *(Hint: Listen to what Antonio says about his family. Then answer the questions.)*

I. ¿Cómo se llama el hermano menor de Antonio?
     a. Alberto   **b.** Andrés

2. ¿Cuántos años tiene Andrés?
     a. 8   **b.** 17

3. ¿Quién es Luisa?
     a. su madre   **b.** su hermana

4. ¿Quiénes son Rosa y Alberto?
     a. sus abuelos   **b.** sus padres

5. ¿Cómo son Marta y Rafael?
     a. viejos y divertidos   **b.** jóvenes y divertidos

ACTIVIDAD 9

¿Cuántos años?

Hablar Pregúntale a otro(a) estudiante cuántos años tiene cada persona. *(Hint: Ask another student how old each person is.)*

modelo

tu madre

Estudiante A: ¿Cuántos años tiene **tu madre**?

Estudiante B: Tiene cuarenta años.

I. tu padre   **4.** tu tío(a)

2. tú   **5.** tu amigo

3. tu abuelo(a)   **6.** tu madre

■ **MÁS COMUNICACIÓN** p. R3

setenta y siete
Etapa 3   **77**

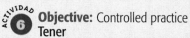

ACTIVIDAD 6

Objective: Controlled practice
Tener

♻ Adjectives: gender/number agreement

Answers

1. Paco tiene una prima cómica.
2. Alma tiene una hermana trabajadora.
3. Verónica tiene una tía bonita.
4. Los señores García tienen un hijo activo.
5. Verónica y Andrés tienen unos primos aburridos.
6. Nosotros tenemos unos padres [pacientes].
7. Yo tengo un tío [divertido].
8. Mi familia y yo tenemos unos abuelos [activos].
9. Tú tienes un(a) hermano(a)[serio(a)].
10. Yo tengo una familia [fenomenal].

ACTIVIDAD 7

Objective: Transitional practice
Tener/numbers

Answers

1. Andrés tiene siete años.
2. Verónica tiene quince años.
3. Javier tiene treinta y nueve años.
4. Yo tengo [catorce] años.
5. Mis padres tienen [cuarenta y dos] años.
6. Mi amigo(a) tiene [diecisiete] años.

Note: Suggesting that students use subject pronouns provides extra practice and helps to reinforce subject/verb agreement.
1. (Él) 2. (Ella) 3. (Él) 4. (Yo) 5. (Ellos) 6. (Él/Ella)

ACTIVIDAD 8

Objective: Transitional practice
Listening comprehension/vocabulary

Answers *(See script p. 67B.)*
1. b	4. a
2. a	5. b
3. b.	

ACTIVIDAD 9

Objective: Open-ended practice
Asking and telling ages

Answers will vary.

▌ Block Schedule

Variety Practice working with numbers by giving students a simple math worksheet containing addition, subtraction, multiplication, and division. Students can read the problems to a partner, do the computation, and write out the answers in Spanish. Have them peer edit their answers. (For additional activities, see **Block Scheduling Copymasters**)

Teaching All Students

Extra Help Have students count various items in the classroom and state the total of each.

Challenge Have volunteers choose a famous person and describe that person using **tener, tener... años,** and **ser** + adjectives. Students should prepare notes ahead of time. The other students guess the identity.

Multiple Intelligences

Musical/Rhythmic Ask students to develop a chant to help recall **los números,** counting by ten.

Logical/Mathematical Provide a list of famous names and birth dates. Students calculate how old that person is.

Teaching Resource Options

Print 📖

Más práctica Workbook PE, p. 30
Para hispanohablantes Workbook PE, p. 28
Block Scheduling Copymasters
Unit 1 Resource Book
  Más práctica Workbook TE, p. 159
  Para hispanohablantes Workbook TE, p. 165

Audiovisual 💻📽️

OHT 32 (Quick Start)

Technology 💻

Intrigas y aventuras CD-ROM, Disc 1

Quick Start Review

 Clothing

Use OHT 32 or write on the board:
Complete the sentences with an article of clothing.

1. No llevo mis j _ _ _ _ a una fiesta formal.
2. Tu blusa está muy bonita con esa f _ _ _ _ .
3. ¿Dónde está mi ch _ _ _ _ _ _ ?
4. No me gusta llevar calcetines con estos z _ _ _ _ _ _ .

Answers
1. jeans   3. chaqueta
2. falda   4. zapatos

Teaching Suggestions
Reinforcing Possession Using de

Point out an article of clothing on a student (**Es la camiseta de...**). Students complete the sentence (**de Ricardo**). Continue with several students. Then point to an article of clothing and have students give the entire sentence.

10 Objective: Controlled practice Possession with **de**

🔄 Clothing

Answers
1. Es el vestido de Verónica.
2. Es el sombrero de Javier.
3. Es la chaqueta de Juan.
4. Es el suéter de Anita.
5. Es la falda de Yolanda.
6. Es la camiseta de David.

GRAMÁTICA

Expressing Possession Using de

In English, you express possession by adding **'s** to the noun that refers to the possessor. In Spanish, you use the preposition **de** to refer to the possessor.

el hermano **de** papá
Dad's brother

los hijos **de** Javier
Javier's children

ACTIVIDAD 10 Gramática

🔄 **La ropa de...**

Hablar Cada persona escoge su ropa para una fiesta. Di de quién es cada cosa. *(Hint: Everyone is choosing clothing for a party. Say whose each item is.)*

modelo

Es **la camisa** de **Andrés.**

Andrés

1. Verónica

2. Javier

3. Juan

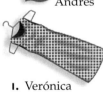
4. Anita

5. Yolanda

6. David

NOTA CULTURAL

The early Spanish settlers of Los Angeles developed land into ranches, or **haciendas**. The names of many **haciendas** have survived as street names, such as **Los Feliz, Verdugos,** and **Sepúlveda**.

Sepulveda

78 setenta y ocho
Unidad 1

Classroom Community

Game Collect one item from each student and line the items up on a table in front of the class. Give each one a number and a label of the word in Spanish. Working in groups of 4, students write in Spanish to whom each item belongs. The group with the most items correctly identified after 5 minutes is the winner. For example: **Es el cuaderno de Miguel.**

Learning Scenario Have students imagine they are organizing the school's Lost and Found. They think they recognize some of the imaginary items as belonging to their classmates. In groups, have them make a list of "unmistakable" items associated with 10 classmates. For example: **Es el sombrero de Antonio.**

ACTIVIDAD **11**

La familia de Rafael Ramos

Hablar/Escribir Explica la relación entre las personas. *(Hint: Explain the relationship between the people.)*

Teresa ---- **Carlos**

Javier ---- **Yolanda**   **Guillermo** ---- **Carolina**

Verónica   **Andrés**   **Rafael**   **Lucía**

modelo

Teresa–Rafael y Lucía   *Javier y Yolanda–Rafael*
Teresa es la abuela de **Rafael y Lucía.**   **Javier y Yolanda** son los tíos de **Rafael.**

1. Carolina–Andrés
2. Carlos–Yolanda y Guillermo
3. Lucía–Verónica
4. Rafael–Lucía
5. Teresa y Carlos–Rafael y Lucía

6. Rafael y Lucía–Guillermo y Carolina
7. Guillermo y Carolina–Rafael y Lucía
8. Rafael y Lucía–Andrés y Verónica

 ACTIVIDAD **12**

¿De quién es?

> **PARA CONVERSAR**
> **STRATEGY: SPEAKING**
> **Rehearse** Practicing with a partner is a rehearsal for real conversation, so make the most of it. Think of real situations where you can use what you are practicing, such as asking about what people in the class are wearing.

Hablar Trabaja con otro(a) estudiante para explicar de quién es la ropa. Cambien de papel. *(Hint: Work with another person to explain whose clothing it is. Change roles.)*

modelo

chaqueta: Francisco

Estudiante A: *¿De quién es la* **chaqueta?**

Estudiante B: *Es de* **Francisco.**

Nota

Use the expression **¿De quién es...?** to ask who owns something. To answer, use **Es de...**

1. falda: Verónica
2. vestido: Anita
3. suéter: Andrés
4. camiseta: Javier
5. blusa: la abuela
6. ¿?

Answers
1. Carolina es la tía de Andrés.
2. Carlos es el padre de Yolanda y Guillermo.
3. Lucía es la prima de Verónica.
4. Rafael es el hermano de Lucía.
5. Teresa y Carlos son los abuelos de Rafael y Lucía.
6. Rafael y Lucía son los hijos de Guillermo y Carolina.
7. Guillermo y Carolina son los padres de Rafael y Lucía.
8. Rafael y Lucía son los primos de Andrés y Verónica.

ACTIVIDAD **12** **Objective:** Open-ended practice Possession with **de** in conversation

Answers
1. A: ¿De quién es la falda?
   B: Es de Verónica.
2. A: ¿De quién es el vestido?
   B: Es de Anita.
3. A ¿De quién es el suéter?
   B: Es de Andrés.
4. A: ¿De quién es la camiseta?
   B: Es de Javier.
5. A: ¿De quién es la blusa?
   B: Es de la abuela.
6. A: ¿De quién es [la camisa]?
   B: Es de [Juan].

Note: For extra practice, have students repeat the noun in their answer.
(Ex: *La falda* es de Verónica.)

Block Schedule

Change of Pace In pairs, have students make a set of cards with all the characters from Unit 1. Have them work together to organize and reorganize the cards into various categories: friends of Francisco, people from San Antonio, relatives of Francisco, etc. See how many combinations they can make and describe in Spanish. (For additional activities, see **Block Scheduling Copymasters.**)

Teaching All Students

Extra Help Hold up a student's item and say it belongs to someone else (**Es el libro de Pablo.**). The class corrects you (**No es el libro de Pablo. Es el libro de Marcelo.**).

Native Speakers If there are street names in Spanish, have students name some in their home communities. What is the significance of the names? Elicit synonyms for **hacienda** (**rancho, finca, estancia**).

Multiple Intelligences

Verbal Describe a family member and have students give the relationship. For example: **Es el hermano de mi padre.** (**Es tu tío.**) **Es la madre de mi madre.** (**Es tu abuela.**) **Ellos son los hijos de mi tío.** (**Son tus primos.**) **Es la hija de mis padres.** (**Es tu hermana.**) Have students add a few.

Teaching Resource Options

Print

Más práctica Workbook PE, p. 31
Para hispanohablantes Workbook PE,
p. 29
Block Scheduling Copymasters
Unit 1 Resource Book
  Más práctica Workbook TE, p. 160
  Para hispanohablantes Workbook
  TE, p. 166

Audiovisual

OHT 33 (Quick Start)

Technology

Intrigas y aventuras CD-ROM, Disc 1

Quick Start Review

♻ Plurals

Use OHT 33 or write on the board:
Make the following words plural:

1. una blusa
2. un vestido
3. un zapato
4. una camiseta
5. una chaqueta
6. un suéter
7. un calcetín
8. una camisa
9. un sombrero
10. una bolsa

Answers *See p. 67B.*

Teaching Suggestions
Teaching Possessive Adjectives

• Point out that there are two ways to
say *my* in Spanish and have students
find them on the chart. Ask them
how many ways there are to say *your*
and to tell what they are.
• Ask students what other words they
know that agree with the noun
(definite articles, indefinite articles,
adjectives).
• Walk around the room and pick up
objects. Using possessive adjectives,
compare the objects: **Mi libro es
grande; tu libro es pequeño.**

GRAMÁTICA
Expressing Possession: Possessive Adjectives

▶ **Possessive adjectives** tell you who owns something or describe a relationship
between people or things. In Spanish, possessive adjectives agree in number with
the nouns they describe.

Singular Possessive Adjectives		Plural Possessive Adjectives	
mi *my*	**nuestro(a)** *our*	**mis** *my*	**nuestros(as)** *our*
tu *your (familiar)*	**vuestro(a)** *your (familiar)*	**tus** *your (familiar)*	**vuestros(as)** *your (familiar)*
su *your (formal)*	**su** *your (formal)*	**sus** *your (formal)*	**sus** *your (formal)*
su *his, her, its*	**su** *their*	**sus** *his, her, its*	**sus** *their*

Francisco would say: —Es **mi** tío.
*He is **my** uncle.*

—Son **mis** abuelos.
*They are **my** grandparents.*

▶ The adjectives **nuestro(a)** and **vuestro(a)** must also agree in gender with the
nouns they describe.

nuestr**o** abuel**o** *agrees*   nuestr**os** abuel**os** *agrees*
nuestr**a** abuel**a** *agrees*   nuestr**as** abuel**as** *agrees*

▶ If you need to emphasize, substitute the adjective with:

de + **pronoun** or the person's name

This also helps to clarify the meaning of **su** and **sus**.

becomes

Es **su** tío.   Es el tío **de él**.

de mí	**de nosotros(as)**
de ti	**de vosotros(as)**
de usted, él, ella	**de ustedes, ellos(as)**

Classroom Community

Paired Activity Have students copy the possessive
adjectives onto individual cards. One student picks a
card and says or writes a statement using that word.
The other student approves or disapproves the
sentence. Partners work together to fix flawed
sentences. If students are having difficulty identifying
and correcting errors, have them write examples on the
board for full-class work.

TPR Divide the class into groups. Each student has a
card labeled with one of the possessive adjectives.
Using the questions from **Actividades 13, 14,** and **15,**
have students stand up when "their" possessive
adjective is needed.

¿De quién es la ropa?

Hablar Ves mucha ropa. No sabes de quién es. Pregúntale a otro(a) estudiante si es de él o ella. Cambien de papel. *(Hint: You see some clothing. You don't know whose it is. Ask another student if it's his or hers. Change roles.)*

modelo

chaqueta (sí)

Estudiante A: *¿Es tu* **chaqueta***?*

Estudiante B: *Sí, es mi* **chaqueta***.*

I. suéter (sí)	**4.** pantalones (no)	**7.** camiseta (no)
2. camisas (sí)	**5.** zapatos (sí)	**8.** calcetines (sí)
3. blusa (no)	**6.** falda (no)	**9.** vestido (no)

¿Quiénes son?

Hablar Estás en la casa de tus amigos para una fiesta. Pregúntale a uno de ellos quién es cada persona. Cambien de papel. *(Hint: You're at your friends' house for a party. Ask one of them who everyone is. Change roles.)*

modelo

abuelo	abuelos
Estudiante A: *¿Quién es?*	**Estudiante B:** *¿Quiénes son?*
Estudiante B: *Es nuestro* **abuelo***.*	**Estudiante A:** *Son nuestros* **abuelos***.*

Nota

When you want to ask who a person is, use the expression **¿Quién es?** When you want to ask who several people are, use **¿Quiénes son?**

I. tía	**4.** padres	**7.** abuela
2. primo	**5.** tío	**8.** vecinos
3. hermanas	**6.** primas	**9.** vecina

■ **MÁS PRÁCTICA** *cuaderno* p. 31
■ **PARA HISPANOHABLANTES** *cuaderno* p. 29

¿De quién es la camisa?

Hablar En tu casa tienes ropa de muchas personas. Otro(a) estudiante te pregunta de quién es. *(Hint: You have many people's clothes in your house. Another student asks you whose they are.)*

modelo

camisa / tu hermano

Estudiante: *¿La camisa es de* **tu hermano***?*

Tú: *Sí, es su camisa.*

1. pantalones / David
2. vestido / tu tía
3. blusas / ellas
4. calcetines / tu padre
5. falda / tu abuela
6. chaquetas / tus abuelos
7. zapatos / Susana
8. camisetas / Rafael

Juego

Marco tiene un hermano. José tiene un año. El hermano de Marco se llama José. ¿Cuántos años tiene el hermano de Marco?

ochenta y uno **81**
Etapa 3

UNIDAD 1 Etapa 3
Vocabulary/Grammar

13 **Objective:** Controlled practice Possessive adjectives in conversation
♻ Clothing

Answers
1. A: ¿Es tu suéter? / B: Sí, es mi suéter.
2. A: ¿Son tus camisas? / B: Sí, son mis camisas.
3. A: ¿Es tu blusa? / B: No, no es mi blusa.
4. A: ¿Son tus pantalones? / B: No, no son mis pantalones.
5. A: ¿Son tus zapatos? / B: Sí, son mis zapatos.
6. A: ¿Es tu falda? / B: No, no es mi falda.
7. A: ¿Es tu camiseta? / B: No, no es mi camiseta.
8. A: ¿Son tus calcetines? / B: Sí, son mis calcetines.
9. A: ¿Es tu vestido? / B: No, no es mi vestido.

14 **Objective:** Controlled practice Possessive adjectives in conversation
♻ Ser

Answers
1. A: ¿Quién es? / B: Es nuestra tía.
2. A: ¿Quién es? / B: Es nuestro primo.
3. A: ¿Quiénes son? / B: Son nuestras hermanas.
4. A: ¿Quiénes son? / B: Son nuestros padres.
5. A: ¿Quién es? / B: Es nuestro tío.
6. A: ¿Quiénes son? / B: Son nuestras primas.
7. A: ¿Quién es? / B: Es nuestra abuela.
8. A: ¿Quiénes son? / B: Son nuestros vecinos.
9. A: ¿Quién es? / B: Es nuestra vecina.

15 **Objective:** Transitional practice Possessive adjectives in conversation
♻ Possession with **de**

Answers
1. A: ¿Los pantalones son de David?
B: Sí, son sus pantalones.
2. A: ¿El vestido es de tu tía?
B: Sí, es su vestido.
3. A: ¿Las blusas son de ellas?
B: Sí, son sus blusas.
4. A: ¿Los calcetines son de tu padre?
B: Sí, son sus calcetines.
5. A: ¿La falda es de tu abuela?
B: Sí, es su falda.
6. A: ¿Las chaquetas son de tus abuelos?
B: Sí, son sus chaquetas.
7. A: ¿Los zapatos son de Susana?
B: Sí, son sus zapatos.
8. A: ¿Las camisetas son de Rafael?
B: Sí, son sus camisetas.

Juego
Answer: El hermano de Marco tiene un año.

■ **Block Schedule**

Process Time Prepare ahead: Newspapers, magazines, brochures, books in Spanish. Give students 5 minutes to skim their chosen item and write a one-sentence "review" for other students.

Teaching All Students

Extra Help Give students a list of clothing. Have them provide sentences saying to whom each item might belong. For example: **Es mi camisa. Es su chaqueta. Son tus zapatos.** Ask students to explain in their own words what **"su"** and **"tus"** mean.

Multiple Intelligences

Interpersonal In pairs, have students each create a list of at least 5 family members and a possession for each. They exchange lists and create sentences using possessive adjectives: la abuela / un suéter → **Es tu abuela. Es su suéter.**

Teaching Resource Options

Print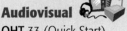

Más práctica Workbook PE, p. 32
Para hispanohablantes Workbook PE, p. 30
Block Scheduling Copymasters
Unit 1 Resource Book
  Más práctica Workbook TE, p. 161
  Para hispanohablantes Workbook TE, p. 167
  Information Gap Activities, pp. 171–172
  Audioscript, pp. 182–183
  Audioscript *Para hispanohablantes*, pp. 182–183

Audiovisual

OHT 33 (Quick Start)
Audio Program Cassette 3B / CD 3
Audio *Para hispanohablantes*
  Cassette 3A / CD 3

Technology

Intrigas y aventuras CD-ROM, Disc 1

Quick Start Review

♻ Numbers

Use OHT 33 or write on the board:
Write out the answers in words:

1. 10 + 10 = ?   6. 16 + 1 = ?
2. 95 − 80 = ?   7. 80 − 15 = ?
3. 14 x 2 = ?   8. 12 x 3 = ?
4. 100 ÷ 20 = ?   9. 100 ÷ 2 = ?
5. ? − 52 = 18   10. ? − 34 = 15

Answers *See p. 67B.*

Teaching Suggestions
Giving Dates: Day and Month

• Have students read the **Gramática** box and look at the vocabulary.
• Use Audio Cassette 3A / CD3 to model the months.
• Ask simple yes/no questions until you are sure students understand the concept and structure. For example: pointing to calendar: ¿Es el (seis de octubre) hoy? (Sí.) ¿Mañana, es el (siete de octubre)? (Sí.) etc.
• Use the TPR activity for additional practice.

16 **Objective:** Transitional practice
Saying how many there is/are

Answers will vary.

82 Vocabulary/Grammar • UNIDAD 1 Etapa 3

ACTIVIDAD **16**

En la clase

Hablar/Escribir Explica cuántas personas de cada tipo hay en la clase. *(Hint: Explain how many of each type of person there are in the class.)*

Nota

The word **hay** is used to mean *there is* or *there are*.

Hay muchos murales en la ciudad de Los Ángeles.
There are many murals in the city of Los Angeles.

Hay un concurso muy interesante.
There is a very interesting contest.

To say that there are none, use
No hay…

1. chicas castañas
2. chicos castaños
3. chicos rubios
4. chicas rubias
5. chicos morenos
6. chicas morenas
7. chicos pelirrojos
8. chicas pelirrojas
9. chicos
10. maestros

 NOTA CULTURAL

In Spanish-speaking countries, the date is written with the number of the day first, then the number of the month.

el dos de mayo = 2/5

82 ochenta y dos
Unidad 1

GRAMÁTICA

Giving Dates: Day and Month

When you want to give the date, use the following phrase:

Es el + **number** + **de** + month.

Alma says:
—Hoy **es el once de** noviembre.
*Today **is the eleventh of** November.*

Notice that the names of months are not capitalized in Spanish.

In Spanish, the only date that does not follow this pattern is the first of the month.

Es el primero de noviembre.
*It is November **first**.*

Vocabulario

Los meses del año

enero	febrero	marzo	abril
mayo	junio	julio	agosto
septiembre	octubre	noviembre	diciembre

¿Cuál es tu mes favorito?

Classroom Community

Group Activity Have students create a wall-sized calendar for the upcoming month. They should decorate the days with special holidays, school sporting or academic events, and birthdays.

TPR Write the months of the year across the board. As you say a month, students born in that month go up and stand under it. When all months have been called out, each student says the date of his/her birthday. Students in each month then line up according to dates.

ACTIVIDAD 17 Gramática

La familia de Francisco

Escribir Explica cuándo son los cumpleaños. *(Hint: Explain when their birthdays are.)*

modelo

Francisco: 15/3

El cumpleaños de **Francisco** es el **quince de marzo**.

1. Alma: 4/1
2. Verónica: 22/10
3. Andrés: 5/5
4. la abuela: 23/7
5. tú: ¿?
6. tu madre: ¿?
7. tu padre: ¿?
8. tu amigo(a): ¿?

■ **MÁS PRÁCTICA** cuaderno p. 32
■ **PARA HISPANOHABLANTES**
  cuaderno p. 30

ACTIVIDAD 18

¿Cuál es la fecha de tu cumpleaños?

Hablar Pregúntales a otros estudiantes la fecha de su cumpleaños. ¿Cuántos cumpleaños hay en cada mes? *(Hint: Ask other students their birthdays. How many are in each month?)*

Nombre	Su cumpleaños es
Ramón	el 13 de junio

ACTIVIDAD 19

¿Cuál es la respuesta?

Escuchar Escoge la respuesta correcta. *(Hint: Choose the correct answer.)*

1. a. Tiene cinco años.
   b. Tiene setenta años.
   c. Tiene veinte años.

2. a. Son viejas.
   b. Son grandes.
   c. Son jóvenes.

3. a. Soy policía.
   b. Soy estudiante.
   c. Soy maestro.

4. a. Llevo un suéter.
   b. Llevo una camiseta.
   c. Llevo una chaqueta.

ACTIVIDAD 20

Mi madre

Escribir Describe a un miembro de tu familia. *(Hint: Describe a family member.)*

modelo

Mi madre se llama Elena. Es alta y castaña. Tiene los ojos verdes. Le gusta cantar y leer. Es muy inteligente. Tiene cuarenta años. Su cumpleaños es el cuatro de mayo.

■ **MÁS COMUNICACIÓN** p. R3

Pronunciación

Trabalenguas

Pronunciación de la *m* y la *n* The letters m and n are pronounced in Spanish just as they are in English. Try the following tongue twisters.

Nueve nenes nadan.   **Mi mamá me mima.**

ochenta y tres
Etapa 3   **83**

Cross Cultural Connections

Point out that many calendars from Spain and Latin America begin the week with Monday, not Sunday.

Supplementary Vocabulary

la primavera	spring
el verano	summer
el otoño	autumn
el invierno	winter

ACTIVIDAD 17
Objective: Transitional practice
Day and month

Answers
1. El cumpleaños de Alma es el cuatro de enero.
2. El cumpleaños de Verónica es el veintidós de octubre.
3. El cumpleaños de Andrés es el cinco de mayo.
4. El cumpleaños de la abuela es el veintitrés de julio.
5. Tu cumpleaños es el...
6. El cumpleaños de tu madre es el...
7. El cumpleaños de tu padre es el...
8. El cumpleaños de tu amigo(a) es el...

ACTIVIDAD 18
Objective: Transitional practice
Day and date in conversation

Answers will vary.
Alternate: Have students ask you your birthday.

ACTIVIDAD 19
Objective: Transitional practice
Listening comprehension/vocabulary

Answers (See script p. 67B.)
1. b   3. b
2. c   4. b

ACTIVIDAD 20
Objective: Open-ended practice
Describing family, telling ages, talking about birthdays in writing

Dictation

After students have read the tongue twisters in the **Pronunciación,** have them close their books. Dictate the tongue twisters in segments while students write them.

■ Block Schedule

Retention Have students write a description of a friend or a famous person, modeled after **Actividad 20.** (For additional activities, see **Block Scheduling Copymasters**)

Teaching All Students

Extra Help Have students list 5 friends or family members with their birthdays, first as a number, then written out in Spanish.

Multiple Intelligences

Kinesthetic Have students make small placards with the months of the year on them. They should decorate them according to the season. Send 12 students, each with a different month in hand, to the front of the class. Have them quickly organize themselves from January to December. The cards can be used for spelling practice.

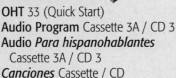
En voces
LECTURA

PARA LEER
STRATEGY: READING
Look for cognates These are words that
look alike and have similar meanings
in both English and Spanish, such as
europeo and **artificiales**. What other
cognates can you find in **"Las
celebraciones del año"**?

Las celebraciones del año

Hay muchas fechas importantes durante el año. Los
países hispanohablantes celebran estas fechas de varias
formas. Algunas[1] celebraciones son iguales que las de
Estados Unidos, pero también hay tradiciones diferentes.

octubre

12/10 El Día de la Raza En este día no
hay trabajo. Hay muchos desfiles[2]. El
día celebra el encuentro[3] del indígena[4]
con el europeo y el africano. Hoy esta
mezcla[5] de razas[6] y tradiciones forma
la cultura latinoamericana.

El Día de la Raza

noviembre

**1/11 El Día de Todos los Santos y 2/11
el Día de los Muertos[7]** En estos días
todos honran a las personas de su
familia. En México las familias
decoran las tumbas de sus
antepasados[8] con flores bonitas.

[1]some	[3]meeting	[5]mixture	[7]Dead
[2]parades	[4]native (Indian)	[6]races	[8]ancestors

84   ochenta y cuatro
     Unidad 1

La Nochevieja

Feliz Año Nuevo Les Desea LA FAMILIA CHAVEZ VEGA

diciembre y enero

31/12 La Nochevieja y 1/1 el Año Nuevo
Hay fuegos artificiales[9], desfiles o celebraciones en todos los países. En Ecuador los años viejos se representan con figuras grandes de personas famosas de ese año. A medianoche[10] los años viejos se queman[11]. En España es tradicional comer doce uvas[12] a la medianoche.

enero

6/1 El Día de los Reyes
Es el día tradicional para dar regalos[13] de Navidad en los países latinos.

TAMBIÉN SE DICE
To talk about U.S. holidays not mentioned in this reading, use these phrases:
Valentine's Day: **Día de los Enamorados, Día de San Valentín**
Mother's Day: **Día de la Madre**
Father's Day: **Día del Padre**
Memorial Day: **Día Conmemorativo**
July 4th: **Día de la Independencia**
Labor Day: **Día del Trabajador**
Halloween: **Noche de Brujas**
Thanksgiving: **Día de Acción de Gracias**
Christmas Eve: **Nochebuena**
Christmas: **Navidad**

¿Comprendiste?

1. ¿Cómo celebran los latinoamericanos el Día de la Raza?
2. ¿Cuáles son las fechas que los mexicanos honran a su familia?
3. Describe dos tradiciones del Año Nuevo.
4. ¿En qué fecha dan regalos de Navidad las personas de los países latinos? ¿Cómo se llama ese día?

¿Qué piensas?

¿Hay una celebración especial en tu casa para un día festivo? ¿Cómo es?

---

[9] fireworks [11] are burned [13] give gifts
[10] midnight [12] grapes

ochenta y cinco
Etapa 3 85

Culture Highlights

● **DÍAS FERIADOS MEXICANOS** There are many holidays celebrated throughout the year in Mexico. Two others are:

- May 5: **Día de la Batalla de Puebla**
- September 16: **Día de la Independencia**

These holidays are usually celebrated with parades and fiestas.

● **EL GRITO DE DOLORES** Considered the first battle for Mexican independence from Spain, **El Grito de Dolores** took place on September 16, 1810. It was a **grito** (uprising) led by the priest Miguel Hidalgo y Costilla that went on for several months. Independence Day in Mexico is celebrated on the anniversary of the **Grito's** beginning and festivities are particularly effusive in **El Zócalo** in Mexico City.

Cross Cultural Connections
Strategy Have students learn more about a holiday in a Spanish-speaking country of their choice and compare it to a similar holiday in the U.S.

¿Comprendiste?
Answers
1. No hay trabajo. Hay muchos desfiles.
2. El primero y el dos de noviembre.
3. (Two of the following) Hay fuegos artificiales; hay desfiles; los años se representan con figuras grandes y los años se queman; comer doce uvas.
4. Dan regalos de Navidad el 6 de enero. Se llama el Día de los Reyes.

Quick Wrap-up
Have students list the holidays that they celebrate in their family.

Block Schedule
Variety Have students prepare the **Lectura** as homework to allow extra time for class discussion of holidays and customs. Give students 5 min. to review the reading, then do the ¿Comprendiste? questions before discussion. (For additional activities, see **Block Scheduling Copymasters**)

Teaching All Students

Extra Help Some students may find it helpful to read each section twice before moving on to the rest of the reading.

Native Speakers Ask students if they celebrate the holidays described in the reading. Have them talk about other important holidays in their cultural community. What is the significance of these days? What are the traditional foods, customs, and dress?

Multiple Intelligences
Musical/Rhythmic Ask volunteers to bring in traditional Hispanic holiday music. Ask other students to bring in music they associate with their family celebrations or holidays. Have students compare and contrast the types of music for each celebration or holiday.

Teaching Resource Options

Print

Unit 1 Resource Book
  Audioscript, p. 185
  Audioscript *Para hispanohablantes*,
    p. 185

Audiovisual

Audio Program Cassette 3A / CD 3
Audio *Para hispanohablantes*
  Cassette 3A / CD 3
OHT 34 (Quick Start)

Quick Start Review

🔁 **Gustar**

Use OHT 34 or write on the board:
Write one complete question and an
answer for each item.

Modelo: Susana / escribir (no)
You write: ¿Le gusta escribir?
        No, no le gusta escribir.

1. tú / leer (sí)
2. María / patinar (no)
3. Jorge / bailar (sí)
4. Ana / trabajar (no)
5. tú / nadar (no)

Answers
1. ¿Te gusta leer?
   Sí, me gusta leer.
2. ¿Le gusta patinar?
   No, no le gusta patinar.
3. ¿Le gusta bailar?
   Sí, le gusta bailar.
4. ¿Le gusta trabajar?
   No, no le gusta trabajar.
5 ¿Te gusta nadar?
   No, no me gusta nadar.

Teaching Suggestions
Presenting Cultura y comparaciones

• Have students look at the pictures on
  pp. 86–87 and make observations.
  They should make note of the
  formality of dress, as well as the age
  range of the guests.
• Have students describe birthday
  traditions with their families. How are
  they similar or different from the one
  shown here?

En colores
CULTURA Y COMPARACIONES

PARA CONOCERNOS
STRATEGY: CONNECTING CULTURES
Compare rites of passage In your community
what are some events, formal or informal,
that mark a young person's transition
from childhood to adulthood? What
are they called and when do they
occur? How are they celebrated?
If you could design your own event,
how would it be celebrated? Use a
word web to record your thoughts.
Think of its components as you read
«La quinceañera».

what   when
      celebration
where   how

La palabra *quinceañera*
se refiere a[1] dos conceptos.
Una quinceañera es una
chica de quince años.
Una quinceañera también
es una fiesta en que se
celebra el cumpleaños de
una chica de quince años.

**La quinceañera lleva
un vestido especial.
Es tradicional llevar
un vestido rosado.**

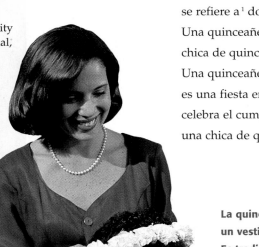

**Hay mucha preparación
para la quinceañera.
Hay muchas decoraciones.**

86 ochenta y seis
Unidad 1

Classroom Community

Group Activity Have students write a short
description of the ideal birthday party. They should
include where the party takes place, in what month,
how many people are invited, what people wear, and
the activities. Provide supplemental vocabulary if
necessary. Have students present their descriptions to
the class.

Portfolio Have students write a description of the
family in the photo on p. 87.

Rubric: Writing

Criteria	Scale	
Logical structure	1 2 3	A = 10–12 pts.
Vocabulary use, expansion	1 2 3	B = 7–9 pts.
Accuracy	1 2 3	C = 5–6 pts.
Creativity	1 2 3	D = 3–4 pts.
		F = < 3 pts.

La quinceañera

¡FELICIDADES!

La tradición más importante es que la familia acompaña a la quinceañera en su día especial.

La quinceañera es una tradición especial de la cultura latina. Representa el momento en que una chica llega a ser[2] una mujer. Las tradiciones son diferentes en cada región. Una tradición es tener una ceremonia religiosa. Algunas fiestas se celebran en la casa de la familia. Otras se celebran en un hotel o un restaurante. La familia de la quinceañera invita a todos sus primos, sus tíos, sus abuelos y sus buenos amigos.

[1] refers to
[2] becomes

¿Comprendiste?

1. ¿Qué es una quinceañera?
2. ¿Cuál es una tradición de la quinceañera?
3. ¿Dónde se celebran las fiestas?
4. ¿Qué lleva la quinceañera?

¿Qué piensas?

1. ¿Qué fiestas hay en tu comunidad?
2. ¿Hay otras fiestas similares para una chica en tu comunidad? ¿Para un chico?

ochenta y siete
Etapa 3 **87**

Reading Strategy

Using the reading strategy students have just learned (Look for cognates, p. 84), have them look for cognates in the **Cultura y comparaciones.**

Culture Highlights

● **LA ÚLTIMA MUÑECA** In Mexico, it has recently become a tradition that when a girl turns fifteen, her parents ask a friend or family member to be the godfather or godmother of a doll that is given to the girl. This last doll symbolizes that the girl has become a woman. Other friends may also give the girl a last doll. These dolls are usually rag dolls.

Supplementary Vocabulary

Descriptions of celebrations:

magnífico(a)	magnificent
desastroso(a)	disastrous
de sorpresa	surprise
triste	sad
emocionante	exciting

¿Comprendiste?

Answers

1. Es una chica de quince años o una fiesta en que se celebra el cumpleaños de una chica de quince años.
2. Una tradición es tener una ceremonia religiosa y una fiesta.
3. Las fiestas se celebran en la casa de la familia, en un hotel o en un restaurante.
4. La quinceañera lleva un vestido especial. Es tradicional llevar un vestido rosado.

▌ Block Schedule

FunBreak In groups, have students propose and design the ideal fun/meaningful birthday celebration and present their proposals to other groups. Have the class vote on the best proposal or combine the best features of several into one celebration. Have a contest to name the celebration. If time permits, prepare and celebrate the "class birthday" in Spanish.

Teaching All Students

Extra Help Have students write a 2–4 sentence summary of the reading in Spanish.

Native Speakers Ask students to talk about the significance of the **quinceañera** and describe any they have attended.

Multiple Intelligences

Visual Have students design an invitation for a **quinceañera** for a friend or relative. Have volunteers present their invitations and display them on the bulletin board.

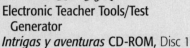
🔔 Quick Start Review

♻ **Tener**

Use OHT 34 or write on the board: Write complete sentences using the correct form of the verb **tener.**

 1. nosotros / 16 años
 2. yo / una hermana bonita
 3. Francisco / 15 años
 4. Raúl y Rosa / un perro
 5. tú / dos primos activos

Answers *See p. 67B.*

✔ Teaching Suggestions
What Have Students Learned?

Have students look at the "Now you can…" notes listed on the left side of pages 88–89. Point out that if they need to review material before doing the activities or taking the test, they should consult the "To review" notes.

ETAPA

3

Now you can...
• describe family.

To review
• vocabulary for family, see p. 70.

Now you can...
• tell ages.

To review
• the verb **tener,** see p. 76.
• vocabulary for numbers, see p. 77.

En uso

REPASO Y MÁS COMUNICACIÓN

ACTIVIDAD **1** Una familia feliz

Mónica, una amiga de Verónica, describe a su familia. Completa el párrafo. *(Hint: Complete Monica's description of her family.)*

modelo

Tengo tres __primos__ . Lucas es mi primo __mayor__ .

Rafael **Esperanza**

Mi familia es muy interesante. Mis __1__ son Gregorio y Berta. Tengo una __2__ que se llama Rosita. Ella es mi hermana __3__. Mi padre tiene un hermano. Es mi __4__ Carlos. Es muy cómico. Sus tres __5__ son Paquita, Lucas y Pepe. Ellos son mis __6__. La __7__ de ellos es mi tía Amalia. Mis primos y yo tenemos unos __8__ muy simpáticos: Rafael y Esperanza Santana.

Gregorio **Berta** **Carlos** **Amalia**

Mónica **Rosita** **Paquita** **Lucas** **Pepe**

ACTIVIDAD **2** ¿Cuántos años tienen?

Di la edad de cada persona que Verónica conoce. *(Hint: Tell the ages of the people Veronica knows.)*

modelo

Yolanda: 44 **Yolanda** tiene **cuarenta y cuatro años.**

 1. Juan y Anita: 42
 2. el señor Uribe: 100
 3. su prima: 28
 4. yo: 15

 5. los amigos de los García: 70
 6. tú: 13
 7. la señora Quiroga: 91
 8. su tío: 67

 9. nosotros: 38
 10. usted: 83
 11. Rafael: 17
 12. Carlota: 21

88 ochenta y ocho
Unidad 1

Classroom Community

Paired Activity Have students choose 2 items from each activity. One student asks a question, the other answers. Problem areas should be reviewed as needed.

Game Divide the class into groups of 4–5, giving each group a 2–3 sentence description in an envelope. For example: **Víctor es de España. Es muy guapo y también muy cómico. Tiene 17 años y su hermana** **tiene 15 años.** After the first student reads the message and whispers it to a neighbor, students begin **Teléfono,** trying to pass on the message correctly. The group's last person says the message aloud; the group closest to its original message wins.

Left column (Now you can...)

Now you can...

• talk about birthdays.

To review

• possession using **de**, see p. 78.

• dates and months, see p. 82.

Now you can...

• give dates.

To review

• dates and months, see p. 82.

Now you can...

• express possession.

To review

• the verb **tener**, see p. 76.

• possessive adjectives, see p. 80.

Main content

ACTIVIDAD 3 ¿Cuándo cumplen años?

¿Cuál es la fecha de cumpleaños de cada persona? *(Hint: What is each person's birthday?)*

modelo

Antonio: 19/7

El cumpleaños de **Antonio** es **el diecinueve de julio.**

1. Rafael: 23/12
2. Francisco: 15/3
3. Rosalinda: 6/2
4. la señora García: 1/10
5. David: 30/6
6. Yolanda: 25/11

Un pastel para la quinceañera

ACTIVIDAD 4 Las fiestas

¿Cuáles son las fechas de estos días festivos? *(Hint: What are the dates of these holidays?)*

modelo

17/3

el diecisiete de marzo

1. 25/12
2. 4/7
3. 1/1
4. 11/11
5. 14/6
6. 12/10
7. 5/5
8. 6/1
9. 19/1
10. 14/2
11. 17/3
12. 31/10

ACTIVIDAD 5 Amigos internacionales

Estas personas tienen amigos y familia de otros países. ¿Cómo son? *(Hint: Describe people's international friends and family members.)*

modelo

Inés: amiga de México (bonito)

Inés tiene **una amiga de México. Su amiga es bonita.**

1. Víctor: vecinos de Cuba (viejo)
2. yo: doctor de Guatemala (joven)
3. ustedes: amigos de Argentina (simpático)
4. nosotras: maestra de la República Dominicana (cómico)
5. tú: tíos de Chile (trabajador)
6. Raquel y Mario: prima de Puerto Rico (moreno)
7. Lisa y yo: amigo de España (guapo)

ochenta y nueve
Etapa 3
89

Right column (Answers)

ACTIVIDAD 1 Answers

1. padres 2. hermana 3. menor 4. tío
5. hijos 6. primos 7. madre 8. abuelos

ACTIVIDAD 2 Answers

1. Juan y Anita tienen cuarenta y dos años.
2. El señor Uribe tiene cien años.
3. Su prima tiene veintiocho años.
4. Yo tengo quince años.
5. Los amigos de los García tienen setenta años.
6. Tú tienes trece años.
7. La señora Quiroga tiene noventa y un años.
8. Su tío tiene sesenta y siete años.
9. Nosotros tenemos treinta y ocho años.
10. Usted tiene ochenta y tres años.
11. Rafael tiene diecisiete años.
12. Carlota tiene veintiún años.

ACTIVIDAD 3 Answers

1. El cumpleaños de Rafael es el veintitrés de diciembre. 2. El cumpleaños de Francisco es el quince de marzo. 3. El cumpleaños de Rosalinda es el seis de febrero. 4. El cumpleaños de la señora García es el primero de octubre. 5. El cumpleaños de David es el treinta de junio. 6. El cumpleaños de Yolanda es el veinticinco de noviembre.

ACTIVIDAD 4 Answers

1. el veinticinco de diciembre 2. el cuatro de julio 3. el primero de enero 4. el once de noviembre 5. el catorce de junio 6. el doce de octubre 7. el cinco de mayo 8. el seis de enero 9. el diecinueve de enero 10. el catorce de febrero 11. el diecisiete de marzo 12. el treinta y uno de octubre

ACTIVIDAD 5 Answers

1. Víctor tiene unos vecinos de Cuba. Sus vecinos son viejos.
2. Yo tengo un doctor de Guatemala. Mi doctor es joven.
3. Ustedes tienen unos amigos de Argentina. Sus amigos son simpáticos.
4. Nosotras tenemos una maestra de la República Dominicana. Nuestra maestra es cómica.
5. Tú tienes unos tíos de Chile. Tus tíos son trabajadores.
6. Raquel y Mario tienen una prima de Puerto Rico. Su prima es morena.
7. Lisa y yo tenemos un amigo de España. Nuestro amigo es guapo.

Block Schedule

Retention Have students do **Actividades 1, 2, 3, 4** as homework to allow more class time for questions and review before the test.

Teaching All Students

Extra Help Some students may need extra review of numbers. Use flashcards to help students work in pairs, or have students make a calendar with months and dates written out in Spanish for review.

Native Speakers Expand **Actividad 4** by having students add a year to each date, then write out the complete date, adding the name of the holiday indicated.

Multiple Intelligences

Logical/Mathematical Have students survey class birthdates, making a chart in Spanish. Students should research and report on the statistical probability of 2 or more people having the same birthdate.

Musical/Rhythmic Have students create a birthday song in Spanish to sing for each month's birthday celebrants.

Teaching Resource Options

Print

Unit 1 Resource Book
 Cooperative Quizzes, pp. 186–187
 Etapa Exam, Forms A and B,
  pp. 188–197
 Para hispanohablantes Etapa Exam,
  pp. 198–202
 Portfolio Assessment, pp. 203–204
 Unit 1 Comprehensive Test,
  pp. 205–212
 Para hispanohablantes Unit 1
  Comprehensive Test, pp. 213–220
 Multiple Choice Test Questions,
  pp. 232–241

Audiovisual

OHT 34 (Quick Start)
Audio Program Testing Cassette T1 /
 CD T1

Technology

Electronic Teacher Tools/Test
 Generator
www.mcdougallittell.com

Rubric: Speaking

Criteria	Scale	
Sentence structure	1 2 3	A = 11–12 pts.
Vocabulary use	1 2 3	B = 9–10 pts.
Originality	1 2 3	C = 7–8 pts.
Fluency	1 2 3	D = 4–6 pts.
		F = < 4 pts.

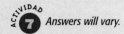
Answers will vary.

 Alternate: Students can draw a "model" family.

 En tu propia voz

Rubric: Writing

Criteria	Scale	
Vocabulary use	1 2 3 4 5	A = 14–15 pts.
Accuracy	1 2 3 4 5	B = 12–13 pts.
Creativity, appearance	1 2 3 4 5	C = 10–11 pts.
		D = 8–9 pts.
		F = < 8 pts.

 ¡Tenemos unas preguntas!

PARA CONVERSAR

STRATEGY: SPEAKING

Practice speaking smoothly Speaking smoothly without starts and stops helps others understand you. So first think about what you want to say, then practice saying it smoothly and naturally.

Trabajando en grupos, escriban preguntas para su maestro(a). Incluyan preguntas sobre su familia y su cumpleaños. *(Hint: Work together to write questions for your teacher. Include questions about his or her family and birthday.)*

modelo

¿Quién es su madre?

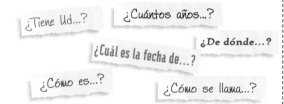
¿Tiene Ud...? ¿Cuántos años...?
¿Cuál es la fecha de...? ¿De dónde...?
¿Cómo es...? ¿Cómo se llama...?

 **Su familia**

Dibuja tu árbol genealógico. Incluye nombres y edades. Usando el árbol genealógico de otro(a) estudiante, descríbele la familia a otro grupo de la clase. *(Hint: Draw your family tree. Include names and ages. Using another student's family tree, describe his or her family to a group from the class.)*

modelo

La familia de Julio es pequeña. Él tiene un hermano mayor. No tiene hermanas. Su padre se llama Víctor y su madre se llama Lisa…

 En tu propia voz

ESCRITURA Usando tu árbol genealógico de la Actividad 7, escribe una descripción de tu familia. *(Hint: Using your family tree from Activity 7, write a description of your family.)*

TÚ EN LA COMUNIDAD

Theresa is a student in Massachusetts. Spanish comes in handy when she and a friend help two fifth-grade Guatemalan girls learn English. At home, she practices speaking Spanish with her brother, who also studies it in school. She also writes letters in Spanish to a little girl in Guatemala, and she is able to read the letters the girl writes back. Do you correspond with anyone in Spanish?

Classroom Community

Cooperative Learning Divide the class into groups. Assign each group one of the **Repaso de vocabulario** sections to illustrate or create flashcards. The work of all groups should be combined to help the class review.

Portfolio Use the family description prepared in **En tu propia voz** as the basis of a larger project including "interviews" (real or imaginary) with selected family members in Spanish. Remind students to use the vocabulary they have learned to ask questions.

Rubric: Writing

Criteria	Scale	
Organization	1 2 3	A = 14–15 pts.
Vocabulary use	1 2 3	B = 12–13 pts.
Sentence structure	1 2 3	C = 10–11 pts.
Accuracy	1 2 3	D = 8–9 pts.
Creativity	1 2 3	F = < 8 pts.

En resumen
REPASO DE VOCABULARIO

DESCRIBING FAMILY

Family Members

la abuela	grandmother
el abuelo	grandfather
los abuelos	grandparents
la hermana	sister
el hermano	brother
los hermanos	brother(s) and sister(s)
la hija	daughter
el hijo	son
los hijos	son(s) and daughter(s), children
la madre	mother
el padre	father
los padres	parents
el (la) primo(a)	cousin
la tía	aunt
el tío	uncle
los tíos	uncle(s) and aunt(s)

Descriptions

joven	young
mayor	older
menor	younger
viejo(a)	old

EXPRESSING POSSESSION

¿De quién es...?	Whose is...?
el (la)... de...	(someone)'s...
Es de...	It's...
mi	my
tu	your (familiar)
su	your (formal), his, her, its, their
nuestro(a)	our
vuestro(a)	your (plural familiar)

ASKING AND TELLING AGES

Asking About Age

la edad	age
¿Cuántos años tiene...?	How old is...?
Tiene... años.	He/She is...years old.

Numbers from 11 to 100

once	eleven
doce	twelve
trece	thirteen
catorce	fourteen
quince	fifteen
dieciséis	sixteen
diecisiete	seventeen
dieciocho	eighteen
diecinueve	nineteen
veinte	twenty
treinta	thirty
cuarenta	forty
cincuenta	fifty
sesenta	sixty
setenta	seventy
ochenta	eighty
noventa	ninety
cien	one hundred

GIVING DATES

Asking the Date

el año	year
la fecha	date
¿Cuál es la fecha?	What is the date?
Es el... de...	It's the...of...

Months

el mes	month
enero	January
febrero	February
marzo	March
abril	April
mayo	May
junio	June
julio	July
agosto	August
septiembre	September
octubre	October
noviembre	November
diciembre	December

TALKING ABOUT BIRTHDAYS

el cumpleaños	birthday
felicidades	congratulations
feliz	happy

OTHER WORDS AND PHRASES

ahora	now
la ciudad	city
con	with
dentro	inside
fuera	outside
hay	there is, there are
más	more
muy	very
¡Qué chévere!	How awesome!
¿Quién es?	Who is it?
¿Quiénes son?	Who are they?
sólo	only
tener	to have
todo(a)	all

Juego

El abuelo tiene 24 años más que su hijo Carlos. Carlos tiene 35 años más que su hijo Antonio. Los tres combinados tienen 100 años. ¿Cuántos años tiene...

1. el abuelo?
2. Carlos?
3. Antonio?

noventa y uno
Etapa 3   **91**

Teaching Resource Options

Print
Block Scheduling Copymasters

Audiovisual
OHT GO1–GO5, 34 (Quick Start)

Technology
Intrigas y aventuras CD-ROM, Disc 1
www.mcdougallittell.com

Quick Start Review

♻ Descriptions

Use OHT 34 or write on the board:
Complete the following:

1. physical description:
   Soy _____ , _____ , _____ .
2. personality description:
   Soy _____ , _____ , _____ .
3. likes and dislikes:
   Me gusta _____ y _____ pero
   no me gusta _____ .

Answers will vary.

Teaching Strategy
Prewriting

- Have students generate a list of words in Spanish that describe themselves.
- Tell students to categorize their words by adjectives, nouns, and verbs.
- Ask students to imagine how another person would describe them. Have them add any new words to the list.
- Point out the **PASS** list at the beginning of the page: **P**urpose, **A**udience, **S**ubject, **S**tructure. This will be their PASS key to a well-structured writing assignment in every unit.

Post-writing

- Have students begin to develop sound proofreading skills. One technique is to read one's own work aloud in order to hear as well as see errors. Another is to to keep the reader in mind when proofreading.

UNIDAD 1

¡Estudia aquí!

𝓘nstituto de español

En tu propia voz
ESCRITURA

¡Estudia en otro país!

You have the opportunity to study in a Spanish-speaking country and live with a family there. The program requires you to write a description of yourself so that you can be placed in a home. Your description will be the family's introduction to their guest, you!

Purpose: Tell others about yourself
Audience: Study-abroad program and Spanish-speaking family
Subject: You
Structure: Descriptive paragraph

PARA ESCRIBIR • STRATEGY: WRITING

Use different kinds of descriptive words Help your readers get to know you and understand what kind of person you are by giving a variety of descriptions. Include biographical data, physical traits, personal characteristics, and interests.

Modelo del estudiante

> The writer begins by offering basic biographical data about herself.

> The author tells what she looks like. This strengthens the portrait she is creating.

> The writer uses descriptive adjectives with **ser** to tell what kind of person she is.

> The author talks about her interests that are relevant to the program. This completes her introduction.

Me llamo Kristin Garza. Soy de Waco, Texas. Tengo 15 años. Soy castaña. Tengo el pelo largo y los ojos verdes. Soy alta y muy fuerte. Soy inteligente y atlética. No soy perezosa. Me gusta correr con mi perro y bailar con mis amigos. Vivo en una casa con mi familia. Tengo dos hermanos y una hermana. Mi padre es policía y mi madre es maestra. Mis abuelos viven en Waco también. Ellos son de México. Yo soy buena estudiante. Me gusta estudiar español y la historia de Latinoamérica.

92 noventa y dos
Unidad 1

Classroom Community

Paired Activity Divide the class into pairs—interviewers and interviewees. Interviewers will prepare a list of questions about personality, family, likes, and dislikes. Interviewees will prepare a list of facts about these categories. They will refer to the list when answering the interviewers' questions. Stress the importance of *listening* in this activity.

Portfolio Have students save this letter for their portfolios. Subsequent writing projects will show their progress in Spanish.

Group Activity Ask students to list what information they think a host family would like to know about a student visitor. Then have them check the **Modelo del estudiante** to see how closely their suggestions match.

Estrategias para escribir

Antes de escribir...

Prepare to write your descriptive paragraph by brainstorming ideas in these categories: biographical data, physical traits, personal characteristics, and interests. Do all of your brainstorming in Spanish. Use a concept web to organize your ideas. Then select the most interesting and descriptive words about yourself from your web. Decide what order to arrange them in your paragraph, and start writing.

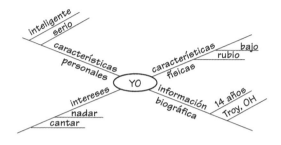

Revisiones

When you finish your first draft, exchange paragraphs with a friend. Then ask:

- *Does the paragraph include name, age and hometown?*
- *Are there enough descriptive adjectives?*
- *Is there a variety of information—family, activities, school, etc.?*

La versión final

Look at your revised paragraph and ask yourself these questions:

- *Are adjectives used correctly?*

Try this: Underline every adjective. Check to make sure that each one agrees in number and gender with its noun.

- *Did I use the right forms of **ser** and **tener**?*

Try this: Circle each form of **ser** and **tener** and their subjects (when given). Check to make sure that they match.

 Share your writing on www.mcdougallittell.com

> Me llamo Jason Potter. Yo tiene *tengo*
> catorce años. Vivo en Troy, Ohio,
> con mis padres. No tengo
> hermanos. Yo soy baja, inteligente
> y serio. Tengo los ojos azules.
> Soy rubia...

Supplementary Vocabulary

artístico(a)	artistic
gregario(a)	gregarious, sociable
reservado(a)	reserved, quiet
dedicado(a)	dedicated
intelectual	intellectual

Rubric: Writing

Let students know ahead of time which elements of their writing you will be evaluating. A global evaluation is more helpful to students than a correction of every mistake made. Consider the following in scoring compositions:

	Sentences
1	Most not logical
2	In logical order
3	Flow purposefully
	Details
1	Few details
2	Sufficient basic details
3	Clear and vivid detail
	Organization
1	Not well organized
2	Some organization
3	Strong organization
	Accuracy
1	Errors prevent comprehension
2	Some spelling and agreement errors throughout
3	Very few errors

Criteria	Scale	
Logical sentence order	1 2 3	A = 10–12 pts.
Clear and vivid detail	1 2 3	B = 7–9 pts.
Organization	1 2 3	C = 4–6 pts.
Accuracy	1 2 3	D = 3 pts.
		F = < 3 pts.

Teaching All Students

Extra Help Review structures with students before writing:
- Use of **ser** to describe physical and personality traits, to talk about professions, and to give place of origin.
- Use of **gustar** + infinitive to say what you like to do.
- Use of **tener** to tell age.
- Use of adjectives that agree in gender and number with the subject.

Native Speakers Have students compose the letter to the host family in its entirety. Included should be a greeting, a personal description, a description of their cultural background, and the reason for wanting to be an exchange student.

Block Schedule

Variety Have students compose a list of questions they would ask the prospective host family. (For additional activities, see **Block Scheduling Copymasters**)

Unit Theme

Going to school in a city (Mexico City, Mexico), discussing classes, and talking about after-school plans.

Communication
- Describing classes, classroom objects, and schedules
- Saying how often you do something
- Asking and telling time
- Requesting snack and lunch food
- Discussing after-school plans
- Talking about places/people you know

Cultures
- Learning about school in Mexico City
- Learning about the history of Mexico City
- Learning about regional vocabulary
- Learning about parks and their importance to life in Mexico

Connections
- Connecting to Mathematics: Using pie charts to summarize survey results in Spanish
- Connecting to Health: Researching the nutritional value of Mexican foods

Comparisons
- Comparing daily schedules of young people in Mexico City and in the U.S.
- Comparing snack foods of Mexico City and the U.S.
- Comparing historical areas in Mexico City and in the U.S.

Communities
- Using Spanish beyond the school experience
- Using Spanish for personal enjoyment

Teaching Resource Options

Print ✎
Block Scheduling Copymasters

Audiovisual 🔊
OHT M1, M2; 35, 36
Canciones Audiocassette/CD
Video Program Videotape 2 / Videodisc 1B

Search Chapter 1, Play to 2
U2 Cultural Introduction

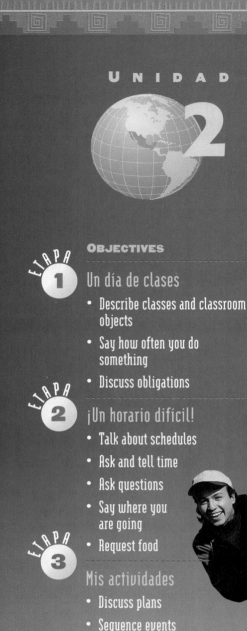

U N I D A D

2

OBJECTIVES

ETAPA **1**
Un día de clases
- Describe classes and classroom objects
- Say how often you do something
- Discuss obligations

ETAPA **2**
¡Un horario difícil!
- Talk about schedules
- Ask and tell time
- Ask questions
- Say where you are going
- Request food

ETAPA **3**
Mis actividades
- Discuss plans
- Sequence events
- Talk about places and people you know

94

ESTADOS UNIDOS

CIUDAD DE MÉXICO MÉXICO

UNA SEMANA TÍPICA

OCÉANO PACÍFICO

GOLFO DE CALIFORNIA

BAJA CALIFORNIA

MÉXICO

GUADALAJARA

TORTILLAS are traditionally made by hand. The price of tortillas is set by the government. What Mexican dishes made with tortillas have you tried?

DIEGO RIVERA (1886–1957) painted *La vendedora de flores* (1942) as well as many other paintings and murals. What paintings by Mexican artists have you seen?

Classroom Community

Paired/Group Activity Have students work in pairs or groups to research another **Persona famosa de México**. Have them list the person's occupation, why the person is famous (famous works of artists, changes effected by political leaders, etc.) and any other information they can find. Students can then compile their findings into a booklet to expand the **Almanaque** on p. 95.

Game Divide the class in half. Have students study all of the information in the **Almanaque** (in addition to the expanded **Almanaque** they have created and shared). Ask questions about the information. The first student to raise his/her hand gets to answer. The team with the most points wins. Have a prize for the winning team.

ALMANAQUE

Población: 16.900.000

Altura: 2.309 metros (7.575 pies)

Clima: 19° C (66° F)

Comida típica: tortillas, frijoles, tacos

Gente famosa de México: Lázaro Cárdenas (político), Carlos Fuentes (escritor), Amalia Hernández (bailarina), Frida Kahlo (pintora), Diego Rivera (pintor)

¿Vas a México, D.F.? Generalmente los mexicanos usan la palabra *México* para hablar del país. Para hablar de la Ciudad de México, usan las frases *la capital, el distrito federal* o simplemente *el D.F.* El distrito federal está en el centro de la ciudad.

 For more information about Mexico, access www.mcdougallittell.com

MONTERREY

PENÍNSULA DE YUCATÁN

MÉXICO, D.F.

BELICE

OAXACA

EL PALACIO DE BELLAS ARTES, begun in 1904 by an Italian architect, was finished 30 years later by a Mexican one. The Ballet Folklórico performs here. What do you think its name means?

EL BALLET FOLKLÓRICO has communicated the spirit of Mexico through dance since 1959. It was founded by Amalia Hernández. What traditional dances of the United States do you know?

SISTEMA DE TRANSPORTE COLECTIVO
RED DEL METRO
CIUDAD DE MEXICO

EL METRO opened in 1969 to combat pollution. It serves over 4 million people a day. To ride it, ask for a **billete!** Why might you ride a subway?

LÁZARO CÁRDENAS (1895–1970), president 1934–1940, made great improvements in Mexico. He created the Department of Tourism and made Mexico internationally influential. Who is the current president of Mexico?

95

Ampliación

These activities may be used at various points in the Unit 2 sequence.

For Block Schedule, you may find that these projects will provide a welcome change of pace while reviewing and reinforcing the material presented in the unit. See the **Block Scheduling Copymasters.**

● PROJECTS

Plan a trip to Mexico. Divide the class into four committees:
1. Air Travel: researches airlines, prices, and schedules to Mexico City.
2. Hotel Reservations: finds out names of hotels, locations, and prices.
3. Sightseeing: investigates places to visit.
4. Itinerary: plans the daily itinerary for the trip.

Committees will need to consult with each other in order to complete their portion of the trip. Each group is responsible for providing posters/visuals to support their information and presenting the results to the class.

> **PACING SUGGESTION:** Have students begin research at the beginning of the unit. Provide a schedule with "milestones" to encourage weekly progress; provide class time for committees to meet. Final projects are completed at the end of Unit 2.

Design a TV guide Plan ahead: Collect old TV guides for reference. Have each student choose a day of the week. For that day, each student plans a schedule of shows, with times written out in words.

> **PACING SUGGESTION:** Upon completion of Etapa 2.

● STORYTELLING

Horarios After reviewing the vocabulary for school subjects and telling time, model a mini-story (using puppets, student actors, or pictures from the text) that students will retell and revise:

> Son las siete y media de la mañana. Ana Luisa está en la escuela. Por la mañana, tiene 3 clases: primero, una clase de música a las ocho menos cuarto, después una de computación a las nueve y luego educación física a las diez y cuarto. Al mediodía tiene el almuerzo en la cafetería.

Pause as the story is being told, giving students a chance to fill in words or act out gestures. Students then write, narrate, and read aloud a longer main story. This new version should include vocabulary from the previous story and add more information about the classes.

Otras clases y actividades Ask students to create their own class schedule stories. They might expand on the model story to include afternoon classes and after-school activities. Suggest that students use the text dialogs as a model and personalize/expand.

> **PACING SUGGESTION:** Upon completion of Etapa 3.

● BULLETIN BOARD/POSTERS

Bulletin Board Have students research early civilizations of the Americas: Olmec, Toltec, Zapotec, Mixtec, Maya, Aztec, Incas. Students should create (a) timelines to show when each civilization existed, and (b) maps to show where they lived.

Posters Have students create •**Travel** posters for Mexico City •**Store fliers** showing computer equipment and school articles •**Schedule** posters of typical class schedules

GAMES

¿Eres artista?

Prepare ahead: Gather pictures of different school and after-school activities and places. Place them facedown in a pile. (You may also use illustrations from the textbook or overhead transparencies.)

Divide the class into two teams. One team member chooses a picture from the pile and tries to draw it for their team to guess. The artist must not use any words. If the team guesses correctly, they get a point. Teams take turns and the team with the most points at the end of 10 minutes wins. **Variation:** Students act out or write the activities instead of drawing them.

PACING SUGGESTION: Upon completion of Etapa 3.

Peces

Prepare ahead: In groups of 4, have students make a set of playing cards using the nouns under the heading "Describing Class Objects" on p. 117. Each student makes 1 card for each of the 17 words; there should be a total of 68 cards.

In the same groups of 4, have students play **Peces** (Go Fish) with their decks of cards.

PACING SUGGESTION: Upon completion of Etapa 1.

MUSIC

Distribute the words to Mexico's **Himno Nacional.** Have students look up key words and discuss the overall meaning of the song. Use the lyrics as a pronunciation practice. You might also have your students begin the next class by singing the anthem. Display the words on an overhead and have one student point to the words to keep the class together. More music samples are available on your *Canciones* Cassette or CD.

HANDS-ON CRAFTS

Ceramic tiles are commonly used in Mexico to decorate the interior of homes and the exterior of buildings. Purchase some plain, inexpensive tiles (or use playdough) and mount them on posterboard. Have students make decorative signs for their home that say either **La habitación de ___** or **La casa de los ___.**

RECIPE

Natilla Students will enjoy this easy-to-make Mexican dessert. In order to serve the custard well chilled, you may want to prepare the custard on one day and serve it the next.

This dessert is very similar to a basic **flan** recipe, another traditional custard dessert served in many restaurants and homes across the Hispanic world.

Receta

Natilla

4 huevos separados	1/4 taza de harina
1 taza de leche	3/4 taza de azúcar
1/8 cucharadita de sal	1 cucharadita de nuez moscada

En una fuente, hacer una pasta con las yemas de los huevos, la harina y 1 taza de leche. En una cacerola mediana, añadir la azúcar y la sal a la leche sobrante y escaldar a temperatura mediana. Añadir la mezcla de yemas a la leche escaldada y continuar cociendo a temperatura mediana hasta que cobre una consistencia cremosa. Retirar la cacerola del fuego y enfriar a temperatura ambiente. Batir las claras de los huevos hasta que se endurezcan pero no se sequen y envolver en la crema. Enfriar antes de servir. Servir porciones con cuchara en platos individuales. Echar una pizca de nuez moscada sobre cada porción. (Sirve a 6.)

Planning Guide CLASSROOM MANAGEMENT

OBJECTIVES

Communication
- Describe classes and classroom objects *pp. 98–99, 112–113*
- Say how often you do something *pp. 100–101*
- Discuss obligations *pp. 100–101, 112–113*

Grammar
- Use present tense of regular **-ar** verbs *pp. 105–107*
- Use adverbs of frequency *pp. 107–108*
- Use **hay que** and **tener que** *pp. 109–111*

Pronunciation
- **y** and **ll** *p. 111*
- Dictation, *TE p. 111*

Culture
- México: its history and culture *pp. 94–95*
- La Universidad Autónoma de México *p. 109*
- **Pluma** and **bolígrafo** *p. 110*

♻ Recycling
- **Hay,** colors, numbers *p. 103*

STRATEGIES

Listening Strategies
- Listen for feelings *p. 100*

Speaking Strategies
- Develop more than one way of expressing an idea *p. 104*
- Expand the conversation *p. 116*

Reading Strategies
- Use context clues *p. 112*

Writing Strategies
- Brainstorm details before writing *p. 116*

Connecting Cultures Strategies
- Learn about the history and culture of Mexico *pp. 94–95*
- Recognize variations in vocabulary *pp. 103, 110*
- Learn about a Mexican university *p. 109*
- Connect and compare what you know about school in your community to help you learn about school in a new community *pp. 98–101, 112–113*

PROGRAM RESOURCES

 Print
- *Más práctica* Workbook PE, *pp. 33–40*
- Block Scheduling Copymasters, *pp. 33–40*
- Unit 2 Resource Book
  Más práctica Workbook TE, *pp. 1–8*
  Para hispanohablantes Workbook TE, *pp. 9–16*

- Information Gap Activities *pp. 17–20*
- Family Involvement *pp. 21–22*
- Video Activities *pp. 23–25*
- Videoscript *pp. 26–28*
- Audioscript *pp. 29–32*
- Assessment Program, Unit 2 Etapa 1 *pp. 33–51; 170–178*
- Answer Keys *pp. 179–194*

 Audiovisual
- **Audio Program** Cassettes 4A, 4B / CD 4
- *Canciones* Cassette / CD
- Video Program Videotape 2 / Videodisc 1B
- Overhead Transparencies M1–M5; 35–36, 38–48

 Technology
- Electronic Teacher Tools/Test Generator
- *Intrigas y aventuras* CD-ROM, Disc 1
- www.mcdougallittell.com

 Assessment Program Options
- **Cooperative Quizzes** (Unit 2 Resource Book)
- **Etapa Exam** Forms A and B (Unit 2 Resource Book)
- *Para hispanohablantes* **Etapa Exam** (Unit 2 Resource Book)
- **Portfolio Assessment** (Unit 2 Resource Book)
- **Multiple Choice Test Questions** (Unit 2 Resource Book)
- **Audio Program** Testing Cassette T1 / CD T1
- **Electronic Teacher Tools/Test Generator**

Native Speakers
- *Para hispanohablantes* Workbook PE, *pp. 33–40*
- *Para hispanohablantes* Workbook TE (Unit 2 Resource Book)
- *Para hispanohablantes* Etapa Exam (Unit 2 Resource Book)
- Audio *Para hispanohablantes* Cassettes 4A, 4B, T1 / CD 4, T1
- Audioscript *Para hispanohablantes* (Unit 2 Resource Book)

Student Text
Listening Activity Scripts

 Videoscript: Diálogo *pages 100–101*

• Videotape 2 • Videodisc 1B

Search Chapter 3, Play to 4
U2E1 • En vivo (Dialog)

• Use the videoscript with **Actividades 1, 2** *page 102*

Isabel:	¡Y la computadora! ¿Qué pasa con la computadora? ¡Y la pantalla! ¡El ratón! ¿Qué pasa con el ratón? Con razón. Hay que conectar el ratón al teclado. Ahora sí. ¡Papel! ¡La impresora no tiene papel!
Mamá:	¡Isabel! ¡Hija! ¡Pronto! ¡Siempre llegas tarde a la escuela! Todos los días lo mismo, Isabel, ¡todos los días!
Isabel:	Sí, mamá, todos los días.
Mamá:	¿Y tu cuaderno? Necesitas tu cuaderno, ¿no?
Isabel:	Sí, mamá, necesito el cuaderno. Gracias.
Mamá:	¿Tus libros? ¿Tienes tus libros?
Isabel:	Sí, mamá, tengo mis libros.
Mamá:	¿Y la calculadora? Usas la calculadora en la clase de matemáticas, ¿no?
Isabel:	Sí, mamá, claro. Necesito la calculadora para la clase de matemáticas. ¡Adiós!
Mamá:	¿Y tu tarea, Isabel? ¿Tu tarea para la clase de ciencias naturales?
Isabel:	Este semestre, necesito sacar una buena nota en esta clase.
Ricardo:	Yo también. Estudio todos los días, pero la clase es difícil.
Isabel:	Me llamo Isabel. ¿Y tú?
Ricardo:	Soy Ricardo. ¡Mucho gusto!
Isabel:	Mucho gusto. Yo siempre preparo la tarea en la computadora, ¿y tú? ¿Cómo preparas tu tarea?
Profesor:	Good morning, class.
Clase:	Good morning, Professor Martínez.
Isabel:	Tengo que sacar una buena nota. ¡Es muy importante!
Profesor:	Miss, would you like to share your ideas with the class?
Isabel:	No, maestro. Lo siento. Yo no hablo más.
Profesor:	In English, Miss. This is English class.
Isabel:	I'm sorry, teacher. I won't talk anymore. ¡Qué vergüenza! Siempre escucho con atención en la clase de inglés.
Ricardo:	Cálmate, Isabel. ¿Qué clases tienes hoy?
Isabel:	Tengo matemáticas y ciencias naturales.
Ricardo:	Yo también tengo ciencias naturales hoy.
Isabel:	Necesito sacar una buena nota en la tarea de ciencias naturales.
Ricardo:	¡Ojalá! ¿Tienes la tarea?
Isabel:	Sí, en mi mochila. ¡Qué horror!
Ricardo:	¿Qué?
Isabel:	¡Mi tarea!
Ricardo:	¿Qué pasa?
Isabel:	¡Mi tarea para la clase de ciencias naturales! ¡Está en la impresora, en mi casa!
Ricardo:	Cálmate, Isabel.
Isabel:	¡Tengo que hablar con la profesora Díaz! ¡Ahora mismo!

 **¡Lógicamente!** *page 107*

1. Ricardo es un buen muchacho.
2. Su amiga estudia mucho.
3. La señora Díaz es maestra.
4. Ricardo prepara su tarea de matemáticas.
5. La clase de ciencias naturales es difícil para Isabel.

19 **La clase de tu amiga** *page 111*

¿Cómo es mi clase de español? Pues, de vez en cuando es difícil, pero siempre es interesante. Mi profesora es la señorita Casas. Ella es de España y es muy simpática. Todos los días habla español en clase. Rara vez habla inglés. Tengo que escuchar bien cuando ella habla. También tengo que estudiar mucho y preparar mi tarea todos los días para sacar una buena nota.

Quick Start Review Answers

p. 96 Meeting and greeting
Answers will vary.
Answers could include:
A: ¡Hola, Miguel!
C: ¡Hola, Susana!
A: Ana, te presento a Miguel.
B: Encantada, Miguel.
C: Igualmente, Ana.
A, B, C: ¡Adiós!

p. 107 -ar verbs
Answers will vary.
Answers could include:
1. hablar
   Yo hablo español y inglés.
2. estudiar
   Nosotros estudiamos mucho.
3. llegar
   Tú llegas tarde a la clase de inglés.
4. mirar
   Isabel mira el pizarrón.
5. usar
   Pedro usa un diccionario en la clase de español.

p. 109 Adverbs and **-ar** verbs
Answers will vary.
Answers could include:
1. nunca llegan tarde a la escuela.
2. siempre sacan buenas notas.
3. siempre escuchan a la maestra.
4. preparan la tarea todos los días.
5. ayudan a los amigos de vez en cuando.

p. 112 Vocabulary review
Answers will vary.
Answers could include:
• verbos: enseñar, llevar, buscar, estudiar, necesitar
• materias: la música, el español, la educación física, el arte, la historia
• objetos de la clase: la computadora, la mochila, el pizarrón, la tiza, el escritorio
• adverbios: nunca, mucho, todos los días, a veces, poco

Sample Lesson Plan - 50 Minute Schedule

DAY 1

Unit Opener
- Anticipate/Activate prior knowledge: Present the *Almanaque* and the cultural notes. Use Map OHTs as needed. **10 MIN.**

Etapa Opener
- Quick Start Review (TE, p. 96) **5 MIN.**
- Have students look at the *Etapa* Opener and answer the questions. **5 MIN.**

En contexto: Vocabulario
- Quick Start Review (TE, p. 98) **5 MIN.**
- Have students use context and pictures to learn *Etapa* vocabulary, then answer the questions, p. 99. Use the Situational OHTs for additional practice. **10 MIN.**

En vivo: Diálogo
- Quick Start Review (TE, p. 100) **5 MIN.**
- Review the Listening Strategy, p. 100. Play audio or show video for the dialog, pp. 100–101. Replay and have students take the roles of the characters. **10 MIN.**

Homework Option:
- Video Activities, Unit 2 Resource Book, pp. 23–25.

DAY 2

En acción: Vocabulario y gramática
- Check homework. **5 MIN.**
- Quick Start Review (TE, p. 102) **5 MIN.**
- Have students open to *En contexto*, pp. 98–99, for reference. Use OHT 39 and 40 to review vocabulary. **5 MIN.**
- Play the video/audio; have students do *Actividades* 1 and 2 orally. **5 MIN.**
- Have students complete *Actividad* 3 in pairs. **5 MIN.**
- Have students complete *Actividad* 4 in writing. Have students exchange papers for peer correction. **10 MIN.**
- Present the *Vocabulario* and have students complete *Actividad* 5 in pairs. **10 MIN.**
- Present the Speaking Strategy, p. 104, and have students complete *Actividad* 6 in pairs. Call on several pairs to present their dialogs. **10 MIN.**

Homework Option:
- Have students write 7 true/false statements about the *Diálogo*.

DAY 3

En acción (cont.)
- Check homework. **5 MIN.**
- Quick Start Review (TE, p. 104) **5 MIN.**
- Present *Gramática:* Saying What You Do: Present of *-ar* Verbs, p. 105. **10 MIN.**
- Ask volunteers to pantomime the verbs in the *Vocabulario*. **5 MIN.**
- Have students complete *Actividad* 7 in writing. Have volunteers write out answers on the board. **10 MIN.**
- Have students complete *Actividades* 8, 9, 10 in pairs. Expand using Information Gap Activities, Unit 2 Resource Book, p. 17; *Más comunicación*, p. R4. **15 MIN.**
- Play the audio; do *Actividad* 11. **5 MIN.**

Homework Option:
- *Más práctica* Workbook, pp. 37–38. *Para hispanohablantes* Workbook, pp. 35–36.

DAY 4

En acción (cont.)
- Check homework. **5 MIN.**
- Quick Start Review (TE, p. 107). **5 MIN.**
- Present *Gramática:* Expressing Frequency with Adverbs, p. 107. **10 MIN.**
- Have students read *Actividad* 12 silently, then answer orally. **10 MIN.**
- Have students do *Actividad* 13 in pairs. Call on volunteers to present their dialogs to the class. **10 MIN.**
- In groups of 3, have students create posters for *Actividad* 14. Suggest that students begin by brainstorming needed vocabulary. **15 MIN.**

Homework Option:
- If necessary, complete posters for *Actividad* 14. *Más práctica* Workbook, p. 39. *Para hispanohablantes* Workbook, p. 37.

DAY 5

En acción (cont.)
- Check homework. **5 MIN.**
- Quick Start Review (TE, p. 109) **5 MIN.**
- Present *Gramática:* Expressing Obligation with *hay que* and *tener que*, p. 109. **10 MIN.**
- Do *Actividades* 15 and 16 orally. **10 MIN.**
- Have students complete *Actividad* 17 in small groups. **5 MIN.**
- Present the *Nota*. Then have students read and complete *Actividad* 18. **5 MIN.**
- Play the audio; do *Actividad* 19. **5 MIN.**
- Have students complete *Actividad* 20. Expand using Information Gap Activities, Unit 2 Resource Book, pp. 18–19; *Más comunicación*, p. R4. **10 MIN.**

Homework Option:
- *Más práctica* Workbook, p. 40. *Para hispanohablantes* Workbook, p. 38.

DAY 6

Pronunciación
- Check homework. **5 MIN.**
- Play the audio and have students practice the *Trabalenguas*. **10 MIN.**

En voces: Lectura
- Quick Start Review (TE, p. 112) **5 MIN.**
- Review the Reading Strategy, p. 112. **5 MIN.**
- Have students read the *Lectura* silently. Then have various students read the *Lectura* aloud. **10 MIN.**
- Call on volunteers to answer the *¿Comprendiste?* questions, p. 113. **5 MIN.**
- Have students complete *¿Qué piensas?*, p. 113. Have several students present their answers. **15 MIN.**

Homework Option:
- Have students write answers to the *¿Comprendiste?* questions, p. 113. Review in preparation for *En uso*.

DAY 7

En uso: Repaso y más comunicación
- Check homework. **5 MIN.**
- Quick Start Review (TE, p. 114) **5 MIN.**
- Present the *Repaso y más comunicación* using the Teaching Suggestions (TE, p. 114). **5 MIN.**
- Have students write *Actividades* 1 and 2, then check answers with the whole class. **10 MIN.**
- Do *Actividades* 3 and 4 orally. **10 MIN.**
- Present the Speaking Strategy, p. 116, and have students do *Actividad* 5 in pairs. **10 MIN.**
- Have students do *Actividad* 6 in groups. Have volunteers perform their dialogs for the class. **10 MIN.**

Homework Option:
- Review for *Etapa* 1 Exam.

DAY 8

En tu propia voz: Escritura
- Do *Actividad* 7 in writing. Ask volunteers to present their descriptions. **10 MIN.**

Conexiones
- Read and discuss *Las matemáticas*, p. 116. **5 MIN.**

En resumen: Repaso de vocabulario
- Quick Start Review (TE, p. 117) **5 MIN.**
- Review grammar questions, etc., as necessary. **10 MIN.**
- Complete *Etapa* 1 Exam. **20 MIN.**

Ampliación
- Optional: Use a suggested project, game, or activity. (TE, pp. 95A–95B) **15 MIN.**

Homework Option:
- Conduct the survey and make a chart for *Conexiones*. Preview *Etapa* 2 Opener.

Sample Lesson Plan - Block Schedule (90 minutes)

DAY 1

Unit Opener
- Anticipate/Activate prior knowledge: Present the *Almanaque* and the cultural notes. Use Map OHTs as needed. 10 MIN.

Etapa Opener
- Quick Start Review (TE, p. 96) 5 MIN.
- Have students look at the *Etapa* Opener and answer the questions. 5 MIN.
- Use Block Scheduling Copymasters. 5 MIN.

En contexto: Vocabulario
- Quick Start Review (TE, p. 98) 5 MIN.
- Have students use context and pictures to learn *Etapa* vocabulary, then answer the questions, p. 99. Use the Situational OHTs for additional practice. 15 MIN.

En vivo: Diálogo
- Quick Start Review (TE, p. 100) 5 MIN.
- Review the Listening Strategy, p. 100. Play audio or show video for the dialog, pp. 100–101. Replay and have students take the roles of the characters. 20 MIN.

En acción: Vocabulario y gramática
- Quick Start Review (TE, p. 102) 5 MIN.
- Have students open to *En contexto,* pp. 98–99, for reference. Use OHT 39 and 40 to review vocabulary. 5 MIN.
- Play the video/audio; do *Actividades* 1 and 2 orally. 10 MIN.

Homework Option:
- Video Activities, Unit 2 Resource Book, pp. 23–25. Have students write 7 true/false statements about the *Diálogo.*

DAY 2

En acción (cont.)
- Check homework. 5 MIN.
- Have students complete *Actividad* 3 in pairs. 5 MIN.
- Have students complete *Actividad* 4 in writing. Have students exchange papers for peer correction. 10 MIN.
- Present the *Vocabulario* and have students complete *Actividad* 5 in pairs. 10 MIN.
- Present the Speaking Strategy, p. 104, and have students complete *Actividad* 6 in pairs. Call on several pairs to present their dialogs. 10 MIN.
- Quick Start Review (TE, p. 104) 5 MIN.
- Present *Gramática:* Saying What You Do: Present of *-ar* Verbs, p. 105. 10 MIN.
- Ask volunteers to pantomime the verbs in the *Vocabulario.* 5 MIN.
- Have students complete *Actividad* 7 in writing. Have volunteers write out answers on the board. 10 MIN.
- Have students complete *Actividades* 8, 9, 10 in pairs. Expand using Information Gap Activities, Unit 2 Resource Book, p. 17; *Más comunicación,* p. R4. 15 MIN.
- Play the audio; do *Actividad* 11. 5 MIN.

Homework Option:
- *Más práctica* Workbook, pp. 37–38. *Para hispanohablantes* Workbook, pp. 35–36.

DAY 3

En acción (cont.)
- Check homework. 5 MIN.
- Quick Start Review (TE, p. 107) 5 MIN.
- Present *Gramática:* Expressing Frequency with Adverbs, p. 107. 10 MIN.
- Have students read *Actividad* 12 silently, then answer orally. 5 MIN.
- Have students do *Actividad* 13 in pairs. 5 MIN.
- In groups of 3, have students begin to create posters for *Actividad* 14. Suggest that students start by brainstorming needed vocabulary. 10 MIN.
- Quick Start Review (TE, p. 109) 5 MIN.
- Present *Gramática:* Expressing Obligation with *hay que* and *tener que,* p. 109. 10 MIN.
- Do *Actividades* 15 and 16 orally. 10 MIN.
- Have students complete *Actividad* 17 in small groups. 5 MIN.
- Have students read and complete *Actividad* 18. 5 MIN.
- Play the audio; do *Actividad* 19. 5 MIN.
- Have students complete *Actividad* 20. Expand using Information Gap Activities, Unit 2 Resource Book, pp. 18–19; *Más comunicación,* p. R4. 10 MIN.

Pronunciación
- Play the audio and have students practice the *Trabalenguas.* 5 MIN.

Homework Option:
- Complete posters for *Actividad* 14. *Más práctica* Workbook, pp. 39–40. *Para hispanohablantes* Workbook, pp. 37–38.

DAY 4

En voces: Lectura
- Check homework. 10 MIN.
- Quick Start Review (TE, p. 112) 5 MIN.
- Review the Reading Strategy, p. 112. 5 MIN.
- Have students read the *Lectura* silently. Then have various students read the *Lectura* aloud. 15 MIN.
- Call on volunteers to answer the questions, p. 113. 5 MIN.

En uso: Repaso y más comunicación
- Quick Start Review (TE, p. 114) 5 MIN.
- Have students write *Actividades* 1 and 2, then check answers with the whole class. 15 MIN.
- Do *Actividades* 3 and 4 orally. 10 MIN.
- Present the Speaking Strategy, p. 116, and have students do *Actividad* 5 in pairs. 10 MIN.
- Have students do *Actividad* 6 in groups. Have volunteers perform their dialogs for the class. 10 MIN.

Homework Option:
- Review for *Etapa* 1 Exam.

DAY 5

En tu propia voz: Escritura
- Do *Actividad* 7 in writing. Ask volunteers to present their descriptions. 15 MIN.

Conexiones
- Read and discuss *Las matemáticas,* p. 116. Have students plan their surveys. 15 MIN.

En resumen: Repaso de vocabulario
- Quick Start Review (TE, p. 117) 5 MIN.
- Review grammar questions, etc., as necessary. 10 MIN.
- Complete *Etapa* 1 Exam. 20 MIN.

Ampliación
- Use one or more suggested projects, games, or activities. (TE, pp. 95A–95B) 25 MIN.

Homework Option:
- Conduct the survey and make a pie chart for *Conexiones.* Preview *Etapa* 2 Opener.

▼ Isabel y Ricardo en la escuela.

Etapa Theme
Talking about school, classes, schedules, and teachers.

Grammar Objectives
- Saying what you do: present tense of **-ar** verbs
- Expressing frequency with adverbs
- Expressing obligation with **hay que** and **tener que**

Teaching Resource Options
Print
Block Scheduling Copymasters

Audiovisual
OHT 36, 45 (Quick Start)

Quick Start Review
🔄 Meeting and greeting
Use OHT 45 or write on board:
Write a mini-dialog involving 3 people and the following scenario:
Friend A and B are out for a walk; A spots another friend (C); A and C greet; A introduces C to B; they all say good-bye.

Answers *See p. 95D.*

Teaching Suggestion
Previewing the Etapa
- Ask students to study the picture on pp. 96–97 (1 min.).
- Close books; ask students to share at least 3 things that they noticed.
- Reopen books and look at the picture again (1 min.); close books and share 3 more details.
- Use the **¿Qué ves?** questions to focus the discussion.

Language Note
You may wish to point out that the word **y** becomes **e** before a word beginning with **i** or **hi**. Thus, if students talk about Ricardo and Isabel, they must say **Ricardo e Isabel.**

UNIDAD 2

ETAPA 1

Un día de clases

- Describe classes and classroom objects
- Say how often you do something
- Discuss obligations

¿Qué ves?

Mira la foto del centro de la Ciudad de México.

1. ¿Tiene pelo corto la chica?
2. ¿Son rubios o morenos los chicos?
3. ¿Es roja o rosada la chaqueta del chico?
4. ¿Isabel tiene clases el sábado?

96

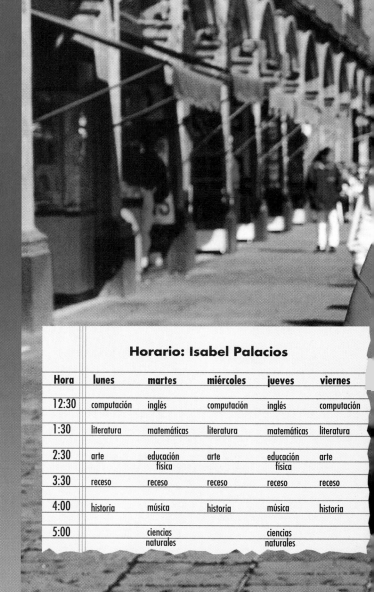

Horario: Isabel Palacios

Hora	lunes	martes	miércoles	jueves	viernes
12:30	computación	inglés	computación	inglés	computación
1:30	literatura	matemáticas	literatura	matemáticas	literatura
2:30	arte	educación física	arte	educación física	arte
3:30	receso	receso	receso	receso	receso
4:00	historia	música	historia	música	historia
5:00		ciencias naturales		ciencias naturales	

Classroom Management

Planning Ahead Have students create their own class schedule in Spanish. You can either hand out a schedule form similar to the one on p. 96 or have students create their own. Have students write any differences they find between their own schedules and that of Isabel Palacios. Alternate: Make up a schedule of the day's classroom activities (for example: **Repaso, Lectura, Grupos,** etc.) to keep students on task.

Streamlining Either make flashcards with simple drawings yourself or assign one flashcard word per student for the vocabulary on pp. 98–99. After you present the vocabulary the following day you can drill students with the flashcards to aid vocabulary retention. Students can also make posters with items labeled in Spanish, or create a "sculpture" of actual objects on a desk with labels.

97

Connecting Cultures

Have students describe any differences they notice between downtown Mexico City and the downtown of their own city or town. Have them also compare the clothing of Isabel and her friend with clothes they typically wear.

Culture Highlights

● **MÉXICO, D.F.** Mexico City was established in 1521 by Hernán Cortés. It is located on the site of the famous Aztec city, Tenochtitlán, which was destroyed by Cortés.

● **AZTECAS** As a nomadic people, the Aztecs had no permanent settlements. According to legend, one day they saw an eagle, perched on a cactus, with a serpent in its beak. They interpreted this as a sign from their gods to settle in one place. This settlement became Tenochtitlán. The symbol of the eagle and serpent is reproduced today on Mexico's flag, its currency, and official government documents.

● **EL ZÓCALO** The **Zócalo,** or Plaza of the Constitution, is the historical center of Mexico City (see pp. 158–159). It occupies the site of the central square of the ancient Aztec city of Tenochtitlán. It is surrounded by the baroque National Cathedral, the Municipal Palace, and the National Palace, where the office of the President and the Senate are located. A major avenue leads from the **Zócalo** to the **Plaza de las Tres Culturas.**

Teaching Note

You may want to tell students that the photograph was taken at **El Zócalo** in downtown Mexico City.

Block Schedule

Previewing To guide students through the format of an **Etapa,** have them predict what things they might learn for the topic "school." Also have them scan the **Etapa** to preview the grammar. (For additional activities, see **Block Scheduling Copymasters.**)

Teaching All Students

Extra Help Ask students a series of yes/no or either/or questions about the photo. For example: ¿Lleva jeans la chica? (Sí.) ¿Lleva un suéter azul el chico? (No.) ¿Es pelirroja la chica? (No.) ¿Es moreno el chico? (Sí.) ¿La camiseta de Isabel es amarilla o rosada? (rosada) Los lunes, ¿Isabel tiene clase de arte o de música? (de arte)

Multiple Intelligences

Visual Divide students into 4 groups, and assign each group 1/4 of the photo (i.e., upper left, upper right, lower left, lower right). Students list as many details as they can recall. Then, compile the four lists to see if the class has formed a complete picture.

Musical/Rhythmic Have students develop a short rap/chant to describe the photo.

Teaching Resource Options

Print

Unit 2 Resource Book
Video Activities, pp. 23–24
Videoscript, p. 26
Audioscript, p. 29
Audioscript *Para hispanohablantes,*
  p. 29

Audiovisual

OHT 39, 40, 41, 41A, 42, 42A, 45 (Quick
Start)
Audio Program Cassette 4A / CD 4
Audio *Para hispanohablantes*
  Cassette 4A / CD 4
Video Program Videotape 2 /
  Videodisc 1B

Search Chapter 2, Play to 3
U2E1 • En contexto (Vocabulary)

Technology
Intrigas y aventuras CD-ROM, Disc 1

Quick Start Review
♻ Clothing

Use OHT 45 or write on board:
Write what Isabel is wearing in the large
picture on p. 98.

Answers
Isabel lleva unos jeans, una camisa azul, una
camiseta rosada y unos zapatos.

Teaching Suggestions
Introducing Vocabulary

• Have students look at pages 98–99.
  Use OHT 39 and 40 and Audio
  Cassette 4A / CD 4 to present the
  vocabulary.
• Ask the Comprehension Questions in
  order of yes/no (questions 1–3),
  either/or (questions 4–6), and simple
  word or phrase (questions 7–10).
  Expand by adding similar questions.
• Use the TPR activity to reinforce the
  meaning of individual words.
• Use the video vocabulary presentation
  for review and reinforcement.

En contexto
VOCABULARIO

Isabel spends most of the week in school. Here Isabel describes
the things she uses there.

A

Bienvenidos a mi **escuela**. En **la clase**
el maestro **habla** mucho. Los estudiantes
escuchan al maestro. Las **lecciones** son
interesantes.

el diccionario   el lápiz   el papel
el escritorio   el cuaderno

B Para **estudiar**, tengo un escritorio.
En mi escritorio, tengo un **cuaderno**,
un **diccionario**, un **lápiz** y **papel**.

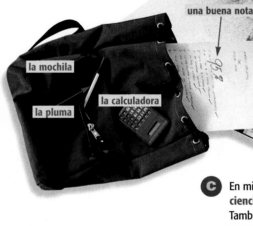

una buena nota
la mochila
la pluma   la calculadora
el libro

C En mi **mochila**, tengo mi **libro** de
ciencias, mi **calculadora** y mi **pluma**.
También tengo mi **tarea**. ¡Siempre
saco una buena nota en la tarea!

98 noventa y ocho
Unidad 2

Classroom Community

TPR Ask students to take out 5–6 school supplies. Ask
questions about who has what supplies: ¿Quién tiene
tres lápices o más? ¿Quién tiene un diccionario de
español? ¿de inglés? ¿Quién tiene una mochila azul?
etc. Students hold up the indicated items, saying
Tengo.../Yo tengo...

Paired Activity Working in pairs, students take
turns hiding a school supply item behind their backs
while their partner guesses what it is. When one
partner guesses correctly, he/she should add one more
sentence to describe the object. For example:
–¿Tienes una mochila? –Sí, tengo una mochila. Es
roja.

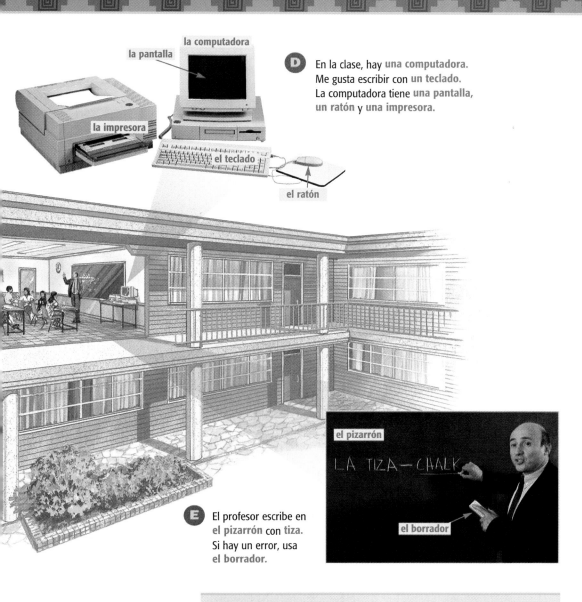

la computadora

la pantalla

la impresora

el teclado

el ratón

D En la clase, hay **una computadora**. Me gusta escribir con **un teclado**. La computadora tiene **una pantalla**, **un ratón** y **una impresora**.

el pizarrón

LA TIZA - CHALK

el borrador

E El profesor escribe en **el pizarrón** con **tiza**. Si hay un error, usa **el borrador**.

Preguntas personales

1. ¿Hay una computadora en tu clase?
2. ¿Te gusta usar la computadora o una pluma?
3. ¿Practicas mucho o no en la clase de español?
4. ¿Qué tienes en tu mochila?
5. ¿Qué tienes en tu escritorio?

noventa y nueve
Etapa 1
99

Comprehension Questions

1. ¿Tiene Isabel una calculadora? (Sí.)
2. ¿Tiene Isabel una mochila azul? (No.)
3. ¿A Isabel le gusta escribir con un teclado? (Sí.)
4. ¿Siempre saca Isabel una buena nota o una mala nota en la tarea? (una buena nota)
5. ¿Habla su maestro mucho o poco? (mucho)
6. ¿Escribe el profesor con el borrador o con la tiza? (con la tiza)
7. ¿Qué tiene Isabel en su escritorio? (un cuaderno, un diccionario, un lápiz y papel)
8. ¿Qué tiene Isabel en su mochila? (un libro de ciencias, una calculadora, una pluma y la tarea)
9. ¿Qué usa el profesor si hay un error en el pizarrón? (un borrador)
10. ¿Qué tiene la computadora? (una pantalla, un teclado, un ratón y una impresora)

Quick Wrap-up

Have various students tell or write what classroom objects they use in class every day (**Uso...**). You may also ask students to narrate as they put items in their backpacks: **Tengo... en mi mochila,** etc.

Block Schedule

Organization One key to continued success in block scheduling is organization. Students should be strongly encouraged to keep a notebook and take notes on class presentations. One section should contain vocabulary lists copied out of the book. Also in this section could be the Reference Lists created in class and Supplementary Vocabulary lists based on class need and interests. The **Block Scheduling Copymasters** contain homework assignment sheets to help students keep track of their work.

Teaching All Students

Extra Help Walk around the room pointing at classroom items. Ask either/or questions. For example: **¿Es un libro o un cuaderno?** Put labels on classroom objects to increase retention.

Native Speakers Ask students if they know other words commonly used for classroom items. For example: **el gis** (chalk), **el bolígrafo** o **boli** (pen), **el ordenador** (computer).

Multiple Intelligences

Visual Have students design an ad for school supplies. They should list items, add art, and give prices.

Logical/Mathematical Have students make signs to identify classroom objects. Then have students sort and color code the signs according to function, size, etc.

Teaching Resource Options

Print

Más práctica Workbook PE, pp. 33–36
Para hispanohablantes Workbook
  PE, pp. 33–34
Block Scheduling Copymasters
Unit 2 Resource Book
  Más práctica Workbook TE, pp. 1–4
  Para hispanohablantes Workbook
    TE, pp. 9–10
  Video Activities, pp. 23–24
  Videoscript, p. 27
  Audioscript, p. 29
  Audioscript *Para hispanohablantes*,
    p. 29

Audiovisual

OHT 43, 44, 45 (Quick Start)
Audio Program Cassette 4A / CD 4
Audio *Para hispanohablantes*
  Cassette 4A / CD 4
Video Program Videotape 2 /
  Videodisc 1B

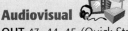

Search Chapter 3, Play to 4
U2E1 • En vivo (Dialog)

Technology

Intrigas y aventuras CD-ROM, Disc 1

Quick Start Review

♻ **Tener**

Use OHT 45 or write on the board:
Complete the following sentences with
the appropriate forms of **tener**:

1. Tú ____ catorce años.
2. Yo ____ una mochila verde.
3. La impresora no ____ papel.
4. Nosotros ____ una computadora.
5. Ana y Luisa ____ un perro.

Answers

1. tienes	4. tenemos
2. tengo	5. tienen
3. tiene	

Gestures

In photo 10, Isabel is grimacing because
she forgot to bring her homework. In
Spanish, there is no verb for *to grimace*.
You would have to say that she is making
a face: **está haciendo una mueca.**

En vivo

 ● **DIÁLOGO**

¡A la escuela!

| Isabel | Mamá | Ricardo | Prof. Martínez |

PARA ESCUCHAR • **STRATEGY: LISTENING**

Listen for feelings Many things happen to Isabel in this
scene. How does she feel? What do you hear that makes
you think she feels that way?

1 ▶ **Isabel:** ¿Qué pasa con la
computadora? ¡Y la pantalla! ¿Qué
pasa con el ratón? Con razón. Hay
que conectar el ratón al teclado.

5 ▶ **Isabel:** Necesito sacar una buena
nota en esta clase.
Ricardo: Yo también. Estudio
todos los días, pero la clase es
difícil.

6 ▶ **Profesor:** Good morning, class.
Clase: Good morning, Professor Martínez.

7 ▶ **Isabel:** Tengo que sacar una buena
nota. ¡Es muy importante!
Profesor: Miss, would you like to
share your ideas with the class?

100   cien
Unidad 2

Classroom Community

Group Activity Working in groups, assign students
the roles of the characters in the dialog (some students
can be non-speaking extras, playing the parts of
students in the classroom scenes). Encourage students
to read their parts with verbal and physical expression.
They should also use props to enhance dramatic effect.
Discuss adjectives of feelings and their corresponding
gestures prior to the dialogs.

Portfolio Have students write 4–5 sentences about
classroom items, items in their school bags, and school
items in their room at home. Include colors to review
vocabulary from Unit 1.

Rubric A = 13–15 pts. B = 10–12 pts. C = 7–9 pts. D = 4–6 pts. F = < 4pts.

Writing criteria	Scale
Vocabulary use	1 2 3 4 5
Logical sentence order	1 2 3 4 5
Grammar/spelling accuracy	1 2 3 4 5

2 ▶ **Isabel:** ¡Papel! ¡La impresora no tiene papel!
Mamá: ¡Pronto! ¡Siempre llegas tarde a la escuela!

3 ▶ **Mamá:** ¿Necesitas tu cuaderno? ¿Y tus libros? ¿Y la calculadora?
Isabel: Sí, mamá, claro.

4 ▶ **Mamá:** ¿Y tu tarea, Isabel? ¿Tu tarea para la clase de ciencias naturales?

8 ▶ **Isabel:** Lo siento. No hablo más.
Profesor: This is English class.
Isabel: I'm sorry, teacher. I won't talk anymore.

9 ▶ **Isabel:** ¡Qué vergüenza! Siempre escucho con atención en la clase de inglés.
Ricardo: Cálmate, Isabel. ¿Qué clases tienes hoy?
Isabel: Tengo matemáticas y ciencias naturales.

10 ▶ **Isabel:** ¡Qué horror!
Ricardo: ¿Qué?
Isabel: ¡Mi tarea para la clase de ciencias naturales! ¡Está en la impresora, en mi casa! ¡Tengo que hablar con la profesora Díaz! ¡Ahora mismo!

ciento uno
Etapa 1   **101**

Teaching Suggestions
Presenting the Dialog
- Prepare students for listening by having them scan the photos. Ask them to guess what is happening just by looking at the characters' facial expressions.
- Ask students to guess why there is English dialog in photos 6, 7, and 8.
- Use the video, audio cassette, or CD to present the dialog. The expanded dialog on video offers additional listening practice opportunities.

Video Synopsis
- Isabel is rushing off to school, only to have a pretty bad day there. For a complete transcript of the video dialog, see p. 95D.

Comprehension Questions

1. ¿Tiene que conectar Isabel el ratón al teclado? (Sí.)
2. ¿Tiene papel la impresora? (No.)
3. ¿Siempre llega tarde Isabel a la escuela? (Sí.)
4. ¿Es la clase de inglés fácil? (No.)
5. ¿Habla el profesor español o inglés en la clase? (inglés)
6. ¿El profesor de inglés se llama el profesor Martínez o el profesor Santiago? (el profesor Martínez)
7. ¿Por qué estudia Ricardo todos los días? (Necesita sacar una buena nota.)
8. ¿Qué clases tiene Isabel hoy? (matemáticas y ciencias naturales)
9. ¿Dónde está la tarea de Isabel para la clase de ciencias naturales? (en la impresora)
10. ¿Cómo se llama la profesora de ciencias naturales? (la profesora Díaz)

Block Schedule

Variety Let students hear the dialog more than once in order to clearly hear accent and intonation. Then have students work in groups of 4 and practice reading the dialog out loud. Give a prize to the group with the most authentic sounding dialog. (For additional activities, see **Block Scheduling Copymasters.**)

Teaching All Students

Extra Help Assign each of the 21 lines of the dialog to a different student to be memorized. Then do a full class dialog with the 21 participants.

Multiple Intelligences

Kinesthetic Describe the photos in the dialog. Have various students touch the photos in their texts as they are being described. For example: **Isabel está frustrada con la computadora.** (1); **El profesor dice buenos días a la clase.** (6) Choose a volunteer to act out/ mime each photo description.

Teaching Resource Options

Print

Unit 2 Resource Book
Video Activities, p. 25
Videoscript, p. 28
Audioscript, p. 29
Audioscript *Para hispanohablantes,*
  p. 29

Audiovisual

OHT 46 (Quick Start)
Audio Program Cassette 4A / CD 4
Audio *Para hispanohablantes*
  Cassette 4A / CD 4
Video Program Videotape 2 /
  Videodisc 1B

Quick Start Review

♻ **Classroom objects**

Use OHT 46 or write on the board:
Make a list of 7–10 objects in the
classroom. When possible, also give
the color.

Answers

Answers will vary. Answers could include:
unos diccionarios negros, unos cuadernos
rojos y verdes, una calculadora, unas plumas
azules, unas mochilas rojas y verdes, unos
escritorios blancos, una computadora, una
impresora, un pizarrón negro, un borrador
verde, un lápiz amarillo

Teaching Suggestions
Comprehension Check

Use **Actividades 1** and **2** to assess
retention after the dialog. Read each
item in **Actividad 1** and pause before
reading a, b, and c to give students a
chance to think of the answer on their
own.

 Objective: Transitional practice
Listening comprehension/vocabulary

Answers (See script, p. 95D.)
1. c   4. b
2. a   5. a
3. b

 Objective: Transitional practice
Listening comprehension/vocabulary

Answers (See script, p. 95D.)
1. a   4. c
2. a   5. a
3. b

En acción
VOCABULARIO Y GRAMÁTICA

OBJECTIVES

• Describe classes and
  classroom objects
• Say how often you do
  something
• Discuss obligations

ACTIVIDAD 1

¿Cuál es?

Escuchar Escoge la respuesta
correcta. (*Hint: Choose the best answer.*)

1. Este semestre Isabel
   necesita sacar una buena
   nota en la clase de _____.
   a. matemáticas
   b. español
   c. inglés

2. Isabel prepara su tarea
   en _____.
   a. la computadora
   b. la clase
   c. el cuaderno

3. Isabel no tiene su tarea
   para la clase de _____.
   a. inglés
   b. ciencias naturales
   c. matemáticas

4. La tarea de Isabel está
   en _____.
   a. su mochila
   b. la impresora
   c. la clase

5. Isabel tiene que hablar
   con _____.
   a. la profesora Díaz
   b. Ricardo
   c. su mamá

ACTIVIDAD 2

¿Qué dicen?

Escuchar Escoge lo que dice cada persona según la foto.
(*Hint: Choose what each person is saying.*)

1. a. ¿Qué pasa con el ratón?
   b. Éste es mi escritorio.
   c. Ésta es la computadora.

2. a. ¡La impresora no tiene papel!
   b. ¡Todos los días lo mismo!
   c. ¡Y la pantalla!

3. a. Usas la calculadora en la clase de
      matemáticas, ¿no?
   b. ¿Necesitas tu cuaderno?
   c. Yo siempre preparo mi tarea en la
      computadora.

4. a. Yo también tengo ciencias naturales hoy.
   b. Preparo mi tarea en la computadora.
   c. Cálmate, Isabel.

5. a. ¡Mi tarea! ¡Está en la impresora en mi
      casa!
   b. Tengo matemáticas y ciencias
      naturales.
   c. Tengo mis libros.

Classroom Management

Peer Review After completing **Actividades 1** and **2**,
have students work in pairs and take turns reading their
answers to each other. Students check to see if they got
the same answer. If not, they should work together to
determine who is correct.

Student Self Checks Have students complete
Actividad 4 in writing. Tell them to list as many items
as they can and to be as specific as possible (describing
colors, etc.). Then give them your detailed list, which
you can create beforehand, of all the items. Have them
check their work to see how well they did.

- Use present tense of regular **-ar** verbs
- Use adverbs of frequency
- Use **tener que, hay que**

ACTIVIDAD 3

 ¿Qué hay en la clase?

Hablar Trabaja con otro(a) estudiante para decir si hay o no hay estas cosas en la clase. Cambien de papel. *(Hint: Say if these things are in the classroom.)*

modelo

Tú: *¿Hay una mochila azul?*

Otro(a) estudiante: *No, no hay una mochila azul. Hay una mochila roja.*

1. un lápiz
2. un cuaderno
3. un pizarrón
4. una mochila roja
5. un escritorio
6. un borrador
7. dos computadoras
8. ¿?

TAMBIÉN SE DICE

Mexico is a country with a lot of distinctive regional vocabulary. Many Mexicans would say **calificaciones** instead of **notas**, **gis** instead of **tiza**, and **libreta** instead of **cuaderno**. You may also hear the word **mouse** instead of **ratón** in many countries. This is a loan word from English.

ACTIVIDAD 4

 ¿Qué hay?

Hablar/Escribir ¿Qué hay en el escritorio de Isabel? *(Hint: What's on Isabel's desk?)*

modelo

Hay tres libros.

ciento tres
Etapa 1   **103**

Objective: Transitional practice
Classroom vocabulary

Hay, colors

Answers
1. A: ¿Hay un lápiz?
   B: No, no hay un lápiz.
2. A: ¿Hay un cuaderno?
   B: Sí, hay un cuaderno.
3. A: ¿Hay un pizarrón?
   B: Sí, hay un pizarrón.
4. A: ¿Hay una mochila roja?
   B: Sí, hay una mochila roja.
5. A: ¿Hay un escritorio?
   B: Sí, hay un escritorio.
6. A: ¿Hay un borrador?
   B: Sí, hay un borrador.
7. A: ¿Hay dos computadoras?
   B: No, no hay dos computadoras.
      Hay una computadora.
8. *Answers will vary.*

Objective: Open-ended practice
Classroom vocabulary

Hay, numbers

Answers will vary.

Quick Wrap-up

Write a list of classroom objects on the board. Students give a sentence for each object they have, including its color. For example: **un cuaderno: Tengo un cuaderno rojo.**

Teaching All Students

Extra Help Hold up or point to various classroom items. Ask yes/no and either/or questions to help students build confidence. If students are ready, ask them to name each item as a culminating activity. Then have a volunteer spell the item in Spanish.

Multiple Intelligences

Visual Have students work in pairs. Each student takes a turn setting up his/her desk with a variety of classroom items. The other students gets 30 seconds to look at the items on the desk, turn away, and write everything he/she remembers. Alternate: Have students draw a desk with items (singular and plural) as homework. Pairs then use the drawings for the retention activity.

Block Schedule

"Plan B" On a tray, place 7–10 classroom objects, using different amounts for each. For example: 2 erasers, 3 pieces of chalk, etc. Show the tray to the class for one minute, then hide it. Have students write down what they saw—the object and the amount.

Teaching Resource Options

Print

Block Scheduling Copymasters

Audiovisual

OHT 46 (Quick Start)

Technology

Intrigas y aventuras CD-ROM, Disc 1

Teaching Suggestions
Reinforcing Las materias

• Have students name their classes and give a description. For example: **el español – Es interesante.**
• Name some professions and careers that students can easily recognize and have them match subject areas and professions.

5 Objective: Transitional practice Class subjects in conversation

Answers will vary.

6 Objective: Open-ended practice Class subjects in conversation

Answers will vary.

🔔 Quick Start Review

♲ **Vocabulary**

Use OHT 46 or write on the board: Fill in the missing letters to review computer vocabulary.

1. el r _ _ _ _
2. la i _ _ _ _ _ _ _ _
3. la p _ _ _ _ ll _
4. la c _ _ _ _ _ _ _ _ _ _
5. el t _ _ _ _ _ _

Answers
1. ratón
2. impresora
3. pantalla
4. computadora
5. teclado

ACTIVIDAD 5

¿Qué clases tienes?

Hablar Habla con otro(a) estudiante sobre las clases que tienes este semestre. Cambien de papel. *(Hint: Talk about your classes.)*

modelo

arte | **Tú:** ¿Tienes clases de **arte** este semestre?
Otro(a) estudiante: *Sí, tengo arte.*
o: *No, no tengo arte.*

1. ciencias
2. literatura
3. matemáticas
4. computación
5. música
6. estudios sociales

ACTIVIDAD 6 **¿Cómo son las clases?**

PARA CONVERSAR

STRATEGY: SPEAKING

Develop more than one way of expressing an idea It adds variety and interest to your speech. For example, in addition to saying what something *is*, you can say what it is *not*.

—**¿Cómo es tu clase de historia?**

—**No es interesante.**

Hablar Descríbele tus clases a otro(a) estudiante. Contesta sus preguntas. Cambien de papel. *(Hint: Describe your classes. Answer the questions.)*

modelo

Tú: *¿Qué clases tienes?*

Otro(a) estudiante: *Tengo historia, español, literatura…*

Tú: *¿Cómo es…?*

Otro(a) estudiante: *Es… No es…*

Tú: *¿Qué te gusta estudiar?*

Vocabulario

Las materias

el arte

la historia

las ciencias

el inglés *(Good morning.)*

la computación

la literatura

la educación física

las matemáticas $x+y=z$

el español *(Buenos días.)*

la música

los estudios sociales

For more class subjects, see p. R20.

Here are other words to talk about classes.

fácil *easy*
difícil *difficult, hard*
el examen *test*
la lección *lesson*
la prueba *quiz*

♲ Remember that you can use these adjectives you've learned, too.

aburrido(a)
interesante
bueno(a)
malo(a)

¿Qué clase tiene mucha tarea?

---

104 ciento cuatro
Unidad 2

Classroom Community

Cooperative Learning Divide the class into groups. Each group sits in a circle. Student 1 writes an infinitive on a piece of paper (**buscar**) and passes it to Student 2. Student 2 writes the first form (**Yo busco [mi libro.]**), then passes the paper on to Student 3, who writes the next form. This continues until all forms are complete. The group reviews the complete conjugation.

TPR Have volunteers act out the meanings of the **-ar** verbs. The rest of the class guesses which verb it is.

Paired Activity Have pairs of students write 5 questions using the **-ar** verbs. Then have them exchange questions with another pair. The pairs should then make up answers to each other's questions. For example: –**¿Qué necesitas?** –**Necesito un lápiz.**

GRAMÁTICA

Saying What You Do: Present of -ar Verbs

To talk about things you do, you use the present tense. To form the present tense of a regular verb that ends in -ar,

drop the -ar and add the appropriate ending.

estudiar ← o, as, a, amos, áis, or an

The verb estudiar means *to study*.

yo	estudio	nosotros(as)	estudiamos
tú	estudias	vosotros(as)	estudiáis
usted, él, ella	estudia	ustedes, ellos(as)	estudian

Isabel's mother says:

—¿Necesitas tu cuaderno?
Do you need your notebook?

Vocabulario

Verbs ending in -ar

ayudar (a) *to help*
buscar *to look for, to search*
contestar *to answer*
enseñar *to teach*
entrar (a, en) *to enter*
esperar *to wait for, to expect*

llegar *to arrive*
llevar *to wear, to carry*
mirar *to look at, to watch*
necesitar *to need*
pasar *to happen, to pass, to pass by*
preparar *to prepare*
usar *to use*

¿Qué haces cada día?

ACTIVIDAD 7 Gramática

¿Qué estudian?

Hablar/Escribir Describe lo que estudia cada persona. *(Hint: Describe what each person studies.)*

modelo

Elena:

Elena estudia **historia**.

1. yo: Buenos días.

2. mis amigos: x + y = z

3. nosotros: Good morning.

4. Federico:

5. tú:

6. Juana y Miguel:

7. ella: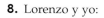

8. Lorenzo y yo:

Teaching Note

You may wish to pre-teach some -ar verbs by having students draw pictures of various activities with the infinitive on the other side before presenting the conjugations.

Teaching Suggestions
Presenting Saying What You Do: Present Tense of Regular -ar Verbs

• Give students two lists: one with conjugated forms of various -ar verbs and one with various subject nouns and pronouns. Have them match the subject nouns/pronouns with the verb forms.

• If students ask, tell them not to be concerned about the two vowels at the end of **estudiar**. Point out that the conjugation does not differ from that of **hablar**.

ACTIVIDAD 7
Objective: Controlled practice Present tense of -ar verbs

Answers
1. Yo estudio español.
2. Mis amigos estudian matemáticas.
3. Nosotros estudiamos inglés.
4. Federico estudia ciencias.
5. Tú estudias estudios sociales.
6. Juana y Miguel estudian arte.
7. Ella estudia música.
8. Lorenzo y yo estudiamos literatura.

Teaching All Students

Native Speakers Have students compare school in their native countries and in the U.S. in terms of schedules, grading, requirements, class load, years of study leading to graduation, second language study, etc.

Multiple Intelligences

Kinesthetic Toss a soft ball to a student as you say an -ar verb infinitive and a subject pronoun (estudiar – yo). The student gives the correct conjugated form, then tosses the ball back to you. Continue with other students.

Naturalist Have students brainstorm a list of scientific elements that stay the same in any language (formulas, chemical notations, Latin plant/animal names, etc.).

Block Schedule

Retention Have students use the verb charts they created in Unit 1 (see TE p. 33) to review **tener** and to practice the new -ar verbs. (For additional activities, see **Block Scheduling Copymasters**.)

Teaching Resource Options

Print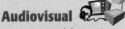

Más práctica Workbook PE, pp. 37–38
Para hispanohablantes Workbook PE,
p. 35–36
Block Scheduling Copymasters
Unit 2 Resource Book
  Más práctica Workbook TE, pp. 5–6
  Para hispanohablantes Workbook
  TE, pp. 11–12
  Information Gap Activities, p. 17
  Audioscript, p. 30
  Audioscript *Para hispanohablantes*,
  p. 30

Audiovisual

OHT 46 (Quick Start)
Audio Program Cassettes 4A, 4B / CD 4
Audio *Para hispanohablantes*
  Cassette 4A / CD 4

Technology

Intrigas y aventuras CD-ROM, Disc 1

ACTIVIDAD 8 Objective: Controlled practice
Using **-ar** verbs in conversation

Answers

Answers will vary.
1. A: Isabel busca su libro. / B: No, no busca su libro. Busca su [pluma].
2. A: Las muchachas esperan a Ricardo. / B: No, no esperan a Ricardo. Esperan a [Isabel].
3. A: Su amigo usa una computadora. / B: No, no usa una computadora. Usa [una calculadora].
4. A: La profesora Díaz enseña historia. / B: No, no enseña historia. Enseña ciencias naturales.
5. A: Los estudiantes sacan malas notas. / B: No, no sacan malas notas. Sacan buenas notas.
6. A: La muchacha mira el libro. / B: No, no mira el libro. Mira [el pizarrón].

ACTIVIDAD 9 Objective: Open-ended practice
Using **-ar** verbs in conversation

Answers
1. A: ¿Hablas mucho? / B: Sí, (No, no) hablo mucho.
2. A: ¿Usas un diccionario? / B: Sí, (No, no) uso un diccionario.
3. A: ¿Escuchas en clase? / B: Sí, (No, no) escucho en clase.
4. A: ¿Preparas la tarea en la computadora? B: Sí, (No, no) preparo la tarea en la computadora.
5. A: ¿Llegas tarde a la clase? / B: Sí, (No, no) llego tarde a la clase.
6. A: ¿Usas una calculadora en la clase de matemáticas? / B: Sí, (No, no) uso una calculadora en la clase de matemáticas.
7. A: ¿Miras el pizarrón? / B: Sí, (No, no) miro el pizarrón.
8. A: ¿Estudias mucho? / B: Sí, (No, no) estudio mucho.

106 Vocabulary/Grammar • UNIDAD 2 Etapa 1

ACTIVIDAD 8  Gramática

¿Qué hacen en la escuela?

Hablar Tu amigo(a) está equivocado(a). Decide lo que hace cada persona en la escuela de Isabel y Ricardo en realidad. Cambien de papel. *(Hint: Your friend is mistaken. Decide what each person is really doing.)*

modelo

Ricardo / estudiar francés (¿?)

Estudiante A: *Ricardo estudia francés.*

Estudiante B: *No, no estudia francés. Estudia inglés.*

1. Isabel / buscar su libro (¿?)
2. las muchachas / esperar a Ricardo (¿?)
3. su amigo / usar una computadora (¿?)
4. la profesora Díaz / enseñar historia (¿?)
5. los estudiantes / sacar malas notas (¿?)
6. la muchacha / mirar el libro (¿?)

■ **MÁS PRÁCTICA** *cuaderno* pp. 37–38
■ **PARA HISPANOHABLANTES** *cuaderno* pp. 35–36

APOYO PARA ESTUDIAR

Verb Conjugations

Using the right ending on a verb is very important. Often verbs are used without subject pronouns (**yo, tú, él, ella, usted,** and so on). To help remember verb endings, practice each **-ar** verb with a partner in a question/answer exercise:

¿Estudias…?	—Sí, estudio…
¿Miran ustedes…?	—Sí, miramos…
¿Enseña ella…?	—Sí, ella enseña…
¿Preparan ellos…?	—Sí, ellos preparan…

ACTIVIDAD 9

¿Qué haces?

Hablar Pregúntale a otro(a) estudiante si hace estas actividades. *(Hint: Ask another student if he or she does these activities.)*

modelo

sacar buenas notas

Tú: *¿Sacas buenas notas?*

Otro(a) estudiante: *Sí, saco buenas notas.*

1. hablar mucho
2. usar un diccionario
3. escuchar en clase
4. preparar la tarea en la computadora
5. llegar tarde a la clase
6. usar una calculadora en la clase de matemáticas
7. mirar el pizarrón
8. estudiar mucho

ACTIVIDAD 10

¿Qué hacen?

Hablar Ahora pregúntale a otro(a) estudiante si él o ella y su amigo(a) hacen las actividades de la Actividad 9. *(Hint: Now ask if he or she and a friend do the activities.)*

modelo

sacar buenas notas

Tú: *¿Tú y tu amigo(a) sacan buenas notas?*

Otro(a) estudiante: *Sí, sacamos buenas notas.*

■ **MÁS COMUNICACIÓN** p. R4

106 ciento seis
Unidad 2

Classroom Community

Group Activity Have students work in groups to create, conduct, and analyze a "how often/activity" survey and report back to the class. For example:

	siempre	mucho	a veces	nunca
estudiar en la biblioteca				
estudiar con amigos				
contestar en la clase de español				

Portfolio Have students write a school journal entry, using adverbs and these expressions: **ayudar al profesor, necesitar, estudiar, usar la calculadora, hablar español, preparar la tarea.** Students may add other expressions.

Rubric A = 13–15 pts. **B** = 10–12 pts. **C** = 7–9 pts. **D** = 4–6 pts. **F** = < 4pts.

Writing criteria	Scale
Adverb use	1 2 3 4 5
Logical sentence order	1 2 3 4 5
Grammar/spelling accuracy	1 2 3 4 5

ACTIVIDAD 11

¡Lógicamente!

Escuchar Escucha la oración e indica la respuesta más lógica.
(Hint: Listen and indicate the most logical response.)

1. a. No estudia.
   b. Ayuda a sus padres.
   c. Necesita un lápiz.

2. a. Tiene un examen mañana.
   b. Habla mucho en clase.
   c. No escucha a la maestra.

3. a. Enseña ciencias naturales.
   b. Necesita estudiar.
   c. Espera a su amigo.

4. a. Usa una calculadora.
   b. No estudia mucho.
   c. Ayuda a su abuelo.

5. a. Necesita estudiar mucho.
   b. Estudia en casa.
   c. Busca su diccionario.

GRAMÁTICA

Expressing Frequency with Adverbs

To talk about how often someone does something, you use expressions of frequency. Expressions of frequency are adverbs or adverbial phrases.

siempre	*always*
todos los días	*every day*
mucho	*often*
a veces	*sometimes*
de vez en cuando	*once in a while*
poco	*a little*
rara vez	*rarely*
nunca	*never*

Ricardo and Isabel might say:
—Estudio **todos los días**.
*I study **every day**.*

—Yo **siempre** estudio.
*I **always** study.*

Different adverbs are placed in different parts of a sentence.

These expressions are usually placed before the **verb**:

siempre	Isabel siempre **llega** tarde a la escuela.
rara vez	Isabel rara vez **habla** español en la clase de inglés.
nunca	Isabel nunca **usa** un diccionario.

These expressions are usually placed after the **verb**:

| **mucho** | Ricardo **estudia** mucho. |
| **poco** | Isabel **habla** poco en la clase. |

Longer phrases can be placed at the beginning or the end of the **sentence**:

todos los días Todos los días Isabel llega tarde.
Isabel llega tarde todos los días.

a veces

de vez en cuando

Teaching All Students

Extra Help Have students write 5 sentences about what they do at school and how often. Then have them exchange papers with a partner for peer correction. Alternate: Make a chart on the board showing **nunca/ a veces/mucho/siempre.** Have students write their names on small notecards. Ask questions and have students post their names under the correct heading. Then have students create their own sentences.

Multiple Intelligences

Interpersonal Working in small groups and using the list of adverbs, have students develop short descriptive sentences for each member of the group. The group descriptions are then presented to the class. You may want to provide students with a beginning, such as: **Los estudiantes de nuestro grupo...**

ACTIVIDAD 10 Objective: Open-ended practice
Using -ar verbs in conversation

Answers
1. A: ¿Tú y tu amigo(a) hablan mucho?
   B: Sí, (No, no) hablamos mucho.
2. A: ¿Tú y tu amigo(a) usan un diccionario?
   B: Sí, (No, no) usamos un diccionario.
3. A: ¿Tú y tu amigo(a) escuchan en clase?
   B: Sí, (No, no) escuchamos en clase.
4. A: ¿Tú y tu amigo(a) preparan la tarea en la computadora?
   B: Sí, (No, no) preparamos la tarea en la computadora.
5. A: ¿Tú y tu amigo(a) llegan tarde a la clase?
   B: Sí, (No, no) llegamos tarde a la clase.
6. A: ¿Tú y tu amigo(a) usan una calculadora en la clase de matemáticas?
   B: Sí, (No, no) usamos una calculadora en la clase de matemáticas.
7. A: ¿Tú y tu amigo(a) miran el pizarrón?
   B: Sí, (No, no) miramos el pizarrón.
8. A: ¿Tú y tu amigo(a) estudian mucho?
   B: Sí, (No, no) estudiamos mucho.

ACTIVIDAD 11 Objective: Transitional practice
Listening comprehension/-ar verbs

Answers (See script, p. 95D.)
1. b   2. a   3. a   4. a   5. a

🔔 Quick Start Review

🔄 **-ar** verbs
Use OHT 46 or write on the board:
Make a list of 5 **-ar** verb infinitives. Then write a sentence using each one.

Answers *See p. 95D.*

Teaching Suggestions
Reinforcing Expressing Frequency with Adverbs

Make 3 columns on the board: subject nouns/pronouns; verb infinitives; adverbs. Have students suggest 6–8 items for each column. Then have them form sentences using one word from each column.

Block Schedule

Peer Teaching Assign each student a "pet verb." Students are responsible for knowing the conjugation of their verbs. Whenever a classmate is having trouble with a verb, the "pet owner" is responsible for helping out. (For additional activities, see **Block Scheduling Copymasters.**)

Teaching Resource Options

Print

Más práctica Workbook PE, pp. 39–40
Para hispanohablantes Workbook
PE, pp. 37–38
Block Scheduling Copymasters
Unit 2 Resource Book
  Más práctica Workbook TE,
    pp. 7–8
  Para hispanohablantes Workbook
    TE, pp. 13–14

Audiovisual

OHT 47 (Quick Start)

Technology

Intrigas y aventuras CD-ROM, Disc 1

Objective: Controlled practice
Using adverbs of frequency

Answers
1. Felipe
2. María
3. María
4. Felipe
5. Felipe
6. Felipe
7. María
8. Felipe

Objective: Transitional practice
Using adverbs of frequency in
conversation

Answers will vary.

Objective: Open-ended practice
Using adverbs of frequency

Answers will vary.

Quick Wrap-up

Based on **Actividad 13**, ask various
students to make true or false
statements to describe themselves.
The class determines if the statement
is true or false.

12 **Gramática**

Los estudiantes diferentes

Leer María es una buena
estudiante. Felipe no es un
buen estudiante. Lee las
oraciones y explica quién dice
probablemente cada una. *(Hint:
Explain if María or Felipe most likely says
each of these sentences.)*

modelo

Estudio mucho.	María

1. Nunca escucho en clase.
2. Rara vez saco malas notas.
3. Preparo mi tarea todos los días.
4. Estudio poco para los exámenes.
5. A veces entro en la clase tarde.
6. Miro poco el pizarrón.
7. Siempre estudio para las pruebas.
8. Estudio de vez en cuando.

MÁS PRÁCTICA *cuaderno* p. 39

PARA HISPANOHABLANTES
cuaderno p. 37

13

¿Siempre o nunca?

Hablar Pregúntale a otro(a) estudiante si hace mucho estas
actividades. *(Hint: Ask another student if he or she does these activities often.)*

modelo

Tú: *¿Usas mucho la computadora?*

Otro(a) estudiante: *Sí, uso la computadora todos los días.*

1. usar la computadora
2. llegar tarde a la escuela
3. estudiar español
4. escuchar a la maestra
5. hablar en clase
6. preparar tu tarea en la computadora
7. sacar una buena nota
8. ayudar a tus amigos
9. necesitar una calculadora

siempre
todos los días
mucho
a veces
de vez en cuando
poco
rara vez
nunca

14

El estudiante ideal

Hablar/Escribir Trabaja en un
grupo de tres para hacer un
póster. Describe al estudiante
ideal. Usa las expresiones
**siempre, todos los días, mucho,
a veces, de vez en cuando,
poco, rara vez, nunca.** *(Hint: Work
in groups of three to make a poster that
describes the ideal student. Use expressions
of frequency.)*

> *Un estudiante ideal*
>
> *Prepara su tarea
> todos los días.
> Nunca llega tarde
> a clase.*

Classroom Community

Peer Teaching Have students write down all the
classes they are taking and then write what they have
to do for those classes this week. Students then
exchange and check papers for spelling, verb forms,
etc. Have students report to the class one or two items
another student has to do.

Learning Scenario Have students imagine that a
new student is coming into their class in a few days.

In groups of 2–3, students write to the new student,
describing the school and particularly the Spanish class.
Ask volunteers to read their letters to the class.

Rubric A = 5 pts. B = 4 pts. C = 3 pts. D = 2 pts. F = < 2pts.

Accurate use of verbs, adjectives, adverbs	5 pts.
Some errors in verbs, limited adj., limited adv.	4 pts.
Some errors in verbs, limited adj., no adv.	3 pts.
Many errors in verbs, little use of adj. and adv.	2 pts.

GRAMÁTICA

Expressing Obligation with hay que and tener que

To talk about things someone must do, you can use two different phrases that express obligation.

- Use the impersonal phrase

  hay que + *infinitive*

  if there is **no specific subject**.

- Use a form of **tener** in the phrase

  tener que + *infinitive*

  if there is a **specific subject**.

—Hay que **conectar** el ratón al teclado.
You have to (one must) **connect** *the mouse to the keyboard.*

—Tengo que **sacar** una buena nota.
I have to **get** *a good grade.*

ACTIVIDAD 15 Gramática

Las necesidades

Hablar/Escribir Explica lo que los amigos de Ricardo tienen que hacer hoy. Di si tú tienes que hacer las mismas cosas. *(Hint: Explain what Ricardo's friends have to do and say if you have to do these things too.)*

modelo

Juan / estudiar

Juan tiene que **estudiar.** Yo (no) tengo que estudiar.

1. Elena / esperar a su hermano
2. Ana y Luis / usar la computadora
3. Antonio / preparar su tarea para mañana
4. Isabel y María / ayudar a su abuela
5. Andrés / hablar con el maestro
6. Felipe y yo / correr

MÁS PRÁCTICA *cuaderno p. 40*

PARA HISPANOHABLANTES *cuaderno p. 38*

NOTA CULTURAL

La Universidad Autónoma de México, founded in 1551, is the oldest university in the Americas. Its modern campus covers almost three square miles.

ciento nueve
Etapa 1
109

Teaching All Students

Extra Help Ask simple yes/no questions using **hay que, tener que,** and **-ar** verbs. For example, ¿Hay que hablar español en la clase de español? ¿Tenemos que estudiar el vocabulario todos los días?

Multiple Intelligences

Kinesthetic Have students act out the two types of students described in **Actividad 12.**

Logical Ask students to make two lists: things a good student does/doesn't do at school and at home and things a poor student does/doesn't do at school and at home.

Quick Start Review

♻ Adverbs and **-ar** verbs

Use OHT 47 or write on the board: Write 5 completions to this sentence:

Los buenos estudiantes...

Answers *See p. 95D.*

Teaching Suggestions
Presenting Expressing Obligation with hay que and tener que

- Explain that **hay que** never changes, but that **tener que** changes depending on who the subject is.
- Have students write original sentences using both **hay que** and **tener que** to be sure they understand the difference.

ACTIVIDAD 15 Objective: Controlled practice
Hay que and tener que

Answers

1. Elena tiene que esperar a su hermano.
2. Ana y Luis tienen que usar la computadora.
3. Antonio tiene que preparar su tarea para mañana.
4. Isabel y María tienen que ayudar a su abuela.
5. Andrés tiene que hablar con el maestro.
6. Felipe y yo tenemos que correr.

Culture Highlight

● **LA UNIVERSIDAD AUTÓNOMA DE MÉXICO** The university is traditionally referred to as "UNAM." The exterior of its library (pictured here) is the distinctive Orozco mural, designed by Juan O'Gorman. This striking building is often used as a symbol of the university.

Enrollment at UNAM is over 100,000. Due to the large number of students there is a day session of classes and an evening session.

Block Schedule

Change of Pace Have students work in pairs and interview each other. They should ask and answer questions about what they do/have to do in school. Then have them present each other to the class. (For additional activities, see **Block Scheduling Copymasters.**)

Teaching Resource Options

Print 📖

Block Scheduling Copymasters
Unit 2 Resource Book
 Information Gap Activities,
  pp. 18–19
 Audioscript, p. 30
 Audioscript *Para hispanohablantes,*
  p. 30

Audiovisual 📼

Audio Program Cassettes 4A, 4B / CD 4
Audio *Para hispanohablantes*
 Cassette 4A / CD 4

Technology 💻

Intrigas y aventuras CD-ROM, Disc 1

 Objective: Transitional practice
16 Hay que

Answers will vary.

Alternate: You may wish to substitute
another class subject for math, such as art
or physical education.

 Objective: Open-ended practice
17 Tener que in conversation

Answers will vary.

 Objective: Controlled practice
18 El/La before titles

Answers
1. la
2. —
3. —
4. La

Buenas notas...

Hablar/Escribir ¿Qué hay que hacer para sacar
buenas notas en la clase de matemáticas?
Menciona un mínimo de cuatro cosas. *(Hint:
Mention at least four things one must do to get a good math grade.)*

> **modelo**
>
> *Hay que escuchar en clase.*

usar   practicar

preparar   escuchar

¿Qué tienes que hacer?

Hablar/Escribir Pregúntales a cinco estudiantes
qué tienen que hacer después de clases. Da un
resumen. *(Hint: Ask five students what they have to do after
classes. Give a summary.)*

> **modelo**
>
> **Tú:** *José, ¿qué tienes que hacer después de clases hoy?*
> **José:** *Tengo que estudiar.*
> **Resumen:** *Tres estudiantes tienen que estudiar.*

Nombre	Tiene que...
José	estudiar
1.	
2.	

¡Pobre Isabel!

Leer Lee sobre Isabel y su profesora de ciencias
naturales. Explica si **el** o **la** es necesario. *(Hint: Read
about Isabel and her science teacher. Explain if **el** or **la** is necessary.)*

Nota

Use **el** and **la** before titles like **profesor(a)** and **señor(a)**
when talking *about* someone.

—¡Tengo que hablar con *la* **profesora Díaz**!

***El* señor Martínez** es el profesor de inglés.

Do not use articles when talking *to* someone.

—No tengo mi tarea, **profesora Díaz.**

Isabel habla con __1__ profesora Díaz, su
profesora de ciencias naturales.

«Buenos días, __2__ profesora Díaz. ¿Cómo está
usted hoy?»

«Muy bien, Isabel, ¿y tú?»

«Pues, no estoy muy bien, __3__ profesora. No
tengo mi tarea para hoy.»

__4__ profesora Díaz no está muy feliz.

«Isabel, para sacar una buena nota, ¡hay que
preparar la tarea todos los días!»

NOTA CULTURAL

Pluma is the word for *feather*. It has come to
mean *pen* because birds' feathers were once used
with ink to serve as pens. **Bolígrafo** is a modern word
for *pen*. Technically **bolígrafo,** or **boli,** refers
to a ball-point pen, but **pluma** is also used.

Classroom Community

Paired Activity On index cards, one word per card,
have students write down 15 words in 3 categories:
5 verbs, 5 classroom objects, 5 adverbs. One student
mixes the cards, then holds them in a fan. The other
student picks one card, says the word, gives its
category, and uses it in a sentence. Partners then switch
and continue.

Group Activity Each person in the group presents
himself/herself as a classroom object, a class subject, or
a verb by acting it out or describing it. The other
students guess what the word is.

La clase de tu amiga

Escuchar Una amiga describe su clase de español. Escucha la descripción. Luego, contesta las preguntas. *(Hint: Listen to a friend describe her Spanish class, and then answer the questions.)*

1. La clase de español es
   _____.
   a. fácil y divertida
   b. difícil pero interesante
   c. fácil pero aburrida

2. La profesora de la clase es
   de _____.
   a. España
   b. México
   c. Estados Unidos

3. La señorita Casas habla
   español en clase _____.
   a. rara vez
   b. de vez en cuando
   c. todos los días

4. Tu amiga tiene que _____
   cuando la señorita Casas
   habla.
   a. escribir
   b. escuchar
   c. estudiar

5. Tiene que preparar su
   tarea todos los días para
   _____.
   a. practicar mucho
   b. sacar una buena nota
   c. usar la computadora

Mi clase favorita es...

Escribir Escribe un párrafo sobre tu clase favorita y qué tienes que hacer para sacar una buena nota. Luego, léele tu párrafo a la clase. *(Hint: Write about your favorite class and what you have to do to get a good grade. Read your paragraph to the class.)*

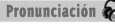

Mi clase favorita es historia. Me gusta escuchar a la maestra. Ella es la señorita Sánchez. Enseña bien. Habla mucho y es muy interesante. Todos los días escuchamos muy bien. Hay que estudiar para sacar una buena nota. Tengo que preparar la tarea todos los días. Siempre preparo la tarea con la computadora.

MÁS COMUNICACIÓN p. R4

Pronunciación

Trabalenguas

Pronunciación de la y y la ll The **ll** and **y** have the same sounds in Spanish. At the beginning and middle of words they sound like the *y* in the English word *yes*. At the end of a word the **y** sounds like the Spanish **i**, as in **muy**. Ll does not occur at the end of words. To practice these sounds, say the tongue twisters.

Yolanda ya vive en una casa amarilla.

¿Cómo se llama la llama llorona?

ciento once
Etapa 1

III

 Objective: Transitional practice
Listening comprehension/vocabulary,
adverbs, **tener que**

Answers (See script, p. 95D.)
1. b
2. a
3. c
4. b
5. b

Objective: Open-ended practice
Vocabulary, adverbs, **hay que,
tener que** in writing

Answers will vary.

Dictation

After students have read the tongue twisters in the **Pronunciación,** have them close their books. Dictate the tongue twisters in segments while students write them.

Quick Wrap-up

Have students list as many words as they can recall that have the letters **y** or **ll.** Tell them to refer back to the Preliminary Unit and Unit 1 for additional words. If time permits, you may wish to use an activity from the **Más comunicación** section.

Teaching All Students

Extra Help Have students read the items in **Actividad 19** before using it as a listening comprehension exercise.

Challenge Ask students if they know any additional **trabalenguas** that would help the class practice vowel sounds, or have students contact a native speaker to ask for another **trabalenguas**.

Multiple Intelligences

Interpersonal After completing **Actividad 18,** have pairs of students prepare short skits of conversing with a favorite teacher in the hallway.

Visual Ask students to draw a picture of the ideal classroom. They should label the objects. In addition, they should draw the ideal student and describe what he/she is wearing.

Block Schedule

Change of Pace Group students together who chose the same favorite course in **Actividad 20.** Have them create a commercial for the course, as if they were promoting it for incoming students. (For additional activities, see **Block Scheduling Copymasters.**)

🔔 Quick Start Review

♻ Vocabulary review

Use OHT 47 or write on the board:
Write at least 5 words in each category:
• verbos
• materias
• objetos de la clase
• adverbios
Answers *See p. 95D.*

Teaching Suggestions

• **Prereading** Review the
  ¿Comprendiste? questions before
  reading so that students will know
  what information to look for.

• **Strategy: Use context clues** Have
  students scan the paragraph on
  p. 112. Then have students look at
  the glossed words to try to guess
  their meanings through context clues.

• **Reading** Ask students to skim the
  reading first. Then have volunteers
  read it aloud as the others follow
  along in their textbooks.

• **Post-reading** Have pairs of
  students work together to tailor the
  survey to their own class, another
  Spanish class, or the school. Each
  student then compiles the survey as
  Ricardo did.

Cross Cultural Connections

Strategy Ask students to use a Venn
diagram to compare and contrast the list
of courses to what is offered at your school.

En voces
LECTURA

PARA LEER
STRATEGY: READING

Use context clues You can use the
context to guess the meaning of
unfamiliar words. Context
includes what is written before
and after the word. Pictures
often contribute to the context
too. What do you think the
highlighted words mean?

• Una encuesta **escolar**
• El papel sale de la impresora
  con los **resultados** de la
  encuesta.

Una encuesta[1] escolar

Ricardo tiene que hacer una encuesta en la escuela.
Él prepara una lista de preguntas. Ricardo habla con los
otros estudiantes y escribe sus respuestas en un cuaderno.
En casa él escribe las respuestas en la computadora. Con
una calculadora suma[2] el total de respuestas. El papel
sale[3] de la impresora con los resultados de la encuesta.
Ricardo usa los resultados de la encuesta para hacer un
proyecto en la clase de matemáticas.

---

[1] survey   [2] adds   [3] comes out

112 ciento doce
Unidad 2

Classroom Community

Storytelling In small groups, have students retell
Ricardo's story from his point of view. Students reread
the sentences on p. 112, but this time they use the **yo**
form of the verbs. They can also add imagined details.

Portfolio Have students choose one of the students
in the picture on p. 112 and write a complete
description. Included should be a physical description,
clothing, personality, class schedule, favorite class, etc.

Rubric **A** = 13–15 pts. **B** = 10–12 pts. **C** = 7–9 pts. **D** = 4–6 pts. **F** = < 4pts.

Writing criteria	Scale
Vocabulary use	1 2 3 4 5
Logical sentence order	1 2 3 4 5
Grammar/spelling accuracy	1 2 3 4 5

Mi clase favorita es...

Soy estudiante de la escuela secundaria _____.

Tengo clases de...
- ❑ arte
- ❑ ciencias
- ❑ computación
- ❑ educación física
- ❑ inglés
- ❑ estudios sociales
- ❑ historia
- ❑ literatura
- ❑ matemáticas
- ❑ música

Tengo mucha tarea en la clase de _____

Saco una buena nota en la clase de _____

Siempre hablo en la clase de _____ .

Nunca hablo en la clase de _____ .

Siempre escucho en la clase de _____

Nunca escucho en la clase de _____

Mi clase más difícil es _____ .

Mi clase más fácil es _____ .

Mi clase favorita es _____

Los resultados
Una encuesta a 50 estudiantes

Clase con más tarea: matemáticas
(25 estudiantes)

Los estudiantes sacan más buenas notas en la clase de: música
(35 estudiantes)

Los estudiantes hablan más en la clase de: literatura
(30 estudiantes)

Los estudiantes nunca hablan en la clase de: inglés
(25 estudiantes)

Los estudiantes escuchan más en la clase de: ciencias
(40 estudiantes)

Los estudiantes nunca escuchan en la clase de: historia
(20 estudiantes)

La clase más difícil es: ciencias
(35 estudiantes)

La clase más fácil es: arte
(45 estudiantes)

La clase favorita es: literatura
(30 estudiantes)

¿Comprendiste?
1. ¿Qué tiene que hacer Ricardo?
2. ¿Qué usa Ricardo para escribir la encuesta?
3. ¿Los estudiantes hablan mucho o poco en la clase de inglés?
4. ¿Es difícil la clase de música o arte en la escuela de Ricardo?
5. ¿Qué clase es la clase favorita de los estudiantes?

¿Qué piensas?

Escribe tus respuestas para la encuesta de Ricardo.

ciento trece
Etapa 1

113

Culture Highlights

● **LA ESCUELA** In Mexico, public school is mandatory until the age of 14. Those who continue beyond this age take college preparatory classes for three more years before applying to the university.

Many students attend private schools, which are often Roman Catholic. It is common in high school for students to attend an all boys or all girls school. At most of these schools students wear uniforms every day.

Interdisciplinary Connection

Mathematics Have students call on their math skills to compile a percentage of students' favorite classes. Use the results from the survey created in the Post-reading activity on TE p. 112. This is also excellent practice for reviewing numbers. For example: 25 students total answered the survey and 5 said that art is their favorite subject: $5 \div 25 = .20 = 20\%$

¿Comprendiste?

Answers
1. Tiene que hacer una encuesta escolar.
2. Usa una computadora.
3. Hablan poco.
4. No, son fáciles.
5. Literatura.

Block Schedule

Change of Pace Have students form groups according to their favorite class. They should brainstorm a list of adjectives or phrases in Spanish describing what they like about the particular subject. On a piece of construction paper, have students write **Mi clase favorita: español. ¿Por qué?: es interesante, ...** Post students' work on class bulletin board.

Teaching All Students

Extra Help Check students' comprehension by asking yes/no questions. For example: **¿Tiene que hacer Ricardo una encuesta escolar? ¿Escribe su encuesta en el pizarrón?**

Multiple Intelligences

Interpersonal Have students choose a different partner than the one with whom they created their survey. Have students interview each other using their surveys in order to practice answering questions orally. As the interviewee answers each question, the interviewer should write down his/her response. Students then reverse roles.

Teaching Resource Options

Print

Para hispanohablantes Workbook PE,
pp. 39–40

Unit 2 Resource Book
Para hispanohablantes Workbook
TE, pp. 15–16
Information Gap Activities, p. 20
Family Involvement, pp. 21–22
Multiple Choice Test Questions,
pp. 170–179

Audiovisual

OHT 48 (Quick Start)
Audio Program Testing Cassette T1 /
CD T1

Technology

Electronic Teacher Tools/Test
Generator
Intrigas y aventuras CD-ROM, Disc 1

Quick Start Review

🔄 **-ar** verbs

Use OHT 48 or write on the board:
Complete the following conjugations:

1. tú / buscar
2. nosotros / estudiar
3. el profesor / enseñar
4. yo / preparar
5. usted / mirar

Answers
1. tú buscas
2. nosotros estudiamos
3. el profesor enseña
4. yo preparo
5. usted mira

Teaching Suggestions
What Have Students Learned?

Point out the Objectives at the top of
the page. Ask students what they most
need to review, and how they plan to
review and practice (making flashcards,
studying with a partner in a question/
answer session, etc.).

ETAPA 1

Now you can...

• describe classes
and classroom
objects.

To review

• vocabulary for
classroom objects,
see p. 98.

• the present tense
of regular **-ar**
verbs, see p. 105.

OBJECTIVES

• Describe classes and
classroom objects
• Say how often you do
something
• Discuss obligations

En uso

REPASO Y MÁS COMUNICACIÓN

ACTIVIDAD 1 En la clase de matemáticas

Mira el dibujo de la clase y corrige las oraciones. *(Hint: Correct the statements to match the drawing.)*

modelo

Hay siete libros en el escritorio de la profesora.
Hay cinco libros en el escritorio de la profesora.

1. Tres muchachas hablan y no escuchan a la profesora.
2. Hay tres cuadernos en el escritorio de la profesora.
3. La profesora usa una calculadora.
4. Hay tres computadoras y dos impresoras.
5. No hay borradores.
6. Las computadoras no tienen ratones.
7. Hay tres pizarrones en la clase.
8. Todos los estudiantes tienen lápices.

114 ciento catorce
Unidad 2

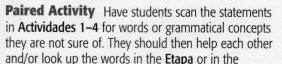

Classroom Community

Paired Activity Have students scan the statements
in **Actividades 1–4** for words or grammatical concepts
they are not sure of. They should then help each other
and/or look up the words in the **Etapa** or in the
glossary.

Group Activity Have students draw a picture of
your classroom and write 8 sentences describing it.
Some of the statements should contain factual errors!
Then have students exchange papers with another
group and correct the factual errors. Variations:
(1) Students draw another classroom and write
sentences describing it. (2) Students write a shopping
list of school supplies.

Now you can...
- describe classes.
- say how often you do something.

To review
- **-ar** verbs, see p. 105.
- adverbs of frequency, see p. 107.

ACTIVIDAD 2 ¿Cómo es cada clase?

Una amiga de Isabel describe las acciones de unos estudiantes. ¿Cómo es cada clase que describe? Escoge la opción apropiada.
(Hint: Choose the option that describes each class.)

1. Nosotros siempre escuchamos en la clase de música.
2. Isabel estudia mucho para la clase de inglés.
3. Isabel y Ricardo sacan buenas notas en la clase de arte.
4. Muchos estudiantes llegan tarde a la clase de matemáticas.

a. Es difícil.
b. Es fácil.
c. Es interesante.
d. Es aburrida.

Now you can...
- say how often you do something.

To review
- the present tense of regular **-ar** verbs, see p. 105.
- adverbs of frequency, see p. 107.

ACTIVIDAD 3 ¡Unos estudiantes excelentes!

Todos estos estudiantes son excelentes. ¿Por qué? *(Hint: Tell why they are excellent.)*

modelo

nosotros / preparar la tarea: ¿siempre o nunca?
Nosotros siempre preparamos la tarea.

1. Isabel y Ricardo / llegar tarde: ¿todos los días o rara vez?
2. tú / sacar buenas notas: ¿siempre o nunca?
3. Alma / ayudar a sus amigos: ¿mucho o poco?
4. yo / escuchar al profesor: ¿de vez en cuando o todos los días?
5. Arturo y yo / hablar inglés en la clase de español: ¿a veces o nunca?
6. ellas / mirar el pizarrón: ¿mucho o poco?

Now you can...
- discuss obligations.

To review
- **tener que**, see p. 109.

ACTIVIDAD 4 Una fiesta pequeña

Explica por qué estas personas no están en la fiesta de Alberto.
(Hint: Tell why these people aren't at Alberto's party.)

modelo

Sonia: habla con su madre   ***Sonia** tiene que **hablar con su madre**.*

1. ustedes: estudian
2. yo: preparo la tarea
3. mis amigos y yo: trabajamos
4. tú: esperas a tus padres
5. Samuel: ayuda a su hermano
6. Soledad y Raúl: usan la computadora

ciente quince | **115**
Etapa 1

Answers

1. Dos muchachos hablan y no escuchan a la profesora.
2. Hay dos cuadernos en el escritorio de la profesora.
3. La profesora usa tiza. *o:* Un estudiante usa una calculadora.
4. Hay una computadora y no hay impresora.
5. Hay dos borradores.
6. La computadora tiene ratón. *o:* La computadora no tiene teclado (impresora).
7. Hay un pizarrón en la clase.
8. Dos estudiantes tienen lápices.

Answers

1. c
2. a
3. b
4. d

Answers

1. Isabel y Ricardo rara vez llegan tarde.
2. Tú siempre sacas buenas notas.
3. Alma ayuda mucho a sus amigos.
4. Yo escucho al profesor todos los días.
5. Arturo y yo nunca hablamos inglés en la clase de español.
6. Ellas miran mucho el pizarrón.

Alternate: Have students rewrite the sentences to describe themselves.

Answers

1. Ustedes tienen que estudiar.
2. Yo tengo que preparar la tarea.
3. Mis amigos y yo tenemos que trabajar.
4. Tú tienes que esperar a tus padres.
5. Samuel tiene que ayudar a su hermano.
6. Soledad y Raúl tienen que usar la computadora.

■ Block Schedule

Retention Have students document **Etapa 1** by creating a study sheet. It can include vocabulary lists, verb charts, sample sentences, and grammatical hints. These study sheets can be used again for review for the unit test, a midterm exam, and a final exam. It can also be used as a reference for games and projects. Students may also use the Bookmarks from their workbooks to focus review.

Teaching All Students

Extra Help Ask students to list 5 things they have to do today. Then they should add a statement saying if this is difficult/easy, good/bad, boring/interesting. Stress the use of **tener que** and **hay que** in addition to the adjectives.

Multiple Intelligences

Intrapersonal Have students write about a time when they had to turn down invitations to everything because they had too much to do.

Teaching Resource Options

Print

Unit 2 Resource Book
Cooperative Quizzes, pp. 33–34
Etapa Exam, Forms A and B,
 pp. 35–44
Para hispanohablantes **Etapa Exam,**
 pp. 45–49
Portfolio Assessment, pp. 50–51
Multiple Choice Test Questions,
 pp. 170–178

Audiovisual

OHT 48 (Quick Start)
Audio Program Testing Cassette T1 /
 CD T1

Technology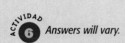

Electronic Teacher Tools/Test
 Generator
www.mcdougallittell.com

ACTIVIDAD 5

Rubric: Speaking

Criteria	Scale	
Sentence structure	1 2 3	A = 11–12 pts.
Vocabulary use	1 2 3	B = 9–10 pts.
Originality	1 2 3	C = 7–8 pts.
Fluency	1 2 3	D = 4–6 pts.
		F = < 4 pts.

ACTIVIDAD 6 *Answers will vary.*

ACTIVIDAD 7 **En tu propia voz**

Rubric: Writing

Criteria	Scale	
Vocabulary use	1 2 3 4 5	A = 14–15 pts.
Accuracy	1 2 3 4 5	B = 12–13 pts.
Creativity, appearance	1 2 3 4 5	C = 10–11 pts.
		D = 8–9 pts.
		F = < 8 pts.

Interdisciplinary Connection

ESL If your school has Spanish-speaking
students in ESL classes, have your students
ask them the survey questions in Spanish.
Then have the ESL students ask your
students the questions in English. This
school/community connection will help
students see the possibilities of further
study of Spanish.

ACTIVIDAD 5 **¿Cómo son tus clases?**

PARA CONVERSAR
STRATEGY: SPEAKING

Expand the conversation How do you keep a
conversation going? Be interested. Find out
more about your partner by asking either/or
questions to prompt him or her when words
don't come. Also, it's hard to keep a
conversation going with just **sí** or **no**
answers. So, say more rather than less.

¿Te gusta… o…?

¿Cómo es…?

Prepara cinco preguntas para hablar con otro(a)
estudiante sobre sus clases. *(Hint: Prepare five questions
to talk with another student about classes.)*

modelo

Tú: *¿Tienes clase de historia?*
Otro(a) estudiante: *Sí, tengo clase de historia.*
Tú: *¿Cómo es la clase?*
Otro(a) estudiante: *Es buena. El profesor enseña bien…*

ACTIVIDAD 6 **Una visita a la clase**

Imagínate que tus compañeros son nuevos
estudiantes. Háblales de ocho cosas que hay
en la clase y de cinco actividades que hacen
los estudiantes. *(Hint: Give new students a "tour" of the
class, pointing out items and discussing activities.)*

modelo

En la clase hay veinte escritorios y un pizarrón…
Los estudiantes estudian y…

ACTIVIDAD 7 **En tu propia voz**

ESCRITURA Describe tu clase favorita con
muchos detalles. Incluye información sobre las
cosas que hay en la clase y las actividades que
hacen los estudiantes. *(Hint: Describe your favorite class.)*

Mi clase favorita es…
Yo a veces…
En la clase hay…
El maestro siempre…
Todos los días hay que…
Nosotros nunca…
La maestra se llama…
Los estudiantes siempre…

CONEXIONES

Las matemáticas Remember Ricardo's survey that polled
students about their classes? Use his survey to interview
students who are studying Spanish at your school.
Interview twenty students to find out which class they
like best, which class they find hardest, and so on.
Summarize your results. Create a pie chart for each
question, showing the percentage of students that voted
for each class named. Compare your survey with Ricardo's.

Clase favorita
Resultados de 20 estudiantes

historia	8
literatura	4
español	4
arte	2
música	2

Classroom Community

TPR Assign a vocabulary word from the **Repaso de
vocabulario** "Classroom Activities and "Actions" lists to
each student. Have students act out the meaning of the
words while the class determines what is being shown.

Game In groups of 4–6, have one student write a
sentence using vocabulary from the **Repaso de
vocabulario.** (The teacher should check the accuracy of
the sentence.) The student hides the paper and then
whispers the sentence to a second student. That
student whispers the sentence to a third student, and
so on. The last student says the sentence out loud. The
group compares the final sentence to the original one.

En resumen
REPASO DE VOCABULARIO

DESCRIBING CLASSES

At School

la clase	class, classroom
la escuela	school
el examen	test
la lección	lesson
la prueba	quiz
la tarea	homework

School Subjects

el arte	art
las ciencias	science
la computación	computer science
la educación física	physical education
el español	Spanish
los estudios sociales	social studies
la historia	history
el inglés	English
la literatura	literature
las matemáticas	mathematics
la materia	subject
la música	music

Classroom Activities

enseñar	to teach
escuchar	to listen (to)
estudiar	to study
hablar	to talk, to speak
mirar	to watch, to look at
preparar	to prepare
sacar una buena nota	to get a good grade

DESCRIBING CLASS OBJECTS

el borrador	eraser
la calculadora	calculator
el cuaderno	notebook
el diccionario	dictionary
el escritorio	desk
el lápiz	pencil
el libro	book
la mochila	backpack
el papel	paper
el pizarrón	chalkboard
la pluma	pen
la tiza	chalk

At the Computer

la computadora	computer
la impresora	printer
la pantalla	screen
el ratón	mouse
el teclado	keyboard

SAYING HOW OFTEN

a veces	sometimes
de vez en cuando	once in a while
mucho	often
nunca	never
poco	a little
rara vez	rarely
siempre	always
todos los días	every day

DISCUSSING OBLIGATIONS

hay que	one has to, one must
tener que	to have to

Actions

ayudar (a)	to help
buscar	to look for, to search
contestar	to answer
entrar (a, en)	to enter
esperar	to wait for, to expect
llegar	to arrive
llevar	to wear, to carry
necesitar	to need
pasar	to happen, to pass, to pass by
usar	to use

OTHER WORDS AND PHRASES

¡Ahora mismo!	Right now!
Con razón.	That's why.
difícil	difficult, hard
fácil	easy
mismo(a)	same
pronto	soon
la razón	reason
tarde	late

Juego

Jorge tiene que preparar la tarea de cada clase. ¿En qué materias tiene tarea?

1. Usa una calculadora.

2. Estudia un libro sobre computadoras.

3. Busca una palabra en inglés en su diccionario.

4. Canta.

Teaching All Students

Extra Help Have students study the first category of words in the **Repaso de vocabulario** for 1 minute. Then tell them to close their books and write down as many words as they can remember in 2 minutes. They should then open their books and check their work. Continue with the other categories.

Multiple Intelligences

Logical/Mathematical Have students mind map the vocabulary by re-dividing the words into 7 groups instead of 5. Students should be creative, but should be sure the words in each group have something in common.

Planning Guide CLASSROOM MANAGEMENT

OBJECTIVES

Communication
- Talk about schedules *pp. 120–121*
- Ask and tell time *pp. 120–121, 122–123*
- Ask questions *pp. 122–123*
- Say where you are going *pp. 122–123*
- Request food *pp. 134–135*

Grammar
- Use the verb **ir** *pp. 126–127*
- Use phrases to tell time *pp. 128–129*
- Use the verb **estar** *pp. 130–131*
- Use interrogative words *pp. 131–133*

Pronunciation
- Pronunciation of **h** and **j** *p. 133*
- Dictation *TE p. 133*

Culture
- Regional vocabulary *pp. 124, 129*
- Public high schools in Mexico City *p. 127*
- Olympic Stadium in Mexico City *p. 132*
- Snack foods in Mexico *pp. 134–135*

♻ **Recycling**
- Using **-ar** verbs *p. 124*
- Days of the week *p. 127*

STRATEGIES

Listening Strategies
- Listen for the main idea *pp. 122–123*

Speaking Strategies
- Take risks *p. 129*
- Help your partner *p. 138*

Reading Strategies
- Scan *p. 134*

Writing Strategies
- When writing questions, brainstorm what you might want to know *p. 138*

Connecting Cultures Strategies
- Recognize regional vocabulary *pp. 124, 129*
- Learn about public high schools in Mexico *p. 127*
- Learn about Olympic Stadium *p. 132*
- Connect and compare what you know about snack foods in your community to help you learn about snack foods in a new community *pp. 134–135*

PROGRAM RESOURCES

 Print
- *Más práctica* Workbook PE, *pp. 41–48*
- Block Scheduling Copymasters, *pp. 41–48*
- Unit 2 Resource Book
  Más práctica Workbook TE, *pp. 52–59*
  Para hispanohablantes Workbook TE, *pp. 60–67*
- Information Gap Activities *pp. 68–71*
- Family Involvement *pp. 72–73*
- Video Activities *pp. 74–76*
- Videoscript *pp. 77–79*
- Audioscript *pp. 80–83*
- Assessment Program, Unit 2 Etapa 2 *pp. 84–102; 170–178*
- Answer Keys *pp. 179–194*

 Audiovisual
- **Audio Program** Cassettes 5A, 5B / CD 5
- *Canciones* Cassette / CD
- **Video Program** Videotape 2 / Videodisc 1B
- **Overhead Transparencies** M1–M5; 47; 49–58

 Technology
- Electronic Teacher Tools/Test Generator
- *Intrigas y aventuras* CD-ROM, Disc 1
- www.mcdougallittell.com

 **Assessment Program Options**
- **Cooperative Quizzes** (Unit 2 Resource Book)
- **Etapa Exam** Forms A and B (Unit 2 Resource Book)
- *Para hispanohablantes* **Etapa Exam** (Unit 2 Resource Book)
- **Portfolio Assessment** (Unit 2 Resource Book)
- **Multiple Choice Test Questions** (Unit 2 Resource Book)
- **Audio Program** Testing Cassette T1 / CD T1
- **Electronic Teacher Tools/Test Generator**

Native Speakers
- *Para hispanohablantes* Workbook PE, *pp. 41–48*
- *Para hispanohablantes* Workbook TE (Unit 2 Resource Book)
- *Para hispanohablantes* Etapa Exam (Unit 2 Resource Book)
- Audio *Para hispanohablantes* Cassettes 5A, 5B, T1 / CD 5, T1
- Audioscript *Para hispanohablantes* (Unit 2 Resource Book)

Student Text Listening Activity Scripts

 Videoscript: Diálogo *pages 122–123*

• Videotape 2 • Videodisc 1B

Search Chapter 5, Play to 6
U2E2 • En vivo (Dialog)

• Use the videoscript with **Actividades 1, 2** *page 124*

Isabel: Perdone... busco a la profesora Díaz.

Maestra: La profesora Díaz no está en este momento.

Isabel: ¿A qué hora llega?

Maestra: Normalmente llega a las diez y media. Generalmente está aquí a esta hora.

Isabel: Bueno, gracias. Perdone, profesora, ¿qué hora es?

Maestra: Son las once menos cuarto. ¡Señorita! A veces la profesora Díaz está en su oficina durante el almuerzo, y a las tres.

Isabel: Muchas gracias, profesora. Hasta luego.

Maestra: Hasta luego.

Ricardo: ¿Qué pasa?

Isabel: ¡Qué problema! La profesora Díaz no está en su oficina. ¿Adónde vas, Ricardo?

Ricardo: Voy a la cafetería. ¿Me acompañas?

Isabel: Sí, vamos. Son las once y media. Tengo tiempo.

Ricardo: ¡Vamos! Quiero comer unas papas fritas, y quiero beber un refresco.

Isabel: Quiero beber un refresco también. ¡Este nuevo semestre es horrible! Tengo un horario muy difícil.

Ricardo: ¡No me digas!

Isabel: Sí. Los lunes, miércoles y viernes tengo inglés, historia, matemáticas y literatura.

Ricardo: ¿Y los martes y jueves? ¿Qué clases tienes?

Isabel: Los martes y jueves tengo música, geografía, computación y ciencias naturales.

Ricardo: Es verdad. Tu horario es muy difícil. ¿A qué hora es tu clase de computación?

Isabel: Tomo la clase de computación a la una de la tarde, con el profesor García.

Ricardo: Mi clase de computación es a las cuatro, con el profesor Anaya.

Isabel: Toma mi refresco. Ya no quiero más. Mira, ¿qué es eso? ¡Qué interesante!

Ricardo: ¡De verdad es interesante! ¿Te gusta escribir?

Isabel: Sí, me gusta mucho escribir.

Ricardo: ¿Por qué no participamos?

Isabel: Quiero participar... pero con mi horario...

Ricardo: Isabel, por la noche hay tiempo para trabajar en el concurso...

Isabel: ¡Por la noche tengo que trabajar en mi tarea! ¡Tengo mucha tarea!

Ricardo: Bueno, ¿por qué no vamos a la cafetería para hablar más tranquilos?

Isabel: ¿Cuándo?

Ricardo: ¿A qué hora terminas hoy?

Isabel: A las cinco.

Ricardo: Entonces, a las cinco y veinte.

Isabel: De acuerdo. Voy a las cinco y veinte. ¡Ay! ¡Ya es tarde! Me voy.

 ¿A qué hora? *page 129*

Tú tienes seis materias. A las siete y media, tienes arte, y a las ocho y cuarto tienes matemáticas. A las nueve, tienes inglés. A las diez menos cuarto tienes receso. Después, a las diez y media tienes ciencias naturales, tu clase más difícil. A las once y cuarto tienes estudios sociales. Al mediodía tienes literatura.

¡Pobre Luis! *page 133*

—Hola, Luis, ¿cómo estás?

—No muy bien. Es un semestre difícil. Tengo ocho materias.

—¿Estudias mucho?

—Sí, con ocho materias, hay que estudiar mucho.

—¿Qué hora es, Luis?

—¡Ay! Es la una y veinticinco. Tengo una cita con la señora García a la una y media.

—¿Con quién?

—Con la señora García, mi profesora de literatura. Tengo un examen de literatura el lunes por la mañana.

Quick Start Review Answers

p. 122 Numbers 13–60
13 trece   15 quince
18 dieciocho   20 veinte
25 veinticinco   30 treinta
35 treinta y cinco   40 cuarenta
45 cuarenta y cinco
50 cincuenta
55 cincuenta y cinco
60 sesenta

p. 124 Classroom activities
1. El profesor Pérez enseña a las dos.
2. Hablamos mucho en la clase de español.
3. Nunca estudio en la biblioteca.
4. Tengo que preparar mi tarea.

p. 126 Possessive adjectives
Answers will vary.
Answers could include:
1. Mis padres escuchan música.
2. Tu hermano es muy alto.
3. Nuestro perro es cómico.
4. Nuestra abuela es paciente.
5. Sus amigos estudian mucho.

p. 130 School locations and activities
Answers will vary.
Answers could include:
1c. La chica busca un libro en la biblioteca.
2a. Isabel y Ricardo toman un refresco en la cafetería.
3d. ¿Usas una calculadora en la clase de matemáticas?
4b. Me gusta ayudar a los maestros de educación física en el gimnasio.

p. 131 Estar
Answers will vary.
Answers could include:
Estoy en la clase de español.
José está en la cafetería.
Mi lápiz está en el escritorio.
Mis libros están en mi mochila.
Isabel está en la oficina.

p. 136 Interrogatives
Answers will vary.
Answers could include:
1. ¿Dónde está la oficina?
2. ¿Cómo se llama tu hermana?
3. ¿Por qué van los muchachos a casa?

Sample Lesson Plan - 50 Minute Schedule

DAY 1

Etapa Opener
- Quick Start Review (TE, p. 118) 5 MIN.
- Anticipate/Activate prior knowledge: Have students look at the *Etapa* Opener and answer the questions. 5 MIN.

En contexto: Vocabulario
- Quick Start Review (TE, p. 120) 5 MIN.
- Have students use context and pictures to learn *Etapa* vocabulary. In pairs, have students answer the questions, p. 121. Use the Situational OHTs for additional practice. 10 MIN.

En vivo: Diálogo
- Quick Start Review (TE, p. 122) 5 MIN.
- Review the Listening Strategy, p. 122. Play audio or show video for the dialog, pp. 122–123. 10 MIN.
- Replay twice. Read aloud, having students take the roles of characters. 10 MIN.

Homework Option:
- Video Activities, Unit 2 Resource Book, pp. 74–76.

DAY 2

En acción: Vocabulario y gramática
- Check homework. 5 MIN.
- Quick Start Review (TE, p. 124) 5 MIN.
- Use OHT 49 and 50 to review *En contexto* vocabulary. Ask students for a summary of the dialog to check recall. 5 MIN.
- Play the video/audio; have students do *Actividades* 1 and 2. 10 MIN.
- Have students read and complete *Actividad* 3. 5 MIN.
- Present the *Nota.* Then have students complete *Actividad* 4 in pairs and *Actividad* 5 orally. 5 MIN.
- Quick Start Review (TE, p. 126) 5 MIN.
- Present *Gramática:* Saying Where You Are Going: The Verb **ir** and the *Vocabulario,* p. 126. 10 MIN.
- Have students read and complete *Actividad* 6. 5 MIN.

Homework Option:
- Have students complete *Actividad* 5 in writing. *Más práctica* Workbook, p. 45. *Para hispanohablantes* Workbook, p. 43.

DAY 3

En acción (cont.)
- Check homework. 5 MIN.
- Present the *Nota* for *Actividad* 7, then do the activity orally. 10 MIN.
- Present the *Nota* for *Actividad* 8, then do the activity in groups. 5 MIN.
- Quick Start Review (TE, p. 128) 5 MIN.
- Present *Gramática:* Telling Time, p. 128. 15 MIN.
- Have students complete *Actividad* 9 in pairs. 5 MIN.
- Present the *Vocabulario,* p. 129. Reinforce by asking simple questions (¿Cuándo estudias? ¿Cuándo llegas a la escuela? ¿Cuándo escuchas música?). 5 MIN.
- Play the audio; do *Actividad* 10. 5 MIN.

Homework Option:
- Have students complete *Actividad* 7 in writing. *Más práctica* Workbook, p. 46. *Para hispanohablantes* Workbook, p. 44.

DAY 4

En acción (cont.)
- Check homework. 5 MIN.
- Present the Speaking Strategy, p. 129, and have students do *Actividad* 11 in pairs. Expand using Information Gap Activities, Unit 2 Resource Book, p. 68; *Más comunicación,* p. R5. 15 MIN.
- Quick Start Review (TE, p. 130) 5 MIN.
- Present *Gramática:* Describing Location with the Verb **estar,** p. 130. 10 MIN.
- Have students read and complete *Actividad* 12 in writing. Ask volunteers to write out answers on the board. 10 MIN.
- Have students do *Actividad* 13 in pairs and *Actividad* 14 orally. 10 MIN.

Homework Option:
- Have students complete *Actividad* 14 in writing. *Más práctica* Workbook, p. 47. *Para hispanohablantes* Workbook, p. 45.

DAY 5

En acción (cont.)
- Check homework. 5 MIN.
- Quick Start Review (TE, p. 131) 5 MIN.
- Present *Gramática:* Asking Questions: Interrogative Words, p. 131. 15 MIN.
- Do *Actividad* 15 orally. 5 MIN.
- Have students read and complete *Actividades* 16 and 17 in writing. Then have them exchange papers for peer correction. 15 MIN.
- Have students complete *Actividad* 18 orally. 5 MIN.
- Play the audio; do *Actividad* 19. 5 MIN.

Homework Option:
- Have students complete *Actividad* 18 in writing. *Más práctica* Workbook, p. 48. *Para hispanohablantes* Workbook, p. 46.

DAY 6

En acción (cont.)
- Check homework. 5 MIN.
- Have students complete *Actividad* 20. Expand using Information Gap Activities, Unit 2 Resource Book, pp. 69–70; *Más comunicación,* p. R5. 15 MIN.

Pronunciación
- Play the audio and have students practice the *Trabalenguas.* 10 MIN.

En colores: Cultura y comparaciones
- Quick Start Review (TE, p. 134) 5 MIN.
- Review the Connecting Cultures Strategy, p. 134. 5 MIN.
- Have volunteers read the selection aloud and answer the questions, p. 135. 15 MIN.

Homework Option:
- Have students complete the *¿Comprendiste?/¿Qué piensas?* questions in writing.

DAY 7

En uso: Repaso y más comunicación
- Check homework. 5 MIN.
- Quick Start Review (TE, p. 136) 5 MIN.
- Have students write *Actividad* 1. Have volunteers write out answers on the board. 10 MIN.
- Do *Actividad* 2 in pairs and *Actividades* 3–5 orally. 10 MIN.
- Present the Speaking Strategy, p. 138, and have students do *Actividad* 6 in pairs. 10 MIN.
- Have students do *Actividad* 7 in groups. 5 MIN.

En tu propia voz: Escritura
- Do *Actividad* 8 in writing. Have several students present their questions. 10 MIN.

Homework Option:
- Review for *Etapa* 2 Exam.

DAY 8

Conexiones
- Present *La salud,* p. 138. 5 MIN.

En resumen: Repaso de vocabulario
- Quick Start Review (TE, p. 139) 5 MIN.
- Review grammar questions, etc. as necessary. 10 MIN.
- Complete *Etapa* 2 Exam. 20 MIN.

Ampliación
- Use a suggested project, game, or activity. (TE, pp. 95A–95B) 10 MIN.

Homework Option:
- Research food and complete the chart as presented in *Conexiones.* Preview *Etapa* 3 Opener.

Sample Lesson Plan - Block Schedule (90 minutes)

DAY 1

Etapa Opener
- Quick Start Review (TE, p. 118) 5 MIN.
- Anticipate/Activate prior knowledge: Have students look at the *Etapa* Opener and answer the questions. 5 MIN.

En contexto: Vocabulario
- Quick Start Review (TE, p. 120) 5 MIN.
- Have students use context and pictures to learn *Etapa* vocabulary. Have students answer the questions, p. 121. 10 MIN.
- Use Block Scheduling Copymasters. 5 MIN.

En vivo: Diálogo
- Quick Start Review (TE, p. 122) 5 MIN.
- Review the Listening Strategy, p. 122. Play audio or show video for the dialog, pp. 122–123. 10 MIN.
- Replay twice. Read aloud, having students take the roles of characters. 10 MIN.

En acción: Vocabulario y gramática
- Quick Start Review (TE, p. 124) 5 MIN.
- Use OHT 49 and 50 to review *En contexto* vocabulary. Ask students for a summary of the dialog to check recall. 5 MIN.
- Play the video/audio; do *Actividades* 1 and 2. 10 MIN.
- Have students read and complete *Actividad* 3. 5 MIN.
- Present the *Nota*. Then have students complete *Actividad* 4 in pairs and *Actividad* 5 orally. 10 MIN.

Homework Option:
- Have students complete *Actividad* 5 in writing. Video Activities, Unit 2 Resource Book, pp. 74–76.

DAY 2

En acción (cont.)
- Check homework. 5 MIN.
- Quick Start Review (TE, p. 126) 5 MIN.
- Present *Gramática:* Saying Where You Are Going: The Verb **ir** and the *Vocabulario,* p. 126. 10 MIN.
- Have students read and complete *Actividad* 6. 5 MIN.
- Present the *Nota* for *Actividad* 7, then do the activity orally. 10 MIN.
- Present the *Nota* for *Actividad* 8, then do the activity in groups. 5 MIN.
- Quick Start Review (TE, p. 128) 5 MIN.
- Present *Gramática:* Telling Time, p. 128. 15 MIN.
- Have students complete *Actividad* 9 in pairs. 5 MIN.
- Present the *Vocabulario,* p. 129. Reinforce by asking simple questions (¿Cuándo estudias? ¿Cuándo llegas a la escuela? ¿Cuándo escuchas música?). 5 MIN.
- Play the audio; do *Actividad* 10. 5 MIN.
- Present the Speaking Strategy, p. 129, and have students do *Actividad* 11 in pairs. Expand using Information Gap Activities, Unit 2 Resource Book, p. 68; *Más comunicación,* p. R5. 15 MIN.

Homework Option:
- Have students complete *Actividad* 7 in writing. *Más práctica* Workbook, pp. 45–46. *Para hispanohablantes* Workbook, pp. 43–44.

DAY 3

En acción (cont.)
- Check homework. 5 MIN.
- Quick Start Review (TE, p. 130) 5 MIN.
- Present *Gramática:* Describing Location with the Verb **estar,** p. 130. 10 MIN.
- Have students read and complete *Actividad* 12 in writing. Ask volunteers to write out answers on the board. 5 MIN.
- Have students do *Actividad* 13 in pairs and *Actividad* 14 orally. 10 MIN.
- Quick Start Review (TE, p. 131) 5 MIN.
- Present *Gramática:* Asking Questions: Interrogative Words, p. 131. 10 MIN.
- Do *Actividad* 15 orally. 5 MIN.
- Have students read and complete *Actividades* 16 and 17 in writing. Then have them exchange papers for peer correction. 15 MIN.
- Have students complete *Actividad* 18 orally. 5 MIN.
- Play the audio; do *Actividad* 19. 5 MIN.
- Have students do *Actividad* 20. Expand using Information Gap Activities, Unit 2 Resource Book, pp. 69–70; *Más comunicación,* p. R5. 10 MIN.

Homework Option:
- Have students complete *Actividades* 14 and 18 in writing. *Más práctica* Workbook, pp. 47–48. *Para hispanohablantes* Workbook, pp. 45–46.

DAY 4

Pronunciación
- Check homework. 5 MIN.
- Play the audio; have students practice the *Trabalenguas.* 10 MIN.

En colores: Cultura y comparaciones
- Quick Start Review (TE, p. 134) 5 MIN.
- Review the Connecting Cultures Strategy, p. 134. 5 MIN.
- Have volunteers read the selection aloud and answer the questions, p. 135. 20 MIN.

En uso: Repaso y más comunicación
- Quick Start Review (TE, p. 136) 5 MIN.
- Have students write *Actividad* 1. Have volunteers write out answers on the board. 10 MIN.
- Do *Actividad* 2 in pairs and *Actividades* 3–5 orally. 15 MIN.
- Present the Speaking Strategy, p. 138, and have students do *Actividad* 6 in pairs. 10 MIN.
- Have students do *Actividad* 7 in groups. 5 MIN.

Homework Option:
- Review for *Etapa* 2 Exam.

DAY 5

En tu propia voz: Escritura
- Do *Actividad* 8 in writing. Have several students present their questions. 20 MIN.

Conexiones
- Present *La salud,* p. 138. 10 MIN.

En resumen: Repaso de vocabulario
- Quick Start Review (TE, p. 139) 5 MIN.
- Review grammar questions, etc. as necessary. 10 MIN.
- Complete *Etapa* 2 Exam. 20 MIN.

Ampliación
- Use a suggested project, game, or activity. (TE, pp. 95A–95B) 25 MIN.

Homework Option:
- Research food and complete the chart as presented in *Conexiones.* Preview *Etapa* 3 Opener.

▼ Isabel y Ricardo toman un refresco.

Etapa Theme
Asking and telling time, saying where you are going after classes in a city (México, D.F.), and requesting snack food.

Grammar Objectives
- Using the verb **ir**
- Using phrases to tell time
- Using the verb **estar**
- Using interrogative words

Teaching Resource Options

Print

Block Scheduling Copymasters

Audiovisual

OHT 37, 55 (Quick Start)

🔔 Quick Start Review

♻️ **Tener que**

Use OHT 55 or write on board: Create sentences using **tener que** and words from columns A and B:

A	B
yo	estudiar mucho hoy
tú	escribir la tarea
mi amigo	usar la computadora
nosotros	preparar la lección
las chicas	buscar un diccionario

Answers
Answers will vary. Answers could include:
Yo tengo que preparar la lección.
Tú tienes que buscar un diccionario.
Mi amigo tiene que estudiar mucho hoy.
Nosotros tenemos que usar la computadora.
Las chicas tienen que escribir la tarea.

Teaching Suggestions
Previewing the Etapa
- Ask students to study the picture on pp. 118–119 (1 min.).
- Have them close their books and share their initial impressions of the scene—the people, weather, clothing, activities, etc.
- Use the **¿Qué ves?** questions to focus the discussion.

UNIDAD 2

ETAPA **2**

¡Un horario difícil!

- Talk about schedules
- Ask and tell time
- Ask questions
- Say where you are going
- Request food

¿Qué ves?

Mira la foto del patio de una escuela mexicana. **¡Ojo!** El símbolo **$** representa pesos mexicanos, **no** dólares.

1. ¿Llevan jeans todos?
2. ¿Hay aguas en el menú?
3. ¿Es verde o azul la mochila de Ricardo?
4. ¿Es roja o rosada la mochila de Isabel?

118

MENÚ de la CAFETERÍA

TORTAS	$12
HAMBURGUESAS	$15
PAPAS FRITAS	$5
REFRESCOS	$3
AGUAS	$2

Classroom Management

Planning Ahead Prepare students to observe and talk about going to a **café** or **cafetería** and ordering snack foods by brainstorming ideas in the following categories:
- places to go after school with friends
- favorite foods and drinks
- topics of conversation

Time Saver Prepare a "mini-menu" ahead of time with snack food vocabulary from this **Etapa.** (Each item should be labeled in Spanish and have a drawing or photo of it. Index cards may also be used.) Make photocopies and distribute. Students should give prices for each item in pesos. Once students have learned vocabulary, these menus can be used for other activities.

Cross Cultural Connections

Ask students to think about what a typical school cafeteria is like in the U.S. Is this similar to what they see on pp. 118–119? Ask them to note similarities and differences.

Culture Highlights

● **CAFÉS Y CAFETERÍAS** Mexican students enjoy spending their free time in **cafés** and **cafeterías.** There, they eat, study, and spend time with friends. In Mexico, **cafés** and **cafeterías** sell a special kind of sandwich called a **torta.** There are different types of **tortas,** such as a traditional one from Guadalajara and Jalisco called **torta ahogada.** This **torta** is filled with beans, meat, and tomato sauce, and it can be partially or totally "drowned" (**ahogada**) in chile.

● **TORTAS Y SÁNDWICHES** A **torta** is a sandwich made using bread such as a bun. A **sándwich** is made using bread similar to sandwich bread in the U.S. The word **sándwich** is only used when the bread is store-bought and square.

Quick Wrap-up

Provide students with a list of items, some of which are shown in the photo and some of which are not. With books closed, have student check the items they recall seeing. Then have them open their books and check their answers. Alternate: Use the OHT and have students list as many words shown in the photo as possible in 3 minutes.

Block Schedule

Streamlining Divide the class into groups of 4. Have students count off within the groups. Student 1 of each group answers question 1 for the group, student 2 answers question 2, and so on. Everyone writes the answers in their notebooks. (For additional activities, see **Block Scheduling Copymasters.**)

Teaching All Students

Extra Help Ask students about the photo using yes/no or either/or questions. For example: ¿Tienen Isabel y Ricardo sus mochilas? ¿Llevan pantalones cortos o jeans? ¿Estudian?

Multiple Intelligences

Visual Have students sketch several pairs of young people or cut out pictures from magazines and arrange them on paper. Have them draw dialog bubbles and fill them in with dialog in Spanish. Have a few volunteers present their scenes, and select a few other scenes to display on the bulletin board.

Teaching Resource Options

Print

Unit 2 Resource Book
  Video Activities, pp. 74–75
  Videoscript, p. 77
  Audioscript, p. 80
  Audioscript *Para hispanohablantes,*
    p. 80

Audiovisual

OHT 49, 50, 51, 51A, 52, 52A, 55 (Quick Start)
Audio Program Cassette 5A / CD 5
Audio *Para hispanohablantes*
  Cassette 5A / CD 5
Video Program Videotape 2 / Videodisc 1B

Search Chapter 4, Play to 5
U2E2 • En contexto (Vocabulary)

Technology

Intrigas y aventuras CD-ROM, Disc 1

Quick Start Review

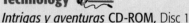

♻ Numbers 1–12

Use OHT 55 or write on board:
Write out the numbers 1–12 in words.

Answers

1 uno 2 dos 3 tres 4 cuatro 5 cinco
6 seis 7 siete 8 ocho 9 nueve 10 diez
11 once 12 doce

Teaching Suggestions
Introducing Vocabulary

• Have students look at pages 120–121. Use OHT 49 and 50 and Audio Cassette 5 / CD 5 to present the vocabulary.

• Ask the Comprehension Questions in order of yes/no (questions 1–3), either/or (questions 4–6), and simple word or phrase (questions 7–10). Expand by adding similar questions.

• Use the TPR activity to reinforce the meaning of individual words.

• Use the video vocabulary presentation for review and reinforcement.

En contexto

VOCABULARIO

Isabel and Ricardo have a lot to do at school today. Let's see where they go at different times during the day.

A

Isabel: Hola, Ricardo. ¿Qué hora es?
Ricardo: Son las once.
Isabel: ¿A qué hora está la maestra en la oficina?
Ricardo: A la una.

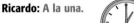

Horario para hoy

11:00 Oficina
11:30 Biblioteca
2:00 Auditorio
4:00 Gimnasio
5:00 Cafetería

B

Son las once y media. Todos los días Ricardo estudia en **la biblioteca.** Hay muchos libros en la biblioteca.

120 ciento veinte
Unidad 2

Classroom Community

Paired Activity Have students make their own **Horario para hoy,** using the vocabulary they have learned thus far. Students write times and places on a sheet of paper and then compare each other's schedule by asking questions.

TPR Hold up a clock (a child's toy clock or one made from a paper plate with movable hands). Say a time on the hour or half hour. Have one student come up and move the hands to that time, then hold the clock up to the class and repeat the time. Continue with several more students.

C

Son las dos. Isabel y Ricardo están en el auditorio. ¡Qué bien actúan!

GIMNASIO

D

Son las cuatro. Ricardo está en el gimnasio de la escuela con unos amigos.

la merienda

las papas fritas

la fruta

el refresco

un vaso de agua

la hamburguesa

la torta

E

Son las cinco. Durante el receso, Isabel y Ricardo toman una merienda en la cafetería.

Isabel: Para la merienda siempre quiero comer una torta o fruta. A veces quiero tomar un refresco.

Ricardo: Para la merienda yo quiero comer una hamburguesa y papas fritas. Quiero beber agua.

Preguntas personales

1. ¿Tu escuela tiene un gimnasio? ¿Un auditorio?
2. ¿Estudias en la biblioteca o en casa?
3. ¿Te gusta comer en la cafetería de la escuela o en casa?
4. ¿Qué te gusta beber: un refresco o agua?
5. Para la merienda, ¿qué te gusta comer?

ciento veintiuno
Etapa 2

121

Comprehension Questions

1. En la foto A, ¿es la una? (No.)
2. ¿Está Ricardo en la biblioteca a las once y media? (Sí.)
3. ¿Actúan bien Isabel y Ricardo? (Sí.)
4. ¿Está la maestra en la oficina a la una o a las dos? (a la una)
5. ¿Estudia Ricardo mucho o poco en la biblioteca? (mucho)
6. A las cuatro, ¿está Ricardo en el auditorio o en el gimnasio? (en el gimnasio)
7. ¿Qué hay en la biblioteca? (muchos libros)
8. ¿Qué toman Isabel y Ricardo en la cafetería? (una merienda)
9. ¿Qué come siempre Isabel para la merienda? (una torta o fruta)
10. ¿A Ricardo, qué le gusta comer? (una hamburguesa y papas fritas)

Supplementary Vocabulary

el desayuno	breakfast
desayunar	to have breakfast
el almuerzo	lunch
almorzar	to have lunch
la cena	dinner
cenar	to have dinner
la merienda	snack
merendar	to have a snack

Language Note

In Latin America, lunch is usually referred to as **el almuerzo** and dinner as **la comida**. In Spain, lunch is called **la comida** and dinner is **la cena**.

Block Schedule

Variety Write a list of times during the school day on the board. Ask students to say the time in Spanish and then say where they are on a typical day at that time. They might also provide additional information. For example: **9:00 / Son las nueve. Estoy en la clase de historia. (Mi profesor es la señora Davis.) 11:30 / Son las once y media. Estoy en la cafetería. Tomo una merienda.**

Teaching All Students

Extra Help Re-read the beginning of sentences from the vocabulary presentation. Have students complete the sentences. For example: TEACHER: **Hola, Ricardo. ¿Qué hora... ?** STUDENT: **es**

Native Speakers Ask students to describe the pictures using any synonyms that are more commonly used in their community.

Multiple Intelligences

Visual Have students sketch a plan of the layout of your school. They should label each room in Spanish. They might also write the name of the teacher/administrator that usually uses that classroom/room.

Teaching Resource Options

Print

Más práctica Workbook PE, pp. 41–44
Para hispanohablantes Workbook PE, pp. 41–42
Block Scheduling Copymasters
Unit 2 Resource Book
  Más práctica Workbook TE, pp. 52–55
  Para hispanohablantes Workbook TE, pp. 60–61
  Video Activities, p. 76
  Videoscript, p. 78
  Audioscript, p. 80
  Audioscript *Para hispanohablantes*, p. 80

Audiovisual

OHT 53, 54, 55 (Quick Start)
Audio Program Cassette 5A / CD 5
Audio *Para hispanohablantes*
  Cassette 5A / CD 5
Video Program Videotape 2 / Videodisc 1B

Search Chapter 5, Play to 6
U2E2 • En vivo (Dialog)

Technology

Intrigas y aventuras CD-ROM, Disc 1

Quick Start Review

♻ Numbers 13–60

Use OHT 55 or write on board:
Write out these numbers in words: 13, 15, 18, 20, 25, 30, 35, 40, 45, 50, 55, 60.

Answers *See p. 117B.*

Teaching Suggestions
Presenting the Dialog

• Prepare students for listening by reintroducing the characters: ¿Cómo se llama el chico? ¿Cómo se llama la chica? ¿Son primos o amigos? ¿Son maestros o estudiantes?

• Use the video, audiocassette, or CD to present the dialog. The expanded dialog on video offers additional listening practice opportunities.

Video Synopsis

• Isabel and Ricardo talk about their busy class schedules over a snack.

En vivo
 DIÁLOGO

Horas y horarios

Isabel   Maestra   Ricardo

PARA ESCUCHAR • STRATEGY: LISTENING

Listen for the main idea It is important first to understand the main idea without getting lost in the details. Here Isabel is looking for a teacher. What do you hear that tells you that?

1▶ Isabel: Busco a la profesora Díaz.
Maestra: No está en este momento.
Isabel: ¿A qué hora llega?
Maestra: A las diez y media.

5▶ Ricardo: Quiero comer unas papas fritas, y quiero beber un refresco.
Isabel: Quiero beber un refresco también.

6▶ Isabel: ¡Este semestre es horrible! Tengo un horario difícil. Los lunes, miércoles y viernes tengo inglés, historia, matemáticas y literatura. Y los martes y jueves música, geografía, computación y ciencias naturales.

7▶ Ricardo: ¿A qué hora es tu clase de computación?
Isabel: A la una de la tarde, con el profesor García.
Ricardo: Mi clase de computación es a las cuatro, con el profesor Anaya.

122 ciento veintidós
Unidad 2

Classroom Community

Game Divide the class into 10 groups (one for each dialog scene). Have each group "storyboard" one of the scenes. Collect, shuffle, and then call up each team to organize the scenes in correct order. The team ordering the storyboards correctly in the shortest period of time wins.

Storytelling After watching the video, divide the class into groups of 3. Have each group choose a portion of the dialog and retell it in their own words, using gestures as necessary to communicate meaning.

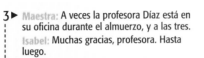

2 ▶ **Isabel:** Profesora, ¿qué hora es?

Maestra: Son las once menos cuarto.

3 ▶ **Maestra:** A veces la profesora Díaz está en su oficina durante el almuerzo, y a las tres.

Isabel: Muchas gracias, profesora. Hasta luego.

4 ▶ **Isabel:** ¿Adónde vas, Ricardo?

Ricardo: Voy a la cafetería. ¿Me acompañas?

Isabel: Sí, vamos. Tengo tiempo.

8 ▶ **Isabel:** Mira, ¿qué es eso?

Ricardo: ¡De verdad es interesante! ¿Te gusta escribir?

Isabel: Sí, me gusta mucho.

Ricardo: ¿Por qué no participamos?

9 ▶ **Isabel:** Quiero participar… pero con mi horario…

Ricardo: Isabel, por la noche hay tiempo para trabajar en el concurso…

Isabel: Por la noche tengo que trabajar en mi tarea. ¡Tengo mucha tarea!

10 ▶ **Ricardo:** ¿Por qué no vamos a la cafetería para hablar más tranquilos?

Isabel: ¿Cuándo?

Ricardo: A las cinco y veinte.

Isabel: De acuerdo. Voy a las cinco y veinte. ¡Ay! ¡Ya es tarde!

ciento veintitrés
Etapa 2

123

Comprehension Questions

1. ¿Busca Isabel a la profesora Díaz? (Sí.)
2. ¿Llega la profesora a las nueve? (No.)
3. En la foto 2, ¿son las once menos cuarto? (Sí.)
4. ¿Está la profesora Díaz en la cafetería durante el almuerzo? (No.)
5. En la foto 4, ¿va Ricardo a clase o a la cafetería? (a la cafetería)
6. ¿Tiene Isabel la clase de inglés los lunes o los martes? (los lunes)
7. ¿Qué clases tiene Isabel los jueves? (música, geografía, computación y ciencias naturales)
8. ¿Cómo se llama el profesor de la clase de computación de Isabel? (el profesor García)
9. ¿Con qué profesor estudia Ricardo computación? (el profesor Anaya)
10. ¿Qué tiene que hacer Isabel por la noche? (trabajar en su tarea)

Culture Highlights

● **EL HORARIO** Once a week in public schools in Mexico, the school day begins with an assembly. On that day, students line up by classes, the flag of Mexico is paraded by, and everyone sings the national anthem.

Quick Wrap-up

Have students close their books. Write 10 sentences on the board—5 that are from the dialog and 5 that are not. Have students decide which ones are from the dialog. This activity could also be done as a true/false quiz.

Block Schedule

Change of Pace Working in groups of 2–3, have students create a continuation of the video. For example, Isabel goes back to Professor Díaz's office. Students should write out the conversation and present it to the class. (For additional activities, see **Block Scheduling Copymasters**.)

Teaching All Students

Extra Help On the board or on a worksheet, write 6–10 statements that the characters say in the dialog. Have students say or write who said each statement.

Multiple Intelligences

Verbal Replay the dialog. Have students write down any **hora** that they hear (10:30, 10:45, 3:00, 1:00, 4:00, 5:20).

Visual After watching the video once, see how much students observed. Ask them to describe what Isabel, Ricardo, and the teacher were wearing, including colors. Was anyone wearing a hat? A watch? Rings? etc.

Teaching Resource Options

Print

Unit 2 Resource Book
  Videoscript, p. 76
  Audioscript, p. 80
  Audioscript *Para hispanohablantes*,
    p. 80

Audiovisual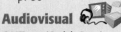

OHT 56 (Quick Start)
Audio Program Cassette 5A / CD 5
Audio *Para hispanohablantes*
  Cassette 5A / CD 5
Video Program Videotape 2 / Videodisc
  1B

🔔 Quick Start Review

♻ Classroom activities

Use OHT 56 or write on board:
Unscramble the following sentences:

1. enseña / profesor / El / las / a
   Pérez / dos
2. mucho / clase / en / español /
   de / Hablamos / la
3. en / biblioteca / Nunca / la /
   estudio
4. que / mi / Tengo / tarea /
   preparar

Answers *See p. 117B.*

Teaching Suggestions
Comprehension Check

Use **Actividades 1** and **2** to assess
retention after the dialog. For **Actividad
1**, have students write a big C **(cierto)**
on one piece of paper and a big F
(falso) on another. As you read
Actividad 1 have them hold up one
sheet or the other.

 Objective: Transitional practice
Listening comprehension/vocabulary

Answers (See script, p. 117B.)
1. Falso. La profesora Díaz no está.
2. Falso. Quiere comer unas papas fritas.
3. Cierto
4. Falso. Ricardo tiene computación con el
   profesor Anaya; Isabel con el profesor García.
5. Cierto

En acción
VOCABULARIO Y GRAMÁTICA

ACTIVIDAD 1

¿Cierto o falso?

Escuchar ¿Es cierto o falso? Si es falso, di lo que es cierto.
(Hint: True or false? If it is false, say what is true.)

1. La profesora Díaz está en su oficina.
2. Ricardo quiere comer una hamburguesa.
3. Isabel tiene un horario muy difícil.
4. Isabel y Ricardo tienen la clase de computación
   con el profesor Anaya.
5. Isabel tiene mucha tarea.

ACTIVIDAD 2

¿Qué pasa?

Escuchar Escoge la respuesta correcta según el diálogo.
(Hint: Choose the correct answer.)

1. Isabel busca _____.
   a. a Ricardo
   b. su libro de matemáticas
   c. a la profesora Díaz
2. La profesora Díaz normalmente llega a su oficina _____.
   a. a las diez y media
   b. tarde
   c. a las dos
3. Ricardo va _____.
   a. a la cafetería
   b. al gimnasio
   c. a la clase
4. Ricardo quiere beber _____.
   a. unas papas fritas
   b. un refresco
   c. agua
5. Isabel va a la cafetería _____.
   a. a las cinco y veinte
   b. a las diez y media
   c. a las tres

ACTIVIDAD 3

♻ Los amigos de Isabel

Leer Isabel dice lo que ella
y sus amigos hacen en clase.
Completa sus oraciones con la
forma correcta del verbo. *(Hint:
Complete Isabel's sentences, telling what she
and her friends do.)*

1. Elena _____ (hablar) poco.
2. Antonio y Marisol siempre
   _____ (ayudar) al profesor.
3. Ana y yo _____ (buscar)
   un libro.
4. Yo _____ (escuchar) la
   computadora en la clase
   de inglés.
5. Nosotros _____ (usar) la
   calculadora en la clase de
   matemáticas.
6. Mis amigos _____ (hablar)
   mucho en la clase de
   inglés.
7. Yo _____ (mirar) la
   pantalla de la
   computadora para leer.
8. Tú _____ (estudiar)
   mucho.

> **TAMBIÉN SE DICE**
>
> In Latin America, a potato is **una
> papa**, but in Spain it is **una
> patata**. **Papas fritas** and **patatas
> fritas** are both french fries and
> potato chips.

124 ciento veinticuatro
Unidad 2

Classroom Management

Streamlining Instead of a homework assignment,
use **Actividad 3** as a quick quiz on **-ar** verbs. Add the
following 2 questions to make it an easy-to-correct,
10-question quiz:

9. Mi amiga _____ (buscar) a la profesora.
10. Elena y Ricardo _____ (llegar) tarde a la clase.

Answers: 9. busca   10. llegan

Time Saver Have copies of answers to Video/
Listening **Actividades 1** and **2** ready. Have students
check their own work.

- *Use the verb **ir***
- *Use phrases to tell time*
- *Use the verb **estar***
- *Use interrogative words*

ACTIVIDAD 4

¡Una buena merienda!

Hablar Trabajas en la cafetería. Un(a) estudiante quiere comprar algo. ¿Qué dicen? Cambien de papel. *(Hint: A student asks for a snack as you work in the cafeteria. Change roles.)*

modelo

Estudiante: *¿Qué hay para la merienda?*

Tú: *¿Quieres comer **una torta** o **fruta**?*

Estudiante: *Una torta, por favor.*

Nota

To ask what someone wants to eat, say **¿Quieres comer...?;** to ask what someone wants to drink say, **¿Quieres beber...?** Use **por favor** when you want to say *please*.

ACTIVIDAD 5

¿Qué es?

Hablar/Escribir Isabel le muestra la escuela a una nueva estudiante. ¿Qué dice? *(Hint: Isabel shows a new student the school. What does she say?)*

modelo

*Es **el gimnasio**.*

ciento veinticinco
Etapa 2

125

ACTIVIDAD 2

Objective: Transitional practice
Listening comprehension/vocabulary

Answers (See script, p. 117B.)
1. c   2. a   3. a   4. b   5. a

ACTIVIDAD 3

Objective: Controlled practice
Saying what you and others do

♻ **-ar** verbs

Answers
1. habla
2. ayudan
3. buscamos
4. escucho
5. usamos
6. hablan
7. miro
8. estudias

ACTIVIDAD 4

Objective: Transitional practice
Vocabulary in conversation

Answers
1. ¿Quieres comer una hamburguesa o unas papas fritas?
2. ¿Quieres beber agua o un refresco?
3. ¿Quieres comer una torta o unas papas fritas?
4. ¿Quieres comer una hamburguesa o una fruta?

ACTIVIDAD 5

Objective: Transitional practice
Vocabulary

Answers
1. Es la biblioteca.
2. Es la cafetería.
3. Es el auditorio.
4. Es la clase.

■ Block Schedule

FunBreak Divide students into teams of 4–5 to play a whole-class game called Video Quiz. Combine the list of Comprehension questions on TE p. 123 with those in **Actividades 1** and **2.** Assign easier questions 1 point, either/or questions 2 points, multiple choice questions 3 points, and short answer questions 4 points. For each turn, the team chooses a level of difficulty and the student answering must consult the entire team before responding. You may also want to prepare bonus questions from **Etapa 1.**

Teaching All Students

Extra Help Modify **Actividad 3** for students who need to review verbs. Ask them to copy the subject and write the conjugated verb form for each sentence. They should not move on to reading the rest of the sentence until after they have completed the verbs correctly.

Native Speakers Ask students to talk about school snacks and meals in their home countries, and how they may have changed their eating habits in the U.S.

Multiple Intelligences

Logical/Mathematical Using plastic food, pictures of food, or empty food containers, have students set up an imaginary fundraiser for the Spanish Club. Fundraisers describe the food they will offer at lunchtime. Students tell the fundraiser how much they will pay for what food. The fundraisers record the offers and determine how much they have raised for the club.

Teaching Resource Options

Print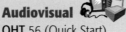

Más práctica Workbook PE, p. 45
Para hispanohablantes Workbook PE,
  p. 43
Block Scheduling Copymasters
Unit 2 Resource Book
  Más práctica Workbook TE, p. 56
  Para hispanohablantes Workbook
  TE, p. 62

Audiovisual

OHT 56 (Quick Start)

Technology

Intrigas y aventuras CD-ROM, Disc 1

Quick Start Review

♻ Possessive adjectives

Use OHT 56 or write on board:
Write a sentence using each possessive
adjective:

1. mis   4. nuestra
2. tu   5. sus
3. nuestro

Answers *See p. 117B.*

Teaching Suggestions
Presenting Saying Where You Are Going: The Verb ir

• Explain that **Yo voy**, for example,
means *I go* and *I am going*. Provide
several examples of each meaning,
using **voy** and other forms.
• Before assigning **Actividad 7**, write a
sample schedule on the board, using
a student's actual schedule for the
week.
• For **Actividad 8**, encourage students
to add information whenever
possible. For example: **Estudio en la
biblioteca. / Nunca estudio en casa.**

Objetive: Controlled practice
The verb **ir**

Answers
1. vas   4. vas
2. Voy   5. vamos
3. voy

GRAMÁTICA

Saying Where You Are Going: The Verb ir

When you talk about where someone is going, use the verb **ir**.

> As a question, **vamos** can mean **Shall we…?** But if stated definitely it means **Let's go!**

The verb **ir** means *to go*.

yo	**voy**	nosotros(as)	**vamos**
tú	**vas**	vosotros(as)	**vais**
usted, él, ella	**va**	ustedes, ellos(as)	**van**

Isabel and Ricardo say:

—¿**Adónde vas**, Ricardo?
  Where are you going, Ricardo?

—**Voy** a la cafetería.
  I'm going to the cafeteria.

Isabel uses the word **adónde** to ask where Ricardo is going.
This word means *where*. **Dónde** also means *where*.

• Use **adónde** to mean *where*
  when there is a verb indicating
  motion, such as **ir**.

  ¿Adónde va Ricardo?
  (To) **Where** is Ricardo going?

• Use **dónde** to ask where
  someone or something is.

  ¿Dónde está Ricardo?
  Where is Ricardo?

> Notice how asking ¿**dónde…?** is similar to asking **to where…?**

Vocabulario

La vida diaria

el almuerzo *lunch*
la cita *appointment*
comprar *to buy*
descansar *to rest*
terminar *to finish*
tomar *to take, to eat or drink*
visitar *to visit*
¿Qué te gusta hacer cada día?

ACTIVIDAD 6 Gramática

¿Adónde van?

Leer Isabel y Ricardo hablan en la escuela. Completa su
conversación con **ir**. *(Hint: Complete what Isabel and Ricardo say, using ir.)*

Isabel: ¡Hola, Ricardo! ¿Adónde __1__?

Ricardo: __2__ a la cafetería a tomar un refresco.

Isabel: Yo __3__ a la oficina de la profesora
  Díaz. Tengo una cita con ella ahora
  mismo.

Ricardo: Y después, ¿adónde __4__?

Isabel: Después, Andrea y yo __5__ a
  la biblioteca para estudiar.

Ricardo: Es un semestre difícil, ¿verdad?

Isabel: ¡Sí! ¡Tengo un horario horrible!

■ **MÁS PRÁCTICA** *cuaderno p. 45*
■ **PARA HISPANOHABLANTES** *cuaderno p. 43*

126 ciento veintiséis
      Unidad 2

Classroom Community

TPR Write destinations, such as going to the cafeteria
or going to the gym, on slips of paper. Have students in
turn draw a slip and act it out, using appropriate props.
The other students must guess where that student is
going.

Learning Scenario Put students in groups of 4–5.
Pretend that a new student in the school is a bit lost.
The group chooses one person to play the role of the
new student. That student asks each of the other group
members where to go for school activities. For
example: where to go to study, where to go to see
teachers, where to go to work on homework, etc. Have
groups present their scenes to the class.

ACTIVIDAD 7

  Un horario difícil

Hablar/Escribir Éste es el horario de Isabel. ¿Qué días va a sus clases? *(Hint: On what days does Isabel go to her classes?)*

modelo

inglés

*Isabel va a la clase de **inglés** los martes y jueves.*

Nota

Use **el** with a day of the week to say an event will happen on a specific day. Use **los** with a day of the week to say an event happens every week on that day. Add an **s** to **sábado** and **domingo** when you use **los**.

El lunes voy a la biblioteca.
On Monday I am going to the library.

Los martes y jueves tengo estudios sociales.
On Tuesdays and Thursdays I have social studies.

Los sábados y domingos no tengo clase.
On Saturdays and Sundays I don't have class.

Horario: Isabel Palacios

lunes	martes	miércoles	jueves	viernes
computación	inglés	computación	inglés	computación
literatura	matemáticas	literatura	matemáticas	literatura
arte	educación física	arte	educación física	arte
receso	receso	receso	receso	receso
historia	música	historia	música	historia
	ciencias naturales		ciencias naturales	

1. educación física
2. historia
3. computación
4. literatura
5. ciencias naturales
6. matemáticas
7. música
8. arte

ACTIVIDAD 8

¿Adónde vas para...?

Hablar Pregúntales a cinco estudiantes adónde van para hacer estas actividades. Léele un resumen de las respuestas a la clase. *(Ask five others where they go to do these things and report your results.)*

modelo

Tú: ¿Adónde vas para **estudiar**?

Estudiante 1: *Voy a **casa**.*

Resumen: *Cuatro estudiantes van a casa para estudiar. Un estudiante va a la biblioteca.*

Nota

When **a** is placed before the definite article **el,** the two words form the contraction **al.**

a + el = al   Voy **al** gimnasio.

Las actividades

1. estudiar
2. visitar al (a la) profesor(a) de español
3. comprar una hamburguesa
4. tomar un refresco
5. descansar
6. usar la computadora
7. buscar un diccionario
8. preparar tu tarea

¿Adónde?

el auditorio
la biblioteca
la cafetería
casa
la clase
la escuela
el gimnasio
su oficina
¿otro lugar?

NOTA CULTURAL

Public high schools in Mexico City have two daily schedules. The students attend classes either during the morning, from around 7:30 to 12:30, or during the afternoon, from around 1:00 to 6:00.

ACTIVIDAD 7

Objective: Transitional practice
The verb **ir**

♻ Days of the week

Answers
1. Isabel va a la clase de educación física los martes y jueves.
2. Isabel va a la clase de historia los lunes, miércoles y viernes.
3. Isabel va a la clase de computación los lunes, miércoles y viernes.
4. Isabel va a la clase de literatura los lunes, miércoles y viernes.
5. Isabel va a la clase de ciencias naturales los martes y jueves.
6. Isabel va a la clase de matemáticas los martes y jueves.
7. Isabel va a la clase de música los martes y jueves.
8. Isabel va a la clase de arte los lunes, miércoles y viernes.

ACTIVIDAD 8

Objective: Open-ended practice
The verb **ir** in conversation

Answers will vary.

🔔 **Quick Wrap-up**

Name a day of the week. Have several students name one place they go during school hours and one place they go after school hours on that day. Continue with other days of the week.

Teaching Note

In order to maximize the usefulness of student schedules, use them throughout the year to practice present, immediate future, and preterite tenses (tell what you are doing today/going to do/did last week), or as a group activity where students compare schedules and make arrangements to meet for an activity.

Block Schedule

Variety Put a volunteer student's schedule on a large poster. Next to it, put a series of statements about the schedule to be completed using the vocabulary and the verb **ir.** (Note that answers may vary.) For example:
1. Los lunes, Manuel... 2. El martes, la primera clase... (For additional activities, see **Block Scheduling Copymasters**.)

Teaching All Students

Extra Help Have students add **ir** to their collection of verb conjugation flashcards. Have students sit in small circles and quiz each other on **ir**, as well as previous verbs.

Challenge Have students modify **Actividad 6**, changing the names, destinations, etc., or expand by making up their own dialogs.

Multiple Intelligences

Visual Put students in small groups to design their schedule for the coming week, using all the days of the week and various times of day. They should make their schedules colorful and include artwork. When the schedules are completed, vote on the 2 or 3 most appealing ones and display them on the bulletin board. Keep the schedules for use in later **Etapas.**

Teaching Resource Options

Print

Más práctica Workbook PE, p. 46
Para hispanohablantes Workbook
  PE, p. 44
Block Scheduling Copymasters
Unit 2 Resource Book
  Más práctica Workbook TE, p. 57
  Para hispanohablantes Workbook
    TE, p. 63
  Information Gap Activities, p. 68
  Audioscript, p. 81
  Audioscript *Para hispanohablantes*,
    p. 82

Audiovisual

OHT 56 (Quick Start)
Audio Program Cassettes 5A, 5B / CD 5
Audio *Para hispanohablantes*
  Cassette 5A / CD 5

Technology

Intrigas y aventuras CD-ROM, Disc 1

Quick Start Review

🔄 **Ir**

Use OHT 56 or write on board:
Complete each sentence with the
correct form of **ir**:

1. Los domingos, yo nunca ____ a la
   escuela.
2. Isabel siempre ____ a la clase de
   computación los miércoles.
3. A veces, tú ____ a la casa de tus
   abuelos los viernes.
4. Nosotros ____ mucho al gimnasio
   los sábados.
5. Uds. ____ al auditorio todos los
   días, ¿no?

Answers
1. voy   2. va   3. vas   4. vamos   5. van

Teaching Suggestions
Teaching Telling Time

• Tell students that **Es la una** uses a
  singular verb because you are talking
  about one hour. With **Son las dos**, you
  are talking about more than one hour.
• To help students distinguish between
  ¿Qué hora es? and **¿A qué hora +
  verb?**, have them listen carefully for
  Qué and **A qué**. The first few times,
  exaggerate these words.

GRAMÁTICA
Telling Time

There are several useful
phrases for talking about
the current time. Use:

¿Qué hora es? to ask what time it is.
Son las + *hour*. to give the time for every hour except one o'clock.
Es la una. to say it is one o'clock.

Son las doce *y minutes*

Use **y** + *minutes* for
the number of minutes
after the hour.

Son las doce. (12:00)
Son las doce y diez. (12:10)
Son las doce y cuarto. (12:15)
Son las doce y media. (12:30)

Es la una menos *minutes*

Use **menos** + *minutes*
for the number of minutes
before the hour.

Es la una. (1:00)
Es la una menos diez. (12:50)
Es la una menos cuarto. (12:45)

> Use **cuarto** for a
> quarter of an hour and
> **media** for half an hour.

To talk about when something will
happen, use:

¿A qué hora + *verb* + *event*?   ¿A qué hora es la clase?
What time is the class?

A las + *hour*   A las (dos, tres).
At (two o'clock, three o'clock).

A la + *one o'clock*   A la una.
At one o'clock.

ACTIVIDAD 9 Gramática

¿Qué hora es?

Hablar El padre de Isabel tiene una colección de relojes.
Trabaja con otro(a) estudiante para preguntar y decir
la hora que da cada uno. Cambien de papel. *(Hint: Isabel's
father has a collection of clocks. Tell the time for each.)*

1.  **2.** **3.**

modelo

Estudiante A: *¿Qué hora es?*
Estudiante B: *Son las siete y veinte.*

4. **5.** **6.**

■ **MÁS PRÁCTICA** *cuaderno* p. 46   ■ **PARA HISPANOHABLANTES** *cuaderno* p. 44

128 ciento veintiocho
Unidad 2

Classroom Community

Paired Activity Have students pretend that for one
day they could do whatever they would like. Students
should write their schedules, explaining what they
would do and at what time. Have several pairs present
their schedules to the class.

TPR Make up a short, fictitious story that includes as
many times (on the clock) in it as you have students.
On slips of paper, write out the times so that every
student receives a slip. Tell the class the story.
Whenever you call out a time, the student with that
time slip should stand up. By the end of the story, the
entire class should be standing.

ACTIVIDAD 10

¿A qué hora?

Escuchar/Escribir Escucha al profesor para completar el horario de Ana, una amiga de Isabel. Luego, escribe cuándo tiene cada clase. *(Hint: Listen and complete Ana's schedule. Then write when each class is.)*

modelo

arte - 7:30

Ana tiene la clase de arte a las siete y media de la mañana.

1. matemáticas
2. inglés
3. receso
4. ciencias naturales
5. estudios sociales
6. literatura

Vocabulario

Para hablar de la hora

Use these phrases when telling time.

A la una de la mañana/tarde/noche *At one in the morning/afternoon/night*

la medianoche *midnight*

el mediodía *noon*

el reloj *clock, watch*

por la mañana/tarde/noche *during the morning/afternoon/night*

¿Cuándo estudias?

ACTIVIDAD 11

Tu horario

PARA CONVERSAR

STRATEGY: SPEAKING

Take risks You learn faster when you are willing to take chances. Don't worry about sounding foolish. Your desire to communicate in Spanish encourages others and helps you.

Hablar Habla con otro(a) estudiante de tu horario, usando las preguntas como guía. Cambien de papel. *(Hint: Take turns with another student to ask questions about your schedules.)*

1. ¿Qué clases tienes por la mañana?
2. ¿Qué clases tienes por la tarde?
3. ¿A qué hora tienes inglés?
4. ¿A qué hora tienes el almuerzo?
5. ¿A qué hora tienes…?
6. ¿Qué días tienes la clase de…?

■ **MÁS COMUNICACIÓN** p. R5

NOTA CULTURAL

In Mexico the word **torta** is used to describe a large sandwich on crusty bread. In Spain **bocadillo** is used to describe this. However, in other countries, **torta** usually means *cake*. In Mexico, the word **pastel** is used to mean *cake*.

pastel

torta
bocadillo

ciento veintinueve
Etapa 2
129

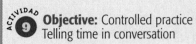
ACTIVIDAD 9

Objective: Controlled practice
Telling time in conversation

Answers
1. Es la una.
2. Son las seis y diez.
3. Son las once y media. *o* Son las once y treinta.
4. Son las cinco menos veinte *o* Son las cuatro y cuarenta.
5. Son las dos menos cinco. *o* Es la una y cincuenta y cinco.
6. Son las ocho y cuarto. *o* Son las ocho y quince.

Teaching Suggestions
Reinforcing Vocabulary

Ask additional simple questions. Students must use the new expressions in their answers: **¿Cuándo/A qué hora tienes el almuerzo? ¿Cuándo/A qué hora preparas tu tarea?** etc.

ACTIVIDAD 10

Objective: Transitional practice
Listening comprehension/Telling time

Answers *(See script, p. 117B.)*
1. matemáticas - 8:15 / Ana tiene la clase de matemáticas a las ocho y cuarto.
2. inglés - 9:00 / Ana tiene la clase de inglés a las nueve.
3. receso - 9:45 /Ana tiene el receso a las diez menos cuarto.
4. ciencias naturales - 10:30 / Ana tiene la clase de ciencias naturales a las diez y media.
5. estudios sociales - 11:15 / Ana tiene la clase de estudios sociales a las once y cuarto.
6. literatura - 12:00 / Ana tiene la clase de literatura al mediodía.

ACTIVIDAD 11

Objective: Open-ended practice
Discussing schedules in conversation

Answers will vary.

■ Block Schedule

Variety Working in pairs, have students imagine that their partner's watch is always 10 minutes fast. Use this model.

> A: ¿Qué hora es?
> B: Son las tres.
> A: No, no son las tres. Son las tres menos diez.

Each partner plays each role for at least 5 rounds. Note that Student B makes up a new time each round. (For additional activities, see **Block Scheduling Copymasters**.)

Teaching All Students

Extra Help Review numbers for telling time, by having students count off in class from 1-60. Then have them (a) count by 2s, (b) count by 5s, and (c) count backwards from 60.

Native Speakers Ask students if the 24-hour clock system is used in their home countries. Is it always used or only in certain cases? Have them explain to the class.

Multiple Intelligences

Logical/Mathematical Write a variety of real events on the board **(almuerzo 11:30–12:15)**. Have students calculate how many minutes each activity lasts.

Musical/Rhythmic Have students write a rap/chant to tell you what they do over the time span 9:00–12:00 (noon) on the hour, the quarter hour, and half hour.

Teaching Resource Options

Print 🖊

Más práctica Workbook PE, p. 47
Para hispanohablantes Workbook PE, p. 45
Block Scheduling Copymasters
Unit 2 Resource Book
  Más práctica Workbook TE, p. 58
  Para hispanohablantes Workbook TE, p. 64

Audiovisual 📼

OHT 57 (Quick Start)

Technology 💻

Intrigas y aventuras CD-ROM, Disc 1

Quick Start Review

♻ School locations and activities

Use OHT 57 or write on the board:
Match the activities with the places and write complete sentences:

Actividades	En...
1. buscar un libro	a. la cafetería
2. tomar un refresco	b. el gimnasio
3. usar una calculadora	c. la biblioteca
4. ayudar a los maestros de educación física	d. la clase de matemáticas

Answers *See p. 117B.*

Teaching Suggestions
Presenting Describing Location with the Verb estar

• Explain that **estar** is used to say where things are located, including things that never move, such as buildings, monuments, and countries.
• Remind students that they already know how to use **estar** to say how they are feeling: **Estoy bien.**
• To say where a function is held, remind students to use **ser: La fiesta es en la escuela.**

Objective: Controlled practice
The verb **estar**

Answers
1. Estamos en la clase de [español].   2. Está en clase de matemáticas.   3. Están en la cafetería.
4. Está en el auditorio.   5. Estás en la biblioteca.
6. Está en el gimnasio.

130 Vocabulary/Grammar • UNIDAD 2 Etapa 2

GRAMÁTICA — Describing Location with the Verb estar

To say where people or things are located, use the verb **estar**. Here are its forms in the present tense.

yo	**estoy**	nosotros(as)	**estamos**
tú	**estás**	vosotros(as)	**estáis**
usted, él, ella	**está**	ustedes, ellos(as)	**están**

The teacher says:
—La profesora Díaz **está** en su oficina durante el almuerzo…
*Professor Díaz **is** in her office during lunch…*

ACTIVIDAD 12 Gramática

¿Dónde están?

Leer/Escribir Lee las oraciones y explica dónde están los estudiantes. *(Hint: Read the sentences and explain where the students are.)*

modelo

Carlos habla español.
Está en la clase de español.

1. Nosotros miramos el pizarrón.
2. Ella usa una calculadora.
3. Ellas toman un refresco.
4. Él escucha música.
5. Tú buscas un libro.
6. Juana corre.

■ **MÁS PRÁCTICA** *cuaderno* p. 47
■ **PARA HISPANOHABLANTES** *cuaderno* p. 45

ACTIVIDAD 13

¡Cuántos lugares!

Hablar Isabel, Ricardo y sus amigos están en varios lugares durante el día. Con otro(a) estudiante, di dónde están.
(Hint: Take turns saying where Isabel, Ricardo, and friends are in the pictures.)

modelo

Tú: *¿Dónde están Isabel y Ricardo?*
Otro(a) estudiante: *Están en la clase.*

130 ciento treinta
Unidad 2

Classroom Community

Group Activity Working in groups of 6, have each group choose a topic, such as clothing, school subjects, school items, time, dates, likes and dislikes, family, etc. Each student in the group forms one question with one of the interrogative words on p. 131. Then have groups exchange questions and answer them.

Learning Scenario Your school was just informed that 5 students from your class were named Students of the Week. Organize a press conference in which the 5 students answer questions from the press about school schedules, when and where they study, etc. After the conference, have the students from the press corps work in groups to compile the answers and write a summary. The 5 Students of the Week will evaluate the articles.

ACTIVIDAD 14

¿Dónde estás?

Hablar/Escribir Son las diez de la mañana del lunes. Explica dónde están estas personas. *(Hint: It's ten o'clock Monday morning. Explain where these people are.)*

1. yo
2. mi maestro(a) de español
3. los maestros de educación física
4. los estudiantes de drama
5. mi hermano(a)
6. los estudiantes de mi clase y yo

GRAMÁTICA

Asking Questions: Interrogative Words

There are many ways to ask questions. This is how you create a simple question that has a *yes* or *no* answer.

Statement	Technique	Question
Isabel va a la escuela.	Use rising intonation to imply a question.	¿Isabel va a la escuela?
Isabel va a la escuela.	Switch the position of the **subject** and **verb**.	¿Va Isabel a la escuela?

You've already learned the interrogative words (a)dónde and cuántos(as).

Here are more interrogative words.

Some questions are formed by putting a **conjugated verb** after the question word.

> Each interrogative word has an **accent** on the appropriate vowel.

cómo	how	¿Cómo está Ricardo?
cuál(es)	which or what	¿Cuál es el libro?
cuándo	when	¿Cuándo estudia Ricardo?
por qué	why	¿Por qué va Ricardo a casa?
qué	what	¿Qué es?
quién(es)	who	¿Quién(es) habla(n) con el profesor?

> All questions are **preceded** by an **inverted question mark** and **followed** by a **question mark**.

Sometimes qué and cuál(es) are followed by words other than verbs. Qué can be followed directly by a **noun**, but cuál or cuáles cannot. Use cuál for one item and cuáles for more than one.

¿Qué **libro** mira Isabel?
*What **book** is Isabel looking at?*

¿Cuáles **de los libros** mira Isabel?
*Which **books** is Isabel looking at?*

ciento treinta y uno
Etapa 2

131

Teaching All Students

Native Speakers Have students dramatize a conversation among friends, one of whom **es muy preguntón/preguntona** (always asking questions). Students try to make plans, but the **preguntón/ preguntona** keeps interrupting with one question after another. Have the rest of the students write down the interrogatives as they hear them.

Multiple Intelligences

Visual Have students design a colorful, useful poster for the classroom showing interrogatives. For example, a flower with one question word in the middle and question sentences using that word on the petals.

Kinesthetic Divide the class into groups and have students act out each interrogative. (For example: pointing to the clock: ¿A qué hora?)

ACTIVIDAD 13 Objective: Transitional practice
The verb **estar** in conversation

Answers
1. A: ¿Dónde están Isabel y Ricardo?
   B: Están en la cafetería.
2. A: ¿Dónde está Ricardo?
   B: Está en la biblioteca.
3. A: ¿Dónde están Ricardo y sus amigos?
   B: Están en el gimnasio.
4. A: ¿Dónde están Isabel y Ricardo?
   B: Están en la oficina.
5. A: ¿Dónde están Isabel, Ricardo y sus amigos?
   B: Están en el auditorio.
6. A: ¿Dónde está Isabel?
   B: Está en casa.

ACTIVIDAD 14 Objective: Open-ended practice
The verb **estar**

Answers will vary.

Quick Start Review

♻ Estar

Use OHT 57 or write on the board: Using **estar,** write the name and location of 5 people or items in the school.

Answers *See p. 117B.*

Teaching Suggestions
Reinforcing Asking Questions: Interrogative Words

Have students write each interrogative (as well as **dónde** and **adónde**) on a flashcard, and use them for practice. Student 1 shows a card to Student 2, who uses that word to form a question.

Block Schedule

Change of Pace Have students cut out pictures from magazines that show people doing things. Tape them on a poster or flip chart and number them. Give students a worksheet that provides an answer to a possible question for each picture. For example: (1) a picture of a girl in a hospital bed might correspond to the answer on the worksheet (1) **Isabel no está bien.** The question students would provide is ¿**Cómo está Isabel?** (For additional activities, see **Block Scheduling Copymasters.**)

Teaching Resource Options

Print

Más práctica Workbook PE, p. 48
Para hispanohablantes Workbook PE, p. 46
Block Scheduling Copymasters
Unit 2 Resource Book
  Más práctica Workbook TE, p. 59
  Para hispanohablantes Workbook TE, p. 65
  Information Gap Activities, pp. 69–70
  Audioscript, p. 81
  Audioscript *Para hispanohablantes*, p. 82

Audiovisual

Audio Program Cassettes 5A, 5B / CD 5
Audio *Para hispanohablantes* Cassette 5A / CD 5

Technology

Intrigas y aventuras CD-ROM, Disc 1

 Objective: Controlled practice Interrogative words

Answers
1. ¿Tienen ellos clases difíciles hoy?
2. ¿Habla Ricardo con su profesora a las dos?
3. ¿Tienen Isabel y Ricardo una prueba?
4. ¿Estudian Isabel y sus amigas en la biblioteca?
5. ¿Terminan ellos las clases a las cinco?

 Objective: Controlled practice Interrogative words

Answers
1. qué	3. Quién	5. Por qué
2. Cómo	4. Cómo	6. Cuándo

Objective: Controlled practice Interrogative words

Answers
1. Qué	4. Cuál	6. Qué
2. Cuál	5. Cuáles	7. Cuáles
3. Qué		

Culture Highlights

● **EL ESTADIO GUILLERMO CAÑEDO**
The Guillermo Cañedo Stadium (Olympic Stadium) was the site of the 1970 and 1986 World Cup of soccer. It has a capacity of 115,000 and provides spectators with unrestricted views of the field from every sector.

Un día típico

Hablar Una amiga de Isabel te habla de un día típico, pero tú no escuchas. Tienes que verificar lo que dice. Cambia la posición del verbo para formar una pregunta. Sigue el modelo. *(Hint: Make sure of what Isabel's friend is telling you. Ask a question by changing the position of the verb.)*

modelo

Isabel y Ricardo van a la escuela a la una.
¿Van Isabel y Ricardo a la escuela a la una?

1. Ellos tienen clases difíciles hoy.
2. Ricardo habla con su profesora a las dos.
3. Isabel y Ricardo tienen una prueba.
4. Isabel y sus amigas estudian en la biblioteca.
5. Ellos terminan las clases a las cinco.

La amiga curiosa

Leer/Escribir Isabel tiene una amiga curiosa. Le hace muchas preguntas sobre su clase de ciencias naturales. Escribe la palabra interrogativa para completar sus preguntas. *(Hint: Write the appropriate question word.)*

1. ¿A _____ hora tienes la clase? A las cuatro.
2. ¿ _____ es la clase? Difícil.
3. ¿ _____ enseña la clase? La profesora Díaz.
4. ¿ _____ es la profesora? Simpática.
5. ¿ _____ tienes que hablar con la profesora? No tengo mi tarea.
6. ¿ _____ preparas tu tarea? Por la noche.

¿Qué o cuál?

Leer Necesitas más información sobre Isabel y Ricardo. Completa las preguntas con **qué** o **cuál(es)** para informarte. *(Hint: Complete each question with qué or cuál(es) to ask for more information.)*

1. Ricardo tiene ocho materias este semestre.
   ¿_____ materia le gusta más?
2. Hoy es el cumpleaños de Isabel.
   ¿_____ es la fecha de hoy?
3. Ricardo tiene una clase a la una.
   ¿_____ clase tiene a la una?
4. Hay dos señores en la clase.
   ¿_____ es el profesor?
5. Hay cinco libros en la clase de matemáticas.
   ¿_____ de los libros son de Ricardo?
6. No es una calculadora.
   ¿_____ es?
7. Paco, Ricardo, Ana y Marcela son estudiantes en la clase de matemáticas.
   ¿_____ de ellos sacan buenas notas?

■ **MÁS PRÁCTICA** *cuaderno* p. 48
■ **PARA HISPANOHABLANTES** *cuaderno* p. 46

Mexico City is located in a valley surrounded by volcanic mountains. Its Olympic Stadium, built for the 1968 Summer Olympics, resembles a volcano with a bowl sunk into its crater.

Classroom Community

Group Activity Have students plan a Review Fair. Divide the information in the **Etapa** into categories: telling time, new verbs, interrogatives, snack food.
• Have groups sign up for the category they feel most prepared in. Be sure categories are equally represented.
• Each group will assemble flash cards, review sheets, information posters, and short quizzes for their booth.
• Each group then sets up a booth for each category where everyone can visit and practice the materials.
• Students will need to trade off booth duty and visiting other booths.

Paired Activity Have students look through all of Unit 1 and **Etapas** 1 and 2 of Unit 2 to find words that begin with **h** or **j**. Have students create a **Trabalenguas** using the words they find. Give a prize to the pair that finds the most words.

ACTIVIDAD 18

¿Quién?

Hablar/Escribir A veces Isabel no escucha cuando sus amigos le hablan. Ayúdala a hacer preguntas basadas en lo que dicen. *(Hint: Help Isabel ask questions based on what her friends say.)*

modelo

Elena estudia español. (¿Quién?)

¿Quién estudia español?

1. El inglés es fácil. (¿Cómo?)
2. Paco y sus amigos tienen el receso a las tres. (¿Cuándo?)
3. La clase de música es divertida. (¿Cuál?)
4. Ana está en clase. (¿Dónde?)
5. Margarita compra una computadora. (¿Qué?)
6. Luisa descansa. (¿Quién?)
7. Estudio por la mañana. (¿Cuándo?)
8. Rita tiene una computadora nueva. (¿Qué?)
9. El libro de arte es interesante. (¿Cuál?)
10. Es un diccionario. (¿Qué?)

ACTIVIDAD 19

¡Pobre Luis!

Escuchar Escucha la conversación entre Ernesto y Luis. Luego, contesta las preguntas. *(Hint: Listen to the conversation. Then answer the questions.)*

1. ¿Por qué no está bien Luis?
   a. Tiene que ayudar a su padre.
   b. Está muy bien.
   c. Tiene un semestre difícil.

2. ¿Qué hora es?
   a. Es la una y veinticinco.
   b. Son las dos y media.
   c. A la una y veinticinco.

3. ¿A qué hora tiene la cita con la señora García?
   a. A las ocho.
   b. A la una y media.
   c. Es la una y media.

4. ¿Cuándo tiene un examen de literatura?
   a. mañana
   b. el lunes
   c. hoy

ACTIVIDAD 20

¿Cómo es tu horario?

Hablar Pregúntale a otro(a) estudiante sobre los detalles de su horario, como los días y las horas de sus clases, cómo son y adónde va para las clases. Cambien de papel. *(Hint: Ask another student about his or her schedule. Change roles.)*

modelo

Tú: *¿Qué clases tienes por la mañana?*

Otro(a) estudiante: *Tengo español, matemáticas y…*

Tú: *¿A qué hora tienes la clase de…?*

Otro(a) estudiante: *A las diez menos cuarto.*

Tú: *¿Adónde vas para esta clase?*

Otro(a) estudiante: *Voy al…*

■ **MÁS COMUNICACIÓN** p. R5

Pronunciación

Trabalenguas

The **h** in Spanish is always silent, like the *h* in the English word *honest.* The j in Spanish sounds like the English *h* in *Ha, ha!* To practice these sounds, try this tongue twister.

Hoy Juanita hace de jinete.

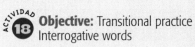

ACTIVIDAD 18
Objective: Transitional practice Interrogative words

Answers
1. ¿Cómo es el inglés?
2. ¿Cuándo tienen el receso Paco y sus amigos?
3. ¿Cuál es divertida?
4. ¿Dónde está Ana?
5. ¿Qué compra Margarita?
6. ¿Quién descansa?
7. ¿Cuándo estudias?
8. ¿Qué tiene Rita?
9. ¿Cuál es interesante?
10. ¿Qué es?

ACTIVIDAD 19
Objective: Transitional practice Listening comprehension/ interrogative words

Answers (See script, p. 117B.)
1. c
2. a
3. b
4. b

ACTIVIDAD 20
Objective: Open-ended practice Interrogative words in conversation

Answers will vary.

Dictation
After students have read the tongue twister in the **Pronunciación,** have them close their books. Dictate the tongue twister in segments while students write it.

■ Block Schedule

Peer Teaching Have each student choose a primary "study buddy" and a secondary "study buddy." Whenever students have questions about their homework assignments or need help with a particular point, they should first ask their primary buddy for help. If that student is not available, they should ask their secondary buddy. (For additional activities, see **Block Scheduling Copymasters.**)

Teaching All Students

Extra Help Have students write a guided paragraph about school. Provide questions to help them organize their paragraph. For example: **¿Cuántas materias tienes? ¿Qué tienes a las ocho de la mañana? ¿Quién enseña la clase? ¿Es un semestre fácil o difícil?**

Native Speakers Ask students to talk about a typical school day in their home countries. How long are classes? Do students or teachers change rooms for each period?

Multiple Intelligences

Interpersonal Working in small groups, have students prepare interview questions to ask you and/or to ask a teacher in another subject area. After carrying out the interview, have the groups present their findings to the class.

Teaching Resource Options

Print

Unit 2 Resource Book
  Audioscript, pp. 82–83
  Audioscript *Para hispanohablantes*,
    pp. 82–83

Audiovisual

Audio Program Cassette 5A / CD 5
Audio *Para hispanohablantes*
  Cassette 5A / CD 5
OHT 57 (Quick Start)
Canciones Cassette / CD

Quick Start Review

♻ Descriptions

Use OHT 57 or write on the board:
List as many foods as you can in
Spanish.

Answers
Answers will vary. Answers could include:
las papas fritas, la fruta, la hamburguesa,
la torta, las tortillas, los tacos, los burritos,
las fajitas, las quesadillas, la paella, el flan

Teaching Suggestions
Presenting Cultura y comparaciones

• Have students look at the pictures
on pp. 134–135 and guess the topic
of the reading. Write the list of
possibilities on the board.

• Ask students for their observations on
the photos. What are the people
doing? Where are they in each
photo? Do these places look similar
to those in the U.S.?

Reading Strategy

Ask students to identify what comes to
mind when they think of snack foods.
Then have them scan the reading to see if
those foods are included in the reading.

Supplementary Vocabulary

¿Cuánto es?   How much is it?
¿Tiene Ud.   Do you have
  cambio?   change?
¡Está rico   It tastes great!
  (delicioso)!

En colores

CULTURA Y COMPARACIONES

PARA CONOCERNOS
STRATEGY: CONNECTING CULTURES
Compare snack foods Make a list of your
favorite snack foods. Then read to find out
about typical snack foods in Mexico City.
Based on this, how would you compare snack
foods in the U.S. with those in Mexico?

Las meriendas populares

Estados Unidos	México
1.	1.
2.	2.
3.	3.

¿Quieres comer una merienda mexicana?

Aquí tenemos dos tipos de meriendas típicas
de México. En México la
merienda grande se llama
una torta. La torta tiene pan
redondo[1] y muchos
ingredientes. La merienda
pequeña se llama **un sándwich.**
En Estados Unidos, ¿cómo se
llama una torta?

Una merienda típica de México es
el taco al pastor. Tiene carne asada[2],
normalmente puerco[3],
en una tortilla de
maíz[4]. ¿Es diferente
de los tacos que tú comes?

[1] round bread   [3] pork
[2] roasted meat   [4] corn

TAQUERIA

Classroom Community

Group Activity Have students read the article in
groups. The first student reads the first paragraph,
pausing after the question at the end. The student who
answers the question correctly gets to read the second
paragraph. The student who answers the question at
the end the second paragraph gets to read the third
paragraph. That student should then make up a
question about the third paragraph.

Storytelling In groups, have students make up a
story that includes a food vendor and a few customers.
(The menus suggested on TE p. 118 could be used
here.) Students should use **Etapa** vocabulary and the
Supplementary Vocabulary. Have several groups
present their stories.

Si te gusta comer fruta para la merienda, hay una variedad increíble. O tal vez te interesa[5] un **agua de fruta** en vez de[6] agua. En México es común beber aguas de frutas tropicales. Hay aguas de papaya, piña[7] y muchas otras frutas. ¡Y si no te gustan las frutas, siempre es posible comprar **una hamburguesa y papas fritas**!

---

[5] you are interested in
[6] instead of
[7] pineapple

¿Comprendiste?

1. ¿Qué diferencia hay entre un sándwich y una torta en México?
2. ¿Cómo es el taco al pastor?
3. ¿Qué hay en un agua de fruta?
4. ¿Cuáles de las meriendas mexicanas comes?

¿Qué piensas?

Estás en México y quieres comer. ¿Qué vas a comprar, una hamburguesa o una merienda típica de México? ¿Por qué?

135

Culture Highlights

● **AGUA DE FRUTA** In Mexico, fruit juices are called **aguas de fruta**. Fruit shakes are called **licuados** because they are made in the **licuadora** (blender). In other places in Latin America, fruit juices are called **jugos de frutas**. In Spain, they are called **zumos de frutas**.

● **LA COMIDA** One result of the arrival of Spaniards to the Americas was an exchange of foods. The Spanish brought onions, wheat, rice, and sugarcane to the New World. They returned with corn, chili peppers, chocolate, tomatoes, and avocados. These products were unknown in Europe.

Language Note

The Spanish settlers adapted the following Nahuatl (Aztec) words:

mahís	maíz (corn)
chillí	chile (chili pepper)
chocolatl	chocolate (chocolate)
tomatl	tomate (tomato)
ahuactl	aguacate (avocado)

Interdisciplinary Connection

Ecology Outdoor vendors are careful to recycle the glass bottles from the soft drinks they sell. Customers drink their soft drinks at the stand and return the bottles to the vendors. Some vendors pour the drink into a baggie. People drink the soda with a straw and throw the baggie away.

¿Comprendiste?

Answers
1. Un sándwich es pequeño; una torta es grande. La torta tiene pan redondo.
2. Tiene carne asada, normalmente puerco, en una tortilla de maíz.
3. Hay frutas tropicales—papaya, piña y muchas otras frutas.
4. *Answers will vary.*

Block Schedule

FunBreak When discussing snack foods, bring in a Hispanic treat for students to try. Some easy and inexpensive snacks are plantain chips, tropical fruit juices, tortilla española, and flan. (See the recipe for **Natilla** in the **Ampliación**, TE p. 95B.)

Teaching All Students

Extra Help Have students list the words that are new to them or for which they can't remember the meaning. Form a class list of new and/or difficult vocabulary items.

Native Speakers Ask students to talk about the **merienda** in their home communities. Do they have a snack at school and at home? Is the **merienda** a "fourth meal" for the family?

Multiple Intelligences

Visual Have students make a poster of one or more typical Mexican snacks to enjoy instead of typical snacks in the U.S.

Teaching Resource Options

Print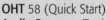

Para hispanohablantes Workbook PE,
  pp. 47–48
Block Scheduling Copymasters
Unit 2 Resource Book
  Para hispanohablantes Workbook
    TE, pp. 66–67
  Information Gap Activities,
    p. 71
  Family Involvement, pp. 72–73
  Multiple Choice Test Questions,
    pp. 170–178

Audiovisual

OHT 58 (Quick Start)
Audio Program Testing Cassette T1 /
  CD T1

Technology

Electronic Teacher Tools/Test
  Generator
Intrigas y aventuras CD-ROM, Disc 1

Quick Start Review

🔄 Interrogatives

Use OHT 58 or write on the board:
Write 3 questions using 3 different
interrogatives and 3 different verbs.

Answers *See p. 117B.*

Teaching Suggestions
What Have Students Learned?

• Have students look at the "Now you
  can…" notes listed on the left side of
  pages 136–137. Tell students to think
  about which areas they might not be
  sure of. For those areas, they should
  consult the "To review" notes.
• Use the video to review vocabulary
  and structures.

Now you can...

• talk about
  schedules.

To review

• telling time, see
  p. 128.

Now you can...

• ask and tell time.

To review

• telling time, see
  p. 128.
• location with the
  verb **estar**, see
  p. 130.

ETAPA 2

En uso
REPASO y MÁS COMUNICACIÓN

OBJECTIVES

• Talk about schedules
• Ask and tell time
• Ask questions
• Say where you are going
• Request food

ACTIVIDAD 1 ¡Qué horario!

Sara habla de su horario. ¿Qué dice?
(Hint: Tell what Sara says about her schedule.)

modelo

inglés

*Tengo inglés los lunes, miércoles y
viernes a las siete y media.*

Sara Blanco	lunes	martes	miércoles	jueves	viernes
7:30	inglés	——	inglés	——	inglés
8:15	——	computación	——	computación	——
9:00	literatura	música	literatura	música	literatura
9:45	receso	receso	receso	receso	receso
10:30	educación física	ciencias naturales	educación física	ciencias naturales	educación física
11:15	historia	——	historia	——	historia
12:00	matemáticas	arte	matemáticas	arte	matemáticas

1. arte   **5.** receso
2. literatura   **6.** historia
3. música   **7.** matemáticas
4. ciencias   **8.** computación
     naturales

ACTIVIDAD 2 Un día ocupado

Hablas por teléfono con un(a) amigo(a). Hablen de la hora y de
dónde están estas personas. Cambien de papel. *(Hint: You're on the
phone. Tell the time and where people are.)*

modelo

9:05: Isabel (cafetería)
Tú: *¿Qué hora es?*
Otro(a) estudiante: *Son las **nueve y cinco** de la mañana.*
Tú: *¿Dónde está **Isabel**?*
Otro(a) estudiante: *Está en **la cafetería**.*

1. 8:15: Gloria (clase de arte)   **5.** 2:40: Isabel (oficina del maestro)
2. 11:30: Ricardo (gimnasio)   **6.** 4:25: ustedes (gimnasio)
3. 12:50: la profesora (oficina)   **7.** 7:30: René (biblioteca)
4. 1:00: Manuel y Eva (auditorio)   **8.** 9:45: tú (casa)

136 | ciento treinta y seis
Unidad 2

Classroom Community

Cooperative Learning Divide the class into groups
of 5. Student 1 is assigned the first of the 5 "Now you
can..." sections, Student 2 the second, and so on. The
group members review the concept of their sections
and plan a short review lesson to present to the rest of
the group. They should include instruction as well as
review practice.

Paired Activity Have students create a list of
articles for a time capsule that would depict a typical
student week at their school. For example: a class
schedule, a map of the school, a list of teachers, a
lunch menu, etc. Have them gather the articles and
translate as much as possible into Spanish.

ACTIVIDAD 3 ¡Muchas preguntas!

Los amigos de Ricardo le hacen preguntas. Complétalas con palabras interrogativas según las respuestas entre paréntesis.
(Hint: Complete Ricardo's friends' questions with the correct interrogative word.)

1. ¿ _____ estudias? (En mi casa.)
2. ¿ _____ es tu clase favorita? (La clase de literatura.)
3. ¿ _____ vas al gimnasio? (Por la tarde.)
4. ¿ _____ estás hoy? (Bien.)
5. ¿ _____ es el profesor de computación? (El profesor Anaya.)
6. ¿ _____ vas? (A la cafetería.)
7. ¿ _____ estudias inglés? (Me gusta el inglés.)
8. ¿ _____ están en la biblioteca? (Isabel y Andrea.)
9. ¿ _____ de estos libros necesitas? (El diccionario y el libro de inglés.)

ACTIVIDAD 4 En la escuela

Es la una de la tarde. ¿Adónde van estas personas? *(Hint: Tell where everyone is going.)*

modelo

Miguel y Ana tienen que correr.   *Van al gimnasio.*

1. Necesito buscar unos libros.
2. Isabel tiene que hablar con sus profesores.
3. Tú quieres comprar una torta.
4. Mis amigos tienen que cantar en un programa.
5. Nosotros tenemos un examen de español.

ACTIVIDAD 5 En la cafetería

¿Que dices cuando quieres una de estas meriendas? *(Hint: What do you say when you want one of these snacks?)*

modelo

Un taco, por favor.

1.   2.   3.   4.   5.   6.

ciento treinta y siete
Etapa 2   **137**

Now you can...
- ask questions.

To review
- interrogative words, see p. 131.

Now you can...
- say where you are going.

To review
- the verb **ir**, see p. 126.

Now you can...
- request food.

To review
- vocabulary for snacks, see p. 121.

ACTIVIDAD 1 Answers

1. Tengo arte los martes y jueves al mediodía (a las doce).
2. Tengo literatura los lunes, miércoles y viernes a las nueve.
3. Tengo música los martes y jueves a las nueve.
4. Tengo ciencias naturales los martes y jueves a las diez y media.
5. Tengo receso los lunes, martes, miércoles, jueves y viernes a las diez menos cuarto.
6. Tengo historia los lunes, miércoles y viernes a las once y cuarto.
7. Tengo matemáticas los lunes, miércoles y viernes al mediodía (a las doce).
8. Tengo computación los martes y jueves a las ocho y cuarto.

ACTIVIDAD 2 Answers

1. Son las ocho y cuarto de la mañana. / Está en la clase de arte.
2. Son las once y media de la mañana. / Está en el gimnasio.
3. Es la una menos diez de la tarde. / Está en la oficina.
4. Es la una de la tarde. / Están en el auditorio.
5. Son las tres menos veinte de la tarde. / Está en la oficina del maestro.
6. Son las cuatro y veinticinco de la tarde. / Estamos en el gimnasio.
7. Son las siete y media de la noche. / Está en la biblioteca.
8. Son las diez menos cuarto de la noche. / Estoy en casa.

ACTIVIDAD 3 Answers

1. Dónde	4. Cómo	6. Adónde	8. Quiénes
2. Cuál	5. Quién	7. Por qué	9. Cuáles
3. Cuándo			

ACTIVIDAD 4 Answers

1. Voy a la biblioteca.
2. Va a la oficina.
3. Vas a la cafetería.
4. Van al auditorio.
5. Vamos a la clase de español.

ACTIVIDAD 5 Answers

1. Fruta, por favor.
2. Un refresco, por favor.
3. Una hamburguesa, por favor.
4. Unas papas fritas, por favor.
5. Un sándwich, por favor.
6. Agua, por favor.

Teaching All Students

Extra Help Ask students to write a personal response to each question in **Actividad 3**.

Native Speakers If students have successfully completed the activities in the **Para hispanohablantes** Workbook, have them each prepare 5 quiz questions (and answers). Then have them exchange papers. Coorperative peer correction in groups will help students prepare for the **Etapa** exam.

Multiple Intelligences

Visual Working in pairs, have students scramble the word order for the sentences in **Actividad 4**. They should then exchange papers and re-order the words.

Kinesthetic Have students look back at the photo on pp. 118–119. Have them arrange a similar scene. Then have them write and present a friendly dialog between Ricardo and Isabel.

Block Schedule

Variety Have students write for 10 minutes on the topic: **Yo, el/la estudiante...".** They should include as much as they can about themselves, using known vocabulary and structures. (For additional activities, see **Block Scheduling Copymasters**.)

Teaching Resource Options

Print

Unit 2 Resource Book
Cooperative Quizzes, pp. 84–85
Etapa Exam, Forms A and B,
  pp. 86–95
Para hispanohablantes Etapa Exam,
  pp. 96–100
Portfolio Assessment, pp. 101–102
Multiple Choice Test Questions,
  pp. 170–178

Audiovisual

OHT 58 (Quick Start)
Audio Program Testing Cassette T1 /
CD T1

Technology

Electronic Teacher Tools/Test
Generator
www.mcdougallittell.com

ACTIVIDAD 6

Rubric: Speaking

Criteria	Scale	
Sentence structure	1 2 3	A = 11–12 pts.
Vocabulary use	1 2 3	B = 9–10 pts.
Originality	1 2 3	C = 7–8 pts.
Fluency	1 2 3	D = 4–6 pts.
		F = < 4 pts.

ACTIVIDAD 7 *Answers will vary.*

ACTIVIDAD 8 *En tu propia voz*

Rubric: Writing

Criteria	Scale	
Vocabulary use	1 2 3 4 5	A = 14–15 pts.
Accuracy	1 2 3 4 5	B = 12–13 pts.
Creativity, appearance	1 2 3 4 5	C = 10–11 pts.
		D = 8–9 pts.
		F = < 8 pts.

Interdisciplinary Connection

Home economics With a home economics class, choose a Mexican recipe from a cookbook and prepare it for both classes to enjoy. On a bulletin board, post the illustrated recipe with a resource list for needed vocabulary so that other curious students can try the recipe.

ACTIVIDAD 6 **El horario**

PARA CONVERSAR

STRATEGY: SPEAKING

Help your partner Make an effort to discover what you have in common. If you think of an activity that you have learned to say but don't remember the word, ask **¿Cómo se dice…?** Help each other out.

Conversa con otro(a) estudiante sobre su horario. *(Hint: Discuss your schedule with a partner.)*

¿A qué hora…?

 estar en la clase de inglés
 ir a la cafetería
 estar en el gimnasio
 preparar la tarea
 usar la computadora
 descansar

ACTIVIDAD 7 **¿Dónde estoy?**

Describe una situación. Incluye información sobre la hora y las actividades de las personas. Tus amigos tienen que adivinar dónde estás. *(Hint: Describe a situation. Your partners have to guess where you are.)*

modelo

Tú: *Son las diez. Uso mi calculadora y escucho al profesor.*

Otro(a) estudiante: *Estás en la clase de matemáticas.*

ACTIVIDAD 8 *En tu propia voz*

ESCRITURA Prepara siete preguntas para un(a) nuevo(a) estudiante. Incluye preguntas sobre su horario, sus clases y sus actividades. *(Hint: List seven questions for a new student.)*

¿A qué hora…? ¿Cuál es…? ¿Qué…?
¿Dónde estás a las…? ¿Cómo es…? ¿Cuándo…?
¿Por qué…? ¿Adónde vas para…? ¿Quién…?

CONEXIONES

La salud You can learn about the nutrition in Mexican food from cookbooks, a menu from a Mexican restaurant, or the grocery store. Choose three foods and a beverage and find out about their nutritional value. Read their packaging, request nutritional information from a restaurant, or check a book that lists nutritional values. Create a chart. Which is the most nutritious? Why?

	Calorías	Grasa	Carbohidratos	Vitaminas
1.				
2.				

Classroom Community

Paired Activity Put students in pairs. One student chooses a vocabulary word from the **Repaso de vocabulario** list and uses it in a game of hangman. Have students play until they have each guessed 5–10 words.

Learning Scenario Divide students into small groups. Assign half of the groups the skit **Horario fantástico** and the other half **Horario horrible.** Each group then describes and dramatizes their imaginary schedule, embellishing with tales of teachers and homework. Students vote at the end for the most convincing skit.

En resumen
REPASO DE VOCABULARIO

TALKING ABOUT SCHEDULES

el almuerzo	lunch
la cita	appointment
el horario	schedule
el receso	break
el semestre	semester

Activities

comprar	to buy
descansar	to rest
estar	to be
terminar	to finish
tomar	to take, to eat or drink
visitar	to visit

ASKING AND TELLING TIME

¿A qué hora es...?	(At) What time is...?
¿Qué hora es?	What time is it?
A la(s)...	At... o'clock.
Es la.../Son las...	It is... o'clock.
de la mañana	in the morning
de la noche	at night
de la tarde	in the afternoon
la medianoche	midnight
el mediodía	noon
menos	to, before
por la mañana	during the morning
por la noche	during the evening
por la tarde	during the afternoon
el reloj	clock, watch
y cuarto	quarter past
y media	half past

ASKING QUESTIONS

adónde	(to) where
cómo	how
cuál(es)	which (ones), what
cuándo	when
dónde	where
por qué	why
qué	what
quién(es)	who

REQUESTING FOOD

¿Quieres beber...?	Do you want to drink...?
¿Quieres comer...?	Do you want to eat...?
Quiero beber...	I want to drink...
Quiero comer...	I want to eat...

Snacks

el agua (fem.)	water
la fruta	fruit
la hamburguesa	hamburger
la merienda	snack
las papas fritas	french fries
el refresco	soft drink
la torta	sandwich
el vaso de	glass of

SAYING WHERE YOU ARE GOING

ir	to go
al	to the

Places

el auditorio	auditorium
la biblioteca	library
la cafetería	cafeteria, coffee shop
el gimnasio	gymnasium
la oficina	office

OTHER WORDS AND PHRASES

durante	during
por favor	please
la verdad	truth

Juego

¿Adónde van?

Marco: Me gusta escuchar música.

Maricarmen: Necesito buscar unos libros.

Josefina: Voy a hablar con la maestra. Ella no está en clase.

¿Adónde va Marco? ¿Maricarmen? ¿Josefina?

 Buenos días.

 Good morning.

 x + y = z

Quick Start Review

🔄 Etapa vocabulary

Use OHT 58 or write on the board. Write a short poem using vocabulary words from this **Etapa.** (This activity may also be assigned as homework.)

Answers will vary.

Teaching Suggestions
Vocabulary Review

• Ask students to list the 10 words they find the most difficult to recall.
• Have them create visuals or mnemonic devices that will help them.

Juego

Answers

Marco va al auditorio.
Maricarmen va a la biblioteca.
Josefina va a la oficina.

Block Schedule

Retention After doing the review exercises, have students think about the types of questions that might be on the **Etapa** exam. In groups, have them write several such questions. A group of students could swap questions with another group. Are they able to answer each other's questions correctly?

Teaching All Students

Extra Help Have students look back at the activities in the **Etapa** and choose one that was challenging for them at the time. They should then redo the exercise to see if it is easier to complete now. If not, they should review the instructional material.

Challenge See who can use the most vocabulary words in one sentence.

Native Speakers For the **Conexiones,** have Spanish-speaking students help the English speakers generate a list of food items from which to choose.

Multiple Intelligences

Intrapersonal Have students write a script for their own 10-frame dialog similar to the dialog on pp. 122–123.

Planning Guide CLASSROOM MANAGEMENT

OBJECTIVES

Communication
- Discuss plans *pp. 142–143, 156–157*
- Sequence events *pp. 144–145*
- Talk about places and people you know *pp. 144–145, 158–59*

Grammar
- Use **ir a** + infinitive *pp. 149–151*
- Use the present tense of regular **-er** and **-ir** verbs *pp. 151–152*
- Use verbs with irregular **yo** forms *p. 153*
- Use the verb **oír** *p. 154*

Pronunciation
- Word stress *p. 155*
- Dictation *TE p. 155*

Culture
- **El Museo Nacional de Antropología** *p. 146*
- Mealtimes in Mexico *p. 152*
- **El Zócalo** *pp. 158–159*

♻ **Recycling**
- **Estar** *p. 147*
- Food and drinks *p. 148*
- Telling time *p. 149*
- **Me gusta, tener que** *p. 151*
- Adverbs of frequency *p. 152*
- People *p. 153*
- Places *p. 154*

STRATEGIES

Listening Strategies
- Listen and observe *pp. 144–145*

Speaking Strategies
- Use all you know *p. 148*
- Ask for clarification *p. 162*

Reading Strategies
- Skim *p. 156*

Writing Strategies
- Brainstorm vocabulary before writing *p. 162*
- Organize information chronologically and by category *pp. 164–165*

Connecting Cultures Strategies
- Learn about a museum in Mexico City *p. 146*
- Compare mealtimes in Mexico and in the U.S. *p. 152*
- Learn about the leisure activities of Mexican young people *pp. 156–157*
- Connect and compare what you know about places in your community to help you learn about places in a new community *pp. 158–159*

PROGRAM RESOURCES

 Print
- *Más práctica* Workbook PE, *pp. 49–56*
- Block Scheduling Copymasters, *pp. 49–56*
- Unit 2 Resource Book
  Más práctica Workbook TE, *pp. 103–110*
  Para hispanohablantes Workbook TE, *pp. 111–118*
- Information Gap Activities *pp. 119–122*
- Family Involvement *pp. 123–124*
- Video Activities *pp. 125–127*
- Videoscript *pp. 128–130*
- Audioscript *pp. 131–134*
- Assessment Program, Unit 2 Etapa 3 *pp. 135–178*
- Answer Keys *pp. 179–194*

 Audiovisual
- Audio Program Cassettes 6A, 6B / CD 6
- *Canciones* Cassette / CD
- Video Program Videotape 2 / Videodisc 1B
- Overhead Transparencies M1–M5; GO1–GO5; 38, 59–68

 **Technology**
- Electronic Teacher Tools/Test Generator
- *Intrigas y aventuras* CD-ROM, Disc 1
- www.mcdougallittell.com

 Assessment Program Options
- Cooperative Quizzes (Unit 2 Resource Book)
- Etapa Exam Forms A and B (Unit 2 Resource Book)
- *Para hispanohablantes* Etapa Exam (Unit 2 Resource Book)
- Portfolio Assessment (Unit 2 Resource Book)
- Unit 2 Comprehensive Test (Unit 2 Resource Book)
- *Para hispanohablantes* Unit 2 Comprehensive Test (Unit 2 Resource Book)
- Multiple Choice Test Questions (Unit 2 Resource Book)
- Audio Program Testing Cassette T1 / CD T1
- Electronic Teacher Tools/Test Generator

Native Speakers
- *Para hispanohablantes* Workbook PE, *pp. 49–56*
- *Para hispanohablantes* Workbook TE (Unit 2 Resource Book)
- *Para hispanohablantes* Etapa Exam (Unit 2 Resource Book)
- *Para hispanohablantes* Unit 2 Comprehensive Test (Unit 2 Resource Book)
- Audio *Para hispanohablantes* Cassettes 6A, 6B, T1 / CD 6, T1
- Audioscript *Para hispanohablantes* (Unit 2 Resource Book)

Student Text
Listening Activity Scripts

 Videoscript: Diálogo *pages 144–145*

• Videotape 2 • Videodisc 1B

Search Chapter 7, Play to 8
U2E3 • En vivo (Dialog)

• Use the videoscript with **Actividades 1, 2** *page 146*

Ricardo:	¡Hola, Isabel! ¿Qué tal?
Isabel:	Pues, bien. No tengo problemas con la clase de ciencias naturales. La profesora Díaz es muy simpática.
Ricardo:	¡Qué bueno!
Isabel:	¿Adónde vamos? Quiero hablar del concurso, pero no aquí.
Ricardo:	¿Tienes hambre?
Isabel:	No, la verdad, no.
Ricardo:	Normalmente, ¿qué haces después de clases?
Isabel:	Pues, veo la televisión. O paso un rato con mis amigos.
Ricardo:	¿Vas al parque?
Isabel:	Sí, también. Vivo cerca de un parque.
Ricardo:	Bueno, ¿por qué no vamos al Parque Hundido?
Isabel:	¡Buena idea! Vamos al parque. Y tú, ¿qué haces después de las clases y antes de cenar?
Ricardo:	Pues, a veces tengo que cuidar a mi hermano. Pero si no tengo que cuidar a mi hermano, ando en bicicleta.
Isabel:	¿Ah, sí? ¿Eres muy atlético?
Ricardo:	Sí. La verdad, sí. Pero también toco el piano.
Isabel:	¡Mira nada más! ¡Qué talento tienes!
Ricardo:	La verdad es que... no toco el piano muy bien.
Isabel:	¡Conozco a alguien muy modesto!
Ricardo:	¿Tienes hambre? ¿Comemos unos chicharrones? Esa señora vende unos chicharrones deliciosos
Isabel:	Sí, buena idea. Voy contigo.
Ricardo:	Bueno, ahora vamos a hablar del concurso. ¿Vas a participar?
Isabel:	Quiero participar en el concurso. Pero, ¡con mi horario! No es posible.
Ricardo:	Mira, Isabel. Si no haces algo muy complicado, no hay problema. No necesitas mucho tiempo.
Isabel:	Comprendo, Ricardo. Pero, ¿qué?, ¿qué hago?
Ricardo:	No te preocupes. Las personas con inspiración no tienen problemas en México. Vivimos en un país fascinante.
Isabel:	Ricardo, ya es tarde. ¡Es hora de ir a casa!
Ricardo:	Sí, es verdad. ¡Bay!
Isabel:	¡La plaza! ¡La plaza! ¡La gente! ¡Los animales! ¡Los muchachos! ¡Las actividades! ¡La gente vive en una plaza! ¡Es mi proyecto para el concurso! La plaza es el corazón de la vida mexicana.
	¡Voy a participar en el concurso! Para conocer a los mexicanos, hay que ir a una plaza. La plaza es un poema.

 **Primero...** *page 151*

Ricardo va a hacer muchas cosas hoy después de las clases y antes de ir a casa. Primero, va a hacer ejercicio en el gimnasio. Luego, va a buscar un libro en la biblioteca. Después, va a pasar un rato con sus amigos. Por fin, va a ir a casa para cenar.

 **¡A oír bien!** *page 155*

1. A Antonio le gusta hacer música. Va a...
2. Alicia tiene hambre. Va a...
3. A José le gusta leer. Va a...
4. Pilar tiene sed. Va a...

Quick Start Review Answers

p. 140 Interrogatives/food
Answers will vary.
Answers could include:
1. Hoy tengo el almuerzo [a la una menos cuarto].
2. Voy a comer [un sándwich].
3. Voy a beber [un refresco].
4. Tomo la merienda [a las cuatro].
5. Para la merienda me gusta comer [papas fritas].

p. 142 Verbs / **me gusta**
1. (No) Me gusta escribir en el pizarrón.
2. (No) Me gusta escuchar al profesor/a la profesora.
3. (No) Me gusta preparar la tarea.
4. (No) Me gusta comer en la cafetería.
5. (No) Me gusta cantar y bailar con mis amigos.

p. 144 Family vocabulary
1. abuela
2. primos
3. tía
4. padre/tío
5. hermana

p. 146 Ser and **estar**
1. es
2. estoy
3. estamos
4. son
5. es

p. 148 After-school activities
1. Me gusta más ir al teatro [ir al museo].
2. Me gusta más caminar con el perro [pasear con los amigos]
3. Me gusta más correr [andar en bicicleta].
4. Me gusta más leer una revista [escribir un poema].
5. Me gusta más tocar la guitarra [pasar un rato con los amigos(as)].

p. 151 Ir a...
Answers will vary.
Answers could include:
1. El lunes, a las siete y media de la mañana, voy a [ir a la escuela].
2. El martes, a las doce menos cuarto de la mañana, voy a [almorzar].
3. El viernes a las tres y media de la tarde, voy a [hacer ejercicio].
4. El sábado, a las ocho de la noche, voy a [ir al teatro].
5. El domingo, a la una de la tarde, voy a [pasar un rato con mis amigos].

p. 153 Verbs
Answers will vary.
Answers could include:
1. pasear, caminar, correr
2. comer, beber, tomar
3. estudiar, preparar, escuchar, leer
4. mirar, pintar, estudiar
5. leer, ver, comer

p. 160 Verb review
Answers will vary.
Answers could include:
-ar verbs: pintar, tocar, mandar
-er verbs: aprender, vender, beber
-ir verbs: recibir, vivir, oír

p. 163 Verbs / places
Answers will vary.
Answers could include:
Ignacio compra una revista en la tienda.
Yo bebo un refresco en la cafetería.
Adriana lee una novela en la biblioteca.
Vamos a andar en bicicleta en el parque.

Sample Lesson Plan - 50 Minute Schedule

DAY 1

Etapa Opener
- Quick Start Review (TE, p. 140) **5 MIN.**
- Anticipate/Activate prior knowledge: Have students look at the *Etapa* Opener and answer the questions. **5 MIN.**

En contexto: Vocabulario
- Quick Start Review (TE, p. 142) **5 MIN.**
- Have students use context and pictures to learn *Etapa* vocabulary. In pairs, have students answer the questions, p. 143. Use the Situational OHTs for additional practice. **10 MIN.**

En vivo: Diálogo
- Quick Start Review (TE, p. 144) **5 MIN.**
- Review the Listening Strategy, p. 144. Play audio or show video for the dialog, pp. 144–145. **10 MIN.**
- Replay twice. Read aloud, having students take the roles of characters. **10 MIN.**

Homework Option:
- Video Activities, Unit 2 Resource Book, pp. 125–127.

DAY 2

En acción: Vocabulario y gramática
- Check homework. **5 MIN.**
- Quick Start Review (TE, p. 146) **5 MIN.**
- Ask students for a summary of the dialog to check recall. **5 MIN.**
- Play the video/audio; have students do *Actividades* 1 and 2 orally. **10 MIN.**
- Have students complete *Actividad* 3 orally and *Actividad* 4 in pairs. **10 MIN.**
- Present the Speaking Strategy. Do *Actividad* 5 in groups. **10 MIN.**
- Present the *Nota* and have students complete *Actividad* 6 in pairs. Ask several pairs to present their mini-dialogs. **10 MIN.**

Homework Option:
- Have students write 10 true/false statements about the *Diálogo*.

DAY 3

En acción
- Check homework. **5 MIN.**
- Quick Start Review (TE, p. 148) **5 MIN.**
- Present *Gramática:* Saying What You Are Going to Do: *ir a...* and the *Vocabulario,* p. 149. **10 MIN.**
- Have students complete *Actividad* 7 orally and *Actividad* 8 in pairs. **5 MIN.**
- Have students do *Actividad* 9 orally. **5 MIN.**
- Present the *Vocabulario,* p. 150. Then play the audio and do *Actividad* 10. **10 MIN.**
- Have students do *Actividad* 11 in writing. Ask volunteers to share their paragraphs with the class. Expand using Information Gap Activities, Unit 2 Resource Book, p. 119; *Más comunicación,* p. R6. **15 MIN.**

Homework Option:
- Have students complete *Actividades* 7 and 9 in writing. *Más práctica* Workbook, p. 53. *Para hispanohablantes* Workbook, p. 51.

DAY 4

En acción (cont.)
- Check homework. **5 MIN.**
- Quick Start Review (TE, p. 151) **5 MIN.**
- Present *Gramática:* Present Tense of Regular *-er* and *-ir* Verbs and the *Vocabulario,* p. 151. **10 MIN.**
- Have students complete *Actividades* 12 and 13 orally. **5 MIN.**
- Have students do *Actividad* 14 in groups. **10 MIN.**
- Quick Start Review (TE, p. 153) **5 MIN.**
- Present *Gramática:* Regular Present Tense Verbs with Irregular *yo* Forms, p. 153. **5 MIN.**
- Have students read and complete *Actividad* 15. **5 MIN.**
- Do *Actividades* 16 and 17 orally. **5 MIN.**

Homework Option:
- Have students complete *Actividades* 13, 16, and 17 in writing. *Más práctica* Workbook, pp. 54–55. *Para hispanohablantes* Workbook, pp. 52–53.

DAY 5

En acción (cont.)
- Check homework. **5 MIN.**
- Quick Start Review (TE, p. 154) **5 MIN.**
- Present *Gramática:* Using the Verb *oír,* p. 154. **5 MIN.**
- Have students do *Actividad* 18 in writing, and then have them exchange papers for peer correction. **10 MIN.**
- Do *Actividad* 19 in pairs. **5 MIN.**
- Play the audio; do *Actividad* 20. **5 MIN.**
- Have students do *Actividad* 21 in writing. Expand using Information Gap Activities, Unit 2 Resource Book, pp. 120–121; *Más comunicación,* p. R6. **15 MIN.**

Pronunciación
- Play the audio and have students practice the *refrán.* **5 MIN.**

Homework Option:
- *Más práctica* Workbook, p. 56. *Para hispanohablantes* Workbook, p. 54.

DAY 6

En voces: Lectura
- Check homework. **5 MIN.**
- Quick Start Review (TE, p. 156) **5 MIN.**
- Present the Reading Strategy, p. 156. **5 MIN.**
- Have volunteers read the selection aloud and answer the questions, p. 157. **10 MIN.**

En colores: Cultura y comparaciones
- Quick Start Review (TE, p. 158) **5 MIN.**
- Discuss the Connecting Cultures Strategy, p. 158. **5 MIN.**
- Have volunteers read the selection aloud and answer the questions, p. 159. Show video culture presentation for expansion. **10 MIN.**
- Review *En uso* for *Etapa* 3 Exam. **10 MIN.**

Homework Option:
- Prepare *En uso Actividades* 1–4. Review for *Etapa* 3 Exam.

DAY 7

En uso: Repaso y más comunicación
- Check homework. **5 MIN.**
- Quick Start Review (TE, p. 160) **5 MIN.**
- Review *Actividades* 1–4 orally. **5 MIN.**
- Present the Speaking Strategy, p. 162. Do *Actividad* 5 in pairs and *Actividad* 6 in groups. **10 MIN.**

En resumen: Repaso de vocabulario
- Complete *Etapa* 3 Exam. **20 MIN.**

En tu propia voz: Escritura
- Do *Actividad* 7 in writing. **5 MIN.**

Tú en la comunidad
- Present *Tú en la comunidad,* p. 162. **5 MIN.**

Homework Option:
- Review for Unit 3 Comprehensive Test.

DAY 8

En resumen: Repaso de vocabulario
- Quick Start Review (TE, p. 163) **5 MIN.**

En tu propia voz: Escritura
- Do the writing activity, pp. 164–165. **10 MIN.**

Unit 2 Comprehensive Test
- Review grammar questions, etc. as necessary. **5 MIN.**
- Complete Unit 2 Comprehensive Test. **30 MIN.**

Ampliación
- Optional: Use a suggested project, game, or activity. (TE, pp. 95A–95B) **15 MIN.**

Homework Option:
- Preview *Unidad 3* Opener: Have students read and study pp. 166–167.

Sample Lesson Plan - Block Schedule (90 minutes)

DAY 1

Etapa Opener
- Quick Start Review (TE, p. 140) 5 MIN.
- Anticipate/Activate prior knowledge: Have students look at the *Etapa* Opener and answer the questions. 5 MIN.

En contexto: Vocabulario
- Quick Start Review (TE, p. 142) 5 MIN.
- Have students use context and pictures to learn *Etapa* vocabulary. In pairs, have students answer the questions, p. 143. 5 MIN.
- Use Block Scheduling Copymasters. 5 MIN.

En vivo: Diálogo
- Quick Start Review (TE, p. 144) 5 MIN.
- Review the Listening Strategy, p. 144. Play audio or show video for the dialog, pp. 144–145. 10 MIN.
- Replay twice. Read aloud, having students take the roles of characters. 10 MIN.

En acción: Vocabulario y gramática
- Quick Start Review (TE, p. 146) 5 MIN.
- Ask students for a summary of the dialog to check recall. 5 MIN.
- Play the video/audio; have students do *Actividades* 1 and 2 orally. 10 MIN.
- Have students complete *Actividad* 3 orally and *Actividad* 4 in pairs. 10 MIN.
- Present the Speaking Strategy. Do *Actividad* 5 in groups. 10 MIN.

Homework Option:
- Have students write 10 true/false statements about the *Diálogo*. Video Activities, Unit 2 Resource Book, pp. 125–127.

DAY 2

En acción (cont.)
- Check homework. 5 MIN.
- Present the *Nota* and have students complete *Actividad* 6 in pairs. Ask a few pairs to present their mini-dialogs. 5 MIN.
- Quick Start Review (TE, p. 148) 5 MIN.
- Present *Gramática:* Saying What You Are Going to Do: *ir a...* and the *Vocabulario,* p. 149. 10 MIN.
- Have students complete *Actividad* 7 orally and *Actividad* 8 in pairs. 5 MIN.
- Have students do *Actividad* 9 orally. 5 MIN.
- Present the *Vocabulario,* p. 150. Then play the audio and do *Actividad* 10. 10 MIN.
- Have students do *Actividad* 11 in writing. Ask volunteers to share their paragraphs with the class. Expand using Information Gap Activities, Unit 2 Resource Book, p. 119; *Más comunicación,* p. R6. 20 MIN.
- Quick Start Review (TE, p. 151) 5 MIN.
- Present *Gramática:* Present Tense of Regular *-er* and *-ir* Verbs and the *Vocabulario,* p. 151. 10 MIN.
- Have students complete *Actividades* 12 and 13 orally. 5 MIN.
- Have students do *Actividad* 14 in groups. 5 MIN.

Homework Option:
- Have students complete *Actividades* 9 and 13 in writing. *Más práctica* Workbook, pp. 53–54. *Para hispanohablantes* Workbook, pp. 51–52.

DAY 3

En acción (cont.)
- Check homework. 5 MIN.
- Quick Start Review (TE, p. 153) 5 MIN.
- Present *Gramática:* Regular Present Tense Verbs with Irregular *yo* Forms, p. 153. 5 MIN.
- Have students read and complete *Actividad* 15. 5 MIN.
- Do *Actividades* 16 and 17 orally. 10 MIN.
- Quick Start Review (TE, p. 154) 5 MIN.
- Present *Gramática:* Using the Verb *oír,* p. 154. 5 MIN.
- Have students do *Actividad* 18 in writing, and then have them exchange papers for peer correction. 10 MIN.
- Do *Actividad* 19 in pairs. 5 MIN.
- Play the audio; do *Actividad* 20. 5 MIN.
- Have students do *Actividad* 21 in writing. Ask volunteers to share their letters with the class. Expand using Information Gap Activities, Unit 2 Resource Book, pp. 120–121; *Más comunicación,* p. R6. 20 MIN.

Ampliación
- Use a suggested project, game, or activity. (TE, pp. 95A–95B) 10 MIN.

Homework Option:
- Have students complete *Actividades* 16 and 17 in writing. *Más práctica* Workbook, pp. 55–56. *Para hispanohablantes* Workbook, pp. 53–54.

DAY 4

Pronunciación
- Check homework. 5 MIN.
- Play the audio and have students practice the *refrán.* 5 MIN.

En voces: Lectura
- Quick Start Review (TE, p. 156) 5 MIN.
- Present the Reading Strategy, p. 156. 5 MIN.
- Have volunteers read the selection aloud and answer the questions, p. 157. 10 MIN.

En colores: Cultura y comparaciones
- Quick Start Review (TE, p. 158) 5 MIN.
- Discuss the Connecting Cultures Strategy, p. 158. 5 MIN.
- Have volunteers read the selection aloud and answer the questions, p. 159. Show video culture presentation for expansion. 10 MIN.

En uso: Repaso y más comunicación
- Quick Start Review (TE, p. 160) 5 MIN.
- Do *Actividades* 1–4 orally. 15 MIN.
- Present the Speaking Strategy, p. 162. Do *Actividad* 5 in pairs and 6 in groups. 10 MIN.
- Do *Actividad* 7 in writing. 10 MIN.

Homework Option:
- Review for *Etapa* 3 Exam.

DAY 5

En resumen: Repaso de vocabulario
- Quick Start Review (TE, p. 163) 5 MIN.
- Review grammar questions, etc. as necessary. 5 MIN.
- Complete *Etapa* 3 Exam. 20 MIN.

Tú en la comunidad
- Present *Tú en la comunidad,* p. 162. 10 MIN.

Unit 2 Comprehensive Test
- Review grammar questions, etc. as necessary. 5 MIN.
- Complete Unit 2 Comprehensive Test. 30 MIN.

En tu propia voz: Escritura
- Do the writing activity, pp. 164–165. 15 MIN.

Homework Option:
- Preview *Unidad 3* Opener: Have students read and study pp. 166–167.

▼ Isabel pasea por el parque.

Etapa Theme
Discussing plans and activities, and talking about places and people you know.

Grammar Objectives
• Using **ir** + **a** + infinitive
• Using the present tense of regular **-er** and **-ir** verbs
• Using verbs with irregular **yo** forms
• Using the verb **oír**

Teaching Resource Options
Print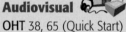
Block Scheduling Copymasters

Audiovisual
OHT 38, 65 (Quick Start)

Quick Start Review
♻ Interrogatives/food
Use OHT 65 or write on board:
Answer the following questions:

1. ¿A qué hora tienes el almuerzo hoy?
2. ¿Qué vas a comer? ¿Un sándwich? ¿Una hamburguesa? ¿Un taco?
3. ¿Qué vas a beber?
4. ¿Cuándo tomas la merienda?
5. ¿Qué te gusta comer para la merienda?

Answers *See p. 139B.*

Teaching Suggestions
Previewing the Etapa
• Ask students to study the picture on pp. 140–141 (1 min.).
• Have them name as many objects as they can in Spanish—people, drinks, colors, clothing, etc.
• Ask students to speculate:
¿Dónde están las personas?
¿Cuántos años tienen las personas?
¿Adónde van?
• Use the **¿Qué ves?** questions to focus the discussion.

UNIDAD 2
ETAPA 3

Mis actividades

• Discuss plans

• Sequence events

• Talk about places and people you know

¿Qué ves?

Mira la foto del centro de Coyoacán, en la Ciudad de México. *Coyoacán* significa «lugar de los coyotes».

1. ¿Hay muchas personas en el parque?
2. ¿La familia de la foto quiere comer o beber?
3. ¿Hay una universidad en la Ciudad de México?

140

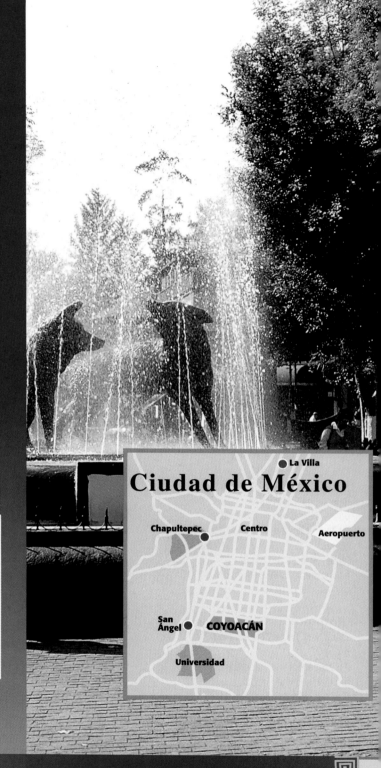

Ciudad de México

La Villa
Chapultepec
Centro
Aeropuerto
San Ángel
COYOACÁN
Universidad

Classroom Management

Planning Ahead Tell students that they will be creating a "class schedule" story to use in a Storytelling activity (see **Ampliación,** TE p. 95A) upon completion of this **Etapa.** Make copies of the suggested story (**Son las siete y media...**) and distribute to the class. Have students maintain logs of their day-to-day schedules. As vocabulary for school subjects and telling time is learned, they should begin writing an initial "class schedule" story.

Peer Teaching Working with partners, ask students to write 3 additional **¿Qué ves?** questions to further discuss this **Etapa** opener.

141

Cross Cultural Connections

Ask students to compare this park in Coyoacán (a neighborhood of Mexico City) to parks in their neighborhoods. Ask them to discuss any similarities and/or differences that they notice.

Culture Highlights

● **COYOACÁN** South of downtown Mexico City, **Coyoacán** is one of the city's most attractive suburbs. It has two parks: the **Jardín Centenario** and the **Palcita de la Conchita**. It also boasts the **Museo Frida Kahlo** (1907–1954), located in the birthplace and home of the famous artist. Her works and those of her husband, Diego Rivera, hang on the walls of the museum, as well as works of other famous artists of the time.

Supplementary Vocabulary

la fuente	fountain
el globo	balloon
el (la) vendedor(a)	vendor
la carretilla de mano	pushcart
la sombrilla	umbrella
el árbol	tree
el poste de alumbrado	streetlamp

Block Schedule

Process Time Use this time to get students settled and concentrating. Have them write the date in their notebooks and then give them 3 minutes to write answers to the ¿Qué ves? questions on p. 140. If they need more time, have them finish the questions as homework. (For additional activities, see **Block Scheduling Copymasters**.)

Teaching All Students

Extra Help Ask yes/no or either/or questions about the photo. For example: **La muchacha y el muchacho, ¿están en la escuela?** (No.) **¿Son las seis de la mañana o de la tarde?** (de la tarde) **¿Tiene Isabel una mochila verde o roja?** (roja) **¿Lleva Ricardo unos jeans?** (Sí.)

Multiple Intelligences

Verbal Have students dramatize a conversation between Isabel and Ricardo in the photo. Encourage them to use words they already know.

Naturalist Have students compare the plants in the photo to plants native to their community. Use a Venn diagram to compare common elements.

Teaching Resource Options

Print 📖

Unit 2 Resource Book
Video Activities, pp. 125–126
Videoscript, p. 128
Audioscript, p. 131
Audioscript *Para hispanohablantes,*
 p. 131

Audiovisual 🎧

OHT 59, 60, 61, 61A, 62, 62A,
65 (Quick Start)
Audio Program Cassette 6A / CD 6
Audio *Para hispanohablantes*
 Cassette 6A / CD 6
Video Program Videotape 2 /
 Videodisc 1B

Search Chapter 6, Play to 7
U2E3 • En contexto (Vocabulary)

Technology 💻 CD-ROM

Intrigas y aventuras **CD-ROM,** Disc 1

🔔 Quick Start Review

♻️ Verbs / **me gusta**

Use OHT 65 or write on board:
Write whether you like or dislike doing
the following activities.

1. escribir en el pizarrón
2. escuchar al profesor/a la
 profesora
3. preparar la tarea
4. comer en la cafetería
5. cantar y bailar con tus amigos

Answers *See p. 139B.*

✳️ Culture Highlights

● **CHICHARRONES** **Chicharrones** are
fried pork rinds that are often prepared in
decorative shapes. They are served hot
and salted. They may also be accompanied
by a salsa made of chile. Although popular
throughout Mexico, **chicharrones** are a
specialty of Nuevo León.

En contexto

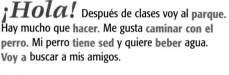

VOCABULARIO

Ricardo is taking a walk through a park where he and his
friends spend a lot of time after school.

¡Hola! Después de clases voy al **parque.**
Hay mucho que **hacer.** Me gusta **caminar con el**
perro. Mi perro **tiene sed** y quiere **beber** agua.
Voy a buscar a mis amigos.

la guitarra

A Me gusta **pasar un rato con**
mis amigos en el parque.
Tocan la guitarra y cantan.

la bicicleta

B A veces me gusta **andar en bicicle[ta]**

142

Classroom Community

Paired Activity The **Preguntas personales** can be
done as a paired oral activity or paired written activity,
where one student asks the questions and the other
writes the answers. (Students should take turns.)

TPR Have various students act out the different
activities. Other students state what they are doing.

Portfolio Have students write 3–5 sentences about
what they like to do on the weekend.

Rubric: Writing

Criteria	Scale
Accuracy	1 2 3 4 5
Vocabulary use	1 2 3 4 5
Creativity, appearance	1 2 3 4 5

A = 14–15 pts.
B = 13 pts.
C = 11–12 pts.
D = 9–10 pts.
F = < 9 pts.

el parque

la tienda

los chicharrones

la revista

el periódico

C La chica **cuida a su hermano.** Ellos **pasean** por el parque.

D A Isabel le gusta leer **una revista.** A mí me gusta leer **el periódico.** ¿Quieres ir al **museo** o al **teatro** por la tarde?

E Cuando **tenemos hambre** y sed, compramos una merienda, como fruta y un refresco, en **la tienda.** ¡También me gusta **comer chicharrones!**

Preguntas personales

1. ¿Hay un parque en tu comunidad?
2. ¿Qué te gusta más, andar en bicicleta o correr?
3. ¿Te gusta leer el periódico o una revista?
4. ¿De vez en cuando vas a un museo o al teatro? ¿Vas con tus padres o con amigos?
5. ¿Tocas la guitarra u otro instrumento? ¿Uno(a) de tus amigos(as) toca un instrumento? ¿Cuál?

ciento cuarenta y tres
Etapa 3

143

Teaching Suggestions
Introducing Vocabulary

- Have students look at pages 142–143. Use OHT 59 and 60 and Audio Cassette 6A / CD 6 to present the vocabulary.
- Ask the Comprehension Questions below in order of yes/no (questions 1–3), either/or (questions 4–6), and simple word or phrase (questions 7–10). Expand by adding similar questions.
- Use the TPR activity to reinforce the meaning of individual words.
- Use the video vocabulary presentation for review and reinforcement.

Comprehension Questions

1. ¿Está Ricardo en la escuela? (No.)
2. ¿Va al parque después de sus clases? (Sí.)
3. ¿Tiene sed el perro? (Sí.)
4. ¿Los amigos de Ricardo bailan o cantan en el parque? (cantan)
5. ¿Los amigos de Ricardo tocan la guitarra o andan en bicicleta? (tocan la guitarra)
6. ¿Cuida la chica a su hermana o a su hermano? (a su hermano)
7. A Isabel, ¿qué le gusta leer? (una revista)
8. A Ricardo, ¿qué le gusta leer? (el periódico)
9. ¿Cuándo compran Isabel y Ricardo una merienda? (cuando tienen hambre)
10. ¿Dónde compran fruta y un refresco? (en la tienda)

Quick Wrap-up

Have students rank the following activities from 1 (favorite) to 10 (least favorite): ir al parque, caminar con el perro, andar en bicicleta, cantar, tocar la guitarra, pasar un rato con mis amigos, ir al museo, ir al teatro, leer una revista, leer el periódico.

Block Schedule

Reference Lists Have students add new vocabulary words to the Supplementary Vocabulary section of their notebooks. As they advance, they can also write synonyms and antonyms next to new words.

Teaching All Students

Extra Help Have students go through the **En contexto** and make a list of all the verbs—conjugated forms and infinitives. If the verb is in a conjugated form, they should also give its infinitive.

Native Speakers Ask students to talk about after-school activities in their home communities, as well as about homework assignments and study time.

Multiple Intelligences

Visual Have students take a piece of paper and first draw a clock at the top. The clock hands should indicate the time school is over. Below the clock, have students list where students go after school and what they do. They should also illustrate these activities.

Teaching Resource Options

Print

Más práctica Workbook PE, pp. 49–52
Para hispanohablantes Workbook PE, pp. 49–50
Block Scheduling Copymasters
Unit 2 Resource Book
  Más práctica Workbook TE, pp. 103–106
  Para hispanohablantes Workbook TE, pp. 111–112
  Video Activities, pp. 125–126
  Videoscript, p. 129
  Audioscript, p. 131
  Audioscript *Para hispanohablantes*, p. 131

Audiovisual

OHT 63, 64, 65 (Quick Start)
Audio Program Cassette 6A / CD 6
Audio *Para hispanohablantes*
  Cassette 6A / CD 6
Video Program Videotape 2 / Videodisc 1B

Search Chapter 7, Play to 8
U2E3 • En vivo (Dialog)

Technology

Intrigas y aventuras CD-ROM, Disc 1

Quick Start Review

Family vocabulary

Use OHT 65 or write on board:
Complete each sentence with the name of a family member.

1. Mi ____ es la madre de mi madre.
2. Los hijos de mis tíos son mis ____.
3. La hermana de mi padre es mi ____.
4. El hijo de mi abuelo es mi ____.
5. La hija de mi madre es mi ____.

Answers *See p. 139B.*

Culture Highlights

● **EL PARQUE HUNDIDO** The **Parque Hundido** is located in the southern part of Mexico City. It has a children's playground as well as an open-air museum that displays copies of many important pre-Columbian sculptures. The **Parque Hundido** also has the largest floral clock in Mexico. Photos 4–8 of the dialog were taken here.

En vivo

DIÁLOGO

Ricardo   Isabel

En el parque

PARA ESCUCHAR • STRATEGY: LISTENING
Listen and observe During a conversation, it is just as important to observe physical actions as it is to listen to the words spoken. Body language supports what is being said and sometimes better expresses meaning. What do you see and hear in this segment that influences Isabel's decision?

1 ► **Ricardo:** ¡Hola, Isabel! ¿Qué tal?
  Isabel: Bien, no tengo problemas con la clase de ciencias naturales.
  Ricardo: ¡Qué bueno!

5 ► **Ricardo:** También toco el piano.
  Isabel: ¡Mira nada más!
  Ricardo: La verdad es que... no toco el piano muy bien.
  Isabel: ¡Conozco a alguien muy modesto!

6 ► **Ricardo:** ¿Tienes hambre? ¿Comemos unos chicharrones? Esa señora vende unos chicharrones deliciosos.
  Isabel: Sí, buena idea. Voy contigo.

7 ► **Ricardo:** Vamos a hablar del concurso. ¿Vas a participar?
  Isabel: ¿Con mi horario?
  Ricardo: Si no haces algo muy complicado, no hay problema.
  Isabel: Pero, ¿qué?, ¿qué hago?

144 ciento cuarenta y cuatro
Unidad 2

Classroom Community

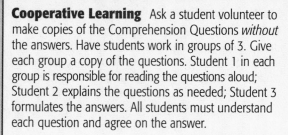

Cooperative Learning Ask a student volunteer to make copies of the Comprehension Questions *without* the answers. Have students work in groups of 3. Give each group a copy of the questions. Student 1 in each group is responsible for reading the questions aloud; Student 2 explains the questions as needed; Student 3 formulates the answers. All students must understand each question and agree on the answer.

Paired Activity Have pairs of students first review the dialog. Then each student lists 5 activities that Isabel and Ricardo mention. Finally, the 2 students compare their lists to come up with a final, longer list.

2 ▶ Isabel: ¿Adónde vamos? Quiero hablar del concurso.
Ricardo: ¿Tienes hambre?
Isabel: No, la verdad, no.

3 ▶ Ricardo: ¿Qué haces después de clases?
Isabel: Veo la televisión o paso un rato con mis amigos.
Ricardo: ¿Por qué no vamos al parque?

4 ▶ Isabel: Y tú, ¿qué haces después de las clases y antes de cenar?
Ricardo: Si no tengo que cuidar a mi hermano, ando en bicicleta.

8 ▶ Ricardo: No te preocupes. Las personas con inspiración no tienen problemas en México.
Isabel: Ricardo, ya es tarde. ¡Es hora de ir a casa!
Ricardo: Sí, es verdad.

9 ▶ Isabel: ¡La plaza! ¡La gente! ¡Los animales! ¡Los muchachos! ¡Las actividades! ¡La gente vive en una plaza! ¡Es mi proyecto para el concurso! La plaza es el corazón de la vida mexicana.

10 ▶ Isabel: ¡Voy a participar en el concurso! Para conocer a los mexicanos, hay que ir a una plaza. La plaza es un poema.

ciento cuarenta y cinco
Etapa 3   **145**

Teaching All Students

Extra Help Write 8–10 sentences from the dialog on the board. Have students identify the speaker as Isabel or Ricardo.

Native Speakers Ask students about where people gather socially in their home communities—in homes or in public places? Does **el paseo** exist as a social custom on a daily or weekly basis? Where do teenagers spend time after school?

Multiple Intelligences

Musical/Rhythmic Bring in Mexican music to play in the background while reading the dialog. Point out that there is always music being played in plazas around Mexico. If student have access to computers, they can also check the Internet for names of groups currently popular among Mexican teenagers.

Teaching Suggestions
Presenting the Dialog

• Prepare students for listening by focusing on the dialog context using yes/no or either/or questions. Reintroduce the characters and the setting: **¿La chica se llama Isabel? ¿Está con Francisco o Ricardo? ¿Están en el parque?**

• Use the video, audiocassette, or CD to present the dialog. The expanded dialog on video offers additional listening practice opportunities.

Video Synopsis

• Isabel and Ricardo go to the park after school and discuss their plans. For a complete transcript of the video dialog, see p. 139B.

Comprehension Questions

1. ¿Van Isabel y Ricardo al parque? (Sí.)
2. ¿Tiene Isabel problemas con su clase de ciencias naturales? (No.)
3. ¿Tiene hambre Isabel? (No.)
4. ¿Quiere Isabel hablar de su horario o del concurso? (del concurso)
5. Después de clase, ¿toca Isabel la guitarra o ve la televisión? (ve la televisión)
6. ¿Son horribles o deliciosos los chicharrones del parque? (deliciosos)
7. ¿Qué hace Ricardo antes de cenar? (Anda en bicicleta o cuida a su hermano.)
8. ¿Cómo toca Ricardo el piano? (no muy bien)
9. ¿Qué tienen que hacer Isabel y Ricardo? (ir a casa)
10. ¿Cuál es el proyecto de Isabel para el concurso? (la plaza mexicana)

▉ Block Schedule

Process Time Prepare ahead: Find a children's book in Spanish about going places. Have students practice their listening skills. Tell them that they may not understand everything, but that they should listen for the main ideas. (For additional activities, see **Block Scheduling Copymasters**.)

Teaching Resource Options

Print 📖

Unit 2 Resource Book
  Video Activities, p. 127
  Videoscript, p. 130
  Audioscript, p. 131
  Audioscript *Para hispanohablantes,*
    p. 131

Audiovisual

OHT 66 (Quick Start)
Audio Program Cassette 6A / CD 6
Audio *Para hispanohablantes*
  Cassette 6A / CD 6
Video Program Videotape 2 / Videodisc
  1B

Quick Start Review

🔁 **Ser** and **estar**

Use OHT 66 or write on the board:
Complete the following sentences
using the appropriate form of **ser** or
estar:

1. Ricardo ____ un chico muy activo.
2. Por la mañana, yo ____ en clase.
3. Nosotros siempre ____ en el
   parque después de las clases.
4. Los hermanos de mi padre ____
   mis tíos.
5. La plaza ____ el corazón de la
   vida mexicana.

Answers *See p. 139B.*

Teaching Suggestions
Comprehension Check

Use **Actividades 1** and **2** to assess
retention after the dialog. For **Actividad
1,** have students think about the
photos of the dialog to help them put
the sentences in order. For **Actividad
2,** point out that there may be more
than one right answer.

Objective: Transitional practice
Listening comprehension/vocabulary

Answers (See script p. 139B.)
a. 3   b. 4   c. 1   d. 5   e. 2

Objective: Transitional practice
Listening comprehension/vocabulary

Answers (See script p. 139B.)
1. b, c   2. a, c   3. b   4. b

146   Vocabulary/Grammar • UNIDAD 2 Etapa 3

OBJECTIVES
• Discuss plans
• Sequence events
• Talk about places and people
  you know

ACTIVIDAD 1

¿En qué orden?

Escuchar ¿Cuándo pasan
estas cosas? Pon las oraciones
en el orden correcto según
el diálogo. *(Hint: Put the sentences
in order.)*

a. Isabel y Ricardo comen
   chicharrones.

b. Isabel pasa por la plaza.

c. Isabel y Ricardo van al
   parque.

d. Isabel decide participar en
   el concurso.

e. Ricardo habla de sus
   actividades después de
   las clases.

TAMBIÉN SE DICE

There are different ways to say
Wow! when you are amazed by
something or someone. Isabel
uses one in the dialog. Do you
recognize which?
• **¡Anda!:** Spain
• **¡Mira nada más!:** Mexico
• **¡Mirá vos!:** Argentina

ACTIVIDAD 2

¿Qué pasa?

Escuchar Escoge la(s) respuesta(s) correcta(s) según el diálogo.
¡Ojo! Algunas oraciones tienen más de una respuesta correcta.
(Hint: Choose the correct answer or answers.)

1. Normalmente, después de
   las clases, Isabel _____.
   a. va al parque
   b. ve la televisión
   c. pasa un rato con los amigos

2. Después de las clases,
   Ricardo _____.
   a. cuida a su hermano
   b. toca la guitarra
   c. anda en bicicleta

3. En el parque, los dos
   comen _____.
   a. papas fritas
   b. chicharrones
   c. tacos

4. El proyecto de Isabel para
   el concurso va a ser sobre
   la vida en _____.
   a. el parque
   b. la plaza
   c. la ciudad

NOTA CULTURAL

El Museo Nacional de Antropología, in Mexico City's **Parque Chapultepec,**
contains objects from Mexico's native cultures. It is a popular place for school
groups to visit.

146 ciento cuarenta y seis
Unidad 2

Classroom Management

Streamlining Before replaying the dialog, have
students read the questions in **Actividades 1** and **2**.
Remind students to focus on these key question areas
as they are listening to/watching the dialog and
completing the activities.

Organizing Paired Work Have a list of infinitives
needed to answer the questions in **Actividad 4** written
on the board. (The infinitives should not be in the
correct order.)

- Use *ir* + *a* + infinitive
- Use the present tense of regular -*er* and -*ir* verbs
- Use verbs with irregular **yo** forms
- Use the verb **oír**

ACTIVIDAD 3

♻ ¿Dónde están?

Hablar ¿Dónde están Isabel y Ricardo?
(Hint: Say where they are.)

modelo

Están en la cafetería.

ACTIVIDAD 4

¿Qué hacen?

Hablar Explica lo que hacen después de las clases. ¿Lo haces también? *(Hint: Say what these people do after class. Do you do it too?)*

modelo

Estudiante A: *La muchacha cuida a su hermano. ¿Cuidas a tu hermano también?*

Estudiante B: *Sí, yo cuido a mi hermano.*

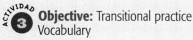

Objective: Transitional practice Vocabulary

♻ **Estar**

Answers
1. Están en el parque.
2. Están en la tienda.
3. Están en la escuela (clase).
4. Está en la biblioteca.

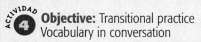

Objective: Transitional practice Vocabulary in conversation

Answers
1. A: El muchacho camina con el perro.
   ¿Caminas con el perro también?
   B: Sí, (No, no) camino con el perro.
2. A: Las muchachas pasean por el parque.
   ¿Paseas por el parque también?
   B: Sí, (No, no) paseo por el parque.
3. A: El muchacho anda en bicicleta.
   ¿Andas en bicicleta también?
   B: Sí, (No, no) ando en bicicleta.
4. A: El muchacho pasa un rato con sus amigos.
   ¿Pasas un rato con tus amigos también?
   B: Sí, (No, no) paso un rato con mis amigos.
5. A: El muchacho toca la guitarra.
   ¿Tocas la guitarra también?
   B: Sí, (No, no) toco la guitarra.

🌐 Culture Highlights

● **EL MUSEO NACIONAL DE ANTROPOLOGÍA** Chapultepec *(Hill of the Grasshopper)* is a rocky height in Mexico City with a castle at the top. The surrounding area is called **Parque Chapultepec.** In addition to the **Museo Nacional de Antropología,** the park contains lakes, fountains, a zoo, an astronomical observatory, and the **Niños héroes** statue. **Chapultepec** was used by the early Aztecs as a park area for recreation.

Teaching All Students

Extra Help Give a dictation of a list of places for in-school and after-school activities: **la escuela, la clase, la cafetería, el auditorio, la biblioteca, el gimnasio, la oficina, el parque, el museo, el teatro, la tienda, la casa, la tienda.**

Challenge Working in pairs, one student says a line that could be overheard in a specific place, such as in **la biblioteca.** The other student guesses the place.

Multiple Intelligences

Kinesthetic Have students first draw or create a collage of pictures from magazines that show places for in-school or after-school activities (see list under Extra Help). Then have volunteers come to the front of the class, display their pictures, and act out what they would do in that place. The class must say where each student is and what he/she is doing there.

■ Block Schedule

Variety Working in small groups, have students write and present a mini-skit based on Ricardo and Isabel's characters. They should also bring in a new character, such as Ricardo's little brother or a cousin of Isabel's from the United States.

Teaching Resource Options

Print
Block Scheduling Copymasters

Audiovisual
OHT 66 (Quick Start)

Technology
Intrigas y aventuras CD-ROM, Disc 1

5 Objective: Open-ended practice
Vocabulary in conversation and
writing

Answers will vary.

6 Objective: Transitional practice
Tener sed/tener hambre in
conversation

♻ Food and drinks

Answers

1. A: ¿Tienes hambre?
   B: Sí, tengo hambre. Voy a comer unas papas fritas.
2. A: ¿Tienes sed?
   B: Sí, tengo sed. Voy a beber un refresco.
3. A: ¿Tienes hambre?
   B: Sí, tengo hambre. Voy a comer unos tacos.
4. A: ¿Tienes hambre?
   B: Sí, tengo hambre. Voy a comer fruta.
5. A: ¿Tienes sed?
   B: Sí, tengo sed. Voy a beber un vaso de agua.
6. A: ¿Tienes hambre?
   B: Sí, tengo hambre. Voy a comer una torta.

Juego

Answer: El perro tiene sed.

🔔 Quick Start Review

♻ After-school activities

Use OHT 66 or write on the board:
Write which activity you like better,
using **Me gusta más...**

1. ¿ir al teatro o ir al museo?
2. ¿caminar con el perro o pasear con los amigos?
3. ¿correr o andar en bicicleta?
4. ¿leer una revista o escribir un poema?
5. ¿tocar la guitarra o pasar un rato con los amigos(as)?

Answers *See p. 139B.*

ACTIVIDAD 5 — ¿Qué haces?

PARA CONVERSAR

STRATEGY: SPEAKING

Use all you know It is easy to rely on what you
learned most recently. But it is important
to reuse what you've learned before. Try to
include activities you learned in Unit 1, such
as **cantar** and **nadar,** in your answers.

Hablar/Escribir Escribe dos cosas que haces
después de clases. Luego, habla con cinco
estudiantes y escribe sus respuestas. *(Hint: Write
two things you do and ask five others what they do.)*

modelo

Tú: *Normalmente, ¿qué haces después de clases, Marco?*

Marco: *Paso un rato con mis amigos.*

Nombre	Actividad
yo	Ando en bicicleta.
	....
Marco	Pasa un rato con sus amigos.
	....

Juego

Paco tiene agua. Pepe tiene sed. ¿Qué tiene el perro?

ciento cuarenta y ocho
Unidad 2

148

ACTIVIDAD 6 — ♻ ¡Qué hambre y sed!

Hablar Trabaja con otro(a) estudiante para hacer
y contestar preguntas basadas en cada dibujo.
Cambien de papel. *(Hint: Take turns answering questions
based on each picture.)*

modelo

Estudiante A: *¿Tienes sed?*

Estudiante B: *Sí, tengo sed. Voy a beber un vaso de agua.*

Estudiante B: *¿Tienes hambre?*

Estudiante A: *Sí, tengo hambre. Voy a comer una hamburguesa.*

Nota

To say that someone is thirsty, use the phrase **tener sed;** if
the person is hungry, use **tener hambre.**

1. 2. 3. 4. 5. 6.

Classroom Community

Paired Activity Have pairs of students make a map
that includes the following places: **el museo, el parque,
el teatro, la escuela, la tienda.** Students then plan an
imaginary trip around their city that includes each
place. They should decide where they are going, at
what time, and what they will do there. Have pairs
present their trips to the class. (This is an excellent
opportunity to review time, location, interrogatives.)

Portfolio Students write 6–10 sentences about what
they are going to do after school today. They should
provide as much information as possible, such as at
what time they will do the activity, people with whom
they will do the activity, or why they are doing the
activity.

GRAMÁTICA

Saying What You Are Going to Do: ir a...

When you talk about things you are planning to do in the future, you say what you are *going to* do. To talk about activities you are going to do, use the phrase:

ir + a + *infinitive*

yo	**voy a...**	nosotros(as)	**vamos a...**
tú	**vas a...**	vosotros(as)	**vais a...**
usted, él, ella	**va a...**	ustedes, ellos(as)	**van a...**

Isabel says:
—¡**Voy a participar** en el concurso!
I'm going to participate in the contest!

ACTIVIDAD 7 Gramática

 ¿A qué hora?

Hablar Isabel y Ricardo tienen mucho que hacer hoy. Explica lo que van a hacer y a qué hora. ¿Cuándo vas a hacer tú estas actividades?
(Hint: Say when they are going to do these things and when you will do them.)

modelo

Isabel y Ricardo / estudiar en la escuela / 10:00
Isabel y Ricardo van a **estudiar en la escuela** a las **diez**.
Yo voy a estudiar a las seis.

---

1. Isabel / usar la computadora / 11:20
2. Ricardo / ir a la biblioteca / 12:45
3. Isabel y Ricardo / tomar un refresco / 1:55
4. Ricardo / hacer ejercicio / 3:00
5. Isabel / pasear con su amiga / 6:30
6. Ricardo / ayudar a su padre / 7:45
7. Ricardo / preparar su tarea / 8:15
8. Isabel y Ricardo / cenar / 9:00
9. Isabel / ver la televisión / 9:35

Vocabulario

Más para hacer después de clases

cuidar (a) *to take care of*
un animal

el pájaro

el pez

mandar una carta

pintar

tocar el piano

ver la televisión

cenar *to have dinner, supper*
hacer ejercicio *to exercise*
ir al supermercado *to go to the supermarket*
preparar *to prepare*
  la cena *supper, dinner*
  (la) comida *food, a meal*

leer *to read*
  una novela *novel*
  un poema *poem*
  (la) poesía *poetry*

See the words for more pets on p. R20.

¿Qué haces tú?

Teaching All Students

Extra Help Break up **Actividad 7** into smaller parts. First have students conjugate the verb portion of each sentence. Then have them work on the time expressions. Finally, have them put the information together.

Native Speakers As a variation of **Actividad 7**, have students revise the list of activities and times to represent what would be true for their home communities.

Multiple Intelligences

Logical/Mathematical Have students design a survey to see when students watch the most TV—before school, in the afternoon, in the evening, or on weekends. Have students conduct the survey, compile the results, and report their findings. They could also expand the survey to include students in other classes, or compare total hours of TV viewing vs. hours spent on study/homework.

Teaching Suggestions
Presenting ir a...

Point out that **voy a** + *place* tells where you are going (**voy a la biblioteca**), while **voy a** + *infinitive* tells what you are going to do (**voy a estudiar**).

ACTIVIDAD 7 Objective: Controlled practice
Ir a...
♻ Telling time

Answers
1. Isabel va a usar la computadora a las once y veinte. Yo voy a usar la computadora a...
2. Ricardo va a ir a la biblioteca a la una menos cuarto. Yo voy a ir a la biblioteca a...
3. Isabel y Ricardo van a tomar un refresco a las dos menos cinco. Yo voy a tomar un refresco a...
4. Ricardo va a hacer ejercicio a las tres. Yo voy a hacer ejercicio a...
5. Isabel va a pasear con su amiga a las seis y media. Yo voy a pasear con mi amiga a...
6. Ricardo va a ayudar a su padre a las ocho menos cuarto. Yo voy a ayudar a mi padre a...
7. Ricardo va a preparar su tarea a las ocho y cuarto. Yo voy a preparar mi tarea a...
8. Isabel y Ricardo van a cenar a las nueve. Yo voy a cenar a...
9. Isabel va a ver la televisión a las diez menos veinticinco. Yo voy a ver la televisión a...

■ Block Schedule

Change of Pace To vary the usual method of presentation of activities, rewrite the items in **Actividad 7** on a large posterboard, leaving space between items. For each item, have 2 students come to the front of the class. One student gives the answer orally and the other writes it on the poster board. (For additional activities, see **Block Scheduling Copymasters**.)

Teaching Resource Options

Print

Más práctica Workbook PE, p. 53
Para hispanohablantes Workbook PE, p. 51
Block Scheduling Copymasters
Unit 2 Resource Book
  Más práctica Workbook TE, p. 107
  Para hispanohablantes Workbook TE, p. 113
  Information Gap Activities, p. 119
  Audioscript, p. 132
  Audioscript *Para hispanohablantes*, p. 132

Audiovisual

OHT M5; 59, 60, 66 (Quick Start)
Audio Program Cassettes 6A, 6B / CD 6
Audio *Para hispanohablantes*
  Cassette 6A / CD 6

Technology

Intrigas y aventuras CD-ROM, Disc 1

ACTIVIDAD 8 **Objective:** Controlled practice
Ir a... in conversation

Answers

1. A: ¿Adónde van ustedes? / B: Vamos al parque. / A: ¿Qué van a hacer allí? / B: Vamos a pasear.
2. A: ¿Adónde vas tú? / B: Voy a casa. / A: ¿Qué vas a hacer allí? / B: Voy a ver la televisión.
3. A: ¿Adónde vas tú? / B: Voy a la biblioteca. A: ¿Qué vas a hacer allí? / B: Voy a estudiar.
4. A: ¿Adónde van ustedes? / B: Vamos a la tienda. / A: ¿Qué van a hacer allí? / B: Vamos a comprar ropa.
5. A: ¿Adónde vas tú? / B: Voy al supermercado. / A: ¿Qué vas a hacer allí? / B: Voy a comprar una merienda.
6. A: ¿Adónde van ustedes? / B: Vamos a la cafetería. / A: ¿Qué van a hacer allí? / B: Vamos a comer chicharrones.
7. A: ¿Adónde vas tú? / B: Voy al gimnasio. / A: ¿Qué vas a hacer allí? / B: Voy a hacer ejercicio.

Teaching Suggestions
Reinforcing Sequencing Events

Visually and orally emphasize the use of sequencing words when talking to the class, particularly when giving instructions. Award a small prize or bonus points when students use one of these words.

ACTIVIDAD 8 Gramática

¿Adónde vas?

Hablar Un(a) estudiante te pregunta sobre las actividades que tú y tus amigos van a hacer después de clases. *(Hint: Say what you and your friends are going to do after school.)*

modelo

tú y tus amigos: museo (¿ver arte o hacer ejercicio?)

Estudiante: *¿Adónde van ustedes?*

Tú: *Vamos al museo.*

Estudiante: *¿Qué van a hacer allí?*

Tú: *Vamos a ver arte.*

1. tú y tus amigos: parque (¿comprar libros o pasear?)
2. tú: casa (¿ver la televisión o hablar con el maestro?)
3. tú: biblioteca (¿estudiar o tocar la guitarra?)
4. tú y tus amigos: tienda (¿caminar con el perro o comprar ropa?)
5. tú: supermercado (¿mandar una carta o comprar una merienda?)
6. tú y tus amigos: cafetería (¿comer chicharrones o usar la computadora?)
7. tú: gimnasio (¿leer una revista o hacer ejercicio?)

■ **MÁS PRÁCTICA** *cuaderno* p. 53
■ **PARA HISPANOHABLANTES** *cuaderno* p. 51

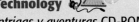

TAMBIÉN SE DICE Plaza is a word that refers to any public square in the Spanish-speaking world. The main square in a city or town might be called the plaza principal or plaza mayor. In Mexico, the main square is called the zócalo. The Zócalo in Mexico City is where the cathedral and many government buildings are.

ACTIVIDAD 9

¡Lógicamente!

Hablar/Escribir ¿Adónde van y qué van a hacer tus amigos y tu familia? *(Hint: What are the people going to do?)*

modelo

Yo voy a la plaza. Voy a caminar con el perro.

¿Quién?	¿Adónde?	¿Qué va a hacer?
1. yo	auditorio	beber un refresco
2. mi amigo(a)	biblioteca	buscar un libro
3. mi amiga y yo	cafetería	pasear
4. mis padres	plaza	comprar una revista
5. ellas	tienda	escuchar música
6. mi hermano(a)	¿otro lugar?	¿otra actividad?

Vocabulario

Sequencing Events

To sequence events, use these words.

primero *first*	**antes** *before*
entonces *then, so*	**después** *after, afterward*
luego *later*	
por fin *finally*	

When a **noun** or an **infinitive** follows **antes** or **después**, use the preposition **de**.

¿Qué haces **después de las clases** y **antes de cenar**?

*What do you do **after** classes and **before** eating dinner?*

¿Qué pasa cada día?

Classroom Community

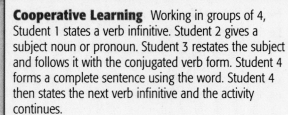

Cooperative Learning Working in groups of 4, Student 1 states a verb infinitive. Student 2 gives a subject noun or pronoun. Student 3 restates the subject and follows it with the conjugated verb form. Student 4 forms a complete sentence using the word. Student 4 then states the next verb infinitive and the activity continues.

Group Activity Divide the class into groups of 3–4. Write a letter of the alphabet on the board. The groups have 60 seconds to write as many Spanish words as they can that begin with that letter. They get a point for each correct word. Continue with other letters. The winning team gets a small prize or extra credit points.

ACTIVIDAD 10

Primero...

Escuchar Lee las oraciones. Luego, escucha el párrafo. ¿En qué orden va a hacer Ricardo estas actividades?
(Hint: Listen and indicate the order in which Ricardo plans to do things.)

a. Va a hacer ejercicio en el gimnasio.
b. Va a cenar.
c. Va a pasar un rato con sus amigos.
d. Va a ir a la biblioteca a buscar un libro.

ACTIVIDAD 11

 Después de clases...

Escribir Escribe un párrafo sobre lo que *te gusta hacer* y lo que *tienes que hacer*. Usa **primero, antes (de), después (de), entonces, luego**. *(Hint: Write about what you like to do and have to do.)*

modelo

Después de las clases, me gusta hacer muchas cosas. Primero, me gusta ir al gimnasio. Luego, paso un rato con mis amigos. Hablamos o escuchamos música. A las seis voy a casa. ¿Y entonces? Siempre tengo que ayudar a mi madre y cuidar a mi hermana. Después de cenar, tengo que preparar mi tarea. ¡Por fin estudio!

■ **MÁS COMUNICACIÓN** p. R6

GRAMÁTICA

Present Tense of Regular -er and -ir Verbs

♻ **¿RECUERDAS?** *p. 105* Remember how to conjugate present tense **-ar** verbs?

estudio	estudiamos
estudias	estudiáis
estudia	estudian

▶ Regular verbs that end in **-er** or **-ir** work similarly. Regular **-er** verbs have the same endings as **-ir** verbs except in the **nosotros(as)** and **vosotros(as)** forms.

The letter change matches the verb ending:
-er verbs = **emos, éis**
-ir verbs = **imos, ís**

com er *to eat*

yo	com o	nosotros(as)	com emos
tú	com es	vosotros(as)	com éis
usted, él, ella	com e	ustedes, ellos(as)	com en

viv ir *to live*

yo	viv o	nosotros(as)	viv imos
tú	viv es	vosotros(as)	viv ís
usted, él, ella	viv e	ustedes, ellos(as)	viv en

Ricardo says:

—Esa señora **vend e** unos chicharrones deliciosos.
*That woman **sells** delicious pork rinds.*

Vocabulario

Verbs Ending in -er and -ir

You have seen the verbs **beber, comer, correr, escribir, leer** before. Here are some others.

Verbs: **-er**

aprender *to learn*	**vender** *to sell*
comprender *to understand*	**ver** *to see* (**yo: veo**)

Verbs: **-ir**

abrir *to open*	**recibir** *to receive*
compartir *to share*	**vivir** *to live*

¿Qué haces después de clases?

ACTIVIDAD 9
Objective: Transitional practice
Ir a...
Answers will vary.

ACTIVIDAD 10
Objective: Transitional practice
Listening comprehension/**ir a...**
Answers (See script p. 139B.)
a. 1   b. 4   c. 3   d. 2

ACTIVIDAD 11
Objective: Open-ended practice
Sequencing events
♻ **Me gusta, tener que**
Answers will vary.

🔔 Quick Start Review

♻ **Ir a...**
Use OHT 66 or write on the board: Write what you are going to do on these days and at these times:

1. lunes, 7:30 de la mañana
2. martes, 11:45 de la mañana
3. viernes, 3:30 de la tarde
4. sábado, 8:00 de la noche
5. domingo, 1:00 de la tarde

Answers *See p. 139B.*

Teaching Suggestions
Reinforcing Present Tense of Regular -er and -ir Verbs

• Have students look back at the **diálogo** on pp. 144–145 and identify the regular **-er** and **-ir** verbs.

• Provide students with a list of conjugated verb forms. Have students identify them as **-ar, -er,** or **-ir** verbs.

■ Block Schedule
Change of Pace For **Actividad 9**, have students work in groups of 2–3. Tell them to copy each word/expression onto a separate slip of paper. Then have them mix and match the words/expressions to make as many sentences as possible within a certain timeframe. (For additional activities, see **Block Scheduling Copymasters**.)

Teaching All Students

Extra Help Help students organize their paragraph for **Actividad 11** by brainstorming activities. Have them make one column for activities they like to do and another for activities they have to do. Then have them put the activities in chronological order.

Native Speakers Have native speakers act out and narrate their morning routines using the vocabulary for sequencing events on p. 150. If necessary, help the

other students with vocabulary by writing unknown words on the board. They can add these words to their Supplementary Vocabulary lists.

Multiple Intelligences

Interpersonal Have students work in small groups to devise a board game or card game that uses all the verb infinitives they have learned up to this point. Remind students to avoid translation games.

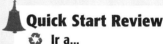

Teaching Resource Options

Print
Más práctica Workbook PE, pp. 54–55
Para hispanohablantes Workbook PE, pp. 52–53
Unit 2 Resource Book
  Más práctica Workbook TE, pp. 108–109
  Para hispanohablantes Workbook TE, pp. 114–115

Audiovisual
OHT 67 (Quick Start)

Technology
Intrigas y aventuras CD-ROM, Disc 1

 Objective: Controlled practice
Regular **-er** and **-ir** verbs

Answers
1. Beatriz lee un libro.
2. Los muchachos leen el diccionario.
3. Tú lees una revista.
4. Horacio escribe un poema.
5. Tú escribes una carta.
6. Sus padres escriben poesía.
7. Yo leo [una novela].
8. Mi amigo(a) escribe [un poema].
9. Mi amigo(a) y yo leemos [el periódico].
10. Yo escribo [la tarea].

 Objective: Transitional practice
Regular **-er** and **-ir** verbs
  ♻ Adverbs of frequency

Answers
1. Yo aprendo mucho (poco).
2. Mis amigos y yo comemos mucho (poco).
3. Mis amigos comparten mucho (poco) las meriendas.
4. Mi amigo(a) vende mucho (poco) periódicos.
5. Yo veo mucho (poco) la televisión.
6. Mi hermano(a) recibe mucho (poco) cartas.
7. Mi padre lee mucho (poco).
8. Los estudiantes abren mucho (poco) los libros.
9. Mis primos comen mucho (poco) y beben mucho (poco).
10. Mi madre comprende mucho (poco).

 Objective: Open-ended practice
Regular **-er** and **-ir** verbs in conversation

Answers will vary.

¿Qué leen y escriben?

Hablar Explica lo que leen y escriben estas personas.
(Hint: Explain what these people are reading and writing.)

modelo
Alberto / leer una novela
Alberto lee una novela.

1. Beatriz / leer un libro
2. los muchachos / leer el diccionario
3. tú / leer una revista
4. Horacio / escribir un poema
5. tú / escribir una carta
6. sus padres / escribir poesía
7. yo / leer ¿?
8. mi amigo(a) / escribir ¿?
9. mi amigo(a) y yo / leer ¿?
10. yo / escribir ¿?

■ **MÁS PRÁCTICA** *cuaderno* p. 54
■ **PARA HISPANOHABLANTES** *cuaderno* p. 52

NOTA CULTURAL

In Mexico mealtimes are much later than in the United States. Lunch is usually between 2:00 and 3:00 in the afternoon and dinner between 9:00 and 10:00 in the evening.

♻ ¿Mucho o poco?

Hablar/Escribir ¿Las personas que tú conoces hacen mucho o poco estas cosas? *(Hint: Do the people you know do these things a lot or a little?)*

1. yo (aprender)
2. mis amigos y yo (comer)
3. mis amigos (compartir las meriendas)
4. mi amigo(a) (vender periódicos)
5. yo (ver la televisión)
6. mi hermano(a) (recibir cartas)
7. mi padre (leer)
8. los estudiantes (abrir los libros)
9. mis primos (comer y beber)
10. mi madre (comprender)

¿Lo hacen o no?

Hablar/Escribir Pregúntales a cinco estudiantes si hacen lo siguiente. Dale un resumen de las respuestas a la clase.
(Hint: Ask five students whether they do the following. Report the results.)

modelo
comer en la cafetería
Tú: *¿Comes en la cafetería?*
Pedro: *No, no como en la cafetería.*

Resumen: *Cristina, Ramón, Lidia y Tomás comen en la cafetería. Pedro no come en la cafetería.*

1. vivir en un apartamento
2. aprender mucho en la escuela
3. ver la televisión todos los días
4. recibir muchas cartas
5. comprender las matemáticas

152   ciento cincuenta y dos
Unidad 2

Classroom Community

Group Activity Have students gather information outside of class about college schedules. Have them write down in-class and after-class activities of friends, neighbors, or relatives who are in college full-time or part-time. Then have them compile what all group members find out and compare the schedules to their own. Ask several groups to present their findings.

Portfolio Have students plan a calendar of their activities for the coming week. For each day, they should include at least one activity that they have to do, like to do, or are going to do. Have them also include times as well as with whom they will do the activities.

Rubric A = 8–9 pts. B = 6–7 pts. C = 4–5 pts. D = 3 pts. F = < 3pts.

Criteria	Scale		
Vocabulary use	1	2	3
Accuracy	1	2	3
Appearance	1	2	3

GRAMÁTICA

Regular Present Tense Verbs with Irregular **yo** Forms

These are verbs that have regular present tense forms except for an irregular **yo** form.

conocer *to know, to be familiar with (a person or a place)*

cono**zco**	conocemos
conoces	conocéis
conoce	conocen

These verbs follow the form for regular -er verbs except in the yo form.

hacer *to do, to make*

ha**go**	hacemos
haces	hacéis
hace	hacen

Isabel says:

—¡Cono**zco** a **alguien** muy modesto!
*I **know** someone very modest!*

Tengo que cuidar a **mi hermano.**
*I have to take care of **my brother.***

Tengo que cuidar mi **gato.**
*I have to take care of **my cat.***

Note that whenever a **person** is the object of a verb, the personal **a** must be used after the **verb** except for the verb **tener**.

A may also be used when talking about animals that are pets, but it is not required.

ACTIVIDAD 15 Gramática

En la biblioteca

Leer Completa la conversación de Isabel y Ricardo con el verbo **hacer**. *(Hint: Practice with the verb hacer.)*

Isabel: Ricardo, ¿qué ___1___?

Ricardo: ___2___ la tarea. Y tú, ¿qué ___3___?

Isabel: Yo también ___4___ la tarea.

Ricardo: ¿Vas a participar en el concurso?

Isabel: ¡Sí, y voy a ___5___ algo muy interesante!

▪ **MÁS PRÁCTICA** *cuaderno* p. 55
▪ **PARA HISPANOHABLANTES** *cuaderno* p. 53

ACTIVIDAD 16

Un día típico

Hablar/Escribir Explica lo que hacen. Usa la **a** personal si es necesario. *(Hint: Explain what they're doing. Use the personal a if needed.)*

1. un amigo / cuidar / ¿?
2. yo / hacer / ¿?
3. nosotros / esperar / ¿?
4. mis padres / visitar / ¿?
5. tú / ayudar / ¿?
6. yo / conocer / ¿?

ACTIVIDAD 17

 ¿A quién conocen?

Hablar/Escribir Tú, tus amigos y tu familia conocen a muchas personas. Explica a quiénes conocen. *(Hint: Explain who they know.)*

1. yo
2. mi amigo(a)
3. mis amigos
4. mi familia y yo
5. mis padres

ciento cincuenta y tres
Etapa 3 | **153**

Teaching All Students

Extra Help Give students a list of 10–12 verb infinitives (some that have regular **yo** forms and some that have irregular forms). Have students provide the **yo** forms.

Native Speakers As a variation of **Actividad 16**, have students provide items for **Un sábado típico** in their cultural communities.

Multiple Intelligences

Musical/Rhythmic Working in groups, have students work on rap songs or chants to the conjugations of **-ar**, **-er**, and **-ir** verbs. Have several groups perform for the class.

Quick Start Review

♻ Verbs
Use OHT 67 or write on the board: List verbs related to each category:

1. en el parque
2. en la cafetería
3. en la escuela
4. en el museo
5. en casa

Answers *See p. 139B.*

Teaching Suggestions
Teaching Regular Present Tense Verbs with Irregular yo Forms

Point out the various uses of **a** that students know: **Voy** *a* la biblioteca *a* las tres. **Voy** *a* buscar un diccionario. ¿Conoces *a* mi mejor hermano?

ACTIVIDAD 15 Objective: Controlled practice Verbs with irregular **yo** forms

Answers
1. haces   4. hago
2. Hago   5. hacer
3. haces

ACTIVIDAD 16 Objective: Transitional practice Verbs with irregular **yo** forms/ the personal **a**

Answers
1. Un amigo cuida...
2. Yo hago...
3. Nosotros esperamos...
4. Mis padres visitan...
5. Tú ayudas...
6. Yo conozco...

ACTIVIDAD 17 Objective: Open-ended practice Verbs with irregular **yo** forms
♻ People

Answers will vary.

Block Schedule

Retention Have students continue using their verb charts to review new types of verbs. You might also compile all the types learned so far on a poster or a flip chart and spend time reviewing.

Teaching Resource Options

Print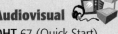

Más práctica Workbook PE, p. 56
Para hispanohablantes Workbook PE,
  p. 54
Block Scheduling Copymasters
Unit 2 Resource Book
  Más práctica Workbook TE, p. 110
  Para hispanohablantes Workbook
    TE, p. 116
  Information Gap Activities,
    pp. 120–121
  Audioscript, p. 132
  Audioscript *Para hispanohablantes*,
    p. 132

Audiovisual

OHT 67 (Quick Start)
Audio Program Cassettes 6A, 6B / CD 6
Audio *Para hispanohablantes*
  Cassette 6A / CD 6

Technology

Intrigas y aventuras CD-ROM, Disc 1

🔔 Quick Start Review

♻ Interrogatives

Use OHT 67 or write on the board:
Complete the following sentences with
an interrogative word/expression:

1. ¿ _____ vas después de clase?
2. ¿ _____ se llama tu perro?
3. ¿ _____ música te gusta más?
4. ¿ _____ vamos al parque?
5. ¿ _____ no está aquí nuestra
   profesora?
6. ¿ _____ viven tus tíos?

Answers
1. Adónde
2. Cómo
3. Qué
4. Cuándo/A qué hora/Por qué
5. Por qué
6. Dónde

Teaching Suggestions
Reinforcing Using the Verb oír

After teaching the forms of the verb
oír, point out all the verbs students
know that have a special **yo** form to
remember: **oigo, soy, voy, estoy,
tengo, hago, conozco, veo.** Have
students use each one in a sentence.

 GRAMÁTICA

Using the Verb oír

▶ Like **hacer** and **conocer**, the verb **oír** *(to hear)* has an irregular
yo form in the present tense.

oigo	oímos
oyes	oís
oye	oyen

* Some of its forms also require a spelling change where
  the **i** becomes a **y.**
* Note that the **nosotros(as)** and **vosotros(as)** forms have accents.

▶ You may hear the expression **¡Oye!** used throughout the dialog. It is
used to get someone's attention, the way *Hey!* is used in English.

To get Isabel's attention Ricardo might say: —**¡Oye,** Isabel!

ACTIVIDAD 18 Gramática

¿A quiénes oyen?

Escribir ¿A quién oye cada
persona? Completa las
oraciones con la forma correcta
del verbo **oír.** *(Hint: Say whom each
person hears.)*

modelo

Isabel / su madre

Isabel oye a **su madre.**

1. Anita / sus amigos
2. los estudiantes /
   la profesora
3. tú / tu amigo
4. yo / mi hermano
5. Felipe y yo / la señora Ruiz
6. ustedes / sus vecinos

■ **MÁS PRÁCTICA** *cuaderno* p. 56
■ **PARA HISPANOHABLANTES**
  cuaderno p. 54

ACTIVIDAD 19

♻ ¿Dónde oyes...?

Hablar Conversa con otro(a) estudiante sobre dónde oyes estas
cosas. *(Hint: Say where you hear these things.)*

modelo

música   **Estudiante A:** ¿Dónde oyes música?

   Estudiante B: Oigo música en el auditorio.

Estudiante A
PREGUNTAS

1. música
2. la profesora
3. tus amigos
4. la guitarra
5. el doctor
6. unos pájaros
7. el piano

Estudiante B
RESPUESTAS

la casa
la clase
el auditorio
la tienda
la escuela
la oficina
el parque

154 ciento cincuenta y cuatro
Unidad 2

Classroom Community 🔲

Group Activity Have students prepare a tape of 10
different sounds, such as those listed in **Actividad 19.**
Have them number each sound. For example: **Número
uno,** *sound of guitar music playing.* Students then play
their tapes for the class and the class identifies where
they hear this sound.

Storytelling In order to review some of the irregular
yo verb forms learned so far, have students work in
small groups and tell a story about themselves. They
should include at least 4 of the following verbs in the
yo form: **conocer, ser, estar, tener, hacer, oír, ver, ir.**

ACTIVIDAD 20

¡A oír bien!

Escuchar Escoge la respuesta más apropiada para cada oración. *(Hint: Choose the best response.)*

1. **a.** caminar con el perro
   b. tocar la guitarra
   c. hacer ejercicio

2. **a.** ir al parque
   b. comer una hamburguesa
   c. abrir el libro

3. **a.** mandar una carta
   b. ir al teatro
   c. comprar una novela

4. **a.** comer una torta
   b. beber un refresco
   c. visitar a los amigos

ACTIVIDAD 21

Una carta

Escribir Tu amigo(a) quiere saber qué haces todos los días. Escríbele una carta. *(Hint: Write a letter to your friend.)*

modelo

Querido Paco:

¿Cómo estás? Yo estoy muy bien. ¿Qué hago todos los días? Pues, hago muchas cosas. Primero, siempre camino con el perro en el parque. Después, paso un rato con mis amigos. A veces, andamos en bicicleta o vamos a casa para escuchar música. De vez en cuando, tengo que cuidar a mi hermano...

¿Y tú? ¿Qué haces después de las clases?

Tu amigo,

Daniel

■ **MÁS COMUNICACIÓN** p. R6

Pronunciación

Refrán

Pronunciación de los acentos

1. Words ending in a vowel, or the letters **n** or **s**, are stressed on the next-to-last syllable.

2. Words ending in a consonant other than **n** or **s** are stressed on the last syllable.

3. Words that have written accents are stressed on the syllable with the accent.

A las diez en la cama estés, mejor antes que después.

ciento cincuenta y cinco
Etapa 3   **155**

Vocabulary/Grammar • UNIDAD 2 Etapa 3   155

Teaching All Students

Extra Help For the **Pronunciación** section, write 10–12 words on the board. Ask volunteers to divide the words into syllables and underline the stressed syllable. You may wish to explain the difference between a stressed syllable and an accented letter.

Multiple Intelligences

Verbal Ask for volunteers to exchange and then read several of the letters submitted for **Actividad 21**. The other students listen and guess who wrote the letters.

Visual Have students draw visuals to illustrate the following verbs: **oír, ver, ir, hacer, tener.**

ACTIVIDAD 18 Objective: Controlled practice
Oír

Answers
1. Anita oye a sus amigos.
2. Los estudiantes oyen a la profesora.
3. Tú oyes a tu amigo.
4. Yo oigo a mi hermano.
5. Felipe y yo oímos a la señora Ruiz.
6. Ustedes oyen a sus vecinos.

ACTIVIDAD 19 Objective: Transitional practice
Oír in conversation
♻ Places

Answers
Answers will vary.
1. A: ¿Dónde oyes música?
   B: Oigo música en el auditorio.
2. A: ¿Dónde oyes a la profesora?
   B: Oigo a la profesora en la clase.
3. A: ¿Dónde oyes a tus amigos?
   B: Oigo a mis amigos en la escuela.
4. A: ¿Dónde oyes la guitarra?
   B: Oigo la guitarra en la tienda.
5. A: ¿Dónde oyes al doctor?
   B: Oigo al doctor en la oficina.
6. A: ¿Dónde oyes unos pájaros?
   B: Oigo unos pájaros en el parque.
7. A: ¿Dónde oyes el piano?
   B: Oigo el piano en la casa.

ACTIVIDAD 20 Objective: Transitional practice
Listening comprehension/vocabulary

Answers (See script p. 139B.)
1. b   3. c
2. b   4. b

ACTIVIDAD 21 Objective: Open-ended practice
Talking about after-school activities in writing

Answers will vary.

Dictation

After presenting the **Pronunciación**, have students close their books. Dictate the **Refrán** in segments while students write it.

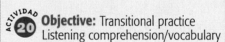

■ Block Schedule

FunBreak In groups have students write one of the **Etapa**'s new vocabulary words on an index card. They should refer to pp. 142–143, 149, 150, 151, 153, and 154. They can then use these cards to play hangman or Pictionary™. (For additional activities, see **Block Scheduling Copymasters**.)

Teaching Resource Options

Print

Block Scheduling Copymasters
Unit 2 Resource Book
  Audioscript, p. 133
  Audioscript *Para hispanohablantes*,
    p. 133

Audiovisual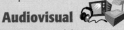

OHT 68 (Quick Start)
Audio Program Cassette 6A / CD 6
Audio *Para hispanohablantes*
  Cassette 6A / CD 6
Canciones Cassette / CD

Quick Start Review

♻ Mexico City

Use OHT 68 or write on the board:
Write 5 sentences about places to see
and things to do in Mexico City.

Answers will vary.

Teaching Suggestions

• **Prereading** Divide the class in 4
  groups. Have each group provide
  descriptions/facts about 1 of the
  photos on pp. 156–157.
• **Strategy: Skim** Have students look
  at the visuals and skim the reading.
  Ask volunteers for some of the clues
  they found that indicate the central
  theme or topic.
• **Reading** Have students first look at
  the ¿Comprendiste? questions to see
  what information they should look for
  when they read.
• **Post-reading** Have students think
  of questions they might ask a young
  person from Mexico about their
  weekday and weekend activities.

Cross Cultural Connections

Strategy Ask students to compare the
information about young people in
Mexico City with young people in your
town/city. Have them list at least 2
similarities and 2 differences.

En voces
LECTURA

México y sus jóvenes

PARA LEER
STRATEGY: READING
Skim Before reading a long
passage, it is helpful to read
quickly to get a general idea of
its content. Skim the paragraphs,
noting clues that indicate the
central theme or topic. By
skimming, you can tell quickly
what a reading is about. Then it
will be easier to do a more
careful reading.

¿Qué hacen los mexicanos jóvenes? De
lunes a viernes los muchachos que tienen
menos de[1] 18 años van a la escuela.
Tienen muchas materias —a veces
tienen hasta ocho clases en un día.
Y también tienen mucha
tarea. Por eso, después
de clases muchos de
los estudiantes van a sus
casas para hacer la tarea y después
descansar.

En la Ciudad de México hay
muchos teatros, museos, tiendas y
parques. En cada[2] lugar es posible
ver a muchos jóvenes, especialmente
los fines de semana.

[1] less than
[2] each, every

156 ciento cincuenta y seis
Unidad 2

Classroom Community

Cooperative Learning Have students work
together in groups of 4 to answer the ¿Comprendiste?
questions. For each question, Student 1 reads the
question aloud, Student 2 answers it, Student 3 writes
the answer, and Student 4 checks it. Students should
exchange roles for each question.

Game On the board, scramble the words from one
sentence in the **Lectura.** Have students unscramble the
words without referring to the text. Call on students to
read the correct sentence. The student who responds
correctly gets to scramble the next sentence. This game
may also be done in groups, with each group
unscrambling a different sentence.

Los viernes por la tarde, los sábados y los domingos son los días principales en que los jóvenes mexicanos están libres³. Los domingos hay mucha gente en los parques. Andan en bicicleta, practican deportes⁴ o tocan un instrumento. De vez en cuando, para el almuerzo, van a un restaurante con sus familias. El domingo es el día principal para pasear y descansar.

³ free
⁴ sports

¿Comprendiste?

1. ¿Qué hacen los jóvenes de lunes a viernes?
2. ¿Adónde van muchos jóvenes los fines de semana en la Ciudad de México?
3. ¿Qué actividades hacen los domingos?
4. ¿Qué hace a veces una familia los domingos?

¿Qué piensas?

Explica si tu vida es como la vida de un joven mexicano.

ciento cincuenta y siete **157**
Etapa 3

Culture Highlights

● **LOS DEPORTES** The sports played in Mexico today have various origins: baseball from the U.S., **jai alai** from the Basques in Spain and France, and soccer and bullfighting from Spain.

¿Comprendiste?
Answers
1. Van a la escuela. Hacen mucha tarea.
2. Van a los teatros, a los museos, a las tiendas y a los parques.
3. Andan en bicicleta, practican deportes o tocan un instrumento.
4. Va a un restaurante para el almuerzo.

Block Schedule
Variety Just as variety is necessary in teaching a block schedule situation, variety is also necessary in homework assignments. Try assigning a combination of written activities along with pre-reading of the **En voces** and **En colores** sections. (For additional activities, see **Block Scheduling Copymasters**.)

Teaching All Students

Extra Help Have students reread the **Lectura** one paragraph at a time. They should provide a brief summary of each paragraph before moving to the next.

Native Speakers Ask students to compare and contrast the information about Mexico City with the social activities in their home communities. Are the same facilities and activities available? What is the social life like?

Multiple Intelligences

Intrapersonal Have students do a library or Internet search to find out more information about daily life in Mexico City. All students should share several facts with the class. Topics such as shopping, transportation, schools, and leisure activities may be used. Have students tell what aspects of life they could easily adapt to, or if there are any that might be difficult.

Teaching Resource Options

Print

Unit 2 Resource Book
  Audioscript, p. 134
  Audioscript *Para hispanohablantes*,
    p. 134

Audiovisual

Audio Program Cassette 6A / CD 6
Audio *Para hispanohablantes*
  Cassette 6A / CD 6
OHT 68 (Quick Start)
Video Program Videotape 2 / Videodisc
  1B

Search Chapter 8, Play to 9
U2E3 • En colores (Culture)

Quick Start Review

♻ Verbs with irregular **yo** forms
Use OHT 68 or write on the board:
Complete each sentence with the **yo**
form of one of these verbs: **hacer /
conocer / ir / estar / tener / ver**

1. A las ocho de la mañana, yo ___
   a mi clase de música.
2. Yo no ___ a mis amigos. ¿Dónde
   están?
3. Yo ___ quince años.
4. Yo no ___ a tu prima. ¿Cómo se
   llama?
5. Yo siempre ___ ejercicio en el
   gimnasio.
6. A veces yo ___ en la biblioteca a
   las cuatro.

Answers

1.	voy	3.	tengo	5.	hago
2.	veo	4.	conozco	6.	estoy

Teaching Suggestions
Presenting Cultura y comparaciones

- Have students make observations
  about the pictures on pp. 158–159.
  How does **El Zócalo** compare to the
  center of a city they are familiar with?
- Ask students if they are more interested
  in ancient history or modern history
  and why. Explain that Mexico City is a
  fascinating combination of both.
- Expand the cultural information by
  showing the video culture presentation.

En colores
CULTURA Y
COMPARACIONES

PARA CONOCERNOS
STRATEGY: CONNECTING CULTURES

Compare places Have you lived in or visited a
place that has a long history? Is there a special
name for that historical area? How old is it?
What can you see—buildings, sculptures,
murals—that reveals its history? What is its
historical importance? What comparisons can
you make between it and places in «**El Zócalo:
centro de México**»?

Conozco este lugar	Lugar histórico de México
Nombre del lugar: Edad del lugar: Pinturas/Murales: Otras cosas:	Nombre del lugar: Edad del lugar: Pinturas/Murales: Otras cosas:

Un canal del imperio azteca

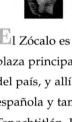

El Zócalo es el centro de México, D.F. Es la
plaza principal de la ciudad. El D.F. es la capital
del país, y allí estaban[1] la vieja capital colonial
española y también la capital azteca de México,
Tenochtitlán. En los días de los aztecas, el
Zócalo fue[2] un centro ceremonial con pirámides
y palacios. Después de conquistar Tenochtitlán
en 1521, los españoles construyeron[3] su capital
encima de[4] la capital de los aztecas. La Catedral
española está aquí, encima del Templo Mayor

[1] there were   [2] was   [3] built   [4] on top of

158
ciento cincuenta y ocho
Unidad 2

Classroom Community

Group Activity Assign sections or photos of the
reading to groups. Each group will research and present
to the class more information about the places
mentioned or shown in their section or photos.

Portfolio Have students research the Aztecs and
create a poster depicting several interesting facts or
images.

Rubric A = 13–15 pts. B = 10–12 pts. C = 7–9 pts. D = 4–6 pts. F = < 4pts.

Criteria	Scale
Details	1 2 3 4 5
Organization	1 2 3 4 5
Creativity, appearance	1 2 3 4 5

En el Zócalo están **la Catedral** y **el Sagrario**. Son dos símbolos religiosos y ejemplos importantes de la arquitectura y el arte colonial de México.

El Templo Mayor es la pirámide principal de Tenochtitlán. De esta excavación vienen descubrimientos[6] importantes sobre los aztecas.

El calendario azteca o la Piedra del Sol[7] fue descubierto[8] debajo del[9] Zócalo en 1790.

centro de México

de los aztecas, una gran pirámide. El Palacio Nacional, el centro del gobierno[5] mexicano, está encima de las ruinas de un palacio azteca. Hoy el Zócalo es el centro de la vida social y religiosa de las personas de esta ciudad.

[5] government
[6] discoveries
[7] Sun Stone
[8] was discovered
[9] beneath

¿Comprendiste?

1. ¿Cómo se llama la capital azteca?
2. ¿Qué está encima de las ruinas de un palacio?
3. ¿Qué descubrimientos importantes hay en el Zócalo?
4. ¿Qué lugar del Zócalo representa la vida política de México?
5. ¿Cuáles representan la vida religiosa?

¿Qué piensas?

1. Si vas a la Ciudad de México, ¿por qué es importante ver el Zócalo?
2. ¿Qué importancia tiene el Zócalo en la historia de México?

ciento cincuenta y nueve
Etapa 3 **159**

Teaching Resource Options

Print

Para hispanohablantes Workbook PE, pp. 55–56
Block Scheduling Copymasters
Unit 2 Resource Book
  Para hispanohablantes Workbook TE, pp. 117–118
  Information Gap Activities, p. 122
  Family Involvement, pp. 123–124
  Multiple Choice Test Questions, pp. 170–178

Audiovisual

OHT 68 (Quick Start)
Audio Program Testing Cassette T1 / CD T1

Technology

Electronic Teacher Tools/Test Generator
Intrigas y aventuras CD-ROM, Disc 1

Quick Start Review

♻ Verb review
Use OHT 68 or write on the board:
Write at least 3 infinitives in each column. Write a sentence for 1 verb each column.

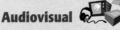

-ar verbs	**-er** verbs	**-ir** verbs

Answers *See p. 139B.*

✔ Teaching Suggestions
What Have Students Learned?

Have students look at the "Now you can…" notes listed on the left side of pages 160–161. Point out that if they need to review material before doing the activities or taking the test, they should consult the "To review" notes.

ETAPA 3

Now you can…
• discuss plans.

To review
• **ir + a +** infinitive, see p. 149.

Now you can…
• talk about places and people you know.

To review
• the verb **conocer**, see verbs with irregular **yo** forms, p. 153.

En uso

REPASO Y MÁS COMUNICACIÓN

ACTIVIDAD 1 ¿Qué vas a hacer tú?

Todos tienen planes para esta tarde. ¿Qué van a hacer? *(Hint: Tell what people's afternoon plans are.)*

modelo

Victoria   *Victoria va a tocar la guitarra.*

1. Juan y Rubén

4. yo

2. la señora Estrada

5. nosotros

3. tú

6. Benjamín

ACTIVIDAD 2 Nuestra comunidad

Todos hablan de las personas y de los lugares que conocen en la comunidad. ¿Qué dicen? *(Hint: Tell who is familiar with the people and places.)*

modelo

nosotros: la familia Méndez
Nosotros conocemos a **la familia Méndez.**

1. ellos: los vecinos
2. yo: el museo de arte
3. tú: la tienda de música
4. Marcela: el doctor
5. nosotras: el teatro
6. yo: las policías

160 | ciento sesenta
Unidad 2

Classroom Community

Group Activity Prepare ahead: flashcards, activities, and short quizzes to review each of the 6 bulleted "To review" sections on pp. 160–161. Divide the class into 6 groups. Have students move in groups from one area to another to review the materials.

Paired Activity After **Actividades 1–4** are completed, have pairs of students write 10 quiz questions. They should exchange questions with another pair and answer the other pair's questions. Then have them peer correct each other's answers.

ACTIVIDAD 3 — Todos los sábados

¿Qué hace Miguel todos los sábados? Usa el horario para completar las oraciones. *(Hint: Tell what Miguel does every Saturday.)*

modelo

Primero , Miguel lee el periódico.

1. _____ correr en el gimnasio, Miguel lee el periódico.
2. _____ correr, él escribe cartas.
3. _____, Miguel come con los amigos.
4. _____ comer, descansa en casa.
5. _____, él pasea en el parque.

10:00	leer el periódico
10:30	correr en el gimnasio
11:30	escribir cartas
1:00	comer con los amigos
3:00	descansar en casa
5:00	pasear en el parque

ACTIVIDAD 4 — ¡Muchas actividades!

¿Dónde hacen estas personas las siguientes actividades?
(Hint: Where do people do these activities?)

modelo

Luz / correr (¿museo o parque?)
Luz corre en el parque.

1. Samuel y Sofía / leer unos libros (¿biblioteca o teatro?)
2. yo / ver la televisión (¿gimnasio o casa?)
3. usted / comer fruta (¿museo o cafetería?)
4. nosotros / hacer la tarea (¿supermercado o biblioteca?)
5. yo / oír música (¿auditorio o museo?)
6. la señora Santana / vender ropa (¿cafetería o tienda?)
7. tú / recibir cartas (¿casa o parque?)
8. yo / hacer ejercicio (¿gimnasio o museo?)
9. nosotros / comer chicharrones (¿parque o biblioteca?)
10. Eduardo / oír los pájaros (¿teatro o parque?)
11. Marcelo / comprender la lección (¿clase de matemáticas o cafetería?)
12. Cristina / aprender historia (¿escuela o gimnasio?)

ciento sesenta y uno
Etapa 3   161

Now you can...
- sequence events.

To review
- vocabulary for sequencing events, see p. 150.

Now you can...
- discuss plans.

To review
- the present tense of regular **-er** and **-ir** verbs, see p. 151.
- verbs with irregular **yo** forms, see p. 153.
- the verb **oír**, see p. 154.

ACTIVIDAD 1 — Answers

1. Juan y Rubén van a andar en bicicleta.
2. La señora Estrada va a pintar.
3. Tú vas a tocar el piano.
4. Yo voy a ver la televisión.
5. Nosotros vamos a pasear (por el parque).
6. Benjamín va a caminar con el perro.

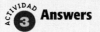

ACTIVIDAD 2 — Answers

1. Ellos conocen a los vecinos.
2. Yo conozco el museo de arte.
3. Tú conoces la tienda de música.
4. Marcela conoce al doctor.
5. Nosotras conocemos el teatro.
6. Yo conozco a las policías.

ACTIVIDAD 3 — Answers

1. Antes de	4. Después de
2. Después de	5. Por fin
3. Luego	

ACTIVIDAD 4 — Answers

1. Samuel y Sofía leen unos libros en la biblioteca.
2. Yo veo la televisión en casa.
3. Usted come fruta en la cafetería.
4. Nosotros hacemos la tarea en la biblioteca.
5. Yo oigo música en el auditorio.
6. La señora Santana vende ropa en la tienda.
7. Tú recibes cartas en casa.
8. Yo hago ejercicio en el gimnasio.
9. Nosotros comemos chicharrones en el parque.
10. Eduardo oye los pájaros en el parque.
11. Marcelo comprende la lección en la clase de matemáticas.
12. Cristina aprende historia en la escuela.

Block Schedule

FunBreak Have students work in pairs and make 18 Match Game cards. Half of the cards should have place names on them and the other half should have activities to be done in those places. It is important that students agree on which 2 cards must go together. Students then shuffle the cards and lay them out facedown. In turn, each partner turns over one card, then tries to find the matching card. If the 2 cards match, the student keeps the cards and plays again. If the second card does not match, both cards are turned facedown again and the next student plays. (For additional activities, see **Block Scheduling Copymasters.**)

Teaching All Students

Challenge For **Actividad 4** have students write a verb phrase for the place *not* chosen. For example:
1. en el teatro: ver el Ballet Folklórico.

Multiple Intelligences

Intrapersonal Have students write a personalized sequence of events in a short paragraph, using the new vocabulary from this **Etapa**.

Verbal Given a verb infinitive, have students make a sentence using the verb and one other vocabulary word from **Etapa 3**.

Teaching Resource Options

Print

Unit 2 Resource Book
Cooperative Quizzes, pp. 135–136
Etapa Exam, Forms A and B,
pp. 137–146
Para hispanohablantes Etapa Exam,
pp. 147–151
Portfolio Assessment, pp. 152–153
Unit 2 Comprehensive Test,
pp. 154–161
Para hispanohablantes Unit 2
Comprehensive Test, pp. 162–169
Multiple Choice Test Questions,
pp. 170–178

Audiovisual

OHT 68 (Quick Start)
Audio Program Testing Cassette T1 /
CD T1

Technology

Electronic Teacher Tools/Test
Generator
www.mcdougallittell.com

ACTIVIDAD 5

Rubric: Speaking

Criteria	Scale	
Vocabulary use	1 2 3	A = 8–9 pts.
Sentence structure	1 2 3	B = 6–7 pts.
Ease, fluency	1 2 3	C = 4–5 pts.
		D = 3 pts.
		F = < 3 pts.

ACTIVIDAD 6 Answers will vary.

ACTIVIDAD 7 En tu propia voz

Rubric: Writing

Criteria	Scale	
Vocabulary use	1 2 3 4 5	A = 14–15 pts.
Accuracy	1 2 3 4 5	B = 12–13 pts.
Creativity, appearance	1 2 3 4 5	C = 10–11 pts.
		D = 8–9 pts.
		F = < 8 pts.

ACTIVIDAD 5  Y luego...

> **PARA CONVERSAR**
>
> **STRATEGY: SPEAKING**
>
> **Ask for clarification** Show your interest by asking for clarification or verification: **Ah, sí, ¿tú vas al museo antes de comer?** Or use other words about the sequence of plans: **entonces, luego, después (de), antes (de),** or a specific time.

Imagínate que eres un(a) turista en una ciudad mexicana. Selecciona cuatro actividades. Luego, conversa con otro(a) estudiante sobre tus planes. *(Hint: You are a tourist. Select four activities and explain your plans.)*

modelo

Primero, voy al Zócalo...

9:00	Excursión al Zócalo
10:30	Museo de Arte Moderno
2:00	Almuerzo
3:30	Tienda de ropa típica
5:00	Paseo en el parque central
8:30	Cena mexicana en el hotel

TÚ EN LA COMUNIDAD

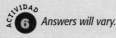

Tim is a high school student in Wisconsin. He volunteers to help children with their homework, and he often speaks with them in Spanish. He also uses Spanish to understand some of the customers at his part-time job at a store. Do you speak Spanish at work?

ACTIVIDAD 6 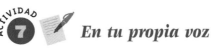 En la plaza

Tú y tus compañeros están en esta plaza mexicana. Hablen sobre lo que ven y oyen y mencionen a las personas que conocen. ¡Usen la imaginación! *(Hint: You and your classmates are in this Mexican plaza. Talk about what you see and hear and the people you know.)*

ACTIVIDAD 7 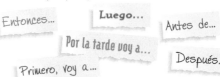 *En tu propia voz*

ESCRITURA Imagínate que el sábado vas a hacer muchas cosas. Describe tus planes. *(Hint: Describe your plans.)*

Entonces...

Luego...

Antes de...

Por la tarde voy a...

Primero, voy a...

Después...

Classroom Community

Cooperative Learning The class will sponsor an essay contest—**Mis actividades favoritas.** Divide the class into 5 committees:

1. Rules Committee: Determine the contest rules: dates of the contest, what needs to be included in the essay, how long it should be, etc.
2. Advertising Committee: Make several posters and a flier to advertise the contest. Include all necessary information provided by the Rules Committee.
3. Distribution Committee: Hang up the posters around the school. Make copies of the fliers and distribute them to all Spanish 1 classes.
4. Awards Committee: Decide on prizes. These can be made by students or purchased by contest sponsors.
5. Judges Committee: Design an evaluation form. Read the essays and determine the top 3 winners.

En resumen

REPASO DE VOCABULARIO

DISCUSSING PLANS

ir a…	to be going to…

After-school Plans

andar en bicicleta	to ride a bike
caminar con el perro	to walk the dog
cenar	to have dinner, supper
comer chicharrones	to eat pork rinds
cuidar (a)	to take care of
el animal	animal
mi hermano(a)	my brother (sister)
el pájaro	bird
el pez	fish
hacer ejercicio	to exercise
ir al supermercado	to go to the supermarket
leer	to read
la novela	novel
el periódico	newspaper
el poema	poem
la poesía	poetry
la revista	magazine
mandar una carta	to send a letter
pasar un rato con los amigos	to spend time with friends
pasear	to go for a walk
pintar	to paint
preparar	to prepare
la cena	supper, dinner
la comida	food, a meal
tocar el piano	to play the piano
tocar la guitarra	to play the guitar
ver la televisión	to watch television

SEQUENCING EVENTS

antes (de)	before
después (de)	after, afterward
entonces	then, so
luego	later
por fin	finally
primero	first

ACTIVITIES

abrir	to open
aprender	to learn
beber	to drink
compartir	to share
comprender	to understand
hacer	to make, to do
oír	to hear
recibir	to receive
tener hambre	to be hungry
tener sed	to be thirsty
vender	to sell
ver	to see
vivir	to live

PLACES AND PEOPLE YOU KNOW

conocer a alguien	to know, to be familiar with someone

Places

el museo	museum
el parque	park
el teatro	theater
la tienda	store

OTHER WORDS AND PHRASES

cada	each, every
el corazón	heart
la gente	people
el problema	problem
la vida	life

Juego

¿Qué actividades hacen las personas?

Adriana: Le gusta hacer ejercicio y tiene un perro.

José: Le gusta tocar un instrumento. Jakob Dylan, Mary Chapin Carpenter y Melissa Etheridge tocan este instrumento.

Jorge: Es un hermano muy responsable. Tiene una familia grande.

ciento sesenta y tres
Etapa 3 **163**

🔔 Quick Start Review

♻ School activities

Use OHT 68 or write on the board:
Complete the following lists:

Mis clases por la mañana	Mis clases por la tarde

Answers
Answers will vary. Answers could include:
Por la mañana: inglés, español, música
Por la tarde: educación física, ciencias
naturales, historia, matemáticas

Teaching Strategy
Prewriting

- Ask students to name their school subjects this semester. Keep a complete list on the board.
- Ask for volunteers to describe one of their courses, as if they were addressing a student new to the school.
- Remind students of the **PASS** list at the beginning of the page: **P**urpose, **A**udience, **S**ubject, **S**tructure. This PASS key will help them complete a well-structured assignment.

Post-writing

- Have students extend their schedule through the evening hours, writing times and brief descriptions of their activities on a typical weekday.

UNIDAD

2

En tu propia voz
ESCRITURA

El horario de la escuela

Alicia and Álvaro are Spanish-speaking students who are coming to your school. Familiarize them with a typical school week by sending them their schedule, which is the same as yours.

Purpose: Acquaint new students with school schedule
Audience: Spanish-speaking students
Subject: School day
Structure: School schedule

PARA ESCRIBIR • STRATEGY: WRITING

Organize information chronologically and by category A clear and detailed schedule is important for any student. Alicia and Álvaro will need to know the school hours, class subjects and times, and after-school activities in chronological order.

Modelo del estudiante

Franklin High School FHS

El horario escolar

The writer organizes information chronologically, using appropriate times.

● **7:40** Llegamos a la escuela.

● **7:45–11:00** Tenemos las clases de historia, música (lunes, miércoles y viernes), arte (martes y jueves), inglés y biología por la mañana.

The author groups classes according to the morning or afternoon, noting that not all classes meet every day.

11:05–12:05 Almuerzo. Comemos en la cafetería.

12:10–2:35 Tenemos las clases de español, matemáticas, educación física (lunes y jueves) y computación (martes, miércoles y viernes) por la tarde.

The writer describes a variety of extracurricular activities (common in American culture but not Hispanic ones) and tells on which days they take place.

● **2:50–4:00** Siempre hay actividades después de las clases. Los lunes vamos al club de español. Los martes y jueves nadamos. Los miércoles usamos las computadoras. Los viernes bailamos en el gimnasio.

164   ciento sesenta y cuatro
Unidad 2

Classroom Community

Paired Activity Have students make up a chart of (1) what students new to the school would *need* to know, and (2) what they would *want* to know. Remind students to use their vocabulary lists to help them when writing.

Group Activity Ask students to first write a brief description of a class they are taking, without naming the class. Then, in groups, have students read their descriptions aloud while the rest of the group tries to guess which class is being described.

Estrategias para escribir

Antes de escribir...

Before you begin the first draft of your schedule, brainstorm the elements of your school week. Good writers always begin by thinking about their audience, the people who will be reading their work. So think about the Spanish-speaking students. What kinds of things would you want to know if you were in their place? Use a chart to help you organize your ideas. Be sure to include your class subjects and times, lunch time, and after-school activities. Then write your schedule in chronological order, including complete-sentence descriptions for each block of time.

mi horario

hora	lunes	martes	miércoles	jueves	viernes
7:45	llegar				
8:00	matemáticas				
8:45	educación física	música	música	educación física	música

Revisiones

Share your draft with a partner. Then ask:

- *Is the schedule complete and accurate?*
- *Is the schedule organized chronologically?*
- *Would any other information be useful?*

La versión final

Review what you have written, asking yourself these questions:

- *Did I use the appropriate verb forms?*

Try this: Circle every verb. Check to make sure that each verb has the appropriate subject.

- *Are articles used correctly?*

Try this: Underline every article/noun combination. Check to make sure that each article agrees in number and gender with its noun.

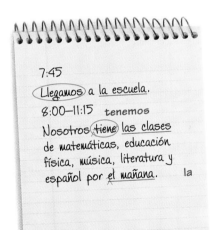

7:45
Llegamos a la escuela.
8:00—11:15 tenemos
Nosotros tiene las clases
de matemáticas, educación
física, música, literatura y
español por el mañana.   la

 Share your writing on www.mcdougallittell.com

ciento sesenta y cinco
Unidad 2   **165**

el francés	el cálculo
el japonés	la geometría
el ruso	la biología
el chino	la geología
el alemán	la contabilidad
la física	(accounting)
la química	

Rubric: Writing

Let students know ahead of time which elements of their writing you will be evaluating. A global evaluation is more helpful to students than a correction of every mistake made. Consider the following in scoring compositions:

Sentences	
1	Most are not logical
2	In logical order
3	Flow purposefully

Details	
1	Few classes/activities
2	Sufficient classes/activities
3	Detailed classes/activities

Organization	
1	Not well organized
2	Some organization
3	Strong organization

Accuracy	
1	Errors prevent comprehension
2	Some spelling and agreement errors throughout
3	Very few errors

Criteria	Scale	
Logical sentence order	1 2 3	A = 10–12 pts.
Detailed classes/activities	1 2 3	B = 7–9 pts.
Organization	1 2 3	C = 4–6 pts.
Accuracy	1 2 3	D = 3 pts.
		F = < 3 pts.

Teaching All Students

Extra Help Have students make flashcards of class subjects, days of the week, and time expressions such as **por la mañana, a las dos y media,** etc. Then have them quiz each other.

Challenge Working in pairs, have students write a short letter of greeting and introduction to Alicia and Álvaro. Students should first brainstorm the contents of their letter.

Native Speakers Have students role-play Alicia and Álvaro and ask the class questions about class schedules, subjects, and after-school activities. Encourage them to use a variety of question formats—yes/no, short answer, and more complex questions.

Block Schedule

Variety Have students role-play introducing Alicia and Álvaro to their friends at school and family members at home. (For additional activities, see **Block Scheduling Copymasters.**)

Unit Theme

Living in and visiting Puerto Rico, discussing weather, and participating in leisure activities

Communication
- Expressing feelings and emotions
- Discussing what just happened
- Talking on the telephone
- Discussing sports
- Talking about clothes and accessories
- Describing the weather
- Stating preferences and opinions

Cultures
- Learning about regional vocabulary
- Learning about leisure activities in Puerto Rico
- Learning about the history, geography, and wildlife of Puerto Rico
- Learning about some important people from Puerto Rico

Connections
- Connecting to Music: Music and dance in Puerto Rico and in the U.S.
- Connecting to Science: Using the Celsius scale in Spanish-speaking countries and learning the conversion formula

Comparisons
- Comparing music and dance in Puerto Rico and in the U.S.
- Comparing sports traditions in Puerto Rico with sports traditions in the U.S.
- Comparing tourist attractions in Puerto Rico and in the U.S.

Communities
- Using Spanish for personal interest
- Using Spanish to help others

Teaching Resource Options

Print
Block Scheduling Copymasters

Audiovisual
OHT M1, M2; 69, 70
Canciones Audiocassette/CD
Video Program Videotape 3 / Videodisc 2A

Search Chapter 1, Play to 2
U3 Cultural Introduction

UNIDAD 3

SAN JUAN
PUERTO RICO
EL FIN DE SEMANA

OBJECTIVES

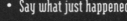

ETAPA 1

¡Me gusta el tiempo libre!
- Extend invitations
- Talk on the phone
- Express feelings
- Say where you are coming from
- Say what just happened

ETAPA 2

¡Deportes para todos!
- Talk about sports
- Express preferences
- Say what you know
- Make comparisons

ETAPA 3

El tiempo en El Yunque
- Describe the weather
- Discuss clothing and accessories
- State an opinion
- Describe how you feel
- Say what is happening

166

GIGI FERNÁNDEZ won the gold medal in women's tennis (doubles) in the 1992 and 1996 Summer Olympics. What other Latin American athletes do you know?

ARECIBO

• MAYAGÜEZ

PONCE •

PASTA DE GUAYABA is a popular dessert. This sweet, thick paste made from the guava fruit is usually eaten with white cheese. What tropical fruits have you eaten?

Classroom Community

Paired Activity Give pairs of students 3–5 minutes to write a list of what they would expect to find on an island that they wouldn't find in their own community.

Group Activity Working in groups, have students do an Internet or library search to find out additional facts that they might include on this Unit opener. They should also illustrate the facts. Let the class select the best additions and display them on the bulletin board.

ALMANAQUE

Población: 3.522.000
Altura: 0 metros (el nivel del mar)
Clima: 27° C (80° F)
Comida típica: pasta de guayaba, tostones, pernil
Gente famosa de Puerto Rico: Gigi Fernández (tenista), Luis Muñoz Marín (político), Luis Rafael Sánchez (escritor), Chayanne (cantante)

¿Vas a Puerto Rico? No necesitas pasaporte. Puerto Rico es una parte de Estados Unidos.

INTERNET For more information about Puerto Rico, access www.mcdougallittell.com

EL MORRO is a fortress that the Spanish began in 1539 and finished in 1787. How could such a fortress protect the city of San Juan?

SAN JUAN

PUERTO RICO

EL YUNQUE

HUMACAO

VIEQUES

LUIS MUÑOZ MARÍN (1898–1980) became the island's first elected governor in 1948. In 1952 he signed an agreement making Puerto Rico a Commonwealth of the U.S. What other U.S. territories do you know that aren't states?

TAÍNOS were natives on the island when Columbus arrived in 1493. They left these glyphs. Their language survived in words like **huracán** *(hurricane)*. What other Native American cultures can you name?

EL CARIBE

Estados Unidos
Islas Bahamas
Cuba
República Dominicana
Jamaica   Haití   Puerto Rico
Antillas Menores

EL LORO PUERTORRIQUEÑO became an endangered species in 1971, when only twenty of these parrots were left. Their numbers have now increased. You might see one in El Yunque, the tropical rain forest. What other animals have been saved from extinction?

167

Teaching All Students

Extra Help Have students identify the following as **persona, lugar, comida o animal:**
1. Luis Muñoz Marín
2. el loro puertorriqueño
3. pasta de guayaba
4. los taínos
5. El Morro
6. Gigi Fernández

Multiple Intelligences
Logical/Mathematical Have students calculate the distance from your area to San Juan, Puerto Rico.

Teaching Suggestion
Previewing the Unit
Tell students that this unit centers on Puerto Rico. Ask students to scan these two pages for 15 seconds, then close their books. Then ask them to tell you what they remember. You may wish to use the introduction to the video to preview the unit.

Culture Highlights

● **ATLETAS LATINOAMERICANOS** A great number of Latin American athletes have been successful in many sports. Some well-known baseball stars are Roberto and Sandy Alomar from Puerto Rico and Sammy Sosa from the Dominican Republic.

● **PASTA DE GUAYABA** Another dessert that is similar to **pasta de guayaba** is **jalea de mango.** It is made with mango pulp and sugar and has a thick, jelly consistency. It is cut into cubes and refrigerated.

● **EL MORRO** This fortress was built to protect the Spanish settlers from pirates and other invaders. Some of its walls are 20 feet thick. It is a popular place to fly kites **(hacer volar una chiringa).**

● **LUIS MUÑOZ MARÍN** In 1942, Marín, head of the Popular Democratic Party in Puerto Rico, launched a development program that greatly improved the manufacturing sector and led to a rise in the general standard of living.

● **TAÍNOS** The **taínos** were hunters, fishers, and farmers. They were enslaved by the Spaniards, and subsequently exterminated. The word **taíno** means *gentle.*

● **EL LORO PUERTORRIQUEÑO** The Puerto Rican Parrot is the only native parrot in Puerto Rico. Its blue wing tips are usually only visible when it is in flight.

Block Schedule

Research Have students compile a list of sports. Then have them research the names of Latin American athletes who participate in those sports, especially those from Puerto Rico. (For additional activities, see **Block Scheduling Copymasters.**)

Ampliación

These activities may be used at various points in the Unit 3 sequence.

For Block Schedule, you may find that these projects will provide a welcome change of pace while reviewing and reinforcing the material presented in the unit. See the **Block Scheduling Copymasters.**

PROJECTS

Plan a seasonal vacation Divide the class into four groups: **el verano, el otoño, el invierno, la primavera.** Each group is responsible for researching a great vacation spot (in Puerto Rico or another Spanish-speaking country) for their season. They should prepare:

- a map showing where the place is
- a poster depicting what the area looks like (buildings, plants, animals, etc.)
- a catalog of pictures of appropriate clothing to bring
- a poster depicting what activities are available

Display the projects in four corners of the room. Have students travel to each season and vote on which vacation spot they prefer.

VEREDA
EL YUNQUE
EL YUNQUE TRAIL
BOSQUE NACIONAL
DEL CARIBE

> **PACING SUGGESTION:** Have students begin research at the beginning of the unit. Final projects are completed at the end of Unit 3.

Record a telephone answering machine message Have students write and record an appropriate phone machine message, using the Ortiz family's message as a model if needed. They may want to accompany it with a background of Latin music.

> **PACING SUGGESTION:** Upon completion of Etapa 1.

STORYTELLING

Poemas After reviewing the vocabulary for all three Etapas, model the following rhyme (using objects or pictures). Tell students that it is used in Puerto Rican schools to teach English to the students.

> Pollito, chicken. Gallina, hen. Lápiz, pencil. Y pluma, pen.
> Ventana, window. Puerta, door. Maestra, teacher. Y piso, floor.

Pause as the rhyme is being told, giving students a chance to fill in words or act out gestures. Students then write and read aloud a rhyme of their own, using vocabulary from this unit. They should continue supplying a Spanish word first, then the English translation.

Más poemas Now have students reverse the order of the words. They should give an English word first, and then try to rhyme the Spanish translations.

> **PACING SUGGESTION:** Upon completion of Etapa 3.

BULLETIN BOARD/POSTERS

Bulletin Board Have students create a "Puerto Rico: Isla del encanto" bulletin board. They should decorate it with brochures from travel agencies, hand-drawn visuals, articles from magazines and newspapers, etc.

Posters Have students create •**Travel** posters for Puerto Rico •**Topographical maps** of Puerto Rico •**Musical instrument** posters •**Ads** for CDs of Puerto Rican music artists •**Lyrics poster** of the words to "La Borinqueña," the Puerto Rican national anthem (For more information, go to www.mcdougallittell.com)

GAMES

Pantomimas

Divide the class into two teams, A and B, and then into pairs. After reviewing the vocabulary from all 3 **Etapas,** have each pair write an original sentence on a slip of paper. Collect the sentences and put them in a separate box for each team. A player from Team A picks a sentence from Team B's box and vice versa. That player must pantomime each word in the sentence until someone on the team guesses it. Place a 3-minute time limit and let students know that using English disqualifies the team for that round. The team with the most correct sentences is the winner.

PACING SUGGESTION: Upon completion of Etapa 3.

Dominós

Domino games are a common sight in the parks and plazas throughout Puerto Rico. Obtain several sets of dominoes and have students learn how to play. On a specified day, hold a double or triple elimination tournament (so that everyone gets to play at least two or three matches). If your class periods are too short to complete the tournament in one day, keep track of the results on a grid and continue play on another day.

PACING SUGGESTION: For use at any point in the unit.

MUSIC

Teach your students the simple folk song **El coquí.** (For more information, go to www.mcdougallittell.com) Discuss if there is an animal that represents or typifies your area or state. Are there others that are associated with different areas of the U.S. or the world? More music samples are available on your *Canciones* Cassette or CD.

HUMACAO

HANDS-ON CRAFTS

- Have students create cardstock dominoes with vocabulary words and pictures from the unit. Pairs of students can play as a review activity.

- Have students create their own **coquí** mascots using papier-mâché, paints, pipe cleaners, and small beads (if available). Work with the art department to make the papier-mâché ahead. Using the **coquí** shown above or the one on p. 228 as a model, form the body and head. Let dry and then paint as desired. Glue beads for eyes and add pipe cleaners for feet.

RECIPE

Piraguas **Piraguas** are sold by **piragüeros** in the parks and on the streets of Puerto Rico. These refreshing treats are similar to snow cones, but with tropical fruit flavors. You can make them right in your classroom with only a blender for equipment.

Encourage students to try the juices of fruits they have not eaten before.

Receta

Piraguas
1 bolsa de hielo
3 o más latas de jugo concentrado congelado de
  sabores tropicales (piña, mango, papaya, etc.)
vasos de cartón pequeños
cucharitas de plástico

En un jarrón, diluir cada lata de jugo concentrado a 1/3 de lo que indican las instrucciones (usualmente una lata de agua en vez de tres). Triturar hielo en la licuadora y ponerlo en pequeños vasos de cartón. Verter el almíbar sobre el hielo y servir con una cucharita.

Planning Guide CLASSROOM MANAGEMENT

OBJECTIVES

Communication
- Extend invitations *pp. 170–171, 172–173*
- Talk on the phone *pp. 172–173*
- Express feelings *pp. 170–171, 172–173*
- Say where you are coming from *pp. 172–173*
- Say what just happened *pp. 172–173*

Grammar
- Use **estar** with adjectives *pp. 176–177*
- Use **acabar de** *pp. 178–179*
- Use the verb **venir** *pp. 179–180*
- Use **gustar** with infinitives *pp. 181–182*

Pronunciation
- **b** and **v** *p. 183*
- Dictation, *TE p. 183*

Culture
- Puerto Rico *pp. 166–167, 179*
- Ricky Martin *p. 180*
- **La bomba y la plena** *pp. 184–185*

♻ Recycling
- Verbs
- **Ir a** + infinitive
- Place vocabulary
- Interrogatives

STRATEGIES

Listening Strategies
- Listen for a purpose *p. 172*

Speaking Strategies
- Personalize *p. 179*
- Use your tone to convey meaning *p. 188*

Reading Strategies
- Scan *p. 184*

Writing Strategies
- Brainstorm details before writing *p. 188*

Connecting Cultures Strategies
- Recognize variations in vocabulary *pp. 175, 183*
- Learn about Puerto Rico *pp. 166–167, 179*
- Learn about a Puerto Rican celebrity *pp. 166, 180*
- Connect and compare what you know about music in your community to help you learn about music in a new community *pp. 181–182, 184–185, 188*

PROGRAM RESOURCES

 Print

- *Más práctica* Workbook PE, *pp. 57–64*
- Block Scheduling Copymasters, *pp. 57–64*
- Unit 3 Resource Book
  Más práctica Workbook TE, *pp. 1–8*
  Para hispanohablantes Workbook TE, *pp. 9–16*

- Information Gap Activities *pp. 17–20*
- Family Involvement *pp. 21–22*
- Video Activities *pp. 23–25*
- Videoscript *pp. 26–28*
- Audioscript *pp. 29–32*
- Assessment Program, Unit 3 Etapa 1 *pp. 33–51; 170–178*
- Answer Keys *pp. 187–202*

 Audiovisual

- **Audio Program** Cassettes 7A, 7B / CD 7
- *Canciones* Cassette / CD
- **Video Program** Videotape 3 / Videodisc 2A
- **Overhead Transparencies** M1–M5; 69, 72–82

 **Technology**

- **Electronic Teacher Tools/Test Generator**
- *Intrigas y aventuras* CD-ROM, Disc 1
- www.mcdougallittell.com

 Assessment Program Options

- **Cooperative Quizzes** (Unit 3 Resource Book)
- **Etapa Exam** Forms A and B (Unit 3 Resource Book)
- *Para hispanohablantes* **Etapa Exam** (Unit 3 Resource Book)
- **Portfolio Assessment** (Unit 3 Resource Book)
- **Multiple Choice Test Questions** (Unit 3 Resource Book)
- **Audio Program** Testing Cassette T1 / CD T1
- **Electronic Teacher Tools/Test Generator**

Native Speakers

- *Para hispanohablantes* Workbook PE, *pp. 57–64*
- *Para hispanohablantes* Workbook TE (Unit 3 Resource Book)
- *Para hispanohablantes* Etapa Exam (Unit 3 Resource Book)
- Audio *Para hispanohablantes* Cassettes 7A, 7B, T1 / CD 7, T1
- Audioscript *Para hispanohablantes* (Unit 3 Resource Book)

Student Text Listening Activity Scripts

Diana   Ignacio   Roberto

 ## Videoscript: Diálogo *pages 172–173*

• Videotape 3 • Videodisc 2A

Search Chapter 3, Play to 4
U3E1 • En vivo (Dialog)

• Use the videoscript with **Actividades 1, 2** *page 174*

Diana: ¿Oye, hermano, voy de compras. ¿Quieres acompañarme?

Ignacio: No, tal vez otro día.

Diana: Anda, Ignacio, vamos. ¿Qué vas a hacer aquí? ¡Qué aburrido!

Ignacio: ¡El teléfono!

Diana: Ay, Ignacio. No tienes que contestar; la máquina contesta.

Mensaje: Es la casa de la familia Ortiz. Deja un mensaje después del tono. ¡Gracias!

Roberto: ¡Oye, Ignacio! Habla tu viejo amigo Roberto. Ignacio, ¿estás allí? Si estás allí, ¡por favor, contesta!

Ignacio: ¡Sí, Roberto, estoy aquí! ¡Qué sorpresa! ¿Cómo estás? ¿Dónde estás? En Minnesota, ¿no?

Roberto: Sí, en Minnesota. Mira, no tengo mucho tiempo para hablar, pero tengo muy buenas noticias. ¡Estoy muy emocionado!

Ignacio: ¿Qué pasa?

Roberto: Mi familia y yo vamos a Puerto Rico, no sólo a visitar, sino ¡a vivir! Llegamos el viernes.

Ignacio: ¡Qué chévere! ¿Estás contento?

Roberto: Sí, súper contento. ¿Cuándo hablamos?

Ignacio: Te invito a mi práctica de béisbol. Es el sábado, a las dos. ¿Te gustaría venir?

Roberto: ¡Claro que sí! En el lugar de siempre, ¿no?

Ignacio: Sí, en el mismo lugar de siempre.

Roberto: Bueno, el sábado a las dos. ¡Adiós!

Ignacio: Adiós, Roberto. Saludos a tu familia.

Diana: ¿Tu pana Roberto? ¿Qué pasa?

Ignacio: Roberto y su familia vienen a vivir a Puerto Rico de nuevo.

Diana: Oye, ¡qué bien! Estás contento, ¿no?

Ignacio: Pues, sí. Pero también estoy un poco nervioso.

Diana: ¿Por qué?

Ignacio: No sé... después de dos años, ¿cómo va a ser Roberto?

Diana: Va a ser el Roberto de siempre. Bueno, ¿quieres ir de compras, o no?

Ignacio: Pues, sí, hermanita. Ya no quiero ver más deportes. Vamos.

Diana: ¡Aquí estás! Acabo de comprar unos zapatos.

Ignacio: Yo vengo del cine. ¿Quieres ver una película después de las compras?

Diana: ¿Hay una película interesante?

Ignacio: Hay muchas. Hay películas de acción, de misterio...

Diana: ¿... y de romance?

Ignacio: A las muchachas sólo les gusta ver las películas de romance, ¿no es verdad? ¿Quieres ver una?

Diana: ¡No, no es verdad! También nos gusta ver las películas de acción y de misterio. ¡Ignacio! ¿Qué pasa? ¿Estás preocupado?

Ignacio: Sí, estoy un poco preocupado.

Diana: ¿Es Roberto? Ay, Ignacio, cálmate.

Ignacio: Es que... dos años en Minnesota... ya no conozco a Roberto.

Diana: ¡No te preocupes! Los buenos amigos son amigos para siempre.

Ignacio: Sí, es verdad.

Diana: Oye, ¿por qué no alquilamos un video?

Ignacio: No, no. Roberto viene a mi práctica de béisbol. ¡Tengo que practicar! ¡Quiero estar listo!

El tiempo libre de su amiga
page 175

Los sábados estoy muy ocupada. Primero, por la mañana, siempre cuido a mi hermano Juan. Después, preparo el almuerzo para la familia. Comemos una torta o una hamburguesa y tomamos un refresco. Por la tarde, hago mi tarea y ayudo a mi madre. Después, paso un rato con mis amigos. Practicamos deportes o vamos de compras. Por la noche, mis amigos y yo vamos al cine o alquilamos un video.

Una conversación telefónica
page 182

Sra. Campos: Hola.

Ignacio: Buenas tardes, señora. ¿Puedo hablar con Roberto?

Sra. Campos: Un momento.

Ignacio: Gracias, señora.

Roberto: Hola, Ignacio, ¿cómo estás?

Ignacio: Bien, gracias. Oye, Roberto, ¿te gustaría ir al cine el sábado?

Roberto: Gracias, Ignacio, pero no puedo. Tengo que ir a casa de mi abuela. Es su cumpleaños.

Ignacio: ¿Y el domingo? ¿Tienes tiempo libre?

Roberto: Sí, tengo tiempo libre el domingo. ¿A qué hora es la película?

Ignacio: La película es a las cuatro y media. Llego a tu casa a las cuatro menos cuarto.

Roberto: Bueno. Entonces, hasta el domingo. Adiós.

Quick Start Review Answers

p. 168 Sequencing events
Answers will vary.
Answers could include:
hacer mi tarea / descansar / veo la televisión / ver la televisión / escucho música / leo una revista / toco el piano

p. 172 Expressing feelings
Answers could vary:
1. cansado(a) 4. contento(a)
2. alegre 5. emocionado(a)
3. triste 6. cansado(a)

p. 174 Video vocabulary
1. acompañarme 4. noticias
2. máquina 5. siempre
3. mensaje

p. 178 Accepting/declining invitations
Answers will vary.
Answers could include:
1. Tal vez otro día.
2. Me gustaría ir contigo.
3. Gracias, pero no puedo.
4. Sí, me encantaría.

p. 179 Acabar de
Answers will vary.
Answers could include:
1. Voy de compras con mi hermana. Acabo de ir de compras con mi hermana.
2. Alquilo un video. Acabo de alquilar un video.
3. Saco fotos. Acabo de sacar fotos.

Sample Lesson Plan - 50 Minute Schedule

DAY 1

Unit Opener
- Anticipate/Activate prior knowledge: Present the *Almanaque* and the cultural notes. Use Map OHTs as needed. 10 MIN.

Etapa Opener
- Quick Start Review (TE, p. 168) 5 MIN.
- Have students look at the *Etapa* Opener and answer the questions. 5 MIN.

En contexto: Vocabulario
- Quick Start Review (TE, p. 170) 5 MIN.
- Have students use context and pictures to learn *Etapa* vocabulary, then answer the questions, p. 171. Use the Situational OHTs for additional practice. 10 MIN.

En vivo: Diálogo
- Quick Start Review (TE, p. 172) 5 MIN.
- Review the Listening Strategy, p. 172. Play audio or show video for the dialog, pp. 172–173. Replay and have students take the roles of the characters. 10 MIN.

Homework Option:
- Video Activities, Unit 3 Resource Book, pp. 23–25.

DAY 2

En acción: Vocabulario y gramática
- Check homework. 5 MIN.
- Quick Start Review (TE, p. 174) 5 MIN.
- Have students open to *En contexto*, pp. 170–171, for reference. Use OHT 73 and 74 to review vocabulary. 10 MIN.
- Play the video/audio; have students do *Actividades* 1 and 2 orally. 10 MIN.
- Have students complete *Actividad* 3 in pairs. 5 MIN.
- Play the audio; do *Actividad* 4. 5 MIN.
- Have students read *Actividad* 5 and give the answers orally. 5 MIN.
- Use an expansion activity from TE, p. 175 for reinforcement and variety. 10 MIN.

Homework Option:
- Have students complete *Actividad* 3 and/or 5 in writing.

DAY 3

En acción (cont.)
- Check homework. 5 MIN.
- Quick Start Review (TE, p. 176) 5 MIN.
- Present *Gramática:* Expressing Feelings with *estar* and Adjectives, p. 176. Review adjectives learned so far. 15 MIN.
- Present the *Nota* and have students complete *Actividad* 6 orally. 5 MIN.
- Have students complete *Actividad* 7 in pairs. Ask for volunteers to present their mini-conversations. 10 MIN.
- Present the *Vocabulario*, p. 177, and have students answer the question *¿Cuándo usas estas frases?* 5 MIN.
- Present the *Nota*. Then have students complete *Actividad* 8 in pairs. 10 MIN.

Homework Option:
- *Más práctica* Workbook, p. 61. *Para hispanohablantes* Workbook, p. 59.

DAY 4

En acción (cont.)
- Check homework. 5 MIN.
- Quick Start Review (TE, p. 178) 5 MIN.
- Present *Gramática:* Saying What Just Happened with *acabar de,* p. 178. 5 MIN.
- Do *Actividad* 9 orally. 5 MIN.
- Have students complete *Actividad* 10 in writing. 5 MIN.
- Present the Speaking Strategy, p. 179. Then have students do *Actividad* 11 in pairs. Expand using Information Gap Activities, Unit 3 Resource Book, p. 17; *Más comunicación*, p. R7. 15 MIN.
- Quick Start Review (TE, p. 179) 5 MIN.
- Present *Gramática:* Saying Where You Are Coming From with *venir*, p. 179. 5 MIN.
- Have students read *Actividad* 12 silently, then answer orally. 5 MIN.

Homework Option:
- *Más práctica* Workbook, pp. 62–63. *Para hispanohablantes* Workbook, pp. 60–61.

DAY 5

En acción (cont.)
- Check homework. 5 MIN.
- Review *venir* and do *Actividad* 13 orally. 5 MIN.
- Present the *Nota* and do *Actividad* 14. 5 MIN.
- Quick Start Review (TE, p. 181) 5 MIN.
- Present *Gramática:* Saying What Someone Likes to Do Using *gustar* + infinitive, p. 181. 10 MIN.
- Have students read and complete *Actividad* 15. 5 MIN.
- Do *Actividades* 16 and 17 orally. 10 MIN.
- Present the *Vocabulario,* p. 182. Then play the audio and do *Actividad* 18. 10 MIN.

Homework Option:
- Have students complete *Actividad* 13 and/or 16 in writing. *Más práctica* Workbook, p. 64. *Para hispanohablantes* Workbook, p. 62.

DAY 6

En acción (cont.)
- Check homework. 5 MIN.
- Have students read and complete *Actividad* 19 in pairs. 5 MIN.
- Have students do *Actividad* 20 in groups. Expand using Information Gap Activities, Unit 3 Resource Book, pp. 18–19; *Más comunicación*, p. R7. 15 MIN.

Pronunciación
- Play the audio and have students practice the *refrán.* 5 MIN.

En voces: Lectura
- Quick Start Review (TE, p. 184) 5 MIN.
- Review the Reading Strategy, p. 184. 5 MIN.
- Have volunteers read the selection aloud and answer the questions, p. 185. 15 MIN.

Homework Option:
- Have students write answers to the *¿Comprendiste?* questions, p. 185. Review in preparation for *En uso.*

DAY 7

En uso: Repaso y más comunicación
- Check homework. 5 MIN.
- Quick Start Review (TE, p. 186) 5 MIN.
- Present the *Repaso y más comunicación* using the Teaching Suggestions (TE, p. 186) 5 MIN.
- Have students write *Actividades* 1 and 2, then check answers with the whole class. 10 MIN.
- Do *Actividades* 3 and 4 orally. 10 MIN.
- Present the Speaking Strategy, p. 188, and have students do *Actividad* 5 in groups. 10 MIN.
- Have students do *Actividad* 6 in pairs. Have volunteers perform their mini-conversations for the class. 10 MIN.

Homework Option:
- Review for *Etapa* 1 Exam.

DAY 8

En tu propia voz: Escritura
- Do *Actividad* 7 in writing. Ask volunteers to present their letters. 10 MIN.

Conexiones
- Read and discuss *La música*, p. 188. 5 MIN.

En resumen: Repaso de vocabulario
- Quick Start Review (TE, p. 189) 5 MIN.
- Review grammar questions, etc., as necessary. 10 MIN.
- Complete *Etapa* 1 Exam. 20 MIN.

Ampliación
- Optional: Use a suggested project, game, or activity. (TE, pp. 167A–167B) 15 MIN.

Homework Option:
- Research and complete the chart for *Conexiones.* Preview *Etapa* 2 Opener.

Sample Lesson Plan - Block Schedule (90 minutes)

DAY 1

Unit Opener
- Anticipate/Activate prior knowledge: Present the *Almanaque* and the cultural notes. Use Map OHTs as needed. 10 MIN.

Etapa Opener
- Quick Start Review (TE, p. 168) 5 MIN.
- Have students look at the *Etapa* Opener and answer the questions. 5 MIN.
- Use Block Scheduling Copymasters. 5 MIN.

En contexto: Vocabulario
- Quick Start Review (TE, p. 170) 5 MIN.
- Have students use context and pictures to learn *Etapa* vocabulary, then answer the questions, p. 171. Use the Situational OHTs for additional practice. 15 MIN.

En vivo: Diálogo
- Quick Start Review (TE, p. 172) 5 MIN.
- Review the Listening Strategy, p. 172. Play audio or show video for the dialog, pp. 172–173. Replay and have students take the roles of the characters. 15 MIN.

En acción: Vocabulario y gramática
- Quick Start Review (TE, p. 174) 5 MIN.
- Have students open to *En contexto*, pp. 170–171, for reference. Use OHT 73 and 74 to review vocabulary. 5 MIN.
- Play the video/audio; do *Actividades* 1 and 2 orally. 10 MIN.
- Have students complete *Actividad* 3 in pairs. 5 MIN.

Homework Option:
- Video Activities, Unit 1 Resource Book, pp. 23–25. Have students complete *Actividad* 3 in writing.

DAY 2

En acción (cont.)
- Check homework. 5 MIN.
- Play the audio; do *Actividad* 4. 5 MIN.
- Have students read and complete *Actividad* 5. 5 MIN.
- Quick Start Review (TE, p. 176) 5 MIN.
- Present *Gramática:* Expressing Feelings with *estar* and Adjectives, p. 176. Review adjectives learned so far. 10 MIN.
- Present the *Nota* and have students complete *Actividad* 6 orally. 5 MIN.
- Have students complete *Actividad* 7 in pairs. Ask for volunteers to present their mini-conversations. 10 MIN.
- Present the *Vocabulario*, p. 177, and have students answer the question *¿Cuándo usas estas frases?* 5 MIN.
- Present the *Nota*. Then have students complete *Actividad* 8 in pairs. 5 MIN.
- Quick Start Review (TE, p. 178) 5 MIN.
- Present *Gramática:* Saying What Just Happened with *acabar de*, p. 178. 5 MIN.
- Do *Actividad* 9 orally. 5 MIN.
- Have students complete *Actividad* 10 in writing. 5 MIN.
- Present the Speaking Strategy, p. 179. Then have students do *Actividad* 11 in pairs. Expand using Information Gap Activities, Unit 3 Resource Book, p. 17; *Más comunicación,* p. R7. 15 MIN.

Homework Option:
- *Más práctica* Workbook, pp. 61–62. *Para hispanohablantes* Workbook, pp. 59–60.

DAY 3

En acción (cont.)
- Check homework. 5 MIN.
- Quick Start Review (TE, p. 179) 5 MIN.
- Present *Gramática:* Saying Where You Are Coming From with *venir*, p. 179. 5 MIN.
- Have students read *Actividad* 12 silently, then answer orally. 5 MIN.
- Have students do *Actividad* 13 orally. 5 MIN.
- Present the *Nota* and do *Actividad* 14. 5 MIN.
- Quick Start Review (TE, p. 181) 5 MIN.
- Present *Gramática:* Saying What Someone Likes to Do Using *gustar* + infinitive, p. 181. 10 MIN.
- Have students read and complete *Actividad* 15. 5 MIN.
- Do *Actividades* 16 and 17 orally. 10 MIN.
- Present the *Vocabulario*, p. 182. Then play the audio and do *Actividad* 18. 10 MIN.
- Have students read and complete *Actividad* 19 in pairs. 5 MIN.
- Have students do *Actividad* 20 in groups. Expand using Information Gap Activities, Unit 3 Resource Book, pp. 18–19; *Más comunicación*, p. R7. 15 MIN.

Homework Option:
- *Más práctica* Workbook, pp. 63–64. *Para hispanohablantes* Workbook, pp. 61–62.

DAY 4

Pronunciación
- Check homework. 5 MIN.
- Play the audio and have students practice the *refrán*. 5 MIN.

En voces: Lectura
- Quick Start Review (TE, p. 184) 5 MIN.
- Review the Reading Strategy, p. 184. 5 MIN.
- Have volunteers read the selection aloud and answer the questions, p. 185. 20 MIN.

En uso: Repaso y más comunicación
- Quick Start Review (TE, p. 186) 5 MIN.
- Have students write *Actividades* 1 and 2, then check answers with the whole class. 15 MIN.
- Do *Actividades* 3 and 4 orally. 10 MIN.
- Present the Speaking Strategy, p. 188, and have students do *Actividad* 5 in groups. 10 MIN.
- Have students do *Actividad* 6 in pairs. Have volunteers perform their mini-conversations for the class. 10 MIN.

Homework Option:
- Review for *Etapa* 1 Exam.

DAY 5

En tu propia voz: Escritura
- Do *Actividad* 7 in writing. Ask volunteers to present their letters. 15 MIN.

Conexiones
- Read and discuss *La música*, p. 188. 10 MIN.

En resumen: Repaso de vocabulario
- Quick Start Review (TE, p. 189) 5 MIN.
- Review grammar questions, etc., as necessary. 15 MIN.
- Complete *Etapa* 1 Exam. 20 MIN.

Ampliación
- Use one or more suggested projects, games, or activities. (TE, pp. 167A–167B) 25 MIN.

Homework Option:
- Research and complete the chart for *Conexiones*. Preview *Etapa* 2 Opener.

▼ Ignacio y Diana van de compras.

Etapa Theme

Extending invitations, talking on the phone, expressing feelings, saying where you are coming from, and saying what just happened.

Grammar Objectives

- Expressing feelings with **estar** and adjectives
- Saying what just happened with **acabar de**
- Saying where you are coming from with **venir**
- Saying what someone likes to do using **gustar** + infinitive

Teaching Resource Options

Print

Block Scheduling Copymasters

Audiovisual

OHT 70, 79 (Quick Start)

Quick Start Review

♻ Sequencing events

Use OHT 79 or write on board:
Complete the following paragraph with information about yourself:

Antes de _____ (infinitive), me gusta ____ (infinitive). Primero, yo ____ (conjugated verb). Después de ____ (infinitive), ____ (conjugated verb). Luego, ____ (conjugated verb). Entonces, ____ (conjugated verb).

Answers See p. 167D.

Teaching Suggestion

Previewing the Etapa

- Ask students to study the photo on pp. 168–169 (1 min.).
- Close books; ask students to share at least 3 things that they noticed.
- Reopen books and look at the picture again (1 min.); close books and share 3 more details.
- Ask students where the two people might be coming from and where they might be going.
- Use the **¿Qué ves?** questions to focus the discussion.

UNIDAD 3

ETAPA 1

¡Me gusta el tiempo libre!

- Extend invitations
- Talk on the phone
- Express feelings
- Say where you are coming from
- Say what just happened

¿Qué ves?

Mira la foto de la calle de San Sebastián en el Viejo San Juan, Puerto Rico.

1. ¿Las casas son viejas?
2. ¿Qué llevan las personas, ropa formal o casual?
3. ¿Cómo se llama la plaza de la calle San Sebastián?

168

VIEJO SAN JUAN

Classroom Management

Planning Ahead In preparation for the grammar in this **Etapa**, review regular -ar, -er, and -ir verbs, as well as **ir, estar,** and **tener.** Do this with flashcards or with a ball. Toss the ball to a student, while naming an infinitive and a subject noun/pronoun. The student catches the ball, gives the conjugation, and tosses the ball back. If the student answers correctly, move on to another verb and student. If not, have another student give the answer.

Time Saver In this unit there are numerous opportunities for Internet searches. Supervise a volunteer who can help you research a list of web sites about Puerto Rico for the class to refer to when necessary.

Cross Cultural Connections

El Viejo San Juan Ask students to compare **el Viejo San Juan** and a central area of your town. What are the differences? What are the similarities?

✴ Culture Highlights

● **PUERTO RICO** The official name of the country is **Estado Libre Asociado de Puerto Rico** (Commonwealth of Puerto Rico). It consists of one main island and several smaller ones. Columbus named the island San Juan Bautista. The settlement already established there was named Puerto Rico. Historians think that the names were accidentally reversed by an early cartographer, resulting in the island being called Puerto Rico. Although no gold or precious stones were ever found on "Rich Port," it was the place where the riches of the New World were gathered before being taken to the European courts.

● **SAN JUAN** San Juan is the capital of Puerto Rico. Its metropolitan population is close to one million, making it the largest city on the island. The city was first settled in 1508–1509 by Ponce de León. It was attacked in the 1590s by English buccaneers and in 1625 by the Dutch. During the Spanish-American War of 1898, American forces took control of it.

● **VIEJO SAN JUAN** Old San Juan is the original section of the city. Portions of the walls that once surrounded it are still visible. The area is seven square miles and contains many historic buildings. Much of the old city has been preserved in its original Spanish architecture and with its cobblestone streets. The photo shows **Calle San Sebastián** in **Viejo San Juan.**

▮ Block Schedule

Variety Have students write down 3–5 things they know about Puerto Rico. Topics can include history, geography, daily life, language, government, etc. Compile the lists to form a more complete **Almanaque.** (For additional activities, see **Block Scheduling Copymasters.**)

Teaching All Students

Extra Help Have students pretend that they live in **Viejo San Juan.** They are looking out the window of their apartment. What are at least 3 things they see?

Multiple Intelligences

Interpersonal Have students work in small groups to write and perform a dialog for the characters in the photo. However, instead of shopping bags, they should have school supplies.

Teaching Resource Options

Print

Unit 3 Resource Book
Video Activities, pp. 23–24
Videoscript, p. 26
Audioscript, p. 29
Audioscript *Para hispanohablantes,*
p. 29

Audiovisual

OHT 73, 74, 75, 75A, 76, 76A,
79 (Quick Start)
Audio Program Cassette 7A / CD 7
Audio *Para hispanohablantes*
Cassette 7A / CD 7
Video Program Videotape 3 /

Search Chapter 2, Play to 3
U3E1 • En contexto (Vocabulary)

Technology

Intrigas y aventuras CD-ROM, Disc 1

Quick Start Review

🔁 After-school activities

Use OHT 79 or write on board:
Complete the following sentences with
an activity:

1. Después de clases, mis amigos y
   yo ____.
2. Cuando tiene hambre, mi
   hermano ____.
3. El sábado, me gusta ____.
4. El domingo, mis padres ____.
5. ¿Te gusta ____?
6. ¿Quieres ____ o ____ por la tarde?

Answers
Answers will vary. Answers could include:
1. paseamos por el parque
2. compra una merienda
3. andar en bicicleta
4. van al teatro
5. tocar la guitarra
6. ir a la biblioteca / ver la televisión

En contexto
 ## VOCABULARIO

Look at the illustrations to see what Diana and Ignacio do in their free time.
This will help you understand the meaning of the words in blue. It will also
help you answer the questions on the next page.

A Ignacio y Diana tienen **tiempo libre.** Hoy van a unas tiendas para **ir de compras.**

Diana: ¿Quieres **acompañarme a** comprar unas cosas?
Ignacio: Sí, me **encantaría.**

B El muchacho de la tienda trabaja mucho. Él está muy **ocupado.**

Diana: ¿Por qué no **alquilamos un video? ¿Te gustaría** ver algo?
Ignacio: ¡**Claro que sí!**

ocupado

C ¡Para Ignacio y Diana es divertido tomar fotos! Expresan muchas emociones. Primero, Diana está **alegre,** pero Ignacio está **triste.** Luego, Diana está **enojada,** pero Ignacio no. Él está **tranquilo.** Al final Ignacio está **preocupado,** pero Diana no. Ella está **contenta.**

alegre
triste
enojada
tranquilo
contenta
preocupado

Classroom Community

TPR In groups of 4, have students pretend that they
are trying out for a play. One student plays the director.
He/she asks the others to express a few of the following
emotions through facial and body language: **alegre,
triste, enojado, contento, tranquilo, preocupado,
nervioso, emocionado, deprimido.** The director must
choose one person for the part. All chosen actors then
perform their emotions for the rest of the class.

Learning Scenario Have students imagine that
their class has been given the afternoon off from
school. Have them decide what they will do as a group.
They should plan a timetable, destinations, and
activities. On a large poster, make an itinerary of the
class's afternoon schedule.

nervioso

enfermo

emocionada

deprimido

D El hombre que trabaja en la tienda está **nervioso**. ¡El cliente de la camisa roja está enojado! La madre cuida a su niño. Él está **enfermo**.

F En el estadio la comunidad **practica deportes**. En Puerto Rico el deporte favorito es el béisbol. Muchas personas miran. Unas están **emocionadas**, otras están **deprimidas**.

el cine

G Ignacio: Te invito a ir a **un concierto**.
Diana: ¡Gracias!

E Ignacio y Diana **van al cine**. Después de ver **la película**, Diana está **cansada**.

cansada

¡TODOS A BAILAR!
Concierto espectacular de
BOMBA y PLENA
¡Músicos sensacionales!

Preguntas personales

1. ¿Tienes mucho tiempo libre?
2. ¿Te gusta más ir al cine o alquilar un video?
3. ¿Te gusta ir de compras o practicar deportes?
4. ¿Te gusta ir a conciertos? ¿Cómo estás cuando escuchas un concierto?
5. ¿Cuál es tu actividad favorita? ¿Cómo estás cuando haces la actividad?

ciento setenta y uno
Etapa 1   **171**

Teaching Suggestions
Introducing Vocabulary

- Have students look at pages 170–171. Use OHT 73 and 74 and Audio Cassette 7A / CD 7 to present the vocabulary.
- Ask the Comprehension Questions in order of yes/no (questions 1–3), either/or (questions 4–6), and simple word or phrase (questions 7–10). Expand by adding similar questions.
- Use the TPR activity to reinforce the meaning of individual words.
- Use the video vocabulary presentation for review and reinforcement.

Comprehension Questions

1. ¿Tienen tiempo libre Ignacio y Diana? (Sí.)
2. ¿Quiere Ignacio ir de compras con Diana? (Sí.)
3. ¿Van a ir con otros amigos? (No.)
4. ¿Trabaja mucho o poco el muchacho de la tienda de videos? (mucho)
5. ¿Ignacio y Diana van a comprar o alquilar un video? (alquilar)
6. Para Ignacio y Diana, ¿es divertido o aburrido tomar fotos? (divertido)
7. En la primera foto, ¿cómo está Diana? (está alegre)
8. ¿Por qué está nervioso el hombre que trabaja en la tienda? (Porque un cliente está enojado.)
9. ¿Cuál es el deporte favorito de Puerto Rico? (el béisbol)
10. ¿Adónde van Ignacio y Diana para ver una película? (Van al cine.)

Teaching All Students

Extra Help Have students construct a chart showing Ignacio and Diana's activities. Columns should read: **Destinación** and **Actividad**.

Native Speakers Ask students to give synonyms for the adjectives presented. For example: **alegre = feliz, enojado(a) = irritado(a)**. Make a list of Supplementary Vocabulary for the class. For each new **Vocabulario** section, you may want to continue adding to the list.

Multiple Intelligences
Logical/Mathematical Ask students to construct a likely timeline for Ignacio and Diana's trip to the mall. They should show the beginning and ending time for each activity and calculate its duration.

Block Schedule
Journal For the next week, have students begin each class by writing how they feel that day and why. At the end of the week, ask students to write a summary.

Teaching Resource Options

Print

Más práctica Workbook PE, pp. 57–60
Para hispanohablantes Workbook
 PE, pp. 57–58
Block Scheduling Copymasters
Unit 3 Resource Book
 Más práctica Workbook TE, pp. 1–4
 Para hispanohablantes Workbook
  TE, pp. 9–10
 Video Activities, p. 25
 Videoscript, p. 27
 Audioscript, p. 29
 Audioscript *Para hispanohablantes*,
  p. 29

Audiovisual

OHT 77, 78, 79 (Quick Start)
Audio Program Cassette 7A / CD 7
Audio *Para hispanohablantes*
 Cassette 7A / CD 7
Video Program Videotape 3 /
 Videodisc 2A

Search Chapter 3, Play to 4
U3E1 • En vivo (Dialog)

Technology

Intrigas y aventuras CD-ROM, Disc 1

Quick Start Review

♻ Expressing feelings

Use OHT 79 or write on the board:
Write how you feel in each of these
situations:

1. ver una película de 3 horas
2. pasar el día con tus amigos(as)
3. sacar una mala nota
4. sacar una buena nota
5. ver los deportes en la televisión
6. cuidar a un niño por un día

Answers *See p. 167D.*

Gestures

People from Latin America have a
reputation for being very expressive with
their hands and bodies. However, there is
a difference between people in different
Spanish-speaking countries and between
people from different regions of the same
country. For example, in Puerto Rico, Cuba,
and Mexico, people from the mountain
areas are said to be more reserved than
those from areas near the beach.

En vivo
DIÁLOGO

La llamada

Diana · Ignacio · Roberto

PARA ESCUCHAR • STRATEGY: LISTENING

Listen for a purpose Listening for specific information is like
scanning when reading. Practice listening for one idea. What is
the exact day and time of an
important event for Ignacio?
Why is it important?

El evento	El día	La hora

1 ▶ Diana: Oye, hermano, voy de
compras. ¿Quieres acompañarme?
Ignacio: No, tal vez otro día.
Diana: ¡Qué aburrido!

5 ▶ Roberto: Tengo muy buenas
noticias. ¡Estoy muy emocionado!
¡Mi familia y yo vamos a Puerto
Rico a vivir! Llegamos el viernes.
¿Cuándo hablamos?

6 ▶ Ignacio: Te invito a mi práctica de béisbol.
Es el sábado, a las dos. ¿Te gustaría venir?
Roberto: ¡Claro que sí! En el lugar de
siempre, ¿no?
Ignacio: Sí, en el mismo lugar de siempre.
Roberto: Bueno, ¡adiós!

7 ▶ Diana: ¿Tu pana Roberto?
Ignacio: Roberto y su familia vienen
a vivir a Puerto Rico de nuevo.
Diana: Estás contento, ¿no?
Ignacio: Sí, pero también estoy
nervioso.

172 ciento setenta y dos
Unidad 3

Classroom Community

Storytelling After watching the video, divide the
class into groups of 3. Have each group choose a
portion of the dialog (scenes 1–2, 3–4, 5–6, 7–8, or
9–10) and retell it in their own words (in Spanish),
using gestures as necessary to communicate meaning.

Group Activity Divide students into groups of 3–4.
Each group chooses one picture on pp. 172–173 and
writes 3 statements about the picture. Two of the
statements must be true and one must be false. As a
whole class, have a member of each group read their
statements aloud. The other groups try to guess which
statement is false.

2 ▶ Ignacio: ¡El teléfono!
Diana: Ay, Ignacio. No tienes que contestar; la máquina contesta.

3 ▶ Mensaje: Es la casa de la familia Ortiz. Deja un mensaje después del tono. ¡Gracias!
Roberto: ¡Oye, Ignacio! Habla tu viejo amigo Roberto. Si estás allí, ¡por favor, contesta!

4 ▶ Ignacio: ¡Sí, Roberto, estoy aquí! ¡Qué sorpresa! ¿Cómo estás? ¿Dónde estás? En Minnesota, ¿no?

8 ▶ Diana: Va a ser el Roberto de siempre. Bueno, ¿quieres ir de compras, o no?
Ignacio: Pues, sí, hermanita. Ya no quiero ver más deportes. Vamos.

9 ▶ Diana: Acabo de comprar unos zapatos.
Ignacio: Yo vengo del cine.
Diana: ¿Hay una película interesante?
Ignacio: A las muchachas sólo les gusta ver las películas de romance, ¿no es verdad?
Diana: ¡No! ¡También nos gusta ver otras!

10 ▶ Diana: ¿Qué pasa? ¿Estás preocupado?
Ignacio: Es que… dos años en Minnesota… ya no conozco a Roberto.
Diana: ¡No te preocupes! Los buenos amigos son amigos para siempre.

ciento setenta y tres
Etapa 1 **173**

Teaching Suggestions
Presenting the Dialog

• Prepare students for listening by focusing on the dialog context. Reintroduce the characters by asking yes/no or simple answer questions, such as: **¿La chica se llama Isabel? ¿El chico se llama Ignacio? ¿Lleva Ignacio una camisa amarilla? ¿Qué lleva Diana? ¿Dónde están Ignacio y Diana?**

• Use the video, audio cassette, or CD to present the dialog. The expanded dialog on video offers additional listening practice opportunities.

Video Synopsis

• Ignacio receives an important phone call from an old friend in Minnesota. For a complete transcript of the video dialog, see p. 167D.

Comprehension Questions

1. En la foto número 1, ¿quiere ir Ignacio con su hermana? (No.)
2. ¿Va Diana al cine? (No.)
3. ¿Tiene la familia Ortiz una máquina para contestar el teléfono? (Sí.)
4. ¿Es la llamada para Diana? (No.)
5. ¿Quiere Diana contestar la llamada o escucharla en la máquina? (escucharla en la máquina)
6. ¿Quién llama —el vecino o el amigo de Ignacio? (el amigo)
7. ¿Cómo se llama el amigo de Ignacio? (Roberto)
8. ¿Cuáles son las buenas noticias de Roberto? (Va a Puerto Rico a vivir.)
9. ¿Cuándo es la práctica de béisbol? (Es el sábado a las dos.)
10. ¿Por qué está nervioso Ignacio? (Porque piensa que ya no conoce a Roberto.)

■ Block Schedule

Variety After presenting the dialog, have students produce a variation of the telephone scene. This new dialog should include a greeting, an invitation to go somewhere, an arrangement of a time and place, and saying good-bye. (For additional activities, see **Block Scheduling Copymasters**.)

Teaching All Students

Extra Help Have students work in pairs to write 5 questions about the dialog. Then have pairs exchange papers and answers the other pair's questions.

Native Speakers Have students act out a typical short dialog between siblings in their home or two Spanish-speaking classmates. Ask the other students what they understood from the dialog.

Multiple Intelligences

Visual Have students watch the video again. Then ask them to write 5–6 sentences about what they saw, or make a list for discussion.

Kinesthetic Have students touch the photo that you describe. For example: **Ignacio contesta el teléfono.** (4) **Ignacio invita a Roberto a su práctica de béisbol.** (6) **Ignacio y Diana hablan de películas.** (9)

OBJECTIVES
- Extend invitations
- Talk on the phone
- Express feelings
- Say where you are coming f[r]
- Say what just happened

En acción
VOCABULARIO Y GRAMÁTICA

ACTIVIDAD 1

¿Cierto o falso?

Escuchar ¿Es cierto o falso? Si
es falso, di lo que es cierto.
(Hint: Say what is true.)

1. Roberto es un viejo amigo.
2. Roberto está en San Juan.
3. Diana compra unos
   calcetines.
4. Ignacio pasa por el cine.
5. A Diana sólo le gusta ver
   las películas de romance.
6. Ignacio está muy
   tranquilo.

ACTIVIDAD 2

¿Quién?

Escuchar ¿Qué persona del
diálogo habla: Diana, Ignacio o
Roberto? *(Hint: Say who speaks.)*

1. «Oye, hermano, voy de
   compras.»
2. «Tengo muy buenas
   noticias.»
3. «¡Mi familia y yo vamos a
   Puerto Rico a vivir!»
4. «Te invito a mi práctica de
   béisbol.»
5. «Yo vengo del cine.»
6. «¡También nos gusta ver
   otras!»

ACTIVIDAD 3

♻ El tiempo libre

Hablar Explica lo que Ignacio y Diana hacen en su tiempo libre.
Pregúntale a otro(a) estudiante si también hace la actividad.
(Hint: Say what they do. Ask another student if he or she does it, too.)

alquilar un video   leer una novela   ver la televisión
escribir una carta
ir al cine   practicar deportes   ir de compras

modelo

Estudiante A: *En su tiempo libre, Ignacio y Diana*
ven la televisión. ¿Te gusta ver la
televisión en tu tiempo libre?

Estudiante B: *Sí, me gusta ver la televisión en mi*
tiempo libre.

174 ciento setenta y cuatro
Unidad 3

Classroom Management

Organizing Paired/Group Work Although time
limits should be set for all paired and group activities,
you might also provide students with a signal for
indicating when they are finished. For example:
students could have a card with a red side and a green
side. While working they would display the red side;
when done, the green side. With one quick glance you
will see when all pairs/groups are finished.

Peer Teaching According to educator William
Glasser's learning scales: "We learn 10% of what we
read; 20% of what we hear; 30% of what we see;
50% of what we both see and hear; 70% of what is
discussed with others; 80% of what we experience
personally; 95% of what we *teach* to someone else."
Therefore, it makes sense to use students to peer teach
whenever possible.

- Use *estar* with adjectives
- Use *acabar de*
- Use the verb *venir*
- Use *gustar* with infinitives

ACTIVIDAD 4

♻ El tiempo libre de su amiga

Escuchar Escucha lo que dice la amiga de Diana. Ella habla de lo que hace los sábados. Luego, indica el orden en que ocurren las actividades. *(Hint: Put Diana's friend's activities in order.)*

a. Alquila un video.

b. Prepara el almuerzo.

c. Hace la tarea.

d. Cuida a su hermano.

e. Va de compras.

TAMBIÉN SE DICE

There are many ways to talk about **un buen amigo.** Diana uses one of them, **pana.**

- **colega:** Spain
- **cuadro:** Colombia
- **cuate:** Mexico
- **pana:** Puerto Rico, Ecuador, parts of Latin America
- **pata:** Peru
- **vale:** Venezuela

Ignacio uses the word **hermanita** when talking to Diana. The ending **-ito(a)** adds meaning to a word. It can mean *very small* or express a special relationship. **Hermanita** means *little sister,* but it also expresses Ignacio's close relationship with his sister. This ending is used in most Spanish-speaking countries.

ACTIVIDAD 5

¿Cómo están?

Leer ¿Cómo están Diana, Ignacio y Roberto en estas situaciones? Completa cada oración con los adjetivos de la lista. *(Hint: How do they feel?)*

alegre   deprimido(a)   nervioso(a)

preocupado(a)   tranquilo(a)   ocupado(a)

triste   enfermo(a)

emocionado(a)   cansado(a)

enojado(a)   contento(a)

1. Cuando Diana trabaja mucho, ella está _____.

2. Cuando Roberto habla con Ignacio, ellos están _____.

3. Cuando Ignacio y Diana sacan una buena nota, ellos están _____.

4. Cuando Ignacio y Diana sacan una mala nota, ellos están _____.

5. Cuando Roberto no está bien, él está _____.

6. Cuando no hay clases, Diana está _____.

7. Cuando Ignacio tiene mucha tarea, él está _____.

8. Cuando Roberto está en la clase y no tiene su tarea, él está _____.

9. Cuando su abuelo está enfermo, Diana está _____.

10. Cuando Ignacio come la comida de Diana, ella está _____.

ACTIVIDAD 3

Objective: Transitional practice Free time activities in conversation

♻ Verbs

Answers

1. A: En su tiempo libre, Ignacio practica deportes. ¿Te gusta practicar deportes en tu tiempo libre?
   B: Sí, (No, no) me gusta practicar deportes en mi tiempo libre.
2. A: En su tiempo libre, Diana lee una novela. ¿Te gusta leer una novela en tu tiempo libre?
   B: Sí, (No, no) me gusta leer una novela en mi tiempo libre.
3. A: En su tiempo libre, Ignacio y Diana van de compras. ¿Te gusta ir de compras en tu tiempo libre?
   B: Sí, (No, no) me gusta ir de compras en mi tiempo libre.
4. A: En su tiempo libre, Ignacio escribe una carta. ¿Te gusta escribir una carta en tu tiempo libre?
   B: Sí, (No, no) me gusta escribir una carta en mi tiempo libre.
5. A: En su tiempo libre, Ignacio y Diana alquilan un video. ¿Te gusta alquilar un video en tu tiempo libre?
   B: Sí, (No, no) me gusta alquilar un video en mi tiempo libre.
6. A: En su tiempo libre, Ignacio y Diana van al cine. ¿Te gusta ir al cine en tu tiempo libre?
   B: Sí, (No, no) me gusta ir al cine en mi tiempo libre.

ACTIVIDAD 4

Objective: Transitional practice Listening comprehension/free time activities

♻ Verbs

Answers (See script, p. 167D.)

a. 5
b. 2
c. 3
d. 1
e. 4

ACTIVIDAD 5

Objective: Transitional practice Vocabulary

Answers will vary.

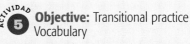

Block Schedule

Gather and Sort Have students review pp. 174–175 and write down all the new vocabulary words they find. Have them continue with this activity as the **Etapa** continues. At the end of the **Etapa,** have them determine categories for the words and sort them accordingly. Then compare their lists with the one on p. 189.

Teaching All Students

Extra Help Using at least 3 of the adjectives in **Actividad 5,** ask students to complete the sentence: Hoy yo estoy... o Hoy yo no estoy...

Challenge Have students complete the following:
1. Estoy alegre cuando...
2. Estoy cansado(a) cuando...
3. Estoy nervioso cuando...
4. Estoy emocionado(a) cuando...

Multiple Intelligences

Visual Have students work in small groups and make a set of sketches to illustrate the adjectives in **Actividad 5.** Then have students use the sketches to practice the adjectives and form original sentences with them.

Teaching Resource Options

Print

Más práctica Workbook PE, p. 61
Para hispanohablantes Workbook PE, p. 59
Block Scheduling Copymasters

Unit 3 Resource Book
  Más práctica Workbook TE, p. 5
  Para hispanohablantes Workbook TE, p. 11

Audiovisual

OHT 80 (Quick Start)

Technology

Intrigas y aventuras CD-ROM, Disc 1

Quick Start Review

🔔 Ser

Use OHT 80 or write on the board:
Complete the sentences with **ser**.

1. La profesora de español ____ muy interesante.
2. Mis primos ____ muy cómicos.
3. Mis amigos y yo ____ muy activos.
4. Yo no ____ muy paciente.
5. Tú ____ simpático.
6. Arturo ____ alto y moreno.

Answers

1. es	4. soy
2. son	5. eres
3. somos	6. es

Teaching Suggestions
Teaching Expressing Feelings with estar and Adjectives

• Point out that the Quick Start Review uses adjectives that describe people's personalities and physical characteristics; therefore, the verb **ser** is used. Explain that the verb **estar** is used to talk about feelings (something that changes).

• Expand the Quick Start Review by having students modify the adjectives to reflect their own situation.

GRAMÁTICA

Expressing Feelings with **estar** and Adjectives

♻ **¿RECUERDAS?** *p. 130* You learned that the verb **estar** is used to say where someone or something is located.

Estar is also used with **adjectives** to describe how someone feels at a given moment.

estoy	estamos
estás	estáis
está	están

agrees
Diana **está** preocupada por Ignacio.
Diana is worried about Ignacio.

agrees
Ignacio **está** preocupado por Roberto.
Ignacio is worried about Roberto.

Remember that **adjectives** must **agree** in gender and number with the nouns they describe.

ACTIVIDAD 6 Gramática

Una reacción típica

Hablar ¿Cómo están estas personas en estas situaciones?
(Hint: How are they?)

modelo

Cuando mi tía está enferma…   ella está deprimida.

Nota

When **cuando** is not used as a question word, it does not have an accent.

1. Cuando mis amigos(as) y yo vamos de compras…
2. Cuando vemos una película muy divertida…
3. Cuando tengo un examen de inglés…
4. Cuando mi amigo(a) saca una mala nota…
5. Cuando no recibes una carta de tu buen amigo…
6. Cuando mis amigos(as) no tienen clases…
7. Cuando oigo música alegre…
8. Cuando es tu cumpleaños…

■ **MÁS PRÁCTICA** *cuaderno* p. 61
■ **PARA HISPANOHABLANTES** *cuaderno* p. 59

ACTIVIDAD 7

¿Cuándo estás…?

Hablar Con otro(a) estudiante, explica cuándo te sientes así.
(Hint: Say when you feel this way.)

modelo

deprimido(a)

Tú: *¿Cuándo estás deprimido(a)?*

Otro(a): *Estoy deprimido(a) cuando no tengo tiempo para pasar un rato con mis amigos. ¿Y tú?*

Tú: *Estoy deprimido(a) cuando tengo mucho trabajo.*

1. alegre	4. cansado(a)
2. triste	5. enojado(a)
3. nervioso(a)	6. contento(a)

---

176 ciento setenta y seis
Unidad 3

Classroom Community

Cooperative Learning Divide the class into groups of 4. Student 1 writes a question using **estar** at the top of a piece of paper. Student 2 writes a response. Student 3 writes a question with **ser**. Student 4 writes a response. Continue for 5 minutes. Have students present their work. Give extra credit for the most correct question/response pairings.

Paired Activity Have pairs of students continue **Actividad 7** by adding more adjectives (**aburrido, emocionado, ocupado, preocupado, deprimido, tranquilo**).

Portfolio Have students write 3 things they like to do, with whom they do each, and how they feel during the activity. For example: **Me gusta… Voy con… Estoy… cuando…**

¿Te gustaría...?

Hablar Pregúntale a otro(a) estudiante si le gustaría hacer estas actividades contigo el sábado. Cambien de papel. *(Hint: Invite a classmate to do things with you.)*

modelo

Estudiante A: ¿Te gustaría ir conmigo al museo el sábado?

Estudiante B: ¡Claro que sí!

Nota

When you use **mí** and **ti** after **con**, they combine with **con** to form the words **conmigo** and **contigo**.

¿Te gustaría venir **conmigo**?
*Would you like to come **with me**?*

Sí, me gustaría ir **contigo**.
*Yes, I'd like to go **with you**.*

Estudiante A
PREGUNTAS

¿Quieres acompañarme a...?
Te invito a...
¿Te gustaría venir conmigo a...?

CENTRO DE BELLAS ARTES
LUIS A. FERRE

2.

3.

¿?

5.

Estudiante B
RESPUESTAS

¡Claro que sí!
Sí, me encantaría.
Me gustaría ir contigo a...

Gracias, pero no puedo.
Tal vez otro día.
¡Qué lástima! Gracias, pero no puedo.

Teaching All Students

Challenge As a variation of **Actividad 6**, have students state the negative for each sentence. For example: **Cuando mis amigos(as) y yo no vamos de compras...**

Multiple Intelligences

Visual Have students design **ser** and **estar** verb charts to help them remember when to use which verb. Encourage creativity and a variety of configurations.

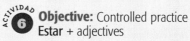
6 **Objective:** Controlled practice
Estar + adjectives

Answers

1. estamos [alegres / contentos(as)].
2. estamos [alegres / contentos(as)].
3. estoy [nervioso(a) / preocupado(a)].
4. él/ella está [deprimido(a) / enojado(a) / preocupado(a)].
5. estás [triste / preocupado(a)].
6. ellos/ellas están [alegres / contentos(as)].
7. estoy [contento(a) / alegre].
8. estás [emocionado(a) / alegre / contento(a)].

7 **Objective:** Transitional practice
Estar + adjectives in conversation

Answers will vary.

Teaching Suggestions
Presenting Vocabulary

Before students use the **Vocabulario** in **Actividad 8**, be sure they answer the question ¿Cuándo usas estas frases? For the 4 accepting/declining expressions, have students provide questions that could precede each response. For the 3 useful words, have students make up original sentences. It is a good idea to model responses before asking students to give their answers.

8 **Objective:** Open-ended practice
Accepting or not accepting an invitation in conversation

Answers will vary.

Block Schedule

FunBreak Reinforce the conjugations of **ser** and **estar** by having students quiz each other playing Verbs of Fortune. Working in groups of 3, one student selects a verb conjugation and draws the appropriate number of blanks on a piece of paper. The other students guess letters until one of them can guess the word. In the bonus round, students use the completed verb conjugations in complete sentences. (For additional activities, see **Block Scheduling Copymasters**.)

Teaching Resource Options

Print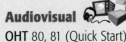

Más práctica Workbook PE, p. 62
Para hispanohablantes Workbook PE, p. 60
Block Scheduling Copymasters

Unit 3 Resource Book
  Más práctica Workbook TE, p. 6
  Para hispanohablantes Workbook TE, p. 12
  Information Gap Activities, p. 17

Audiovisual

OHT 80, 81 (Quick Start)

Technology

Intrigas y aventuras CD-ROM, Disc 1

Quick Start Review

♻ Accepting/declining invitations
Use OHT 80 or write on the board:
Write a response to these invitations:
1. ¿Te gustaría ir de compras?
2. Te invito al concierto mañana.
3. ¿Quieres acompañarme al cine?
4. ¿Quieres ver un video conmigo?
Answers See p. 167D.

Teaching Suggestions
Teaching Saying What Just Happened with acabar de

Point out that English uses the past tense to say what just happened *(I just rented a video).*

9 Objective: Controlled practice
Acabar de
♻ Verbs

Answers
1. Ignacio y Pedro acaban de escuchar un concierto.
2. Yo acabo de correr en el parque.
3. Raquel acaba de bailar con Juan.
4. Lucía y Pilar acaban de alquilar un video.
5. Tú acabas de comprar una novela nueva.
6. Mi hermano y yo acabamos de visitar a nuestro primo.
7. Ana acaba de sacar una buena nota en el examen.
8. Alma y Dorotea acaban de comer tacos.

 GRAMÁTICA

Saying What Just Happened with acabar de

When you want to say that something just happened, use the present tense of

acabar + **de** + *infinitive*

acabo **de comer** *I just ate*	acabamos **de comer** *we just ate*
acabas **de comer** *you just ate*	acabáis **de comer** *you just ate*
acaba **de comer** *he, she, you just ate*	acaban **de comer** *they, you just ate*

Diana says:
—**Acabo de comprar** unos zapatos.
I just bought some shoes.

ACTIVIDAD 9 Gramática

♻ ¿Qué acaban de hacer?

Hablar Ignacio y sus amigos acaban de hacer muchas cosas. ¿Qué acaban de hacer? *(Hint: Say what they just did.)*

modelo

Ignacio y yo: ver una película interesante
Ignacio y yo acabamos de **ver una película interesante.**

1. Ignacio y Pedro: escuchar un concierto
2. yo: correr en el parque
3. Raquel: bailar con Juan
4. Lucía y Pilar: alquilar un video
5. tú: comprar una novela nueva
6. mi hermano y yo: visitar a nuestro primo
7. Ana: sacar una buena nota en el examen
8. Alma y Dorotea: comer tacos

 **MÁS PRÁCTICA** *cuaderno* p. 62
PARA HISPANOHABLANTES *cuaderno* p. 60

ACTIVIDAD 10

¿Por qué están así?

Escribir Diana explica cómo están sus amigos. Escribe por qué están así. *(Hint: Diana explains how her friends are. Tell why they feel that way.)*

modelo

Ignacio y yo / triste
Ignacio y yo estamos **tristes** porque acabamos de **leer una novela triste.**

1. Roberto / ocupado(a)
2. unas amigas / preocupado(a)
3. yo / tranquilo(a)
4. Antonio / cansado(a)
5. ellos / enojado(a)
6. Ana / enfermo(a)
7. Ignacio / contento(a)
8. mis amigas y yo / emocionado(a)

leer una novela triste
sacar una mala nota
ir a un concierto
llegar a San Juan
comer mucho
terminar un examen
ver su programa favorito
trabajar mucho
leer poesía

178 ciento setenta y ocho
Unidad 3

Classroom Community

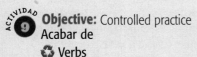

Paired Activity One student tells the other where he/she is coming from and what he/she just finished doing. For example: **Vengo del gimnasio. Acabo de hacer ejercicio.** The partner comments on how the other student must feel: **Estás muy cansado, ¿no?**

TPR In front of the class, a volunteer first acts out an emotion. After students guess the emotion correctly, the volunteer then acts out the reason for the emotion. For example: **Estás triste. / Sacas una mala nota en la clase de español.**

ACTIVIDAD 11  ¿Cómo están?

PARA CONVERSAR • STRATEGY: SPEAKING

Personalize After completing this activity, make the expressions your own by describing how you feel after doing these things.

Hablar ¿Cómo están estas personas cuando acaban de hacer lo siguiente? *(Hint: How are these people when they just did the following?)*

modelo

¿Cómo está tu padre...? (trabajar mucho)

Estudiante A: *¿Cómo está tu padre cuando acaba de trabajar mucho?*

Estudiante B: *Está cansado.*

1. ¿Cómo está tu amigo(a)...? (estudiar mucho)
2. ¿Cómo está tu amigo(a)...? (pasear por el parque)
3. ¿Cómo estás tú...? (terminar un examen)
4. ¿Cómo están tus padres...? (escuchar un concierto)
5. ¿Cómo estás tú...? (leer una revista)
6. ¿Cómo está tu maestro(a)...? (hablar mucho)

■ **MÁS COMUNICACIÓN** p. R7

NOTA CULTURAL

The name **Puerto Rico** was given to the island by the Spanish. Its port is one of the world's busiest. Guess what **Puerto Rico** means in English.

GRAMÁTICA Saying Where You Are Coming From with venir

 ¿RECUERDAS? *p. 76* Do you remember the forms of the verb **tener**?

tengo	tenemos
tienes	tenéis
tiene	tienen

Venir *(to come)* is similar to **tener**, except that the **nosotros(as)** and **vosotros(as)** forms have **-ir** endings, while **tener** uses **-er** endings.

vengo	ven**imos**
vienes	ven**ís**
viene	vienen

You use **venir** when you want to say that someone is coming.

Ignacio says: —Roberto y su familia **vienen**...
*Roberto and his family **are coming**...*

Later he says: —Yo **vengo** del cine.
*I'm **coming** from the movie theater.*

Teaching All Students

Extra Help First, have students add **venir** to their collection of verb flashcards. Then have them work in small groups to review and practice conjugations.

Native Speakers Ask students if other expressions are used synonymously or instead of **acabar de** in their cultural community. For example: **recién** + preterite form.

Multiple Intelligences

Verbal Provide students with the opportunity to practice conversation skills. In pairs, have one student initiate a conversation (for example: **Acabo de ver una película interesante**). The other student asks a follow-up question (**¿Cómo se llama la película?**), and the conversation continues from there.

ACTIVIDAD 10 Objective: Transitional practice Acabar de

Answers
1. Roberto está ocupado porque acaba de [llegar a San Juan].
2. Unas amigas están preocupadas porque acaban de [terminar un examen].
3. Yo estoy tranquilo(a) porque acabo de [leer poesía].
4. Antonio está cansado porque acaba de [trabajar mucho].
5. Ellos están enojados porque acaban de [sacar una mala nota].
6. Ana está enferma porque acaba de [comer mucho].
7. Ignacio está contento porque acaba de [ver su programa favorito].
8. Mis amigas y yo estamos emocionadas(os) porque acabamos de [ir a un concierto].

ACTIVIDAD 11 Objective: Open-ended practice Acabar de in conversation

Answers will vary.

Quick Start Review

♻ **Acabar de**

Use OHT 81 or write on the board: Write 3 sentences about things you do. Then re-write the sentences saying you just did these things, using **acabar de**.

Answers *See p. 167D.*

Teaching Suggestions
Teaching Saying Where You Are Coming From with venir

Have students practice the conjugations of **tener** and **venir** by saying them aloud. Emphasize the differences in the **nosotros** and **vosotros** forms.

■ Block Schedule

Change of Pace Divide the class into groups of 4. Give each group a set of index cards. The set should include cards with several subject nouns and pronouns, 6 with the forms of **venir**, several with the word **de**, and several with place names. Hold a timed race to see how fast students in each group can choose cards from the set and then line up holding one card each to form a sentence. (For additional activities, see **Block Scheduling Copymasters**.)

Teaching Resource Options

Print

Más práctica Workbook PE, pp. 63–64
Para hispanohablantes Workbook
PE, pp. 61–62
Block Scheduling Copymasters
Unit 3 Resource Book
  Más práctica Workbook TE,
   pp. 7–8
  Para hispanohablantes Workbook
   TE, pp. 13–14

Audiovisual

OHT 81 (Quick Start)

Technology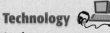

Intrigas y aventuras CD-ROM, Disc 1

ACTIVIDAD 12 **Objective:** Controlled practice
Venir

Answers
1. vengo
2. viene
3. venimos
4. vienes
5. vienen

ACTIVIDAD 13 **Objective:** Transitional practice
Venir
  ♻ **Ir a**

Answers
1. Tú no vienes conmigo porque [vas a practicar deportes].
2. Ignacio no viene conmigo porque [va a hacer la tarea].
3. Mis primos no vienen conmigo porque [van a ver la televisión].
4. Emiliana no viene conmigo porque [va a preparar la cena].
5. Ana no viene conmigo porque [va a cuidar a su hermano].

ACTIVIDAD 14 **Objective:** Open-ended practice
Venir
  ♻ **Place vocabulary**

Answers
1. Vienen del gimnasio.
2. Vienen del museo.
3. Vienen de la cafetería.
4. Vengo de la biblioteca.
5. Vienes de la tienda.
6. Viene del cine.
7. Vienes de la escuela.
8. Vengo del parque.

ACTIVIDAD 12 Gramática

Vienen de...

Leer Roberto está en el aeropuerto de San Juan. Él viene de Minneapolis. ¿De dónde vienen los otros pasajeros? *(Hint: Where are these passengers coming from?)*

modelo

Tomás **viene** de Miami.

1. Yo _____ de Nueva York.
2. Antonio _____ de Quito, Ecuador.
3. Nosotros _____ de San Antonio.
4. Tú _____ de la Ciudad de México.
5. Las señoras _____ de Los Ángeles.

■ **MÁS PRÁCTICA** *cuaderno* p. 63
■ **PARA HISPANOHABLANTES** *cuaderno* p. 61

ACTIVIDAD 13

♻ ¿Por qué no vienen?

Hablar/Escribir Diana va al cine, pero sus amigos no van. Ella explica por qué. *(Hint: What does Diana say about her friends not coming with her?)*

modelo

Julio

Julio no viene conmigo porque va a **practicar deportes**.

1. tú
2. Ignacio
3. mis primos
4. Emiliana
5. Ana

| hacer la tarea |
| preparar la cena |
| cuidar a su hermano |
| ver la televisión |
| practicar deportes |

ACTIVIDAD 14

♻ ¿De dónde vienen?

Hablar/Leer Lee las oraciones. Explica de dónde vienen estas personas. *(Hint: Explain where the people are coming from.)*

tienda	cine	gimnasio
museo	concierto	parque
cafetería	biblioteca	escuela

modelo

Ignacio y Diana acaban de escuchar música.
Vienen del concierto.

Nota

Remember how **a** contracts with **el** to form **al**? The preposition **de** also contracts with **el** to form **del**.

1. Mis amigos acaban de hacer ejercicio.
2. Ustedes acaban de ver una exhibición de arte.
3. Ignacio y Diana acaban de comer.
4. Acabo de buscar un libro.
5. Acabas de comprar una falda.
6. Roberto acaba de ver una película.
7. Acabas de tomar un examen de historia.
8. Acabo de caminar con el perro.

NOTA CULTURAL

Ricky Martin, born in Puerto Rico in 1971, sang with the pop group Menudo at the age of twelve. He has also recorded solo albums, spent three years on the daytime drama "General Hospital," and starred in *Les Misérables* on Broadway!

Classroom Community

Paired Activity Working in pairs, have students refer back to the verbs and activities listed at the end of each **Etapa** in Units 1 and 2. Have them ask each other whether they like to do these things.

Portfolio Have students make a two-column chart of likes and dislikes. The chart heads could be illustrations of happy and sad faces. Have students fill in the chart. Then have them write a short paragraph using the information from their charts and **gustar** + infinitive. They can also illustrate their paragraphs if desired.

Rubric **A** = 13–15 pts. **B** = 10–12 pts. **C** = 7–9 pts. **D** = 4–6 pts. **F** = < 4 pts.

Writing criteria	Scale
Vocabulary use	1 2 3 4 5
Grammar/spelling accuracy	1 2 3 4 5
Creativity	1 2 3 4 5

GRAMÁTICA

Saying What Someone Likes to Do Using gustar + infinitive

 ¿RECUERDAS? *p. 37* You learned to use me gusta, te gusta, and le gusta + *infinitive* to talk about how a person feels about the activities he or she likes to do.

me gusta **correr**
te gusta **correr**
le gusta **correr**

Here are more phrases to talk about what more than one person likes to do.

nos gusta **correr** *we like to run*
os gusta **correr** *you (familiar) like to run*
les gusta **correr** *they/you (formal) like to run*

When you want to emphasize or identify the person that you are talking about, use:

a +

name	**A Diana** le gusta **ir** de compras.
	Diana likes to shop.
noun	**A su hermana** le gusta **ir** de compras.
	*His **sister** likes to shop.*
pronoun	**A ella** le gusta **ir** de compras.
	She likes to shop.

These are the **pronouns** that follow **a**.

a mí →	me gusta		**a nosotros(as)** →	nos gusta
a ti →	te gusta		**a vosotros(as)** →	os gusta
a usted, él, ella →	le gusta		**a ustedes, ellos(as)** →	les gusta

ACTIVIDAD 15 Gramática

¿A quién le gusta?

Leer Diana le escribe una carta a su amiga Elena, contándole las actividades que ella y sus amigos hacen. Completa su carta con **a mí, a ti, a él, a ella, a nosotros, a ustedes.** *(Hint: Complete Diana's letter to her friend.)*

■ **MÁS PRÁCTICA** *cuaderno* p. 64

■ **PARA HISPANOHABLANTES** *cuaderno* p. 62

Querida Elena:
¿Qué hago aquí en San Juan? Bueno, primero estudio mucho porque __1__ me gusta sacar buenas notas. Después de las clases, normalmente voy a la cafetería con mis amigos Pablo y Linda. Pablo siempre compra dos hamburguesas. ¡ __2__ le gusta mucho comer!
Cuando tenemos tiempo libre, vamos al cine. __3__ nos gusta ver películas de acción. A veces, Pablo y yo vamos al museo. Linda no va porque __4__ no le gusta el arte.
Y tú, ¿qué haces? ¿ __5__ te gusta estudiar? ¿Qué haces con tus amigos? ¿ __6__ les gusta ir al cine o a un museo?
Bueno, espero tu carta.
Tu amiga,
Diana

Teaching All Students

Extra Help Have students write the names of 4–5 family members or friends. Then have them write one thing each person does or does not like to do.

Challenge Have students write their own original version of **Actividad 15.** Provide them with a few alternate closings: **Abrazos de tu amigo(a), Con afecto, Un beso de.**

Multiple Intelligences

Musical/Rhythmic Have students write lyrics to a popular tune using a grammar form they have learned recently. For example, using the tune to **Feliz Navidad,** they could sing **Me gusta correr...**

Intrapersonal Ask students to write about two of their favorite activities for a free day: one activity that they do with friends or family and one they like to do alone.

Teaching Resource Options

Print

Block Scheduling Copymasters
Unit 3 Resource Book
  Information Gap Activities, pp. 18–19
  Audioscript, p. 30
  Audioscript *Para hispanohablantes,*
    p. 30

Audiovisual

Audio Program Cassettes 7A, 7B / CD 7
Audio *Para hispanohablantes*
  Cassette 7A / CD 7

Technology

Intrigas y aventuras **CD-ROM,** Disc 1

 Objective: Transitional practice
16 Gustar + infinitive

Answers will vary.

 Objective: Transitional practice
17 Gustar + infinitive in conversation
    ♻ Verbs

Answers will vary.

Teaching Suggestions
Teaching Vocabulary

- When introducing vocabulary and simulating phone conversations, try to use toy telephones or old telephones. You might also want to have students sit back-to-back so that facial expressions and gestures do not provide clues to meaning.
- Have students practice phone etiquette using formal vs. informal greetings.

 Objective: Controlled practice
18 Listening comprehension/accepting
    or not accepting an invitation/
    telephone vocabulary

Answers (See script, p. 167D.)
1. Falso. La señora Campos contesta el teléfono.
2. Falso. Roberto está en casa.
3. Falso. Ignacio invita a Roberto a ir al cine.
4. Cierto.
5. Falso. Es el cumpleaños de su abuela.
6. Cierto.
7. Falso. La película es a las cuatro y media.

ACTIVIDAD 16
¿A quién le gusta ir a...?

Hablar/Escribir ¿A quién le gusta hacer estas actividades? *(Hint: Who likes to do the following?)*

  a mis abuelos   **a mi amigo y a mí**
  a mis padres   a mi amigo(a)   **a mí**
  a mi profesor(a) de...   a mis amigos(as)
        a mi hermano(a)

modelo

ir a los museos
*A mis padres les gusta **ir a los museos.***

1. ir a los museos
2. ir de compras
3. hacer la tarea
4. ir al cine
5. bailar
6. llegar temprano
7. ir a conciertos
8. alquilar videos
9. practicar deportes
10. cantar solo(a)

ACTIVIDAD 17
♻ ¿Qué les gusta hacer?

Hablar Pregúntales a otros estudiantes lo que a ellos y a sus amigos les gusta hacer. *(Hint: Ask others what they and their friends like to do.)*

modelo

nadar
Tú: *¿A ustedes les gusta **nadar?***
Otro(a): *No, no nos gusta **nadar**, pero nos gusta bailar.*

1. andar en bicicleta
2. escribir poesía
3. practicar deportes
4. alquilar videos
5. patinar
6. leer novelas
7. ir de compras
8. ¿?

182 ciento ochenta y dos
Unidad 3

ACTIVIDAD 18
Una conversación telefónica

Escuchar Escucha la conversación de Ignacio y Roberto. Luego, di si las oraciones son ciertas o falsas. Corrige las falsas. *(Hint: Say if the sentences are true or false. Correct the false ones.)*

1. El señor Campos contesta el teléfono.
2. Roberto no está en casa.
3. Ignacio invita a Roberto a ir a un concierto.
4. Roberto no tiene tiempo libre el sábado.
5. El sábado es el cumpleaños de su hermano.
6. Ignacio y Roberto van al cine el domingo.
7. La película es a las cuatro.

Vocabulario

El teléfono

contestar *to answer*
dejar un mensaje *to leave a message*
la guía telefónica *phone book*
la llamada *call*
llamar *to call*
la máquina contestadora *answering machine*
marcar *to dial*
Speaking on the phone:

¿Puedo hablar con...?	*May I speak with...?*
Un momento.	*One moment.*
Regresa más tarde.	*He/She will return later.*
Dile/Dígale que me llame.	*Tell (familiar/formal) him or her to call me.*
Quiero dejar un mensaje para...	*I want to leave a message for...*
Deje un mensaje después del tono.	*Leave a message after the tone.*

¿Qué dices cuando hablas por teléfono?

Classroom Community

Group Activity To continue practice of **gustar** + infinitive, have students in groups make up quotes from characters in this and previous **Etapas.** The quotes must use **gustar** + infinitive. Have them present their quotes to the class. The other students guess who said it. For example: **Estoy contento en Miami, pero me gusta mucho vivir en San Antonio.** (Francisco)

Paired Activity Have pairs of students make up a variation of the conversation in **Actividad 19.** Then have them role play their conversation for the class.

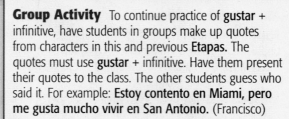

ACTIVIDAD **19**

♻ **¿Puedo hablar con...?**

Hablar/Leer Practica con otro(a) estudiante la llamada de Diana. Contesta las preguntas. *(Hint: Practice the conversation and answer the questions.)*

Señor Ruiz: Hola.

Diana: Buenas tardes, señor Ruiz. Soy Diana.

Señor Ruiz: ¡Ah! Diana, ¿cómo estás?

Diana: Muy bien, gracias, señor. ¿Puedo hablar con Gloria, por favor?

Señor Ruiz: Pues, Gloria no está en este momento. Está en la biblioteca. Regresa más tarde.

Diana: Dígale que me llame, por favor.

Señor Ruiz: Sí, cómo no.

Diana: Gracias, adiós.

Señor Ruiz: Hasta luego.

1. ¿Quién hace la llamada?
2. ¿Quién contesta?
3. ¿Cómo está Diana?
4. ¿Dónde está Gloria?
5. ¿Cuándo regresa Gloria?

TAMBIÉN SE DICE

There are many ways to answer the phone.
- **Hola:** Puerto Rico
- **Aló:** Chile, Colombia, Venezuela
- **Bueno:** Mexico
- **Diga:** Spain
- **Hable:** Argentina
- **Oigo:** Uruguay

ACTIVIDAD **20**

Te invito a...

Hablar/Escribir Trabaja en un grupo de tres. Tú llamas a casa de un(a) amigo(a) para hablar de su tiempo libre y hacerle una invitación. *(Hint: Work in a group of three to create two telephone conversations.)*

Conversación 1:
Tu amigo(a) no puede aceptar tu invitación. Explica por qué.

Conversación 2:
Tu amigo(a) acepta tu invitación. Deciden la hora y el día.

modelo

Señor Cano: *Hola.*

Luis: *Buenas tardes. Soy Luis. ¿Puedo hablar con Ana?*

Señor Cano: *Sí, Luis. Un momento.*

Ana: *Hola, Luis…*

■ **MÁS COMUNICACIÓN** p. R7

Pronunciación

Refrán

Pronunciación de la *b* y la *v* The b and v are pronounced alike. At the beginning of a phrase and after the letters **m** or **n**, they are pronounced like the English *b* in the word *boy*. In the middle of a word, a softer sound is made by vibrating the lips. Practice the following words.

bueno   vamos   acaba   novela   hombre

La **b** es de **burro**.   La **v** es de **vaca**.

Now try this **refrán**. Can you guess what it means?

No hay mal que por bien no venga.

ciento ochenta y tres **183**
Etapa 1

ACTIVIDAD 19 Objective: Transitional practice
Telephone vocabulary in conversation
♻ Interrogatives

Answers
1. Diana hace la llamada.
2. El señor Ruiz contesta.
3. Está muy bien.
4. Está en la biblioteca.
5. Regresa más tarde.

ACTIVIDAD 20 Objective: Open-ended practice
Telephone vocabulary in conversation

Answers will vary.

Dictation
After students have read the **refrán** in the **Pronunciación,** have them close their books. Dictate the **refrán** in segments while students write it.

🔔 **Quick Wrap-up**
Have students list as many words as they can recall that have the letters **b** or **v**. Tell them to refer back to the Preliminary Unit and Units 1 and 2 for additional words. You may want to limit the work to words that begin with **b** or **v**.

Block Schedule
Challenge Have students work in pairs to create a follow-up telephone conversation to **Actividad 19** between Diana and Gloria. Have students memorize the dialog and perform it for the class. (For additional activities, see **Block Scheduling Copymasters**.)

Teaching All Students

Extra Help Have pairs of students memorize and present to the class the conversation in **Actividad 19.**

Native Speakers Ask students to bring in an actual tape of a phone message in Spanish. (Be sure they have the person's permission to record.) Have the class listen to the tape and write down key information. Alternate: Ask students to model phone etiquette and provide a list of any new words or expressions.

Multiple Intelligences

Verbal Have students choose one of the following situations and role play leaving a message on a telephone answering machine: (1) inviting a friend to a party; (2) asking a friend if he/she wants to go shopping with you; (3) telling a friend you cannot go to the movies and why; (4) asking a friend to come watch a video with you; (5) a situation of the student's choosing.

Teaching Resource Options

Print 📖

Unit 3 Resource Book
Audioscript, p. 31
Audioscript *Para hispanohablantes*,
   p. 31

Audiovisual 🎧💻📖

Audio Program Cassette 7A / CD 7
Audio *Para hispanohablantes*
   Cassette 7A / CD 7
OHT M2, M3, 82 (Quick Start)
Canciones Cassette / CD

🔔 Quick Start Review

♻ Gustar

Use OHT 82 or write on the board:
Complete the sentences logically:

1. _____ le gusta hablar español.
2. _____ les gusta practicar béisbol.
3. _____ nos gusta ir de paseo.
4. _____ te gusta bailar y cantar.
5. _____ le gusta ir de compras.

Answers
Answers will vary. Answers could include:
1. A la profesora Díaz   4. A ti
2. A Miguel y Carlos   5. A Diana
3. A nosotros

Teaching Suggestions

- **Prereading** Have students study the pictures on pp. 184–185 for 1 min. Then have them close their books and share what they can recall seeing. Based on this information, what do they think the reading is about?

- **Strategy: Scan** Have students scan the poster on p. 184. Ask them to list the type of information shown (type of event, performers, date, time, place).

- **Reading** Have one volunteer read aloud the information on the poster. He/she should remember that the goal is to entice the reader to attend the concert. Have other volunteers read the rest of the selection.

- **Post-reading** Ask students to summarize the reading in 2–3 sentences.

En voces

LECTURA

PARA LEER
STRATEGY: READING
Scan Reading very quickly to get a specific piece of information, like a football score or a movie time, is called scanning. Scan this poster and decide whether Ignacio and Roberto can attend the festival. (Remember their plans for Saturday.)

¡TODOS A BAILAR!
Concierto espectacular de
BOMBA y PLENA
¡Músicos sensacionales!

Claudio de Mata: *maracas*
Rubén López: *cuatro*
Lucio Escobar: *tamborín*

¡Y la actuación especial de los bailarines
Lilián y Alberto!

*Sábado 16 de octubre
a las 5 de la tarde
en el Instituto de Cultura*

184   ciento ochenta y cuatro
Unidad 3

Classroom Community

Paired Activity Have pairs of students review the paragraph on p. 185. Then have them list all the words in the following categories: nouns; verbs (conjugated forms and infinitives); adjectives.

Group Activity In small groups, have students research another aspect of Puerto Rican music, dance, or art. They should write a short paragraph and use illustrations. Then have them present their reports to the class.

Bomba y plena

La bomba y la plena son danzas típicas de Puerto Rico. Tienen sus orígenes en la música africana. Los instrumentos originales para tocar esta música alegre son los tambores[1], las panderetas[2], las maracas y el cuatro. El cuatro es un tipo de guitarra española pequeña, originalmente con cuatro cuerdas[3]. Las personas que bailan estas danzas llevan ropa de muchos colores. La música tiene mucho ritmo[4] y las personas ¡mueven todo el cuerpo[5]!

---

[1] drums
[2] type of tambourine
[3] strings
[4] rhythm
[5] body

¿Comprendiste?

1. ¿Cuándo es el concierto?
2. ¿En qué tienen sus orígenes la bomba y la plena?
3. ¿Es una música triste o alegre?
4. ¿Qué es el cuatro?
5. ¿Qué otros instrumentos hay?
6. ¿Qué ropa llevan las personas que bailan?

¿Qué piensas?

1. Hoy hay un concierto de bomba y plena en tu ciudad. ¿Qué ropa llevas y por qué?
2. ¿Un concierto de bomba y plena es divertido? ¿Por qué sí o por qué no?

Teaching Resource Options

Print
Para hispanohablantes Workbook PE, pp. 63–64
Unit 3 Resource Book
Para hispanohablantes Workbook TE, pp. 15–16
Information Gap Activities, p. 20
Family Involvement, pp. 21–22
Multiple Choice Test Questions, pp. 170–178

Audiovisual
OHT 82 (Quick Start)
Audio Program Testing Cassette T1 / CD T1

Technology
Electronic Teacher Tools/Test Generator
Intrigas y aventuras CD-ROM, Disc 1

🔔 Quick Start Review
♻ **Gustar** + infinitive

Use OHT 82 or write on the board:
Write 3 things you like to do and 3 things you don't like to do, using **gustar** + infinitive:
Answers will vary. Answers could include:
Me gusta practicar deportes, ir de compras y pasar un rato con mis amigos.
No me gusta caminar con el perro, ir al museo y tocar la guitarra.

✔ Teaching Suggestions
What Have Students Learned?

Plan time for a Reviewers' Workshop. Have students work in small groups to review according to "Now you can.../To review." If one member of the group is having trouble with a point, the others are responsible for clarifying it.

🅐 Answers

1. Puedo	4. Dígale	7. Tal vez
2. Regresa	5. conmigo	8. lástima
3. mensaje	6. Gracias	9. contigo

ETAPA 1

En uso
REPASO Y MÁS COMUNICACIÓN

Now you can...
• extend invitations.
• talk on the phone.

To review
• vocabulary for invitations, see p. 170 and p. 177.
• vocabulary for talking on the phone, see p. 182.

Now you can...
• express feelings.

To review
• **gustar** with infinitives, see p. 181.

OBJECTIVES
• Extend invitations
• Talk on the phone
• Express feelings
• Say where you are coming from
• Say what just happened

🅐 1 Una invitación por teléfono

Mateo, un amigo de Ignacio, habla por teléfono. Completa las dos conversaciones con las palabras apropiadas. *(Hint: Complete Mateo's conversations.)*

conmigo contigo lástima mensaje tal vez
puedo gracias dígale regresa

Sra. Ruiz: Hola.

    Mateo: Buenas tardes, señora. Soy Mateo. ¿ __1__ hablar con Laura?

Sra. Ruiz: No está en este momento. __2__ más tarde. ¿Quieres dejar un __3__ ?

    Mateo: Sí, gracias. __4__ que me llame, por favor.

Más tarde...

Mateo: Hola.

    Laura: Hola, Mateo. Soy Laura.

Mateo: Oye, ¿te gustaría ir al cine __5__ mañana?

    Laura: __6__ , pero no puedo. Tengo que trabajar. __7__ otro día.

Mateo: ¡Qué __8__ ! ¿Y el sábado?

    Laura: Sí, me encantaría ir __9__ .

🅐 2 Están contentos

Todos están contentos porque hacen las actividades que les gusta hacer. ¿Qué les gusta hacer? *(Hint: Say what they like to do.)*

modelo

Carlos: pasear

*A **Carlos** le gusta **pasear**.*

1. mis padres: alquilar un video
2. tú: escuchar un concierto
3. mis hermanos y yo: practicar deportes
4. la vecina: ir al cine
5. yo: ver la televisión
6. Berta y José: ir de compras
7. Ignacio: pasear
8. nosotros: hablar por teléfono

Classroom Community

Group Activity Have students work in groups of 3 to complete **Actividad 1**. Then have each student select a role (**Sra. Ruiz, Mateo, Laura**) and act out the conversation. Have a few groups present their conversations to the class.

Paired Activity In pairs, have students write a variation of **Actividad 2**. They should substitute a different noun subject for each item. The subjects should be friends and family members. Then have them complete their new activity.

ACTIVIDAD 3 Un festival internacional

Hay un festival internacional el sábado. ¿Cómo reaccionan estas personas? *(Hint: Tell how these people are feeling.)*

alegre   emocionado(a)   triste   nervioso(a)   enojado(a)

modelo

Julia: le gusta bailar

Julia está alegre porque **le gusta bailar.**

1. Ignacio y Diana: tienen que estudiar

2. Rogelio: sus amigos no van

3. tú: vas a cantar

4. yo: tengo que trabajar

5. ustedes: su grupo favorito va a tocar

6. nosotros: vamos a ver a nuestros amigos

ACTIVIDAD 4 Muchas actividades

Todos estos amigos de Diana están muy ocupados hoy. ¿Qué acaban de hacer? ¿De dónde vienen? *(Hint: Tell what these people have just done and where they are coming from.)*

modelo

mis amigos: hacer ejercicio

Mis amigos acaban de **hacer ejercicio.** *Vienen del gimnasio.*

1. yo: ver una exhibición de arte

2. tú: practicar deportes

3. Ernesto: leer revistas y periódicos

4. Hugo y Raquel: escuchar música

5. mi madre y yo: comprar comida

6. los Fernández: ver una película

7. usted: ir de compras

8. nosotros: comer papas fritas

ciente ochenta y siete **187**
Etapa I

Now you can...
• express feelings.

To review
• **estar** with adjectives, see p. 176.

Now you can...
• say what just happened.
• say where you are coming from.

To review
• **acabar de,** see p. 178.
• the verb **venir**, see p. 179.

ACTIVIDAD 2 Answers

1. A mis padres les gusta alquilar un video.
2. A ti te gusta escuchar un concierto.
3. A mis hermanos y a mí nos gusta practicar deportes.
4. A la vecina le gusta ir al cine.
5. A mí me gusta ver la televisión.
6. A Berta y a José les gusta ir de compras.
7. A Ignacio le gusta pasear.
7. A nosotros nos gusta hablar por teléfono.

ACTIVIDAD 3 Answers

1. Ignacio y Diana están enojados porque tienen que estudiar.
2. Rogelio está triste porque sus amigos no van.
3. Tú estás nerviosa porque vas a cantar.
4. Yo estoy triste porque tengo que trabajar.
5. Ustedes están emocionados porque su grupo favorito va a tocar.
6. Nosotros estamos alegres porque vamos a ver a nuestros amigos.

ACTIVIDAD 4 Answers

1. Yo acabo de ver una exhibición de arte. Vengo del museo.
2. Tú acabas de practicar deportes. Vienes del parque (del gimnasio).
3. Ernesto acaba de leer revistas y periódicos. Viene de la biblioteca.
4. Hugo y Raquel acaban de escuchar música. Vienen del concierto (del auditorio).
5. Mi madre y yo acabamos de comprar comida. Venimos del supermercado.
6. Los Fernández acaban de ver una película. Vienen del cine.
7. Usted acaba de ir de compras. Viene de la tienda.
8. Nosotros acabamos de comer papas fritas. Venimos de la cafetería.

Teaching All Students

Extra Help Based on the activities listed in **Actividad 2,** have students choose 3 that they like to do and write complete sentences.

Native Speakers Have students work with youth magazines in Spanish to expand the additional/supplementary vocabulary lists related to new activities.

Multiple Intelligences

Visual Have students cut out magazine pictures to depict the activities listed in **Actividad 4** and other activities they have learned to describe. Students can create a collage with the pictures and label them.

Block Schedule

Variety Have students write their own version of **Actividad 3.** They should sketch faces and emotions and provide names and activities. Have students exchange papers with a partner and complete each other's activity.

Teaching Resource Options

Print

Unit 3 Resource Book
Cooperative Quizzes, pp. 33–34
Etapa Exam, Forms A and B,
   pp. 35–44
Para hispanohablantes Etapa Exam,
   pp. 45–49
Portfolio Assessment, pp. 50–51
Multiple Choice Test Questions,
   pp. 170–178

Audiovisual

OHT 82 (Quick Start)
Audio Program Testing Cassette T1 /
CD T1

Technology

Electronic Teacher Tools/Test
   Generator
www.mcdougallittell.com

ACTIVIDAD 5

Rubric: Speaking

Criteria	Scale	
Sentence structure	1 2 3	A = 11–12 pts.
Vocabulary use	1 2 3	B = 9–10 pts.
Originality	1 2 3	C = 7–8 pts.
Fluency	1 2 3	D = 4–6 pts.
		F = < 4 pts.

ACTIVIDAD 6 *Answers will vary.*

ACTIVIDAD 7 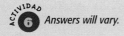 **En tu propia voz**

Rubric: Writing

Criteria	Scale	
Vocabulary use	1 2 3 4 5	A = 14–15 pts.
Accuracy	1 2 3 4 5	B = 12–13 pts.
Creativity, appearance	1 2 3 4 5	C = 10–11 pts.
		D = 8–9 pts.
		F = < 8 pts.

Community Connections

Tell students to scan the radio to see if there are any stations that play Hispanic music. They could also check the TV for Hispanic music programs.

ACTIVIDAD 5  **Por teléfono**

PARA CONVERSAR
STRATEGY: SPEAKING
Use your tone to convey meaning Words alone do not reveal meaning. Your tone of voice makes a difference. In both your invitations and answers, express different feelings (happy, nervous, worried, angry, etc.).

Imagínate que vas a invitar a un(a) amigo(a) a hacer algo contigo. Llama a dos amigos. Un(a) amigo(a) no acepta la invitación, pero el (la) otro(a) sí. Decidan la hora y el día. *(Hint: Call two friends. One refuses your invitation, but the other accepts. Agree on the time and day.)*

ACTIVIDAD 6  **¡De visita!**

Imagínate que estás de visita en Puerto Rico en la casa de una amiga. Los amigos de tu amiga vienen a conocerte. Conversen para aprender quiénes son, cómo están, por qué y de dónde vienen. *(Hint: Find out more about the people your friend knows.)*

modelo

Tú: *¿Quién es la muchacha?*

Tu amigo(a): *Es mi amiga Rosa. Está cansada porque acaba de practicar deportes. Viene del gimnasio.*

¿Quién es?	¿Cómo está?	¿Por qué?	¿De dónde viene?
un(a) amigo(a)	alegre	acaba de ¿ ?	la escuela
¿ ?	¿ ?		¿ ?

ACTIVIDAD 7  **En tu propia voz**

ESCRITURA Imagínate que tienes un(a) amigo(a) puertorriqueño(a) por correspondencia. Escribe una carta sobre tus actividades y pregúntale sobre sus actividades. Sigue las instrucciones. *(Hint: Write a letter about your leisure activities to your pen pal.)*

• ¿Cuáles son tres de tus actividades favoritas?
• Pregúntale a tu amigo(a) sobre tres actividades específicas.

CONEXIONES

La música Would you like to hear **bomba y plena** music? Check your local library or the international section of a music store for recordings. You can probably find many kinds of music with Spanish influences. What other kinds of music do you like? You can check the Internet to find out what is popular in Spain. Listen to five songs from any source and complete the following chart. Then say why you do or don't like the songs.

Título	Sí, me gusta/No, no me gusta	¿Por qué?

Classroom Community

Group Activity Divide the class into small groups and assign each group one of the sections in the **Repaso de vocabulario:** (1) Extending Invitations, (2) Expressing Feelings, and (3) Talking on the Phone. Each group creates a short story or skit that incorporates the vocabulary from that list. Have groups present their stories/skits to the class, using props as necessary.

Paired Activity First, have students write 3 different invitations to a friend. Then have them exchange invitations with a partner and write a response to each one. Finally, have them act out all 6 invitations and responses.

En resumen
REPASO DE VOCABULARIO

EXTENDING INVITATIONS

¿Quieres acompañarme a…?	Would you like to come with me to…?
Te invito.	I'll treat you. I invite you.
¿Te gustaría…?	Would you like…?

Accepting

¡Claro que sí!	Of course.
Me gustaría…	I would like…
Sí, me encantaría.	Yes, I would love to.

Declining

Gracias, pero no puedo.	Thanks, but I can't.
¡Qué lástima!	What a shame!
Tal vez otro día.	Maybe another day.

Activities

alquilar un video	to rent a video
el concierto	concert
ir al cine	to go to a movie theater
ir de compras	to go shopping
la película	movie
practicar deportes	to play sports
el tiempo libre	free time

EXPRESSING FEELINGS

alegre	happy
cansado(a)	tired
contento(a)	content, happy, pleased
deprimido(a)	depressed
emocionado(a)	excited
enfermo(a)	sick
enojado(a)	angry
nervioso(a)	nervous
ocupado(a)	busy
preocupado(a)	worried
tranquilo(a)	calm
triste	sad

TALKING ON THE PHONE

contestar	to answer
dejar un mensaje	to leave a message
la guía telefónica	phone book
la llamada	call
llamar	to call
la máquina contestadora	answering machine
marcar	to dial
el teléfono	telephone

Phrases for talking on the phone

Deje un mensaje después del tono.	Leave a message after the tone.
Dile/Dígale que me llame.	Tell (familiar/formal) him or her to call me.
¿Puedo hablar con…?	May I speak with…?
Quiero dejar un mensaje para…	I want to leave a message for…
Regresa más tarde.	He/She will return later.
Un momento.	One moment.

WHERE YOU ARE COMING FROM

del	from the
venir	to come

SAYING WHAT JUST HAPPENED

acabar de…	to have just…

OTHER WORDS AND PHRASES

conmigo	with me
contigo	with you
cuando	when, whenever
¡No te preocupes!	Don't worry!
porque	because
solo(a)	alone
temprano	early
ya no	no longer

Juego

¿Adónde van en su tiempo libre?

1. A Miguel le gusta escuchar música.
2. A Mariela le gusta ver las películas de Antonio Banderas.
3. A Martina y a Martín les gusta comprar ropa.

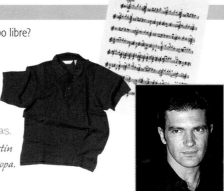

Teaching All Students

Extra Help For **Actividad 7**, have students exchange letters with a partner. Have them make comments and suggestions for improvement. Have each student check for grammar, spelling, vocabulary, and use of expressions by going back through the **Etapa** presentations.

Native Speakers In addition to using tone to convey meaning, people also use gestures. Ask students to demonstrate gestures used to express feelings in their home communities.

Quick Start Review

♻ Etapa vocabulary

Use OHT 82 or write on the board: Write 3 words/expressions for each of the following categories:

1. Extending invitations
2. Expressing feelings
3. Talking on the phone

Answers

Answers will vary. Answers could include:
1. ¿Quieres acompañarme a… ? / Me gustaría… / ¡Qué lástima!
2. alegre / enojado(a) / triste
3. dejar un mensaje / la máquina contestadora / Un momento.

Teaching Suggestions
Vocabulary Review

Have each student make flashcards for 10 different vocabulary words/expressions. In groups of 3–4, have students quiz each other with their cards. Save the cards for future use.

Juego

Answers
1. Miguel va a un concierto.
2. Mariela va al cine.
3. Martina y Martín van de compras (a la tienda).

Block Schedule

FunBreak Using the list of "Expressing Feelings," in the **Repaso de vocabulario**, have students circulate and poll their classmates to find out which of these emotions their classmates are feeling. When done, have them count how many people felt each emotion. Were any emotions left out?

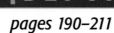
Planning Guide CLASSROOM MANAGEMENT

OBJECTIVES

Communication
- Talk about sports *pp. 192–193, 194–195, 206–207*
- Express preferences *pp. 194–195*
- Say what you know *pp. 194–195*
- Make comparisons *pp. 194–195, 206–207*

Grammar
- Use the verb **jugar** *pp. 198–199*
- Use stem-changing verbs: **e→ie** *pp. 199–200*
- Use the verb **saber** *pp. 201–202*
- Use phrases for making comparisons *pp. 202–204*

Pronunciation
- Pronunciation of **ñ** *p. 205*
- Dictation *TE p. 205*

Culture
- Regional vocabulary *p. 197*
- **La Fortaleza** *p. 201*
- Relationship of Puerto Rico to the U.S. *p. 203*
- Baseball in Puerto Rico *pp. 206–207*
- Roberto Clemente *p. 207*

♻ Recycling
- Sports vocabulary
- Adjectives

STRATEGIES

Listening Strategies
- Listen for "turn-taking" tactics *p. 194*

Speaking Strategies
- Monitor yourself *p. 200*
- Give reasons for your preferences *p. 210*

Reading Strategies
- Scan *p. 206*

Writing Strategies
- Brainstorm details, then organize your information *p. 210*

Connecting Cultures Strategies
- Recognize regional vocabulary *p. 197*
- Learn about a historical residence in Puerto Rico *p. 201*
- Learn about Puerto Rico's relationship with the U.S. *p. 203*
- Learn about a great Puerto Rican baseball player and humanitarian *p. 207*
- Connect and compare what you know about sports traditions in your community to help you learn about sports traditions in a new community *pp. 206–207*

PROGRAM RESOURCES

 Print
- *Más práctica* Workbook PE, *pp. 65–72*
- Block Scheduling Copymasters, *pp. 65–72*
- Unit 3 Resource Book
  Más práctica Workbook TE, *pp. 52–59*
  Para hispanohablantes Workbook TE, *pp. 60–67*

- Information Gap Activities *pp. 68–71*
- Family Involvement *pp. 72–73*
- Video Activities *pp. 74–76*
- Videoscript *pp. 77–79*
- Audioscript *pp. 80–83*
- Assessment Program, Unit 3 Etapa 2 *pp. 84–102; 170–178*
- Answer Keys *pp. 187–202*

 Audiovisual
- **Audio Program** Cassettes 8A, 8B / CD 8
- *Canciones* Cassette / CD
- **Video Program** Videotape 3 / Videodisc 2A
- **Overhead Transparencies** M1–M5; 71; 83–92

 **Technology**
- Electronic Teacher Tools/Test Generator
- *Intrigas y aventuras* CD-ROM, Disc 1
- www.mcdougallittell.com

 Assessment Program Options
- **Cooperative Quizzes** (Unit 3 Resource Book)
- **Etapa Exam** Forms A and B (Unit 3 Resource Book)
- *Para hispanohablantes* **Etapa Exam** (Unit 3 Resource Book)
- **Portfolio Assessment** (Unit 3 Resource Book)
- **Multiple Choice Test Questions** (Unit 3 Resource Book)
- **Audio Program** Testing Cassette T1 / CD T1
- **Electronic Teacher Tools/Test Generator**

Native Speakers
- *Para hispanohablantes* Workbook PE, *pp. 65–72*
- *Para hispanohablantes* Workbook TE (Unit 3 Resource Book)
- *Para hispanohablantes* Etapa Exam (Unit 3 Resource Book)
- Audio *Para hispanohablantes* Cassettes 8A, 8B, T1 / CD 8, T1
- Audioscript *Para hispanohablantes* (Unit 3 Resource Book)

Student Text Listening Activity Scripts

 Videoscript: Diálogo *pages 194–195*

• Videotape 3 • Videodisc 2A

Search Chapter 5, Play to 6
U3E2 • En vivo (Dialog)

• Use the videoscript with **Actividades 1, 2** *page 196*

Claudio:	Oye, ¿qué haces? ¿No ves que va a empezar la práctica?
Ignacio:	Sí, ya veo. Pero es que espero a mi amigo de Minneapolis.
Claudio:	¿De Minneapolis? ¿Viene de Minneapolis a ver la práctica?
Ignacio:	No, hombre. Él y su familia vienen a Puerto Rico a vivir.
Claudio:	Ah. ¿Sabe él a qué hora empieza la práctica?
Ignacio:	Sí, Roberto sabe que la práctica empieza a las dos.
Claudio:	¿Quieres practicar un poco conmigo?
Ignacio:	No, gracias. Prefiero esperar a Roberto aquí.
Claudio:	Ya sabes que la práctica empieza en menos de cinco minutos.
Ignacio:	Sí, ya sé. No espero más de dos o tres minutos.
Roberto:	¡Ignacio! ¡Qué gusto!
Ignacio:	¡Roberto! ¡Cuánto tiempo!
Roberto:	¿Qué tal?
Ignacio:	Bien, ¿y tú?
Roberto:	Muy contento. ¡Ahora tengo un amigo para hablar de deportes! Bien, a ver tu guante. Tienes un guante bien chévere. A ver tus bates. ¿Prefieres este bate o éste?
Ignacio:	Yo prefiero este bate. ¿Juegas al béisbol en Minneapolis?
Roberto:	Sí, pero no estoy en un buen equipo de béisbol.
Sr. Castillo:	Vamos, Ignacio. La práctica empieza en unos minutos.
Ignacio:	Sr. Castillo, le presento a mi amigo Roberto. Viene de Minneapolis.
Sr. Castillo:	Mucho gusto, Roberto.
Roberto:	Igualmente, Sr. Castillo.
Sr. Castillo:	¿Qué deportes juegan en Minneapolis?
Roberto:	Hay mucho fútbol americano. ¡Son locos con el fútbol americano!
Sr. Castillo:	¡Como nosotros! Aquí en Puerto Rico somos locos con el béisbol.

Roberto:	Sí, exactamente.
Ignacio:	¿Les gusta jugar al fútbol?
Roberto:	Sí, pero el fútbol no es tan popular como el fútbol americano.
Sr. Castillo:	Es interesante, ¿no? Cada país prefiere diferentes deportes.
Roberto:	Sí, mucha gente en los Estados Unidos piensa que el fútbol americano es más interesante que el fútbol.
Ignacio:	Y tú, ¿cuál es tu deporte favorito?
Roberto:	A mí me gusta jugar al baloncesto, y un poco al tenis también. Pero pienso que el tenis es menos divertido que el baloncesto. También me gusta nadar.
Ignacio:	Me gusta correr más que nadar.
Sr. Castillo:	¿Piensas jugar en el equipo de baloncesto de la escuela?
Roberto:	Sí, me gustaría mucho. Pero también quiero jugar en el equipo de béisbol. Veo que usted tiene un equipo muy bueno. ¿Puedo practicar con ustedes?
Sr. Castillo:	Pero, ¡claro, hombre! ¡Vamos, muchachos! ¡A practicar!
Ignacio:	¿Sabes? Necesito tu ayuda.
Roberto:	¿Para qué?
Ignacio:	Quiero participar en un concurso. Es para la revista *Onda internacional*.
Roberto:	Y ¿qué piensas hacer?
Ignacio:	Pues, no sé todavía. Tengo una idea, pero me gustaría hablar contigo sobre el proyecto.
Roberto:	Claro, está bien. ¿Por qué no vienes a casa mañana por la mañana?
Ignacio:	Gracias. Así también saludo a tu familia.
Roberto:	¡Perfecto!... Oye, me gustaría ver a tu hermana. ¿Por qué no invitas a Diana también?
Ignacio:	Está bien. Diana y yo vamos a tu casa mañana por la mañana. Nos vemos como a las diez. ¿Dónde está tu casa?

13 **Los deportistas** *page 202*

Mis amigos saben jugar a muchos deportes. Gisela y César saben esquiar en el agua. Pablo no sabe esquiar, pero sabe jugar al tenis. Mi hermano y yo sabemos jugar al béisbol. Roberto y su hermano saben jugar al baloncesto. Practican mucho. Y yo sé jugar al voleibol. ¿A qué sabes jugar tú?

18 **¡Lógicamente!** *page 205*

1. Son las dos menos cuatro. El partido empieza a las dos.
2. Me gusta practicar el tenis. Voy a jugar después de las clases.
3. Voy a la piscina. ¿Quieres venir conmigo?
4. Marco quiere jugar al fútbol americano. No tiene casco.
5. A Édgar le gusta levantar pesas más que nadar.

Quick Start Review Answers

p. 196 Dialog review
1. ¿Quieres practicar un poco conmigo?
2. Son locos con el fútbol americano.
3. Pienso que el tenis es menos divertido que el baloncesto.
4. Me gustaría hablar contigo sobre el proyecto.

p. 206 Comparisons
Answers will vary.
Answers could include:
1. El baloncesto es más interesante que el tenis. (El tenis es más interesante que el baloncesto.)
2. Levantar pesas es más interesante que nadar. (Nadar es más interesante que levantar pesas.)

3. El surfing es más interesante que el voleibol. (El voleibol es más interesante que el surfing.)
4. El fútbol es más interesante que el fútbol americano. (El fútbol americano es más interesante que el fútbol.)
5. El hockey es más interesante que el baloncesto. (El baloncesto es más interesante que el hockey.)

p. 208 Sports vocabulary
1. el béisbol
2. el fútbol americano, andar en patineta, el hockey, el béisbol
3. levantar pesas
4. el béisbol
5. el tenis

Sample Lesson Plan - 50 Minute Schedule

DAY 1

Etapa Opener
- Quick Start Review (TE, p. 190) **5** MIN.
- Anticipate/Activate prior knowledge: Have students look at the *Etapa* Opener and answer the questions. **5** MIN.

En contexto: Vocabulario
- Quick Start Review (TE, p. 192) **5** MIN.
- Have students use context and pictures to learn *Etapa* vocabulary. In pairs, have students answer the questions, p. 193. Use the Situational OHTs for additional practice. **10** MIN.

En vivo: Diálogo
- Quick Start Review (TE, p. 194) **5** MIN.
- Review the Listening Strategy, p. 194. Play audio or show video for the dialog, pp. 194–195. **10** MIN.
- Replay twice. Read aloud, having students take the roles of characters. **10** MIN.

Homework Option:
- Video Activities, Unit 3 Resource Book, pp. 74–76.

DAY 2

En acción: Vocabulario y gramática
- Check homework. **5** MIN.
- Quick Start Review (TE, p. 196) **5** MIN.
- Use OHT 83 and 84 to review *En contexto* vocabulary. Ask students for a summary of the dialog to check recall. **5** MIN.
- Play the video/audio; have students do *Actividades* 1 and 2. **10** MIN.
- Have students do *Actividad* 3 in writing. Review answers orally. **5** MIN.
- Have students complete *Actividad* 4 orally. **5** MIN.
- Quick Start Review (TE, p. 198) **5** MIN.
- Present *Gramática:* Talking About Playing a Sport: The Verb *jugar* and the *Vocabulario*, p. 198. **10** MIN.
- Have students read and complete *Actividad* 5. **5** MIN.

Homework Option:
- Have students complete *Actividad* 4 in writing. *Más práctica* Workbook, p. 69. *Para hispanohablantes* Workbook, p. 67.

DAY 3

En acción (cont.)
- Check homework. **5** MIN.
- Review *jugar* and then do *Actividad* 6 orally and *Actividad* 7 in groups. **10** MIN.
- Quick Start Review (TE, p. 199) **5** MIN.
- Present *Gramática:* Stem-Changing Verbs: *e → ie* and the *Vocabulario*, p. 199. **10** MIN.
- Have students complete *Actividad* 8 orally. **5** MIN.
- Present the Speaking Strategy, p. 200. Then have students complete *Actividad* 9 orally. **5** MIN.
- Have students complete *Actividad* 10 orally. **5** MIN.
- Have students do *Actividad* 11 in writing. Then have them exchange papers for peer correction. **10** MIN.

Homework Option:
- Have students complete *Actividad* 9 in writing. *Más práctica* Workbook, p. 70. *Para hispanohablantes* Workbook, p. 68.

DAY 4

En acción (cont.)
- Check homework. **5** MIN.
- Quick Start Review (TE, p. 201) **5** MIN.
- Present *Gramática:* Saying What You Know: The Verb *saber,* p. 201. **10** MIN.
- Have students read and complete *Actividad* 12 in writing. Ask volunteers to write out answers on the board. **10** MIN.
- Use a suggested expansion activity (TE, pp. 200–201) to review verbs. **5** MIN.
- Play the audio; do *Actividad* 13. **5** MIN.
- Have students do *Actividad* 14 in pairs. Expand using Information Gap Activities, Unit 3 Resource Book, p. 68; *Más comunicación*, p. R8. **15** MIN.

Homework Option:
- Have students complete *Actividad* 14 in writing. *Más práctica* Workbook, p. 71. *Para hispanohablantes* Workbook, p. 69.

DAY 5

En acción (cont.)
- Check homework. **5** MIN.
- Quick Start Review (TE, p. 202) **5** MIN.
- Present *Gramática:* Phrases for Making Comparisons, p. 202. **15** MIN.
- Have students complete *Actividad* 15 in writing. Then have them exchange papers for peer correction. **10** MIN.
- Do *Actividad* 16 orally. **10** MIN.
- Have students do *Actividad* 17 in pairs. **5** MIN.
- Play the audio; do *Actividad* 18. **5** MIN.

Homework Option:
- Have students complete *Actividad* 16 in writing. *Más práctica* Workbook, p. 72. *Para hispanohablantes* Workbook, p. 70.

DAY 6

En acción (cont.)
- Check homework. **5** MIN.
- Have students complete *Actividad* 19 in groups. Expand using Information Gap Activities, Unit 3 Resource Book, pp. 69–70; *Más comunicación*, p. R8. **20** MIN.

Pronunciación
- Play the audio and have students practice the *Trabalenguas.* **5** MIN.

En colores: Cultura y comparaciones
- Quick Start Review (TE, p. 206) **5** MIN.
- Review the Connecting Cultures Strategy, p. 206. Have volunteers read the selection aloud and answer the questions, p. 207. Show video culture presentation for expansion. **20** MIN.

Homework Option:
- Have students complete the *¿Comprendiste?/¿Qué piensas?* questions in writing.

DAY 7

En uso: Repaso y más comunicación
- Check homework. **5** MIN.
- Quick Start Review (TE, p. 208) **5** MIN.
- Have students write *Actividad* 1. Have volunteers write out answers on the board. **10** MIN.
- Do *Actividad* 2 in pairs and *Actividades* 3 and 4 orally. **10** MIN.
- Present the Speaking Strategy, p. 210, and have students do *Actividad* 5 in pairs. **5** MIN.
- Have students do *Actividad* 6 in groups. **5** MIN.

En tu propia voz: Escritura
- Do *Actividad* 7 in writing. Have a few students present their brochures. **15** MIN.

Homework Option:
- Review for *Etapa* 2 Exam.

DAY 8

Tú en la comunidad
- Present *Sarah*, p. 210. **5** MIN.

En resumen: Repaso de vocabulario
- Quick Start Review (TE, p. 211) **5** MIN.
- Review grammar questions, etc. as necessary. **10** MIN.
- Complete *Etapa* 2 Exam. **20** MIN.

Ampliación
- Use a suggested project, game, or activity. (TE, pp. 167A–167B) **10** MIN.

Homework Option:
- Preview *Etapa* 3 Opener.

Sample Lesson Plan - Block Schedule (90 minutes)

DAY 1

Etapa Opener
- Quick Start Review (TE, p. 190) 5 MIN.
- Anticipate/Activate prior knowledge: Have students look at the *Etapa* Opener and answer the questions. 5 MIN.
- Use Block Scheduling Copymasters, pp. 65–66. 5 MIN.

En contexto: Vocabulario
- Quick Start Review (TE, p. 192) 5 MIN.
- Have students use context and pictures to learn *Etapa* vocabulary. Have students answer the questions, p. 193. 10 MIN.

En vivo: Diálogo
- Quick Start Review (TE, p. 194) 5 MIN.
- Review the Listening Strategy, p. 194. Play audio or show video for the dialog, pp. 194–195. 10 MIN.
- Replay twice. Read aloud, having students take the roles of characters. 10 MIN.

En acción: Vocabulario y gramática
- Quick Start Review (TE, p. 196) 5 MIN.
- Use OHT 83 and 84 to review *En contexto* vocabulary. Ask students for a summary of the dialog to check recall. 10 MIN.
- Play the video/audio; have students do *Actividades* 1 and 2. 10 MIN.
- Have students do *Actividad* 3 in writing. Review answers orally. 5 MIN.
- Have students complete *Actividad* 4 orally. 5 MIN.

Homework Option:
- Video Activities, Unit 3 Resource Book, pp. 74–76. Have students complete *Actividad* 4 in writing.

DAY 2

En acción (cont.)
- Check homework. 5 MIN.
- Quick Start Review (TE, p. 198) 5 MIN.
- Present *Gramática:* Talking About Playing a Sport: The Verb *jugar* and the *Vocabulario,* p. 198. 10 MIN.
- Have students read and complete *Actividad* 5. 5 MIN.
- Do *Actividad* 6 orally and *Actividad* 7 in groups. 10 MIN.
- Quick Start Review (TE, p. 199) 5 MIN.
- Present *Gramática:* Stem-Changing Verbs: *e → ie* and the *Vocabulario,* p. 199. 10 MIN.
- Have students complete *Actividad* 8 orally. 5 MIN.
- Present the Speaking Strategy, p. 200. Then have students complete *Actividad* 9 orally. 10 MIN.
- Have students complete *Actividad* 10 orally. 5 MIN.
- Have students do *Actividad* 11 in writing. Then have them exchange papers for peer correction. 10 MIN.
- Use one or more suggested expansion activities (TE, pp. 200–201) to review verbs. 10 MIN.

Homework Option:
- Have students complete *Actividad* 9 in writing. *Más práctica* Workbook, pp. 69–70. *Para hispanohablantes* Workbook, pp. 67–68.

DAY 3

En acción (cont.)
- Check homework. 5 MIN.
- Quick Start Review (TE, p. 201) 5 MIN.
- Present *Gramática:* Saying What You Know: The Verb *saber,* p. 201. 5 MIN.
- Have students read and complete *Actividad* 12 in writing. Ask volunteers to write out answers on the board. 10 MIN.
- Play the audio; do *Actividad* 13. 5 MIN.
- Have students do *Actividad* 14 in pairs. Expand using Information Gap Activities, Unit 3 Resource Book, p. 68; *Más comunicación,* p. R8. 10 MIN.
- Quick Start Review (TE, p. 202) 5 MIN.
- Present *Gramática:* Phrases for Making Comparisons, p. 202. 10 MIN.
- Have students complete *Actividad* 15 in writing. Then have them exchange papers for peer correction. 5 MIN.
- Do *Actividad* 16 orally. 5 MIN.
- Have students do *Actividad* 17 in pairs. 5 MIN.
- Play the audio; do *Actividad* 18. 5 MIN.
- Have students complete *Actividad* 19 in groups. Expand using Information Gap Activities, Unit 3 Resource Book, pp. 69–70; *Más comunicación,* p. R8. 15 MIN.

Homework Option:
- Have students complete *Actividad* 16 in writing. *Más práctica* Workbook, pp. 71–72. *Para hispanohablantes* Workbook, pp. 69–70.

DAY 4

Pronunciación
- Check homework. 5 MIN.
- Play the audio and have students practice the *Trabalenguas.* 5 MIN.

En colores: Cultura y comparaciones
- Quick Start Review (TE, p. 206) 5 MIN.
- Review the Connecting Cultures Strategy, p. 206. Have volunteers read the selection aloud and answer the questions, p. 207. Show video culture presentation for expansion. 25 MIN.

En uso: Repaso y más comunicación
- Quick Start Review (TE, p. 208) 5 MIN.
- Have students write *Actividad* 1. Have volunteers write out answers on the board. 10 MIN.
- Do *Actividad* 2 in pairs and *Actividades* 3 and 4 orally. 15 MIN.
- Present the Speaking Strategy, p. 210, and have students do *Actividad* 5 in pairs. 10 MIN.
- Do *Actividad* 6 in groups. 10 MIN.

Homework Option:
- Review for *Etapa* 2 Exam.

DAY 5

En tu propia voz: Escritura
- Do *Actividad* 7 in writing. Have a few students present their brochures. 20 MIN.

Tú en la comunidad
- Present *Sarah,* p. 210. 5 MIN.

En resumen: Repaso de vocabulario
- Quick Start Review (TE, p. 211) 5 MIN.
- Review grammar questions, etc. as necessary. 15 MIN.
- Complete *Etapa* 2 Exam. 20 MIN.

Ampliación
- Use a suggested project, game, or activity. (TE, pp. 167A–167B) 25 MIN.

Homework Option:
- Preview *Etapa* 3 Opener.

▼ Ignacio y Roberto en la práctica de béisbol.

Etapa Theme
Discussing sports and identifying sports equipment, expressing preferences, and making comparisons

Grammar Objectives
- Using the verb **jugar**
- Using stem-changing verbs: e → ie
- Using the verb **saber**
- Using phrases for comparisons

Teaching Resource Options
Print
Block Scheduling Copymasters

Audiovisual
OHT 71, 89 (Quick Start)

Quick Start Review
♻ **Gustar**/activities/places
Use OHT 89 or write on board:
Using **gustar**, say what these people like to do and where:

1. A mí...
2. A ti...
3. A mi amigo(a)...
4. A mi profesor(a) de música
5. A usted...
6. A nosotros...
7. A mi profesor(a) de educación física...

Answers
Answers will vary. Answers could include:
1. me gusta pasear por el parque
2. te gusta leer una novela en la biblioteca
3. le gusta ver la televisión en casa
4. le gusta ir a conciertos al teatro
5. le gusta hacer la tarea en la biblioteca
6. nos gusta ver una película en el cine
7. le gusta practicar deportes en el gimnasio

Teaching Suggestions
Previewing the Etapa
- Ask students to study the picture on pp. 190–191 (1 min.).
- Have them close their books and share their initial impressions of the scene—the people, weather, clothing, activities, etc.
- Use the **¿Qué ves?** questions to focus the discussion.

UNIDAD 3

ETAPA **2**

¡Deportes para todos!

- **Talk about sports**
- **Express preferences**
- **Say what you know**
- **Make comparisons**

¿Qué ves?

Mira la foto de un campo de béisbol en San Juan.

1. Para ti, ¿el béisbol es interesante?
2. ¿Quién practica, Ignacio o Roberto?
3. ¿Cuál es la fecha del campeonato de béisbol?
4. ¿En qué día de la semana es el campeonato?

190

Campeonato de béisbol

Los Toros Valientes

vs.

Los Huracanes

domingo
17 de abril
a las 6 de la tarde
en el campo de deportes

Entrada: $3

Classroom Management

Planning Ahead Have each student bring in at least one piece of equipment from their favorite sport. Keep a list to avoid too much duplication. Be sure items are labelled with students' names. You can use the equipment throughout the **Etapa** for practicing vocabulary and grammar. Also bring in brochures/fliers from sporting goods stores.

Organizing Paired/Group Work When students work in pairs or groups it is important to set time limits. You may want to set a timer to go off 30 seconds before the end of the specified time so that students know to start wrapping up their work.

191

Cross Cultural Connections

Point out that this photo was taken in San Juan. In what other countries might students see people playing baseball? Where wouldn't they see people playing baseball? What sports might be played internationally?

Culture Highlights

● **LOS DEPORTES EN PUERTO RICO** Weather and geographical conditions make Puerto Rico a great place to take part in all kinds of sports. The sandy beaches and beautiful waters are ideal for swimming, fishing, and boating. There are numerous golf courses and tennis courts throughout the island. Baseball, basketball, and boxing are also very popular sports.

● **EL BÉISBOL EN PUERTO RICO** Many famous American Major League baseball players came from Puerto Rico; for example: Juan Gonzalez, Javi Lopez, and Bernie Williams. The baseball season in Puerto Rico begins as the one in the U.S. ends. Many of the Puerto Rican players who play in the American Major League return to play in Puerto Rico, giving them year-round practice.

Supplementary Vocabulary

el uniforme	uniform
el (la) bateador(a)	batter
el (la) lanzador(a)	pitcher
el catcher	catcher
el casco	helmet
la pelota	ball
el bate	bat
el equipo	team
los (las) jugadores(as)	players

Block Schedule

Process Time Students need to stop approximately every 10 minutes to process the information they have learned. You might plan your activities in 10 minute sessions. Then stop and ask students to write down one thing they just learned. (For additional activities, see **Block Scheduling Copymasters**.)

Teaching All Students

Extra Help Have students write 3 questions about the photo. Then have them exchange papers with a partner and answer each other's questions.

Native Speakers Ask students to draw and label in Spanish a baseball diamond. The drawing should include the team members on the field as well as the batter. The rest of the class may want to add words to their supplementary vocabulary lists.

Multiple Intelligences

Visual Tell students to look carefully at the people in the photo. Then ask them to provide possible information about them: age, name, physical description, personality, etc.

Teaching Resource Options

Print ✎

Unit 3 Resource Book
  Video Activities, pp. 74–75
  Videoscript, p. 77
  Audioscript, p. 80
  Audioscript *Para hispanohablantes,*
    p. 80

Audiovisual

OHT 83, 84, 85, 85A, 86, 86A,
  89 (Quick Start)
Audio Program Cassette 8A / CD 8
Audio *Para hispanohablantes*
  Cassette 8A / CD 8
Video Program Videotape 3 / Videodisc
  2A

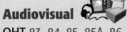

Search Chapter 4, Play to 5
U3E2 • En contexto (Vocabulary)

Technology 💻

Intrigas y aventuras CD-ROM, Disc 1

🔔 Quick Start Review

♻ Free time activities

Use OHT 89 or write on board:
List 5 free time activities.

Answers .
Answers will vary. Answers could include:
pasear por el parque
ir al cine
tocar la guitarra
pasar un rato con los amigos
practicar deportes

Teaching Suggestions
Introducing Vocabulary

• Have students look at pages 192–193.
  Use OHT 83 and 84 and Audio Cassette
  8A /CD 8 to present the vocabulary.
• Ask the Comprehension Questions in
  order of yes/no (questions 1–3),
  either/or (questions 4–6), and simple
  word or phrase (questions 7–10).
  Expand by adding similar questions.
• Use the TPR activity to reinforce the
  meaning of individual words.
• Use the video vocabulary presentation
  for review and reinforcement.

En contexto
VOCABULARIO

Diana and Ignacio are looking at equipment in a sporting
goods store. Look at the illustrations to understand the
meaning of the words in blue. This will help you answer
the questions on the next page.

¡Hola!   Ignacio y yo estamos en la tienda
de deportes. ¡Vamos a ver qué hay!

A

A mí me gusta andar en patineta. Uso
un casco cuando ando en patineta y
cuando uso patines.

la patineta

el casco

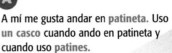

los patines

las bolas

B

Aquí hay de todo para
practicar deportes como
el baloncesto, el
voleibol, el fútbol y el
fútbol americano. ¡Y hay
una bola especial para
cada deporte! El
baloncesto y el voleibol
se practican en una
cancha. El fútbol y el
fútbol americano se
practican en un campo.
A veces se practican
en un estadio.

¡los deportes!

El baloncesto   las canchas   El voleibol

el estadio

El fútbol
americano   los campos   El fútbol

192   ciento noventa y dos
    Unidad 3

Classroom Community

TPR Have 3 students come to the front of the class.
As you say a vocabulary word, the students act it out.
The class determines who is the most dramatic or
accurate. That person stays at the front of the class.
Then 2 more students come up and the activity
continues.

Group Activity Divide the class into 6 groups and
give each group a sport: **el baloncesto, el voleibol, el
fútbol, el fútbol americano, el tenis, el béisbol.** Using
outside sources as necessary, groups list the equipment
needed for their sport, where the sport is popular, and
some famous players.

D ¿Te gusta **levantar pesas**?

la pesa

ienda de Deportes Peña

la raqueta

E Para practicar **el tenis** usas **una raqueta** y una bola.

F En Puerto Rico, es divertido **esquiar** en el agua o practicar **el surfing**.

esquiar

el surfing

C Practicas **el béisbol** con un **guante**, un **bate** y una **pelota**. Ésta es una foto del **equipo** de béisbol de Ignacio.

el guante

la pelota

el bate

el equipo

Preguntas personales

1. ¿Practicas deportes?
2. ¿Practicas el baloncesto o el voleibol?
3. ¿Te gusta más mirar el fútbol o el fútbol americano?
4. ¿Cuál es tu deporte favorito?
5. ¿Qué usas cuando practicas tu deporte favorito?

ciento noventa y tres
Etapa 2 | **193**

Comprehension Questions

1. ¿Está Diana en el supermercado? (No.)
2. ¿A Diana le gusta andar en patineta? (Sí.)
3. ¿Usa Diana un casco? (Sí.)
4. En la tienda, ¿hay todo para la escuela o para los deportes? (para los deportes)
5. ¿Se practica el fútbol en un campo o en una cancha? (en una cancha)
6. Se practica el fútbol americano en un estadio o en un gimnasio? (en un estadio)
7. ¿Dónde se practica el baloncesto? (en una cancha)
8. ¿Con qué practicas el béisbol? (con un guante, un bate y una pelota)
9. ¿Con qué equipo practica Ignacio? (el equipo de béisbol)
10. ¿Qué deportes acuáticos son populares en Puerto Rico? (esquiar en el agua y practicar el surfing)

Culture Highlights

● **EL SURFING EN PUERTO RICO** With its 272 miles of coastline with clear blue water, the island of Puerto Rico is an ideal place for water sports, such as swimming, snorkeling, windsurfing, and surfing. The island has sponsored several international surfing competitions. The best surfing areas are on the Atlantic coast. The best season for surfing is October through April.

Supplementary Vocabulary

el esquí	skiing
el esquí acuático	waterskiing
patinar en el hielo	to ice-skate
patinar sobre ruedas	to roller-skate
patinar en línea	to in-line skate

Block Schedule

FunBreak Have students divide up into groups according to their favorite sport. (You may need to do some rearranging.) First, each group looks up the vocabulary needed to describe the sport in more detail. Then, they use these words to write and present a skit demonstrating the sport to the class.

Teaching All Students

Extra Help Point to the pictures and ask yes/no questions: For example: ¿Es un bate? ¿Es un equipo? ¿Es una tienda de videos?

Native Speakers Ask students about favorite sports in their cultural communities. What equipment is needed for these sports? Have these students provide supplementary vocabulary for the rest of the class.

Multiple Intelligences

Visual Have students design an ad for a store that sells sports equipment. They can sketch the articles or use cut-outs from magazines/fliers. They should label the equipment and give a price.

Teaching Resource Options

Print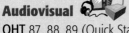

Más práctica Workbook PE, pp. 65–68
Para hispanohablantes Workbook PE,
  pp. 65–66
Block Scheduling Copymasters
Unit 3 Resource Book
  Más práctica Workbook TE,
    pp. 52–55
  Para hispanohablantes Workbook
    TE, pp. 60–61
  Video Activities, p. 76
  Videoscript, p. 78
  Audioscript, p. 80
  Audioscript *Para hispanohablantes*,
    p. 80

Audiovisual

OHT 87, 88, 89 (Quick Start)
Audio Program Cassette 8A / CD 8
Audio *Para hispanohablantes*
  Cassette 8A / CD 8
Video Program Videotape 3 / Videodisc
2A

Search Chapter 5, Play to 6
U3E2 • En vivo (Dialog)

Technology

Intrigas y aventuras CD-ROM, Disc 1

Quick Start Review

♻ Sports vocabulary

Use OHT 89 or write on board:
Write 2 words associated with each sport:

1. el tenis   4. el fútbol
2. el béisbol   americano
3. el baloncesto   5. el voleibol

Answers
Answers will vary. Answers could include:
1. una raqueta, una bola
2. un bate, un guante
3. una bola, una cancha
4. un estadio, un campo
5. una bola, una cancha

Gestures

In Puerto Rico, as in other Spanish-
speaking countries, it is not uncommon
for male friends to give each other a
quick hug or slap on the back when
meeting after a long time.

En vivo

 DIÁLOGO

 Ignacio   Claudio   Roberto    Sr. Castillo

PARA ESCUCHAR • STRATEGY: LISTENING
Listen for "turn-taking" tactics In English conversation
we often say *uh, yeah, well, say,* or *listen* to signal
that we are getting ready to speak. Listen carefully
to the Spanish. What words or expressions do you
hear that signal, "It's my turn to talk"?

El campo de béisbol

1▶ Claudio: Oye, ¿qué haces?
Ignacio: Espero a mi amigo.
Claudio: ¡Ah! ¿Sabe él a qué hora
empieza la práctica?
Ignacio: Sí.

5▶ Ignacio: Sr. Castillo, le presento a
Roberto. Viene de Minneapolis.
Sr. Castillo: Mucho gusto. ¿Qué
deportes juegan en Minneapolis?
Roberto: ¡Son locos con el fútbol
americano!

6▶ Ignacio: ¿Les gusta jugar al fútbol?
Roberto: Sí, pero no es tan popular como
el fútbol americano. Mucha gente en los
Estados Unidos piensa que el fútbol
americano es más interesante que el fútbol.

7▶ Roberto: Me gusta jugar al baloncesto
y al tenis. Pienso que el tenis es
menos divertido que el baloncesto.
También me gusta nadar.
Ignacio: Me gusta correr más que
nadar.

194 ciento noventa y cuatro
Unidad 3

Classroom Community

Paired Activity Working in pairs, have students
look at the illustration and caption to each scene of the
dialog. Then have them write an appropriate title for
each one. Have various pairs share their titles with the
class.

Game ¿Cierto o falso? Have each student prepare
either a true or a false statement about the dialog. Then
divide the class in half and have them face each other.
In turn, each team tries to trick the other. The team
guessing true or false correctly gets one point. If they
can correct the false statement, they get a bonus point.
When all students have read statements, the team with
the most points wins.

2► **Claudio:** ¿Quieres practicar un poco conmigo?
Ignacio: No, gracias. Prefiero esperar a Roberto aquí.

3► **Roberto:** ¡Ignacio! ¡Qué gusto!
Ignacio: ¡Roberto! ¡Cuánto tiempo!
Roberto: ¡Ahora tengo un amigo para hablar de deportes!

4► **Roberto:** ¿Prefieres este bate o éste?
Ignacio: Yo prefiero este bate. ¿Juegas al béisbol en Minneapolis?
Roberto: Sí.

8► **Sr. Castillo:** ¿Piensas jugar en el equipo de baloncesto?
Roberto: Sí. También quiero jugar en el equipo de béisbol. ¿Puedo practicar con ustedes?
Sr. Castillo: ¡Claro! ¡Vamos!

9► **Ignacio:** Necesito tu ayuda. Quiero participar en un concurso.
Roberto: ¿Y qué piensas hacer?
Ignacio: Tengo una idea. Me gustaría hablar contigo sobre el proyecto.

10► **Roberto:** Claro, está bien. ¿Por qué no vienes a casa mañana por la mañana?
Ignacio: Así también saludo a tu familia.
Roberto: ¿Por qué no invitas a Diana?
Ignacio: Está bien. Nos vemos como a las diez.

ciento noventa y cinco
Etapa 2 **195**

Teaching Suggestions
Presenting the Dialog
- Prepare students for listening by reintroducing the characters and setting: **¿Cómo se llama el chico, Ignacio o Roberto? ¿Quién viene a ver la práctica, Diana o Roberto? ¿Practica el equipo en Minneapolis?**
- Use the video, audiocassette, or CD to present the dialog. The expanded dialog on video offers additional listening practice opportunities.

Video Synopsis
- Ignacio meets his old friend Roberto at baseball practice. Roberto discusses sports in Minneapolis. For a complete transcript of the video dialog, see p. 189B.

Comprehension Questions
1. ¿Están los chicos en el campo de béisbol? (Sí.)
2. ¿Espera Ignacio a Diana? (No.)
3. ¿Sabe Roberto a qué hora empieza la práctica? (Sí.)
4. ¿Prefiere Ignacio practicar con Claudio o esperar a Roberto? (esperar a Roberto)
5. ¿Está Ignacio alegre o triste cuando llega Roberto? (alegre)
6. ¿Van a hablar los muchachos de la escuela o de deportes? (de deportes)
7. ¿Qué deporte juega Roberto en Minneapolis? (béisbol)
8. ¿Por qué es más popular en Minneapolis el fútbol americano que el fútbol? (porque muchos americanos piensan que es más interesante)
9. ¿Qué otros deportes practica Roberto? (baloncesto, tenis, nadar)
10. ¿Adónde invita Roberto a Ignacio? (a su casa)

Block Schedule
Peer Review Divide the class into groups of 4 and provide each group a cassette recorder. After practicing, have students record the dialog, each person reading one part. Then have them exchange tapes with another group. Groups should rate each other on comprehensibility, tone, and accent. (For additional activities, see **Block Scheduling Copymasters**.)

Teaching All Students

Extra Help Have students make a chart with drawings of 3 people: Ignacio, Robert, Señor Castillo. They should list 3 facts about each.

Challenge In groups of 3, have students write a mini-dialog of the conversation between Roberto, Ignacio, and Diana when they meet at Roberto's house the next morning.

Multiple Intelligences

Verbal Have students look just at the photos of the dialog. Using familiar vocabulary, have them create logical dialogs.

Interpersonal Working in pairs, have students take turns asking and answering one question about each scene of the dialog.

Teaching Resource Options

Print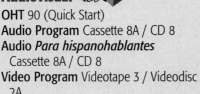

Unit 3 Resource Book
  Videoscript, p. 76
  Audioscript, p. 80
  Audioscript *Para hispanohablantes,*
    p. 80

Audiovisual

OHT 90 (Quick Start)
Audio Program Cassette 8A / CD 8
Audio *Para hispanohablantes*
  Cassette 8A / CD 8
Video Program Videotape 3 / Videodisc
  2A

🔔 Quick Start Review

♻ Dialog review

Use OHT 90 or write on board:
Unscramble the following sentences,
adding the necessary punctuation:

1. un poco / Quieres / conmigo / practicar

2. locos / el / con / americano / fútbol / Son

3. tenis / Pienso / es / que / el / divertido / el / menos / que / baloncesto

4. contigo / sobre / gustaría / el / Me / hablar / proyecto

Answers *See p. 189B.*

Teaching Suggestions
Comprehension Check

Use **Actividades** 1 and 2 to assess
retention after the dialog. Also point
out the use of the personal **a** in
Actividad 1, items 1.b and 3.c, and in
Actividad 2, item 1.

 Objective: Transitional practice
Listening comprehension/vocabulary

Answers (See script, p. 189B.)
1. a   2. b   3. c   4. a

Objective: Transitional practice
Listening comprehension/vocabulary

Answers (See script, p. 189B.)
1. b   2. a   3. b   4. b   5. c

En acción
VOCABULARIO Y GRAMÁTICA

OBJECTIVES
- Talk about sports
- Express preferences
- Say what you know
- Make comparisons

¿Qué dicen?

Escuchar ¿Qué dice una de las personas de la foto? Escoge
la oración correcta. *(Hint: Choose what they would be saying.)*

a. ¡Ignacio! ¡Qué gusto!
b. Espero a mi amigo.
c. Necesito tu ayuda.

a. No, gracias.
b. Necesito tu ayuda.
c. Sr. Castillo, le presento
   a Roberto.

a. ¡Cuánto tiempo!
b. ¡Vamos a jugar!
c. ¿Piensas jugar al
   baloncesto?

a. ¿Prefieres este bate o éste?
b. ¿Y qué piensas hacer?
c. ¿Qué deportes juegan
   en Minneapolis?

¿Qué pasa?

Escuchar Explica lo que hacen
las personas del diálogo.
Escoge la respuesta correcta.
(Hint: Explain what they do.)

1. Ignacio espera _____.
   a. a Diana
   b. a su amigo Roberto
   c. al señor Castillo

2. Roberto viene de _____.
   a. Minneapolis
   b. Miami
   c. Puerto Rico

3. Roberto piensa que el
   _____ es muy popular en
   Minneapolis.
   a. béisbol
   b. fútbol americano
   c. baloncesto

4. A Ignacio le gusta _____
   más que nadar.
   a. jugar al béisbol
   b. correr
   c. patinar

5. Ignacio necesita la ayuda
   de Roberto para el _____.
   a. béisbol
   b. tenis
   c. concurso

Classroom Management 🔲

Planning Ahead Have volunteers research names
of famous Spanish-speaking athletes. They should list
the name, country of origin, and sport. These names
will be used in a later activity (see TE p. 200, Group
Activity).

Student Checks When beginning a new grammar
topic, write the objective on the board. Also indicate to
students how they would use this topic in a real-life
situation. At the end of the grammar unit, repeat the
objective. Ask students if they feel that they have
achieved it.

- Use the verb **jugar**
- Use stem-changing verbs: **e→ie**
- Use the verb **saber**
- Use phrases for comparisons

ACTIVIDAD 3

¡Los deportes son buenos!

Escribir Completa el póster para tu clase de educación física. Da el nombre del deporte correspondiente a cada foto. *(Hint: Give the name of each sport.)*

¡Los deportes son buenos!

1.
2.
3.
4.
5.
6.

TAMBIÉN SE DICE

There are different ways to say *ball*.
- **bola:** Puerto Rico
- **balón:** Spain
- **pelota:** Latin America, Spain

In Puerto Rico, **una pelota** is a baseball. **Balón** and **cesto** (basket) are combined as **baloncesto** to mean *basketball*. **Básquetbol** is also sometimes used as a name for this sport.

ACTIVIDAD 4

¡Organízalos!

Hablar Trabajas en una tienda de deportes. Explícale a otro(a) trabajador(a) dónde poner los artículos. ¡Ojo! Algunos artículos van en más de una sección. *(Hint: Tell your coworker the appropriate section for each article.)*

modelo

los bates

Los bates *van en la sección de béisbol.*

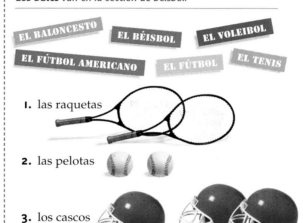

EL BALONCESTO   EL BÉISBOL   EL VOLEIBOL
EL FÚTBOL AMERICANO   EL FÚTBOL   EL TENIS

1. las raquetas

2. las pelotas

3. los cascos

4. los guantes

5. las bolas

ciento noventa y siete
Etapa 2   **197**

Answers
1. el fútbol
2. el tenis
3. el fútbol americano
4. el surfing
5. el voleibol
6. el béisbol

ACTIVIDAD 4
Objective: Transitional practice
Vocabulary

Answers
1. Las raquetas van en la sección de tenis.
2. Las pelotas van en la sección de béisbol.
3. Los cascos van en la sección de fútbol americano.
4. Los guantes van en la sección de béisbol.
5. Las bolas van en la sección de tenis, de voleibol, de fútbol y de baloncesto.

🔔 Quick Wrap-up

Ask students what they prefer to do during an important sports event, such as the World Cup or the Super Bowl. Note that they may prefer to watch the event or they may prefer to do another activity.

■ Block Schedule

Variety Have students prepare a list of questions for you about your interests in sports. Encourage them to use a variety of vocabulary and grammar constructions. Have them take notes during the question/answer session. Then have them write a summary of your answers.

Teaching All Students

Extra Help Ask students to say which sports they like to watch and which sports they like to play.

Native Speakers Ask students to list sports played with balls. Then have them say what the ball is called for each sport. Also ask students to name any internationally known athletes from their home countries or from the Spanish-speaking world.

Multiple Intelligences

Logical/Mathematical Have students collect sports statistics from the newspaper or Internet (player rankings, team rankings, game scores, game statistics, etc.). Have them present some of the information to the class.

Musical/Rhythmic Using sports music/chants as a basis, have students insert the new vocabulary to the rhythm.

Teaching Resource Options

Print 📖

Más práctica Workbook PE, p. 69
Para hispanohablantes Workbook PE, p. 67
Block Scheduling Copymasters

Unit 3 Resource Book
  Más práctica Workbook TE, p. 56
  Para hispanohablantes Workbook TE, p. 72

Audiovisual 🖥️

OHT 90 (Quick Start)

Technology 💿

Intrigas y aventuras CD-ROM, Disc 1

🔔 Quick Start Review

♻️ Sports vocabulary

Use OHT 90 or write on board:
Answer the following questions:
1. ¿Cuál es tu deporte favorito?
2. ¿Dónde se practica?
3. ¿Cuántas personas juegan?/
   ¿Cuántas personas hay en un equipo?
4. ¿Con qué se practica?
5. ¿Qué deporte no te gusta?

Answers
Answers will vary. Answers could include:
1. Mi deporte favorito es el baloncesto.
2. Se practica en una cancha.
3. Hay 5 personas en el equipo.
4. Se practica con una bola de baloncesto.
5. No me gusta el fútbol americano.

Teaching Suggestions
Presenting Talking About Playing a Sport: The Verb jugar

Have students pay particular attention to the vowels in the conjugation of **jugar**. Point out the boot (shoe) shape around the 4 forms with the vowels **ue**. Tell students that this is called a "boot" or "shoe" verb.

 Objective: Controlled practice
The verb **jugar**

Answers
1. jugamos
2. juego
3. jugar
4. juego
5. juegan
6. juega
7. juegas

GRAMÁTICA

Talking About Playing a Sport: The Verb jugar

When you talk about playing a sport, you use the verb **jugar**. The forms of **jugar** are unique. In some of them, the **u** changes to **ue**.

jugar *to play*

juego	**jug**amos
juegas	**jug**áis
juega	**juega**n

When you use **jugar** with the name of a sport, you must use

jugar a + *sport*

Ignacio asks Roberto:
—¿**Juegas al** béisbol en Minneapolis?
*Do **you play** baseball in Minneapolis?*

Coach Castillo asks:
—¿Qué deportes **juegan** en Minneapolis?
*What sports do **they play** in Minneapolis?*

Vocabulario

Más sobre los deportes

al aire libre *outdoors*
andar en patineta *to skateboard*
ganar *to win*
el gol *goal*
la gorra *baseball cap*
el hockey *hockey*
el partido *game*
la piscina *pool*
sobre hielo *on ice*

Use these adjectives and others you know to describe sports.

favorito(a) *favorite*
peligroso(a) *dangerous*

¿Qué frase usas para hablar de tu deporte favorito?

ACTIVIDAD 5 — Gramática

¿A qué juegan?

Leer La nueva amiga de Diana quiere saber a qué deportes juegan ella y sus amigos. Completa sus oraciones con una forma de **jugar**. *(Hint: Use the correct form of **jugar**.)*

Mis amigos y yo __1__ a muchos deportes. Yo __2__ al voleibol. No ganamos siempre, pero me gusta mucho __3__. Yo también __4__ al baloncesto, y ¡sí! ganamos mucho. Antonio y Marco __5__ al fútbol americano y al béisbol. Andrea __6__ al tenis y al voleibol conmigo. Bueno, ¿a qué __7__ tú?

■ **MÁS PRÁCTICA** *cuaderno* p. 69
■ **PARA HISPANOHABLANTES** *cuaderno* p. 67

ACTIVIDAD 6

¿Quién juega a qué?

Hablar ¿A qué deportes juegan tú, tus amigos y tus familiares? *(Hint: What sports do you and your friends and family play?)*

modelo

mi hermana
Mi hermana *juega al voleibol.*

1. yo
2. mi hermano(a)
3. mis amigos(as)
4. mi amigo(a)
5. mis amigos(as) y yo
6. mi primo(a)
7. mis primos(as)
8. ¿ ?

---

 198 ciento noventa y ocho
Unidad 3

Classroom Community

Learning Scenario Turn your classroom into a sporting goods store using the equipment students brought in (see TE p. 190, Planning Ahead). Designate some students as customers and others as salespeople. Salespeople should greet the customers and ask about customers' sports interests and needs. Customers ask about the equipment. Each customer must purchase at least one item.

Paired Activity Using the list of stem-changing verbs on p. 199, as well as **jugar**, one student asks a question and the other answers using the same verb. Then they exchange roles. They both must ask a question using each verb.

ACTIVIDAD 7

La tienda de deportes

Hablar Acabas de recibir este anuncio de una tienda de deportes. Habla con tres estudiantes sobre los artículos que van a comprar. Luego, da un resumen de cuatro de los artículos. *(Hint: Discuss with several classmates what they want to buy.)*

modelo

Tú: *¿Juegas al fútbol?*

Sara: *Sí, juego al fútbol.*

Tú: *¿Vas a comprar una bola nueva?*

Sara: *No, no necesito una bola nueva.*

Resumen: *Sara y Pablo juegan al fútbol. Carlos no juega al fútbol. Pablo va a comprar una bola de fútbol nueva.*

¡VENDEMOS DE TODO PARA TODOS LOS DEPORTES!

Bolas de fútbol $50

Raquetas de tenis $95

Cascos de fútbol americano $75

Bolas de voleibol $40

Bolas de baloncesto $35

Guantes de béisbol $70

Deportes Rodríguez
Calle Santurce, 134 • San Juan • tel: 321-4226 • fax 321-4230

GRAMÁTICA

Stem-Changing Verbs: e → ie

You learned that the **u** in **jugar** sometimes changes to **ue**. When you use the verb **pensar** (*to think, to plan*), the **e** in its **stem** sometimes changes to **ie**.

stem changes to

p**e**nsar → p**ie**nso

In stem-changing verbs, it is always the next-to-last syllable that changes.

pensar *to think, to plan*

pienso	**pens**amos
piensas	**pens**áis
piensa	**pie**nsan

Roberto says:

—Yo **pref ie ro** este bate.
I prefer this bat.

The coach asks:

—¿**Pie nsas** jugar en el equipo de baloncesto?
Do you plan to play on the basketball team?

Note that when one verb follows another, the first verb is **conjugated** and the second is in its **infinitive** form.

Vocabulario

Stem-Changing Verbs: e → ie

cerrar *to close*
empezar *to begin*
entender *to understand*
merendar *to have a snack*
querer *to want*
perder *to lose*
preferir *to prefer*

¿Cuándo usas una de estas palabras?

ciento noventa y nueve
Etapa 2 **199**

ACTIVIDAD 6

Objective: Transitional practice
The verb **jugar**

Answers
1. Yo juego [al fútbol americano].
2. Mi hermano(a) juega [al baloncesto].
3. Mis amigos(as) juegan [al tenis].
4. Mi amigo(a) juega [al fútbol].
5. Mis amigos(as) y yo jugamos [al voleibol].
6. Mi primo(a) juega [al béisbol].
7. Mis primos(as) juegan [al baloncesto].
8. *Answers will vary.*

ACTIVIDAD 7

Objective: Open-ended practice
The verb **jugar**/Sports vocabulary in conversation

Answers will vary.

Quick Start Review

🔔 Subject/verb agreement
Use OHT 90 or write on board:
Give the subject pronoun(s) for each verb form; give all possibilities.

1. ____ practicas 5. ____ vende
2. ____ juegan 6. ____ vivimos
3. ____ veo 7. ____ conozco
4. ____ ganamos 8. ____ haces

Answers
Answers will vary. Answers could include:
1. tú 5. él/ella/usted
2. ellos/ellas/ustedes 6. nosotros/nosotras
3. yo 7. yo
4. nosotros/nosotras 8. tú

Teaching Suggestions
Presenting Stem-Changing Verbs: e → ie

• Point out that these verbs are also "boot" or "shoe" verbs.
• Have students provide original sentences using **pensar/querer/preferir** + infinitive.

Block Schedule

Retention Provide students with a complete list of verbs learned so far. Then, have students work in groups to write and perform skits using as many verbs as possible. Grade the groups on the variety of verbs used. Groups could also make posters of the dialogs they write. (For additional activities, see **Block Scheduling Copymasters**.)

Teaching All Students

Extra Help Give the infinitive form of a stem-changing verb. One student gives a subject noun or pronoun. Another student gives the correct verb form. Alternate: Divide the class into rows of 5; give each group a piece of paper with a verb at the top. Each student in the "Verb Race" writes one form and passes the paper on. The first group to finish with correct forms wins.

Multiple Intelligences

Visual Have students draw visual hooks to recall the meaning of each verb: for example: **cerrar** / a picture of a closing door.

Logical/Mathematical Have students go to a sporting goods store and find out what it could cost to outfit a baseball player, hockey player, soccer player, etc., including uniforms and equipment.

Teaching Resource Options

Print

Más práctica Workbook PE, pp. 70–71
Para hispanohablantes Workbook PE,
  pp. 68–69
Block Scheduling Copymasters
Unit 3 Resource Book
  Más práctica Workbook TE,
    pp. 57–58
  Para hispanohablantes Workbook
    TE, pp. 63–64

Audiovisual

OHT 91 (Quick Start)

Technology

Intrigas y aventuras CD-ROM, Disc 1

8 **Objective:** Controlled practice
Stem-changing verbs: **e → ie**

Answers
1. Diana piensa jugar.
2. Yo pienso jugar.
3. Ella piensa jugar.
4. Los chicos piensan jugar.
5. Nosotros pensamos jugar.
6. Tú piensas jugar.
7. Ignacio piensa jugar.
8. Usted piensa jugar.

9 **Objective:** Controlled practice
Stem-changing verbs: **e → ie**

Answers
1. Los estudiantes cierran el libro.
2. Nosotras perdemos el partido.
3. El equipo quiere hacer un gol.
4. Tú quieres jugar al tenis.
5. Yo entiendo las matemáticas.
6. El partido empieza a las cuatro.
7. Ellos meriendan en la cafetería.
8. Yo prefiero nadar en la piscina.

10 **Objective:** Transitional practice
Stem-changing verbs: **e → ie**

Answers
Answers will vary. Answers could include:
1. La chica no entiende bien. Prefiere patinar sobre hielo.
2. El partido de baloncesto empieza a las cuatro. Juegan en el gimnasio.
3. Los muchachos no entienden las matemáticas. Quieren aprender [entender, saber más].
4. El hombre cierra la tienda a las nueve. Quiere regresar a casa [descansar, pasar un rato con su familia].

11 **Objective:** Open-ended practice
Stem-changing verbs: **e → ie**

Answers will vary.

¡Todos piensan jugar!

Hablar Explícale a un(a) amigo(a) quién piensa jugar a la pelota. *(Hint: Explain who plans to play ball.)*

modelo

ustedes	**Ustedes** piensan jugar.

1. Diana
2. yo
3. ella
4. los chicos
5. nosotros
6. tú
7. Ignacio
8. usted

¿Qué hacen?

> **PARA CONVERSAR**
> **STRATEGY: SPEAKING**
> **Monitor yourself** Listen to yourself. How do you sound? Do you hear errors? If so, stop and correct yourself. It is OK to do so.

Hablar/Escribir Explica lo que pasa un día en la escuela. *(Hint: Say what's happening.)*

1. los estudiantes / cerrar / libro
2. nosotras / perder / partido
3. el equipo / querer hacer / gol
4. tú / querer jugar / tenis
5. yo / entender / matemáticas
6. el partido / empezar / a las cuatro
7. ellos / merendar / cafetería
8. yo / preferir nadar / piscina

 MÁS PRÁCTICA *cuaderno* p. 70
PARA HISPANOHABLANTES *cuaderno* p. 68

¿Qué pasa aquí?

Hablar/Escribir Describe los dibujos con dos oraciones, usando las palabras. *(Hint: Use the words to describe what is happening.)*

entender/preferir

entender/querer

empezar/jugar

cerrar/querer

Un día de clases

Escribir Describe tu día de clases. Usa las palabras como guía. *(Hint: Describe your day, using the words as a guide.)*

1. yo / querer
2. mi maestro(a) / preferir
3. yo / empezar
4. mi amigo(a) / pensar
5. la clase de… / empezar
6. mis amigos y yo / merendar
7. el equipo de… / perder
8. los estudiantes / entender

 doscientos
Unidad 3

Classroom Community

Game In a container, place slips of paper with infinitives on them. Mark each one with an instruction (give the conjugation, give a complete sentence, ask a question, etc.) and assign each one a point value. Also put in a few blank slips with free bonus points. Have students play in teams. Each team takes a turn drawing a slip and answering. The team with the most points at the end of a time limit wins.

Group Activity Using the list of Spanish-speaking athletes (see TE p. 196, Planning Ahead), have students each choose one. Then, working in small groups, have students role play that athlete. The other students ask questions about name, country of origin, sport, likes and dislikes, etc. The athlete can also provide (or even make up) additional information, such as what he/she has just done, if he/she is thirsty, etc.

GRAMÁTICA

Saying What You Know: The Verb saber

 ¿RECUERDAS? *pp. 153, 154* You learned that some verbs have irregular yo forms.

Saber is another verb that has an irregular yo form. You use **saber** when you talk about factual information you know.

conocer → conozco
hacer → hago
oír → oigo

saber *to know*

sé	sabemos
sabes	sabéis
sabe	saben

Claudio asks Ignacio:

—¿**Sabe** él a qué hora empieza la práctica?
*Does **he know** what time practice starts?*

To say that someone knows how to do something, use: **saber** + *infinitive*.

Sé patinar muy bien.
I know how to skate very well.

NOTA CULTURAL

La Fortaleza is the oldest continuously inhabited executive mansion in the Americas. Built in 1532 to protect the island against invasion by sea, it is the residence of Puerto Rico's governor. Can you guess what **fortaleza** means?

ACTIVIDAD 12 Gramática

 ¡Saben hacer mucho!

Leer Estas personas saben hacer muchas cosas. Completa las oraciones con la forma correcta del verbo **saber.** *(Hint: Complete each sentence with the correct form of saber.)*

1. María _____ jugar al tenis.
2. Tú _____ nadar.
3. Nosotros _____ hablar español.
4. Yo _____ patinar.
5. Ustedes _____ bailar.
6. Él _____ cantar.
7. Los chicos _____ jugar al voleibol.
8. Ella _____ tocar el piano.

■ **MÁS PRÁCTICA** *cuaderno* p. 71

■ **PARA HISPANOHABLANTES** *cuaderno* p. 69

doscientos uno
Etapa 2   **201**

Teaching Resource Options

Print

Más práctica Workbook PE, p. 72
Para hispanohablantes Workbook PE, p. 70
Block Scheduling Copymasters
Unit 3 Resource Book
  Más práctica Workbook TE, p. 59
  Para hispanohablantes Workbook TE, p. 65
  Information Gap Activities, p. 68
  Audioscript, p. 81
  Audioscript *Para hispanohablantes*, p. 82

Audiovisual

OHT 91 (Quick Start)
Audio Program Cassettes 8A, 8B / CD 8
Audio *Para hispanohablantes*
  Cassette 8A / CD 8

Technology

Intrigas y aventuras CD-ROM, Disc 1

ACTIVIDAD 13 Objective: Transitional practice
Listening comprehension/**Saber**

Answers (See script, p. 189B.)
1. Saben esquiar en el agua.
2. Sabe jugar al tenis.
3. Saben jugar al béisbol.
4. Saben jugar al baloncesto.
5. Sabe jugar al voleibol.

ACTIVIDAD 14 Objective: Open-ended practice
Saber in conversation

Answers will vary.

Quick Start Review

♻ School locations and activities
Use OHT 91 or write on the board:
Write 2 possible adjectives for each noun.

1. el gato	4. la computación
2. el béisbol	5. la muchacha
3. la película	6. el surfing

Answers
Answers will vary. Answers could include:
1. gordo / contento
2. aburrido / popular
3. interesante / aburrida
4. difícil / fácil
5. seria / trabajadora
6. peligroso / divertido

Los deportistas

Escuchar Muchos amigos de Diana saben jugar a varios deportes. Escucha las descripciones de Diana y explica a lo que saben jugar.
(Hint: Explain what sports her friends know.)

1. Gisela y César
2. Pablo
3. ella y su hermano
4. Roberto y su hermano
5. Diana

¿Qué saben hacer?

Hablar ¿Qué saben hacer las personas que tú conoces?
(Hint: Say what they know how to do.)

modelo

tu hermano(a)

Tú: ¿Qué sabe hacer **tu hermana**?

Otro(a) estudiante: *Mi hermana sabe cantar y bailar.*

1. tu amigo(a)
2. tus amigos(as)
3. tú
4. tú y tus amigos(as)
5. tu maestro(a) de español

■ **MÁS COMUNICACIÓN** p. R8

GRAMÁTICA

Phrases for Making Comparisons

▶ Several phrases are used to compare things. Roberto and Ignacio use these when they discuss sports.

- **más... que**
  more... than
  ...el fútbol americano es **más** interesante **que** el fútbol.
  *...football is **more** interesting **than** soccer.*

- **menos... que**
  less... than   **agrees**
  ...**el tenis** es **menos** divertid**o que** el baloncesto.
  *...tennis is **less** entertaining **than** basketball.*

> Adjectives must agree in gender and number with the **nouns** that precede them.

- **tan... como**
  as... as
  ...el fútbol no es **tan** popular **como** el fútbol americano.
  *...soccer is not **as** popular **as** football.*

▶ These phrases are also used to compare things.

- **más que...**
  more than...
  Me gusta correr **más que** nadar.
  *I like to run **more than** (I like to) swim.*

- **menos que...**
  less than...
  Me gusta usar un guante nuevo **menos que** un bate nuevo.
  *I like to use a new glove **less than** a new bat.*

- **tanto como...**
  as much as...
  A él le gusta jugar al fútbol **tanto como** al béisbol.
  *He likes to play soccer **as much as** baseball.*

▶ When you talk about numbers, you must use **más de** or **menos de**.

más de dos o tres minutos	en **menos de** cinco minutos
more than two or three minutes	in **less than** five minutes

▶ There are a few irregular comparative words.

mayor	**menor**	**mejor**	**peor**
older	*younger*	*better*	*worse*

Classroom Community

Group Activity Assign groups of students to become experts in one category of comparisons: **más... que; menos... que; tan... como; más que...; menos que...; tanto como...; más de/menos de; mayor/menor/mejor/peor.** Have students write and present several examples of their category and explain how it works to the rest of the class.

Paired Activity Have students work in pairs and write 5 comparison statements. Then, on another sheet of paper, have them scramble the words of the sentences. They should then exchange these papers with another pair. Students work together to unscramble the other pair's sentences and then check their work.

ACTIVIDAD 15 Gramática

¿De o que?

Escribir Usa la palabra apropiada para describir los deportistas de la escuela.
(Hint: Describe the athletes.)

1. Hay más _____ siete personas en el equipo de béisbol.

2. Los chicos corren más _____ las chicas.

3. Las chicas saben jugar mejor _____ las maestras.

4. Hay menos _____ ocho personas en el equipo de baloncesto.

5. La chica rubia quiere jugar menos _____ la morena.

6. Ignacio tiene más _____ cinco bates.

7. Roberto juega peor _____ Diana.

8. Todas las semanas Ignacio practica más _____ cinco veces.

NOTA CULTURAL

Puerto Ricans periodically vote on the relationship they want with the U.S.: to be a commonwealth, a state, or an independent country. They chose to remain a commonwealth in 1993.

ACTIVIDAD 16 Gramática

♻ Las comparaciones

Hablar/Escribir Haz comparaciones usando **más que, menos que, tan... como** o **tanto como.** *(Hint: Use the correct phrase for making comparisons.)*

1. El gato es _____ gordo _____ el perro.

2. Le gusta estudiar _____ bailar.

3. Las muchachas son _____ altas _____ los chicos.

4. Paco es _____ trabajador _____ María Luisa.

5. Las camisetas azules son _____ grandes _____ las camisetas rojas.

6. Carmen es _____ seria _____ José.

7. Le gusta comer un sándwich _____ un taco.

8. yo / mi amigo(a): ¿?

■ **MÁS PRÁCTICA** *cuaderno* p. 72

■ **PARA HISPANOHABLANTES** *cuaderno* p. 70

doscientos tres
Etapa 2 | **203**

When presenting comparisons, try to provide a variety of visually stimulating examples of comparisons. The more extreme or silly, the better.

ACTIVIDAD 15 Objective: Controlled practice
Making comparisons

Answers

1. de	5. que
2. que	6. de
3. que	7. que
4. de	8. de

ACTIVIDAD 16 Objective: Controlled practice
Making comparisons
♻ Adjectives

Answers

1. más... que	5. tan... como
2. menos que...	6. menos... que
3. tan... como	7. tanto como
4. más... que	8. *Answers will vary.*

🔔 Quick Wrap-up

Write a list of sports on the board. Have students compare 2 of them. For example: **Me gusta practicar el baloncesto más que el fútbol.**

■ Block Schedule

Change of Pace Have students each create a set of 20 cards. The cards should have 10 pairs of people/objects that can be compared (similar to the pictures in **Actividad 16**). For example: a tall boy and a short boy, a happy dog and a sad dog, two nervous girls, etc. Students can then use the cards for practicing comparisons with a partner or for playing a memory game. (For additional activities, see **Block Scheduling Copymasters**.)

Teaching All Students

Extra Help Have students refer back to the dialog on pp. 194–195 and find examples of comparisons.

Native Speakers Ask students to make comparison statements about their friends or family members. When they use a word unknown to the rest of the class, write it on the board.

Multiple Intelligences

Logical/Mathematical Make a list of schedule scenarios to present to students. Have them decide how much time they have to complete each activity using **más de** or **menos de**. For example: **Son las 2:00. A las 2:15 vamos a la clase de historia. / Tenemos menos de 20 minutos.** o **Tenemos más de 10 minutos.**

Objective: Transitional practice
Making comparisons

Answers

1. A: Para ti, ¿qué deporte es más divertido, el
   béisbol o el fútbol?
   B: *Answers will vary.*
   A: *Answers will vary.*
2. A: Para ti, ¿qué deporte es más peligroso, el
   fútbol americano o el baloncesto?
   B: *Answers will vary.*
   A: *Answers will vary.*
3. A: Para ti, ¿qué deporte es más difícil, el
   voleibol o el tenis?
   B: *Answers will vary.*
   A: *Answers will vary.*
4. A: Para ti, ¿qué deporte es peor, el baloncesto
   o el béisbol?
   B: *Answers will vary.*
   A: *Answers will vary.*
5. A: Para ti, ¿qué deporte es mejor, el fútbol o el
   fútbol americano?
   B: *Answers will vary.*
   A: *Answers will vary.*
6. A: Para ti, ¿qué deporte es más interesante, el
   voleibol o el surfing?
   B: *Answers will vary.*
   A: *Answers will vary.*

¿Qué piensas tú?

Hablar Trabaja con otro(a) estudiante para comparar los deportes.
Cambien de papel. *(Hint: Compare sports with a classmate.)*

interesante

modelo

Estudiante A: *Para ti, ¿qué deporte es más **interesante, el tenis** o **el béisbol**?*
Estudiante B: *Para mí, el tenis es más interesante que el béisbol.*
Estudiante A: *Para mí, el tenis es tan interesante como el béisbol.*

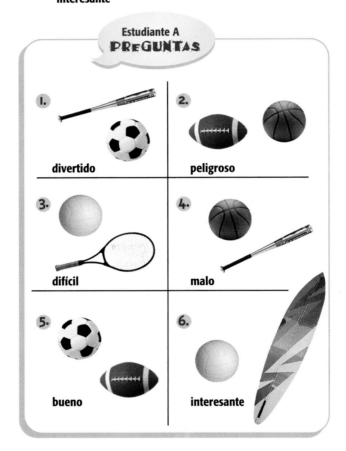

Estudiante A
PREGUNTAS

1. divertido
2. peligroso
3. difícil
4. malo
5. bueno
6. interesante

Estudiante B
RESPUESTAS

Para mí, ... es más... que...
Para mí, ... es menos... que...
Para mí, ... es tan... como...

**APOYO PARA
ESTUDIAR**

Comparatives

When comparing, picture these visual cues:
  (+) más que   (−) menos que
      (=) tan como

Think about extremes that would illustrate **más**
and **menos**, such as **UN ELEFANTE [(+) más
grande]** and **un ratón [(−) menos grande]**.
Now think of two very different athletes or
performers about whom you have an opinion.
How would you compare them?

Classroom Community

Group Activity Have students work in small groups
and compare this school year to last school year. They
should write all their statements and present their
opinions to the class. Comparisons may include
courses, schedule, sports activities, and social activities.

Paired Activity For **Actividad 17**, have students
continue working in pairs. Have them repeat how they
felt about the 2 sports, this time asking and answering
the question ¿**Por qué?**

¡Lógicamente!

Escuchar Todos hablan de los deportes. Escucha lo que dicen. Luego, indica la respuesta más lógica. *(Hint: Listen and indicate the most logical response.)*

1. **a.** ¡Qué bien! Tenemos más de cinco minutos.
   b. ¡Ay! Tenemos menos de cinco minutos.

2. **a.** ¿Tienes tu raqueta?
   b. ¿Tienes tu tarea?

3. **a.** Sí, me gusta nadar.
   b. ¡Claro que sí! Me gusta patinar.

4. **a.** No necesita un guante.
   b. ¿Va a la tienda de deportes?

5. **a.** Prefiere nadar.
   b. Prefiere levantar pesas.

♻ ¿Cuál es tu deporte favorito?

Hablar/Escribir Habla con otros estudiantes sobre los deportes. Escribe sus respuestas. Prepara un resumen para la clase.
(Hint: Ask classmates about sports. Record responses and report them.)

La encuesta	Estudiante 1	Estudiante 2
1. ¿A qué deportes sabes jugar?		
2. ¿A qué deportes juegas mucho?		
3. ¿A qué deporte prefieres jugar?		
4. ¿Cómo es?		
5. ¿Qué deporte prefieres ver?		
6. Compara el deporte que prefieres ver con el deporte que prefieres jugar.		
7. ¿Cuál es tu equipo favorito?		
8. ¿Cómo es?		
9. ¿Pierde mucho?		

■ **MÁS COMUNICACIÓN** p. R8

Pronunciación

Trabalenguas

Pronunciación de la ñ The letter **ñ** does not exist in English, but the sound does. It is the sound made by the combination of the letters *ny* in the English word *canyon*. To practice the sound, pronounce the following tongue twister.

ñ

La ñ es la n con bigote.

¡La araña se baña mañana!

doscientos cinco **205**
Etapa 2

 Objective: Transitional practice Listening comprehension/Sports vocabulary

Answers (See script, p. 189B.)
1. b
2. a
3. a
4. b
5. b

 Objective: Open-ended practice Interrogative words

♻ Sports vocabulary

Answers will vary.

🔔 Quick Wrap-up

Have students each make one true comparison statement about a topic of their choosing. For example, today's weather, 2 friends, how much time is left in the class, how many girls and boys are in the class, etc.

Dictation

After students have read the tongue twister in the **Pronunciación,** have them close their books. Dictate the tongue twister in segments while students write them.

■ Block Schedule

Survey Using comparisons, have each student pick a point to poll the class on; for example, what sport do students prefer, running or swimming. After formulating the question, asking all classmates, and compiling the data, have students use a paper plate to make a pie chart or bar graph. Students should then present their data in a comparative sentence. For example: **A las chicas les gusta nadar más que correr.** (For additional activities, see **Block Scheduling Copymasters.**)

Teaching All Students

Extra Help After presenting the **Apoyo para estudiar,** have students continue with similar comparisons: 2 very different singers, 2 very different actors, 2 very different teachers, etc.

Multiple Intelligences

Interpersonal In pairs, have students look back at the photos in previous **Etapas** to see what comparison statements they can make. Encourage them to use the characters' names and a variety of vocabulary. Each pair chooses its most creative comparison to share. The class votes on the most creative entry; the winning "team" receives a small prize.

Teaching Resource Options

Print

Unit 3 Resource Book
  Audioscript, p. 81
  Audioscript *Para hispanohablantes*,
    p. 81

Audiovisual

Audio Program Cassette 8A / CD 8
Audio *Para hispanohablantes*
  Cassette 8A / CD 8
OHT 92 (Quick Start)
Canciones Cassette / CD

Quick Start Review

♻ Comparisons

Use OHT 92 or write on the board:
Say which activity you think is more
interesting.

1. el baloncesto / el tenis
2. levantar pesas / nadar
3. el surfing / el voleibol
4. el fútbol / el fútbol americano
5. el hockey /el baloncesto

Answers *See p. 189B.*

Teaching Suggestions
Presenting Cultura y comparaciones

• Ask students if they think the United
  States has a national sport and
  encourage discussion in their answers.
• Ask why they think baseball is so
  popular in Puerto Rico.

Reading Strategy

Remind students that scanning for specific
information can help them understand
what a reading is about. Have them scan
this **En colores** for proper nouns. What do
these words tell them about the reading?

En colores
CULTURA Y COMPARACIONES

PARA CONOCERNOS
STRATEGY: CONNECTING CULTURES

Reflect on sports traditions Can you
think of any sports in the U.S.
that have players from other
countries? What sports are they?
Are some countries associated
with certain sports more than
others? Why do you think that
might be true? Use this chart to
organize your answers.

Deporte	País 1	País 2	País 3
el béisbol	Cuba	Japón	
el hockey	Canadá	Rusia	

Do you associate other countries
with areas such as science, music,
or art? If so, which ones? Why?

Béisbol

El pasatiempo nacional

En Puerto Rico el béisbol es muy popular. La temporada[1] de
béisbol es de octubre a marzo. Los equipos que juegan forman
la liga de invierno[2] y hay un partido casi todos los días.

Cada ciudad principal tiene un equipo. Unos jugadores[3]
de las ligas mayores y menores[4] de Estados Unidos participan
junto con los jugadores puertorriqueños.

---

[1] season   [2] winter league   [3] players   [4] major and minor leagues

206 doscientos seis
Unidad 3

Classroom Community

Group Activity In groups, have students talk about
how important or unimportant baseball is in (a) their
community, and (b) their personal lives. Ask them to
complete the sentences **Me gusta mucho el béisbol
porque...** or **No me gusta el béisbol porque...** They
should also respond to any group member's comments.

Portfolio Have students choose one sport to follow
for a week in the newspaper. They should clip articles,
statistics, etc. and create a collage with labels and
headlines in Spanish. In addition, they should write a
short summary of the sport in Spanish.

Rubric A = 13–15 pts. B = 10–12 pts. C = 7–9 pts. D = 4–6 pts. F = < 4 pts.

Writing criteria	Scale
Clear detail	1 2 3 4 5
Vocabulary use	1 2 3 4 5
Appearance	1 2 3 4 5

Roberto Clemente (1934–1972), jugador de los Piratas de Pittsburgh, es el puertorriqueño más famoso del béisbol. El primer latino elegido[5] para el Salón de la Fama[6] en 1973, Clemente empezó[7] su carrera con el equipo de Santurce, Puerto Rico. Hoy, en la ciudad de San Juan, el estadio principal de béisbol se llama Coliseo Roberto Clemente.

En el resto del Caribe el béisbol es tan importante como en Puerto Rico. Muchos jugadores importantes vienen de esta región. Juan Marichal de la República Dominicana está en el Salón de la Fama. Andrés Galarraga de Venezuela, Edgar Rentería de Colombia, Liván Hernández de Cuba y Fernando Valenzuela de México son otras figuras latinoamericanas importantes de las ligas mayores de béisbol de Estados Unidos.

[5] elected
[6] Hall of Fame
[7] began

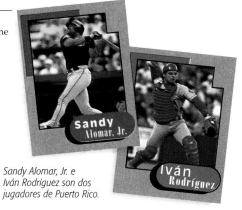

Sandy Alomar, Jr. e Iván Rodríguez son dos jugadores de Puerto Rico.

¿Comprendiste?

1. ¿En qué meses juegan los equipos de la liga de invierno?
2. ¿De dónde vienen los jugadores de la liga de invierno?
3. ¿Quién es el primer latino elegido para el Salón de la Fama?
4. ¿Qué países latinos tienen jugadores en las ligas mayores?

¿Qué piensas?

1. ¿Por qué juegan en Puerto Rico los jugadores de las ligas mayores y menores de Estados Unidos?
2. ¿Por qué vienen a Estados Unidos los jugadores de otros países?

Culture Highlights

● **BERNIE WILLIAMS** Bernie Williams (Bernabe Figueroa Williams) is a well-known Puerto Rican baseball player who plays with the New York Yankees. He was voted the most valuable player of the 1996 American League playoffs.

● **SAMMY SOSA** Sammy Sosa, from the Dominican Republic, set the record for the most home runs in a single month when he hit 20 in June 1998. Both Sosa and Mark McGwire broke the home run record of Roger Maris (61)—Sosa with 66 and McGwire with 70 home runs in the 1998 season.

Interdisciplinary Connections

Physics Have students research and explain how the laws of motion pertain to the game of baseball.

Social Studies Students can research the origin and the spread of the game of baseball.

¿Comprendiste?

Answers
1. Juegan de octubre a marzo.
2. Unos jugadores vienen de las ligas mayores y menores de Estados Unidos. Otros son de Puerto Rico.
3. Roberto Clemente es el primer latino elegido para el Salón de la Fama.
4. La República Dominicana, Venezuela, Colombia, Puerto Rico, Cuba y México

■ Block Schedule

Research Have students consult the Internet or the library for information about salary ranges for professional athletes in the U.S. and abroad. They should compare salaries between countries (for example: baseball in the U.S. and Puerto Rico or Cuba). Students then present their findings, using at least one comparison statement.

Teaching All Students

Extra Help After students have read through the selection once, have them read it again, paragraph by paragraph. After each paragraph, have students suggest a title for it.

Native Speakers Ask students about professional sports in their home countries. Which sports are popular? How are the leagues divided? What is the national championship called?

Multiple Intelligences

Intrapersonal Have students make sports or academic trading cards of themselves. On one side of a small piece of cardboard they should either draw a picture of themselves or use a photo. On the back, they should write autobiographical information and list outstanding statistics/achievements.

Teaching Resource Options

Print

Para hispanohablantes Workbook PE, pp. 71–72

Block Scheduling Copymasters
Unit 3 Resource Book
  Para hispanohablantes Workbook
    TE, pp. 66–67
  Information Gap Activities,
    p. 71
  Family Involvement, pp. 72–73
  Multiple Choice Test Questions,
    pp. 170–178

Audiovisual

OHT 92 (Quick Start)
Audio Program Testing Cassette T1 /
  CD T1

Technology

Electronic Teacher Tools/Test
  Generator
Intrigas y aventuras CD-ROM, Disc 1

Quick Start Review

♻ Sports vocabulary

Use OHT 92 or write on the board:
Write all sports related to:

1. un guante
2. un casco
3. unas pesas
4. una pelota
5. una raqueta

Answers *See p. 189B.*

✓ Teaching Suggestions
What Have Students Learned?

• Have students look at the "Now you can…" notes listed on the left side of pages 208–209. Tell students to think about which areas they might not be sure of. For those areas, they should consult the "To review" notes.
• Use the video to review vocabulary and structures.

ETAPA **2**

En uso
REPASO Y MÁS COMUNICACIÓN

OBJECTIVES
• Talk about sports
• Express preferences
• Say what you know
• Make comparisons

Now you can...
• talk about sports.

To review
• the verb **jugar**, see p. 198.

ACTIVIDAD 1 ¿Dónde juegas?

Todos hablan de su deporte favorito. ¿Dónde lo juegan?
(Hint: Tell where people play their favorite sports.)

modelo

mi padre: tenis (¿en la piscina o en la cancha?)
Mi padre juega al **tenis** en la cancha.

1. tú: baloncesto
   (¿en el campo o en la cancha?)
2. usted: voleibol
   (¿en la cancha o sobre hielo?)
3. yo: fútbol
   (¿en la cancha o en el campo?)
4. los vecinos: béisbol
   (¿al aire libre o en el gimnasio?)
5. Tomás y yo: fútbol americano
   (¿en el estadio o en la piscina?)
6. mi hermano: hockey
   (¿en la cancha o sobre hielo?)

Now you can...
• express preferences.

To review
• stem-changing verbs: **e→ie**, see p. 199.

ACTIVIDAD 2 ¡Vamos a jugar!

Las amigas de Diana hablan de los deportes. Completa su conversación con los verbos apropiados en la forma correcta.
(Hint: Complete the conversation with the appropriate verbs in the correct form.)

cerrar pensar querer entender preferir empezar

Eva: Rita, ¿ __1__ ir a un partido de béisbol conmigo mañana? El partido __2__ a las siete.

Rita: Gracias, pero no me gusta ver el béisbol. Yo __3__ los deportes individuales, como el surfing. Para mí, el béisbol es aburrido. No __4__ por qué te gusta.

Eva: Pues, yo __5__ que el béisbol es muy interesante. Y mañana mi equipo favorito, los Cardenales, va a jugar.

Rita: Mis hermanos también __6__ ver jugar a los Cardenales mañana, pero yo no. Mi mamá y yo __7__ pasar los sábados en las tiendas. Pero, a veces vamos al nuevo gimnasio. Abre a las siete de la mañana y __8__ a las nueve de la noche.

208 doscientos ocho
Unidad 3

Classroom Community

Cooperative Learning Divide the class into groups of 4. With books closed and for 1 minute, the group brainstorms sports-related words. Student 1 writes the list. Student 2 writes a complete statement using several of the words. Student 3 writes a question using different words. Student 4 proofs the sentences. The groups present their work to the class and receive points for number of words and correctness of sentences.

Paired Activity Have students role play the dialog between Eva and Rita in **Actividad 2**. They should memorize the lines and present the dialog to the class.

Now you can...
• say what you know.

To review
• the verb **saber**, see p. 201.

ACTIVIDAD 3 Somos deportistas

¿A qué deportes saben jugar estas personas? ¿Qué usan para jugar? *(Hint: Describe the sports these people know.)*

modelo

Bárbara

Bárbara

sabe patinar. Usa **patines**.

ustedes

Ustedes

saben jugar al voleibol. Usan **una bola**.

1. Guillermo
2. nosotros
3. yo
4. mis amigos
5. tú
6. yo

Now you can...
• make comparisons.

To review
• phrases for making comparisons, see p. 202.

ACTIVIDAD 4 Comparaciones

Expresa tus opiniones acerca de los deportes. *(Hint: Express your opinions about sports.)*

modelo

correr / nadar (menos / divertido)

Correr es menos divertido que nadar.

o: Nadar es menos divertido que correr.

o: Correr es tan divertido como nadar.

1. el baloncesto / el tenis (menos / interesante)
2. el surfing / el béisbol (más / aburrido)
3. nadar / levantar pesas (más / bueno)
4. esquiar / patinar (más / peligroso)
5. el fútbol americano / el baloncesto (más / popular)
6. el voleibol / el fútbol (menos / difícil)
7. el tenis / el béisbol (más / malo)
8. patinar / levantar pesas (menos / fácil)

doscientos nueve
Etapa 2
209

ACTIVIDAD 1 Answers

1. Tú juegas al baloncesto en la cancha.
2. Usted juega al voleibol en la cancha.
3. Yo juego al fútbol en el campo.
4. Los vecinos juegan al béisbol al aire libre.
5. Tomás y yo jugamos al fútbol americano en el estadio.
6. Mi hermano juega al hockey sobre hielo.

ACTIVIDAD 2 Answers

1. quieres
2. empieza
3. prefiero
4. entiendo
5. pienso
6. quieren (piensan)
7. preferimos
8. cierra

ACTIVIDAD 3 Answers

1. Guillermo sabe jugar al béisbol. Usa un bate, un guante y una pelota.
2. Nosotros sabemos jugar al fútbol americano. Usamos cascos.
3. Yo sé andar en patineta. Uso una patineta y un casco.
4. Mis amigos saben jugar al fútbol. Usan una bola.
5. Tú sabes levantar pesas. Usas pesas.
6. Yo sé jugar al tenis. Uso una raqueta.

ACTIVIDAD 4 Answers

1. El baloncesto es menos interesante que el tenis. *o:* El tenis es menos interesante que el baloncesto. *o:* El baloncesto es tan interesante como el tenis.
2. El surfing es más aburrido que el béisbol. *o:* El béisbol es más aburrido que el surfing. *o:* El surfing es tan aburrido como el béisbol.
3. Nadar es mejor que levantar pesas. *o:* Levantar pesas es mejor que nadar. *o:* Nadar es tan bueno como levantar pesas.
4. Esquiar es más peligroso que patinar. *o:* Patinar es más peligroso que esquiar. *o:* Esquiar es tan peligroso como patinar.
5. El fútbol americano es más popular que el baloncesto. *o:* El baloncesto es más popular que el fútbol americano. *o:* El fútbol americano es tan popular como el baloncesto.
6. El voleibol es menos difícil que el fútbol. *o:* El fútbol es menos difícil que el voleibol. *o:* El voleibol es tan difícil como el fútbol.
7. El tenis es peor que el béisbol. *o:* El béisbol es peor que el tenis. *o:* El tenis es tan malo como el béisbol.
8. Patinar es menos fácil que levantar pesas. *o:* Levantar pesas es menos fácil que patinar. *o:* Patinar es tan fácil como levantar pesas.

Teaching All Students

Extra Help Ask students to refer back to the dialog on pp. 194–195 and find all instances of stem-changing verbs and list them. If the verb is in the conjugated form, they should write the infinitive next to it.

Multiple Intelligences

Kinesthetic Have students work in pairs. One student acts out a sport. The other states one fact about the sport and then expresses his/her opinion of it. Students then reverse roles and continue for a few turns each.

Block Schedule

Variety Have students design a flier for students who are *not* interested in upcoming sporting events at your school. Have them suggest alternative activities using known grammar and vocabulary. (For additional activities, see **Block Scheduling Copymasters**.)

Teaching Resource Options

Print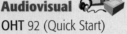

Unit 3 Resource Book
  Cooperative Quizzes, pp. 84–85
  Etapa Exam, Forms A and B,
    pp. 86–95
  Para hispanohablantes Etapa Exam,
    pp. 96–100
  Portfolio Assessment, pp. 101–102
  Multiple Choice Test Questions,
    pp. 170–178

Audiovisual

OHT 92 (Quick Start)
Audio Program Testing Cassette T1 /
  CD T1

Technology

Electronic Teacher Tools/Test
  Generator
www.mcdougallittell.com

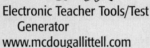

Rubric: Speaking

Criteria	Scale	
Sentence structure	1 2 3	A = 11–12 pts.
Vocabulary use	1 2 3	B = 9–10 pts.
Originality	1 2 3	C = 7–8 pts.
Fluency	1 2 3	D = 4–6 pts.
		F = < 4 pts.

 Answers will vary.

 En tu propia voz

Rubric: Writing

Criteria	Scale	
Vocabulary use	1 2 3 4 5	A = 14–15 pts.
Accuracy	1 2 3 4 5	B = 12–13 pts.
Creativity, appearance	1 2 3 4 5	C = 10–11 pts.
		D = 8–9 pts.
		F = < 8 pts.

Community Connection

What people in your community use
Spanish in their jobs? Have students look
through the Help Wanted section of the
newspaper to see what jobs require
knowledge of Spanish.

ACTIVIDAD 5 ¿Qué opinas tú?

PARA CONVERSAR

STRATEGY: SPEAKING

Give reasons for your preferences Support your
choices in different ways. Compare (1) how
you feel about the sports, (2) what you know
or don't know about them, or (3) basic
similarities and differences among them.
Think of different ways of explaining your
choices.

Habla con otro(a) estudiante sobre los deportes.
Explícale cuáles son tus preferencias y por qué.
(Hint: Talk about sports.)

modelo

Tú: *¿Prefieres levantar pesas o jugar al voleibol?*

Otro(a) estudiante: *Prefiero jugar al voleibol. El voleibol es
más interesante que levantar pesas.*

Tú: *Para mí, levantar pesas es más divertido.*

ACTIVIDAD 6 Un paseo por el club

Imagínate que trabajas en un nuevo club de
deportes. Muéstrales el club a tus amigos,
describiendo las actividades. *(Hint: Show your
friends the new sports club where you work.)*

Hay equipos de...   Muchas personas juegan al...

Tenemos cancha de...   El club abre...

Para jugar al voleibol, hay...

Los sábados jugamos al...

Al aire libre jugamos...   Los viernes hay clases de...

Para las personas que les gusta nadar, hay...

ACTIVIDAD 7 *En tu propia voz*

ESCRITURA Imagínate que tienes que preparar
un folleto para promover el club nuevo de la
Actividad 6. Incluye información sobre las
actividades y el horario del club. *(Hint: Write
a brochure promoting the new sports club.)*

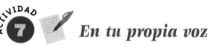 TÚ EN LA COMUNIDAD

Sarah is a Florida student who uses Spanish at her job as
a restaurant hostess and sends e-mails in Spanish. She also
used her Spanish when she went to Venezuela as a volunteer
with a medical mission group. Sarah spoke Spanish to the
patients and translated doctors' questions and instructions.
Do you use Spanish to help others?

Classroom Community

Paired Activity Working in pairs, have students list
the sports offered at your school. Next to each sport,
they should then write words associated with it:
equipment, place played, season, schedule, etc. Have
students share their information with another pair.

Game **Prepare ahead:** Gather photos or pictures of
places where sports are played (see "Locations" in the
Repaso de vocabulario). Divide the class into 2 teams.

Display the photos/pictures of the places for sports. In
turn, call on teams and name a word from the "Sports"
and "Equipment" lists in the **Repaso de vocabulario**.
The team gets 1 point when they correctly categorize
the sport or piece of equipment in the right location.
The team with the most points at the end of 5 minutes
wins.

En resumen
REPASO DE VOCABULARIO

TALKING ABOUT SPORTS

el equipo	team
ganar	to win
el gol	goal
jugar	to play
el partido	game
la tienda de deportes	sporting goods store

Sports

andar en patineta	to skateboard
el baloncesto	basketball
el béisbol	baseball
esquiar	to ski
el fútbol	soccer
el fútbol americano	football
el hockey	hockey
levantar pesas	to lift weights
el surfing	surfing
el tenis	tennis
el voleibol	volleyball

Equipment

el bate	bat
la bola	ball
el casco	helmet
la gorra	baseball cap
el guante	glove
los patines	skates
la patineta	skateboard
la pelota	baseball
la raqueta	racket

Locations

al aire libre	outdoors
el campo	field
la cancha	court
el estadio	stadium
la piscina	swimming pool
sobre hielo	on ice

EXPRESSING PREFERENCES

preferir	to prefer
querer	to want

SAYING WHAT YOU KNOW

saber	to know

MAKING COMPARISONS

más de	more than
más... que	more…than
mayor	older
mejor	better
menor	younger
menos de	less than
menos... que	less…than
peor	worse
tan... como	as…as
tanto como	as much as

OTHER WORDS AND PHRASES

cerrar	to close
empezar	to begin
entender	to understand
favorito(a)	favorite
loco(a)	crazy
merendar	to have a snack
peligroso(a)	dangerous
pensar	to think, to plan
perder	to lose

Juego

A Ángela, a Marco y a Juanito les gusta practicar diferentes deportes. ¿Cuáles son? Busca sus nombres. Con las otras letras, identifica su deporte preferido.

1. ALSAEGSPENARALEVANT
2. GINAMURFSOCR
3. NIAUJOTTBLOFU

doscientos once
Etapa 2
211

Planning Guide CLASSROOM MANAGEMENT

OBJECTIVES

Communication	• Describe the weather *pp. 214–215, 216–217* • Discuss clothing and accessories *pp. 214–215* • Describe the geography of a place, its plants and animals *pp. 216–217, 228–229, 230–231*
Grammar	• Use weather expressions *pp. 220–222* • Use **tener** expressions *pp. 223–224* • Use direct object pronouns *pp. 224–226* • Use present progressive *pp. 226–227*
Pronunciation	• j and g *p. 227* • Dictation *TE p. 227*
Culture	• **El Yunque** *p. 224* • **El coquí** *pp. 228–229* • Tourism in Puerto Rico *pp. 230–231*
♻ **Recycling**	• **Hay** • **Preferir** • **Ir a** • **Tener** • Sports vocabulary • **Estar**

STRATEGIES

Listening Strategies	• Sort and categorize details *p. 216*
Speaking Strategies	• Say how often *p. 222* • Get specific information *p. 234*
Reading Strategies	• Distinguish details *p. 228* • Look at graphics *p. 230*
Writing Strategies	• Brainstorm and organize information by category *p. 234* • Appeal to the senses *pp. 236–237*
Connecting Cultures Strategies	• Recognize variations in vocabulary *pp. 218, 222* • Learn about rain forests *pp. 224, 228–229* • Connect and compare what you know about travel and tourism in your community to help you learn about travel and tourism in a new community *pp. 230–231*

PROGRAM RESOURCES

 Print

• *Más práctica* Workbook PE, *pp. 73–80*
• Block Scheduling Copymasters, *pp. 73–80*
• Unit 3 Resource Book
   Más práctica Workbook TE, *pp. 103–110*
   Para hispanohablantes Workbook TE, *pp. 111–118*

Information Gap Activities *pp. 119–122*
Family Involvement *pp. 123–124*
Video Activities *pp. 125–127*
Videoscript *pp. 128–130*
Audioscript *pp. 131–134*
Assessment Program, Unit 3 Etapa 3 *pp. 135–186*
Answer Keys *pp. 187–202*

 Audiovisual

• **Audio Program** Cassettes 9A, 9B / CD 9
• *Canciones* Cassette / CD
• **Video Program** Videotape 3 / Videodisc 2A
• **Overhead Transparencies** M1–M5; GO1–GO5; 72, 93–102

 Technology

• Electronic Teacher Tools/Test Generator
• *Intrigas y aventuras* CD-ROM, Disc 1
• www.mcdougallittell.com

 Assessment Program Options

• **Cooperative Quizzes** (Unit 3 Resource Book)
• **Etapa Exam** Forms A and B (Unit 3 Resource Book)
• *Para hispanohablantes* Etapa Exam (Unit 3 Resource Book)
• **Portfolio Assessment** (Unit 3 Resource Book)
• **Unit 3 Comprehensive Test** (Unit 3 Resource Book)
• *Para hispanohablantes* **Unit 3 Comprehensive Test** (Unit 3 Resource Book)
• **Midterm Test** (Unit 3 Resource Book)
• **Multiple Choice Test Questions** (Unit 3 Resource Book)
• **Audio Program** Testing Cassette T1 / CD T1
• **Electronic Teacher Tools/Test Generator**

Native Speakers

• *Para hispanohablantes* Workbook PE, *pp. 73–80*
• *Para hispanohablantes* Workbook TE (Unit 3 Resource Book)
• *Para hispanohablantes* Etapa Exam (Unit 3 Resource Book)
• *Para hispanohablantes* **Unit 3 Comprehensive Test** (Unit 3 Resource Book)
• **Audio** *Para hispanohablantes* Cassettes 9A, 9B, T1 / CD 9, T1
• **Audioscript** *Para hispanohablantes* (Unit 3 Resource Book)

Student Text
Listening Activity Scripts

 Videoscript: Diálogo *pages 216–217*

• Videotape 3 • Videodisc 2A

Search Chapter 7, Play to 8
U3E3 • En vivo (Dialog)

• Use the videoscript with **Actividades 1, 2** *page 218*

Diana: ¡Qué mona tu bufanda! Me gusta tu gorro. ¿Hace mucho frío en Minneapolis?

Roberto: En el invierno, sí, ¡hace mucho frío! ¡Brrr! Tengo frío cuando pienso en los inviernos de Minneapolis. Los detesto.

Diana: ¿Nieva mucho?

Ignacio: Diana, ¡qué pregunta! Claro que nieva mucho en Minnesota.

Diana: Pues, yo no sé.

Roberto: Bueno, en el invierno, nieva casi todas las semanas. Pero en verano, es como aquí. Hace mucho calor.

Ignacio: ¿Y qué vas a hacer con este abrigo? ¿Y con toda esta ropa de invierno? Aquí nadie la necesita.

Roberto: Tienes razón. Voy a necesitar shorts, trajes de baño y gafas de sol.

Diana: ¡Ay! Pues ya tienes ropa de verano.

Roberto: Claro que la tengo. ¡En Minneapolis no es invierno todo el año!

¡Qué día bonito! Hace muy buen tiempo. ¿Sabes qué, Ignacio? Tengo muchas ganas de ir a El Yunque.

Ignacio: ¡Perfecto!

Roberto: ¿Por qué perfecto?

Diana: Perfecto porque el proyecto de Ignacio para el concurso es sobre el bosque tropical. Y está preparando el proyecto este mes.

Ignacio: Sí, y necesito sacar fotos del bosque. Y las quiero sacar hoy mismo.

Roberto: ¡Qué chevere! Tengo suerte, ¿no lo creen? ¡Yo los acompaño con mucho gusto! ¡Vamos a El Yunque!

Diana: Creo que sí. Creo que tienes mucha suerte.

Ignacio: Tengo prisa. Es buena hora para sacar fotos porque hay sol. ¡Tenemos que ir ahora mismo a El Yunque! ¡Avancen!

¡Qué bonito! Los árboles, las flores...

Roberto: Sí, muy bonita.

Ignacio: No es como Minneapolis, ¿verdad, Roberto?

Roberto: Tienes razón, Ignacio. No es para nada como Minneapolis.

Ignacio: Mi proyecto va a estar bien chévere, ¿no creen?

¿No creen? ¿Dónde está el paraguas? Lo necesito.

...Sí, Ignacio, creo que tu proyecto va a ser muy impresionante.

¡Está lloviendo! ¡Y no tengo paraguas!

Roberto: Te estamos esperando, hombre.

 **El tiempo** *page 221*

1. Hace fresco. Llueve mucho. Las flores son bonitas.
2. Hace mucho frío. Nieva. Quiero patinar sobre hielo.
3. Hace frío y hay mucho viento. Es divertido ir a un partido de fútbol americano.
4. Hace calor. La temperatura es de noventa grados. Voy a la piscina.

¿Qué pasa? *page 225*

María: ¡Hola, Raúl! Llueve mucho, ¿verdad?

Raúl: Sí. Yo veo la televisión cuando llueve.

María: Yo también la veo, pero no es mi actividad favorita. Prefiero leer unas revistas.

Raúl: A mí me gusta leer las revistas. A veces las leo cuando llueve.

María: Me gusta caminar en la lluvia.

Raúl: ¿Llevas paraguas?

María: No, no lo llevo.

Raúl: ¡Ay! Cuando quiero nadar, ¡voy a la playa!

María: ¡Buena idea! ¿Va a llover mañana?

Raúl: Creo que no.

María: Entonces, ¿vamos a la playa? Tengo muchas ganas de nadar.

Raúl: Sí. Pero tengo que comprar gafas de sol. Las necesito para ir a la playa.

María: ¿Necesito llevar bronceador?

Raúl: No. Yo lo tengo.

Quick Start Review Answers

p. 214 Adjectives of feeling
Answers will vary.
Answers could include:
1. tengo un partido de béisbol muy importante más tarde
2. saco buenas notas en matemáticas
3. va a un concierto
4. tienen un examen de español
5. no tenemos mucha tarea

p. 218 Dialog review
1. Ahora Roberto vive en Puerto Rico.
2. En Minnesota en el invierno hace mucho frío.
3. En Minnesota y Puerto Rico en el verano hace calor.
4. Roberto tiene ganas de ir a El Yunque.

p. 220 Seasons/sports
Answers will vary.
Answers could include:
1. el béisbol, el tenis, el surfing
2. el fútbol, el fútbol americano
3. el hockey, esquiar
4. el baloncesto, el voleibol

p. 223 Tener
1. tiene   3. tenemos   5. tiene
2. tienes   4. tengo

p. 224 Gender
1. el   3. el   5. el   7. los
2. los   4. las   6. la   8. el

p. 226 Direct object pronouns
1. las revistas / Sí, las tengo.
2. la camisa con rayas / Sí, la lleva.
3. las pelotas / Sí, las compra.
4. los bates /Sí, los buscan.
5. el libro / Sí, lo lee.
6. el bronceador / Sí, lo necesito.

p. 235 Seasons/weather/clothing
Answers will vary.
Answers could include:
otoño
• Hace fresco y hace viento.
• un suéter
• el fútbol americano
• tengo ganas de bailar

Sample Lesson Plan - 50 Minute Schedule

DAY 1

Etapa Opener
- Quick Start Review (TE, p. 212) 5 MIN.
- Anticipate/Activate prior knowledge: Have students look at the *Etapa* Opener and answer the questions. 5 MIN.

En contexto: Vocabulario
- Quick Start Review (TE, p. 214) 5 MIN.
- Have students use context and pictures to learn *Etapa* vocabulary. In pairs, have students answer the questions, p. 215. Use the Situational OHTs for additional practice. 10 MIN.

En vivo: Diálogo
- Quick Start Review (TE, p. 216) 5 MIN.
- Review the Listening Strategy, p. 216. Play audio or show video for the dialog, pp. 216–217. 10 MIN.
- Replay twice. Read aloud, having students note similarities and differences between Minneapolis and San Juan. 10 MIN.

Homework Option:
- Video Activities, Unit 3 Resource Book, pp. 125–127.

DAY 2

En acción: Vocabulario y gramática
- Check homework. 5 MIN.
- Quick Start Review (TE, p. 218) 5 MIN.
- Have students open to *En contexto,* pp. 214–215, for reference. Use OHT 93 and 94 to review vocabulary by asking yes/no questions (*¿Es un[a]...?*). 5 MIN.
- Play the audio; have students do *Actividades* 1 and 2 orally. 10 MIN.
- Students complete *Actividad* 3 in writing. Go over answers orally. Have volunteers write out answers on the board. 10 MIN.
- Present *Vocabulario,* p. 219. Model pronunciation. 5 MIN.
- Have students do *Actividad* 4 orally. 5 MIN.
- Have students complete *Actividad* 5 in writing, then exchange papers for peer correction. 10 MIN.

Homework Option:
- Have students complete *Actividad* 4 in writing.

DAY 3

En acción (cont.)
- Check homework. 5 MIN.
- Quick Start Review (TE, p. 220) 5 MIN.
- Present *Gramática:* Describing the Weather, p. 220. 10 MIN.
- Play the audio; have students do *Actividad* 6. 5 MIN.
- Do *Actividad* 7 orally. 5 MIN.
- In pairs, have students do *Actividad* 8. They should take turns asking and answering the questions. Call on several pairs to present their answers. 10 MIN.
- Present the Speaking Strategy, p. 222. Have students do *Actividad* 9 in pairs. 5 MIN.
- Have students complete *Actividad* 10. Choose one or two groups to present their work to the class. 10 MIN.

Homework Option:
- Have students complete *Actividad* 7 in writing. *Más práctica* Workbook, p. 77. *Para hispanohablantes* Workbook, p. 75.

DAY 4

En acción (cont.)
- Check homework. 5 MIN.
- Quick Start Review (TE, p. 223) 5 MIN.
- Present *Gramática:* Special Expressions Using *tener,* p. 223. 5 MIN.
- Have students complete *Actividad* 11 in writing, then go over the answers orally. 5 MIN.
- Do *Actividad* 12 orally. 5 MIN.
- Have students complete *Actividad* 13 in pairs. Expand using Information Gap Activities, Unit 3 Resource Book, p. 119; *Más comunicación,* p. R9. 10 MIN.
- Quick Start Review (TE, p. 224) 5 MIN.
- Present *Gramática:* Direct Object Pronouns, p. 224. 5 MIN.
- Have students work in pairs to complete *Actividad* 14. 5 MIN.
- Have students read and complete *Actividad* 15. 5 MIN.

Homework Option:
- *Más práctica* Workbook, pp. 78–79. *Para hispanohablantes* Workbook, pp. 76–77.

DAY 5

En acción (cont.)
- Check homework. 5 MIN.
- Do *Actividad* 16 in pairs. 5 MIN.
- Play the audio; have students do *Actividad* 17. 5 MIN.
- Do *Actividad* 18 in pairs. 5 MIN.
- Quick Start Review (TE, p. 226) 5 MIN.
- Present *Gramática:* Present Progressive, p. 226. 10 MIN.
- Do *Actividades* 19 and 20 orally. 5 MIN.
- Do *Actividad* 21 in writing. Expand using Information Gap Activities, Unit 3 Resource Book, pp. 120–121; *Más comunicación,* p. R9. 10 MIN.

Pronunciación
- Play the audio and have students practice the *Trabalenguas.* 5 MIN.

Homework Option:
- *Más práctica* Workbook, p. 80. *Para hispanohablantes* Workbook, p. 78.

DAY 6

En voces: Lectura
- Check homework. 5 MIN.
- Quick Start Review (TE, p. 228) 5 MIN.
- Present the Reading Strategy, p. 228. 5 MIN.
- Have volunteers read the selection aloud and answer the questions, p. 229. 10 MIN.

En colores: Cultura y comparaciones
- Quick Start Review (TE, p. 230) 5 MIN.
- Discuss the Connecting Cultures Strategy, p. 230. 5 MIN.
- Have volunteers read the selection aloud and answer the questions, p. 231. 10 MIN.
- Review *En uso* for *Etapa* 3 Exam. 10 MIN.

Homework Option:
- Prepare *En uso Actividades* 1–5. Review for *Etapa* 3 Exam.

DAY 7

En uso: Repaso y más comunicación
- Check homework. 5 MIN.
- Quick Start Review (TE, p. 232) 5 MIN.
- Review *Actividades* 1–5 orally. 5 MIN.
- Present the Speaking Strategy, p. 234. Do *Actividad* 6 in groups and *Actividad* 7 in pairs. 10 MIN.

En resumen: Repaso de vocabulario
- Complete *Etapa* 3 Exam. 20 MIN.

En tu propia voz: Escritura
- Do *Actividad* 8 in writing. 5 MIN.

Conexiones
- Present *Las ciencias,* p. 234. 5 MIN.

Homework Option:
- Review for Unit 3 Comprehensive Test.

DAY 8

En resumen: Repaso de vocabulario
- Quick Start Review (TE, p. 235) 5 MIN.

En tu propia voz: Escritura
- Do the writing activity, pp. 236–237. 10 MIN.

Unit 3 Comprehensive Test
- Review grammar questions, etc. as necessary. 5 MIN.
- Complete Unit 3 Comprehensive Test. 30 MIN.

Ampliación
- Optional: Use a suggested project, game, or activity. (TE, pp. 167A–167B) 15 MIN.

Homework Option:
- Preview *Unidad* 4 Opener: Have students read and study pp. 238–239.

Sample Lesson Plan - Block Schedule (90 minutes)

DAY 1

Etapa Opener
- Quick Start Review (TE, p. 212) 5 MIN.
- Anticipate/Activate prior knowledge: Have students look at the *Etapa* Opener and answer the questions. 5 MIN.
- Use Block Scheduling Copymasters. 5 MIN.

En contexto: Vocabulario
- Quick Start Review (TE, p. 214) 5 MIN.
- Have students use context and pictures to learn *Etapa* vocabulary. In pairs, have students answer the questions, p. 215. Use the Situational OHTs for additional practice. 10 MIN.

En vivo: Diálogo
- Quick Start Review (TE, p. 216) 5 MIN.
- Review the Listening Strategy, p. 216. Play audio or show the video for the dialog, pp. 216–217. 10 MIN.
- Replay twice. Read aloud, having students note similarities and differences between Minneapolis and San Juan. 10 MIN.

En acción: Vocabulario y gramática
- Quick Start Review (TE, p. 218) 5 MIN.
- Play the audio; have students do *Actividades* 1 and 2. 10 MIN.
- Have students do *Actividad* 3 in writing, and go over answers orally. 5 MIN.
- Present *Vocabulario*, p. 219. 5 MIN.
- Have students do *Actividad* 4 orally and *Actividad* 5 in writing. 10 MIN.

Homework Option:
- Video Activities, Unit 3 Resource Book, pp. 125–127. Have students complete *Actividad* 4 in writing.

DAY 2

En acción (cont.)
- Check homework. 5 MIN.
- Quick Start Review (TE, p. 220) 5 MIN.
- Present *Gramática:* Describing the Weather, p. 220. 10 MIN.
- Replay dialog to demonstrate usage. 5 MIN.
- Play the audio; have students do *Actividad* 6. 5 MIN.
- Have students do *Actividad* 7 orally. 5 MIN.
- In pairs, have students do *Actividad* 8. They should take turns asking and answering the questions. Call on several pairs to present their answers. 10 MIN.
- Present the Speaking Strategy, p. 222. Have students do *Actividad* 9 in pairs. 5 MIN.
- Have students complete *Actividad* 10. Choose one or two groups to present their work to the class. 5 MIN.
- Quick Start Review (TE, p. 223) 5 MIN.
- Present *Gramática:* Special Expressions Using *tener,* p. 223. 10 MIN.
- Have students complete *Actividad* 11 in writing, then go over the answers orally. 5 MIN.
- Do *Actividad* 12 orally. 5 MIN.
- Have students complete *Actividad* 13 in pairs. Expand using Information Gap Activities, Unit 3 Resource Book, p. 119; *Más comunicación*, p. R9. 10 MIN.

Homework Option:
- Have students write 10 original sentences using weather/season vocabulary. *Más práctica* Workbook, pp. 77–78. *Para hispanohablantes* Workbook, pp. 75–76.

DAY 3

En acción (cont.)
- Check homework. 5 MIN.
- Quick Start Review (TE, p. 224) 5 MIN.
- Present *Gramática:* Direct Object Pronouns, p. 224. 10 MIN.
- Have students work in pairs to complete *Actividad* 14. 5 MIN.
- Have students read and complete *Actividad* 15. Go over answers orally. 10 MIN.
- Do *Actividad* 16 in pairs. 5 MIN.
- Play the audio; have students do *Actividad* 17. 10 MIN.
- Have students do *Actividad* 18 in pairs. Call on a few pairs to present their answers. 10 MIN.
- Quick Start Review (TE, p. 226) 5 MIN.
- Present *Gramática:* Saying What Is Happening: Present Progressive, p. 226. 10 MIN.
- Do *Actividades* 19 and 20 orally. 5 MIN
- Do *Actividad* 21 in writing. Expand using Information Gap Activities, Unit 3 Resource Book, pp. 120–121; *Más comunicación,* p. R9. 10 MIN.

Pronunciación
- Play the audio and have students practice the *Trabalenguas.* 5 MIN.

Homework Option:
- *Más práctica* Workbook, pp. 79–80. *Para hispanohablantes* Workbook, pp. 77–78.

DAY 4

En voces: Lectura
- Check homework. 5 MIN.
- Quick Start Review (TE, p. 228) 5 MIN.
- Present the Reading Strategy, p. 228. 5 MIN.
- Have volunteers read the selection aloud and answer the questions, p. 229. 10 MIN.

En colores: Cultura y comparaciones
- Quick Start Review (TE, p. 230) 5 MIN.
- Present the Connecting Cultures Strategy, p. 230. 5 MIN.
- Have volunteers read the selection aloud and answer the questions, p. 231. 15 MIN.

En uso: Repaso y más comunicación
- Quick Start Review (TE, p. 232) 5 MIN.
- Do *Actividades* 1–5 orally. 15 MIN.
- Present the Speaking Strategy, p. 234. Do *Actividad* 6 in groups and *Actividad* 7 in pairs. 10 MIN.
- Do *Actividad* 8 in writing. 10 MIN.

Homework Option:
- Review for *Etapa* 3 Exam.

DAY 5

En resumen: Repaso de vocabulario
- Quick Start Review (TE, p. 235) 5 MIN.
- Review grammar questions, etc. as necessary. 5 MIN.
- Complete *Etapa* 3 Exam. 20 MIN.

Conexiones
- Read and discuss *Las ciencias,* p. 234. 10 MIN.

Unit 3 Comprehensive Test
- Review grammar questions, etc. as necessary. 5 MIN.
- Complete Unit 3 Comprehensive Test. 30 MIN.

En tu propia voz: Escritura
- Do the writing activity, pp. 236–237. 15 MIN.

Ampliación
- Optional: Use a suggested project, game, or activity. (TE, pp. 167A–167B) 15 MIN.

Homework Option:
- Preview *Unidad* 4 Opener: Have students read and study pp. 238–239.

▼ Ignacio, Diana y Roberto en El Yunque.

Etapa Theme
Describing the weather, discussing clothes, and stating opinions and feelings.

Grammar Objectives
- Using weather expressions
- Using **tener** expressions
- Using direct object pronouns
- Using present progressive

Teaching Resource Options
Print
Block Scheduling Copymasters

Audiovisual
OHT 72, 99 (Quick Start)

Quick Start Review

♻ Free time activities

Use OHT 99 or write on board:
Complete the following sentences with an activity:

Modelo: Mañana queremos ____.
You write: **esquiar en el agua**

1. El sábado prefiero ____.
2. Mis padres quieren ____.
3. A mis amigos y a mí nos gusta ____.
4. Mi hermano siempre quiere ____.
5. ¿Te gusta ____?
6. ¿Quieres ____?

Answers
Answers will vary. Answers could include:
1. ir de compras
2. visitar a mis abuelos
3. andar en patineta
4. jugar al béisbol
5. practicar deportes
6. ver la televisión

Teaching Suggestions
Previewing the Etapa
- Ask students to study the picture on pp. 212–213 (1 min.).
- Close books; ask students to share at least 3 items that they noticed.
- Reopen books and look at the picture again (1 min.); close books and share 3 more details.
- Use the **¿Qué ves?** questions to focus the discussion.

UNIDAD 3

ETAPA 3

El tiempo en El Yunque

- Describe the weather
- Discuss clothing and accessories
- State an opinion
- Describe how you feel
- Say what is happening

¿Qué ves?

Mira la foto de El Yunque, el bosque tropical.

1. ¿Hay muchas plantas verdes?
2. ¿Ignacio está ocupado o no?
3. ¿Diana y Roberto están alegres o preocupados?
4. ¿Cómo se llama el lugar?

212

Classroom Management

Planning Ahead Prepare to discuss the weather by collecting weather-related information from local newspapers and the Internet. Gather weather maps of regions students have studied so that they can compare them to their own area. Make weather symbol visuals (one per card) and laminate them for continued use.

Time Saver Assign a place in the classroom where students pick up handouts at the beginning of class and hand in any in-class assignments at the end of class.

BAÑO GRANDE
CUERPOS CIVILES DE CONSERVACIÓN
CIVILIAN CONSERVATION CORPS

213

Cross Cultural Connections

Have students look at the sign at the top of p. 213. Ask them where else they would expect to see signs in more than one language.

Culture Highlights

● **EL YUNQUE** El Bosque Nacional del Caribe (the Caribbean National Forest) is also known as **El Yunque.** This name comes from the name of the major mountain in the forest, **El Yunque,** which is 3,493 feet high. The forest is located 25 miles southeast of San Juan in the Sierra de Luquillo and is approximately 28,000 acres in size. It is the only tropical forest in the U.S. National Forest System and contains 240 different species of trees, 30 of which are unique to this area. There are also 50 species of native orchids and over 150 species of ferns. Within the forest, there are many trees known to be over 1000 years old.

The photo on pp. 212–213 was taken in **El Yunque.**

Language Notes

The word **yunque** means *anvil.* The mountain **El Yunque** is called this because its peak resembles an anvil when viewed from a nearby town.

Mention to students that many Puerto Ricans know English and Spanish, which makes travelling between Puerto Rico and the United States much easier. English is mandatory in schools from kindergarten through high school.

Block Schedule

Process Time Have students spend 3 minutes on their own looking at the photo and writing 2–3 sentences about it. Then have them share their observations with the class. (For additional activities, see **Block Scheduling Copymasters.**)

Teaching All Students

Extra Help Ask yes/no or simple answer questions about the photo. For example: **¿Hay tres o cuatro personas en la foto? ¿Lleva la muchacha un vestido? ¿Están en Canadá o Puerto Rico? ¿Están tristes o contentos?**

Challenge Recreate the scene in the classroom and have students prepare mini-dialogs among the 3 people.

Multiple Intelligences

Naturalist Ask students to study the photo and name similar geographic areas or preserves they have visited, seen on TV, or read about. Make a list of the places and have students describe geographical details and information about plants, animals, or other natural phenomena. Variation: Plan an ecotour of the area.

Teaching Resource Options

Print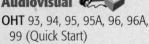

Unit 3 Resource Book
  Video Activities, pp. 125–126
  Videoscript, p. 128
  Audioscript, p. 131
  Audioscript *Para hispanohablantes*,
    p. 131

Audiovisual

OHT 93, 94, 95, 95A, 96, 96A,
  99 (Quick Start)
Audio Program Cassette 9A / CD 9
Audio *Para hispanohablantes*
  Cassette 9A / CD 9
Video Program Videotape 3 / Videodisc
  2A

Search Chapter 6, Play to 7
U3E3 • En contexto (Vocabulary)

Technology
Intrigas y aventuras CD-ROM, Disc 1

Quick Start Review

♻ Adjectives of feeling

Use OHT 99 or write on board:
Write a logical completion to each:

1. Estoy preocupado(a) porque...
2. Mis padres están contentos
   porque...
3. Mi hermana está emocionada
   porque...
4. Los estudiantes están nerviosos
   porque...
5. Hoy estamos tranquilos porque...

Answers *See p. 211B.*

Culture Highlights

● **EL TIEMPO** Puerto Rico enjoys sub-tropical weather all year round. Its proximity to the equator along with steady tradewinds from the northeast keep temperatures at about 80°F in the summer and 70°F in the winter.

En contexto
VOCABULARIO

Roberto has experienced all kinds of weather in Minnesota and Puerto Rico. Take a look at the pictures in his scrapbook to understand the meaning of the words in blue. This will also help you answer the questions on the next page.

A ¿Qué tiempo hace en Minnesota? En el invierno hace mal tiempo. ¡Hace frío y hay mucha nieve! Cuando va a nevar, necesitas un gorro, una bufanda y un abrigo.

yo en el invierno
el gorro
la bufanda
el abrigo
la nieve

B Cuando va a llover, necesitas un paraguas. A la madre de Roberto le gusta caminar bajo la lluvia con su paraguas de cuadros.

mamá con paraguas
el paraguas
de cuadros

C En Puerto Rico, en el verano hace calor. Cuando hay sol, es divertido ir a la playa y nadar en el mar.

mi primo en el verano
el mar
el traje de baño
la playa

214 doscientos catorce
Unidad 3

Classroom Community

TPR Bring in assorted items and pictures related to **el invierno, el verano, cuando va a llover,** and **el bosque tropical.** Designate one area of the classroom for each of these situations. As you show the items and pictures to the class and name them, have various students repeat the names, say where they belong, and then place them in the appropriate area.

Learning Scenario Divide the class into 4 groups. Provide students with clothing catalogs. Have each group cut out and make a poster of clothing for one of the following situations: **en el invierno, en el verano, cuando va a llover, cuando estás en el bosque tropical.** Each group must then present their scenario and what people would wear.

las gafas de sol

E Estas gafas de sol son para el verano.

mi amiga María

con rayas

F En el bosque tropical El Yunque, hay árboles, plantas y flores muy interesantes.

el bosque

la planta   la flor

EL YUNQUE

el árbol

D La chica lleva una camisa con rayas. Es verano.

EL TIEMPO

el sol

Temperaturas
9 de marzo

	ALTA	BAJA
San Juan	87°	73°
Minneapolis	30°	15°

Preguntas personales

1. ¿Usas un paraguas cuando llueve?
2. En el lugar donde vives, ¿hace calor o hace frío en el invierno?
3. ¿Prefieres ropa de cuadros o ropa con rayas?
4. ¿Qué ropa llevas en el invierno?
5. ¿Qué hay en un bosque tropical?

doscientos quince
Etapa 3   **215**

Teaching Suggestions
Introducing Vocabulary

- Have students look at pages 214–215. Use OHT 93 and 94 and Audiocassette 9A / CD 9 to present the vocabulary.
- Ask the Comprehension Questions below in order of yes/no (questions 1–3), either/or (questions 4–6), and simple word or phrase (questions 7–10). Expand by adding similar questions.
- Use the TPR activity to reinforce the meaning of individual words.
- Use the video vocabulary presentation for review and reinforcement.

Comprehension Questions

1. En Minnesota, ¿hace buen tiempo en el invierno? (No.)
2. ¿Hace frío y hay mucha nieve? (Sí.)
3. Cuando va a llover, ¿necesitas un paraguas? (Sí.)
4. ¿A la madre de Roberto le gusta caminar bajo la lluvia o prefiere estar en casa? (caminar bajo la lluvia)
5. ¿Es divertido ir a la playa en Puerto Rico cuando llueve o cuando hay sol? (cuando hay sol)
6. ¿La chica en la foto D lleva pantalones con rayas o una camisa con rayas? (una camisa con rayas)
7. ¿Qué hay en el bosque tropical? (Hay árboles, plantas y flores.)
8. ¿Cómo se llama el bosque tropical de Puerto Rico? (El Yunque)
9. ¿Cuál es la temperatura más alta en San Juan el 9 de marzo? (87°)
10. ¿Qué artículo usamos mucho en el verano? (las gafas de sol)

Teaching All Students

Challenge Use the **Preguntas personales** as a basis for students to create surveys. They may add additional questions. Students then conduct their surveys with at least 5 people and compile the results.

Native Speakers Ask students to describe the weather in their home countries. How does the weather influence lifestyle? Are there severe weather conditions that require safety precautions?

Multiple Intelligences

Interpersonal In pairs, have students draw on a card a representation of their favorite weather and an item that they would wear/use. Then they tell their partner in one sentence about the card.

Verbal Working in pairs, have students re-read each section of the **En contexto.** Have them ask each other one question about each section.

Block Schedule

Change of Pace Have students sign up for the day when they will be the weather forecaster. Each day a different student will start class with the day, date, season, temperature, and weather report.

Teaching Resource Options

Print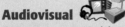

Más práctica Workbook PE, pp. 73–76
Para hispanohablantes Workbook PE, pp. 73–74
Block Scheduling Copymasters
Unit 3 Resource Book
  Más práctica Workbook TE, pp. 103–106
  Para hispanohablantes Workbook TE, pp. 111–112
  Video Activities, pp. 125–126
  Videoscript, p. 128
  Audioscript, p. 131
  Audioscript *Para hispanohablantes*, p. 131

Audiovisual

OHT 97, 98, 99 (Quick Start)
Audio Program Cassette 9A / CD 9
Audio *Para hispanohablantes* Cassette 9A / CD 9
Video Program Videotape 3 / Videodisc 2A

Search Chapter 7, Play to 8
U3E3 • En vivo (Dialog)

Technology

Intrigas y aventuras CD-ROM, Disc 1

🔔 Quick Start Review

♻ Clothing

Use OHT 99 or write on board:
List 2 things associated with each situation:

1. en el invierno
2. en el verano
3. cuando va a llover
4. en el bosque tropical
5. en el desierto

Answers
Answers will vary. Answers could include:
1. el abrigo, la nieve
2. el traje de baño, la playa
3. el paraguas, la lluvia
4. la camiseta, el árbol
5. las gafas de sol, el sombrero

Gestures

Point out the gestures used in pictures 1, 3, 4, and 7. Have students read and act out the dialog for those pictures, emphasizing the gestures. Point out the importance of nonverbal expression in conversation.

En vivo

 DIÁLOGO

 Diana
 Roberto
 Ignacio

¡Qué tiempo!

ROPA DE INVIERNO

PARA ESCUCHAR • STRATEGY: LISTENING

Sort and categorize details Minneapolis and San Juan are a world apart, yet in at least one way they are similar. How? What does Roberto say? What differences are mentioned? Use a Venn diagram to sort these details.

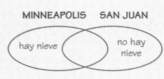

MINNEAPOLIS   SAN JUAN

hay nieve   no hay nieve

1 ▶ Diana: ¡Qué mona tu bufanda! Me gusta tu gorro. ¿Hace mucho frío en Minneapolis?

ROPA

5 ▶ Diana: ¡Ay! Pues, ya tienes ropa de verano.
Roberto: Claro que la tengo. ¡En Minneapolis no es invierno todo el año!

6 ▶ Roberto: ¡Qué día bonito! Hace muy buen tiempo. Tengo ganas de ir a El Yunque.
Diana: Perfecto, porque el proyecto de Ignacio para el concurso es sobre el bosque tropical. Y está preparando el proyecto este mes.

7 ▶ Ignacio: Sí, y necesito sacar fotos del bosque. Y las quiero sacar hoy mismo.
Roberto: Tengo suerte, ¿no lo creen?
Diana: Creo que tienes mucha suerte.
Ignacio: Tengo prisa. Es buena hora para sacar fotos porque hay sol.

216 doscientos dieciséis
Unidad 3

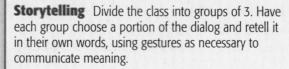

Classroom Community

Storytelling Divide the class into groups of 3. Have each group choose a portion of the dialog and retell it in their own words, using gestures as necessary to communicate meaning.

Paired Activity Have students work in pairs to find all the verbs used in the dialog and list them. If the verb is in the conjugated form, they should also give the infinitive.

Teaching Suggestions
Presenting the Dialog

- Prepare students for listening by focusing on the dialog context using yes/no or either/or questions. Reintroduce the characters and the setting: **¿Están en Minnesota o Puerto Rico? ¿La chica se llama Diana? ¿El chico de Minnesota se llama Roberto? ¿Cómo se llama el otro chico, Francisco o Ignacio?**
- Use the video, audiocassette, or CD to present the dialog. The expanded dialog on video offers additional listening practice opportunities.

Video Synopsis

- Roberto and his friends discuss the weather in Minnesota. Afterwards, they go to visit **El Yunque.** For a complete transcript of the video dialog, see p. 211B.

2 ▶ Roberto: En el invierno, sí, ¡hace mucho frío! ¡Brrr! Tengo frío cuando pienso en los inviernos de Minneapolis.

3 ▶ Diana: ¿Nieva mucho?
Roberto: Bueno, en el invierno, nieva casi todas las semanas. Pero en verano, es como aquí. Hace mucho calor.

4 ▶ Ignacio: ¿Qué vas a hacer con toda esta ropa de invierno? Aquí nadie la necesita.
Roberto: Tienes razón. Voy a necesitar shorts, trajes de baño y gafas de sol.

8 ▶ Ignacio: ¡Qué bonito! Los árboles, las flores…
Roberto: Sí, muy bonita.
Ignacio: No es como Minneapolis, ¿verdad, Roberto?
Roberto: Tienes razón, Ignacio.

9 ▶ Ignacio: Mi proyecto va a estar bien chévere, ¿no creen?… ¿No creen?…
…Sí, Ignacio, creo que tu proyecto va a ser muy impresionante.

10 ▶ Ignacio: ¡Está lloviendo! ¡Y no tengo paraguas!
Roberto: Te estamos esperando, hombre.

doscientos diecisiete
Etapa 3 | **217**

Comprehension Questions

1. ¿A Diana le gustan la bufanda y el gorro de Roberto? (Sí.)
2. ¿Hace calor en invierno en Minneapolis? (No.)
3. ¿A Roberto le gustan mucho los inviernos de Minneapolis? (No.)
4. ¿Nieva mucho o poco en Minnesota? (mucho)
5. ¿Hace frío o calor en verano en Minnesota? (Hace calor.)
6. En Puerto Rico, ¿usan la ropa de verano o la ropa de invierno? (la ropa de verano)
7. ¿Qué necesita Roberto para el verano? (shorts, trajes de baño y gafas de sol)
8. ¿Adónde quiere ir Roberto? (a El Yunque)
9. ¿Por qué quiere ir Ignacio también? (Necesita sacar fotos del bosque.)
10. ¿Qué tiempo hace en El Yunque? (Hay sol. Más tarde está lloviendo.)

◼ Block Schedule

Retention After making the Venn diagram, have students write 3–5 complete sentences comparing the two cities. They can share them with a partner or compile them as a class. (For additional activities, see **Block Scheduling Copymasters.**)

Teaching All Students

Extra Help Read 8–10 sentences from the dialog. Have students identify the speaker as Roberto, Diana, or Ignacio.

Native Speakers Ask students to describe modes of dress for different situations/social settings for a man, a woman, a male teenager, and a female teenager in their home country.

Multiple Intelligences

Visual Have students draw a caricature or cartoon of one of the dialog pictures with speech bubbles or a caption.

Verbal Have students look at each picture of the dialog. Ask them to provide 1–3 statements about each. Compile all the statements to form a descriptive passage of the dialog.

OBJECTIVES
- Describe the weather
- Discuss clothing and accessories
- State an opinion
- Describe how you feel
- Say what is happening

En acción
VOCABULARIO Y GRAMÁTICA

¿Qué lugar?

Escuchar ¿Qué lugar describe cada oración,
Puerto Rico o Minnesota? ¡Ojo! Algunas
oraciones describen los dos lugares. *(Hint: Which
place is described?)*

1. En el invierno, hace mucho frío.
2. La gente no necesita ropa de invierno.
3. Nieva casi todas las semanas en el invierno.
4. En el verano, hace calor.
5. Necesitas shorts, traje de baño y gafas
   de sol.
6. Hay un bosque tropical.

Oraciones revueltas

Escuchar Completa las siguientes oraciones
según el diálogo, combinando frases de las
dos columnas. *(Hint: Complete the sentences by matching.)*

1. El proyecto de Ignacio
   para el concurso es
   sobre _____.
2. Tengo frío cuando
   pienso en _____.
3. ¿Qué vas a hacer
   con _____?
4. Es buena hora
   para _____.

a. sacar fotos
b. toda esta ropa
   de invierno
c. el bosque
   tropical
d. los inviernos de
   Minneapolis

♻ ¿Qué hay en la maleta?

Hablar/Escribir Describe lo que hay en la maleta
de Roberto. *(Hint: Describe what's in Roberto's suitcase.)*

modelo

Hay un abrigo marrón.

TAMBIÉN SE DICE

There are different ways to say *cute*.

- **bonito:** Mexico and other countries
- **mono(a):** Puerto Rico, Spain
- **lindo(a):** many countries

Classroom Management

Time Saver Focus on a quick whole-class review of
the dialog. Begin by saying: **Ahora Roberto vive en
Puerto Rico.** Ask students to recount the series of
events by adding sentences in turn about what
happened next. Alternate: Give a short listening
comprehension quiz in True/False format.

Peer Review Divide the class into 4–8 groups.
Ask each group to complete 1–2 descriptions from
Actividad 4. All members of the group are responsible
for the accuracy of their sentences. Then have each
group share its description. Have the rest of the class
evaluate its accuracy.

- Use weather expressions
- Use **tener** expressions
- Use direct object pronouns
- Use present progressive

Vocabulario

Las estaciones

el verano

el otoño

tomar el sol

el viento

la montaña

el desierto

el broncedor

los shorts

el río

el invierno

la primavera

el lago

la tormenta

cero grados

el impermeable

¿Qué actividad te gusta hacer en cada estación?

ACTIVIDAD **4**

¡Todos van de vacaciones!

Hablar/Escribir Todas las personas van de vacaciones. Explica adónde van, usando elementos de cada columna. ¿Qué van a llevar y qué van a hacer? *(Hint: Explain where people are vacationing, what they're taking with them, and what they'll be doing.)*

modelo

Yo voy a la playa en el verano.

Voy a llevar un traje de baño, gafas de sol y bronceador para tomar el sol.

Ignacio y Diana
Roberto
tú
yo
mi amigo(a)
mis amigos
mi familia y yo

la playa
las montañas
el desierto
el lago
el bosque tropical
¿otro lugar?

primavera
verano
otoño
invierno

la bufanda
el traje de baño
el paraguas
las gafas de sol
el abrigo
el bronceador
los shorts
el gorro
el impermeable

tomar el sol
andar en bicicleta
nadar
jugar a (¿qué deporte?)
esquiar
patinar sobre hielo
descansar
ver las plantas y las flores
sacar fotos
¿?

doscientos diecinueve
Etapa 3 **219**

ACTIVIDAD **3** **Objective:** Transitional practice Clothing vocabulary

♻ **Hay**

Answers

1. Hay un abrigo marrón.
2. Hay una bufanda azul de cuadros.
3. Hay una gorra roja.
4. Hay un traje de baño con rayas negras y blancas.
5. Hay unos jeans.
6. Hay unas gafas de sol moradas.
7. Hay una camisa roja de cuadros.
8. Hay un suéter amarillo.
9. Hay unos zapatos marrones.
10. Hay una camiseta con rayas azules y blancas.
11. Hay un paraguas verde.

Teaching Suggestions
Reinforcing Las estaciones

After presenting the vocabulary for **Las estaciones**, name various articles of clothing. Have students say in what season they would most likely wear each article.

ACTIVIDAD **4** **Objective:** Transitional practice Seasons vocabulary

Answers will vary.

 Quick Wrap-up

Write the 4 seasons on the board. Have students choose their favorite one and provide 2–3 sentences, orally or in writing, to describe what they typically do during that season.

Teaching All Students

Extra Help Focus on reviewing vocabulary associated with the seasons. Have students brainstorm a list of known vocabulary (clothing, sports, other leisure activities, school activities, places) related to each one. This activity can be done in groups in either oral or written form, as a Round Table/Round Robin activity.

Multiple Intelligences
Verbal Have students describe what they will wear in one of the following situations: **Alaska en el invierno; Puerto Rico en el verano; California en la primavera; Vermont en el otoño.**

 Block Schedule

Variety Divide the class into small groups. Give each group a season. Groups must devise a visual (collage, poster, mural, diorama, brochure, etc.) to represent their season.

Teaching Resource Options

Print 📖

Más práctica Workbook PE, p. 77
Para hispanohablantes Workbook PE, p. 75
Block Scheduling Copymasters
Unit 3 Resource Book
  Más práctica Workbook TE, p. 107
  Para hispanohablantes Workbook TE, p. 113
  Audioscript, pp. 131–132
  Audioscript *Para hispanohablantes*, pp. 131–132

Audiovisual 🎧

OHT 100 (Quick Start)
Audio Program Cassettes 9A, 9B / CD 9
Audio *Para hispanohablantes*
  Cassette 9A / CD 9

Technology 💻

Intrigas y aventuras CD-ROM, Disc 1

 Objective: Transitional practice Seasons vocabulary

Answers

1. Las gafas de sol van en la sección de verano.
2. Los shorts van en la sección de verano.
3. El bronceador va en la sección de verano.
4. Los abrigos van en la sección de invierno (otoño/primavera).
5. Los trajes de baño van en la sección de verano.
6. Los paraguas van en la sección de primavera (otoño).
7. Los gorros van en la sección de invierno.
8. Las bufandas van en la sección de invierno.
9. Los impermeables van en la sección de primavera (otoño).

🔔 Quick Start Review

♻ **Seasons/sports**

Use OHT 100 or write on the board: List the sports people would usually participate in during each season.

1. el verano   3. el invierno
2. el otoño   4. la primavera

Answers See p. 211B.

Teaching Suggestions
Teaching Describing the Weather

Begin by asking yes/no or either/or questions. As a final step, use flashcards of the weather expressions and have students form sentences using each one.

ACTIVIDAD 5

¡Organízalos!

Escribir Trabajas en una tienda. Organiza los artículos según la estación. *(Hint: Group the articles according to the season.)*

modelo

Las gorras van en la sección de verano.

LA PRIMAVERA   EL OTOÑO

EL VERANO   EL INVIERNO

1.

2.

3.

4.

5.

6.

7.

8.

9.

220 doscientos veinte
Unidad 3

GRAMÁTICA — Describing the Weather

▶ To talk about weather, you will often use the verb **hacer**.

¿Qué tiempo hace?	**Hace...**	**(mucho) calor.**
What's it like out?	*It's...*	*(very) hot.*
		(mucho) frío.
		(very) cold.
		(mucho) sol.
		(very) sunny.
		(mucho) viento.
		(very) windy.
		(muy) buen tiempo.
		(very) nice outside.
		(muy) mal tiempo.
		(very) bad outside.
		(mucho) fresco.
		(very) cool.

Diana asks Roberto:

—¿**Hace mucho frío** en Minneapolis?
*Is it **very cold** in Minneapolis?*

Roberto replies:

—En el invierno, sí, ¡**hace mucho frío**!
*In the winter, yes, **it's very cold**!*

▶ When you talk about wind or sun, you can also use **hay**.

Hay...	**(mucho) sol.**
It's...	*(very) sunny.*
	(mucho) viento.
	(very) windy.

▶ Use the verbs **llover** and **nevar** to say it is raining or snowing. They are verbs with stem changes, just like **jugar** and **pensar**.

Llueve mucho en el bosque tropical.
*It **rains** a lot in the tropical rain forest.*

Nieva mucho en Minnesota.
*It **snows** a lot in Minnesota.*

▶ To say that it's cloudy, use the expression **está nublado**.

No vamos a la playa porque **está nublado**.
*We're not going to the beach because **it's cloudy**.*

Classroom Community

TPR Have students act out the weather conditions. Classmates guess what they are representing.

Learning Scenario Have students write and perform skits in which they try to convince a friend from a different country/region to come and visit. They should describe the great weather and weather-related activities.

Portfolio Have students adapt and expand on **Actividad 7** to provide a description of their region during the season of their choice.

Rubric A = 13–15 pts. B = 10–12 pts. C = 7–9 pts. D = 4–6 pts. F = < 4 pts.

Writing criteria	Scale
Vocabulary use	1 2 3 4 5
Logical sentence order	1 2 3 4 5
Grammar/spelling accuracy	1 2 3 4 5

El tiempo

Escuchar Escucha las descripciones. ¿Qué estación es? Escoge el número de la oración que corresponde a cada estación. *(Hint: Match the number of the description with the season.)*

a. la primavera   **c.** el otoño
b. el verano   **d.** el invierno

¿Qué tiempo hace?

Hablar/Escribir Usa un mínimo de dos expresiones para describir el tiempo en cada dibujo. ¿Qué estación es? *(Hint: Describe the weather and season.)*

modelo

Hace frío. Hay sol. Es invierno.

■ **MÁS PRÁCTICA** *cuaderno* p. 77
■ **PARA HISPANOHABLANTES** *cuaderno* p. 75

♻ ¿Qué prefieres hacer?

Hablar Trabaja con otro(a) estudiante para explicar tus preferencias. Cambien de papel. *(Hint: Take turns giving your preferences.)*

modelo

preferir / hacer frío: ¿ir a la playa o patinar sobre hielo?

Estudiante A: ¿Qué **prefieres** hacer cuando **hace frío**, ir a la playa o patinar sobre hielo?

Estudiante B: Prefiero **patinar sobre hielo.**

1. querer / hay sol: ¿jugar al tenis o ver la televisión?
2. preferir / hacer mucho calor: ¿nadar en el mar o cuidar a tu hermano?
3. preferir / llover: ¿ir a la montaña o tocar la guitarra?
4. querer / nevar: ¿esquiar en las montañas o correr en el parque?
5. querer / hacer buen tiempo: ¿ir al cine o sacar fotos en el parque?
6. preferir / hacer mal tiempo: ¿ir de compras o pasear por el parque?
7. ¿?

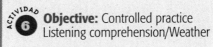

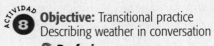

Objective: Controlled practice
Listening comprehension/Weather

Answers (See script p. 211B.)
1. a   2. d   3. c   4. b

Objective: Controlled practice
Describing weather

Answers
1. Hace/Hay (mucho) viento. Hace fresco. Hace buen tiempo. Es otoño.
2. Hace (mucho) calor. Hace/Hay (mucho) sol. Hace (muy) buen tiempo. Es verano.
3. Hace (muy) mal tiempo. Hace fresco. Llueve. Está nublado. Es primavera.
4. Hace/Hay (mucho) viento. Hace fresco. Hace buen tiempo. Es otoño.

Objective: Transitional practice
Describing weather in conversation
♻ **Preferir**

Answers
1. A: ¿Qué quieres hacer cuando hay sol, jugar al tenis o ver la televisión?
   B: Quiero jugar al tenis [ver la televisión].
2. A: ¿Qué prefieres hacer cuando hace mucho calor, nadar en el mar o cuidar a tu hermano?
   B: Prefiero nadar en el mar [cuidar a mi hermano].
3. A: ¿Qué prefieres hacer cuando llueve, ir a la montaña o tocar la guitarra?
   B: Prefiero tocar la guitarra [ir a la montaña].
4. A: ¿Qué quieres hacer cuando nieva, esquiar en las montañas o correr en el parque?
   B: Quiero esquiar en las montañas [correr en el parque].
5. A: ¿Qué quieres hacer cuando hace buen tiempo, ir al cine o sacar fotos en el parque?
   B: Quiero sacar fotos en el parque [ir al cine].
6. A: ¿Qué prefieres hacer cuando hace mal tiempo, ir de compras o pasear por el parque?
   B: Prefiero ir de compras [pasear por el parque].
7. *Answers will vary.*

■ Block Schedule

Change of Pace Using paper plates, have students divide their plates into 8 sections. They should decorate each section with a weather condition and a person wearing appropriate clothing. Then have them attach a spinner. Use the weather plates for practice and review. Students move the spinner and then describe what is happening on the spot where the spinner lands. Or other students may ask questions (**¿Qué tiempo hace? ¿Qué lleva la chica?**). (For additional activities, see **Block Scheduling Copymasters.**)

Teaching All Students

Extra Help Display a 12-month calendar. Provide students with adhesive buttons with pictures and labels for the different weather conditions. Have students place the buttons at various points on the calendar, depending on the weather in your area.

Native Speakers Have students watch a weather report in Spanish and list 5–10 new vocabulary terms to teach to the class.

Multiple Intelligences

Intrapersonal Have students list the various weather conditions. Then, next to each one, they should write how they feel. For example: **Llueve. Estoy cansado(a).**

Musical/Rhythmic Have students devise sound effects to represent different seasons and weather conditions.

Teaching Resource Options

Print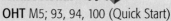

Más práctica Workbook PE, p. 78
Para hispanohablantes Workbook PE, p. 76
Block Scheduling Copymasters
Unit 3 Resource Book
  Más práctica Workbook TE, p. 108
  Para hispanohablantes Workbook TE, p. 114

Audiovisual

OHT M5; 93, 94, 100 (Quick Start)

Technology

Intrigas y aventuras CD-ROM, Disc 1

Teaching Suggestions
Reinforcing vocabulary

• Before assigning **Actividad 9** for pair work, use OHT 93 and 94 to review clothing vocabulary.
• Display a world map or OHT M5 in the classroom. After students read **Actividad 10**, have them locate each of the cities listed.

 9 Objective: Open-ended practice Describing weather and clothing in conversation

Answers will vary.

Alternate: You may wish to introduce the following expressions:
  —¿Cómo te vas a **vestir** hoy?
  —¿Qué te vas a **poner**?

 10 Objective: Open-ended practice Describing weather in conversation

Answers will vary.

Culture Highlights

● **PUERTO RICO** Due to its beautiful scenery and tropical climate, Puerto Rico is also known as **Isla del encanto.** Each year thousands of tourists visit Puerto Rico, bringing in $1.4 billion annually.

 ACTIVIDAD 9

♻ ¿Qué vas a llevar?

> **PARA CONVERSAR**
> **STRATEGY: SPEAKING**
> **Say how often** Generalize by saying how often you wear an item in this weather. **(Siempre / A veces) llevo shorts cuando hace calor.**

Hablar La ropa que llevas depende mucho del tiempo. Trabaja con otro(a) estudiante para explicar qué vas a llevar según el tiempo. *(Hint: Explain what you'll be wearing.)*

modelo

hace calor

Estudiante A: *Hace calor. ¿Qué vas a llevar hoy?*

Estudiante B: *Voy a llevar una camiseta y shorts. Siempre llevo shorts cuando hace calor.*

1. hace mucho frío
2. hace fresco
3. hace mucho calor
4. hay sol
5. llueve
6. ¿?

 **ACTIVIDAD 10**

El tiempo hoy

Hablar/Leer Tienes un periódico de San Juan. Tus amigos quieren saber qué tiempo hace en varias ciudades. Trabaja en un grupo de tres para hacer y contestar las preguntas sobre el tiempo. *(Hint: Say what the weather is in various places)*

¿Qué tiempo hace en…?
¿Cuál es la temperatura en…?
¿Hace buen/mal tiempo en…?
¿Dónde hace/hay…?

EL TIEMPO 4 de enero	Tiempo	Temperatura mínima	máxima
San Juan	sol	70°	82°
Buenos Aires	sol	75°	90°
Los Ángeles	lluvia	50°	64°
Madrid	nublado	37°	46°
México	nublado	48°	61°
Miami	sol	59°	70°
Nueva York	nieve	28°	32°
Quito	sol	50°	59°
San Antonio	viento	39°	51°

Clave: sol ☀ lluvia 🌧 nieve ❄ nublado ☁ viento 🌬

TAMBIÉN SE DICE There are different ways to say the following:

sunglasses
• **gafas de sol:** Puerto Rico, Spain, Ecuador
• **lentes de sol:** many countries

T-shirt
• **camiseta:** Puerto Rico and many countries
• **playera:** Mexico
• **polera:** Chile
• **remera:** Argentina

shorts
• **shorts:** Puerto Rico
• **pantalones cortos:** many countries
• **pantalonetas:** Colombia, Ecuador

Classroom Community

Storytelling Each student will state a sentence in order to form a short story entitled **Vamos de vacaciones.** The first student starts with one sentence about the things they need to pack for their vacation; each student adds one sentence. Alternate: **Vamos de vacaciones y vamos a llevar...** [article of clothing]. Each student must remember all previous articles and add a new one. This activity may also be done in groups.

Portfolio Have students write the date, the season, the weather, and what they are wearing. They might also write what they are going to do and wear after school.

Group Activity Divide the class into groups of 4. Have each group write an explanation for the difference between **tener** and **tener ganas de,** including two or three model sentences. Ask several groups to present their explanations to the class.

GRAMÁTICA

Special Expressions Using tener

 **¿RECUERDAS?** *p. 148* You learned to say that someone is hungry or thirsty using the verb *tener*. You also learned how to tell age using *tener*.

tener **hambre**

tener **sed**

tener... **años**

You can use the verb *tener* in many expressions.

tener... *to be...*		tener ganas de... *to feel like...*	**bailar** *dancing*
calor *hot*			**cantar** *singing*
cuidado *careful*			
frío *cold*			
miedo *afraid*	Roberto says:		
prisa *in a hurry*	—Tengo **suerte.** *I'm lucky.*		
razón *right*			
sueño *sleepy*	Ignacio says:		
suerte *lucky*	—Tengo **prisa.** *I'm in a hurry.*		

ACTIVIDAD 11 · Gramática

♻ Tiene ganas de...

Hablar/Escribir ¿Qué tienen ganas de hacer estas personas?
(Hint: What do they feel like doing?)

modelo

Diana: ir a la playa

Diana tiene ganas de ir a la playa.

1. nosotras: caminar
2. usted: ver la televisión
3. ellos: practicar deportes
4. tú: patinar
5. yo: ¿?

■ **MÁS PRÁCTICA** *cuaderno* p. 78

■ **PARA HISPANOHABLANTES** *cuaderno* p. 76

ACTIVIDAD 12

¿Qué pasa aquí?

Hablar ¿Cómo se sienten estas personas? Describe cada dibujo, usando una expresión con **tener**. *(Hint: Describe each picture with a tener expression.)*

1. la amiga de Roberto

2. su prima

3. su hermana

4. su vecino

5. su amigo

doscientos veintitrés
Etapa 3 **223**

Teaching Resource Options

Print

Más práctica Workbook PE, p. 79
Para hispanohablantes Workbook PE, p. 77
Unit 3 Resource Book
  Más práctica Workbook TE, p. 109
  Para hispanohablantes Workbook TE, p. 115
  Information Gap Activities, p. 119
  Audioscript, pp. 131–132
  Audioscript *Para hispanohablantes*, pp. 131–132

Audiovisual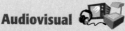

OHT 101 (Quick Start)
Audio Program Cassettes 9A, 9B / CD 9
Audio *Para hispanohablantes*
  Cassette 9A / CD 9

Technology

Intrigas y aventuras CD-ROM, Disc 1

ACTIVIDAD 13 **Objective:** Open-ended practice
Expressions using **tener**

Answers
1. A: ¿Cómo estás cuando corres a la escuela?
   B: ¡Tengo [prisa]!
2. A: ¿Cómo estás cuando juegas al tenis en el sol?
   B: ¡Tengo [calor]!
3. A: ¿Cómo estás cuando ves una película de horror?
   B: ¡Tengo [miedo]!
4. A: ¿Cómo estás cuando caminas en la nieve?
   B: ¡Tengo [frío]!
5. A: ¿Cómo estás cuando sabes hacer un examen?
   B: ¡Tengo [razón]!
6. A: ¿Cómo estás cuando ganas mucho?
   B: ¡Tengo [suerte]!

Quick Start Review

♻ **Gender**

Use OHT 101 or write on the board:
Write the definite article for each noun.

1. ___ abrigo   5. ___ bosque
2. ___ shorts   6. ___ bufanda
3. ___ paraguas   7. ___ árboles
4. ___ plantas   8. ___ bronceador

Answers *See p. 211B.*

ACTIVIDAD 13

Yo tengo...

Hablar Dile a otro(a) estudiante cómo te sientes en cada situación. Usa estas palabras: **calor, frío, miedo, prisa, razón, suerte.** Cambien de papel. *(Hint: Say how you feel.)*

modelo

no comer por muchas horas

Tú: *¿Cómo estás cuando **no comes por muchas horas**?*

Otro(a) estudiante: *¡Tengo hambre!*

1. correr a la escuela
2. jugar al tenis en el sol
3. ver una película de horror
4. caminar en la nieve
5. saber hacer un examen
6. ganar mucho

■ **MÁS COMUNICACIÓN** p. R9

NOTA CULTURAL

El Yunque is a rain forest. All rain forests have four zones. They are (from lowest to highest) the floor, the understory, the canopy, and the emergent layer. Some zones are more humid than others; some get more sunlight. Each is a habitat for different kinds of animals and plants.

GRAMÁTICA — Direct Object Pronouns

▶ The **direct object** in a sentence receives the action of the verb. Direct objects answer the question *who?* or *what?* Nouns used as **direct objects** can be replaced by **pronouns.**

Singular		Plural	
me	me	**nos**	us
te	you (familiar)	**os**	you (familiar)
lo → masculine	you (formal), him, it	**los** → masculine	you (formal), them
la → feminine	you (formal), her, it	**las** → feminine	you (formal), them

▶ The **direct object** noun is placed after the **conjugated verb**.

Diana says: Roberto answers:

replaced by

—Pues, ya **tienes ropa de verano.**   —Claro que **la tengo**.
*You already have **summer clothing**.*   *Of course I have **it**.*

▶ The direct object **pronoun** is placed directly **before** the **conjugated verb**.

▶ When an infinitive follows the conjugated verb, the direct object **pronoun** can be placed:

before the **conjugated verb** or **attached** to the **infinitive**

Ignacio says: *replaced by*

—Necesito sacar **fotos** del bosque. Y **las quiero sacar** hoy mismo.
*I need to take pictures of the rain forest. I want to take **them** today.*

He could also have said: *replaced by*

—Necesito sacar **fotos** del bosque. Y **quiero sacarlas** hoy mismo.

---

224 doscientos veinticuatro
Unidad 3

Classroom Community

Paired Activity Tell students to pretend that they are cleaning out their backpacks. As they remove each article, they ask their partners if they want it. The partner answers yes or no. For example: —¿Quieres mi libro de matemáticas? —Sí, lo quiero. *o* No, no lo quiero.

Cooperative Learning Have students work in groups of 4. Student 1 writes a verb **(tener)**. Student 2 writes a logical direct object noun **(perro)**. Student 3 writes a logical sentence **(Marta tiene un perro)**. Student 4 writes a follow-up sentence using a direct object pronoun **(Lo tiene en el parque hoy)**. The group evaluates the 2 sentences. Then Student 2 writes a verb and the activity continues.

¿Qué compran?

Hablar Habla con otro(a) estudiante para explicar qué compran. *(Hint: Say what they buy.)*

modelo

Roberto: el guante de béisbol

Tú: *¿Roberto compra el guante de béisbol?*

Otro(a) estudiante: *Sí, lo compra.*

1. Diana: los patines
2. Ignacio: la raqueta
3. Roberto: las pelotas
4. Diana: las pesas
5. Roberto: el casco
6. Roberto: los bates
7. Diana: la patineta
8. Diana: el traje de baño

La fiesta

Leer Diana y su amiga se escriben por Internet. Completa su conversación con el pronombre apropiado. *(Hint: Complete their conversation.)*

Diana: Sara, ¿Juan _____ invita a ti a su fiesta?

Sara: Sí, _____ invita. ¿A ustedes _____ invita?

Diana: Sí, _____ invita.

Sara: ¿Invita a Tina y a Graciela?

Diana: No, no _____ conoce.

Sara: ¿Y a Roberto?

Diana: Sí, _____ invita.

Sara: ¿Invita a Julio y a Fernando?

Diana: Sí, _____ invita. Son sus mejores amigos.

Sara: ¿Y a Mónica?

Diana: No, no _____ invita. Ella es su hermana.

■ **MÁS PRÁCTICA** *cuaderno p. 79*

■ **PARA HISPANOHABLANTES** *cuaderno p. 77*

Una visita

Hablar Tú y un(a) amigo(a) van a San Juan. Pregúntense qué van a llevar en el viaje. *(Hint: Tell your friend what you are taking on the trip.)*

modelo

tu traje de baño　　**Tú amigo(a):** *¿Vas a llevar tu traje de baño?*

　　　　　　　　Tú: *Sí, voy a llevarlo. o*
　　　　　　　　　　Sí, lo voy a llevar.

Nota

You learned that **llevar** means *to wear*. In this example, **llevar** means *to take along*.

1. tus gafas de sol
2. tu abrigo
3. tu bufanda
4. tus shorts
5. tu gorro
6. tu impermeable
7. tu raqueta de tenis
8. tus camisetas
9. tus libros de español
10. ¿?

¿Qué pasa?

Escuchar Escucha la conversación. Luego, decide si las oraciones son ciertas o falsas. Corrige las falsas. *(Hint: True or false?)*

1. Cuando llueve, Raúl ve la televisión.
2. Raúl lee revistas. Las lee cuando llueve.
3. María lleva paraguas. Lo lleva cuando llueve.
4. Raúl necesita gafas de sol para ir a la playa.
5. María tiene bronceador. Va a llevarlo a la playa.

doscientos veinticinco
Etapa 3　**225**

UNIDAD 3 Etapa 3
Vocabulary/Grammar

Teaching Suggestions
Teaching Direct Object Pronouns
Make statements using direct object nouns. State the object in a whisper so that students can ask *¿Qué...?* For example: Quiero [la revista]. Necesito [las fotos]. Students ask: *¿Qué quiere Ud.? ¿Qué necesita Ud.?* Tell students that the "missing word" is a direct object noun. Point out that when you don't want to repeat the word, you substitute it with a pronoun.

14 Objective: Controlled practice
Direct object pronouns in conversation
♻ Sports equipment vocabulary

Answers
1. A: ¿Diana compra los patines? / B: Sí, los compra.　2. A: ¿Ignacio compra la raqueta? / B: Sí, la compra.　3. A: ¿Roberto compra las pelotas? / B: Sí, las compra.　4. A: ¿Diana compra las pesas? / B: Sí, las compra.　5. A: ¿Roberto compra el casco? / B: Sí, lo compra.
6. A: ¿Roberto compra los bates? / B: Sí, los compra.　7. A: ¿Diana compra la patineta? / B: Sí, la compra.　8. A: ¿Diana compra el traje de baño? / B: Sí, lo compra.

15 Objective: Controlled practice
Direct object pronouns

Answers
te / me / los / nos / las / lo / los / la

16 Objective: Transitional practice
Direct object pronouns in conversation

Answers
1. A: ¿Vas a llevar tus gafas de sol? / B: Sí, voy a llevarlas. *o* Sí, las voy a llevar.　2. A: ¿Vas a llevar tu abrigo? / B: No, no voy a llevarlo. *o* No, no lo voy a llevar.　3. A: ¿Vas a llevar tu bufanda? / B: No, no voy a llevarla. *o* No, no la voy a llevar.
4. A: ¿Vas a llevar tus shorts? / B: Sí, voy a llevarlos. *o* Sí, los voy a llevar.　5. A: ¿Vas a llevar tu gorro? / B: No, no voy a llevarlo. *o* No, no lo voy a llevar.
6. A: ¿Vas a llevar tu impermeable? / B: Sí, voy a llevarlo. *o* Sí, lo voy a llevar.　7. A: ¿Vas a llevar tu raqueta de tenis? / B: Sí, voy a llevarla. *o* Sí, la voy a llevar.　8. A: ¿Vas a llevar tus camisetas? / B: Sí, voy a llevarlas. *o* Sí, las voy a llevar.
9. A: ¿Vas a llevar tus libros de español? / B: Sí, voy a llevarlos. *o* Sí, los voy a llevar.
10. *Answers will vary.*

17 Objective: Transitional practice
Listening comprehension/Direct object pronouns

Answers (See script p. 211B.)
1. Cierto.　2. Cierto.　3. Falso. No lo lleva cuando llueve.　4. Cierto.　5. Falso. Raúl va a llevarlo.

Teaching All Students

Extra Help Have students look back at the **Diálogo** on pp. 216–217 and find the instances of direct object pronouns. Then have them say what direct object nouns they replaced.

Multiple Intelligences
Kinesthetic For **Actividad 14**, have students make a flashcard for each part of the 2 sentences in each item: (A) subject / verb / d.o. noun, (B) **Sí** / d.o. pronoun / verb. Distribute each item's 6 cards to 6 different students. These students come to the front of the class and hold up the cards in scrambled order. Two other students come up and arrange the students/cards in the correct order.

Vocabulary/Grammar • UNIDAD 3 Etapa 3　225

Teaching Resource Options

Print

Más práctica Workbook PE, p. 80
Para hispanohablantes Workbook PE, p. 78
Block Scheduling Copymasters
Unit 3 Resource Book
  Más práctica Workbook TE, p. 110
  Para hispanohablantes Workbook TE, p. 116
  Information Gap Activities, pp. 120–121

Audiovisual
OHT 101 (Quick Start)

Technology
Intrigas y aventuras CD-ROM, Disc 1

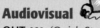 **Objective:** Open-ended practice
Direct object pronouns/**creer que sí/no**

Answers
1. A: Hace/Hay sol.
   B: ¿Necesito gafas de sol?
   A: Creo que sí. Las necesitas.
2. A: Llueve.
   B: ¿Necesito bronceador?
   A: Creo que no. No lo necesitas.
3./4. *Answers will vary.*

Additional cues:
frío / abrigo; nevar / el gorro

Juego
Answer: b.

 Quick Start Review

♻ Direct object pronouns

Use OHT 101 or write on the board:
Copy each question and underline the direct object. Then, answer the question using **Sí** + direct object pronoun.

1. ¿Tiene Ud. las revistas?
2. ¿Lleva tu madre la camisa con rayas?
3. ¿Compra María las pelotas?
4. ¿Buscan los muchachos los bates?
5. ¿Lee Ignacio el libro?
6. ¿Necesitas el bronceador?

Answers *See p. 211B.*

 ACTIVIDAD 18

Creo que...

Hablar Tienes que pensar en el tiempo. ¿Qué necesitas llevar? Cambien de papel. *(Hint: Say if you think so.)*

modelo

calor (chaqueta)

Tú: *Hace calor.*

Tu amigo(a): *¿Necesito chaqueta?*

Tú: *Creo que no. No la necesitas.*

Nota

Creer *(to think, to believe)* can be used to state an opinion.
Creo que sí.   Creo que no.

1. sol (gafas de sol)
2. llover (bronceador)
3. sol (¿?)
4. llover (¿?)

Juego

¿Qué describe la oración?
Hace buen tiempo.

a.

b.

 GRAMÁTICA

Saying What Is Happening: Present Progressive

When you want to say that an action is happening now, use the present progressive.

estoy **esperando**	estamos **esperando**
estás **esperando**	estáis **esperando**
está **esperando**	están **esperando**

Ignacio says: —¡Está **lloviendo**!
    It's raining!

Roberto replies: —Te estamos **esperando**…
    We're waiting for you…

▸ To form this tense, use:

the present tense of estar + **present participle**

▸ To form the present participle of a verb, drop the **ending** of the infinitive and add **-ando** or **-iendo**.

-ar verbs	esperar ~~ar~~	◂ ando	esperando
-er verbs	comer ~~er~~	◂ iendo	comiendo
-ir verbs	escribir ~~ir~~	◂ iendo	escribiendo

▸ When the **stem** of an **-er** or **-ir** verb ends in a vowel, change the **-iendo** to **-yendo**.

leer ⟶ le**y**endo
oír ⟶ o**y**endo
creer ⟶ cre**y**endo

---

226 doscientos veintiséis
Unidad 3

Classroom Community

Group Activity Have students prepare short skits about vacationing somewhere (the beach, the mountains, the lake, the rain forest). Each skit should include 3 verb anomalies–things that you would not see or do at that place. As students present their skits, the rest of the class writes down the mistakes and reports them at the end.

Paired Activity Have students bring in 3–4 pictures of people doing activities for which they have learned the vocabulary. In pairs, student discuss what is happening in each picture using the present progressive form. As a class, students display their pictures. They then describe just one picture. The rest of the class indicates which picture is being described. As a Time Saver, laminate and save the pictures in a class file for re-use.

ACTIVIDAD 19 Gramática

 ¡Están ocupados!

Hablar Todos están haciendo sus actividades favoritas. ¿Qué están haciendo? *(Hint: Say what everyone is doing.)*

1. Diana: comprar ropa
2. Roberto y su hermano: hablar
3. Luis: abrir un libro
4. Paco y yo: pasar un rato con los amigos
5. tú: bailar con tus amigos
6. nosotros: leer una novela
7. yo: ver la televisión
8. sus amigos: oír música
9. Carlos: escribir una carta
10. la familia: comer

■ **MÁS PRÁCTICA** *cuaderno* p. 80

■ **PARA HISPANOHABLANTES** *cuaderno* p. 78

ACTIVIDAD 20

¿Qué están haciendo?

Hablar Es sábado por la tarde. ¿Qué están haciendo estas personas? *(Hint: Say what everyone's doing.)*

1. tus padres
2. tú y tus amigos
3. tu hermano(a)
4. tu amigo(a)
5. tú

ACTIVIDAD 21

¡Qué buenas vacaciones!

Escribir Elena y su familia están de vacaciones en la playa. Describe lo que está pasando. Usa las preguntas como guía.
(Hint: Describe what is happening. Use the questions as a guide.)

la señora Álvarez
el señor Álvarez
Pablo
Ana
Elena
Marta

- ¿Qué tiempo hace?
- ¿Qué están haciendo las personas?
- ¿Cómo están? ¿Tienen frío? ¿Tienen hambre?

■ **MÁS COMUNICACIÓN** p. R9

Pronunciación

Trabalenguas

Pronunciación de la *j* y la *g* The letter **j** is pronounced somewhat like the *h* in the English word *hope*, but a bit stronger. Before the letters **e** and **i**, the Spanish **g** is pronounced just like the **j**. Listen to this tongue twister, then try it yourself to practice.

«Ji, ji, ji» ríen Javier y Jorge cuando miran a Jazmín la jirafa ingerir jarabe.

doscientos veintisiete
Etapa 3 | **227**

Teaching Suggestions
Teaching Saying What is Happening: Present Progressive

- Emphasize that the present progressive in Spanish is used only to say what is in progress at the moment. Whereas in English we might say *I'm studying in Ecuador next year,* in Spanish we must say **Voy a estudiar en Ecuador el año que viene.**
- Point out that nothing ever comes between **estar** and the present participle.

ACTIVIDAD 19 Objective: Controlled practice Present progressive

♻ **Estar**

Answers
1. Diana está comprando ropa.
2. Roberto y su hermano están hablando.
3. Luis está abriendo un libro.
4. Paco y yo estamos pasando un rato con los amigos.
5. Tú estás bailando con tus amigos.
6. Nosotros estamos leyendo una novela.
7. Yo estoy viendo la televisión.
8. Sus amigos están oyendo música.
9. Carlos está escribiendo una carta.
10. La familia está comiendo.

ACTIVIDAD 20 Objective: Transitional practice Present progressive

Answers will vary.

ACTIVIDAD 21 Objective: Open-ended practice Describing weather/expressions using **tener**/present progressive in writing

Answers will vary.

Dictation

After presenting the **Pronunciación**, have students close their books. Dictate the **Trabalenguas** in segments while students write it.

■ Block Schedule

Variety Have students use the present progressive to write a poem that includes 3 things that they are doing and 3 things that they are not doing. (For additional activities, see **Block Scheduling Copymasters**.)

Teaching All Students

Extra Help Give students a list of 10 regular -ar, -er, and -ir verbs. Students first write the present participle next to each verb. Then they write sentences for 5 of the verbs using the present progressive form.

Multiple Intelligences

Kinesthetic Have volunteers act out various activities using known vocabulary. The rest of the class uses the present progressive to say what the person is doing. As an alternate, have students choose verb infinitives from a container and act them out.

Teaching Resource Options

Print 📖

Block Scheduling Copymasters
Unit 3 Resource Book
  Audioscript, p. 133
  Audioscript *Para hispanohablantes*,
    p. 133

Audiovisual 📼

OHT 101 (Quick Start)
Audio Program Cassette 9A / CD 9
Audio *Para hispanohablantes*
  Cassette 9A / CD 9
Canciones Cassette / CD

🔔 Quick Start Review

♻ **El Yunque**

Use OHT 101 or write on the board:
Write 3 facts about **El Yunque.**

Answers
Answers will vary. Answers could include:
Está en Puerto Rico. / Es un bosque tropical. /
Hace calor. /Hay árboles, plantas y flores
interesantes. /Tiene cuatro zonas. / El loro
puertorriqueño vive aquí.

Teaching Suggestions

• **Prereading** Have students look at
the photo of the **coquí** and discuss
other popular images of frogs—in
stories, commercials, etc. How
common are frogs in your area?

• **Strategy: Distinguish details** Have
students complete the word web for
the **coquí.** You could also have them
do a similar web for **El Yunque.**

• **Reading** Have 13 student volunteers
read 1 of the 13 sentences in the
reading. Then sit back and have the
students take over the reading of the
selection.

• **Post-reading** Ask students to
provide a short description of the
coquí in the photo based on the
information they have just read.

Cross Cultural Connections

Strategy Have students compare a
national park in your region with **el
Bosque Nacional del Caribe.** They should
list information about geography, plants,
and animals. Are there any plants or
animals that are endangered species?

En voces
LECTURA

PARA LEER • STRATEGY: READING

Distinguish details Find out what **coquíes**
are. What features do they have? Use the
word web to describe a **coquí** and name
its identifying characteristics.

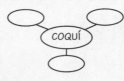

VEREDA NATURAL
BAÑO GRANDE
NATURE TRAIL

El coquí

No muy lejos de[1] San Juan está el Bosque
Nacional del Caribe. En este bosque tropical,
El Yunque, hay animales y plantas que no ves
en ninguna otra parte[2] del mundo. El coquí,
el animal más conocido de todo Puerto Rico,
vive protegido[3] en El Yunque.

[1] Not far from   [2] any other part   [3] protected

228 doscientos veintiocho
Unidad 3

Classroom Community

Group Activity Divide students into 13 groups and
have each group choose 1 one of the 13 sentences in
the reading. Each group writes the words from that
sentence on individual slips of paper. First, they mix up
the papers and then try to unscramble them. Finally, in
correct sentence order, have the groups come to the
front of the class and line up with the words in correct
order. The class therefore forms the complete reading.

Paired Activity Have pairs of students choose a
Spanish-speaking country. Then have them prepare a
short report on an animal or bird that is native to that
country. Pairs should present their reports to the class,
along with visuals.

*El Yunque, el Bosque
Nacional del Caribe*

Si visitas Puerto Rico, vas a ver imágenes del coquí en muchos lugares —en nombres de tiendas, artículos de promoción y libros. La tradición puertorriqueña es que si ves un coquí vas a tener mucha suerte. Y si quieres tener un bonito recuerdo⁹ de Puerto Rico es posible comprar un coquí verde de juguete¹⁰, símbolo de la isla.

---

⁹ souvenir   ¹⁰ toy

El coquí es una rana⁴ de tamaño⁵ pequeño que vive en los árboles. Los coquíes son de diferentes colores. Hay coquíes grises⁶, marrones, amarillos y verdes. Reciben su nombre por su canto⁷ característico. Hay 16 especies de coquíes en Puerto Rico, pero sólo dos producen el canto típico «coquí». Dos están en peligro⁸ de extinción. Casi todos los coquíes empiezan a cantar cuando llega la noche.

---

⁴ frog   ⁶ grey   ⁸ danger
⁵ size   ⁷ song

¿Comprendiste?

1. ¿Dónde vive el coquí?
2. ¿Qué es el coquí? ¿Por qué se llama coquí?
3. ¿Cómo es el coquí?
4. ¿Cuándo canta el coquí?
5. ¿Por qué es bueno ver un coquí?

¿Qué piensas?

¿Por qué piensas que dos especies de coquí están en peligro de extinción?

Hazlo tú

Estudia más sobre el coquí y dibuja o describe las plantas típicas que hay donde vive.

doscientos veintinueve
Etapa 3

229

Culture Highlights

● **EL BAÑO GRANDE** Another important attraction in **El Yunque** is **El Baño Grande,** a large man-made pool built by the Civilian Conservation Corps in the 1930s.

● **ANIMALES EN PUERTO RICO** No dangerous or poisonous wild animals are indigenous to Puerto Rico. The only potentially harmful creature is a large centipede, found in the sugarcane fields, whose bite is very painful.

Language Note

Point out the accent mark at the end of **coquí.** Explain that few nouns in Spanish end with an accented vowel. Another animal that ends with an accented vowel is **jabalí,** a wild boar.

Nouns ending in an accented vowel usually add **-es** to form the plural.

Supplementary Vocabulary

el renacuajo	tadpole
el sapo	toad
las verrugas	warts
el grillo	cricket
el chapulín }	grasshopper
el saltamontes }	

¿Comprendiste?

Answers

1. Vive en El Yunque.
2. El coquí es una rana. Recibe su nombre por su canto característico.
3. Es de tamaño pequeño. Hay coquíes grises, marrones, amarillos y verdes.
4. Canta cuando llega la noche.
5. La tradición puertorriqueña es que si ves un coquí vas a tener mucha suerte.

Block Schedule

Variety Have students write a similar piece about another animal of their own choosing. They should say where the animal is found, describe the weather conditions there, describe the animal's size and color, and say why they like the animal. (For additional activities, see **Block Scheduling Copymasters.**)

Teaching All Students

Extra Help In small groups, have students help each other figure out the meanings of the questions on p. 229. Then have them help each other by pointing out in the text where the answers are found.

Native Speakers Have students provide the names of various animals in Spanish. Categorize them as wild animals or pets. Have the native speakers lead the class in practicing the pronunciation of the new words.

Multiple Intelligences

Naturalist Ask students to find a place away from traffic where they can listen to the sounds of nature. They should write down what animals, insects, or birds they hear and look up the names in a Spanish dictionary. Have them present their findings to the class.

Teaching Resource Options

Print 📖

Unit 3 Resource Book
  Audioscript, p. 134
  Audioscript *Para hispanohablantes,*
    p. 134

Audiovisual 📻

Audio Program Cassette 9A / CD 9
Audio *Para hispanohablantes*
  Cassette 9A / CD 9
OHT 102 (Quick Start)
Video Program Videotape 3 / Videodisc
  2A

Search Chapter 8, Play to 9
U3E3 • En colores (Culture)

🔔 Quick Start Review

♻ Puerto Rico

Use OHT 102 or write on the board:
Write a list of as many items as
possible that you would pack for a
trip to Puerto Rico.

Answers
Answers will vary. Answers could include:
un traje de baño, unas gafas de sol, el
bronceador, unos shorts, unas camisetas,
un sombrero, una raqueta de tenis

Teaching Suggestions
Presenting Cultura y comparaciones

• Have students read the Connecting
  Cultures strategy and discuss.
• Ask students what parts of the
  reading particularly attract their
  attention. Do the photos make them
  want to visit Puerto Rico?
• Ask students if they have ever been
  to a place similar to Puerto Rico.
  What challenges might they expect in
  Puerto Rico that they wouldn't find
  traveling in their area of the country?
  What would they look forward to in
  Puerto Rico?

Reading Strategy

Remind students to look at the graphics
to predict the subject of the article. Based
on their observations, what do they think
is the topic of the cultural reading? Write
the list of possibilities on the board.

En colores
CULTURA Y COMPARACIONES

PARA CONOCERNOS
STRATEGY: CONNECTING CULTURES

Define travel and tourism Look at a travel brochure.
(Get one from a travel agency or hotel.) What
does it contain? What does it *not* contain? Do you
think there is a difference between being a *traveler*
and being a *tourist*? List the interests of each.
Explain your ideas.

Viajero	Turista

Una excursión por la isla

Roberto tiene ganas de
pasear por Puerto Rico
otra vez. Diana e Ignacio
lo llevan de excursión
por la isla. En la Oficina
de Turismo ven
este folleto[1].

----
[1] brochure

230 doscientos treinta
Unidad 3

Descubra la isla de Puerto Rico

¡La hija del mar y del sol!

El mar y Puerto Rico tienen una unión
fuerte. Las primeras personas de la
isla. los taínos. llegan en canoas.
Cristóbal Colón también llega a la isla
por el mar. Y por el mar Puerto Rico
sufre[2] ataques por muchos años.
Los españoles construyen[3] El Morro en
el siglo XV[4] como protección contra los
ingleses. los holandeses y los piratas.
Hoy una excursión por San Juan
siempre incluye[5] una visita a esta
gran fortaleza.

----
[2] suffers
[3] build
[4] 15th century
[5] includes
[6] waves
[7] national anthem
[8] indigenous. native
[9] land

Classroom Community

Group Activity Have students write and present
short skits where one student is a travel guide in Puerto
Rico and the others are tourists. The guide greets the
tourists, tells them about Puerto Rico, asks them what
they want to do, etc.

Storytelling Display a globe at the front of the
classroom. (A pie chart made from a paper plate with a
spinner can also be used.) Have students come up
one-by-one, close their eyes, spin the globe, then stop
it by putting a finger on it. They open their eyes and
name the country they are going to visit, what the weather
is probably like there, what they will wear, what they
might visit, and what activities they will participate in.

Puerto Rico: Diversión para todos

El himno nacional[7] de Puerto Rico, «La Borinqueña», habla de Borinquen, una palabra que viene del nombre indígena[8] de la isla. Sus palabras explican la relación entre la tierra[9], el mar y el sol.

> «Ésta es la linda tierra,
> que busco yo.
> Es Borinquen la hija,
> la hija del mar y el sol.»

Tanto para el turista como para el puertorriqueño, el mar ofrece muchas actividades. En las playas es posible practicar muchos deportes: nadar, practicar el surfing o esquiar. El surfing es muy popular. En Puerto Rico hay playas que tienen olas[6] grandes, donde hay competiciones internacionales.

¿Comprendiste?

1. ¿Cuál es el grupo que llega primero a Puerto Rico?
2. ¿De quiénes vienen los ataques contra los españoles de Puerto Rico?
3. ¿Cuáles son unos deportes populares en las playas de Puerto Rico?
4. ¿De qué deporte hacen competiciones internacionales?
5. En el himno nacional de Puerto Rico, ¿qué es Borinquen?

¿Qué piensas?

1. Si algún día vas a Puerto Rico, ¿qué vas a hacer? ¿Te gustaría visitar lugares históricos o pasar toda tu visita en la playa? ¿Por qué?
2. ¿Cómo imaginas tu vacación perfecta? ¿Adónde vas? ¿Qué tiempo hace?

Hazlo tú

¿Cuáles son los deportes más populares en tu comunidad? Trabaja con otro(a) estudiante para preparar un folleto sobre las atracciones de tu estado.

doscientos treinta y uno
Etapa 3 | **231**

☀ Culture Highlights

● **OTRAS ATRACCIONES DE PUERTO RICO** One tourist attraction in Puerto Rico is **Phosphorescent Bay,** a natural phenomenon off the southeast coast. There are millions of tiny organisms in the water that cause the bay to glow green at night.

Every year the town of Guayamo holds the **Paso Fino Horse Show.** This breed of horses is descended from the horses the Spanish brought with them in the 16th century. They are small in stature and are know for their graceful, flowing gait, even when galloping.

The **Arecibo Observatory,** run by Cornell University, has a reflector with a 1000-foot diameter. The first discovery of planets beyond our solar system was made here in 1992.

Cross Cultural Connections

Have students name popular sports that young people in your town participate in. Also name important attractions in your area or state. Have students make a Venn diagram to compare and contrast local activities and those shown in the reading.

Interdisciplinary Connection

Geography Have students create 3-D topographical maps of Puerto Rico. They can also decorate the maps with palm trees, people, animals, etc.

¿Comprendiste?

Answers
1. Los taínos llegan primero a Puerto Rico.
2. Los ataques vienen de los ingleses, los holandeses y los piratas.
3. nadar, practicar el surfing, esquiar
4. Hacen competiciones internacionales del surfing.
5. Borinquen es el nombre indígena de Puerto Rico.

▮ Block Schedule

Peer Teaching Have pairs of students work together to compile a list of the key words used in the reading. Then have them make flashcards of the words and quiz each other. In addition, they could work together to write original sentences using the words.

Teaching All Students

Extra Help In pairs, have students write 5–8 true/false statements about the reading. Then have them work with another pair and determine the validity of each other's statements.

Native Speakers Ask students to present a short report on the geography (vegetation, animals, climate zones, interesting attractions) of their home countries. They may also add some important historical facts.

Multiple Intelligences

Logical/Mathematical Have students research and present various statistics about Puerto Rico. For example: total population, population of San Juan, area in square miles, life expectancy of men and women, literacy rate, televisions per person, etc. They might also research comparable statistics for the U.S.

Teaching Resource Options

Print
Para hispanohablantes Workbook PE,
  pp. 79–80
Block Scheduling Copymasters
Unit 3 Resource Book
  Para hispanohablantes Workbook
  TE, pp. 117–118
  Information Gap Activities, p. 122
  Family Involvement, pp. 123–124
  Multiple Choice Test Questions,
  pp. 170–178

Audiovisual
OHT 102 (Quick Start)
Audio Program Testing Cassette T1 /
CD T1

Technology
Electronic Teacher Tools/Test
  Generator
Intrigas y aventuras CD-ROM, Disc 1

Quick Start Review

 Weather

Use OHT 102 or write on the board:
Write the probable weather for the
following places and months:

1. Nova Scotia, mayo
2. El Yunque, agosto
3. Chicago, enero
4. Colorado, octubre
5. México, D.F., junio

Answers
Answers will vary. Answers could include:
1. Hace fresco. Llueve.
2. Hace mucho calor. Llueve.
3. Hace mucho frío. Nieva. Hace/Hay viento.
4. Hace fresco. Hace/Hay viento.
5. Hace calor. Hace buen tiempo.

Teaching Suggestions
What Have Students Learned?

Have students look at the "Now you
can…" notes listed on the left side of
pages 232–233. Remind them to
review the material in the "To review"
notes before doing the activities or
taking the test.

ETAPA 3

Now you can...
- describe the weather.

To review
- weather expressions, see p. 220.

Now you can...
- describe the weather.
- discuss clothing and accessories.

To review
- direct object pronouns, see p. 224.

Now you can...
- state an opinion.

To review
- weather expressions, see p. 220.

En uso
REPASO Y MÁS COMUNICACIÓN

OBJECTIVES
- Describe the weather
- Discuss clothing and accessories
- State an opinion
- Describe how you feel
- Say what is happening

ACTIVIDAD 1 ¿Qué tiempo hace?

Estás leyendo el periódico. Explica qué tiempo hace en cada
lugar. *(Hint: Explain what the weather is like.)*

 1. Miami 92°   3.  Boston 31°   5. Portland 34°

2. San Juan 85°   4. Washington 67°   6. Los Ángeles 75°

ACTIVIDAD 2 ¿Cuándo lo usas?

Otro(a) estudiante quiere saber cuándo usas las siguientes cosas.
¿Qué le dices? Cambien de papel. *(Hint: Tell when you use the following items.)*

modelo

¿el traje de baño?: verano

Tú: *¿Cuándo usas **el traje de baño?***

Otro(a) estudiante: *Lo uso en el **verano** porque hace calor.*

1. ¿los shorts?: verano   3. ¿los suéteres?: otoño   5. ¿el paraguas?: primavera
2. ¿el gorro?: invierno   4. ¿la bufanda?: invierno   6. ¿las gafas de sol?: verano

ACTIVIDAD 3 Opiniones

¿Qué sabes de Puerto Rico? Expresa tu opinión. *(Hint: Express your opinion.)*

modelo

Hace mal tiempo todo el año.   *Hay playas bonitas.*
Creo que no.   *Creo que sí.*

1. En el invierno hay mucha nieve.   3. Cuando está nublado, los
2. En El Yunque hay plantas y   puertorriqueños toman el sol.
   animales muy interesantes.   4. El surfing es popular en Puerto Rico.

Classroom Community

Group Activity Divide the class into 5 groups.
Assign each group a "Now you can…/To review"
section. Have each group review the grammar and
vocabulary taught in that section and reteach it to the
class.

Portfolio Have students create a variation of the
drawing in **Actividad 5**. This time, the picture should
depict school or any other place. Label all people and
write what each person is doing.

Rubric A = 13–15 pts. B = 10–12 pts. C = 7–9 pts. D = 4–6 pts. F = < 4 pts.

Writing criteria	Scale
Clear detail	1 2 3 4 5
Vocabulary use	1 2 3 4 5
Originality/humor	1 2 3 4 5

ACTIVIDAD 4 Los problemas de Roberto

Roberto siempre tiene problemas. Descríbelos. *(Hint: Describe Roberto's problems.)*

calor   frío   ganas   **prisa**   sed

hambre   **miedo**   sueño   razón   suerte

1. Cuando Roberto tiene _____, nunca hay comida.
2. Roberto siempre tiene _____, pero siempre llega tarde.
3. Cuando hay una tormenta, Roberto tiene mucho _____.
4. En invierno en Minnesota, Roberto no lleva un abrigo y siempre tiene _____.
5. Cuando Roberto tiene _____ de nadar, siempre llueve.
6. Roberto tiene mucha _____, pero no hay agua.
7. Cuando camina en el desierto, Roberto tiene mucho _____.
8. Cuando Roberto participa en un concurso, nunca tiene _____.
9. Roberto piensa que 2 + 2 = 5. No tiene _____.
10. Cuando Roberto va a un concierto, siempre tiene _____.

ACTIVIDAD 5 ¡Está lloviendo!

La familia de Josefina, una amiga de Diana, está en casa. Según Josefina, ¿qué están haciendo ahora? *(Hint: What are they doing?)*

1. Emilio y yo
2. Dani y Pati
3. mi padre
4. yo
5. mi madre
6. Emilio

Now you can...
- describe how you feel.

To review
- **tener** expressions, see p. 223.

Now you can...
- say what is happening.

To review
- the present progressive, see p. 226.

ACTIVIDAD 1 Answers

1. Hay sol y hace mucho calor.
2. Está lloviendo. Hace calor.
3. Está nevando y hace frío.
4. Está nublado y hace fresco.
5. Hace viento y hace frío.
6. Hay sol y hace buen tiempo.

ACTIVIDAD 2 Answers

1. A: ¿Cuándo usas los shorts?
   B: Los uso en el verano porque [hace calor].
2. A: ¿Cuándo usas el gorro?
   B: Lo uso en el invierno porque [nieva].
3. A: ¿Cuándo usas los suéteres?
   B: Los uso en el otoño porque [hace fresco].
4. A: ¿Cuándo usas la bufanda?
   B: La uso en el invierno porque [hace viento].
5. A: ¿Cuándo usas el paraguas?
   B: Lo uso en la primavera porque [llueve].
6. A: ¿Cuándo usas las gafas de sol?
   B: Las uso en el verano porque [hay sol].

ACTIVIDAD 3 Answers

1. Creo que no.
2. Creo que sí.
3. Creo que no.
4. Creo que sí.

ACTIVIDAD 4 Answers

1. hambre
2. prisa
3. miedo
4. frío
5. ganas
6. sed
7. calor
8. suerte
9. razón
10. sueño

ACTIVIDAD 5 Answers

1. Emilio y yo estamos viendo la televisión.
2. Dani y Pati están haciendo la tarea.
3. Mi padre está leyendo el periódico.
4. Yo estoy bebiendo.
5. Mi madre está tocando el piano.
6. Emilio está comiendo una merienda.

Block Schedule

Variety Variety can be provided not only by changing the activity; it can be provided by changing the classroom set-up. Instead of having students sit in rows facing forward, have them turn their desks 90 degrees to face the students in the next row. Have them give activity responses to their new neighbors rather than to you. (For additional activities, see **Block Scheduling Copymasters**.)

Teaching All Students

Extra Help Modify **Actividad 2** for students having trouble with direct object pronouns. First have them write out just the questions and underline the direct object nouns. Then have them write the direct object pronoun over each noun. Finally, have them answer the questions using the pronouns.

Multiple Intelligences

Intrapersonal Have students pretend it's a rainy day and they are staying home. Have them make a sketch of their home, their family members, any visitors, etc. and describe what each person is doing.

Teaching Resource Options

Print

Unit 3 Resource Book
  Cooperative Quizzes, pp. 135–136
  Etapa Exam, Forms A and B,
    pp. 137–146
  Para hispanohablantes Etapa Exam,
    pp. 147–151
  Portfolio Assessment, pp. 152–153
  Unit 3 Comprehensive Test,
    pp. 154–161
  Para hispanohablantes Unit 3
    Comprehensive Test, pp. 162–169
  Midterm Test, pp. 179–186
  Multiple Choice Test Questions,
    pp. 170–178

Audiovisual

OHT 102 (Quick Start)
Audio Program Testing Cassette T1 /
  CD T1

Technology

Electronic Teacher Tools/Test
  Generator
www.mcdougallittell.com

ACTIVIDAD 6

Rubric: Speaking

Criteria	Scale	
Vocabulary use	1 2 3	A = 8–9 pts.
Sentence structure	1 2 3	B = 6–7 pts.
Ease, fluency	1 2 3	C = 4–5 pts.
		D = 3 pts.
		F = < 3 pts.

Community Connections

Ask students to look for various places where they might see the Celsius scale used in their community. For example: on thermometers, on signs that display the temperature, in the newspaper weather report, on food packages, etc.

ACTIVIDAD 6  ¿Adónde voy?

PARA CONVERSAR

STRATEGY: SPEAKING

Get specific information To find out someone's vacation plans ask questions about all the specifics. Ask about weather (**el tiempo**), clothing (**la ropa**), or activities (**actividades y deportes**) at their destination. The model shows you how.

Imagínate que vas a uno de estos lugares. Los otros estudiantes tienen que adivinar adónde vas. Contesta sus preguntas. *(Hint: Answer your classmates' questions as they try to guess where you are going.)*

el desierto
el bosque
  tropical
la playa en
  verano
las montañas
  en invierno
el lago en
  otoño

modelo

Otro(a): ¿Va a nevar?

Tú: No, no va a nevar.

Otro(a): ¿Vas a llevar el traje de baño?

Tú: Sí, voy a llevarlo.

Otro(a): ¿Vas a practicar el surfing?

Tú: Sí, voy a practicarlo.

Otro(a): ¿Vas a la playa?

Tú: Sí, voy a la playa.

ACTIVIDAD 7 Por teléfono

Estás de vacaciones. Hablas con tu amigo(a) por teléfono. Describe el tiempo que hace, cómo estás y lo que está haciendo tu familia en ese momento. *(Hint: Describe the weather, how you feel, and what your family is doing on your vacation.)*

ACTIVIDAD 8 *En tu propia voz*

ESCRITURA Tu amigo(a) puertorriqueño(a) viene a vivir con tu familia por un año. Escríbele una carta describiendo qué tiempo hace durante cada estación del año, la ropa que necesita llevar y las actividades que él o ella puede hacer en cada estación. *(Hint: Write your Puerto Rican friend a letter describing the weather and items he or she should bring when visiting.)*

En la primavera hace...

Para el frío, necesitas llevar...

En el verano hace...

Llueve mucho en...

CONEXIONES

Las ciencias The Fahrenheit temperature scale is used in Puerto Rico. However, most Spanish-speaking countries use the Celsius scale. On this scale, water freezes at 0° and boils at 100°. To convert, use these formulas.

$100°C \times 9/5 + 32 = 212°F$ $212°F - 32 \times 5/9 = 100°C$

Convert the temperatures in the chart and write what seasons they might represent. Explain the other weather conditions. Choose a location in the Spanish-speaking world. Find out its average temperature and weather conditions in each season.

C	F	Estación	Tiempo
0°			
10°			
	68°		
25°			
30°			
	95°		

Classroom Community

Paired Activity Have students research a Spanish-speaking country they would like to visit. They will need to find out the weather in each season and some typical activities/sports they can do. Then with their partners, they ask and answer questions similar to **Actividad 6**. Have students report to the class on the information they find.

Group Activity Have students work in groups of 3–4. The groups will modify **Actividad 8** by preparing a video that they will send along with the letter they wrote. The video should demonstrate some of the weather conditions, clothing, and activities mentioned in the letter.

En resumen

REPASO DE VOCABULARIO

DESCRIBING THE WEATHER

¿Qué tiempo hace?	What is the weather like?
Está nublado.	It is cloudy.
Hace…	It is…
buen tiempo	nice outside
calor	hot
fresco	cool
frío	cold
mal tiempo	bad outside
sol	sunny
viento	windy
Hay…	It's…
sol	sunny
viento	windy
el grado	degree
llover	to rain
la lluvia	rain
nevar	to snow
la nieve	snow
el sol	sun
la temperatura	temperature
el tiempo	weather
la tormenta	storm
el viento	wind

Seasons

las estaciones	seasons
el invierno	winter
el otoño	fall
la primavera	spring
el verano	summer

DESCRIBING HOW YOU FEEL

tener…	to be…
calor	hot
cuidado	careful
frío	cold
miedo	afraid
prisa	in a hurry
razón	right
sueño	sleepy
suerte	lucky
tener ganas de…	to feel like…

STATING AN OPINION

creer	to think, to believe
Creo que sí/no.	I think so. / I don't think so.

CLOTHING AND ACCESSORIES

Clothing

el abrigo	coat
la bufanda	scarf
el gorro	cap
el impermeable	raincoat
los shorts	shorts
el traje de baño	bathing suit

Styles

con rayas	striped
de cuadros	plaid, checked

Accessories

el bronceador	suntan lotion
las gafas de sol	sunglasses
el paraguas	umbrella

OTHER WORDS AND PHRASES

sacar fotos	to take pictures
tomar el sol	to sunbathe

Places

el bosque	forest
el desierto	desert
el lago	lake
el mar	sea
la montaña	mountain
la playa	beach
el río	river

Vegetation

el árbol	tree
la flor	flower
la planta	plant

Juego

Es julio. Hace frío y nieva mucho. Mucha gente esquía en las montañas. ¿En qué país están?

a. **México**

b. **Estados Unidos**

c. **Chile**

doscientos treinta y cinco
Etapa 3

235

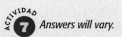

 7 Answers will vary.

 8 ✏️ **En tu propia voz**

Rubric: Writing

Criteria	Scale	
Vocabulary use	1 2 3 4 5	A = 14–15 pts.
Accuracy	1 2 3 4 5	B = 12–13 pts.
Creativity, appearance	1 2 3 4 5	C = 10–11 pts.
		D = 8–9 pts.
		F = < 8 pts.

Quick Start Review

♻️ Seasons/weather/clothing

Use OHT 102 or write on the board: Write down your favorite season. Then write one appropriate thing from each of the following categories:

- typical weather
- typical clothing
- typical activity/sport
- how you feel (expression using **tener**)

Answers See p. 211B.

Teaching Suggestions
Vocabulary Review

Have students name the 2 vocabulary words they find the easiest to remember and why. Then they should name the 2 words they find the hardest to remember. Have them create visuals to help them remember the meanings.

Supplementary Vocabulary

el esquí	skiing

Juego

Answer: c. Chile

▨ Block Schedule

Peer Teaching Have students work in pairs. One person reads 5 vocabulary words. The partner spells them and gives the meanings. Then students switch roles. Continue until all words are reviewed.

Teaching All Students

Extra Help Have students refer back to the **Diálogo**, pp. 216–217. First, have them just listen to the vocabulary words in context. Then, in their textbooks, have them point out where the words are used in each scene.

Multiple Intelligences

Visual Have students choose one of the groups of vocabulary words and make a collage to represent it. The collage can include pictures as well as illustrative depictions of the words themselves.

Teaching Resource Options

Print

Block Scheduling Copymasters

Audiovisual

OHT GO1–GO5, 102 (Quick Start)

Technology

Intrigas y aventuras CD-ROM, Disc 1
www.mcdougallittell.com

Quick Start Review

🔅 School activities

Use OHT 102 or write on the board:
List 10 things related to Puerto Rico.

Answers

Answers will vary. Answers could include:
pasta de guayaba, el loro puertorriqueño,
El Morro, Luis Muñoz Marín, los taínos, San
Juan, El Yunque, el coquí, la bomba y la plena,
la Fortaleza, el béisbol, Roberto Clemente

Teaching Strategy
Prewriting

• Discuss the importance of appealing
to the senses in writing. Have pairs of
students compile their lists from the
Quick Start Review.

• Explain to students why they do peer
editing of their writing projects. It is
more difficult to find errors in your
own writing because you tend to see
what you meant to write, rather than
what you actually did write.

• Remind students of the **PASS** list at
the beginning of the page: **P**urpose,
Audience, **S**ubject, **S**tructure. This
PASS key will help them complete a
well-structured assignment.

Post-writing

• Have students evaluate each other's
posters for attractiveness. Have them
suggest improvements if necessary.

UNIDAD

3

En tu propia voz
ESCRITURA

Una fiesta puertorriqueña

The Spanish classes at your school are sponsoring an all-school
celebration of Puerto Rican culture. It is your job to design the
posters. Use the student model as your guide.

Purpose: Invite others to an all-school party
Audience: Students and faculty
Subject: Puerto Rico
Structure: Poster-sized invitation

PARA ESCRIBIR • STRATEGY: WRITING

Appeal to the senses A well-constructed poster will entice people
to attend the party. One way to do so is to include details that
appeal to the senses: sight **(la vista)**, hearing **(el oído)**, touch **(el
tacto)**, taste **(el gusto)**, and smell **(el ofato)**.

Modelo del estudiante

The writer keeps herself focused by
generating categories (**fecha, hora,**
etc.) under which specific information
will be listed.

The writer appeals to **sight** when she
shows that students will "tour" Puerto
Rico via photos.

The writer addresses the students'
sense of **hearing** by mentioning music.

¿Estás aburrido?   ¿Te gusta comer la comida
de otros lugares?

¿Te gusta bailar?   ¿Tienes frío?

¿Quieres ir a una
isla tropical?

¡Te invitamos a una fiesta puertorriqueña!

FECHA: 12 de diciembre   HORA: 12:00   LUGAR: el auditorio
ACTIVIDADES: MENÚ:

• Conocer Puerto Rico: • Pasta de guayaba
ver fotos de las playas,   • Tostones
la capital, El Yunque   • Refrescos tropicales

• Escuchar música
puertorriqueña
• Comer cosas típicas
• Aprender a bailar
bomba y plena
• Participar en un juego
de trivia puertorriqueña

Puerto Rico es un lugar tropical. ¿Qué ropa vas a llevar?

The invitation appeals
to **taste** and **smell** by
mentioning various
Puerto Rican foods.

236

Classroom Community

Group Activity In small groups, have students
brainstorm a list of party-related items and activities.
Then have them determine which sense each item or
activity makes them think of.

Paired Activity Have pairs of students exchange
posters and check for language and spelling accuracy.
You might give extra credit points for errors detected.
As an alternative, you may wish to have pairs of
students develop posters together.

Estrategias para escribir

Antes de escribir...

With another student, discuss what you have learned about Puerto Rico. Use an observation chart to help organize your thoughts. Short on ideas? Review this unit, or use the library or Internet to find more information. Then bring the details together to make an exciting poster (and party). Be sure to include: date, time, and place of the party; activities; food and drink; suggested dress; decorations.

Una fiesta puertorriqueña

la vista	el oído	el tacto	el gusto	el olfato
el sol	música bomba y plena	la playa	tostones	las flores
el Viejo San Juan	el mar			la comida

Revisiones

Once you have a draft, share it with a partner. Then ask:

- *Can you tell where/when the party takes place?*
- *Does the poster appeal to the senses?*
- *Does it make you want to go to the party?*
- *Does it communicate the island theme?*

La versión final

Before you create the final draft of your invitation, look over your work with the following questions in mind:

- *Did I use gustar correctly?*

Try this: Underline each use of **gustar.** Check to make sure that it is used with an infinitive and the correct pronoun: **me, te, le, nos, os,** or **les.**

- *Are adjectives used correctly?*

Try this: Circle every noun/adjective combination. Check to make sure that each adjective matches the gender and number of the noun it modifies.

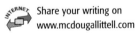
Share your writing on
www.mcdougallittell.com

237

Supplementary Vocabulary

oler	to smell
probar	to taste
oír	to hear
tocar	to touch
ver	to see

Rubric: Writing

Let students know ahead of time which elements of their writing you will be evaluating. A global evaluation is more helpful to students than a correction of every mistake made. Consider the following in scoring compositions:

	Appeal to senses
1	Appeals to only 1–2 senses
2	Appeals to 3–4 senses
3	Appeals to all 5 senses

	Details
1	Few details
2	Sufficient basic details
3	Clear and vivid detail

	Organization
1	Not well organized
2	Some organization
3	Strong organization

	Accuracy
1	Errors prevent comprehension
2	Some spelling and agreement errors throughout
3	Very few errors

Criteria	Scale	
Appeal to senses	1 2 3	A = 10–12 pts.
Clear and vivid detail	1 2 3	B = 7–9 pts.
Organization	1 2 3	C = 4–6 pts.
Accuracy	1 2 3	D = 3 pts.
		F = < 3 pts.

Teaching All Students

Extra Help Have students look at readings in this unit and find examples of each of the five senses.

Challenge Have students write a brief review of the advertised party for the school newspaper.

Native Speakers Ask students to describe parties they attended in their home countries/communities. These students can write their invitations based on parties they have attended. Discuss whether written invitations are common for informal parties.

Block Schedule

Variety Have students make an invitation for a party they are going to have for their friends, such as a birthday party or holiday party. (For additional activities, see **Block Scheduling Copymasters.**)

Unit Theme
Visiting a city (Oaxaca, Mexico), making purchases, and ordering in a restaurant.

Communication
• Asking for and giving directions
• Identifying places to visit in the city
• Choosing means of transportation
• Talking about shopping
• Making purchases and bargaining
• Discussing gift ideas
• Ordering food
• Saying where you went

Cultures
• Learning about the history of Oaxaca and its surroundings
• Learning about traditional arts, crafts, and architecture in Oaxaca
• Learning about regional foods
• Learning about bargaining in a marketplace

Connections
• Connecting to Physical Education: Mexican folk dancing
• Connecting to Mathematics: Calculating prices in a Mexican mercado

Comparisons
• Comparing shopping in Mexico and in the U.S.
• Comparing modes of transportation
• Comparing city/town structure

Communities
• Using Spanish in the workplace
• Using Spanish in volunteer activities

Teaching Resource Options

Print
Block Scheduling Copymasters

Audiovisual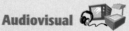
OHT M1, M2; 103, 104
Canciones Audiocassette/CD
Video Program Videotape 4 / Videodisc 2B

Search Chapter 1, Play to 2
U4 Cultural Introduction

UNIDAD 4

OAXACA MÉXICO
ESTADOS UNIDOS

¡DE VISITA!

OBJECTIVES

ETAPA 1
¡A visitar a mi prima!
• Identify places
• Give addresses
• Choose transportation
• Request directions
• Give instructions

ETAPA 2
En el mercado
• Talk about shopping
• Make purchases
• Talk about giving gifts
• Bargain

ETAPA 3
¿Qué hacer en Oaxaca?
• Order food
• Request the check
• Talk about food
• Express extremes
• Say where you went

CHIHUAHUA •
OCÉANO PACÍFICO
GOLFO DE CALIFORNIA
MÉXICO
BAJA CALIFORNIA
GUADALAJARA •

ANIMALITOS are popular forms for Oaxacan wood carvings. Notice the colorful painting. What other Oaxacan carving is on this page?

238

Classroom Community

Paired Activity Divide the class into pairs. Give students a time limit of 5 minutes to discuss and write a short list of things they would hope to see and/or experience in a Spanish-speaking country. Examples include monuments, holidays, regional food, music. Bring the class together to share lists; one student acts as the recorder to compile a master list on the board. Then have students group them into categories.

Group Activity Have students work together in groups of 3 for 2 minutes and try to think of as many Mexican cities as they can. Refer to the map on p. xxix in the student text and have students find the cities on the map, or assign for homework.

ALMANAQUE

Población: 212.943

Altura: 1.550 metros (5.084 pies)

Clima: 21° C (69.1° F)

Comida típica: mole negro, tasajo

Gente famosa de Oaxaca: Francisco Toledo (pintor), Benito Juárez (político), Rufino Tamayo (pintor)

¿Vas a Oaxaca? La gente de México usa la palabra *Oaxaca* para referirse al estado de Oaxaca, la ciudad de Oaxaca y el valle de Oaxaca. Cuando escuches «Oaxaca», pregunta a qué parte se refiere.

INTERNET For more information about Oaxaca, access www.mcdougallittell.com

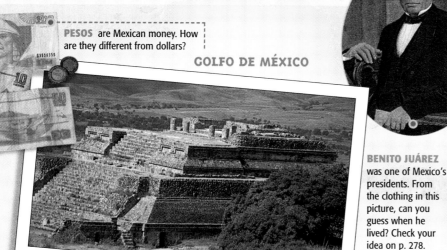

PESOS are Mexican money. How are they different from dollars?

GOLFO DE MÉXICO

MONTE ALBÁN

BENITO JUÁREZ was one of Mexico's presidents. From the clothing in this picture, can you guess when he lived? Check your idea on p. 278.

BAHÍA DE CAMPECHE

PENÍNSULA DE YUCATÁN

★ MÉXICO, D.F.

ESTADO DE OAXACA

● OAXACA

MONTE ALBÁN This city was built by the Zapotecs around 600 B.C. high upon a hill. What do you think the word **monte** means?

BELICE

HONDURAS

GUATEMALA

EL SALVADOR

NICARAGUA

MOLE NEGRO Many ingredients, including chiles and chocolate, make up black **mole** sauce. What have you eaten that is made from chocolate?

RUFINO TAMAYO (1899–1991), Oaxacan artist, completed *Mujer tendiendo la mano a la luna* in 1946. Can you guess what that means?

239

Check your idea on p. 278.

Teaching Suggestion
Previewing the Unit

Tell students that this unit centers on Oaxaca, Mexico. Ask students to scan these two pages for 15 seconds, then close their books. Then ask them to tell you what they remember. You may wish to use the introduction to the video to preview the unit.

Culture Highlights

● **ARTESANÍAS DE OAXACA** The wood carvings seen here are called **alebrije**. Pottery, jewelry, and **tapetes** (rugs) are also made in Oaxaca.

● **PESOS** The name **peso** is also used for currency in Argentina, Chile, Colombia, the Dominican Republic, and Uruguay.

● **MOLE NEGRO** Oaxaca's traditional cuisine is a fusion of Spanish and Native American flavors. **Mole negro** contains **chiles mulatos, chiles chilhuacles,** chocolate, oregano, and onions.

● **BENITO JUÁREZ** Benito Juárez is among the most revered presidents in Mexican history. In 1857, he implemented major reforms in Mexico's constitution. During his presidency, he led Mexico's fight against the French in the 1860s. **El Cinco de Mayo**, a Mexican holiday also celebrated by Mexican-Americans, commemorates Juárez's victory over the French at the Battle of Puebla in 1862.

● **MONTE ALBÁN** Monte Albán offers the best view of the city of Oaxaca. Monte Albán contains temples, tombs, a ball court, and areas that might have been used for astronomical observation.

● **RUFINO TAMAYO** Rufino Tamayo, born in Oaxaca, gave his personal collection of pre-Columbian art to Oaxaca in 1974.

Block Schedule

Variety Bring Mexican money into class to familiarize students with the peso. Have available the current exchange rate between the peso and the dollar. Students can then try to convert prices in dollars into pesos. (For additional activities, see **Block Scheduling Copymasters.**)

Teaching All Students

Native Speakers If any of your Spanish-speaking students have family from Mexico, ask them to speak about their particular region of the country. Ask them to bring any handicrafts and/or regional food specialties to the class for extra credit.

Multiple Intelligences

Logical/Mathematical Have students compare and contrast the population and geography of Oaxaca with their own city or town.

Musical/Rhythmic Have students bring in a cassette or a CD of authentic Mexican music to share with the class.

Ampliación

These activities may be used at various points in the Unit 4 sequence.

📖 For Block Schedule, you may find that these projects will provide a welcome change of pace while reviewing and reinforcing the material presented in the unit. See the **Block Scheduling Copymasters.**

ESTADOS UNIDOS

PROJECTS

Create a tourist guide for Oaxaca. Divide the class into groups, assigning each group research on a particular aspect of the guide:

1. Geography   4. Main tourist attractions
2. History   5. Art and music
3. Museums   6. Crafts

Each group is responsible for writing and illustrating its section of the guide. The completed project may be duplicated and published for display, or shared with other Spanish classes or family members.

> PACING SUGGESTION: Have students begin research at the beginning of the unit. Final projects are completed at the end of Unit 4.

Film or record an audiovisual guide for bargaining in a **mercado.** Include at least four different dialogs scripted by the students showing both successful and unsuccessful bargaining interactions.

> PACING SUGGESTION: Upon completion of Etapa 2.

MÉXICO

STORYTELLING

Rosa al mercado After reviewing bargaining vocabulary, model a mini-story (using puppets, student actors, or pictures from the text) that students will retell and revise:

> Rosa va al mercado. Mañana es el cumpleaños de su mamá. Rosa le pregunta al vendedor, "¿Me deja ver un anillo de plata?" El vendedor le deja ver un anillo de plata. Rosa pregunta, "¿Cuánto cuesta el anillo?" El vendedor dice, "100 pesos." Rosa regatea con el vendedor. Rosa le dice, "Quiero comprar el anillo pero es muy caro. Le puedo ofrecer 90 pesos." El vendedor acepta.

★ MÉXICO, D.F.

Pause as the story is being told so that students may fill in words and act out gestures. Students then write, narrate, and read aloud a longer main story. This new version should include vocabulary from the previous story.

Tú al mercado Ask students to create their own shopping stories. They may imagine shopping in a mall, a market, small shops, or even by phone.

> PACING SUGGESTION: Upon completion of Etapa 2.

OAXACA

BULLETIN BOARD/POSTERS

Bulletin Board Plan ahead: Contact local travel agencies for maps and brochures on Oaxaca. To begin the unit, ask students to create mind maps to activate prior knowledge after looking at the bulletin board for 2 minutes. Add the mind maps to the bulletin board.

Posters Have students create •**Travel** posters for Oaxaca •**Museum** or artisan posters •**Magazine/newspaper** posters for stores with items and prices •**Garage sale** posters with items listed

OAXACA
la ciudad y sus alrededores

GAMES

¿Me lo vendes?

Divide the class in half. Give half of the students in the class a total of 100 pesos in play money (bills). Give the other half pictures of items to sell. Have students call a local bank or check the Internet for the current exchange rate. Tell students they must establish a price for each item. The sellers should try to get as much money for their items as possible, while the buyers should try to buy as many items as possible. Give the class 10 minutes to circulate and bargain with one another. At the end of 10 minutes, the seller with the most money and the buyer with the most objects win.

PACING SUGGESTION: Upon completion of Etapa 2.

El tesoro del centro comercial

Photocopy a map of a local shopping center and give each student a copy. Decide, as a class, on a common starting point (usually the entrance to the mall). Divide the class into pairs. Instruct one of the players in each pair to draw (in pencil) a treasure chest somewhere on the map, without letting the partner see the map or the location of the treasure. Tell the partner who "hid" the treasure that he/she must now guide his/her partner to the treasure by giving directions in Spanish. Once students are familiar with the game, they can erase the original treasure chests and play again as a timed competition between pairs.

PACING SUGGESTION: Use as review of directions at any point in the unit.

MUSIC

An important festival of music and dance is held in Oaxaca every July. The **Guelaguetza** (gay·ła·gay·tzah), which means "deep and sincere offering" in the Zapotec language, celebrates a ceremony that brought together the people of the seven regions of the state in times of great need. Music samples are available on your *Canciones* Cassette or CD. Videos and recordings are available through the Tourist Board of Oaxaca. Contact www.mcdougallittell.com for more information.

HANDS-ON CRAFTS

Work with the art department to make **animalitos** in clay or homemade playdough. As students paint and decorate their creations, review colors in Spanish, adding new vocabulary if needed. Completed projects may be displayed at your school, at a local elementary school, or at the local library.

RECIPE

Chocolate oaxaqueño is a well-known specialty of Oaxaca. It is sold in the form of powder, sticks, or bars and used in cooking as well as in making hot chocolate. Although you may not be able to purchase authentic Oaxacan chocolate locally, you can still prepare a tasty version of **chocolate oaxaqueño** with your students.

Receta

Chocolate oaxaqueño
225 g (1/2 lb.) de chocolate amargo en trozos
2 litros (2 quarts) de leche
1/4 taza de agua
azúcar y canela al gusto

Ponga el agua a hervir en una cacerola pequeña. Añada el chocolate y derrítalo a fuego lento, sin dejar de mezclar. Eche la leche, siga calentando y con una batidora, bata hasta que se forme espuma. Añada azúcar y canela al gusto. Sirva inmediatamente en tazas pequeñas. ¡Mmmmm!—¡qué rico!

Planning Guide CLASSROOM MANAGEMENT

OBJECTIVES

Communication
- Identify places *pp. 242–243, 256–257*
- Give addresses *pp. 244–245*
- Choose transportation *pp. 244–245*
- Request directions *pp. 244–245*
- Give instructions *pp. 244–245, 256–257*

Grammar
- Use the verb **decir** *pp. 248–249*
- Use prepositions of location *pp. 250–251*
- Use regular affirmative **tú** commands *pp. 252–255*

Pronunciation
- Pronunciation of **r** *p. 255*
- Dictation, *TE p. 255*

Culture
- Oaxaca, Mexico–its history and culture *pp. 238–239, 251, 253, 256–257*

♻ Recycling
- **Hay** *p. 246*
- Seasons, weather *p. 247*
- Free-time activities *p. 252*
- Direct object pronouns *pp. 252, 253*
- Sequencing events *p. 253*

STRATEGIES

Listening Strategies
- Listen and follow directions *p. 244*

Speaking Strategies
- Recognize and use set phrases *p. 251*
- Use variety to give directions *p. 260*

Reading Strategies
- Combine strategies *p. 256*

Writing Strategies
- Organize information by category *TE p. 260*

Connecting Cultures Strategies
- Recognize variations in vocabulary *p. 248*
- Learn about Oaxaca, Mexico *pp. 238–239, 251, 253, 256–257*
- Learn about Native American groups in Oaxaca, Mexico *p. 251*
- Connect and compare what you know about streets and places in your community to help you learn about streets and places in a new community *pp. 242–243, 256–257, TE p. 257*

PROGRAM RESOURCES

 Print

- *Más práctica* Workbook PE *pp. 81–88*
- Block Scheduling Copymasters *pp. 81–88*
- Unit 4 Resource Book
  Más práctica Workbook TE *pp. 1–8*
  Para hispanohablantes Workbook TE *pp. 9–16*

- Information Gap Activities *pp. 17–20*
- Family Involvement *pp. 21–22*
- Video Activities *pp. 23–25*
- Videoscript *pp. 26–28*
- Audioscript *pp. 29–32*
- Assessment Program, Unit 4 Etapa 1 *pp. 33–51; 170–178*
- Answer Keys *pp. 179–200*

 Audiovisual

- **Audio Program** Cassettes 10A, 10B / CD 10
- *Canciones* Cassette / CD
- **Video Program** Videotape 4 / Videodisc 2B
- **Overhead Transparencies** M1–M5; 103–104, 107–116

 **Technology**

- Electronic Teacher Tools/Test Generator
- *Intrigas y aventuras* CD-ROM, Disc 1
- www.mcdougallittell.com

 Assessment Program Options

- **Cooperative Quizzes** (Unit 4 Resource Book)
- **Etapa Exam** Forms A and B (Unit 4 Resource Book)
- *Para hispanohablantes* **Etapa Exam** (Unit 4 Resource Book)
- **Portfolio Assessment** (Unit 4 Resource Book)
- **Multiple Choice Test Questions** (Unit 4 Resource Book)
- **Audio Program** Testing Cassette T2 / CD T2
- **Electronic Teacher Tools/Test Generator**

Native Speakers
- *Para hispanohablantes* Workbook PE, *pp. 81–88*
- *Para hispanohablantes* Workbook TE (Unit 4 Resource Book)
- *Para hispanohablantes* Etapa Exam (Unit 4 Resource Book)
- Audio *Para hispanohablantes* Cassettes 10A, 10B, T2 / CD 10, T2
- Audioscript *Para hispanohablantes* (Unit 4 Resource Book)

Student Text Listening Activity Scripts

Rosa   Carlos   Sofía

 Videoscript: Diálogo *pages 244–245*

• Videotape 4 • Videodisc 2B

Search Chapter 3, Play to 4
U4E1 • En vivo (Dialog)

• Use the videoscript with **Actividades 1, 2** *page 246*

Rosa: Perdone, ¿puede usted decirme dónde queda la calle Morelos?

Hombre: ¿Cómo dice, señorita?

Rosa: ¿Si sabe dónde está la calle Morelos?

Hombre: No, señorita. Perdone, pero no sé dónde queda esa calle.

Rosa: Gracias.
¡Disculpe!

Carlos: ¿Sí? Buenos días.

Rosa: Buenos días. Vengo de la Ciudad de México para visitar a mi prima y su familia. No sé donde queda su nueva casa. Ella no sabe que vengo. No quiero llamar. Busco esta dirección.

Carlos: Ah, sí, claro, la calle Morelos. Desde aquí es muy fácil llegar.

Rosa: ¡Ay, qué bueno! ¿Queda lejos de aquí?

Carlos: No, no está lejos. Son unas cuatro o cinco cuadras. A pie, llegas en diez minutos. Pero llegas más rápido en taxi.

Rosa: Como es un día bonito, prefiero caminar. ¿Puedes decirme cómo llego?

Carlos: ¡Sí, claro que sí!
Ésta es la avenida Constitución. Camina derecho una cuadra por esta calle. Allí vas a ver un banco.

Rosa: ¿Dices que hay un banco?

Carlos: Sí, hay un banco al lado de una farmacia.

Rosa: Y ahí, ¿qué hago?

Carlos: Vas a llegar a un parque. Cruza el parque. Enfrente de la estatua está la calle Morelos.

Rosa: Muchas gracias, eh...

Carlos: Carlos, me llamo Carlos.

Rosa: Muchas gracias, Carlos.

Carlos: De nada, eh...

Rosa: Rosa, soy Rosa.

Carlos: Encantado, Rosa.

Rosa: Igualmente, Carlos.

Carlos: Si tienes tiempo durante tu visita, pasa por la tienda. Salgo del trabajo a las siete. Si quieres, salimos a comer con tu prima.

Rosa: Me gustaría. Bueno, si hay tiempo. A ver qué dice mi prima. ¡Ah! ¿Puedo llevar el mapa?

Carlos: Sí, claro que sí. ¡Hasta luego, Rosa!

Rosa: Hasta luego. ¡Gracias!

Sofía: ¡Rosa!

Rosa: ¡Sofía, prima! ¿Cómo estás?

Sofía: ¡Qué sorpresa! ¿Qué haces por aquí?

Rosa: ¡Vengo a visitarte!

Sofía: ¡Qué gusto de verte! Pasa, pasa, prima.

Rosa: ¡Qué bonita es la nueva casa de tu familia!

Sofía: Gracias.

Rosa: ¿Dónde está mi tía?

Sofía: Está haciendo algunas compras.

Rosa: Ah, yo también quiero ir de compras. Es el cumpleaños de mi mamá y quiero comprar algo bonito para ella aquí en Oaxaca.

Sofía: Yo digo que el mercado tiene las cosas más bonitas. ¿Por qué no vamos mañana por la mañana? ¿Qué dices?

Rosa: Me encantaría. Además, tú sabes dónde venden cosas buenas y bonitas.

Sofía: Entonces, mañana, ¡al mercado! Y después, salimos a pasear por la plaza.

Rosa: ¡Ay, qué bueno! ¿Y qué más podemos hacer?

Sofía: Podríamos ir al cine.

🎧 **¿En qué estación?** *page 247*

5

1. Rosa está de vacaciones. Visita a su amiga Ana en Vermont. Van a las montañas con la familia de Ana a esquiar. Hace mucho frío y nieva mucho.

2. Ana manda una carta. Describe sus vacaciones. Es julio. Hace mucho calor. Va a la playa por dos semanas. Nada mucho y toma el sol.

3. Llega otra carta de Ana. Describe el tiempo. Unos días hay mucha lluvia y hace fresco. Otros días hay mucho sol y también hace fresco. Hay unas flores muy bonitas.

4. Ana describe el tiempo en otra carta. Hace fresco y hay mucho viento. Unos días llueve, otros no. No hay muchas flores. Los colores de los árboles son bonitos.

🎧 **¿Puede usted decirme...?** *page 255*

19

Rosa: Perdone, señor. ¿Puede usted decirme dónde está la librería?

Policía: ¡Sí! ¡Cómo no! Queda muy cerca. Camina derecho una cuadra por la calle Reforma. Allí vas a ver una plaza.

Rosa: ¿Veo una plaza?

Policía: Sí. Allí, dobla a la derecha y camina una cuadra más. La librería está a la izquierda en la esquina de la avenida Juárez.

Rosa: ¿Y puede usted decirme si hay una papelería cerca de aquí?

Policía: Sí. Cuando sales de la librería, dobla a la derecha y camina dos cuadras. La papelería está a la izquierda.

Rosa: Ah, por favor, ¿puede usted decirme si el correo está por aquí?

Policía: Sí, está a la derecha de la papelería en la misma cuadra.

Rosa: ¡Qué bueno! Muchas gracias, señor.

Quick Start Review Answers

p. 246 Video review
1. queda   4. al lado de
2. dirección   5. Enfrente de
3. A pie

p. 250 Transportation
Answers will vary.
Answers could include:
en autobús, en carro, en taxi,
a pie, en metro

1. Voy a la escuela en autobús.
2. Voy al centro commercial en carro.
3. Voy al aeropuerto en taxi.
4. Voy a la tienda de videos a pie.
5. Voy a la joyería en metro.

p. 252 Vocabulary
caminar, correr, pasear,
ir a pie

Sample Lesson Plan - 50 Minute Schedule

DAY 1

Unit Opener
- Anticipate/Activate prior knowledge: Present the *Almanaque* and the cultural notes. Use Map OHTs as needed. 10 MIN.

Etapa Opener
- Quick Start Review (TE, p. 240) 5 MIN.
- Have students look at the *Etapa* Opener and answer the questions. 5 MIN.

En contexto: Vocabulario
- Quick Start Review (TE, p. 242) 5 MIN.
- Have students use context and pictures to learn *Etapa* vocabulary, then answer the questions, p. 243. Use the Situational OHTs for additional practice. 10 MIN.

En vivo: Diálogo
- Quick Start Review (TE, p. 244) 5 MIN.
- Review the Listening Strategy, p. 244. Play audio or show video for the dialog, pp. 244–245. Replay and have students take the roles of the characters. 10 MIN.

Homework Option:
- Video Activities, Unit 4 Resource Book, pp. 23–25.

DAY 2

En acción: Vocabulario y gramática
- Check homework. 5 MIN.
- Quick Start Review (TE, p. 246) 5 MIN.
- Have students open to *En contexto*, pp. 242–243, for reference. Use OHT 107 and 108 to review vocabulary. 10 MIN.
- Play the video/audio; have students do *Actividades* 1 and 2 orally. 10 MIN.
- Present the *Nota* and have students complete *Actividad* 3 orally. 5 MIN.
- Present the *Vocabulario*, p. 247, and ask students to use each word in a sentence. 5 MIN.
- Do *Actividad* 4 orally. 5 MIN.
- Play the audio; do *Actividad* 5. 5 MIN.
- Use an expansion activity from TE, pp. 246–247, for reinforcement and variety. 5 MIN.

Homework Option:
- Have students make flashcards of the vocabulary on p. 247. Have them complete *Actividades* 3 and 4 in writing.

DAY 3

En acción (cont.)
- Check homework. 5 MIN.
- Quick Start Review (TE, p. 248) 5 MIN.
- Present *Gramática:* The Verb *decir*, p. 248. 5 MIN.
- Have students do *Actividad* 6 orally. 5 MIN.
- Present the *Nota*. Then have students complete *Actividad* 7 in writing. Go over answers orally. 10 MIN.
- Present the *Vocabulario*, p. 249, and have students answer the question *¿Cómo prefieres viajar?* Have students make flashcards of the words. 10 MIN.
- Have students complete *Actividad* 8 orally. 5 MIN.
- Have students complete *Actividad* 9 in pairs. Ask a few pairs to present their mini-conversations. 10 MIN.

Homework Option:
- Have students complete *Actividad* 8 in writing. *Más práctica* Workbook, p. 85. *Para hispanohablantes* Workbook, p. 83.

DAY 4

En acción (cont.)
- Check homework. 5 MIN.
- Quick Start Review (TE, p. 250) 5 MIN.
- Present *Gramática:* Using Prepositional Phrases to Express Location, p. 250. 5 MIN.
- Have students do *Actividad* 10 in writing, then go over answers orally. 10 MIN.
- Have students complete *Actividad* 11 in pairs. Ask a few pairs to present their mini-conversations. 10 MIN.
- Present the Speaking Strategy, p. 251, then do *Actividad* 12 orally. Expand using Information Gap Activities, Unit 4 Resource Book, p. 17; *Más comunicación*, p. R10. 15 MIN.
- Have a volunteer draw a quick scene on the board with labeled buildings, cars, people, etc. Ask students to talk about where things are located in the pictures, using prepositions. 5 MIN.

Homework Option:
- *Más práctica* Workbook, pp. 86–87. *Para hispanohablantes* Workbook, pp. 84–85.

DAY 5

En acción (cont.)
- Check homework. 5 MIN.
- Quick Start Review (TE, p. 252) 5 MIN.
- Present *Gramática:* Regular Affirmative *tú* Commands and the *Vocabulario*, p. 252. 10 MIN.
- Have students do *Actividad* 13 in writing. Go over answers orally. 10 MIN.
- Have students do *Actividades* 14, 15, 16 in pairs. 10 MIN.
- Do *Actividad* 17 orally. 5 MIN.
- Present the *Vocabulario*, p. 254. Then have students do *Actividad* 18 in groups. 10 MIN.

Homework Option:
- Have students complete *Actividad* 17 in writing. *Más práctica* Workbook, p. 88. *Para hispanohablantes* Workbook, p. 86.

DAY 6

En acción (cont.)
- Check homework. 5 MIN.
- Play the audio; do *Actividad* 19. 5 MIN.
- Have students do *Actividad* 20 in writing. Expand using Information Gap Activities, Unit 4 Resource Book, pp. 18–19; *Más comunicación*, p. R10. 15 MIN.

Pronunciación
- Play the audio and have students practice the *refrán*. 5 MIN.

En voces: Lectura
- Quick Start Review (TE, p. 256) 5 MIN.
- Review the Reading Strategy, p. 256. 5 MIN.
- Have volunteers read the selection aloud and answer the questions, p. 257. 15 MIN.

Homework Option:
- Have students write answers to the *¿Comprendiste?* questions, p. 257. Review in preparation for *En uso*.

DAY 7

En uso: Repaso y más comunicación
- Check homework. 5 MIN.
- Quick Start Review (TE, p. 258) 5 MIN.
- Present the *Repaso y más comunicación* using the Teaching Suggestions (TE, p. 258). 5 MIN.
- Have students write *Actividades* 1 and 2, then check answers with the whole class. 10 MIN.
- Do *Actividades* 3 and 4 orally. 10 MIN.
- Present the Speaking Strategy, p. 260, and have students do *Actividad* 5 in pairs. 10 MIN.

En tu propia voz: Escritura
- Do *Actividad* 6 in writing. Ask volunteers to present their recommendations. 10 MIN.

Homework Option:
- Review for *Etapa* 1 Exam.

DAY 8

Conexiones
- Read and discuss *La educación física*, p. 260. 5 MIN.

En resumen: Repaso de vocabulario
- Quick Start Review (TE, p. 261) 5 MIN.
- Review grammar questions, etc., as necessary. 10 MIN.
- Complete *Etapa* 1 Exam. 20 MIN.

Ampliación
- Use a suggested project, game, or activity. (TE, pp. 239A–239B) 10 MIN.

Homework Option:
- Research Mexican folk dances as outlined in the *Conexiones*. Preview *Etapa* 2 Opener.

Sample Lesson Plan - Block Schedule (90 minutes)

DAY 1

Unit Opener
- Anticipate/Activate prior knowledge: Present the *Almanaque* and the cultural notes. Use Map OHTs as needed. **10 MIN.**

Etapa Opener
- Quick Start Review (TE, p. 240) **5 MIN.**
- Have students look at the *Etapa* Opener and answer the questions. **5 MIN.**
- Use Block Scheduling Copymasters. **5 MIN.**

En contexto: Vocabulario
- Quick Start Review (TE, p. 242) **5 MIN.**
- Have students use context and pictures to learn *Etapa* vocabulary, then answer the questions, p. 243. Use the Situational OHTs for additional practice. **15 MIN.**

En vivo: Diálogo
- Quick Start Review (TE, p. 244) **5 MIN.**
- Review the Listening Strategy, p. 244. Play audio or show video for the dialog, pp. 244–245. Replay and have students take the roles of characters. **10 MIN.**

En acción: Vocabulario y gramática
- Quick Start Review (TE, p. 246) **5 MIN.**
- Have students open to *En contexto,* pp. 242–243, for reference. Use OHT 107 and 108 to review vocabulary. **10 MIN.**
- Play the video/audio; do *Actividades* 1 and 2 orally. **10 MIN.**
- Present the *Nota* and do *Actividad* 3 orally. **5 MIN.**

Homework Option:
- Have students complete *Actividad* 3 in writing. Video Activities, Unit 4 Resource Book, pp. 23–25.

DAY 2

En acción (cont.)
- Check homework. **5 MIN.**
- Present the *Vocabulario,* p. 247, and ask students to use each word in a sentence. **5 MIN.**
- Do *Actividad* 4 orally. **5 MIN.**
- Play the audio; do *Actividad* 5. **5 MIN.**
- Quick Start Review (TE, p. 248) **5 MIN.**
- Present *Gramática:* The Verb *decir,* p. 248. **5 MIN.**
- Have students do *Actividad* 6 orally. **5 MIN.**
- Present the *Nota.* Then have students complete *Actividad* 7 in writing. Go over answers orally. **10 MIN.**
- Present the *Vocabulario,* p. 249, and have students answer the question *¿Cómo prefieres viajar?* Have students make flashcards of the words. **10 MIN.**
- Have students complete *Actividad* 8 orally. **5 MIN.**
- Have students complete *Actividad* 9 in pairs. Ask a few pairs to present their mini-conversations. **10 MIN.**
- Quick Start Review (TE, p. 250) **5 MIN.**
- Present *Gramática:* Using Prepositional Phrases to Express Location, p. 250. **5 MIN.**
- Have students do *Actividad* 10 in writing, then go over answers orally. **10 MIN.**

Homework Option:
- Have students complete *Actividad* 8 in writing. *Más práctica* Workbook, pp. 85–87. *Para hispanohablantes* Workbook, pp. 83–85.

DAY 3

En acción (cont.)
- Check homework. **5 MIN.**
- Have students complete *Actividad* 11 in pairs. Ask a few pairs to present their mini-conversations. **10 MIN.**
- Present the Speaking Strategy, p. 251, then do *Actividad* 12 orally. Expand using Information Gap Activities, Unit 4 Resource Book, p. 17; *Más comunicación,* p. R10. **15 MIN.**
- Have a volunteer draw a quick scene on the board with labeled buildings, cars, people, etc. Ask students to talk about where things are located in the pictures, using prepositions. **5 MIN.**
- Quick Start Review (TE, p. 252) **5 MIN.**
- Present *Gramática:* Regular Affirmative *tú* Commands and the *Vocabulario,* p. 252. **10 MIN.**
- Have students do *Actividad* 13 in writing. Go over answers orally. **10 MIN.**
- Have students do *Actividades* 14, 15, 16 in pairs. **15 MIN.**
- Do *Actividad* 17 orally. **5 MIN.**
- Present the *Vocabulario,* p. 254. Then have students do *Actividad* 18 in groups. **10 MIN.**

Homework Option:
- Have students complete *Actividades* 12 and 17 in writing. *Más práctica* Workbook, p. 88. *Para hispanohablantes* Workbook, p. 86.

DAY 4

En acción (cont.)
- Check homework. **5 MIN.**
- Play the audio; do *Actividad* 19. **5 MIN.**
- Have students do *Actividad* 20 in writing. Expand using Information Gap Activities, Unit 4 Resource Book, pp. 18–19; *Más comunicación,* p. R10. **20 MIN.**

Pronunciación
- Play the audio and have students practice the *refrán.* **5 MIN.**

En voces: Lectura
- Quick Start Review (TE, p. 256) **5 MIN.**
- Present the Reading Strategy, p. 256. Have volunteers read the selection aloud and answer the questions, p. 257. **20 MIN.**

En uso: Repaso y más comunicación
- Quick Start Review (TE, p. 258) **5 MIN.**
- Present the *Repaso y más comunicación* using the Teaching Suggestions (TE, p. 258). **5 MIN.**
- Have students write *Actividades* 1 and 2, then check answers with the whole class. **10 MIN.**
- Do *Actividades* 3 and 4 orally. **10 MIN.**

Homework Option:
- Review for *Etapa* 1 Exam.

DAY 5

En uso: Repaso y más comunicación (cont.)
- Present the Speaking Strategy, p. 260, and have students do *Actividad* 5 in pairs. **10 MIN.**

En tu propia voz: Escritura
- Do *Actividad* 6 in writing. Ask volunteers to present their recommendations. **15 MIN.**

Conexiones
- Read and discuss *La educación física,* p. 260. **10 MIN.**

En resumen: Repaso de vocabulario
- Quick Start Review (TE, p. 261) **5 MIN.**
- Review grammar questions, etc., as necessary. **10 MIN.**
- Complete *Etapa* 1 Exam. **20 MIN.**

Ampliación
- Use a suggested project, game, or activity. (TE, pp. 239A–239B) **20 MIN.**

Homework Option:
- Research Mexican folk dances as outlined in the *Conexiones.* Preview *Etapa* 2 Opener.

▼ Carlos le explica a Rosa dónde queda la calle Morelos.

Etapa Theme
Identifying places in a city, choosing transportation, and asking for and giving directions.

Grammar Objectives
- Using the verb **decir**
- Using prepositions of location
- Using regular affirmative **tú** commands

Teaching Resource Options
Print

Block Scheduling Copymasters

Audiovisual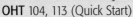

OHT 104, 113 (Quick Start)

Quick Start Review
♻ Vocabulary review

Use OHT 113 or write on board: Write at least 3 items/expressions associated with these geographic regions (weather, clothing, activities, etc.):

1. la playa
2. las montañas
3. el bosque
4. el desierto

Answers
Answers will vary. Answers could include:
1. el verano, el traje de baño, esquiar en el agua, tomar el sol
2. hace frío, la nieve, esquiar, los árboles
3. hace calor, los shorts, sacar fotos, las plantas
4. hace/hay sol, el sombrero, las gafas de sol, tener sed

Teaching Suggestion
Previewing the Etapa
- Ask students to study the photo on pp. 240–241 (1 min.).
- Close books; ask students to share at least 3 things that they noticed.
- Reopen books and look at the picture again (1 min.); close books and share 3 more details.
- Ask students where the girl might be coming from and where she might be going.
- Use the **¿Qué ves?** questions to focus the discussion.

UNIDAD 4

ETAPA 1

¡A visitar a mi prima!

- Identify places
- Give addresses
- Choose transportation
- Request directions
- Give instructions

¿Qué ves?

Mira la foto del Zócalo de Oaxaca.

1. ¿La chica vive en Oaxaca o está visitando Oaxaca?
2. ¿Qué tiempo hace?
3. ¿Cuántos museos ves en el mapa?

240

OAXACA

- Museo Rufino Tamayo
- Museo de Arte Contemporáneo
- Av. Morelos
- Av. Independencia
- Catedral de Oaxaca
- 5 de Mayo
- Av. Juárez
- Tinoco y Palacios
- Zócalo
- Las Casas
- Palacio de Gobierno
- Mercado Juárez
- a Monte Albán

Classroom Management

Planning Ahead In preparation for giving directions using maps, collect town/city maps of your area as well as areas of Mexico. You might use the Internet as a source. Also bring in pesos for students to observe. Make price tags and label common items with typical prices (for example: **cuaderno = 10 pesos**). Students will begin to understand the value of the peso compared to the U.S. dollar.

Time Saver Ask students to prepare flashcards of all the new vocabulary words from the **En contexto** on pp. 242–243. You will be able to use these in simple vocabulary review exercises later.

241

Cross Cultural Connections

El mapa de Oaxaca Ask students to compare the map of Oaxaca to a map of their town. How does the street organization compare? Which buildings are the same? Which are different?

Culture Highlights

● **OAXACA** The region of Oaxaca, located in southeast Mexico, has a population of more than 3 million people, including many native groups. During pre-Columbian times, the region was inhabited by diverse ethnic groups, such as the Mixtecs and Zapotecs. Toward the middle of the 15th century, the Aztecs conquered the area and established a number of military points to control the transportation of merchandise.

● **LA CATEDRAL DE OAXACA** Construction of the cathedral in Oaxaca began in 1640, but suffered a series of setbacks and reconstructions after earthquakes and pillages. Inside the cathedral, there is an altar made of bronze imported from Italy, an antique pipe organ, and paintings from the 18th century.

● **MUSEO DE ARTE CONTEMPORÁNEO** The Museum of Contemporary Art, which opened in 1992, is located in a house that once belonged to an aristocratic family in Oaxaca. It contains the most important collections of Mexican modern art, including a retrospective of the work of the Oaxacan artist Rufino Tamayo.

Supplementary Vocabulary

la fuente	fountain
el mirador	gazebo
los globos	balloons
el (la) vendedor(a)	vendor
la maleta	suitcase

Teaching All Students

Extra Help Ask yes/no questions about the photo, or make statements about the photo and have students respond with **Sí/No.** Have students correct the incorrect statements. For example: ¿Hay chicos en la foto? (Sí.) **La muchacha lleva un vestido.** (No. Lleva pantalones, una camisa y un suéter.)

Challenge Have students sketch the girl in the photo and draw a thought bubble over her head. Have them write what she might be thinking.

Multiple Intelligences

Visual Have students name objects in the photo (see the Supplementary Vocabulary) and their colors. Then have them make complete sentences with this information and compose a description of the whole photo.

Block Schedule

Retention Have students write down as many things as they can remember about Mexico from **Unidad 2.** Compile the lists to form a more complete review of Mexico. (For additional activities, see **Block Scheduling Copymasters.**)

Teaching Resource Options

Print

Unit 4 Resource Book
  Video Activities, pp. 23–24
  Videoscript, p. 26
  Audioscript, p. 29
  Audioscript *Para hispanohablantes,*
    p. 29

Audiovisual

OHT 107, 108, 109, 109A, 110, 110A,
113 (Quick Start)
Audio Program Cassette 10A / CD 10
Audio *Para hispanohablantes*
  Cassette 10A / CD 10
Video Program Videotape 4 / Videodisc
2B

Search Chapter 2, Play to 3
U4E1 • En contexto (Vocabulary)

Technology

Intrigas y aventuras CD-ROM, Disc 1

Quick Start Review

♻ Verb review

Use OHT 113 or write on the board:
Complete each sentence with the
correct form of the verb:

1. Mañana, yo ____ al bosque. (ir)
2. ¿Cuándo ____ Alma el museo?
   (visitar)
3. ¿A qué hora ____ las niñas? (llegar)
4. Nosotros ____ todos los días por
   el parque. (pasear)
5. ¿Te gusta ____ en el parque?
   (caminar)
6. ¿ ____ usted dónde está el teatro?
   (saber)
7. La maestra ____ la puerta. (cerrar)
8. Yo ____ de San Antonio. (venir)

Answers
1. voy   3. llegan   5. caminar 7. cierra
2. visita 4. paseamos 6. Sabe   8. vengo

Language Note

Point out that the word **farmacia** is like
familia, with the stress on the next-to-last
syllable. Both words end in a -*ya* sound,
unlike the word **día,** in which you hear
both vowels separately.

En contexto

🎧💿 VOCABULARIO

Rosa is taking a walk through the city of Oaxaca. She looks at a map
in order to find her way around.

A Hay mucho que ver en Oaxaca.
¡Mira **el mapa**! Es divertido
pasear. Primero, voy a **una
plaza.** Después, descanso en
un café y tomo un refresco.

B Allí está **el correo**, de donde mando
cartas. **La iglesia** es muy bonita.

C Si estoy enferma y necesito medicina, voy a
la farmacia. Está en **la calle** Bustamante.

la plaza
el café
el correo
la iglesia
la farmacia
MAPA
oaxaca • Huatulco

242   doscientos cuarenta y dos
Unidad 4

Classroom Community

TPR Have students work in pairs or small groups to
act out scenes (verbal or pantomime) that take place in
the various locations in the city. The class guesses the
locations.

Paired Activity Have students generate Supplementary Vocabulary lists related to the places mentioned
in the **En contexto**. They should aim for 3 new words
for each place and look up the words in the dictionary.
For example, for **el correo: los timbres/las estampillas/
los sellos** (stamps), **el buzón** (mailbox), **el cartero**
(mail carrier). Each pair presents their lists. Compile a
class list. Use the words in bonus questions on quizzes.

el banco

el hotel

D Voy al **banco** por la tarde. Si quieres visitar la ciudad, hay **un hotel** muy bonito para pasar la noche.

la estación de autobuses

E Llego a **la estación de autobuses** de Oaxaca. Acabo de venir de la capital.

la esquina

F Para ir del **centro** al **aeropuerto** voy por esta **avenida**. Hay un taxi en **la esquina**.

Preguntas personales

1. ¿Te gusta ir al centro?
2. ¿Usas la estación de autobuses o el aeropuerto?
3. ¿Prefieres pasar un rato en un café o en una plaza?
4. ¿Dónde compras medicina?
5. ¿Adónde vas si estás en otra ciudad y tienes sueño?

doscientos cuarenta y tres
Etapa 1 **243**

Teaching All Students

Extra Help Randomly call out words from the new vocabulary. Have students point to what you are saying in the pictures.

Native Speakers Ask students to give synonyms for **autobús (bus, ómnibus, camioneta, colectivo, guagua)**. Is the bus a common form of transportation in their cultural community? What are other common modes of transportation?

Multiple Intelligences

Visual Ask students to draw and label a map of their town/city center. Have volunteers present and describe their maps to the class.

Interpersonal Have students ask you the **Preguntas personales**.

Teaching Suggestions
Introducing Vocabulary

- Have students look at pages 242–243. Use OHT 107 and 108 and Audio Cassette 10A / CD 10 to present the vocabulary.
- Ask the Comprehension Questions in order of yes/no (questions 1–3), either/or (questions 4–6), and simple word or phrase (questions 7–10). Expand by adding similar questions.
- Use the TPR activity to reinforce the meaning of individual words.
- Use the video vocabulary presentation for review and reinforcement.

Comprehension Questions

1. ¿Hay mucho que ver en Oaxaca? (Sí.)
2. ¿Es posible pasear en Oaxaca? (Sí.)
3. ¿Va Rosa primero a un café? (No.)
4. ¿Quiere Rosa tomar una merienda o un refresco? (un refresco)
5. ¿De dónde manda cartas, del correo o de la iglesia? (del correo)
6. Cuando Rosa está enferma, ¿va a la farmacia o a la plaza? (a la farmacia)
7. ¿En qué calle está la farmacia? (en la calle Bustamante)
8. ¿Adónde va Rosa por la tarde? (al banco)
9. Si quieres visitar a Oaxaca, ¿dónde puedes pasar la noche? (en un hotel)
10. ¿Cómo puedes ir del centro al aeropuerto? (en un taxi)

Supplementary Vocabulary

el edificio	building
la acera	sidewalk
el semáforo	traffic light
la estación de policía	police station
la estación de bomberos	fire station
el hospital	hospital
la estación de metro	subway station
la estación de tren	train station

Block Schedule

Retention Expand the vocabulary by having students write definitions in Spanish for the new words. For example: **el correo es donde mando cartas.**

🔔 Quick Start Review

♻ **Greetings**

Use OHT 113 or write on the board:
Write a brief dialog between 2 people
meeting for the first time:

Answers
Answers will vary. Answers could include:
A: Hola, me llamo Carlos.
B: Encantada, Carlos.
A: Y tú, ¿cómo te llamas?
B: Me llamo Elena.
A: Mucho gusto, Elena.
B: El gusto es mío, Carlos.

Gestures

Before reading the **Diálogo,** have students
pay close attention to scenes 3, 4, 5, 6, 8,
and 10. Ask them if the gestures pictured
help them predict what is going to be
said in the **Diálogo.** Discuss students'
predictions.

En vivo

 DIÁLOGO

Rosa

Carlos

Sofía

Visita a Oaxaca

PARA ESCUCHAR • STRATEGY: LISTENING

Listen and follow directions How you remember directions gives
clues about the ways you prefer to learn. Listen to Carlos's
directions. Which is most natural for you, to (1) repeat key words,
(2) write key words, (3) use gestures, (4) draw a map, or (5) do
something else? Your choices indicate how you prefer to learn.
Use them to help you follow directions as you listen.

1 ► **Rosa:** Perdone, ¿puede usted
decirme dónde queda la calle
Morelos?
Hombre: No, señorita. Perdone,
pero no sé dónde queda esa calle.

5 ► **Carlos:** Ésta es la avenida
Constitución. Camina por esta
calle. Allí vas a ver un banco.
Rosa: ¿Dices que hay un banco?
Carlos: Sí, hay un banco al lado
de una farmacia.

6 ► **Carlos:** Vas a llegar a un parque. Cruza
el parque. Enfrente de la estatua está la
calle Morelos.
Rosa: Muchas gracias, eh…
Carlos: Carlos, me llamo Carlos.
Rosa: Rosa, soy Rosa.

7 ► **Carlos:** Salgo del trabajo a las siete.
Si quieres, salimos a comer con tu
prima.
Rosa: Me gustaría. A ver qué dice
mi prima. ¿Puedo llevar el mapa?
Carlos: Sí, claro que sí.

244 doscientos cuarenta y cuatro
Unidad 4

Classroom Community

Group Activity After watching the video, divide the
class into small groups. Give each group 28 index
cards—one for each dialog line. Students should copy
one dialog line on each card. First, have them shuffle
the cards. Then have them reorganize the cards in the
correct order, reading the lines aloud as they do so.

Learning Scenario Have students rewrite the
dialog using information pertinent to their town/city.
They should substitute place and street names. Then
have volunteers act out the new dialog.

2 ▶ Rosa: Buenos días. Vengo a visitar a mi prima. No sé dónde queda su nueva casa. Busco esta dirección.

3 ▶ Carlos: ¡Ah, sí!, claro, la calle Morelos. Desde aquí es muy fácil llegar.
Rosa: ¡Ay, qué bueno! ¿Queda lejos de aquí?

4 ▶ Carlos: A pie llegas en diez minutos. Pero llegas más rápido en taxi.
Rosa: Prefiero caminar. ¿Puedes decirme cómo llego?

8 ▶ Sofía: ¡Rosa!
Rosa: ¡Sofía! ¿Cómo estás?
Sofía: ¡Qué sorpresa! ¿Qué haces por aquí?
Rosa: ¡Vengo a visitarte!
Sofía: Pasa, pasa, prima.

9 ▶ Rosa: ¡Qué bonita es la nueva casa de tu familia! ¿Dónde está mi tía?
Sofía: Está haciendo algunas compras.
Rosa: Yo también quiero ir de compras. Es el cumpleaños de mi mamá y quiero comprar algo bonito para ella.

10 ▶ Sofía: Yo digo que el mercado tiene las cosas más bonitas. ¿Por qué no vamos mañana por la mañana? ¿Qué dices?
Rosa: Me encantaría.
Sofía: Entonces, mañana, ¡al mercado! Y después, salimos a pasear por la plaza.

doscientos cuarenta y cinco
Etapa 1
245

Teaching All Students

Extra Help Have students listen to the dialog again and pretend that they are taking notes for Rosa. They should write down the key information about getting to Sofía's house. Then have several students give Rosa the directions.

Challenge Have students write a continuation of the dialog in which Rosa describes Carlos to Sofía and they decide whether or not to accept his dinner invitation.

Multiple Intelligences

Kinesthetic With books closed, re-read the dialog to students. Have various students act out the scenes as you read, using gestures to correspond to what they hear. Alternate: Have students listen to the dialog and draw a path to Rosa's house on a map.

Teaching Suggestions
Presenting the Dialog

• Prepare students for listening by focusing on the dialog context. Reintroduce the characters and the setting by asking yes/no, either/or, or simple answer questions, such as: **¿Cómo se llama la chica? ¿Está Rosa en la Ciudad de México? ¿De dónde viene Rosa, de Miami o de la Ciudad de México?**

• Use the video, audio cassette, or CD to present the dialog. The expanded dialog on video offers additional listening practice opportunities.

Video Synopsis

• Rosa goes to Oaxaca to visit her cousin Sofía. She asks people for directions to Sofía's house. For a complete transcript of the video dialog, see p. 239D.

Comprehension Questions

1. ¿Sabe el hombre dónde queda la calle Morelos? (No.)
2. ¿Viene Rosa a visitar a su prima? (Sí.)
3. ¿Es difícil llegar a la calle Morelos desde la tienda? (No.)
4. ¿Llegas en diez minutos a pie? (Sí.)
5. ¿Prefiere Rosa ir en taxi o a pie? (a pie)
6. ¿Está el banco en la avenida Constitución o en la calle Morelos? (en la avenida Constitución)
7. ¿Qué hay al lado del banco, un hotel o una farmacia? (una farmacia)
8. ¿Qué hay en el parque? (una estatua)
9. ¿Dónde está la tía de Rosa? (Está haciendo algunas compras.)
10. ¿Por qué quiere Rosa ir de compras con Sofía? (Porque es el cumpleaños de su mamá.)

▌Block Schedule

Variety First, have students write a 2-sentence description of each character: Rosa, Carlos, and Sofía. Then have them write a 3–5 sentence summary of the dialog. Combine the best descriptions and summaries to come up with a dialog résumé. (For additional activities, see **Block Scheduling Copymasters.**)

Teaching Resource Options

Print
Unit 4 Resource Book
Video Activities, p. 25
Videoscript, p. 28
Audioscript, pp. 29–30
Audioscript *Para hispanohablantes,*
pp. 29–30

Audiovisual
OHT 114 (Quick Start)
Audio Program Cassettes 10A, 10B /
CD 10
Audio *Para hispanohablantes*
Cassette 10A / CD 10
Video Program Videotape 4 /
Videodisc 2B

Quick Start Review

♻ Video review

Use OHT 114 or write on the board:
Complete the sentences according to
the video.
1. ¿Puede usted decirme dónde ____
la calle Morelos?
2. No sé dónde queda su nueva
casa. Busco esta ____.
3. ____ ____ llegas en diez minutos.
4. Sí, hay un banco ____ ____ ____
una farmacia.
5. ____ ____ la estatua está la calle
Morelos.
Answers *See p. 239D.*

Teaching Suggestions
Comprehension Check
Use **Actividades 1** and **2** to assess
retention after the dialog. After
students have successfully completed
both activities, have them add items to
Actividad 1 and quiz each other.

ACTIVIDAD 1 Objective: Transitional practice
Listening comprehension/vocabulary

Answers (See script, p. 239D.)
1. Cierto   2. Cierto   3. Falso. Es fácil llegar a la
casa de Sofía.   4. Falso. Las dos quieren ir al
mercado.   5. Falso. Rosa quiere comprar algo
para su madre.

ACTIVIDAD 2 Objective: Transitional practice
Listening comprehension/vocabulary

Answers (See script, p. 239D.)
b, e, a, f, c, d

OBJECTIVES
• Identify places
• Give addresses
• Choose transportation
• Request directions
• Give instructions

En acción
VOCABULARIO Y GRAMÁTICA

¿Cierto o falso?

Escuchar ¿Es cierto o falso?
Si es falso, di lo que es cierto.
(*Hint: Say what is true.*)

1. Sofía no sabe que Rosa
viene a visitarla.
2. El hombre de la calle no
sabe dónde vive Sofía.
3. Es difícil llegar a la casa de
Sofía.
4. Rosa quiere ir al mercado,
pero Sofía no quiere ir.
5. Rosa quiere comprar algo
para su padre.

¿En qué orden?

Escuchar Di en qué orden
pasan los sucesos. (*Hint: Give
the order of events.*)

a. Rosa habla con Carlos.
b. Rosa llega a Oaxaca.
c. Rosa camina a la casa de
su prima.
d. Sofía habla con Rosa sobre
el mercado.
e. Rosa habla con un hombre
en la calle.
f. Rosa recibe el mapa de
Carlos.

♻ La nueva comunidad

Hablar Una muchacha quiere saber qué hay en
su nueva comunidad. ¿Qué pregunta?
(*Hint: Ask about places.*)

modelo

¿Hay un correo por aquí?

Nota

The word **por**, which most often means *for*, has many uses and meanings.

Camina **por** esta calle.	Walk **along/down** this street.
Pasa **por** la tienda.	Come (Pass) **by** the store.
¿Qué haces **por** aquí?	What are you doing **around** here?

246   doscientos cuarenta y seis
Unidad 4

Classroom Management

Peer Review Upon completion of **Actividades 1–3**,
have students exchange papers. Review answers with
the class and have students make any necessary
corrections.

Organizing Group Work Students should
brainstorm as many items as possible that they could
expect to purchase in the stores presented on p. 247.
If necessary, they should refer to a dictionary for
unknown words. Have each group share their lists with
the rest of the class.

- Use the verb **decir**
- Use prepositions of location
- Use regular affirmative **tú** commands

ACTIVIDAD 4

¿Adónde van?

Hablar Rosa y Sofía van de compras. Di adónde van para comprar las siguientes cosas. *(Hint: Say where they go to buy things.)*

modelo

Van a la pastelería.

1. 2. 3. 4. 5.
6. 7. 8. 9. 10.

ACTIVIDAD 5

♻ ¿En qué estación?

Escuchar Escucha las descripciones. ¿Qué estación describe cada una? *(Hint: Say which season.)*

a. la primavera
b. el verano
c. el otoño
d. el invierno

Vocabulario

Las tiendas

el centro comercial

CARNICERÍA — **la carnicería**
Joyería ◊ Joyería — **la joyería**
LIBRERÍA — **la librería**
Panadería — **la panadería**

papelería — **la papelería**
Pastelería — **la pastelería**
TIENDA DE música y videos — **la tienda de música y videos**
ZAPATERÍA — **la zapatería**

¿A qué tiendas vas de compras?

doscientos cuarenta y siete
Etapa 1 **247**

Teaching All Students

Extra Help In pairs, have students review store vocabulary. One student says they need something (**Necesito un libro.**); the other says where they can go to buy it (**Vamos a la librería.**).

Native Speakers If you have students from the southern hemisphere, ask them to name the months for each season in their home countries. Also have them give a general weather description for each.

Multiple Intelligences

Visual Have each student make an advertisement or flier for one store. They should draw and label a picture of the store and items sold in it. For the names of the items, they will need to use their dictionaries or the help of native speakers in the class. Display the advertisements/fliers on the bulletin board.

ACTIVIDAD 3 **Objective:** Transitional practice
Places in a city

🔄 **Hay**

Answers
1. ¿Hay una farmacia por aquí?
2. ¿Hay una estación de autobuses por aquí?
3. ¿Hay una plaza por aquí?
4. ¿Hay un banco por aquí?
5. ¿Hay una iglesia por aquí?
6. ¿Hay un hotel por aquí?

Teaching Suggestions
Teaching Vocabulary

Have students practice the **Vocabulario** in pairs. One student names a familiar store in their town/city. The other says what kind of store it is.

Language Note

Point out to students that the names of these stores come from the items they sell. **La librería** sells **libros**, **la papelería** sells **papel**, **la zapatería** sells **zapatos**, and so on. Students will learn: **joyas** *(jewelry)* in **Unidad 4, Etapa 2**; **carne** *(meat)*, **pan** *(bread)*, and **pastel** *(cake)* in **Unidad 4, Etapa 3**.

ACTIVIDAD 4 **Objective:** Transitional practice
Places in a city

Answers
1. Van a la tienda de música.   2. Van a la joyería.
3. Van a la zapatería.   4. Van a la carnicería.
5. Van a la librería.   6. Van a la farmacia.
7. Van al correo.   8. Van a la papelería.
9. Van al café.   10. Van a la panadería.

ACTIVIDAD 5 **Objective:** Transitional practice
Listening comprehension

🔄 **Seasons, weather**

Answers (See script, p. 239D.)
1. d   2. b   3. a   4. c

▪ Block Schedule

Variety Do a variation of **Actividad 3** related to your town/city. Working in pairs, one student plays a Spanish-speaking visitor. He/she asks the other student whether certain places/stores are found in your town/city. Students should take turns playing each role.

Quick Start Review

🔔 Verbs with irregular **yo** forms
Use OHT 114 or write on the board:
Write sentences using the elements given:

1. yo / saber / hablar español
2. yo / hacer / mi tarea en la biblioteca
3. yo / oír / a mi hermano
4. yo / tener / quince años
5. yo / conocer / a un muchacho de Puerto Rico
6. yo / venir / del cine

Answers
1. Yo sé hablar español.
2. Yo hago mi tarea en la biblioteca.
3. Yo oigo a mi hermano.
4. Yo tengo quince años.
5. Yo conozco a un muchacho de Puerto Rico.
6. Yo vengo del cine.

Teaching Suggestions
Teaching the Verb decir

- Review regular and irregular verbs.
- Point out that **decir** means *to say* or *to tell.* Give one example of each: **A ver qué dice mi prima. ¿Puede usted decirme dónde queda la calle Morelos?**
- Introduce and practice the verb **salir** before doing **Actividad 7.**

GRAMÁTICA

The Verb decir

To talk about what someone says, use the verb **decir**. The verb **decir** means *to say* or *to tell*. It has several irregular forms in the present tense.

di**go**	**d**e**cimos**
di**ces**	**d**e**cís**
di**ce**	**d**i**cen**

Only the **nosotros(as)** and **vosotros(as)** forms are regular.

Note that **decir que** means *to say that...*

Sofía says: —Yo **d**i**go que** el mercado tiene las cosas más bonitas.
I say that the market has the prettiest things.

6 Gramática

¿Quién lo dice?

Hablar Muchos dicen que Oaxaca tiene mucho de interés. ¿Quién lo dice? *(Hint: Who says what?)*

modelo

yo / la ciudad / calles bonitas
Yo digo que **la ciudad** tiene **calles bonitas.**

1. Carlos / las iglesias / arte regional
2. Rosa y Sofía / el Zócalo / gente interesante
3. tú / las joyerías / cosas bonitas
4. Roberto y yo / los cafés / comida regional
5. yo / los museos / artículos interesantes

TAMBIÉN SE DICE

There are different ways to talk about a car.

- **el auto(móvil):** many countries
- **el coche:** Spain, parts of South America
- **el carro:** Mexico, Central America

7 Gramática

¿De dónde salen?

Escribir Rosa y Sofía ven a muchas personas. ¿De dónde salen todos? Usa la forma correcta de **salir.** *(Hint: Say from where people are leaving.)*

Nota

Salir means *to leave* or *to go out.* It has an irregular **yo** form: **salgo.** Its other forms are regular.

1. Rosa y Sofía _____ del café.
2. Carlos _____ de la tienda de música y videos.
3. Yo _____ de la panadería.
4. Nosotros _____ de la farmacia.
5. Juan y Pedro _____ de la librería.
6. Beatriz _____ del cine.
7. Tú _____ del correo.
8. Ustedes _____ del banco.

■ **MÁS PRÁCTICA** *cuaderno* p. 85
■ **PARA HISPANOHABLANTES** *cuaderno* p. 83

---

248 doscientos cuarenta y ocho
Unidad 4

Classroom Community

Paired Activity First, have students write topics of interest on slips of paper—movies, sports, school events, etc. Collect the slips and put them in a container. Then have pairs of students select a slip of paper and discuss what various people say about the topic. Encourage them to include a variety of people in their discussions.

Group Activity Have students plan a trip to Oaxaca in which they must use at least 5 different modes of transportation. Some useful verbs are **salir, llegar, viajar, ir, venir.** Have each group present its plans to the class.

ACTIVIDAD 8

De viaje

Hablar/Escribir Todos salen. ¿Para dónde salen y qué transporte van a usar? *(Hint: Say where they are headed and what transportation they use.)*

modelo

Sofía / el café

Sofía sale para **el café**. Va en **taxi**.

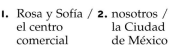

1. Rosa y Sofía / el centro comercial
2. nosotros / la Ciudad de México
3. tú / San Juan
4. ellos / Miami

5. Félix / el banco
6. ustedes / el correo
7. Carlos / Monte Albán
8. yo / ¿?

ACTIVIDAD 9

¿Qué dicen?

Hablar Pregúntale a un(a) amigo(a) cómo les gusta viajar a estas personas. Cambien de papel. *(Hint: Explain what they say about traveling.)*

modelo

tus padres

Tú: ¿Cómo les gusta viajar a **tus padres**?

Tu amigo(a): *Mis padres siempre dicen que les gusta viajar en avión.*

1. tu hermano(a)
2. tus abuelos
3. tú
4. tus amigos
5. tú y tu familia

Vocabulario

De viaje

manejar *to drive*
viajar *to travel*
el viaje *trip*

 a pie

 en autobús

 en avión

 en barco

 en carro

 en metro

 en moto(cicleta)

 en taxi

 en tren

¿Cómo prefieres viajar?

Teaching All Students

Extra Help Have students create verb flashcards for **decir** and **salir,** and add them to the flashcards they have made for other verbs. In pairs, have them quiz each other on all verb forms.

Multiple Intelligences

Interpersonal Have students ask each other which mode of transportation the other prefers, following this model: **¿Te gusta más viajar en avión o en barco?** Each student should give at least 3 either/or statements.

Naturalist Have students describe a hike to a place of interest in their town/city. Ask them to describe the natural phenomena and buildings they see along the way.

ACTIVIDAD 6

Objective: Controlled practice
Decir

Answers

1. Carlos dice que las iglesias tienen arte regional.
2. Rosa y Sofía dicen que el Zócalo tiene gente interesante.
3. Tú dices que las joyerías tienen cosas bonitas.
4. Roberto y yo decimos que los cafés tienen comida regional.
5. Yo digo que los museos tienen artículos interesantes.

ACTIVIDAD 7

Objective: Controlled practice
Salir in writing

Answers

1. salen 3. salgo 5. salen 7. sales
2. sale 4. salimos 6. sale 8. salen

ACTIVIDAD 8

Objective: Transitional practice
Salir/transportation vocabulary

Answers

1. Rosa y Sofía salen para el centro comercial. Van en autobús.
2. Nosotros salimos para la Ciudad de México. Vamos en tren.
3. Tú sales para San Juan. Vas en barco.
4. Ellos salen para Miami. Van en avión.
5. Félix sale para el banco. Va en moto(cicleta).
6. Ustedes salen para el correo. Van a pie.
7. Carlos sale para Monte Albán. Va en carro.
8. Yo salgo para [el café]. Voy [en metro].

ACTIVIDAD 9

Objective: Open-ended practice
Decir/transportation vocabulary in conversation

Answers will vary.

Language Notes

- Students may use the word **motocicleta** or the shortened form **moto** to refer to a motorcycle. Both are feminine.
- **Manejar** is usually used to talk about driving in Latin America. **Conducir** is usually used in Spain. **Guiar** is used in Puerto Rico.

Block Schedule

Change of Pace Have students draw a map with their house/apartment as the central location. The map can be of your town/city, of your state, or even of the world. Have them add pictures and labels of stores, monuments, places they are interested in going to, etc. Then have them write sentences saying how they go to each place. For example: **Voy al centro comercial a pie. Voy a Argentina en avión.** (For additional activities, see **Block Scheduling Copymasters**.)

Teaching Resource Options

Print

Más práctica Workbook PE, pp. 86–87
Para hispanohablantes Workbook PE,
 pp. 84–85
Block Scheduling Copymasters
Unit 4 Resource Book
 Más práctica Workbook TE, pp. 6–7
 Para hispanohablantes Workbook
  TE, pp. 12–13
 Information Gap Activities, p. 17

Audiovisual
OHT 114 (Quick Start)

Technology
Intrigas y aventuras CD-ROM, Disc 1

Quick Start Review
🔄 Transportation

Use OHT 114 or write on the board:
List 5 modes of transportation. Then,
using each expression, write a complete
sentence saying where you go.

Modelo: a pie
 Voy al parque a pie.

Answers *See p. 239D.*

Teaching Suggestions
**Teaching Using Prepositional
Phrases to Express Location**

Explain that these words are important
for communicating where things are.
Use manipulatives to reinforce the
meanings of the prepositions.

Objective: Controlled practice
Prepositional phrases to express location

Answers
1. a la derecha
2. cerca
3. detrás
4. lejos
5. a la izquierda
6. entre

GRAMÁTICA

Using Prepositional Phrases to Express Location

When you talk about where things are located, use **prepositions**.
Here are some common ones.

- Rosa está **cerca del taxi.**
 *Rosa is **near** the taxi.*

- El banco está **detrás del taxi.**
 *The bank is **behind** the taxi.*

- El taxi está **enfrente del banco.**
 *The taxi is **in front of** the bank.*

- El policía está **al lado del banco.**
 *The policeman is **beside** the bank.*

- La farmacia está **a la izquierda de la carnicería.**
 *The pharmacy is **to the left of** the butcher's shop.*

- La carnicería está **entre la farmacia y la panadería.**
 *The butcher's shop is **between** the pharmacy and the bakery.*

- La panadería está **a la derecha de la carnicería.**
 *The bakery is **to the right of** the butcher's shop.*

- El aeropuerto está **lejos de esta calle.**
 *The airport is **far from** this street.*

> Use **de** when the preposition is followed by a **specific location**.

ACTIVIDAD 10 Gramática

¿Dónde está?

Hablar/Escribir Explica dónde están las tiendas
de la foto. *(Hint: Explain where they are.)*

1. La carnicería está (a la izquierda / a la
 derecha) de la farmacia.
2. El taxi está (cerca / lejos) de Rosa.
3. El banco está (enfrente / detrás) del taxi.
4. La panadería está (cerca / lejos) del
 aeropuerto.
5. La carnicería está (a la izquierda / a la
 derecha) de la panadería.
6. La farmacia está (entre / al lado de) la
 carnicería y el banco.

MÁS PRÁCTICA *cuaderno* pp. 86–87
PARA HISPANOHABLANTES *cuaderno* pp. 84–85

Classroom Community

Group Activity Have students work in small
groups. The first student names a place in their
town/city. The others use prepositions to say where it
is located. Continue around the group.

Paired Activity In this activity, one partner tries to
get the other to name the right store. For example:
**Trabajo en una tienda entre la escuela y la biblioteca.
¿Qué es?** Students provide more clues as needed.

Game Give students the location of 10 different
people in the class. For example: **Esta persona está
lejos de la profesora. Está entre Raúl y Paulina.**
Student write down the names of the people. The
student(s) with the most correct answers gets extra
credit points.

ACTIVIDAD 11

En el centro comercial

Hablar Rosa y Sofía van al centro comercial. Sofía explica dónde están las tiendas. *(Hint: Say where the stores are.)*

modelo

la farmacia

Rosa: *¿Dónde está la farmacia?*

Sofía: *La farmacia está enfrente del café. Está a la derecha de la pastelería y a la izquierda de la papelería. (o: Está entre la pastelería y la papelería.) Está detrás del correo.*

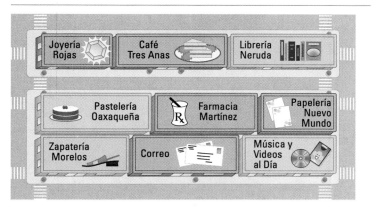

Joyería Rojas	Café Tres Anas	Librería Neruda
Pastelería Oaxaqueña	Farmacia Martínez	Papelería Nuevo Mundo
Zapatería Morelos	Correo	Música y Videos al Día

1. correo
2. librería
3. café
4. papelería
5. zapatería
6. joyería
7. pastelería
8. tienda de música y videos

NOTA CULTURAL

The Zapotecs, Mixtecs, and 16 other Native American groups live in Oaxaca, each with its own language and culture. In July they celebrate the **Guelaguetza,** wearing their native costumes, dancing, and exchanging gifts. **Guelaguetza** is a Zapotec word that means *gift.*

ACTIVIDAD 12 Las tiendas

PARA CONVERSAR

STRATEGY: SPEAKING

Recognize and use set phrases Think of the expressions you use as a whole instead of constructing them a word at a time. This helps you think in Spanish instead of translating from English.

Hablar/Escribir Explica dónde están las tiendas de tu comunidad. ¿Cómo vas? *(Hint: Explain where stores are and how you go there.)*

a pie	en carro
en autobús	en moto
en metro	en bicicleta
en taxi	

modelo

la librería

***La librería** está lejos de mi casa. Está al lado de una farmacia grande. Voy a la librería en autobús.*

1. farmacia
2. librería
3. zapatería
4. joyería
5. pastelería
6. centro comercial
7. tienda de música y videos

■ **MÁS COMUNICACIÓN** p. R10

doscientos cincuenta y uno
Etapa 1

251

UNIDAD 4 Etapa 1
Vocabulary/Grammar

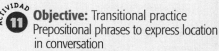

ACTIVIDAD 11

Objective: Transitional practice Prepositional phrases to express location in conversation

1. El correo está entre la zapatería y la tienda de música y videos. (o: Está a la derecha de la zapatería y a la izquierda de la tienda de música y videos.) Está enfrente de la farmacia.
2. La librería está a la derecha del café. Está enfrente de la papelería.
3. El café está entre la joyería y la librería. (o: Está a la derecha de la joyería y a la izquierda de la librería.) Está enfrente de la farmacia.
4. La papelería está a la derecha de la farmacia. Está enfrente de la librería.
5. La zapatería está a la izquierda del correo. Está enfrente de la pastelería.
6. La joyería está a la izquierda del café. Está enfrente de la pastelería.
7. La pastelería está enfrente de la joyería. Está a la izquierda de la farmacia. Está detrás de la zapatería.
8. La tienda de música y videos está a la derecha del correo. Está enfrente de la papelería.

ACTIVIDAD 12

Objective: Open-ended practice Prepositional phrases to express location

Answers will vary.

Culture Highlights

● **LA GUELAGUETZA** La Guelaguetza, one of the most popular fiestas of Oaxaca, takes place on the third and fourth Monday of July. The 3-hour-long folk dance performed during the fiesta features groups representing each of the 7 regions of Oaxaca and their indigenous groups.

Block Schedule

FunBreak In groups, have students create 3-D cities to use throughout the **Etapa.** Use posterboard for the base and have students draw the streets and empty spots for buildings, parks, etc. For the buildings, use either houses from board games or cutouts. For the parks, student can make trees from art supplies. They should also make labels for each building, park, etc. Use the cities to practice vocabulary and giving directions. Students can change the location of the buildings and the labels to add variety to their activities. (For additional activities, see **Block Scheduling Copymasters.**)

Teaching All Students

Extra Help Have students arrange a pencil and 5 small pieces of paper of different colors in front of them. Tell them where to place the pencil in relation to the pieces of paper. For example: **Pongan el lápiz entre el papel azul y el amarillo.**

Native Speakers For **Actividad 11,** ask students to sketch a map of stores in their home communities. Have them teach the other students any new names of shops. For example: **la mercería, la churrería, la droguería,** etc.

Multiple Intelligences

Kinesthetic Call on various students and send them to different locations around the room. Use prepositional phrases. For example: **María, tú vas al lado del pizarrón. Javier, tú vas a la derecha de mi escritorio.**

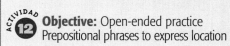

Teaching Resource Options

Print

Más práctica Workbook PE, p. 88
Para hispanohablantes Workbook PE, p. 86
Block Scheduling Copymasters
Unit 4 Resource Book
 Más práctica Workbook TE, p. 8
 Para hispanohablantes Workbook TE, p. 9

Audiovisual

OHT 115 (Quick Start)

Technology

Intrigas y aventuras CD-ROM, Disc 1

Quick Start Review

 Vocabulary

Use OHT 115 or write on the board: Write the words from the following list that refer to traveling on foot.

caminar / correr / cerrar / pasear / decir / nadar / manejar / ir a pie

Answers *See p. 239D.*

Teaching Suggestions
Regular Affirmative tú Commands

Affirmative **tú** command forms of one syllable do not need an accent when a pronoun is attached: **velo** *(see it)*.

Language Note

Emphasize the difference between **derecho** *(straight ahead)* and **derecha** *(right)*.

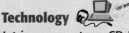 **Objective:** Controlled practice Regular affirmative **tú** commands

 Free-time activities

Answers
1. Corre.
2. Saca fotos.
3. Habla con Carlos.
4. Escribe una carta.
5. Escucha música.
6. Pasea por la plaza.
7. Lee revistas.
8. Visita el museo.

14 Objective: Controlled practice Regular affirmative **tú** commands

Direct object pronouns

Answers
1. A: ¿Invito a Sandra? / B: Sí, ¡invítala!
2. A: ¿Invito a las muchachas? / B: Sí, ¡invítalas!
3. A: ¿Invito a Jorge, Pepe y Alicia? / B: Sí, ¡invítalos!
4. A: ¿Invito a Julio? / B: Sí, ¡invítalo!
5. A: ¿Invito a Juan y Diego? / B: Sí, ¡invítalos!
6. A: ¿Invito a Amalia? / B: Sí, ¡invítala!

GRAMÁTICA
Regular Affirmative tú Commands

To tell a person to do something, use an affirmative command. **Tú commands** are used with friends or family. The regular affirmative **tú command** is the same as the **él/ella** form of the present tense.

Infinitive	Present	Affirmative tú Command
caminar	(él, ella) **camina**	¡Camina!
comer	(él, ella) **come**	¡Come!
abrir	(él, ella) **abre**	¡Abre!

Carlos says:

—**Camina** por esta calle… **Cruza** el parque…
***Walk** down this street… **Cross** the park…*

If you use a **command** with a **direct object pronoun**, attach the pronoun to the end of the command.

Cruza el parque. ⟶ ¡Crúza**lo**!
***Cross** the park. ⟶ **Cross** it!*

*If needed, add an **accent** when you attach a pronoun to retain the original stress.*

Vocabulario

Las direcciones

cruzar *to cross*
doblar *to turn*
quedar (en) *to stay, to be (in a specific place), to agree on*
la cuadra *city block*
derecho *straight ahead*
desde *from*
hasta *until, as far as*
¿Cómo vas a la escuela?

 **13 Gramática**

 ¿Qué hacer en Oaxaca?

Escribir Sofía le explica a Rosa qué hacer en Oaxaca. *(Hint: Explain what Sofía suggests Rosa should do.)*

modelo

jugar al tenis
Juega al tenis.

1. correr
2. sacar fotos
3. hablar con Carlos
4. escribir una carta
5. escuchar música
6. pasear por la plaza
7. leer revistas
8. visitar el museo

14 Gramática

¡Invita a todos!

Hablar La amiga de Sofía organiza una fiesta y quiere saber a quién invitar. Sofía le dice su opinión. *(Hint: Tell who Sofía says to invite.)*

modelo

Carlos	**Su amiga:** ¿Invito a **Carlos**?
	Sofía: Sí, ¡invítalo!

1. Sandra
2. las muchachas
3. Jorge, Pepe y Alicia
4. Julio
5. Juan y Diego
6. Amalia

MÁS PRÁCTICA *cuaderno* p. 88
PARA HISPANOHABLANTES *cuaderno* p. 86

Classroom Community

TPR Call on individual students and give them a command. For example: **Marcos, escribe en el pizarrón, por favor. Rosa, abre el libro, por favor.**

Paired Activity Have students imagine that they are having difficulty in school. In turn, each student gives the other a piece of advice, using an affirmative command. Continue for 3–5 rounds.

Cooperative Learning Have students work in groups of 4. Student 1 writes a verb infinitive on a piece of paper. Student 2 writes the affirmative **tú** command form. Student 3 writes a sentence using the form. Student 4 reads it aloud. The group makes any necessary corrections. Then Student 2 writes the verb infinitive and the activity continues.

ACTIVIDAD 15

♻ ¿Qué hago primero?

Hablar Carlos tiene que hacer muchas cosas hoy. Le pregunta a Rosa qué debe hacer primero. *(Hint: Say what Rosa tells Carlos to do.)*

modelo

¿trabajar en la tienda o comer?

Carlos: *¿Qué hago primero, **trabajo en la tienda o como**?*

Rosa: *Primero, come. Después, trabaja.*

1. ¿escribir una carta o estudiar para un examen?
2. ¿leer el periódico o abrir la tienda?
3. ¿correr en el parque o cenar?
4. ¿ver la televisión o terminar mi tarea?

ACTIVIDAD 16

♻ ¡Mañana es otro día!

Hablar Tu amigo(a) quiere hacer muchas cosas, pero no tiene tiempo. Tú le dices cuándo hacer todo. *(Hint: Say when your friend should do things.)*

modelo

comprar unos jeans

Tu amigo(a): *Quiero **comprar unos jeans**, pero no tengo tiempo.*

Tú: *¡Cómpralos el lunes!*

1. buscar las gafas de sol
2. visitar el museo del centro
3. leer un libro sobre un viaje
4. vender los libros
5. preparar el almuerzo para la familia
6. escribir una carta

ACTIVIDAD 17

¡A la fiesta!

Hablar/Escribir Sofía explica cómo llegar a su casa para una fiesta. Su amiga Amalia la llama para confirmar las direcciones. Completa su conversación, usando un pronombre si es posible. *(Hint: Give directions.)*

modelo

Amalia: *¿Primero camino derecho tres cuadras por la calle González Ortega? ¿Cruzo la calle?*

Sofía: *Sí, camina derecho tres cuadras por la calle González Ortega. Crúzala.*

1. **Amalia:** ¿Entonces doblo a la izquierda y camino seis cuadras más?
2. **Amalia:** Allí veo una plaza. ¿Cruzo la plaza y camino una cuadra más por la calle Guerrero?
3. **Amalia:** ¿Entonces doblo a la derecha y camino una cuadra por la calle 20 de Noviembre?
4. **Amalia:** Entonces, llego a la avenida Hidalgo. ¿La cruzo?
5. **Amalia:** Entonces, veo el Parque Alameda. ¿Cruzo el parque?

N O T A CULTURAL

Oaxaca means "place of the **guaje**" in Nahuatl, a language of Mexico. The **guaje** is a large tree with pods and flowers. The pods sometimes look like gourds. Some say *Oaxaca* means "place of the gourds."

ACTIVIDAD 15

Objective: Transitional practice Regular affirmative **tú** commands in conversation

♻ Sequencing events

Answers

1. A: ¿Qué hago primero, escribo una carta o estudio para un examen? / B: Primero, escribe una carta (o: estudia para un examen).
2. A: ¿Qué hago primero, leo el periódico o abro la tienda? / B: Primero, lee el periódico (o: abre la tienda).
3. A: ¿Qué hago primero, corro en el parque o ceno? / B: Primero, corre en el parque (o: cena).
4. A: ¿Qué hago primero, veo la televisión o termino mi tarea? / B: Primero, ve la televisión (o: termina tu tarea).

ACTIVIDAD 16

Objective: Transitional practice Regular affirmative **tú** commands in conversation

♻ Direct object pronouns

Answers

Answers will vary.

1. A: Quiero buscar las gafas de sol.
   B: ¡Búscalas... !
2. A: Quiero visitar el museo del centro.
   B: ¡Visítalo... !
3. A: Quiero leer un libro sobre un viaje.
   B: ¡Léelo... !
4. A: Quiero vender los libros.
   B: ¡Véndelos... !
5. A: Quiero preparar el almuerzo para la familia.
   B: ¡Prepáralo... !
6. A: Quiero escribir una carta.
   B: ¡Escríbela... !

ACTIVIDAD 17

Objective: Transitional practice Regular affirmative **tú** commands

Answers

1. Sofía: Sí, dobla a la izquierda y camina seis cuadras más.
2. Sofía: Sí, crúzala y camina una cuadra más por la calle Guerrero.
3. Sofía: Sí, dobla a la derecha y camina una cuadra por la calle 20 de Noviembre.
4. Sofía: Sí, crúzala.
5. Sofía: Sí, crúzalo.

▣ Block Schedule

Variety In pairs, have students make a list of affirmative **tú** commands they would hear at a variety of locations, such as at home, at school, or around town. Then have them work with another pair. One pair reads their items and the other pair guesses the possible location. (For additional activities, see **Block Scheduling Copymasters**.)

Teaching All Students

Extra Help Ask students either/or questions (for example: **¿Practico el piano o estudio para mi examen?**) and have them respond orally or in writing using affirmative **tú** command forms.

Native Speakers Have students write an original version of **Actividad 13,** using their home communities instead of Oaxaca. Put the activities on an overhead transparency and have the class complete them.

Multiple Intelligences

Kinesthetic Take one student out of the classroom and put a blindfold on him/her. Rearrange the desks in rows and have the class decide where they will have the student go. When the blindfolded student returns, the class directs him/her around the room to a designated desk. Continue with other students.

Teaching Resource Options

Print

Block Scheduling Copymasters
Unit 4 Resource Book
  Information Gap Activities, pp. 18–19
  Audioscript, p. 30
  Audioscript *Para hispanohablantes,*
    p. 30

Audiovisual

Audio Program Cassettes 10A, 10B /
  CD 10
Audio *Para hispanohablantes*
  Cassette 10A / CD 10

Technology

Intrigas y aventuras CD-ROM, Disc 1

Teaching Suggestions
Teaching Vocabulary

Have students look back at the **Diálogo**
to find where and in what context
some of these expressions are used.

Language Note

Perdona is the familiar form. **Perdone** is
the formal form.

 Objective: Transitional practice
Giving directions

Answers
Answers will vary. Answers could include:
1. Joven 2: Cómo no. Camina derecho una
   cuadra por la avenida Hidalgo hasta la calle 5
   de Mayo. Dobla a la izquierda y camina tres
   cuadras más hasta la calle Murguía. La tienda
   de artesanías está en la esquina.
2. Joven 2: Cómo no. Camina derecho dos
   cuadras por la calle 5 de Mayo hasta la
   avenida Independencia. Dobla a la derecha y
   camina tres cuadras más hasta la calle 20 de
   Noviembre. El correo está en la esquina.
3. Joven 2: Cómo no. Camina derecho tres
   cuadras por la calle 20 de Noviembre hasta la
   calle Las Casas. Dobla a la izquierda. El
   mercado está a la derecha.
4. Joven 2: Cómo no. Camina derecho por la
   calle Las Casas hasta la calle Miguel Cabrera.
   Dobla a la izquierda y camina dos cuadras
   hasta la avenida Hidalgo. Dobla a la derecha y
   la catedral está a la izquierda.
5. Joven 2: Cómo no. Camina derecho por la
   avenida Hidalgo hasta la calle Miguel Cabrera.
   Dobla a la izquierda y camina una cuadra más
   hasta la calle Guerrero. La iglesia está en la
   esquina.
6. Joven 2: Cómo no. Camina derecho una
   cuadra por la calle Miguel Cabrera hasta la
   avenida Hidalgo. El parque está en la esquina
   a la izquierda.

254 Vocabulary/Grammar • UNIDAD 4 Etapa 1

Una visita a Oaxaca

Hablar Estás de visita en Oaxaca. Quieres saber cómo llegar a
varios lugares. Hablas con dos jóvenes. ¿Qué dicen? Cambien
de papel. *(Hint: Ask directions to various places.)*

modelo

el parque → el teatro *(Estás en el parque. Vas al teatro.)*

Tú: *Perdona. ¿Cómo llego al teatro?*

Joven 1: *Lo siento, pero no sé. No vivo por aquí.*

Tú: *Perdona. ¿Puedes decirme dónde queda el teatro?*

Joven 2: *Cómo no. Camina derecho dos cuadras por la avenida Independencia
hasta la calle 5 de Mayo. El teatro está en la esquina.*

1. el Zócalo → la tienda
   de artesanías
2. la tienda de artesanías
   → el correo
3. el correo → el mercado
4. el mercado → la catedral
5. la catedral → la iglesia
6. la iglesia → el parque

Vocabulario

Direcciones, por favor

Perdona(e), ¿cómo llego a…?
Pardon, how do I get to…?

**¿Puedes (Puede usted) decirme
dónde queda…?** *Could you tell
me where…is?*

¿Queda lejos? *Is it far?*

Las respuestas

¡Cómo no! *Of course!*

Lo siento… *I'm sorry…*

acá/aquí *here*

allá/allí *there*

el camino *road*

la dirección *address, direction*

¿Cómo explicas las direcciones?

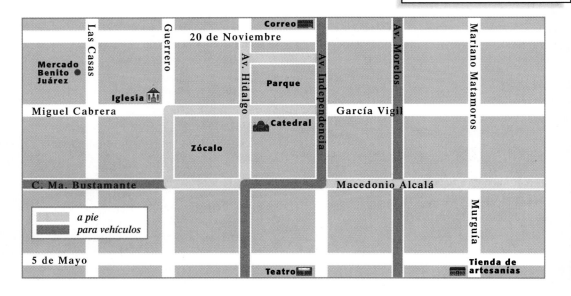

254 | doscientos cincuenta y cuatro
Unidad 4

Classroom Community

Cooperative Learning Have students work in
groups of 4 and do **Actividad 18** in a cooperative
learning format. Student 1 plays the role of **Tú;** Student
2 is **Joven 1;** Student 3 is **Joven 2;** Student 4 is the
monitor. The monitor checks for statements that do not
make sense. That person identifies the problem and the
group works together to correct it. Students switch roles
for each activity item.

Storytelling Working in pairs, have students write a
story or mini-dialog using as many of the new
expressions from **Etapa 1** as possible. Have several
pairs present their work to the class.

ACTIVIDAD 19

¿Puede usted decirme...?

Escuchar Rosa le pregunta a un policía cómo llegar a la librería. Escucha su conversación. Indica en qué cuadra del mapa están la librería, la papelería y el correo. *(Hint: Say where each place is.)*

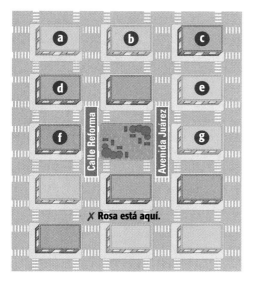

Calle Reforma

Avenida Juárez

✗ **Rosa está aquí.**

ACTIVIDAD 20

Tu comunidad

Escribir Vas a dar una fiesta. Escribe las direcciones para ir a tu casa desde la escuela. *(Hint: Give directions to your house from school.)*

modelo

Mi casa está a seis cuadras de la escuela. Camina dos cuadras por la calle Wilson. Vas a ver un banco. Dobla a la izquierda y camina dos cuadras por la calle Metropolitan. Hay una farmacia en la esquina. Dobla a la derecha y camina una cuadra. En la avenida Connecticut, dobla a la izquierda y camina una cuadra más. Yo vivo en la avenida Connecticut 284. Mi casa está enfrente de la pastelería.

Nota

Addresses with numbers that have more than two digits can be expressed by pairing digits.

284 Connecticut Avenue

—Vivo en la avenida Connecticut, dos ochenta y cuatro.

1340 Main Street

—Vivo en la calle Main, trece cuarenta.

■ **MÁS COMUNICACIÓN** p. R10

Pronunciación

Refrán

Pronunciación de la r When the letter **r** occurs in the middle of a word and between two vowels, it is pronounced by a single tap of your tongue just behind your teeth. It feels like the English *d* when you say the words *buddy* or *ladder*. To practice the tap **r**, pronounce these words. Then try the **refrán**. Can you guess what it means?

la joyería la panadería la papelería la pastelería la zapatería

Hay que ver para creer.

doscientos cincuenta y cinco
Etapa 1 **255**

Teaching All Students

Extra Help Use the maps you collected at the beginning of this **Etapa;** see "Planning Ahead," TE, p. 240. Use these maps for additional practice in asking for and giving directions.

Multiple Intelligences

Verbal Have students draw a simple map of a town with a town square, several buildings, a park, and a lake. Then have students work in pairs. One student describes his/her drawing. The other student attempts to reproduce it on paper, asking questions if necessary. Then students switch roles. Upon completion, students compare the finished products.

ACTIVIDAD 19 **Objective:** Transitional practice Listening comprehension/giving directions

Answers (See script, p. 239D.)
la librería: g
la papelería: b
el correo: b

ACTIVIDAD 20 **Objective:** Open-ended practice Giving directions in writing

Answers will vary.

Language Note

Point out that **calle** and **avenida** are not capitalized even when they are used to identify specific streets.

Critical Thinking

Have students exchange written directions from **Actividad 20,** draw a map according to the instructions, then return the map to be checked by the original writer.

Dictation

After students have read the **refrán** in the **Pronunciación,** have them close their books. Dictate the **refrán** in two segments while students write it.

Quick Wrap-up

Have students list all the words from the **Vocabulario,** pp. 242–243, and the **Diálogo,** pp. 244–245, that have the letter **r** in the middle of a word and between two vowels. Then have them practice pronouncing them.

Block Schedule

Research Have students research the history of Mexico and Oaxaca to find the significance of some of the street names on the map of Oaxaca on p. 254. Some are historical events and others are important people. (For additional activities, see **Block Scheduling Copymasters.**)

Teaching Resource Options

Print

Unit 4 Resource Book
  Audioscript, p. 31
  Audioscript *Para hispanohablantes*,
    p. 31

Audiovisual

Audio Program Cassette 10A / CD 10
Audio *Para hispanohablantes*
  Cassette 10A / CD 10
OHT M4; 115 (Quick Start)
Canciones Cassette / CD

Quick Start Review

♻ Oaxaca

Use OHT 115 or write on the board:
Make a list of at least 10 places or
buildings you would expect to see on
a visit to Oaxaca.

Answers
Answers will vary. Answers could include:
el Zócalo, Monte Albán, un parque, un correo,
un mercado, una farmacia, una iglesia, un
banco, un hotel, un aeropuerto, una estación
de autobuses, una carnicería, una joyería,
una librería, una panadería, una papelería,
una pastelería, una tienda de música y videos,
una zapatería

Teaching Suggestions

• **Prereading** Have students study the
pictures on pp. 256–257 for 1 min.
Then have them close their books and
share what they can recall seeing.
Based on this information, what do
they think the reading is about?

• **Strategy: Combine strategies**
Have students follow the steps in the
Strategy. Then have them complete
the chart.

• **Reading** Have a volunteer read
each paragraph. Then have the class
decide on a 2–4 word title for each
one.

• **Post-reading** Ask students to
summarize the entire reading in 2–3
sentences.

En voces
LECTURA

PARA LEER

STRATEGY: READING

Combine strategies Put together
the reading strategies you
have practiced.

1. Look at the title, photos,
   and graphics to predict the
   reading's theme.
2. Skim the reading to get a
   general idea of the content.
3. Use context clues to help
   you make intelligent
   guesses about new words.

These steps make it easier for
you to read Spanish.

Predict	Theme:
Skim	General Idea:
Use context clues	New Words:

¡VISITA OAXACA!
UN PASEO[1] A PIE

La ciudad de Oaxaca es
un monumento histórico
nacional. Hay arquitectura
colonial, iglesias y museos
muy importantes. Para
verla mejor tienes que
conocer Oaxaca a pie.

❶ Empieza en el Zócalo,
el centro de Oaxaca. Es el
lugar ideal para ver a los
oaxaqueños. Hay muchos
cafés y restaurantes aquí.

❷ Ahora cruza la calle
Guerrero y entra en el Palacio
de Gobierno[2]. Mira el mural
sobre la historia y la cultura
de Oaxaca.

Classroom Community

Paired Activity Have one student act as narrator,
while the partner imagines he/she is listening to a tape
about visiting Oaxaca. The narrator reads p. 256 of the
text with enthusiasm, while the partner listens. Partners
switch roles for p. 257. Then each student writes down
everything he/she remembers from the entire reading,
and they compare notes.

Portfolio Have students rewrite the reading,
adapting it to their town/city. Along with the text, they
should include photos or drawings.

Rubric A = 13–15 pts. **B** = 10–12 pts. **C** = 7–9 pts. **D** = 4–6 pts. **F** = < 4 pts.

Writing criteria	Scale
Vocabulary use	1 2 3 4 5
Grammar/spelling accuracy	1 2 3 4 5
Creativity, appearance	1 2 3 4 5

③ Al salir del Palacio, camina hasta llegar a la avenida Hidalgo. Cruza la avenida para ver la catedral. A veces hay conciertos aquí.

④ Detrás de la catedral está la avenida Independencia. Sigue por la avenida y dobla a la izquierda en la calle Macedonio Alcalá. Allí hay unas tiendas excelentes y varias casas coloniales. Sigue derecho cuatro cuadras para ver la iglesia de Santo Domingo. Mira el interior.

⑤ Al lado de la iglesia queda el Museo Regional de Oaxaca. En el museo hay objetos arqueológicos de Monte Albán. También hay ropa, artículos textiles y otros artículos de las primeras culturas de la región.

CALLE NICOLÁS BRAVO

CALLE IGNACIO ALLENDE

CALLE GARCÍA VIGIL

CALLE MACEDONIO ALCALÁ

⑥ Regresa al Zócalo. Si hace buen tiempo, hay conciertos aquí a las siete de la tarde. ¿Tienes hambre? Entonces, cena en uno de los restaurantes oaxaqueños. ¡Come algo típico y pasa un rato con tus amigos!

¹ walk   ² Government Palace, State Capitol

¿Comprendiste?

1. ¿Por qué es importante visitar Oaxaca?
2. ¿Dónde empieza el paseo?
3. ¿Dónde ves un mural sobre la historia y la cultura de Oaxaca?
4. ¿Dónde está la catedral?
5. ¿Qué hay en la calle Macedonio Alcalá?
6. ¿Dónde está el Museo Regional de Oaxaca?

¿Qué piensas?

Eres un(a) turista en Oaxaca, pero tienes sólo cuatro horas para visitarla. ¿Qué es lo más interesante para ti? ¿Por qué? ¿Qué vas a hacer primero? ¿Adónde vas después? Describe tu visita.

doscientos cincuenta y siete
Etapa 1   **257**

Teaching All Students

Extra Help Have students work together to answer the ¿Comprendiste? questions. They should first figure out the meaning of the questions, and then locate the answers in the text.

Multiple Intelligences

Intrapersonal Have students plan an itinerary for a trip to Oaxaca based on the descriptions in the reading that interest them the most. They should also look back at the maps on pp. 240 and 254.

Culture Highlights

● **EL ZÓCALO** El Zócalo in Oaxaca is a very large plaza where a great variety of entertaining activities take place every day and night. Bands play music every evening, and there are sometimes several bands playing at the same time in different corners of the plaza.

● **EL MUSEO REGIONAL DE OAXACA** This museum is located in a 16th century building that was once a convent. It displays a large collection of artifacts made by the Zapotec and Mixtec cultures, including funerary objects found in Tomb 7 of Monte Albán.

Cross Cultural Connections

Strategy Have students connect and compare what they know about their community to help them learn about new communities. Ask them to research basic information about some of the oldest important buildings in your state, the state Capitol building, or a museum in your state or region. How do these places compare to those in Oaxaca? Do they contain important cultural/historical artifacts or murals?

¿Comprendiste?

Answers

1. Porque es un monumento histórico. o: Hay arquitectura colonial, iglesias y museos importantes.
2. El paseo empieza en el Zócalo, el centro de Oaxaca.
3. Ves un mural sobre la historia y la cultura de Oaxaca en el Palacio de Gobierno.
4. La catedral está en la avenida Hidalgo.
5. En la calle Macedonio Alcalá hay unas tiendas excelentes y varias casas coloniales.
6. El Museo Regional de Oaxaca está al lado de la iglesia de Santo Domingo.

▇ Block Schedule

Change of Pace In small groups, have students gather additional information about Oaxaca, either from library resources or the Internet. Each group should add at least 3 more paragraphs to the reading. One paragraph should be entitled **Especialmente para los jóvenes.**

Teaching Resource Options

Print

Para hispanohablantes Workbook PE, pp. 87–88

Unit 4 Resource Book
Para hispanohablantes Workbook TE, pp. 15–16
Information Gap Activities, p. 20
Family Involvement, pp. 21–22
Multiple Choice Test Questions, pp. 170–178

Audiovisual

OHT 116 (Quick Start)
Audio Program Testing Cassette T2 / CD T2

Technology

Electronic Teacher Tools/Test Generator
Intrigas y aventuras **CD-ROM,** Disc 1

🔔 Quick Start Review

♻ Requesting directions

Use OHT 116 or write on the board: Write 5 questions you would ask while finding your way around a Spanish-speaking city for the first time.

Answers will vary. Answers could include:

¿Puede usted decirme dónde está [el banco]?
¿Hay [un hotel] cerca de aquí?
¿Cómo llego [al correo]?
¿Queda lejos?
¿Dónde está [el centro comercial]?
¿Cruzo la calle?

✓ Teaching Suggestions
What Have Students Learned?

Have students look at the "Now you can…" notes and give examples of each category. Have them spend extra time reviewing categories they feel they are weak in, by consulting the "To review" notes.

ETAPA 1

Now you can…

• identify places.
• give addresses.

To review

• prepositions of location, see p. 250.

Now you can…

• give instructions.

To review

• regular affirmative **tú** commands, see p. 252.

OBJECTIVES

• Identify places
• Give addresses
• Choose transportation
• Request directions
• Give instructions

En uso

REPASO Y MÁS COMUNICACIÓN

ACTIVIDAD 1 ¡Al centro!

Hay un nuevo estudiante en la comunidad. Usando el mapa, explícale adónde vas cuando quieres hacer las siguientes cosas. *(Hint: Say where to go.)*

modelo

comprar zapatos (detrás de)

Cuando quiero **comprar zapatos,** *voy a la zapatería. Está* **detrás de** *la tienda de música y videos. La dirección es avenida Flores setenta y nueve.*

Avenida Flores

| Farmacia 77 | Zapatería 79 | Café 81 | Correo 83 |

| Tienda de ropa 34 | Tienda de música y videos 36 | Papelería 38 | Librería 40 |

Calle Colón

1. comprar papel (a la derecha de)
2. comprar jeans (a la izquierda de)
3. tomar un refresco (entre)
4. comprar medicina (detrás de)
5. mandar una carta (al lado de)
6. comprar un libro (a la derecha de)
7. alquilar un video (entre)
8. comprar zapatos (a la izquierda de)

ACTIVIDAD 2 Para sacar buenas notas…

Tu amigo(a) quiere sacar buenas notas. Contesta sus preguntas con mandatos afirmativos. *(Hint: Say what to do.)*

modelo

¿Uso el diccionario?   *Sí, úsalo.*

1. ¿Preparo la tarea?
2. ¿Leo el libro?
3. ¿Miro los videos?
4. ¿Aprendo el vocabulario?
5. ¿Estudio las lecciones?
6. ¿Escribo un poema?
7. ¿Compro una calculadora?
8. ¿Tomo los exámenes?

258 doscientos cincuenta y ocho
Unidad 4

Classroom Community

Learning Scenario Working in groups, have students prepare and present to the class a skit about traveling. Have them introduce and solve a problem as part of their skit. Be sure students assign a narrator to set the scene.

Paired Activity Have students do **Actividad 2** in pairs as an oral exercise. One student asks the first 4 questions, and the partner responds (books closed). Students switch for questions 5–8. Have each student also add one additional question of their own.

Now you can...
• request directions.

To review
• prepositions of location, see p. 250.

ACTIVIDAD 3 ¿Dónde queda?

Estás visitando un pueblo y necesitas direcciones para llegar a un banco. Hablas con un policía. Completa la conversación con las expresiones correctas. *(Hint: Ask for directions.)*

Tú: (**Oye / Perdone**). Señor, ¿(**puede / puedo**) usted decirme dónde está el banco?

Policía: ¡Cómo (**no / sí**)! El banco no queda (**cerca / lejos**). Está a sólo tres (**lados / cuadras**) de aquí. Primero, hay que caminar (**derecho / detrás**) por la avenida Olmos hasta llegar a la plaza. Allí, (**dobla / llega**) a la derecha en la calle San Juan y (**queda / camina**) una cuadra. Entonces, (**cruza / camina**) la calle Sonora. El banco queda en la esquina.

Tú: Muchas gracias, señor. ¿Y (**hay / puede**) un café cerca del banco?

Policía: Sí. El Café Romano está (**al lado / entre**) del banco. Es excelente. Y si necesitas mandar cartas, el correo queda (**derecho / a la izquierda**) del café.

Now you can...
• choose transportation.

To review
• the verb **salir**, see p. 248.
• the verb **decir**, see p. 248.

ACTIVIDAD 4 ¡Salgo hoy!

Todos salen para diferentes lugares. Explica adónde van, qué dicen del lugar adónde van y cómo van a viajar. *(Hint: Tell where they go, what they say, and how they go.)*

modelo

mi vecino: México (es muy interesante)

Mi vecino sale para México. Dice que **es muy interesante.** Va en carro.

1. mi primo: España (es muy especial)

2. nosotros: Los Ángeles (es fantástico)

3. ustedes: la Ciudad de México (es muy divertida)

4. yo: Puerto Rico (es muy bonito)

5. Marta y Ramón: la playa (es divertida)

6. usted: el centro (no es aburrido)

doscientos cincuenta y nueve
Etapa 1
259

ACTIVIDAD 1 Answers

1. Cuando quiero comprar papel, voy a la papelería. Está a la derecha de la tienda de música y videos. La dirección es calle Colón, treinta y ocho.
2. Cuando quiero comprar jeans, voy a la tienda de ropa. Está a la izquierda de la tienda de música y videos. La dirección es calle Colón, treinta y cuatro.
3. Cuando quiero tomar un refresco, voy al café. Está entre la zapatería y el correo. La dirección es avenida Flores, ochenta y uno.
4. Cuando quiero comprar medicina, voy a la farmacia. Está detrás de la tienda de ropa. La dirección es avenida Flores, setenta y siete.
5. Cuando quiero mandar una carta, voy al correo. Está al lado del café. La dirección es avenida Flores, ochenta y tres.
6. Cuando quiero comprar un libro, voy a la librería. Está a la derecha de la papelería. La dirección es calle Colón, cuarenta.
7. Cuando quiero alquilar un video, voy a la tienda de música y videos. Está entre la tienda de ropa y la papelería. La dirección es calle Colón, treinta y seis.
8. Cuando quiero comprar zapatos, voy a la zapatería. Está a la izquierda del café. La dirección es avenida Flores, setenta y nueve.

ACTIVIDAD 2 Answers

1. Sí, prepárala.
2. Sí, léelo.
3. Sí, míralos.
4. Sí, apréndelo.
5. Sí, estúdialas.
6. Sí, escríbelo.
7. Sí, cómprala.
8. Sí, tómalos.

ACTIVIDAD 3 Answers

Tú: Perdone / puede
Policía: no / lejos / cuadras / derecho / dobla / camina / cruza
Tú: hay
Policía: al lado / a la izquierda

ACTIVIDAD 4 Answers

1. Mi primo sale para España. Dice que es muy especial. Va en avión.
2. Nosotros salimos para Los Ángeles. Decimos que es fantástico. Vamos en tren.
3. Ustedes salen para la Ciudad de México. Dicen que es muy divertida. Van en autobús.
4. Yo salgo para Puerto Rico. Digo que es muy bonito. Voy en barco.
5. Marta y Ramón salen para la playa. Dicen que es divertida. Van en moto(cicleta).
6. Usted sale para el centro. Dice que no es aburrido. Va en taxi.

Block Schedule

Variety Alternate between giving the **Repaso** as homework and having students do it in class. In either case, go over the answers with the group.

Teaching All Students

Extra Help For **Actividad 2**, first have students identify the verb infinitive for each sentence. Then have them identify the direct objects and what corresponding direct object pronoun should be used.

Multiple Intelligences

Intrapersonal Have students practice **Actividad 2** as if they were having a conversation with themselves. Have them also add 5 more items. In addition, you may wish to have them record their sentences and submit the tapes as a quiz grade.

Teaching Resource Options

Print

Unit 4 Resource Book
  Cooperative Quizzes, pp. 33–34
  Etapa Exam, Forms A and B,
    pp. 35–44
  Para hispanohablantes Etapa Exam,
    pp. 45–49
  Portfolio Assessment, pp. 50–51
  Multiple Choice Test Questions,
    pp. 170–178

Audiovisual

OHT 116 (Quick Start)
Audio Program Testing Cassette T2 /
  CD T2

Technology

Electronic Teacher Tools/Test
  Generator
www.mcdougallittell.com

ACTIVIDAD 5

Rubric: Speaking

Criteria	Scale	
Sentence structure	1 2 3	A = 11–12 pts.
Vocabulary use	1 2 3	B = 9–10 pts.
Originality	1 2 3	C = 7–8 pts.
Fluency	1 2 3	D = 4–6 pts.
		F = < 4 pts.

ACTIVIDAD 6 En tu propia voz

Rubric: Writing

Criteria	Scale	
Vocabulary use	1 2 3 4 5	A = 14–15 pts.
Accuracy	1 2 3 4 5	B = 12–13 pts.
Creativity, appearance	1 2 3 4 5	C = 10–11 pts.
		D = 8–9 pts.
		F = < 8 pts.

Teaching Note: En tu propia voz

Have students use a town map to indicate where the activities take place, using the writing strategy "Organize information by category" to group contiguous activities.

ACTIVIDAD 5 ¿Cómo llego?

PARA CONVERSAR • STRATEGY: SPEAKING

Use variety to give directions When you give directions, don't just speak. Make your directions clear by using gestures, pointing to a map, and repeating key information. This helps others make sense of your words.

Trabajas en la tienda de música y videos. Explícale a un(a) joven turista cómo llegar a tres lugares. Antes de explicar, haz un mapa como ayuda. Cambien de papel. *(Hint: Say how to get to three places.)*

modelo

Turista: *Perdone, señor(ita), ¿cómo llego a la iglesia?*

Tú: *Camina tres cuadras por la avenida Juárez. La iglesia está a la izquierda en la esquina.*

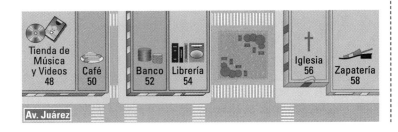

Tienda de Música y Videos 48 | Café 50 | Banco 52 | Librería 54 | Iglesia 56 | Zapatería 58

Av. Juárez

CONEXIONES

La educación física Different regions in Mexico have their own special folk music, dances, and costumes. For example, in one Oaxacan folk dance, women balance filled glasses on their heads! Research other Mexican folk dances in the library and/or on the Internet. Then teach a dance to your class. Answer these questions about the dance.

- ¿De qué región es la danza?
- ¿Qué representa la danza?
- ¿En qué ocasión la bailan?
- ¿Cómo es la música?
- ¿Qué ropa llevan los danzantes?

260 doscientos sesenta
Unidad 4

ACTIVIDAD 6 En tu propia voz

ESCRITURA Hay una nueva estudiante que no conoce tu comunidad. Usa las siguientes expresiones para darle siete recomendaciones. *(Hint: Write recommendations for a new student.)*

comer	caminar
visitar	practicar deportes
nadar	jugar
correr	ver películas
patinar	alquilar videos
comprar	mandar cartas
pasear	buscar libros

modelo

Compra ropa en el centro comercial Park Plaza.

Classroom Community

Pair Activity Have each student draw a quick sketch of their favorite store/building/place and label it. Then working in pairs, have students ask for and give directions to go to each other's favorite place.

Group Activity Working in small groups, have students quiz each other on the **Repaso de vocabulario** by category. One student names a category and the others give words/expressions in the category, until all have been given. The person quizzing may need to give hints to elicit all words.

En resumen
REPASO DE VOCABULARIO

IDENTIFYING PLACES

el aeropuerto	airport
el banco	bank
el café	café
la carnicería	butcher's shop
el centro	center, downtown
el centro comercial	shopping center
el correo	post office
la estación de autobuses	bus station
la farmacia	pharmacy, drugstore
el hotel	hotel
la iglesia	church
la joyería	jewelry store
la librería	bookstore
la panadería	bread bakery
la papelería	stationery store
la pastelería	pastry shop
la plaza	town square
la tienda de música y videos	music and video store
la zapatería	shoe store

GIVING ADDRESSES

la avenida	avenue
la calle	street
el camino	road
la dirección	address, direction

CHOOSING TRANSPORTATION

a pie	on foot
el autobús	bus
el avión	airplane
el barco	ship
el carro	car
el metro	subway
la moto(cicleta)	motorcycle
el taxi	taxi, cab
el tren	train

REQUESTING DIRECTIONS

Requesting

Perdona(e), ¿cómo llego a…?	Pardon, how do I get to…?
¿Puedes (Puede usted) decirme dónde queda…?	Could you tell me where … is?
¿Queda lejos?	Is it far?
acá/aquí	here
allá/allí	there

Replying

¡Cómo no!	Of course!
Lo siento…	I'm sorry…
cerca (de)	near (to)
cruzar	to cross
la cuadra	city block
a la derecha (de)	to the right (of)
derecho	straight ahead
desde	from
detrás (de)	behind
doblar	to turn
enfrente (de)	in front (of)
entre	between
la esquina	corner
hasta	until, as far as
a la izquierda (de)	to the left (of)
al lado (de)	beside, next to
lejos (de)	far (from)
quedar (en)	to stay, to be (in a specific place), to agree on

OTHER WORDS AND PHRASES

la cosa	thing
decir	to say, to tell
manejar	to drive
el mapa	map
por	for, by, around
salir	to go out, to leave
viajar	to travel
el viaje	trip

Juego

¿Adónde van los jóvenes?

Viajo en avión. ¿Adónde voy?

Adriana

No estoy bien y necesito medicina. ¿Adónde voy?

Andrés

Necesito pesos. No tengo suficiente en casa. ¿Adónde voy?

Arturo

Planning Guide CLASSROOM MANAGEMENT

OBJECTIVES

Communication
- Talk about shopping *pp. 264–265*
- Make purchases *pp. 266–267*
- Talk about giving gifts *pp. 266–267*
- Bargaining *pp. 264–265, 266–267, 278–279*

Grammar
- Stem-changing verbs: **o → ue** *pp. 270–272*
- Indirect object pronouns *pp. 273–275*
- Placement of indirect object pronouns *pp. 276–277*

Pronunciation
- Pronunciation of **rr** *p. 277*
- Dictation *TE p. 277*

Culture
- The **artesanías** of Oaxaca *pp. 264–265*
- **El Museo Regional de Oaxaca** *p. 274*
- Shopping and making purchases *pp. 278–279*
- Benito Juárez *p. 278*

♻ **Recycling**
- Numbers *p. 269*
- Places *p. 271*
- Telling time *p. 271*
- Transportation *p. 271*

STRATEGIES

Listening Strategies
- Observe as you listen *p. 266*

Speaking Strategies
- Express emotion *p. 272*
- Disagree politely *p. 282*

Reading Strategies
- Preview graphics *TE p. 278*

Writing Strategies
- Brainstorm details, then organize your information *TE p. 282*

Connecting Cultures Strategies
- Recognize variations in regional vocabulary *p. 268*
- Learn about a museum in Oaxaca *p. 274*
- Learn about an important person in Mexican history *p. 278*
- Connect and compare what you know about bargaining customs in your community to help you learn about bargaining customs in a new community *pp. 264–265, 266–267, 278–279*

PROGRAM RESOURCES

 Print
- *Más práctica* Workbook PE *pp. 89–96*
- Block Scheduling Copymasters *pp. 89–96*
- Unit 4 Resource Book
  Más práctica Workbook TE *pp. 52–59*
  Para hispanohablantes Workbook TE *pp. 60–67*
- Information Gap Activities *pp. 68–71*
- Family Involvement *pp. 72–73*
- Video Activities *pp. 74–76*
- Videoscript *pp. 77–79*
- Audioscript *pp. 80–83*
- Assessment Program, Unit 4 Etapa 2 *pp. 84–102; 170–178*
- Answer Keys *pp. 188–202*

 Audiovisual
- **Audio Program** Cassettes 11A, 11B / CD 11
- *Canciones* Cassette / CD
- **Video Program** Videotape 4 / Videodisc 2B
- **Overhead Transparencies** M1–M5; 105; 117–126

 Technology
- Electronic Teacher Tools/Test Generator
- *Intrigas y aventuras* CD-ROM, Disc 1
- www.mcdougallittell.com

 Assessment Program Options
- **Cooperative Quizzes** (Unit 4 Resource Book)
- **Etapa Exam** Forms A and B (Unit 4 Resource Book)
- *Para hispanohablantes* **Etapa Exam** (Unit 4 Resource Book)
- **Portfolio Assessment** (Unit 4 Resource Book)
- **Multiple Choice Test Questions** (Unit 4 Resource Book)
- **Audio Program** Testing Cassette T2 / CD T2
- **Electronic Teacher Tools/Test Generator**

Native Speakers
- *Para hispanohablantes* Workbook PE, *pp. 89–96*
- *Para hispanohablantes* Workbook TE (Unit 4 Resource Book)
- *Para hispanohablantes* Etapa Exam (Unit 4 Resource Book)
- Audio *Para hispanohablantes* Cassettes 11A, 11B, T2 / CD 11, T2
- Audioscript *Para hispanohablantes* (Unit 4 Resource Book)

Student Text Listening Activity Scripts

Videoscript: Diálogo *pages 266–267*

• Videotape 4 • Videodisc 2B

Search Chapter 5, Play to 6
U4E2 • En vivo (Dialog)

• Use the videoscript with **Actividades 1, 2** *page 268*

Sofía: Bueno, ¿qué le vas a comprar a tu mamá?

Rosa: Quiere una olla de barro negro. ¡Qué mercado tan bonito, Sofía! Venden de todo. En la ciudad voy a los centros comerciales, no a los mercados.

Sofía: ¿Y cuál prefieres?

Rosa: No sé... los centros comerciales son más modernos, pero los mercados son muy interesantes y puedes regatear.
Mira, es el nuevo disco compacto de mi grupo favorito.

Sofía: Pero tienes que comprarle un regalo a tu mamá. ¿Tienes suficiente dinero para un disco compacto?

Rosa: No sé. Vuelvo si me queda dinero.

Carlos: ¡Sofía!

Sofía: ¡Carlos! ¡Qué sorpresa! Carlos, te presento a mi prima Rosa. Es de la Ciudad de México. ¡Carlos!

Carlos: Sí, ya lo sé. Hola, Rosa. ¿Qué onda?

Sofía: Tú... ¿Tú conoces a Rosa? ¿Cómo?

Carlos: Es nuestro secreto, ¿verdad?

Rosa: Sí, es nuestro secreto.

Carlos: Bueno, tengo que ir a trabajar. Pero ¿almorzamos juntos mañana? Podemos ir a mi restaurante favorito para comer sus especialidades oaxaqueñas. Almuerzo allí cada ocho días.

Rosa: Nos encantaría, ¿no, Sofía?

Sofía: Claro que sí.

Carlos: Voy a participar en un concurso y quiero sus opiniones.

Rosa: Me parece ideal.

Carlos: Entonces hasta mañana, a la una, en el restaurante La Madre Tierra. Está cerca de la tienda donde trabajo. ¿Recuerdas cómo llegar al restaurante, Sofía?

Sofía: Sí, Carlos, recuerdo dónde está. Hasta mañana.

Carlos: ¡Adiós!

Rosa: ¡Hasta mañana! ¡Ah! ¡Y te doy el mapa!

Sofía: ¿Qué mapa?

Vendedor: Tenemos de todo... ollas, platos, jarras. Tenemos aquí una selección muy grande. Aquí usted encuentra el regalo perfecto...

Rosa: ¿Me deja ver esta olla grande?

Vendedor: Sí, cómo no.

Rosa: Es muy bonita. ¿Cuánto cuesta?

Vendedor: Las ollas grandes cuestan 70 pesos cada una.

Sofía: Son preciosas, ¿no?

Rosa: ¡Es muy cara! Le puedo ofrecer 50 pesos.

Vendedor: Ay, señorita, tengo que ganarme la vida, ¿no? Le dejo la olla en 65.

Rosa: ¿Por qué no me da la olla por 60?

Vendedor: Muy bien, señorita. Quedamos en 60.

Rosa: Muchísimas gracias, muy amable.

Vendedor: De nada.

Sofía: Muy bien, Rosa. Ahora tienes el regalo para tu mamá. ¿Tienes dinero suficiente para el disco compacto?

Rosa: Sí, creo que sí. ¿Sabes? Quiero comprarle un regalo a Carlos. Le doy el disco compacto mañana. ¿Por qué no volvemos a esa tienda de música?

 ¿Qué usa? *page 271*

Como está cerca, voy a la escuela a pie.

Si tengo prisa, voy a mi clase de piano en taxi.

El Parque Chapultepec es muy bonito. Voy allí los domingos en metro.

Mi familia y yo visitamos a mis abuelos en carro.

Hay un museo interesante en el centro. Para ir, voy en autobús.

Regalos para todos *page 275*

La tienda de música y videos es el lugar ideal para comprar regalos. A mis hermanas les gusta ver videos. Por eso les compro dos. A mi hermano le compro un videojuego. Juega todo el fin de semana. Para mis amigos, los mejores regalos están en la sección de música. A mi amiga Amanda le gusta mucho bailar, entonces le compro un disco compacto de salsa. Mi amigo Pablo va a celebrar su cumpleaños. Le compro un radio. ¡A la profesora Díaz le compro un casete de rock en español! ¡No te preocupes, Sofía! ¡Te compro un casete a ti también!

Quick Start Review Answers

p. 266 Shopping vocabulary
artículos de cuero:
  el cinturón / las botas / la cartera / la bolsa
joyas:
  la pulsera / el collar / los aretes / el anillo
cerámica:
  la olla / la jarra / el plato

p. 268 Dialog review
1. Rosa y Sofía son primas.
2. Sofía y Carlos son amigos.
3. Rosa quiere un regalo para su madre.
4. Rosa quiere comprarle un regalo a Carlos.

p. 278 Bargaining vocabulary
6. Muy bien, quedamos en 80. Muchas gracias.
2. Cuesta 100 pesos.
3. ¡Es demasiado! Le puedo ofrecer 70.
4. ¡Es demasiado barato! Se la dejo en 90.
1. Es muy bonita esta jarra. ¿Cuánto cuesta?
5. No puedo. ¿Me la deja en 80?

Sample Lesson Plan - 50 Minute Schedule

DAY 1

Etapa Opener
- Quick Start Review (TE, p. 262) 5 MIN.
- Anticipate/Activate prior knowledge: Have students look at the *Etapa* Opener and answer the questions. 5 MIN.

En contexto: Vocabulario
- Quick Start Review (TE, p. 264) 5 MIN.
- Have students use context and pictures to learn *Etapa* vocabulary. In pairs, have students answer the questions, p. 265. Use the Situational OHTs for additional practice. 10 MIN.

En vivo: Diálogo
- Quick Start Review (TE, p. 266) 5 MIN.
- Review the Listening Strategy, p. 266. Play audio or show video for the dialog, pp. 266–267. 10 MIN.
- Replay twice. Read aloud, having students take the roles of characters. 10 MIN.

Homework Option:
- Video Activities, Unit 4 Resource Book, pp. 74–76.

DAY 2

En acción: Vocabulario y gramática
- Check homework. 5 MIN.
- Quick Start Review (TE, p. 268) 5 MIN.
- Use OHT 117 and 118 to review *En contexto* vocabulary. Ask students for a summary of the dialog to check recall. 10 MIN.
- Play the video/audio; have students do *Actividades* 1 and 2. 10 MIN.
- Present the *Nota.* Then have students read and complete *Actividad* 3 in writing. Review answers orally. 5 MIN.
- Have students complete *Actividad* 4 in pairs. 5 MIN.
- Present the *Nota.* Then have students read and complete *Actividad* 5 in pairs. 5 MIN.
- Use a suggested expansion activity (TE, pp. 268–269) to reinforce retention of vocabulary and dialog structures. 10 MIN.

Homework Option:
- Have students write 5 True/False statements about the dialog and complete *Actividad* 5 in writing.

DAY 3

En acción (cont.)
- Check homework. 5 MIN.
- Quick Start Review (TE, p. 270) 5 MIN.
- Present *Gramática:* Stem-Changing Verbs: *o → ue* and the *Vocabulario,* p. 270. 15 MIN.
- Have students complete *Actividad* 6 in writing. Have volunteers write their answers on the board. 5 MIN.
- Have students read and complete *Actividad* 7 in writing. Then have them exchange papers for peer correction. 10 MIN.
- Have students complete *Actividad* 8 in groups. 5 MIN.
- Have students complete *Actividad* 9 in pairs. Ask several pairs to present their mini-dialogs. 10 MIN.

Homework Option:
- Have students make flashcards of the *Vocabulario,* p. 270. *Más práctica* Workbook, p. 93. *Para hispanohablantes* Workbook, p. 91.

DAY 4

En acción (cont.)
- Check homework. 5 MIN.
- Play the audio; do *Actividad* 10. 5 MIN.
- Present the Speaking Strategy, p. 272. Then present the *Vocabulario,* p. 272. Have students complete *Actividad* 11 in pairs. Expand using Information Gap Activities, Unit 4 Resource Book, p. 68; *Más comunicación,* p. R11. 15 MIN.
- Quick Start Review (TE, p. 273) 5 MIN.
- Present *Gramática:* Indirect Object Pronouns, p. 273. 10 MIN.
- Have students read and complete *Actividad* 12 in writing. Ask volunteers to write out the sentences on the board. 5 MIN.
- Present the *Nota.* Then have students complete *Actividad* 13 in writing. Review answers orally. 10 MIN.

Homework Option:
- *Más práctica* Workbook, pp. 94–95. *Para hispanohablantes* Workbook, pp. 92–93.

DAY 5

En acción (cont.)
- Check homework. 5 MIN.
- Present the *Vocabulario,* p. 275. Then play the audio and do *Actividad* 14. 10 MIN.
- Have students do *Actividad* 15 in pairs. Have several pairs present their mini-dialogs. 10 MIN.
- Quick Start Review (TE, p. 276) 5 MIN.
- Present *Gramática:* Placement of Indirect Object Pronouns, p. 276. 10 MIN.
- Have students complete *Actividad* 16 in writing. Then have them exchange papers for peer correction. 10 MIN.
- Do *Actividad* 17 orally. 5 MIN.

Homework Option:
- Have students complete *Actividad* 17 in writing. *Más práctica* Workbook, p. 96. *Para hispanohablantes* Workbook, p. 94.

DAY 6

En acción (cont.)
- Check homework. 5 MIN.
- Have students complete *Actividad* 18 in pairs. Expand using Information Gap Activities, Unit 4 Resource Book, pp. 69–70; *Más comunicación,* p. R11. 20 MIN.

Pronunciación
- Play the audio and have students practice the *Trabalenguas.* 5 MIN.

En colores: Cultura y comparaciones
- Quick Start Review (TE, p. 278) 5 MIN.
- Review the Connecting Cultures Strategy, p. 278. Have volunteers read the selection aloud and answer the questions, p. 279. 20 MIN.

Homework Option:
- Have students complete the *¿Comprendiste?/¿Qué piensas?* questions in writing.

DAY 7

En uso: Repaso y más comunicación
- Check homework. 5 MIN.
- Quick Start Review (TE, p. 280) 5 MIN.
- Have students write *Actividad* 1. Have volunteers write out answers on the board. 5 MIN.
- Do *Actividad* 2 in groups of 3, *Actividad* 3 orally and *Actividad* 4 in pairs. 15 MIN.
- Present the Speaking Strategy, p. 282, and have students do *Actividad* 5 in pairs. 5 MIN.
- Have students do *Actividad* 6 in groups. 5 MIN.

En tu propia voz: Escritura
- Do *Actividad* 7 in writing. Have a few students present their paragraphs. 15 MIN.

Homework Option:
- Review for *Etapa* 2 Exam.

DAY 8

Conexiones
- Present *Las matemáticas,* and make plans for the *mercado.* p. 282. 5 MIN.

En resumen: Repaso de vocabulario
- Quick Start Review (TE, p. 283) 5 MIN.
- Review grammar questions, etc. as necessary. 10 MIN.
- Complete *Etapa* 2 Exam. 20 MIN.

Ampliación
- Use a suggested project, game, or activity. (TE, pp. 239A–239B) 10 MIN.

Homework Option:
- Gather objects as described in *Conexiones,* p. 282. Preview *Etapa* 3

Sample Lesson Plan - Block Schedule (90 minutes)

DAY 1

Etapa Opener
- Quick Start Review (TE, p. 262) 5 MIN.
- Anticipate/Activate prior knowledge: Have students look at the *Etapa* Opener and answer the questions. 5 MIN.
- Use Block Scheduling Copymasters. 10 MIN.

En contexto: Vocabulario
- Quick Start Review (TE, p. 264) 5 MIN.
- Have students use context and pictures to learn *Etapa* vocabulary. In pairs, have students answer the questions, p. 265. Use the Situational OHTs for additional practice. 10 MIN.

En vivo: Diálogo
- Quick Start Review (TE, p. 266) 5 MIN.
- Review the Listening Strategy, p. 266. Play audio or show video for the dialog, pp. 266–267. 10 MIN.
- Replay twice. Read aloud, having students take the roles of characters. 10 MIN.

En acción: Vocabulario y gramática
- Quick Start Review (TE, p. 268) 5 MIN.
- Use OHT 117 and 118 to review *En contexto* vocabulary. Ask students for a summary of the dialog to check recall. 10 MIN.
- Play the video/audio; have students do *Actividades* 1 and 2. 10 MIN.
- Present the *Nota.* Then have students read and complete *Actividad* 3 in writing. Review answers orally. 5 MIN.

Homework Option:
- Video Activities, Unit 4 Resource Book, pp. 74–76.

DAY 2

En acción (cont.)
- Check homework. 5 MIN.
- Have students complete *Actividad* 4 in pairs. 5 MIN.
- Present the *Nota.* Then have students read and complete *Actividad* 5 in pairs. 5 MIN.
- Quick Start Review (TE, p. 270) 5 MIN.
- Present *Gramática:* Stem-Changing Verbs: *o → ue* and the *Vocabulario,* p. 270. 15 MIN.
- Have students complete *Actividad* 6 in writing. Have volunteers write their answers on the board. 5 MIN.
- Have students read and complete *Actividad* 7 in writing. Then have them exchange papers for peer correction. 10 MIN.
- Have students complete *Actividad* 8 in groups. 5 MIN.
- Have students complete *Actividad* 9 in pairs. Ask several pairs to present their mini-dialogs. 10 MIN.
- Play the audio; do *Actividad* 10. 5 MIN.
- Present the Speaking Strategy, p. 272. Then present the *Vocabulario,* p. 272. Have students complete *Actividad* 11 in pairs. Expand using Information Gap Activities, Unit 4 Resource Book, p. 68; *Más comunicación,* p. R11. 20 MIN.

Homework Option:
- Have students make flashcards of the *Vocabulario,* pp. 270 and 272. *Más práctica* Workbook, p. 93. *Para hispanohablantes* Workbook, p. 91.

DAY 3

En acción (cont.)
- Check homework. 5 MIN.
- Quick Start Review (TE, p. 273) 5 MIN.
- Present *Gramática:* Indirect Object Pronouns, p. 273. 10 MIN.
- Have students read and complete *Actividad* 12 in writing. Ask volunteers to write out the sentences on the board. 5 MIN.
- Present the *Nota.* Then have students complete *Actividad* 13 in writing. Review answers orally. 5 MIN.
- Present the *Vocabulario,* p. 275. Then play the audio and do *Actividad* 14. 10 MIN.
- Have students do *Actividad* 15 in pairs. Have several pairs present their mini-dialogs. 10 MIN.
- Quick Start Review (TE, p. 276) 5 MIN.
- Present *Gramática:* Placement of Indirect Object Pronouns, p. 276. 10 MIN.
- Have students complete *Actividad* 16 in writing. Then have them exchange papers for peer correction. 5 MIN.
- Do *Actividad* 17 orally. 5 MIN.
- Have students complete *Actividad* 18 in pairs. Expand using Information Gap Activities, Unit 4 Resource Book, pp. 69–70; *Más comunicación,* p. R11. 15 MIN.

Homework Option:
- Have students complete *Actividad* 17 in writing. *Más práctica* Workbook, pp. 94–96. *Para hispanohablantes* Workbook, pp. 92–94.

DAY 4

Pronunciación
- Check homework. 5 MIN.
- Play the audio and have students practice the *Trabalenguas.* 5 MIN.

En colores: Cultura y comparaciones
- Quick Start Review (TE, p. 278) 5 MIN.
- Review the Connecting Cultures Strategy, p. 278. Have volunteers read the selection aloud and answer the questions, p. 279. 25 MIN.

En uso: Repaso y más comunicación
- Quick Start Review (TE, p. 280) 5 MIN.
- Have students write *Actividad* 1. Have volunteers write out answers on the board. 10 MIN.
- Do *Actividad* 2 in groups of 3, *Actividad* 3 orally and *Actividad* 4 in pairs. 20 MIN.
- Present the Speaking Strategy, p. 282, and have students do *Actividad* 5 in pairs. 10 MIN.
- Have students do *Actividad* 6 in groups. 5 MIN.

Homework Option:
- Review for *Etapa* 2 Exam.

DAY 5

En tu propia voz: Escritura
- Do *Actividad* 7 in writing. Have a few students present their paragraphs. 20 MIN.

Conexiones
- Present *Las matemáticas,* p. 282, and make plans for the *mercado.* 10 MIN.

En resumen: Repaso de vocabulario
- Quick Start Review (TE, p. 283) 5 MIN.
- Review grammar questions, etc. as necessary. 10 MIN.
- Complete *Etapa* 2 Exam. 20 MIN.

Ampliación
- Use one or more suggested projects, games, or activities. (TE, pp. 239A–239B) 25 MIN.

Homework Option:
- Gather objects as described in *Conexiones,* p. 282. Preview *Etapa* 3 Opener.

▼ Rosa regatea con el vendedor.

Etapa Theme
Making purchases in Oaxaca and bargaining in the Mercado Benito Juárez.

Grammar Objectives
- Using stem-changing verbs: **o → ue**
- Using indirect object pronouns

Teaching Resource Options
Print

Block Scheduling Copymasters

Audiovisual

OHT 105, 123 (Quick Start)

Quick Start Review
♻ Places

Use OHT 123 or write on board:
List at least 5 items in each category:
1. Places in a city
2. Modes of transportation
3. Prepositions to express location
4. Giving directions/addresses

Answers
Answers will vary. Answers could include:
1. el banco, el café, el centro comercial, la farmacia, la iglesia, la plaza
2. a pie, en autobús, en barco, en carro, en metro, en taxi
3. cerca (de), detrás (de), a la derecha (de), a la izquierda (de), al lado (de), lejos (de)
4. la calle, la dirección, cruzar, la cuadra, derecho, doblar, la esquina

Teaching Suggestions
Previewing the Etapa
- Ask students to study the picture on pp. 262–263 (1 min.).
- Have them close their books and share at least 3 items that they noticed.
- Have them reopen their books and look at the picture again (1 min.). Have them close their books again and share 3 more details.
- Use the **¿Qué ves?** questions to focus the discussion.

UNIDAD 4

ETAPA 2

En el mercado

- Talk about shopping
- Make purchases
- Talk about giving gifts
- Bargain

¿Qué ves?

Mira la foto del centro de Oaxaca.
1. ¿Hace buen tiempo?
2. ¿Quiénes llevan camisetas azules?
3. ¿Quiénes llevan vestidos?
4. ¿Qué hace la mujer?

262

Classroom Management

Planning Ahead Prepare to introduce the communicative theme of bargaining. Begin by collecting objects, photographs, and play money for students to use in upcoming role-play activities. You may wish to use the game **¿Me lo vendes?** in the **Ampliación** on page 239B as a final wrap-up activity for this **Etapa**.

Peer Teaching Have students form pairs. Each student writes 2 additional **¿Qué ves?** questions. Have them ask and answer each other's questions. They can then share their new questions and answers with the rest of the class.

Cross Cultural Connections

Ask students to read the restaurant sign in the upper left corner of the photo: **La Casa de la Abuela.** What kind of cooking might they expect at this restaurant? **(La Casa de la Abuela** serves traditional Oaxacan dishes.)

Culture Highlights

● **EL MERCADO** The **mercados** in Oaxaca have become popular tourist attractions. Artisans sell their products, such as rugs, pottery, wood carvings, and jewelry. **Mercados** are also good places to eat and try out a great variety of Oaxacan traditional dishes.

Explain that there are several types of markets in Latin American cities; there are artisans' markets, produce markets, and flower markets. Ask students if they can guess what **supermercado** or **hipermercado** mean.

● **ALEBRIJE** Wood carving has been practiced since Zapotec times by artisans and their families. You might mention that **alebrije** means "something that is jumbled, confused, or fantastic." The carvings are usually done with a knife, then painted to create imaginary figures such as **cabras** (goats), **armadillos**, **asnos** (donkeys), **coyotes**, **serpientes** (snakes), **unicornios** (unicorns), and even **marcianos** (Martians)!

Supplementary Vocabulary

el dulce de algodón	cotton candy
el líquido para pompas (burbujas) de jabón	bubble soap
el cangrejo	crab
la jirafa	giraffe
el ciervo	deer

Teaching All Students

Extra Help Ask students about the picture on pp. 262–263 using yes/no or either/or questions, such as ¿Está el mercado en el centro de Oaxaca? ¿Qué vende la mujer, animales o vestidos? ¿Tiene el muchacho un animal azul o rosado?

Challenge Encourage students to describe the picture using words they already know. One student creates a sentence and others follow in turn. Ask them to elaborate by adding adjectives where possible.

Multiple Intelligences

Logical/Mathematical Ask students to compare shopping at the **Mercado Benito Juárez** and shopping in their own city or town, making a topic-oriented chart.

Block Schedule

Setting the Theme Play Mexican music and ask students to close their eyes and pretend they are in Oaxaca. Have them describe what they might see and what they imagine themselves to be doing. (For additional activities, see **Block Scheduling Copymasters.**)

Teaching Resource Options

Print

Unit 4 Resource Book
Video Activities, pp. 74–75
Videoscript, p. 77
Audioscript, p. 80
Audioscript *Para hispanohablantes*,
p. 80

Audiovisual 🔊💻

OHT 117, 118, 119, 119A, 120, 120A,
123 (Quick Start)
Audio Program Cassette 11A / CD 11
Audio *Para hispanohablantes*
Cassette 11A / CD 11
Video Program Videotape 4 / Videodisc
2B

Search Chapter 4, Play to 5
U4E2 • En contexto (Vocabulary)

Technology 🎧💻 CD-ROM

Intrigas y aventuras CD-ROM, Disc 1

Quick Start Review

🔄 **Stores**

Use OHT 123 or write on board:
List at least 5 types of stores.

Answers .
Answers will vary. Answers could include:
la carnicería, la farmacia, la joyería, la librería,
la panadería, la papelería, la tienda de música
y videos, la zapatería

Teaching Suggestions
Introducing Vocabulary

- Have students look at pages 264–265.
  Use OHT 117 and 118 and Audio
  Cassette 11A /CD 11 to present the
  vocabulary.
- Ask the Comprehension Questions in
  order of yes/no (questions 1–3),
  either/or (questions 4–6), and simple
  word or phrase (questions 7–10).
  Expand by adding similar questions.
- Use the TPR activity to reinforce the
  meaning of individual words.
- Use the video vocabulary presentation
  for review and reinforcement.

En contexto
VOCABULARIO

ARTESANÍAS

Sofía is going shopping at the market in Oaxaca. She sees all
kinds of things. Find out what items interest her the most.

el mercado

A

¡Hola! Voy al **Mercado**
Benito Juárez. Allí compro **el regalo**
perfecto.

el regalo

los artículos de cuero

las botas

la bolsa

el cinturón

la cartera

B Hay **artículos de cuero**, como
botas, una bolsa, un cinturón y una
cartera. ¿Qué voy a comprar?

las joyas

las pulseras

plata

los anillos

los aretes

oro

el collar

C Me gusta usar **las joyas** de **oro** y de
plata. Voy a **poder** comprar **aretes,
anillos, pulseras** y **collares** aquí.

264 doscientos sesenta y cuatro
Unidad 4

Classroom Community

TPR Ask each student to bring in an example of the
items on pp. 264–265, or find pictures of them. Assign
imaginary values to the objects in pesos and make
price tags. Then have students arrange themselves in a
line according to the value of their items. First, ask
them to identify which classmate is holding each item:
¿Quién tiene la cartera? ¿Quién tiene el anillo? As the
class answers, the classmate with the appropriate object

steps forward. Then have students compare objects in
terms of price: **¿Cuál es más caro, la cartera o el
anillo?**

Paired Activity The **Preguntas personales** can
also be done as a paired activity. The main objective is
to create a context for oral communication while
practicing new vocabulary. (Note that they may also
be assigned as a written activity.)

CERÁMICA

la cerámica

el plato

la jarra

la olla

el precio

$60

D Hay muchas **artesanías** aquí. Hay **cerámica**, como **jarras, ollas** y **platos. El precio** de la jarra es 60 pesos.

pagar

el dinero

JARRAS $75

E En el mercado es divertido **regatear**.

Sofía: ¿**Me deja ver** la jarra? ¿**Cuánto cuesta**?
Vendedor: Cincuenta pesos.
Sofía: ¡**Es muy cara!** No tengo suficiente **dinero**. **Le puedo ofrecer** treinta y cinco pesos.
Vendedor: Le dejo la jarra **en** cuarenta pesos.
Sofía: Bueno.
Vendedor: ¿Cómo va a **pagar**?

Preguntas personales

1. ¿Te gustan las artesanías?
2. ¿Prefieres las joyas o las artesanías?
3. Cuando vas a un mercado, ¿regateas o pagas el precio?
4. ¿Qué joya quieres comprar?
5. ¿Tienes un artículo de cuero? ¿Cuál?

doscientos sesenta y cinco
Etapa 2

265

Comprehension Questions

1. ¿Busca Sofía el regalo perfecto? (Sí.)
2. ¿Ella va al correo? (No.)
3. ¿Es una cartera un artículo de cuero? (Sí.)
4. ¿Es el collar de plata o de oro? (de plata)
5. En la foto C, ¿hay un anillo o dos anillos? (dos)
6. ¿Cuál es el precio de la jarra en la foto D, sesenta pesos o setenta pesos? (sesenta pesos)
7. ¿Qué es divertido hacer en el mercado? (regatear)
8. ¿Cuánto cuesta la jarra originalmente? (cincuenta pesos)
9. ¿Cuánto ofrece Sofía? (treinta y cinco pesos)
10. ¿Cuánto paga? (cuarenta pesos)

Culture Highlights

● **JOYERÍA DE OAXACA** Oaxacan jewelry reflects Mesoamerican traditions dating back to 1500 B.C. In pre-Columbian times, Mixtec and Zapotec jewelry was used for religious purposes and burial ceremonies. Mixtec jewelry can be found in the Museum of the American Indian in New York. Reproductions of the valuable gold, silver, jade, and pearl artifacts that Dr. Alfonso Caso discovered at Monte Albán in 1932 are in the Museum of Oaxaca.

Language Notes

• In **joyas de oro y de plata,** the word **de** is used to say what the jewelry is made of.
• There are other Spanish words for the different kinds of jewelry. **Sortija** is another word for *ring.* **Pendiente(s)** also means *earring(s).* Another way to say *bracelet* is **brazalete.**

Teaching All Students

Extra Help Point to pictures and ask simple yes/no questions about the vocabulary, such as ¿**Es un anillo?** ¿**Es un collar?**

Native Speakers You might ask native speakers if they can suggest additional words for **tiendas.** Some examples might be **colmado** in Puerto Rico, or **bodega** in Ecuador, which both mean "grocery store." A **botica** can be a pharmacy or a small store or stall. In Argentina, **almacén** can refer to a grocery store while in other countries it may be a department store.

Multiple Intelligences

Visual Prepare ahead: construction paper, magazines, markers, tape or glue. Ask students to design an ad for a store that sells leather goods, jewelry, clothing, or ceramics.

Block Schedule

Variety Try to offer students as many different intelligence approaches as possible. Note which students respond to which approaches. It is not necessary to do each approach yourself; encourage individual students to choose their own intelligence preference.

Teaching Resource Options

Print

Más práctica Workbook PE, pp. 89–92
Para hispanohablantes Workbook PE,
 pp. 89–90
Block Scheduling Copymasters
Unit 4 Resource Book
 Más práctica Workbook TE, pp. 52–55
 Para hispanohablantes Workbook
 TE, pp. 60–61
 Video Activities, p. 76
 Videoscript, p. 78
 Audioscript, p. 80
 Audioscript *Para hispanohablantes*,
 p. 80

Audiovisual

OHT 121, 122, 123 (Quick Start)
Audio Program Cassette 11A / CD 11
Audio *Para hispanohablantes*
 Cassette 11A / CD 11
Video Program Videotape 4 / Videodisc
 2B

Search Chapter 5, Play to 6
U4E2 • En vivo (Dialog)

Technology

Intrigas y aventuras CD-ROM, Disc 1

Quick Start Review

♻ Shopping vocabulary

Use OHT 123 or write on board:
Write each word in the correct column:

la olla / la pulsera / el collar /
el cinturón / la jarra / las botas /
los aretes / la cartera / el plato /
el anillo / la bolsa

artículos de cuero	joyas	cerámica

Answers See p. 261B.

Gestures

Ask students to look at scenes 8–9 and identify facial expressions that show how the vendor feels about Rosa's offer. Remind students that nonverbal communication clues can increase comprehension.

En vivo
DIÁLOGO

Rosa

Sofía

Carlos

Vendedor

PARA ESCUCHAR • STRATEGY: LISTENING

Observe as you listen Look carefully as you listen to understand meaning from visual cues. Look for items that belong in specific categories. Write the items in the appropriate column in a chart.

cerámica	cuero	música	joyas

¡A regatear!

1 ▶ **Sofía:** ¿Qué le vas a comprar a tu mamá?
 Rosa: Quiere una olla de barro negro. Los mercados son muy interesantes y puedes regatear.

5 ▶ **Carlos:** ¿Almorzamos juntos mañana? Podemos ir a mi restaurante favorito. Almuerzo allí cada ocho días. Voy a participar en un concurso y quiero sus opiniones.
 Rosa: Me parece ideal.

6 ▶ **Carlos:** Entonces hasta mañana, a la una, en el restaurante La Madre Tierra. ¿Recuerdas cómo llegar al restaurante?
 Sofía: Sí, Carlos, recuerdo dónde está.
 Carlos: ¡Adiós!
 Rosa: ¡Hasta mañana!

7 ▶ **Vendedor:** ¡Ollas, platos, jarras! Aquí encuentra el regalo perfecto…
 Rosa: ¿Me deja ver esta olla grande? ¿Cuánto cuesta?
 Vendedor: Las ollas grandes cuestan 70 pesos cada una.

266 doscientos sesenta y seis
Unidad 4

Classroom Community

Storytelling After watching the video, divide the class into groups of 3. Have each group choose a portion of the dialog and retell it in their own words, using gestures as necessary to communicate meaning.

Game ¿Cierto o falso? Divide students into groups of 3–4. Each group chooses a picture on p. 266 or p. 267 and writes 3 detailed statements about it. Two of the statements are true and one is false. A member of each group reads the statements aloud. The other groups try to guess which statement is false.

2 ▶ Rosa: Mira, es el nuevo disco compacto de mi grupo favorito.
Sofía: Tienes que comprarle un regalo a tu mamá.

3 ▶ Rosa: Vuelvo si me queda dinero.
Sofía: ¡Carlos! ¡Qué sorpresa! Te presento a mi prima. Es de la Ciudad de México.

4 ▶ Carlos: Sí, ya lo sé. Hola, Rosa. ¿Qué onda?
Sofía: ¿Tú conoces a Rosa? ¿Cómo?
Carlos: Es nuestro secreto, ¿verdad?

8 ▶ Rosa: ¡Es muy cara! Le puedo ofrecer 50 pesos.
Vendedor: Ay, señorita, tengo que ganarme la vida, ¿no? Le dejo la olla en 65.

9 ▶ Rosa: ¿Por qué no me da la olla por 60?
Vendedor: Muy bien. Quedamos en 60.
Rosa: Muchísimas gracias, muy amable.
Vendedor: De nada.
Sofía: Muy bien, Rosa. Ahora tienes el regalo para tu mamá.

10 ▶ Sofía: ¿Tienes dinero suficiente para el disco compacto?
Rosa: Sí, creo que sí. ¿Sabes?, quiero comprarle un regalo a Carlos. Le doy el disco compacto mañana. ¿Por qué no volvemos a esa tienda de música?

doscientos sesenta y siete **267**
Etapa 2

Teaching Suggestions
Presenting the Dialog
• Prepare students for listening by focusing on the dialog context using yes/no or either/or questions. Reintroduce the characters and the setting: **¿El muchacho se llama Carlos? ¿La muchacha que lleva el vestido azul se llama Rosa? ¿Cuál es el nombre de la otra muchacha, Ana o Rosa? ¿Quién lleva un sombrero, el vendedor o Carlos?**
• Use the video, audio cassette, or CD to present the dialog. The expanded dialog on video offers additional listening practice opportunities.

Video Synopsis
• Rosa and Sofía meet Carlos while shopping at the open-air market. For a complete transcript of the video dialog, see p. 261B.

Comprehension Questions
1. ¿Están Rosa y Sofía en el mercado? (Sí.)
2. ¿Rosa va de compras? (Sí.)
3. ¿Quiere Rosa un disco compacto para su madre? (No.)
4. ¿Compra Rosa el disco compacto o espera hasta más tarde? (Espera hasta más tarde.)
5. ¿Es Rosa la prima o la hermana de Sofía? (la prima)
6. ¿Es Rosa de Oaxaca o de la Ciudad de México? (de la Ciudad de México)
7. ¿Quiénes tienen un secreto, Carlos y Rosa o Carlos y Sofía? (Carlos y Rosa)
8. ¿Adónde van Carlos y las muchachas mañana? (al restaurante La Madre Tierra)
9. ¿Qué cosas tiene el vendedor? (ollas, platos, jarras)
10. ¿Cuánto cuestan las ollas grandes? (setenta pesos)

■ Block Schedule
Process Time Watch out for that overloaded look! Remind students that they don't have to understand every word. To facilitate comprehension, suggest that they concentrate on the dialog in sections. (For additional activities, see **Block Scheduling Copymasters**.)

Teaching All Students

Extra Help For students who may not get the general gist of the dialog, break the dialog into 2 sections: scenes 1–6 and 7–10. Have students act out these two sections using their own words. Correct mistakes only if they impede comprehension.

Challenge As a follow-up activity, point to one of the individual scenes and ask students, in their own words, to explain what was happening in that scene.

Multiple Intelligences
Kinesthetic Have students touch the picture being described, saying, **Toquen las fotos que describo:**
1. **Rosa ve un disco compacto nuevo.** (2)
2. **Rosa quiere ver una olla.** (7)
3. **Carlos invita a Rosa y Sofía al restaurante.** (5)

Teaching Resource Options

Print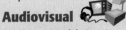

Unit 4 Resource Book
Videoscript, p. 76
Audioscript, p. 80
Audioscript *Para hispanohablantes,*
p. 80

Audiovisual

OHT 124 (Quick Start)
Audio Program Cassette 11A / CD 11
Audio *Para hispanohablantes*
Cassette 11A / CD 11
Video Program Videotape 4 / Videodisc
2B

Quick Start Review

 Dialog review

Use OHT 124 or write on board:
Students unscramble the words to make
sentences about the dialog.

1. primas / y / Rosa / Sofía / son
2. amigos / Sofía / son / y / Carlos
3. para / Rosa / regalo / madre /
   un / quiere / su
4. un / comprarle / regalo /quiere /
   a / Rosa / Carlos

Answers *See p. 261B.*

Teaching Suggestions
Comprehension Check

Use **Actividades 1** and **2** to assess
retention after the dialog. Have students
close their books. Act out the phrases
in **Actividad 2** and see if students can
comprehend and answer correctly.

 Objective: Transitional practice
Listening comprehension/vocabulary

Answers (See script, p. 261B.)
1. Falso. Rosa quiere comprar un regalo para su
   mamá.
2. Falso. La mamá de Rosa quiere una olla de
   barro negro.
3. Cierto
4. Cierto
5. Falso. Rosa paga sesenta pesos por la olla.

Objective: Transitional practice
Listening comprehension/vocabulary

Answers (See script, p. 261B.)
1. Sofía   2. Sofía   3. Carlos
4. el vendedor   5. Rosa

268   Vocabulary/Grammar • UNIDAD 4 Etapa 2

En acción
VOCABULARIO Y GRAMÁTICA

OBJECTIVES
• Talk about shopping
• Make purchases
• Talk about giving gifts
• Bargain

¿Cierto o falso?

Escuchar ¿Es cierto o falso? Si es falso, di lo que
es cierto. *(Hint: Say what is true.)*

1. Rosa quiere comprar un regalo para Sofía.
2. La mamá de Rosa quiere un disco
   compacto.
3. Rosa cree que los mercados son interesantes.
4. Rosa, Sofía y Carlos van a comer juntos
   mañana.
5. Rosa paga cincuenta pesos por la olla.

¿Quién habla?

Escuchar ¿Quién habla: Rosa, Sofía, Carlos o
el vendedor? *(Hint: Say who speaks.)*

1. «¿Qué le vas a comprar a tu mamá?»
2. «Te presento a mi prima.»
3. «Podemos ir a mi restaurante favorito.»
4. «¡Ollas, platos, jarras!»
5. «Quiero comprarle un regalo a Carlos.»

TAMBIÉN SE DICE There are many ways to
ask people what's happening or what's going on.
In many countries you may hear
• ¿Qué hay?   • ¿Qué pasa?   • ¿Qué tal?
In Mexico you may hear
• ¿Qué hubo?   • ¿Qué onda?

Los planes

Leer/Escribir Completa la carta de Rosa con una
de las expresiones. *(Hint: Complete Rosa's letter.)*

artículos de cuero	mercado	para
cartera	olla	precio
cinturón	pagar	regalo

Nota

Use **para** *(for, in order to)* to indicate…

• the recipient of items	…el regalo **para** tu mamá.
• purpose	Vamos al restaurante **para** comer.
• implied purpose	Tengo dinero **para** [comprar] algo.

Querida Emiliana:

Hoy voy al ___1___ con mi prima Sofía.
Tengo que comprar un ___2___ de cumpleaños ___3___
mi mamá. Ella quiere una ___4___ negra. No sé qué
___5___ tiene una olla, pero Sofía dice que no voy
a ___6___ más de setenta pesos. Si Sofía tiene
razón, voy a tener suficiente dinero ___7___ comprar
algo para mi papá también. Él prefiere los ___8___.
Entonces, voy a comprar una ___9___ o un ___10___
para él. ¡Ay! Son las ocho. Me tengo que ir. Sofía
me está esperando.

Hasta pronto,

Rosa

---

268   doscientos sesenta y ocho
Unidad 4

Classroom Management

Time Saver Focus on a quick whole-class review of
the dialog. Begin by saying, **Rosa y Sofía van al
mercado.** Ask students to recount the sequence of
events by adding sentences in turn about what
happened next. Then do **Actividades 1** and **2** orally.

Streamlining Before replaying the video/audio for
use in **Actividades 1** and **2,** have students scan the two
exercises. Have them note what kind of information
they should be listening for.

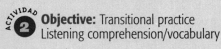

- *Use stem-changing verbs: o→ue*
- *Use indirect object pronouns*

ACTIVIDAD 4

La tienda

Hablar Trabajas en una tienda grande. Acaban de llegar algunos artículos nuevos. Dile a otro(a) vendedor(a) adónde llevar los artículos. Cambien de papel. *(Hint: Tell where the items go.)*

modelo

botas

Tú: ¿Adónde llevo **las botas**?

Otro(a): *Al departamento de **artículos de cuero**, por favor.*

ROPA

ARTÍCULOS DE CUERO

JOYAS

COSAS PARA LA CASA

1. carteras	**7.** pantalones
2. pulseras de oro	**8.** collares de oro
3. jarras	**9.** bolsas
4. ollas	**10.** platos
5. aretes de plata	**11.** anillos de plata
6. cinturones	

ACTIVIDAD 5

♻ ¿Cuánto cuestan?

Hablar Rosa quiere saber los precios de unas joyas. ¿Qué dice el vendedor? Cambien de papel. *(Hint: Ask prices.)*

modelo

Rosa: ¿Cuánto cuesta **el anillo**?

Vendedor: Cuesta **cuarenta y ocho** pesos.

Nota

When asking or giving the price of a single item, use **cuesta.** When asking or giving the price of more than one item, use **cuestan.**

¿**Cuánto cuesta** el anillo? ¿**Cuánto cuestan** los aretes?

1. $65
2. $84
3. $98
4. $48
5. $76
6. $60

Teaching All Students

Extra Help Focus on reviewing the content of the dialog on pp. 266–267. Ask students simple yes/no questions to verify their comprehension of the story line, such as, ¿Quiere comprar Rosa un regalo para su padre? ¿No? ¿Para su madre? ¿Sí? and so on.

Multiple Intelligences

Visual Have students draw their own cartoons to illustrate the dialog, putting the conversation in bubbles.

Rubric A = 13–15 pts. B = 10–12 pts. C = 7–9 pts. D = 4–6 pts. F = < 4 pts.

Writing criteria	Scale
Vocabulary use	1 2 3 4 5
Grammar/spelling accuracy	1 2 3 4 5
Creativity/appearance	1 2 3 4 5

ACTIVIDAD 3
Objective: Transitional practice
Vocabulary/**para**

Answers

1. mercado	6. pagar
2. regalo	7. para
3. para	8. artículos de cuero
4. olla	9. cartera
5. precio	10. cinturón

ACTIVIDAD 4
Objective: Transitional practice
Vocabulary in conversation

Answers

1. A: ¿Adónde llevo las carteras? / B: Al departamento de artículos de cuero, por favor.
2. A: ¿Adónde llevo las pulseras de oro? / B: Al departamento de joyas, por favor.
3. A: ¿Adónde llevo las jarras? / B: Al departamento de cosas para la casa, por favor.
4. A: ¿Adónde llevo las ollas? / B: Al departamento de cosas para la casa, por favor.
5. A: ¿Adónde llevo los aretes de plata? / B: Al departamento de joyas, por favor.
6. A: ¿Adónde llevo los cinturones? / B: Al departamento de artículos de cuero, por favor.
7. A: ¿Adónde llevo los pantalones? / B: Al departamento de ropa, por favor.
8. A: ¿Adónde llevo los collares de oro? / B: Al departamento de joyas, por favor.
9. A: ¿Adónde llevo las bolsas? / B: Al departamento de artículos de cuero, por favor.
10. A: ¿Adónde llevo los platos? / B: Al departamento de cosas para la casa, por favor.
11. A: ¿Adónde llevo los anillos de plata? / B: Al departamento de joyas, por favor.

ACTIVIDAD 5
Objective: Transitional practice
Vocabulary in conversation

♻ **Numbers**

Answers

1. Rosa: ¿Cuánto cuestan los aretes?
   Vendedor: Cuestan sesenta y cinco pesos.
2. Rosa: ¿Cuánto cuesta la pulsera?
   Vendedor: Cuesta ochenta y cuatro pesos.
3. Rosa: ¿Cuánto cuesta el collar?
   Vendedor: Cuesta noventa y ocho pesos.
4. Rosa: ¿Cuánto cuesta la pulsera?
   Vendedor: Cuesta cuarenta y ocho pesos.
5. Rosa: ¿Cuánto cuestan los aretes?
   Vendedor: Cuestan setenta y seis pesos.
6. Rosa: ¿Cuánto cuesta el anillo?
   Vendedor: Cuesta sesenta pesos.

▮ Block Schedule

Variety Have each student choose a Spanish-speaking country. Then have them research the currency of that country and find out the exchange rate. They should find out the names of the bills and coins, and draw illustrations of them.

Teaching Resource Options

Print 📖

Más práctica Workbook PE, p. 93
Para hispanohablantes Workbook PE, p. 91
Block Scheduling Copymasters
Unit 4 Resource Book
  Más práctica Workbook TE, p. 56
  Para hispanohablantes Workbook TE, p. 62
  Audioscript, p. 81
  Audioscript *Para hispanohablantes*, p. 82

Audiovisual 🎧

OHT 124 (Quick Start)
Audio Program Cassettes 11A, 11B / CD 11
Audio *Para hispanohablantes* Cassette 11A / CD 11

Technology 💻

Intrigas y aventuras CD-ROM, Disc 1

🔔 Quick Start Review

♻ **e → ie** verbs
Use OHT 124 or write on board:
Write the correct form of the verb.

1. María ____ comprar unos aretes. (querer)
2. Ellos ____ ir al concierto. (pensar)
3. Yo ____ la jarra roja. (preferir)
4. ¿A qué hora ____ la clase de historia? (empezar)
5. Tú siempre ____ la lección de matemáticas. (entender)

Answers
1. quiere
2. piensan
3. prefiero
4. empieza
5. entiendes

Teaching Suggestions
Presenting Stem-Changing Verbs: o → ue

Activating prior knowledge: Focus on the ¿Recuerdas? note. Ask students to write or draw a description of the new **o → ue** verbs using their own words. Point out that **o → ue** stem-changing verbs are also "boot" verbs. Remind students to double-check infinitive endings when conjugating.

GRAMÁTICA

Stem-Changing Verbs: o → ue

♻ **¿RECUERDAS?** *p. 199* Remember verbs like **pensar**, where the stem alternates between **e** and **ie**?

pensar *to think, to plan*

pienso	**pensamos**
piensas	**pensáis**
piensa	**piensan**

▶ Something similar happens with verbs like **almorzar** *(to eat lunch)*. The stem alternates between **o** and **ue**.

The stem doesn't change for the **nosotros** *(we)* or **vosotros** *(you)* form.

almorzar *to eat lunch*

almuerzo	**almorzamos**
almuerzas	**almorzáis**
almuerza	**almuerzan**

Carlos says:
—**Almuerzo** allí cada ocho días.
I eat lunch there every week.

▶ Many other verbs have this same kind of change in their stem.

The vendor says:

—Aquí **encuentra** el regalo perfecto.
*Here **you'll find** the perfect gift.*

—Las ollas grandes **cuestan** 70 pesos…
*The big pots **cost** 70 pesos…*

ACTIVIDAD 6 — Gramática

¿Qué pueden hacer?

Escribir Escribe lo que estas personas pueden hacer. Completa las frases con la forma correcta de **poder.**
(Hint: Write what they can do.)

modelo
los chicos: jugar al béisbol
Los chicos** pueden **jugar al béisbol.

1. tú: tocar el piano
2. Rosa y Sofía: patinar
3. Carlos: manejar
4. yo: hablar español
5. Andrea y yo: nadar
6. ellos: escribir poesía
7. nosotros: correr
8. Rodrigo: bailar

Vocabulario

Stem-Changing Verbs: o → ue

almorzar *to eat lunch*
contar *to count, to tell or retell*
costar *to cost*
devolver *to return (an item)*
dormir *to sleep*
encontrar *to find, to meet*
poder *to be able, can*
recordar *to remember*
volver *to return, to come back*

¿Qué haces cada día? ¿Cada semana?

Classroom Community

Learning Scenario For **Actividad 9**, expand each interchange by having **mamá** refuse permission to go out. Students must convince her. Sample dialog: **1. yo – centro comercial:** Mamá, ¿puedo ir al mercado? / No, no puedes ir. / Quiero comprar un regalo para el cumpleaños de papá. / Bueno, pero ¿a qué hora vuelves? / Vuelvo a las tres y media.

TPR Act out the meaning of each stem-changing verb.

Cooperative Learning Divide the class into groups of 5. On a piece of paper, Student 1 writes a question using a stem-changing verb and Student 2 writes a response. Then Student 3 writes a question and Student 4 writes a response. Group members continue passing the paper around the circle, writing questions, then responses. At the end of the time period (5 min.), the group with the most correct exchanges wins.

ACTIVIDAD 7 Gramática

♻ ¡Al mercado!

Leer/Escribir Sofía y Rosa hablan con la madre de Sofía antes de ir al mercado. Completa su conversación con la forma correcta de cada verbo. *(Hint: Complete what they say.)*

| almorzar | encontrar | recordar |
| devolver | poder | volver |

Rosa: Vamos al mercado para ver si yo __1__ un regalo para mamá.

Mamá: ¿ __2__ ustedes para almorzar?

Sofía: No. Nosotras __3__ en un café.

Mamá: Entonces yo voy a la zapatería para __4__ mis zapatos nuevos.

Sofía: ¿Por qué los __5__ ?

Mamá: Porque son pequeños.

Rosa: Tía, si yo __6__ bien, la zapatería está cerca del correo, ¿no?

Mamá: Sí, tú __7__ muy bien.

Rosa: ¿ __8__ mandar una carta?

Mamá: ¡Sí! ¡Cómo no!

■ **MÁS PRÁCTICA** *cuaderno* p. 93
■ **PARA HISPANOHABLANTES** *cuaderno* p. 91

ACTIVIDAD 8

♻ ¿A qué hora almuerzas tú?

Hablar Pregúntales a cuatro estudiantes a qué hora almuerzan. *(Hint: Ask when they eat lunch.)*

Nombre	Hora
1. María	12:00

ACTIVIDAD 9

♻ ¿Podemos ir?

Hablar Tus primas están de visita. Ustedes quieren ir a varios lugares. Tú le preguntas a tu mamá si pueden ir. Sigue el modelo. *(Hint: Ask for permission.)*

modelo

mis primas y yo → cine (9:30)

Tú: *¿Mamá, podemos ir al cine?*

Mamá: *¿A qué hora vuelven?*

Tú: *Volvemos a las nueve y media.*

1. yo → centro comercial (4:00)
2. Elena → joyería (2:30)
3. Ana y yo → librería (4:30)
4. nosotros(as) → café (8:30)
5. Ana y Elena → tienda de ropa (1:30)

ACTIVIDAD 10

♻ ¿Qué usa?

Escuchar Rosa le explica a Sofía cómo va a varios lugares en la capital. ¿Qué transporte usa para ir a cada lugar? *(Hint: Say what transportation she uses.)*

1. carro
2. metro
3. taxi
4. a pie
5. autobús

a. la escuela
b. la clase de piano
c. el parque
d. el museo
e. la casa de los abuelos

doscientos setenta y uno
Etapa 2
271

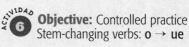

ACTIVIDAD 6

Objective: Controlled practice
Stem-changing verbs: o → ue

Answers
1. Tú puedes tocar el piano.
2. Rosa y Sofía pueden patinar.
3. Carlos puede manejar.
4. Yo puedo hablar español.
5. Andrea y yo podemos nadar.
6. Ellos pueden escribir poesía.
7. Nosotros podemos correr.
8. Rodrigo puede bailar.

ACTIVIDAD 7

Objective: Controlled practice
Stem-changing verbs: o → ue
♻ Places

Answers
1. encuentro   4. devolver   7. recuerdas
2. Vuelven   5. devuelves   8. Puedes
3. almorzamos   6. recuerdo

ACTIVIDAD 8

Objective: Transitional practice
Stem-changing verbs: o → ue
♻ Telling time
Answers will vary.

ACTIVIDAD 9

Objective: Transitional practice
Stem-changing verbs: o → ue
♻ Telling time

Answers
1. Tú: Mamá, ¿puedo ir al centro comercial?
   Mamá: ¿A qué hora vuelves?
   Tú: Vuelvo a las cuatro.
2. Tú: Mamá, ¿puede ir a la joyería?
   Mamá: ¿A qué hora vuelve?
   Tú: Vuelve a las dos y media.
3. Tú: Mamá, ¿podemos ir a la librería?
   Mamá: ¿A qué hora vuelven?
   Tú: Volvemos a las cuatro y media.
4. Tú: Mamá, ¿podemos ir al café?
   Mamá: ¿A qué hora vuelven?
   Tú: Volvemos a las ocho y media.
5. Tú: Mamá, ¿pueden ir a la tienda de ropa?
   Mamá: ¿A qué hora vuelven?
   Tú: Vuelven a la una y media.

ACTIVIDAD 10

Objective: Transitional practice
Listening comprehension
♻ Places/transportation

Answers (See script, p. 261B.)
1. e   2. c   3. b   4. a   5. d

■ Block Schedule

Change of Pace Have one student pantomime a simple sentence using a stem-changing verb (**Él/Ella almuerza a las once y media.**) while the rest of class guesses. The student who guesses, pantomimes a new sentence. (For additional activities, see **Block Scheduling Copymasters**.)

Teaching All Students

Extra Help To reinforce learning of stem-changing o → ue verbs, have student pairs create flashcards with infinitives on one side and sample sentences on the other. Pairs exchange cards and drill each other.

Native Speakers Have students write a "rap" to practice stem-changing o → ue verbs, i.e., **Yo recuerdo la información cuando duermo en mi habitación,...**

Multiple Intelligences

Visual Have students use colored markers or pencils to create their own verb "boots."

Musical/Rhythmic Have students record the sample sentences they wrote in "Extra Help" to a rock beat.

Kinesthetic Have students create "puzzle pieces" for the new verbs to highlight stems and changes.

Teaching Resource Options

Print

Block Scheduling Copymasters
Unit 4 Resource Book
  Information Gap Activities, p. 68

Audiovisual

OHT 125 (Quick Start)

Technology

Intrigas y aventuras CD-ROM, Disc 1

🔔 Quick Wrap-up

Using **poder,** have students work in pairs and tell each other 3 things they can do well and 3 things they cannot do well.

Teaching Suggestions
Presenting Vocabulary

- Before assigning **Actividad 11,** have students work in pairs and use the new vocabulary to comment on the photos of the items and their prices. Remember that the prices represent pesos, not dollars.
- Have students repeat the new vocabulary words. Encourage them to use associated gestures when appropriate.

Objective: Open-ended practice
Stem-changing verbs: o → ue/
bargaining vocabulary

Answers will vary.

Culture Highlights

● **LA CERÁMICA** The region of Oaxaca is famous for its pottery. Several towns make their own special kind of pottery that is easy to differentiate by the way it is decorated and the colors of the pieces. For example, the town of Santa María Atzompa makes green pottery; San Bartolo Coyotepec makes black pottery; San Marcos Tlapazola makes orange pottery.

ACTIVIDAD **11**  **Le puedo ofrecer...**

> ### PARA CONVERSAR
> **STRATEGY: SPEAKING**
> **Express emotion** Bargaining is the art of compromise with a little emotion.
>
> **React:** ¡Qué bonito! ¡Qué chévere! ¡Qué bien!
>
> **Get someone's attention:** Perdone…
>
> **Agree:** Creo que sí. Claro que sí. Está bien.
>
> **Disagree:** Creo que no. Gracias, pero no puedo.

Hablar Estás en un mercado. Necesitas comprar unas cosas. Con otro(a) estudiante, regatea. Cambien de papel. ¡La conversación puede variar mucho! *(Hint: Bargain.)*

modelo

Tú: *¿Me deja ver los aretes? ¿Cuánto cuestan?*

Vendedor(a): *Ochenta pesos.*

Tú: *¡Es demasiado! Le puedo ofrecer setenta pesos.*

Vendedor(a): *¡Son muy baratos! Son de buena calidad. Le dejo los aretes en setenta y cinco pesos.*

Tú: *Bueno, los llevo.*

Vendedor(a): *¿Cómo paga usted?*

Tú: *En efectivo.*

Vendedor(a): *¡Perfecto!*

■ **MÁS COMUNICACIÓN** p. R11

Vocabulario

Expresiones para regatear

barato(a) *cheap, inexpensive*	**demasiado(a)** *too much*
la calidad *quality*	**el dólar** *dollar*
cambiar *to change, to exchange*	**el efectivo** *cash*
el cambio *change, money exchange*	**perfecto(a)** *perfect*
caro(a) *expensive*	**la tarjeta de crédito** *credit card*

¿Qué palabras usas cuando regateas?

272 doscientos setenta y dos
Unidad 4

Classroom Community

Game Have students make two sets of cards. The first set will consist of subjects: **yo, mi mejor amigo(a), ustedes, tú, nosotros, el (la) profesor(a) de español.** The second set will contain the names or pictures of gift items. In small groups, students take turns turning over one card from each stack and telling what they are buying for that person: **tú / un disco compacto = Te compro un disco compacto.**

Learning Scenario Have students imagine they and a sibling have only enough money to buy one gift together for their grandmother, but have chosen different items. Discuss the problem and try to come to an agreement using only Spanish.

Portfolio Students may want to choose their best bargaining conversation from **Actividad 11** or the scenario to record on cassette or video for their portfolios.

GRAMÁTICA

Indirect Object Pronouns

¿**RECUERDAS?** *p. 224* You learned that direct object pronouns can be used to avoid repetition of the noun and answer the question *who?* or *what?*

replaces

—Pues, ya tienes **ropa** de verano. —Claro que la tengo.
*You already have summer **clothing**.* *Of course I have **it**.*

Indirect objects are **nouns** that tell *to whom/what* or *for whom/what*. Indirect object pronouns replace or accompany **indirect objects**.

Singular	Plural
me	nos
me	*us*
te	os
you (familiar)	*you (familiar)*
le	les
you (formal), him, her	*you (formal), them*

Notice that indirect object pronouns use the same words as direct object pronouns except for le and les.

accompanies *replaces*

Rosa le compra una olla **a su madre.** Rosa le compra una olla.
*Rosa buys a pot **for her mother**.* *Rosa buys a pot **for her**.*

The pronouns le and les can refer to different **indirect objects**. To clarify what they mean, they are often accompanied by:

a + name, noun, or **pronoun**

Rosa le compra una olla.
*Rosa buys a pot **for her**.*

Rosa le compra una olla **a su madre.**
*Rosa buys a pot **for her mother**.*

Teaching All Students

Extra Help Use OHT 121 and 122, **(En vivo Diálogo).** Have students find sentences with indirect object pronouns, then identify the subject and indirect object.

Native Speakers Ask native speakers to mention other currency. **Níquel,** used in Puerto Rico and Cuba, and **vellón,** from Puerto Rico, are both terms for a 5-cent coin. The **peseta** is the monetary unit of Spain.

Multiple Intelligences

Naturalist Ask students to bring in coins from Spanish-speaking countries. Have them research the material the coins are made of (copper, bronze, silver, etc.), and have them explain to the class.

Quick Start Review

♻ **Direct object pronouns**

Use OHT 125 or write on board: Write the direct object pronouns you would use to answer these questions.

1. ¿Necesitas el mapa?
2. ¿Vas a comprar las botas?
3. ¿Quieres el disco compacto de Selena?
4. ¿Recibe Julia los regalos de cumpleaños?
5. ¿Tenemos la jarra de mamá?

Answers
1. lo 2. las 3. lo 4. los 5. la

Teaching Suggestions
♻ **Direct object pronouns**

- Focus students' attention on the note on direct object pronouns. Ask for 5 sample sentences.

Presenting Indirect Object Pronouns

- Using gestures, present the verb **dar** *(to give).* Then pass out some classroom objects to students, describing as you go: **Le doy un lápiz verde a Carolina. Les doy papeles a Juan y Chucho.** Reaching for someone's book, ask: **¿Me das tu libro? Gracias.** Have students pass the items to other students and describe: **Carolina te da el lápiz verde, Dani.**
- Point out that there are only two basic differences between direct object pronouns and indirect object pronouns: the key questions, *to whom?* or *for whom?* and the two pronouns **le** and **les.** Also point out that there must be an indirect object pronoun in a sentence with an indirect object.
- Remind students that they have already used indirect object pronouns with **gustar.**

Block Schedule

Process Time To give students more processing time before presenting indirect object pronouns, try the storytelling activity from **Ampliación,** p. 239A. (For additional activities, see **Block Scheduling Copymasters.**)

Teaching Resource Options

Print

Más práctica Workbook PE, pp. 94–95
Para hispanohablantes Workbook PE,
  pp. 92–93
Block Scheduling Copymasters
Unit 4 Resource Book
  Más práctica Workbook TE, pp. 57–58
  Para hispanohablantes Workbook
    TE, pp. 63–64
  Audioscript, p. 81
  Audioscript *Para hispanohablantes*,
    p. 82

Audiovisual

Audio Program Cassettes 11A, 11B /
  CD 11
Audio *Para hispanohablantes*
  Cassette 11A / CD 11

Technology

Intrigas y aventuras CD-ROM, Disc 1

Teaching Suggestions
Reinforcing Object Pronouns

For additional practice, write these sentences on the board: **Rosa le compra una olla a su mamá.** *Buys what?* **(una olla)** *To whom or for whom?* **(su mamá)** Sí, Rosa le compra una olla a su mamá. Yo les busco zapatos nuevosa mis primos. *Looks for what?* **(zapatos nuevos)** *To whom or for whom?* **(mis primos)** ¡Bueno! Les busco zapatos nuevos a mis primos.

12 Objective: Controlled practice Indirect object pronouns

Answers
1. le	3. nos	5. le	7. les
2. me	4. le	6. les	8. te

13 Objective: Controlled practice Indirect object pronouns/**dar**

Answers
1. Su esposo le da un collar de oro.
2. Nosotros le damos una bolsa.
3. Sus hijos le dan una pulsera.
4. Su hermano le da una jarra de barro negro.
5. Yo le doy un disco compacto.
6. Tú le das un video.
7. Sofía le da unos aretes.

Juego

Answer: Lola quiere darle la lila a Lidia.

274 Vocabulary/Grammar • UNIDAD 4 Etapa 2

ACTIVIDAD 12 Gramática

El mercado

Leer Los padres de Sofía van al mercado. Completa las oraciones de Sofía con **me, te, le, les** o **nos.** *(Hint: Say for whom they buy things.)*

1. Mis padres _____ compran unas botas de cuero a mi hermano.
2. Ellos _____ compran unos aretes a mí.
3. Ellos _____ compran unos discos compactos a mi hermano y a mí.
4. Mi mamá _____ compra una cartera a mi papá.
5. Mi papá _____ compra una pulsera a mi mamá.
6. Mis padres _____ compran un plato a mis abuelos.
7. Ellos _____ compran una jarra a sus amigos.
8. Rosa, ¡ellos _____ compran algo a ti también!

Juego

¿Lidia le da la lila a Lola, o quiere darle Lola la lila a Lidia?

274 doscientos setenta y cuatro
Unidad 4

ACTIVIDAD 13 Gramática

¡Cuántos regalos!

Escribir Es el cumpleaños de la mamá de Rosa. Muchas personas le dan regalos. ¿Qué le dan? *(Hint: What do they give her?)*

modelo

Rosa: una olla

Rosa le da **una olla.**

Nota

Dar means *to give.* It has an irregular **yo** form: **doy.** Its other forms are regular, except the **vosotros** form has no accent.

1. su esposo: un collar de oro
2. nosotros: una bolsa
3. sus hijos: una pulsera
4. su hermano: una jarra de barro negro
5. yo: un disco compacto
6. tú: un video
7. Sofía: unos aretes

■ **MÁS PRÁCTICA** *cuaderno* pp. 94–95
■ **PARA HISPANOHABLANTES** *cuaderno* pp. 92–93

NOTA CULTURAL

El Museo Regional de Oaxaca contains gold jewelry from tomb 7 at Monte Albán. Mexican archaeologists Alfonso Caso and Ignacio Bernal discovered the tomb in 1932. You can buy reproductions of the jewelry at the museum or at shops in Oaxaca.

*Figura mixteca
de la tumba 7*

Classroom Community

TPR Use pictures of the vocabulary items or objects in the classroom, if available. Have students pretend they are on a home shopping TV show. One student describes an item and its price, another student holds it up and demonstrates the item.

Group Activity Working in groups of 3, have students create a skit that uses the grammar and vocabulary from this **Etapa.** Two students can be shopping for a gift; the third student is the salesperson. Allow 10 minutes to create and practice, then 2 minutes to perform the skit.

Regalos para todos

Escuchar Rosa va a la tienda de música y videos. ¡Compra muchos regalos! Escucha a Rosa y escribe lo que les compra a las personas. *(Hint: Say for whom Rosa buys what.)*

modelo
*Rosa le compra **un casete** a la profesora Díaz.*

a.

d.

b.

e.

c.

¿Qué te dan a ti?

Hablar ¿Qué te dan estas personas para tu cumpleaños?
(Hint: Who gives what?)

modelo
tus padres

Tú: *¿Qué te dan **tus padres** para tu cumpleaños?*

Otro(a): *Mis padres me dan un radiocasete.*

1. tu hermano(a)
2. tus primos
3. tus abuelos
4. tus tíos
5. tus amigos
6. tu mejor amigo(a)

Vocabulario

En la tienda de música y videos

el casete

el disco compacto

el radio

el radiocasete

el video

la videograbadora

el videojuego

¿Qué te gusta usar?

---

doscientos setenta y cinco
Etapa 2

275

Teaching Suggestions
Presenting Vocabulary
Present the vocabulary using the text or objects in the classroom, if available. Ask questions. Progress from yes/no questions (¿Escuchas música con un casete? ¿Tienes muchos discos compactos?), to either/or questions (¿Te gusta escuchar música con un casete o un disco compacto?), to questions using interrogatives (¿En cuál pones videos, en un videograbadora o en un radiocasete? ¿Dónde pones casetes?).

14 Objective: Transitional practice Listening comprehension/Indirect object pronouns/Music and video vocabulary

Answers (See script, p. 261B.)
a. Rosa les compra dos videos a sus hermanas.
b. Rosa le compra un disco compacto a su amiga Amanda.
c. Rosa le compra un videojuego a su hermano.
d. Rosa le compra un radio a su amigo Pablo.
e. Rosa le compra un casete a Sofía.

15 Objective: Open-ended practice Indirect object pronouns/Music and video vocabulary in conversation

Answers will vary.

Quick Wrap-up
Have students name items they would like to buy in the following stores:
una joyería / una tienda de cerámica / una tienda de música y videos / una tienda de artículos de cuero

Block Schedule
Change of Pace Have students work in pairs. One student closes his/her eyes while the other places an object (identifiable in Spanish) in the partner's hands, saying: **¿Qué te doy?** The partner guesses, responding **Me das...** Variation: Have students hand you objects to guess. (For additional activities, see **Block Scheduling Copymasters**.)

Teaching All Students

Extra Help First have students list verbs that use direct objects, such as **leer, comprar, vender, enseñar,** etc. Then have them add 5 items to this chart:

VERBO	OBJETO DIRECTO	OBJETO INDIRECTO	ORACIÓN COMPLETA
leer	un libro	mi hermano	Le leo un libro a mi hermano.

Multiple Intelligences

Logical/Mathematical Give students play money or a credit limit and have them bid on various items. The teacher or a student can act as auctioneer. Hold up pictures of items and say, **¿Cuánto me pagan por el radiocasete? Es de muy buena calidad.** Students respond with, **Le pago cincuenta dólares.** Give the picture to the highest bidder, and begin with a new item.

🔔 Quick Start Review

♻️ **Indirect object pronouns**

Use OHT 125 or write on the board:
Match the indirect object pronoun with
its corresponding phrase:

1. les	a. a mí
2. nos	b. a ella
3. te	c. a Juan y a mí
4. le	d. a los niños
5. me	e. a ti

Answers
1. d   2. c   3. e   4. b   5. a

Teaching Suggestions
Reinforcing Placement of Indirect Object Pronouns

For additional practice, have students
complete these sentences:

1. Mi mejor amigo acaba de salir
   de vacaciones. Voy a escribir___
   pronto.
2. Tengo información interesante
   para ti. Voy a decir___ esta noche.
3. Mi cumpleaños es mañana. Mis
   padres van a comprar___ un
   radiocasete.
4. Nuestro profesor de español es
   excelente. Va a enseñar___ una
   canción mexicana.
5. Mis primos buscan un coche.
   Quiero vender___ mi coche viejo.

Answers
1. escribirle
2. decirte
3. comprarme
4. enseñarnos
5. venderles

GRAMÁTICA

Placement of Indirect Object Pronouns

How do you know where indirect object pronouns go in a sentence? They work
just like **direct object pronouns.**

- When the pronoun accompanies
  a **conjugated verb**, the pronoun
  comes before the verb.

  before

  Rosa le **quiere comprar**
  una olla a su madre.
  Rosa wants to buy her mother a pot.

- But when the pronoun accompanies a sentence with an
  infinitive, it can either go before the **conjugated verb**
  or be attached to the end of the **infinitive**:

  attached

  Rosa **quiere comprarle**
  una olla a su madre.
  Rosa wants to buy her mother a pot.

ACTIVIDAD 16 — Gramática

¿Qué quieres darles?

Escribir Ya sabes qué les gusta hacer a varias
personas. ¿Qué quieres darles? *(Hint: Say what you
want to give.)*

modelo

mamá / llevar joyas

A mi **mamá** le gusta **llevar joyas.** Quiero darle un collar.
        o: Le quiero dar un collar.

1. papá / llevar artículos de cuero
2. hermano / jugar al béisbol
3. hermana / usar la cerámica
4. abuela / escuchar música
5. mejor amigo / ver videos
6. prima / jugar al tenis

 **MÁS PRÁCTICA** *cuaderno* p. 96
PARA HISPANOHABLANTES *cuaderno* p. 94

ACTIVIDAD 17

En la tienda

Hablar/Escribir Carlos está muy ocupado hoy.
Acaba de vender muchas cosas en la tienda de
su papá. ¿A quiénes les vendió cosas? *(Hint: To
whom has Carlos sold things?)*

modelo

Carlos acaba de venderle una revista a Rosa.

o: Carlos le acaba de vender una revista a Rosa.

un refresco	Rosa
un mapa	Rosa y Sofía
un periódico	mí
una revista	su vecino
¿?	¿?

276

doscientos setenta y seis
Unidad 4

Classroom Community

Paired Activity Have students act out a situation in
which someone buys a gift and presents it to another
person, but there is a problem with it (too big, too
small, wrong color, etc.). Allow pairs 3 minutes to work
together. Model the appropriate use of object pronouns.

Portfolio Have students record the **Trabalenguas.**
Record other pronunciation activities during the year to
show students' improvement.

Cooperative Learning In groups of 3, each student
writes a sentence with a direct and an indirect object
(**Mi padre me compra el radio**). Students then pass
their papers to the right. The next student rewrites the
sentence using an infinitive (**Mi padre va a comprarme
el radio**). The next student rewrites the sentence with
the indirect object pronoun in a different position (**Mi
padre me va a comprar el radio**). Continue with
another sentence, but now pass the papers to the left.

ACTIVIDAD 18

Almacén SuperGanga

Hablar Tú y un(a) amigo(a) van de compras. ¿Cuál es un buen regalo para cada persona de la familia? ¿Cuánto cuesta? ¿Es caro o barato? Hablen de las posibilidades.
(Hint: Choose gifts.)

modelo

hermanito

Tú: *Quiero comprarle un regalo a mi* **hermanito.**

Tu amigo(a): *¿Por qué no le compras el videojuego "El dragón gigante"?*

Tú: *Busco algo más barato.*

Tu amigo(a): …

1. hermano(a)
2. amigo(a)
3. primo(a)

■ **MÁS COMUNICACIÓN** p. R11

ALMACÉN SUPERGANGA

mayo

Especiales

Video
El futuro del planeta
94 pesos

Disco compacto
Las tortugas locas
40 pesos

Reloj
Galaxia
85 pesos

Radio Juvenil
Arco iris
94 pesos

Casete
Super Estrella
35 pesos

Videojuego
El dragón gigante
67 pesos

Pronunciación

Trabalenguas

Pronunciación de la rr The sound of rr in Spanish is produced by rapidly tapping the roof of the mouth with the tip of the tongue. Practice **rr** by repeating this tongue twister aloud. Use the pictures to help you figure out what it means.

Erre con erre, guitarra,

erre con erre, barril;

¡qué rápido corren los carros, los carros del ferrocarril!

doscientos setenta y siete
Etapa 2
277

Answers

1. A mi papá le gusta llevar artículos de cuero. Quiero darle [una cartera *o:* un cinturón, unas botas]. *o:* Le quiero dar [una cartera *o:* un cinturón, unas botas].
2. A mi hermano le gusta jugar al béisbol. Quiero darle [un guante *o:* un bate, una gorra]. *o:* Le quiero dar [un guante *o:* un bate, una gorra].
3. A mi hermana le gusta usar la cerámica. Quiero darle [una jarra *o:* un plato, una olla]. *o:* Le quiero dar [una jarra *o:* un plato, una olla].
4. A mi abuela le gusta escuchar música. Quiero darle [un disco compacto *o:* un casete]. *o:* Le quiero dar [un disco compacto *o:* un casete].
5. A mi mejor amigo le gusta ver videos. Quiero darle [un video]. *o:* Le quiero dar [un video].
6. A mi prima le gusta jugar al tenis. Quiero darle [una raqueta]. *o:* Le quiero dar [una raqueta].

ACTIVIDAD 17
Objective: Transitional practice
Placement of indirect object pronouns

Answers will vary.

ACTIVIDAD 18
Objective: Open-ended practice
Placement of indirect object pronouns/
Etapa vocabulary

Answers will vary.

🔔 Quick Wrap-up

Dictation: To reinforce comprehension of indirect object pronoun placement, dictate the following four items.
1. Mi tío me compra un libro.
2. Mi tío quiere comprarme un libro.
3. Raúl le escribe una carta a María.
4. Raúl va a escribirle una carta a María.

Dictation

After students have read the tongue twister in the **Pronunciación,** have them close their books. Dictate the tongue twister in segments while students write them.

▣ Block Schedule

Peer Teaching Now that you are at the end of the **En acción** activities, have students choose a concept that they are struggling with. Divide the class into groups. Have students brainstorm for 5 minutes to come up with suggestions for an easy way to remember the concept. Have groups share ideas with the class. (For additional activities, see **Block Scheduling Copymasters.**)

Teaching All Students

Extra Help Some students find it hard to memorize tongue twisters. To facilitate memorization, write the **Trabalenguas** on the board and have the class repeat it. Begin erasing the words from the end of the sentence to the beginning as students repeat it.

Native Speakers Ask students if they or their parents know of other **trabalenguas** for the **rr** sound.

Multiple Intelligences

Verbal Write a list of gift recipients: **mi tío, mis padres, mi amigo(a), tú, nosotros,** etc. Then have the class decide on a gift. Have one student write down a recipient for the gift and give it to the teacher. Students take turns guessing the recipient: **¿Les compras las botas a tu amigo?** (No.) **¿Me compras las botas?** (No.) When someone guesses correctly, they write down a recipient for another gift.

Teaching Resource Options

Print

Unit 4 Resource Book
  Audioscript, p. 81
  Audioscript *Para hispanohablantes,*
    p. 82

Audiovisual

Audio Program Cassette 11A / CD 11
Audio *Para hispanohablantes*
  Cassette 11A / CD 11
OHT 125 (Quick Start)
Canciones Cassette / CD

Quick Start Review

♻ Bargaining vocabulary

Use OHT 125 or write on the board:
Reassemble the following bargaining
conversation by numbering the
following sentences in a logical order.

____ Muy bien, quedamos en 80.
Muchas gracias.

____ Cuesta 100 pesos.

____ ¡Es demasiado! Le puedo
ofrecer 70.

____ ¡Es demasiado barato! Se la
dejo en 90.

____ Es muy bonita esta jarra.
¿Cuánto cuesta?

____ No puedo. ¿Me la deja en 80?

Answers See p. 261B.

Teaching Suggestions
Presenting Cultura y comparaciones

- Begin by asking students to guess the
topic of the culture section. Write the
list of possibilities on the board.
- Then have students suggest their own
strategies for working on the material.
- Note that in **Para conocernos,**
creating a Venn diagram is a retrieval
strategy that assists in learning and
remembering.

Reading Strategy

Preview graphics Based on what
students see in the visuals, have them
predict the subject of this article. After
reading the passage, have them decide if
their prediction was on target.

En colores
CULTURA Y COMPARACIONES

PARA CONOCERNOS
STRATEGY: CONNECTING CULTURES

Compare bargaining customs Where does bargaining
take place? How do people act when they
bargain? Use a Venn diagram to compare
bargaining in the United States to the kind of
bargaining that Rosa did in the Mercado Benito
Juárez in Oaxaca.

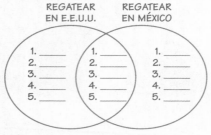

REGATEAR EN E.E.U.U.   REGATEAR EN MÉXICO

1. _____   1. _____   1. _____
2. _____   2. _____   2. _____
3. _____   3. _____   3. _____
4. _____   4. _____   4. _____
5. _____   5. _____   5. _____

What do they have in common?

NOTA CULTURAL

Benito Juárez (1806–1872) is
the most famous Oaxacan in
the history of Mexico. Of Zapotec
origin, he was elected governor
of Oaxaca and later president
of Mexico. The market is named
in his honor.

278 doscientos setenta y ocho
Unidad 4

El Mercado Benito Juárez

El mercado tiene una gran variedad de
cerámica y otras artesanías regionales.
También hay plantas medicinales,
productos textiles, frutas, verduras[1] y
carnes[2]. El mercado es un festival de
colores, texturas y aromas. Como[3] todos
los mercados, el Benito Juárez es un
lugar ideal para regatear.

_____

[1] vegetables   [2] meats   [3] As, Like

Classroom Community

TPR Ask students to act out each **regla.** First, teach
the following commands by acting them out: **levántate,
haz, rechaza, acepta, compra, siéntate.** Have students
perform a bargaining dialog based on the **cinco reglas.**
_____, **levántate. / Haz una oferta a** (another
student). / **Rechaza la oferta con regla #3. / Haz otra
oferta con regla #5. / Acepta la oferta. / Compra (el
objeto).**

Paired Activity Have students create their own **Las
cinco reglas...** for topics such as the following: **para
sacar una "A" en español; para encontrar el mejor
regalo para tu amigo(a).** Have pairs present their rules
to the class.

Las cinco reglas [4] fundamentales para regatear

Regatear es un arte que necesitas practicar.
Estas reglas te van a ayudar.

1 *Habla sólo español.*

2 *Actúa [5] como un(a) estudiante con poco dinero, no como un(a) turista rico(a) [6].*

3 *Escucha el primer precio. Después contesta: «¡Es demasiado!»*

4 *Pasa por otras tiendas para comparar los precios.*

5 *Siempre sonríe [7] al regatear. No cuesta dinero y a veces recibes mejores precios.*

[4] rules   [5] Act   [6] rich   [7] smile

¿Comprendiste?

1. ¿Qué hay para comprar en el Mercado Benito Juárez?
2. ¿Cómo es el mercado?
3. ¿Cómo compras en este mercado?

¿Qué piensas?

1. En tu opinión, ¿cuál es la regla más importante para recibir un buen precio? ¿Por qué?
2. ¿Cuáles de estas reglas son efectivas? ¿Piensas que algunas reglas no son efectivas? Explica tu opinión.
3. Ya sabes unas reglas para regatear. Mira tu diagrama de Venn. ¿Quieres escribir algo más? ¿Quieres cambiar algo?

Hazlo tú

Con otro(a) estudiante prepara un diálogo. Van a regatear. Una persona puede ser el (la) vendedor(a). La otra puede ser el (la) cliente(a).

Teaching All Students

Extra Help Have students read the **cinco reglas** out loud. While one student is reading a rule aloud, have another student act it out. Then reverse roles.

Native Speakers Ask native speakers if they have had experiences bargaining. Can they describe other places or situations where they would use bargaining strategies other than a market? Some suggestions: taking a cab, negotiating a service (repair to a shoe, bike, car). Are there situations where bargaining would be inappropriate?

Supplementary Vocabulary

¿Cuánto vale?	How much is it?
No puedo.	I can't.
Sólo tengo __ pesos.	I only have ____ pesos.
¡Es una ganga!	It's a bargain!

Cross Cultural Connections

Explain to students that if they visit a market, they should ask if they may touch items for sale before doing so. Some vendors do not want the customers touching the merchandise! (This includes foods.) Ask if students have had similar experiences at stores/markets in the U.S.

Interdisciplinary Connections

Social Studies Have students list places in their town/city or state that are named after famous Americans. Then have them list places in other parts of the U.S.

Critical Thinking

Ask students to think of a bargaining situation from their own lives and either say which of the **Cinco reglas** they used, or write a new rule that was effective.

¿Comprendiste?

Answers
1. Hay una gran variedad de cerámica y otras artesanías regionales, plantas medicinales, productos textiles, frutas, verduras y carne.
2. Es un festival de colores, texturas y aromas.
3. Es un lugar para regatear.

Hazlo tú

Students may refer to the video dialog, but should try to expand on it incorporating the "rules" given here. Remind students to think about previous dialogs they have practiced before beginning to write.

Block Schedule

FunBreak Try out the recipe for **Chocolate oaxaqueño** found in the **Ampliación** on p. 239B.

Teaching Resource Options

Print

Para hispanohablantes Workbook PE,
  pp. 95–96
Block Scheduling Copymasters
Unit 4 Resource Book
  Para hispanohablantes Workbook
    TE, pp. 66–67
  Information Gap Activities,
    p. 71
  Family Involvement, pp. 72–73
  Multiple Choice Test Questions,
    pp. 170–178

Audiovisual 🎧

OHT 126 (Quick Start)
Audio Program Testing Cassette T2 /
  CD T2

Technology 💻

Electronic Teacher Tools/Test
  Generator
Intrigas y aventuras CD-ROM, Disc 1

Quick Start Review

♻ Stem-changing verbs

Use OHT 126 or write on the board:
Write out the conjugation of 3 stem-
changing verbs. Then outline the
"boot" shape of each.

Answers will vary.

Teaching Suggestions
What Have Students Learned?

• Have students look at the "Now you
can…" notes listed on the left side of
pages 280–281. Tell students to think
about which areas they might not be
sure of. For those areas, they should
consult the "To review" notes.

• Use the video to review vocabulary
and structures.

ETAPA 2

Now you can...

• talk about
  shopping.

To review

• indirect object
  pronouns, see
  p. 273 and p. 276.

Now you can...

• make purchases.

To review

• stem-changing
  verbs: o → ue,
  see p. 270.

OBJECTIVES
• Talk about shopping
• Make purchases
• Talk about giving
  gifts
• Bargain

En uso
REPASO Y MÁS COMUNICACIÓN

ACTIVIDAD 1 ¿Qué nos va a comprar?

La abuela de Carlos conoce bien a su familia. ¿Qué les va a
comprar a todos? *(Hint: Say what she'll buy.)*

modelo

Héctor y Eloísa: ver películas

A **Héctor y a Eloísa** les gusta **ver películas.** Entonces, ella
va a comprarles un video. Cuesta **cincuenta y tres pesos.**

I. yo: usar artículos de cuero
2. mamá: llevar joyas
3. nosotros: escuchar música

4. tú: leer
5. papá: jugar al béisbol
6. los vecinos: tener cosas de cerámica

ACTIVIDAD 2 ¡De compras!

Rosa y Sofía están de compras. Completa su conversación con
el vendedor. *(Hint: Complete the conversation.)*

Rosa: ¿Cuánto __1__ (costar) los aretes?

Vendedor: __2__ (recordar, yo) el precio. Los aretes __3__ (costar) sólo
75 pesos.

Sofía: Rosa, ¿por qué no __4__ (volver, nosotras) más tarde? __5__
(poder, nosotras) almorzar en el café Sol.

Rosa: ¿El café Sol otra vez? Tú y yo siempre __6__ (almorzar) allí.

Vendedor: Yo les __7__ (poder) recomendar el nuevo café Florida.

Rosa: Gracias, señor. Compro los aretes.

Sofía: ¡Qué suerte! Tú siempre __8__ (encontrar) regalos baratos.

280 doscientos ochenta
Unidad 4

Classroom Community

TPR Do a quick review of vocabulary on pp. 280–281.
Say the names of the items pictured and have students
point to them in the book.

Group Activity Have students memorize and
present **Actividad 2** or **4** to the class. Students may
make changes and improvisations in the presentations,
as long as they make sense.

Learning Scenario Select a person who has an
upcoming birthday. Other members of the class will
make and label **regalos** for the student, using known
vocabulary. Each student will announce his/her gift
(**Voy a darle...**) and then speak to the recipient
(**Martina, te doy...**). The recipient must respond in
Spanish.

Now you can...

• talk about giving gifts.

To review

• the verb **dar**, see p. 274.

• indirect object pronouns, see p. 273 and p. 276.

ACTIVIDAD 3 ¡Feliz cumpleaños!

Hoy la señora Juárez celebra su cumpleaños. ¿Qué le dan todos? *(Hint: Say what people give.)*

modelo

Gustavo

Gustavo le da **una bolsa.**

I. yo

2. su esposo

3. tú

4. Sara y yo

5. sus hijos

6. nosotros

Now you can...

• bargain.

To review

• vocabulary for bargaining, see p. 265 and p. 272.

• stem-changing verbs: **o → ue**, see p. 270.

• indirect object pronouns, see p. 273 and p. 276.

ACTIVIDAD 4 ¡A regatear!

Tú quieres comprar un cinturón en el mercado y tienes que regatear. Completa la conversación. *(Hint: Bargain.)*

Tú: Perdone, señora. ¿(Te / Me) deja ver el cinturón de cuero, por favor?

Vendedora: ¡Cómo no! Usted (podemos / puede) ver que es de muy buena (calidad / oro).

Tú: Es muy bonito. Busco un (precio / regalo) para mi papá, a quien (les / le) gusta usar artículos de cuero. ¿Cuánto (cuesta / cuestan) el cinturón?

Vendedora: Para usted, joven, sólo cien pesos.

Tú: ¡Uy! ¡Es muy (barato / caro)! (Le / Nos) puedo ofrecer setenta pesos.

Vendedora: Bueno, (me / le) dejo el cinturón en ochenta y cinco.

Tú: No (puedes / puedo) pagar tanto. ¿Por qué no (me / les) da el cinturón por ochenta?

Vendedora: Está bien. Quedamos en ochenta.

doscientos ochenta y uno
Etapa 2 **281**

ACTIVIDAD 1 Answers

1. A mí me gusta usar artículos de cuero. Entonces, ella va a comprarme una cartera. Cuesta setenta y seis pesos.
2. A mamá le gusta llevar joyas. Entonces, ella va a comprarle una pulsera. Cuesta ochenta y siete pesos.
3. A nosotros nos gusta escuchar música. Entonces, ella va a comprarnos un disco compacto. Cuesta noventa y cuatro pesos.
4. A ti te gusta leer. Entonces, ella va a comprarte un libro. Cuesta sesenta pesos.
5. A papá le gusta jugar al béisbol. Entonces, ella va a comprarale una gorra. Cuesta cuarenta y dos pesos.
6. A los vecinos les gusta tener objetos de cerámica. Entonces, ella va a comprarles una olla. Cuesta setenta y dos pesos.

ACTIVIDAD 2 Answers

1. cuestan	5. Podemos
2. Recuerdo	6. almorzamos
3. cuestan	7. puedo
4. volvemos	8. encuentras

ACTIVIDAD 3 Answers

1. Yo le doy unos aretes.
2. Su esposo le da un anillo.
3. Tú le das un cinturón.
4. Sara y yo le damos una olla.
5. Sus hijos le dan un radiocasete.
6. Nosotros le damos un plato.

ACTIVIDAD 4 Answers

Me / puede / calidad / regalo / le / cuesta / caro / Le / le / puedo / me

■ Block Schedule

Change of Pace Bingo with stem changing verbs o→ue Review verb forms with the class. Before playing, write all of the possible infinitives to be used on the board. Have students fill out their cards with conjugated verb forms. Give clues as follows: subject pronoun, infinitive. (Ex: **yo** form of **poder**) When a student says "bingo", ask him/her to recite the conjugated verbs. (For additional activities, see **Block Scheduling Copymasters.**)

Teaching All Students

Extra Help Have students who are experiencing difficulty with stem-changing verbs and indirect object pronouns re-do the **Gramática** activities in each section for additional practice. Then have students explain the concepts to you in their own words, using examples.

Multiple Intelligences

Visual Have students find pictures of Oaxacan crafts on the Internet or in the library. Ask them to create their own catalog page, describing the items and pricing them.

Interpersonal Assign one minute reflections done in a group format. Students share the most interesting/most beneficial/most difficult section of the **Etapa** with their group.

Teaching Resource Options

Print

Unit 4 Resource Book
  Cooperative Quizzes, pp. 84–85
  Etapa Exam, Forms A and B,
    pp. 86–95
  Para hispanohablantes Etapa Exam,
    pp. 96–100
  Portfolio Assessment, pp. 101–102
  Multiple Choice Test Questions,
    pp. 170–178

Audiovisual

OHT 126 (Quick Start)
Audio Program Testing Cassette T2 /
  CD T2

Technology

Electronic Teacher Tools/Test
  Generator
www.mcdougallittell.com

ACTIVIDAD 5

Rubric: Speaking

Criteria	Scale	
Sentence structure	1 2 3	A = 11–12 pts.
Vocabulary use	1 2 3	B = 9–10 pts.
Originality	1 2 3	C = 7–8 pts.
Fluency	1 2 3	D = 4–6 pts.
		F = < 4 pts.

ACTIVIDAD 6 *Answers will vary.*

ACTIVIDAD 7 *En tu propia voz*

Rubric: Writing

Criteria	Scale	
Vocabulary use	1 2 3 4 5	A = 14–15 pts.
Accuracy	1 2 3 4 5	B = 12–13 pts.
Creativity, appearance	1 2 3 4 5	C = 10–11 pts.
		D = 8–9 pts.
		F = < 8 pts.

Teaching Note: En tu propia voz

Suggest that students make a chart similar to the one in **Actividad 6** in order to implement the writing strategy "Brainstorm details, then organize your information" in the paragraph they will write for the visitor from Oaxaca.

ACTIVIDAD 5  **El mercado**

PARA CONVERSAR

STRATEGY: SPEAKING

Disagree politely Find ways to disagree with the seller about the quality of the article or how it compares with another one. You can contradict politely or express a negative opinion in these ways: **no me gusta/gustaría…, no puedo…, no pienso…**

Estás en un mercado al aire libre. Compra tres cosas. Regatea para pagar el mejor precio. Después, cambien de papel. *(Hint: Bargain for three items.)*

¿Cuánto cuesta(n)?

¿Me deja ver…?

Le dejo… en…

¡Es muy caro!
Le puedo ofrecer…

ACTIVIDAD 6  **¡A comprar regalos!**

Completa la tabla con los regalos que vas a comprar para estas personas. No puedes pagar más de cien dólares. Luego, en grupos de tres, hablen de sus compras. *(Hint: Say what you'll buy.)*

modelo

Voy a comprarle un videojuego a mi amigo Daniel. Lo puedo encontrar en la tienda Super Max. Cuesta veinte dólares.

¿Para quién?	¿Qué?	¿Dónde?	¿Cuánto?
mi amigo(a) Daniel	un videojuego	Super Max	$20
todos mis amigos			
el (la) profesor(a)			
mi familia y yo			
yo			

ACTIVIDAD 7 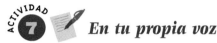 *En tu propia voz*

ESCRITURA Una joven de Oaxaca está de visita en tu comunidad. En un párrafo, explícale dónde y cómo comprar regalos para cinco miembros de su familia. *(Hint: Explain where and how to shop.)*

modelo

¿A tu mamá le gusta usar joyas? Puedes encontrar joyas bonitas en la joyería Sparkles. Queda en la calle Main. Venden collares muy baratos. Cuestan veinte dólares. No puedes regatear, pero puedes pagar con tarjeta de crédito…

CONEXIONES

Las matemáticas Create your own **mercado** in your Spanish classroom with objects donated by your classmates. You will **regatear**. Make a chart of the objects for sale and the prices they sell for. Calculate the total amount of money raised. Donate all proceeds to a community organization on behalf of the Spanish classes in your school.

Objeto	Precio
disco compacto	$5

282 doscientos ochenta y dos
Unidad 4

Classroom Community

Storytelling A student begins to tell a story using the **Vocabulario** on p. 283. The next student continues with the story by repeating the first sentence and adding another. Continue until the story is complete.

Paired Activity Divide students into pairs. One student chooses a vocabulary word from the **Vocabulario** on p. 283 and uses it in a game of hangman. Students play until they have each guessed 2 words correctly.

Group Activity Have students work in groups of 3 and do a variation of **Actividad 5**. This time, the 3 friends are shopping together. One friend is buying something, and the others are providing suggestions and comments.

En resumen
REPASO DE VOCABULARIO

MAKING PURCHASES

Jewelry

el anillo	ring
el arete	earring
el collar	necklace
las joyas	jewelry
el oro	gold
la plata	silver
la pulsera	bracelet

Music and Videos

el casete	cassette
el disco compacto	compact disc
el radio	radio
el radiocasete	radio-tape player
el video	video
la videograbadora	VCR
el videojuego	video game

Handicrafts

la artesanía	handicraft
los artículos de cuero	leather goods
la bolsa	handbag
las botas	boots
la cartera	wallet
la cerámica	ceramics
el cinturón	belt
la jarra	pitcher
la olla	pot
el plato	plate

BARGAINING

¿Cuánto cuesta(n)...?	How much is (are) ...?
¡Es muy caro(a)!	It's very expensive!
Le dejo... en...	I'll give ... to you for ...
Le puedo ofrecer...	I can offer you ...
¿Me deja ver...?	May I see ...?
regatear	to bargain

TALKING ABOUT GIVING GIFTS

dar	to give
el regalo	gift

TALKING ABOUT SHOPPING

barato(a)	cheap, inexpensive
la calidad	quality
cambiar	to change, to exchange
caro(a)	expensive
demasiado(a)	too much
el mercado	market
perfecto(a)	perfect

Money and Payment

el cambio	change, money exchange
el dinero	money
el dólar	dollar
el efectivo	cash
pagar	to pay
el precio	price
la tarjeta de crédito	credit card

OTHER WORDS AND PHRASES

juntos	together
para	for, in order to

Stem-Changing Verbs: o → ue

almorzar	to eat lunch
contar	to count, to tell or retell
costar	to cost
devolver	to return (an item)
dormir	to sleep
encontrar	to find, to meet
poder	to be able, can
recordar	to remember
volver	to return, to come back

Juego

¿Qué cosa compras por pocos pesos, una olla de plata o un plato barato?

Teaching All Students

Extra Help
- Using the video and videoscript, have students listen for the vocabulary words and circle them on the script.
- Have students write 5–7 questions to ask a salesclerk; for example: ¿Cuánto cuesta... ?, Yo quiero comprar...

Challenge Have students study the first column of words in the **Vocabulario** for 2 minutes. Close books. Allow each student 2 minutes to list all the words they can remember.

Exchange papers. Cross out words that are misspelled or incorrect. Exchange papers with a third person for checking. Return papers to the original student for final checking.

Multiple Intelligences
Visual Have students draw items from the **Vocabulario**. Hang them by category on strings around the classroom, or tack them on a bulletin board.

Interdisciplinary Connection
Math Give students a list of currencies for several Spanish-speaking countries. Have them look up the exchange rate for these currencies in the financial pages of a newspaper. Then have them convert the prices in **Actividad 1,** p. 280, into various currencies.

Community Connections
Have students look around their homes for articles (jewelry, handicrafts, etc.) made in Spanish-speaking countries and make a list. Compile a class list and categorize the items.

Quick Start Review
♻ Etapa vocabulary
Use OHT 126 or write on the board. Make flashcards of the **Repaso de vocabulario.** These will be used later as vocabulary review.

Teaching Suggestions
Vocabulary Review
Using flashcards of the words from the Quick Start, break students into groups of 3. Deal 5 cards per group. In 3 minutes, see how many sentences they can make using one card per sentence. The team with the most grammatically correct sentences wins.

Juego
Answer: Compro un plato barato.

Block Schedule
Projects
Assign the following out-of-class projects:
- Check the current exchange rate for the Mexican peso/U.S. dollar in the newspaper.
- Find a Mexican recipe.
- Find out about at least one current event in Mexico (Internet, etc.).
- Find realia (travel agencies, etc.).

Rubric: Project

Current exchange rate	1 pt.
Recipe	2 pts.
Current event	3 pts.
Realia (hands-on material)	4 pts.
Activity total:	10 pts.

Planning Guide CLASSROOM MANAGEMENT

OBJECTIVES

Communication
- Order food and request the check *pp. 288–289*
- Talk about food *pp. 286–287*
- Express extremes *pp. 288–289, 295*
- Say where you went *pp. 288–289, 292*

Grammar
- Use the verb **poner** *p. 291*
- Use **gustar** to talk about things you like *pp. 292–293*
- Use affirmative and negative words *pp. 294–295*
- Use stem-changing verbs: e → i *pp. 296–297*

Pronunciation
- Pronunciation of **g** *p. 299*
- Dictation *TE p. 299*

Culture
- Oaxacan cuisine *p. 292*
- Oaxacan artistic heritage *pp. 296, 300–301*
- Zapotec Indians *p. 302*
- Monte Albán *pp. 302–303*

♻ Recycling
- Prepositions of location *p. 291*
- Stores *p. 292*
- Clothing *p. 293*
- Direct object pronouns *p. 298*

STRATEGIES

Listening Strategies
- Integrate your skills *p. 288*

Speaking Strategies
- Vary ways to express preferences *p. 290*
- Borrow useful expressions *p. 306*

Reading Strategies
- Gather and sort information as you read *p. 300*
- Look for cognates *TE p. 303*

Writing Strategies
- Use different kinds of descriptive words *TE p. 234*
- Tell who, what, where, when, why, and how *pp. 308–309*

Connecting Cultures Strategies
- Recognize variations in vocabulary *p. 291*
- Consider the effects of tourism from the point of view of the inhabitants *pp. 302–303*
- Connect and compare what you know about jobs in your community to help you learn about jobs in a new community *pp. 300–301, 302–303, 306*

PROGRAM RESOURCES

 Print
- *Más práctica* Workbook PE *pp. 97–104*
- Block Scheduling Copymasters *pp. 97–104*
- Unit 4 Resource Book
  Más práctica Workbook TE *pp. 103–110*
  Para hispanohablantes Workbook TE *pp. 111–118*
- Information Gap Activities *pp. 119–122*
- Family Involvement *pp. 123–124*
- Video Activities *pp. 125–127*
- Videoscript *pp. 128–130*
- Audioscript *pp. 131–134*
- Assessment Program, Unit 4 Etapa 3 *pp. 135–178*
- Answer Keys *pp. 179–200*

 Audiovisual
- **Audio Program** Cassettes 12A, 12B / CD 12
- *Canciones* Cassette / CD
- **Video Program** Videotape 4 / Videodisc 2B
- **Overhead Transparencies** M1–M5; GO1–GO5; 106, 127–136

 Technology
- **Electronic Teacher Tools/Test Generator**
- *Intrigas y aventuras* CD-ROM, Disc 1
- www.mcdougallittell.com

 Assessment Program Options
- **Cooperative Quizzes** (Unit 4 Resource Book)
- **Etapa Exam** Forms A and B (Unit 4 Resource Book)
- *Para hispanohablantes* **Etapa Exam** (Unit 4 Resource Book)
- **Portfolio Assessment** (Unit 4 Resource Book)
- **Unit 4 Comprehensive Test** (Unit 4 Resource Book)
- *Para hispanohablantes* **Unit 4 Comprehensive Test** (Unit 4 Resource Book)
- **Multiple Choice Test Questions** (Unit 4 Resource Book)
- **Audio Program** Testing Cassette T2 / CD T2
- **Electronic Teacher Tools/Test Generator**

Native Speakers
- *Para hispanohablantes* **Workbook PE**, *pp. 97–104*
- *Para hispanohablantes* **Workbook TE** (Unit 4 Resource Book)
- *Para hispanohablantes* **Etapa Exam** (Unit 4 Resource Book)
- *Para hispanohablantes* **Unit 4 Comprehensive Test** (Unit 4 Resource Book)
- **Audio** *Para hispanohablantes* Cassettes 12A, 12B, T2 / CD 12, T2
- **Audioscript** *Para hispanohablantes* (Unit 4 Resource Book)

Student Text
Listening Activity Scripts

Sofía　Rosa　Carlos　Mesero

 Videoscript: Diálogo *pages 288–289*

• Videotape 4　• Videodisc 2B

Search Chapter 7, Play to 8
U4E3 • En vivo (Dialog)

• Use the videoscript with **Actividades 1, 2** *page 290*

Sofía: Tienes que decirme. ¿Cómo conoces a Carlos?

Rosa: ¡Es un secreto!

Sofía: ¡Por favor, Rosa!

Rosa: No puedo decirte. Las promesas son promesas.

Sofía: ¡Pero soy tu prima, Rosa! ¡Me tienes que decir!

Rosa: Está bien, está bien. Conozco a Carlos porque fui a la tienda de su papá para pedir direcciones para llegar a tu casa.

Sofía: ¡Ah!, ¿es todo? ¿No son amigos por Internet?

Rosa: No, ¡qué va! Qué imaginación tienes.

Mesero: Buenas tardes, Carlos. Buenas tardes, señoritas. Bienvenidos al restaurante La Madre Tierra. Aquí tienen el menú.

Carlos: ¿Nos puede traer pan, por favor?

Mesero: Sí, cómo no. Enseguida se lo traigo.

Rosa: Yo quiero un plato tradicional de Oaxaca. ¿Qué pido?

Carlos: La especialidad de la casa es una combinación de algunos platos regionales. Tiene mole negro y tasajo. Es riquísima.

Sofía: Yo voy a pedir una ensalada mixta y pollo.

Rosa: Y tú, Carlos, ¿qué pides normalmente?

Carlos: Me gustan las enchiladas, pero ahora tengo ganas de comer carne. Voy a pedir bistec asado. Viene con arroz y frijoles.

Mesero: ¿Listos para pedir?

Sofía: Sí, señor. Para mí, una ensalada mixta y pollo.

Rosa: Para mí, la especialidad de la casa.

Mesero: ¿Y para el señor?

Carlos: Un bistec asado.

Mesero: ¿Algo de tomar?

Sofía: Una limonada para mí.

Rosa: Agua mineral, por favor.

Carlos: Un refresco de naranja.

Mesero: Muy bien. ¿Y de postre? Los postres ricos son otra especialidad de la casa. Son buenísimos.

Sofía: Por ahora, nada más. El postre lo pedimos después, gracias.

Mesero: Para servirles.

Rosa: Oye, Carlos, ¿cómo va tu proyecto para el concurso?

Carlos: Muy bien. Mi proyecto para el concurso es sobre las ruinas de Monte Albán. Es fascinante la historia de México.

Rosa: ¿Ya fuiste a Monte Albán?

Carlos: Sí, fui a Monte Albán el otro día para sacar fotos. Hay mucho que ver: tumbas, altares ceremoniales y pirámides. El Centro Ceremonial es algo increíble. Desde arriba, hay unas vistas fabulosas. Los Danzantes son unas figuras muy curiosas. Y el Juego de Pelota es antiguo e interesante. El Palacio es maravilloso. Las ruinas de Monte Albán son impresionantes. ¡Es un lugar mágico!

Rosa: Estoy segura de que tú vas a ganar el concurso. Tu proyecto va a presentar el pasado fascinante de los mexicanos. Me gusta mucho tu idea para el concurso.

Mesero: ¿Algo más, jóvenes?

Sofía: Qué crees, Rosa, ¿pido un postre y lo compartimos?

Rosa: Bueno, si pedimos algo pequeño.

Mesero: ¿Un flan, señoritas? Lo sirvo en dos platos con dos cucharas.

Sofía: Perfecto, señor. Muchas gracias.

Mesero: ¿Y para usted?

Carlos: No quiero ningún postre, pero ¿me puede traer la cuenta, por favor? Tengo prisa.

Mesero: Sí, cómo no.

Sofía: El mesero es muy amable y sirve muy bien.

Carlos: Sí, el mesero es muy amable. Me gusta la gente de este restaurante. ¡Quisiera comer aquí todos los días!

Rosa: ¡Ah! ¡Un momento! Aquí tienes tu mapa. Gracias.

Carlos: Al contrario.

 **¿Qué pasa?** *page 291*

1. Le gusta comer los postres. Está comiendo un flan.
2. No tiene mucha hambre. Prefiere comer sólo fruta.
3. Está enfermo. Quiere comer sopa de pollo.
4. Tiene mucha sed. Está tomando una limonada.

 **¿A quién?** *page 298*

Carlos: ¡Qué hambre tengo! ¿Qué vas a pedir, Elena?

Elena: Voy a pedir unas enchiladas de carne.

Carlos: Tú siempre pides enchiladas.

Elena: Sí, tienes razón. Siempre las pido. Me gustan mucho y son riquísimas aquí. ¿Y tú?

Carlos: Voy a pedir un bistec y papas fritas.

Elena: ¿Y para beber?

Carlos: Voy a tomar algún refresco.

Elena: Y yo un té.

Carlos: De postre, voy a pedir un flan. ¿Y tú?

Elena: No tengo tanta hambre como tú. No voy a pedir ningún postre.

🔔 **Quick Start Review Answers**

p. 288 Food vocabulary
1. el plato, el tenedor, el cuchillo, la taza
2. el arroz, el bistec, el pollo, una enchilada
3. la limonada, el café, el té, el refresco

p. 290 Dialog review
1. tienda
2. mole
3. ensalada
4. postres
5. ningún

p. 294 Likes and dislikes
Answers will vary.
Answers could include:
1. A mi hermano le gusta la comida picante.
2. A mis padres les gusta la sopa vegetariana.
3. A mi mejor amiga le gustan las papas fritas.
4. A mi tía Ana le gusta el pan dulce.
5. A Tomás le gustan las enchiladas.

p. 296 Affirmative and negative words
1. nadie
2. alguien
3. algo
4. tampoco
5. algún

p. 302 In a restaurant
Answers will vary.
Answers could include:
1. el pan
2. la especialidad de la casa
3. la propina
4. la comida picante
5. la carne

Sample Lesson Plan - 50 Minute Schedule

DAY 1

Etapa Opener
- Quick Start Review (TE, p. 284) 5 MIN.
- Anticipate/Activate prior knowledge: Have students look at the *Etapa* Opener and answer the questions. 5 MIN.

En contexto: Vocabulario
- Quick Start Review (TE, p. 286) 5 MIN.
- Have students use context and pictures to learn *Etapa* vocabulary. In pairs, have students answer the questions, p. 287. Use the Situational OHTs for additional practice. 10 MIN.

En vivo: Diálogo
- Quick Start Review (TE, p. 288) 5 MIN.
- Review the Listening Strategy, p. 288. Play audio or show video for the dialog, pp. 288–289. 10 MIN.
- Replay twice. Read aloud, having students take the roles of the characters. 10 MIN.

Homework Option:
- Video Activities, Unit 4 Resource Book, pp. 125–127.

DAY 2

En acción: Vocabulario y gramática
- Check homework. 5 MIN.
- Quick Start Review (TE, p. 290) 5 MIN.
- Have students open to *En contexto*, pp. 286–287, for reference. Use OHT 127 and 128 to review vocabulary by asking yes/no questions (*¿Es un[a]...?*). 10 MIN.
- Play the audio; have students do *Actividades* 1 and 2 orally. 10 MIN.
- Present the *Vocabulario*, p. 290. Model pronunciation. Then have students complete *Actividad* 3 orally. 10 MIN.
- Play the audio; have students do *Actividad* 4. 5 MIN.
- Present the *Nota*. Have students complete *Actividad* 5 in pairs. 5 MIN.
- Present the *Nota*. Have students complete *Actividad* 6 in pairs. Have a few pairs present their work to the class. 5 MIN.

Homework Option:
- Have students complete *Actividades* 3 and 5 in writing.

DAY 3

En acción (cont.)
- Check homework. 5 MIN.
- Quick Start Review (TE, p. 292) 5 MIN.
- Present *Gramática:* Using *gustar* to Talk About Things You Like, p. 292. 10 MIN.
- Do *Actividad* 7 orally. 5 MIN.
- In groups, have students do *Actividad* 8. Call on a few groups to present their answers. 5 MIN.
- Do *Actividad* 9 orally. Expand using Information Gap Activities, Unit 4 Resource Book, p. 119; *Más comunicación*, p. R12. 10 MIN.
- Quick Start Review (TE, p. 294) 5 MIN.
- Present *Gramática:* Affirmative and Negative Words, p. 294. 10 MIN.

Homework Option:
- Have students complete *Actividades* 7 and 9 in writing. *Más práctica* Workbook, p. 101. *Para hispanohablantes* Workbook, p. 99.

DAY 4

En acción (cont.)
- Check homework. 5 MIN.
- Review Affirmative and Negative Words. Then present the *Nota* and have students read and complete *Actividad* 10. 10 MIN.
- Have students complete *Actividad* 11 in pairs. 5 MIN.
- Do *Actividad* 12 orally. 5 MIN.
- Have students complete *Actividad* 13 in writing. Have students exchange papers for peer correction. 10 MIN.
- Present the *Nota*. Have students complete *Actividad* 14 orally. 5 MIN.
- Quick Start Review (TE, p. 296) 5 MIN.
- Present *Gramática:* Stem-Changing Verbs: *e → i* and *Vocabulario*, p. 296. 5 MIN.
- Have students read and complete *Actividad* 15. Go over answers orally. 5 MIN.

Homework Option:
- Have students complete *Actividades* 12 and 14 in writing. *Más práctica* Workbook, pp. 102–103. *Para hispanohablantes* Workbook, pp. 100–101.

DAY 5

En acción (cont.)
- Check homework. 5 MIN.
- Do *Actividad* 16 orally. 5 MIN.
- Present the *Nota*. Then do *Actividad* 17 in pairs. 5 MIN.
- Present the *Vocabulario*, p. 298. Then play the audio and do *Actividad* 18. 10 MIN.
- Present the *Nota*. Then do *Actividad* 19 in pairs and *Actividades* 20 and 21 in groups. 15 MIN.
- Do *Actividad* 22 in groups. Expand using Information Gap Activities, Unit 4 Resource Book, pp. 120–121; *Más comunicación*, p. R12. 10 MIN.

Pronunciación
- Play the audio and have students practice the *Trabalenguas*. 5 MIN.

Homework Option:
- *Más práctica* Workbook, p. 104. *Para hispanohablantes* Workbook, p. 102.

DAY 6

En voces: Lectura
- Check homework. 5 MIN.
- Quick Start Review (TE, p. 300) 5 MIN.
- Present the Reading Strategy, p. 300. Have volunteers read the selection aloud and answer the questions, p. 301. 15 MIN.

En colores: Cultura y comparaciones
- Quick Start Review (TE, p. 302) 5 MIN.
- Discuss the Connecting Cultures Strategy, p. 302. Have volunteers read the selection aloud and answer the questions, p. 303. Show video culture presentation for expansion. 20 MIN.
- Review *En uso* for *Etapa* 3 Exam. 5 MIN.

Homework Option:
- Prepare *En uso Actividades* 1–5. Review for *Etapa* 3 Exam.

DAY 7

En uso: Repaso y más comunicación
- Check homework. 5 MIN.
- Quick Start Review (TE, p. 304) 5 MIN.
- Review *Actividades* 1–5 orally. 5 MIN.
- Present the Speaking Strategy, p. 306. Do *Actividad* 6 in pairs and *Actividad* 7 in groups. 10 MIN.

En resumen: Repaso de vocabulario
- Complete *Etapa* 3 Exam. 20 MIN.

En tu propia voz: Escritura
- Do *Actividad* 8 in writing. 5 MIN.

Tú en la comunidad
- Present *Tú en la comunidad*, p. 306. 5 MIN.

Homework Option:
- Review for Unit 4 Comprehensive Test.

DAY 8

En resumen: Repaso de vocabulario
- Quick Start Review (TE, p. 307) 5 MIN.

En tu propia voz: Escritura
- Present the Writing Strategy, p. 308. Do the writing activity, pp. 308–309. 10 MIN.

Unit 4 Comprehensive Test
- Review grammar questions, etc. as necessary. 5 MIN.
- Complete Unit 4 Comprehensive Test. 30 MIN.

Ampliación
- Optional: Use a suggested project, game, or activity. (TE, pp. 239A–239B) 15 MIN.

Homework Option:
- Preview *Unidad* 5 Opener: Have students read and study pp. 310–311.

Sample Lesson Plan - Block Schedule (90 minutes)

DAY 1

Etapa Opener
- Quick Start Review (TE, p. 284) 5 MIN.
- Anticipate/Activate prior knowledge: Have students look at the *Etapa* Opener and answer the questions. 5 MIN.
- Use Block Scheduling Copymasters. 5 MIN.

En contexto: Vocabulario
- Quick Start Review (TE, p. 286) 5 MIN.
- Have students use context and pictures to learn *Etapa* vocabulary. In pairs, have students answer the questions, p. 287. Use the Situational OHTs for additional practice. 10 MIN.

En vivo: Diálogo
- Quick Start Review (TE, p. 288) 5 MIN.
- Review the Listening Strategy, p. 288. Play audio or show video for the dialog, pp. 288–289. 10 MIN.
- Replay twice. Read aloud, having students take the roles of the characters. 10 MIN.

En acción: Vocabulario y gramática
- Quick Start Review (TE, p. 290) 5 MIN.
- Play the audio; do *Actividades* 1 and 2 orally. 10 MIN.
- Present the *Vocabulario*, p. 290. Then have students complete *Actividad* 3 orally. 10 MIN.
- Play the audio; have students do *Actividad* 4. 5 MIN.
- Present the *Nota.* Have students do *Actividad* 5 in pairs. 5 MIN.

Homework Option:
- Have students complete *Actividades* 3 and 5 in writing. Video Activities, Unit 4 Resource Book, pp. 125–127.

DAY 2

En acción (cont.)
- Check homework. 5 MIN.
- Present the *Nota.* Have students complete *Actividad* 6 in pairs. Have a few pairs present their work to the class. 5 MIN.
- Quick Start Review (TE, p. 292) 5 MIN.
- Present *Gramática:* Using *gustar* to Talk About Things You Like, p. 292. 10 MIN.
- Do *Actividad* 7 orally. 5 MIN.
- In groups, have students do *Actividad* 8. Call on a few groups to present their answers. 5 MIN.
- Do *Actividad* 9 orally. Expand using Information Gap Activities, Unit 4 Resource Book, p. 119; *Más comunicación,* p. R12. 15 MIN.
- Quick Start Review (TE, p. 294) 5 MIN.
- Present *Gramática:* Affirmative and Negative Words, p. 294. 10 MIN.
- Present the *Nota* and have students read and complete *Actividad* 10. 5 MIN.
- Have students complete *Actividad* 11 in pairs. 5 MIN.
- Do *Actividad* 12 orally. 5 MIN.
- Have students complete *Actividad* 13 in writing. Have students exchange papers for peer correction. 10 MIN.

Homework Option:
- Have students complete *Actividades* 9 and 12 in writing. *Más práctica* Workbook, pp. 101–103. *Para hispanohablantes* Workbook, pp. 99–101.

DAY 3

En acción (cont.)
- Check homework. 5 MIN.
- Present the *Nota.* Have students complete *Actividad* 14 orally. 5 MIN.
- Quick Start Review (TE, p. 296) 5 MIN.
- Present *Gramática:* Stem-Changing Verbs: *e → i* and *Vocabulario,* p. 296. 5 MIN.
- Have students read and complete *Actividad* 15. Go over answers orally. 5 MIN.
- Have students do *Actividad* 16 orally. 5 MIN.
- Present the *Nota.* Then have students complete *Actividad* 17 in pairs. 5 MIN.
- Present the *Vocabulario,* p. 298. Then play the audio and do *Actividad* 18. 10 MIN.
- Present the *Nota.* Then have students do *Actividad* 19 in pairs. 5 MIN.
- Do *Actividades* 20 and 21 in groups. 10 MIN.
- Have students do *Actividad* 22 in groups. Expand using Information Gap Activities, Unit 4 Resource Book, pp. 120–121; *Más comunicación,* p. R12. 15 MIN.

Ampliación
- Use a suggested project, game, or activity. (TE, pp. 239A–239B) 10 MIN.

Pronunciación
- Play the audio and have students practice the *Trabalenguas.* 5 MIN.

Homework Option:
- Have students complete *Actividades* 14 and 16 in writing. *Más práctica* Workbook, p. 104. *Para hispanohablantes* Workbook, p. 102.

DAY 4

En voces: Lectura
- Check homework. 5 MIN.
- Quick Start Review (TE, p. 300) 5 MIN.
- Present the Reading Strategy, p. 300. Have volunteers read the selection aloud and answer the questions, p. 301. 20 MIN.

En colores: Cultura y comparaciones
- Quick Start Review (TE, p. 302) 5 MIN.
- Discuss the Connecting Cultures Strategy, p. 302. Have volunteers read the selection aloud and answer the questions, p. 303. Show video culture presentation for expansion. 20 MIN.

En uso: Repaso y más comunicación
- Quick Start Review (TE, p. 304) 5 MIN.
- Do *Actividades* 1–5 orally. 10 MIN.
- Present the Speaking Strategy, p. 306. Do *Actividad* 6 in pairs and *Actividad* 7 in groups. 10 MIN.
- Do *Actividad* 8 in writing. 10 MIN.

Homework Option:
- Review for *Etapa* 3 Exam.

DAY 5

En resumen: Repaso de vocabulario
- Quick Start Review (TE, p. 307) 5 MIN.
- Review grammar questions, etc. as necessary. 5 MIN.
- Complete *Etapa* 3 Exam. 20 MIN.

Tú en la comunidad
- Present *Tú en la comunidad,* p. 306. 10 MIN.

Unit 4 Comprehensive Test
- Review grammar questions, etc. as necessary. 5 MIN.
- Complete Unit 4 Comprehensive Test. 30 MIN.

En tu propia voz: Escritura
- Present the Writing Strategy, p. 308. Do the writing activity, pp. 308–309. 15 MIN.

Homework Option:
- Preview *Unidad* 5 Opener: Have students read and study pp. 310–311.

▼ Carlos, Sofía y Rosa almuerzan en el restaurante.

Etapa Theme
Ordering food in a restaurant, talking about food, and requesting the check.

Grammar Objectives
- Using the verb **gustar** with nouns
- Using affirmative and negative words
- Using stem-changing verbs: **e → i**

Teaching Resource Options
Print

Block Scheduling Copymasters

Audiovisual

OHT 106, 133 (Quick Start)

Quick Start Review
♻ **Gustar**/Free-time activities

Use OHT 133 or write on board: Complete the following sentences with **gustar** and activities that you and your friends like to do after school and on weekends.

1. A mí...
2. A mi mejor amigo(a)...
3. A ti...
4. A mi mejor amigo(a) y a mí...
5. A muchos de mis amigos...

Answers
Answers will vary. Answers could include:
1. me gusta practicar deportes
2. le gusta ver la televisión
3. te gusta andar en patineta
4. nos gusta jugar al tenis
5. les gusta ir al cine

Teaching Suggestions
Previewing the Etapa
- Ask students to study the picture on pp. 284–285 (1 min.).
- Close books; ask students to talk about what the people are wearing, what they are doing, where they are, etc.
- Reopen books and look at the picture again (1 min.); close books and share 3 details about the picture.
- Use the **¿Qué ves?** questions to focus the discussion.

UNIDAD 4

ETAPA 3

¿Qué hacer en Oaxaca?

- Order food
- Request the check
- Talk about food
- Express extremes
- Say where you went

¿Qué ves?

Mira la foto de Monte Albán.

1. ¿Alguien lleva una gorra?
2. ¿Quién es la persona principal?
3. ¿Qué hace?
4. ¿Cuánto cuesta un refresco en el restaurante?

284

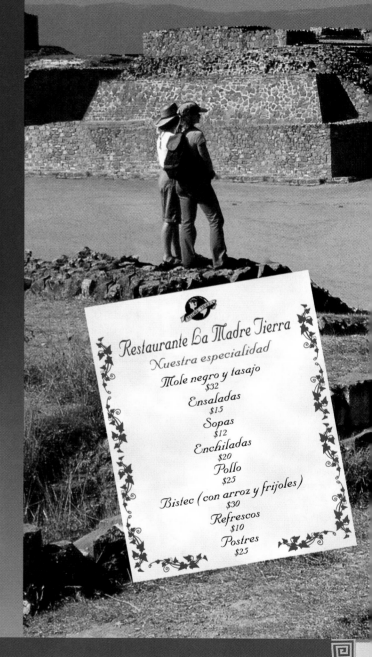

Restaurante La Madre Tierra
Nuestra especialidad

Mole negro y tasajo
$32

Ensaladas
$15

Sopas
$12

Enchiladas
$20

Pollo
$25

Bistec (con arroz y frijoles)
$30

Refrescos
$10

Postres
$25

Classroom Management

Planning Ahead Have authentic menus in Spanish on hand for students to observe. (Ask students to visit or write to Mexican/Spanish restaurants and request their menus.) Display the menus. Additionally, ask students to bring in simple recipes for Mexican foods. You can create a class recipe box and begin thinking of a possible "Mexican Food Party" (students prepare items!) upon completion of the unit.

Time Saver To save time when presenting vocabulary and doing the activities, prepare ahead of time magazine cutouts/simple drawings of the food items/tableware presented in the **En contexto** on pp. 286–287. You might also collect an assortment of plastic food and tableware.

285

Cross Cultural Connections

Have students talk about ethnic restaurants that are popular in your area. What similarities and differences do they notice between those restaurants and typical U.S. restaurants? Would they be willing to go to a Mexican restaurant and order in Spanish?

Culture Highlights

● **MONTE ALBÁN** The photo on these pages is of Monte Albán. Archaeological excavations, begun in 1931, revealed that an advanced civilization flourished here around 200 B.C. At one time, there were 25,000 inhabitants. No one knows why the city was abandoned about 1400 A.D.

In the South Platform of Monte Albán, archaeologists discovered hidden carvings. The foundation stones in the four corners of the building have carvings on their bottom ends. They were seen only by those who carved them and those who worked on their placement. They were not intended for public enjoyment, but were offerings to the Earth.

Supplementary Vocabulary

una pirámide	pyramid
una excavación	archaeological dig
unas ruinas	ruins
una cámara	camera
una diapositiva	slide
una videocámara	video camera

Critical Thinking

Ask students if they recall any information about Monte Albán from the Unit Opener. Assign research groups to gather additional information and present to the class. What are the theories about why the city was abandoned?

Block Schedule

Preview Have students leaf through the **Etapa.** What do they already know related to what they see? What do they expect to learn? Have them write down their expectations. At the end of the **Etapa,** have them look back and see if they learned what they had expected to. (For additional activities, see **Block Scheduling Copymasters.**)

Teaching All Students

Extra Help Have students study the picture for 1 minute. Give them a list that contains 5 items that are found in the picture and 5 that are not. Have them check the items that are in the picture.

Multiple Intelligences

Naturalist Have students look at the photo and list elements that indicate what kind of physical environment is shown (vegetation, sky conditions, temperature indicated by clothing, etc.). Have students list similarities and differences between the area shown and students' local area. Have they ever been to a place similar to the one shown?

Teaching Resource Options

Print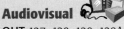

Unit 4 Resource Book
Video Activities, pp. 125–126
Videoscript, p. 128
Audioscript, p. 131
Audioscript *Para hispanohablantes*,
p. 131

Audiovisual

OHT 127, 128, 129, 129A, 130, 130A,
133 (Quick Start)
Audio Program Cassette 12A / CD 12
Audio *Para hispanohablantes*
Cassette 12A / CD 12
Video Program Videotape 4 /
Videodisc 2B

Search Chapter 6, Play to 7
U4E3 • En contexto (Vocabulary)

Technology

Intrigas y aventuras CD-ROM, Disc 1

Quick Start Review

♻ Food vocabulary

Use OHT 133 or write on board:
Make a list of 5 snacks and drinks in
Spanish.

Answers
Answers will vary. Answers could include:
la fruta, la hamburguesa, las papas fritas,
la torta, los chicharrones, el agua, el refresco,
los tacos, el sándwich, las tortillas

Culture Highlights

● **LA COCINA DE OAXACA** The names
of traditional Oaxacan dishes are as
creative as the dishes themselves. There is,
for example, **caldo de gato** (Cat broth),
which is made with beef and vegetables.
The names of other dishes come from the
Indian tradition that influenced them; for
example, **tlayudas** (giant tortillas).

En contexto

VOCABULARIO

Carlos is at a restaurant in Oaxaca. Take
a look at what he likes to eat.

A

Carlos tiene mucha hambre y va a **un
restaurante**. Lee **el menú** y decide
comer **una enchilada**. Es **deliciosa**.
¡Pero **la salsa** es **picante**! **El mesero**
va a **servirle una limonada**.

el restaurante
el mesero
la enchilada
la limonada

CASA LINDA

ENSALADAS Y SOPAS

Ensalada mixta	$25
Sopa de pollo	$20

COMIDAS

Servidas con arroz y frijoles

Arroz con pollo	$45
Bistec asado	$60
Enchiladas	$40
Pollo	$50
Tacos	$35
Tamales	$40
Tortas	$35

el bistec
el arroz
el tenedor
el cuchillo

B

Otras personas comen en el restaurante
también. Una persona come **arroz** y **bistec**.
Usa **un tenedor** y **un cuchillo** para comer.

286   doscientos ochenta y seis
Unidad 4

Classroom Community

TPR Have vocabulary items or pictures arranged on a
table at the front of the classroom. Call students
individually to come up and take the item you name.
Have them hold the item up and repeat the name.

Paired Activity First, review adverbs of frequency
(siempre, a veces, nunca, etc.). Then have students
work in pairs and tell each other how often they eat or
drink the items shown and those listed in the menu.

D Una persona quiere café con azúcar. Otra quiere una taza de té.

el café

las tazas

el té

el azúcar

LA ESPECIALIDAD DE LA CASA

Mole negro y tasajo $40

BEBIDAS

Agua mineral	$10
Café	$12
Limonada	$15
Refrescos	$15
Té	$12

POSTRES

Flan	$20
Fruta	$15
Pastel	$20

la sopa

E ¿Qué tienen de postre? ¡Un flan muy rico!

el flan

el pollo

la ensalada

la cuchara

C Otra persona come sopa, pollo y ensalada. Usa una cuchara para tomar la sopa.

Preguntas personales

1. ¿Te gusta comer comida picante?
2. ¿Prefieres comer en un restaurante o en casa?
3. ¿Prefieres un bistec o pollo?
4. ¿Qué te gusta más: la sopa, la ensalada o el postre?
5. ¿Cuál es tu comida favorita?

doscientos ochenta y siete
Etapa 3 **287**

Teaching Suggestions
Introducing Vocabulary

- Have students look at pages 286–287. Use OHT 127 and 128 and Audio Cassette 12A / CD 12 to present the vocabulary.
- Ask the Comprehension Questions below in order of yes/no (questions 1–3), either/or (questions 4–6), and simple word or phrase (questions 7–10). Expand by adding similar questions.
- Use the TPR activity to reinforce the meaning of individual words.
- Use the video vocabulary presentation for review and reinforcement.

Comprehension Questions

1. ¿Tiene hambre Carlos? (Sí.)
2. ¿Va Carlos a una cafetería? (No.)
3. ¿Tiene el restaurante un menú? (Sí.)
4. ¿Va Carlos a comer una enchilada o un sándwich? (una enchilada)
5. ¿Va el mesero a servirle un vaso de agua o una limonada? (una limonada)
6. ¿Está Carlos solo en el restaurante o hay otras personas? (Hay otras personas.)
7. ¿Qué come una persona con su bistec? (arroz y frijoles)
8. ¿Qué usa otra persona para tomar la sopa? (una cuchara)
9. ¿Qué pone otra persona en su café? (azúcar)
10. ¿Qué tienen de postre? (flan)

Supplementary Vocabulary

el jugo de naranja	orange juice
los huevos fritos	fried eggs
los huevos revueltos	scrambled eggs
el cereal	cereal
la leche	milk

Teaching All Students

Extra Help Have students work in groups of 5 on the **Preguntas personales.** Students first read each question, discuss its meaning, and write an answer. Ask each student in the group one of the five questions.

Native Speakers Ask students about table etiquette in their home countries. How do they hold the fork and knife? What should one *not* do at the table? What does one do with the napkin at the end of the meal?

Multiple Intelligences

Visual Have students design a menu for a Mexican snack bar in the school cafeteria.

Verbal Students will test their memories as waiters. Working in groups of 3, the "customer" orders a meal (food from the **Vocabulario),** and the "waiter" turns to the "cook" and repeats the order. The "cook" confirms the order with the "customer."

Block Schedule

Change of Pace Have students draw a picture of the meal they would have at **Casa Linda** (all courses). Then have them describe their meals to a partner.

Teaching Resource Options

Print

Más práctica Workbook PE, pp. 97–100
Para hispanohablantes Workbook PE, pp. 97–98
Block Scheduling Copymasters
Unit 4 Resource Book
  Más práctica Workbook TE, pp. 103–106
  Para hispanohablantes Workbook TE, pp. 111–112
  Video Activities, pp. 125–126
  Videoscript, p. 129
  Audioscript, p. 131
  Audioscript *Para hispanohablantes*, p. 131

Audiovisual

OHT 131, 132, 133 (Quick Start)
Audio Program Cassette 12A / CD 12
Audio *Para hispanohablantes*
  Cassette 12A / CD 12
Video Program Videotape 4 / Videodisc 2B

Search Chapter 7, Play to 8
U4E3 • En vivo (Dialog)

Technology

Intrigas y aventuras CD-ROM, Disc 1

🔔 Quick Start Review

♻ Food vocabulary
Use OHT 133 or write on board:
List 4 items for each category:
1. Place setting
2. Food
3. Drinks
Answers *See p. 283B.*

Language Note

Point out that the waiter addresses the customers formally, using **usted**. The customers do the same when speaking to the waiter. Have students use **usted** when role-playing scenes in restaurants, stores, etc.

Gestures

In most Spanish-speaking countries, it is considered impolite to lean over others at the table and reach for something. You should ask for items and wait for them to be passed.

En vivo

 DIÁLOGO

¡Al restaurante!

| Sofía | Rosa | Carlos | Mesero |

PARA ESCUCHAR • STRATEGY: LISTENING

Integrate your skills Combine what you know.
1. Identify the main idea. Is it (1) explaining relationships, (2) ordering in a restaurant, or (3) learning about Oaxaca?
2. Listen for specifics. What word(s) describe(s) Monte Albán?
3. Listen for feelings. Who expresses curiosity? Pleasure? Other emotions?

1 ▶ Sofía: Tienes que decirme. ¿Cómo conoces a Carlos?
Rosa: ¡Es un secreto!
Sofía: ¡Por favor, Rosa!

5 ▶ Carlos: Un bistec asado.
Mesero: ¿Algo de tomar?
Sofía: Una limonada para mí.
Rosa: Agua mineral, por favor.
Carlos: Un refresco de naranja.

6 ▶ Mesero: Muy bien. ¿Y de postre? Los postres ricos son otra especialidad de la casa. Son buenísimos.
Sofía: Por ahora, nada más. El postre lo pedimos después, gracias.
Mesero: Para servirles.

7 ▶ Sofía: Oye, Carlos, ¿cómo va tu proyecto para el concurso?
Carlos: Muy bien. Es sobre las ruinas de Monte Albán.
Rosa: ¿Ya fuiste a Monte Albán?
Carlos: Sí, fui para sacar fotos.

288 doscientos ochenta y ocho
Unidad 4

Classroom Community

TPR Replay the video. Have students raise their hand when they hear a food mentioned. Have them stand up when they hear a drink mentioned.

Group Activity Have students work in groups of 3 or 4. Write the categories **Antes, Durante,** and **Después** on the board. In turn, each student reads a line at random from the dialog. The other group members decide if it was spoken before, during, or after the meal.

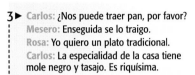

2 ▶ **Rosa:** Está bien. Conozco a Carlos porque fui a la tienda de su papá para pedir direcciones para llegar a tu casa.

3 ▶ **Carlos:** ¿Nos puede traer pan, por favor?
Mesero: Enseguida se lo traigo.
Rosa: Yo quiero un plato tradicional.
Carlos: La especialidad de la casa tiene mole negro y tasajo. Es riquísima.

4 ▶ **Carlos:** Me gustan las enchiladas, pero voy a pedir bistec. Viene con arroz y frijoles.
Mesero: ¿Listos para pedir?
Sofía: Para mí, una ensalada mixta y pollo.
Rosa: Para mí, la especialidad.

8 ▶ **Carlos:** Hay unas vistas fabulosas. Y el juego de pelota es antiguo e interesante.
Rosa: ¡Me gusta mucho tu idea para el concurso!

9 ▶ **Mesero:** ¿Algo más, jóvenes?
Sofía: ¿Pido un postre y lo compartimos?
Mesero: ¿Un flan, señoritas? Lo sirvo en dos platos con dos cucharas.
Sofía: Perfecto, señor. Muchas gracias.
Mesero: ¿Y para usted?

10 ▶ **Carlos:** No quiero ningún postre, pero ¿me puede traer la cuenta, por favor?
Mesero: Sí, cómo no.
Sofía: El mesero sirve muy bien.
Carlos: Me gusta este restaurante. ¡Quisiera comer aquí todos los días!

doscientos ochenta y nueve **289**
Etapa 3

Teaching Suggestions
Presenting the Dialog

• Prepare students for listening by focusing on the dialog context using simple questions. Reintroduce the characters: **¿Cómo se llaman las dos chicas? ¿Son amigas, primas o hermanas? ¿Cómo se llama el chico? ¿Conoce él a las dos chicas?**

• Use the video, audio cassette, or CD to present the dialog. The expanded dialog on video offers additional listening practice opportunities.

Video Synopsis

• Sofía and Rosa meet Carlos for lunch at a restaurant. Carlos discusses his plans for the contest. For a complete transcript of the video dialog, see p. 283B.

Comprehension Questions

1. ¿Van las primas a un restaurante? (Sí.)
2. ¿Conoce Rosa a Carlos por Internet? (No.)
3. ¿Quieren pan los jóvenes? (Sí.)
4. ¿Quiere Carlos la especialidad de la casa o un bistec? (un bistec)
5. ¿Viene el bistec con arroz o con papas fritas? (con arroz)
6. ¿Quién quiere una ensalada mixta, Rosa o Sofía? (Sofía)
7. ¿Qué prefiere tomar Rosa? (agua mineral)
8. ¿Cómo son los postres? (Son ricos y buenísimos.)
9. ¿Sobre qué es el proyecto de Carlos? (sobre las ruinas de Monte Albán)
10. ¿Quiénes quieren postre? (Rosa y Sofía)

■ Block Schedule

Time Saver The day before working with the **Diálogo,** assign previewing it for homework. Students should look at the photos and read the text, trying to get the general idea. Have them write a 2–3 sentence description. (For additional activities, see **Block Scheduling Copymasters.**)

Teaching All Students

Extra Help Have students list and/or sketch what Carlos, Sofía, and Rosa ordered at the restaurant.

Native Speakers Elicit recommendations from students about traditional restaurants and/or foods one would try when visiting their home communities. What would the decor of the restaurant probably be like? What items would be found on the menu?

Multiple Intelligences

Intrapersonal Ask students to make a list of foods they would definitely like to order and foods they would not order. They should try to understand the reasons behind their choices and decide if they see themselves as adventurous or cautious about foods.

Verbal Have students cover the words under the scenes. Read the words under one of them. Students give the number of the scene.

Teaching Resource Options

Print

Unit 4 Resource Book
Video Activities, p. 127
Videoscript, p. 130
Audioscript, pp. 131–132
Audioscript *Para hispanohablantes,*
   pp. 131–132

Audiovisual

OHT 134 (Quick Start)
Audio Program Cassettes 12A, 12B /
   CD 12
Audio *Para hispanohablantes*
   Cassette 12A / CD 12
Video Program Videotape 4 / Videodisc
   2B

Quick Start Review

♻ Dialog review

Use OHT 134 or write on the board:
Complete the following sentences from
the dialog:

1. Conozco a Carlos porque fui a la
   ____ de su papá.
2. La especialidad de la casa tiene
   ____ negro y tasajo.
3. Para mí, una ____ mixta y pollo.
4. Los ____ ricos son otra
   especialidad de la casa.
5. No quiero ____ postre.

Answers *See p. 283B.*

Teaching Suggestions
Comprehension Check

Use **Actividades 1** and **2** to assess
retention after the dialog. Have
students close their books. Read the
items and see if students can answer
correctly. Use as many gestures as
necessary to help students.

Objective: Transitional practice
Listening comprehension/vocabulary

Answers (See script p. 283B.)
1. Sofía 2. Rosa 3. Carlos 4. el mesero 5. Carlos

Objective: Transitional practice
Listening comprehension/vocabulary

Answers (See script p. 283B.)
1. Rosa 2. Sofía 3. Rosa 4. Carlos
5. Carlos 6. Sofía 7. Sofía y Rosa

En acción
VOCABULARIO Y GRAMÁTICA

OBJECTIVES
- Order food
- Request the check
- Talk about food
- Express extremes
- Say where you went

ACTIVIDAD 1

¿Quién habla?

Escuchar ¿Quién habla: Sofía,
Carlos, Rosa o el mesero?
(Hint: Say who speaks.)

1. «¿Cómo conoces a
   Carlos?»
2. «Yo quiero un plato
   tradicional.»
3. «Me gustan las enchiladas,
   pero voy a pedir bistec.»
4. «¿Un flan, señoritas? Lo
   sirvo en dos platos…»
5. «No quiero ningún postre,
   pero ¿me puede traer la
   cuenta, por favor?»

ACTIVIDAD 2

¿Quién lo come?

Escuchar ¿Quién come o bebe
estas cosas: Rosa, Sofía o
Carlos? ¡Ojo! Dos personas
comparten una cosa. *(Hint: Who
orders what?)*

1. el mole negro y tasajo
2. una ensalada mixta y pollo
3. un agua mineral
4. un bistec
5. un refresco de naranja
6. una limonada
7. un flan

ACTIVIDAD 3 En la cafetería

> **PARA CONVERSAR** • **STRATEGY: SPEAKING**
> **Vary ways to express preferences** Use **querer** or **preferir** to vary
> your sentences about their choices.

Hablar Carlos y sus amigos van a comer. ¿Qué va a comer cada
persona? Piensa en las palabras que sabes, las de esta etapa y las
del siguiente vocabulario. *(Hint: Say what each one eats.)*

modelo

Ana: postre

Ana *prefiere comer flan, pan dulce o pastel.*

1. Carlos: comida mexicana
2. Diego: carne
3. Elena: comida picante
4. Marta: comida vegetariana
5. Daniel: algo típico de
   Estados Unidos

Vocabulario

La comida

las bebidas    **el pan dulce**

la carne   **el pastel**

la lechuga   **el queso**

el pan   **caliente** *hot, warm*
dulce *sweet*
sin *without*
vegetariano(a) *vegetarian*

¿Prefieres una cena con carne o sin carne? ¿Qué te gusta comer?

---

290 doscientos noventa
Unidad 4

Classroom Management

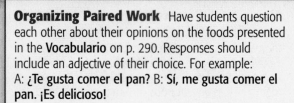

Organizing Paired Work Have students question
each other about their opinions on the foods presented
in the **Vocabulario** on p. 290. Responses should
include an adjective of their choice. For example:
A: **¿Te gusta comer el pan?** B: **Sí, me gusta comer el
pan. ¡Es delicioso!**

Peer Review Before doing **Actividad 5,** have
students form groups and generate a list of
prepositions of location. Refer them to the **Repaso de
vocabulario,** p. 261, if necessary. Have each group
write 5 original sentences using 5 different prepositions.
Each group should present their sentences, using
gestures to indicate placement.

- *Use the verb **gustar** with nouns*
- *Use affirmative and negative words*
- *Use stem-changing verbs: **e→i***

ACTIVIDAD 4

¿Qué pasa?

Escuchar Escucha las descripciones. ¿Qué foto se relaciona con cada descripción? *(Hint: Which description matches each photo?)*

a.

b.

c.

d.

ACTIVIDAD 5

♻ A poner la mesa

Hablar Trabajas en un restaurante. El (La) nuevo(a) mesero(a) no sabe cómo poner la mesa. Ayúdalo(a). *(Hint: Help the waiter/waitress set the table.)*

modelo

el tenedor

Mesero(a): ¿Dónde pongo **el tenedor**?

Tú: *Al lado del plato, a la izquierda.*

Nota

Poner means *to put*. It has an irregular **yo** form: **pongo**. The expression **poner la mesa** means *to set the table*.

1. el cuchillo
2. la cuchara
3. el vaso
4. la taza
5. el plato

TAMBIÉN SE DICE

Spanish speakers use different words for *waiter/waitress*.

- **mesero(a):** Mexico, Puerto Rico
- **camarero(a):** Spain
- **mozo(a):** Argentina, Puerto Rico
- **caballero/señorita:** many countries

To describe Mexico's spicy cuisine, **picante** is used by all Spanish speakers. In Mexico, **picoso(a)** describes especially spicy food!

salsa picante

Teaching Suggestions
Presenting Vocabulary

After presenting the vocabulary for **La comida**, name various foods and drinks. Have students classify them as **Es dulce** or **No es dulce**.

ACTIVIDAD 3
Objective: Transitional practice Food vocabulary

Answers
1. Carlos prefiere comer [una torta, un taco, unas enchiladas de carne o pollo].
2. Diego prefiere comer [un bistec o una enchilada de carne].
3. Elena prefiere comer [enchiladas con salsa picante].
4. Marta prefiere comer [una ensalada de lechuga con queso].
5. Daniel prefiere comer [una hamburguesa y papas fritas].

ACTIVIDAD 4
Objective: Transitional practice Listening comprehension/vocabulary

Answers (See script p. 283B.)
1. b   2. d   3. a   4. c

ACTIVIDAD 5
Objective: Transitional practice Vocabulary/**poner** in conversation
♻ **Prepositions of location**

Answers
1. A: ¿Dónde pongo el cuchillo?
   B: Entre el plato y la cuchara.
2. A: ¿Dónde pongo la cuchara?
   B: Al lado del cuchillo, a la derecha.
3. A: ¿Dónde pongo el vaso?
   B: Detrás del plato, a la izquierda de la taza.
4. A: ¿Dónde pongo la taza?
   B: Al lado del vaso, a la derecha.
5. A: ¿Dónde pongo el plato?
   B: Entre el tenedor y el cuchillo.

▪ Block Schedule

Variety Have students research Mexican restaurants in your area. They should obtain menus and calculate the total cost of a class lunch at several of the restaurants. If possible, plan a class trip to one of the restaurants. If a class trip is not possible, plan a potluck supper with a Mexican theme.

Teaching All Students

Extra Help Have students make illustrated menus using all known food vocabulary.

Native Speakers Have students expand the list of items presented in the **Vocabulario.** They might give types of meat, cheese, cake, etc. They should model pronunciation for the other students.

Multiple Intelligences

Logical/Mathematical Using the Internet, have students look up restaurant menus in Mexico and in your area. Have them convert the Mexican prices to dollars. Then have them compare prices in Mexican and U.S. restaurants. Variation: Have students calculate the total cost of a class lunch at a popular Mexican restaurant in your area and report to the class.

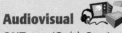
Teaching Note

Students will learn the complete conjugation of **ir** in the preterite tense in **Unidad 6, Etapa 1.**

 Objective: Transitional practice
Fui/fuiste in conversation
♻ Stores

Answers

Answers will vary.
1. Sofía: ¿Fuiste a la zapatería?
   Rosa: Sí, fui para comprar [unos zapatos].
2. Sofía: ¿Fuiste a la joyería?
   Rosa: Sí, fui para comprar [una pulsera].
3. Sofía: ¿Fuiste a la librería?
   Rosa: Sí, fui para comprar [un libro].
4. Sofía: ¿Fuiste a la pastelería?
   Rosa: Sí, fui para comprar [un pastel].
5. Sofía: ¿Fuiste a la carnicería?
   Rosa: Sí, fui para comprar [carne].
6. Sofía: ¿Fuiste a la panadería?
   Rosa: Sí, fui para comprar [pan].

🔔 Quick Start Review

♻ Foods and drinks

Use OHT 134 or write on the board:
Unscramble the following words:

1. elugcha
2. soeuq
3. tosper
4. psoa
5. crúaaz
6. ercan
7. lseapt
8. zrora

Answers
1. lechuga
2. queso
3. postre
4. sopa
5. azúcar
6. carne
7. pastel
8. arroz

ACTIVIDAD 6

♻ ¿Fuiste?

Hablar Sofía y Rosa hablan de muchas tiendas. Trabaja con otro(a) estudiante. Cambien de papel. *(Hint: Talk about where they went.)*

modelo

tienda de música

Sofía: ¿Fuiste a la **tienda de música**?

Rosa: *Sí, fui para comprar un disco compacto.*

Nota

Fui and **fuiste** are past tense forms of the verb **ir**. **Fui** means *I went*; **fuiste** means *you* (**tú**) *went*.

1. zapatería
2. joyería
3. librería
4. pastelería
5. carnicería
6. panadería

NOTA CULTURAL

Oaxaca's cuisine blends pre-Hispanic and Spanish traditions. Visitors should try the many **mole** sauces, the string cheese **quesillo,** the giant tortillas known as **tlayudas,** and **tasajo,** strips of grilled spicy meat.

292   doscientos noventa y dos
Unidad 4

GRAMÁTICA — Using **gustar** to Talk About Things You Like

♻ **¿RECUERDAS?** *p. 181* Remember how to express what **activities** people like to do? You use these phrases with an infinitive.

me gusta…	nos gusta…
te gusta…	os gusta…
le gusta…	les gusta…

When you want to talk about **things** that people like, change the form of **gustar** to match the **singular** or **plural** nouns for those things.

Singular

me gusta **la idea**	nos gusta **la idea**
te gusta **la idea**	os gusta **la idea**
le gusta **la idea**	les gusta **la idea**

Plural

me gustan **las personas**	nos gustan **las personas**
te gustan **las personas**	os gustan **las personas**
le gustan **las personas**	les gustan **las personas**

Rosa says: *matches singular noun*
—¡**Me gusta** mucho tu **idea** para el concurso!
I like your idea for the contest a lot!

> Notice that the form of **gustar** matches the **noun,** not the speaker.

Carlos says: *matches plural noun*
—**Me gustan** las **enchiladas.**
I like enchiladas.

Classroom Community

Paired Activity Working in pairs, have one student tell 5 places he/she went during the last week (**Fui al cine**). The partner then asks if they went 5 more places (**¿Fuiste a la librería?**). Students then reverse roles.

Portfolio Have students write what foods and drinks they like to have for lunch and for dinner. They should use a dictionary to look up unfamiliar words, and plan and describe complete meals.

Rubric   A = 13–15 pts. **B** = 10–12 pts. **C** = 7–9 pts. **D** = 4–6 pts. **F** = < 4 pts.

Writing criteria	Scale				
Vocabulary use	1	2	3	4	5
Logical sentence order	1	2	3	4	5
Grammar/spelling accuracy	1	2	3	4	5

¿Qué les gusta(n)?

Hablar Rosa habla de la comida que a ella y a sus amigos les gusta. ¿Qué dice? *(Hint: Say what food people like.)*

modelos

a mí: las enchiladas

*Me gustan **las enchiladas**.*

A Pedro y a Juan: el flan

*Les gusta **el flan**.*

1. a Diego: el arroz
2. a Arturo: las papas fritas
3. a mí: el flan
4. a ustedes: los postres
5. a nosotros: la comida picante
6. a Paco y a Enrique: el pollo
7. a nosotras: el pan dulce
8. a ti: las ensaladas
9. a Carlos: el mole negro
10. a los chicos: los tacos

■ **MÁS PRÁCTICA** *cuaderno* p. 101
■ **PARA HISPANOHABLANTES** *cuaderno* p. 99

APOYO PARA ESTUDIAR

¿Me gusta o me gustan?

How do you say *I like it* or *I like them* when talking about nouns? When you use **gustar** with nouns, think of the phrase *to please* in English. *I like something* means *Something is pleasing to me.* So, how do you say *I like it* or *I like them*? Look at the title of this study hint!

¿Te gusta(n)...?

Hablar Pregúntales a cinco estudiantes si les gustan estas comidas. Da un resumen de los resultados. *(Hint: Say who likes what.)*

modelo

las enchiladas

Tú: *¿Te gustan **las enchiladas**?*

Otro(a) estudiante: *Sí, me gustan mucho.*

Resumen: *A cuatro personas les gustan las enchiladas. A una persona no le gustan.*

1. las hamburguesas
2. los postres
3. el arroz con pollo
4. las papas fritas
5. el flan
6. la carne
7. la salsa
8. los tacos

¡Nos gusta la ropa!

Hablar/Escribir Estás en una tienda de ropa. Explica a quién le gusta cada prenda. *(Hint: Say what they like.)*

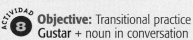

zapatos **camisa** **blusa** **camiseta**
pantalones **falda** calcetines **suéter**

modelo

a mí   Me gustan los zapatos negros.

1. a mí
2. a mi hermano(a)
3. a mi amigo(a)
4. a mis padres
5. a mis amigos

■ **MÁS COMUNICACIÓN** p. R12

Teaching All Students

Extra Help Have students label index cards with the following: **A mí, A ti,** etc.; indirect object pronouns; **gusta; gustan;** singular nouns; plural nouns. Have students use the cards to form a variety of complete sentences.

Multiple Intelligences

Kinesthetic As you hold up a food item/picture of a food item, ask: ¿A quién le gusta [el pastel]? The first to respond **A mí me gusta [el pastel]** gets to retrieve and hold on to the item. After all items have been retrieved, follow up with the questions again: ¿A quién le gusta [el pastel]? Students must point to the person with the item and say: **A [Juana] le gusta [el pastel]**.

Teaching Suggestions
Teaching Using gustar to Talk About Things You Like

Point out that **le** and **les + gusta/ gustan** can be ambiguous. Therefore, it is helpful to specify to whom an item is pleasing by using the appropriate clause; for example: **A mi amigo, A mis padres,** etc.

ACTIVIDAD 7 Objective: Controlled practice Gustar + noun

Answers

1. A Diego le gusta el arroz.
2. A Arturo le gustan las papas fritas.
3. A mí me gusta el flan.
4. A ustedes les gustan los postres.
5. A nosotros nos gusta la comida picante.
6. A Paco y a Enrique les gusta el pollo.
7. A nosotras nos gusta el pan dulce.
8. A ti te gustan las ensaladas.
9. A Carlos le gusta el mole negro.
10. A los chicos les gustan los tacos.

ACTIVIDAD 8 Objective: Transitional practice Gustar + noun in conversation

Answers will vary.

ACTIVIDAD 9 Objective: Open-ended practice Gustar + noun
♻ Clothing

Answers will vary.

🔔 Quick Wrap-up

Using **gustar** + noun, have students say what they like in each of the following categories: school subjects, places, seasons, sports.

■ Block Schedule

Change of Pace Have students poll their classmates regarding their favorite foods. To report their findings, have them create a visual, such as a paper plate pie chart. Using **Actividad 7** as a model, they should also write 5–7 sentences to accompany their visual. (For additional activities, see **Block Scheduling Copymasters.**)

Teaching Resource Options

Print

Más práctica Workbook PE,
  pp. 102–103
Para hispanohablantes Workbook PE,
  pp. 100–101
Block Scheduling Copymasters
Unit 4 Resource Book
  Más práctica Workbook TE,
    pp. 108–109
  Para hispanohablantes Workbook
    TE, pp. 114–115

Audiovisual

OHT 134 (Quick Start)

Technology

Intrigas y aventuras CD-ROM, Disc 1

Quick Start Review

🔔 **Likes and dislikes**

Use OHT 134 or write on the board:
Tell which of your friends or relatives
like the following foods. Write complete
sentences using **gustar**.

1. la comida picante
2. la sopa vegetariana
3. las papas fritas
4. el pan dulce
5. las enchiladas

Answers *See p. 283B.*

Teaching Suggestions
Presenting Affirmative and Negative Words

• Refer to the **Diálogo,** pp. 288–289.
  Have students identify the affirmative
  and negative words.
• Make up a short scenario using
  several of the words. When students
  hear one of these words, they should
  raise their hands or write down the
  word.

Objective: Controlled practice
Affirmative and negative words

Answers

1. algún	5. alguna	9. algunas
2. ningún	6. ninguna	10. ninguna
3. alguna	7. algunos	11. algunos
4. ninguna	8. ningún	12. ningún

294 Vocabulary/Grammar • UNIDAD 4 Etapa 3

 GRAMÁTICA

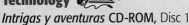

Affirmative and Negative Words

▶ When you want to talk about an indefinite or negative situation,
you use an **affirmative** or a negative word.

Affirmative Words	Negative Words
algo *something*	nada *nothing*
alguien *someone*	nadie *no one*
algún/alguno(a) *some*	ningún/ninguno(a) *none, not any*
siempre *always*	nunca *never*
también *also*	tampoco *neither, either*

The waiter asks:
—¿**Algo** de tomar?
Something to drink?

Sofía says:
—Por ahora, nada más.
*For now, **nothing** more.*

▶ Notice that **alguno(a)** and ninguno(a) must match the gender of
the noun they replace or modify. **Alguno** and ninguno have
different forms when used before masculine singular nouns.

  alguno ➡ **algún**   ninguno ➡ ningún

  Las chicas quieren **algún** postre, pero Carlos no
  quiere ningún postre.
  *The girls want **some** dessert, but Carlos **doesn't** want **any** dessert.*

▶ When a verb is preceded by **no,** words that follow it must also be
negative. A **double negative** is required in Spanish when **no** comes
before the verb.

  No quiero nada.   Carlos **no** quiere ninguno
  *I **don't** want **anything**.*   (de los postres).
                              *Carlos does **not** want **any** (of the desserts).*

▶ However, if a sentence **begins** with a negative word, such as
nunca or nadie, a second negative is not needed.

  Nadie quiere postre.   Nunca comen en casa.
  No one *wants dessert.*   *They **never** eat at home.*

294 doscientos noventa y cuatro
Unidad 4

ACTIVIDAD 10 Gramática

De mal humor

Leer Estás de mal humor. Tu
amigo(a) te hace muchas
invitaciones pero no quieres
hacer nada. Completa el
diálogo con la forma correcta
de **alguno(a)** o **ninguno(a)**.
(Hint: Complete the conversation.)

Nota

Ningunos(as) is almost never used. It
is used only with items that are usually
plural, such as **pantalones**.

No tengo **ningunos** pantalones.

1. ¿Quieres ir a _____ restaurante?
2. No quiero ir a _____ restaurante.
3. ¿Quieres comer _____ fruta?
4. No quiero comer _____ fruta.
5. ¿Quieres ir a _____ tienda?
6. No quiero ir a _____ tienda.
7. ¿Quieres alquilar _____ videos?
8. No, no quiero alquilar _____ video.
9. ¿Quieres leer _____ revistas?
10. No quiero leer _____ revista.
11. ¿Quieres escuchar _____ discos compactos?
12. No quiero escuchar _____ disco compacto.

Classroom Community

Paired Activity Have students write affirmative and
negative words on slips of paper and put them in a
bag. Students take turns reaching in and making up
sentences using the words. They should first give each
sentence orally, then write it down. After both students
have written 5 sentences, have them check the
sentences for spelling/grammatical accuracy.

Portfolio Students write 10 true statements about
their lives using **siempre, también, alguien, nada, nadie,**
and **nunca.** Have them date their list and review it later
in the year to see what has changed and what has not.

Rubric A = 13–15 pts. B = 10–12 pts. C = 7–9 pts. D = 4–6 pts. F = < 4 pts.

Writing criteria	Scale
Vocabulary use	1 2 3 4 5
Grammar accuracy	1 2 3 4 5
Spelling accuracy	1 2 3 4 5

ACTIVIDAD 11 Gramática

El sábado por la noche

Hablar Pregúntale a otro(a) estudiante si va a hacer varias cosas el sábado por la noche. Te dice que no las va a hacer. *(Hint: Ask what someone will do.)*

modelos

invitar a alguien al cine

Tú: *¿Vas a **invitar a alguien al cine**?*

Otro(a) estudiante: *No, no voy a invitar a nadie.*

leer algo

Tú: *¿Vas a **leer algo**?*

Otro(a) estudiante: *No, no voy a leer nada.*

1. visitar a alguien	**4.** ver a alguien
2. hablar con alguien	**5.** estudiar algo
3. escribir algo	**6.** llamar a alguien

■ **MÁS PRÁCTICA** *cuaderno pp. 102–103*

■ **PARA HISPANOHABLANTES** *cuaderno pp. 100–101*

ACTIVIDAD 12

¿Sí o no?

Hablar/Escribir Usa una palabra de cada columna para decir si van a hacer algo o no. *(Hint: Say if someone will do something or not.)*

modelo

Yo voy a beber algo.

yo	algo
mi hermano(a)	alguien
mi amigo(a)	nada
mis padres	nadie
mis amigos	

ACTIVIDAD 13

¡No lo hago!

Escribir Lee la lista de Rosa. Luego, escribe cinco cosas que tú no haces, usando estas palabras. *(Hint: Write what you don't do.)*

		Las cosas que no hago
1.	nada	No como nada picante.
2.	nadie	No conozco a nadie aburrido.
3.	ninguno(a)	No tengo ningún libro interesante.
4.	nunca	Nunca hablo en clase.
5.	tampoco	Tampoco escribo en mis libros.

ACTIVIDAD 14

¡Es buenísimo!

Hablar/Escribir Todos describen algo hoy. ¿Qué dicen? Sigue el modelo. *(Hint: Describe each item.)*

modelo

el postre (bueno)   ***El postre* es *buenísimo*.**

Nota

To express extremes with most adjectives, drop the final vowel and add the ending **-ísimo(a)**. The adjective must agree in gender and number with the noun it modifies.

La idea de Rosa es **interesantísima**.

*Rosa's idea is **very (extremely) interesting**.*

When the last consonant is **c**, the **c** changes to **qu**.

rico(a) → **ri**qu**ísimo(a)**

1. la maestra (bueno)	**4.** la película (triste)
2. las enchiladas (rico)	**5.** las joyas (caro)
3. el perro (malo)	**6.** el libro (aburrido)

Teaching All Students

Extra Help Using **Actividad 10** as a model, have students write 3 more questions with affirmative words and 3 more answers with negative words.

Native Speakers Ask students to talk about what young people do on Saturday night in their home communities. Then have them present a variation of **Actividad 11** where they substitute the affirmative and negative expressions with appropriate activities.

Multiple Intelligences

Visual Have students draw cartoons in which one character makes a suggestion and another gives a negative response. For example: (1) ¡Vamos a estudiar! (2) ¡No quiero estudiar nunca!

Musical/Rhythmic Have students develop a short rap or chant to practice the affirmative and negative words.

ACTIVIDAD 11 Objective: Controlled practice
Affirmative and negative words in conversation

Answers
1. A: ¿Vas a visitar a alguien?
   B: No, no voy a visitar a nadie.
2. A: ¿Vas a hablar con alguien?
   B: No, no voy a hablar con nadie.
3. A: ¿Vas a escribir algo?
   B: No, no voy a escribir nada.
4. A: ¿Vas a ver a alguien?
   B: No, no voy a ver a nadie.
5. A: ¿Vas a estudiar algo?
   B: No, no voy a estudiar nada.
6. A: ¿Vas a llamar a alguien?
   B: No, no voy a llamar a nadie.

ACTIVIDAD 12 Objective: Transitional practice
Affirmative and negative words

Answers will vary.

ACTIVIDAD 13 Objective: Open-ended practice
Affirmative and negative words in writing

Answers will vary.

ACTIVIDAD 14 Objective: Open-ended practice
Expressing extremes with **-ísimo(a)**

Answers will vary.

Language Note

To express extremes with adjectives, there is another spelling change. When the last consonant is **g**, the **g** changes to **gu**: largo(a) → larguísimo(a).

■ Block Schedule

Recycle Have students look back through units 1–3 for sentences using adjectives. Have them rewrite and illustrate the sentences using exaggeration. For example, p. 193, photo D: En Puerto Rico, es divertidísimo esquiar en el agua. (For additional activities, see **Block Scheduling Copymasters**.)

Teaching Resource Options

Print
Más práctica Workbook PE, p. 104
Para hispanohablantes Workbook PE, p. 102
Unit 4 Resource Book
  Más práctica Workbook TE, p. 110
  Para hispanohablantes Workbook TE, p. 116

Audiovisual
OHT 135 (Quick Start)

Technology
Intrigas y aventuras CD-ROM, Disc 1

Quick Start Review
🔔 **Affirmative and negative words**
Use OHT 135 or write on the board:
Rewrite the sentences using the correct word:

1. No hay ____ aquí hoy. (alguien / nadie)
2. ¿Hay ____ en tu clase que no tiene hermanos? (alguien / nadie)
3. Quiero darte ____ después de clase. (alguno / algo)
4. Yo no quiero ir ____. (tampoco / también)
5. ¿Quieres ____ postre? (alguna / algún)

Answers *See p. 283B.*

Teaching Suggestions
Teaching Stem-Changing Verbs: e → i

• Review stem-changing **e → ie** verbs. List the verbs and have students provide original sentences of each.
• Practice **e → ie** and **e → i** verbs with a soft ball. Toss the ball to a student as you say a verb infinitive and a subject noun/pronoun. The student must give the correct conjugated form as he/she tosses the ball back.

Objective: Controlled practice Stem-changing verbs: **e → i**

Answers
1. piden
2. pedir
3. pedimos
4. pides
5. pido

GRAMÁTICA
Stem-Changing Verbs: e → i

♻️ **¿RECUERDAS?** *p. 199* You have already learned about **e → ie** stem-changing verbs like **pensar**.

pensar *to think, to plan*

pienso	**pens**amos
piensas	**pens**áis
piensa	**piens**an

▶ The verb **pedir** also has a stem change. The stem alternates between **e** and **i**.

pedir *to ask for, to order*

pido	**ped**imos
pides	**ped**ís
pide	**pid**en

The stem doesn't change for the **nosotros** *(we)* or **vosotros** *(you)* form.

Sofía says:
—¿**Pid**o un postre y lo compartimos?
*Should **I order** dessert and we'll share it?*

Vocabulario

Stem-Changing Verbs: e → i
pedir *to ask for, to order*
servir *to serve*
Other verbs that follow the pattern:
repetir *to repeat*
seguir *to follow, to continue*
The **yo** form of **seguir** drops the **u: yo sigo.**
¿Qué pides en un restaurante?

ACTIVIDAD 15   Gramática

En el restaurante

Leer Rosa, Carlos y Sofía van a un restaurante. Completa su conversación con la forma correcta de **pedir**. *(Hint: Complete the conversation.)*

Carlos: Las enchiladas son riquísimas aquí. ¿Las __1__ ustedes?

Chicas: ¡Claro que sí!

Mesero: ¿Listos para __2__ ?

Carlos: Sí, queremos las enchiladas de carne para los tres.

Mesero: ¿Y de postre?

Rosa: Sofía, ¿ __3__ tú y yo un pastel y lo compartimos?

Sofía: Buenísima idea. Y tú, Carlos, ¿qué __4__ ?

Carlos: Yo __5__ un flan, ¡y no lo comparto con nadie!

🌿 **NOTA CULTURAL**
The artistic heritage of Oaxaca is known worldwide. There are baskets, pottery, hand-loomed clothing, and rugs with pre-Hispanic designs.

Classroom Community

Paired Activity Have students write grammar activities using **pedir** and **servir**. Put the best ones on transparencies/worksheets for the rest of the class to complete.

Cooperative Learning Students work in groups of 4. Student 1 writes a subject noun/pronoun (**Mi amiga Yolanda**). Student 2 writes a stem-changing verb (**servir**). Student 3 writes a logical sentence (**Mi amiga Yolanda sirve tacos para la merienda**). Student 4 reads the sentence aloud. The group evaluates the sentence and makes necessary corrections. Student 2 begins the next round. Continue for 4 rounds.

ACTIVIDAD 16 Gramática

Sirven...

Hablar/Escribir Carlos almuerza mucho en las casas de sus amigos. ¿Qué sirven? *(Hint: Say what they serve.)*

modelo

Antonio: hamburguesas

Antonio sirve **hamburguesas.**

1. Patricia y Carla: ensalada
2. yo: enchiladas
3. nosotros: fruta
4. usted: tortas
5. tú: mole negro
6. mi hermana y yo: tacos
7. ustedes: pollo
8. la señora Ruiz: bistec

■ MÁS PRÁCTICA *cuaderno* p. 104

■ PARA HISPANOHABLANTES *cuaderno* p. 102

ACTIVIDAD 17

Pido...

Hablar Pregúntale a otro(a) estudiante qué bebida pide normalmente. Cambien de papel. *(Hint: Say what drink you ask for.)*

modelo

desayunas

Estudiante A: *¿Qué bebida pides cuando* **desayunas***?*

Estudiante B: *Pido una taza de té.*

Nota

Desayunar means *to have breakfast*. **El desayuno** is *breakfast*.

ESTUDIANTE A

¿Qué bebida pides cuando...?
1. desayunas
2. tienes mucha sed
3. estás enfermo(a)
4. no puedes dormir
5. cenas con tu familia en un restaurante
6. tienes frío
7. tienes calor

ESTUDIANTE B

Pido...

ACTIVIDAD 16 Objective: Controlled practice
Stem-changing verbs: **e → i**

Answers
1. Patricia y Carla sirven ensalada.
2. Yo sirvo enchiladas.
3. Nosotros servimos fruta.
4. Usted sirve tortas.
5. Tú sirves mole negro.
6. Mi hermana y yo servimos tacos.
7. Ustedes sirven pollo.
8. La señora Ruiz sirve bistec.

ACTIVIDAD 17 Objective: Transitional practice
Stem-changing verbs: **e → i** in conversation

Answers will vary.

Variation: Have students use the question **¿Qué comida pides cuando... ?** and substitute food words for the drinks.

Quick Wrap-up

Have students list 3 things that you order (**pedir**) and 3 things that you serve (**servir**).

Interdisciplinary Connection

Art Work with the art department and have students first research pre-Hispanic designs, then create some simple weaving projects.

Teaching All Students

Extra Help Have students make flashcards of the e → i stem-changing verbs. Working in pairs, have them quiz each other and make sample sentences.

Native Speakers Ask students about customary beverages at the various meals in their home communities. Compile a list of drinks for each meal. Have all students add any new words to their Supplementary Vocabulary list.

Multiple Intelligences

Intrapersonal Have students write a paragraph describing a typical or imaginary trip to a restaurant. Ask them to name the restaurant, when they go, what's on the menu, who orders what, etc. Students should then describe their personal reactions to the food, decor, service, etc.

Block Schedule

Change of Pace Write all stem-changing verbs on individual cards and put them in a bag. Have students pull out 2 cards. Have them write mini-paragraphs using both words. Ask volunteers to present their work.

Teaching Resource Options

Print 📖

Block Scheduling Copymasters
Unit 4 Resource Book
Information Gap Activities, pp. 120–121
Audioscript, p. 132
Audioscript *Para hispanohablantes,*
p. 132

Audiovisual 💻

Audio Program Cassettes 12A, 12B /
CD 12
Audio *Para hispanohablantes*
Cassette 12A / CD 12

Technology 💻

Intrigas y aventuras **CD-ROM,** Disc 1

Teaching Suggestions
Presenting Vocabulary

Before beginning the activities, you
might wish to conduct "mesero(a)
training." Each trainee must
demonstrate his/her knowledge of the
typical questions and statements that a
server needs to know. Include props.

Language Note

Aparte is an adverb, not an adjective, so
its form does not change.

Objective: Transitional practice
Listening comprehension/Restaurant
vocabulary

Answers (See script p. 283B.)
1. Cierto
2. Falso. Va a pedir enchiladas de carne.
3. Cierto
4. Falso. Carlos va a pedir algún refresco; Elena
   va a pedir un té.
5. Falso. Carlos va a pedir un flan.

¿A quién?

Escuchar Lee las oraciones.
Carlos y su amiga Elena están
en un restaurante. Escucha y
decide si cada oración es cierta
o falsa. Corrige las falsas.
(Hint: Say if each sentence is true or false.)

1. Carlos tiene hambre.
2. Elena va a pedir
   enchiladas de pollo.
3. Carlos va a pedir un
   bistec.
4. Los dos van a pedir algún
   refresco.
5. Carlos no va a pedir
   ningún postre.

Vocabulario

En el restaurante

Para pedir comida

¿Me ayuda a pedir? *Could you
help me order?*

¿Me trae...? *Could you bring
me...?*

Quisiera... *I would like...*

Para pedir la cuenta

¿Cuánto es? *How much is it?*

La cuenta, por favor. *The check,
please.*

Es aparte. *Separate checks.*

¿Está incluido(a)...? *Is ...
included?*

¿Cuánto le doy de propina?
How much do I tip?

¿Cómo pides en un restaurante?

♻ La fiesta

Hablar Estás organizando una fiesta. Tu amigo(a) te pregunta
quién trae ciertas cosas. *(Hint: Who brings what?)*

modelo

Antonio: platos

Tu amigo(a): *Antonio* trae los *platos*, ¿verdad?

Tú: *Sí, él los trae.*

Nota

Traer means *to bring.* It has an irregular **yo** form: **traigo.** Its other forms
are regular.

1. tú: tenedores
2. Marta: postre
3. la señorita Díaz: refrescos
4. Margarita y yo: ensalada
5. Enrique y Pablo: pollo
6. yo: enchiladas

¿Listos para pedir?

Hablar Eres mesero(a) en un restaurante mexicano. Tres personas
llegan y quieren comer. ¿Qué dicen? Trabaja con tres estudiantes
para representar la escena. Cambien de papel. *(Hint: Order food.)*

modelo

Mesero(a): *¿Listos para pedir?*

Persona A: *Sí, quisiera un bistec asado con papas fritas.*

Mesero(a): *¿Algo para tomar?*

Persona A: *Una limonada, por favor.*

Mesero(a): *¿Y usted?*

Persona B: *¿Me trae una enchilada de pollo y un refresco?*

Mesero(a): *¿Y usted, señorita?*

Persona C: *Me gustaría...*

298

doscientos noventa y ocho
Unidad 4

Classroom Community

TPR Display restaurant/food props at the front of the
classroom (menus, tableware, plastic food or pictures
of food, etc.). Tell students that they are waiters and
you are a customer in their restaurant. Ask students to
bring you the items (**¿Me trae... ?**).

Paired Activity Using the menus from "Planning
Ahead" on TE, p. 284, tell students to list any unknown
vocabulary. Have them look up the words in the
dictionary. Then have each pair teach 5–6 of these new
words to the class.

¡La cuenta, por favor!

Hablar Acaban de comer y quieren la cuenta. ¿Qué dicen? La conversación puede variar. *(Hint: Request the check.)*

modelo

Persona A: *Perdone. La cuenta, por favor.*

Mesero(a): *¿Para los dos?*

Persona B: *No, mi cuenta es aparte.*

Persona A: *¿Está incluida la propina?*

Mesero(a): *No, señor. Bueno, ahora traigo las dos cuentas.*

1. Las cuentas son aparte.
2. Las cuentas no son aparte.
3. La propina está incluida.
4. La propina no está incluida.

¡A comer!

Hablar/Escribir Vas a un restaurante con unos amigos. Trabaja en un grupo de cuatro para escribir un diálogo en tres partes, usando las expresiones de la lista. Luego, presenten los diálogos a la clase. *(Hint: Write a restaurant dialog.)*

Parte 1: Llegan al restaurante. El (La) mesero(a) les trae el menú. Piden la comida.

Parte 2: El (La) mesero(a) les trae la comida. Hablan de la calidad de la comida y del servicio.

Parte 3: Acaban de comer. Piden la cuenta. Pagan la cuenta y dan una propina.

modelo

Persona A: *¿Nos puede traer el menú, por favor?*

Mesero(a): *Sí, ahora mismo lo traigo.*

Persona B: *Bueno, ¿qué vamos a pedir?*

Persona C: *¿Sirven buenas enchiladas de pollo aquí?*

Persona A: *Creo que sí.*

Persona C: *Entonces, voy a pedirlas.*

Persona B: *A mí no me gustan las enchiladas. Yo voy a pedir arroz con pollo.*

Persona A: *Y yo bistec.*

Mesero(a): *¿Listos para pedir?…*

■ **MÁS COMUNICACIÓN** p. R12

Pronunciación

Trabalenguas

Pronunciación de la *g* The letter **g** in Spanish has a soft sound before the vowels **i** and **e**. It sounds somewhat like the *h* in the English word *he*, but a little harder. Practice by pronouncing the following words:

gimnasio   biolo**gí**a   **ge**neral   **Ge**raldo

When it precedes other vowels, the **g** has a different sound, like in the word *go*. To produce this sound with **i** or **e**, a **u** must be inserted. Practice the following words:

gato   **gu**sto   **go**rdo   abri**go**   **gui**tarra   hambur**gue**sa

Now try the tongue twister.

> Cuando digo «digo» digo «Diego». Cuando digo «Diego» digo «digo».

Diego

doscientos noventa y nueve
Etapa 3   **299**

Teaching All Students

Extra Help Give statements or questions typically heard in a restaurant. Have students say whether the **mesero(a)** or the **cliente** is speaking.

Multiple Intelligences

Visual Using drawings or photos, have one student order a meal and the other students put out the correct visual representation of the order.

Logical/Mathematical Using the menus from "Planning Ahead" on TE, p. 284, have students plan a complete meal. Have them first calculate the price of the meal, then a 15% tip, and finally the total cost of the meal.

---

19 **Objective:** Transitional practice **Traer**/vocabulary in conversation

♻ Direct object pronouns

Answers

1. A: ¿Tú traes los tenedores?
   B: Sí, yo los traigo.
2. A: ¿Marta trae el postre?
   B: Sí, ella lo trae.
3. A: ¿La señorita Díaz trae los refrescos?
   B: Sí, ella los trae.
4. A: ¿Margarita y yo traemos la ensalada?
   B: Sí, ustedes la traen.
5. A: ¿Enrique y Pablo traen el pollo?
   B: Sí, ellos lo traen.
6. A: ¿Yo traigo las enchiladas?
   B: Sí, tú las traes.

20 **Objective:** Open-ended practice Ordering in a restaurant

Answers will vary.

21 **Objective:** Open-ended practice Asking for the check

Answers will vary.

22 **Objective:** Open-ended practice Ordering in a restaurant and asking for the check

Answers will vary.

Dictation

After presenting the **Pronunciación,** have students close their books. Dictate the **Trabalenguas** in segments while students write it.

■ Block Schedule

Variety Have the class plan a Mexican lunch for students and/or staff. Students will select and prepare food items, design a menu, write invitations, provide decorations, and supply appropriate music. (For additional activities, see **Block Scheduling Copymasters.**)

Teaching Resource Options

Print

Block Scheduling Copymasters
Unit 4 Resource Book
  Audioscript, p. 133
  Audioscript *Para hispanohablantes,*
    p. 133

Audiovisual

OHT 135 (Quick Start)
Audio Program Cassette 12A / CD 12
Audio *Para hispanohablantes*
  Cassette 12A / CD 12
Canciones Cassette / CD

Quick Start Review

♻ School and after-school activities

Use OHT 135 or write on the board:
Write 3 activities that you participate in
during school and 3 activities that you
participate in after school.

Answers
Answers will vary. Answers could include:
Voy a mis clases. Hablo con mis profesores.
Estudio en la biblioteca.
Voy al centro comercial. Juego al fútbol
americano. Paso un rato con mis amigos.

Teaching Suggestions

- **Prereading** Have students scan the
reading and write down a guess as to
what it will be about. Have volunteers
share their ideas with the class.

- **Strategy: Gather and sort
information as you read** Before
reading the selection, have students
complete the chart with information
about 2 of their classmates.

- **Reading** In order to focus students'
reading, have them look at the
¿Comprendiste? questions first. Then
have volunteers read each paragraph.

- **Post-reading** Ask students to give a
title to each of the 3 paragraphs of
the reading.

Cross Cultural Connections

Strategy Have students compare
Andrés's after-school job with jobs they
or their classmates hold. What jobs might
require an apprenticeship?

En voces
LECTURA

PARA LEER
STRATEGY: READING

Gather and sort information as you read
Do you and your friends have jobs
after school or on weekends? Fill out
this chart about jobs by interviewing
two people. Then use this chart to
gather information about Andrés
as you read.

Preguntas	Yo	Estudiante 1	2
¿Dónde trabajas?			
¿Cuándo?			
¿Qué haces?			
¿Trabajas en algo que te puede servir en el futuro?			

300 trescientos
Unidad 4

Andrés, joven aprendiz de alfarero[1]

¡Hola! Me llamo Andrés Real. Vivo en San Bartolo
Coyotepec, un pueblo cerca de la ciudad de Oaxaca.
Coyotepec significa[2] «montaña de los coyotes». La
verdad es que ya no hay muchos de estos animales.
Mi pueblo no es muy grande, pero es muy famoso.
La cerámica negra que ves en tiendas y mercados por
todo México es de aquí. Si algún día ves una olla de
barro[3] negro que parece[4] metal, probablemente es de
San Bartolo Coyotepec.

La *Alfarería Doña Rosa* es donde yo trabajo
después de salir de la escuela. En la alfarería hacemos
la cerámica de barro. Esta alfarería se llama *Doña Rosa*
en honor a mi abuela doña Rosa Valente Nieto de
Real. Ella inventó[5] este tipo de cerámica. Mi abuela
murió[6] en 1979, pero mi familia todavía[7] usa su
método para hacer la cerámica.

---

[1] potter	[4] that looks like	[6] died
[2] means	[5] invented	[7] still
[3] clay		

Classroom Community

Paired Activity One partner plays the role of
Andrés Real. The other partner acts as an exchange
student and asks "Andrés" questions based on the
reading, such as ¿De dónde eres? ¿Quién es doña
Rosa?

Group Activity One person plays the role of Andrés
Real and two others play reporters from a local
television station. The reporters interview "Andrés."

Storytelling Have groups of students write the
sentences of the reading on index cards—one sentence
per card. Have them shuffle the cards and then try to
put them back in order. Finally, have students retell the
story in their own words, striving for two sentences per
paragraph. Advanced students may add imagined
details.

Culture Highlights

● **LA CERÁMICA DE SAN BARTOLO COYOTEPEC** The pottery made in San Bartolo Coyotepec has a unique black color. In the special process designed by doña Rosa, the surface of the pottery is rubbed with quartz. When the pottery is fired, it develops a shine that makes it look like metal.

Some of doña Rosa's pieces, which have won many prizes, may be seen in **San Bartolo Coyotepec** at the **Museo del Barro Negro de Coyotepec.**

Language Note

Words that begin with **al-** in Spanish represent the Arabic influence in the Spanish language, as a result of the coexistence of the Christians and the Moors in Spain prior to the 15th century. There are approximately 14,000 Arabic words in the Spanish language; for example, **albaricoque** (apricot), **albahaca** (basil), **almohada** (pillow).

Yo soy aprendiz, o estudiante, de alfarero. Mi papá, mi mamá y mis tíos me enseñan este arte. No hago ollas grandes pero hago animalitos, como coyotes. Mis animalitos no siempre salen bien porque estoy aprendiendo. Como mi abuela, algún día voy a vender los artículos de barro negro de Coyotepec por todo el mundo.

¿Comprendiste?

1. ¿Dónde vive Andrés?
2. ¿Por qué es famoso su pueblo?
3. ¿Quién es su abuela? ¿Por qué es famosa?
4. ¿Qué hace Andrés en la alfarería?
5. ¿Qué quiere hacer Andrés algún día?

¿Qué piensas?

Usa tu imaginación. En otra hoja de papel, escribe lo que hace Andrés en un día típico. También escribe lo que tú haces antes o después de clases.

¿Qué hace Andrés? | ¿Qué haces tú?

trescientos uno
Etapa 3 301

¿Comprendiste?

Answers
1. Andrés vive en el pueblo de San Bartolo Coyotepec.
2. El pueblo es famoso por la cerámica negra.
3. Su abuela es doña Rosa Valente Nieto de Real. Es famosa porque ella inventó un método para hacer la cerámica de barro negro.
4. En su trabajo, Andrés aprende a hacer la cerámica. Hace animalitos.
5. Algún día va a vender los artículos de barro negro de Coyotepec por todo el mundo.

Teaching All Students

Extra Help Encourage students to read sentences from the story out loud. As each sentence is read, a volunteer tries to act out its meaning for the class.

Native Speakers Assign 1 of the 3 paragraphs to each student. (Group students by number if there is more than one.) These students become "experts," knowing what facts and details are important in their paragraphs and helping other students in the class.

Multiple Intelligences

Interpersonal Have students imagine that Andrés can be contacted by e-mail. Ask them to write a list of questions they would ask and describe their own school and community.

Block Schedule

Time Saver Assign the reading as homework so that students can get a head start on comprehension. (For additional activities, see **Block Scheduling Copymasters.**)

Teaching Resource Options

Print

Unit 4 Resource Book
 Audioscript, p. 133
 Audioscript *Para hispanohablantes,*
  p. 133

Audiovisual

Audio Program Cassette 12A / CD 12
Audio *Para hispanohablantes*
  Cassette 12A / CD 12
OHT 135 (Quick Start)
Video Program Videotape 4 / Videodisc
  2B

Search Chapter 8, Play to 9
U4E3 • En colores (Culture)

Quick Start Review

♻ In a restaurant

Use OHT 135 or write on the board:
You and a friend are customers in a
Mexican restaurant. Complete the
following sentences:

Al mesero/A la mesera
 1. ¿Me trae... ?
 2. Quisiera...
 3. ¿Está incluido(a)... ?

A tu amigo(a)
 4. Me gusta mucho...
 5. No me gusta...

Answers *See p. 283B.*

Teaching Suggestions
Presenting Cultura y comparaciones

• Have students read the Connecting
 Cultures Strategy and discuss.
• Have students read the passage to
 themselves, listing any words they
 don't know. Then have volunteers
 read the passage aloud. Ask students
 to see if they might be able to guess
 the meanings of the words on their
 lists. Go over context clues to help
 them with any they still do not know.
• Expand the cultural information by
 showing the video culture presentation.

En colores
CULTURA Y
COMPARACIONES

PARA CONOCERNOS
STRATEGY: CONNECTING CULTURES
Analyze and recommend Some areas depend
on tourism for income, but sometimes local
people are against it. Why is that so?
Think of reasons for and against tourism.

Turismo: no	Turismo: sí
1.	1.
2.	2.
3.	3.

Based on your analysis, write three or more
rules for being a good tourist.

N O T A CULTURAL

Today many Zapotec Indians
support themselves through
farming and traditional
handicrafts such as weaving.

Monte Albán:

*Para el concurso de Onda Internacional,
Carlos visita Monte Albán. Saca fotos y escribe
este artículo sobre una de las primeras culturas
de Oaxaca.*

El estado de Oaxaca es una importante
región arqueológica. El lugar más famoso es
Monte Albán, una de las primeras ciudades
de Mesoamérica[1] y la vieja capital de los
zapotecas[2]. Sabemos que la civilización de
Monte Albán empieza por el año 500 a.C.[3]
Pero los orígenes y el fin de esta civilización
son un misterio fascinante.

---

[1] Middle America (Mexico and Central America)
[2] Zapotec Indians
[3] B.C.

302 trescientos dos
Unidad 4

Classroom Community

Group Activity Have students work in groups to
come up with a short story that explains why the
Zapotecs abandoned Monte Albán. You may suggest
that students use a web diagram to organize their
brainstorming and writing. Each group presents its story
to the class. The class votes on which story seems to be
the most logical.

Portfolio Have students research and develop a
timeline comparing events in Monte Albán with 10 other
worldwide events to gain a perspective on the culture.

Rubric A = 13–15 pts. B = 10–12 pts. C = 7–9 pts. D = 4–6 pts. F = < 4 pts.

Writing criteria	Scale
Clear detail	1 2 3 4 5
Logical organization	1 2 3 4 5
Creativity	1 2 3 4 5

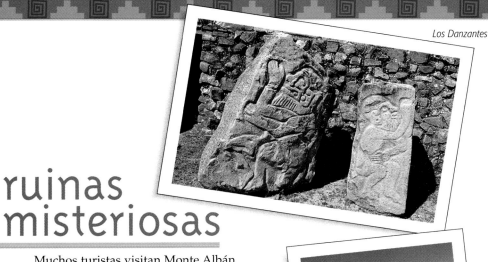

Los Danzantes

ruinas misteriosas

Muchos turistas visitan Monte Albán todos los años para conocer sus pirámides, terrazas, tumbas y esculturas. La parte donde hay más exploración es la Plaza Central, centro de la vida social y religiosa de los zapotecas. Allí hay grandes plataformas, como el Juego de Pelota y la Galería de los Danzantes. Los arqueólogos no saben mucho sobre el Juego de Pelota. Tampoco saben qué representan los Danzantes. ¿Son figuras de hombres que danzan o son prisioneros[4]?

El Juego de Pelota

Aproximadamente entre los años 700 y 800 d.C.[5], los zapotecas abandonan Monte Albán. Luego, los mixtecas[6] usan el lugar. Hoy, descendientes de los dos grupos viven en las montañas y el valle de Oaxaca. Su cultura sigue presente en la lengua y las costumbres[7].

[4] prisoners
[5] A.D.
[6] Mixtec Indians
[7] customs

¿Comprendiste?

1. ¿Qué importancia tiene Monte Albán?
2. ¿Qué sabemos del fin de la civilización de Monte Albán?
3. ¿Qué pueden ver los turistas aquí?
4. ¿Qué saben los arqueólogos del Juego de Pelota o de los Danzantes?
5. ¿Hay zapotecas hoy en Oaxaca?

¿Qué piensas?

Eres un(a) turista en Monte Albán. En una hoja de papel, describe tu visita y tus reacciones. Mira las fotos para inspirarte.

trescientos tres
Etapa 3   **303**

Language Note
The abbreviations **a.C.** and **d.C.** stand for **antes de Cristo** and **después de Cristo.**

Reading Strategy
Ask students to look for and list all cognates in the reading. Compile a class list. Do students notice any spelling patterns for close cognates (for example, **-ción** = *-tion,* **-oso[a]** = *-ous)?*

Culture Highlights

● **LAS TUMBAS DE MONTE ALBÁN**
During the excavations performed in Monte Albán, nearly 170 tombs were found. Some of these tombs were decorated by mural paintings, and most contained many rich offerings. The famous Tomb 7 was filled with marvelous objects made by the Mixtec Indians.

Cross Cultural Connections
Strategy Have students think again about the differences between travel and tourism. If there are archaeological sites in your area, ask students to think about their own reactions to visitors and compare them to possible Zapotec and Mixtec reactions in Monte Albán.

¿Comprendiste?
Answers
1. Monte Albán es una de las primeras ciudades de Mesoamérica y la vieja capital de los zapotecas.
2. El fin de la civilización de Monte Albán es un misterio.
3. Los turistas pueden ver pirámides, terrazas, tumbas y esculturas.
4. Los arqueólogos no saben mucho del Juego de Pelota o de los Danzantes.
5. Sí, hay hoy en Oaxaca.

Teaching All Students

Native Speakers Ask students to present a short report on an important site in their home countries (especially an archaeological one).

Multiple Intelligences
Visual Have students create a travel poster for Monte Albán. They should remember that a well-constructed poster includes details that appeal to the 5 senses.

Naturalist Have students recall a visit to the mountains or to a site where ruins are located. Ask them to describe what they saw (plants, trees, rocks, dirt), using as many senses as possible. What did the plants look and smell like? etc.

Block Schedule
Research Have students research more information about Monte Albán, using the Internet or library resources. Some students might also research Mitla, another major archaeological site located 24 miles southwest of Oaxaca.

Teaching Resource Options

Print

Para hispanohablantes Workbook PE, pp. 103–104
Block Scheduling Copymasters
Unit 4 Resource Book
  Para hispanohablantes Workbook TE, pp. 117–118
  Information Gap Activities, p. 122
  Family Involvement, pp. 123–124
  Multiple Choice Test Questions, pp. 170–178

Audiovisual

OHT 136 (Quick Start)
Audio Program Testing Cassette T2 / CD T2

Technology

Electronic Teacher Tools/Test Generator
Intrigas y aventuras CD-ROM, Disc 1

Quick Start Review

♻ Verb review

Use OHT 136 or write on the board:
Give the correct present tense forms of the following verbs:

1. (yo) poner   4. (nosotros) servir
2. (tú) traer   5. (ustedes) pensar
3. (usted) pedir

Answers
1. pongo   4. servimos
2. traes   5. piensan
3. pide

Teaching Suggestions
What Have Students Learned?

Have students look at the "Now you can…" notes listed on the left side of pages 304–305. Remind them to review the material in the "To review" notes before doing the activities or taking the test.

 Answers

1. alguien   5. algo
2. nadie   6. nada
3. ningún   7. algún
4. algunos   8. alguna

ETAPA 3

En uso
REPASO Y MÁS COMUNICACIÓN

Now you can...
• order food.
• request the check.

To review
• affirmative and negative words, see p. 294.

Now you can...
• talk about food.

To review
• stem-changing verbs: **e → i**, see p. 296.

OBJECTIVES
• Order food
• Request the check
• Talk about food
• Express extremes
• Say where you went

ACTIVIDAD 1 En el restaurante

Lucía y Emilio están en un restaurante. Completa su diálogo con el mesero con la forma correcta de las siguientes palabras: **alguno, ninguno, algo, nada, alguien, nadie.** *(Hint: Complete the conversation.)*

Lucía: Emilio, conozco a ___1___ que trabaja en este restaurante.

Emilio: ¿De verdad? Yo no conozco a ___2___ aquí. ¿Quién es?

Lucía: Un vecino. Prepara los postres.

Mesero: La especialidad es el bistec. No hay ___3___ bistec tan delicioso como el nuestro. Les doy ___4___ minutos para mirar el menú.

Mesero: ¿Están listos para pedir?

Emilio: Sí, para mí, la especialidad.

Lucía: Y yo quisiera las enchiladas y una ensalada.

Mesero: ¿Quieren ___5___ de tomar?

Emilio: Por ahora, ___6___ más. Después, vamos a compartir ___7___ postre.

Emilio: La cuenta, por favor.

Mesero: Sí, señor. Un momento.

Lucía: ¿Le dejamos ___8___ propina?

Emilio: No. Está incluida.

ACTIVIDAD 2 El nuevo mesero

El nuevo mesero está aprendiendo. ¿Qué sirve?
(Hint: Say what he serves.)

modelo

Isabel: arroz (lechuga)

*Cuando **Isabel** pide **arroz**, el mesero le sirve **lechuga**.*

1. Andrés y yo: enchiladas (pollo)
2. tú: una ensalada (pastel)
3. los señores Gálvez: un flan (pan)
4. yo: carne (un postre)
5. ella: una sopa (un sándwich)
6. nosotros: té (café)

Classroom Community

TPR Prepare ahead: Have students bring in the items listed in **Actividad 5**. Have students work in pairs to complete **Actividad 5**. Then have the pairs present their questions and answers to the class. Students should pantomime buying the items as if they were in the stores mentioned.

Portfolio Have students answer the following question in a short paragraph: ¿Adónde fuiste ayer? ¿Por qué?

Rubric   A = 13–15 pts. B = 10–12 pts. C = 7–9 pts. D = 4–6 pts. F = < 4 pts.

Writing criteria	Scale
Vocabulary use	1 2 3 4 5
Grammar/spelling accuracy	1 2 3 4 5
Logical organization	1 2 3 4 5

Now you can...
• talk about food.
• express extremes.

To review
• the verb **gustar** +
nouns, see p. 292.
• extremes, see
p. 295.

ACTIVIDAD 3 ¡La comida es buenísima!

A todos les gusta comer. ¿Qué opinan de la comida?
(Hint: Describe their reactions.)

modelo

yo / enchiladas / bueno
A mí me gustan **las enchiladas.** Son **buenísimas.**

1. mis hermanos / flan / rico
2. Jaime / papas fritas / bueno
3. tú / salsa / rico
4. yo / limonada / bueno
5. la señorita Anaya / arroz / bueno
6. nosotros / tacos / rico

Now you can...
• talk about food.

To review
• the verb **traer**, see
p. 298.

ACTIVIDAD 4 ¡Una fiesta mexicana!

Hay una fiesta mexicana hoy. ¿Qué traen todos?
(Hint: Say what people bring.)

modelo

Dolores: salsa
Dolores trae **la salsa.**

1. yo: tenedores
2. Salvador: platos
3. nosotros: enchiladas
4. el profesor: arroz
5. Alex y Tito: ensalada
6. la directora: flan
7. tú: pastel
8. René y yo: limonada

Now you can...
• say where you
went.

To review
• **fui/fuiste**, see
p. 292.

ACTIVIDAD 5 ¿Adónde fuiste?

Tu amigo(a) acaba de ir de compras. Escribe tus preguntas y sus respuestas según el modelo. Tiene las siguientes cosas: **un disco compacto, pan, un collar, carne, un pastel, unos artículos de cuero** y **una novela.** *(Hint: Say where you went.)*

modelo

pastelería
Tú: *¿Fuiste a la **pastelería**?*
Tu amigo(a): *Sí, fui para comprar un pastel.*

1. joyería
2. librería
3. panadería
4. carnicería
5. tienda de música
6. mercado

ACTIVIDAD 2 Answers
1. Cuando Andrés y yo pedimos enchiladas, el mesero nos sirve pollo.
2. Cuando tú pides una ensalada, el mesero te sirve un pastel.
3. Cuando los señores Gálvez piden un flan, el mesero les sirve pan.
4. Cuando yo pido carne, el mesero me sirve un postre.
5. Cuando ella pide una sopa, el mesero le sirve un sándwich.
6. Cuando nosotros pedimos té, el mesero nos sirve café.

ACTIVIDAD 3 Answers
1. A mis hermanos les gusta el flan. Es riquísimo.
2. A Jaime le gustan las papas fritas. Son buenísimas.
3. A ti te gusta la salsa. Es riquísima.
4. A mí me gusta la limonada. Es buenísima.
5. A la señorita Anaya le gusta el arroz. Es buenísimo.
6. A nosotros nos gustan los tacos. Son riquísimos.

ACTIVIDAD 4 Answers
1. Yo traigo los tenedores.
2. Salvador trae los platos.
3. Nosotros traemos las enchiladas.
4. El profesor trae el arroz.
5. Alex y Tito traen la ensalada.
6. La directora trae el flan.
7. Tú traes el pastel.
8. René y yo traemos la limonada.

ACTIVIDAD 5 Answers
1. A: ¿Fuiste a la joyería?
   B: Sí, fui para comprar un collar.
2. A: ¿Fuiste a la librería?
   B: Sí, fui para comprar una novela.
3. A: ¿Fuiste a la panadería?
   B: Sí, fui para comprar pan.
4. A: ¿Fuiste a la carnicería?
   B: Sí, fui para comprar carne.
5. A: ¿Fuiste a la tienda de música?
   B: Sí, fui para comprar un disco compacto.
6. A: ¿Fuiste al mercado?
   B: Sí, fui para comprar unos artículos de cuero.

Block Schedule
FunBreak Have students work in groups of 3–4 to play a scavenger hunt. Provide each group with a different list of items, using vocabulary from units 1–4. Be sure you have these items (or pictures of these items) in your classroom. The first group to gather all items gets extra credit points or a small prize. (For additional activities, see **Block Scheduling Copymasters**.)

Teaching All Students

Extra Help After students have completed **Actividad 1**, give them a dictation of one of the three sections. Have 2–3 student volunteers write their work on the board for class review and correction.

Multiple Intelligences

Visual In small groups, have students create and illustrate an invitation for ¡**Una fiesta mexicana!** They should list the date, time, foods they will serve, activities, etc. Have the class vote on the most creative party.

Teaching Resource Options

Print

Unit 4 Resource Book
Cooperative Quizzes, pp. 135–136
Etapa Exam, Forms A and B,
  pp. 137–146
Para hispanohablantes Etapa Exam,
  pp. 147–151
Portfolio Assessment, pp. 152–153
Unit 4 Comprehensive Test,
  pp. 154–161
Para hispanohablantes Unit 4
  Comprehensive Test, pp. 162–169
Multiple Choice Test Questions,
  pp. 170–178

Audiovisual

OHT 136 (Quick Start)
Audio Program Testing Cassette T2 /
  CD T2

Technology

Electronic Teacher Tools/Test
  Generator
www.mcdougallittell.com

ACTIVIDAD 6

Rubric: Speaking

Criteria	Scale	
Vocabulary use	1 2 3	A = 8–9 pts.
Sentence structure	1 2 3	B = 6–7 pts.
Ease, fluency	1 2 3	C = 4–5 pts.
		D = 3 pts.
		F = < 3 pts.

ACTIVIDAD 7 Answers will vary.

ACTIVIDAD 8 **En tu propia voz**

Rubric: Writing

Criteria	Scale	
Vocabulary use	1 2 3 4 5	A = 14–15 pts.
Accuracy	1 2 3 4 5	B = 12–13 pts.
Creativity, appearance	1 2 3 4 5	C = 10–11 pts.
		D = 8–9 pts.
		F = < 8 pts.

Teaching Note: En tu propia voz

Remind students to review the writing strategy "Use different kinds of descriptive words" before beginning the paragraph describing the Mexican restaurant.

ACTIVIDAD 6 **¡Tengo hambre!**

PARA CONVERSAR

STRATEGY: SPEAKING
Borrow useful expressions Here are some useful expressions for agreeing and accepting (**está bien, perfecto**) and for refusing (**no quiero…, por ahora nada más**). Use them in your conversation in the restaurant.

Estás en un restaurante. Pide un mínimo de tres cosas. Después, habla de la comida y pide la cuenta. Otro(a) estudiante va a ser el (la) mesero(a). Cambien de papel. *(Hint: Order food.)*

Quisiera…

¿Me trae…?

Me gustaría…

¿Está incluido(a)…?

ACTIVIDAD 7 **¡Una fiesta!**

Trabajando en grupos, hablen de dos cosas que cada persona va a traer a una fiesta.
(Hint: Plan a party.)

modelo

Sara: *Me gusta la limonada. Traigo limonada y algunos vasos.*

José: *Me gustan las enchiladas y la música. Traigo enchiladas y una guitarra.*

ACTIVIDAD 8 **En tu propia voz**

ESCRITURA Trabajas en un restaurante mexicano. Escribe un párrafo para una guía turística. *(Hint: Describe a Mexican restaurant.)*

modelo

Restaurante Azteca *¿Le gusta la salsa picante? En el restaurante Azteca servimos una salsa deliciosa y muy picante. La especialidad de la casa es…*

TÚ EN LA COMUNIDAD

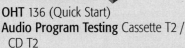

Grendale is a high school student in Nevada. He sometimes speaks Spanish with coworkers when he volunteers at a nursing home. At his part-time job, he uses Spanish with Mexican, South American, and Spanish tourists who come to the store. He has a friend from Uruguay who is an exchange student, and they often speak in Spanish. Do you speak Spanish with any of your friends?

306 trescientos seis
Unidad 4

Classroom Community

Paired Activity Working in pairs, have students sort the food and drink items in the **Repaso de vocabulario** into categories of how they can be consumed: **Con los dedos** (fingers), **Con una cuchara, Con un tenedor y un cuchillo, En un vaso o una taza.**

Group Activity In groups of 3–4, have students create menus in Spanish for an imaginary Mexican restaurant. They can use the menus on pp. 284 and 286–287 as a starting point and add other food items. Have them decide on prices and illustrate their menus for display.

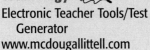

En resumen
REPASO DE VOCABULARIO

ORDERING FOOD

¿Me ayuda a pedir?	Could you help me order?
¿Me trae...?	Could you bring me...?
el menú	menu
pedir	to ask for, to order
Quisiera...	I would like...

At the Restaurant

el (la) mesero(a)	waiter (waitress)
el restaurante	restaurant
servir	to serve
traer	to bring

Place Setting

la cuchara	spoon
el cuchillo	knife
la taza	cup
el tenedor	fork

EXPRESSING EXTREMES

riquísimo(a)	very tasty

REQUESTING THE CHECK

¿Cuánto es?	How much is it?
¿Cuánto le doy de propina?	How much do I tip?
la cuenta	bill, check
La cuenta, por favor.	The check, please.
Es aparte.	Separate checks.
¿Está incluido(a)...?	Is... included?
la propina	tip

SAYING WHERE YOU WENT

Fui.../Fuiste...	I went.../You went...

TALKING ABOUT FOOD

caliente	hot, warm
delicioso(a)	delicious
dulce	sweet
picante	spicy
rico(a)	tasty
vegetariano(a)	vegetarian

Food

el arroz	rice
el azúcar	sugar
el bistec	steak
la carne	meat
la enchilada	enchilada
la ensalada	salad
la lechuga	lettuce
el pan	bread
el pollo	chicken
el queso	cheese
la salsa	salsa
la sopa	soup

Beverages

la bebida	beverage, drink
el café	coffee
la limonada	lemonade
el té	tea

Desserts

el flan	caramel custard dessert
el pan dulce	sweet roll
el pastel	cake
el postre	dessert

OTHER WORDS AND PHRASES

algo	something
alguien	someone
alguno(a)	some
desayunar	to have breakfast
el desayuno	breakfast
la lengua	language
listo(a)	ready
nada	nothing
nadie	no one
ninguno(a)	none, not any
poner	to put
poner la mesa	to set the table
el pueblo	town, village
sin	without
tampoco	neither, either
todavía	still, yet

Juego

Cada miembro de la familia Martínez quiere algo diferente. ¡Pobre Pablo, el mesero! Pablo es inteligente y trae lo que quieren. ¿Qué les sirve a 1) Marco, 2) Martina y 3) Marisol?

Marco Martínez: Quiero algo líquido y caliente con proteínas.

Martina Martínez: Quiero algo verde y vegetariano.

Marisol Martínez: Quiero algo dulce para mi café.

Marco   Martina   Marisol

trescientos siete
Etapa 3   **307**

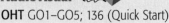

Teaching Resource Options

Print
Block Scheduling Copymasters

Audiovisual
OHT GO1–GO5; 136 (Quick Start)

Technology
Intrigas y aventuras CD-ROM, Disc 1
www.mcdougallittell.com

Quick Start Review

♻ Vacation activities

Use OHT 136 or write on the board:
Write 3 sentences about things you like
to do on vacation and 3 sentences
about things you do *not* like to do on
vacation.

Answers
Answers will vary. Answers could include:
Me gusta viajar en avión. Me gusta sacar
fotos. Me gusta ir de compras.
No me gusta viajar en tren. No me gusta
visitar los museos. No me gusta caminar
mucho.

Teaching Strategy
Prewriting

• Ask students to create a semantic
map using the key question words as
headings around **"Mi viaje"** or
"Mi carta." Encourage them to
generate as many details as possible.

• Remind students of the **PASS** list at
the beginning of the page: Purpose,
Audience, Subject, Structure. This
PASS key will help them complete a
well-structured assignment.

Post-writing

• Have students evaluate each other's
letters. Remind them to keep the
reader in mind and to use different
kinds of descriptive words.

Supplementary Vocabulary

Querido(a)...	Dear...
el primer día	the first day
el segundo día	the second day
el tercer día	the third day

En tu propia voz
ESCRITURA

¡A viajar!

You and your family are planning a vacation. Write a letter to
a Spanish-speaking friend, detailing your plans for the trip.

Purpose: Explain plans for a trip
Audience: A friend
Subject: Your destination
Structure: Personal letter

> **PARA ESCRIBIR** • STRATEGY: WRITING
>
> **Tell who, what, where, when, why, and how** A well-written, friendly
> letter uses many details to communicate information. Cover all
> the details by answering these interrogatives: **¿Quién? ¿Qué?
> ¿Dónde? ¿Cuándo? ¿Por qué? ¿Cómo?**

Modelo del estudiante

> **Who** is indicated by the salutation. Friendly
> letters usually start with **Querido(a)** *(dear)*,
> followed by a colon.

Querida Ana:

• ¿Cómo estás? Yo estoy muy emocionada. ¡Mi familia y yo vamos
de vacaciones a México en agosto! Vamos a estar en Oaxaca por tres
días. Estamos estudiando México en mi clase de español y ayer fui a la
biblioteca para aprender más. Nuestros planes para el viaje son muy
interesantes. ¡Vamos a hacer muchas cosas!

> In the first paragraph,
> the writer tells **where,
> when,** and **why** she is
> going.

• **Día 1:** Salimos en avión por la mañana y llegamos al Hostal de La Noria
al mediodía. Por la tarde hacemos una excursión por la ciudad. Cenamos
en el restaurante La Casa de la Abuela, en el centro de Oaxaca.

> In the remaining paragraphs,
> the writer tells **what** she will do
> on each day of her trip. She also
> says **how** she will be traveling.

• **Día 2:** Por la mañana vamos en autobús a Monte Albán. ¡Voy a sacar
muchas fotos! Por la tarde vamos de compras al Mercado Benito Juárez.
¿Prefieres un collar o unos aretes?

> The author keeps herself organized
> and on task by constructing each
> paragraph around what she will do
> on a specific day.

• **Día 3:** Quiero conocer los museos y caminar por la ciudad. No tenemos
planes especiales.

¿Qué haces tú durante las vacaciones? ¡Escríbeme!

> She adds a closing, followed by
> a comma, and signs her name.

• Hasta luego,

Susana

308 trescientos ocho
Unidad 4

Classroom Community

Group Activity Divide the class into groups of 3.
One student role-plays a student from Oaxaca, and the
other 2 are students from the U.S. The students from
the U.S. write (in Spanish) a list of questions to ask the
student from Oaxaca. After they write out the questions,
they conduct an interview.

Portfolio Have students save their letters as a
selection for their portfolios.

Paired Activity Divide the class into pairs. Have
students exchange the letters that they wrote. Each
student will write a brief response to their partner's
letter.

Estrategias para escribir

Antes de escribir…

Think about a trip you will take, or one that you'd like to take. Remember that you will need to tell who, what, where, when, why, and how. To help you organize your details, fill in a chart like this one.

Revisiones

Read your letter aloud to a partner. Then ask:

- *How did I make my letter clear?*
- *When, where, and how are we going on vacation?*
- *What, if anything, is confusing?*
- *What other details may be helpful?*

La versión final

Before you create the final draft of your letter, look over your work with the following questions in mind:

- *Are verbs correct? Have I included necessary stem changes?*

Circle the verbs in your letter. Remember the special spellings of stem-changing verbs.

- *Is punctuation accurate?*

Underline all punctuation. Check that the salutation has a colon, the closing has a comma, sentences end with periods, and question marks and exclamation points are in place.

To insert or delete words, letters, or punctuation, use the editorial marks shown.

 Share your writing on www.mcdougallittell.com

¿A quién le escribes? **a mi amigo Carlos**

¿Adónde van de viaje? **a Oaxaca**

¿Cómo van a llegar? _____

¿Qué van a hacer allí? _____

    ¿Día 1? _____

    ¿Día 2? _____

    ¿Día 3? _____

Querido Carlos,
¿Qué tal? Estoy muy feliz.
Mañana voy a viajar a México y volvo vuelvo en dos semanas. ¡No puedo creerlo! Viajo con mi hermano mayor. Primero, vamos a la Ciudad de México. Después quiero haser una excursión en autobús a Oaxaca.

Día 1
Primero, pensamos ir al Mercado Benito Juárez…

EDITORIAL MARKS

∧ = **insert**   ∧̇ = **insert colon**

⌐ = **delete**

Rubric: Writing

Let students know ahead of time which elements of their writing you will be evaluating. A global evaluation is more helpful to students than a correction of every mistake made. Consider the following in scoring compositions:

Sentences	
1	Most are not logical
2	In logical order
3	Flow purposefully

Details	
1	Few details
2	Sufficient basic details
3	Clear and vivid detail

Organization	
1	Not well organized
2	Some organization
3	Strong organization

Accuracy	
1	Errors prevent comprehension
2	Some spelling and agreement errors throughout
3	Very few errors

Criteria	Scale	
Logical sentence order	1 2 3	A = 10–12 pts.
Clear and vivid detail	1 2 3	B = 7–9 pts.
Organization	1 2 3	C = 4–6 pts.
Accuracy	1 2 3	D = 3 pts.
		F = < 3 pts.

Teaching All Students

Extra Help Students may be concerned about having to write a whole letter for this assignment. If so, have students write several short postcards, each card representing one place to visit on vacation. Encourage students to focus upon one event or one aspect of their trip for each card.

Native Speakers For extra credit, ask students to bring into class an original letter or postcard in Spanish. Ask them to read it aloud to the class, and have them answer short questions about the contents.

Block Schedule

Online Ask students to submit their work (anonymously, if they are nervous) to the website and see if they get posted. (For additional activities, see **Block Scheduling Copymasters**.)

Unit Theme
Carrying out one's daily routine in Barcelona, doing chores, and planning a party.

Communication
- Describing daily routines, grooming, and chores
- Telling others to do something
- Saying what people are doing
- Persuading others
- Describing a house
- Negotiating responsibilities
- Planning a party and purchasing food
- Describing past activities
- Expressing extremes

Cultures
- Learning about Barcelona and its architecture
- Learning about well-known people from Barcelona
- Learning about regional foods
- Learning how to cook

Connections
- Connecting to Art: Comparing painting styles
- Connecting to Health: Planning a meal

Comparisons
- Comparing daily routines and chores in Spain and in the U.S.
- Comparing homes in Spain and in the U.S.
- Comparing appetizers

Communities
- Using Spanish in the workplace
- Using Spanish with family and friends

Teaching Resource Options

Print
Block Scheduling Copymasters

Audiovisual
OHT M5; 137, 138
Canciones Audiocassette/CD
Video Program Videotape 5 / Videodisc 3A

Search Chapter 1, Play to 2
U5 Cultural Introduction

UNIDAD 5

BARCELONA
ESPAÑA

PREPARACIONES ESPECIALES

OBJECTIVES

ETAPA 1
¿Cómo es tu rutina?
- Describe daily routine
- Talk about grooming
- Tell others to do something
- Discuss daily chores

ETAPA 2
¿Qué debo hacer?
- Say what people are doing
- Persuade others
- Describe a house
- Negotiate responsibilities

ETAPA 3
¡Qué buena celebración!
- Plan a party
- Describe past activities
- Express extremes
- Purchase food

310

MIGUEL DE CERVANTES SAAVEDRA (1574–1616) is the most well-known Spanish author. His classic *Don Quijote de la Mancha* is considered to be the first modern novel. What plays or movies are based on this book?

Océano Atlántico

ISLAS CANARIAS

PORTUGAL

JOAN MIRÓ (1893–1983) is one of Barcelona's most famous artists. You can see his surrealist works at the **Fundación Miró.** How would you describe this piece by Miró?

Tapestry of the Foundation, Miró Foundation on Montjuic

Classroom Community

Group Activity Divide the class into groups of 3–4. Have them write information in 2 columns: (1) what we know about Spain and (2) what we want to learn about Spain. As a class, compile the lists and categorize them: geography, government, food, music, authors, artists, etc.

Paired Activity Have students work in pairs and discuss the question at the end of each photo description. Then have each group present their answers to the class.

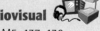

ALMANAQUE

Población: 1.630.867
Altura: 12 metros (39 pies)
Clima: 10°C (54°F), invierno; 25°C (75°F), verano
Comida típica: mariscos, tapas, paella
Gente famosa de Barcelona: José Carreras (cantante), Antonio Gaudí (arquitecto), Joan Miró (pintor), Pablo Picasso (pintor), Arantxa Sánchez Vicario (tenista)

¿Vas a Barcelona? Barcelona es la capital de Cataluña, una región de España. Tiene una identidad catalana muy fuerte. La gente habla catalán y español.

For more information about Barcelona, access www.mcdougallittell.com

EL MONUMENTO DE CRISTÓBAL COLÓN commemorates Columbus's meeting with the king and queen of Spain after his first voyage to the Americas. They met in Barcelona in 1493. Who were the king and queen of Spain then?

FRANCIA

ANDORRA

ESPAÑA

ACEITUNAS are one of Spain's most important products. Their oil is used to cook Spanish specialties such as **paella** and **tortilla española.** They are also often eaten as **tapas.** What dishes made with olives or olive oil have you eaten?

BARCELONA ·

★ MADRID

LA SAGRADA FAMILIA is a church begun by architect Antonio Gaudí (1852–1926). It is not yet finished. What do you think about the style of architecture you see in the photo?

VALENCIA ·

ISLAS BALEARES

SEVILLA

LAS RAMBLAS is a well-known street in the heart of Barcelona that has it all! Artisans, performers, and vendors sell everything from parakeets to newspapers here. Where might you find something similar in the U.S.?

· GIBRALTAR (R.U.)
CEUTA

Mar
Mediterráneo

ARGELIA

MELILLA
MARRUECOS

311

Teaching All Students

Native Speakers Ask students to compare Gaudí's **Sagrada Familia** with churches in their home communities. How is the architecture different? Are there modern churches in their communities? What do they look like?

Multiple Intelligences

Visual Ask students to use color markers to create drawings that simulate Joan Miró's style. Have volunteers present their creations and explain what they represent.

Musical/Rhythmic Have students research a short biography of José Carreras and/or bring in one of his recordings. They might also research a list of other musicians/singers from Spain.

Teaching Suggestion
Previewing the Unit
Tell students that this unit centers on Barcelona, Spain. Ask students to scan these two pages for 15 seconds, then close their books. Then ask them to tell you what they remember. You may wish to use the introduction to the video to preview the unit.

Culture Highlights

● **CERVANTES** The tumultuous life of Cervantes was the inspiration for his humor and satire. He lost the use of his left hand in battle, he was captured by pirates and held as a slave for 5 years, and he was imprisoned by the Spanish government for suspicious tax-collecting activities. It was during his imprisonment that he conceived the idea for *Don Quijote.*

● **JOAN MIRÓ** The surrealist style of Joan Miró is based on subject matters from the realm of memory and fantasy.

● **EL MONUMENTO DE CRISTÓBAL COLÓN** This monument is a tribute to the adventuresome spirit as well as to Christopher Columbus. The design on the column includes the continents of Europe, Asia, Africa, and the Americas.

● **ACEITUNAS** Olives, one of Spain's major exports, are harvested both when they are green and later when they turn black.

● **LA SAGRADA FAMILIA** This great church, a blend of neo-Gothic and Art Nouveau styles, was Gaudí's greatest project and dream. He wanted it to be large enough for a choir of 1500 singers, 700 children, and 5 organs.

● **LAS RAMBLAS** Rambla means *torrent* in Arabic. The location of the current street is thought to be a former stream bed outside the old city walls.

Block Schedule
Preview Have students look through the unit to see what they will be learning. As they do this, they should write a list of words they know that apply to what they see. Compile a class list for reference as students work through the unit. (For additional activities, see **Block Scheduling Copymasters.**)

Ampliación

These activities may be used at various points in the Unit 5 sequence.

■ For Block Schedule, you may find that these projects will provide a welcome change of pace while reviewing and reinforcing the material presented in the unit. See the **Block Scheduling Copymasters.**

● PROJECTS

Organize tours of Barcelona. Have students work in groups of 4–5 to organize a tour of Barcelona for one of the following groups:
- a group of high school students from the U.S.
- a group of senior citizens from the U.S.
- a group interested in science
- a group interested in art or theater

Each group should plan the length of each tour, an itinerary, the transportation, meals, and the estimated costs. Each group will create a brochure, including a map, and prepare a presentation.

> PACING SUGGESTION: Have students begin research at the beginning of the unit. Final projects are completed at the end of Unit 5.

Film a self-help video with suggestions for being organized, especially for getting ready quickly in the morning. The video should include at least 4 scenes scripted by students showing what to do as well as what not to do.

> PACING SUGGESTION: Upon completion of Etapa 1.

● STORYTELLING

Diego desastre After reviewing vocabulary for daily routines and chores, model a mini-story (using puppets, student actors, or photos from the text) that students will retell and revise:

> Diego no es muy organizado y es un poco perezoso en casa. Sus padres siempre tienen que darle órdenes: «Diego, lávate los dientes antes de ir a la escuela.» «Diego, quita la mesa después de la cena.» Un día llega tarde a clase para un examen. No hace el examen. Sus amigos también le dan órdenes a Diego. «Diego, ordena tu habitación. ¡Es un desastre!»

Pause as the story is being told so that students may fill in words and act out gestures. Students then write, narrate, and read aloud a longer main story. This new version should include vocabulary from the previous story.

Otros quehaceres y rutinas Have students create their own routine/chore stories. They might expand on the model story by centering it around a specific day or event, or they can create their own characters.

> PACING SUGGESTION: Upon completion of Etapa 2.

● BULLETIN BOARD/POSTERS

Bulletin Board Have students research the history of Barcelona to create timelines that show different civilizations, cultures, architecture, events, etc., related to the development of the city. Students should illustrate their timelines with Internet printouts and/or drawings.

Posters Have students create •**Museum** posters for museums in Barcelona •**Restaurant** fliers showing hours, specialties, and prices of Barcelona restaurants •**Chore charts** for a typical household

GAMES

FRANCIA

Dibujorama

Prepare ahead: Bring in a timer, an easel, a large writing pad, and markers. Prepare 20–30 index cards with grooming and chore commands. Each card should include 1 command; some should be negative commands. Divide the class into 2–3 teams. Give a member of the first team a card. He/she silently reads the card. Set the timer to 30 seconds. The group member draws—no speaking or gestures allowed!—to elicit the command on the card. When guessing, only Spanish may be used or the team forfeits its turn. If students on the team guess the command correctly before the time is up, they score, and the next team has a turn. If not, the next team picks a new card. If that team guesses the correct command, they score, and they get another turn.

PACING SUGGESTION: Upon completion of Etapa 2.

RECIPE

Postre con naranjas

is an attractive dessert served around the end-of-year holidays. Ask students what special foods they eat on occasions such as Thanksgiving, the Fourth of July, etc. Have them brainstorm foods that are closely linked to special holidays.

Prepare ahead: Prepare the filling the day before. Bring the filling, cream, cherries, and chilled orange halves to class and allow students to prepare their desserts as you read the final instructions. Point out the importance of color and presentation when preparing foods.

Monopolio

Prepare ahead: Bring to class pieces of sturdy cardboard, slips of paper to make fake money, odds and ends for tokens. Have students work in groups of 4 to create Monopoly®-style boards featuring attractions and streets in Barcelona. Encourage them to be creative with the kinds of spaces they create for the board (shopping, restaurants, etc.), and to include spaces with real estate purchases, expenses (shopping, eating out), fines, and prizes. Then have them make pesetas. Each group can make up their own rules for purchasing, selling, and winning, but the rules should be straightforward and simple. Have students play their game in groups of 4.

PACING SUGGESTION: Upon completion of Etapa 3.

MUSIC

Show students photos of people dancing the **sardana**—the regional dance of Cataluña. Point out that outside cathedrals in that region on Sunday afternoons, circles of people, young and old, hold hands with raised arms and step in unison to the beat of a **sardana** song. Play a **sardana** in class and have students join hands with raised arms and move in a circle, following the steps of a designated leader. More music samples are available on your *Canciones* Cassette or CD.

HANDS-ON CRAFTS

Display examples of paintings in the following styles: realism, surrealism, impressionism, and cubism. Have students formulate a description of each style. Then have students do an art study on one person. They will paint that person in the four different styles. Choose one medium and provide supplies for all students (large posterboards and paint) or have students bring their own supplies. Set up a museum to display the studies.

Receta

Postre con naranjas
6 naranjas tipo «navel» grandes
un poco de azúcar
2 cucharadas de harina de maíz (la típica Maizena)
nata montada

Parta las naranjas. Exprima el zumo cuidadosamente, sin romper la cáscara. Añada al zumo, un poco de agua, azúcar al gusto y 2 cucharadas de harina de maíz. Cocine la mezcla a fuego muy bajo y remuévela mientras va espesando. Cuando la mezcla está espesa, como una crema, retírela del fuego y póngala en la nevera. Rellene las medias naranjas vacías con la crema enfriada. Encima ponga un poco de nata y una cereza confitada. (Sirve a 12.)

Planning Guide CLASSROOM MANAGEMENT

OBJECTIVES

Communication	• Describe daily routine *pp. 314–315*
	• Talk about grooming *pp. 314–315, 316–317*
	• Tell others to do something *pp. 316–317*
	• Discuss daily chores *pp. 316–317*
Grammar	• Use reflexive verbs *pp. 320–321*
	• Use irregular affirmative **tú** commands *pp. 322–323*
	• Use negative **tú** commands *pp. 324–325*
	• Use correct pronoun placement with commands *pp. 325–326*
Pronunciation	• Pronunciation of **s, z, c** *p. 327*
	• Dictation, *TE p. 327*
Culture	• History and culture of Barcelona, Spain *pp. 310–311*
	• **Catalán** *p. 324*
	• **Rock con raíces** *p. 326*
	• Pablo Picasso *pp. 328–329*
♻ **Recycling**	• Telling time *p. 318*
	• Object pronouns *p. 326*

STRATEGIES

Listening Strategies	• Listen for a mood or a feeling *p. 316*
Speaking Strategies	• Sequence events *p. 321*
	• Use gestures *p. 332*
Reading Strategies	• Scan for crucial details *p. 328*
Writing Strategies	• Organize information chronologically and by category *TE p. 332*
Connecting Cultures Strategies	• Learn about Barcelona, Spain *pp. 310–311*
	• Recognize variations in vocabulary *pp. 318, 324*
	• Learn about the Spanish **rock con raíces** *p. 326*
	• Learn about Pablo Picasso *pp. 328–329*
	• Connect and compare what you already know about artists and art styles to help you learn about different artists and art styles *pp. 310–311, 328–329, 332*

PROGRAM RESOURCES

 Print

• *Más práctica* Workbook PE, *pp. 105–112*
• Block Scheduling Copymasters, *pp. 105–112*
• Unit 5 Resource Book
  Más práctica Workbook TE, *pp. 1–8*
  Para hispanohablantes Workbook TE, *pp. 9–16*

Information Gap Activities *pp. 17–20*
Family Involvement *pp. 21–22*
Video Activities *pp. 23–25*
Videoscript *pp. 26–28*
Audioscript *pp. 29–32*
Assessment Program, Unit 5 Etapa 1 *pp. 33–51; 170–178*
Answer Keys *pp. 179–200*

 Audiovisual

• **Audio Program** Cassettes 13A, 13B / CD 13
• *Canciones* Cassette / CD
• Video Program Videotape 5 / Videodisc 3A
• Overhead Transparencies M1–M5; 137, 140–150

 Technology

• Electronic Teacher Tools/Test Generator
• *Intrigas y aventuras* CD-ROM, Disc 1
• www.mcdougallittell.com

 Assessment Program Options

• Cooperative Quizzes (Unit 5 Resource Book)
• Etapa Exam Forms A and B (Unit 5 Resource Book)
• *Para hispanohablantes* Etapa Exam (Unit 5 Resource Book)
• Portfolio Assessment (Unit 5 Resource Book)
• Multiple Choice Test Questions (Unit 5 Resource Book)
• Audio Program Testing Cassette T2 / CD T2
• Electronic Teacher Tools/Test Generator

Native Speakers

• *Para hispanohablantes* Workbook PE, *pp. 105–112*
• *Para hispanohablantes* Workbook TE (Unit 5 Resource Book)
• *Para hispanohablantes* Etapa Exam (Unit 5 Resource Book)
• Audio *Para hispanohablantes* Cassettes 13A, 13B, T2 / CD 13, T2
• Audioscript *Para hispanohablantes* (Unit 5 Resource Book)

Student Text
Listening Activity Scripts

 Videoscript: Diálogo *pages 316–317*

•Videotape 5 • Videodisc 3A

Search Chapter 3, Play to 4
U5E1 • En vivo (Dialog)

•Use the videoscript with **Actividades 1, 2** *page 318*

Juan Carlos: ¡Luis, Luis! ¡Mercedes llega en diez minutos!

Luis: ¡Sí, ya lo sé! ¡Ahora me ducho y salgo!

Juan Carlos: ¡Vale!

Lourdes: ¡Luis! ¡Mercedes llega en cinco minutos!

Luis: ¡Sí, sí, ya lo sé, mamá! ¡Pero primero necesito lavarme los dientes!

Carmen: ¡Luis! ¡Luis! ¡Mercedes está aquí!

Luis: ¡Sí, sí, sí! ¡Pero primero me pongo la ropa! ¡Ya voy!
¡Hola, Mercedes! ¿Cómo estás?

Mercedes: Bien, Luis. ¡Y feliz cumpleaños! ¿Qué tal tu mañana?

Luis: Muy tranquila, gracias. Mercedes, ¿qué haces? ¿Por qué me estás sacando fotos? ¡No hagas eso!

Mercedes: No te pongas así. Las fotos son para un concurso.

Luis: ¿Un concurso? Pues dime, ¿para qué concurso son?

Mercedes: Luego, te digo luego. Bueno, Álvaro nos espera en una hora. ¿Estás listo?

Luis: No, no estoy listo. Todavía necesito secarme el pelo. Salgo en diez minutos. Espérame aquí.

Carmen: ¡Ponte otra camisa! ¡Mírate en el espejo, ¡esta camisa es muy fea!

Luis: Muchas gracias, Carmen.

Carmen: Ah, y ¡no uses mi secador de pelo! ¡Por favor, no lo uses!

Luis: Bueno, ya estoy listo. ¿Vamos?

Juan Carlos: Hijo.

Luis: ¿Sí, papá?

Juan Carlos: Necesito tu ayuda. Por favor, haz todo lo que está en esta lista.

Luis: Pero, papá, yo voy a salir. ¿Tengo que hacerlo todo hoy?

Juan Carlos: Sí, hijo. Primero haz los quehaceres.

Luis: ¡Pero, papá!

Lourdes: Luis, necesitamos leche y varias cosas. Ve a la tienda. Aquí tienes mi lista.

Luis: Papá, mamá, es que tengo otros planes. Me espera Álvaro.

Lourdes: Sí, hijo, ya lo sabemos, pero esto es importante.

Luis: ¡No es justo! ¡Es mi cumpleaños!

Juan Carlos: Sí, pero también puedes celebrarlo después. Aquí tienes. Ah, también, cuida a tu hermana.

Luis: ¡No puede ser!

Carmen: ¡Ja, ja! ¡Me tienes que cuidar!

Luis: Voy a llamar a Álvaro. Nunca vamos a llegar a tiempo.

Mercedes: No te preocupes. Él nos espera. ¡Pobre Luis! ¡No seas tan dura con él! Es su cumpleaños.

Carmen: ¡Le quiero ver la cara al llegar a su fiesta!

Luis: Está ocupado. Lo llamo más tarde. Bueno, vamos. Tenemos muchas cosas que hacer. Carmen, Mercedes, ¿me ayudáis con los quehaceres?

Se lavan... *page 320*

1. Carmen se lava la cabeza.
2. Mis padres se lavan las manos.
3. Mercedes y yo nos lavamos los pies.
4. Yo me lavo las piernas.
5. Álvaro se lava la cara.

19 La rutina de Álvaro *page 327*

Andrés: Oye, Álvaro, ¿a qué hora te despiertas los sábados?

Álvaro: Bueno, normalmente me despierto entre las ocho y las ocho y media.

Andrés: ¿Usas un despertador?

Álvaro: No, no me gustan los despertadores.

Andrés: ¿Y a qué hora te levantas?

Álvaro: Pues, como me gusta quedarme un rato en la cama, no me levanto antes de las nueve y media.

Andrés: ¿Qué haces después de levantarte?

Álvaro: Me lavo la cara y los dientes.

Andrés: ¿No te bañas los sábados?

Álvaro: ¡Claro que sí! Me baño por la noche antes de salir. También me afeito y me lavo la cabeza.

Quick Start Review
Answers

p. 316 Morning routine
Answers will vary.
Answers could include:
1. Antes de las siete.
2. Después de las siete.
3. Sí, uso un despertador.
4. Uso dos mantas.
5. Mi champú favorito se llama "Pert Plus." Mi jabón favorito se llama "Dove."

p. 318 Dialog review
1. Carmen   4. Luis
2. Luis   5. Mercedes
3. Lourdes   6. Juan Carlos

p. 322 Reflexive verbs
1. se lava   4. lavarnos
2. te despiertas   5. Me acuesto
3. secarme

p. 324 Affirmative **tú** commands
1. Haz tu tarea.
2. Pon el libro en tu escritorio.
3. Di la verdad a tu madre.
4. Ponte otra camisa.
5. Ven aquí.

p. 325 Negative **tú** commands
1. No escribas tu nombre aquí.
2. No hagas la cena esta noche.
3. No pongas el jabón al lado de la toalla.
4. No compres el regalo hoy.
5. No des los libros al profesor.

p. 333 Etapa vocabulary
Answers will vary.
Answers could include:
1. Me despierto a las seis y cuarto pero me levanto a las seis y media.
2. Me ducho todos los días.
3. Me lavo la cabeza con champú.
4. Me lavo los dientes.
5. Me pongo una camisa y unos jeans.

Sample Lesson Plan - 50 Minute Schedule

DAY 1

Unit Opener
- Anticipate/Activate prior knowledge: Present the *Almanaque* and the cultural notes. Use Map OHTs as needed. **10** MIN.

Etapa Opener
- Quick Start Review (TE, p. 312) **5** MIN.
- Have students look at the *Etapa* Opener and answer the questions. **5** MIN.

En contexto: Vocabulario
- Quick Start Review (TE, p. 314) **5** MIN.
- Have students use context and pictures to learn *Etapa* vocabulary, then answer the questions, p. 315. Use the Situational OHTs for additional practice. **10** MIN.

En vivo: Diálogo
- Quick Start Review (TE, p. 316) **5** MIN.
- Review the Listening Strategy, p. 316. Play audio or show video for the dialog, pp. 316–317. Replay and have students take the roles of the characters. **10** MIN.

Homework Option:
- Video Activities, Unit 5 Resource Book, pp. 23–25.

DAY 2

En acción: Vocabulario y gramática
- Check homework. **5** MIN.
- Quick Start Review (TE, p. 318) **5** MIN.
- Have students open to *En contexto*, pp. 314–315, for reference. Use OHT 141 and 142 to review vocabulary. **10** MIN.
- Play the video/audio; have students do *Actividades* 1 and 2 orally. **10** MIN.
- Have students complete *Actividad* 3 orally. **5** MIN.
- Have students complete *Actividades* 4 and 5 in pairs. For each activity, have a few pairs present their dialogs. **20** MIN.

Homework Option:
- Have students create 7 true/false statements for the *Diálogo.* Have them complete *Actividad* 3 in writing.

DAY 3

En acción (cont.)
- Check homework. **5** MIN.
- Quick Start Review (TE, p. 320) **5** MIN.
- Present *Gramática:* Describing Actions That Involve Oneself: Reflexive Verbs and the *Vocabulario,* p. 320. Have students act out the verbs. **15** MIN.
- Play the audio; do *Actividad* 6. **5** MIN.
- Have students complete *Actividades* 7 and 8 in pairs. For each activity, have a few pairs present their dialogs. **20** MIN.
- Present the Speaking Strategy, p. 321, then do *Actividad* 9 orally. **5** MIN.

Homework Option:
- Have students complete *Actividad* 9 in writing. *Más práctica* Workbook, p. 109. *Para hispanohablantes* Workbook, p. 107.

DAY 4

En acción (cont.)
- Check homework. **5** MIN.
- Quick Start Review (TE, p. 322) **5** MIN.
- Present *Gramática:* Irregular Affirmative *tú* Commands, p. 322. **10** MIN.
- Have students complete *Actividad* 10 orally. **5** MIN.
- Present the *Vocabulario,* p. 323. Then have students do *Actividad* 11 in pairs. **10** MIN.
- Do *Actividad* 12 orally. Expand using Information Gap Activities, Unit 5 Resource Book, p. 17; *Más comunicación,* p. R13. **15** MIN.
- Use an expansion activity from TE, pp. 322–323, for reinforcement and variety. **5** MIN.

Homework Option:
- Have students complete *Actividades* 10 and 12 in writing. *Más práctica* Workbook, p. 110. *Para hispanohablantes* Workbook, p. 108.

DAY 5

En acción (cont.)
- Check homework. **5** MIN.
- Quick Start Review (TE, p. 324) **5** MIN.
- Present *Gramática:* Negative *tú* Commands, p. 324. **5** MIN.
- Do *Actividades* 13 and 14 orally. **10** MIN.
- Have students do *Actividad* 15 in groups. Have groups present their findings to the class. **10** MIN.
- Quick Start Review (TE, p. 325) **5** MIN.
- Present *Gramática:* Using Correct Pronoun Placement with Commands, p. 325. **5** MIN.
- Do *Actividad* 16 orally, *Actividad* 17 in pairs, and *Actividad* 18 in groups. **10** MIN.

Homework Option:
- Have students complete *Actividades* 13, 14, and 16 in writing. *Más práctica* Workbook, pp. 111–112. *Para hispano-hablantes* Workbook, pp. 109–110.

DAY 6

En acción (cont.)
- Check homework. **5** MIN.
- Play the audio; do *Actividad* 19. **5** MIN.
- Have students do *Actividad* 20 in writing. Expand using Information Gap Activities, Unit 5 Resource Book, pp. 18–19; *Más comunicación,* p. R13. **15** MIN.

Pronunciación
- Play the audio and have students practice the *trabalenguas.* **5** MIN.

En voces: Lectura
- Quick Start Review (TE, p. 328) **5** MIN.
- Review the Reading Strategy, p. 328. **5** MIN.
- Have volunteers read the selection aloud and answer the questions, p. 329. **15** MIN.

Homework Option:
- Have students write answers to the *¿Comprendiste?* questions, p. 329. Review in preparation for *En uso.*

DAY 7

En uso: Repaso y más comunicación
- Check homework. **5** MIN.
- Quick Start Review (TE, p. 330) **5** MIN.
- Present the *Repaso y más comunicación* using the Teaching Suggestions (TE, p. 330) **5** MIN.
- Have students write *Actividades* 1 and 2; check answers with the whole class. **10** MIN.
- Do *Actividades* 3 and 4 orally. **5** MIN.
- Present the Speaking Strategy, p. 332; have students do *Actividad* 5 in pairs. **10** MIN.
- Have students complete *Actividad* 6 in groups. **5** MIN.

En tu propia voz: Escritura
- Do *Actividad* 7 in writing. Ask volunteers to present their descriptions. **10** MIN.

Homework Option:
- Review for *Etapa* 1 Exam.

DAY 8

Conexiones
- Read and discuss *El arte,* p. 332. **5** MIN.

En resumen: Repaso de vocabulario
- Quick Start Review (TE, p. 333) **5** MIN.
- Review grammar questions, etc., as necessary. **5** MIN.
- Complete *Etapa* 1 Exam. **20** MIN.

Ampliación
- Use a suggested project, game, or activity. (TE, pp. 311A–311B) **15** MIN.

Homework Option:
- Have students paint a portrait and discuss it with a homework partner as outlined in *Conexiones.* Preview *Etapa* 2 Opener.

Sample Lesson Plan - Block Schedule (90 minutes)

DAY 1

Unit Opener
- Anticipate/Activate prior knowledge: Present the *Almanaque* and the cultural notes. Use Map OHTs as needed. 10 MIN.

Etapa Opener
- Quick Start Review (TE, p. 312) 5 MIN.
- Have students look at the *Etapa* Opener and answer the questions. 5 MIN.
- Use Block Scheduling Copymasters. 10 MIN.

En contexto: Vocabulario
- Quick Start Review (TE, p. 314) 5 MIN.
- Have students use context and pictures to learn *Etapa* vocabulary, then answer the questions, p. 315. Use the Situational OHTs for additional practice. 10 MIN.

En vivo: Diálogo
- Quick Start Review (TE, p. 316) 5 MIN.
- Review the Listening Strategy, p. 316. Play audio or show video for the dialog, pp. 316–317. Replay and have students take the roles of the characters. 10 MIN.
- Quick Start Review (TE, p. 318) 5 MIN.
- Have students open to *En contexto,* pp. 314–315, for reference. Use OHT 141 and 142 to review vocabulary. 10 MIN.
- Play the video/audio; have students do *Actividades* 1 and 2 orally. 10 MIN.
- Have students complete *Actividad* 3 orally. 5 MIN.

Homework Option:
- Have students complete *Actividad* 3 in writing. Video Activities, Unit 5 Resource Book, pp. 23–25.

DAY 2

En acción (cont.)
- Check homework. 5 MIN.
- Have students complete *Actividades* 4 and 5 in pairs. For each activity, have a few pairs present their dialogs. 15 MIN.
- Quick Start Review (TE, p. 320) 5 MIN.
- Present *Gramática:* Describing Actions That Involve Oneself: Reflexive Verbs and the *Vocabulario,* p. 320. Have students act out the verbs. 15 MIN.
- Play the audio; do *Actividad* 6. 5 MIN.
- Have students complete *Actividades* 7 and 8 in pairs. For each activity, have a few pairs present their dialogs. 15 MIN.
- Present the Speaking Strategy, p. 321, then do *Actividad* 9 orally. 10 MIN.
- Quick Start Review (TE, p. 322) 5 MIN.
- Present *Gramática:* Irregular Affirmative *tú* Commands, p. 322. 10 MIN.
- Have students complete *Actividad* 10 orally. 5 MIN.

Homework Option:
- Have students complete *Actividades* 9 and 10 in writing. *Más práctica* Workbook, pp. 109–110. *Para hispanohablantes* Workbook, pp. 107–108.

DAY 3

En acción (cont.)
- Check homework. 5 MIN.
- Present the *Vocabulario,* p. 323. Then have students do *Actividad* 11 in pairs. 10 MIN.
- Do *Actividad* 12 orally. Expand using Information Gap Activities, Unit 5 Resource Book, p. 17; *Más comunicación,* p. R13. 15 MIN.
- Quick Start Review (TE, p. 324) 5 MIN.
- Present *Gramática:* Negative *tú* Commands, p. 324. 5 MIN.
- Do *Actividad* 13 in writing. Have students exchange papers for peer correction. 5 MIN.
- Do *Actividad* 14 in writing. Go over answers orally. 5 MIN.
- Have students do *Actividad* 15 in groups. Have groups present their findings to the class. 10 MIN.
- Quick Start Review (TE, p. 325) 5 MIN.
- Present *Gramática:* Using Correct Pronoun Placement with Commands, p. 325. 5 MIN.
- Do *Actividad* 16 orally, *Actividad* 17 in pairs, and *Actividad* 18 in groups. 15 MIN.
- Play the audio; do *Actividad* 19. 5 MIN.

Homework Option:
- Have students complete *Actividades* 12 and 16 in writing. *Más práctica* Workbook, pp. 111–112. *Para hispanohablantes* Workbook, pp. 109–110.

DAY 4

En acción (cont.)
- Check homework. 5 MIN.
- Have students do *Actividad* 20 in writing. Expand using Information Gap Activities, Unit 5 Resource Book, pp. 18–19; *Más comunicación,* p. R13. 20 MIN.

Pronunciación
- Play the audio and have students practice the *trabalenguas.* 5 MIN.

En voces: Lectura
- Quick Start Review (TE, p. 328) 5 MIN.
- Review the Reading Strategy, p. 328. 5 MIN.
- Have volunteers read the selection aloud and answer the questions, p. 329. 15 MIN.

En uso: Repaso y más comunicación
- Quick Start Review (TE, p. 330) 5 MIN.
- Have students write *Actividades* 1 and 2; check answers with the whole class. 10 MIN.
- Do *Actividades* 3 and 4 orally. 5 MIN.
- Present the Speaking Strategy, p. 332; have students do *Actividad* 5 in pairs. 10 MIN.
- Do *Actividad* 6 in groups. 5 MIN.

Homework Option:
- Review for *Etapa* 1 Exam.

DAY 5

En tu propia voz: Escritura
- Do *Actividad* 7 in writing. Ask volunteers to present their descriptions. 15 MIN.

Conexiones
- Read *El arte,* p. 332, and do the activity. 15 MIN.

En resumen: Repaso de vocabulario
- Quick Start Review (TE, p. 333) 5 MIN.
- Review grammar questions, etc., as necessary. 10 MIN.
- Complete *Etapa* 1 Exam. 20 MIN.

Ampliación
- Use a suggested project, game, or activity. (TE, pp. 311A–311B) 25 MIN.

Homework Option:
- Preview *Etapa* 2 Opener.

▼ Mercedes saca fotos de Luis para el concurso.

Etapa Theme
Talking about one's daily routine, grooming, and chores.

Grammar Objectives
- Using reflexive verbs
- Using irregular affirmative **tú** commands
- Using negative **tú** commands
- Using correct pronoun placement with commands

Teaching Resource Options

Print

Block Scheduling Copymasters

Audiovisual

OHT 138, 147 (Quick Start)

Quick Start Review

♻ Vocabulary review

Use OHT 147 or write on the board: Write what means of transportation you might use to get to each place:

1. la escuela
2. el centro comercial
3. San Antonio, Texas
4. Oaxaca, México
5. España

Answers
Answers will vary. Answers could include:
1. a pie, en autobús
2. en carro, en metro
3. en carro, en avión
4. en tren, en avión
5. en barco, en avión

Teaching Suggestion
Previewing the Etapa
- Ask students to study the photo on pp. 312–313 (1 min.).
- Close books; ask students to share at least 3 things that they noticed.
- Reopen books and look at the picture again (1 min.); close books and share 3 more details.
- Have students describe the people in the photo and the weather.
- Use the **¿Qué ves?** questions to focus the discussion.

UNIDAD 5

ETAPA 1

¿Cómo es tu rutina?

- Describe daily routine
- Talk about grooming
- Tell others to do something
- Discuss daily chores

¿Qué ves?

Mira la foto del Parque Güell en Barcelona.

1. ¿Es interesante o no el parque?
2. ¿Qué hace la chica?
3. ¿Qué lleva la mujer?
4. ¿De qué color es el animal?
5. ¿Cómo se llama el parque de atracciones de Barcelona?

Barcelona

Parque Güell

Sagrada Familia

Avenida Diagonal

Parque de Joan Miró

Estación del Norte

Estación Barcelona Sants

BARRIO GÓTICO

Gran Vía de las Cortes Catalanas

Las Ramblas

Avenida del Paralelo

PLAYA

Parque de atracciones de Montjuïc

Puerto

Paseo de Colón

312

Classroom Management

Planning Ahead Collect and bring in items from Spain: newspapers, magazines, photos, music, museum guides, crafts, metro passes, brochures, etc. This will help students to develop an understanding of peninsular Spanish culture and to differentiate between Mexican and Spanish culture.

Organizing Paired/Group Work Many of the activities in this unit are to be done in pairs and groups. Have students practice moving quickly into these pairs and groups so that class time can be used efficiently later on.

Cross Cultural Connections

Survey students to see how many read the international news in the newspaper and/or watch international news programs. Explain that, in general, Spaniards tend to know more about U.S. culture than people in the U.S. know about Spain. Discuss why that might be. Ask students what they could do to learn more about Spain.

Culture Highlights

● **BARCELONA** Barcelona has 4 major sections: **Montjuic, Las Ramblas, El Ensanche,** and **El Barrio Gótico. Montjuic** is a high hill outside the city proper. It has been the site of a temple, a lighthouse, and a military fort. Today it is popular for its amusement park, museums (one displaying works by Joan Miró), the 1992 Olympic Stadium, and a botanical garden.

The city of Barcelona has a great interest in the enjoyment of the outdoors. In the last 20 years, close to 100 parks and plazas have been constructed or remodeled.

● **EL PARQUE GÜELL** El Parque Güell was created by Antonio Gaudí and named after his patron, industrialist Eusebio Güell. The park contains stone trees, reptilian fountains, and mosaics of broken ceramic pieces set in concrete.

● **ANTONIO GAUDÍ** Some of Gaudí's other works include **Casa Vicens** (a private home in Barcelona), **Casa Batlló** and **Casa Milá** (2 apartment buildings), and **Palacio Güell.**

Supplementary Vocabulary

la estatua	statue
el lagarto	lizard
la escalera	stairway
subir	to go up

Block Schedule

Variety Have students sketch and color an **Etapa** opener for their town/city. Have them share their artwork by telling the location, its significance, and what any people in their pictures are doing. (For additional activities, see **Block Scheduling Copymasters.**)

Teaching All Students

Extra Help Have students make a list of people (**chica, mujer, hombre,** etc.), a list of descriptors (hair color, height, clothing, etc.), and a list of verb infinitives. Then have them use these lists to write complete sentences describing the people in the photo.

Multiple Intelligences

Logical/Mathematical Have students calculate the distance between the following places: their town/city and Barcelona; Mexico City and Barcelona; Los Angeles and Barcelona; and Madrid and Barcelona. Also have them research the time of an airplane flight from the nearest international airport to Barcelona. Where would they have to change planes?

Teaching Resource Options

Print

Unit 5 Resource Book
Video Activities, pp. 23–24
Videoscript, p. 26
Audioscript, p. 29
Audioscript *Para hispanohablantes*,
   p. 29

Audiovisual

OHT 141, 142, 143, 143A, 144, 144A,
147 (Quick Start)
Audio Program Cassette 13A / CD 13
Audio *Para hispanohablantes*
Cassette 13A / CD 13
Video Program Videotape 5 / Videodisc
3A

Search Chapter 2, Play to 3
U5E1 • En contexto (Vocabulary)

Technology

Intrigas y aventuras CD-ROM, Disc 1

Quick Start Review

♻ Verb review

Use OHT 147 or write on the board:
Use the verb **ir** and a word from each
column to create 5 original sentences:

Modelo: Todos los días, mi mamá va
a la panadería.

los viernes	la panadería
los sábados	el parque
los domingos	el centro comercial
todos los días	la playa
los lunes	el banco
los jueves	la iglesia
	la tienda de vídeos

Answers

Answers will vary. Answers could include:
Los sábados voy al centro comercial.
Los domingos mi tía va a la iglesia.
Todos los días mi hermano va al parque.
Los viernes Arturo va a la tienda de vídeos.
Los jueves mi papá va al banco.

Teaching Note

Students are not expected to produce the
reflexive construction at this point. For the
Preguntas personales, they may answer
with phrases rather than complete sentences.

En contexto

📺🎧 VOCABULARIO

Luis is following his morning routine. Watch him get
ready for the day.

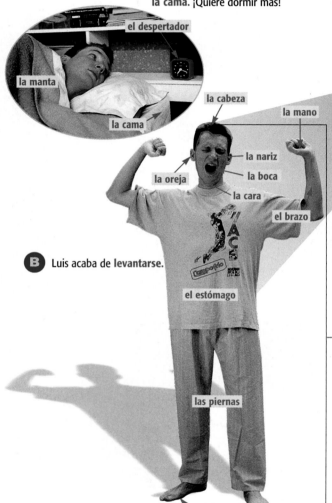

A Luis oye **el despertador**. Pero está en
la cama. ¡Quiere dormir más!

el despertador
la manta
la cama

la cabeza
la mano
la nariz
la oreja
la boca
la cara
el brazo

B Luis acaba de **levantarse**.

el estómago
el cuerpo
las piernas
los pies

314 trescientos catorce
Unidad 5

Classroom Community

TPR Have students imagine that they are Luis. As you
read sections A–E aloud, have students act out what
you say.

Game Have students stand up and play **Simón dice.**
For example: you say, **Simón dice «Toca los brazos».**
Students must touch their arms. Students who do not
react, react incorrectly, or react when the words **Simón
dice** are not included must sit down. The last student
standing is the winner.

C Luis va a lavarse. Se lava la cara con jabón y va a secarse con una toalla.

el jabón

la toalla

D Esta mañana Luis tiene tiempo para ducharse y lavarse la cabeza con champú.

el espejo

el secador de pelo

el champú

la pasta de dientes

LICOR-POLO·3

E Luis se lava los dientes con el cepillo de dientes. Después, va a peinarse con un peine. ¡Ya está listo!

los dientes

el cepillo de dientes

el peine

Preguntas personales

1. ¿Usas un despertador?
2. ¿Te lavas la cara por la mañana o por la noche?
3. ¿Usas un secador de pelo o una toalla para secarte el pelo?
4. ¿A qué hora te levantas?
5. ¿Cuándo te lavas los dientes?

trescientos quince
Etapa 1   **315**

Teaching Suggestions
Introducing Vocabulary

- Have students look at pages 314–315. Use OHT 141 and 142 and Audio Cassette 13A / CD 13 to present the vocabulary.
- Ask the Comprehension Questions in order of yes/no (questions 1–3), either/or (questions 4–6), and simple word or phrase (questions 7–10). Expand by adding similar questions.
- Use the TPR activity to reinforce the meaning of individual words.
- Use the video vocabulary presentation for review and reinforcement.

Comprehension Questions

1. En la foto 1, ¿está Luis en la cama? (Sí.)
2. ¿Oye Luis el despertador? (Sí.)
3. ¿Tiene Luis 3 mantas? (No.)
4. ¿Quiere Luis levantarse o dormir más? (dormir más)
5. ¿Luis va a lavarse o comer? (lavarse)
6. ¿Usa una camisa o una toalla para secarse? (una toalla)
7. ¿Con qué se lava Luis la cara? (con jabón)
8. ¿Con qué se lava Luis la cabeza? (con champú)
9. ¿Con qué se lava Luis los dientes? (con un cepillo de dientes)
10. ¿Con qué va a peinarse? (con un peine)

Supplementary Vocabulary

el mentón, la barbilla	chin
el codo	elbow
la rodilla	knee
los dedos	fingers
la muñeca	wrist
el tobillo	ankle
la frente	forehead
la barba	beard
el bigote	mustache

Block Schedule

FunBreak Working in groups, have students play a word association game. The first student gives a word (**los dientes**) and the next student gives a related word (**lavarse**). The next student gives a word associated with the second word (**jabón**), and so on.

Teaching All Students

Extra Help Make true/false statements about Luis's morning routine. Have students hold up cards showing **Cierto** or **Falso.**

Native Speakers Ask students to supply additional vocabulary pertaining to grooming. Have them model the pronunciation for the other students. Have the class add these words to their Supplementary Vocabulary Lists.

Multiple Intelligences

Interpersonal Working in pairs, have students first write predictions about their partner's answers to the **Preguntas personales.** They then ask each other the questions and check their predictions. Then have each student make up one more **Pregunta personal** to ask their partner.

Teaching Resource Options

Print

Más práctica Workbook PE,
pp. 105–108

Para hispanohablantes Workbook PE,
pp. 111–112

Block Scheduling Copymasters

Unit 5 Resource Book

Más práctica Workbook TE, pp. 1–4

Para hispanohablantes Workbook
TE, pp. 9–10

Video Activities, pp. 23–24

Videoscript, p. 27

Audioscript, p. 29

Audioscript *Para hispanohablantes*,
p. 29

Audiovisual

OHT 145, 146, 147 (Quick Start)

Audio Program Cassette 13A / CD 13

Audio *Para hispanohablantes*
Cassette 13A / CD 13

Video Program Videotape 5 / Videodisc
3A

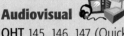

Search Chapter 3, Play to 4
U5E1 • En vivo (Dialog)

Technology

Intrigas y aventuras CD-ROM, Disc 1

Quick Start Review

♻ Morning routine

Use OHT 147 or write on the board:
Answer the following questions about
your morning routine:

1. ¿Cuándo te levantas los lunes—
   antes o después de las siete?
2. ¿Cuándo te levantas los sábados—
   antes o después de las siete?
3. ¿Usas un despertador?
4. ¿Cuántas mantas usas en la cama?
5. ¿Cómo se llama tu champú
   favorito? ¿Tu jabón favorito?

Answers *See p. 311D.*

Gestures

Assign groups of students specific
characters from the dialog. As you read
the dialog, have them make the gestures
that correspond to their characters.

En vivo

 DIÁLOGO

Muchos quehaceres

Luis Carmen Mercedes Juan Carlos Lourdes

PARA ESCUCHAR • STRATEGY: LISTENING

Listen for a mood or a feeling Nothing is going right for Luis.
What does he say to show frustration? Jot down some of his
expressions for protesting. When would you use them?

1▶ **Juan Carlos:** ¡Luis! ¡Mercedes llega
en diez minutos!
Luis: ¡Sí, ya lo sé! ¡Ahora me ducho
y salgo! ¡Necesito lavarme los
dientes!

5▶ **Luis:** Necesito secarme el pelo.
Carmen: ¡Ponte otra camisa!
Mírate en el espejo, ¡esta camisa
está muy fea! ¡Y no uses mi
secador de pelo! ¡Por favor, no
lo uses!

6▶ **Juan Carlos:** Hijo. Por favor, haz todo lo
que está en esta lista.
Luis: Pero, ¿tengo que hacerlo todo hoy?
Juan Carlos: Sí, hijo. Primero haz los
quehaceres.
Luis: ¡Pero, papá!

7▶ **Lourdes:** Necesitamos varias cosas.
Ve a la tienda. Aquí tienes mi lista.
Luis: Mamá, me espera Álvaro.
Lourdes: Pero esto es importante.
Luis: ¡No es justo! ¡Es mi
cumpleaños!

316 trescientos dieciséis
Unidad 5

Classroom Community

Cooperative Learning Have students work in
groups of 5. Each student chooses 2 different scenes
from the dialog and writes a short description of each.
Student 1 presents his/her first description. Student 2
gives the scene number. Student 3 confirms. Student 4
presents his/her first description, and so on until all
descriptions are complete. The group then puts all the
descriptions in order and presents a full-dialog summary.

Learning Scenario Have students work in groups.
Half the groups will create and present skits depicting a
typical morning at home before school. The other half
will depict a typical weekend morning. Encourage
students to use verbal and physical expression.

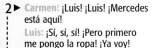

2▶ Carmen: ¡Luis! ¡Luis! ¡Mercedes está aquí!
Luis: ¡Sí, sí, sí! ¡Pero primero me pongo la ropa! ¡Ya voy!

3▶ Luis: ¡Hola, Mercedes! ¿Cómo estás?
Mercedes: Bien, Luis. ¡Y feliz cumpleaños! ¿Qué tal tu mañana?
Luis: Muy tranquila, gracias.

4▶ Luis: ¿Qué haces? ¿Por qué me estás sacando fotos? ¡No hagas eso!
Mercedes: Son para un concurso.
Luis: ¿Para qué concurso son?
Mercedes: Te digo luego. Álvaro nos espera en una hora. ¿Estás listo?

8▶ Juan Carlos: Sí, pero también puedes celebrarlo después. También cuida a tu hermana.
Luis: ¡No puede ser!
Carmen: ¡Ja, ja! ¡Me tienes que cuidar!

9▶ Luis: Voy a llamar a Álvaro. Nunca vamos a llegar a tiempo.
Mercedes: ¡Pobre Luis! ¡No seas tan dura con él! Es su cumpleaños.
Carmen: ¡Le quiero ver la cara al llegar a su fiesta!

10▶ Luis: Está ocupado. Lo llamo más tarde. Bueno, vamos. Tenemos muchas cosas que hacer. ¡Carmen, Mercedes!, ¿me ayudáis con los quehaceres?

trescientos diecisiete
Etapa 1 **317**

Teaching Resource Options

Print

Unit 5 Resource Book
  Video Activities, p. 25
  Videoscript, p. 28
  Audioscript, p. 29
  Audioscript *Para hispanohablantes,*
    p. 29

Audiovisual

OHT 148 (Quick Start)
Audio Program Cassette 13A / CD 13
Audio *Para hispanohablantes*
  Cassette 13A / CD 13
Video Program Videotape 5 /
  Videodisc 3A

🔔 Quick Start Review

 Dialog review

Use OHT 148 or write on the board:
Identify the speaker of each quote:

1. Mírate en el espejo, ¡esta camisa está muy fea!
2. ¿Por qué me estás sacando fotos?
3. Aquí tienes mi lista.
4. ¡Necesito lavarme los dientes!
5. Álvaro nos espera en una hora.
6. Primero haz los quehaceres.

Answers *See p. 311D.*

Teaching Suggestions
Comprehension Check

Use **Actividades** 1 and 2 to assess retention after the dialog. After students have successfully completed both activities, have them add items to **Actividad 2** and quiz each other.

Objective: Transitional practice
Listening comprehension/vocabulary

Answers (See script, p. 311D.)
1. e 2. d 3. b 4. a 5. c

Objective: Transitional practice
Listening comprehension/vocabulary

Answers (See script, p. 311D.)
1. ... saca fotos.
2. ... un concurso.
3. ... ducharse y lavarse los dientes.
4. ... Mercedes y Álvaro.
5. ... tiene que cuidar a su hermana, hacer algunos quehaceres e ir de compras para su mamá.

OBJECTIVES
• Describe daily routine
• Talk about grooming
• Tell others to do something
• Discuss daily chores

En acción
VOCABULARIO Y GRAMÁTICA

 ACTIVIDAD 1

Frases revueltas

Escuchar Explica lo que pasa en el diálogo. Completa las oraciones, combinando frases de las dos columnas. *(Hint: Explain what happens.)*

1. Cuando Mercedes llega, Luis…
2. Mercedes…
3. Álvaro…
4. A Luis no le gusta…
5. Cuando Luis llama a Álvaro…

a. cuidar a su hermana.
b. no está en casa de Luis.
c. está ocupado.
d. está sacando fotos.
e. no está listo para salir.

ACTIVIDAD 2

¿Qué pasa?

Escuchar Completa las oraciones para describir lo que pasa en el diálogo. *(Hint: Describe what happens.)*

1. Cuando Mercedes va a casa de Luis, ella…
2. Mercedes saca fotos para…
3. Cuando Mercedes llega, Luis acaba de…
4. Luis tiene planes para salir con…
5. Luis no está contento porque…

ACTIVIDAD 3

♻ Antonio va a...

Hablar/Escribir Hoy va a ser un día típico para Antonio, un amigo de Carmen. Explica a qué hora va a hacer cada actividad, según los dibujos. *(Hint: Explain when he is going to do each activity.)*

modelo

*Antonio va a **levantarse** a las **siete y cuarto.***

1.

2.

3.

4.

TAMBIÉN SE DICE In this unit you will see and hear language that is typical of Spain.

Did you notice that Luis uses the word **ayudáis**? Remember that in Spain the **vosotros(as)** form of verbs is usually used with people one knows well.

In Spain people use certain expressions for daily routine.

to wash one's hair
• **lavarse la cabeza:** Spain
• **lavarse el pelo/el cabello:** many countries

to brush one's teeth
• **lavarse los dientes:** Spain
• **cepillarse los dientes:** many countries

Classroom Management

Organizing Pair Work Assign pairs of students to work together on correcting the answers to **Actividades** 1 and 2. Then have these same pairs work together to complete **Actividades 3–5**. Students will be responsible for helping each other.

Time Saver If time is short, for **Actividades 4** and **5,** assign the odd numbers to half the class and the even numbers to the other half. Check answers as a group.

- Use reflexive verbs
- Use irregular affirmative **tú** commands
- Use negative **tú** commands
- Use correct pronoun placement with commands

En la droguería

Hablar Los padres de Luis están de compras y ven este anuncio. Hablan de lo que necesitan Luis y Carmen. ¿Qué dicen? *(Hint: Say what they need.)*

modelo

Luis (¿?): lavarse

Papá: *¿Necesita **Luis** jabón?*

Mamá: *Sí, lo necesita para **lavarse**.*

¡DROGUERÍA LAS RAMBLAS ABRE EL LUNES
21 de abril!

750 ptas

200 ptas

2.000 ptas

350 ptas

300 ptas

600 ptas

1.000 ptas

300 ptas

¡Vende de todo! Artículos de alta calidad a precios bajos!

1. Luis (¿?): lavarse los dientes
2. Luis y Carmen (¿?): peinarse
3. Carmen (¿?): lavarse la cabeza
4. Luis y Carmen (¿?): secarse
5. Carmen (¿?): secarse el pelo

Para correr...

Hablar Imagínate que un extraterrestre llega a tu casa. Pregúntale cómo hace las siguientes actividades.
(Hint: Ask how the extraterrestrial does these activities.)

modelo

correr

Tú: *¿Cómo **corres**?*

Extraterrestre: *Para **correr**, uso seis piernas y seis pies.*

1. comer
2. bailar
3. oír
4. escribir
5. pensar
6. nadar
7. caminar
8. tocar el piano
9. ver la televisión
10. jugar al béisbol

Language Notes

- Students should be aware that a **farmacia** in Spain is not the same as a pharmacy in the U.S. A **farmacia** only sells medicines and items used for medicinal purposes. A **droguería** sells a variety of items, as a pharmacy in the U.S. might.
- Note that in most Spanish-speaking countries numbers over 1,000 use decimal points instead of commas. For example: 1.258; 32.547; 498.000.

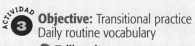

3 Objective: Transitional practice
Daily routine vocabulary
♻ **Telling time**

Answers

1. Antonio va a ducharse a las siete y veinte.
2. Antonio va a secarse a las siete y media.
3. Antonio va a peinarse a las ocho menos cuarto.
4. Antonio va a lavarse los dientes a las ocho.

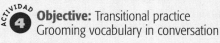

4 Objective: Transitional practice
Grooming vocabulary in conversation

Answers

1. Papá: ¿Necesita Luis pasta de dientes y un cepillo de dientes?
   Mamá: Sí, los necesita para lavarse los dientes.
2. Papá: ¿Necesitan Luis y Carmen peines?
   Mamá: Sí, los necesitan para peinarse.
3. Papá: ¿Necesita Carmen champú?
   Mamá: Sí, lo necesita para lavarse la cabeza.
4. Papá: ¿Necesitan Luis y Carmen toallas?
   Mamá: Sí, las necesitan para secarse.
5. Papá: ¿Necesita Carmen un secador de pelo?
   Mamá: Sí, lo necesita para secarse el pelo.

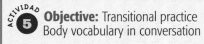

5 Objective: Transitional practice
Body vocabulary in conversation

Answers

1. Para comer, uso dos bocas.
2. Para bailar, uso seis pies, seis piernas, cuatro brazos y cuatro manos.
3. Para oír, uso dos orejas.
4. Para escribir, uso cuatro manos [una mano].
5. Para pensar, uso dos cabezas.
6. Para nadar, uso seis pies, seis piernas, cuatro brazos y cuatro manos.
7. Para caminar, uso seis piernas y seis pies.
8. Para tocar el piano, uso cuatro manos.
9. Para ver la televisión, uso cuatro ojos.
10. Para jugar al béisbol, uso seis pies, seis piernas, cuatro brazos y cuatro manos.

Block Schedule

FunBreak Have students create Bingo cards with words for parts of the body, personal care items, and daily routine vocabulary. Instead of calling out the words, provide clues. For example: **Es para lavarse los dientes = la pasta de dientes.**

Teaching All Students

Extra Help Have students make flashcards of personal care items and daily routine activities. Have them work in pairs and quiz each other. Variation: Have students create a poster similar to the one in **Actividad 4,** adding labels for the items.

Multiple Intelligences

Kinesthetic Prepare ahead: Bring in personal care items. Put the items in a bag. Call on individual students to close their eyes, pull out an item, and identify it by touch. For a challenge, add other known items from the classroom, such as pencils, notebooks, etc.

Teaching Resource Options

Print

Más práctica Workbook PE, p. 109
Para hispanohablantes Workbook PE, p. 107
Block Scheduling Copymasters
Unit 5 Resource Book
  Más práctica Workbook TE, p. 5
  Para hispanohablantes Workbook TE, p. 11
  Audioscript, p. 30
  Audioscript *Para hispanohablantes*, p. 30

Audiovisual

OHT 148 (Quick Start)
Audio Program Cassettes 13A, 13B / CD 13
Audio *Para hispanohablantes* Cassette 13A / CD 13

Technology

Intrigas y aventuras CD-ROM, Disc 1

Quick Start Review

♻ Personal care items

Use OHT 148 or write on the board:
List 5 items you use when getting ready in the morning. Tell what part of the body is involved with each one.

Answers
Answers will vary. Answers could include:
1. el jabón: las manos, la cara
2. el champú: la cabeza
3. el cepillo de dientes: los dientes
4. el espejo: la cara, el pelo
5. la toalla: el cuerpo

Teaching Suggestions
Teaching Reflexive Verbs

• Explain to students that they have been using one reflexive verb for a long time: **llamarse (Me llamo...)**.
• Point out that many reflexive verbs describe physical actions.

Objective: Controlled practice
Listening comprehension/ reflexive verbs

Answers (See script, p. 311D.)
1. Carmen se lava la cabeza.
2. Los padres de Luis se lavan las manos.
3. Mercedes y Luis se lavan los pies.
4. Luis se lava las piernas.
5. Álvaro se lava la cara.

GRAMÁTICA

Describing Actions That Involve Oneself: Reflexive Verbs

To describe people doing things for themselves, use reflexive verbs. Examples of reflexive actions are *brushing one's teeth* or *combing one's hair*. **Reflexive pronouns** are used with **reflexive verbs** to indicate that the subject of the sentence receives the action of the verb.

lavarse *to wash oneself*

me lavo	**nos** lavamos
te lavas	**os** laváis
se lava	**se** lavan

Many verbs can be used with or without **reflexive pronouns**. When there is **no** reflexive pronoun, the person doing the action does **not** receive the action.

reflexive
Pepa **se** lava.
Pepa washes herself.

not reflexive
Pepa **lava** el carro.
Pepa washes the car.

Luis says:
—¡Primero **me pongo** la ropa!
First I put on my clothes!

Notice he says **la ropa**, not **mi ropa**, because reflexive pronouns include the concept of possession.

When you use the **infinitive form** of a reflexive verb **after** a **conjugated verb**, be sure to use the correct **reflexive pronoun**.

Quiero levantar**me** temprano.
I want to get up early.

Me quiero levantar temprano.

You can also put the **reflexive pronoun** **in front** of the **conjugated verb.**

Some verbs have different meanings when used reflexively.

dormir *to sleep*	**dormirse** *to fall asleep*
ir *to go*	**irse** *to leave, to go away*
poner *to put*	**ponerse** *to put on (clothes)*

Vocabulario

Reflexive Verbs

acostarse: o→ue

lavarse la cabeza

afeitarse

lavarse los dientes

bañarse

maquillarse

despertarse: e→ie

ponerse la ropa

Notice that **acostarse** and **despertarse** are stem-changing verbs.

¿Cuándo haces estas actividades, por la mañana o por la noche?

Classroom Community

Paired Activity Have each pair make a simple clock with a spinner. Then have one student set the clock to a time and show it to his/her partner. The partner responds by saying what he/she normally does at that time. Students continue taking turns, showing different times of the day.

Portfolio Have students complete **Actividad 9** as a 3-paragraph essay: paragraph 1 = the morning routine; paragraph 2 = the afternoon routine; paragraph 3 = the evening routine. Students should use reflexive verbs as well as previously learned verbs.

Rubric A = 13–15 pts. **B** = 10–12 pts. **C** = 7–9 pts. **D** = 4–6 pts. **F** = < 4 pts.

Writing criteria	Scale
Vocabulary use	1 2 3 4 5
Grammar/spelling accuracy	1 2 3 4 5
Creativity, appearance	1 2 3 4 5

Se lavan...

Escuchar/Escribir Luis explica que todos tienen que lavarse después de trabajar mucho. ¿Qué se lavan? *(Hint: What is being washed?)*

1. Carmen / lavarse / ¿?
2. los padres de Luis / lavarse / ¿?
3. Mercedes y Luis / lavarse / ¿?
4. Luis / lavarse / ¿?
5. Álvaro / lavarse / ¿?

No están listos

Hablar Luis y sus amigos van a una fiesta. Nadie está listo. ¿Qué tiene que hacer cada uno? *(Hint: Say what they have to do.)*

modelo

Marta: lavarse la cabeza

Estudiante A: *¿Por qúe no está lista **Marta**?*

Estudiante B: ***Marta** tiene que **lavarse la cabeza.***
    o: ***Marta** se tiene que **lavar la cabeza.***

1. Luis: afeitarse
2. vosotros(as): secarse el pelo
3. Álvaro y su hermano: lavarse los dientes
4. tú: ducharse
5. Emiliana: maquillarse
6. sus primos: ponerse la ropa nueva
7. Mercedes y Elena: peinarse
8. tu hermana: lavarse la cara

■ **MÁS PRÁCTICA** *cuaderno* p. 109
■ **PARA HISPANOHABLANTES** *cuaderno* p. 107

Primero...

Hablar Pregúntale a otro(a) estudiante qué hace primero. *(Hint: Which activity do you do first?)*

modelo

¿ducharse o lavarse los dientes?

Estudiante A: *¿Qué haces primero, **te duchas** o **te lavas los dientes?***

Estudiante B: *Primero **me ducho** y luego **me lavo los dientes.***

1. ¿lavarse la cabeza o lavarse la cara?
2. ¿bañarse o lavarse los dientes?
3. ¿afeitarse/maquillarse o peinarse?
4. ¿lavarse la cara o ponerse la ropa?
5. ¿ponerse la ropa o peinarse?

ACTIVIDAD 9 — Tu día típico

> **PARA CONVERSAR**
> **STRATEGY: SPEAKING**
> **Sequence events** When telling about several events, make the order in which they occurred clear. Remember these expressions: **primero, entonces, luego, después, antes de..., después de..., por la mañana/tarde.**
>
> To show your acting talents, mime the activities of your daily routine in order.

Hablar/Escribir Describe tu día típico. Usa los verbos reflexivos que conoces. *(Hint: Describe a typical day.)*

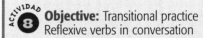

Objective: Controlled practice
Reflexive verbs in conversation

Answers
1. A: ¿Por qué no está listo Luis? B: Luis tiene que afeitarse. *o:* Luis se tiene que afeitar.
2. A: ¿Por qué no estáis listos vosotros? B: Nosotros tenemos que secarnos el pelo. *o:* Nosotros nos tenemos que secar el pelo.
3. A: ¿Por qué no están listos Álvaro y su hermano? B: Álvaro y su hermano tienen que lavarse los dientes. *o:* Álvaro y su hermano se tienen que lavar los dientes.
4. A: ¿Por qué no estás listo(a) tú? B: Yo tengo que ducharme. *o:* Yo me tengo que duchar.
5. A: ¿Por qué no está lista Emiliana? B: Emiliana tiene que maquillarse. *o:* Emiliana se tiene que maquillar.
6. A: ¿Por qué no están listos sus primos? B: Sus primos tienen que ponerse la ropa nueva. *o:* Sus primos se tienen que poner la ropa nueva.
7. A: ¿Por qué no están listas Mercedes y Elena? B: Mercedes y Elena tienen que peinarse. *o:* Mercedes y Elena se tienen que peinar.
8. A: ¿Por qué no está lista tu hermana? B: Mi hermana tiene que lavarse la cara. *o:* Mi hermana se tiene que lavar la cara.

Objective: Transitional practice
Reflexive verbs in conversation

Answers
1. A: ¿Qué haces primero, te lavas la cabeza o te lavas la cara? B: Primero me lavo la cabeza y luego me lavo la cara. *o:* Primero me lavo la cara y luego me lavo la cabeza.
2. A: ¿Qué haces primero, te bañas o te lavas los dientes? B: Primero me baño y luego me lavo los dientes. *o:* Primero me lavo los dientes y luego me baño.
3. A: ¿Qué haces primero, te afeitas (te maquillas) o te peinas? B: Primero me afeito (me maquillo) y luego me peino. *o:* Primero me peino y luego me afeito (me maquillo).
4. A: ¿Qué haces primero, te lavas la cara o te pones la ropa? B: Primero me lavo la cara y luego me pongo la ropa. *o:* Primero me pongo la ropa y luego me lavo la cara.
5. A: ¿Qué haces primero, te pones la ropa o te peinas? B: Primero me pongo la ropa y luego me peino. *o:* Primero me peino y luego me pongo la ropa.

Objective: Open-ended practice
Reflexive verbs

Answers will vary.

Teaching All Students

Extra Help In one box, put slips of paper with subject pronouns on them. In another box, put slips of paper with reflexive verbs in them. Have students draw a slip from each box, then create a sentence using both words.

Native Speakers Have students dramatize a typical morning at home, using props and gestures. Have them write any new reflexive verbs they use on the board and model pronunciation for the other students.

Multiple Intelligences

Musical/Rhythmic Have students bring in music they listen to while getting ready for school. Have them play the music and act out their morning routines while they tell what they are doing. Remind students to use sequencing vocabulary, such as **primero, después,** etc.

■ Block Schedule

Change of Pace Have students create small posters depicting related reflexive and nonreflexive actions, such as **Me baño por la mañana** and **Baño al perro los domingos.** (For additional activities, see **Block Scheduling Copymasters.**)

Teaching Resource Options

Print

Más práctica Workbook PE, p. 110
Para hispanohablantes Workbook PE, p. 108
Block Scheduling Copymasters
Unit 5 Resource Book
 Más práctica Workbook TE, p. 6
 Para hispanohablantes Workbook TE, p. 12
 Information Gap Activities, p. 17

Audiovisual 🎧

OHT 148 (Quick Start)

Technology 💻

Intrigas y aventuras CD-ROM, Disc 1

🔔 Quick Start Review

♻ **Reflexive verbs**

Use OHT 148 or write on the board:
Complete each sentence with the appropriate form of a reflexive verb:

1. Mi amigo ___ la cabeza con el champú.
2. Tú ___ con un despertador, ¿no?
3. A mí me gusta ___ con una toalla grande.
4. Necesitamos un cepillo de dientes para ___ los dientes.
5. Yo ___ todos los días a las diez de la noche.

Answers *See p. 311D.*

Teaching Suggestions
Teaching Irregular Affirmative tú Commands

Point out to students that they can now use all regular and irregular verbs in their affirmative **tú** command forms. In other words, they can tell a friend or a family member what to do.

ACTIVIDAD 10 Objective: Controlled practice Affirmative **tú** commands

Answers
1. Sé buena.   2. Di la verdad.   3. Haz la tarea.
4. Ven a casa a las seis.   5. Sal para comprar pan.   6. Ten paciencia.   7. Ve a la tienda.
8. Pon el libro en la mochila.

Juego

Answer: Necesita peinarse.

Gramática
Irregular Affirmative **tú** Commands

♻ **¿RECUERDAS?** *p. 252* You've already learned how to give instructions to someone by using the **affirmative tú commands** of regular verbs.

caminar	¡Camina!
comer	¡Come!
abrir	¡Abre!

▶ Some verbs have **irregular affirmative tú commands.** Here are the irregular affirmative **tú** commands of some verbs you know.

Infinitive	Affirmative tú Command
decir	di
hacer	haz
ir	ve
poner	pon
salir	sal
ser	sé
tener	ten
venir	ven

Luis's father says:

—Primero **haz** los quehaceres.
*First **do** the chores.*

▶ Remember that when you use a **pronoun** with an **affirmative command,** the **pronoun attaches** to the **command.**

Carmen says:

—¡**Pon te** otra camisa!
Put on (yourself) another shirt!

ACTIVIDAD 10 Gramática

¡Pobre Carmen!

Hablar/Escribir Luis siempre le dice a su hermana qué hacer. ¿Qué le dice? *(Hint: Give Luis's commands.)*

modelo

poner la mesa
Pon la mesa.

1. ser buena
2. decir la verdad
3. hacer la tarea
4. venir a casa a las seis
5. salir para comprar pan
6. tener paciencia
7. ir a la tienda
8. poner el libro en la mochila

■ **MÁS PRÁCTICA** *cuaderno* p. 110

■ **PARA HISPANOHABLANTES** *cuaderno* p. 108

Juego

Beto se despierta, se levanta, se ducha, desayuna y sale para la escuela. ¿Qué más necesita hacer esta mañana?

Classroom Community

TPR Have students imagine that they are robots who respond to your every command. Rapidly give each student a different command until all students are performing a task simultaneously. For example: **pon la mesa, haz la cama, lava los platos.**

Storytelling Working in pairs, have students write and perform a skit: **¡Tengo demasiado que hacer!** One student will play various roles of people giving orders throughout the day. The other student plays the hassled person and acts out the various commands.

ACTIVIDAD 11

¿Qué hago primero?

Hablar Tienes mucho que hacer hoy. Le preguntas a tu mamá qué debes hacer primero. ¿Qué te dice? *(Hint: Talk about chores.)*

modelo

¿poner la mesa o hacer las camas?

Tú: *¿Qué hago primero? ¿Pongo la mesa o hago las camas?*

Mamá: *Primero haz las camas. Después pon la mesa.*

1. ¿hacer la cama o preparar el desayuno?
2. ¿limpiar el cuarto o comprar comida?
3. ¿ir a la tienda o hacer los otros quehaceres?
4. ¿quitar la mesa o lavar los platos?
5. ¿hacer ejercicio o lavar la ropa sucia?

ACTIVIDAD 12

Los amigos ayudan

Hablar/Escribir Mercedes les pide mucho a sus amigos. ¿Qué les pide? *(Hint: What does Mercedes ask?)*

modelo

Ángela: poner ¿?

Ángela, pon los libros en mi mochila, por favor.

1. Luis: ser ¿?
2. Andrés: salir para ¿?
3. Marta: venir a ¿?
4. Álvaro: poner ¿?
5. Lucía: hacer ¿?
6. Paco: decir ¿?
7. Linda: ir ¿?
8. Carmen: tener ¿?

 MÁS COMUNICACIÓN p. R13

Vocabulario

Para hablar de los quehaceres

hacer la cama

lavar los platos

limpiar el cuarto

quitar la mesa

estar limpio(a)

estar sucio(a)

En tu familia, ¿quién hace estos quehaceres?

trescientos veintitrés
Etapa 1 **323**

Teaching All Students

Extra Help Have students make flashcards of regular and irregular **tú** commands, with an infinitive on one side and the command on the other. Have them study the cards alone, and then quiz a partner.

Native Speakers Discuss domestic roles in students' home communities. How are household chores distributed among family members? Who does the majority of the housekeeping? Who does the cooking?

Multiple Intelligences

Interpersonal Have students work in pairs and give each other advice for making improvements in the following situations: at school, at home, relationships with friends, eating habits.

Intrapersonal Have students list the chores they do at home in order from least to most favorite. Have them also explain why they prefer their favorite chore.

Teaching Suggestions
Presenting Vocabulary

Personalize the chores by asking students who does what chores at home. For example: **En tu casa, ¿quién quita la mesa? ¿Haces tu cama? ¿La haces todos los días?**

ACTIVIDAD 11 **Objective:** Transitional practice Affirmative **tú** commands/Chores in conversation

Answers

1. Tú: ¿Qué hago primero? ¿Hago la cama o preparo el desayuno?
   Mamá: Primero haz la cama. Después prepara el desayuno. *o:* Primero prepara el desayuno. Después haz la cama.
2. Tú: ¿Qué hago primero? ¿Limpio el cuarto o compro comida?
   Mamá: Primero limpia el cuarto. Después compra comida. *o:* Primero compra comida. Después limpia el cuarto.
3. Tú: ¿Qué hago primero? ¿Voy a la tienda o hago los otros quehaceres?
   Mamá: Primero ve a la tienda. Después haz los otros quehaceres. *o:* Primero haz los otros quehaceres. Después ve a la tienda.
4. Tú: ¿Qué hago primero? ¿Quito la mesa o lavo los platos?
   Mamá: Primero quita la mesa. Después lava los platos. *o:* Primero lava los platos. Después quita la mesa.
5. Tú: ¿Qué hago primero? ¿Hago ejercicio o lavo la ropa sucia?
   Mamá: Primero haz ejercicio. Después lava la ropa sucia. *o:* Primero lava la ropa sucia. Después haz ejercicio.

ACTIVIDAD 12 **Objective:** Open-ended practice Affirmative **tú** commands

Answers

Answers will vary.

1. Luis, sé...
2. Andrés, sal para...
3. Marta, ven a...
4. Álvaro, pon...
5. Lucía, haz...
6. Paco, di...
7. Linda, ve...
8. Carmen, ten...

Block Schedule

Variety First have students write a series of 3 affirmative **tú** commands, using regular and irregular verbs. The commands should follow one theme (getting ready in the morning, doing chores, etc.). Then have students work in pairs and take turns giving each other the orders and acting them out. Then have the pairs give their commands to another pair of students. (For additional activities, see **Block Scheduling Copymasters.**)

Teaching Resource Options

Print

Más práctica Workbook PE, p. 111
Para hispanohablantes Workbook PE, p. 109
Block Scheduling Copymasters
Unit 5 Resource Book
  Más práctica Workbook TE, p. 7
  Para hispanohablantes Workbook TE, p. 13

Audiovisual

OHT 149 (Quick Start)

Technology

Intrigas y aventuras CD-ROM, Disc 1

Quick Start Review

♻ Affirmative **tú** commands

Use OHT 149 or write on the board:
Write **tú** command sentences using the following elements:

1. hacer / tu tarea
2. poner / el libro en tu escritorio
3. decir / la verdad a tu madre
4. ponerse / otra camisa
5. venir / aquí

Answers *See p. 311D.*

Teaching Suggestions
Teaching Negative tú Commands

Note that when verbs ending in **-car**, **-gar**, and **-zar** are used in negative **tú** commands, they require spelling changes: **practiques, juegues, cruces.** Exercises avoid the production of these forms. If students attempt to use verbs with these endings in open discussion, they should be made aware of this.

Objective: Controlled practice
Negative **tú** commands

Answers
1. Carmen, no corras en la casa.
2. Carmen, no veas la televisión antes de hacer la tarea.
3. Carmen, no hables mucho por teléfono.
4. Carmen, no abras el libro de papá.
5. Carmen, no mires mis videos.
6. Carmen, no comas muchos dulces.
7. Carmen, no uses mis discos compactos.
8. Carmen, no bebas tantos refrescos.
9. Carmen, no vayas al parque muy tarde.
10. Carmen, no vengas tarde a comer.

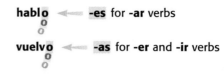

GRAMÁTICA — Negative tú Commands

When you tell someone what **not** to do, use a **negative command**. **Negative tú commands** are formed by taking the **yo** form of the present tense, dropping the **-o**, and adding the appropriate ending.

hablo ← **-es** for **-ar** verbs

vuelvo ← **-as** for **-er** and **-ir** verbs

Infinitive	Yo Form	Negative tú Command
hablar	**hablo**	**¡No hables!**
volver	**vuelvo**	**¡No vuelvas!**
venir	**vengo**	**¡No vengas!**

Carmen says:
—¡Y **no uses** mi secador de pelo!
*And **don't use** my hair dryer!*

A few verbs have **irregular negative tú commands**. Notice that none of the **yo** forms of these verbs end in **-o**.

Infinitive (yo form)	Negative tú Command
dar (doy)	**No le des** mi dirección a nadie. ***Don't give** my address to anyone.*
estar (estoy)	**No estés** triste. ***Don't be** sad.*
ir (voy)	**No vayas** a la tienda. ***Don't go** to the store.*
ser (soy)	**No seas** mala. ***Don't be** bad.*

ACTIVIDAD 13 — Gramática

¡No, no, no!

Hablar/Escribir Cuando Luis cuida a su hermana menor, ella hace cosas que no debe hacer. Luis siempre le dice que no.
(Hint: What does Luis say?)

modelo

patinar en la calle
*Carmen, no **patines en la calle.***

1. correr en la casa
2. ver la televisión antes de hacer la tarea
3. hablar mucho por teléfono
4. abrir el libro de papá
5. mirar mis videos
6. comer muchos dulces
7. usar mis discos compactos
8. beber tantos refrescos
9. ir al parque muy tarde
10. venir tarde a comer

■ **MÁS PRÁCTICA** *cuaderno* p. 111
■ **PARA HISPANOHABLANTES** *cuaderno* p. 109

NOTA CULTURAL

Many people in Barcelona speak **catalán**. Can you guess what these **catalán** words mean?

Bon dia
        Benvinguts
    museu

Classroom Community

Paired Activity After completing **Actividad 13** orally, have students work in pairs and give each other a dictation based on the answers. Student 1 dictates the answers to the even-numbered items to Student 2. Student 2 dictates the odd-numbered items to Student 1.

Game Play **Simón dice** again (see TE p. 314). This time, use the **tú** command forms that have been learned. For example: you say, **Simón dice «Pon la mano en el estómago».** Commands could also include movements that must be mimed, such as **Simón dice «Lava los platos».**

ACTIVIDAD 14

Las instrucciones

Hablar/Escribir Estás cuidando a un niño de seis años. ¿Qué instrucciones le das? *(Hint: What do you say to a six-year-old?)*

modelo

correr en la casa

No corras en la casa. *Corre en el parque.*

1. poner los libros en el gimnasio
2. ser malo
3. salir de la casa solo
4. comer dulces antes de cenar
5. estar triste
6. decir malas palabras
7. llevar mi chaqueta
8. dormir en el sofá

ACTIVIDAD 15

Cuando salgo, mis padres me dicen...

Hablar/Escribir ¿Cuáles son las instrucciones que te dan tus padres cuando sales? Habla con los otros estudiantes de la clase. Cada estudiante dice un mínimo de dos instrucciones. ¿Cuáles son las cinco instrucciones más comunes? *(Hint: What instructions do your parents give you?)*

modelo

Tú: *Ana, ¿qué te dicen tus padres cuando sales?*

Ana: *Haz la tarea antes de salir. No salgas sola. Sé buena. No vayas lejos. Regresa a las ocho.*

Persona	Instrucciones afirmativas	Instrucciones negativas
Ana	Haz la tarea.	No salgas sola.
	Sé buena.	No vayas lejos.
	Regresa a las ocho.	

GRAMÁTICA

Using Correct Pronoun Placement with Commands

♻ **¿RECUERDAS?** *p. 252* Remember that when you use an **object pronoun** with an **affirmative command**, you **attach** the pronoun to the end of the command.

> Cruza el parque. ➞ ¡Crúza**lo**!
> *Cross the park.* ➞ *Cross it!*

Object pronouns precede *negative commands*, just as with other conjugated verbs.

Carmen says:

—¡**No lo** uses!
Don't use it (the hair dryer)!

Remember, you may need to add an **accent** when you attach a pronoun.

Teaching All Students

Extra Help Have students refer back to the **Diálogo,** pp. 316–317, find all instances of commands, and list them. Then have students write the verb infinitive next to each one.

Native Speakers Ask students about official languages in their home countries. Is Spanish the only official language? What other languages/dialects are spoken?

Multiple Intelligences

Verbal Have groups of students write 10 realistic affirmative and negative commands. Then, in turn, have the groups read their commands. Have the other students guess in what situation this command might be heard; for example: **en la escuela, en casa, en la tienda de música.**

ACTIVIDAD 14

Objective: Transitional practice Affirmative and negative **tú** commands

Answers

Answers will vary.
1. No pongas los libros en el gimnasio. Ponlos...
2. No seas malo. Sé...
3. No salgas de la casa solo. Sal...
4. No comas dulces antes de cenar. Come...
5. No estés triste. Está...
6. No digas malas palabras. Di...
7. No lleves mi chaqueta. Lleva...
8. No duermas en el sofá. Duerme...

ACTIVIDAD 15

Objective: Open-ended practice Affirmative and negative **tú** commands in conversation

Answers will vary.

🔔 Quick Start Review

♻ Negative **tú** commands
Use OHT 149 or write on the board: Change the following to negative commands:

1. Escribe tu nombre aquí.
2. Haz la cena esta noche.
3. Pon el jabón al lado de la toalla.
4. Compra el regalo hoy.
5. Da los libros al profesor.

Answers *See p. 311D.*

Teaching Suggestions
Reinforcing Correct Pronoun Placement with Commands

Have students give examples of verbs that take direct and indirect object nouns (**escribir, hablar, mirar, leer, poner,** etc.). Have students provide sample sentences. Then have them substitute the nouns with pronouns.

Block Schedule

Change of Pace Have groups of 3 present "good guy/bad guy" skits. Two students stand on either side of the third student, who is trying to make a decision (**¿Hago la tarea?**). The "good guy" side tells him/her a good thing to do (**Haz tu tarea**). The "bad guy" side tells him/her the opposite (**No hagas tu tarea. Ve al parque.**). (For additional activities, see **Block Scheduling Copymasters.**)

Teaching Resource Options

Print

Más práctica Workbook PE, p. 112
Para hispanohablantes Workbook PE, p. 110
Block Scheduling Copymasters
Unit 5 Resource Book
  Más práctica Workbook TE, p. 8
  Para hispanohablantes Workbook TE, p. 14
  Information Gap Activities, pp. 18–19
  Audioscript, p. 30
  Audioscript *Para hispanohablantes*, p. 30

Audiovisual

Audio Program Cassettes 13A, 13B / CD 13
Audio *Para hispanohablantes* Cassette 13A / CD 13

Technology

Intrigas y aventuras CD-ROM, Disc 1

ACTIVIDAD 16 **Objective:** Controlled practice Pronoun placement with commands
  ♻ Object pronouns

Answers

Answers will vary.
1. Sí, léelo.
2. Sí, cómelo.
3. No. No los compartas.
4. No. No lo pidas.
5. Sí, págala.
6. No. No la dejes.

ACTIVIDAD 17 **Objective:** Controlled practice Pronoun placement with commands

Answers
1. Tú: Tengo que limpiar el cuarto.
   Tu amigo(a): No lo limpies ahora. Límpialo más tarde.
2. Tú: Tengo que poner la mesa.
   Tu amigo(a): No la pongas ahora. Ponla más tarde.
3. Tú: Tengo que lavar los platos.
   Tu amigo(a): No los laves ahora. Lávalos más tarde.
4. Tú: Tengo que preparar la cena.
   Tu amigo(a): No la prepares ahora. Prepárala más tarde.
5. Tú: Tengo que comprar pan.
   Tu amigo(a): No lo compres ahora. Cómpralo más tarde.
6. Tú: Tengo que hacer la tarea.
   Tu amigo(a): No la hagas ahora. Hazla más tarde.
7. Tú: Tengo que cuidar las plantas.
   Tu amigo(a): No las cuides ahora. Cuídalas más tarde.
8. Tú: Tengo que escribir una carta.
   Tu amigo(a): No la escribas ahora. Escríbela más tarde.

ACTIVIDAD 16 Gramática

♻ En el restaurante

Hablar/Escribir Tu amigo(a) no puede decidir qué hacer en el restaurante. Contesta sus preguntas.
(Hint: Answer your friend's questions.)

modelo

¿Bebo limonada? (sí)	*¿Pido enchiladas? (no)*
Sí, bébela.	*No. No las pidas.*

1. ¿Leo el menú? (sí)
2. ¿Como el arroz? (sí)
3. ¿Comparto los frijoles? (no)
4. ¿Pido un postre? (no)
5. ¿Pago la cuenta? (sí)
6. ¿Dejo la propina? (no)

ACTIVIDAD 17 Gramática

¡No lo hagas ahora!

Hablar Tu amigo(a) quiere salir pero tú tienes muchos quehaceres hoy. ¿Qué te dice?
(Hint: Give commands.)

modelo

hacer la cama

Tú: *Tengo que **hacer la cama**.*

Tu amigo(a): *No **la hagas** ahora. **Hazla** más tarde.*

1. limpiar el cuarto
2. poner la mesa
3. lavar los platos
4. preparar la cena
5. comprar pan
6. hacer la tarea
7. cuidar las plantas
8. escribir una carta

■ **MÁS PRÁCTICA** *cuaderno* p. 112
■ **PARA HISPANOHABLANTES** *cuaderno* p. 110

ACTIVIDAD 18

¡Las decisiones!

Hablar Quieres hacer algo, pero tienes que hacer otra cosa. Escoge una situación y pregúntales a cinco estudiantes qué hacer. *(Hint: Ask five students what to do.)*

modelo

Quieres ver la televisión pero tienes tarea.

Tú: *¿Veo la televisión o hago la tarea?*

Estudiante 1: *No veas la televisión. Haz la tarea.*

Estudiante 2: *Ve la televisión pero haz la tarea primero.*

1. Quieres alquilar un video pero tienes que visitar a tus abuelos.
2. Quieres descansar pero tus amigos quieren andar en bicicleta.
3. Quieres cenar en un restaurante pero tienes que preparar la cena.
4. Quieres acostarte pero tienes que estudiar para un examen.
5. Quieres ir a una tienda pero puedes regatear en el mercado.

NOTA CULTURAL

Rock con raíces, or Root-Rock, has become popular with urban youth in Spain. It blends traditional elements of **flamenco,** such as castanets and hand claps, with electric guitars and synthesizers. Rosario's music has many flamenco influences.

326 trescientos veintiséis
Unidad 5

Classroom Community

Paired Activity If time is short, have students do **Actividad 18** in pairs. Remind them that their questions will be based on the verb infinitives, not on **quieres.**

Group Activity Have groups of students write 5 affirmative and 5 negative commands telling a new student what to do and what not to do to be happy and successful in your school. Have groups share their ideas with the class. Compile the results in a class *do's* and *dont's* list.

ACTIVIDAD 19

La rutina de Álvaro

Escuchar Lee las oraciones. Luego, escucha el diálogo y di si las oraciones son ciertas o falsas. Corrige las falsas. *(Hint: Say what is true.)*

1. Álvaro se despierta a las nueve los sábados.
2. Álvaro se queda en la cama un rato después de despertarse.
3. Álvaro se lava la cara y los dientes después de levantarse.
4. Álvaro no se baña los sábados.
5. Álvaro se afeita y se lava la cabeza por la noche.

ACTIVIDAD 20

La Farmacia VendeTodo

Escribir Trabajas en una farmacia. Escribe un anuncio sobre algunos productos. Usa los verbos reflexivos para describir los productos. Usa los mandatos (afirmativos y negativos) para decirles a los clientes qué comprar. *(Hint: Write an ad for a pharmacy.)*

■ **MÁS COMUNICACIÓN** p. R13

Pronunciación

Trabalenguas

Pronunciación de la *s*, la *z* y la *c* In the Spanish spoken in Latin America and southern Spain, the **s** and **z** always sound like the *s* in the English word *miss*. When **c** is followed by the vowel **i** or **e**, it has the same sound. In central and northern Spain, the **z** and **c** are not pronounced like an *s*, but like the *th* sound in the English word *thin,* when they are followed by **i** or **e**. So if you go to Barcelona, you may want to try the *th* sound! Practice the sounds by repeating the following words. Then try the tongue twister! From the picture, can you guess what it means?

cabeza	pasta de dientes
cepillo	secador
lápiz	

¡El sapo del centro sirve zumo sabroso!

trescientos veintisiete
Etapa 1 **327**

ACTIVIDAD 18

Objective: Transitional practice Affirmative and negative **tú** commands in conversation

Answers will vary.

Variation: Convert the activity into a writing activity by having students note answers and report back to the class.

ACTIVIDAD 19

Objective: Transitional practice Listening comprehension/reflexive verbs

Answers (See script, p. 311D.)
1. Falso. Se despierta entre las ocho y las ocho y media.
2. Cierto.
3. Cierto.
4. Falso. Se baña los sábados por la noche antes de salir.
5. Cierto.

ACTIVIDAD 20

Objective: Open-ended practice Reflexive verbs/commands in writing

Answers will vary.

🔔 Quick Wrap-up

Have students look back at the **Etapa** opener, pp. 312–313, and give 3 commands Mercedes might give to Luis and 3 commands Luis might give to Mercedes.

Dictation

After students have read the **trabalenguas** in the **Pronunciación,** have them close their books. Dictate the **trabalenguas** in two segments while students write it.

📖 Block Schedule

Variety Have students write their own **trabalenguas.** They should refer to the **Repaso de vocabulario** at the end of each **Etapa** for help in remembering vocabulary. Have students present their **trabalenguas** and see how well the class does at pronouncing them. (For additional activities, see **Block Scheduling Copymasters.**)

Teaching All Students

Extra Help Have students make a 4-column chart of the verbs used in **Actividades 16** and **17.** The columns should read: infinitive, **yo** form, + **tú** command, − **tú** command.

Native Speakers Give students an opportunity to read the audioscript to **Actividad 19** to small groups of students and provide help when necessary.

Multiple Intelligences

Musical/Rhythmic Bring in a recording of **flamenco** music and several sets of castanets. First, have students describe the sound of the music and give their opinion of it. Then let students practice using the castanets and play along with the recording.

Teaching Resource Options

Print 📖

Unit 5 Resource Book
  Audioscript, p. 31
  Audioscript *Para hispanohablantes,*
    p. 31

Audiovisual 🎧📀

Audio Program Cassette 13A / CD 13
Audio *Para hispanohablantes*
  Cassette 13A / CD 13
OHT 149 (Quick Start)
Canciones Cassette / CD

🔔 Quick Start Review

♻ Barcelona

Use OHT 149 or write on the board:
Imagine that you are on vacation in
Barcelona. Write 2 activities you could
do at each of the following locations:

1. un mercado
2. un parque
3. un restaurante
4. la playa

Answers
Answers will vary. Answers could include:
1. regatear, comprar regalos
2. dar un paseo, sacar fotos
3. tomar un refresco, cenar
4. nadar, tomar el sol

Teaching Suggestions

• **Prereading** Have students pool
their knowledge about Pablo Picasso.
Write the information on the board.

• **Strategy: Scan for crucial details**
Have students follow the steps in the
Strategy. Go over the answers to the
questions as a class.

• **Reading** Have students read each
paragraph silently, then have a
volunteer read it aloud. As a class,
decide on a 1-sentence summary of
each paragraph.

• **Post-reading** Ask students for their
impressions of the paintings shown
here. Have them describe the
subjects, the colors, and whether they
like the paintings or not.

En voces
LECTURA

Una exhibición especial de Picasso

PARA LEER • STRATEGY: READING

Scan for crucial details Before you decide to
visit the exhibit **«Picasso y los retratos»**
there is some practical information you need
to know. Look quickly to pick up certain
details. Can you find the answers in the
article? If you can, jot them down.

1. **¿En qué museo está la exhibición?**
2. **¿Cuándo termina?**
3. **¿Cuáles son las horas de visita?**

NOTA CULTURAL

Pablo Ruiz Picasso (1881–1973) was born in Málaga.
In 1895 he moved with his family to Barcelona. He
studied classical art there and
later painted on his own. After
several trips to France, Picasso
moved there in 1904. This is
one of his self-portraits.

En catalán la palabra
museo se dice **museu.**

Si te levantas el sábado y tienes ganas de ir a
un museo, hay una exhibición especial en el
Museo Picasso de Barcelona. Es una colección
de retratos[1] de Pablo Picasso. La exhibición se
llama «Picasso y los retratos». Es posible verla
hasta el 31 de julio.

Las pinturas de la exhibición «Picasso y
los retratos» son de varios estilos. En algunos
retratos, por ejemplo *Retrato de Jaime Sabatés*,
usa un estilo tradicional. En otros retratos
vemos el desarrollo[2] de la pintura moderna
en la composición de las partes del
cuerpo: la cara, las orejas, los brazos y
las piernas. Un ejemplo es *Maya con
una muñeca.*

---

[1] portraits   [2] development

328 trescientos veintiocho
Unidad 5

Classroom Community

Learning Scenario Have students research the life
of Pablo Picasso and his art, and then have a Pablo
Picasso Appreciation Day. Students should bring in
samples of Picasso's art (as shown in books, copied
from library materials, or downloaded from Internet
sites). Display the artwork and have students talk about
what they learned.

Portfolio Have students choose one work of art by
Picasso that they like. They should make a photocopy
of the work, describe it, and tell why they like it.

Rubric A = 13–15 pts. B = 10–12 pts. C = 7–9 pts. D = 4–6 pts. F = < 4 pts.

Writing criteria	Scale
Details	1 2 3 4 5
Grammar/spelling accuracy	1 2 3 4 5
Creativity, appearance	1 2 3 4 5

Retrato de Jaime Sabatés, *1899–1900 Un retrato de Jaime Sabatés, gran amigo de Picasso. Sabatés le dio[5] su importante colección de obras[6] de Picasso al museo.*

Maya con una muñeca, 1938

Los retratos de Picasso también nos dan una idea de su vida privada. Hay retratos de sus amigos, sus hijos y las mujeres importantes en su vida.

Si vas a la exhibición, aprovecha[3] tu visita para ver otras obras de este pintor español en nuestro Museo Picasso. ¡Hay más de tres mil[4]!

---

[3] take advantage of
[4] thousand
[5] gave
[6] works

¿Comprendiste?

1. ¿Cómo se llama la exhibición especial del Museo Picasso de Barcelona?
2. ¿Cuáles son dos estilos de retratos de la exhibición?
3. ¿De quiénes son los retratos de la exhibición?
4. ¿Cómo se llama el amigo que Picasso pintó?
5. ¿Cuántas obras de Picasso hay normalmente en el Museo Picasso de Barcelona?

¿Qué piensas?

Mira los dos retratos que están al lado del artículo. ¿Qué diferencias hay entre los dos? ¿Cuál tiene un estilo moderno? ¿Por qué?

trescientos veintinueve
Etapa 1   **329**

Culture Highlights

● **PABLO PICASSO** Pablo Picasso was a painter and a sculptor. He mastered many styles and media. His favorite subjects were musical instruments, still-life objects, and his friends. In 1971, he became the first living artist to have an exhibition at the Louvre in Paris. He is one of the most prolific artists in history, with more than 20,000 works.

Cross Cultural Connections

Strategy Have students reflect on famous artists from the U.S. Who are students familiar with from colonial times? Who are they familiar with from modern times? Do any of these artists use the same styles as Picasso? Do any have museums named after them?

Interdisciplinary Connection

History Have students research the Spanish Civil War and its impact on artists, authors, musicians, and film directors in Spain. Have them include information about the U.S. involvement in the war.

¿Comprendiste?

Answers
1. Se llama «Picasso y los retratos».
2. El estilo traditional y el estilo moderno.
3. Los retratos son de sus amigos, sus hijos y las mujeres importantes en su vida.
4. Se llama Jaime Sabatés.
5. Hay más de tres mil.

Teaching Note

You may want to have students create a Venn diagram to support/illustrate their answers to the ¿**Qué piensas?** questions.

Teaching All Students

Extra Help Have students scan the reading for words they are not sure of. Have them work with a partner to identify the meanings from context.

Native Speakers Invite students to talk about famous artists from their cultural communities. Are the artists primarily painters or sculptors? Where are their works displayed?

Multiple Intelligences

Visual Have students create a time line of Picasso's life and the various periods of his art. If possible, students should also include important world events that influenced many of his works. For example, *Guernica* was influenced by the Spanish Civil War.

Block Schedule

Research Have students research where in the world there is currently a Picasso exhibit. Find out what paintings are in that exhibit and, if possible, print out copies of these works.

Teaching Resource Options

Print 📖

Para hispanohablantes Workbook PE, pp. 111–112

Unit 5 Resource Book
Para hispanohablantes Workbook TE, pp. 15–16
Information Gap Activities, p. 20
Family Involvement, pp. 21–22
Multiple Choice Test Questions, pp. 170–178

Audiovisual 📼

OHT 150 (Quick Start)
Audio Program Testing Cassette T2 / CD T2

Technology 💻

Electronic Teacher Tools/Test Generator
Intrigas y aventuras CD-ROM, Disc 1

🔔 Quick Start Review

♻ **Daily routine**

Use OHT 150 or write on the board: Answer the following questions in complete sentences:

1. ¿A qué hora te levantas los lunes? ¿los sábados?
2. ¿Te despiertas con un despertador?
3. ¿Comes el desayuno antes o después de bañarte?
4. ¿Te secas el pelo con un secador de pelo?
5. ¿A qué hora te acuestas normalmente?

Answers
Answers will vary. Answers could include:
1. Los lunes me levanto a las seis. Los sábados me levanto a las nueve.
2. Sí, me despierto con un despertador.
3. Como el desayuno después de bañarme.
4. No, no me seco el pelo con un secador de pelo.
5. Normalmente me acuesto a las diez.

✔ Teaching Suggestions
What Have Students Learned?

Have students look at the "Now you can…" notes and give examples of each category. Have them spend extra time reviewing categories they feel they are weak in, by consulting the "To review" notes.

Now you can...

• describe daily routine.

To review

• reflexive verbs, see p. 320.

En uso

REPASO Y MÁS COMUNICACIÓN

OBJECTIVES

• Describe daily routine
• Talk about grooming
• Tell others to do something
• Discuss daily chores

ACTIVIDAD 1 Nuestra rutina diaria

Un amigo de Luis describe la rutina diaria de su familia. ¿Qué dice? *(Hint: Describe his family's daily routine.)*

modelo

Todos los días yo __me despierto__ a las siete.

1. Mis padres _____ a las seis y media.

2. Yo _____ después de levantarme.

3. Papá _____ a las siete menos cuarto.

4. Mamá _____ antes de prepararnos el desayuno.

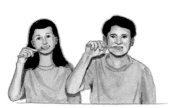

5. Nosotros _____ los dientes después del desayuno.

6. Mi hermana _____ por la noche.

330 trescientos treinta
Unidad 5

Classroom Community

Paired Activity   Have students do **Actividades 1–4** in pairs. One student does the odd-numbered items and the other does the even-numbered items. Be sure that students discuss when they disagree about an answer.

Group Activity   Have students work in groups of 4–5. Assign each group a location: school, home, restaurant, library, daycare, etc. The groups must write 3 affirmative and 3 negative **tú** commands that would be heard in that location. Then have the groups read their commands as the other groups guess the location.

Now you can...

• talk about grooming.

To review

• reflexive verbs, see p. 320.

reflexive verbs, see p. 320.

ACTIVIDAD
2 ¡De viaje!

Luis y su familia van a hacer un viaje. ¿Qué necesitan llevar todos? *(Hint: Say what they need.)*

1. maquillarse (mamá)
2. lavarse los dientes (tú)
3. despertarse (nosotros)
4. secarse (tú)
5. lavarse la cabeza (yo)
6. secarse el pelo (Carmen y yo)
7. peinarse (papá)
8. lavarse las manos (ustedes)

modelo

lavarse la cara (yo)

Yo necesito jabón para lavarme la cara.

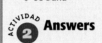

ACTIVIDAD
1 Answers

1. se levantan
2. me ducho
3. se afeita
4. se peina
5. nos lavamos
6 se baña

ACTIVIDAD
2 Answers

1. Mamá necesita el espejo para maquillarse.
2. Tú necesitas el cepillo de dientes y la pasta de dientes para lavarte los dientes.
3. Nosotros necesitamos el despertador para despertarnos.
4. Tú necesitas la toalla para secarte.
5. Yo necesito el champú para lavarme la cabeza.
6. Carmen y yo necesitamos el secador de pelo para secarnos el pelo.
7. Papá necesita el peine para peinarse.
8. Ustedes necesitan jabón para lavarse las manos.

Now you can...

• tell others to do something.

To review

• irregular affirmative **tú** commands, see p. 322.

• negative **tú** commands, see p. 324.

ACTIVIDAD
3 A casa de los abuelos

Vas a pasar el fin de semana con tus abuelos. ¿Qué te dice tu mamá? *(Hint: What does your mother say?)*

modelo

ser simpático(a)   *levantarte muy tarde*

Sé simpático(a).   *No te levantes muy tarde.*

1. hacer los quehaceres
2. ser perezoso(a)
3. salir con tus abuelos y no con tus amigos
4. ir a fiestas con tus amigos
5. decir cosas interesantes
6. ser bueno(a)
7. ponerte otra camisa
8. llevar ropa sucia
9. ir al supermercado con tu abuela
10. tener paciencia con tus abuelos

ACTIVIDAD
3 Answers

Answers will vary.
1. Haz los quehaceres.
2. No seas perezoso(a).
3. Sal con tus abuelos y no con tus amigos.
4. No vayas a fiestas con tus amigos.
5. Di cosas interesantes.
6. Sé bueno(a).
7. Ponte otra camisa.
8. No lleves ropa sucia.
9. Ve al supermercado con tu abuela.
10. Ten paciencia con tus abuelos.

Now you can...

• tell others to do something.
• discuss daily chores.

To review

• pronoun placement with commands, see p. 325.

ACTIVIDAD
4 ¡A trabajar!

Un(a) amigo(a) quiere ayudarte con los quehaceres. Contesta sus preguntas. *(Hint: Answer a friend's questions.)*

modelo

¿Compro los refrescos? (sí)   *¿Preparo la cena? (no)*

Sí, cómpralos.   *No, no la prepares.*

1. ¿Hago las camas? (sí)
2. ¿Lavo los platos sucios? (sí)
3. ¿Cuido a tu hermano? (no)
4. ¿Quito la mesa? (no)
5. ¿Mando las cartas? (sí)
6. ¿Contesto el teléfono? (no)

ACTIVIDAD
4 Answers

1. Sí, hazlas.
2. Sí, lávalos.
3. No, no lo cuides.
4. No, no la quites.
5. Sí, mándalas.
6. No, no lo contestes.

Teaching All Students

Extra Help Before completing **Actividad 2**, have students review the grooming and daily routine items on pp. 314–315.

Challenge Have students extend **Actividad 4** with more questions.

Multiple Intelligences

Visual Have students create **día/noche** posters. Each part of the poster should be decorated and labeled with appropriate activities and times. Students should use as many reflexive verbs as possible.

Naturalist Have students research water resources/water use associated with daily routine activities and suggest conservation ideas on a poster in Spanish.

▪ Block Schedule

Variety Use a toy clock or draw a clock on the board. Use a sun and moon to indicate day and night. Give students a time and elicit commands they might hear at that time of day. For example, for 8 A.M.: **Son las ocho de la mañana. ¡Ve a clase!**

Teaching Resource Options

Print

Unit 5 Resource Book
  Cooperative Quizzes, pp. 33–34
  Etapa Exam, Forms A and B,
    pp. 35–44
  Para hispanohablantes Etapa Exam,
    pp. 45–49
  Portfolio Assessment, pp. 50–51
  Multiple Choice Test Questions,
    pp. 170–178

Audiovisual

OHT 150 (Quick Start)
Audio Program Testing Cassette T2 /
CD T2

Technology

Electronic Teacher Tools/Test
  Generator
www.mcdougallittell.com

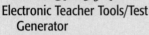

ACTIVIDAD 5

Rubric: Speaking

Criteria	Scale	
Sentence structure	1 2 3	A = 11–12 pts.
Vocabulary use	1 2 3	B = 9–10 pts.
Originality	1 2 3	C = 7–8 pts.
Fluency	1 2 3	D = 4–6 pts.
		F = < 4 pts.

ACTIVIDAD 6 *Answers will vary.*

ACTIVIDAD 7   **En tu propia voz**

Rubric: Writing

Criteria	Scale	
Vocabulary use	1 2 3 4 5	A = 14–15 pts.
Accuracy	1 2 3 4 5	B = 12–13 pts.
Creativity, appearance	1 2 3 4 5	C = 10–11 pts.
		D = 8–9 pts.
		F = < 8 pts.

Teaching Note: En tu propia voz

Suggest that students brainstorm a list of
activities and times in order to implement
the writing strategy "Organize information
chronologically and by category" in the
paragraph describing their typical Saturday.

ACTIVIDAD 5 **Todos los días...**

PARA CONVERSAR

STRATEGY: SPEAKING

Use gestures Physical actions, gestures, and
body language convey meaning too. Watch
your partner's actions. Do they convey
meaning? Observe others, especially native
speakers, and mimic body language to
enhance meaning when you speak.

Describe tu rutina diaria. Explica a qué hora
haces las actividades. Mientras hablas, otro(a)
estudiante tiene que hacer las acciones. Cambien
de papel. *(Hint: Describe your routine as your partner acts it out.)*

modelo

*Me levanto a las seis de la mañana. Después de
levantarme, siempre me ducho. A las seis y media…*

despertarse   **bañarse**   afeitarse

levantarse   **lavarse la cabeza**   maquillarse

ducharse   peinarse   ponerse la ropa

ACTIVIDAD 6 **¡Necesito consejos!**

Imagínate que tienes uno de los problemas de la
lista. ¿Qué consejo van a darte tus compañeros?
(Hint: What advice do they give?)

modelo

Tú: *Siempre tengo sueño en mis clases. Estoy cansado
todo el día.*

Estudiante 1: *Acuéstate más temprano.*

Estudiante 2: *No te levantes hasta las siete.*

- Tu casa es un desastre y tus padres tienen una
  fiesta esta noche.
- Estás enfermo(a).
- Siempre tienes sueño en tus clases.
- Sacas malas notas en la clase de español.
- Comes mucho y no haces ejercicio.
- Estás muy sucio(a) después de trabajar
  mucho.
- ¿?

ACTIVIDAD 7 *En tu propia voz*

ESCRITURA Describe un sábado típico en tu
casa. Incluye las rutinas y los quehaceres de los
miembros de tu familia. *(Hint: Describe a Saturday.)*

CONEXIONES

El arte Which kind of art do you prefer? Modern?
Traditional? Still life? Portraits? Who is your
favorite painter? Paint (or draw) a portrait
(**un retrato**) or a still life (**una naturaleza
muerta**) in the style you prefer. Then explain
to a partner what is in your painting. Compare
your painting (in terms of style, subject, and colors)
with your partner's. Complete a Venn diagram.

Mi cuadro   El cuadro
              de Teresa

Classroom Community

Pair Activity Have students modify **Actividad 5** by
using the chores given on p. 323 in the **Vocabulario**
and in **Actividad 11**.

Group Activity Working in small groups, have one
student pantomime a daily routine. The rest of the
group watches and writes down what they see. At the
end of each person's pantomime, have students
compare their interpretations.

En resumen
REPASO DE VOCABULARIO

DESCRIBING DAILY ROUTINE

acostarse	to go to bed
afeitarse	to shave oneself
bañarse	to take a bath
despertarse	to wake up
dormirse	to fall asleep
ducharse	to take a shower
lavarse	to wash oneself
lavarse la cabeza	to wash one's hair
lavarse los dientes	to brush one's teeth
levantarse	to get up
maquillarse	to put on makeup
peinarse	to comb one's hair
ponerse la ropa	to get dressed
secarse	to dry oneself

TALKING ABOUT GROOMING

Items

el cepillo (de dientes)	brush (toothbrush)
el champú	shampoo
el espejo	mirror
el jabón	soap
la pasta de dientes	toothpaste
el peine	comb
el secador de pelo	hair dryer
la toalla	towel

Parts of the Body

la boca	mouth
el brazo	arm
la cabeza	head
la cara	face
el cuerpo	body
el diente	tooth
el estómago	stomach
la mano	hand
la nariz	nose
la oreja	ear
el pie	foot
la pierna	leg

DISCUSSING DAILY CHORES

hacer la cama	to make the bed
lavar los platos	to wash the dishes
limpiar el cuarto	to clean the room
limpio(a)	clean
los quehaceres	chores
quitar la mesa	to clear the table
sucio(a)	dirty

OTHER WORDS AND PHRASES

la cama	bed
el despertador	alarm clock
duro(a)	hard, tough
irse	to leave, to go away
la manta	blanket
ponerse	to put on (clothes)

Juego

Ya son las siete. ¿Qué necesitan estos chicos para prepararse y llegar a tiempo a la escuela?

1.

2.

3.

4.

trescientos treinta y tres
Etapa 1   333

Teaching All Students

Extra Help Have students study the **Repaso de vocabulario** for 5 minutes. Then have them close their books. Give a category (describing daily routine, grooming items, parts of the body, daily chores) and see how many words students can list from memory in that category.

Native Speakers Have students talk about frequently-used gestures in their communities. What gestures are used when talking? Are there any gestures that would be considered inappropriate in their communities that are not considered as such in the U.S.?

Critical Thinking
Ask students to discuss the reasons behind their art preferences. Did they go to museums when they were young? Do personal color preferences play a role?

Community Connections
Have students look in the arts/cultural section of major area newspapers. Can they find any exhibits of Spanish-speaking artists? They might also look on the Internet.

Interdisciplinary Connection
Art Work with the Art department to help students compile a list of well-known Spanish-speaking artists. Have each student choose one artist to research and present.

Quick Start Review
♻ Etapa vocabulary

Use OHT 150 or write on the board: Use reflexive verbs to write 5 things you do in the morning before school.

Answers *See p. 311D*

Teaching Suggestions
Vocabulary Review

First, name items associated with different parts of the body and have students identify what part (**el champú = la cabeza**). Then give commands and have students identify the parts of the body associated with them (**Ponte los zapatos. = los pies**)

Juego
Answers: **un despertador, un secador de pelo, un peine, un espejo**

Block Schedule
Retention Without looking back at the **Diálogo**, first have students write a summary of Luis's day. Then tell them to open their books to pp. 316–317 to see how accurate they were. They should correct any errors. Then have students write a paragraph about what might happen after scene 10.

Planning Guide CLASSROOM MANAGEMENT

OBJECTIVES

Communication
- Saying what people are doing *pp. 336–337*
- Persuading others *pp. 338–339*
- Describing a house *pp. 336–337*
- Negotiating responsibilities *pp. 338–339*

Grammar
- Pronouns with the present progressive *pp. 342–344*
- The verb **deber** *pp. 345–346*
- Adverbs that end in **-mente** *pp. 347–348*

Pronunciation
- Pronunciation of **c, p, t** *p. 349*
- Dictation *TE p. 349*

Culture
- Regional vocabulary *pp. 340, 348*
- Spanish **tortillas** *p. 341*
- **Tapas** *pp. 350–351*

♻ Recycling
- Affirmative **tú** commands *pp. 340, 346*
- Reflexive verbs *p. 343*
- Expressing extremes *p. 347*
- Daily chores *p. 348*

STRATEGIES

Listening Strategies
- Note and compare *p. 338*

Speaking Strategies
- Negotiate *p. 342*
- Detect misunderstandings *p. 354*

Reading Strategies
- Scan for crucial details *TE p. 350*

Writing Strategies
- Use different kinds of descriptive words *TE p. 354*

Connecting Cultures Strategies
- Recognize variations in regional vocabulary *pp. 340, 348*
- Learn about **tortillas** in Spain *p. 341*
- Predict reactions about restaurants *p. 350*
- Connect and compare what you know about eating experiences in your community to help you learn about eating experiences in a new community *pp. 350–351*

PROGRAM RESOURCES

 Print
- *Más práctica* Workbook PE *pp. 113–120*
- Block Scheduling Copymasters *pp. 113–120*
- Unit 5 Resource Book
  Más práctica Workbook TE *pp. 52–59*
  Para hispanohablantes Workbook TE *pp. 60–67*

- Information Gap Activities *pp. 68–71*
- Family Involvement *pp. 72–73*
- Video Activities *pp. 74–76*
- Videoscript *pp. 77–79*
- Audioscript *pp. 80–83*
- Assessment Program, Unit 5 Etapa 2 *pp. 84–102; 170–178*
- Answer Keys *pp. 179–200*

 Audiovisual
- **Audio Program** Cassettes 14A, 14B / CD 14
- *Canciones* Cassette / CD
- **Video Program** Videotape 5 / Videodisc 3A
- **Overhead Transparencies** M1–M5; 139; 151–160

 Technology
- Electronic Teacher Tools/Test Generator
- *Intrigas y aventuras* CD-ROM, Disc 1
- www.mcdougallittell.com

 Assessment Program Options
- **Cooperative Quizzes** (Unit 5 Resource Book)
- **Etapa Exam** Forms A and B (Unit 5 Resource Book)
- *Para hispanohablantes* **Etapa Exam** (Unit 5 Resource Book)
- **Portfolio Assessment** (Unit 5 Resource Book)
- **Multiple Choice Test Questions** (Unit 5 Resource Book)
- **Audio Program** Testing Cassette T2 / CD T2
- **Electronic Teacher Tools/Test Generator**

Native Speakers
- *Para hispanohablantes* Workbook PE, *pp. 113–120*
- *Para hispanohablantes* Workbook TE (Unit 5 Resource Book)
- *Para hispanohablantes* Etapa Exam (Unit 5 Resource Book)
- Audio *Para hispanohablantes* Cassettes 14A, 14B, T2 / CD 14, T2
- Audioscript *Para hispanohablantes* (Unit 5 Resource Book)

Student Text
Listening Activity Scripts

 Videoscript: Diálogo *pages 338–339*

• Videotape 5 • Videodisc 3A

Search Chapter 5, Play to 6
U5E2 • En vivo (Dialog)

• Use the videoscript with **Actividades 1, 2** *page 340*

Luis: Carmen, Mercedes, ¿me ayudáis con los quehaceres?

Carmen: ¿Por qué te debo ayudar?

Luis: A ver. ¿Porque eres una hermana muy maja?
Porque si limpias la sala, te llevo al cine mañana.

Carmen: ¿Eso es todo?

Luis: Te doy un regalo.

Carmen: ¿Qué me vas a dar? ¡Dámelo ahora!

Luis: No, no, después. Primero quita el polvo de la mesa.

Carmen: Ya, ya, estoy quitándolo.

Luis: Mercedes, ¿todavía estás sacando fotos?

Mercedes: Sí, estoy sacándolas para algo muy importante.

Luis: ¿No ves que estoy barriendo el suelo?

Mercedes: Claro, veo que estás barriéndolo. Pero necesito las fotos.

Luis: En vez de sacar fotos, debes ayudarme. Si no me ayudas, vamos a llegar tarde a casa de Álvaro. ¡Me estás volviendo loco con esa cámara!

Mercedes: Está bien, Luis. Ahora te estoy ayudando.

Luis: Carmen, ¿qué estás haciendo? ¿Por qué no estás pasando la aspiradora?

Carmen: Sí, sí, mira, estoy pasándola.

Luis: Pero, Carmen, debes pasarla cuidadosamente. Mira, hazlo como lo estoy haciendo yo, lentamente.

Carmen: Ay, pero Luis, quiero terminar rápidamente.

Luis: Lentamente.
Todavía hay que lavar los platos y sacar la basura.

Mercedes: Tú debes sacar la basura. Yo ayudo a Carmen a lavar los platos. ¿Está bien, Carmen?

Carmen: ¡Sí, perfecto!

Luis: Bueno. Y después vamos a la tienda.
Pero, ¿qué hacéis? ¿Y los platos?

Carmen: Estamos lavándolos, ¿no ves?

9 ¡Qué inteligente! *page 343*

Álvaro: ¡Hola! Ana. ¿Quieres ir al cine esta tarde?

Ana: Gracias, Álvaro, pero no puedo. Estoy ayudando a mi mamá.

Álvaro: ¿Qué están haciendo?

Ana: Estamos limpiando la casa.

Álvaro: ¡Ay! ¡Qué trabajo! ¿Están ayudándote tus hermanos?

Ana: ¡Claro que están ayudándome!

Álvaro: ¿Qué están haciendo?

Ana: Pues, Felipe y Paco están barriendo el suelo.

Álvaro: ¿Y tus hermanas?

Ana: Marta está quitando el polvo y Lucía está pasando la aspiradora.

Álvaro: ¿Y tú? ¿Qué estás haciendo?

Ana: Yo... pues... yo estoy ¡diciéndoles qué hacer!

15 ¿En qué orden? *page 346*

Mi familia y yo vamos a hacer una fiesta para mi abuelo. Él va a cumplir setenta años. ¡Ay! ¡Es mucho trabajo! ¿Cómo empezamos? Bueno, primero debemos mandar las invitaciones. Luego, debo comprar un regalo. A mi abuelo le gustan los artículos de cuero. Le compro una cartera o un cinturón. Después, mi mamá debe hacer una tarta. Y como a él le gustan los dulces, ¡le va a hacer una tarta muy grande! Luego, el día de la fiesta, debemos preparar la comida: chorizo, calamares, jamón... ¡Sí! ¡Va a ser una fiesta fenomenal!

Quick Start Review Answers

p. 340 Dialog review
1. Primero quita el polvo de la mesa.
2. Tú debes sacar la basura.
3. ¿Porque eres una hermana muy maja?
4. Estoy barriendo el suelo.

p. 342 Household chores
1. barrer el suelo
2. sacar la basura
3. quitar el polvo
4. hacer la cama
5. pasar la aspiradora

p. 347 Vocabulary review
1. llave
2. reciente
3. tapas
4. deber
5. baño

Sample Lesson Plan - 50 Minute Schedule

DAY 1

Etapa Opener
- Quick Start Review (TE, p. 334) **5 MIN.**
- Anticipate/Activate prior knowledge: Have students look at the *Etapa* Opener and answer the questions. **5 MIN.**

En contexto: Vocabulario
- Quick Start Review (TE, p. 336) **5 MIN.**
- Have students use context and pictures to learn *Etapa* vocabulary. In pairs, have students answer the questions, p. 337. Use the Situational OHTs for additional practice. **10 MIN.**

En vivo: Diálogo
- Quick Start Review (TE, p. 338) **5 MIN.**
- Review the Listening Strategy, p. 338. Play audio or show video for the dialog, pp. 338–339. **10 MIN.**
- Replay twice. Read aloud, having students take the roles of characters. **10 MIN.**

Homework Option:
- Video Activities, Unit 5 Resource Book, pp. 74–76.

DAY 2

En acción: Vocabulario y gramática
- Check homework. **5 MIN.**
- Quick Start Review (TE, p. 340) **5 MIN.**
- Use OHT 151 and 152 to review *En contexto* vocabulary. Ask students for a summary of the dialog to check recall. **10 MIN.**
- Play the video/audio; have students do *Actividades* 1 and 2. **10 MIN.**
- Have students complete *Actividad* 3 in pairs. **5 MIN.**
- Have students read and complete *Actividad* 4 in writing. Have them exchange papers for peer correction. **5 MIN.**
- Do *Actividad* 5 orally. **5 MIN.**
- Present the Speaking Strategy, p. 342. Then present the *Nota* and have students do *Actividad* 6 in pairs. **10 MIN.**

Homework Option:
- Have students write 5 true/false statements about the dialog and complete *Actividad* 5 in writing.

DAY 3

En acción (cont.)
- Check homework. **5 MIN.**
- Quick Start Review (TE, p. 342) **5 MIN.**
- Present *Gramática:* Using Pronouns with the Present Progressive, p. 342. **10 MIN.**
- Present the *Vocabulario,* p. 343. Then have students complete *Actividad* 7 in pairs. **10 MIN.**
- Present the *Nota.* Then have students do *Actividad* 8 in pairs. Have a few pairs present their mini-dialogs. **10 MIN.**
- Play the audio; do *Actividad* 9. **5 MIN.**
- Have students complete *Actividad* 10 in pairs. Have volunteer pairs present the various items. **10 MIN.**

Homework Option:
- Have students make flashcards of the *Vocabulario,* p. 343. *Más práctica* Workbook, pp. 117–118. *Para hispanohablantes* Workbook, pp. 115–116.

DAY 4

En acción (cont.)
- Check homework. **5 MIN.**
- Have students complete *Actividad* 11 in writing. Have students exchange papers for peer correction. Expand using Information Gap Activities, Unit 5 Resource Book, p. 68; *Más comunicación,* p. R14. **20 MIN.**
- Quick Start Review (TE, p. 345) **5 MIN.**
- Present *Gramática:* Using the Verb *deber,* p. 345. **5 MIN.**
- Present the *Vocabulario,* p. 345. Then do *Actividad* 12 orally. **5 MIN.**
- Have students complete *Actividades* 13 and 14 in pairs. Have several pairs present their mini-dialogs. **10 MIN.**
- Play the audio; do *Actividad* 15. **5 MIN.**

Homework Option:
- Have students complete *Actividad* 12 in writing. *Más práctica* Workbook, p. 119. *Para hispanohablantes* Workbook, p. 117.

DAY 5

En acción (cont.)
- Check homework. **5 MIN.**
- Have students do *Actividad* 16 in writing. Have volunteers write answers on the board. **10 MIN.**
- Quick Start Review (TE, p. 347) **5 MIN.**
- Present *Gramática:* Using Adverbs That End in *-mente,* p. 347. **10 MIN.**
- Have students read and complete *Actividad* 17. **5 MIN.**
- Do *Actividad* 18 orally. **5 MIN.**
- Have students read and complete *Actividad* 19. **5 MIN.**
- Have students do *Actividad* 20 in pairs. **10 MIN.**

Homework Option:
- Have students complete *Actividad* 18 in writing. *Más práctica* Workbook, p. 120. *Para hispanohablantes* Workbook, p. 118.

DAY 6

En acción (cont.)
- Check homework. **5 MIN.**
- Have students complete *Actividad* 21 in groups. Expand using Information Gap Activities, Unit 5 Resource Book, pp. 69–70; *Más comunicación,* p. R14. **20 MIN.**

Pronunciación
- Play the audio and have students practice the *trabalenguas.* **5 MIN.**

En colores: Cultura y comparaciones
- Quick Start Review (TE, p. 350) **5 MIN.**
- Review the Connecting Cultures Strategy, p. 350. Have volunteers read the selection aloud and answer the questions, p. 351. Show video culture presentation for expansion. **20 MIN.**

Homework Option:
- Have students complete the *¿Comprendiste?/¿Qué piensas?* questions in writing.

DAY 7

En uso: Repaso y más comunicación
- Check homework. **5 MIN.**
- Quick Start Review (TE, p. 352) **5 MIN.**
- Have students do *Actividad* 1 in pairs. **5 MIN.**
- Have students do *Actividad* 2 in writing. Go over answers as a class. **5 MIN.**
- Do *Actividad* 3 orally and *Actividad* 4 in pairs. **10 MIN.**
- Present the Speaking Strategy, p. 354. Have students do *Actividad* 5 in pairs. **5 MIN.**
- Have students do *Actividad* 6 in groups. **5 MIN.**

En tu propia voz: Escritura
- Do *Actividad* 7 in writing. Have a few students present their descriptions. **15 MIN.**

Homework Option:
- Review for *Etapa* 2 Exam.

DAY 8

Tú en la comunidad
- Read and discuss *Tú en la comunidad,* p. 354. **5 MIN.**

En resumen: Repaso de vocabulario
- Quick Start Review (TE, p. 355) **5 MIN.**
- Review grammar questions, etc. as necessary. **10 MIN.**
- Complete *Etapa* 2 Exam. **20 MIN.**

Ampliación
- Use a suggested project, game, or activity. (TE, pp. 311A–311B) **10 MIN.**

Homework Option:
- Preview *Etapa* 3 Opener.

Sample Lesson Plan - Block Schedule (90 minutes)

DAY 1

Etapa Opener
- Quick Start Review (TE, p. 334) 5 MIN.
- Anticipate/Activate prior knowledge: Have students look at the *Etapa* Opener and answer the questions. 5 MIN.
- Use Block Scheduling Copymasters. 10 MIN.

En contexto: Vocabulario
- Quick Start Review (TE, p. 336) 5 MIN.
- Have students use context and pictures to learn *Etapa* vocabulary. In pairs, have students answer the questions, p. 337. Use the Situational OHTs for additional practice. 10 MIN.

En vivo: Diálogo
- Quick Start Review (TE, p. 338) 5 MIN.
- Review the Listening Strategy, p. 338. Play audio or show video for the dialog, pp. 338–339. Replay and have students take the roles of characters. 20 MIN.

En acción: Vocabulario y gramática
- Quick Start Review (TE, p. 340) 5 MIN.
- Use OHT 151 and 152 to review *En contexto* vocabulary. Ask students for a summary of the dialog to check recall. 10 MIN.
- Play the video/audio; have students do *Actividades* 1 and 2. 10 MIN.
- Have students complete *Actividad* 3 in pairs. 5 MIN.

Homework Option:
- Have students write 5 true/false statements about the dialog. Video Activities, Unit 5 Resource Book, pp. 74–76.

DAY 2

En acción (cont.)
- Check homework. 5 MIN.
- Have students read and complete *Actividad* 4 in writing. Have them exchange papers for peer correction. 5 MIN.
- Do *Actividad* 5 orally. 5 MIN.
- Present the Speaking Strategy, p. 342. Then present the *Nota* and have students do *Actividad* 6 in pairs. 10 MIN.
- Quick Start Review (TE, p. 342) 5 MIN.
- Present *Gramática:* Using Pronouns with the Present Progressive, p. 342. 10 MIN.
- Present the *Vocabulario,* p. 343. Then have students complete *Actividad* 7 in pairs. 10 MIN.
- Present the *Nota.* Then have students do *Actividad* 8 in pairs. Have a few pairs present their mini-dialogs. 10 MIN.
- Play the audio; do *Actividad* 9. 5 MIN.
- Have students complete *Actividad* 10 in pairs. Have volunteer pairs present the various items. 5 MIN.
- Have students complete *Actividad* 11 in writing. Have students exchange papers for peer correction. Expand using Information Gap Activities, Unit 5 Resource Book, p. 68; *Más comunicación,* p. R14. 20 MIN.

Homework Option:
- Have students complete *Actividad* 5 in writing. Have students make flashcards of the *Vocabulario,* p. 343. *Más práctica* Workbook, pp. 117–118. *Para hispanohablantes* Workbook, pp. 115–116.

DAY 3

En acción (cont.)
- Check homework. 5 MIN.
- Quick Start Review (TE, p. 345) 5 MIN.
- Present *Gramática:* Using the Verb *deber,* p. 345. 5 MIN.
- Present the *Vocabulario,* p. 345. Then do *Actividad* 12 orally. 5 MIN.
- Have students complete *Actividades* 13 and 14 in pairs. Have several pairs present their mini-dialogs. 10 MIN.
- Play the audio; do *Actividad* 15. 5 MIN.
- Have students do *Actividad* 16 in writing. Have volunteers write answers on the board. 10 MIN.
- Quick Start Review (TE, p. 347) 5 MIN.
- Present *Gramática:* Using Adverbs That End in *-mente,* p. 347. 10 MIN.
- Have students read and complete *Actividad* 17. 5 MIN.
- Do *Actividad* 18 orally. 5 MIN.
- Have students read and complete *Actividad* 19. Discuss answers as a class. 10 MIN.
- Have students do *Actividad* 20 in pairs. 10 MIN.

Homework Option:
- Have students complete *Actividades* 12 and 18 in writing. *Más práctica* Workbook, pp. 119–120. *Para hispanohablantes* Workbook, pp. 117–118.

DAY 4

En acción (cont.)
- Check homework. 5 MIN.
- Have students complete *Actividad* 21 in groups. Expand using Information Gap Activities, Unit 5 Resource Book, pp. 69–70; *Más comunicación,* p. R14. 20 MIN.

Pronunciación
- Play the audio and have students practice the *trabalenguas.* 5 MIN.

En colores: Cultura y comparaciones
- Quick Start Review (TE, p. 350) 5 MIN.
- Review the Connecting Cultures Strategy, p. 350. Have volunteers read the selection aloud and answer the questions, p. 351. Show video culture presentation for expansion. 25 MIN.

En uso: Repaso y más comunicación
- Check homework. 5 MIN.
- Quick Start Review (TE, p. 352) 5 MIN.
- Have students do *Actividad* 1 in pairs. 5 MIN.
- Have students do *Actividades* 2–4 in writing. Go over answers as a class. 15 MIN.

Homework Option:
- Review for *Etapa* 2 Exam.

DAY 5

En uso: Repaso y más comunicación (cont.)
- Present the Speaking Strategy, p. 354. Have students do *Actividad* 5 in pairs. 5 MIN.
- Have students do *Actividad* 6 in groups. 5 MIN.

En tu propia voz: Escritura
- Do *Actividad* 7 in writing. Have a few students present their descriptions. 20 MIN.

Tú en la comunidad
- Read and discuss *Tú en la comunidad,* p. 354. 5 MIN.

En resumen: Repaso de vocabulario
- Quick Start Review (TE, p. 355) 5 MIN.
- Review grammar questions, etc. as necessary. 10 MIN.
- Complete *Etapa* 2 Exam. 20 MIN.

Ampliación
- Use a suggested project, game, or activity. (TE, pp. 311A–311B) 20 MIN.

Homework Option:
- Preview *Etapa* 3 Opener.

▼ Carmen y Mercedes le ayudan a Luis con los quehaceres.

Etapa Theme
Doing chores at home and negotiating responsibilities

Grammar Objectives
- Using pronouns with the present progressive
- Using the verb **deber**
- Using adverbs that end in **-mente**

Teaching Resource Options
Print

Block Scheduling Copymasters

Audiovisual

OHT 139, 157 (Quick Start)

Quick Start Review
♻ **Commands**

Use OHT 157 or write on the board: Your friend made the following statements. Give some advice, using a **tú** command:

1. Estoy muy cansado.
2. Necesito un libro sobre Picasso.
3. Esta comida no me gusta.
4. Hay una fiesta esta noche pero no quiero ir.
5. No sé dónde está mi libro.

Answers
Answers will vary. Answers could include:
1. Duerme más.
2. Ve a la biblioteca.
3. No la comas.
4. No vayas a la fiesta.
5. Búscalo.

Teaching Suggestions
Previewing the Etapa
- Ask students to study the picture on pp. 334–335 (1 min.).
- Have them close their books and share at least 3 items that they noticed.
- Have students identify the location of the 3 people and describe what they see.
- Use the **¿Qué ves?** questions to focus the discussion.

UNIDAD 5

ETAPA
2

¿Qué debo hacer?

- Say what people are doing
- Persuade others
- Describe a house
- Negotiate responsibilities

¿Qué ves?

Mira la foto de la tienda.

1. ¿La tienda vende muchas o pocas frutas?
2. ¿Quién compra muchas frutas: Carmen, Mercedes o Luis?
3. ¿Cuánto cuesta el pan?

334

Ofertas del día
Arroz
95 ptas.
Pan
50 ptas.
Leche - 100 ptas

Classroom Management

Planning Ahead Set up a doll house or other toy house with furniture in your classroom for use in working with the vocabulary in this **Etapa.**

Time Saver Assign the **¿Qué ves?** questions the night before. Review the answers in class.

Student Self-checks Before beginning the new material, have students write a list of items they might see in a market. Then have them check their accuracy with the **Repaso de vocabulario** lists at the end of each **Etapa.** You might also refer them to the **Vocabulario adicional** on p. R21.

335

Ask students what similarities and differences they notice between the market in this picture and those in the U.S. Also have them notice Mercedes' shopping basket. Would they see this kind of basket in the U.S.?

Culture Highlights

● **BARCELONA** Legend says that Barcelona was founded as Barcina about 2300 B.C. by General Hamilcar Barca, a Carthaginian. In the third century B.C., it became part of the Roman Empire. It was conquered by the Moors in 713, and then captured by Charlemagne in 801.

The modern center of Barcelona, known as **El Ensanche** (meaning "extension"), was built between 1870 and 1936. Some famous landmarks located here are **Sagrada Familia,** the University of Barcelona, and the **Plaza de Toros.**

Supplementary Vocabulary

la banana, el plátano	banana
la naranja	orange
la sandía	watermelon
el tomate	tomato
la canasta	basket

Teaching All Students

Extra Help Make true/false statements about the picture. If the statement is false, have students correct it. For example: **Hay dos muchachas en la foto. (Cierto) El muchacho se llama Álvaro. (Falso. Se llama Luis.) Los muchachos están en el mercado. (Cierto) El arroz cuesta 50 pesetas. (Falso. El arroz cuesta 95 pesetas.)**

Multiple Intelligences

Intrapersonal Have students write a list of what they would buy at the market in the photo. Have native speakers help with vocabulary and/or refer students to the **Vocabulario adicional** on p. R21.

Logical/Mathematical Have students research the exchange rate of the Spanish peseta. Then have them convert the prices in the sign on p. 334 into U.S. dollars.

Block Schedule

Extension In small groups, have students write and perform skits dealing with Luis, Mercedes, and Carmen in the market. The skits should include discussions about what to buy and bargaining with vendors. (For additional activities, see **Block Scheduling Copymasters.**)

Teaching Resource Options

Print

Unit 5 Resource Book
Video Activities, pp. 74–75
Videoscript, p. 77
Audioscript, p. 80
Audioscript *Para hispanohablantes*,
  p. 80

Audiovisual

OHT 151, 152, 153, 153A, 154, 154A,
157 (Quick Start)
Audio Program Cassette 14A / CD 14
Audio *Para hispanohablantes*
  Cassette 14A / CD 14
Video Program Videotape 5 / Videodisc
3A

Search Chapter 4, Play to 5
U5E2 • En contexto (Vocabulary)

Technology CD ROM

Intrigas y aventuras CD-ROM, Disc 1

Quick Start Review

♻ Activities

Use OHT 157 or write on the board:
List at least 3 activities for each place:

1. en casa
2. en la escuela
3. al aire libre (outside)

Answers

Answers will vary. Answers could include:
1. dormir, ver la televisión, comer
2. estudiar, hablar, escuchar
3. practicar deportes, ir de compras, sacar
   fotos

Language Note

Point out that the suffix **-ón** is used to
imply that something is large. **Un sillón** is
a large **silla**.

En contexto

VOCABULARIO

Luis and Carmen have a lot of chores to do!
See what they do to clean up their house.

A Luis **barre el suelo** de la cocina.

la cocina
la ventana
la pared
el suelo

el baño

B En **la habitación** de
Luis hay **una lámpara**
y **un armario**. Aquí
todo ya está limpio.

la habitación
la lámpara
el armario

336 trescientos treinta y seis
Unidad 5

Classroom Community

TPR Write the various chores and items in the home
on individual slips of paper. Distribute the slips to
students. Have students act out the activities or pretend
they are one of the items as the rest of the class
guesses what they are doing or what they are.

Paired Activity In pairs, have students ask and
answer questions about the chores they do at home.
They should use vocabulary from pp. 336–337, as well
as from **Etapa 1**, p. 323. As a class, ask students what
chores their partners are responsible for.

el jardín

el comedor

la mesa

la silla

quitar el polvo

D Luis **quita el polvo** de **la mesa** del **comedor.** También tiene que quitar el polvo de **las sillas.**

la puerta

la llave

la aspiradora

E Cuando terminan, Luis cierra **la puerta** de la casa con la **llave** y sale con Carmen.

la sala

los muebles

el sillón

el sofá

C

En **la sala** Carmen **pasa la aspiradora.** Aquí hay **unos muebles,** como **el sofá** y **el sillón.** También hay un televisor.

Preguntas personales

1. ¿Tienes jardín?
2. ¿Prefieres barrer el suelo o pasar la aspiradora?
3. ¿Quitas el polvo en la sala o en tu habitación?
4. ¿Dónde hay una mesa en tu casa?
5. ¿Qué muebles hay en tu habitación?

trescientos treinta y siete
Etapa 2 **337**

Teaching Suggestions
Introducing Vocabulary

- Have students look at pages 336–337. Use OHT 151 and 152 and Audio Cassette 14A / CD 14 to present the vocabulary.
- Ask the Comprehension Questions in order of yes/no (questions 1–3), either/or (questions 4–6), and simple word or phrase (questions 7–10). Expand by adding similar questions.
- Use the TPR activity to reinforce the meaning of individual words.
- Use the video vocabulary presentation for review and reinforcement.

Comprehension Questions

1. ¿Barre Luis el suelo de la cocina? (Sí.)
2. ¿Quita Luis el polvo de la pared? (No.)
3. ¿Tiene que quitar el polvo de las sillas? (Sí.)
4. ¿Tiene Luis un armario o dos armarios? (un armario)
5. ¿Ahora está sucia o limpia la habitación de Luis? (limpia)
6. ¿Tiene la casa jardín o no tiene jardín? (tiene jardín)
7. ¿Qué hace Carmen en la sala? (pasa la aspiradora)
8. ¿Qué hay en la sala? (un televisor, un sofá y un sillón)
9. ¿Qué usa Luis para cerrar la puerta de la casa? (una llave)
10. ¿Con quién sale Luis? (con Carmen)

Block Schedule
Categorize Have students work in pairs and make a complete list of chores (things to do in the house and outside). Then have them categorize the chores into those that need doing every day, twice a week, and once a week. Students could also then make a schedule and divide up the chores equally among the group members.

Teaching All Students

Extra Help Have students write down all the verbs on pp. 336–337. For those that are conjugated forms, they should also provide the infinitives. Then have them categorize the list into old verbs and new verbs.

Native Speakers Ask students about houses and apartments in their home communities. Do they look like those in the U.S.? What are the similarities and the differences?

Multiple Intelligences

Verbal Have students work in pairs to do the **Preguntas personales.** One student reads the question while the other listens with his/her book closed. He/she repeats the question, using the **yo** form of the verb, then answers it. For example: A: **¿Tienes jardín?** B: **¿Tengo jardín? Sí, tengo jardín.** Students then reverse roles.

Teaching Resource Options

Print
Más práctica Workbook PE,
pp. 113–116
Para hispanohablantes Workbook PE,
pp. 113–114
Block Scheduling Copymasters
Unit 5 Resource Book
Más práctica Workbook TE, pp. 52–55
Para hispanohablantes Workbook
TE, pp. 60–61
Video Activities, p. 76
Videoscript, p. 78
Audioscript, p. 80
Audioscript *Para hispanohablantes,*
p. 80

Audiovisual
OHT 155, 156, 157 (Quick Start)
Audio Program Cassette 14A / CD 14
Audio *Para hispanohablantes*
Cassette 14A / CD 14
Video Program Videotape 5 / Videodisc
3A

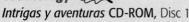

Search Chapter 5, Play to 6
U5E2 • En vivo (Dialog)

Technology
Intrigas y aventuras CD-ROM, Disc 1

🔔 Quick Start Review

♻️ **Household chores**

Use OHT 157 or write on the board:
List at least 5 household chores.

Answers
Answers will vary. Answers could include:
barrer el suelo, pasar la aspiradora, quitar el
polvo, hacer la cama, quitar la mesa, lavar los
platos, limpiar el cuarto

Gestures

Imitate some of the gestures used by the
characters in the dialog. Have students
identify the person and the scene number.
For example: Carmen standing with her
arms crossed in scene 2.

En vivo

  DIÁLOGO

¡A limpiar la casa!

| Luis | Carmen | Mercedes |

PARA ESCUCHAR • STRATEGY: LISTENING

Note and compare Jot down what you do to help around the house.
Then listen and note what Luis, Carmen, and Mercedes are doing.
How are your lists similar? How are they different? Who does
more? What do you think of Carmen's approach to her chores?

Yo	Luis, Carmen y Mercedes

1 ▶ Luis: Carmen, Mercedes, ¿me
ayudáis con los quehaceres?
Carmen: ¿Por qué te debo ayudar?
Luis: A ver. ¿Porque eres una
hermana muy maja?

5 ▶ Luis: En vez de sacar fotos, debes
ayudarme. Si no me ayudas,
vamos a llegar tarde a casa de
Álvaro.
Mercedes: Está bien, Luis. Ahora
te estoy ayudando.

6 ▶ Luis: Carmen, ¿qué estás haciendo? ¿Por
qué no estás pasando la aspiradora?
Carmen: Sí, sí, mira, estoy pasándola.

7 ▶ Luis: Pero, Carmen, debes pasarla
cuidadosamente. Mira, hazlo como
lo estoy haciendo yo, lentamente.
Carmen: ¡Ay, pero Luis! Quiero
terminar rápidamente.

338 trescientos treinta y ocho
Unidad 5

Classroom Community

Group Activity Have students work in groups of 3
to act out the **Diálogo.** Encourage students to use
appropriate gestures and intonation. Have the class
vote on the best presentation.

Paired Activity Have pairs of students contact a
cleaning service (they can check for ads in local
newspapers or on the Internet) and find out what
chores the service performs and the cost. Students
should report findings (in Spanish!) to the class. They
might also convert the cost in U.S. dollars to pesetas,
using the current exchange rate.

2 ▶ Luis: Porque si limpias la sala, te llevo al cine mañana.
Carmen: ¿Eso es todo?
Luis: Te doy un regalo.

3 ▶ Carmen: ¿Qué me vas a dar? ¡Dámelo ahora!
Luis: No, no, después. Primero quita el polvo de la mesa.
Carmen: Ya, ya, estoy quitándolo.

4 ▶ Luis: ¿Todavía estás sacando fotos?
Mercedes: Sí, estoy sacándolas para algo muy importante.
Luis: Estoy barriendo el suelo.
Mercedes: Claro, veo que estás barriéndolo. Pero necesito las fotos.

8 ▶ Luis: Todavía hay que lavar los platos y sacar la basura.
Mercedes: Tú debes sacar la basura. Yo ayudo a Carmen a lavar los platos. ¿Está bien, Carmen?

9 ▶ Carmen: ¡Sí, perfecto!
Luis: Bueno. Y después vamos a la tienda.

10 ▶ Luis: Pero, ¿qué hacéis? ¿Y los platos?
Mercedes: Estamos lavándolos, ¿no ves?

trescientos treinta y nueve
Etapa 2

339

Teaching All Students

Extra Help Have students write a list of household chores and tell who normally takes care of each task in their house.

Native Speakers Ask students about floor coverings in the houses/apartments in their home communities. Is it common to have carpeting?

Multiple Intelligences

Logical/Mathematical Have students price a variety of cleaning products and report their findings to the class. Also have students compare prices at two or more stores.

Naturalist Have students report on cleaning products that are environmentally safe. If some products have labels in Spanish, display them in class.

Teaching Suggestions
Presenting the Dialog

• Prepare students for listening by focusing on the dialog context using yes/no or either/or questions. Reintroduce the characters and the setting: **¿Dónde están los muchachos? ¿Cómo se llama el muchacho? ¿Cómo se llama la muchacha que saca fotos—Carmen o Mercedes? ¿Son hermanas Carmen y Mercedes?**

• Use the video, audio cassette, or CD to present the dialog. The expanded dialog on video offers additional listening practice opportunities.

Video Synopsis

• Luis, his little sister Carmen, and his friend Mercedes complete a list of chores. For a complete transcript of the video dialog, see p. 333B.

Comprehension Questions

1. ¿Quiere Carmen ayudar a Luis con los quehaceres? (No.)
2. ¿Dice Luis que Carmen es una hermana muy mala? (No.)
3. ¿Si Carmen limpia la sala, va a ir al cine? (Sí.)
4. ¿Quién les ayuda a Carmen y a Luis—Mercedes o Álvaro? (Mercedes)
5. ¿Va a recibir Carmen dinero o un regalo para limpiar la sala? (un regalo)
6. ¿Está Mercedes sacando fotos de Carmen o de Luis? (de Luis)
7. ¿Qué hace Luis cuando Mercedes saca fotos? (barre el suelo)
8. ¿Cómo pasa Carmen la aspiradora? (rápidamente)
9. ¿Quién va a sacar la basura? (Luis)
10. ¿Adónde van después de lavar los platos y sacar la basura? (a la tienda)

▣ Block Schedule

Change of Pace Before beginning the grammar presentations, have students begin work on some bulletin boards or posters from **Ampliación,** TE p. 311A. (For additional activities, see **Block Scheduling Copymasters.**)

Teaching Resource Options

Print

Unit 5 Resource Book
  Videoscript, p. 76
  Audioscript, p. 80
  Audioscript *Para hispanohablantes,*
  p. 80

Audiovisual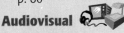

OHT 158 (Quick Start)
Audio Program Cassette 14A / CD 14
Audio *Para hispanohablantes*
  Cassette 14A / CD 14
Video Program Videotape 5 / Videodisc
  3A

Quick Start Review

♻ Dialog review

Use OHT 158 or write on the board:
Unscramble the words to make sentences
from the dialog.

1. quita / polvo / Primero / de /
   mesa / la / el
2. sacar / la / Tú / basura / debes
3. maja? / hermana / eres / muy /
   una / ¿Porque
4. barriendo / suelo / el / Estoy

Answers *See p. 333B.*

Teaching Suggestions
Comprehension Check

Use **Actividades 1** and **2** to assess
retention after the dialog. Have students
close their books. Act out the phrases
in **Actividad 1** and see if students can
comprehend and answer correctly.

 Objective: Transitional practice
Listening comprehension/vocabulary

Answers (See script, p. 333B.)
1. Carmen   4. Luis
2. Luis   5. Carmen y Mercedes
3. Carmen (y Luis)

 Objective: Transitional practice
Listening comprehension/vocabulary

Answers (See script, p. 333B.)
1. Cierto.
2. Falso. Carmen ayuda con los quehaceres.
3. Cierto.
4. Falso. Van a la casa de Álvaro.
5. Cierto.

En acción
VOCABULARIO Y GRAMÁTICA

OBJECTIVES
• Say what people are (
• Persuade others
• Describe a house
• Negotiate responsibili

ACTIVIDAD 1

¿Quién hace qué?

Escuchar ¿Quién(es) hace(n) cada quehacer
según el diálogo: Carmen, Mercedes o Luis?
(Hint: Say who does each chore.)

1. quita el polvo   4. saca la basura
2. barre el suelo   5. lava los platos
3. pasa la aspiradora

ACTIVIDAD 2

¿Cierto o falso?

Escuchar ¿Es cierto o falso? Corrige las falsas.
(Hint: True or false? Correct the false ones.)

1. Luis tiene muchos quehaceres.
2. Carmen no ayuda a Luis con los quehaceres.
3. Mercedes está sacando fotos.
4. Mercedes y Luis no van a salir esta tarde.
5. Mercedes ayuda a Carmen a lavar los
   platos.

> **TAMBIÉN SE DICE**
> There are different ways to describe a really wonderful
> person in Spanish. Luis uses one of them: **una hermana
> muy maja.**
> **Es muy maja:** Spain
> **Es muy buena onda:** Mexico
> **Es muy buena gente:** many countries

ACTIVIDAD 3

♻ ¿Dónde pongo...?

Hablar La señorita Díaz acaba de entrar en una
nueva casa. El trabajador le pregunta dónde
poner los muebles y otras cosas. ¿Qué dicen?
(Hint: Say in which room these things belong.)

modelo
Trabajador: ¿Dónde pongo **la mesa**?
Señorita Díaz: Ponla en la cocina.

1.

6.

2.

7.

3.

8.

4.

9.

5.

10.

340 trescientos cuarenta
Unidad 5

Classroom Management

Student Self-checks Assign **Actividades 4** and **5**
as homework. Hand out answers to the activities during
the next class and have students check their own work.

Organizing Group Work Plan to put students of
varying skills and abilities into groups to design a house
later in the unit. Each group should have students
skilled in art, creativity, language, and leadership skills.
(See TE p. 352.)

- Use pronouns with the present progressive
- Use the verb **deber**
- Use adverbs that end in **-mente**

ACTIVIDAD 4

La casa

Leer/Escribir Todos hablan de la casa. ¿Qué dicen? Escoge la respuesta más apropiada para cada oración. *(Hint: Choose the appropriate answer.)*

1. Siempre dormimos en _____.
   a. el baño
   b. el comedor
   c. las habitaciones

2. Normalmente, veo la televisión en _____.
   a. la sala
   b. el baño
   c. el jardín

3. Mi abuela prepara un almuerzo rico en la _____.
   a. pared
   b. cocina
   c. puerta

4. Abro la puerta con _____.
   a. el suelo
   b. la llave
   c. la ventana

5. Comemos en el _____.
   a. baño
   b. suelo
   c. comedor

6. Hay flores y plantas bonitas en _____.
   a. el jardín
   b. la pared
   c. la puerta

ACTIVIDAD 5

El plano de la casa

Hablar/Escribir Imagínate que eres arquitecto(a). Indícale a tu cliente cada cuarto o lugar en el plano de la casa. *(Hint: What is in the house?)*

modelo

Aquí está la sala. La sala tiene una puerta y tres ventanas.

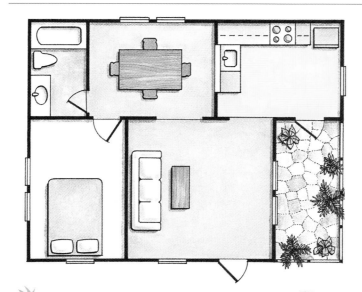

N O T A CULTURAL

When you ask for a **tortilla** in a restaurant in Spain, don't expect the kind of **tortilla** you eat in Mexico! In Spain, a **tortilla** is a dish made with eggs that is a lot like an omelet.

trescientos cuarenta y uno
Etapa 2 341

Objective: Transitional practice
House vocabulary in conversation
♻ Affirmative **tú** commands

Answers
1. Trabajador: ¿Dónde pongo el sofá?
   Señorita Díaz: Ponlo en la sala.
2. Trabajador: ¿Dónde pongo la mesa?
   Señorita Díaz: Ponla en el comedor.
3. Trabajador: ¿Dónde pongo las sillas?
   Señorita Díaz: Ponlas en la cocina.
4. Trabajador: ¿Dónde pongo la cama?
   Señorita Díaz: Ponla en la habitación.
5. Trabajador: ¿Dónde pongo la lámpara?
   Díaz: Ponla en la sala.
6. Trabajador: ¿Dónde pongo la mesa?
   Señorita Díaz: Ponla en la sala.
7. Trabajador: ¿Dónde pongo la ropa?
   Señorita Díaz: Ponla en la habitación.
8. Trabajador: ¿Dónde pongo el champú, el jabón y la pasta de dientes?
   Señorita Díaz: Ponlos en el baño.
9. Trabajador: ¿Dónde pongo el sillón?
   Señorita Díaz: Ponlo en la sala.
10. Trabajador: ¿Dónde pongo el televisor?
    Señorita Díaz: Ponlo en la sala.

Objective: Transitional practice
House vocabulary in reading

Answers
1. c 2. a 3. b 4. b 5. c 6. a

Objective: Transitional practice
House vocabulary

Answers
Answers will vary. Sample answer.
La sala tiene dos ventanas para ver el jardín. En otra pared hay otra ventana y una puerta. Al lado de la sala hay una habitación. La habitación tiene dos ventanas y una puerta. Al lado de la habitación está el baño. No tiene ventanas, pero tiene una puerta para ir al comedor. El comedor tiene dos puertas y dos ventanas. Al lado del comedor está la cocina. Tiene una puerta para ir al jardín y una ventana.

Teaching All Students

Extra Help Have students go back and combine the tasks in **Actividades 3** and **5**. As they repeat each of Señorita Díaz's commands in **Actividad 3,** have them point to the room in the house in **Actividad 5** where the item belongs.

Multiple Intelligences

Visual Have students create pairs of cards with drawings of rooms and household items on one and the Spanish words on the other. They can then use these cards to play a memory game, where they place the cards upside-down and take turns trying to turn over 2 matching cards.

Block Schedule

Variety First have each student draw a house floor plan and include the household items in the wrong rooms. Then have students exchange drawings with a partner. Each student tells the other how to rearrange the house. For example: **Pon la cama en la habitación.**

Teaching Resource Options

Print

Más práctica Workbook PE, pp. 117–118
Para hispanohablantes Workbook PE, pp. 115–116
Block Scheduling Copymasters
Unit 5 Resource Book
  Más práctica Workbook TE, pp. 56–57
  Para hispanohablantes Workbook TE, pp. 62–63
  Audioscript, p. 81
  Audioscript *Para hispanohablantes*, p. 82

Audiovisual

OHT 158 (Quick Start)
Audio Program Cassettes 14A, 14B / CD 14
Audio *Para hispanohablantes* Cassette 14A / CD 14

Technology

Intrigas y aventuras CD-ROM, Disc 1

ACTIVIDAD 6 **Objective:** Transitional practice
House vocabulary/*si* in conversation

Answers

First "tú" is given. Rest of answers will vary.
1. Si tú quitas la mesa, yo lavo los platos.
2. Si tú haces las camas, yo preparo el almuerzo.
3. Si tú pasas la aspiradora, yo barro el suelo.
4. Si tú lavas la ropa, yo quito el polvo.
5. Si tú cuidas al hermano, yo voy al supermercado.

🔔 Quick Start Review

♻ Household chores

Use OHT 158 or write on the board:
Fill in the missing letters to review vocabulary for household chores:

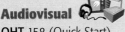

1. _ _ r _ _ _ el _ _ e _ _
2. _ _ c _ _ la _ _ s _ _ _
3. _ _ _ t _ _ el _ _ l _ _
4. _ a _ _ _ la c _ m _
5. _ _ s _ _ la _ s _ _ _ _ d _ _ _

Answers *See p. 333B.*

Teaching Suggestions
Presenting Using Pronouns with the Present Progressive

Tell students to return to the **Diálogo** on pp. 338–339 and find examples of the present progressive with pronouns.

ACTIVIDAD 6
Si tú pones la mesa...

PARA CONVERSAR
STRATEGY: SPEAKING
Negotiate Choose the chore you'd rather do. Then talk with your partner, who will express a preference. Decide who will do each.

Hablar Habla con un(a) amigo(a) sobre los quehaceres y escoge entre dos. *(Hint: Choose a chore.)*

modelo

poner la mesa / preparar la cena

Tú: *Si tú pones la mesa, yo preparo la cena.*

Amigo(a): *Prefiero preparar la cena.*

Tú: *Está bien. Yo pongo la mesa y tú preparas la cena.*

Nota

Use **si** (with no accent!) to say *if*.
Si tú pones la mesa, yo preparo la cena. *If you set the table, I'll make dinner.*

1. quitar la mesa / lavar los platos
2. hacer las camas / preparar el almuerzo
3. pasar la aspiradora / barrer el suelo
4. lavar la ropa / quitar el polvo
5. cuidar al hermano / ir al supermercado

342 trescientos cuarenta y dos
Unidad 5

GRAMÁTICA Using Pronouns with the Present Progressive

♻ **¿RECUERDAS?** *p. 226* Remember how you use the **present progressive** to describe actions in progress?

estoy **esperando**	estamos **esperando**
estás **esperando**	estáis **esperando**
está **esperando**	están **esperando**

▶ When you use **pronouns** with the **present progressive**, you can put them in one of two places.

- Put pronouns **before** the conjugated form of *estar*...
- or **attach** them to the end of the **present participle**.

Mercedes says: **attached**
—**Estoy sacándolas** para algo muy importante.
I'm taking them (the pictures) for something very important.

She could have said:
before
—**Las estoy sacando** para algo muy importante.

You need to add an **accent** when you attach a pronoun.
barriéndolo

▶ Some verbs you know have **irregular present participle forms.**

- When the **stem** of an **-er** or **-ir** verb ends in a vowel, change the **-iendo** to **-yendo** to form the present participle.
- **e → i** stem-changing verbs have a vowel change in the stem.
- Some other verbs also have a vowel change in the stem.

Verb	Irregular Present Participle
le**er**	le**y**endo
o**ír**	o**y**endo
tra**er**	tra**y**endo
p**e**dir	p**i**diendo
s**e**rvir	s**i**rviendo
d**e**cir	d**i**ciendo
d**o**rmir	d**u**rmiendo
v**e**nir	v**i**niendo

Classroom Community

Learning Scenario Have students work in groups to write and present a skit about a family getting ready for company. The parents give the children orders (¡Lava los platos! ¡Limpia tu habitación!). The children respond (¡Estoy lavándolos! ¡Estoy limpiándola ahora!). Encourage them to use vocabulary for telling time, rooms of the house, etc. as well as commands and pronouns with the present progressive.

Cooperative Learning Divide the class into groups of 5. On a piece of paper, Student 1 draws a floor plan of a house. Student 2 labels the rooms. Student 3 draws the outlines of furniture. Student 4 labels the furniture. Student 5 writes one chore for each room. All students review the work and suggest changes before turning in the drawing for a grade.

De compras

Hablar Mercedes y sus amigos están en un supermercado. Están comprando comida para una fiesta. Una prima la encuentra y quiere saber quién está comprando la comida con ella. *(Hint: Say who's buying the food.)*

modelo

las aceitunas (María)

Su prima: *¿Quién está comprando las aceitunas?*

Mercedes: *María las está comprando.*
    o: María está comprándolas.

1. el jamón (Enrique y Pedro)
2. la tortilla española (Marta)
3. los calamares (Isabel y Rocío)
4. el chorizo (Ana y yo)
5. el pan (Álvaro)

Vocabulario

Las tapas

el chorizo *sausage*

las aceitunas *olives*

los calamares *squid*

el jamón *ham*

la tortilla española *potato omelet*

Las tapas son porciones pequeñas de comida. ¿Cuáles te gustan?

♻ ¡Todos están ocupados!

Hablar Tu mamá te deja una lista de quehaceres. Pides ayuda, pero todos están ocupados. *(Hint: Ask for help.)*

modelo

preparar la comida (lavarse la cabeza)

Estudiante A: *¿Me puedes ayudar a preparar la comida?*

Estudiante B: *No puedo. Estoy lavándome la cabeza.*
    o: No puedo. Me estoy lavando la cabeza.

Nota

When using the present progressive, place reflexive pronouns as you would place direct and indirect object pronouns.

1. hacer la cama
   (lavarse la cabeza)
2. poner la mesa
   (afeitarse)
3. pasar la aspiradora
   (secarse el pelo)
4. barrer el suelo
   (ponerse la ropa)
5. lavar la ropa
   (peinarse)
6. limpiar la cocina
   (ponerse la ropa)
7. hacer el almuerzo
   (lavarse las manos)
8. lavar los platos
   (maquillarse)

■ **MÁS PRÁCTICA** *cuaderno* pp. 117–118

■ **PARA HISPANOHABLANTES** *cuaderno* pp. 115–116

¡Qué inteligente!

Escuchar Álvaro llama a una amiga para invitarla a salir. Escucha su conversación. Luego, explica lo que están haciendo las personas. *(Hint: Say what they are doing.)*

1. la madre de Ana
2. sus hermanos
3. sus hermanas
4. Ana

Teaching Resource Options

Print

Block Scheduling Copymasters
Unit 5 Resource Book
  Information Gap Activities, p. 68

Audiovisual

OHT 159 (Quick Start)

Technology

Intrigas y aventuras CD-ROM, Disc 1

---

10 **Objective:** Transitional practice
Pronouns with the present progressive
in conversation

Answers

1. Su madre: ¿Isabel y Rocío van a hacer las camas?
   Álvaro: Las están haciendo ahora.
   o: Están haciéndolas ahora.
2. Su madre: ¿Bárbara va a planchar las camisas?
   Álvaro: Las está planchando ahora.
   o: Está planchándolas ahora.
3. Su madre: ¿Leticia va a ordenar las flores?
   Álvaro: Las está ordenando ahora.
   o: Está ordenándolas ahora.
4. Su madre: ¿Andrés va a barrer el suelo?
   Álvaro: Lo está barriendo ahora.
   o: Está barriéndolo ahora.
5. Su madre: ¿Jorge va a sacar la basura?
   Álvaro: La está sacando ahora.
   o: Está sacándola ahora.
6. Su madre: ¿Linda va a pasar la aspiradora?
   Álvaro: La está pasando ahora.
   o: Está pasándola ahora.
7. Su madre: ¿Paco va a quitar el polvo?
   Álvaro: Lo está quitando ahora.
   o: Está quitándolo ahora.
8. Su madre: ¿Samuel y Pedro van a mover los muebles?
   Álvaro: Los están moviendo ahora.
   o: Están moviéndolos ahora.

---

11 **Objective:** Open-ended practice
Pronouns with the present progressive

Answers will vary.

Teaching Suggestions
Presenting Vocabulary

After presenting the new chores, have students recall those already learned. Call on volunteers to act out the various chores, while the rest of the class guesses.

¡Lo está haciendo ahora!

Hablar Álvaro y unos amigos están limpiando su casa. Su madre le pregunta si van a hacer algunos quehaceres. *(Hint: Say who's doing what.)*

modelo

vosotros

Su madre: ¿**Vosotros** vais a **limpiar el cuarto**?

Álvaro: **Lo estamos limpiando** ahora.
  o: **Estamos limpiándolo** ahora.

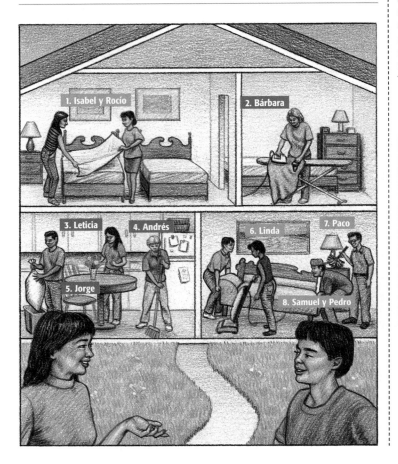

1. Isabel y Rocío
2. Bárbara
3. Leticia
4. Andrés
5. Jorge
6. Linda
7. Paco
8. Samuel y Pedro

344 trescientos cuarenta y cuatro
Unidad 5

El sábado

Escribir Imagínate que es sábado a las nueve de la mañana. ¿Qué está haciendo cada miembro de tu familia? ¿Dónde están? *(Hint: Say what people are doing and where.)*

modelo

Mi mamá está preparando el desayuno. Lo está preparando en la cocina. Mi hermana mayor está leyendo una novela. La está leyendo en su habitación. Mi papá está trabajando en el jardín…

■ **MÁS COMUNICACIÓN** p. R14

Vocabulario

Más quehaceres

mover (o → ue) los muebles
to move the furniture

ordenar (las flores, los libros)
to arrange (the flowers, books)

planchar (la ropa) *to iron (the clothes)*

sacar la basura *to take out the trash*

¿Quién hace estos quehaceres en tu casa?

Classroom Community

Group Activity Convert **Actividad 11** into a group activity. Have each group prepare questions about possible family Saturday activities and interview several students. Groups then report to the class their most common or unusual findings.

Portfolio Have students pretend that they want to earn some extra money by opening a spring cleaning service. They should write and decorate a flier that lists services and prices.

Rubric A = 13–15 pts. B = 10–12 pts. C = 7–9 pts. D = 4–6 pts. F = < 4 pts.

Writing criteria	Scale
Organization	1 2 3 4 5
Grammar/spelling accuracy	1 2 3 4 5
Creativity/appearance	1 2 3 4 5

GRAMÁTICA

Using the Verb deber

The verb **deber** means *should* or *ought to*. To say what people should do, use a **conjugated form of deber** with the **infinitive** of another verb.

deber	*should, ought to*
debo	debemos
debes	debéis
debe	deben

Debo **barrer** el suelo.
I should sweep the floor.

Debes **limpiar** la cocina.
You should clean the kitchen.

Debe **sacar** la basura.
He should take out the trash.

Carmen asks Luis: ← *before*
—¿Por qué **te** debo **ayudar**?
Why should I help you?

Luis tells Mercedes: *attached* ↘
—En vez de sacar fotos, debes **ayudarme**.
Instead of taking pictures, you should help me.

> Remember you can put a **pronoun** in front of a conjugated verb or attach it to an infinitive.

ACTIVIDAD 12 Gramática

¿Qué deben hacer todos para la fiesta?

Hablar/Escribir Mercedes explica lo que deben hacer sus amigos para una fiesta. *(Hint: Explain what they should do.)*

modelo

Luis / comprar platos **Luis debe comprar platos.**

1. Álvaro y sus amigos / limpiar la casa
2. Isabel / ordenar las flores
3. yo / hacer una tarta
4. mis amigos / comprar la comida
5. Yolanda y yo / escribir las invitaciones
6. tú / mandar las invitaciones

Vocabulario

La fiesta

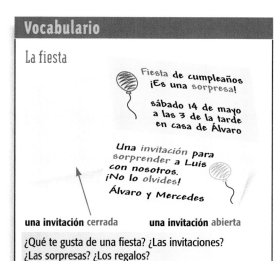

Fiesta de cumpleaños
¡Es una sorpresa!

sábado 14 de mayo
a las 3 de la tarde
en casa de Álvaro

Una invitación para
sorprender a Luis
con nosotros.
¡No lo olvides!

Álvaro y Mercedes

una invitación cerrada   **una invitación abierta**

¿Qué te gusta de una fiesta? ¿Las invitaciones?
¿Las sorpresas? ¿Los regalos?

trescientos cuarenta y cinco
Etapa 2   **345**

🔔 Quick Start Review

♻ Pronouns with the present progressive

Use OHT 159 or write on the board: Respond to these requests by saying that you are doing them.

Modelo: Limpia la cocina, por favor.
You write: **Estoy limpiándola.** *o:*
                 La estoy limpiando.

1. Prepara la cena, por favor.
2. Pon la mesa, por favor.
3. Cuida a los niños, por favor.
4. Lava los platos, por favor.
5. Barre el suelo, por favor.

Answers
1. Estoy preparándola. *o:* La estoy preparando.
2. Estoy poniéndola. *o:* La estoy poniendo.
3. Estoy cuidándolos. *o:* Los estoy cuidando.
4. Estoy lavándolos. *o:* Los estoy lavando.
5. Estoy barriéndolo. *o:* Lo estoy barriendo.

Teaching Suggestions
Presenting Using the Verb deber

Point out that the use of **deber** + infinitive is a gentler alternative to a direct command. Ask students in what contexts they would use a direct command and when they would prefer to use **Debes** + infinitive.

ACTIVIDAD 12 Objective: Controlled practice
The verb **deber**

Answers
1. Álvaro y sus amigos deben limpiar la casa.
2. Isabel debe ordenar las flores.
3. Yo debo hacer una tarta.
4. Mis amigos deben comprar la comida.
5. Yolanda y yo debemos escribir las invitaciones.
6. Tú debes mandar las invitaciones.

▪ Block Schedule

FunBreak Have students each create a drawing, similar to the one in the **Juego** on p. 322, where someone should do something **(Beto debe peinarse).** Display the drawings and have the class say what should happen for each one. (For additional activities, see **Block Scheduling Copymasters.**)

Teaching All Students

Extra Help Use the picture in **Actividad 10**. Describe an activity and have students point to the person performing the chore.

Multiple Intelligences

Intrapersonal Have students write a note to themselves about what they should do this week. Then have them write if they are going to do each thing or not.

Kinesthetic Write questions similar to those in **Actividad 10** on the board. Then give groups of 4 students sheets of paper with each word of an answer, plus an accent card. Groups must arrange words to answer the questions.

Teaching Resource Options

Print

Más práctica Workbook PE, pp. 119–120
Para hispanohablantes Workbook PE, pp. 117–118
Block Scheduling Copymasters
Unit 5 Resource Book
  Más práctica Workbook TE, pp. 58–59
  Para hispanohablantes Workbook TE, pp. 64–65
  Audioscript, p. 81
  Audioscript *Para hispanohablantes*, p. 82

Audiovisual

OHT 159 (Quick Start)
Audio Program Cassettes 14A, 14B / CD 14
Audio *Para hispanohablantes* Cassette 14A / CD 14

Technology

Intrigas y aventuras CD-ROM, Disc 1

Objective: Controlled practice
The verb **deber** in conversation
♻ Affirmative **tú** commands

Answers
1. Ana: ¿Debo ir a la tienda para comprar pan?
   Tú: Sí, ve a la tienda para comprar pan, por favor.
2. Raúl: ¿Debo decirle a Pepe cómo llegar a la casa?
   Tú: Sí, dile cómo llegar a la casa, por favor.
3. Elena: ¿Debo hacer las tapas?
   Tú: Sí, haz las tapas, por favor.
4. Diego: ¿Debo venir a la casa a las cinco?
   Tú: Sí, ven a la casa a las cinco, por favor.
5. Luisa: ¿Debo poner la mesa?
   Tú: Sí, pon la mesa, por favor.
6. Ramón: ¿Debo salir para comprar tenedores?
   Tú: Sí, sal para comprar tenedores, por favor.

Objective: Transitional practice
The verb **deber** in conversation

Answers
1. A: ¿Debo nadar después de comer?
   B: No, no debes nadar después de comer.
2. A: ¿Debo estudiar mucho para sacar buenas notas?
   B: Sí, debes estudiar mucho para sacar buenas notas.
3. A: ¿Debo lavarme las manos antes de comer?
   B: Sí, debes lavarte las manos antes de comer.
4. A: ¿Debo lavarme los dientes después de comer?
   B: Sí, debes lavarte los dientes después de comer.
5. A: ¿Debo llevar un casco en bicicleta?
   B: Sí, debes llevar un casco en bicicleta.
6. A: ¿Debo acostarme tarde?
   B: No, no debes acostarte tarde.

ACTIVIDAD 13 Gramática

♻ ¿Me puedes ayudar?

Hablar Estás organizando una cena y necesitas la ayuda de unos amigos. Los llamas por teléfono. ¿Qué dicen? *(Hint: What do you say?)*

modelo

Carmen: salir para comprar el postre

Carmen: ¿Debo **salir para comprar el postre**?

Tú: Sí, sal para comprar el postre, por favor.

1. Ana: ir a la tienda para comprar pan
2. Raúl: decirle a Pepe cómo llegar a la casa
3. Elena: hacer las tapas
4. Diego: venir a la casa a las cinco
5. Luisa: poner la mesa
6. Ramón: salir para comprar tenedores

MÁS PRÁCTICA *cuaderno* p. 119

PARA HISPANOHABLANTES *cuaderno* p. 117

ACTIVIDAD 14

¿Qué debes hacer?

Hablar Un(a) amigo(a) te pregunta si debe hacer algo o no. Contéstale. *(Hint: Say if a friend should do these things.)*

modelo

hacer la cama por la mañana

Estudiante A: ¿Debo **hacer la cama por la mañana**?

Estudiante B: Sí, debes hacer la cama por la mañana.

1. nadar después de comer
2. estudiar mucho para sacar buenas notas
3. lavarse las manos antes de comer
4. lavarse los dientes después de comer
5. llevar un casco en bicicleta
6. acostarse tarde

ACTIVIDAD 15

¿En qué orden?

Escuchar Liliana y su familia preparan una fiesta para su abuelo. Escucha lo que dice. Luego, indica el orden en que deben hacer las actividades. *(Hint: In what order should they do things?)*

a. preparar la comida
b. mandar las invitaciones
c. hacer la tarta
d. comprar el regalo

ACTIVIDAD 16

Para hacer una buena fiesta...

Escribir Un(a) amigo(a) te pregunta qué debe hacer para preparar una buena fiesta. Explícale todo. *(Hint: Explain what a friend should do.)*

> Para hacer una buena fiesta...
> 1. Debes invitar a muchos amigos.
> 2. Debes servir comida rica.

---

346 trescientos cuarenta y seis
Unidad 5

Classroom Community

Paired Activity Working in pairs, have students give each other suggestions. One students states a problem situation (**Estoy cansado[a]**) and the other offers a remedy (**Debes dormir más**). Each student must make at least 5 statements.

Group Activity Have small groups of students expand **Actividad 16** to include what one needs to do to prepare for the party (clean, buy food, select music, invite guests, etc.). Then have them design a student guide to a successful party, including a list of do's and don'ts. Display the guides in the classroom.

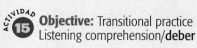

GRAMÁTICA

Using Adverbs That End in -mente

To describe how something is done, use **adverbs.** Many adverbs in Spanish are made by changing an existing **adjective.**

- When an adjective ends in **e, l,** or **z,** simply add **-mente** to the end.

Adjective	Adverb
reciente *recent*	**recientemente** *recently, lately*
frecuente *frequent*	**frecuentemente** *frequently, often*
fácil *easy*	**fácilmente** *easily*
normal *normal*	**normalmente** *normally*
especial *special*	**especialmente** *specially, especially*
feliz *happy*	**felizmente** *happily*

- For adjectives with **-o** or **-a** endings, add **-mente** to the **feminine** form.

Adjective	Adverb
cuidadoso(a) *careful*	**cuidadosamente** *carefully*
rápido(a) *fast, quick*	**rápidamente** *quickly*
lento(a) *slow*	**lentamente** *slowly*
tranquilo(a) *calm*	**tranquilamente** *calmly*

Luis says:

—Pero, Carmen, debes pasarla **cuidadosamente.**

*But Carmen, you should vacuum **carefully.***

Notice that you must keep an **accent** when an adjective is changed to an adverb.

rápido → **rápidamente**
fácil → **fácilmente**

When you use two adverbs, **drop** the **-mente** from the **first** one.

lenta y **tranquilamente**

ACTIVIDAD 17 Gramática

En un restaurante

Leer Luis describe un restaurante. Completa sus oraciones con adverbios. Forma los adverbios de los adjetivos entre paréntesis.
(Hint: Complete the sentences with adverbs.)

Fui __1__ (reciente) con mi familia al restaurante Casa Paco. Es un restaurante buenísimo cerca de mi casa. Comemos allí __2__ (frecuente), ¡pues allí sirven cosas riquísimas! A mí me gustan __3__ (especial) los calamares y el chorizo. Ahora voy a Casa Paco con mis amigos. Vamos __4__ (rápido) porque tenemos mucha hambre. Allí todos comemos __5__ (tranquilo).

MÁS PRÁCTICA *cuaderno* p. 120

PARA HISPANOHABLANTES *cuaderno* p. 118

Teaching All Students

Extra Help After completing **Actividad 17,** have students write 3 true/false "quiz" statements about the paragraph. Have them work with a partner and take each other's "quiz."

Multiple Intelligences

Musical/Rhythmic Have students make up chants or raps using adverbs ending in **-mente.** For example: **Yo trabajo cuidadosamente. Voy a la escuela frecuentemente. No me gusta manejar rápidamente. Porque quiero vivir tranquilamente.**

ACTIVIDAD 15 **Objective:** Transitional practice
Listening comprehension/**deber**

Answers (See script, p. 333B.)
1. b 2. d 3. c 4. a

ACTIVIDAD 16 **Objective:** Open-ended practice
The verb **deber**

Answers will vary.

Quick Start Review

Vocabulary review

Use OHT 159 or write on the board: Write the word that does *not* belong with the other two words:

1. jamón	llave	aceitunas
2. reciente	suelo	pared
3. silla	mesa	tapas
4. planchar	deber	ordenar
5. baño	fiesta	sorpresa

Answers *See p. 333B.*

Teaching Suggestions
Reinforcing Using Adverbs That End in -mente

Point out to students that using adverbs will add vitality to their sentences when they speak and write. Have them give examples of sentences with and without adverbs.

ACTIVIDAD 17 **Objective:** Controlled practice
Adverbs with **-mente**

Expressing extremes

Answers
1. recientemente
2. frecuentemente
3. especialmente
4. rápidamente
5. tranquilamente

Block Schedule

Variety Photocopy some articles from Spanish magazines and distribute them to students. Have students look for adverbs and underline them. Then have students tell what adjectives they think the adverbs came from. Variation: Have students underline the adjectives in the articles and change them to adverbs. (For additional activities, see **Block Scheduling Copymasters.**)

18 **Objective:** Transitional practice
Adverbs with -**mente**

Answers

Answers will vary. They will contain the following adverbs:
seriamente, tranquilamente, pacientemente, frecuentemente, cuidadosamente, rápidamente, lentamente, felizmente, fácilmente

19 **Objective:** Transitional practice
Adverbs with -**mente** in reading
  Daily chores

Answers
1. El servicio limpia fácilmente.
2. Llegan rápidamente a la casa.
3. Ofrecen un servicio completo de limpieza: quitan el polvo, pasan la aspiradora y limpian todos los cuartos.
4. Pasan lentamente la aspiradora.
5. Limpian los baños y la cocina especialmente bien.

ACTIVIDAD **18**

¿Cómo lo hacen?

Hablar/Escribir Todos hacen algo hoy. ¿Cómo lo hacen?
(Hint: Say how everyone does each activity.)

serio   tranquilo   paciente
  frecuente   cuidadoso   fácil
rápido   lento   feliz

modelo

Carmen / barrer el suelo
Carmen barre el suelo *rápidamente.*

1. Luis / hablar
2. Mercedes / trabajar
3. Álvaro / esperar
4. Jorge / terminar la tarea
5. Beto y Marta / cantar
6. Enrique / pasar la aspiradora
7. Rocío y Ana / quitar el polvo
8. Catalina / ir de compras
9. Pedro / desayunar
10. todos / bailar

ACTIVIDAD **19**

♻ ¡La buena limpieza!

Leer/Escribir Imagínate que recibes este anuncio de la compañía Buena Limpieza. Lee el anuncio y después contesta las preguntas.
(Hint: Answer the questions.)

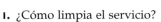
Buena Limpieza

¡Con diez años de experiencia, limpiamos fácilmente todo tipo de hogar!

Llegamos rápidamente a su hogar para ofrecerle un servicio completo de limpieza.

➤ Quitar completamente el polvo
➤ Pasar lentamente la aspiradora
➤ Limpiar cuidadosamente todos los cuartos, especialmente los baños y la cocina

¡Llámenos hoy al 86-25-54 para tener una casa bien limpia mañana!

1. ¿Cómo limpia el servicio?
2. ¿Cómo llegan a la casa?
3. ¿Qué servicios ofrecen?
4. ¿Cómo pasan la aspiradora?
5. ¿Qué cuartos limpian especialmente bien?

TAMBIÉN SE DICE

Many words are used to mean *bedroom*. Almost all are used in all countries. A few are used a bit more often in specific countries.

• **la alcoba:** many countries
• **el cuarto:** many countries
• **el dormitorio:** many countries
• **la habitación:** Spain
• **la pieza:** Argentina, Chile
• **la recámara:** Mexico

---

348 trescientos cuarenta y ocho
Unidad 5

Mi casa ideal

¡Una buena fiesta!

Hablar/Escribir Haz un plano de tu casa ideal. Después, muéstrale el plano a otro(a) estudiante y descríbele la casa. *(Hint: Design and describe your dream house.)*

modelo

Mi casa ideal es grande y bonita. Tiene un jardín con muchas flores y plantas. También tiene una piscina y una cancha de tenis. Hay una sala donde vemos la televisión. Hay una cocina muy grande donde comemos todos los días. La casa también tiene…

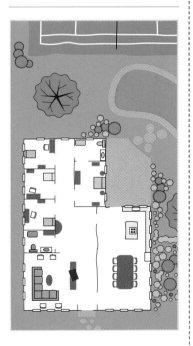

Hablar/Escribir Trabaja en un grupo de tres para planear una fiesta. Luego, dale una invitación a cada estudiante de la clase. Para saber cuál es la mejor fiesta, haz una encuesta. ¿Cuántos estudiantes aceptan tu invitación? ¿Cuántos aceptan las invitaciones de los otros grupos? *(Hint: Plan a party.)*

• ¿Qué tipo de fiesta van a hacer?   • ¿Qué comida van a servir?
• ¿Qué van a celebrar?   • ¿Qué van a hacer en la fiesta?

¡Ven a la fiesta para celebrar el primer día de la primavera!

Servimos…
¡Comida riquísima!
(jamón, chorizo, aceitunas… ¡y mucho más!)
¡Postres deliciosos!
(flan, pasteles… ¡y mucho más!)
Ofrecemos…
¡Juegos divertidísimos!
(videojuegos… ¡y muchos otros!)
¡Música y baile!
(¡discos compactos y casetes de todos tus grupos favoritos!)

■ **MÁS COMUNICACIÓN** p. R14

Pronunciación

Trabalenguas

Pronunciación de la *c*, la *p* y la *t* When a **c** is followed by an **a**, **o**, or **u**, it sounds like the *c* in the English word *cat*. The letter combination **qu**, when followed by **e** or **i**, also makes this sound. This **c** sound and the letters **p** and **t** are pronounced similarly in Spanish and English. However, when you say them in English, a puff of air comes out of your mouth. In Spanish there is no puff of air. Try saying the following tongue twisters to practice these sounds.

Quince quiteños comen papas picantes.

No son tantas las tontas ni tantos los tontos muchachos.

trescientos cuarenta y nueve
Etapa 2 **349**

Vocabulary/Grammar • UNIDAD 5 Etapa 2   **349**

Objective: Open-ended practice
Describing a house

Answers will vary.

Objective: Open-ended practice
Planning a party

Answers will vary.

🔔 Quick Wrap-up

Toss a soft ball to a student as you say an adjective. The student says the corresponding adverb. If you say **Sí,** he/she tosses the ball back to you. If you say **No,** he/she tosses the ball to another student who attempts the adverb.

Dictation

After students have read the tongue twisters in the **Pronunciación,** have them close their books. Dictate the tongue twisters in segments while students write them.

■ Block Schedule

Project Modify **Actividad 21** by having students plan an informational party for incoming students selecting a foreign language in the fall. Have students suggest necessary committees (publicity, invitations, food, music, decorating, clean-up, etc.) Students sign up for committees and produce an outline saying what they need to do and prepare. (For additional activities, see **Block Scheduling Copymasters.**)

Teaching All Students

Challenge Students who are motivated to use the computer may want to prepare their home diagrams with appropriate software.

Native Speakers Ask students if houses in their home communities usually have gardens. Are they for practical or esthetic purposes? Do people living in apartment buildings have plants on their balconies?

Multiple Intelligences

Visual Have a volunteer read his/her **Casa ideal** (**Actividad 20**) as artistic volunteers sketch it in front of the class on the board or an overhead. When the artist makes an error, the class should say ¡**Alto!** (Stop!) or ¡**Para!** (Stop!–more common in Spain) and explain the error.

Teaching Resource Options

Print

Unit 5 Resource Book
  Audioscript, p. 81
  Audioscript *Para hispanohablantes*,
    p. 82

Audiovisual

Audio Program Cassette 14A / CD 14
Audio *Para hispanohablantes*
  Cassette 14A / CD 14
OHT 159 (Quick Start)
Canciones Cassette / CD

Quick Start Review

♻ En el restaurante

Use OHT 159 or write on the board:
Write 5 things you should or should
not do in a nice restaurant. Begin your
sentences with **Debes...** or **No debes...**

Answers
Answers will vary. Answers could include:
Debes llevar ropa limpia.
No debes peinarte en la mesa.
Debes lavarte las manos antes de comer.
No debes cantar.
No debes jugar con la comida.

Teaching Suggestions
Presenting Cultura y comparaciones

• Begin by asking students to look at
  the pictures and tell if they have
  eaten anything like the foods
  pictured. Which dishes appeal to
  them? Do they like to try new foods?
• Have students complete the Strategy
  task. Then have them predict how
  Luis or Mercedes might feel about
  their favorite fast food restaurant.

Reading Strategy

Scan for crucial details Have students
scan the reading to pick up certain details.
Have them find answers to the following
questions: ¿Qué es una tapa? ¿Cuáles
son unos ingredientes? ¿Cuál es la
especialidad de la casa?

En colores

CULTURA Y
COMPARACIONES

PARA CONOCERNOS
STRATEGY: CONNECTING CULTURES
Predict reactions about restaurants Fast food chains
are a U.S. invention being exported to other
countries. Think about a favorite one and
write down your answers to the questions in
the chart.

	comida rápida	tapas
¿Qué comida sirven?		
¿Por qué vamos?		
¿Con quién vamos?		

As you read, answer the same questions
about a place that serves **tapas.** Compare
the two eating experiences. How do you
think Luis or Mercedes would feel on their
first trip to your favorite fast food restaurant?

Las tapas

¿**T**e gustarían unas tapas? Son muy típicas de España. ¿Sabes
qué son? Una tapa es una porción pequeña de comida que la
gente normalmente come con una bebida antes de la cena.
¡Vamos a probar[1] unas!

En el café ponen todas las tapas en el
mostrador[2]. Hay tantas tapas diferentes.
Mucha gente está buscando mesa, pero
no hay. No es un problema porque es
muy común comer las tapas de pie.
Pagas un precio más barato si comes así[3].

---

[1] to try   [2] counter   [3] in this way

350 trescientos cincuenta
Unidad 5

Classroom Community

Group Activity Divide the class into groups of
8–10. Assign 2 students in each group to be servers
and the rest are patrons. The servers will carry paper
plates decorated to look like various **tapas.** The patrons
will mingle and converse in Spanish, perhaps talking
about the "café" or their classes. The servers will offer
their **tapas** and answer questions about them. Provide
typical Spanish music in the background.

Learning Scenario Tell students that their families
are having visitors from Spain at their homes before
they all go out to a restaurant together. Have students
tell what sort of **tapas** they would serve to familiarize
the guests with traditional appetizers in the U.S.

una experiencia muy española

Unos chicos están comiendo aceitunas, jamón y queso. Otros comen chorizo con pan. Las aceitunas, el jamón, el queso y el chorizo son tapas naturales[4]. También hay tapas cocidas[5], como la tortilla española y los calamares. La tortilla española es muy popular y es uno de los platos más famosos. Pero la especialidad de la casa es un plato típico de Barcelona y de toda Cataluña, el cocido catalán[6]. ¡Está riquísimo!

Comer tapas es una buena actividad para la familia o los amigos. A muchas personas les gusta conversar mientras comen las deliciosas tapas.

---

[4] served unheated   [5] cooked   [6] Catalonian stew

¿Comprendiste?

1. ¿Qué sirven en este café?
2. ¿Por qué no hay problema si todas las mesas están ocupadas?
3. ¿Qué son las tapas naturales?
4. ¿Qué tapa cocida piden muchas personas? ¿Qué otras tapas cocidas hay?
5. ¿Cómo se llama la especialidad de la casa?

¿Qué piensas?

En España comer tapas es una actividad social. ¿Hay una actividad similar en Estados Unidos? Descríbela.

Hazlo tú

Eres camarero(a) en un café español. Dos personas llegan y piden tapas. ¿Qué dicen? ¿Qué les sirves?

Culture Highlights

● **TAPAS** **Tapas** help tide over Spanish appetites until their traditional late supper hour. The type of snack varies from region to region. They can be served hot or cold, and might include vegetables, seafood, or meat.

Cross Cultural Connections

Ask students to talk about times when they eat appetizers, both in restaurants and at home. Have they ever been served an appetizer at a restaurant as they waited for a table to become available or as they waited for the main meal to be served?

Interdisciplinary Connections

Social Studies Have students research eating customs in Spanish-speaking countries. They should try to find out at what time each meal is typically served, what is typically served, and which is the main meal of the day.

Critical Thinking

Point out to students that in Spain, restaurants allow people to remain at a table for as long as they wish. Do they think that this is a good policy? How does the policy affect other people wanting to eat in the restaurant, the waiters, and the restaurant's finances?

¿Comprendiste?

Answers
1. Sirven tapas.
2. Porque es muy común comer las tapas de pie.
3. Las aceitunas, el jamón, el queso y el chorizo son tapas naturales.
4. Muchos piden la tortilla española. También hay los calamares.
5. La especialidad de la casa es el cocido catalán.

Block Schedule

Research recipes Have students do research in cookbooks and/or on the Internet for recipes for **tapas**. Survey the ingredients and directions to see which might be easy for students to make. If possible, make them in school. If not, ask for volunteers to make them at home for the class to enjoy.

Teaching All Students

Extra Help Have students work with a partner and ask each other a **sí/no** question about each paragraph.

Native Speakers Ask students if these **tapas** are also found in their home communities. Are there other favorite foods that are not common in the U.S.?

Multiple Intelligences

Visual Have students design menus for a **tapas** café. They should list the items, along with a small drawing, and the prices—for consumption at a table and standing at a counter. They should also include a list of drinks.

Teaching Resource Options

Print

Para hispanohablantes Workbook PE,
pp. 95–96
Block Scheduling Copymasters
Unit 5 Resource Book
Para hispanohablantes Workbook
TE, pp. 66–67
Information Gap Activities,
p. 71
Family Involvement, pp. 72–73
Multiple Choice Test Questions,
pp. 170–178

Audiovisual

OHT 160 (Quick Start)
Audio Program Testing Cassette T2 /
CD T2

Technology

Electronic Teacher Tools/Test
Generator
Intrigas y aventuras CD-ROM, Disc 1

Quick Start Review

♻ **Deber**

Use OHT 160 or write on the board:
You have been granted 5 wishes. Using
the verb **deber**, tell your genie 5 things
that he/she should do for you.

Modelo: Debes limpiar mi habitación.

Answers will vary.

Teaching Suggestions
What Have Students Learned?

• Have students look at the "Now you
can…" notes listed on the left side of
pages 352–353. Tell students to think
about which areas they might not be
sure of. For those areas, they should
consult the "To review" notes.

• Use the video to review vocabulary
and structures.

ETAPA 2

En uso
REPASO Y MÁS COMUNICACIÓN

OBJECTIVES

• Say what people are
doing
• Persuade others
• Describe a house
• Negotiate
responsibilities

Now you can...

• say what people
are doing.

To review

• pronouns with the
present progressive,
see p. 342.

ACTIVIDAD 1 ¡A limpiar!

Luis habla con su madre por teléfono.
¿Qué le dice sobre los quehaceres?
(Hint: Tell who is doing what.)

modelo

¿quitar el polvo de la mesa? (yo)
Mamá: *¿Quién está **quitando el polvo de la mesa**?*
Luis: *Yo estoy quitándolo. o: Yo lo estoy quitando.*

1. ¿barrer el suelo? (yo)
2. ¿pasar la aspiradora? (Carmen)
3. ¿lavar los platos?
   (Mercedes y Carmen)
4. ¿sacar la basura? (yo)
5. ¿poner la mesa? (Carmen)
6. ¿limpiar los baños? (Mercedes y yo)
7. ¿hacer las camas? (yo)
8. ¿preparar las tapas? (nosotros)

Now you can...

• persuade others.

To review

• the verb **deber,** see
p. 345.
• adverbs that end in
-mente, see p. 347.

ACTIVIDAD 2 ¡Una fiesta!

Tú y tus amigos van a hacer una fiesta en tu casa en una hora.
¿Qué deben o no deben hacer todos? *(Hint: Tell what everyone should
or should not do.)*

modelo

yo: poner la mesa (lento)
No debo poner la mesa lentamente.

1. ustedes: ordenar la casa
   (cuidadoso)
2. tú: hablar por teléfono (frecuente)
3. mis amigos y yo: preparar las
   tapas (rápido)
4. yo: ducharme (lento)
5. nosotros: hacer los quehaceres
   (tranquilo)
6. mis amigos: ayudarme (rápido)

Classroom Community

Game Prepare ahead: Make about 30 cards that give
a verb and an appropriate adverb (for example: **correr
rápidamente**). Put the cards in a box. Divide the class
into 4–5 teams. Have one team select a card and act
out what it says. The first team to raise their hands and
correctly identify the verb and the adverb gets a point.

Group Activity Have students work in the groups
planned on TE p. 340. Students are to build a 3-D
home, castle, beach house, cabin in the woods, etc.
They may use materials of their choosing—cardboard,
plastic blocks, toy logs, etc. Each group will present its
construction and describe it.

Now you can...
• describe a house.

To review
• house and furniture vocabulary, see pp. 336–337.

ACTIVIDAD 3 ¡Una nueva casa!

Imagínate que tú y tu familia acaban de llegar a esta nueva casa. Describe lo que hay en estos cuartos. *(Hint: Tell what is in these rooms.)*

modelo

En el baño hay una ventana y un armario.

Now you can...
• negotiate responsibilities.

To review
• **si** clauses with the present tense, see p. 342.

ACTIVIDAD 4 Si tú limpias...

Luis está hablando con Carmen sobre los quehaceres. ¿Qué le dice? *(Hint: Tell what Luis says.)*

modelo

quitar la mesa / lavar los platos
*Si tú **quitas la mesa,** yo **lavo los platos.***

1. lavar la ropa / planchar la ropa
2. barrer el suelo / sacar la basura
3. quitar el polvo / pasar la aspiradora
4. limpiar la sala / limpiar la cocina
5. poner la mesa / hacer las camas
6. limpiar las ventanas / ordenar los muebles

ACTIVIDAD 1 Answers

1. Yo estoy barriéndolo. *o:* Yo lo estoy barriendo.
2. Carmen está pasándola. *o:* Carmen la está pasando.
3. Mercedes y Carmen están lavándolos. *o:* Mercedes y Carmen los están lavando.
4. Yo estoy sacándola. *o:* Yo la estoy sacando.
5. Carmen está poniéndola. *o:* Carmen la está poniendo.
6. Mercedes y yo estamos limpiándolos. *o:* Mercedes y yo los estamos limpiando.
7. Yo estoy haciéndolas. *o:* Yo las estoy haciendo.
8. Nosotros estamos preparándolas. *o:* Nosotros las estamos preparando.

ACTIVIDAD 2 Answers

1. Ustedes deben ordenar la casa cuidadosamente.
2. Tú no debes hablar por teléfono frecuentemente.
3. Mis amigos y yo debemos preparar las tapas rápidamente.
4. Yo no debo ducharme lentamente.
5. Nosotros debemos hacer los quehaceres tranquilamente.
6. Mis amigos deben ayudarme rápidamente.

ACTIVIDAD 3 Answers

En la sala hay dos ventanas, un sofá, un sillón, un televisor y una lámpara.
En el comedor hay una mesa, cuatro sillas y una ventana.
En mi habitación hay un armario, una ventana y una cama.
En el baño hay una ventana y un armario.
En la habitación de mis padres hay dos ventanas, dos armarios, una cama, dos mesas y dos lámparas.

ACTIVIDAD 4 Answers

1. Si tú lavas la ropa, yo plancho la ropa.
2. Si tú barres el suelo, yo saco la basura.
3. Si tú quitas el polvo, yo paso la aspiradora.
4. Si tú limpias la sala, yo limpio la cocina.
5. Si tú pones la mesa, yo hago las camas.
6. Si tú limpias las ventanas, yo ordeno los muebles.

Teaching All Students

Extra Help Using the picture in **Actividad 3**, describe the rooms and their contents. Have students point to each room as they hear its description.

Native Speakers Ask students to brainstorm the names of rooms/places not usually found in the average home, such as **la biblioteca, el cuarto de billares, el recibidor, los establos.**

Multiple Intelligences

Intrapersonal You recently won 4 hours of housecleaning for your home. Make a chart of each room and the work that you want done in it.

Block Schedule

Authentic Materials Prepare ahead: Bring in real estate brochures with floor plans. Do a variation of **Actividad 3**, where students describe what is in each house. (For additional activities, see **Block Scheduling Copymasters**.)

Teaching Resource Options

Print

Unit 5 Resource Book
  Cooperative Quizzes, pp. 84–85
  Etapa Exam, Forms A and B,
    pp. 86–95
  Para hispanohablantes **Etapa Exam,**
    pp. 96–100
  Portfolio Assessment, pp. 101–102
  Multiple Choice Test Questions,
    pp. 170–178

Audiovisual

OHT 160 (Quick Start)
Audio Program Testing Cassette T2 /
  CD T2

Technology

Electronic Teacher Tools/Test
  Generator
www.mcdougallittell.com

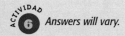

Rubric: Speaking

Criteria	Scale	
Sentence structure	1 2 3	A = 11–12 pts.
Vocabulary use	1 2 3	B = 9–10 pts.
Originality	1 2 3	C = 7–8 pts.
Fluency	1 2 3	D = 4–6 pts.
		F = < 4 pts.

 Answers will vary.

En tu propia voz

Rubric: Writing

Criteria	Scale	
Vocabulary use	1 2 3 4 5	A = 14–15 pts.
Accuracy	1 2 3 4 5	B = 12–13 pts.
Creativity, appearance	1 2 3 4 5	C = 10–11 pts.
		D = 8–9 pts.
		F = < 8 pts.

Teaching Note: En tu propia voz

Suggest that students brainstorm a list of
descriptive words appropriate for a **fiesta**
in order to implement the writing strategy
"Use different kinds of descriptive words"
in the paragraph they will write.

 **ACTIVIDAD 5** — Mi casa es así

PARA CONVERSAR

STRATEGY: SPEAKING

Detect misunderstandings Ask your partner
questions about what he or she said to make
sure you understand. To find out if you
understand each other, you can restate what
was said, do what was said, or draw what
was said. Draw what is described, then
compare your drawings. Together, identify
where any misunderstandings occurred.

Dibuja un cuarto. Descríbeselo a otro(a)
estudiante. Él o ella tiene que dibujar el
cuarto que tú describes y decir qué cuarto
es. *(Hint: Draw and describe a room.)*

modelo

Tú: *Hay una ventana grande a la derecha de la puerta.
Cerca de la ventana hay un sofá y dos sillones. Hay
una mesa entre los sillones…*

Otro(a) estudiante: *Es la sala.*

 **ACTIVIDAD 6** — ¡Límpialo tú!

Tú y tus amigos tienen que preparar la casa
para una fiesta esta noche. Hagan una lista de
los quehaceres y después decidan quiénes van
a hacerlos. *(Hint: List chores and decide who does what.)*

modelo

Tú: *Si ustedes limpian el baño, yo paso la aspiradora.*

Persona A: *¡No! Tú debes limpiar el baño. Yo prefiero
pasar la aspiradora.*

Persona B: *Yo puedo limpiar el baño rápidamente si tú
me ayudas.*

Tú: *Bueno. Yo te ayudo a limpiar el baño.*

 ACTIVIDAD 7 — *En tu propia voz*

ESCRITURA Imagínate que estás en una fiesta
del Club de Español. Escribe una descripción
de lo que están haciendo todos. *(Hint: Describe what
people are doing.)*

modelo

*La fiesta es muy alegre. Gregorio está tocando la guitarra
y todos estamos cantando. La profesora está en la cocina.
Está preparando las tapas cuidadosamente…*

TÚ EN LA COMUNIDAD

Noemi is a high school student in New Jersey.
A native Spanish speaker, she helps out Spanish-
speaking customers in the clothing store where
she works. She also speaks Spanish with family
and friends. With whom do you speak Spanish?

Classroom Community

Learning Scenario Have students present their
negotiations for **Actividad 6,** dramatizing as much as
possible.

Paired Activity Have students work in pairs and
dictate words from the **Repaso de vocabulario** to each
other. They then check their spelling together.

En resumen
REPASO DE VOCABULARIO

PERSUADING OTHERS

cuidadosamente	carefully
cuidadoso(a)	careful
deber	should, ought to
especial	special
especialmente	specially, especially
fácilmente	easily
felizmente	happily
frecuente	frequent
frecuentemente	often, frequently
lentamente	slowly
lento(a)	slow
normal	normal
normalmente	normally
rápidamente	quickly
rápido(a)	fast, quick
reciente	recent
recientemente	lately, recently
tranquilamente	calmly

DESCRIBING A HOUSE

The House

el baño	bathroom
la cocina	kitchen
el comedor	dining room
la habitación	bedroom
el jardín	garden
la pared	wall
la puerta	door
la sala	living room
el suelo	floor
la ventana	window

Furniture

el armario	closet
la lámpara	lamp
la mesa	table
los muebles	furniture
la silla	chair
el sillón	armchair
el sofá	sofa, couch
el televisor	television set

WHAT PEOPLE ARE DOING

barrer el suelo	to sweep the floor
mover los muebles	to move the furniture
ordenar (las flores, los libros)	to arrange (the flowers, books)
pasar la aspiradora	to vacuum
planchar (la ropa)	to iron (the clothes)
quitar el polvo	to dust
sacar la basura	to take out the trash

OTHER WORDS AND PHRASES

abierto(a)	open
cerrado(a)	closed
la llave	key
olvidar	to forget
si	if

Food

las aceitunas	olives
los calamares	squid
el chorizo	sausage
el jamón	ham
las tapas	appetizers
la tortilla española	potato omelet

Invitations

la fiesta	party
la invitación	invitation
sorprender	to surprise
la sorpresa	surprise

Juego

¿En qué cuarto están?
1. Sofía come.
2. Felipe ve la televisión.
3. Cristina lava los platos.

Community Connections

Have students brainstorm a list of people they might possibly speak Spanish with in your area. They could contact the local Chamber of Commerce to see if any local businesses are owned by Spanish-speakers or employ Spanish-speakers. Students might visit these businesses and practice their Spanish.

Quick Start Review

🔄 Etapa vocabulary

Use OHT 160 or write on the board: Write complete sentences describing what someone is doing in each room.
Modelo: la cocina
You write: **Mi padre está preparando la cena.**

1. el baño   4. la cocina
2. el comedor   5. la sala
3. la habitación

Answers
Answers will vary. Answers could include:
1. Mi hermano está lavándose los dientes.
2. Mi madre está quitando la mesa.
3. Yo estoy estudiando.
4. Mi abuela está ordenando las flores.
5. Mi hermana está pasando la aspiradora.

Teaching Suggestions
Vocabulary Review

Have students make flashcards of the vocabulary words. Put the cards in a box. Have 3 students at a time choose 2 words from the box and write a sentence using the words on the board.

Juego

Answers
1. Sofía está en el comedor.
2. Felipe está en la sala.
3. Cristina está en la cocina.

Block Schedule

Variety Have students write up **Actividad 7** as a school newspaper article. Students introduce the article by explaining that they are providing a minute-by-minute account of the great party for those students who were unable to be there. Students may change the **Club de Español** to another focus.

Teaching All Students

Extra Help Have students work in pairs. Students alternate reading a word from the **Repaso de vocabulario** list and making up a sentence using the word.

Multiple Intelligences

Visual Have students draw a cartoon that summarizes the **Etapa,** putting the conversation in bubbles.
Rubric A = 13–15 pts. B = 10–12 pts. C = 7–9 pts. D = 4–6 pts. F = < 4 pts.

Writing criteria	Scale
Vocabulary use	1 2 3 4 5
Grammar/spelling accuracy	1 2 3 4 5
Creativity/appearance	1 2 3 4 5

Planning Guide CLASSROOM MANAGEMENT

OBJECTIVES

Communication
- Plan a party *pp. 358–359, 360–361*
- Describe past activities *pp. 360–361, 374–375*
- Express extremes *pp. 360–361*
- Purchase foods *pp. 360–361*

Grammar
- Use superlatives *pp. 364–365*
- Use regular preterite **-ar** verbs *pp. 366–367*
- Use preterite of **-car, -gar, -zar** verbs *pp. 368–371*

Pronunciation
- Linking words *p. 371*
- Dictation *TE p. 371*

Culture
- Regional vocabulary *p. 362*
- The Spanish **peseta** *p. 369*
- **Paella valenciana** *pp. 372–373*
- Barcelona's architecture *pp. 374–375*

♻ Recycling
- Adjective agreement *p. 365*
- Chores *p. 367*

STRATEGIES

Listening Strategies
- Listen and take notes *p. 360*

Speaking Strategies
- Say what is the best and worst *p. 365*
- Maintain conversational flow *p. 378*

Reading Strategies
- Reorganize information to check understanding *p. 372, TE p. 375*

Writing Strategies
- Tell who, what, where, when, why, and how *TE p. 378*
- Engage the reader by addressing him or her personally *p. 380*

Connecting Cultures Strategies
- Recognize variations in vocabulary *p. 362*
- Spanish cooking and ingredients *pp. 372–373*
- Compare Spanish and North American ingredients *TE p. 373*
- Make a historical time line *p. 374*
- Connect and compare what you know about architecture in your community to help you learn about architecture in a new community *pp. 374–375*

PROGRAM RESOURCES

Print

- *Más práctica* Workbook PE *pp. 121–128*
- Block Scheduling Copymasters *pp. 121–128*
- Unit 5 Resource Book
  Más práctica Workbook TE *pp. 103–110*
  Para hispanohablantes Workbook TE *pp. 111–118*

- Information Gap Activities *pp. 119–122*
- Family Involvement *pp. 123–124*
- Video Activities *pp. 125–127*
- Videoscript *pp. 128–130*
- Audioscript *pp. 131–134*
- Assessment Program, Unit 5 Etapa 3 *pp. 135–178*
- Answer Keys *pp. 179–200*

Audiovisual

- **Audio Program** Cassettes 15A, 15B / CD 15
- *Canciones* Cassette / CD
- **Video Program** Videotape 5 / Videodisc 3A
- **Overhead Transparencies** M1–M5; GO1–GO5; 140, 161–170

Technology

- Electronic Teacher Tools/Test Generator
- *Intrigas y aventuras* CD-ROM, Disc 1
- www.mcdougallittell.com

Assessment Program Options

- **Cooperative Quizzes** (Unit 5 Resource Book)
- **Etapa Exam** Forms A and B (Unit 5 Resource Book)
- *Para hispanohablantes* **Etapa Exam** (Unit 5 Resource Book)
- **Portfolio Assessment** (Unit 5 Resource Book)
- **Unit 5 Comprehensive Test** (Unit 5 Resource Book)
- *Para hispanohablantes* **Unit 5 Comprehensive Test** (Unit 5 Resource Book)
- **Multiple Choice Test Questions** (Unit 5 Resource Book)
- **Audio Program** Testing Cassette T2 / CD T2
- **Electronic Teacher Tools/Test Generator**

Native Speakers

- *Para hispanohablantes* Workbook PE, *pp. 121–128*
- *Para hispanohablantes* Workbook TE (Unit 5 Resource Book)
- *Para hispanohablantes* Etapa Exam (Unit 5 Resource Book)
- *Para hispanohablantes* Unit 5 Comprehensive Test (Unit 5 Resource Book)
- Audio *Para hispanohablantes* Cassettes 15A, 15B, T2 / CD 15, T2
- Audioscript *Para hispanohablantes* (Unit 5 Resource Book)

Student Text
Listening Activity Scripts

 Videoscript: Diálogo *pages 360–361*

• Videotape 5 • Videodisc 3A

Search Chapter 7, Play to 8
U5E3 • En vivo (Dialog)

• Use the videoscript with **Actividades 1, 2** *page 362*

Luis:	No lo puedo creer. Limpié la cocina, saqué la basura y tú, Carmen, pasaste la aspiradora...
Mercedes:	¿Y qué, Luis? ¿Qué es lo que no puedes creer?
Luis:	Bueno, que es mi cumpleaños.
Mercedes:	Sí, lo sé.
Luis:	¡El día empezó con demasiados quehaceres! ¿Por qué?
Mercedes:	No lo sé, Luis..
Carmen:	¡Yo te ayudé, Luis!
Luis:	Sí, Carmen, tú me ayudaste y Mercedes también me ayudó. Muchas gracias a vosotras. Lo más increíble es que son las dos y ¡todavía no terminamos!
Mercedes:	No te preocupes, Luis. ¿Por qué no llamas a Álvaro?
Luis:	Buena idea. Os veo en la tienda. Hola, Álvaro, soy Luis.
Álvaro:	¡Chht! ¡Es Luis! ¡Hola, Luis! ¿Dónde estás?
Luis:	Estoy en la Plaza de San José. Voy a la tienda con Mercedes y Carmen.
Álvaro:	¿Qué haces allí?
Luis:	Pues, no lo vas a creer pero tengo que hacer unas compras para mamá.
Álvaro:	¿Ahora? Hombre, te estoy esperando.
Luis:	Ya lo sé, ya lo sé. Es una larga historia. Trabajé en casa toda la mañana. Tengo que hacer compras. Y ¡también tengo que cuidar a Carmen!
Álvaro:	¡Qué mala suerte! Pero, hombre, no te preocupes. Ven a casa con Mercedes. Y trae a Carmen también. Ella puede jugar con mis videojuegos.
Luis:	Gracias, Álvaro. Nos vemos pronto.
Álvaro:	¡Adiós! Luis no tiene ni idea.
Marta:	¡La tarta está lista, Álvaro! ¡Mírala! Quedó perfecta.
Álvaro:	¡Quedó deliciosa! ¡Es la más deliciosa de Barcelona!
Marta:	¡Álvaro!
Álvaro:	¡Iván! ¡Gran Cocinero! ¿Está lista la carne de res?

Iván:	Sí, claro.
Álvaro:	Mmmm. ¡Excelente, como siempre! ¡Beto! ¿Qué haces?
Beto:	Estoy preparando un plato de verduras. ¡Ay, Álvaro! ¡No te comas las zanahorias! ¿No ves que hay pocas? Oye, Álvaro... una pregunta. Marta preparó la tarta. Iván cocinó la carne. Y yo preparé las patatas y las verduras. ¿Qué cocinaste tú?
Álvaro:	¿Yo? ¡Yo no sé cocinar!
Beto:	Entonces ¡tú vas a lavar los platos!
Todos:	¡Eso!
Luis:	Hablé con Álvaro. Ahora él lo sabe todo.
Mercedes:	Qué bien. Ahora, ¿qué tienes que comprar?
Luis:	A ver. Buenas tardes. Necesito comprar leche, zumo, huevos y mantequilla.
Carmen:	¡Y el helado! ¡No olvides el helado! ¡El helado es lo más rico del mundo!
Mercedes:	Y unas galletas.
Luis:	¿Cuánto es?
Carmen:	¿Cómo pagaste, Luis?
Luis:	Pagué con el dinero de papá. Haces muchas preguntas, Carmen. Primero tenemos que llevar estas cosas a casa. Vamos, pronto.
Álvaro:	Luis está a punto de llegar.
Beto:	¡Ssshhhh! ¡Cállate, Álvaro! ¡Silencio! ¡Callaos todos! ¡Ahí viene Luis!
Luis:	Álvaro, ¿dónde estás?
Todos:	¡Feliz cumpleaños, Luis!
Luis:	¿Cómo puede ser? ¡Mercedes! ¡Álvaro!
Álvaro:	Sí, amigo. Lo planeamos todo.
Luis:	Pues, por fin, dime, Mercedes, ¿para qué son esas fotos?
Mercedes:	Son para un concurso para la revista *Onda internacional*. ¡Y tú eres la estrella de mi proyecto! Y el título de mi proyecto es "Un día especial en la vida de un joven español".
Luis:	¡Te voy a decir definitivamente que este día es muy especial!

¿Por qué no me invitaste?
page 367

Juana:	¡Qué bien lo pasamos en mi casa el viernes pasado! ¡La mejor fiesta sorpresa del año!
Miguel:	¿Qué celebraron?
Juana:	Celebramos el cumpleaños de Yolanda.
Miguel:	¿Y por qué no me invitaste?
Juana:	Porque invité sólo a chicas.
Miguel:	¿A cuántas chicas invitaste?
Juana:	A diez.
Miguel:	¿Y a qué hora empezó la fiesta?
Juana:	Bueno, todas llegaron entre las siete y media y las ocho. Yolanda llegó a las ocho y media. ¡Qué sorpresa para ella!
Miguel:	¿Cómo pasaron la noche?
Juana:	Escuchamos música, cantamos, miramos fotos y... ¡hablamos!

¿Cuánto pagaron? *page 370*

1. Elena compró una pulsera por 3.000 pesetas.
2. Yo compré aretes de oro por 8.600 pesetas.
3. Marta compó un collar por 5.500 pesetas.
4. Ana compró una cartera por 1.300 pesetas.
5. Linda compró un libro por 800 pesetas.

Quick Start Review Answers

p. 360 Kitchen/cooking vocabulary
Answers will vary.
Answers could include:
1. harina, huevos, mantequilla
2. las zanahorias, los tomates
3. un frigorífico, una estufa
4. helado

p. 366 Superlatives
1. Sofía es la más alta.
2. Jaime es el más inteligente.
3. El sofá es el más caro.
4. El Sr. Ricardo es el más viejo.

p. 368 Preterite of **-ar** verbs
1. pasó
2. plancharon
3. limpiamos
4. sacaste
5. olvidé

Sample Lesson Plan - 50 Minute Schedule

DAY 1

Etapa Opener
- Quick Start Review (TE, p. 356) **5 MIN.**
- Anticipate/Activate prior knowledge: Have students look at the *Etapa* Opener and answer the questions. **5 MIN.**

En contexto: Vocabulario
- Quick Start Review (TE, p. 358) **5 MIN.**
- Have students use context and pictures to learn *Etapa* vocabulary. In pairs, have students answer the questions, p. 359. Use the Situational OHTs for additional practice. **10 MIN.**

En vivo: Diálogo
- Quick Start Review (TE, p. 360) **5 MIN.**
- Review the Listening Strategy, p. 360. Play audio or show video for the dialog, pp. 360–361. **10 MIN.**
- Replay twice. Read aloud, having students take the roles of the characters. **10 MIN.**

Homework Option:
- Video Activities, Unit 5 Resource Book, pp. 125–127.

DAY 2

En acción: Vocabulario y gramática
- Check homework. **5 MIN.**
- Quick Start Review (TE, p. 362) **5 MIN.**
- Have students open to *En contexto,* pp. 358–359, for reference. Use OHT 161 and 162 to review vocabulary. **5 MIN.**
- Play the audio; have students do *Actividades* 1 and 2 orally. **5 MIN.**
- Do *Actividad* 3 orally. **5 MIN.**
- Present the *Vocabulario,* p. 363. Model pronunciation. Then have students complete *Actividad* 4 orally. **5 MIN.**
- Have students read and complete *Actividad* 5. Go over answers orally. **5 MIN.**
- Quick Start Review (TE, p. 364) **5 MIN.**
- Present *Gramática:* Talking About Extremes: Superlatives, p. 364. **10 MIN.**
- Have students read and complete *Actividad* 6 in writing. **5 MIN.**

Homework Option:
- *Más práctica* Workbook, p. 125. *Para hispanohablantes* Workbook, p. 123.

DAY 3

En acción (cont.)
- Check homework. **5 MIN.**
- Have students do *Actividad* 7 in writing. Go over answers orally. **5 MIN.**
- Present the Speaking Strategy, p. 365. Then have students do *Actividad* 8 in pairs. Expand using Information Gap Activities, Unit 5 Resource Book, p. 119; *Más comunicación,* p. R15. **15 MIN.**
- Quick Start Review (TE, p. 366) **5 MIN.**
- Present *Gramática:* Talking About the Past: The Preterite of Regular -ar Verbs and the *Vocabulario,* p. 366. **15 MIN.**
- Have students read and complete *Actividad* 9. Go over answers orally. **5 MIN.**
- Do *Actividad* 10 orally. **5 MIN.**

Homework Option:
- Have students complete *Actividad* 10 in writing. *Más práctica* Workbook, pp. 126–127. *Para hispanohablantes* Workbook, pp. 124–125.

DAY 4

En acción (cont.)
- Check homework. **5 MIN.**
- Play the audio; have students do *Actividad* 11. **5 MIN.**
- Have students do *Actividad* 12 in groups. Ask several students to present their findings. **10 MIN.**
- Quick Start Review (TE, p. 368) **5 MIN.**
- Present *Gramática:* Preterite of Verbs Ending in -car, -gar, and -zar, p. 368. **5 MIN.**
- Have students read and complete *Actividad* 13 in writing. Have students exchange papers for peer correction. **10 MIN.**
- Do *Actividad* 14 orally. **5 MIN.**
- Have students complete *Actividad* 15 in groups. **10 MIN.**

Homework Option:
- Have students complete *Actividad* 14 in writing. *Más práctica* Workbook, p. 128. *Para hispanohablantes* Workbook, p. 126.

DAY 5

En acción (cont.)
- Check homework. **5 MIN.**
- Present the *Vocabulario,* p. 369. Name items *(un televisor, un carro)* and have students provide an average price. **5 MIN.**
- Play the audio; do *Actividad* 16. **5 MIN.**
- Present the *Vocabulario,* p. 370. **5 MIN.**
- Present the *Nota.* Then do *Actividad* 17 in pairs. **5 MIN.**
- Do *Actividades* 18 and 19 orally. **10 MIN.**
- Have students do *Actividad* 20 in writing. Expand using Information Gap Activities, Unit 5 Resource Book, pp. 120–121; *Más comunicación,* p. R15. **15 MIN.**

Pronunciación
- Play the audio and have students practice the *refranes.* **5 MIN.**

Homework Option:
- Have students complete *Actividades* 18 and 19 in writing.

DAY 6

En voces: Lectura
- Check homework. **5 MIN.**
- Quick Start Review (TE, p. 372) **5 MIN.**
- Present the Reading Strategy, p. 372. Have volunteers read the selection aloud and answer the questions, p. 373. **15 MIN.**

En colores: Cultura y comparaciones
- Quick Start Review (TE, p. 374) **5 MIN.**
- Discuss the Connecting Cultures Strategy, p. 374. Have volunteers read the selection aloud and answer the questions, p. 375. Show video culture presentation for expansion. **20 MIN.**
- Review *En uso* for *Etapa* 3 Exam. **5 MIN.**

Homework Option:
- Prepare *En uso Actividades* 1–4. Review for *Etapa* 3 Exam.

DAY 7

En uso: Repaso y más comunicación
- Check homework. **5 MIN.**
- Quick Start Review (TE, p. 376) **5 MIN.**
- Review *Actividades* 1–4 orally. **5 MIN.**
- Present the Speaking Strategy, p. 378. Do *Actividad* 5 in pairs and *Actividad* 6 in groups. **10 MIN.**

En resumen: Repaso de vocabulario
- Complete *Etapa* 3 Exam. **20 MIN.**

En tu propia voz: Escritura
- Do *Actividad* 7 in writing. **5 MIN.**

Conexiones
- Present *La salud,* p. 378. **5 MIN.**

Homework Option:
- Review for Unit 5 Comprehensive Test.

DAY 8

En resumen: Repaso de vocabulario
- Quick Start Review (TE, p. 379) **5 MIN.**

En tu propia voz: Escritura
- Present the Writing Strategy, p. 380. Do the writing activity, pp. 380–381. **10 MIN.**

Unit 5 Comprehensive Test
- Review grammar questions, etc. as necessary. **5 MIN.**
- Complete Unit 5 Comprehensive Test. **30 MIN.**

Ampliación
- Optional: Use a suggested project, game, or activity. (TE, pp. 311A–311B) **15 MIN.**

Homework Option:
- Preview *Unidad* 6 Opener: Have students read and study pp. 382–383.

Sample Lesson Plan - Block Schedule (90 minutes)

DAY 1

Etapa Opener
- Quick Start Review (TE, p. 356) 5 MIN.
- Anticipate/Activate prior knowledge: Have students look at the *Etapa* Opener and answer the questions. 5 MIN.
- Use Block Scheduling Copymasters. 10 MIN.

En contexto: Vocabulario
- Quick Start Review (TE, p. 358) 5 MIN.
- Have students use context and pictures to learn *Etapa* vocabulary. In pairs, have students answer the questions, p. 359. Use the Situational OHTs for additional practice. 10 MIN.

En vivo: Diálogo
- Quick Start Review (TE, p. 360) 5 MIN.
- Review the Listening Strategy, p. 360. Play audio or show video for the dialog, pp. 360–361. 10 MIN.
- Replay twice. Read aloud, having students take the roles of the characters. 10 MIN.

En acción: Vocabulario y gramática
- Quick Start Review (TE, p. 362) 5 MIN.
- Have students open to *En contexto,* pp. 358–359, for reference. Use OHT 161 and 162 to review vocabulary. 5 MIN.
- Play the audio; have students do *Actividades* 1 and 2 orally. 10 MIN.
- Do *Actividad* 3 orally. 5 MIN.
- Present the *Vocabulario,* p. 363. Then have students complete *Actividad* 4 orally. 5 MIN.

Homework Option:
- Video Activities, Unit 5 Resource Book, pp. 125–127.

DAY 2

En acción (cont.)
- Check homework. 5 MIN.
- Have students read and complete *Actividad* 5. Go over answers orally. 5 MIN.
- Quick Start Review (TE, p. 364) 5 MIN.
- Present *Gramática:* Talking About Extremes: Superlatives, p. 364. 10 MIN.
- Have students read and complete *Actividad* 6 in writing. 5 MIN.
- Have students do *Actividad* 7 in writing. Go over answers orally. 5 MIN.
- Present the Speaking Strategy, p. 365. Then have students do *Actividad* 8 in pairs. Expand using Information Gap Activities, Unit 5 Resource Book, p. 119; *Más comunicación,* p. R15. 15 MIN.
- Quick Start Review (TE, p. 366) 5 MIN.
- Present *Gramática:* Talking About the Past: The Preterite of Regular *-ar* Verbs and the *Vocabulario,* p. 366. 10 MIN.
- Have students read and complete *Actividad* 9. Go over answers orally. 5 MIN.
- Do *Actividad* 10 orally. 5 MIN.
- Play the audio; have students do *Actividad* 11. 5 MIN.
- Have students do *Actividad* 12 in groups. Ask several students to present their findings. 10 MIN.

Homework Option:
- Have students complete *Actividades* 7 and 10 in writing. *Más práctica* Workbook, pp. 125–127. *Para hispanohablantes* Workbook, pp. 123–125.

DAY 3

En acción (cont.)
- Check homework. 5 MIN.
- Quick Start Review (TE, p. 368) 5 MIN.
- Present *Gramática:* Preterite of Verbs Ending in *-car, -gar,* and *-zar,* p. 368. 5 MIN.
- Have students read and complete *Actividad* 13 in writing. Have students exchange papers for peer correction. 10 MIN.
- Do *Actividad* 14 orally. 5 MIN.
- Have students complete *Actividad* 15 in groups. 10 MIN.
- Present the *Vocabulario,* p. 369. Name items *(un televisor, un carro)* and have students provide an average price. 5 MIN.
- Play the audio; do *Actividad* 16. 5 MIN.
- Present the *Vocabulario,* p. 370. 5 MIN.
- Present the *Nota.* Then do *Actividad* 17 in pairs. 5 MIN.
- Do *Actividades* 18 and 19 orally. 10 MIN.
- Have students do *Actividad* 20 in writing. Expand using Information Gap Activities, Unit 5 Resource Book, pp. 120–121; *Más comunicación,* p. R15. 15 MIN.

Pronunciación
- Play the audio and have students practice the *refranes.* 5 MIN.

Homework Option:
- Have students complete *Actividades* 14, 18, and 19 in writing. *Más práctica* Workbook, p. 128. *Para hispanohablantes* Workbook, p. 126.

DAY 4

En voces: Lectura
- Check homework. 5 MIN.
- Quick Start Review (TE, p. 372) 5 MIN.
- Present the Reading Strategy, p. 372. Have volunteers read the selection aloud and answer the questions, p. 373. 15 MIN.

En colores: Cultura y comparaciones
- Quick Start Review (TE, p. 374) 5 MIN.
- Discuss the Connecting Cultures Strategy, p. 374. Have volunteers read the selection aloud and answer the questions, p. 375. Show video culture presentation for expansion. 20 MIN.
- Review *En uso* for *Etapa* 3 Exam. 5 MIN.

En uso: Repaso y más comunicación
- Quick Start Review (TE, p. 376) 5 MIN.
- Do *Actividades* 1–4 orally. 10 MIN.
- Present the Speaking Strategy, p. 378. Do *Actividad* 5 in pairs and *Actividad* 6 in groups. 10 MIN.
- Do *Actividad* 8 in writing. 10 MIN.

Homework Option:
- Review for *Etapa* 3 Exam.

DAY 5

En resumen: Repaso de vocabulario
- Quick Start Review (TE, p. 376) 5 MIN.
- Review grammar questions, etc. as necessary. 5 MIN.
- Complete *Etapa* 3 Exam. 20 MIN.

Conexiones
- Present *La salud,* p. 378. 5 MIN.

Unit 5 Comprehensive Test
- Review grammar questions, etc. as necessary. 5 MIN.
- Complete Unit 5 Comprehensive Test. 30 MIN.

En tu propia voz: Escritura
- Present the Writing Strategy, p. 308. Do the writing activity, pp. 308–309. 20 MIN.

Ampliación
- Optional: Use a suggested project, game, or activity. (TE, pp. 311A–311B) 15 MIN.

Homework Option:
- Preview *Unidad* 6 Opener: Have students read and study pp. 382–383.

▼ Mercedes, Carmen y Luis van de compras.

Etapa Theme
Planning a party and talking about past activities

Grammar Objectives
- Using superlatives
- Using regular preterite **-ar** verbs
- Using preterite of **-car, -gar, -zar** verbs

Teaching Resource Options
Print
Block Scheduling Copymasters

Audiovisual
OHT 140, 167 (Quick Start)

Quick Start Review
♻ Commands/chores
Use OHT 167 or write on the board:
You and your friend Isabel are preparing for a party. Tell her 4 things she can do to help:

Modelo: Prepara la comida.

Answers
Answers will vary. Answers could include:
1. Escribe las invitaciones.
2. Ve de compras.
3. Haz las tapas.
4. Barre el suelo.
5. Compra un disco compacto.

Teaching Suggestions
Previewing the Etapa
- Ask students to study the picture on pp. 356–357 (1 min.).
- Close books; ask students to share at least 3 things they remember.
- Reopen books and look at the picture again. Have students describe the people and the setting.
- Use the **¿Qué ves?** questions to focus the discussion.

UNIDAD 5

ETAPA 3

¡Qué buena celebración!

- Plan a party

- Describe past activities

- Express extremes

- Purchase food

¿Qué ves?

Mira la foto de la fiesta para Luis.
1. ¿Está contento Luis?
2. ¿Qué hay en la mesa?
3. ¿Cuántas personas están en la fiesta?
4. ¿En qué cuarto de la casa están?

356

Classroom Management

Planning Ahead Bring in party decorations (balloons, decorations, wrapping paper, ribbon, etc.) to use as props in this **Etapa**. Also bring in as many items as possible (real or toy items) from p. 358–359. If this is not possible, have students draw and color them on paper plates.

Peer Review/Peer Teaching Assign partners (or groups of 3, if necessary) to be "editors" for each other throughout this **Etapa**. Editors will proofread partners' writing and give suggestions before the work is turned in.

357

Extra Help Have students work in pairs. One student gives a description of one person in the photo (physical characteristics, clothing, actions). The other student must guess who it is. Students should alternate turns.

Multiple Intelligences

Musical/Rhythmic Have students sing "Happy Birthday" in Spanish. (See Supplementary Vocabulary.)

Intrapersonal Have students imagine what their "dream" birthday celebration is like. Remind them that this celebration should fulfill all their hopes. They should write a short paragraph about who is there and what is happening.

Cross Cultural Connections

Ask students to compare the photo of the party here with birthday celebrations they have been to. Have students talk about birthday traditions in the U.S.

Culture Highlights

● **LA COCINA** The cuisine of Barcelona includes a variety of cakes and tarts made with fruits. Some examples are: **tarta de frutas** (fruit tart), **torta de manzanas** (apple cake), **torta de naranjas** (orange cake), and **pan de banana** (banana bread).

● **EL TURRÓN** Turrón is a delicious gourmet sweet that is very popular in Spain. It consists of peeled toasted almonds mixed with wild honey, sugar, and glucose. It has a chewy consistency.

Supplementary Vocabulary

los adornos	decorations
los globos	balloons
la bandera	banner
el papel de envolver	wrapping paper
la cinta	ribbon
los regalos	gifts

Following are the words to "Happy Birthday":

**Cumpleaños feliz
Te deseamos a ti.
Cumpleaños feliz
Te deseamos a ti.**

Block Schedule

Streamlining Assign one of the **¿Qué ves?** questions to each student. They will be responsible for not only answering the question, but expanding on it. For example: for question #1, students should also talk about how the other people feel. (For additional activities, see **Block Scheduling Copymasters.**)

Teaching Resource Options

Print

Unit 5 Resource Book
  Video Activities, pp. 125–126
  Videoscript, p. 128
  Audioscript, p. 131
  Audioscript *Para hispanohablantes*,
    p. 131

Audiovisual

OHT 161, 162, 163, 163A, 164, 164A,
167 (Quick Start)
Audio Program Cassette 15A / CD 15
Audio *Para hispanohablantes*
  Cassette 15A / CD 15
Video Program Videotape 5 /
  Videodisc 3A

Search Chapter 6, Play to 7
U5E3 • En contexto (Vocabulary)

Technology
Intrigas y aventuras CD-ROM, Disc 1

Quick Start Review

♻ Food vocabulary

Use OHT 167 or write on the board:
Write 5 food items you have eaten
recently.

Answers
Answers will vary. Answers could include:
una hamburguesa, unas papas fritas,
una torta, unos tacos, un sándwich,
unas tortillas, un bistec, una ensalada,
una enchilada, un pastel

Language Notes

• In Spain, the word **tarta** is often used
for cake. In earlier **Etapas,** students
learned the words **pastel** (Mexico) and
torta (Latin America).

• **Patatas alioli** is a dish that is similar to
potato salad. Two ingredients are garlic
and olive oil, from which it derives its
name. In **catalán, ali** is garlic and **oli** is
oil.

En contexto

🎧📺 VOCABULARIO

Luis's friends are finishing their preparations for his
surprise birthday party. Look at all of the food!

A Hay mucha comida para la fiesta. En
el frigorífico hay **una lata de zumo** y
crema. ¿Y en **el congelador?** ¡**Helado!**

el congelador

el helado

el frigorífico

el horno

la crema

la lata de zumo

B Para hacer la tarta, Marta usa
harina, huevos, mantequilla y
leche. Acaba de hacer **galletas.**

los huevos

la leche

las galletas

la mantequilla

la harina

las verduras

las salchichas

los tomates

las zanahorias

C Hay **verduras, tomates** y **zanahorias.**
También hay **salchichas.**

358 trescientos cincuenta y ocho
Unidad 5

Classroom Community

TPR Give students commands using the vocabulary
and the props collected ahead of time (see TE p. 356).
For example: **Apaga la luz. Pon una cebolla en tu
escritorio.**

Storytelling Have students use this **En contexto** as
a model and tell similar stories of preparing for a party.
They should also refer back to pp. 286–287 for
additional ideas.

cocinar

D

Iván **cocina en la estufa.**
Cocina **carne de res** con
cebollas.

las cebollas

la carne de res

la estufa

el microondas

el lavaplatos

las patatas

la botella de aceite

la pimienta   la sal

E Para **las patatas** alioli, Beto usa patatas, un
poco de **aceite, sal** y **pimienta.** También
usa mayonesa y otros ingredientes.

¡Cállate!

apagar la luz

F Cuando Luis llega, Marta **apaga la luz.**
Beto le dice a Marta «**¡Cállate!**».
¡Quieren silencio para darle la sorpresa a Luis!

Preguntas personales

1. ¿Te gusta cocinar?
2. ¿Qué postre prefieres, helado o galletas?
3. ¿Cuál usas más, la estufa o el microondas?
4. ¿Qué preparas?
5. ¿Qué hay en tu frigorífico?

trescientos cincuenta y nueve
Etapa 3   **359**

Teaching Suggestions
Introducing Vocabulary

- Have students look at pages
  358–359. Use OHT 161 and 162
  and Audio Cassette 15A / CD 15
  to present the vocabulary.
- Ask the Comprehension Questions
  below in order of yes/no (questions
  1–3), either/or (questions 4–6), and
  simple word or phrase (questions
  7–10). Expand by adding similar
  questions.
- Use the TPR activity to reinforce the
  meaning of individual words.
- Use the video vocabulary presentation
  for review and reinforcement.

Comprehension Questions

1. ¿Hay poca comida para la fiesta? (No.)
2. ¿Usa Marta verduras para hacer la torta?
   (No.)
3. ¿Acaba de hacer Marta las galletas? (Sí.)
4. ¿Hay crema o leche en la tarta?
   (crema)
5. ¿Usa Beto mantequilla o mayonesa en
   las patatas? (mayonesa)
6. ¿Usa Iván la estufa o el horno? (la
   estufa)
7. ¿Qué prepara Iván? (carne de res con
   cebollas)
8. ¿Qué hay en el congelador? (helado)
9. ¿Qué hace Marta cuando llega Luis?
   (apaga la luz)
10. ¿Por qué quieren todos callarse? (para
    darle la sorpresa a Luis)

Supplementary Vocabulary

la taza de medir	measuring cup
la cuchara de madera	wooden spoon
el tazón	bowl
el abrelatas	can opener
la espátula	spatula
la cacerola	cooking pot
el sartén	frying pan

■ Block Schedule

Process Time To allow students time
to process the information, have them
draw a picture of their kitchen or an
imaginary kitchen and label it. They
should include items out on the counter
or table.

Teaching All Students

Extra Help Arrange as many vocabulary items as
possible on a large table. Use drawings or photos
where necessary. Put a number on each item. Have
students walk around and identify the items on a sheet
of paper. After several minutes, have students return to
their seats. Hold up each item in order and have a
volunteer identify it. Have students check their papers.

Multiple Intelligences

Visual Have students design a menu for an upcoming
birthday celebration.
Kinesthetic One-by-one, hand students a food item
(use props, drawings, photos). Have them name the
item, then come up to the front of the room and put it
into one of three boxes marked: **el congelador, el
frigorífico, el armario.**

Teaching Resource Options

Print

Más práctica Workbook PE, pp. 121–124
Para hispanohablantes Workbook PE, pp. 121–122
Block Scheduling Copymasters
Unit 5 Resource Book
  Más práctica Workbook TE, pp. 103–106
  Para hispanohablantes Workbook TE, pp. 111–112
  Video Activities, pp. 125–126
  Videoscript, p. 129
  Audioscript, p. 131
  Audioscript *Para hispanohablantes*, p. 131

Audiovisual

OHT 165, 166, 167 (Quick Start)
Audio Program Cassette 15A / CD 15
Audio *Para hispanohablantes*
  Cassette 15A / CD 15
Video Program Videotape 5 / Videodisc 3A

Search Chapter 7, Play to 8
U5E3 • En vivo (Dialog)

Technology

Intrigas y aventuras CD-ROM, Disc 1

Quick Start Review

♻ Kitchen/cooking vocabulary
Use OHT 167 or write on the board:
Complete the following sentences logically:

1. Voy a hacer galletas. Necesito
   ____ , ____ y ____ .
2. Mis verduras favoritas son ____ y
   ____ .
3. En mi cocina no hay lavaplatos,
   pero si hay ____ y ____ .
4. En nuestro congelador, siempre
   tenemos ____ .

Answers *See p. 355B.*

Gestures

In scene 4, Álvaro says, **Hombre..**
Although the stress is usually on the next-to-last syllable, an exasperated Spaniard will stress the last syllable and throw up his/her hands at the same time: **¡Hom<u>bre</u>!**

En vivo

 DIÁLOGO

¡De compras!

 Álvaro   Marta   Iván   Beto

PARA ESCUCHAR • STRATEGY: LISTENING

Listen and take notes There are many different ways to celebrate a birthday. Luis's friends have prepared a meal for him. Listen and write down the menu. Were all categories mentioned?

Bebidas	Carne	Verduras	Postre

1 ► **Luis:** No lo puedo creer. Limpié la cocina, saqué la basura y tú, Carmen, pasaste la aspiradora.
Mercedes: ¿Y qué, Luis? ¿Qué es lo que no puedes creer?
Luis: Que es mi cumpleaños.

5 ► **Luis:** Trabajé en casa toda la mañana. Y ¡también tengo que cuidar a Carmen!
Álvaro: Ven a casa con Mercedes. Y trae a Carmen también.
Luis: Gracias. Nos vemos pronto.

6 ► **Marta:** ¡La tarta está lista, Álvaro! ¡Mírala!
Álvaro: ¡Quedó deliciosa! ¡Es la más deliciosa de Barcelona!
Marta: ¡Álvaro!
Álvaro: ¡Iván! ¿Está lista la carne de res?
Iván: Sí, claro.

7 ► **Álvaro:** ¡Beto! ¿Qué haces?
Beto: Estoy preparando un plato de verduras. ¡No te comas las zanahorias! ¿No ves que hay pocas?

 360 trescientos sesenta
Unidad 5

Classroom Community

Paired Activity Make copies of the Comprehension Questions (TE p. 361) and have students work in pairs to answer them. For any "No" answer, students should supply the correct information. Have each pair make up one additional question to ask the class.

Group Activity Have students work in groups of 3 or 4. Only one student at a time has the book open. That student quotes one person from one of the scenes. The other students guess who it is. The student who guesses correctly, supplies the next quote.

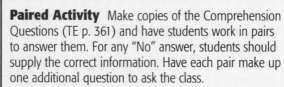

2▸ Luis: ¡El día empezó con demasiados quehaceres!
Carmen: ¡Yo te ayudé, Luis!
Luis: Sí, Carmen, tú me ayudaste y Mercedes también me ayudó.

3▸ Luis: Lo más increíble es que son las dos y ¡todavía no terminamos!
Mercedes: No te preocupes, Luis. ¿Por qué no llamas a Álvaro?
Luis: Buena idea. Os veo en la tienda.

4▸ Luis: Hola, Álvaro, soy Luis.
Álvaro: ¡Hola, Luis! ¿Dónde estás?
Luis: Voy a la tienda con Mercedes y Carmen. Tengo que hacer unas compras.
Álvaro: ¿Ahora? Hombre, te estoy esperando.

8▸ Luis: Necesito comprar leche, zumo, huevos y mantequilla.
Carmen: ¡No olvides el helado! ¡Es lo más rico del mundo!
Luis: Tenemos que llevar estas cosas a casa. Vamos, pronto.

9▸ Todos: ¡Feliz cumpleaños, Luis!
Luis: ¿Cómo puede ser? ¡Mercedes! ¡Álvaro!
Álvaro: Sí, amigo. Lo planeamos todo.
Luis: Pues, por fin, dime, Mercedes, ¿para qué son esas fotos?

10▸ Mercedes: Son para un concurso. ¡Y tú eres la estrella de mi proyecto! Y el título de mi proyecto es «Un día especial en la vida de un joven español».
Luis: ¡Te voy a decir definitivamente que este día es muy especial!

trescientos sesenta y uno
Etapa 3 | 361

Teaching All Students

Extra Help Give a 1-sentence description of each scene. Have students say which scene is being described. For example: **Luis llama a Álvaro.** (4)

Native Speakers Inquire about parties in students' home communities. What kinds of foods would be served? Is there a custom similar to our potluck suppers, where every guest brings a dish or a beverage?

Multiple Intelligences

Verbal First have students watch and listen to the video. Then ask students to listen to the audio only. Instruct students to close their eyes and imagine the character and the action as they hear each character's voice.

Teaching Suggestions
Presenting the Dialog

• Prepare students for listening by focusing on the dialog context using yes/no or either/or questions. Reintroduce the characters and setting: **¿Es Luis el hermano de Carmen? ¿Es hoy el cumpleaños de Mercedes o de Luis? ¿Hace Álvaro los quehaceres con sus amigos?**

• Use the video, audio cassette, or CD to present the dialog. The expanded dialog on video offers additional listening practice opportunities.

Video Synopsis

• Luis, Carmen, and Mercedes have more errands to run while Álvaro and other friends get ready for Luis's birthday party. For a complete transcript of the video dialog, see p. 355B.

Comprehension Questions

1. ¿Están de paseo Luis, Carmen y Mercedes? (No.)
2. ¿Sacó Luis la basura? (Sí.)
3. ¿Empezó el día con muchos quehaceres? (Sí.)
4. En la foto 3, ¿son las dos o son las dos y media? (son las dos)
5. ¿Quién va a llamar a Álvaro, Mercedes o Luis? (Luis)
6. ¿Está preparando la tarta Marta o Álvaro? (Marta)
7. ¿Qué está preparando Beto? (un plato de verduras)
8. ¿Qué quiere Carmen en la tienda? (helado)
9. ¿Cuál es la sorpresa para Luis? (una fiesta de cumpleaños)
10. ¿Por qué sacó Mercedes tantas fotos de Luis? (para el concurso)

Block Schedule

Previewing Point out to students that in this **Etapa** they will learn how to talk about events that have already happened. Tell them that there are several verbs in the dialog in the past tense. Have students try to identify them using context. (For additional activities, see **Block Scheduling Copymasters**.)

Teaching Resource Options

Print 📖

Unit 5 Resource Book
Video Activities, p. 127
Videoscript, p. 130
Audioscript, p. 131
Audioscript *Para hispanohablantes,*
p. 131

Audiovisual 📽️

OHT 168 (Quick Start)
Audio Program Cassette 15A / CD 15
Audio *Para hispanohablantes*
Cassette 15A / CD 15
Video Program Videotape 5 / Videodisc
3A

🔔 Quick Start Review

♻️ Dialog review

Use OHT 168 or write on the board:
Complete the following sentences from
the dialog:

1. El día empezó con demasiados
   ____ .
2. ¡Iván! ¿Está lista la ____ ?
3. Necesito comprar leche, zumo,
   ____ y mantequilla.
4. Estoy preparando un plato de
   ____ .
5. ¡Y tú eres la estrella de mi ____ !

Answers
1. quehaceres
2. carne de res
3. huevos
4. verduras
5. proyecto

Teaching Suggestions
Comprehension Check

Use **Actividades 1** and **2** to assess
retention after the dialog. Have
students close their books. Read the
items and see if students can
comprehend. Have students add 3
items to **Actividad 1.**

Objective: Transitional practice
Listening comprehension/vocabulary

Answers (See script p. 355B.)
1. e   2. d   3. a   4. b   5. c

En acción
VOCABULARIO Y GRAMÁTICA

ACTIVIDAD 1

Frases revueltas

Escuchar Completa las oraciones para describir lo que pasa en el
diálogo. *(Hint: Complete the sentences.)*

1. Luis tiene que cuidar a
2. Luis va a hacer
3. Carmen quiere comprar
4. Marta está feliz con
5. Los amigos de Luis están
   preparando

a. helado
b. su tarta
c. la comida
d. compras para su mamá
e. su hermana Carmen

ACTIVIDAD 2

¿En qué orden?

Escuchar ¿En qué orden pasan estas cosas? *(Hint: In what order do
they happen?)*

a. Luis entra en la tienda.
b. Luis, Mercedes y Carmen llegan a la casa de Álvaro.
c. Mercedes le dice a Luis que las fotos son para un concurso.
d. Los amigos de Luis le dicen «¡Feliz cumpleaños!».
e. Luis llama a Álvaro por teléfono.

TAMBIÉN SE DICE

Sometimes **el frigorífico** is used in Spain to talk about the refrigerator.
Other words are also used for this appliance.

• **la nevera**: Ecuador, Puerto Rico,
  parts of Spain
• **la heladera**: Argentina
• **el refrigerador**: Mexico

Spaniards say **zumo** for *juice.*
Latin Americans use **jugo.**

ACTIVIDAD 3

Marta necesita...

Hablar Marta está haciendo
una tarta para la fiesta de
Luis. ¿Qué necesita? *(Hint: Say
what Marta needs.)*

1.

2.

3.

4.

5.

Classroom Management

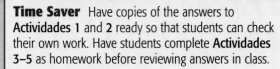

Time Saver Have copies of the answers to
Actividades 1 and **2** ready so that students can check
their own work. Have students complete **Actividades
3–5** as homework before reviewing answers in class.

Peer Review Have students recycle flashcards for
foods and drinks learned in earlier units. Then have
them make flashcards for the new foods in this **Etapa.**
Have students work in pairs to quiz each other on all
the cards. Each time they give a word, students should
also provide a sample sentence.

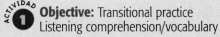

- *Use superlatives*
- *Use regular preterite -ar verbs*
- *Use preterite of -car, -gar, -zar verbs*

ACTIVIDAD 4

¿Qué cosa no debe estar?

Hablar Trabajas en un restaurante y tienes que poner todo en su lugar. Indica la cosa que no debe estar con las otras cosas. *(Hint: Say which item doesn't belong.)*

1. zumo	leche	agua	harina
2. galleta	cebolla	helado	flan
3. chorizo	salchicha	aceite	carne de res
4. crema	lechuga	tomate	zanahoria
5. azúcar	sal	huevos	pimienta
6. pescado	carne	puerco	zanahoria
7. cereal	pasta	leche	arroz
8. leche	puerco	yogur	crema

ACTIVIDAD 5

¡Lógicamente!

Leer Todos están muy ocupados con las preparaciones para la fiesta de Luis. Explica lo que hacen. *(Hint: Explain what they do.)*

1. Álvaro pone el helado en (el congelador, la mantequilla, la pimienta).

2. Marta saca la leche (de la estufa, del frigorífico, del lavaplatos).

3. Iván empieza a cocinar (el helado, el zumo, la carne de res) a la una.

4. Marta hace (unos huevos, unas patatas, unas galletas) porque a Luis le gustan las cosas dulces.

5. La carne está muy (caliente, picante, dulce) porque Iván acaba de cocinarla.

6. Álvaro pone los platos sucios en (el lavaplatos, el microondas, la estufa).

Vocabulario

La comida

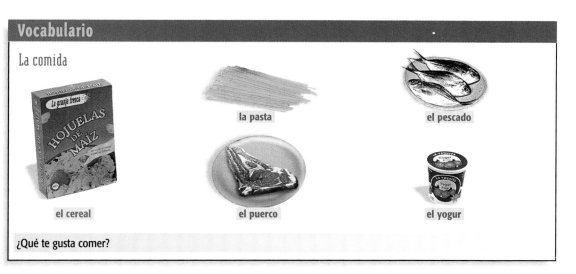

el cereal   la pasta   el pescado

el puerco   el yogur

¿Qué te gusta comer?

trescientos sesenta y tres
Etapa 3
363

Teaching All Students

Extra Help Have students write 5 more items for **Actividad 4** and quiz a partner.

Native Speakers Refer students to the pictures in **Actividad 3**. Does the packaging/presentation of the items look similar to what they have seen in their home communities? Ask them to describe similarities and differences.

Multiple Intelligences

Naturalist Have students investigate and report on the best places in their town/city to buy fresh produce. Have them visit a (super)market and make a list in Spanish of available items and prices. If possible, ask them to compare prices with a (super)market offering organic produce.

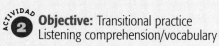

ACTIVIDAD 2 **Objective:** Transitional practice
Listening comprehension/vocabulary

Answers (See script p. 355B.)
e, a, b, d, c

ACTIVIDAD 3 **Objective:** Transitional practice
Food vocabulary

Answers
1. la leche
2. el azúcar
3. la mantequilla
4. los huevos
5. la harina

Teaching Suggestions
Presenting Vocabulary

Present the food vocabulary on p. 363 and review the food vocabulary on pp. 358–359 and 286–287. Then have students sort and classify the foods as **Carne/Pescado, Producto lácteo, Grano, Fruta/Verdura,** or **Dulce.**

ACTIVIDAD 4 **Objective:** Transitional practice
Food vocabulary

Answers

1. harina	5. huevos
2. cebolla	6. zanahoria
3. aceite	7. leche
4. crema	8. puerco

ACTIVIDAD 5 **Objective:** Transitional practice
Cooking vocabulary

Answers

1. el congelador	4. unas galletas
2. del frigorífico	5. caliente
3. la carne de res	6. el lavaplatos

Block Schedule

Expansion Expand **Actividad 3** into an activity using real recipes. Have students bring in their favorite recipes and tell the class what is needed. For additional vocabulary, they may consult dictionaries or native speakers in the classroom.

Teaching Resource Options

Print

Más práctica Workbook PE, p. 125
Para hispanohablantes Workbook PE, p. 123
Block Scheduling Copymasters
Unit 5 Resource Book
  Más práctica Workbook TE, p. 107
  Para hispanohablantes Workbook TE, p. 113
  Information Gap Activities, p. 119

Audiovisual

OHT 168 (Quick Start)

Technology

Intrigas y aventuras CD-ROM, Disc 1

Quick Start Review

⟳ Comparisons

Use OHT 168 or write on the board: Complete the following comparison sentences with a logical adjective:

1. Mi mejor amiga es más ____ que yo.
2. El béisbol es más ____ que el tenis.
3. Carmen estudia todo el tiempo. Es más ____ que Anita.
4. Las botas cuestan mucho. Son más ____ que los zapatos.

Answers
Answers will vary. Answers could include:
1. alta
2. divertido
3. trabajadora
4. caras

Teaching Suggestions
Teaching Talking About Extremes: Superlatives

Show 3 of the same article (**tres libros**). First make comparisons with them. (El libro de español es más nuevo que el libro de historia. El libro de historia es más nuevo que el libro de matemáticas.) Then state the superlative. (El libro de español es el más nuevo.)

GRAMÁTICA

Talking About Extremes: Superlatives

♻ **¿RECUERDAS?** *p. 202* Remember how you make comparisons? These phrases say that one item has more or less of a certain quality than another item has.

más... que
menos... que

When you want to say that something has the most or the least of a certain quality, use a **superlative.**

el más...	el menos...
los más...	los menos...
la más...	la menos...
las más...	las menos...

Luis es **el** más **alto.** Carmen es **la** más **pequeña.** Mercedes es **la** menos **cansada.**
Luis is the tallest. Carmen is the smallest. Mercedes is the least tired.

To use a **noun** with the superlative form, put it **after** the article.

matches

Luis es **el chico** más **alto.** Mercedes es **la chica** menos **cansada.**
Luis is the tallest boy. Mercedes is the least tired girl.

matches

Iván prepara **las comidas** más **sabrosas.**
Iván makes the tastiest meals.

Be sure the adjective matches the noun in both gender and number.

When you refer to an idea or concept, which has no gender, use the neuter article **lo**.

Luis says: — **Lo** más **increíble** es que son las dos...
The most incredible (thing) is that it's two o'clock...

Remember to use these **irregular** forms you learned with comparatives when referring to the *best, worst, oldest,* and *youngest.*

| **el mejor** | **el peor** | **el mayor** | **el menor** |

Luis es **el mayor.** Carmen es **la menor.**
Luis is the oldest. Carmen is the youngest.

Mayor and **menor** are used only when describing people.

Las comparaciones

Leer/Escribir ¿Qué decide Luis después de comparar todo? Lee la pregunta y contéstala. *(Hint: Explain what Luis decides.)*

modelo

La galleta no es sabrosa, la fruta es sabrosa y la tarta es muy sabrosa. (¿Cuál es la más sabrosa?)

La tarta es la más sabrosa.

1. Mercedes tiene 16 años, Carmen tiene 12 años y Marta tiene 17 años. (¿Quién es la menor?)
2. La casa de Luis tiene diez cuartos, la casa de Marta tiene ocho cuartos y la casa de Beto tiene seis cuartos. (¿Quién tiene la casa más pequeña?)
3. Antonio no es muy alto, Andrés es alto y Álvaro es muy alto. (¿Quién es el más alto?)
4. Las zanahorias cuestan 60 pesetas, los huevos cuestan 229 pesetas y la leche cuesta 103 pesetas. (¿Qué es lo menos caro?)
5. Iván saca una A en arte, Enrique saca una B y Pepe saca una C. (¿Quién es el mejor estudiante?)

■ **MÁS PRÁCTICA** *cuaderno* p. 125
■ **PARA HISPANOHABLANTES** *cuaderno* p. 123

Classroom Community

Game Have students work in groups of 3 and prepare 12 sets of cards. The sets should be modeled after **Actividad 7** and contain 3 similar items + adjectives. Then have students play a game where they each draw 1 of the 3 cards from each set. They must compare themselves to their opponents. The person who has the superlative of the group gets 3 points; the person with the middle gets 2 points; and the least gets 1 point.

Portfolio Have students write **Actividad 8** as a component of a time capsule representing teens' most and least favorite in these categories. They can add information about each category as well.

Rubric A = 13–15 pts. B = 10–12 pts. C = 7–9 pts. D = 4–6 pts. F = < 4 pts.

Writing criteria	Scale
Accuracy of superlatives	1 2 3 4 5
Other grammar/spelling accuracy	1 2 3 4 5
Creativity/appearance	1 2 3 4 5

ACTIVIDAD 7

♻ Cosas para la casa

Hablar/Escribir Los padres de Luis van a un mercado al aire libre para comprar cosas para la casa. Comparan lo que ven. ¿Qué dicen? *(Hint: Compare the items.)*

> *modelo*
>
> pequeño, grande
>
> La silla roja es la más **pequeña**.
>
> La silla azul es la más **grande**.

1. caro, barato

2. largo, corto

3. alto, bajo

4. limpio, sucio

5. viejo, nuevo

ACTIVIDAD 8

En mi opinión...

PARA CONVERSAR

STRATEGY: SPEAKING

Say what is the best and worst Decide **el mejor** or **el peor** of any of these: **equipo de baloncesto o béisbol, cantante, actor o actriz, grupo musical, película del año,** or any other categories you want to make.

Hablar Todos tienen opiniones. Da tu opinión sobre las siguientes cosas. *(Hint: Give your opinion.)*

> *modelo*
>
> la comida más rica
>
> **Estudiante A:** ¿Cuál es **la comida más rica** para tí?
>
> **Estudiante B:** El bistec es **la comida más rica**.

1. la música más popular

2. el deporte menos divertido

3. la clase menos difícil

4. el peor quehacer

5. el lugar más bonito

6. la película menos interesante

7. el actor más guapo

8. la actriz más bonita

■ **MÁS COMUNICACIÓN** p. R15

trescientos sesenta y cinco
Etapa 3

365

ACTIVIDAD 6 **Objective:** Controlled practice Superlatives

Answers
1. Carmen es la menor.
2. Beto tiene la casa más pequeña.
3. Álvaro es el más alto.
4. Las zanahorias son las menos caras.
5. Iván es el mejor estudiante.

ACTIVIDAD 7 **Objective:** Transitional practice Superlatives

♻ Adjective agreement

Answers
1. El sillón rojo es el más caro. El sillón blanco es el más barato.
2. La mesa marrón es la más larga. La mesa blanca es la más corta.
3. El frigorífico verde es el más alto. El frigorífico blanco es el más bajo.
4. La lámpara negra es la más sucia. La lámpara blanca es la más limpia.
5. La manta roja es la más nueva. La manta verde es la más vieja.

ACTIVIDAD 8 **Objective:** Open-ended practice Superlatives in conversation

Answers will vary.

🔔 Quick Wrap-up

Say a category and a person/thing in that category (**día de la semana/lunes**). Students say whether or not that person/thing is the best (**El lunes es el mejor día de la semana./El lunes no es el mejor día de la semana.**)

Teaching All Students

Extra Help Have students write down 5 adjectives and build comparative/superlative statements for each. For example: **inteligente. Ricardo es inteligente. Ignacio es más inteligente. Luis es el más inteligente.**

Native Speakers Give students 5–10 themes (home, travel, vacation, books, etc.) and have them make superlative statements about each.

Multiple Intelligences

Logical/Mathematical Have students gather statistics about their areas of interest. They should have at least 3 examples. Have them draw conclusions from the statistics to say who/what is the "most." For example: **Mo Vaughn es fuerte. Sammy Sosa es más fuerte. Pero Mark McGwire es el jugador de béisbol más fuerte.**

■ Block Schedule

Change of Pace Prepare a set of cards with categories on them similar to those in **Actividad 8.** Have students draw a card and talk for at least 30 seconds about 3 members of the group and rank them. (For additional activities, see **Block Scheduling Copymasters.**)

Teaching Resource Options

Print

Más práctica Workbook PE, pp. 126–127
Para hispanohablantes Workbook PE,
pp. 124–125
Block Scheduling Copymasters
Unit 5 Resource Book
  Más práctica Workbook TE,
   pp. 108–109
  Para hispanohablantes Workbook
   TE, pp. 114–115
  Audioscript, p. 132
  Audioscript *Para hispanohablantes*,
   p. 132

Audiovisual

OHT 168 (Quick Start)
Audio Program Cassettes 15A, 15B /
CD 15
Audio *Para hispanohablantes*
Cassette 15A / CD 15

Technology

Intrigas y aventuras CD-ROM, Disc 1

Quick Start Review

♻ Superlatives

Use OHT 168 or write on the board:
Write a superlative statement based on
the following information.

1. Carlos, 5 ft. 7 in. / Ana, 5 ft. 3 in. /
   Sofía, 5 ft. 8 in.
2. Roberto, D (nota) / Jaime, A /
   Miguel, C
3. el sofá, $375 / el sillón, $60 /
   la mesa, $200
4. Sr. Ruíz, 75 años / Sr. Ricardo, 80
   años / Sr. Fernández, 60 años

Answers *See p. 355B.*

Teaching Suggestions
Presenting The Preterite of Regular -ar Verbs

• Make up a short scenario using **-ar**
  verbs to say what you did before school
  today. (**Preparé el desayuno...**)
• Present the vocabulary words in
  sample sentences using a calendar.
  Mark an X for today. Then point to
  each appropriate day, week, month,
  year as you give each sentence.

GRAMÁTICA

Talking About the Past: The Preterite of Regular -ar Verbs

▶ When you want to talk about actions completed in the past, use the
preterite tense. To form the preterite of a regular **-ar** verb, add the
appropriate preterite **ending** to the verb's **stem**.

limpiar *to clean*

Notice that the first and
third person singular
forms have an **accent**
over the final vowel.

limpi**é**	limpi**amos**
limpi**aste**	limpi**asteis**
limpi**ó**	limpi**aron**

The **nosotros(as)**
form is the same in
the **preterite** as in
the **present** tense.

Luis says:
—**Limpié** la cocina…
—Sí, Carmen, tú me **ayudaste** y Mercedes también
me **ayudó**.
I cleaned the kitchen…
Yes, Carmen, you helped me and Mercedes helped me also.

ACTIVIDAD 9 Gramática

Las compras

Leer Álvaro le explica a Beto qué compraron para la fiesta.
Completa sus oraciones con la forma correcta de **comprar**.
(Hint: Complete what Álvaro explains.)

Nosotros __1__ cosas riquísimas para la fiesta de Luis,
¿verdad? Marta __2__ los huevos, la harina, la mantequilla y la
leche para hacer la tarta. Iván __3__ la carne de res y las
cebollas para hacer su plato riquísimo. Tú __4__ las patatas y el
aceite para hacer las patatas alioli. Bárbara y Luisa __5__ los
refrescos. ¿Y yo? Pues, yo __6__ lo más rico de todo, ¡el
helado!

Vocabulario

El pasado

anoche *last night*

anteayer *the day before
yesterday*

el año pasado *last year*

ayer *yesterday*

el mes pasado *last month*

la semana pasada *last week*

¿Cuándo patinaste (nadaste,
cocinaste)?

Classroom Community

Group Activity As a class, brainstorm a list of
regular **-ar** verbs and write them on the board or
overhead. Then have students work in groups of 5–6.
Each student says one thing they did last night,
yesterday, etc., using the new **Vocabulario**. Group
members must then ask one additional question about
that activity.

Storytelling In pairs, have students use a list of **-ar**
verbs and prepare a story (realistic or imaginative)
about what someone did over the past week. Have
each pair present their story to the class, using
intonation and gestures.

ACTIVIDAD 10 Gramática

¿Qué terminaron ayer?

Hablar/Escribir Luis habla de los quehaceres que él y sus amigos terminaron ayer. ¿Qué dice? *(Hint: Explain what they finished yesterday.)*

1. Ana y Marta **2.** tú **3.** Álvaro

4. Sara y yo **5.** ellos **6.** Juana

■ **MÁS PRÁCTICA** *cuaderno* pp. 126–127

■ **PARA HISPANOHABLANTES** *cuaderno* pp. 124–125

APOYO PARA ESTUDIAR

Preterite Tense

Since the **nosotros** form of a regular **-ar** verb is the same in both the preterite and the present tenses, how can you determine the tense? Use context clues to help you. Look for time indicators, like those in the vocabulary box, and the tense of other verbs.

ACTIVIDAD 11

¿Por qué no me invitaste?

Escuchar Juana y su amigo Miguel hablan de una fiesta. Escucha su conversación. Luego, contesta las preguntas. *(Hint: Answer the questions.)*

1. ¿Qué celebraron las chicas?

2. ¿Cuándo celebraron?

3. ¿Por qué Juana no invitó a Miguel?

4. ¿A cuántas chicas invitó?

5. ¿Cómo pasaron la noche?

ACTIVIDAD 12

¿Cuándo...?

Hablar/Escribir Pregúntales a cinco estudiantes cuándo hicieron estas actividades. Haz una lista. *(Hint: Ask when others did these activities.)*

modelo

terminar la tarea

Tú: *¿Cuándo **terminaste la tarea**?*

Pablo: ***Terminé la tarea** anteayer.*

Actividad	Pablo
1. terminar la tarea	anteayer
2. preparar una comida	
3. lavar los platos	
4. patinar sobre hielo	
5. usar la computadora	
6. escuchar un disco compacto	
7. limpiar tu habitación	

trescientos sesenta y siete
Etapa 3 | **367**

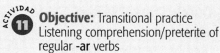

ACTIVIDAD 9
Objective: Controlled practice
Preterite of regular **-ar** verbs

Answers
1. compramos
2. compró
3. compró
4. compraste
5. compraron
6. compré

ACTIVIDAD 10
Objective: Controlled practice
Preterite of regular **-ar** verbs
♻ Chores

Answers
1. Ana y Marta lavaron los platos.
2. Tú pasaste la aspiradora.
3. Álvaro cocinó.
4. Sara y yo quitamos el polvo.
5. Ellos quitaron la mesa.
6. Juana planchó.

ACTIVIDAD 11
Objective: Transitional practice
Listening comprehension/preterite of regular **-ar** verbs

Answers (See script p. 355B.)
1. Las chicas celebraron el cumpleaños de Yolanda con una fiesta sorpresa para ella.
2. Celebraron el viernes pasado.
3. Porque invitó sólo a chicas.
4. Invitó a diez chicas.
5. Escucharon música, cantaron, miraron fotos y hablaron.

ACTIVIDAD 12
Objective: Open-ended practice
Preterite of regular **-ar** verbs in conversation

Answers
Student B answers will vary.
1. A: ¿Cuándo terminaste la tarea?
   B: Terminé la tarea...
2. A: ¿Cuándo preparaste una comida?
   B: Preparé una comida...
3. A: ¿Cuándo lavaste los platos?
   B: Lavé los platos...
4. A: ¿Cuándo patinaste sobre hielo?
   B: Patiné sobre hielo...
5. A: ¿Cuándo usaste la computadora?
   B: Usé la computadora...
6. A: ¿Cuándo escuchaste un disco compacto?
   B: Escuché un disco compacto...
7. A: ¿Cuándo limpiaste tu habitación?
   B: Limpié mi habitación...

■ Block Schedule

Interviews Have students write a series of interview questions to ask a partner. Suggest a common theme, such as "what you studied last year" or "what you cooked last week." Have students take notes and report findings to the class. (For additional activities, see **Block Scheduling Copymasters**.)

Teaching All Students

Extra Help On index cards, have students write subject nouns and pronouns, **-ar** verb stems, and preterite endings. Then have them work in pairs, make combinations with the cards, and create sentences.

Native Speakers Ask students to talk about what young people do on Saturday night in their home communities.

Multiple Intelligences

Verbal Use the preterite of regular **-ar** verbs in questions that would be answered with a direct object. Have students answer quickly with the **yo** form of the verb. For example: **¿Qué lavaste anoche? / Yo lavé el carro.**

Teaching Resource Options

Print

Más práctica Workbook PE, p. 128
Para hispanohablantes Workbook PE, p. 126
Unit 5 Resource Book
  Más práctica Workbook TE, p. 110
  Para hispanohablantes Workbook TE, p. 116

Audiovisual

OHT 169 (Quick Start)

Technology

Intrigas y aventuras CD-ROM, Disc 1

Quick Start Review

♻ Preterite of **-ar** verbs

Use OHT 169 or write on the board:
Complete the following sentences with the appropriate preterite forms:

1. Ayer Tomás ____ la aspiradora en casa. (pasar)
2. Anoche Susana y Sylvia ____ todas sus camisas. (planchar)
3. El mes pasado Eduardo y yo ____ la casa de nuestra abuela. (limpiar)
4. Esta mañana tú ____ la basura, ¿no? (sacar)
5. Anteayer, yo ____ mi libro de español en casa. (olvidar)

Answers *See p. 355B.*

Teaching Suggestions
Teaching Preterite of Verbs Ending in -car, -gar, and -zar

• Emphasize that these spelling changes take place only in the **yo** form. Have students write out and say aloud the entire conjugations.
• Dictate short sentences using some of these verbs and have students underline them.

 Objective: Controlled practice Preterite of verbs ending in **-car, -gar,** and **-zar**

Answers
1. empecé	5. llegué
2. jugué	6. toqué
3. busqué	7. saqué
4. practiqué	8. almorcé

GRAMÁTICA

Preterite of Verbs Ending in -car, -gar, and -zar

Regular verbs that end in **-car**, **-gar**, or **-zar** have a spelling change in the **yo form** of the preterite.

		becomes	
sa**car**	**c**	**qu**	(yo) sa**qu**é
pa**gar**	**g**	**gu**	(yo) pa**gu**é
empe**zar**	**z**	**c**	(yo) empe**c**é

Luis says:

—…sa**qu**é la basura…
…**I took out** the trash…

ACTIVIDAD 13 · Gramática

¡Una semana llena!

Leer Mercedes habla de sus actividades de la semana pasada. ¿Qué dice? Completa sus oraciones con el pretérito de cada verbo.
(Hint: Complete what Mercedes says.)

El lunes __1__ (empezar) a leer un libro de historia muy largo. El martes __2__ (jugar) al voleibol con mis amigas. El miércoles fui al centro comercial con mi mamá y __3__ (buscar) unos jeans nuevos para la fiesta del sábado. El jueves __4__ (practicar) el tenis con Elena. El viernes __5__ (llegar) tarde a la escuela. ¡Por fin llegó el sábado! Fui a una fiesta donde __6__ (tocar) la guitarra y __7__ (sacar) muchas fotos. El domingo __8__ (almorzar) en casa de mis abuelos.

ACTIVIDAD 14 · Gramática

¿Qué pasó en la fiesta?

Hablar/Escribir Álvaro explica lo que pasó en la fiesta. ¿Qué dice? *(Hint: What does Álvaro explain?)*

modelo

Luis / llegar / **3:00**   Luis llegó a las tres.

1. yo / apagar /
2. Mercedes / sacar /
3. yo / tocar /
4. Carmen y Samuel / jugar con /
5. todos / almorzar /
6. yo / empezar a /

🟦 **MÁS PRÁCTICA** *cuaderno* p. 128
🟦 **PARA HISPANOHABLANTES** *cuaderno* p. 126

Classroom Community

Paired Activity Have students use **más** (+), **menos** (–), **por** (x), and **dividido por** (÷) to make up several math problems for each other. One person reads a problem aloud, both write the answer it, and partners then compare answers.

Cooperative Learning Have groups of 4 students first review the **Repaso de vocabulario** section in all **Etapas** to compile a complete list of **-car, -gar,** and **-zar** verbs. Then have them write a group story. Student 1 writes a subject noun/pronoun. Student 2 writes a form of a **-car, -gar,** or **-zar** verb. Student 3 completes a logical sentence. Student 4 reads the sentence aloud. The group evaluates the sentence and makes necessary corrections. Student 2 begins the next round. The second sentence must continue the story of the first sentence. Continue for 4 sentences.

NOTA CULTURAL

When shopping in Spain, take along many **pesetas**. The **peseta** is the currency, and you will need a lot of them when you shop! To find out their exchange rate, check a current newspaper. Sometimes you will see the word **pesetas** abbreviated as **ptas**.

ACTIVIDAD 15

¿Tienes buena memoria?

Hablar/Escribir Pregúntales a cinco estudiantes sobre sus actividades. Escribe sus respuestas. *(Hint: Ask about activities.)*

modelo

Tú: *¿A qué hora llegaste a la escuela ayer?*

Otro(a) estudiante: *Llegué a la escuela a las siete y veinte.*
      o: *No sé a qué hora llegué.*

	Estudiante 1	Estudiante 2
1. ¿Qué deporte practicaste el año pasado?		
2. ¿Qué buscaste en el centro comercial este año?		
3. ¿Qué almorzaste anteayer?		
4. ¿Cuándo empezaste a estudiar español?		
5. ¿Qué fotos sacaste en tus últimas vacaciones?		

Vocabulario

Los números de 200 a 1.000.000

doscientos(as) 200
trescientos(as) 300
cuatrocientos(as) 400
quinientos(as) 500
seiscientos(as) 600
setecientos(as) 700
ochocientos(as) 800
novecientos(as) 900
mil 1.000
un millón 1.000.000

¿Qué cuesta más de cien dólares?

Periods are used instead of commas for thousands and millions. The word **y** is used as you previously learned. It is *not* used after hundreds, thousands, or millions.

148 = ciento cuarenta **y** ocho   1.968 = mil novecientos sesenta **y** ocho

250 = doscientos cincuenta   1.000.562 = un millón quinientos sesenta **y** dos

The word **ciento** is used instead of **cien** before numbers greater than 100.

La bicicleta costó **cien** dólares.   El radio costó **ciento cincuenta** dólares.

Numbers ending in 200–900 agree in gender and number with nouns.

Costó doscient**os dólares.**   Pagué doscient**as pesetas.**

Un millón is followed by **de** before nouns.   **un millón de** dólares

trescientos sesenta y nueve
Etapa 3   **369**

Teaching All Students

Extra Help Have students write various numerals on cards. Then have them work in small groups and practice saying the numbers out loud.

Native Speakers Ask students to use **Actividad 14** as a model to describe a typical fiesta in their home communities.

Multiple Intelligences

Logical/Mathematical Have students calculate how much money they spent yesterday, last month, and last year. Ask them to tell what they bought. Remind students to use the past tense.

ACTIVIDAD 14 **Objective:** Open-ended practice Preterite of verbs ending in **-car**, **-gar**, and **-zar**

Answers
1. Yo apagué la luz.
2. Mercedes sacó fotos.
3. Yo toqué la guitarra.
4. Carmen y Samuel jugaron con los videojuegos.
5. Todos almorzaron salchicha.
6. Yo empecé a cantar.

ACTIVIDAD 15 **Objective:** Transitional practice Preterite of verbs ending in **-car**, **-gar**, and **-zar** in conversation

Answers will vary.

Teaching Suggestions
Presenting Vocabulary

• Have students practice numbers by counting by 10s, 20s, 50s, etc. Have them count backwards from 1000 to 100 by 100s, 50s, etc.
• Dictate 4-digit numbers and have students write the numerals on the board.

Culture Highlights

● **LAS PESETAS** Looking at **peseta** coins can help determine when they were minted. Old coins display a likeness of Franco; newer ones show King Juan Carlos. **Peseta** bills have the king on one side and pictures of famous Spaniards on the other.

Interdisciplinary Connection

History Bring in examples of **peseta** coins and bills. Make a list of people pictured on them. Have students research these people and why they are important.

 Block Schedule

Process Time Have students use as many of the **-car**, **-gar**, and **-zar** verbs in the **yo** form as possible. For example, **Saqué la basura. Empecé la tarea.** Limit their time to 3–5 minutes. Have volunteers read some of their sentences to the class.

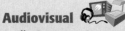
ACTIVIDAD 16 **Objective:** Transitional practice
Listening comprehension/preterite of
verbs ending in -car, -gar, and -zar/
Numbers

Answers (See script p. 355B.)
1. 3.000 (tres mil) pesetas
2. 8.600 (ocho mil) seiscientas pesetas
3. 5.500 (cinco mil) quinientas pesetas
4. 1.300 (mil trescientas) pesetas
5. 800 (ochocientas) pesetas

Teaching Suggestions
Presenting Vocabulary

Present the words for quantities in
familiar contexts. For example: **una
docena de huevos, un litro de leche,
un paquete de azúcar.** Have students
add more examples.

ACTIVIDAD 17 **Objective:** Open-ended practice
Quantities and numbers

Answers will vary.

¿Cuánto pagaron?

Escuchar Alicia, una amiga de Luis, habla de las
cosas que ella y sus amigas compraron. Escucha
lo que dice. ¿Cuánto pagaron por cada cosa?
(Hint: Say what it cost.)

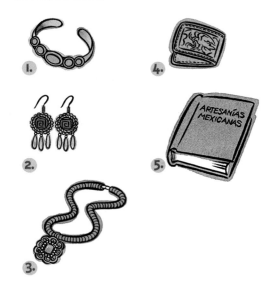

1.
2.
3.
4.
5.

Vocabulario

Las cantidades

la docena *dozen*	**el paquete** *package*
el gramo *gram*	**el pedazo** *piece*
el kilo *kilogram*	**cuarto(a)** *quarter*
el litro *liter*	**medio(a)** *half*

Use the definite article when talking about the price of a
specific quantity of food.

  Los huevos cuestan 200 pesetas **la** docena.

  El pescado cuesta 1.500 pesetas **el** kilo.

¿Cuándo usas estas cantidades?

Compras para la fiesta

Hablar/Leer Imagínate que estás en España.
Tú y un(a) amigo(a) van a hacer una fiesta.
Tienen 7.500 pesetas para comprar comida y
refrescos. Lee el anuncio. ¿Qué van a comprar?
(Hint: Say what you'll buy.)

modelo

Estudiante A: *¿Compramos salchicha?*

Estudiante B: *¿A cuánto está?*

Estudiante A: *Está a setecientas cincuenta pesetas el kilo.*

Estudiante B: *Bueno, vamos a comprar dos kilos.*

Nota

¿A cuánto está(n)…? is an expression used to ask how
much something costs. It is often used with food items that
may increase or decrease in price given a good or bad
harvest. It may also indicate changing prices during a sale.

¡SuperEspeciales! 210 ptas/2 botellas · 500 ptas

Supermercado BuenPrecio

750 ptas/kilo · 550 ptas/kilo
285 ptas/kilo · 250 ptas/kilo
125 ptas/kilo · 550 ptas/6 botellas
400 ptas/3 latas · ¡Especiales de la semana!

Classroom Community

Paired Activity After completing **Actividad 16,**
have pairs discuss items (real or imaginary) they have
recently purchased. Ask them to tell what they bought,
how much they paid, where they bought the items, and
when.

Group Activity **Prepare ahead:** Ask students to
bring in supermarket ads similar to the one on p. 370.
Have students do a variation of **Actividad 17.** They will
pretend that they are going to purchase food for the
group for one week. They must establish a budget and
a food list. Have groups report back to the class. Did
they stay within their budgets? Did they purchase food
for well-balanced meals?

ACTIVIDAD 18

Los regalos

Hablar/Escribir Todos le compraron a Luis un regalo de cumpleaños. ¿Cuánto pagaron? *(Hint: How much did they pay?)*

Álvaro

modelo

Álvaro pagó ochocientas pesetas por el disco compacto.

1. Mercedes

3. Iván y Beto

2. los padres de Luis

4. yo

ACTIVIDAD 19

¿Qué van a comprar?

Hablar/Escribir Imagínate que vives en España. ¿Qué van a comprar tú y estas personas con el dinero que tienen? *(Hint: Say what they'll buy.)*

modelo

yo / 500 ptas

Tengo quinientas pesetas. Voy a comprar un libro.

1. yo / 500 ptas.

2. mi hermano(a) / 200 ptas.

3. mi madre / 800 ptas.

4. mis tíos / 80.000 ptas.

5. mis padres / 25.000 ptas.

6. mi amigo(a) / 750 ptas.

7. mi vecino / 1.500 ptas.

ACTIVIDAD 20

Una fiesta

Escribir Describe una fiesta real o imaginaria. Incluye la siguiente información. *(Hint: Describe a party.)*

- ¿Cuándo y dónde celebraron la fiesta?
- ¿Cómo prepararon la fiesta?
- ¿Quiénes ayudaron para hacer la fiesta?
- ¿Cómo pasaron la noche?

modelo

El año pasado celebramos el cumpleaños de mi abuela con una fiesta en mi casa. Muchos ayudaron. Mis hermanos limpiaron la casa. Mi mamá preparó la comida: salchichas, verduras y carne de res. Yo preparé un pastel riquísimo. Apagué la luz y cuando mi abuela llegó por fin a la casa, todos le cantamos «Cumpleaños feliz». Saqué muchas fotos. Bailamos toda la noche y…

■ **MÁS COMUNICACIÓN** p. R15

Pronunciación

Refranes

Linking words Native speakers may seem to speak quickly when they link their words together in breath groups. Instead of pronouncing each word separately, they run some words together. This is common in all languages. Practice linking words in the following sentences.

Él que algo quiere, algo le cuesta.

Aceite de oliva, todo el mal quita.

La larga experiencia, más que los libros enseña.

ACTIVIDAD 18
Objective: Controlled practice Preterite of verbs ending in **-car**, **-gar**, and **-zar**/Numbers

Answers

1. Mercedes pagó mil doscientas pesetas por la camiseta.
2. Los padres de Luis pagaron quince mil pesetas por el radiocasete.
3. Iván y Beto pagaron dos mil quinientas pesetas por el videojuego.
4. Yo pagué setecientas cincuenta pesetas por la cartera.

ACTIVIDAD 19
Objective: Transitional practice Numbers

Answers

Answers will vary.

1. Tengo quinientas pesetas. Voy a comprar…
2. Mi hermano(a) tiene doscientas pesetas. Va a comprar…
3. Mi madre tiene ochocientas pesetas. Va a comprar…
4. Mis tíos tienen ochenta mil pesetas. Van a comprar…
5. Mis padres tienen veinticinco mil pesetas. Van a comprar…
6. Mi amigo(a) tiene setecientas cincuenta pesetas. Va a comprar…
7. Mi vecino tiene mil quinientas pesetas. Va a comprar…

ACTIVIDAD 20
Objective: Open-ended practice Planning a party

Answers will vary.

Dictation

After presenting the **Pronunciación**, have students close their books. Dictate the **refranes** in segments while students write them.

■ Block Schedule

FunBreak Pass out self-stick slips of paper to half the class. These students will label their clothing, jewelry, books, etc. and add prices. They will also cut out pictures of expensive items from magazines, label these, and display them. Pass out several thousand dollars in play money to the other half of the class. These students will walk around the room and practice the art of **el regateo**. When a sale is made, the buyer counts out the money to the seller and collects the price tag. At the end of "market day," find out who spent the most, sold the most, sold the least, etc. (For additional activities, see **Block Scheduling Copymasters**.)

Teaching All Students

Extra Help Bring in Spanish newspaper articles that include high numbers. Have students read the numbers out loud in Spanish. Give extra credit to anyone who can also summarize the article.

Multiple Intelligences

Kinesthetic Have students make play **pesetas** (coins and bills). Then have them design "paychecks" to be cashed. Assign 4–5 students to be bank tellers. The other students go to the bank and cash their "paychecks." They must tell the teller the amount. The teller counts out the cash for the customer.

Teaching Resource Options

Print

Block Scheduling Copymasters
Unit 5 Resource Book
  Audioscript, p. 133
  Audioscript *Para hispanohablantes,*
    p. 133

Audiovisual

OHT 169 (Quick Start)
Audio Program Cassette 15A / CD 15
Audio *Para hispanohablantes*
  Cassette 15A / CD 15
Canciones Cassette / CD

Quick Start Review

🔁 Quantities

Use OHT 169 or write on the board:
Complete the sentences with an
appropriate quantity:

1. Los huevos cuestan 200 pesetas
   ___ .
2. Ayer compré ___ de galletas.
3. Este pescado cuesta 1.500
   pesetas ___ .
4. ¿Cuántos ___ de pimienta quiere
   usted?
5. Diego, cómprame ___ de
   limonada

Answers
1. la docena   4. gramos
2. un paquete   5. un litro
3. el kilo

Teaching Suggestions

• **Prereading** Have students scan the
  reading and describe what they see.

• **Strategy: Reorganize information
  to check understanding** Discuss
  the reading strategy and have
  students complete a recipe card.
  Are students familiar with all these
  ingredients?

• **Reading** Have students first look at
  the ¿Comprendiste? questions. Then
  have them read the selection with
  these questions in mind.

• **Post-reading** Ask students to give a
  description of the photo on p. 373.

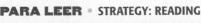

En voces
LECTURA

PARA LEER • **STRATEGY: READING**

Reorganize information to check understanding A family
friend gave you a copy of this recipe from her
favorite cookbook. She has asked you to write
it down as a recipe for her card file. Read «**Los
favoritos de la cocina española**» and fill out the
recipe card for her.

La paella valenciana			
Paso	Ingredientes	Cantidad	Instrucciones
1.	Aceite	1/4 taza	Pon en la sartén
2.			
3.			
4.			

Ésta es la receta[1] de un plato muy especial, la paella
valenciana. Es importante usar los ingredientes más
frescos[2] posibles. Y busca el mejor azafrán[3]. El azafrán
da sabor[4] y color a la paella. Si no hay azafrán, no hay
paella. A todo el mundo le gusta tanto la paella que
generalmente no queda[5] nada. Pero si queda algo,
ponlo en el frigorífico para mañana.

[1] recipe   [3] saffron   [5] remains   [7] cloves of garlic   [9] sweet red pepper
[2] freshest [4] flavor   [6] chef   [8] green peas   [10] shrimp

372 trescientos setenta y dos
Unidad 5

LOS FAVORITOS
de la cocina española

De la cocina de Maruja Serrat,
cocinera[6] del restaurante
Tibidabo de Barcelona

Paella valenciana
para cuatro personas
Ingredientes

  1/4 taza de aceite de oliva
  1/2 kilo de pollo
  1/4 kilo de salchicha
  1 cebolla
  2 dientes de ajo[7]
  1 tomate
  1/2 taza de guisantes[8]
  1 pimentón[9]
  1/4 kilo de calamares
  200 gramos de gambas[10]
  sal y pimienta
  1 1/2 taza de arroz
  1/2 cucharadita de azafrán
  3 tazas de agua

Classroom Community

Group Activity If your school has cooking facilities,
have students sign up to bring in as many paella
ingredients as possible. Fill in with any others needed.
Groups of students will work together to prepare and
serve the dish. If cooking in school is not possible, ask
groups of students to work together at home to
prepare the dish and bring it to school for the class to
enjoy.

Learning Scenario Have students write and
perform commercials for their favorite foods. They may
also invent a food product. Encourage them to use
props and gestures, as well as **tú** commands.

Instrucciones

Primero pon el aceite de oliva en la sartén [11]. Corta [12] el pollo y la salchicha en pedazos. Fríelos [13] por diez minutos. Luego corta la cebolla, el ajo, el tomate y el pimentón. Ponlos en la sartén junto con los guisantes. Ahora añade [14] los calamares y las gambas, la sal y la pimienta. En otra sartén o en una paellera [15], cocina el arroz en el agua. Luego añade el pollo, la salchicha, los calamares, las gambas, las verduras y el azafrán. Cocínalo otros veinte minutos. Sirve la paella en la paellera.

---

[11] frying pan [12] cut [13] fry them [14] add [15] paella pan

NOTA CULTURAL

Paella is a typical dish of Valencia, a region next to Cataluña. It is found throughout Spain.

¿Comprendiste?

1. ¿Por qué es importante el azafrán?
2. Si hay demasiada paella, ¿qué debes hacer?
3. ¿Qué haces con el pollo y la salchicha?
4. ¿Qué pones en la segunda sartén?
5. Después de poner el azafrán, ¿cuánto tiempo cocinas la paella?

¿Qué piensas?

1. ¿Es fácil o difícil hacer esta receta? ¿Por qué?
2. ¿Te gustaría comer paella? ¿Por qué?

Hazlo tú

¿Tienes una receta especial de tu familia? Explica cómo preparas este plato en tu casa.

Cross Cultural Connections

Strategy Have students compare the ingredients in this typical Spanish recipe with ingredients in typical North American dishes or dishes from your area of the U.S.

Critical Thinking

Ask students to think about how to approach a recipe. Does it make sense to read the list of ingredients first or the instructions? Does it help them to have a photograph to look at as well? Would they try a recipe that was not accompanied by a photo?

Culture Highlights

● **LA GASTRONOMÍA DE BARCELONA** Many traditional dishes of Barcelona have **catalán** names; for example, **escudella I carn d'olla,** a soup made of vegetables, rice, and potatoes. Other traditional dishes are **cocido con judías blancas, favas a la catalana,** and **arroz a la cazuela.**

The spice **azafrán** (saffron) is a common spice in Spanish cooking. It gives the rice its yellow color.

¿Comprendiste?

Answers
1. Porque da sabor y color a la paella. Si no hay azafrán, no hay paella.
2. Debes ponerlo en el frigorífico para mañana.
3. Los cortas en pedazos.
4. Pones el arroz en el agua.
5. Cocinas la paella otros veinte minutos.

Teaching All Students

Extra Help Have students learn ingredients first by consulting the recipe and the glosses, and then by finding each ingredient in the instructions. Next, have students close their books and name as many ingredients as they can from memory. Then pass out a worksheet on which you list the ingredients, but with letters missing from each word.

Native Speakers Ask students if there are any traditional dishes from their home communities that they particularly enjoy or associate with certain occasions. Have them bring in recipes in Spanish and share them with the class.

Block Schedule

Variety Have students find all the commands used for cooking instructions in the reading and write them on cards. Then have them use each command in a cooking demonstration of their own choosing. (For additional activities, see **Block Scheduling Copymasters.**)

Teaching Resource Options

Print

Unit 5 Resource Book
Audioscript, p. 133
Audioscript *Para hispanohablantes*,
    p. 133

Audiovisual

Audio Program Cassette 15A / CD 15
Audio *Para hispanohablantes*
    Cassette 15A / CD 15
OHT 169 (Quick Start)
Video Program Videotape 5 / Videodisc
    3A

Search Chapter 8, Play to 9
U5E3 • En colores (Culture)

🔔 Quick Start Review

♻️ Places in a city

Use OHT 169 or write on the board:
List at least 10 places/buildings you
would find in a typical city.

Answers

Answers will vary. Answers could include:
un centro, una plaza, un museo, un parque,
una iglesia, un restaurante, un café, un banco,
una farmacia, una tienda, un correo, una
biblioteca, un cine, un teatro, un calle, una
avenida, un hotel, un aeropuerto

Teaching Suggestions
Presenting Cultura y comparaciones

• Have students read the Connecting
  Cultures Strategy and discuss how
  students will create their time lines.

• Have students look at the buildings in
  the photos. Ask them to suggest
  adjectives that describe them. Write
  their suggestions on the board.

• Show students a street map of
  Barcelona and point out where these
  buildings are. Have students count
  the number of blocks between them.
  Do they recommend walking or
  taking a bus?

• Expand the cultural information by
  showing the video culture presentation.

En colores
CULTURA Y COMPARACIONES

Casa Amatller

PARA CONOCERNOS
STRATEGY: CONNECTING CULTURES
Make a historical time line Place Barcelona's
rich architectural history on a time line from
ancient times to the present. First label each
period with a word or two to identify it.
Next add a word or pictorial symbol of
an important detail from that time.
Finally, use your time line to
summarize for a classmate the
main points of «Barcelona:
Joya de arquitectura».

Barcelona
Joya de arquitectura

*Escena típica del
Barrio Gótico*

NOTA CULTURAL

Barcelona's Gothic Quarter was built when the
Spanish Empire was at its height. The profits from
Spain's colonies funded the construction of
palaces, churches, and public buildings.

Barcelona es una ciudad de muchos barrios[1] y de
una gran variedad de estilos de arquitectura. Los
romanos fueron los primeros en construir una
ciudad aquí en el año 15 a.C.[2] Hoy no hay casi
nada de la ciudad romana. Hay sólo unas ruinas y
murallas[3] en el Barrio Gótico[4].

El Barrio Gótico de Barcelona es la ciudad
vieja, un barrio de calles estrechas[5] y plazas
pequeñas. Tiene muchos edificios[6] y monumentos
impresionantes de los siglos XIII, XIV y XV, época[7]
de la arquitectura gótica. Si caminas por la calle
Montcada puedes ver las casas y los palacios de las

[1] districts	[3] walls	[5] narrow	[7] period
[2] B.C.	[4] Gothic Quarter	[6] buildings	

374 trescientos setenta y cuatro
Unidad 5

Classroom Community

Paired Activity Have students work in pairs and
research the word *Gothic* as it refers to architecture,
literature, etc. Have them bring in photos of other
Gothic structures and list samples of Gothic literature.

Portfolio Have students write a 1-paragraph essay
called **Barcelona: Ciudad de contrastes.** Remind them
to use a compare/contrast approach to their description.

Rubric A = 13–15 pts. B = 10–12 pts. C = 7–9 pts. D = 4–6 pts. F = < 4 pts.

Writing criteria	Scale				
Clear detail	1	2	3	4	5
Logical organization	1	2	3	4	5
Grammar/spelling accuracy	1	2	3	4	5

Casa Battló

Casa Viçens

La Pedrera–apartamentos

Parque Güell

familias principales de Barcelona de la época medieval. Hoy estas casas están convertidas en museos y galerías de arte.

La ciudad moderna tiene grandes avenidas, como Las Ramblas. El arquitecto catalán Antonio Gaudí (1852–1926) construyó[8] edificios originales de estilo modernista. Trabajó con formas y estructuras experimentales. Gaudí trabajó primero en el Parque de la Ciudadela, donde actualmente[9] está el Museo de Arte Moderno. Años más tarde diseñó el Parque Güell, ciudad y parque dentro de Barcelona. Gaudí también diseñó casas privadas, cada una con un diseño único. Su obra maestra[10], nunca terminada, es una iglesia, La Sagrada Familia[11].

---

[8]built   [9]nowadays   [10]masterpiece   [11]The Holy Family

¿Comprendiste?

1. ¿Queda algo de la ciudad romana en Barcelona? Explica.
2. ¿Cómo se llama la ciudad vieja de Barcelona? ¿Por qué?
3. ¿Qué lugares de interés puedes ver en el Barrio Gótico?
4. ¿Cómo es la ciudad moderna?
5. ¿Qué importancia tiene Gaudí?

¿Qué piensas?

¿Es cierto que la historia de Barcelona empieza en la época medieval? Explica tus razones.

Hazlo tú

Eres un(a) guía y tienes que hablar de Barcelona. ¿Qué dices?

Reading Strategy

Ask students to use the Reading Strategy they learned on p. 372: Reorganize information to check understanding. Have them make a chart that organizes the information about architecture in Barcelona. In the left column, they should list the 3 **epocas (romana, medieval, moderna),** then list what buildings are found in Barcelona from each one.

Culture Highlights

● **EL BARRIO GÓTICO DE BARCELONA**
At the heart of the **Barrio Gótico** is the **Plaza de San Jaume,** which dates back to the time of the Roman occupation of Spain. This plaza used to be a Roman forum. Other points of interest in the **Barrio Gótico** are the **Plaza del Rei,** the **Palacio Real Mayor,** and the **Iglesia de Santa Agata.**

Quick Wrap-up

Have students identify the following:
1. Antonio Gaudí   3. Las Ramblas
2. el Barrio Gótico   4. el Parque Güell

Teaching Note

Antoni is the **catalán** version of Gaudí's first name.

¿Comprendiste?

Answers
1. Hoy no hay casi nada de la ciudad romana. Hay sólo unas ruinas y murallas en el Barrio Gótico.
2. Se llama el Barrio Gótico porque tiene edificios y monumentos de la época de la arquitectura gótica.
3. Puedes ver las casas y los palacios de las familias principales de Barcelona de la época medieval.
4. Tiene grandes avenidas.
5. Gaudí construyó edificios originales de estilo modernista. Su obra maestra es La Sagrada Familia.

Block Schedule

Research Have students select another city in Spain to research and/or create a travel brochure. They should include a map, an **Almanaque,** some historical facts, some well-known people, some important sites, etc.

Teaching All Students

Extra Help Ask students to create an outline of the reading using a Roman numeral for each paragraph and capital letters for sections within. For example:
I. Barcelona
   A. Los romanos
   B. Hoy
etc.

Multiple Intelligences

Visual Have students select a famous or familiar structure (such as the White House, their school, or the Eiffel Tower), and redesign it in a Gaudí style.

Teaching Resource Options

Print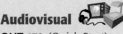

Para hispanohablantes Workbook PE,
  pp. 127–128
Block Scheduling Copymasters
Unit 5 Resource Book
  Para hispanohablantes Workbook
  TE, pp. 117–118
  Information Gap Activities, p. 122
  Family Involvement, pp. 123–124
  Multiple Choice Test Questions,
  pp. 170–178

Audiovisual

OHT 170 (Quick Start)
Audio Program Testing Cassette T2 /
CD T2

Technology

**Electronic Teacher Tools/Test
Generator**
Intrigas y aventuras CD-ROM, Disc 1

Quick Start Review

♻ **Preterite of regular -ar verbs**
Use OHT 170 or write on the board:
First, match the verbs in column A with
the objects in column B. Then use the
pairs to write sentences with the **yo**
preterite form of the verbs.

A	B
1. __ escuchar	a. el piano
2. __ lavar	b. el pescado
3. __ tocar	c. los platos
4. __ cocinar	d. música
5. __ sacar	e. la luz
6. __ apagar	f. fotos

Answers
1. d. Escuché música.
2. c. Lavé los platos.
3. a. Toqué el piano.
4. b. Cociné el pescado.
5. f. Saqué fotos.
6. e. Apagué la luz.

Teaching Suggestions
What Have Students Learned?

Have students look at the "Now you
can…" notes listed on the left side of
pages 376–377. Remind them to review
the material in the "To review" notes
before doing the activities or taking the
test.

ETAPA 3

Now you can...
• plan a party.

To review
• regular preterite
-ar verbs, see
p. 366.

Now you can...
• describe past
activities.

To review
• preterite of **-car,
-gar, -zar** verbs,
see p. 368.

OBJECTIVES
• Plan a party
• Describe past
activities
• Express extremes
• Purchase food

En uso
REPASO Y MÁS COMUNICACIÓN

 **1 ¡A preparar!**

Explica quiénes ayudaron y quiénes no ayudaron
a preparar la fiesta en la casa de Álvaro.
(Hint: Tell who helped and who didn't help prepare for the party.)

modelo

Luis: cuidar a Carmen
Luis no ayudó. **Cuidó a Carmen.**
tú: lavar los platos
Tú ayudaste. **Lavaste los platos.**

1. Álvaro: limpiar la casa
2. yo: nadar en la piscina
3. Iván: cocinar la carne de res
4. Elena y Arturo: escuchar música
5. tú: patinar en el parque
6. Beto: preparar las patatas y verduras
7. nosotros: hablar por teléfono
8. Marta: preparar la tarta

 2 ¡Una fiesta terrible!

Carmen habla con Luis sobre una fiesta muy mala que celebraron
en su casa el mes pasado. ¿Qué dice? *(Hint: Tell what Carmen says about a
terrible party.)*

modelo

yo (buscar) los vasos y no los (encontrar)
Yo busqué los vasos y no los encontré.

1. nadie (sacar) la basura antes de la fiesta
2. yo (pagar) todas las compras con mi dinero
3. pocas personas (llegar)
4. yo (tocar) el piano muy mal
5. yo no (almorzar) nada el día de la fiesta
6. nosotros (jugar) con unos videojuegos aburridos
7. yo (sacar) unas fotos terribles
8. tú (apagar) la luz durante la fiesta

376 trescientos setenta y seis
Unidad 5

Classroom Community

Group Activity Have students work in small groups
to produce a balanced menu of meals and snacks for
one day. Menus should list foods, quantities, and cost.
Have groups share their work with the class. Evaluate
the menus for health and budget consciousness.

Paired Activity Have students do a variation of
Actividad 1 in pairs.

Modelo: A: ¿Ayudó Luis?
  B: No, no ayudó. Cuidó a Carmen.
  A: ¿Tú ayudaste?
  B: Sí, ayudé. Lavé los platos.

Now you can...
• express extremes.

To review
• superlatives, see p. 364.

ACTIVIDAD 3 Opiniones

Luis expresa sus opiniones sobre las siguientes cosas. ¿Qué dice? *(Hint: Give Luis's opinions.)*

modelo

Carmen: más / joven (de mi familia)
Carmen *es la* **menor.**

1. Mercedes: más / bonito (de mis amigas)
2. helado: más / bueno (de los postres)
3. papá: más / viejo (de mi familia)
4. zanahorias: menos / delicioso (de las verduras)
5. tarta: más / sabroso (de los postres)
6. tenis: más / malo (de los deportes)
7. limonada: más / dulce (de las bebidas)
8. calamares: menos / rico (de las tapas)

Now you can...
• purchase food.

To review
• numbers, see p. 369.

ACTIVIDAD 4 ¡Buenos precios!

Imagínate que estás comprando comida en España. ¿Cuáles son los precios de hoy? *(Hint: Tell prices of foods.)*

modelo

Las zanahorias están a doscientas veinticinco pesetas el kilo.

trescientos setenta y siete
Etapa 3 **377**

ACTIVIDAD 1 Answers

1. Álvaro ayudó. Limpió la casa.
2. Yo no ayudé. Nadé en la piscina.
3. Iván ayudó. Cocinó la carne de res.
4. Elena y Arturo no ayudaron. Escucharon música.
5. Tú no ayudaste. Patinaste en el parque.
6. Beto ayudó. Preparó las patatas y verduras.
7. Nosotros no ayudamos. Hablamos por teléfono.
8. Marta ayudó. Preparó la tarta.

ACTIVIDAD 2 Answers

1. Nadie sacó la basura antes de la fiesta.
2. Yo pagué todas las compras con mi dinero.
3. Pocas personas llegaron.
4. Yo toqué el piano muy mal.
5. Yo no almorcé nada el día de la fiesta.
6. Nosotros jugamos con unos videojuegos aburridos.
7. Yo saqué unas fotos terribles.
8. Tú apagaste la luz durante la fiesta.

ACTIVIDAD 3 Answers

1. Mercedes es la más bonita.
2. El helado es el mejor.
3. Papá es el mayor.
4. Las zanahorias son las menos deliciosas.
5. La tarta es la más sabrosa.
6. El tenis es el peor.
7. La limonada es la más dulce.
8. Los calamares son los menos ricos.

ACTIVIDAD 4 Answers

1. Las patatas están a ciento treinta y cinco pesetas el kilo.
2. La salchicha está a setecientas cuarenta pesetas el kilo.
3. El zumo está a ciento setenta y cinco pesetas la lata.
4. El aceite está a quinientas pesetas la botella.
5. Las galletas están a cuatrocientas diez pesetas el paquete.
6. Las cebollas están a trescientas pesetas el kilo.
7. La carne de res está a novecientas cinco pesetas el kilo.
8. Los huevos están a doscientas quince pesetas la docena.

▪ Block Schedule

Change of Pace Have students write and present some Top Five lists; for example, best classes in school, best athletes, best actresses, best musical groups, etc. Students should use comparatives and superlatives in their presentations. (For additional activities, see **Block Scheduling Copymasters**.)

Teaching All Students

Extra Help Check students' knowledge of preterite forms before completing **Actividad 2**. First, write all the verbs on the board and have volunteers conjugate them completely. Then have students do the activity orally. Have other volunteers write answers on the board.

Multiple Intelligences

Intrapersonal Have students write a short paragraph called **Un día malo** (real or imaginary) similar to **Actividad 2**. Remind students of the word **fui** (I went).

Teaching Resource Options

Print

Unit 5 Resource Book
Cooperative Quizzes, pp. 135–136
Etapa Exam, Forms A and B,
pp. 137–146
Para hispanohablantes Etapa Exam,
pp. 147–151
Portfolio Assessment, pp. 152–153
Unit 5 Comprehensive Test,
pp. 154–161
Para hispanohablantes Unit 5
Comprehensive Test, pp. 162–169
Multiple Choice Test Questions,
pp. 170–178

Audiovisual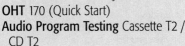

OHT 170 (Quick Start)
Audio Program Testing Cassette T2 /
CD T2

Technology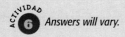

Electronic Teacher Tools/Test
Generator
www.mcdougallittell.com

ACTIVIDAD 5

Rubric: Speaking

Criteria	Scale	
Vocabulary use	1 2 3	A = 8–9 pts.
Sentence structure	1 2 3	B = 6–7 pts.
Ease, fluency	1 2 3	C = 4–5 pts.
		D = 3 pts.
		F = < 3 pts.

ACTIVIDAD 6

Answers will vary.

ACTIVIDAD 7

En tu propia voz

Rubric: Writing

Criteria	Scale	
Vocabulary use	1 2 3 4 5	A = 14–15 pts.
Accuracy	1 2 3 4 5	B = 12–13 pts.
Creativity, appearance	1 2 3 4 5	C = 10–11 pts.
		D = 8–9 pts.
		F = < 8 pts.

Teaching Note: En tu propia voz

Remind students to review the writing
strategy ""Tell who, what, where, when, why,
and how" before beginning the description
of the party. A well-written paragraph uses
many details to communicate information.

ACTIVIDAD 5 El fin de semana pasado

> **PARA CONVERSAR**
>
> **STRATEGY: SPEAKING**
> **Maintain conversational flow** To keep continuity
> in a conversation, acknowledge what was
> said, then add your own ideas. The model
> shows how this is done. You can build
> interest by withholding information: **Compré**
> **algo bonito. ¿Sabes qué es?**

Usando las actividades de la lista, habla con
otro(a) estudiante sobre sus actividades del
fin de semana pasado. *(Hint: Talk about what you
did last weekend.)*

> almorzar en un restaurante
> limpiar la casa
> comprar algo interesante
> alquilar un video
> tocar algún instrumento
> practicar algún deporte
> trabajar

modelo

Tú: *Compré algo interesante.*

Otro(a) estudiante: *¿Qué compraste?*

Tú: *Compré…*

ACTIVIDAD 6  En el supermercado

Imagínate que tú y un(a) amigo(a) están
comprando comida en España. Hay tres
papeles: un(a) comprador(a) optimista, un(a)
comprador(a) pesimista y una persona que
trabaja en el supermercado. Cambien de papel.
*(Hint: Shop in the supermarket. One person is an optimist, another
is a pessimist, and the third works at the supermarket.)*

modelo

Optimista: *¿A cuánto están los tomates?*

Trabajador(a): *Nuestros tomates son los más sabrosos de
la comunidad. Hoy están a…*

Optimista: *¡Qué bien! Los compro.*

Pesimista: *¡No los compres! Los tomates de aquí son…*

ACTIVIDAD 7 *En tu propia voz*

ESCRITURA Imagínate que tú y tus amigos
celebraron una fiesta el sábado pasado.
¿Cómo participaron todos? *(Hint: Describe how
everyone participated in a class party.)*

modelo

*Antes de la fiesta, todos limpiamos la casa. Sara pasó la
aspiradora y yo lavé los platos. Durante la fiesta, Marcos
tocó la guitarra y…*

CONEXIONES

La salud What kind of food do you like the most?
Which ethnic foods do you prefer? Is there a special dish from
your region? Survey ten people at your school to find out their
favorite food. Then create a menu featuring the foods chosen.
Add prices and indicate the dishes that are good for your health.

Persona	La comida favorita

378 trescientos setenta y ocho
Unidad 5

Classroom Community

Peer Review Working in pairs, have students peer edit
the party description for **Actividad 7.** Tell students to look
particularly for preterite verb forms and superlatives.

Paired Activity Have students write true statements
about when they or another person did something.
Then have them read the statements to a partner. The
partner has to guess when the action took place
(**anoche, anteayer, el año pasado,** etc.).

En resumen
REPASO DE VOCABULARIO

PLANNING A PARTY

apagar la luz	to turn off the light
¡Cállate!	Be quiet!

PURCHASING FOOD

¿A cuánto está(n)…?	How much is (are)…?

Food

el aceite	oil
la carne de res	beef
la cebolla	onion
el cereal	cereal
la crema	cream
la galleta	cookie, cracker
la harina	flour
el helado	ice cream
el huevo	egg
la leche	milk
la mantequilla	butter
la pasta	pasta
la patata	potato
el pescado	fish
la pimienta	pepper
el puerco	pork
la sal	salt
la salchicha	sausage
el tomate	tomato
la verdura	vegetable
el yogur	yogurt
la zanahoria	carrot
el zumo	juice

Packaging

la botella	bottle
la lata	can
el paquete	package

REQUESTING QUANTITIES

cuarto(a)	quarter
la docena	dozen
el gramo	gram
el kilo	kilogram
el litro	liter
medio(a)	half
el pedazo	piece
doscientos(as)	two hundred
trescientos(as)	three hundred
cuatrocientos(as)	four hundred
quinientos(as)	five hundred
seiscientos(as)	six hundred
setecientos(as)	seven hundred
ochocientos(as)	eight hundred
novecientos(as)	nine hundred
mil	one thousand
un millón	one million

DESCRIBING PAST ACTIVITIES

anoche	last night
anteayer	the day before yesterday
el año pasado	last year
ayer	yesterday
el mes pasado	last month
la semana pasada	last week

OTHER WORDS AND PHRASES

la estrella	star
sabroso(a)	tasty

In the Kitchen

cocinar	to cook
el congelador	freezer
la estufa	stove
el frigorífico	refrigerator
el horno	oven
el lavaplatos	dishwasher
el microondas	microwave

Juego

¿Qué son estas cosas? ¿Dónde las pones?

1. laheod
2. suplacitosos
3. elhce
4. neredecasr

Teaching All Students

Extra Help Before doing **Actividad 5,** have students provide the **yo** and **tú** forms of each verb.

Native Speakers Ask students to look at the list of food items in the **Repaso de vocabulario.** Then have them go through the list, saying in what packaging and/or in what quantity measurement they would buy each item in their home communities.

Multiple Intelligences

Logical/Mathematical Have students find the equivalents of **gramo, kilo,** and **litro** in U.S. measurements. Provide students with a list of measurements (3 pounds, 10 ounces, 1 gallon, etc.). Have students convert the items in the list to **gramo, kilo,** and **litro.**

Interdisciplinary Connections

Health Have students research the average caloric content of several of the foods learned in this and other **Etapas.** Have them make a chart with pictures of the foods and the number of calories in an average serving. Variation: Have students research the latest nutritional guidelines and prepare posters showing a balanced breakfast, lunch, and dinner with pictures and labels in Spanish.

Quick Start Review

♻ **Etapa vocabulary**

Use OHT 170 or write on the board: Write 3 complete sentences. Each sentence must contain one word from each of the following categories: Purchasing Food, Requesting Quantities, Describing Past Activities.
Answers will vary.

Teaching Suggestions
Vocabulary Review

Have students make flashcards of the vocabulary. Put students in groups of 3. Deal 5 cards per group. In 3 minutes, see how many sentences they can make using 2 cards per sentence.

Juego

Answers
1. helado: en el congelador
2. platos sucios: en el lavaplatos
3. leche: en el frigorífico
4. carne de res: en la estufa

Block Schedule

Time Saver Assign **Actividad 7** for immediately after the **Etapa** exam. This way, students who finish first have something to work on while other students complete the test. The assignment can then be finished at home.

Teaching Resource Options

Print
Block Scheduling Copymasters

Audiovisual
OHT GO1–GO5; 170 (Quick Start)

Technology
Intrigas y aventuras CD-ROM, Disc 1
www.mcdougallittell.com

Quick Start Review

♻ Reflexive verbs/commands
Use OHT 170 or write on the board:
Write the affirmative **tú** command and the negative **tú** command for each of the following:

1. acostarse   4. limpiarse
2. levantarse   5. dormirse
3. bañarse

Answers
1. acuéstate   no te acuestes
2. levántate   no te levantes
3. báñate   no te bañes
4. límpiate   no te limpies
5. duérmete   no te duermas

Teaching Strategy
Prewriting
- Ask students what a "healthy lifestyle" means to them. Do they, in general, get enough sleep? Eat nutritious foods? Exercise daily?
- Have students skim the **Modelo del estudiante**, close their books, and say what they remember. Did they get the feeling that they were being addressed personally?
- Remind students of the PASS list at the beginning of the page: **P**urpose, **A**udience, **S**ubject, **S**tructure. This PASS key will help them complete a well-structured assignment.

Post-writing
- Discuss where students get most of their information about healthy living from—home, peers, TV, school, magazines, etc.

UNIDAD 5

En tu propia voz
ESCRITURA

Una buena rutina diaria

For a contest, design an educational pamphlet in Spanish for teens and young adults. Depict healthful habits, such as eating nutritious food and exercising. The winning pamphlets will be used in recreational facilities across the country.

Purpose: Inform teens about healthful habits
Audience: Spanish-speaking young adults
Subject: Healthful routines and nutrition
Structure: Educational pamphlet

PARA ESCRIBIR • STRATEGY: WRITING

Engage the reader by addressing him or her personally Address your reader directly. Use commands that personally address the reader. Your educational pamphlet will tell the reader what to do and what not to do for a healthy lifestyle.

Modelo del estudiante

Friendly words add a personal touch to your pamphlet.

The writer addresses the reader personally with **questions** directed to him or her.

Here the writer uses **tú commands** to tell the reader exactly what to do.

Negative tú commands work well, too, to tell the reader what not to do.

¿Te despiertas cansadísimo? ¿Preocupado? ¿Deprimido? Tal vez no duermes bien. Para levantarte de buen humor, sigue esta lista:

➤ Prepara toda tu tarea antes de acostarte.
➤ Haz los quehaceres por la noche; no esperes hasta la mañana.
➤ Lee un poco, acuéstate y duerme 8 horas.

Vas a levantarte contentísimo.

Oye, amigo, ¿cómo estás después de comer? Por favor, ¡come mejor!

➤ Limpia bien los platos.
➤ Come comida buena, como pollo o pescado, fruta fresca, verduras y pan.
➤ Come tranquilamente.
➤ Toma mucha agua durante el día. Toma leche, agua o jugo con tus comidas.

¡Vas a estar fabuloso!

¿No tienes tiempo para hacer ejercicio?

➤ Organiza tus quehaceres.
➤ Reserva una hora cada día para practicar un deporte o hacer ejercicio.
➤ Llama a un amigo para hacer ejercicio contigo. Es mucho más divertido así.
➤ ¡No seas perezoso! Usa la hora que reservaste.

Vas a tener muchísima energía.

380 trescientos ochenta
Unidad 5

Classroom Community

Group Activity First, have students individually complete this chart in terms of their lifestyle:

<u>siempre</u>   <u>a veces</u>   <u>rara vez</u>   <u>nunca</u>

Then, have students work in groups and compare their answers. Have them discuss which activities *should* be in different columns.

Portfolio Have students take special care when preparing their pamphlets. When pamphlets are in their final form, students will decorate them and put them in their portfolios.

Estrategias para escribir

Antes de escribir...

With another student, brainstorm the details of your pamphlet:

- *Possible health issues to address*
- *Personal questions*
- *What your reader should do*
- *What your reader should avoid doing*

Discuss issues of nutrition, energy, stress management, etc., that people your age might like to know more about. Then choose one or more issues to focus on in your pamphlet. Use a chart like this one to organize your ideas.

Una buena rutina diaria

Recomendación	Preguntas personales	Qué hacer	Qué no hacer
comer mejor	¿Comes muchos postres?	Compra fruta fresca.	No vayas a la pastelería.
organizar tu tiempo	¿Estás nervioso porque nunca terminas tu tarea?		

Revisiones

Share your draft with a partner. Then ask:

- *How are health issues addressed?*
- *How does the pamphlet "speak" directly to the reader?*
- *What phrases clearly tell the reader what to do?*

La versión final

Before you create the final draft, look over your work with the following questions in mind:

- *Are affirmative **tú** commands used correctly?*

Try this: Underline all affirmative commands. Check that each verb is regular. If not, use the appropriate irregular form. Do reflexive verbs include their pronouns?

- *Are negative commands constructed properly?*

Try this: Circle all negative commands and check their construction. Do they include appropriate stems? Note the marks you can use to insert a period or a comma.

 Share your writing on www.mcdougallittell.com

¡Oye, amigo! ¿Tienes muy poca energía? ¿Pasas mucho tiempo viendo la televisión? ¿Estás perezoso y aburrido? ¡Mira, tengo algunas ideas fabulosas para ti!

- Apaga la televisión y no la ~~pone~~ más esta semana. pongas
- te Levanta y llama a tu mejor Dile amigo. ~~Dícele~~ que van a jugar a su deporte favorito⊙
- ¡Saca las cosas necesarias y hazlo!

EDITORIAL MARKS

⊙ = **period**   ⌃ = **comma**

Let students know ahead of time which elements of their writing you will be evaluating. A global evaluation is more helpful to students than a correction of every mistake made. Consider the following in scoring compositions:

Sentences	
1	Most are not logical
2	In logical order
3	Flow purposefully

Details	
1	Few details
2	Sufficient basic details
3	Clear and vivid detail

Organization	
1	Not well organized
2	Some organization
3	Strong organization

Accuracy	
1	Errors prevent comprehension
2	Some spelling and agreement errors throughout
3	Very few errors

Criteria	Scale	
Logical sentence order	1 2 3	A = 10–12 pts.
Clear and vivid detail	1 2 3	B = 7–9 pts.
Organization	1 2 3	C = 4–6 pts.
Accuracy	1 2 3	D = 3 pts.
		F = < 3 pts.

◼ Block Schedule

Variety Have students look for pictures in magazines that show people doing things that might not be considered healthy (someone watching TV, someone eating at a fast-food restaurant, etc.). They should mount each picture on a piece of cardboard. Below each picture, students should write one thing they would tell that person to do and one thing not to do to improve their health. (For additional activities, see **Block Scheduling Copymasters**.)

Teaching All Students

Extra Help Have students skim the **Modelo del estudiante**, the graphic organizer, and the final draft sample, and write down unfamiliar words. Help them derive the meanings from context. Then ask them to read the **Modelo del estudiante** again and add their own ideas.

Multiple Intelligences

Visual Ask students to submit an outline of their pamphlet ideas:

- Theme: nutrition, exercise, personal care?
- Format: columns, question/answer, picture, description?
- Details: What will you tell your readers to do? Not to do?
- Appeal: How will you address your reader in a friendly way?

Unit Theme
Comparing life in the city (Quito, Ecuador) and in the country (Otavalo, Ecuador)

Communication
- Talking about the past
- Describing city buildings
- Talking about professions
- Pointing out people and things and where they are located
- Discussing the present and future
- Giving instructions

Cultures
- Learning about Quito, Ecuador, and its buildings
- Learning about the people of Otavalo, Ecuador
- Learning about other interesting places to visit in Ecuador
- Learning about international foods

Connections
- Connecting to Science: Finding out about animals
- Connecting to Health: Preparing a typical meal from a Spanish-speaking country

Comparisons
- Comparing place names in Ecuador and in the U.S.
- Comparing cultural groups in Ecuador and in the U.S.
- Comparing foods and what your family eats

Communities
- Using Spanish in the workplace
- Using Spanish to help others

Teaching Resource Options

Print

Block Scheduling Copymasters

Audiovisual

OHT M4; 171, 172
Canciones Audiocassette/CD
Video Program Videotape 6 / Videodisc 3B

Search Chapter 1, Play to 2
U6 Cultural Introduction

UNIDAD

6

QUITO
ECUADOR
LA CIUDAD Y EL CAMPO

OBJECTIVES

ETAPA 1

La vida de la ciudad
- Tell what happened
- Make suggestions to a group
- Describe city buildings
- Talk about professions

ETAPA 2

A conocer el campo
- Point out specific people and things
- Tell where things are located
- Talk about the past

ETAPA 3

¡A ganar el concurso!
- Talk about the present and future
- Give instructions to someone
- Discuss the past

382

LA CASA DE SUCRE was once the home of independence leader Mariscal Antonio José de Sucre. It houses items from Quito's colonial and independence periods. What historic museums have you visited?

ISLAS GALÁPAGOS

OCÉANO PACÍFICO

PAPAS, a staple of the Ecuadorian diet, have been cultivated in the Andes since before the time of the Incas. This New World food was introduced by Spain to the European diet. What dishes made with potatoes do you eat?

Classroom Community

Group Activity Have students work in groups of 3 and select the cultural topic presented on pp. 382–383 that interests them the most. Have them research more information and present it to the class.

Paired Activity Have students work in pairs to discuss similarities and differences between what they know about Ecuador and their own area. Have them outline what information they would substitute if they were to write a similar Cultural Opener about their area of the country.

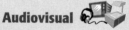

ALMANAQUE

Población: 1.500.000

Altura: 2.700 metros (8.775 pies)

Clima: 21° C (70° F) de día, 12° C (54° F) de noche

Comida típica: llapingachos, locros, fritada, humitas

Gente famosa de Quito: Oswaldo Guayasamín (pintor), Jorge Icaza (escritor), Carlota Jaramillo (cantante)

¿Vas a Quito? Quito es la capital de Ecuador. Su nombre viene de los indígenas quituas, un grupo muy antiguo.

For more information about Quito, access www.mcdougallittell.com

VENEZUELA

Ecuador

LA MITAD DEL MUNDO is a monument built where the equator was measured. Ecuador's name comes from the fact that the equator (**el ecuador**) runs through it. What other countries of the world lie along the equator?

TAPICES are woven wall hangings and rugs made from sheep or alpaca wool. You will find these multicolored wall hangings in stores and outdoor markets. Where have you seen weavings?

OTAVALO

★ **QUITO**

ECUADOR

GUAYAQUIL

CUENCA

COLOMBIA

PERÚ

BRASIL

ATAHUALPA (1500–1533), son of the Incan king Huanya-Capac and grandson of Duchicela, king of Quito, is considered the first great Ecuadorian. He was heir to the kingdom of Quito and became leader of the Incan empire. Can you think of other Native American leaders?

UN RONDADOR is a wind instrument that has been used for more than 2000 years. It is made of cane or bamboo pieces of different widths and lengths. Each produces a distinct musical note. What other wind instruments do you know?

383

Teaching Suggestion
Previewing the Unit
Tell students that this unit centers on the city and the country in Ecuador. Ask students to scan these two pages for 15 seconds, then close their books. Then ask them to tell you what they remember. You may wish to use the introduction to the video to preview the unit.

Culture Highlights

● **ANTONIO JOSÉ DE SUCRE** General Sucre led the revolutionary forces of Ecuador in a battle that took place on the slopes of Mt. Pichincha in 1822. The anniversary of this battle is May 24, a national holiday. Plaza Santo Domingo in Quito has a statue of General Sucre. The figure points to the site of this battle.

● **PAPAS** When the New World explorers introduced the potato to Europe, the Europeans refused to eat it because they thought it was ugly. They were unaccustomed to eating something that came from a tuber rather than a seed.

● **LA MITAD DEL MUNDO** This monument is located a half hour north of Quito, in San Antonio de Pichincha.

● **ATAHUALPA** Atahualpa was the last Inca ruler. He was taken prisoner and executed by the Spanish explorer Francisco Pizarro.

● **TAPICES** The art of weaving is practiced throughout the Americas. The use of cloaks covered by feathers of rare birds woven into them was not unusual among the Aztecs and the Incas.

● **EL RONDADOR** El rondador is a single-row panpipe. Other traditional instruments are the **antara** and **siku** (single- and double-row panpipes) and the **quena** (vertical end-notched flute).

▇ Block Schedule
Sort and Organize After looking at the Unit 6 Cultural Opener, have students look back at the Cultural Openers for Units 1–5 and compare what they see. Have them compile a list of categories, then sort and organize the informational paragraphs. (For additional activities, see **Block Scheduling Copymasters.**)

Teaching All Students

Challenge Working in pairs, have students pretend to be talking on the phone about beginning the last unit of their Spanish book. They should talk about what they see on pp. 382–383 and what they saw in other units.

Native Speakers Ask students to talk about the equivalent of Atahualpa and/or Mariscal Antonio José de Sucre in their home countries. What did the person do? How is the person remembered?

Multiple Intelligences

Kinesthetic Have students take turns walking to a map, globe, or OHT and pointing out the countries that lie on the equator.

Musical/Rhythmic Play recordings of Andean music and have students listen for familiar and unfamiliar instruments. Ask them to identify the instruments as wind instruments, string instruments, etc.

Ampliación

These activities may be used at various points in the Unit 6 sequence.

📖 For Block Schedule, you may find that these projects will provide a welcome change of pace while reviewing and reinforcing the material presented in the unit. See the **Block Scheduling Copymasters.**

● PROJECTS

Create a nature travel guide of Ecuador. Divide the class into 4 groups and assign one of the following regions of Ecuador to each:

- the highlands
- the coast
- the rain forests
- the Galápagos Islands

Each group should research and collect information about the flora and fauna of their region. Within each group, students may be assigned specific animals or plants. Using drawings or photos, have each group write a travel guide entry of their region. Collect and bind the 4 reports to share with other classes.

> PACING SUGGESTION: Upon completion of Etapa 2.

Interview Have students work in groups of 5 to role-play people of different professions, including 1 journalist. The journalist will tape interviews (video or audio) with each person, asking questions about what they did to prepare for the profession, why they chose it, etc.

> PACING SUGGESTION: Upon completion of Etapa 2.

● STORYTELLING

Cinquain poems After reviewing vocabulary for professions, model a cinquain (5-line) poem for students. Write guidelines on the board for students to follow as you read:

OTAVALO
●
★
QUITO

GUIDELINES	CINQUAIN
noun (subject of poem)	Maestro(a)
2 adjectives or 1 noun and 1 adjective	Inteligente, exigente
3-word sentence or 3 infinitives	Preguntar, responder, calificar
4-word sentence expressing an emotion	Quiere a los alumnos
noun or adjective restating the subject	Confidente

ECUADOR

Have each student write a cinquain poem about 3 different professions. Variation: Have students all write about the same 3 professions to contrast ideas.

Otros temas Have students write 2 cinquain poems about contrasting subjects; for example, city vs. country, horse vs. car, etc.

PERÚ

> PACING SUGGESTION: Upon completion of Etapa 3.

● BULLETIN BOARD/POSTERS

Bulletin Board Have students create maps of Ecuador. Each map should depict a different aspect of the country: topography, rainfall, agriculture, animals, crafts, landmarks, etc. Students can decorate their maps with drawings, photos, or small objects.

Posters Have students create •**Advertisement** posters for the market and crafts in Otavalo •**Job fair** fliers announcing booths for different professions •**Travel posters** for the main attractions in Ecuador (the equator, the Galápagos Islands, etc.)

GAMES

La pregunta es...

Prepare ahead: Create Jeopardy!™-style clues and questions for several categories: **profesiones, el campo, la ciudad, los animales,** etc. For example: clue = **Escribe artículos para el periódico.** Question = **¿Quién es un periodista?** To play, divide the class into 3 or 4 teams. Choose a category. After reading a clue from that category, call on the first student who raises his/her hand. The student must provide an appropriate question. If the student answers correctly, the team gets one point and the student chooses the next category. If the student answers incorrectly, the first student from another team to raise his/her hand may try to provide the correct question. The team with the most points at the end of a predetermined time limit wins.

PACING SUGGESTION: Upon completion of Etapa 2.

En la ciudad

Prepare ahead: Make 5 gameboard maps of a city with specific locations numbered, and a corresponding set of numbered cards. Divide the class into 5 groups. Each group receives a map and the corresponding set of numbers. Students pick numbers, then take turns giving directions to a particular building or location. The group completing all directions in the shortest time wins.

PACING SUGGESTION: Upon completion of Etapa 3.

MUSIC

Andean music has gained in popularity throughout the world. Many contemporary groups have recorded traditional songs and new compositions that are a fusion of Andean music and other rhythms. Play recordings by groups such as Inti Illimani, Viento de los Andes, and Ecuador Manta. Have students describe the sounds. Refer them to p. 383 and also show them photos of instruments such as the **quena** (single-row reed flute) and the **siku** (multiple-row reed flute). More music samples are available on your *Canciones* Cassette or CD.

HANDS-ON CRAFTS

Display the flag of Ecuador. Point out that the coat of arms includes palm and laurel branches (symbolizing victory), the condor with outstretched wings (symbolizing shelter and protection), and an image of Chimborazo (the highest mountain in the Andes) and the Guayas River (representing unity between the coast and mountains). The yellow band symbolizes abundance and fertility of crops and land; the blue symbolizes sea and sky; and the red symbolizes bloodshed during independence battles. Have students design flags on posterboards. The flags can represent their school, city, state, etc. Have students present their flags and explain them.

RECIPE

Quimbolitos are sweet biscuits made with corn flour, wrapped in leaves, and steamed. The traditional recipe calls for achira leaves. However, since these leaves are not exported to the U.S., plantain leaves have been substituted. You can also use bamboo leaves, cornhusks, or even wax paper.

BRASIL

Receta

Quimbolitos

2 tazas de harina de maíz tostado	1 taza de leche
1 cucharadita de polvo de hornear	2 huevos
1 taza de mantequilla	1 taza de azúcar
1 taza de jugo de naranja	1 taza de uvas pasas
1 cucharadita de esencia de vainilla	12 hojas de plátano

Mezcle la harina con el polvo de hornear, la mantequilla, el jugo de naranja, la esencia de vainilla y la leche. Separe los huevos. Bata las claras a punto de nieve. Agregue el azúcar y las yemas. Mezcle las dos preparaciones anteriores hasta formar una masa suave y homogénea. Lave las hojas de plátano y coloque la masa en el centro de cada una. Luego añada las uvas pasas. Cierre las hojas. Cocine los quimbolitos al vapor por 20 minutos.

Planning Guide CLASSROOM MANAGEMENT

OBJECTIVES

Communication
- Tell what happened *pp. 388–389, 400–401*
- Make suggestions to a group *pp. 388–389*
- Describe city buildings *pp. 386–387, 400–401*
- Talk about professions *pp. 386–387, 388–389*

Grammar
- Use preterite of regular **-er** and **-ir** verbs *pp. 392–393*
- Use preterite of verbs with a **y** spelling change *pp. 394–395*
- Use preterite of **hacer, ir, ser** *pp. 395–399*

Pronunciation
- Pronunciation of **d** *p. 399*
- Dictation, *TE p. 399*

Culture
- History and culture of Quito, Ecuador *pp. 382–383, 395, 400–401*
- The **sucre** *p. 397*
- Regional vocabulary *p. 398*
- Colonial Ecuador *p. 400*

 Recycling
- Superlatives *p. 392*
- Expressions indicating the past *p. 393*

STRATEGIES

Listening Strategies
- Distinguish between what is said and not said *p. 388*

Speaking Strategies
- Exaggerate and react to exaggerations *p. 392*
- Relate details *p. 404*

Reading Strategies
- Recognize place names *p. 400*

Writing Strategies
- Use different kinds of descriptive words *TE p. 404*

Connecting Cultures Strategies
- Learn about Quito, Ecuador *pp. 382–383, 395, 400–401*
- Learn about the currency of Ecuador *p. 397*
- Recognize regional vocabulary *p. 398*
- Learn about Colonial Ecuador *p. 400*
- Connect and compare what you already know about place names in your community to help you learn about place names in a new community *pp. 400–401*

PROGRAM RESOURCES

 Print
- *Más práctica* Workbook PE, *pp. 129–136*
- Block Scheduling Copymasters, *pp. 129–136*
- Unit 6 Resource Book
  Más práctica Workbook TE, *pp. 1–8*
  Para hispanohablantes Workbook TE, *pp. 9–16*
- Information Gap Activities *pp. 17–20*
- Family Involvement *pp. 21–22*
- Video Activities *pp. 23–25*
- Videoscript *pp. 26–28*
- Audioscript *pp. 29–32*
- Assessment Program, Unit 6 Etapa 1 *pp. 33–51; 170–178*
- Answer Keys *pp. 187–202*

 **Audiovisual**
- Audio Program Cassettes 16A, 16B / CD 16
- *Canciones* Cassette / CD
- Video Program Videotape 6 / Videodisc 3B
- Overhead Transparencies M1–M5; 171, 174–184

Technology
- Electronic Teacher Tools/Test Generator
- *Intrigas y aventuras* CD-ROM, Disc 1
- www.mcdougallittell.com

Assessment Program Options
- Cooperative Quizzes (Unit 6 Resource Book)
- Etapa Exam Forms A and B (Unit 6 Resource Book)
- *Para hispanohablantes* Etapa Exam (Unit 6 Resource Book)
- Portfolio Assessment (Unit 6 Resource Book)
- Multiple Choice Test Questions (Unit 6 Resource Book)
- Audio Program Testing Cassette T2 / CD T2
- Electronic Teacher Tools/Test Generator

Native Speakers
- *Para hispanohablantes* Workbook PE, *pp. 129–136*
- *Para hispanohablantes* Workbook TE (Unit 6 Resource Book)
- *Para hispanohablantes* Etapa Exam (Unit 6 Resource Book)
- Audio *Para hispanohablantes* Cassettes 16A, 16B, T2 / CD 16, T2
- Audioscript *Para hispanohablantes* (Unit 6 Resource Book)

Student Text Listening Activity Scripts

 Videoscript: Diálogo *pages 388–389*

- Videotape 6 • Videodisc 3B

Search Chapter 3, Play to 4
U6E1 • En vivo (Dialog)

- Use the videoscript with **Actividades 1, 2** *page 390*

Patricia:	Decidí participar en el concurso porque leí que los ganadores van a viajar a otros países y van a trabajar como periodistas para la revista *Onda Internacional*.
Miguel:	¿Y por qué necesitas mi ayuda?
Patricia:	Pues, quiero hacer entrevistas con personas que viven en la ciudad y personas que viven en el campo. Tú tienes familia en el campo, ¿no?
Miguel:	Sí. Mi tío, y también la prima de mi madre. ¿Los llamo para ver si puedes hablar con ellos?
Patricia:	¡Sí, muchas gracias, Miguel! Oye, vamos a pedir algo, ¿no? En un rato tengo que entrevistar a unas personas y no quiero llegar tarde.
Patricia:	Buenos días, señora.
Sra. Martínez:	Buenos días.
Patricia:	¿Puede darme algunos minutos de su tiempo? Me llamo Patricia López Carrera. Estoy preparando un artículo para un concurso de la revista *Onda Internacional*.
Sra. Martínez:	Claro que sí.
Patricia:	Muchas gracias. A ver, ¿dónde empezamos? Muy bien, ¿cómo se llama y cuál es su profesión?
Sra. Martínez:	Me llamo Ana Martínez. Soy una mujer de negocios. Trabajo en un banco aquí, en Quito.
Patricia:	¿Le gusta vivir en la ciudad?
Sra. Martínez:	Sí, mucho. Pero también tiene sus problemas.
Patricia:	¿Cómo qué?
Sra. Martínez:	La contaminación del aire, el tráfico, como en todas las ciudades grandes.
Patricia:	Me puede decir, ¿cómo se preparó para ser una mujer de negocios?
Sra. Martínez:	Bueno, hice todo lo necesario. Primero, fui a la universidad. Después me ofrecieron un trabajo en la oficina del banco. Y después de muchos años, llegué a ser gerente.

Patricia:	¿Y siempre vivió en Quito?
Sra. Martínez:	Sí. Mis padres abrieron una panadería aquí.
Sr. González:	Pase, por favor.
Patricia:	Buenas tardes, arquitecto González.
Sr. González:	Buenas tardes, señorita López Carrera. Tome asiento, por favor.
Patricia:	Gracias por su tiempo.
Sr. González:	Es un placer. ¿Para qué es la entrevista?
Patricia:	Estoy participando en un concurso. Voy a escribir sobre el contraste entre la vida en la ciudad y en el campo.
Sr. González:	Ah, sí. ¿Qué quiere saber?
Patricia:	¿Le gusta vivir en la ciudad?
Sr. González:	La ciudad es interesante, y nunca aburrida. Sí, me gusta. Pero sabe, la vida en el campo es mucho más tranquila.
Patricia:	¿Vivió usted alguna vez en el campo?
Sr. González:	De niño viví en el campo, en la casa de mis abuelos en la Argentina. Pero ahora, por mi trabajo, tengo que vivir en Quito, es decir en la ciudad.
Patricia:	¿Y cuándo decidió venir a la ciudad?
Sr. González:	Cuando entré a la universidad. Luego, cuando recibí mi título de arquitecto, vi que en la ciudad hay más oportunidades profesionales que en el campo.
Miguel:	¿Aló?
Patricia:	¿Miguel? Soy Patricia.
Miguel:	¡Hola, Patricia! ¿Cómo fueron las entrevistas?
Patricia:	Excelente. Ya hice dos. ¿Llamaste a tu familia?
Miguel:	Sí. Todo está listo para el sábado. El autobús sale a las ocho. ¿Nos vemos en la estación?
Patricia:	Perfecto. ¡Hasta el sábado entonces!
Miguel:	¡Adiós!

 **¿Cómo son?** *page 391*

Esta ciudad tiene muchos estilos de arquitectura. Los edificios altos son los más modernos de Quito. Las oficinas de muchas compañías internacionales están allí. A la derecha hay un banco con un estilo de arquitectura tradicional en un edificio bajo. Mis edificios favoritos son los antiguos como la iglesia colonial al lado de la farmacia. Es bonita, ¿no? De vez en cuando la ciudad tiene que destruir unos edificios viejos, como el edificio grande y feo al final de la calle.

18 Un sábado especial *page 398*

Patricia:	Hola, Andrea, ¿qué hiciste el sábado?
Andrea:	Por la mañana, le escribí una carta a mi amigo Raúl. Después, fui a un partido de fútbol donde vi a muchos amigos.
Patricia:	Y tú, Marta, ¿hiciste algo interesante?
Marta:	Sí. Por la tarde, fui de compras con Lucía. Luego, salí con Pedro.
Andrea:	¿Adónde fueron?
Marta:	Fuimos a Casa Linda. Comimos una comida riquísima.
Andrea:	Y tú, Patricia, ¿qué hiciste?
Patricia:	Por la mañana corrí en el parque con algunos amigos. Por la noche, salí para el cine con Antonio.
Andrea:	¿Qué vieron?
Patricia:	Vimos una película de acción buenísima.
Andrea:	¡Creo que fue un sábado interesante para todas!

🔔 **Quick Start Review Answers**

p. 388 Professions
1. un(a) taxista
2. un(a) arquitecto(a)
3. un hombre/una mujer de negocios
4. un(a) periodista
5. un(a) cartero(a)
6. un(a) fotógrafo(a)

p. 394 Preterite of **-er** and **-ir** verbs
Answers will vary.
Answers could include:
1. Yo aprendí a cocinar.
2. Tú escribiste una carta a tu abuela.
3. Tomás corrió 5 kilómetros.
4. Mis amigos me ofrecieron una merienda.
5. Nosotros decidimos comer a las ocho.

p. 402 Preterite
Answers will vary.
Answers could include:
1. fui en autobús
2. llegaron tarde
3. salieron a las seis
4. fuiste al parque
5. no me hizo ninguno

Pacing Guide

Sample Lesson Plan - 50 Minute Schedule

DAY 1

Unit Opener
- Anticipate/Activate prior knowledge: Present the *Almanaque* and the cultural notes. Use Map OHTs as needed. 10 MIN.

Etapa Opener
- Quick Start Review (TE, p. 384) 5 MIN.
- Have students look at the *Etapa* Opener and answer the questions. 5 MIN.

En contexto: Vocabulario
- Quick Start Review (TE, p. 386) 5 MIN.
- Have students use context and pictures to learn *Etapa* vocabulary, then answer the questions, p. 387. Use the Situational OHTs for additional practice. 10 MIN.

En vivo: Diálogo
- Quick Start Review (TE, p. 388) 5 MIN.
- Review the Listening Strategy, p. 388. Play audio or show video for the dialog, pp. 388–389. Replay and have students take the roles of the characters. 10 MIN.

Homework Option:
- Video Activities, Unit 6 Resource Book, pp. 23–25.

DAY 2

En acción: Vocabulario y gramática
- Check homework. 5 MIN.
- Quick Start Review (TE, p. 390) 5 MIN.
- Have students open to *En contexto*, pp. 386–387, for reference. Use OHT 175 and 176 to review vocabulary. 10 MIN.
- Play the video/audio; have students do *Actividades* 1 and 2 orally. 10 MIN.
- Have students complete *Actividad* 3 in pairs. 5 MIN.
- Play the audio; do *Actividad* 4. 5 MIN.
- Present the *Vocabulario*, p. 391. Then have students do *Actividad* 5 orally. 10 MIN.
- Discuss the directions for *Actividad* 6. 5 MIN.

Homework Option:
- Have students complete *Actividad* 6 in writing.

DAY 3

En acción (cont.)
- Check homework. 5 MIN.
- Have several volunteers present their descriptions for *Actividad* 6. 5 MIN.
- Present the Speaking Strategy, p. 392, and the *Nota*. Then have students do *Actividad* 7 in pairs. 10 MIN.
- Quick Start Review (TE, p. 392) 5 MIN.
- Present *Gramática:* Talking About the Past: The Preterite of -er and -ir Verbs and the *Vocabulario*, p. 392. Have students act out the verbs. 10 MIN.
- Have students complete *Actividad* 8 in writing, then exchange papers for peer correction. 10 MIN.
- Do *Actividad* 9 in groups. 5 MIN.
- Present the *Nota* and do *Actividad* 10 orally. 5 MIN.

Homework Option:
- Have students complete *Actividad* 10 in writing. *Más práctica* Workbook, pp. 133–134. *Para hispanohablantes* Workbook, pp. 131–132.

DAY 4

En acción (cont.)
- Check homework. 5 MIN.
- Quick Start Review (TE, p. 394) 5 MIN.
- Present *Gramática:* Talking About the Past: Verbs with a y Spelling Change, p. 394. 5 MIN.
- Have students read and complete *Actividad* 11 in writing. Go over answers orally. 5 MIN.
- Have students complete *Actividad* 12 orally. 5 MIN.
- Do *Actividad* 13 in pairs. Expand using Information Gap Activities, Unit 6 Resource Book, p. 17; *Más comunicación*, p. R16. 20 MIN.
- Use an expansion activity from TE pp. 394–395 for reinforcement and variety. 10 MIN.

Homework Option:
- Have students complete *Actividad* 12 in writing. *Más práctica* Workbook, p. 135. *Para hispanohablantes* Workbook, p. 133.

DAY 5

En acción (cont.)
- Check homework. 5 MIN.
- Quick Start Review (TE, p. 395) 5 MIN.
- Present *Gramática:* Using Irregular Verbs in the Preterite: hacer, ir, ser, p. 395. 5 MIN.
- Have students read and complete *Actividad* 14 orally. 5 MIN.
- Present the *Vocabulario*, p. 396. Have students mime the professions. 5 MIN.
- Have students read and complete *Actividad* 15 in writing. Go over answers orally. 15 MIN.
- Do *Actividad* 16 orally and *Actividad* 17 in pairs. 10 MIN.
- Play the audio; do *Actividad* 18. 5 MIN.

Homework Option:
- Have students complete *Actividad* 16 in writing. *Más práctica* Workbook, p. 136. *Para hispanohablantes* Workbook, p. 134.

DAY 6

En acción (cont.)
- Check homework. 5 MIN.
- Present the *Nota*, then do *Actividad* 19 orally. 5 MIN.
- Have students do *Actividades* 20 and 21 in pairs. Expand using Information Gap Activities, Unit 6 Resource Book, pp. 18–19; *Más comunicación*, p. R16. 15 MIN.

Pronunciación
- Play the audio and have students practice the *trabalenguas*. 5 MIN.

En voces: Lectura
- Quick Start Review (TE, p. 400) 5 MIN.
- Review the Reading Strategy, p. 400. 5 MIN.
- Have volunteers read the selection aloud and answer the questions, p. 401. 15 MIN.

Homework Option:
- Have students complete the *Hazlo tú* assignment, p. 401.

DAY 7

En uso: Repaso y más comunicación
- Check homework. 5 MIN.
- Quick Start Review (TE, p. 402) 5 MIN.
- Present the *Repaso y más comunicación* using the Teaching Suggestions (TE, p. 402). 5 MIN.
- Have students write *Actividades* 1 and 2; check answers with the whole class. 10 MIN.
- Do *Actividades* 3 and 4 orally. 5 MIN.
- Present the Speaking Strategy, p. 404; have students do *Actividad* 5 in pairs. 10 MIN.
- Have students complete *Actividad* 6 in groups. 5 MIN.

En tu propia voz: Escritura
- Do *Actividad* 7 in writing. Ask volunteers to present their descriptions. 10 MIN.

Homework Option:
- Review for *Etapa* 1 Exam.

DAY 8

Tú en la comunidad
- Read and discuss *Tú en la comunidad*, p. 404. 5 MIN.

En resumen: Repaso de vocabulario
- Quick Start Review (TE, p. 405) 5 MIN.
- Review grammar questions, etc., as necessary. 5 MIN.
- Complete *Etapa* 1 Exam. 20 MIN.

Ampliación
- Use a suggested project, game, or activity. (TE, pp. 383A–383B) 15 MIN.

Homework Option:
- Preview *Etapa* 2 Opener.

Sample Lesson Plan - Block Schedule (90 minutes)

DAY 1

Unit Opener
- Anticipate/Activate prior knowledge: Present the *Almanaque* and the cultural notes. Use Map OHTs as needed. **10 MIN.**

Etapa Opener
- Quick Start Review (TE, p. 384) **5 MIN.**
- Have students look at the *Etapa* Opener and answer the questions. **5 MIN.**
- Use Block Scheduling Copymasters. **5 MIN.**

En contexto: Vocabulario
- Quick Start Review (TE, p. 386) **5 MIN.**
- Have students use context and pictures to learn *Etapa* vocabulary, then answer the questions, p. 387. Use the Situational OHTs for additional practice. **10 MIN.**

En vivo: Diálogo
- Quick Start Review (TE, p. 388) **5 MIN.**
- Review the Listening Strategy, p. 388. Play audio or show video for the dialog, pp. 388–389. Replay and have students take the roles of the characters. **10 MIN.**

En acción: Vocabulario y gramática
- Quick Start Review (TE, p. 390) **5 MIN.**
- Have students open to *En contexto*, pp. 386–387, for reference. Use OHT 175 and 176 to review vocabulary. **10 MIN.**
- Play the video/audio; do *Actividades* 1 and 2 orally. **10 MIN.**
- Have students complete *Actividad* 3 in pairs. **5 MIN.**
- Play the audio; do *Actividad* 4. **5 MIN.**

Homework Option:
- Video Activities, Unit 6 Resource Book, pp. 23–25.

DAY 2

En acción (cont.)
- Check homework. **5 MIN.**
- Present the *Vocabulario*, p. 391. Then have students do *Actividad* 5 orally. **10 MIN.**
- Have students complete *Actividad* 6 in writing. Have volunteers present their descriptions. **15 MIN.**
- Present the Speaking Strategy, p. 392, and the *Nota*. Then have students do *Actividad* 7 in pairs. **10 MIN.**
- Quick Start Review (TE, p. 392) **5 MIN.**
- Present *Gramática:* Talking About the Past: The Preterite of *-er* and *-ir* Verbs and the *Vocabulario*, p. 392. Have students act out the verbs. **10 MIN.**
- Have students complete *Actividad* 8 in writing, then exchange papers for peer correction. **10 MIN.**
- Do *Actividad* 9 in groups. **5 MIN.**
- Present the *Nota* and do *Actividad* 10 orally. **5 MIN.**
- Quick Start Review (TE, p. 394) **5 MIN.**
- Present *Gramática:* Talking About the Past: Verbs with a *y* Spelling Change, p. 394. **5 MIN.**
- Have students read and complete *Actividad* 11 in writing. Go over answers orally. **5 MIN.**

Homework Option:
- Have students complete *Actividad* 10 in writing. *Más práctica* Workbook, pp. 133–134. *Para hispanohablantes* Workbook, pp. 131–132.

DAY 3

En acción (cont.)
- Check homework. **5 MIN.**
- Have students complete *Actividad* 12 orally. **5 MIN.**
- Do *Actividad* 13 in pairs. Expand using Information Gap Activities, Unit 6 Resource Book, p. 17; *Más comunicación,* p. R16. **20 MIN.**
- Use an expansion activity from TE pp. 394–395 for reinforcement and variety. **10 MIN.**
- Quick Start Review (TE, p. 395) **5 MIN.**
- Present *Gramática:* Using Irregular Verbs in the Preterite: *hacer, ir, ser,* p. 395. **5 MIN.**
- Have students read and complete *Actividad* 14 orally. **5 MIN.**
- Present the *Vocabulario*, p. 396. Have students mime the professions. **5 MIN.**
- Have students read and complete *Actividad* 15 in writing. Go over answers orally. **10 MIN.**
- Do *Actividad* 16 orally and *Actividad* 17 in pairs. **10 MIN.**
- Play the audio; do *Actividad* 18. **5 MIN.**
- Present the *Nota,* then do *Actividad* 19 orally. **5 MIN.**

Homework Option:
- Have students complete *Actividades* 12, 16, and 19 in writing. *Más práctica* Workbook, pp. 135–136. *Para hispanohablantes* Workbook, pp. 133–134.

DAY 4

En acción (cont.)
- Check homework. **5 MIN.**
- Have students do *Actividades* 20 and 21 in pairs. Expand using Information Gap Activities, Unit 6 Resource Book, pp. 18–19; *Más comunicación,* p. R16. **20 MIN.**

Pronunciación
- Play the audio and have students practice the *trabalenguas.* **5 MIN.**

En voces: Lectura
- Quick Start Review (TE, p. 400) **5 MIN.**
- Review the Reading Strategy, p. 400. **5 MIN.**
- Have volunteers read the selection aloud and answer the questions, p. 401. **20 MIN.**

En uso: Repaso y más comunicación
- Quick Start Review (TE, p. 402) **5 MIN.**
- Have students write *Actividades* 1 and 2; check answers with the whole class. **10 MIN.**
- Do *Actividades* 3 and 4 orally. **5 MIN.**
- Present the Speaking Strategy, p. 404; have students do *Actividad* 5 in pairs. **10 MIN.**

Homework Option:
- Review for *Etapa* 1 Exam.

DAY 5

En uso (cont.)
- Have students do *Actividad* 6 in groups. Have a few groups present their conversations. **10 MIN.**

En tu propia voz: Escritura
- Do *Actividad* 7 in writing. Ask volunteers to present their descriptions. **20 MIN.**

Tú en la comunidad
- Read and discuss *Tú en la comunidad,* p. 404. **5 MIN.**

En resumen: Repaso de vocabulario
- Quick Start Review (TE, p. 405) **5 MIN.**
- Review grammar questions, etc., as necessary. **10 MIN.**
- Complete *Etapa* 1 Exam. **20 MIN.**

Ampliación
- Use a suggested project, game, or activity. (TE, pp. 383A–383B) **20 MIN.**

Homework Option:
- Preview *Etapa* 2 Opener.

▼ Patricia y Miguel hablan del concurso.

Etapa Theme
Describing a city and talking about professions

Grammar Objectives
• Using preterite of regular -er and -ir verbs
• Using preterite of verbs with a **y** spelling change
• Using preterite of **hacer, ir, ser**

Teaching Resource Options

Print 📖

Block Scheduling Copymasters

Audiovisual 🎧📖

OHT 172, 181 (Quick Start)

🔔 Quick Start Review
♻ Preterite of **-ar** verbs

Use OHT 181 or write on board:
Write 1 thing that happened at each of these times, using an **-ar** verb in the preterite:

1. ayer
2. anoche
3. el mes pasado
4. el año pasado

Answers
Answers will vary. Answers could include:
1. Empecé a leer una novela.
2. Mi hermano preparó la comida.
3. Celebré mi cumpleaños.
4. Mis padres compraron una videograbadora.

Teaching Suggestion
Previewing the Etapa
• Ask students to study the photo on pp. 384–385 (1 min.).
• Close books; ask students to share at least 3 things that they noticed.
• Reopen books and look at the picture again. Give students the beginning of statements for them to finish; for example: **Las dos mujeres...**
• Use the **¿Qué ves?** questions to focus the discussion.

Supplementary Vocabulary

el edificio	building
el edificio de departamentos	apartment building

UNIDAD 6
ETAPA 1

La vida de la ciudad

• Tell what happened

• Make suggestions to a group

• Describe city buildings

• Talk about professions

¿Qué ves?

Mira la foto de un parque de Quito.

1. ¿Las montañas están cerca o lejos del parque?
2. ¿Qué hacen los dos jóvenes?
3. ¿Qué joyas lleva la señora?
4. ¿Cuántos parques hay en el mapa?

384

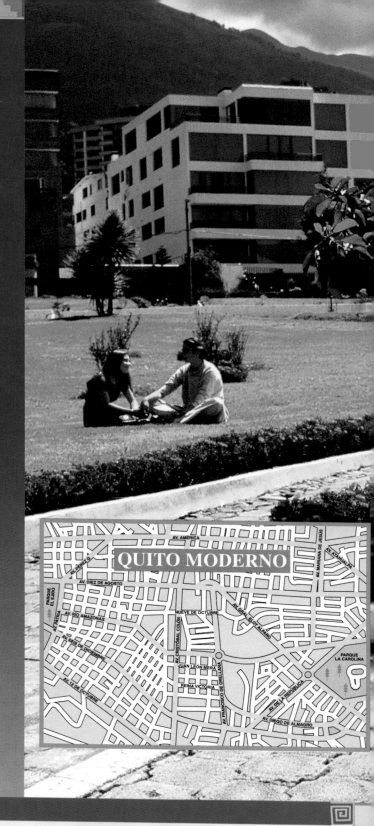

QUITO MODERNO

Classroom Management

Planning Ahead   Collect and bring in photos and posters of urban and rural scenes of Latin American countries. Display them around the classroom. Also collect city maps and subway maps for possible use in giving directions.

Time Saver   If time is short, have students write a description of the photo and do the **¿Qué ves?** questions as homework.

385

Cross Cultural Connections

Have students talk about local or national parks they have been to and how they compare to this one. Ask if they prefer trips to the country or city and why.

Culture Highlights

● **QUITO** Quito, the capital of Ecuador and the Pichincha Province, is located in a valley on the lower slopes of the Pichincha volcano of the Andes Mountains. It is the oldest South American capital.

The architecture of most of Quito's buildings is in the Spanish Baroque style. The most well-known buildings are the Cathedral and the churches of San Francisco, San Agustín, La Compañía, and Santo Domingo.

There are many parks and flower gardens in Quito. The one shown in this photo is the **Parque Sueco,** a small park in **el Quito Moderno.** Two others are **La Carolina** and **El Ejido.**

● **EL TIEMPO EN QUITO** The weather in Quito is changeable. It can go from sunny to rainy to foggy in the course of one day. The temperature can drop 15 degrees on a sunny day when clouds pass overhead.

● **LAS DIRECCIONES EN QUITO** In Quito, all streets that run from east to west are called **calles.** Those that go north to south are **carreras.** If the address you are looking for is **Calle 108-20,** this means the building is on 10th Street, 20 meters from the intersection with **Carrera 8.**

Teaching All Students

Extra Help Have students list as many words as possible for the photo in the following categories: **personas, ropa, números, acciones, naturaleza.**

Multiple Intelligences

Verbal Have students improvise and present a conversation that might be taking place between the 2 women on the bench, the man and woman sitting on the grass, or the 3 teens in the background.

Naturalist Tell students to imagine that they have 1 hour to sit in this park. Then have them talk about all the things they see and hear around them.

Block Schedule

Change of Pace Set up a park scene similar to the one in the photo. Have roaming "news reporters" move from one person to the next, describing the scene and asking the people questions. (For additional activities, see **Block Scheduling Copymasters.**)

Teaching Resource Options

Print 📖

Unit 6 Resource Book
Video Activities, pp. 23–24
Videoscript, p. 26
Audioscript, p. 29
Audioscript *Para hispanohablantes*,
  p. 29

Audiovisual 💻

OHT 175, 176, 177, 177A, 178, 178A,
181 (Quick Start)
Audio Program Cassette 16A / CD 16
Audio *Para hispanohablantes*
  Cassette 16A / CD 16
Video Program Videotape 6 / Videodisc
3B

Search Chapter 2, Play to 3
U6E1 • En contexto (Vocabulary)

Technology 💻

Intrigas y aventuras CD-ROM, Disc 1

🔔 Quick Start Review

♻️ Present progressive

Use OHT 181 or write on the board:
Tell what the following people are
doing right now in the locations
indicated:

Modelo: Eva / la cocina
You write: **Eva está lavando los platos.**

1. los estudiantes / la cafetería
2. los maestros / el departamento
   de español
3. Miguel / la biblioteca
4. la Sra. Ruiz / el supermercado
5. Susana / su habitación

Answers
Answers will vary. Answers could include:
1. Los estudiantes están comiendo.
2. Los maestros están hablando español.
3. Miguel está leyendo una novela.
4. La Sra. Ruiz está comprando la comida.
5. Susana está durmiendo.

En contexto

🎧💿 VOCABULARIO

Patricia is interviewing different people in Quito about their
jobs. As she walks through old and new Quito, she describes
different professions.

(A) **¡Hola!** Me llamo Patricia y voy a explicarles
cómo son las profesiones de varias personas. Ahora
estoy hablando con **un bombero**. Quiero saber algo de
su trabajo. Con mi **grabadora** le hago **una entrevista.**

el edificio moderno

el edificio antiguo y tradicional

la cámara

la fotógrafa

la grabadora

(B) Ella es **fotógrafa**. Saca fotos
con **una cámara**. Está sacando
una foto de **un edificio** muy
antiguo y **tradicional.**

el bombero

el cartero

el taxista

(C) **El cartero** lleva cartas a
todos los edificios. A veces
trabaja en el correo.

(D) Él es **taxista**. En su taxi lleva
a la gente por toda la ciudad.

386 trescientos ochenta y seis
Unidad 6

Classroom Community

TPR Begin by telling the class that many people
change jobs often. Say that you are going to name a
profession and they will act out doing that job until you
name another one. Also use the **Vocabulario adicional**
on p. R21 **(Más profesiones).**

Paired Activity Have students choose 2 of the 7
professions presented on pp. 386–387. Then ask them
to write as many related words as possible under each
one. You may also want to let them use a dictionary.
Have pairs present their lists to the class.

E Mujer de negocios:
Me gusta vender y comprar productos. Ser una mujer de negocios es el trabajo perfecto para mí.

Hombre de negocios:
Siempre leo todas las revistas de economía. Para ser un hombre de negocios hay que saber mucho.

el hombre de negocios

la mujer de negocios

F Él trabaja para un periódico. Le gusta escribir y hacer entrevistas. Por eso es periodista.

el periodista

el arquitecto

G Él es arquitecto. Hace planos de construcción. El edificio que planea aquí es el más grande de Quito. ¡Su oficina está en un edificio enorme y muy moderno!

Preguntas personales

1. ¿Te gusta hacer entrevistas?
2. ¿Prefieres edificios tradicionales o modernos?
3. ¿Tienes una cámara o una grabadora?
4. ¿Quién te lleva cartas?
5. ¿Cuál de estos trabajos te gustaría hacer?

trescientos ochenta y siete
Etapa 1 **387**

Teaching Suggestions
Introducing Vocabulary

• Have students look at pages 386–387. Use OHT 175 and 176 and Audio Cassette 16A / CD 16 to present the vocabulary.
• Ask the Comprehension Questions in order of yes/no (questions 1–3), either/or (questions 4–6), and simple word or phrase (questions 7–10). Expand by adding similar questions.
• Use the TPR activity to reinforce the meaning of individual words.
• Use the video vocabulary presentation for review and reinforcement.

Comprehension Questions

1. ¿Está Patricia hablando con un policía? (No.)
2. ¿Saca fotos la fotógrafa de un edificio antiguo? (Sí.)
3. ¿Trabaja el cartero en el correo a veces? (Sí.)
4. ¿Pasa el taxista el día caminando o manejando? (manejando)
5. ¿Le gusta a la mujer de negocios vender o hacer productos? (vender)
6. ¿Qué lee siempre el hombre de negocios: novelas o revistas de economía? (revistas de economía)
7. ¿Qué hace el periodista? (Escribe y hace entrevistas.)
8. ¿Quién hace planos de construcción? (el arquitecto)
9. ¿Cómo es el edificio que planea el arquitecto en Quito? (Es el más grande de Quito.)
10. ¿En qué tipo de edificio está la oficina del arquitecto? (Es un edificio enorme y muy moderno.)

Block Schedule

Change of Pace Have each student choose 1 profession from pp. 386–387, or a profession listed in the **Vocabulario adicional** on p. R21 (**Más profesiones**). They should write down 2 questions they might ask a person in this profession. You then play the roles of these professionals and students ask you their questions.

Teaching All Students

Extra Help Have students select 1 profession from pp. 386–387, write down the description, memorize it, then tell it to a partner.

Native Speakers Ask students to name and describe professions/trades found in their home communities that are not mentioned here. For example: **gestor(a)** (manager), **afilador de cuchillos** (knife sharpener).

Multiple Intelligences

Intrapersonal Expand student answers to question 5 of the **Preguntas personales** by asking ¿**Por qué?**

Naturalist Have students list, then discuss the advantages and disadvantages of jobs that require outdoor work and those that require indoor work. Then have them explain which type of profession they prefer.

Quick Start Review

♻ Professions

Use OHT 181 or write on the board:
Write the profession associated with
each of the following activities:

1. manejar un taxi
2. hacer planos de construcción
3. estudiar economía
4. escribir y hacer entrevistas
5. llevar cartas
6. sacar fotos

Answers *See p. 383D.*

Gestures

Point out the eye contact and open-hand
gestures in scenes 2, 4, 5, 8, 9. These, and
the handshake in 7, are nonverbal ways of
affirming connection between speakers.
What does it mean when speakers don't
look at each other or make any gestures?

En vivo

📺💿 DIÁLOGO

Patricia — Miguel — Sra. Martínez — Sr. González

PARA ESCUCHAR • STRATEGY: LISTENING

Distinguish between what is said and not said Being a good listener
means being careful and accurate. Which of these are mentioned
in Patricia's interviews about city life? Which are not?

los trabajos	sí	mucha gente
la calidad del aire		muchos vehículos
el crimen		la vida aburrida

En la ciudad

1▶ Patricia: Decidí participar en el
concurso porque leí que los
ganadores van a viajar. Quiero
hacer entrevistas con personas en
la ciudad y personas en el campo.
Tú tienes familia en el campo, ¿no?

5▶ Sra. Martínez: Sí, pero también
tiene sus problemas. La
contaminación del aire, el
tráfico…
Patricia: ¿Cómo se preparó para
ser una mujer de negocios?

6▶ Sra. Martínez: Hice todo lo necesario. Fui
a la universidad. Después me ofrecieron
trabajo en el banco. Y llegué a ser gerente.
Patricia: ¿Y siempre vivió en Quito?
Sra. Martínez: Sí. Mis padres abrieron una
panadería aquí.

7▶ Patricia: Buenas tardes, arquitecto
González. Voy a escribir sobre el
contraste entre la vida en la ciudad
y en el campo.
Sr. González: ¿Qué quiere saber?
Patricia: ¿Le gusta vivir en la ciudad?

388 trescientos ochenta y ocho
Unidad 6

Classroom Community

Paired Activity Have students discuss and
complete a chart with these heads: **El campo: lo
bueno y lo malo / La ciudad: lo bueno y lo malo.**
Have the pairs share their responses with the rest of
the class. Keep a list of ideas on the board.

Game Have students work in groups of 3. Each
student chooses 1 character from the **Vocabulario** or
from the **Diálogo.** Two of the students will write a true
statement about their identity; the other a false
statement. Groups then stand in front of the class. Each
person gives his/her statement. The rest of the class
must guess who is not telling the truth.

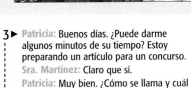

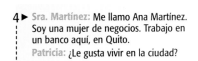

2 ▶ Miguel: Sí. ¿Los llamo?
Patricia: ¡Sí, muchas gracias, Miguel! Oye, vamos a pedir algo, ¿no? En un rato tengo que entrevistar a unas personas y no quiero llegar tarde.

3 ▶ Patricia: Buenos días. ¿Puede darme algunos minutos de su tiempo? Estoy preparando un artículo para un concurso.
Sra. Martínez: Claro que sí.
Patricia: Muy bien. ¿Cómo se llama y cuál es su profesión?

4 ▶ Sra. Martínez: Me llamo Ana Martínez. Soy una mujer de negocios. Trabajo en un banco aquí, en Quito.
Patricia: ¿Le gusta vivir en la ciudad?

8 ▶ Sr. González: La ciudad es interesante. Pero la vida en el campo es mucho más tranquila.
Patricia: ¿Vivió en el campo?
Sr. González: De niño viví en el campo, en casa de mis abuelos.

9 ▶ Patricia: ¿Y cuándo decidió venir a la ciudad?
Sr. González: Cuando entré a la universidad. Cuando recibí mi título de arquitecto, vi que en la ciudad hay más oportunidades que en el campo.

10 ▶ Patricia: ¿Miguel? Soy Patricia.
Miguel: ¿Cómo fueron las entrevistas?
Patricia: Excelente. Ya hice dos. ¿Llamaste a tu familia?
Miguel: Sí. Todo está listo para el sábado.

trescientos ochenta y nueve
Etapa 1   **389**

Teaching Suggestions
Presenting the Dialog
• Prepare students for listening by reintroducing the characters using simple questions: ¿Cómo se llama la chica? ¿Cuál es la profesión de la Sra. Martínez? ¿Cómo se llama el arquitecto?
• Use the video, audio cassette, or CD to present the dialog. The expanded dialog on video offers additional listening practice opportunities.

Video Synopsis
• Patricia tells her friend Miguel about her project for the contest. She is going to interview peopie in the city and in the country. For a complete transcript of the video dialog, see p. 383D.

Comprehension Questions

1. ¿Van a viajar los ganadores del concurso? (Sí.)
2. ¿Tiene Miguel familia en el campo? (Sí.)
3. ¿Tiene Patricia mucho tiempo antes de su próxima entrevista? (No.)
4. ¿Trabaja la Sra. Martínez en el campo o en la ciudad? (en la ciudad)
5. ¿Abrieron sus padres una panadería o un banco? (una panadería)
6. ¿Escribe Patricia sobre las profesiones o sobre el contraste entre la vida en la ciudad y el campo? (sobre el contraste entre la vida en la ciudad y el campo)
7. ¿Qué adjetivo usa el Sr. González para describir la vida en la ciudad? (interesante)
8. ¿Qué adjetivo usa el Sr. González para describir la vida en el campo? (tranquila)
9. ¿Cuándo vivió en el campo? (de niño)
10. ¿Por qué es mejor buscar trabajo en la ciudad? (Hay más oportunidades.)

Block Schedule

Variety Working in pairs, have students make 2 lists of words: those associated with the city and those with the country. They should include professions, clothing, landscape, buildings, etc. Then have them share their lists with another pair and see if the new pair can guess "city" or "country" based on the words in the list. (For additional activities, see **Block Scheduling Copymasters.**)

Teaching All Students

Extra Help Have students draw a time line of Patricia's day. They should fill in her appointments and pertinent information.

Native Speakers Ask students about the biggest cities in their home countries. Are they inland or coastal? Do the inhabitants have a distinctive accent? Are there nicknames for people from the city or from the capital?

Multiple Intelligences

Visual Have students design and write an ad for a beautiful location in the city. Remind them to appeal to the 5 senses. Display the ads in the room.

Rubric   A = 13–15 pts. **B** = 10–12 pts. **C** = 7–9 pts. **D** = 4–6 pts. **F** = < 4 pts.

Writing criteria	Scale				
Grammar/spelling accuracy	1	2	3	4	5
Appeal to the 5 senses	1	2	3	4	5
Creativity, appearance	1	2	3	4	5

Teaching Resource Options

Print
Unit 6 Resource Book
Video Activities, p. 25
Videoscript, p. 28
Audioscript, pp. 29–30
Audioscript *Para hispanohablantes,*
  pp. 29–30

Audiovisual
OHT 182 (Quick Start)
Audio Program Cassettes 16A, 16B /
  CD 16
Audio *Para hispanohablantes*
  Cassette 16A / CD 16
Video Program Videotape 6 /
  Videodisc 3B

Quick Start Review

🔄 Dialog review

Use OHT 182 or write on the board:
Identify the speaker of each quote:

1. Trabajo en un banco aquí en
   Quito.
2. Quiero hacer entrevistas con
   personas en la ciudad y personas
   en el campo.
3. Todo está listo para el sábado.
4. De niño viví en el campo...
5. ¿Llamaste a tu familia?

Answers
1. Sra. Martínez   4. Sr. González
2. Patricia   5. Patricia
3. Miguel

Teaching Suggestions
Comprehension Check

Use **Actividades 1** and **2** to assess
retention after the dialog. After
completing the activities, have students
write out **Actividad 1** in paragraph form
and insert at least 2 more events.

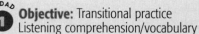
En acción
VOCABULARIO Y GRAMÁTICA

OBJECTIVES
- Tell what happened
- Make suggestions to a group
- Describe city buildings
- Talk about professions

¿En qué orden?

Escuchar Según el diálogo, ¿en qué orden hace Patricia estas cosas? *(Hint: Put events in order.)*

a. Patricia llama por teléfono a Miguel.

b. Patricia le dice a Miguel por qué quiere participar en el concurso.

c. Patricia va a la oficina del arquitecto.

d. Patricia le hace una entrevista a la mujer de negocios.

e. Patricia habla con Miguel sobre su familia del campo.

¿Por qué?

Escuchar Explica por qué cada persona hace lo siguiente.
(Hint: Explain why.)

1. ¿Por qué quiere Patricia participar en el concurso?

2. ¿Por qué habla Patricia con la mujer de negocios?

3. ¿Por qué vive el arquitecto en la ciudad?

4. ¿Por qué le gusta el campo al arquitecto?

¿Cuál es su profesión?

Hablar Todas estas personas trabajan en la ciudad. Tu amigo(a) quiere saber cuáles son sus profesiones. Cambien de papel.
(Hint: Say each profession.)

modelo

Tú: *¿Cuál es la profesión del hombre?*
Tu amigo(a): *Es arquitecto.*

1.

2.

3.

4.

5.

6.

390 trescientos noventa
Unidad 6

Classroom Management

Time Saver If time is short, put the sentences for **Actividades 1** and **2** on the board and have students work on the activities in pairs.

Student Self-check Plan time for students to review their portfolios. They should check for their progress since the beginning of the course. Encourage students to feel proud of their success, and remind them they can look forward to more progress and more fun next year.

- *Use preterite of regular -er and -ir verbs*
- *Use preterite of verbs with a y spelling change*
- *Use preterite of hacer, ir, ser*

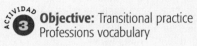

ACTIVIDAD 4

¿Cómo son?

Escuchar Imagínate que haces una excursión de Quito. El guía describe los edificios. Indica el orden en que describe los edificios. *(Hint: Give the order.)*

Vocabulario

La ciudad

ancho(a) *wide*	**formal** *formal*	**lujoso(a)** *luxurious*
estrecho(a) *narrow*	**informal** *informal*	**ordinario(a)** *ordinary*
		sencillo(a) *simple, plain*

¿Cómo son los edificios y las calles donde tú vives?

ACTIVIDAD 5

Un edificio interesante

Hablar Haz un dibujo de un edificio interesante de tu comunidad. Descríbelo.
(Hint: Draw a building and describe it.)

modelo

La iglesia de mi comunidad es interesante. Es enorme y antigua. Cuando entras a la iglesia, ves que también es lujosa. Tiene muchos artículos de oro y ventanas de muchos colores.

ACTIVIDAD 6

Una ciudad grande

Escribir Imagínate que vas a visitar una ciudad grande. ¿Qué ciudad quieres visitar? ¿Qué sabes de la ciudad? Escribe un mínimo de seis oraciones para describirla.
(Hint: Describe a city.)

modelo

Me gustaría visitar la ciudad de Nueva York. Sé que es una ciudad muy grande y divertida. En Nueva York hay muchos edificios enormes. Algunos son viejos y otros son muy modernos. Hay cosas interesantes en Nueva York. Hay…

trescientos noventa y uno
Etapa 1 **391**

ACTIVIDAD 2 Objective: Transitional practice
Listening comprehension/vocabulary

Answers (See script, p. 383D.)
1. Los ganadores van a viajar y trabajar para la revista.
2. Quiere hacer entrevistas con personas que viven en la ciudad.
3. Porque hay más oportunidades para su trabajo en la ciudad.
4. Porque la vida en el campo es tranquila.

ACTIVIDAD 3 Objective: Transitional practice
Professions vocabulary

Answers
1. Tú: ¿Cuál es la profesión de la mujer?
Tu amigo(a): Es mujer de negocios.
2. Tú: ¿Cuál es la profesión del hombre?
Tu amigo(a): Es cartero.
3. Tú: ¿Cuál es la profesión de la mujer?
Tu amigo(a): Es fotógrafa.
4. Tú: ¿Cuál es la profesión del hombre?
Tu amigo(a): Es periodista.
5. Tú: ¿Cuál es la profesión del hombre?
Tu amigo(a): Es taxista.
6. Tú: ¿Cuál es la profesión del hombre?
Tu amigo(a): Es bombero.

ACTIVIDAD 4 Objective: Transitional practice
Listening comprehension/city vocabulary

Answers (See script, p. 383D.)
d, c, b, a

Teaching Suggestions
Reinforcing Vocabulary

Have various students name buildings or streets in your town/city. The other students describe these places using an adjective from the **Vocabulario.**

ACTIVIDAD 5 Objective: Open-ended practice
City vocabulary

Answers will vary.

ACTIVIDAD 6 Objective: Open-ended practice
City vocabulary in writing

Answers will vary.

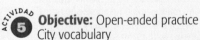

Block Schedule

Research Have students research a Latin American city of their choosing. Have them sketch a map of the city and write a description of it. They should also plan a walking tour, using directions and names of buildings, monuments, parks, etc. Have them present their work.

Teaching All Students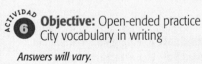

Extra Help Describe each of the 11 photos on pp. 390–391 in random order. Students point to the correct photo and say the corresponding number or letter.

Native Speakers Discuss women as professionals in students' home countries. Is it common to find a woman architect or journalist? Is it common to find women in the fire or police department?

Multiple Intelligences

Visual Have students prepare a set of sketches to illustrate the city adjectives in the **Vocabulario.** Then have students use the sketches to practice the adjectives and form original sentences with them.

Teaching Resource Options

Print 📖

Más práctica Workbook PE,
 pp. 133–134
Para hispanohablantes Workbook PE,
 pp. 131–132
Block Scheduling Copymasters
Unit 6 Resource Book
 Más práctica Workbook TE, pp. 5–6
 Para hispanohablantes Workbook
 TE, pp. 11–12

Audiovisual

OHT 182 (Quick Start)

Technology

Intrigas y aventuras CD-ROM, Disc 1

ACTIVIDAD 7

Objective: Open-ended practice
Giving opinions in conversation
♻ Superlatives
Answers will vary.

🔔 Quick Start Review

♻ **Preterite of -ar verbs**

Use OHT 182 or write on the board:
Use the following verbs to tell 5 things
that happened in the past week:

1. estudiar   4. sacar
2. limpiar   5. empezar
3. levantarse

Answers
Answers will vary. Answers could include:
1. Tú estudiaste para el examen de inglés.
2. Mi madre limpió mi habitación.
3. Hoy me levanté a las siete.
4. Ayer mi hermano sacó la basura.
5. Anoche el concierto empezó a las ocho.

Teaching Suggestions
Teaching the Preterite of -er and -ir Verbs

• Review the preterite of **-ar** verbs so
that students can conjugate them as
quickly as they can say their math facts.
• Explain to students that by learning
the preterite of **-er** and **-ir** verbs, they
will be able to more fully use the past
tense and therefore be able to
communicate better in Spanish.

ACTIVIDAD 7 ♻ **¿Cuál es tu opinión?**

PARA CONVERSAR • STRATEGY: SPEAKING

Exaggerate and react to exaggerations As you discuss your
opinions, you can be truthful or you can exaggerate. If you
question the truth of what you hear, you can use these ways of
expressing disbelief: **¿de veras?, ¿verdad?, ¡increíble!, ¡no me
digas!, ¡no lo creo!** Use them when necessary.

Hablar Da tu opinión sobre las siguientes cosas. Luego, pregúntale
a otro(a) estudiante cuál es su opinión. *(Hint: Give your opinion.)*

modelo

los edificios más interesantes

Tú: *Los edificios más interesantes* son modernos. ¿Estás de acuerdo?

Otro(a) estudiante: No estoy de acuerdo. Para mí *los edificios más
interesantes* son antiguos.

Nota

Estar de acuerdo means *to agree*.
To say *I agree*, say **estoy de acuerdo**.

1. el edificio más bonito
2. la profesión más peligrosa
3. el actor más popular
4. el deporte menos aburrido
5. el mejor lugar para vivir
6. la profesión más interesante
7. el edificio más feo
8. la comida más rica
9. la peor estación del año

GRAMÁTICA

Talking About the Past: The Preterite of -er and -ir Verbs

 ¿RECUERDAS? *p. 366* You've already
learned to talk about completed past
actions using regular **-ar** verbs.

Regular **-er** and **-ir** verbs follow a similar
pattern. Notice that in the preterite, **-er**
and **-ir** verb endings **match** each other.

The **yo** forms
and the **usted, él,
ella** forms take
accents.

Patricia asks: —¿**Viv**ió en el campo?
Did you live in the country?

limpiar *to clean*

limpi**é**	limpi**amos**
limpi**aste**	limpi**asteis**
limpi**ó**	limpi**aron**

ofrecer *to offer*

ofrec**í**	ofrec**imos**
ofrec**iste**	ofrec**isteis**
ofrec**ió**	ofrec**ieron**

decidir *to decide*

decid**í**	decid**imos**
decid**iste**	decid**isteis**
decid**ió**	decid**ieron**

Vocabulario

These verbs you know are
regular in the preterite tense:

-er verbs

aprender	**devolver**
barrer	**entender**
beber	**mover**
comer	**perder**
comprender	**vender**
correr	**volver**

-ir verbs

abrir	**recibir**
compartir	**salir**
escribir	**vivir**

392   trescientos noventa y dos
Unidad 6

Classroom Community

Storytelling Tell students a story about what you or
someone else did over the past week. As you tell the
story, students write down the past tense verbs they
hear. Repeat the story and have them check their work.
Then go over answers as a class.

Cooperative Learning Write a variety of regular
verb infinitives on small cards and distribute them to
groups of 4 students. Student 1 takes the first card

(aprender) and makes a statement using **yo** +
preterite. **(Yo aprendí 5 palabras hoy.)** Student 2
retells the statement, using the person's name. **(Rosa
aprendió 5 palabras hoy.)** Then he/she adds his/her
own **yo** information. **(Yo aprendí una canción.)**
Student 3 continues in this manner. Student 4 repeats
what each person says. The group confirms or corrects.
Then Student 2 begins the next round with a new verb.

ACTIVIDAD 8 Gramática

¿Dónde vivieron?

Escribir Los amigos de Patricia comentan sobre las ciudades donde estudiaron durante un semestre. ¿Dónde vivieron? *(Hint: Where did they live?)*

modelo

Sam y Carlota: Barcelona

Sam y Carlota vivieron en **Barcelona.**

1. Enrique: Nueva York
2. nosotros: San Juan
3. tú: la Ciudad de México
4. Anita y yo: Miami
5. yo: San Antonio
6. ustedes: Los Ángeles

■ **MÁS PRÁCTICA** *cuaderno* pp. 133–134

■ **PARA HISPANOHABLANTES** *cuaderno* pp. 131–132

ACTIVIDAD 9

¿Qué comiste?

Hablar Pregúntales a cinco estudiantes qué comieron y bebieron ayer. Preséntale a la clase un resumen de las respuestas. *(Hint: Ask what they ate and drank.)*

modelo

Tú: ¿Qué comiste y bebiste para el desayuno?

Estudiante 1: Comí cereal y bebí jugo.

Resumen: Para el desayuno, tres personas comieron cereal y dos comieron yogur. Cuatro personas bebieron jugo y una bebió leche.

La comida	Estudiante 1	Estudiante 2
el desayuno	cereal, jugo	
el almuerzo		
la merienda		
la cena		

ACTIVIDAD 10

 El otro día

Hablar/Escribir Explica qué hicieron tus amigos, tu familia y tú, usando las palabras indicadas como guía. *(Hint: Say what they did.)*

Nota

The verb **ver** is regular in the preterite but does not have accents in any of its forms.

modelo

| Yo | salí | con mis amigos | anoche. |

1. yo
2. mi hermano(a)
3. mis padres
4. mi amigo(a)
5. mis amigos y yo
6. ¿?

aprender
compartir
escribir
recibir
salir
ver

¿?

anoche
ayer
anteayer
la semana pasada
el año pasado
¿?

trescientos noventa y tres
Etapa 1 **393**

Language Note
Point out that the verb **ofrecer** has an irregular **yo** form in the present: **ofrezco.**

ACTIVIDAD 8
Objective: Controlled practice
Preterite of **-er** and **-ir** verbs in writing

Answers
1. Enrique vivió en Nueva York.
2. Nosotros vivimos en San Juan.
3. Tú viviste en la Ciudad de México.
4. Anita y yo vivimos en Miami.
5. Yo viví en San Antonio.
6. Ustedes vivieron en Los Ángeles.

ACTIVIDAD 9
Objective: Transitional practice
Preterite of **-er** and **-ir** verbs in conversation

Answers will vary.

ACTIVIDAD 10
Objective: Open-ended practice
Preterite of **-er** and **-ir** verbs

♻ Expressions indicating the past

Answers will vary.

Teaching All Students

Extra Help Have students make preterite flashcards of the verbs on p. 392, and practice conjugating the verbs with a partner. Have partners keep a separate pile of verbs that were difficult for their partner, and run through them again.

Multiple Intelligences

Visual Create a worksheet that contains all the necessary words for many complete sentences about the past. Have students use a colored pencil or pen to draw lines from word to word to create a complete sentence. Then have them change to another color for the next sentence, and so on. Ask volunteers to write their sentences on the board.

■ Block Schedule

Change of Pace Have students write a "children's book" about **una semana excelente** or **una semana horrible,** using the preterite tense. They should also illustrate the book. (For additional activities, see **Block Scheduling Copymasters.**)

Teaching Resource Options

Print

Más práctica Workbook PE, p. 135
Para hispanohablantes Workbook PE,
  p. 133
Block Scheduling Copymasters
Unit 6 Resource Book
  Más práctica Workbook TE, p. 7
  Para hispanohablantes Workbook
  TE, p. 13
  Information Gap Activities, p. 17

Audiovisual

OHT 182 (Quick Start), 183 (Quick Start)

Technology

Intrigas y aventuras CD-ROM, Disc 1

Quick Start Review

🔄 Preterite of **-er** and **-ir** verbs

Use OHT 182 or write on the board:
Write complete past tense sentences
using the following words:

1. yo / aprender
2. tú / escribir
3. Tomás / correr
4. mis amigos / ofrecer
5. nosotros / decidir

Answers *See p. 383D.*

Teaching Suggestions
Teaching Verbs with a y Spelling Change

After teaching the preterite forms with
a **y** spelling change, tell students facts
about yourself and about another
person, using **oír, leer,** and **creer.** For
example: **Anoche leí una novela. Mi
hijo leyó una revista.**

 Objective: Controlled practice
Verbs with a **y** spelling change

Answers

1. Leyó	4. oímos	7. oíste
2. creyó	5. oyeron	8. oí
3. leyó	6. Oímos	9. leí

GRAMÁTICA

Talking About the Past: Verbs with a y Spelling Change

To write the third person **preterite** forms of **-er** and **-ir** verbs with stems
that **end in a vowel**, change the **i** to **y**. Notice that all of these preterite
forms require an accent, except the **ustedes, ellos(as)** forms.

o**ír** *to hear*	
o**í**	o**ímos**
o**íste**	o**ísteis**
o**yó**	o**yeron**

le**er** *to read*	
le**í**	le**ímos**
le**íste**	le**ísteis**
le**yó**	le**yeron**

cre**er** *to believe*	
cre**í**	cre**ímos**
cre**íste**	cre**ísteis**
cre**yó**	cre**yeron**

Patricia le**yó** algo del
concurso.
*Patricia read something about
the contest.*

ACTIVIDAD 11 Gramática

Una conversación

Leer Dos amigos de Patricia están hablando
de ella. Para saber lo que dicen, completa su
conversación con la forma correcta del verbo
leer, oír o **creer.** *(Hint: Complete their conversation.)*

Linda: ¿Por qué quiere participar Patricia en
el concurso?

Raúl: ___1___ en la revista que las personas que
ganan van a viajar a diferentes países.

Linda: ¿Y ___2___ ella lo que ___3___ ?

Raúl: ¡Claro que sí! Mi hermana y yo también
___4___ algo en la radio sobre el concurso.

Linda: ¿Qué ___5___ ustedes?

Raúl: ___6___ que las personas que ganan
también van a trabajar como periodistas
para la revista. ¿Y tú no ___7___ nada en
la radio sobre el concurso?

Linda: No, no ___8___ nada en la radio ni ___9___
nada en la revista.

🟥 **MÁS PRÁCTICA** *cuaderno* p. 135

🟥 **PARA HISPANOHABLANTES** *cuaderno* p. 133

ACTIVIDAD 12

¡A leer!

Hablar/Escribir ¿Qué leyeron estas personas?
(Hint: What did they read?)

la revista   el poema
              el menú   el periódico
la novela
              el libro
        la tarea

modelo

mi madre

Mi madre leyó una revista.

1. yo	**5.** mi amigo(a) y yo
2. mi amigo(a)	**6.** mis amigos
3. mis padres	**7.** mi hermano(a)
4. mi padre	**8.** mi maestro(a)

394 trescientos noventa y cuatro
Unidad 6

Classroom Community

Paired Activity Have students work in pairs. Tell
them to choose a **Vocabulario** or **Diálogo** from a
previous **Etapa** and retell the story using the preterite.
For example, for p. 314, students would begin: **Luis oyó
el despertador. Pero, él se quedó en la cama.**

Storytelling Have students work in groups of 4–5 to
tell a story to the class. One group member stands up
and begins with: **Yo oí que.. ,** and makes up a story
from there. Each member must speak coherently for 20
seconds. If the student falters, the next group member
takes over and continues, making up the next segment
of the story.

ACTIVIDAD 13

¿Qué oyeron?

Hablar Todos fueron a un banquete y oyeron muchas cosas. Pregúntale a otro(a) estudiante lo que oyeron estas personas. *(Hint: Say what they heard.)*

modelo

tu amigo

Tú: *¿Qué oyó **tu amigo**?*

Otro(a) estudiante: *Oyó que Pedro no va a la fiesta.*

1. tu hermano(a)
2. tus amigos
3. tú
4. tu madre
5. tú y tu familia
6. tu padre
7. tus padres
8. tu maestro(a)

■ **MÁS COMUNICACIÓN** p. R16

NOTA CULTURAL

Quito is the second highest capital city in the world after La Paz, Bolivia. It is surrounded by mountains and volcanoes. The old city has colonial buildings with whitewashed walls and red-tiled roofs. The new city has many modern buildings.

GRAMÁTICA

Using Irregular Verbs in the Preterite: hacer, ir, ser

♻ **¿RECUERDAS?** *p. 292* Remember how to say *I went* and *you went* in Spanish?

fui   fuiste

The verb **ir** is irregular in the **preterite.** Its preterite forms are exactly the **same** as the preterite forms of **ser. Hacer** also has irregular **preterite** forms. These verbs don't have any accents in the preterite.

ir/ser *to be/to go*		**hacer** *to make, to do*	
fui	fuimos	hice	hicimos
fuiste	fuisteis	hiciste	hicisteis
fue	fueron	hizo	hicieron

Notice that the **c** becomes **z** before **o.**

The businesswoman says:

—**Hice** todo lo necesario. **Fui** a la universidad…

I did everything necessary. ***I went*** to the university…

trescientos noventa y cinco
Etapa 1 **395**

Teaching All Students

Extra Help Give students a list of interrogatives (see p. 139) and have them write 5–8 questions using **oír, leer,** and **creer** in the past tense. Have volunteers ask their questions and have the class answer them.

Native Speakers Ask students to bring in and discuss any popular magazines they might have from their home communities, especially magazines for teenagers.

Multiple Intelligences

Interpersonal Give students 5 minutes to circulate around the room asking each other where they went and what they did yesterday. Students should note the information and also ask follow-up questions as needed. Then ask volunteers to present interesting information to the class.

ACTIVIDAD 12

Objective: Transitional practice
Verbs with a **y** spelling change

Answers

Answers will vary.
1. Yo leí…
2. Mi amigo(a) leyó…
3. Mis padres leyeron…
4. Mi padre leyó…
5. Mi amigo(a) y yo leímos…
6. Mis amigos leyeron…
7. Mi hermano(a) leyó…
8. Mi maestro(a) leyó…

ACTIVIDAD 13

Objective: Open-ended practice
Verbs with a **y** spelling change in conversation

Answers

Student responses will vary.
1. Tú: ¿Qué oyó tu hermano(a)?
2. Tú: ¿Qué oyeron tus amigos?
3. Tú: ¿Qué oíste tú?
4. Tú: ¿Qué oyó tu madre?
5. Tú: ¿Qué oyeron tú y tu familia?
6. Tú: ¿Qué oyó tu padre?
7. Tú: ¿Qué oyeron tus padres?
8. Tú: ¿Qué oyó tu maestro(a)?

🔔 Quick Start Review

♻ **Oír, leer, creer**

Use OHT 183 or write on the board:
Answer the following questions:
1. ¿Oíste algo interesante ayer?
2. ¿Qué revista leíste recientemente? ¿Le gustó?
3. De niño(a), ¿creíste en Santa Claus? ¿Hasta qué año?

Answers will vary.

Teaching Suggestions
Teaching Irregular Verbs in the Preterite: hacer, ir, ser

Point out that **hacer** in a question is usually replaced by another verb in the answer: **¿Qué hiciste ayer? / Fui al cine.** Have students ask and answer original questions using these 3 verbs.

■ Block Schedule

Expansion Have students expand on **Actividad 12** by supplying titles and additional information to their answers, such as where they bought or found each item, etc. (For additional activities, see **Block Scheduling Copymasters.**)

Teaching Resource Options

Print

Más práctica Workbook PE, p. 136

Para hispanohablantes Workbook PE, p. 134

Block Scheduling Copymasters

Unit 6 Resource Book

 Más práctica Workbook TE, p. 8

 Para hispanohablantes Workbook TE, p. 14

Technology

Intrigas y aventuras CD-ROM, Disc 1

 14 **Objective:** Controlled practice Preterite of **hacer**

Answers
1. hiciste
2. hice
3. hicimos
4. hicieron
5. hice
6. hizo

 15 **Objective:** Controlled practice Preterite of **ser**/professions

1. Fue cartero.
2. Fue recepcionista.
3. Fue fotógrafo.
4. Fuiste arquitecto.
5. Fueron taxistas.
6. Fue editora.
7. Fueron contadores.
8. Fui secretario(a).
9. Fuimos operadores.
10. Fueron periodistas.

Language Note

In **Actividad 15,** note the use of **e** in the direction line. The word **e** is used instead of **y** before a word beginning with **i** or **hi.**

Teaching Suggestions
Teaching Vocabulary

Have each student select a profession from this **Vocabulario** or from pp. 386–387 and write down 3 nouns or verbs associated with it. Call on students to read their lists. Have the class try to guess the profession.

 **ACTIVIDAD 14** **Gramática**

Hoy no, pero ayer sí

Leer Patricia explica lo que hacen hoy y lo que hicieron antes todas las personas. Para saber qué hicieron, usa el pretérito del verbo **hacer.** *(Hint: Use the preterite of* ***hacer****.)*

modelo

Hoy no hago mi cama, pero ayer la ___kice___ .

1. Tú normalmente haces la tarea después de la cena, pero anoche la _____ antes.
2. Yo no voy a hacer la entrevista hoy porque la _____ ayer.
3. Anita y yo siempre hacemos ejercicio en el gimnasio, pero ayer no _____ nada.
4. Mamá y papá siempre me hacen un sándwich para el almuerzo, pero ayer no lo _____.
5. Normalmente no hago pasteles muy buenos, pero la semana pasada _____ uno riquísimo.
6. Mi mamá normalmente me hace vestidos muy bonitos, pero el año pasado no me _____ ninguno.

 **ACTIVIDAD 15** **Gramática**

¿Qué fueron?

Leer/Escribir Todos hablan hoy de sus antiguas profesiones. Lee las oraciones e indica qué profesión tuvo cada persona. *(Hint: Say what each person was.)*

modelo

Escribí una novela de romance.

Fui escritor(a).

1. Alfredo llevó muchísimas cartas.
2. La señora Rivera contestó el teléfono en la oficina y habló con los clientes que llegaron.
3. El señor Cano sacó muchas fotos de personas importantes.
4. Hiciste planos de casas buenísimos.
5. Llevaron a muchas personas al aeropuerto.
6. La señora Flores leyó los manuscritos de muchos escritores.
7. Ustedes trabajaron todo el día con números.
8. Escribí más de mil cartas para mi jefe.
9. Contestamos los teléfonos de toda la compañía.
10. Ellos hicieron muchas entrevistas.

■ **MÁS PRÁCTICA** *cuaderno* p. 136

■ **PARA HISPANOHABLANTES** *cuaderno* p. 134

Vocabulario

Las profesiones

la arquitectura *architecture*

la compañía *company*

el (la) contador(a) *accountant*

el (la) editor(a) *editor*

el (la) escritor(a) *writer*

el (la) gerente *manager*

el (la) jefe(a) *boss*

el (la) operador(a) *operator*

el (la) recepcionista *receptionist*

el (la) secretario(a) *secretary*

¿Cuándo visitas a estas personas?

396 trescientos noventa y seis
Unidad 6

Classroom Community

Cooperative Learning Have students work in groups of 5. Tell them that the school is publishing a bilingual edition of its newsletter and wants an article about Spanish I. Student 1 is the reporter and interviews 3 group members about class activities during the past school year. Student 5 records the answers. Then the group works together to compile the article and present it to the class.

Portfolio Have students record a funny or interesting story on tape/video, being sure to use the preterite. Play the tapes/videos for the class. Have students raise their hands when they hear a verb in the past tense.

Rubric A = 13–15 pts. B = 10–12 pts. C = 7–9 pts. D = 4–6 pts. F = < 4 pts.

Criteria	Scale
Accurate use of preterite	1 2 3 4 5
Pronunciation	1 2 3 4 5
Creativity	1 2 3 4 5

ACTIVIDAD 16

¿Adónde fueron?

Hablar/Escribir Todos salieron ayer. Explica adónde fue cada persona y cómo fue el día. *(Hint: Explain where they went.)*

modelo

Patricia: interesante

Patricia *fue a la oficina del arquitecto. Fue **interesante**.*

1. Miguel: divertido

4. ustedes: ¿?

2. tú: aburrido

5. yo: ¿?

3. Miguel y yo: ¿?

6. mi familia: ¿?

ACTIVIDAD 17

¿Adónde fuiste?

Hablar Pregúntale a otro(a) estudiante adónde fueron y qué hicieron estas personas el fin de semana pasado. *(Hint: Ask where these people went and what they did.)*

modelo

tus amigos

Tú: *¿Adónde fueron y qué hicieron **tus amigos** el fin de semana pasado?*

Otro(a): *El sábado mis amigos fueron a la cancha. Vieron un partido de baloncesto. El domingo no salieron.*

1. tu hermano(a)

2. tus padres

3. tú

4. tus amigos

5. tú y tu mejor amigo(a)

6. tus hermanos

7. tu mejor amigo(a)

8. ¿?

NOTA CULTURAL

The currency of Ecuador is the **sucre**. Where does its name come from? Check p. 382.

Teaching All Students

Extra Help Have students look back at pp. 388–389 and list all the past tense forms. They should also list each form's infinitive.

Multiple Intelligences

Intrapersonal Have students write an end-of-week entry in a Spanish diary. Ask them to characterize the week with a familiar adjective and write supporting details.

Logical/Mathematical Have students research the current exchange rate of the **sucre**. Then have them find out the various bill denominations and calculate the approximate value of each in U.S. dollars.

ACTIVIDAD 16

Objective: Transitional practice
Preterite of **ir** and **ser**

Answers

1. Miguel fue al campo de fútbol. Fue divertido.
2. Tú fuiste al centro comercial. Fue aburrido.
3. Miguel y yo fuimos al cine. Fue...
4. Ustedes fueron a la fiesta. Fue...
5. Yo fui al gimnasio. Fue..
6. Mi familia fue al restaurante. Fue...

ACTIVIDAD 17

Objective: Open-ended practice
Preterite in conversation

Answers

Student responses will vary.

1. Tú: ¿Adónde fue y qué hizo tu hermano(a) el fin de semana pasado?
   Otro(a): El sábado mi hermano(a) fue...
2. Tú: ¿Adónde fueron y qué hicieron tus padres el fin de semana pasado?
   Otro(a): El sábado mis padres fueron...
3. Tú: ¿Adónde fuiste y qué hiciste tú el fin de semana pasado?
   Otro(a): El sábado yo fui...
4. Tú: ¿Adónde fueron y qué hicieron tus amigos el fin de semana pasado?
   Otro(a): El sábado mis amigos fueron...
5. Tú: ¿Adónde fueron y qué hicieron tú y tu mejor amigo(a) el fin de semana pasado?
   Otro(a): El sábado yo y mi mejor amigo(a) fuimos...
6. Tú: ¿Adónde fueron y qué hicieron tus hermanos el fin de semana pasado?
   Otro(a): El sábado mis hermanos fueron...
7. Tú: ¿Adónde fue y qué hizo tu mejor amigo(a) el fin de semana pasado?
   Otro(a): El sábado mi mejor amigo(a) fue...
8. *Answers will vary.*

Culture Highlights

● **EL SUCRE** The Cultural Opener on p. 382 explains that Mariscal Antonio José de Sucre led the movement for the independence of Ecuador. The currency is named after him.

Block Schedule

Project Tell students to contact 2–3 friends and family members of different professions. For each person, they should report on the profession, where the person studied, where he/she worked before, where he/she works now, and how much the person enjoys his/her work. (For additional activities, see **Block Scheduling Copymasters**.)

Teaching Resource Options

Print
Block Scheduling Copymasters
Unit 6 Resource Book
  Information Gap Activities, pp. 18–19
  Audioscript, p. 30
  Audioscript *Para hispanohablantes,*
  p. 30

Audiovisual
Audio Program Cassettes 16A, 16B /
CD 16
Audio *Para hispanohablantes*
Cassette 16A / CD 16

Technology
Intrigas y aventuras CD-ROM, Disc 1

 18 Objective: Transitional practice
Listening comprehension/preterite

Answers (See script, p. 383D.)
1. Patricia   4. Marta
2. Patricia   5. Andrea
3. Andrea   6. Marta

 19 Objective: Transitional practice
Vamos a + infinitive

Answers
1. ¡Vamos a hacer ejercicio! (¡Vamos a jugar al baloncesto!)
2. ¡Vamos a nadar!
3. ¡Vamos a ir de compras!
4. ¡Vamos a jugar al fútbol!

Language Note
The words **chompa** and **saco** may be used in slightly different ways than the English words *jacket* and *sweater.* A **chompa** is any jacket-like outerwear that opens in the front. Woven woolen outerwear with buttons or a zipper up the front would be called a **chompa.** All leather and cloth jackets would also be called **chompas.** Only sweaters that pull on over the head or cardigans are called **sacos.**

Un sábado especial

Escuchar Lee lo que hicieron Patricia, Marta y Andrea. Luego, escucha la conversación y explica quién hizo cada actividad. *(Hint: Indicate who did what.)*

1. Vio una película de acción.
2. Corrió en el parque.
3. Escribió una carta.
4. Comió en el restaurante Casa Linda.
5. Fue a un partido de fútbol.
6. Fue de compras.

TAMBIÉN SE DICE
Ecuador has its own regionalisms for many of the items you already know in Spanish.
- **chompa:** chaqueta
- **departamento:** apartamento
- **esfero:** pluma, bolígrafo
- **saco:** suéter

Vamos a...

Hablar/Escribir Ana siempre quiere hacer algo con sus amigos. ¿Cómo los invita? *(Hint: What does she say?)*

modelo
¡Vamos a comer!

Nota
When you want to say *Let's...!* use **Vamos a** + an infinitive.

1.

2.

3.

4.

398 trescientos noventa y ocho
Unidad 6

Classroom Community

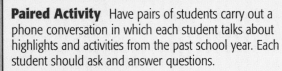

Paired Activity Have pairs of students carry out a phone conversation in which each student talks about highlights and activities from the past school year. Each student should ask and answer questions.

Group Activity Divide the class into 4 groups. Each group represents 1 character's family: Patricia's family, Miguel's family, Sra. Martínez's family, and Sr. González's family. Each student should choose the role of a particular family member. The families then sit around the dinner table and talk about the day's events, including Patricia's interviews.

Tu calendario

Hablar/Escribir Haz un calendario imaginario o real de la semana pasada. Habla con otro(a) estudiante sobre lo que hicieron. *(Hint: Say what you did.)*

modelo

Estudiante A: ¿Qué hiciste el lunes?

Estudiante B: Aprendí un poema.

lunes - aprendí un poema

martes -

miércoles -

jueves -

viernes -

sábado -

domingo -

APOYO PARA ESTUDIAR

Preterite of *ir* and *ser*

Since these verbs are the same in the preterite, how can you tell which is meant? Look at the context. If you see words that say *where*, *ir* is intended; if you see a *description*, *ser* is intended.

—¿Adónde **fuiste** anoche?

—**Fui** al *cine*. *Vi* una película de Antonio Banderas.

—¿**Fue** interesante?

—Sí, y también **fue** muy divertida.

Una entrevista

Hablar/Escribir Imagínate que eres periodista y otro(a) estudiante es profesional. Haz una entrevista, según las instrucciones. Escribe un resumen. *(Hint: Interview someone.)*

Estudiante A: Imagínate que eres una persona profesional y que acabas de empezar un nuevo trabajo. Escoge una profesión. Contesta las preguntas del periodista.

Estudiante B: Imagínate que eres periodista y que estás escribiendo un artículo sobre los profesionales de la ciudad. Haz las preguntas necesarias.

¿Cuál es su profesión?

¿Dónde trabaja usted?

¿Siempre trabajó usted como…?

¿Qué hizo…?

¿Adónde fue para…?

¿Cómo se preparó para ser…?

¿Qué es lo que más le gusta del trabajo?

¿Qué es lo que menos le gusta del trabajo?

■ **MÁS COMUNICACIÓN** p. R16

Pronunciación

Trabalenguas

Pronunciación de la *d* When *d* begins a word or follows the letters **n** or **l**, it is pronounced with a hard sound, as it is in English. When *d* is between two vowels or at the end of a word, it is pronounced like the *th* in the English word *they*. To practice the *d*, try the following tongue twister.

Alcalde Machado   Alcalde Amador

Dos alcaldes, David Machado y Daniela Amador, danzan el fandango el sábado.

trescientos noventa y nueve
Etapa 1 **399**

 Objective: Open-ended practice
Saying what you did in conversation

Answers will vary.

 Objective: Open-ended practice
Talking about professions and what you did

Answers will vary.

Quick Wrap-up

Have students complete the following:
Quiero ser ____ (profesión) porque me gusta ____ (infinitivo).

Dictation

After students have read the **trabalenguas** in the **Pronunciación,** have them close their books. Dictate the **trabalenguas** in two segments while students write it.

Critical Thinking

After reviewing the **Apoyo para estudiar,** ask students to write 5 sentences using **ir** in the preterite and 5 sentences using **ser** in the preterite. Each sentence should be on a separate slip of paper. Collect the slips of paper and scramble them. Then read the sentences aloud. Have the whole class indicate when **ir** or when **ser** is used.

Teaching All Students

Extra Help Prepare a worksheet with lists of verb forms in the present and the preterite. Have students circle the preterite forms and write the person each represents next to it.

Native Speakers Ask students to make up more tongue twisters with the letter **d,** and teach them to the other students.

Multiple Intelligences

Musical/Rhythmic Have students create a rap/chant using verbs in the preterite.

Kinesthetic Working in pairs or groups, have students mime an action or situation. The other students guess what he/she *was* or *did.*

Visual Have students create an original cartoon character and depict its Monday–Friday activities using the preterite.

Block Schedule

Variety Have pairs of students interview each other for a "Who's Who in Our School" column in the Spanish Club newsletter. Students must ask for biographical information, past events, a special activity, a hobby, or an interest. (For additional activities, see **Block Scheduling Copymasters.**)

Teaching Resource Options

Print 📖

Unit 6 Resource Book
 Audioscript, p. 31
 Audioscript *Para hispanohablantes*,
  p. 31

Audiovisual 🎧

Audio Program Cassette 16A / CD 16
Audio *Para hispanohablantes*
 Cassette 16A / CD 16
OHT 183 (Quick Start)
Canciones Cassette / CD

Quick Start Review

 Los edificios

Use OHT 183 or write on the board:
Use these adjectives to write sentences
about famous buildings you have
visited or read about:

1. antiguo(a)   4. lujoso(a)
2. enorme   5. moderno(a)
3. formal   6. tradicional

Answers will vary.

Teaching Suggestions

- **Prereading** Have students discuss
  the kind of information people
  usually include on a postcard.

- **Strategy: Recognize place names**
  Have students follow the steps in the
  Strategy. Go over the chart as a class.

- **Reading** Have students read each
  postcard silently, then have a
  volunteer read it aloud. As a class,
  decide on a 1-sentence summary of
  each paragraph.

- **Post-reading** Have students briefly
  summarize the experiences of the 3
  postcard writers.

En voces
LECTURA

PARA LEER
STRATEGY: READING
Recognize place names It is easy to
be confused by unfamiliar place
names, but often there are
simple words nearby to explain
them. As you read each of the
following place names, identify
the word nearby that explains
what it is.

NOMBRE	LUGAR
Amazonas	
La Carolina	
La Compañía	
El Ejido	
Pichincha	volcán

NOTA CULTURAL

Colonial comes from the word
colonia, just as the word
colonial in English comes from
the word *colony*. In the U.S. we
think of colonial times as when
the colonies were ruled by
England. Ecuador was a colony
of what country? What group
designed its colonial areas?

Saludos desde Quito

Un grupo de estudiantes está de visita en Quito,
Ecuador. Aquí hay unas tarjetas que ellos les
escribieron a sus amigos.

Quito

¡Hola! Hoy llegamos a Quito.
¡Estamos a sólo 24 kilómetros de
la línea ecuatorial[1]! Fuimos en taxi
al Cerro[2] Panecillo. Allí fue posible
ver toda la ciudad. La ciudad es
bonita y el paisaje[3] es maravilloso.
Quito queda al lado del volcán
Pichincha. Hoy, la cima se cubrió[4]
de nieve, ¡pero en la ciudad la
temperatura fue de 80 grados!

Alfonso

John Vivas
4231 Avenue M
Galveston, TX 77550
E.E.U.U.

[1] equator   [3] landscape
[2] hill   [4] the peak was covered

400 cuatrocientos
Unidad 6

Classroom Community

Learning Scenario Have students select a building
or an area mentioned in the postcards and use library
or Internet sources to find out more information about
it. Each student should find at least 5 additional facts
and report them to the class.

Portfolio Pass out large, blank index cards. Have
students select an area of Latin America or Spain and
pretend to send a postcard from there. They should
decorate the front and write a note on the back.

Rubric A = 13–15 pts. B = 10–12 pts. C = 7–9 pts. D = 4–6 pts. F = < 4 pts.

Writing criteria	Scale
Vocabulary	1 2 3 4 5
Grammar/spelling accuracy	1 2 3 4 5
Creativity, appearance	1 2 3 4 5

La Compañía

¡Saludos desde Quito! Ayer paseamos por el Quito Colonial. Fue bonito caminar por las calles estrechas y ver las casas antiguas. Fuimos a la Plaza de la Independencia para ver la Catedral y el Palacio de Gobierno. ¡Allí sacamos muchas fotos! Después fuimos a la iglesia jesuita de la Compañía. Es famosa por su arte y su decoración de oro. Luego, en el Museo Arqueológico aprendí mucho sobre el arte precolombino[5]. Mañana vamos al sector moderno. ¡Hasta pronto!
Lucila

Elena M
59 Col
Coron
E.E.U

¿Qué tal? Hoy paseamos por el norte de Quito. ¡Qué diferencia! Las avenidas son anchas y hay parques grandes, como El Ejido y La Carolina. En el sector de la avenida Amazonas está la mayor parte de los hoteles, bancos, restaurantes caros y tiendas finas. Mañana vamos a visitar la Mitad del Mundo, un complejo turístico en la línea ecuatorial. Allí hay un museo, tiendas y restaurantes. Los domingos hay música típica de los Andes. Me encanta escuchar la música andina.
¡Hasta luego!
Marisa

Jennifer Herrera
131 Edgewater Drive
Orlando, FL 32804
E.E.U.U.

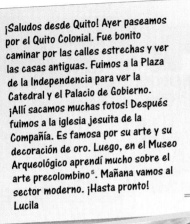
Parque Carolina

¿Comprendiste?

1. ¿Dónde queda Quito?
2. ¿Cómo es el Quito Colonial?
3. ¿Qué lugares puedes visitar en el Quito Colonial?
4. ¿Dónde está la parte moderna de Quito?
5. ¿Adónde vas para caminar por la línea ecuatorial?

¿Qué piensas?

1. ¿Qué diferencias hay entre el Quito Colonial y la ciudad moderna?
2. ¿Qué influencias crees que hay en la arquitectura del Quito Colonial?

Hazlo tú

Lee sobre el Quito Colonial y la ciudad moderna de Quito en la biblioteca o en Internet. Describe una excursión por el Quito Colonial. Indica los monumentos y edificios más importantes.

pre-Columbian

cuatrocientos uno
Etapa 1
401

Culture Highlights

● **LA CATEDRAL** The Cathedral was built in the 16th century. There is a set of stones in the shape of a cloverleaf at its entrance. The church suffered damages due to earthquakes in the city and is in the process of restoration.

● **LA COMPAÑÍA** In 1586, the Jesuit Order sent a group of priests to settle in Quito. In 1587, they bought some houses in the area in front of the University and established a learning center and a church.

Cross Cultural Connections

Strategy Have students think about a city in the U.S. that they would encourage a foreigner to visit. What images would appear on postcards of that city? What is unique about the city? What activities would be fun and interesting? How do these images and ideas compare to those in the reading about Quito? Save the information to share with exchange students.

Interdisciplinary Connection

Science Have students research the weather conditions in various regions of Ecuador and what affects each region's climate.

¿Comprendiste?

Answers
1. Queda al lado del volcán Pichincha.
2. Es bonito y tiene calles estrechas y casas antiguas.
3. Puedes visitar la Catedral, el Palacio de Gobierno, la iglesia jesuita de la Compañía y el Museo Arqueológico.
4. Está en el norte de Quito.
5. Vas a la Mitad del Mundo, un complejo turístico.

Teaching All Students

Extra Help Have students read the ¿Comprendiste? questions. Then have them skim the postcards and write down in which postcard they will find the answer to each question.

Native Speakers Ask students to bring in postcards from their home countries. Have them describe the picture on the front and the stamp(s).

Multiple Intelligences

Kinesthetic Display a large map of the city of Quito. As you reread the postcards, have volunteers trace the route of the students visiting Quito and point out the buildings on the map.

Logical/Mathematical Have students calculate in miles how far Quito is from the equator. Also have them calculate how far your town/city is from the equator.

Block Schedule

Change of Pace Have students begin work on a Project, Bulletin Board/Poster, or Hands-On Craft from the **Ampliación** on TE pp. 383A–383B.

Teaching Resource Options

Print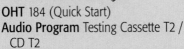

Para hispanohablantes Workbook PE, pp. 135–136

Unit 6 Resource Book
  Para hispanohablantes Workbook TE, pp. 15–16
  Information Gap Activities, p. 20
  Family Involvement, pp. 21–22
  Multiple Choice Test Questions, pp. 170–178

Audiovisual

OHT 184 (Quick Start)
Audio Program Testing Cassette T2 / CD T2

Technology

Electronic Teacher Tools/Test Generator
Intrigas y aventuras CD-ROM, Disc 1

Quick Start Review

♻ **Preterite**

Use OHT 184 or write on the board:
Complete the following sentences with a logical verb in the preterite and any other necessary words:

1. Normalmente, voy a pie a la escuela, pero ayer _____ .
2. Mis amigos siempre llegan a tiempo a clase, pero esta mañana, _____ .
3. Mis padres casi siempre salen de la oficina a las cinco, pero anoche _____ .
4. Frecuentemente, te gusta ir a la biblioteca después de clases, pero ayer tú _____ .
5. En general, mi madre me hace un sándwich, pero hoy _____ .

Answers *See p. 383D.*

✔ Teaching Suggestions
What Have Students Learned?

Have students look at the "Now you can…" notes and give examples of each category. Have them spend extra time reviewing categories they feel they are weak in by consulting the "To review" notes.

ETAPA **1**

Now you can...

• tell what happened.

To review

• preterite of regular **-er** and **-ir** verbs, see p. 392.

Now you can...

• tell what happened.

To review

• preterite of verbs with a **y** spelling change, see p. 394.

En uso
REPASO Y MÁS COMUNICACIÓN

OBJECTIVES

• Tell what happened
• Make suggestions to a group
• Describe city buildings
• Talk about professions

ACTIVIDAD **1** ¡Muy ocupados!

Todos participaron en un festival internacional el domingo pasado. ¿Qué hicieron? *(Hint: Tell what people did at the international festival.)*

modelo

usted: barrer el suelo después del festival
Usted barrió el suelo después del festival.

1. tú: recibir un regalo
2. mis amigos y yo: aprender algunos bailes mexicanos
3. mi madre: vender unas tapas
4. los periodistas: escribir muchos artículos sobre el festival
5. yo: compartir un postre enorme con mis hermanos
6. nosotros: beber mucha limonada
7. los niños: correr por todas partes
8. el fotógrafo: decidir sacar fotos de todas las actividades
9. tú: comer muchos tacos
10. yo: ver artesanías muy interesantes

ACTIVIDAD **2** ¿Lo creíste tú?

Imagínate que Patricia ganó el concurso, pero nadie lo creyó. ¿Dónde oyeron o leyeron el anuncio? *(Hint: Tell where people heard or read about the contest winner.)*

modelo

Miguel: por teléfono
Miguel *lo oyó* **por teléfono,** *pero no lo creyó.*

el arquitecto: en el periódico
El arquitecto *lo leyó* **en el periódico,** *pero no lo creyó.*

1. Patricia: en una carta
2. tú: en la televisión
3. la mujer de negocios: en la radio
4. los tíos de Miguel: por teléfono
5. yo: en la revista
6. nosotros: en el periódico

Classroom Community

Paired Activity Have students do a variation of **Actividad 1** in pairs. One student reads the answer. The other contradicts the answer and changes it. For example, for item #1: A: **Tú recibiste un regalo.** B: **No, yo no recibí un regalo. Recibí una carta.**

Game Two students at a time choose one profession, have it approved by the teacher, and stand in front of the class. The class will ask yes/no or either/or questions and the pair collaborates on the answers until the profession is guessed.

3 ¿Qué fuiste tú?

Todos hablan de sus antiguas profesiones. ¿Qué dicen?
(Hint: Talk about people's former jobs.)

modelo

ella / gerente de un restaurante lujoso: ¿trabajar en un edificio formal o informal?
Ella fue gerente de un restaurante lujoso. Trabajó en un edificio formal.

1. ellos / hombres de negocios: ¿hacer contratos o ejercicio?
2. nosotros / bomberos: ¿ir a muchos conciertos o edificios?
3. tú / recepcionista de una compañía grande: ¿trabajar en un edificio pequeño o enorme?
4. tú y yo / periodistas: ¿hacer muchas tareas o entrevistas?
5. él / taxista: ¿ir a muchos o pocos lugares diferentes?
6. yo / escritor(a): ¿escribir cartas o novelas?
7. tú / cartero(a): ¿ir a muchos parques o muchas casas?
8. usted / arquitecto(a): ¿hacer planos o preguntas?

4 ¡Vamos a divertirnos!

Tú amigo(a) te invita a participar en varias actividades hoy.
¿Qué dice? *(Hint: Suggest activities.)*

modelo

nadar

*¡Vamos a **nadar**!*

1. levantar pesas
2. ir al cine
3. escuchar música
4. comer en un restaurante lujoso
5. jugar al tenis
6. ver la televisión
7. escribirle una carta al editor del periódico
8. pasear en el parque

cuatrocientos tres
Etapa 1 **403**

1 Answers

1. Tú recibiste un regalo.
2. Mis amigos y yo aprendimos algunos bailes mexicanos.
3. Mi madre vendió unas tapas.
4. Los periodistas escribieron muchos artículos sobre el festival.
5. Yo compartí un postre enorme con mis hermanos.
6. Nosotros bebimos mucha limonada.
7. Los niños corrieron por todas partes.
8. El fotógrafo decidió sacar fotos de todas las actividades.
9. Tú comiste muchos tacos.
10. Yo vi artesanías muy interesantes.

2 Answers

1. Patricia lo leyó en una carta, pero no lo creyó.
2. Tú lo oíste en la televisión, pero no lo creíste.
3. La mujer de negocios lo oyó en la radio, pero no lo creyó.
4. Los tíos de Miguel lo oyeron por teléfono, pero no lo creyeron.
5. Yo lo leí en la revista, pero no lo creí.
6. Nosotros lo leímos en el periódico, pero no lo creímos.

3 Answers

1. Ellos fueron hombres de negocios. Hicieron contratos.
2. Nosotros fuimos bomberos. Fuimos a muchos edificios.
3. Tú fuiste recepcionista de una compañía grande. Trabajaste en un edificio enorme.
4. Tú y yo fuimos periodistas. Hicimos muchas entrevistas.
5. Él fue taxista. Fue a muchos lugares diferentes.
6. Yo fui escritor(a). Escribí novelas.
7. Tú fuiste cartero(a). Fuiste a muchas casas.
8. Usted fue arquitecto(a). Hizo planos.

4 Answers

1. ¡Vamos a levantar pesas!
2. ¡Vamos a ir al cine!
3. ¡Vamos a escuchar música!
4. ¡Vamos a comer en un restaurante lujoso!
5. ¡Vamos a jugar al tenis!
6. ¡Vamos a ver la televisión!
7. ¡Vamos a escribirle una carta al editor del periódico!
8. ¡Vamos a pasear en el parque!

Teaching All Students

Extra Help Prepare ahead: 10–12 sets of 10 subject noun/pronoun cards and 10 verb infinitive cards. Give a set of cards to pairs or small groups of students. Have each student pick one subject card and one verb card from each set and make up a sentence using the words.

Challenge Have students extend **Actividad 1** with more items.

Multiple Intelligences

Interpersonal Have students work with a partner and expand **Actividad 4**. One student proposes the activity to the other who accepts or declines, stating a reason in either case.

Block Schedule

FunBreak Have students work in small groups to create sets of cards of the various professions (4 for each of 13 professions). Then have them play **Peces** (Go Fish!) with their cards.

Teaching Resource Options

Print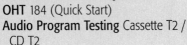

Unit 6 Resource Book
Cooperative Quizzes, pp. 33–34
Etapa Exam, Forms A and B,
  pp. 35–44
Para hispanohablantes Etapa Exam,
  pp. 45–49
Portfolio Assessment, pp. 50–51
Multiple Choice Test Questions,
  pp. 170–178

Audiovisual

OHT 184 (Quick Start)
Audio Program Testing Cassette T2 /
  CD T2

Technology

Electronic Teacher Tools/Test
  Generator
www.mcdougallittell.com

ACTIVIDAD 5

Rubric: Speaking

Criteria	Scale	
Sentence structure	1 2 3	A = 11–12 pts.
Vocabulary use	1 2 3	B = 9–10 pts.
Originality	1 2 3	C = 7–8 pts.
Fluency	1 2 3	D = 4–6 pts.
		F = < 4 pts.

ACTIVIDAD 6 *Answers will vary.*

Variation: Have students take turns going
around the room instead of having the person
who guesses correctly invent a profession.

ACTIVIDAD 7 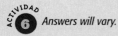 En tu propia voz

Rubric: Writing

Criteria	Scale	
Vocabulary use	1 2 3 4 5	A = 14–15 pts.
Accuracy	1 2 3 4 5	B = 12–13 pts.
Creativity, appearance	1 2 3 4 5	C = 10–11 pts.
		D = 8–9 pts.
		F = < 8 pts.

Teaching Note: En tu propia voz

Suggest that students brainstorm a list of
appropriate descriptive words (basic
details, points of interest, descriptive
adjectives) in order to implement the
writing strategy "Use different kinds of
descriptive words" in their descriptions.

ACTIVIDAD 5 ¿Qué hiciste ayer?

PARA CONVERSAR
STRATEGY: SPEAKING
Relate details When retelling a past event, tell
more than what you did (**¿qué hiciste?**).
People like to know details, such as where
(**¿dónde?**), with whom (**¿con quién?**), and
how it was (**¿cómo fue?**). If your partner
doesn't tell you all of the details, ask for them
by using these questions.

Quieres saber lo que hizo otro(a) estudiante
ayer. Usando los verbos de la lista, hazle
preguntas. *(Hint: Talk about yesterday's activities.)*

comer   ir   leer   oír
ver   escribir   hacer   salir

modelo

Tú: ¿Hiciste ejercicio ayer?

Otro(a) estudiante: Sí, hice ejercicio en el parque. Caminé
con mi perro. ¿Y tú?

Tú: Yo jugué al tenis.

Otro(a) estudiante: ¿Qué comiste anoche?

Tú: Comí…

ACTIVIDAD 6 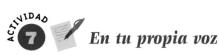 Profesiones interesantes

Eres una persona profesional que ya no trabaja.
Ahora estás visitando la clase de español. Los
estudiantes te hacen preguntas para identificar
tu profesión. La persona que identifica la
profesión correcta es el (la) nuevo(a) profesional.
(Hint: Classmates ask questions to determine professions.)

modelo

Estudiante 1: ¿Sacó usted fotos en su trabajo?

Profesional: No, no saqué fotos.

Estudiante 2: ¿Trabajó usted en una oficina?

Profesional: Sí. Trabajé en una oficina muy lujosa.

Estudiante 2: ¿Fue usted jefe(a)?

Profesional: Sí. Fui jefe(a) de una compañía enorme.

ACTIVIDAD 7 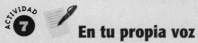 *En tu propia voz*

ESCRITURA ¿Cómo es la ciudad ideal para ti?
Dibújala y descríbela con un mínimo de seis
oraciones. *(Hint: Draw and describe the ideal city.)*

modelo

En la ciudad ideal…

TÚ EN LA COMUNIDAD

Maynor, a native speaker of Spanish, is a high school student in
California. He sometimes interprets for Spanish-speaking people who
don't speak English when he's at his part-time job with a construction
company. He also uses Spanish at his volunteer job at a Boy Scout
camp. This helps boys who are more comfortable speaking in their
native language. Additionally, he helps his friends who are learning
Spanish to practice speaking the language. When do you use Spanish?

404 cuatrocientos cuatro
Unidad 6

Classroom Community

Group Activity Allow students the option to do
Actividad 7 as a group. Each student must contribute
ideas for the design and description. Ask for a
minimum of 10 sentences instead of 6.

Storytelling Working in small groups, have students
prepare to tell the class about an exciting real or
imagined event that took place. In their descriptions of
people and places, have them act out adjectives instead
of saying them. The class helps by filling in appropriate
adjectives.

En resumen
REPASO DE VOCABULARIO

DESCRIBING CITY BUILDINGS

ancho(a)	wide
antiguo(a)	old, ancient
el edificio	building
enorme	huge, enormous
estrecho(a)	narrow
formal	formal
informal	informal
lujoso(a)	luxurious
moderno(a)	modern
ordinario(a)	ordinary
sencillo(a)	simple, plain
tradicional	traditional

TELLING WHAT HAPPENED

la cámara	camera
la entrevista	interview
la grabadora	tape recorder

TALKING ABOUT PROFESSIONS

el (la) arquitecto(a)	architect
la arquitectura	architecture
el bombero	firefighter
el (la) cartero(a)	mail carrier
la compañía	company
el (la) contador(a)	accountant
el (la) editor(a)	editor
el (la) escritor(a)	writer
el (la) fotógrafo(a)	photographer
el (la) gerente	manager
el hombre de negocios	businessman
el (la) jefe(a)	boss
la mujer de negocios	businesswoman
el (la) operador(a)	operator
el (la) periodista	journalist
la profesión	profession
el (la) recepcionista	receptionist
el (la) secretario(a)	secretary
el (la) taxista	taxi driver

MAKING SUGGESTIONS TO A GROUP

Vamos a…	Let's…

OTHER WORDS AND PHRASES

la contaminación del aire	air pollution
decidir	to decide
estar de acuerdo	to agree
el (la) ganador(a)	winner
ofrecer	to offer
el tráfico	traffic

Juego

¿Qué hacen sus padres?

El padre de Susana usa una cámara.
El Sr. Rodríguez tiene un trabajo
peligroso. Al papá de Adriana le
gusta trabajar con los números.

1. ¿Quién es contador?

2. ¿Quién es fotógrafo?

3. ¿Quién es bombero?

cuatrocientos cinco
Etapa 1 **405**

Planning Guide CLASSROOM MANAGEMENT

OBJECTIVES

Communication	• Point out specific people and things *pp. 408–409, 422–423*
	• Tell where things are located *pp. 408–409, 410–411, 422–423*
	• Talk about the past *pp. 410–411*
Grammar	• Use location words *pp. 414–415*
	• Use demonstratives *pp. 416–417*
	• Use ordinal numbers *pp. 418–419*
	• Use irregular verbs in the preterite *pp. 419–421*
Pronunciation	• Pronunciation of **l** *p. 421*
	• Dictation *TE p. 421*
Culture	• Regional vocabulary *p. 415*
	• An indigenous language *p. 420*
	• **Los otavaleños** *pp. 422–423*
Recycling	• Professions *p. 413*
	• School and personal items *p. 415*
	• **Gustar, preferir** *p. 417*
	• Comparatives *p. 417*
	• Places, preterite *p. 420*

STRATEGIES

Listening Strategies	• Listen for implied statements *p. 410*
Speaking Strategies	• Recall what you know *p. 415*
	• Use words that direct others' attention *p. 426*
Reading Strategies	• Recognize place names *TE p. 422*
Writing Strategies	• Organize information chronologically and by category *TE p. 426*
Connecting Cultures Strategies	• Recognize variations in regional vocabulary *p. 415*
	• Learn about an indigenous language in Ecuador *p. 420*
	• Learn about the artisans of Otavalo *pp. 422–423*
	• Connect and compare what you know about cultural groups in your community to help you learn about cultural groups in a new community *pp. 422–423*

PROGRAM RESOURCES

Print

• *Más práctica* Workbook PE *pp. 137–144*
• Block Scheduling Copymasters *pp. 137–144*
• Unit 6 Resource Book
  Más práctica Workbook TE *pp. 52–59*
  Para hispanohablantes Workbook TE *pp. 60–67*

Information Gap Activities *pp. 68–71*
Family Involvement *pp. 72–73*
Video Activities *pp. 74–76*
Videoscript *pp. 77–79*
Audioscript *pp. 80–83*
Assessment Program, Unit 6 Etapa 2 *pp. 84–102; 170–178*
Answer Keys *pp. 187–202*

 Audiovisual

• **Audio Program** Cassettes 17A, 17B / CD 17
• *Canciones* Cassette / CD
• **Video Program** Videotape 6 / Videodisc 3B
• **Overhead Transparencies** M1–M5; 173; 185–194

Technology

• Electronic Teacher Tools/Test Generator
• *Intrigas y aventuras* CD-ROM, Disc 1
• www.mcdougallittell.com

Assessment Program Options

• **Cooperative Quizzes** (Unit 6 Resource Book)
• **Etapa Exam** Forms A and B (Unit 6 Resource Book)
• *Para hispanohablantes* **Etapa Exam** (Unit 6 Resource Book)
• **Portfolio Assessment** (Unit 6 Resource Book)
• **Multiple Choice Test Questions** (Unit 6 Resource Book)
• **Audio Program** Testing Cassette T2 / CD T2
• **Electronic Teacher Tools/Test Generator**

Native Speakers

• *Para hispanohablantes* Workbook PE, *pp. 137–144*
• *Para hispanohablantes* Workbook TE (Unit 6 Resource Book)
• *Para hispanohablantes* Etapa Exam (Unit 6 Resource Book)
• Audio *Para hispanohablantes* Cassettes 17A, 17B, T2 / CD 17, T2
• Audioscript *Para hispanohablantes* (Unit 6 Resource Book)

Student Text Listening Activity Scripts

 Videoscript: Diálogo *pages 410–411*

• Videotape 6 • Videodisc 3B

Search Chapter 5, Play to 6
U6E2 • En vivo (Dialog)

• Use the videoscript with **Actividades 1, 2** *page 412*

Miguel:	¡Buenos días, tía Bárbara!
Bárbara:	¡Miguel! ¡Bienvenidos! ¿Y tú eres Patricia?
Patricia:	Sí. Es un placer, señora Olivera.
Bárbara:	Ay, hija, llámame Bárbara. ¿Te gusta mi taller?
Patricia:	Sí, mucho.
Bárbara:	Vengan, pasen. Siéntate.
Patricia:	Gracias. Tengo esta grabadora. ¿Me permite usarla?
Bárbara:	Cómo no, hija.
Patricia:	Muchas gracias. Bárbara, ¿cuándo vino usted a vivir aquí?
Bárbara:	Vine en el año 1990 con mi esposo y mi hijo.
Patricia:	¿Y le gusta vivir en el campo, en este pueblo pequeño?
Bárbara:	Sí, mucho. Es muy tranquilo aquí. A ver... ¿dónde están las tijeras? Ah, sí, allí están. Miguel, ¿me das las tijeras que están sobre la mesa?
Miguel:	Claro.
Patricia:	¿Cómo fueron sus primeros años aquí?
Bárbara:	Uy, tuvimos que trabajar muchísimo. Fue muy difícil hasta el tercer año.
Patricia:	¿Y venden los sacos y los gorros en los mercados?
Bárbara:	Sí, claro. El mejor mercado es el mercado de Otavalo. Estuvimos ahí el domingo pasado.
Miguel:	¡A mí me gusta mucho ese mercado! La última vez que estuve allí, compré una mochila fenomenal. Vamos hoy después de visitar a mi tío Julio.
Bárbara:	Ya lo sé. Julio nos llamó anoche y nos dijo. ¡Ay!, perdóname, Patricia. Viniste para hacerme preguntas.
Patricia:	No se preocupe. Sólo tengo una pregunta más. En su opinión, ¿cuál es la diferencia más grande entre la vida en la ciudad y la vida en el campo?
Bárbara:	Creo que todo va más lento en el campo. No tenemos tanta prisa como la gente de la ciudad.
Patricia:	Muchas gracias, Bárbara. Me ayudó mucho.

Bárbara:	No hay de qué, hija. Miguel, ¿me bajas aquel saco? Está allí arriba. Te lo doy como recuerdo de tu visita.
Patricia:	¡Ay, Bárbara! ¡No es necesario!
Bárbara:	Claro que no es necesario. Miguel... busca un saco para ti también.
Miguel:	Gracias, tía Bárbara...
Julio:	Sí, soy de una familia de ganaderos. Esta granja fue de mi abuelo.
Patricia:	¿Sus hijos lo ayudan con el trabajo?
Julio:	Sí. Todos los días mi hijo les da de comer a las gallinas y a las vacas. Mi hija, la menor, cuida los cerdos y los caballos. Y hablando de caballos... Miguel, ¿recuerdas la primera vez que viniste a visitarnos?
Miguel:	Ay, tío Julio, por favor... Patricia no quiere oír esas viejas historias.
Patricia:	¡Sí, las quiero oír!
Julio:	Pues, fue al corral para ver al caballo. Abrió la cerca y el caballo se escapó. Lo buscamos por todas partes.
Miguel:	¡Tío Julio!
Julio:	Luego les dio de comer a las gallinas. ¡Les dio una bolsa de comida! Fue suficiente comida para toda una semana...
Miguel:	Tío Julio, por favor...
Julio:	Está bien, está bien. Sabes, Patricia, hay gente que debe vivir en la ciudad y gente que debe vivir en el campo. ¡Miguel debe vivir en la ciudad!
Patricia:	¿Qué piensa Ud. de la ciudad?
Julio:	Vamos a Quito todos los meses para visitar a mi hija mayor y su familia. Es muy interesante y hay mucho trabajo. Pero vivimos aquí y estamos felices.
Patricia:	Gracias, Julio.
Julio:	Dice Miguel que ustedes van a Otavalo esta tarde.
Patricia:	Sí.
Julio:	¿Te contó Miguel de la segunda vez que él nos acompañó a Otavalo?
Miguel:	¡Tío Julio!

¿Qué son? *page 413*

1. Soy artesana. Trabajo en un taller haciendo sacos.
2. Soy pastor. Cuido las llamas y otros animales.
3. Soy secretario. Escribo muchas cartas.
4. Soy arquitecta. Hago los planos de las casas nuevas.

Un día bonito *page 421*

El domingo pasado, Luisa y su amiga Amalia hicieron un viaje a la granja de los abuelos de Luisa. Cuando llegaron allí, fueron primero al establo para ver los caballos. A Luisa le gustan mucho los caballos. Después, Luisa les dio de comer a las gallinas. Y Amalia les dio de comer a los cerdos. ¡Cuánto comieron los cerdos! Al mediodía las amigas almorzaron con los abuelos. ¡Qué simpáticos! ¡Y qué rica fue la comida! Después del almuerzo, fueron al mercado. Amalia compró un saco bonito. Luisa no compró nada porque no tuvo dinero. Las amigas volvieron a la ciudad a las siete de la noche. En el autobús, las amigas dijeron al mismo tiempo: «¡Qué día bonito tuvimos en el campo!».

Quick Start Review Answers

p. 412 Dialog review
1. ganaderos
2. sobre
3. este
4. viniste

p. 416 Prepositions of location
1. Las gallinas están dentro del corral.
2. Los animales que están lejos son llamas.
3. El gallo está encima de la cerca.
4. Patricia quiere un gorro de abajo.
5. Los cerdos están fuera del corral.

p. 418 Vocabulary review
1. arriba
2. saco
3. esto
4. caballo
5. lana

p. 419 Preterite of **hacer, ir, ser**
1. fue
2. hicimos
3. fui
4. fue
5. hiciste

Sample Lesson Plan - 50 Minute Schedule

DAY 1

Etapa Opener
- Quick Start Review (TE, p. 406) 5 MIN.
- Anticipate/Activate prior knowledge: Have students look at the *Etapa* Opener and answer the questions. 5 MIN.

En contexto: Vocabulario
- Quick Start Review (TE, p. 408) 5 MIN.
- Have students use context and pictures to learn *Etapa* vocabulary. In pairs, have students answer the questions, p. 409. Use the Situational OHTs for additional practice. 10 MIN.

En vivo: Diálogo
- Quick Start Review (TE, p. 410) 5 MIN.
- Review the Listening Strategy, p. 410. Play audio or show video for the dialog, pp. 410–411. 10 MIN.
- Replay twice. Read aloud, having students take the roles of characters. 10 MIN.

Homework Option:
- Video Activities, Unit 6 Resource Book, pp. 74–76.

DAY 2

En acción: Vocabulario y gramática
- Check homework. 5 MIN.
- Quick Start Review (TE, p. 412) 5 MIN.
- Use OHT 185 and 186 to review *En contexto* vocabulary. Ask students for a summary of the dialog to check recall. 10 MIN.
- Play the video/audio; have students do *Actividades* 1 and 2. 10 MIN.
- Have students complete *Actividad* 3 orally. 5 MIN.
- Have students read and complete *Actividad* 4 in writing. Have them exchange papers for peer correction. 10 MIN.
- Play the audio; do *Actividad* 5. 5 MIN.
- Use an expansion activity from TE p. 413 for reinforcement and variety. 5 MIN.

Homework Option:
- Have students write 5 true/false statements about the dialog and complete *Actividad* 3 in writing.

DAY 3

En acción (cont.)
- Check homework. 5 MIN.
- Quick Start Review (TE, p. 414) 5 MIN.
- Present *Gramática:* Saying Where Things Are Located, p. 414. 5 MIN.
- Have students do *Actividad* 6 in writing. Go over answers orally. 5 MIN.
- Present the Speaking Strategy, p. 415. Then do *Actividad* 7 in pairs. 5 MIN.
- Have students do *Actividad* 8 in writing. Have a few volunteers present their work to the class. 10 MIN.
- Quick Start Review (TE, p. 416) 5 MIN.
- Present *Gramática:* Pointing Out Specific Things Using Demonstratives, p. 416. 10 MIN.
- Have students read and complete *Actividad* 9 in writing. Go over answers orally. 5 MIN.

Homework Option:
- *Más práctica* Workbook, pp. 141–142. *Para hispanohablantes* Workbook, pp. 139–140.

DAY 4

En acción (cont.)
- Check homework. 5 MIN.
- Have students complete *Actividad* 10 in pairs. Have volunteer pairs present the various items. 5 MIN.
- Have students complete *Actividad* 11 in groups. Expand using Information Gap Activities, Unit 6 Resource Book, p. 68; *Más comunicación*, p. R17. 15 MIN.
- Quick Start Review (TE, p. 418) 5 MIN.
- Present *Gramática:* Ordinal Numbers, p. 418. 5 MIN.
- Do *Actividad* 12 in pairs and *Actividad* 13 orally. 10 MIN.
- Have students complete *Actividad* 14 in writing. Have them exchange papers for peer correction. 10 MIN.

Homework Option:
- Have students complete *Actividad* 13 in writing. *Más práctica* Workbook, p. 143. *Para hispanohablantes* Workbook, p. 141.

DAY 5

En acción (cont.)
- Check homework. 5 MIN.
- Quick Start Review (TE, p. 419) 5 MIN.
- Present *Gramática:* Irregular Preterite Verbs, p. 419. 10 MIN.
- Present the *Nota,* then have students do *Actividad* 15 in writing. Have volunteers write answers on the board. 5 MIN.
- Have students do *Actividad* 16 in pairs. Have several pairs present their mini-dialogs. 10 MIN.
- Have students do *Actividad* 17 in groups, then present their work. 10 MIN.
- Do *Actividad* 18 orally. 5 MIN.
- Play the audio; do *Actividad* 19. 5 MIN.

Homework Option:
- Have students complete *Actividad* 18 in writing. *Más práctica* Workbook, p. 144. *Para hispanohablantes* Workbook, p. 142.

DAY 6

En acción (cont.)
- Check homework. 5 MIN.
- Have students complete *Actividad* 20 in writing. Expand using Information Gap Activities, Unit 6 Resource Book, pp. 69–70; *Más comunicación*, p. R17. 20 MIN.

Pronunciación
- Play the audio and have students practice the *trabalenguas*. 5 MIN.

En colores: Cultura y comparaciones
- Quick Start Review (TE, p. 422) 5 MIN.
- Review the Connecting Cultures Strategy, p. 422. Have volunteers read the selection aloud and answer the questions, p. 423. 20 MIN.

Homework Option:
- Have students complete the *¿Comprendiste?/¿Qué piensas?* questions in writing.

DAY 7

En uso: Repaso y más comunicación
- Check homework. 5 MIN.
- Quick Start Review (TE, p. 424) 5 MIN.
- Have students do *Actividad* 1 in pairs. 5 MIN.
- Have students do *Actividad* 2 in writing. Go over answers as a class. 5 MIN.
- Do *Actividad* 3 orally and *Actividad* 4 in writing. 10 MIN.
- Present the Speaking Strategy, p. 426. Have students do *Actividad* 5 in pairs. 5 MIN.
- Have students do *Actividad* 6 in groups. 5 MIN.

En tu propia voz: Escritura
- Do *Actividad* 7 in writing. Have a few students present their lists. 15 MIN.

Homework Option:
- Review for *Etapa* 2 Exam.

DAY 8

Conexiones
- Read and discuss *Las ciencias*, p. 426. 5 MIN.

En resumen: Repaso de vocabulario
- Quick Start Review (TE, p. 427) 5 MIN.
- Review grammar questions, etc. as necessary. 10 MIN.
- Complete *Etapa* 2 Exam. 20 MIN.

Ampliación
- Use a suggested project, game, or activity. (TE, pp. 383A–383B) 10 MIN.

Homework Option:
- Have student complete the assignment in *Conexiones.* Review *Etapa* 3 Opener.

Sample Lesson Plan - Block Schedule (90 minutes)

DAY 1

Etapa Opener
- Quick Start Review (TE, p. 406) 5 MIN.
- Anticipate/Activate prior knowledge: Have students look at the *Etapa* Opener and answer the questions. 5 MIN.
- Use Block Scheduling Copymasters. 10 MIN.

En contexto: Vocabulario
- Quick Start Review (TE, p. 408) 5 MIN.
- Have students use context and pictures to learn *Etapa* vocabulary. In pairs, have students answer the questions, p. 409. Use the Situational OHTs for additional practice. 10 MIN.

En vivo: Diálogo
- Quick Start Review (TE, p. 410) 5 MIN.
- Review the Listening Strategy, p. 410. Play audio or show video for the dialog, pp. 410–411. 10 MIN.
- Replay twice. Read aloud, having students take the roles of characters. 10 MIN.

En acción: Vocabulario y gramática
- Quick Start Review (TE, p. 412) 5 MIN.
- Use OHT 185 and 186 to review *En contexto* vocabulary. Ask students for a summary of the dialog to check recall. 10 MIN.
- Play the video/audio; have students do *Actividades* 1 and 2. 10 MIN.
- Have students complete *Actividad* 3 orally. 5 MIN.

Homework Option:
- Video Activities, Unit 6 Resource Book, pp. 74–76.

DAY 2

En acción (cont.)
- Check homework. 5 MIN.
- Have students read and complete *Actividad* 4 in writing. Have them exchange papers for peer correction. 10 MIN.
- Play the audio; do *Actividad* 5. 5 MIN.
- Quick Start Review (TE, p. 414) 5 MIN.
- Present *Gramática:* Saying Where Things Are Located, p. 414. 5 MIN.
- Have students do *Actividad* 6 in writing. Go over answers orally. 5 MIN.
- Present the Speaking Strategy, p. 415. Then do *Actividad* 7 in pairs. 5 MIN.
- Have students do *Actividad* 8 in writing. Have a few volunteers present their work to the class. 10 MIN.
- Quick Start Review (TE, p. 416) 5 MIN.
- Present *Gramática:* Pointing Out Specific Things Using Demonstratives, p. 416. 10 MIN.
- Have students read and complete *Actividad* 9 in writing. Go over answers orally. 5 MIN.
- Have students complete *Actividad* 10 in pairs. Have volunteer pairs present the various items. 5 MIN.
- Have students complete *Actividad* 11 in groups. Expand using Information Gap Activities, Unit 6 Resource Book, p. 68; *Más comunicación,* p. R17. 15 MIN.

Homework Option:
- *Más práctica* Workbook, pp. 141–142. *Para hispanohablantes* Workbook, pp. 139–140.

DAY 3

En acción (cont.)
- Check homework. 5 MIN.
- Quick Start Review (TE, p. 418) 5 MIN.
- Present *Gramática:* Ordinal Numbers, p. 418. 5 MIN.
- Do *Actividad* 12 in pairs and *Actividad* 13 orally. 10 MIN.
- Have students complete *Actividad* 14 in writing. Have them exchange papers for peer correction. 5 MIN.
- Quick Start Review (TE, p. 419) 5 MIN.
- Present *Gramática:* Irregular Preterite Verbs, p. 419. 10 MIN.
- Present the *Nota,* then have students do *Actividad* 15 in writing. Have volunteers write answers on the board. 5 MIN.
- Have students do *Actividad* 16 in pairs. 5 MIN.
- Have students do *Actividad* 17 in groups, then present their work. 10 MIN.
- Do *Actividad* 18 orally. 5 MIN.
- Play the audio; do *Actividad* 19. 5 MIN.
- Have students complete *Actividad* 20 in writing. Expand using Information Gap Activities, Unit 6 Resource Book, pp. 69–70; *Más comunicación,* p. R17. 15 MIN.

Homework Option:
- Have students complete *Actividades* 13 and 18 in writing. *Más práctica* Workbook, pp. 143–144. *Para hispanohablantes* Workbook, pp. 141–142.

DAY 4

Pronunciación
- Check homework. 5 MIN.
- Play the audio and have students practice the *trabalenguas.* 5 MIN.

En colores: Cultura y comparaciones
- Quick Start Review (TE, p. 422) 5 MIN.
- Review the Connecting Cultures Strategy, p. 422. Have volunteers read the selection aloud and answer the questions, p. 423. 25 MIN.

En uso: Repaso y más comunicación
- Quick Start Review (TE, p. 424) 5 MIN.
- Have students do *Actividad* 1 in pairs and *Actividad* 2 in writing. Go over answers. 15 MIN.
- Do *Actividad* 3 orally and *Actividad* 4 in writing. Have volunteers write answers on the board. 15 MIN.
- Present the Speaking Strategy, p. 426. Have students do *Actividad* 5 in pairs. 5 MIN.
- Have students do *Actividad* 6 in groups. 10 MIN.

Homework Option:
- Review for *Etapa* 2 Exam.

DAY 5

En tu propia voz: Escritura
- Do *Actividad* 7 in writing. Have several students present their lists. 20 MIN.

Conexiones
- Read and discuss *Las ciencias,* p. 426, and have students begin their research. 10 MIN.

En resumen: Repaso de vocabulario
- Quick Start Review (TE, p. 427) 5 MIN.
- Review grammar questions, etc. as necessary. 10 MIN.
- Complete *Etapa* 2 Exam. 20 MIN.

Ampliación
- Use a suggested project, game, or activity. (TE, pp. 383A–383B) 25 MIN.

Homework Option:
- Have student complete the assignment in *Conexiones.* Review *Etapa* 3 Opener.

▼ Patricia y Miguel visitan a Bárbara en su taller.

Etapa Theme
Visiting the country, pointing things out, and talking about the past

Grammar Objectives
• Using location words
• Using demonstratives
• Using ordinal numbers
• Using irregular verbs in the preterite

Teaching Resource Options

Print
Block Scheduling Copymasters

Audiovisual
OHT 173, 191 (Quick Start)

🔔 Quick Start Review
♻ Preterite review

Use OHT 191 or write on the board: Answer the following questions, using complete sentences in the preterite:

1. ¿Qué hiciste ayer antes de la escuela?
2. ¿Qué hiciste ayer en la escuela?
3. ¿Qué hiciste ayer después de la escuela?
4. ¿Qué hiciste anoche?

Answers
Answers will vary. Answers could include:
1. Me lavé los dientes.
2. Aprendí mucho en la clase de matemáticas.
3. Fui al parque con mis amigos.
4. Hice la tarea.

Teaching Suggestions
Previewing the Etapa
• Ask students to study the picture on pp. 406–407 (1 min.).
• Have them close their books and share at least 3 items that they noticed.
• Have students open their books and look at the **Etapa** title. Ask what they think the relationship is between the title and the photo.
• Use the **¿Qué ves?** questions to focus the discussion.

UNIDAD 6

ETAPA 2

A conocer el campo

• Point out specific people and things

• Tell where things are located

• Talk about the past

¿Qué ves?

Mira la foto de un taller en el campo de Ecuador.

1. ¿Las personas de la foto están contentas o tristes?
2. ¿Hay muchos o pocos sacos?
3. ¿De qué colores son los sacos?
4. ¿Cuál es el teléfono del taller?

406

CENTRO ARTESANAL

Juan León Mera 804   Fax 502-301
Telf. 548-235

Classroom Management

Planning Ahead Collect toy animals and photos of the countryside to teach and practice the **Etapa** vocabulary. Bags of small plastic animals and fences are widely available in toy stores and discount stores. Ask students to bring in materials as well.

Time Saver If time is short, for each activity have students do the odd-numbered items in class and the even-numbered items for homework.

407

Cross Cultural Connections

Ask students to notice the labels in their clothing. Point out that often they will see **Hecho en...** Have them look at their clothing labels at home to see if any were made in a Spanish-speaking country. Also have them look for cleaning instructions in Spanish and copy them down to read in class.

Culture Highlights

● **LOS QUECHUA** The Quechua people are the native people of the South American Andes. Quechua was the official language of the Inca Empire and is currently spoken by more than 10 million people. The Quechua language and culture are found in the countryside and in some towns of the Andean highlands, especially in Otavalo. In Ecuador, the language is usually referred to as "Quichua," but it is derived from the same language base. Quechua people built bridges and roads throughout the Andes and many routes are still in use today. The Quechua artisans produce high quality textiles and pottery.

● **OTAVALO** The most famous place in Otavalo is its market. On Saturdays, people begin trading animals and crafts early in the morning before dawn. There are other interesting places to visit, such as the **Instituto Otavaleño de Antropología** and the **Museo Arqueológico.**

Supplementary Vocabulary

el telar	loom
tejer	to weave
trabajar/tejer a punto de aguja	to knit
tejer con aguja de gancho	to crochet

Block Schedule

Bulletin Board Display a map of South America on the bulletin board. Have each student research an interesting fact, animal, place, person, etc. from one area of South America. Then have each student make a visual for that information, display it near the map, and stretch a piece of color yarn from the visual to the country. (For additional activities, see **Block Scheduling Copymasters.**)

Teaching All Students

Extra Help Tell students that you are going to make false statements about the photo. As you make the statements, students will rewrite them to make them true.

Multiple Intelligences

Naturalist Allow students to form their own working partnerships or groups according to environmental issues that interest them (animals, birds, rain forest, mountains, etc.). Have the groups meet throughout the rest of the unit to research and discuss their areas of interest.

Quick Start Review

♻ Descriptions, Colors

Use OHT 191 or write on the board:
Describe 5 people or items, including a
color in your description

Modelos: Jeff lleva una camiseta azul.
  Tengo tres lápices amarillos.

Answers will vary.

Teaching Suggestions
Introducing Vocabulary

• Have students look at pages 408–409.
  Use OHT 185 and 186 and Audio
  Cassette 17A / CD 17 to present the
  vocabulary.
• Ask the Comprehension Questions in
  order of yes/no (questions 1–3),
  either/or (questions 4–6), and simple
  word or phrase (questions 7–10).
  Expand by adding similar questions.
• Use the TPR activity to reinforce the
  meaning of individual words.
• Use the video vocabulary presentation
  for review and reinforcement.

En contexto
VOCABULARIO

Patricia has left the city and is visiting the country. Look at
the sights she sees and the people she meets.

A Aquí, en **el taller**, **la artesana** hace mucha ropa. Usa
lana de muchos colores. La lana azul está **encima de**
la mesa. La lana roja está **debajo de** la mesa.

B La mujer quiere el saco de
arriba. Patricia quiere un
gorro de **abajo**.

C En **la granja** hay varios animales. **El ganadero**
cuida **estas vacas** que están aquí muy cerca. **Ese**
animal, que está al otro lado de **la cerca**, es
un toro.

Classroom Community

TPR On a table, set up a small plastic fence and put
toy animals to one side. Have students come up to the
table and individually tell each student what to do. For
example: **Eduardo, pon el caballo dentro del corral.**

Storytelling Have students list their favorite animal
stories or movies from their childhood. Next to each
title, have them write the featured animal(s). You may
also want to refer students to the **Vocabulario
adicional** on p. R20. Then have students tell 1 or 2
events from the stories.

las llamas

el pastor

E Aquellas animales, que están lejos, son **llamas**. **El pastor** cuida las llamas.

la granja

los cerdos

las gallinas

allo

D Aquí hay **unas gallinas** y **un gallo**. Las gallinas están **dentro del corral**. El gallo está **fuera**.

F Aquí hay unos **cerdos**. El ganadero también tiene **un caballo**.

el caballo

Preguntas personales

1. ¿Te gustan los caballos?
2. ¿Vives en el campo o en la ciudad?
3. ¿Te gustaría trabajar en una granja o en un taller?
4. ¿Qué hay encima de tu escritorio? ¿Debajo de tu escritorio?
5. ¿Qué ropa de lana tienes?

cuatrocientos nueve
Etapa 2
409

Comprehension Questions

1. ¿Está la artesana en el taller? (Sí.)
2. ¿Usa la artesana lana de un sólo color? (No.)
3. ¿Está la lana roja encima de la mesa? (No.)
4. ¿Quiere la mujer el saco de abajo o de arriba? (de arriba)
5. ¿Quién quiere el gorro de abajo, Patricia o la artesana? (Patricia)
6. ¿Están la gallinas dentro o fuera del corral? (dentro)
7. ¿Qué hace el pastor? (Cuida las llamas.)
8. ¿Quién trabaja en la granja y qué hace? (El ganadero trabaja en la granja. Cuida los animales.)
9. ¿Dónde está el toro? (al otro lado de la cerca)
10. ¿Cuántos caballos tiene el ganadero? (un caballo)

Teaching Note

You may want to expand on questions 1 and 3 of the **Preguntas personales** with a follow-up question, such as **¿Dónde ves caballos?**

Block Schedule

Categorize Have students make flashcards of the vocabulary for animals on pp. 408–409 and the **Vocabulario adicional** on p. R20. Then have them determine categories for them (mammals/birds, domestic/wild, 1-color/multi-colored, etc.) and sort the cards according to the categories.

Teaching All Students

Extra Help Make statements about the various scenes on pp. 408–409 and have students point to or write the letter of the scene being described.

Native Speakers Ask students to provide additional vocabulary for the farm and farm animals. Have them model pronunciation for the other students, while drawing sketches on the board.

Multiple Intelligences

Interpersonal Have each student make up 2 additional **Preguntas personales,** and then ask a partner the questions.

Naturalist Using the vocabulary on pp. 408–409 and the **Vocabulario adicional** on p. R20, have students keep track of the kinds and number of animals they see throughout the rest of the day, live or on TV.

🔔 Quick Start Review

♻️ Vocabulary review
Use OHT 191 or write on the board:
List at least 3 items you find in each
place:
• el taller de artículos de lana
• la granja

Answers
Answers will vary. Answers could include:
• un saco, un gorro, una manta, unos guantes
• una vaca, un caballo, un cerdo, unas gallinas

Language Note

Point out that Patricia addresses Bárbara in
the **usted** form as a sign of respect for
Miguel's older relative. Bárbara, however,
addresses Patricia as **tú** because Patricia is
much younger.

En vivo

🎧💿 DIÁLOGO

 Patricia   Miguel   Bárbara   Julio

PARA ESCUCHAR • STRATEGY: LISTENING

Listen for implied statements Some things are said directly; others are
suggested, but not stated. They are implied. Listen and decide
which of the following are implied:

1. A slow, quiet life is boring.
2. Farm life requires hard work.
3. Life in both the city and the country is interesting.

What did you hear that influenced your decision?

En el campo

1▶ Miguel: ¡Buenos días, tía Bárbara!
Bárbara: ¡Miguel! ¡Bienvenidos! ¿Y
tú eres Patricia?
Patricia: Sí. Es un placer.
Bárbara: ¿Te gusta mi taller?
Patricia: Sí, mucho.

5▶ Bárbara: Sí, ya lo sé. Miguel, ¿me
bajas aquel saco? Está allí arriba.
Patricia: ¡Ay! No es necesario.
Bárbara: Miguel, busca un saco
para ti también.
Miguel: Gracias, tía Bárbara.

6▶ Julio: Soy de una familia de ganaderos.
Esta granja fue de mi abuelo. Todos los
días mi hijo les da de comer a las gallinas
y a las vacas. Mi hija menor cuida los
cerdos y los caballos. Y hablando de
caballos…

7▶ Julio: Miguel, ¿recuerdas la primera
vez que viniste a visitarnos?
Miguel: Patricia no quiere oír esas
viejas historias.
Julio: Pues, fue al corral, abrió la
cerca y el caballo se escapó.

410 cuatrocientos diez
Unidad 6

Classroom Community

Group Activity Divide the class into 10 groups and
assign 1 scene of the dialog to each. Have each group
sketch and elaborate on the picture for their scene and
learn the dialog lines. Then have each group come up
in sequential order and present their work.

Paired Activity Have pairs of students write a
1-sentence summary of each scene on an index card.
Then have them shuffle the cards and put them back in
order.

2 ▶ Patricia: ¿Cuándo vino usted a vivir aquí?
Bárbara: Vine en el año 1990.
Patricia: ¿Y le gusta vivir en el campo, en este pueblo pequeño?
Bárbara: Sí, es muy tranquilo.

3 ▶ Bárbara: A ver… ¿dónde están las tijeras? Ah, sí, allí están. Miguel, ¿me das las tijeras que están sobre la mesa?
Patricia: ¿Cómo fueron sus primeros años aquí?
Bárbara: Tuvimos que trabajar muchísimo.

4 ▶ Patricia: ¿Y venden los sacos y los gorros?
Bárbara: Sí, el mejor mercado es el mercado de Otavalo. Estuvimos ahí el domingo pasado.
Miguel: ¡A mí me gusta mucho ese mercado! ¡Vamos hoy!

8 ▶ Julio: Luego les dio de comer a las gallinas. ¡Les dio una bolsa de comida!
Miguel: ¡Tío Julio, por favor!
Julio: ¿Sabes, Patricia? ¡Miguel debe vivir en la ciudad!

9 ▶ Patricia: ¿Qué piensa usted de la ciudad?
Julio: Vamos a Quito todos los meses para visitar a mi hija mayor y su familia. Es muy interesante y hay mucho trabajo, pero vivimos aquí y estamos felices.
Patricia: Gracias, Julio.

10 ▶ Julio: Dice Miguel que ustedes van a Otavalo esta tarde.
Patricia: Sí.
Julio: ¿Te contó Miguel de la segunda vez que él nos acompañó a Otavalo?
Miguel: ¡Tío Julio!

cuatrocientos once
Etapa 2 411

Teaching All Students

Extra Help Have students work in pairs. One students reads the lines in a dialog scene. The other student covers the words in his/her book, listens to the partner, and then points to the picture of the scene.

Native Speakers Ask students to differentiate between **granja** and **rancho** in their cultural communities. What are the physical characteristics of each?

Multiple Intelligences

Visual Have students draw their own farm scenes, label the items, animals, etc., and write 3 sentences about the scene.

Verbal Ask students to give a verbal description of each character in the dialog. They should provide physical descriptions and personality traits.

Teaching Suggestions
Presenting the Dialog
• Prepare students for listening by focusing on the dialog context and the characters. Ask who Patricia and Miguel are and why they have come to Bárbara's workshop.
• Use the video, audio cassette, or CD to present the dialog. The expanded dialog on video offers additional listening practice opportunities.

Video Synopsis
• Patricia interviews Miguel's relatives about their life in the country. For a complete transcript of the video dialog, see p. 405B.

Comprehension Questions

1. ¿Es Bárbara la tía de Patricia? (No.)
2. ¿Quiere Patricia hacerle una entrevista a Bárbara? (Sí.)
3. ¿Fueron fáciles los primeros años de Bárbara en el campo? (No.)
4. ¿Participó Bárbara en el mercado de Otavalo el domingo pasado o el sábado pasado? (el domingo pasado)
5. ¿Qué les da Bárbara a Patricia y a Miguel, unos gorros o unos sacos? (unos sacos)
6. ¿Quién es Julio, el tío o el abuelo de Miguel? (el tío)
7. ¿Qué trabajo hace el hijo de Julio? (Les da de comer a las gallinas y a las vacas.)
8. ¿Qué trabajo hace la hija menor de Julio? (Cuida los cerdos y los caballos.)
9. ¿Qué pasó cuando Miguel fue al corral y abrió la cerca? (El caballo se escapó.)
10. ¿Por qué va Julio a Quito todos los meses? (Va para visitar a su hija mayor y su familia.)

Block Schedule

FunBreak Have students work in groups of 4. Tape the name of an animal on each student's back. Students then ask the other group members questions in order to determine what animal they are. At the end of 5 minutes, group members tell who they think they are and why. (For additional activities, see **Block Scheduling Copymasters.**)

Teaching Resource Options

Print 📖

Unit 6 Resource Book
  Videoscript, p. 76
  Audioscript, pp. 80–81
  Audioscript *Para hispanohablantes,*
    pp. 80–81

Audiovisual 📠

OHT 192 (Quick Start)
Audio Program Cassettes 17A, 17B /
  CD 17
Audio *Para hispanohablantes*
  Cassette 17A / CD 17
Video Program Videotape 6 / Videodisc
  3B

🔔 **Quick Start Review**

♻ Dialog review

Use OHT 192 or write on the board:
Complete the sentences from the dialog:

1. Soy de una familia de ___.
2. Miguel, ¿me das las tijeras que
   están ___ la mesa?
3. ¿Y le gusta vivir en el campo, en
   ___ pueblo pequeño?
4. Miguel, ¿recuerdas la primera vez
   que ___ a visitarnos?

Answers *See p. 405B.*

Teaching Suggestions
Comprehension Check

Use **Actividades** 1 and 2 to assess
retention after the dialog. Have students
close their books. Act out the sentences
in **Actividad** 1 and see if students can
comprehend and answer correctly.

Objective: Transitional practice
Listening comprehension/vocabulary

Answers (See script, p. 405B.)
e, d, a, b, c

Objective: Transitional practice
Listening comprehension/vocabulary

Answers (See script, p. 405B.)
1. Porque es muy tranquilo.
2. Bárbara vende la ropa que hace en el
   mercado de Otavalo.
3. Trabajaron muchísimo.
4. La granja del tío Julio fue de su abuelo.
5. Sus hijos ayudan al tío Julio con su trabajo.
6. Van a Otavalo.

En acción
VOCABULARIO Y GRAMÁTICA

OBJECTIVES
• Point out specific people
  and things
• Tell where things are located
• Talk about the past

¿En qué orden?

Escuchar ¿En qué orden pasaron estas cosas
según el diálogo? *(Hint: Indicate the correct order.)*

  a. Bárbara les da a Patricia y a Miguel unos
     sacos.
  b. Patricia le hace una entrevista al tío Julio.
  c. Patricia y Miguel van al mercado.
  d. Patricia le hace una entrevista a Bárbara.
  e. Patricia y Miguel llegan al campo.

¿Qué pasa?

Escuchar Contesta las preguntas según el
diálogo. *(Hint: Answer the questions.)*

  1. ¿Por qué le gusta a Bárbara vivir en
     el campo?
  2. ¿Dónde vende Bárbara la ropa que
     hace en su taller?
  3. ¿Cómo fueron los primeros años de
     Bárbara en el campo?
  4. ¿De quién fue la granja del tío Julio?
  5. ¿Quiénes ayudan al tío Julio con su trabajo?
  6. ¿Adónde van Patricia y Miguel después
     de visitar al tío Julio?

Los animales de la granja

Hablar Patricia y Miguel vieron varios animales
en el campo. ¿Qué vieron? *(Hint: Name the animals.)*

modelo

Vieron un caballo.

Classroom Management

Time Saver Have students complete **Actividades**
1–5 in small groups rather than individually.

Peer Review Have students work in groups of 4.
Give the answers to **Actividad 1** to 2 students and the
answers to **Actividad 2** to the other 2 students. Each
student then corrects 2 papers. For any wrong answers,
the student correcting the paper is responsible for
helping the other student understand his/her error.

• Use location words
• Use demonstratives
• Use ordinal numbers
• Use irregular verbs in the preterite

ACTIVIDAD 4

Animales felices

Leer Patricia y Miguel ven este anuncio de alimento (comida) para animales en el camino al campo. Lee el anuncio y contesta las preguntas según la información. *(Hint: Answer questions.)*

Tienda Villagómez

Vendemos alimento para todos los animales.

¡Alimento bueno, animales felices!

Avenida Chimborazo 138
Otavalo, Ecuador
Días: lunes a sábado
Horas: 7:00 a 6:00
tel: 23-83-69

1. ¿Quién compra artículos de esta tienda?
2. ¿Qué vende la tienda?
3. ¿Qué animales ves en el anuncio?
4. ¿Qué días y horas está abierta la tienda?
5. ¿Dónde queda la tienda?

ACTIVIDAD 5

♻ ¿Qué son?

Escuchar Todos hablan de su profesión. Escucha lo que dice cada persona e indica qué es, escogiendo la foto apropiada. *(Hint: Choose the correct picture.)*

a.

b.

c.

d.

Answers
1. Vieron una llama.
2. Vieron un toro.
3. Vieron un gallo.
4. Vieron un cerdo.

4 Objective: Transitional practice
Vocabulary in reading

Answers
1. Los ganaderos compran artículos de esta tienda.
2. La tienda vende alimento para todos los animales.
3. Veo una vaca, un cerdo, un gallo y un caballo.
4. La tienda está abierta de lunes a sábado desde las siete de la mañana hasta las seis de la tarde.
5. La tienda queda en la avenida Chimborazo 138, Otavalo, Ecuador.

5 Objective: Transitional practice
Listening comprehension
♻ Professions

Answers (See script, p. 405B.)
1. c   2. a   3. d   4. b

Critical Thinking

Ask students what they think farm animals need to be healthy. How does this compare to what household pets need? What about animals in the wild or animals in a zoo? Which needs are common to all animals and which are special to one group?

Language Note

Point out how animals "talk" in Spanish. Have students give the English equivalents.

el perro	guau guau
el gato	miau
la vaca	mu
el pollito	pío pío
el gallo	quiquiriquí

Block Schedule

Change of Pace Have students write 3-stanza poems. Stanza 1 describes city life; stanza 2 describes country life; stanza 3 says which type the student prefers. Have volunteers read their poems. Discuss the reasons for preferring one type of life over the other. (For additional activities, see **Block Scheduling Copymasters**.)

Teaching All Students

Extra Help Have students write **Patricia, Miguel, Bárbara,** and **Julio** across the top of a paper. Under each name, students write everything they know about the person. Have students compare charts with a partner.

Native Speakers Ask students to bring in Spanish periodicals they have at home. Have the class look for animal-related ads and compare them to the one in **Actividad 4**.

Multiple Intelligences

Musical/Rhythmic Have students search in the library or on the Internet for children's music in Spanish. Have them scan for songs about animals and then print/copy the words and music. Ask musically talented volunteers to sing or play the songs.

Teaching Resource Options

Print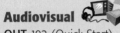

Más práctica Workbook PE, p. 141
Para hispanohablantes Workbook PE,
 p. 139
Block Scheduling Copymasters
Unit 6 Resource Book
  Más práctica Workbook TE, p. 56
  Para hispanohablantes Workbook
  TE, p. 62

Audiovisual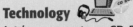

OHT 192 (Quick Start)

Technology

Intrigas y aventuras CD-ROM, Disc 1

Quick Start Review

🔄 **Prepositions of location**

Use OHT 192 or write on the board:
Complete the sentences to make true
statements about your classroom:

1. _____ está cerca _____ .
2. _____ y _____ están detrás _____ .
3. _____ y yo estamos lejos de _____ .
4. _____ está al lado de la
   profesora/del profesor.
5. _____ está enfrente de la clase.

Answers
Answers will vary. Answers could include:
1. La puerta está cerca del pizarrón.
2. Rosa y Beto están detrás de Juan.
3. Yolanda y yo estamos lejos de la
   computadora.
4. La videograbadora está al lado de la
   profesora/del profesor.
5. El pizarrón está enfrente de la clase.

Teaching Suggestions
**Presenting Saying Where
Things Are Located**

• Review recycled prepositions of
  location and teach the new ones
  using manipulatives.
• Call on students by their relative
  positions rather than by names. Have
  them stand up to show understanding.

 Objective: Controlled practice
Prepositions of location

Answers
1. dentro   4. arriba
2. encima   5. debajo
3. fuera

414   Vocabulary/Grammar • UNIDAD 6 Etapa 2

GRAMÁTICA

Saying Where Things Are Located

♻️ **¿RECUERDAS?** *p. 250* Remember
prepositions of location?

You can also talk about the location
of things using these words that you
learned in **En contexto:**

cerca (de)	entre
a la derecha (de)	a la izquierda (de)
detrás (de)	al lado (de)
enfrente (de)	lejos (de)

The words **arriba**
and **abajo** are never
followed by de.

abajo	debajo (de)	encima (de)
arriba	dentro (de)	fuera (de)

Use de only when a
specific location follows
the expression.

Están dentro del taller.
*They are **inside** the workshop.*

—Miguel, ¿me bajas aquel saco? Está allí **arriba.**
*Miguel, (will you) get down that sweater for me? It's **up** there.*

 **Gramática**

¿Dónde están?

Escribir Explica dónde están las
personas y los animales.
Completa cada oración con la
palabra apropiada, según el
dibujo. *(Hint: Explain where they are.)*

1. El cerdo está _____ del
   corral.

2. El gato está _____ de la
   cerca.

3. El artesano está _____ de
   su taller.

4. El pastor está _____ .

5. El perro está _____ de la
   mesa.

🔲 **MÁS PRÁCTICA** *cuaderno* p. 141   🔲 **PARA HISPANOHABLANTES** *cuaderno* p. 139

414   cuatrocientos catorce
Unidad 6

Classroom Community

Paired Activity Have students identify people in
the classroom by describing their locations to a partner.
The partner guesses who is being described. Students
should each take at least 3 turns.

Game Play "I Spy" by having students say where
something is and providing 1 detail. The class tries to
guess what the object is. The student keeps adding
details until the object is guessed.

ACTIVIDAD 7 ♻ Para el viaje

PARA CONVERSAR • STRATEGY: SPEAKING

Recall what you know When describing where items are located, remember to use phrases that you learned earlier, such as **al lado de** and **a la derecha de**, as well as those you just learned.

Hablar Mira las cosas que Patricia va a llevar en su viaje al campo. Trabaja con otro(a) estudiante para preguntar dónde está cada cosa según el dibujo. Cambien de papel. *(Hint: Ask where things are.)*

modelo

1. la grabadora

Estudiante A: ¿Dónde está **la grabadora**?

Estudiante B: Está encima del escritorio.

ACTIVIDAD 8

Mi habitación

Escribir Piensa en tu habitación. ¿Qué hay allí? ¿Dónde está todo? Haz un dibujo y escribe un párrafo para describirla. *(Hint: Draw and describe your bedroom.)*

modelo

Hay muchísimas cosas en mi habitación. Hay muchos zapatos debajo de la cama y muchos libros encima del escritorio. Abajo, en el armario, hay ropa sucia y arriba hay…

TAMBIÉN SE DICE

There are several words for *farm*.

- **la chacra:** many countries
- **la finca:** Colombia, Puerto Rico
- **la granja:** Argentina, Ecuador, Spain
- **la hacienda:** many countries
- **el rancho:** Mexico

cuatrocientos quince
Etapa 2 **415**

UNIDAD 6 Etapa 2
Vocabulary/Grammar

Gestures

Have students use appropriate gestures when asking and answering questions in **Actividad 7**.

ACTIVIDAD 7 Objective: Transitional practice Prepositions of location ♻ School and personal items

Answers
1. A: ¿Dónde está la grabadora?
   B: Está encima del escritorio.
2. A: ¿Dónde está el casete?
   B: Está dentro de la grabadora.
3. A: ¿Dónde está la cartera?
   B: Está encima de la cama.
4. A: ¿Dónde está el dinero?
   B: Está al lado de la cartera (encima de la cama).
5. A: ¿Dónde está la mochila?
   B: Está debajo del escritorio.
6. A: ¿Dónde está la gorra?
   B: Está arriba en el armario.
7. A: ¿Dónde está el cuaderno?
   B: Está encima del escritorio.
8. A: ¿Dónde está el lápiz?
   B: Está encima del cuaderno.
9. A: ¿Dónde está la bolsa?
   B: Está abajo en el armario.

ACTIVIDAD 8 Objective: Open-ended practice Prepositions of location in writing

Answers will vary.

Culture Highlights

● **LA LLAMA** The llama is raised on farms in Ecuador because it is a very useful animal. Its wool is used for clothing, its hide provides leather, and its dung is burned for fuel. They are also excellent pack animals. Llamas can carry more than their weight in cargo and can go several days without food.

Quick Wrap-up

Have students name 2 things on top of your desk and 2 things inside your desk.

Block Schedule

Variety Have students sketch their bedrooms or imaginary bedrooms. Then have them list the objects in the bedroom and where they are located. Next, have them exchange papers with a partner and ask and answer questions about each other's bedroom.

Teaching All Students

Extra Help For **Actividad 8**, students may find it helpful to write out a list of the objects in the picture first.

Multiple Intelligences

Visual First, have students draw a farm scene in the middle of a piece of paper and animals around the edge. Then have them work with a partner and tell the partner where to place the animals. The partner draws lines from the animals to the locations.

Vocabulary/Grammar • UNIDAD 6 Etapa 2 **415**

Teaching Resource Options

Print

Más práctica Workbook PE, p. 142
Para hispanohablantes Workbook
  PE, p. 140
Block Scheduling Copymasters
Unit 6 Resource Book
  Information Gap Activities, p. 68
  Más práctica Workbook TE, p. 57
  Para hispanohablantes Workbook
   TE, p. 63

Audiovisual

OHT 192 (Quick Start)

Technology

Intrigas y aventuras CD-ROM, Disc 1

Quick Start Review

♻ Prepositions of location

Use OHT 192 or write on the board:
Unscramble the following words to
make logical sentences:

1. dentro / las / del / gallinas /
   corral /están
2. lejos / animales / los / llamas /
   que / están / son
3. cerca / está / gallo / encima / el /
   de / la
4. un / Patricia / gorro / abajo / de /
   quiere
5. corral / están / cerdos / los /
   del / fuera

Answers *See p. 405B.*

Teaching Suggestions
Presenting Pointing Out Specific Things Using Demonstratives

• Point out that demonstrative
  adjectives "demonstrate" which items
  you are talking about.
• Use gestures and demonstrative
  adjectives as you pick up items
  around the room and tell to whom
  they belong.
• Find 2 objects of the same category
  and use a demonstrative adjective to
  describe the first one, and a
  demonstrative pronoun for the
  second.

Pointing Out Specific Things Using Demonstratives

When you point out specific things, you use **demonstrative** adjectives and **pronouns.** In **En contexto** you saw how demonstrative adjectives are used. A **demonstrative** adjective describes the location of a **noun** in relation to a person.

Masculine		Feminine	
Singular	**Plural**	**Singular**	**Plural**
este **cerdo**	estos **cerdos**	esta **mesa**	estas **mesas**
this pig	*these pigs*	*this table*	*these tables*
ese **cerdo**	esos **cerdos**	esa **mesa**	esas **mesas**
that pig	*those pigs*	*that table*	*those tables*
aquel **cerdo**	aquellos **cerdos**	aquella **mesa**	aquellas **mesas**
that pig (over there)	*those pigs (over there)*	*that table (over there)*	*those tables (over there)*

*Adjective **relates location**
of the noun to a person*

Bárbara says:
—Miguel, ¿me bajas aquel **saco**?
*Miguel, (will you) get down **that sweater** for me?*

Demonstrative pronouns are used in place of the **adjective** and the **noun.** They are the same as the demonstrative adjectives except that they have an accent.

Masculine		Feminine	
Singular	**Plural**	**Singular**	**Plural**
éste *this one*	éstos *these*	ésta *this one*	éstas *these*
ése *that one*	ésos *those*	ésa *that one*	ésas *those*
aquél *that one (over there)*	aquéllos *those (over there)*	aquélla *that one (over there)*	aquéllas *those (over there)*

Bárbara might have said: —Miguel, ¿me bajas aquél que está arriba?
*Miguel, would you get down **that one** up there for me?*

There are also **demonstrative** pronouns that refer to ideas or unidentified things that do not have a specific gender.

Esto es importante.	¿Qué es eso?	¿Qué es aquello?
***This** is important.*	*What's **that**?*	*What's **that** over there?*

416 cuatrocientos dieciséis
Unidad 6

Classroom Community

Learning Scenario Divide the class into buyers and sellers. Using articles from p. 283 of Unit 4 (jewelry, handicrafts, music articles) or even classroom items, hold a market and bargaining session. Sellers give the bargainers choices: ¿Quieres este collar de oro o ése? Buyers use the demonstratives to respond: ¿Cuánto cuesta este collar? ¿Y ése?

Group Activity Extend **Actividad 11** by having the groups of students add information about their personal items. Suggest that they tell where they bought them, what they cost, etc. Monitor students' use of demonstratives, comparatives, and preterite.

ACTIVIDAD 9 Gramática

En el mercado

Leer Patricia y Miguel están en una tienda. Completa sus oraciones con un pronombre o adjetivo demostrativo. *(Hint: Complete what they say.)*

Patricia: ¿Te gusta ___1___ bufanda amarilla?

Miguel: Prefiero ___2___ bufanda blanca.

Patricia: ¿Y ___3___ saco marrón?

Miguel: No es mi color favorito. Prefiero ___4___ saco verde.

Patricia: Bueno, si te gusta el color verde, ¿por qué no compras ___5___ mochila verde?

Miguel: La verdad es que prefiero ___6___ mochila marrón.

Patricia: Ay, Miguel, ¡no te entiendo!

■ **MÁS PRÁCTICA** *cuaderno* p. 142

■ **PARA HISPANOHABLANTES** *cuaderno* p. 140

ACTIVIDAD 10

♻ **De compras**

Hablar Imagínate que tú y un(a) amigo(a) van de compras. Habla de las cosas que ven según el modelo. Tú decides si están cerca o lejos. Cambien de papel. *(Hint: Talk about what you see.)*

modelo

las raquetas

Estudiante A: *¿Te gustan estas **raquetas**?*

Estudiante B: *Sí, pero prefiero ésas.*

1. la pelota	**5.** la falda
2. los pantalones	**6.** el abrigo
3. las gorras	**7.** las gafas
4. el guante de béisbol	**8.** los zapatos

ACTIVIDAD 11

♻ **En la clase**

Hablar/Escribir En grupos de tres, compara las cosas que tiene cada persona. Escribe las oraciones de tu grupo. *(Hint: Compare your possessions.)*

modelo

libro(s)

Estudiante A: *Estos **libros** son más grandes que ésos.*

1. libro(s)	**5.** mochila(s)
2. pluma(s)	**6.** escritorio(s)
3. silla(s)	**7.** borrador(es)
4. cuaderno(s)	**8.** ¿?

■ **MÁS COMUNICACIÓN** p. R17

Teaching Note

You may want to teach students this mnemonic device for remembering the difference between **este** and **ese**: *"This and these have the t's."*

ACTIVIDAD 9

Objective: Controlled practice Demonstratives in reading

Answers
1. esta
2. esa
3. este
4. aquel
5. esa
6. aquella

ACTIVIDAD 10

Objective: Transitional practice Demonstratives in conversation

♻ **Gustar, preferir**

Answers

Answers will vary.
1. A: ¿Te gusta esta pelota?
   B: Sí, pero prefiero ésa.
2. A: ¿Te gustan estos pantalones?
   B: Sí, pero prefiero ésos.
3. A: ¿Te gustan estas gorras?
   B: Sí, pero prefiero ésas.
4. A: ¿Te gusta este guante de béisbol?
   B: Sí, pero prefiero ése.
5. A: ¿Te gusta esta falda?
   B: Sí, pero prefiero ésa.
6. A: ¿Te gusta este abrigo?
   B: Sí, pero prefiero ése.
7. A: ¿Te gustan estas gafas?
   B: Sí, pero prefiero ésas.
8. A: ¿Te gustan estos zapatos?
   B: Sí, pero prefiero ésos.

ACTIVIDAD 11

Objective: Open-ended practice Demonstratives in conversation

♻ **Comparatives**

Answers will vary.

■ **Block Schedule**

Change of Pace Have pairs of students plan and present skits in which 1 person wants certain articles and the other person keeps giving the wrong ones. For example, a little child asking his/her mother for something, a customer asking for articles in a store, or a couch potato asking a friend to get everything he/she wants. (For additional activities, see **Block Scheduling Copymasters**.)

Teaching All Students

Extra Help Have students prepare for **Actividad 10** by first writing the list of articles. Next to each one they should write the appropriate demonstrative adjective, then the appropriate demonstrative pronoun.

Multiple Intelligences

Interpersonal Have students personalize **Actividad 10** by asking each other real questions about their school supplies: **¿Te gustan estas plumas?**

Naturalist Have students collect items from outside (flowers, leaves, stones, etc.) and talk about them using demonstrative adjectives and pronouns. Provide a dictionary for students to look up unknown vocabulary.

Teaching Resource Options

Print ✎

Más práctica Workbook PE, p. 143
Para hispanohablantes Workbook PE, p. 141
Block Scheduling Copymasters
Unit 6 Resource Book
  Más práctica Workbook TE, p. 58
  Para hispanohablantes Workbook TE, p. 64

Audiovisual 🎧

OHT 193 (Quick Start)

Technology 💻

Intrigas y aventuras CD-ROM, Disc 1

🔔 Quick Start Review

♻ **Vocabulary review**

Use OHT 193 or write on the board: Write the word that does *not* belong with the other two words:

1. aquella   arriba   aquel
2. llama   cerdo   saco
3. fuera de   abajo   esto
4. caballo   taller   artesana
5. ésta   lana   aquélla

Answers *See p. 405B.*

Teaching Suggestions
Teaching Ordinal Numbers

Ask students what they know about adjectives. Write their responses and examples on the board. Point out that ordinal numbers are also adjectives and follow the same rules.

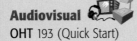
Objective: Controlled practice Ordinal numbers in conversation

Answers
*The **Tú** answers follow the **modelo** pattern.*
1. Tu amigo(a): Él es el sexto.
2. Tu amigo(a): Él es el primero.
3. Tu amigo(a): Él es el quinto.
4. Tu amigo(a): Él es el tercero.
5. Tu amigo(a): Ella es la octava.
6. Tu amigo(a): Ella es la séptima.
7. Tu amigo(a): Él es el noveno.
8. Tu amigo(a): Ella es la décima.
9. Tu amigo(a): Ella es la cuarta.

GRAMÁTICA — Ordinal Numbers

When you talk about the order of items, use ordinal numbers. These are the first ten ordinal numbers.

¥ When used with nouns, they must agree in number and gender.
¥ Ordinals are placed before **nouns**.
¥ Primer o and tercer o drop the o before a **masculine singular** noun.

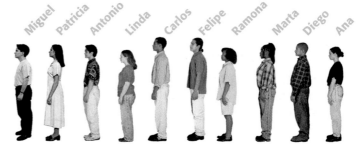

primera segunda tercera cuarta quinta sexta séptima octava novena décima

Patricia asks: *before the noun*
—¿Cómo fueron sus primeros **años** aquí?
*How were your **first** years here?*

Bárbara might say: *drops the o*
—Fue muy difícil hasta el tercer año.
*It was very difficult until the **third** year.*

To say *last,* use último(a).   La última vez que Miguel fue a Otavalo…
*The **last** time Miguel went to Otavalo…*

ACTIVIDAD 12 — Gramática

El orden

Hablar Patricia está con un grupo de amigos. Hacen cola para ver una película. Tú le preguntas a tu amigo(a) quiénes son. *(Hint: Ask who they are.)*

___modelo___

Patricia

Tú: *¿Quién es **Patricia**?*

Tu amigo(a): *Ella es la segunda.*

Miguel Patricia Antonio Linda Carlos Felipe Ramona Marta Diego Ana

1. Felipe   4. Antonio   7. Diego
2. Miguel   5. Marta   8. Ana
3. Carlos   6. Ramona   9. Linda

■ **MÁS PRÁCTICA** *cuaderno* p. 143   ■ **PARA HISPANOHABLANTES** *cuaderno* p. 141

418   cuatrocientos dieciocho
Unidad 6

Classroom Community

TPR Using toy animals, school items, etc., tell students where to position an item in a line. Students place the items according to your orders.

Group Activity In groups of 3–4, have students talk about their memories of first grade (**el primer año de la escuela**), second grade, etc. Each student must tell 1 thing for each grade.

ACTIVIDAD 13

¿Quién llegó primero?

Hablar/Escribir Patricia y sus amigos participaron en una carrera. ¿En qué orden llegaron? *(Hint: Give their order in the race.)*

modelo

Patricia: 2   ***Patricia** fue la **segunda** chica en llegar.*

1. Elena: 7
2. Antonio: 1
3. Ramón: 3
4. Linda: 8
5. Carlos: 10
6. Miguel: 4
7. Marta: 6
8. Alfredo: 9
9. Diego: 5

ACTIVIDAD 14

El primer día...

Escribir Explica en qué día hiciste las cosas durante las vacaciones. *(Hint: In what order did you do things?)*

modelo

***El segundo** día fui a un museo.*

1. primero(a)
2. segundo(a)
3. tercero(a)
4. cuarto(a)
5. quinto(a)
6. último(a)

GRAMÁTICA

Irregular Preterite Verbs

You've learned that **hacer, ir,** and **ser** are irregular in the preterite. Here are some other irregular preterite verbs. Notice that the forms for **dar** are similar to **ver. Decir** and **venir** have their own special forms.

dar *to give*	
di	dimos
diste	disteis
dio	dieron

decir *to say, to tell*	
dije	dijimos
dijiste	dijisteis
dijo	dijeron

venir *to come*	
vine	vinimos
viniste	vinisteis
vino	vinieron

Although the verbs **tener** and **estar** have irregular endings in the preterite, their forms follow similar patterns.

tener *to have*	
tuve	tuvimos
tuviste	tuvisteis
tuvo	tuvieron

estar *to be*	
estuve	estuvimos
estuviste	estuvisteis
estuvo	estuvieron

Bárbara says:

—**Vine** en el año 1990.
I came in 1990.

—**Tuvimos** que trabajar muchísimo.
We had to work a whole lot.

—**Estuvimos** ahí el domingo pasado.
We were there last Sunday.

Estar is never used in the preterite to express feelings.

cuatrocientos diecinueve
Etapa 2   **419**

Teaching All Students

Extra Help Have students make a 2-column poster with 1°, 2°, 3°, etc. down the left column and the ordinals in Spanish down the right column. Have them fold back the right column and randomly practice the words for the numerals in the left column.

Native Speakers Ask students to tell as many ordinals beyond **décimo** they know.

Multiple Intelligences

Visual Have students work in pairs to create a large cut-away drawing of an 11-story apartment building and label the floors. Point out that the ground floor is **la planta baja** and **el primer piso** is above that. Have them include people and write what activities they are participating in. **Variation:** Have students draw an 11-story department store and what is sold on each floor.

ACTIVIDAD 13

Answers
1. Elena fue la séptima chica en llegar.
2. Antonio fue el primer chico en llegar.
3. Ramón fue el tercer chico en llegar.
4. Linda fue la octava chica en llegar.
5. Carlos fue el décimo chico en llegar.
6. Miguel fue el cuarto chico en llegar.
7. Marta fue la sexta chica en llegar.
8. Alfredo fue el noveno chico en llegar.
9. Diego fue el quinto chico en llegar.

ACTIVIDAD 14

Objective: Open-ended practice
Ordinal numbers in writing

Answers
Answers will vary.
1. El primer día...
2. El segundo día...
3. El tercer día...
4. El cuarto día...
5. El quinto día...
6. El último día...

🔔 Quick Start Review

♻ Preterite of **hacer, ir, ser**

Use OHT 193 or write on the board: Complete the sentences with the preterite of the indicated verb:

1. Ayer Eva ____ al campo. (ir)
2. Primero, nosotros ____ un viaje por la ciudad. (hacer)
3. Yo ____ al corral para ver los animales. (ir)
4. El señor Rivera ____ editor. (ser)
5. ¿Qué ____ tú anoche? (hacer)

Answers *See p. 405B.*

Teaching Suggestions
Reinforcing Irregular Preterite Verbs

Tell a story about something interesting you did recently, using the irregular preterites on p. 419. Have students raise their hands when they hear the forms.

Block Schedule

Variety Divide the class into 3 or 4 groups. Assign each student in each group an ordinal number from 1–10. Then have groups come to the front of the class, and by talking amongst themselves, determine how to line up in order. Then have each student state his/her position. (For additional activities, see **Block Scheduling Copymasters**.)

Teaching Resource Options

Print ✎

Más práctica Workbook PE, p. 144
Para hispanohablantes Workbook PE,
   p. 142
Block Scheduling Copymasters
Unit 6 Resource Book
   Information Gap Activities, pp. 69–70
   Más práctica Workbook TE, p. 59
   Para hispanohablantes Workbook
      TE, p. 65
   Audioscript, p. 81
   Audioscript *Para hispanohablantes*,
      p. 82

Audiovisual 🎧📺

Audio Program Cassettes 17A / CD 17
Audio *Para hispanohablantes*
   Cassette 17A / CD 17

Technology 🎧💻

Intrigas y aventuras CD-ROM, Disc 1

 Objective: Controlled practice
Irregular preterite verbs

Answers
1. Yo le di de comer al toro.
2. Ustedes les dieron de comer a los gatos.
3. Miguel les dio de comer a las llamas.
4. Tú le diste de comer al gallo.
5. Mi hija les dio de comer a los caballos.
6. Mis hijos y yo les dimos de comer a las vacas.

 Objective: Controlled practice
Irregular preterite verbs in conversation

Answers
1. Miguel: ¿Por qué no viniste tú?
   Patricia: Yo no vine porque tuve que hacer unos quehaceres.
2. Miguel: ¿Por qué no vinieron Carlos y Alicia?
   Patricia: Carlos y Alicia no vinieron porque tuvieron que trabajar.
3. Miguel: ¿Por qué no vinieron tu hermana y tú?
   Patricia: Mi hermana y yo no vinimos porque tuvimos que limpiar la casa.
4. Miguel: ¿Por qué no vino Ana?
   Patricia: Ana no vino porque tuvo que ir a una fiesta de cumpleaños.
5. Miguel: ¿Por qué no vino Felipe?
   Patricia: Felipe no vino porque tuvo que hacer su tarea.
6. Miguel: ¿Por qué no vinieron Juan y Jorge?
   Patricia: Juan y Jorge no vinieron porque tuvieron que visitar a sus abuelos.

ACTIVIDAD **15** Gramática

Todos ayudaron en la granja

Escribir Hay muchos animales en la granja del tío Julio. Muchas personas lo ayudaron con el trabajo. ¿A qué animales les dieron de comer cada persona? *(Hint: Which animals did they feed?)*

modelo

Patricia: los cerdos   **Patricia les dio de comer a los cerdos.**

Nota

The expression **darle(s) de comer** means *to feed.*
Les di de comer a mis gatos.   *I **fed** my cats.*

1. yo: el toro
2. ustedes: los gatos
3. Miguel: las llamas
4. tú: el gallo
5. mi hija: los caballos
6. mis hijos y yo: las vacas

ACTIVIDAD **16** Gramática

¿Por qué no vinieron?

Hablar Miguel invitó a varios amigos al campo el domingo, pero muchos no vinieron. Le pregunta a Patricia por qué. Cambien de papel. *(Hint: Explain why they didn't come.)*

modelo

Enrique (estudiar)   **Miguel:** ¿Por qué no vino **Enrique**?
                       Patricia: *Enrique no vino porque tuvo que **estudiar.***

1. tú (hacer unos quehaceres)
2. Carlos y Alicia (trabajar)
3. tu hermana y tú (limpiar la casa)
4. Ana (ir a una fiesta de cumpleaños)
5. Felipe (hacer su tarea)
6. Juan y Jorge (visitar a sus abuelos)

▓ **MÁS PRÁCTICA** *cuaderno* p. 144
▓ **PARA HISPANOHABLANTES** *cuaderno* p. 142

ACTIVIDAD **17**

♻ ¿Dónde estuvo?

Hablar Pregúntales a tres estudiantes dónde estuvieron y qué hicieron estas personas el domingo. Luego, haz un resumen para la clase. *(Hint: Say where they were.)*

modelo

tu hermana

Tú: ¿Dónde estuvo y qué hizo **tu hermana** el domingo?

Estudiante 1: *Estuvo en la cancha. Jugó al tenis.*

Resumen: *Un estudiante dijo que su hermana estuvo en la cancha el domingo. Jugó al tenis. Dos dijeron que sus hermanas estuvieron en la iglesia.*

	Estudiante 1
1. tú	
2. tu hermano(a)	
3. tus padres	
4. tú y tus amigos(as)	

NOTA CULTURAL

Quichua, an indigenous language, is still commonly spoken in certain regions of Ecuador, particularly in the mountains. Here is a Quichua expression used in Ecuador today.

¡Achachái!
(¡Qué frío!)

Classroom Community

Paired Activity Each student writes a list of 10 things he/she did in the last 2 weeks. Pairs then trade lists and write follow-up questions for each item. Partners take turns asking and answering their questions.

Portfolio Have students write about an interesting dream or an imaginary event that took place. Tell them to relate what happened, not what people were doing. They can also illustrate the events.

Rubric A = 13–15 pts. B = 10–12 pts. C = 7–9 pts. D = 4–6 pts. F = < 4 pts.

Writing criteria	Scale				
Organization	1	2	3	4	5
Grammar/spelling accuracy	1	2	3	4	5
Creativity/appearance	1	2	3	4	5

ACTIVIDAD 18

Las cosas que nos pasan

Hablar/Escribir Describe algo que te pasó. Usa una forma de cada verbo por lo menos una vez. ¡Usa tu imaginación si es necesario!
(Hint: Describe something that happened.)

dar	tener	
ver	hacer	decir
estar	venir	ser

modelo

Mis primas vinieron a visitarme. Me dieron un regalo. ¡Nunca vi nada tan bonito! Fue una falda azul larga. Dijeron que…

ACTIVIDAD 19

Un día bonito

Escuchar Escucha el párrafo sobre el viaje que hizo Luisa. Luego, ordena las fotos según lo que escuchaste. *(Hint: Put the pictures in order.)*

ACTIVIDAD 20

Un día en el campo

Escribir Escribe un párrafo sobre un viaje real o imaginario que hiciste al campo o a otro lugar. Usa las preguntas como ayuda.
(Hint: Write about a trip.)

¿Adónde fuiste?
¿Qué oíste?
¿Qué viste?
¿Qué hiciste?
¿Con quién fuiste?

MÁS COMUNICACIÓN p. R17

Pronunciación

Trabalenguas

Pronunciación de la l The letter l is pronounced like the *l* in the English word *lucky*. Practice its sound by saying this tongue twister.

Lana, Lena, Lina y Lulú
van y ven al león con el balón.
Al león con el balón ven
Lana, Lena, Lina y Lulú.

Teaching All Students

Extra Help If students are overwhelmed by the irregular preterites, assign 2 "pet" verbs a night. Students must master those 2 by memorizing the forms and writing sample sentences for each.

Multiple Intelligences

Intrapersonal Have students write their previous day's actions in chronological order. Ask them to begin with the time they woke up and fill in every detail possible.

Culture Highlights

● **QUICHUA** The words **quechua** and **quichua** are both used for the native language of the Andes mountains. In Ecuador, it is more common to use the word **quichua**.

ACTIVIDAD 17 **Objective:** Transitional practice
Irregular preterite verbs in conversation
♻ **Places, preterite**

Answers will vary.

ACTIVIDAD 18 **Objective:** Open-ended practice
Irregular preterite verbs in conversation

Answers will vary.

ACTIVIDAD 19 **Objective:** Transitional practice
Listening comprehension/irregular preterite verbs

Answers (See script, p. 405B.)
d, a, c, b

ACTIVIDAD 20 **Objective:** Open-ended practice
Describing a trip

Answers will vary.

Dictation

After students have read the tongue twister in the **Pronunciación,** have them close their books. Dictate the tongue twister in segments while students write it.

Block Schedule

FunBreak Prepare ahead: sets of 12–15 cards with a variety of past actions, using the **yo** form of the verb, written on them. (Be sure to use known preterite forms.) Students work in teams of 5–6. Give each team a set of cards. One team member selects a card and has 1 minute to draw the activity on the board while the team guesses, using the **tú** form of the verb. (For additional activities, see **Block Scheduling Copymasters**.)

Teaching Resource Options

Print

Unit 6 Resource Book
  Audioscript, p. 81
  Audioscript *Para hispanohablantes*,
    p. 82

Audiovisual

Audio Program Cassette 17A / CD 17
Audio *Para hispanohablantes*
  Cassette 17A / CD 17
OHT 193 (Quick Start)
Video Program Videotape 6 /
  Videodisc 3B

Search Chapter 6, Play to 7
U6E2 • En colores (Culture)

Quick Start Review

🔔 El mercado

Use OHT 193 or write on the board:
Write at least 5 words or expressions
that you associate with **el mercado:**

Answers
Answers will vary. Answers could include:
la artesanía, regatear, el (la) vendedor(a),
el precio, ¿Cuánto cuesta(n)...?, ¡Es muy caro!,
Le puede ofrecer...

Teaching Suggestions
Presenting Cultura y comparaciones

• Begin by asking students to compare
  the photos on pp. 422–423 and
  make 2 observations for each.
• Have students complete the Strategy
  task. Have several students present
  their questions.
• Expand the cultural information by
  showing the video culture presentation.

Reading Strategy

Recognize place names Have students
identify the following place names by
looking for words nearby that explain what
they are: **Imbabura y Cotacachi, Otavalo,
Peguche, Carabuela.**

En colores
CULTURA Y COMPARACIONES

PARA CONOCERNOS
STRATEGY:
CONNECTING CULTURES
Research cultural groups The term
indigenous people is used to refer
to the original or native
inhabitants of a region. Who
were or are the indigenous
people where you live? When
researching, make sure to ask
the five W questions: who?,
what?, when?, where?, why?
Make up five research
questions about the original
people of your area, using
these words as prompts.

¿Quién?	
¿Qué?	
¿Cuándo?	
¿Dónde?	
¿Por qué?	

Use these questions to gather
information as you read
«Los otavaleños».

LOS OTAVALEÑOS

Si sales de Quito por la Carretera Panamericana[1] hacia el norte
del país, vas a ver un paisaje[2] impresionante. Hay espléndidas
vistas de montañas, volcanes y lagos. Entre Quito y la frontera[3]
con Colombia hay un valle entre las montañas Imbabura y
Cotacachi. Allí queda el pueblo de Otavalo.

   Aquí viven los otavaleños. Este grupo indígena se conoce[4]
por su artesanía, su éxito[5] económico y la preservación de sus
costumbres folclóricas. Los sábados, los otavaleños organizan un
mercado tradicional. Hay frutas y verduras, animales y lo más
interesante para los turistas: tejidos[6] y artesanías. En este mercado

---

[1] Pan-American Highway	[3] border	[5] success
[2] landscape	[4] is known	[6] textiles

422 cuatrocientos veintidós
Unidad 6

Classroom Community

Cooperative Learning Have students work in
groups of 4 and review the reading. Student 1 finds
prepositions of location in the reading; student 2 finds
demonstratives; student 3 finds past tense verb forms;
student 4 records the information. The group then
verifies the information before submitting the paper for
a grade.

Paired Activity Have pairs of students select
another indigenous group from South America,
research information about it, and present their findings
to the class.

puedes comprar ponchos, chompas
y tapices de lana hechos[7] por los
otavaleños. Los otavaleños también
venden sombreros hechos a medida[8].
Como en todo mercado, ¡es importante
regatear!

Hacer tejidos es una tradición de
los indígenas de Otavalo. En 1917
empezaron a imitar los casimires[9]
ingleses y así nació[10] la industria textil.
Las personas que hacen los tejidos son
de Otavalo y los pueblos cercanos,
como Peguche, Ilumán, Carabuela y
Quinchuqui.

Si visitas Otavalo, debes conocer
la Plaza Bolívar, donde está la estatua
del general inca Rumiñahui. También
puedes aprender un poco de la historia
y la arqueología de esta región en el
Instituto Otavaleño de Antropología.

---

[7] made
[8] custom-made
[9] tweeds
[10] was born

Ropa tradicional otavaleña

¿Comprendiste?

1. ¿Dónde queda Otavalo? ¿Cómo llegas?
2. ¿Qué importancia tiene Otavalo?
3. ¿Qué cosas venden en el mercado de Otavalo?
4. ¿Cómo y cuándo empezó la industria textil?
5. ¿Qué lugares puedes conocer en Otavalo?

¿Qué piensas?

1. ¿Por qué debes regatear si visitas Otavalo?
2. ¿Qué puedes hacer para aprender más de la vida de los otavaleños de hoy?

Hazlo tú

¿Hay artesanos en tu comunidad? Explica qué hacen. Si no hay, investiga alguna artesanía de Estados Unidos y haz un reportaje sobre esto.

Culture Highlights

● **LA RUTA DE LOS VOLCANES** The Cordillera de los Andes passes across Ecuador. This mountain chain has the most concentrated area of active volcanoes in the world. It includes 2 parallel mountain chains, 1 eastern and 1 western. The valleys formed between them have fertile soil.

Cross Cultural Connections

Ask students to compare the market in Otavalo with shopping places in the U.S.: outdoor markets, supermarkets, shopping malls. How do they compare in terms of physical layout and what goes on at each one?

Interdisciplinary Connections

Economics Have students choose one traditional craft and try to name and calculate the costs involved in it: for example, equipment, supplies, packaging, etc.

¿Comprendiste?

Answers

1. Queda entre Quito y la frontera con Colombia, en un valle entre las montañas Imbabura y Cotacachi.
2. Otavalo se conoce por su artesanía, su éxito económico y la preservación de sus costumbres folclóricas. Tiene un mercado tradicional.
3. Venden frutas y verduras, animales, tejidos y artesanías.
4. Empezó en 1917 cuando los indígenas de Otavalo empezaron a imitar los casimires ingleses.
5. Puedes conocer la Plaza Bolívar y el Instituto Otavaleño de Antropología.

Block Schedule

Research Have students visit local stores or on-line stores that sell international crafts. Have them list all the items from Spanish-speaking countries, the countries of origin, and the prices. Compile a list of items in class. Is there any one kind of item that is more prevalent than others?

Teaching All Students

Extra Help Have students reread the passage, sentence-by-sentence, being sure to use commas as resting points. At the end of each paragraph, have students give a 1-sentence summary.

Native Speakers Ask students to compare and contrast one indigenous group in their native land to the **otavaleños** as described in the reading.

Multiple Intelligences

Visual Have students design tapestries based on one of the designs in the photo on p. 423. Variation: Have students design a "traditional" costume for students from your school. Students then describe their designs and how they are like/unlike those in the photos.

Teaching Resource Options

Print

Para hispanohablantes Workbook PE,
pp. 95–96
Block Scheduling Copymasters
Unit 6 Resource Book
  Para hispanohablantes Workbook
  TE, pp. 66–67
  Information Gap Activities,
  p. 71
  Family Involvement, pp. 72–73
  Multiple Choice Test Questions,
  pp. 170–178

Audiovisual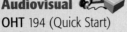

OHT 194 (Quick Start)
Audio Program Testing Cassette T2 /
  CD T2

Technology

Electronic Teacher Tools/Test
  Generator
Intrigas y aventuras CD-ROM, Disc 1

Quick Start Review

🔄 Vocabulary and preterite review
Use OHT 194 or write on the board:
Write 3 sentences saying what Miguel's
Uncle Julio did this morning.

Answers
Answers will vary. Answers could include:
Cuidó las vacas.
Les dio de comer a las gallinas.
Visitó a Bárbara en su taller.
Habló con el pastor.
Le dio de comer al caballo.

Teaching Suggestions
What Have Students Learned?

• Have students look at the "Now you
  can…" notes listed on the left side of
  pages 424–425. Tell students to think
  about which areas they might not be
  sure of. For those areas, they should
  consult the "To review" notes.
• Use the video to review vocabulary
  and structures.

ETAPA 2

Now you can...

• tell where things
  are located.

To review

• location words,
  see p. 414.

Now you can...

• point out specific
  people and things.

To review

• ordinal numbers,
  see p. 418.

OBJECTIVES
• Point out specific people
  and things
• Tell where things are
  located
• Talk about the past

En uso

REPASO Y MÁS COMUNICACIÓN

ACTIVIDAD 1 En el campo

Imagínate que estás en el campo. ¿Qué ves? *(Hint: Tell what you see in the country.)*

modelo

dentro del corral, con los cerdos
*El ganadero está **dentro del corral, con los cerdos.***

1. debajo del árbol
2. arriba, con las llamas
3. encima de la cerca
4. abajo
5. fuera de su casa
6. dentro del corral, con el ganadero

ACTIVIDAD 2 ¿En qué carro?

Estas personas participaron en una carrera. ¿En qué carro manejó cada uno? *(Hint: Say who drove what car in the race.)*

modelo

Campos: 4
***Campos** manejó el cuarto carro.*

1. Molina: 2
2. Anaya: 7
3. Valencia: 9
4. Ibarra: 1
5. Quintana: 5
6. Blanco: 10
7. Rojas: 8
8. Espinoza: 3
9. Santana: 6

424   cuatrocientos veinticuatro
Unidad 6

Classroom Community

Paired Activity Have students sketch a farm scene on a piece of paper. Then have them work in pairs. Each student describes his/her scene to the partner, who attempts to draw it. Students then compare drawings.

Group Activity Have students work in groups of 5 to prepare and present a skit that takes place at the market in Otavalo. One student will be the narrator, first telling what happened. Then the other 4 students play the roles of Patricia, Miguel, Bárbara, and Julio and act out the skit.

Now you can...
• point out specific people and things.

To review
• demonstratives, see p. 416.

ACTIVIDAD 3 ¿Quiénes son?

Hay una fiesta de disfraces hoy. ¿Quiénes son estas personas?
(Hint: Identify the people at the costume party.)

modelo

maestra   Esa mujer es **maestra.**

1. policías
2. fotógrafa
3. bomberos
4. periodista
5. cartero
6. taxista
7. mujeres de negocios
8. doctor

Now you can...
• talk about the past.

To review
• irregular preterite verbs, see p. 419.

ACTIVIDAD 4 Un día especial

Patricia se encuentra con una amiga en Otavalo. Completa lo que dice con la forma correcta de los verbos **decir, estar, tener** o **venir.** *(Hint: Complete with the preterite of the correct verb.)*

Hoy Miguel y yo __1__ en el campo toda la mañana. Yo __2__ tiempo de hacer algunas entrevistas para mi proyecto. Los parientes de Miguel me __3__ muchas cosas interesantes sobre la vida en el campo. El tío Julio también me __4__ algunas cosas cómicas sobre Miguel. Al final de la entrevista con Bárbara, ella me __5__ un regalo: este saco bonito. Después de la segunda entrevista, el tío Julio y su esposa nos __6__ de comer. Luego, nosotros __7__ aquí a Otavalo.

cuatrocientos veinticinco
Etapa 2   425

ACTIVIDAD 1 **Answers**

1. Las gallinas están debajo del árbol.
2. El pastor está arriba, con las llamas.
3. El gallo está encima de la cerca.
4. Las vacas están abajo.
5. El perro está fuera de su casa.
6. Los cerdos están dentro del corral, con el ganadero.

ACTIVIDAD 2 **Answers**

1. Molina manejó el segundo carro.
2. Anaya manejó el séptimo carro.
3. Valencia manejó el noveno carro.
4. Ibarra manejó el primer carro.
5. Quintana manejó el quinto carro.
6. Blanco manejó el décimo carro.
7. Rojas manejó el octavo carro.
8. Espinoza manejó el tercer carro.
9. Santana manejó el sexto carro.

ACTIVIDAD 3 **Answers**

1. Estas mujeres son policías.
2. Aquella mujer es fotógrafa.
3. Esos hombres son bomberos.
4. Este hombre es periodista.
5. Aquel hombre es cartero.
6. Este hombre es taxista.
7. Aquellas mujeres son mujeres de negocios.
8. Ese hombre es doctor.

ACTIVIDAD 4 **Answers**

1. estuvimos
2. tuve
3. dijeron
4. dijo
5. dio
6. dieron
7. vinimos

Teaching All Students

Extra Help Review vocabulary and ordinal numbers by having students draw and cut out animals you list on the board. Then tell them the order in which to line up the animals on their desks. For example: **Pon el cerdo primero. El caballo es segundo,** etc.

Multiple Intelligences

Logical/Mathematical Have students bring in actual statistics from a recent sports competition and tell who finished first, second, etc.

Block Schedule

Change of Pace Have students act out the general scene in **Actividad 3** in groups of 8–9. One student plays a TV commentator, introduces the various professionals, and asks each one a few questions. You may wish to videotape the activity. (For additional activities, see **Block Scheduling Copymasters.**)

UNIDAD 6 Etapa 2
Review

Teaching Resource Options

Print

Unit 6 Resource Book
  Cooperative Quizzes, pp. 84–85
  Etapa Exam, Forms A and B,
    pp. 86–95
  Para hispanohablantes Etapa Exam,
    pp. 96–100
  Portfolio Assessment, pp. 101–102
  Multiple Choice Test Questions,
    pp. 170–178

Audiovisual

OHT 194 (Quick Start)
Audio Program Testing Cassette T2 /
  CD T2

Technology

Electronic Teacher Tools/Test
  Generator
www.mcdougallittell.com

ACTIVIDAD 5

Rubric: Speaking

Criteria	Scale	
Sentence structure	1 2 3	A = 11–12 pts.
Vocabulary use	1 2 3	B = 9–10 pts.
Originality	1 2 3	C = 7–8 pts.
Fluency	1 2 3	D = 4–6 pts.
		F = < 4 pts.

ACTIVIDAD 6 Answers will vary.

ACTIVIDAD 7 En tu propia voz

Rubric: Writing

Criteria	Scale	
Vocabulary use	1 2 3 4 5	A = 14–15 pts.
Accuracy	1 2 3 4 5	B = 12–13 pts.
Creativity, appearance	1 2 3 4 5	C = 10–11 pts.
		D = 8–9 pts.
		F = < 8 pts.

Teaching Note: En tu propia voz

Suggest that students first brainstorm a list of events, then make a list of the months of the year. This way they can implement the writing strategy "Organize information chronologically and by category" by putting each event next to the appropriate month.

ACTIVIDAD 5  ¿Y aquel caballo?

PARA CONVERSAR

STRATEGY: SPEAKING

Use words that direct others' attention You now have many ways to indicate one person, animal, or object among several. Remember to use them all.

- Indicate location (**al lado de,** etc.).
- Indicate order (**el segundo, el último**).
- Indicate distance (**este, ese, aquel**).

Imagínate que tienes dos mil dólares para comprar animales de la granja de un(a) ganadero(a). Regatea para recibir el mejor precio. *(Hint: Bargain for farm animals.)*

modelo

Tú: *¿Cuánto cuesta aquella vaca?*

Ganadero(a): *Aquélla es muy buena. Da mucha leche. Cuesta mil dólares.*

Tú: *¡Es demasiado! Le puedo ofrecer ochocientos.*

Ganadero(a): *No puedo vender aquélla por menos de novecientos, pero le dejo esta vaca más pequeña en setecientos.*

Tú: *Está bien. ¿Y ese cerdo que está en el corral?…*

ACTIVIDAD 6 ¿Dónde está?

Tus amigos buscan algo en la clase. Sólo tú sabes qué es y dónde está. Contesta sus preguntas. *(Hint: Classmates ask questions to find and identify objects.)*

modelo

Estudiante 1: *¿Está encima del escritorio de la maestra?*

Tú: *No, no está encima del escritorio de la maestra.*

Estudiante 2: *¿Está dentro de tu mochila?*

Tú: *Sí, está dentro de mi mochila.*

Estudiante 2: *¿Es tu libro de inglés?*

Tú: *Sí, es mi libro de inglés.*

ACTIVIDAD 7 *En tu propia voz*

ESCRITURA Haz una lista de diez cosas que pasaron en la escuela este año. Pon los sucesos en orden cronológico y escribe oraciones explicando cada uno. *(Hint: List ten things that happened at school this past year in chronological order.)*

modelo

Primero, las clases comenzaron en agosto y todos los estudiantes vinieron a la escuela. Segundo, tuvimos que aprender los nombres de los estudiantes en español durante la primera semana de clases. Tercero, en octubre…

Las ciencias Choose an animal whose name you've learned, such as the **llama,** or find out the Spanish name for another animal that is found in Ecuador. (**Vicuñas** and **alpacas** are close relatives of the **llama.**) Do some research on the animal. Draw a picture of it and write a short paragraph that answers the questions in the chart.

¿Cómo es el animal?
¿De qué color(es) es?
¿Dónde vive?
¿Qué come?
¿Es útil para la gente? ¿Para qué?

Classroom Community

Paired Activity Have partners exchange papers for Actividad 7. Ask them to write comments and suggestions for changes on a separate sheet of paper. Then have students review the comments and do a second draft of their paper.

Game Actividad 6 can be played as a whole class game. The student who is "it" writes the name of the object on a piece of paper and shows it to the teacher. Then the game begins. Emphasize that students can only ask yes/no questions and must use complete questions and answers.

En resumen
REPASO DE VOCABULARIO

POINTING OUT SPECIFIC PEOPLE AND THINGS

Indicating Which One

aquel(la)	that (over there)
aquél(la)	that one (over there)
aquello	that (over there)
ese(a)	that
ése(a)	that one
eso	that
este(a)	this
éste(a)	this one
esto	this

Ordinal Numbers

primero(a)	first
segundo(a)	second
tercero(a)	third
cuarto(a)	fourth
quinto(a)	fifth
sexto(a)	sixth
séptimo(a)	seventh
octavo(a)	eighth
noveno(a)	ninth
décimo(a)	tenth

People

el (la) artesano(a)	artisan
el (la) ganadero(a)	farmer
el (la) pastor(a)	shepherd(ess)

At the Farm

el caballo	horse
la cerca	fence
el cerdo	pig
el corral	corral, pen
la gallina	hen
el gallo	rooster
la granja	farm
la llama	llama
el toro	bull
la vaca	cow

TELLING WHERE THINGS ARE LOCATED

abajo	down
arriba	up
debajo (de)	underneath, under
dentro (de)	inside (of)
encima (de)	on top (of)
fuera (de)	outside (of)

OTHER WORDS AND PHRASES

el campo	countryside, country
darle(s) de comer	to feed
la lana	wool
el taller	workshop
las tijeras	scissors
último(a)	last

Juego

¿En qué orden terminaron la carrera?

cuatrocientos veintisiete
Etapa 2 427

Interdisciplinary Connection
Science Have students do research on the potato, a staple of the Ecuadorian diet. They should first write appropriate variations of the 5 questions in the **Conexiones.** The research should provide answers to these questions, as well as the nutritional value of the potato.

Quick Start Review
♻ Etapa vocabulary
Use OHT 194 or write on the board: Choose 5 new vocabulary words from this **Etapa** and write a short paragraph using the words.
Answers will vary.

Teaching Suggestions
Vocabulary Review
Divide the class into groups of 3–4. See how many sentences students can make using 3 vocabulary words per sentence.

Juego
Answers
1. El cerdo llegó primero.
2. La llama llegó segunda.
3. La vaca llegó tercera.

Block Schedule
Variety Prepare ahead: Cut out pictures from magazines, trying to find several with farm animals in them. You should have enough pictures so that each group in class has 5 pictures. Divide the class into groups of 4. Give each group 5 pictures. Students must try to tie all the pictures together in a story. They should paste the pictures on a posterboard and present the visual and the story to the class.

Teaching All Students

Extra Help Quiz students on vocabulary. For "Ordinal Numbers," hold up 1 finger, 2 fingers, etc. and ask for the ordinal numbers. For "People" and "At the Farm," show pictures or toy animals. For "Telling Where Things Are Located," point to objects in the classroom.

Multiple Intelligences
Musical/Rhythmic Have students make up a farm song, using the tune to "Old MacDonald."

Planning Guide CLASSROOM MANAGEMENT

OBJECTIVES

Communication
- Talk about the present and future *pp. 430–431*
- Give instructions to someone *pp. 431, 432–433*
- Discuss the past *pp. 431, 432–433, 444–445, 446–447*

Grammar
- Review: Present progressive and **ir a...** *pp. 436–438*
- Review: Affirmative **tú** commands *pp. 438–439*
- Review: Preterite tense *pp. 439–443*

Pronunciation
- Pronunciation of **x** *p. 443*
- Dictation *TE p. 443*

Culture
- Regional vocabulary *pp. 434, 445*
- The Galápagos Islands *p. 438*
- The habitats of Ecuador *p. 442*
- The sites of Ecuador *pp. 444–445*
- New World foods *pp. 446–447*

♻ Recycling
- Text vocabulary *p. 434*
- Activities *p. 435*
- Family, daily routine, preferences *p. 435*
- Professions, the farm *p. 436*

STRATEGIES

Listening Strategies
- Listen and take notes *p. 432*

Speaking Strategies
- Use storytelling techniques *p. 437*
- Rely on the basics *p. 450*

Reading Strategies
- Reflect on journal writing *p. 444*
- Combine strategies *TE p. 447*

Writing Strategies
- Tell who, what, where, when, why, and how *TE p. 450*
- Support a general statement with informative details *p. 452*

Connecting Cultures Strategies
- Recognize variations in vocabulary *pp. 434, 445*
- Getting to know Ecuador *pp. 438, 442, 444–445*
- Compare places *TE p. 445*
- Identify international foods *p. 446*
- Connect and compare what you know about foods that are regularly part of your diet to help you learn about foods from other countries *pp. 446–447, 450*

PROGRAM RESOURCES

 Print

- *Más práctica* Workbook PE *pp. 145–152*
- Block Scheduling Copymasters *pp. 145–152*
- Unit 6 Resource Book
  Más práctica Workbook TE *pp. 103–110*
  Para hispanohablantes Workbook TE *pp. 111–118*
- Information Gap Activities *pp. 119–122*
- Family Involvement *pp. 123–124*
- Video Activities *pp. 125–127*
- Videoscript *pp. 128–130*
- Audioscript *pp. 131–134*
- Assessment Program, Unit 6 Etapa 3 *pp. 135–186*
- Answer Keys *pp. 187–202*

 Audiovisual

- Audio Program Cassettes 18A, 18B / CD 18
- *Canciones* Cassette / CD
- Video Program Videotape 6 / Videodisc 3B
- Overhead Transparencies M1–M5; GO1–GO5; 174, 195–204

 Technology

- Electronic Teacher Tools/Test Generator
- *Intrigas y aventuras* CD-ROM, Disc 1
- www.mcdougallittell.com

 Assessment Program Options

- Cooperative Quizzes (Unit 6 Resource Book)
- Etapa Exam Forms A and B (Unit 6 Resource Book)
- *Para hispanohablantes* Etapa Exam (Unit 6 Resource Book)
- Portfolio Assessment (Unit 6 Resource Book)
- Unit 6 Comprehensive Test (Unit 6 Resource Book)
- *Para hispanohablantes* Unit 6 Comprehensive Test (Unit 6 Resource Book)
- Final Test (Unit 6 Resource Book)
- Multiple Choice Test Questions (Unit 6 Resource Book)
- Audio Program Testing Cassette T2 / CD T2
- Electronic Teacher Tools/Test Generator

Native Speakers

- *Para hispanohablantes* Workbook PE, *pp. 145–152*
- *Para hispanohablantes* Workbook TE (Unit 6 Resource Book)
- *Para hispanohablantes* Etapa Exam (Unit 6 Resource Book)
- *Para hispanohablantes* Unit 6 Comprehensive Test (Unit 6 Resource Book)
- Audio *Para hispanohablantes* Cassettes 18A, 18B, T2 / CD 18, T2
- Audioscript *Para hispanohablantes* (Unit 6 Resource Book)

Patricia   **Miguel**

Student Text Listening Activity Scripts

Videoscript: Diálogo *pages 432–433*

• Videotape 6 • Videodisc 3B

Search Chapter 8, Play to 9
U6E3 • En vivo (Dialog)

• Use the videoscript with **Actividades 1, 2** *page 434*

Miguel: ¿Y estás feliz con tus entrevistas?
Patricia: Sí, estoy muy feliz. Hice entrevistas con un arquitecto, la gerente de un banco, un hombre de negocios, un taxista y también con tu tío Julio y Bárbara.
Miguel: ¿Cuál fue la mejor entrevista?
Patricia: No sé... Creo que fue la entrevista con tu tío Julio.
Miguel: ¿Y por qué? ¿Porque te habló de la vida en una granja?
Patricia: No, porque me dijo qué hiciste tú la primera vez que estuviste en la granja.
Miguel: ¡Patricia!... ¿Y aprendiste algo de tus entrevistas?
Patricia: Sí, mucho. Sobre todo aprendí que la gente que vive en el campo no es tan diferente de la gente que vive en la ciudad. Es sólo el estilo de vida que es diferente. ¡A cada pájaro le gusta su nido! Pero aprendí algo mucho más importante también...
Miguel: ¿Sí? Dime.
Patricia: Aprendí que no tienes ni idea de lo que hay que hacer en una granja. Abriste la cerca del corral! ¡Mira, Miguel! ¡Es un mercado fenomenal! Voy a comprarle un regalo a mi hermana. Su cumpleaños es el veintidós de este mes.
Miguel: Cómprale una bolsa o un artículo de cuero. La artesanía de Otavalo es excelente.
Patricia: No sé si tengo suficiente dinero... a ver... tengo 40 mil sucres en efectivo. ¿Crees que puedo regatear aquí?
Miguel: ¡Claro que sí! Es un mercado, ¿no? ¡Ven! ¿Cuándo mandas tu proyecto a la revista?
Patricia: Después del fin de semana. Todavía tengo que escribir mucho.
Miguel: Hazme un favor... ¿Puedo leerlo antes?
Patricia: ¿Por qué?
Miguel: ¿Por qué? ¡Porque creo que va a salir muy bien y lo quiero ver!
Patricia: ¿Crees que va a salir bien? Gracias, Miguel. Eres un buen amigo.
Miguel: Y también...
Patricia: ¿Sí?
Miguel: ¡Quiero ver si escribiste algo de mi experiencia con la cerca y el caballo!
Patricia: Hice todo lo posible. Trabajé mucho. Espero tener buena suerte.

Videoscript: Epílogo *page 428 (optional, p. 443)*

• Videotape 6 • Videodisc 3B

Search Chapter 9, Play to 10
Epilogue

¡Por fin! Recibí mi copia de *Onda Internacional.* Vamos a ver quiénes ganaron el concurso... a ver... aquí. Ah, yo no gané. Qué lástima. ¿Pero quieren saber ustedes quiénes ganaron? ¡Hay dos ganadores! Un muchacho... y una muchacha. El muchacho se llama Francisco García Flores... y ¡es de Miami, Florida! Francisco va a viajar a Puerto Rico y a Costa Rica. La muchacha se llama Isabel Palacios... ¡y es de la Ciudad de México! Isabel va a viajar a España y a Ecuador. ¡Felicidades, Francisco e Isabel!

Actividad 4 — Las actividades *page 435*

1. Alma escribe.
2. Ricardo juega al baloncesto.
3. Isabel lee una revista.
4. Iván cocina algo riquísimo.
5. Diana e Ignacio alquilan un video.
6. Patricia hace una entrevista.
7. Luis se peina.
8. Ignacio y Diana van de compras.
9. Rosa, Sofía y Carlos piden la comida.
10. Luis y Carmen limpian la casa.

Actividad 17 — Un buen fin de semana *page 442*

María: ¡Hola, Rosa! ¿Qué hiciste el fin de semana?
Rosa: Fui al campo para visitar a mis abuelos.
María: ¿Cómo fue?
Rosa: Pues, fenomenal. Me gusta mucho ir al campo.
María: ¿Qué hiciste?
Rosa: Pues, llegué a la granja el viernes a las ocho y media. Cenamos a las nueve.
María: ¿Y el sábado?
Rosa: El sábado me levanté a las siete. Después de desayunar, ayudé a mi abuelo a darles de comer a las gallinas. ¡Qué cómicas fueron las gallinas y qué ruido hicieron!
María: Y por la tarde, ¿qué hiciste?
Rosa: Fui al mercado con mi prima.
María: ¿Viste cosas interesantes?
Rosa: Sí, vi un saco que me gustó mucho.
María: ¿Lo compraste?
Rosa: No. Me encontré con una amiga y salimos a tomar un refresco.
María: ¡Qué divertido! ¿Y qué hicieron esa noche?
Rosa: No hicimos nada especial. Vi la televisión, leí una revista y me acosté temprano. Fue un fin de semana muy tranquilo.
María: ¿Cuándo vas a volver?
Rosa: Mi madre dijo que vamos a volver en dos semanas.
María: ¿Puedo ir con ustedes?
Rosa: ¡Claro que sí!

Quick Start Review Answers
p. 448 Hacer, ir
Answers will vary.
Answers could include:
<u>hacer</u>
1. Ayer hizo muchos quehaceres.
2. Patricia hace entrevistas.
3. Vamos a hacer un viaje en Ecuador.
<u>ir</u>
1. Anoche fui al cine.
2. Voy a la biblioteca a las cuatro.
3. Vamos a poner la mesa.

Sample Lesson Plan - 50 Minute Schedule

DAY 1

Etapa Opener
- Quick Start Review (TE, p. 428) **5 MIN.**
- Anticipate/Activate prior knowledge: Have students look at the *Etapa* Opener and answer the questions. **5 MIN.**

En contexto: Vocabulario
- Quick Start Review (TE, p. 430) **5 MIN.**
- Have students use context and pictures to review text vocabulary. Use the Situational OHTs for additional practice. **10 MIN.**

En vivo: Diálogo
- Quick Start Review (TE, p. 432) **5 MIN.**
- Review the Listening Strategy, p. 432. Play audio or show video for the dialog, pp. 432–433. **10 MIN.**
- Replay twice. Read aloud, having students take the roles of the characters. **10 MIN.**

Homework Option:
- Video Activities, Unit 6 Resource Book, pp. 125–127.

DAY 2

En acción: Vocabulario y gramática
- Check homework. **5 MIN.**
- Quick Start Review (TE, p. 434) **5 MIN.**
- Have students open to *En contexto*, pp. 430–431, for reference. Use OHT 195 and 196 to review. **5 MIN.**
- Play the audio; have students do *Actividades* 1 and 2 orally. **5 MIN.**
- Do *Actividad* 3 orally. **5 MIN.**
- Play the audio; have students do *Actividad* 4. **5 MIN.**
- Have students complete *Actividad* 5 in pairs and *Actividad* 6 orally. **10 MIN.**
- Quick Start Review (TE, p. 436) **5 MIN.**
- Present *Repaso:* Review: Present Progressive and *ir a* + infinitive, p. 436. **10 MIN.**

Homework Option:
- Have students complete *Actividad* 6 in writing and write 2 sentences for each of the following: simple present, present progressive, *ir a* + infinitive.

DAY 3

En acción (cont.)
- Check homework. **5 MIN.**
- Have students do *Actividades* 7 and 8 orally. **10 MIN.**
- Present the Speaking Strategy, p. 437. Then have students do *Actividad* 9 in pairs. Call on a few pairs to present their answers. **10 MIN.**
- Have students do *Actividad* 10 in writing. Then have them exchange papers for peer correction. **10 MIN.**
- Quick Start Review (TE, p. 438) **5 MIN.**
- Present *Repaso:* Review: Affirmative *tú* Commands, p. 438. **10 MIN.**
- Have students do *Actividad* 11 orally. **5 MIN.**

Homework Option:
- Have students complete *Actividades* 7, 8, and 11 in writing. *Más práctica* Workbook, pp. 149–150. *Para hispanohablantes* Workbook, pp. 147–148.

DAY 4

En acción (cont.)
- Check homework. **5 MIN.**
- Have students do *Actividad* 12 in pairs. **5 MIN.**
- Have students do *Actividad* 13 in writing. Expand using Information Gap Activities, Unit 6 Resource Book, p. 119; *Más comunicación*, p. R18. **15 MIN.**
- Quick Start Review (TE, p. 439) **5 MIN.**
- Present *Repaso:* Review: Regular Preterite, p. 439. **10 MIN.**
- Have students read and complete *Actividad* 14 in writing. Go over answers orally. **5 MIN.**
- Have students do the oral part of *Actividad* 15 in groups. **5 MIN.**
- Do *Actividad* 16 orally. **5 MIN.**

Homework Option:
- Have students complete the *Resumen* for *Actividad* 15 in writing. *Más práctica* Workbook, p. 151. *Para hispanohablantes* Workbook, p. 149.

DAY 5

En acción (cont.)
- Check homework. **5 MIN.**
- Quick Start Review (TE, p. 441) **5 MIN.**
- Present *Repaso:* Review: Irregular Preterite, p. 441. **5 MIN.**
- Play the audio; do *Actividad* 17. **5 MIN.**
- Have students do *Actividad* 18 in writing and *Actividad* 19 in pairs. **10 MIN.**
- Do *Actividad* 20 orally. Expand using Information Gap Activities, Unit 6 Resource Book, pp. 120–121; *Más comunicación*, p. R18. **15 MIN.**
- Do *Actividad* 21 orally. **5 MIN.**

Pronunciación
- Play the audio; practice the *refrán*. **5 MIN.**

Homework Option:
- *Más práctica* Workbook, p. 152. *Para hispanohablantes* Workbook, p. 150.

DAY 6

En voces: Lectura
- Check homework. **5 MIN.**
- Quick Start Review (TE, p. 444) **5 MIN.**
- Present the Reading Strategy, p. 444. Have volunteers read the selection aloud and answer the questions, p. 445. **15 MIN.**

En colores: Cultura y comparaciones
- Quick Start Review (TE, p. 446) **5 MIN.**
- Discuss the Connecting Cultures Strategy, p. 446. Have volunteers read the selection aloud and answer the questions, p. 447. **15 MIN.**

En uso: Repaso y más comunicación
- Play the Video Epilogue. **5 MIN.**
- Review *En uso* for *Etapa* 3 Exam. **5 MIN.**

Homework Option:
- Prepare *En uso Actividades* 1–4. Review for *Etapa* 3 Exam.

DAY 7

En uso (cont.)
- Check homework. **5 MIN.**
- Quick Start Review (TE, p. 448) **5 MIN.**
- Review *Actividades* 1–4 orally. **5 MIN.**
- Present the Speaking Strategy, p. 450. Do *Actividad* 5 in pairs and *Actividad* 6 in groups. **10 MIN.**

Etapa 3 Exam
- Complete *Etapa* 3 Exam. **20 MIN.**

En tu propia voz: Escritura
- Do *Actividad* 7 in writing. **5 MIN.**

Conexiones
- Present *La salud*, p. 450. **5 MIN.**

Homework Option:
- Review for Unit 6 Comprehensive Test.

DAY 8

En resumen: Ya sabes
- Quick Start Review (TE, p. 451) **5 MIN.**

En tu propia voz: Escritura
- Present the Writing Strategy, p. 452. Do the writing activity, pp. 452–453. **10 MIN.**

Unit 6 Comprehensive Test
- Review grammar questions, etc. as necessary. **5 MIN.**
- Complete Unit 6 Comprehensive Test. **30 MIN.**

Ampliación
- Optional: Use a suggested project, game, or activity. (TE, pp. 383A–383B) **15 MIN.**

Homework Option:
- Have students complete the report outlined in *Conexiones*. Review for Final Test.

Sample Lesson Plan - Block Schedule (90 minutes)

DAY 1

Etapa Opener
- Quick Start Review (TE, p. 428) 5 MIN.
- Anticipate/Activate prior knowledge: Have students look at the *Etapa* Opener and answer the questions. 5 MIN.
- Use Block Scheduling Copymasters. 10 MIN.

En contexto: Vocabulario
- Quick Start Review (TE, p. 430) 5 MIN.
- Have students use context and pictures to review text vocabulary. In pairs, have students answer the questions, p. 431. Use the Situational OHTs for additional practice. 10 MIN.

En vivo: Diálogo
- Quick Start Review (TE, p. 432) 5 MIN.
- Review the Listening Strategy, p. 432. Play audio or show video for the dialog, pp. 432–433. 10 MIN.
- Replay twice. Read aloud, having students take the roles of the characters. 10 MIN.

En acción: Vocabulario y gramática
- Quick Start Review (TE, p. 434) 5 MIN.
- Have students open to *En contexto,* pp. 430–431, for reference. Use OHT 195 and 196 to review. 5 MIN.
- Play the audio; have students do *Actividades* 1 and 2 orally. 10 MIN.
- Do *Actividad* 3 orally. 5 MIN.
- Play the audio; have students do *Actividad* 4. 5 MIN.

Homework Option:
- Video Activities, Unit 6 Resource Book, pp. 125–127.

DAY 2

En acción (cont.)
- Check homework. 5 MIN.
- Have students complete *Actividad* 5 in pairs and *Actividad* 6 orally. 10 MIN.
- Quick Start Review (TE, p. 436) 5 MIN.
- Present *Repaso:* Review: Present Progressive and *ir a* + infinitive, p. 436. 10 MIN.
- Have students do *Actividades* 7 and 8 orally. 10 MIN.
- Present the Speaking Strategy, p. 437. Then have students do *Actividad* 9 in pairs. Call on a few pairs to present their answers. 10 MIN.
- Have students do *Actividad* 10 in writing. Then have them exchange papers for peer correction. 15 MIN.
- Quick Start Review (TE, p. 438) 5 MIN.
- Present *Repaso:* Review: Affirmative *tú* Commands, p. 438. 10 MIN.
- Have students do *Actividad* 11 orally. 5 MIN.
- Have students do *Actividad* 12 in pairs. 5 MIN.

Homework Option:
- Have students complete *Actividades* 6, 7, 8, and 11 in writing. *Más práctica* Workbook, pp. 149–150. *Para hispanohablantes* Workbook, pp. 147–148.

DAY 3

En acción (cont.)
- Check homework. 5 MIN.
- Have students do *Actividad* 13 in writing. Expand using Information Gap Activities, Unit 6 Resource Book, p. 119; *Más comunicación,* p. R18. 15 MIN.
- Quick Start Review (TE, p. 439) 5 MIN.
- Present *Repaso:* Review: Regular Preterite, p. 439. 5 MIN.
- Have students read and complete *Actividad* 14 in writing. Go over answers orally. 5 MIN.
- Have students do *Actividad* 15 in groups. 5 MIN.
- Do *Actividad* 16 orally. 5 MIN.
- Quick Start Review (TE, p. 441) 5 MIN.
- Present *Repaso:* Review: Irregular Preterite, p. 441. 5 MIN.
- Play the audio; do *Actividad* 17. 5 MIN.
- Have students do *Actividad* 18 in writing and *Actividad* 19 in pairs. 10 MIN.
- Do *Actividad* 20 orally. Expand using Information Gap Activities, Unit 6 Resource Book, pp. 120–121; *Más comunicación,* p. R18. 15 MIN.
- Do *Actividad* 21 orally. 5 MIN.

Homework Option:
- Have students complete *Actividad* 16 in writing. *Más práctica* Workbook, pp. 151–152. *Para hispanohablantes* Workbook, pp. 149–150.

DAY 4

Pronunciación
- Check homework. 5 MIN.
- Play the audio; practice the *refrán.* 5 MIN.

En voces: Lectura
- Quick Start Review (TE, p. 444) 5 MIN.
- Present the Reading Strategy, p. 444. Have volunteers read the selection aloud and answer the questions, p. 445. 15 MIN.

En colores: Cultura y comparaciones
- Quick Start Review (TE, p. 446) 5 MIN.
- Discuss the Connecting Cultures Strategy, p. 446. Have volunteers read the selection aloud and answer the questions, p. 447. 15 MIN.

En uso: Repaso y más comunicación
- Play the Video Epilogue. 5 MIN.
- Quick Start Review (TE, p. 448) 5 MIN.
- Do *Actividades* 1–4 orally. 10 MIN.
- Present the Speaking Strategy, p. 450. Do *Actividad* 5 in pairs and *Actividad* 6 in groups. 10 MIN.
- Do *Actividad* 7 in writing. 10 MIN.

Homework Option:
- Review for *Etapa* 3 Exam.

DAY 5

En resumen: Ya sabes
- Quick Start Review (TE, p. 451) 5 MIN.
- Review grammar questions, etc. as necessary. 5 MIN.
- Complete *Etapa* 3 Exam. 20 MIN.

Conexiones
- Present *La salud,* p. 450. 5 MIN.

Unit 6 Comprehensive Test
- Review grammar questions, etc. as necessary. 5 MIN.
- Complete Unit 6 Comprehensive Test. 30 MIN.

En tu propia voz: Escritura
- Present the Writing Strategy, p. 452. Do the writing activity, pp. 452–453. 20 MIN.

Ampliación
- Optional: Use a suggested project, game, or activity. (TE, pp. 383A–383B) 15 MIN.

Homework Option:
- Have students complete the report outlined in *Conexiones.* Review for Final Test.

▼ Patricia quiere comprarle un regalo a su hermana en el mercado.

Etapa Theme
Remembering what you have learned and summing up the magazine contest

Grammar Objectives
- Reviewing the present progressive and **ir a...**
- Reviewing affirmative **tú** commands
- Reviewing the preterite tense

Teaching Resource Options
Print
Block Scheduling Copymasters

Audiovisual
OHT 174, 201 (Quick Start)

Quick Start Review
♻ Otavalo
Use OHT 201 or write on board:
Write at least 3 things you know about Otavalo, Ecuador:

Answers
Answers will vary. Answers could include:
Queda en Ecuador, entre Quito y la frontera con Colombia.
La gente se llama los otavaleños.
Los sábados hay un mercado tradicional.
Puedes visitar el Instituto Otavaleño de Antropología.
En la Plaza Bolívar hay una estatua del general inca Rumiñahui.

Teaching Suggestions
Previewing the Etapa
- Ask students to study the picture on pp. 428–429 (1 min.).
- Close books; ask students to share at least 3 things they remember.
- Reopen books and look at the picture again. Have students describe the people and the setting.
- Use the **¿Qué ves?** questions to focus the discussion.

UNIDAD 6

ETAPA
3

¡A ganar el concurso!

- **Talk about the present and future**
- **Give instructions to someone**
- **Discuss the past**

¿Qué ves?
Mira la foto del mercado de Otavalo.
1. ¿Las vendedoras sólo venden ropa?
2. ¿Hace mucho calor o no? ¿Cómo lo sabes?
3. ¿De qué color es la blusa tradicional de las mujeres de Otavalo?
4. ¿Para qué es la carta que Patricia escribió?

428

Patricia López Carrera
Calle Oriente 253 y P. Fermín Cevallos
Quito

Revista Onda Internacional
Concurso latino
Apartado 126
Quito

Classroom Management

Planning Ahead Plan to spend 5 minutes every day reviewing verb forms. On a bulletin board, place a large chart with 4 columns: present progressive, affirmative **tú** commands, and preterite. Give the class a few verbs a day. Have student volunteers write in the correct forms on the chart, and have others check and correct them. Be sure that the verbs are regular in the preterite or among the irregular ones students have learned.

Peer Review/Peer Teaching Assign groups to spend a few minutes every class reviewing cultural issues they have studied throughout the year. In their groups, students should look at the **Etapa** openers and compare the scenes to scenes they might see in their community.

429

Cross Cultural Connections

Ask students to compare the address, the stamps, and the handwriting on Patricia's envelope to one they would see in the U.S.

Culture Highlights

● **LOS TEJIDOS DE OTAVALO** Otavalo is renowned for its textiles. The market in Otavalo, where this photo was taken, is filled with beautiful weavings by the skilled people from Otavalo.

● **EL SOMBRERO DE PAJA TOQUILLA** Otavalo is also known for other craft specialties, including woodcarving, leatherworking, and the so-called "Panama" hats. The name comes from the fact that workers on the Panama Canal wore them. A Panama hat is a natural-colored, hand-woven straw hat made from the fibers of the jipijapa plant (named after Jipijapa, a city in western Ecuador). Panama hats were once Ecuador's biggest export item and have maintained their reputation as a fashion item throughout the years.

Supplementary Vocabulary

un sello	stamp
un sobre	envelope
una muñeca	doll
los tejidos	textiles
un tapiz	tapestry
un tapete	rug
un poncho	poncho

Block Schedule

Expansion Have students count off from 1 to 4. That number represents the ¿Qué ves? question that they are responsible for. They must answer the question and expand on it for 3–4 sentences more by adding more description or explanation. They can also add a personal comment. (For additional activities, see **Block Scheduling Copymasters**.)

Teaching All Students

Extra Help Have students work in pairs. One student names a color and the other student names something in the photo on pp. 428–429 that has that color.

Multiple Intelligences

Intrapersonal Have students pretend they are at a the market pictured on pp. 428–429. Have them write what they are going to buy for themselves, a friend, and a family member.

Teaching Resource Options

Print ✎

Unit 6 Resource Book
Video Activities, pp. 125–126
Videoscript, p. 128
Audioscript, p. 131
Audioscript *Para hispanohablantes*,
  p. 131

Audiovisual 📼

OHT M1–M5; 195, 196, 197, 197A, 198,
198A, 201 (Quick Start)
Audio Program Cassette 18A / CD 18
Audio *Para hispanohablantes*
Cassette 18A / CD 18
Video Program Videotape 6 /
Videodisc 3B

Search Chapter 7, Play to 8
U6E3 • En contexto (Vocabulary)

Canciones Cassette / CD

Technology 💻 CD-ROM

Intrigas y aventuras CD-ROM, Disc 1

🔔 Quick Start Review

♻ **Character descriptions**
Use OHT 201 or write on the board:
Write 1 true statement about 5 of the
main characters in this book:

**Alma, Francisco, Isabel, Ricardo,
Diana, Ignacio, Roberto, Carlos, Rosa,
Sofía, Luis, Mercedes, Miguel, Patricia**
Answers will vary.

Teaching Suggestions
Reviewing Vocabulary

• Have students look at pages 430–431.
Use OHT 195 and 196 and Audio
Cassette 18A / CD 18 to review the
vocabulary.
• Ask the Comprehension Questions in
order of yes/no (questions 1–3),
either/or (questions 4–6), and simple
word or phrase (questions 7–10).
Expand by adding similar questions.
• Use the TPR activity to reinforce the
meaning of individual words.
• Use the video vocabulary presentation
for review and reinforcement.

En contexto

🎧📺 VOCABULARIO ♻

Do you remember all that you have learned this year? You have learned to talk
about the present, the future, and the past, and to give instructions. Take a look
at these people and places for a quick review of what you have learned.

¡Hola! Aprendiste mucho este año.
¿Recuerdas todo lo que ves aquí?

MIAMI

 A Talk about the present
Alma: Arturo, te **presento** a
Francisco García. Él **es** mi vecino.
Arturo: Francisco, **es** un placer.
Francisco: Igualmente, Arturo.

Canadá
AMÉRICA
DEL NORTE
Estados Unidos
México
MIAMI
CIUDAD DE
MÉXICO
PUERTO RICO
OAXACA
QUITO
Ecuador
OCÉANO
PACÍFICO

CIUDAD DE MÉXICO

B Talk about the future
Isabel: ¡Voy a participar en el
concurso! Para conocer a los
mexicanos, hay que ir a una
plaza. La plaza es un poema.

Classroom Community

TPR Read each lettered section on pp. 430–431 aloud
while assigned "actors" act out what you are saying.

Group Activity Have students share successful
techniques for learning and remembering vocabulary.
Ask each group to present their best ideas to the class.

Learning Scenario Write names of cities and
countries on cards and put them in a small box. Have
students pull a card out of the box and pretend to be a
teenager from that region and tell the class about
themselves.

PUERTO RICO

OAXACA

BARCELONA

C Say what is happening

Ignacio: ¡Está lloviendo! ¡Y no tengo paraguas!

Roberto: Te estamos esperando, hombre.

D Give instructions

Carlos: Vas a llegar a un parque. **Cruza** el parque. Enfrente de la estatua está la calle Morelos.

Rosa: Muchas gracias…

E Discuss the past

Luis: ¡El día empezó con demasiados quehaceres!

Carmen: ¡Yo te ayudé, Luis!

Luis: Sí, Carmen, tú me ayudaste y Mercedes también me ayudó.

BARCELONA

QUITO

F Discuss the past

Miguel: ¿Cómo fueron las entrevistas?

Patricia: Excelente. Ya hice dos.

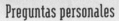

Preguntas personales

1. ¿Quién es tu mejor amigo? ¿amiga?
2. ¿Qué vas a hacer este fin de semana?
3. ¿Qué está pasando en tu clase?
4. Explica cómo llegar a tu casa.
5. ¿Qué hiciste este año?

cuatrocientos treinta y uno
Etapa 3
431

Comprehension Questions

1. ¿Son hermanos Alma y Francisco? (No.)
2. ¿Está Isabel en la plaza? (Sí.)
3. ¿Va a participar Isabel en el concurso? (Sí.)
4. En la foto C, ¿necesita Ignacio unas gafas de sol o un paraguas? (un paraguas)
5. ¿Está la calle Morelos enfrente de o detrás de la estatua? (enfrente)
6. ¿Quién ayudó a Luis con los quehaceres, Rosa o Carmen? (Carmen)
7. ¿Quién es Francisco? (el vecino de Alma)
8. En la foto C, ¿qué tiempo hace? (Está lloviendo.)
9. ¿Cómo empezó el día de Luis? (Empezó con demasiados quehaceres.)
10. ¿Cómo fueron las entrevistas de Patricia? (excelente)

Critical Thinking

Have students decide what should be included in a first-year English textbook used by students in Latin America or Spain.

Supplementary Vocabulary

el globo	globe
el atlas	atlas
la longitud	longitude
la latitud	latitude
un continente	continent

Block Schedule

Change of Pace Ask students to choose a commercial from TV and prepare a similar one in Spanish. Have them present their commercials to the class. Videotape the commercials and have students critique their performances on the basis of language accuracy, pronunciation, acting, and creativity.

Teaching All Students

Extra Help Use OHTs M1–M5 to review geographic areas. Have students point out the areas they have studied and cite a few interesting facts about each.

Native Speakers Have students include in their portfolios a statement in Spanish about where they see the most improvement in their language skills. Have them include a statement about their future goals for Spanish.

Multiple Intelligences

Musical/Rhythmic Devote a portion of class to music from around the Spanish-speaking world. Music samples are available on your **Canciones** Cassette or CD. Play a variety of pieces from many regions and have students identify the regions. Ask them which music was new to them this year and which is their favorite.

Teaching Resource Options

Print

Más práctica Workbook PE, pp. 145–148
Para hispanohablantes Workbook PE,
   pp. 145–146
Block Scheduling Copymasters
Unit 6 Resource Book
   Más práctica Workbook TE,
      pp. 103–106
   Para hispanohablantes Workbook
      TE, pp. 111–112
   Video Activities, pp. 125–126
   Videoscript, p. 129
   Audioscript, p. 131
   Audioscript *Para hispanohablantes*,
      p. 131

Audiovisual

OHT 199, 200, 201 (Quick Start)
Audio Program Cassette 18A / CD 18
Audio *Para hispanohablantes*
   Cassette 18A / CD 18
Video Program Videotape 6 / Videodisc
   3B

Search Chapter 8, Play to 9
U6E3 • En vivo (Dialog)

Technology

Intrigas y aventuras CD-ROM, Disc 1

🔔 Quick Start Review

♻ Miguel and Patricia

Use OHT 201 or write on the board:
Write 3 true statements about Miguel
and 3 true statements about Patricia:

Answers
Answers will vary. Answers could include:
Miguel vive en Quito, Ecuador.
Miguel tiene familia en el campo.
La primera vez que Miguel visitó a su tío Julio,
   fue al corral, abrió la cerca y el caballo se
   escapó.
Patricia decidió participar en el concurso.
Patricia les hizo entrevistas a una mujer de
   negocios y a un arquitecto.
Patricia visitó a Bárbara en su taller.

Gestures

Have volunteers mime the various scenes
in the **Diálogo,** trying to imitate the body
language of Miguel and Patricia. Ask them
to compare this body language to what
they might do in a similar situation.

En vivo

📻 DIÁLOGO

¡Vamos a Otavalo!

Patricia   Miguel

PARA ESCUCHAR • STRATEGY: LISTENING

Listen and take notes This conversation sums up Patricia's work
on her project. What does she think about her work? As you jot
down her ideas, listen for answers to *who? what? when? where?*
and *why?* Use your notes to make a summary statement about
Patricia's project.

1 ▶ **Miguel:** ¿Estás feliz con tus
entrevistas?
Patricia: Sí, estoy muy feliz. Hice
entrevistas con un arquitecto, la
gerente de un banco, y también
con tu tío Julio y Bárbara.

5 ▶ **Patricia:** Pero aprendí algo mucho
más importante también.
Miguel: ¿Sí? Dime.
Patricia: Aprendí que no tienes ni
idea de lo que hay que hacer en
una granja. ¡Abriste la cerca!

6 ▶ **Patricia:** ¡Mira, Miguel! ¡Es un mercado
fenomenal! Voy a comprarle un regalo a
mi hermana. Su cumpleaños es este mes.
Miguel: Cómprale una bolsa o un artículo
de cuero. La artesanía de Otavalo es
excelente.

7 ▶ **Patricia:** No sé si tengo suficiente
dinero... a ver... tengo 40 mil
sucres en efectivo. ¿Crees que
puedo regatear aquí?
Miguel: ¡Claro que sí! Es un
mercado, ¿no? ¡Ven!

432   cuatrocientos treinta y dos
Unidad 6

Classroom Community

Paired Activity Gives pairs of students a copy of
the Comprehension Questions (TE p. 433) and have
them collaborate on the answers. For questions 1–3,
students should supply the correct information for any
No answers.

Game Have students work in groups of 3 or 4. Each
student takes on the identity of a character from Units
1–6. They then describe themselves in 3–5 sentences,
without giving their names. The other students guess
the person's identity.

2 ▶ **Miguel:** ¿Cuál fue la mejor entrevista?
Patricia: No sé… Creo que fue la entrevista con tu tío Julio.
Miguel: ¿Y por qué? ¿Porque te habló de la vida en una granja?

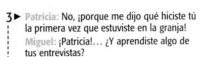

3 ▶ **Patricia:** No, ¡porque me dijo qué hiciste tú la primera vez que estuviste en la granja!
Miguel: ¡Patricia!… ¿Y aprendiste algo de tus entrevistas?

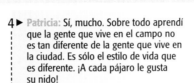

4 ▶ **Patricia:** Sí, mucho. Sobre todo aprendí que la gente que vive en el campo no es tan diferente de la gente que vive en la ciudad. Es sólo el estilo de vida que es diferente. ¡A cada pájaro le gusta su nido!

8 ▶ **Miguel:** ¿Cuándo mandas tu proyecto a la revista?
Patricia: Después del fin de semana. Todavía tengo que escribir mucho.

9 ▶ **Miguel:** Hazme un favor… ¿Puedo leerlo antes? ¡Creo que va a salir muy bien y lo quiero ver! Y también…
Patricia: ¿Sí?
Miguel: ¡Quiero ver si escribiste algo de mi experiencia con la cerca y el caballo!

10 ▶ **Patricia:** Hice todo lo posible. Trabajé mucho. Espero tener buena suerte.

cuatrocientos treinta y tres
Etapa 3   **433**

Teaching All Students

Extra Help Read various quotes from the **Diálogo** and have students identify who said each one.

Native Speakers Ask students to describe country markets and city markets in their home countries. Which are more extensive? What types of purchases does one make at each?

Multiple Intelligences

Kinesthetic Have students notice how close Miguel and Patricia are standing. Have pairs of students role play the characters and note whether or not they feel comfortable at the same distance. Have them experiment with speaking at various distances to see where they feel comfortable and why.

Teaching Suggestions
Presenting the Dialog

• Prepare students for listening by focusing on the dialog context. Have them tell you who the characters are, where they are coming from, where they are going, and why.

• Use the video, audio cassette, or CD to present the dialog. The expanded dialog on video offers additional listening practice opportunities.

Video Synopsis

• Patricia talks to Miguel about what she has learned while interviewing people in the city and the country. For a complete transcript of the video dialog, see p. 427B.

Comprehension Questions

1. ¿Está Patricia feliz con sus entrevistas? (Sí.)
2. ¿Hizo Patricia cuatro entrevistas? (Sí.)
3. ¿Fue la mejor entrevista con el arquitecto? (No.)
4. ¿Aprendió Patricia mucho o poco de sus entrevistas? (mucho)
5. ¿Hay gran diferencia o poca diferencia entre la gente del campo y la gente de la ciudad? (poca diferencia)
6. ¿Cuál es la diferencia entre la vida del campo y la vida de la ciudad, la gente o el estilo de vida? (el estilo de vida)
7. ¿Por qué dice Patricia que Miguel no sabe nada de vivir en una granja? (Porque Miguel abrió la cerca y el caballo se escapó.)
8. ¿Por qué quiere Patricia comprarle un regalo a su hermana? (Porque su cumpleaños es este mes.)
9. ¿Por qué está Patricia preocupada? (Porque no sabe si tiene suficiente dinero.)
10. ¿Cuándo va Patricia a mandar su proyecto a la revista? (después del fin de semana)

Block Schedule

Variety Have 2 students play the roles of Miguel and Patricia, who have come to spend a week at your school. Have the class ask them questions. (For additional activities, see **Block Scheduling Copymasters.**)

Teaching Resource Options

Print

Unit 6 Resource Book
Video Activities, p. 127
Videoscript, p. 130
Audioscript, pp. 131–132
Audioscript *Para hispanohablantes,*
pp. 131–132

Audiovisual

OHT 202 (Quick Start)
Audio Program Cassettes 18A, 18B /
CD 18
Audio *Para hispanohablantes*
Cassette 18A / CD 18
Video Program Videotape 6 / Videodisc
3B

Quick Start Review

 Dialog review

Use OHT 202 or write on the board:
Complete the following sentences from
the dialog:

1. Pero ____ algo mucho más
   importante también.
2. ¿Estás feliz con tus ____ ?
3. ¡Creo que va a ____ muy bien y lo
   quiero ver!
4. Espero tener buena ____ .
5. ____ tengo que escribir mucho.
6. Es ____ el estilo de vida que es
   diferente.

Answers

1. aprendí	4. suerte
2. entrevistas	5. Todavía
3. salir	6. sólo

Teaching Suggestions
Comprehension Check

Use **Actividades 1** and **2** to assess
retention after the dialog. Have
students close their books. Read the
items and see if students can
comprehend. Have students add 3
items to **Actividad 2**.

ACTIVIDAD 1 **Objective:** Transitional practice
Listening comprehension/dialog

Answers (See script p. 427B.)
b, d, c, a

434 Vocabulary/Grammar • UNIDAD 6 Etapa 3

En acción
 **VOCABULARIO Y GRAMÁTICA**

ACTIVIDAD 1

¿En qué orden?

Escuchar ¿En qué orden pasaron estas cosas
según el diálogo? *(Hint: What is the order?)*

a. Patricia mandó su proyecto a la revista.
b. Patricia y Miguel llegaron a Otavalo.
c. Patricia habló del cumpleaños de su
   hermana.
d. Patricia y Miguel entraron al mercado.

ACTIVIDAD 2

Frases revueltas

Escuchar Combina las frases para hacer
oraciones basadas en el diálogo.
(Hint: Make sentences.)

1. Patricia está
   contenta con
2. Miguel no tiene
3. Patricia va a
   comprarle
4. Patricia no sabe si
   tiene suficiente
5. Miguel quiere ver
   si Patricia escribe

a. dinero para
   comprar un regalo.
b. las entrevistas
   que hizo.
c. sobre su experiencia
   con el caballo.
d. ni idea de lo que
   hay que hacer en
   una granja.
e. un regalo a su
   hermana.

ACTIVIDAD 3

Juego de palabras

Hablar Patricia y Miguel juegan a este juego
de palabras. Tú también puedes jugar. Di qué
palabra no debe estar en cada grupo y por qué.
(Hint: Why doesn't one word belong?)

modelo

abrigo	bufanda	gorro	revista

Una revista no es ropa.

1.	cerdo	jefe	vaca	gallo
2.	raqueta	bola	patines	cansado
3.	anillo	arete	casete	collar
4.	casco	cuchara	cuchillo	tenedor
5.	plato	bota	olla	jarra
6.	cancha	contento	campo	estadio
7.	hombre	chico	mujer	suelo
8.	café	té	cuenta	limonada
9.	espejos	orejas	piernas	brazos
10.	cepillo	jabón	jamón	champú

TAMBIÉN SE DICE

There are many ways to say "To each his own." Each is
used in many countries.

• «A cada pájaro le gusta su nido.» *Every bird
  likes its nest.*
• «Zapatero, a tus zapatos.» *Shoemaker, (attend)
  to your shoes!*
• «A cada cual lo suyo.» *To each his own.*
• «Cada oveja con su pareja.» *Every sheep has its mate.*

434 cuatrocientos treinta y cuatro
Unidad 6

Classroom Management

Time Saver If time is short, have students do
Actividad 5 as a paired homework assignment.

Planning Ahead Have students bring in all the
vocabulary and verb flashcards they made during the
school year. They will be able to use these cards for
additional practice throughout the **Etapa.**

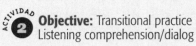

- Review: Present progressive and *ir a...*
- Review: Affirmative *tú* commands
- Review: Preterite tense

♻ Las actividades

Escuchar Todas estas personas están ocupadas. ¿Qué oración describe lo que hace cada una? *(Hint: Describe each picture.)*

♻ Entrevistas

Hablar/Escribir Imagínate que trabajas para una revista y que estás escribiendo un artículo sobre los jóvenes de hoy. Haz una entrevista con un(a) estudiante. Escribe las respuestas. *(Hint: Interview a student.)*

La vida familiar

1. ¿Cuántas personas hay en tu familia? ¿Quiénes son?

2. ¿Quién hace los quehaceres en tu casa?

3. ¿Cuál es la fecha de tu cumpleaños? ¿Cómo lo celebras normalmente?

La vida diaria

4. ¿A qué hora te levantas todos los días? ¿Qué haces después de levantarte?

5. ¿A qué hora te acuestas todos los días?

6. ¿Cómo es tu horario este semestre? ¿Cuántas materias tienes?

Los gustos

7. ¿Qué te gusta hacer después de las clases?

8. ¿Qué te gusta comer y beber?

9. ¿Cuál es tu deporte favorito? ¿Por qué?

10. ¿?

cuatrocientos treinta y cinco
Etapa 3 **435**

Answers (See script p. 427B.)
1. b   2. d   3. e   4. a   5. c

♻ Text vocabulary

Answers
1. Un jefe no es un animal.
2. Cansado no es una cosa que usas para practicar deportes.
3. Un casete no es una joya.
4. Un casco no es una cosa que usas para comer.
5. Una bola no es cerámica.
6. Contento no es un lugar donde puedes practicar deportes.
7. Un suelo no es una persona.
8. Una cuenta no es una bebida.
9. Unos espejos no son parte del cuerpo.
10. Un jamón es comida. Las otras cosas no son comida.

♻ Activities

Answers (See script p. 427B.)
1. d	6. j
2. a	7. b
3. f	8. c
4. e	9. h
5. g	10. i

♻ Family, daily routine, preferences

Answers will vary.

Teaching All Students

Extra Help Before doing **Actividad 3,** have students look up any words they don't remember in the **Glosario** at the back of the book.

Challenge Have students expand the interview in **Actividad 5** by adding questions to each category.

Native Speakers Have students interview and, if possible, record a Spanish-speaking relative about his/her profession.

Multiple Intelligences

Verbal Review vocabulary with categories. Provide a category and have students name as many words/expressions as possible within that category. A sample category is: **Por la mañana.** This would include reflexive verbs, breakfast foods, chores in the house or on the farm, transportation to school, etc.

■ Block Schedule

Change of Pace Have students work in small groups. Using the photos in **Actividad 4,** students write a dialog or monolog that might be overheard at each place. Then have groups share their dialogs/monologs with another group, who guesses where they might be heard.

Teaching Resource Options

Print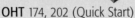

Más práctica Workbook PE, p. 149
Para hispanohablantes Workbook PE, p. 147
Block Scheduling Copymasters
Unit 6 Resource Book
  Más práctica Workbook TE, p. 107
  Para hispanohablantes Workbook TE, p. 113

Audiovisual

OHT 174, 202 (Quick Start)

Technology

Intrigas y aventuras CD-ROM, Disc 1

Objective: Open-ended practice
Vocabulary review

♻ Professions, the farm

Answers

Answers will vary.
1. El pastor cuida las llamas.
2. El caballo está dentro del corral.
3. La mujer de negocios camina por la calle.
4. Estos animales son cerdos.
5. El arquitecto está en su oficina.
6. El taxista está en su taxi.

Quick Start Review

 Present tense

Use OHT 202 or write on the board:
Write the appropriate present tense
form for each subject pronoun:

1. ir: yo ____   4. ser: nosotros ____
2. decir: tú ____   5. hacer: yo ____
3. tener: él ____   6. estar: ustedes ____

Answers

1. voy   4. somos
2. dices   5. hago
3. tiene   6. están

Teaching Suggestions
Reviewing the Present Progressive

Remind students that Spanish does not use the present progressive as often as English. In Spanish, the simple present is used to describe routine actions. The present progressive is for something happening right at this very moment.

♻ **La ciudad y el campo**

Hablar/Escribir Mira las fotos que sacó Patricia y describe lo que ves en cada una. *(Hint: Describe each picture.)*

REPASO

Review: Present Progressive and *ir a* + infinitive

You have learned to use verbs in the present tense three different ways:
* **simple present** tense
* **present progressive** tense
* *ir a* + *infinitive*

♻ **¿RECUERDAS?** *pp. 226, 342* Remember the present progressive? The present progressive is used only to talk about actions that are happening. It is never used to refer to the future.

estoy	**habl ando**	estamos	**habl ando**
estás	**com iendo**	estáis	**com iendo**
está	**escrib iendo**	están	**escrib iendo**

Miguel y Patricia **están** **camin ando** y **habl ando**.
*Miguel and Patricia **are walking** and **talking**.*

♻ **¿RECUERDAS?** *p. 149* To talk about what you are going to do, use *ir a* + *infinitive*. Although this is a present tense, you are talking about something that is going to happen in the **future**.

voy a	**hablar**	vamos a	**hablar**
vas a	**comer**	vais a	**comer**
va a	**escribir**	van a	**escribir**

Patricia says:
—**Voy a comprar**le un regalo a mi hermana.
*I'm **going to buy** a gift for my sister.*

Remember to change -**endo** to -**yendo** when the **stem** of an **-er** or an **-ir** verb ends in a vowel.   cr**e**er → cre**yendo**   l**e**er → le**yendo**   o**í**r → o**yendo**

436   cuatrocientos treinta y seis
Unidad 6

Classroom Community

Group Activity Have students work in groups and expand on **Actividad 7**. They should look for more photos in the book and describe what is happening using the present progressive.

Portfolio Use the Fine Art Transparency (OHT 174) for this **Etapa** as the basis for a short descriptive paragraph.

Rubric A = 13–15 pts. B = 10–12 pts. C = 7–9 pts. D = 4–6 pts. F = < 4 pts.

Writing criteria	Scale
Vocabulary use	1 2 3 4 5
Grammar accuracy	1 2 3 4 5
Spelling accuracy	1 2 3 4 5

¿Qué están haciendo?

Hablar/Escribir Patricia y Miguel hacen muchas cosas. ¿Qué están haciendo en estas fotos? (*Hint: What are they doing?*)

modelo

Patricia y Miguel están caminando.

1.

2.

3.

4.

¿Qué van a hacer?

Hablar/Escribir Todos van a hacer algo. ¿Qué van a hacer?
(*Hint: Explain what they're going to do.*)

modelo

Patricia quiere hacer una entrevista con el tío Julio.
Va a viajar a la granja.

1. Los chicos piensan ver una película en casa.
2. Yo tengo un examen de matemáticas mañana.
3. Miguel quiere una mochila.
4. Tú quieres ir a la playa mañana.
5. Andrea y yo tenemos mucha sed.
6. Felipe y Enrique no quieren estar en casa.
7. Ustedes tienen hambre.
8. Diego piensa ir al gimnasio.

■ **MÁS PRÁCTICA** *cuaderno* p. 149
■ **PARA HISPANOHABLANTES** *cuaderno* p. 147

 **Los planes para el sábado**

PARA CONVERSAR • STRATEGY: SPEAKING

Use storytelling techniques Unexpected contrasts add interest to stories. Imagine an upside-down Saturday in which everyone decides to do spur-of-the-moment things. Example: **Mis padres no van a limpiar la casa. Van a buscar una nueva casa.**

Hablar ¿Qué van a hacer tú y estas personas el sábado por la mañana? Habla con otro(a) estudiante. Cambien de papel.
(*Hint: What are they going to do?*)

1. tu mejor amigo(a)
2. tus padres
3. tu hermano(a)
4. tus amigos y tú
5. tú
6. ¿?

cuatrocientos treinta y siete
Etapa 3 **437**

Answers
Answers will vary.
1. Patricia y Miguel están hablando con Bárbara.
2. Patricia está regateando. (Está comprando algo.)
3. Patricia está mandando su proyecto.
4. Miguel está hablando con Patricia en el mercado.

Answers
Answers will vary.
1. Van a alquilar un video.
2. Voy a estudiar.
3. Va a ir de compras.
4. Vas a nadar y/o tomar el sol.
5. Vamos a beber.
6. Van a salir.
7. Van a comer.
8. Va a hacer ejercicio.

Answers will vary.

🔔 **Quick Wrap-up**

Call out verb infinitives. One student gives the present progressive form. Another student uses it in a sentence. Do the same for **ir a** + infinitive.

■ **Block Schedule**

Change of Pace First, have students brainstorm a list of locations. Next, have them brainstorm a list of people (names, professions, etc.). Finally, have students write 10 sentences, matching up people and locations and saying what the people are doing, using the present progressive. (For additional activities, see **Block Scheduling Copymasters.**)

Teaching All Students

Extra Help Have students say what various people in the classroom are doing, using the present progressive.

Native Speakers Initiate a discussion on similarities and differences between city and country life throughout the Spanish-speaking world, eliciting input from native speakers. Which aspects are the same? Which are different?

Multiple Intelligences

Kinesthetic Have various students act out activities for the class. The class guesses what they are doing, using the present progressive. Variation: The class assumes that the student is going to do these activities tomorrow and uses **ir a** + infinitive in their responses.

Teaching Resource Options

Print

Más práctica Workbook PE, p. 150
Para hispanohablantes Workbook
  PE, p. 148
Block Scheduling Copymasters
Unit 6 Resource Book
  Más práctica Workbook TE, p. 108
  Para hispanohablantes Workbook
   TE, p. 114
Information Gap Activities, p. 119

Audiovisual

OHT 202, 203 (Quick Start)

Technology

Intrigas y aventuras CD-ROM, Disc 1

Language Note

The word **u** is used instead of **o** before words beginning with **o** or **ho**.

ACTIVIDAD 10 Objective: Open-ended practice
Present progressive/**ir a** + infinitive in writing
Answers will vary.

Quick Start Review

♻ Affirmative **tú** commands

Use OHT 202 or write on the board:
Write 5 commands your Spanish teacher might give you:

Answers
Answers will vary. Answers could include:
Mira la foto.
Trabaja con (Claudia).
Contesta las preguntas.
Lee el diálogo.
Levanta la mano.

Teaching Suggestions
Reviewing Affirmative **tú** Commands

Have the first student in each row turn and give a command to the second student. That student acts out the command, then turns to the third student and gives another command, and so on. The last student in each row gives a command to the first student.

ACTIVIDAD 10

Una carta

Escribir Estás de vacaciones en el campo u otro lugar. Escríbele una carta a un(a) amigo(a) describiendo tus actividades. *(Hint: Write a letter.)*

- ¿Dónde estás?
- ¿Cómo es?
- ¿Qué están haciendo tu familia y tú?
- ¿Qué van a hacer mañana?

modelo

Querido Carlos:

Estamos en el campo. ¡Qué tranquilo es! Mis padres están tomando un refresco…

Mañana mis hermanos y yo vamos a…

NOTA CULTURAL

The Galápagos Islands contain some of the most unusual flora and fauna in the world. Their remote location off the coast of mainland Ecuador creates a unique habitat that is home to unusual animals, such as the **blue-footed booby.**

REPASO

Review: Affirmative **tú** Commands

♻ **¿RECUERDAS?** *pp. 252, 322* Remember that **tú commands** are used to give instructions to a friend or family member. The **affirmative tú command** form of a regular verb is the same as the **third person singular** of the simple present tense.

hablar → **Habla.**   **comer** → **Come.**   **escribir** → **Escribe.**

Remember to attach **direct object**, **indirect object**, and **reflexive pronouns** to **affirmative commands**. When you do, you usually need to add an accent.

Háblame.   **Cómelo.**   **Escríbeles.**
Speak to me.   Eat it.   Write to them.

Miguel says: —**Compra le** una bolsa…
Buy her a handbag…

You also learned eight irregular **affirmative tú commands.**

decir → di	**ir** → ve	**salir** → sal	**tener** → ten
hacer → haz	**poner** → pon	**ser** → sé	**venir** → ven

ACTIVIDAD 11 Gramática

¡Cuántas órdenes!

Hablar/Escribir La mamá de Miguel le da muchas órdenes hoy. ¿Qué le dice? *(Hint: What does she say?)*

modelo

salir temprano para la escuela   *Sal temprano para la escuela.*

1. venir a casa temprano
2. ir a la tienda
3. comer las verduras
4. ser bueno con tu hermano
5. lavar los platos
6. compartir con tu hermano
7. decir a qué hora vuelves
8. tener cuidado

■ **MÁS PRÁCTICA** *cuaderno* p. 150
■ **PARA HISPANOHABLANTES** *cuaderno* p. 148

---

438 cuatrocientos treinta y ocho
Unidad 6

Classroom Community

Cooperative Learning Have students work in groups of 4. Student 1 names a place; student 2 gives a command that might be heard at that place; student 3 writes it down; student 4 names the next place; and so on until each student has named a place. The group reviews the written commands and makes corrections as necessary.

Storytelling Have students work in pairs to write and relate a story in which one person keeps telling another person what to do. Students should use their imagination and sense of humor.

¡Mañana es otro día!

Hablar Tu amigo(a) te invita al campo pero tienes otros planes. ¿Qué te dice tu amigo(a)? Cambien de papel. *(Hint: Say what to do.)*

modelo

escribir

Tú: *Quiero **escribir** unas cartas hoy.*

Tu amigo(a): *¡Escríbelas mañana!*

1. leer	**5.** poner
2. visitar	**6.** ver
3. preparar	**7.** hablar
4. hacer	**8.** ¿?

Review: Regular Preterite

 ¿RECUERDAS? *pp. 366, 368, 392, 394* To talk about completed actions in the past, use the **preterite tense.**

-ar verbs		-er verbs		-ir verbs	
hablé	**hablamos**	**comí**	**comimos**	**escribí**	**escribimos**
hablaste	**hablasteis**	**comiste**	**comisteis**	**escribiste**	**escribisteis**
habló	**hablaron**	**comió**	**comieron**	**escribió**	**escribieron**

- Remember that the verb **ver** is regular in the **preterite** but has no accents.

- Remember that verbs ending in **-car**, **-gar**, and **-zar** have a spelling change in the **yo** form of the **preterite**.

  marcar → marqué   **llegar → llegué**   **cruzar → crucé**

- Third person forms of **-er** and **-ir** verbs with **stems** that end in a **vowel** require a **y** in the **preterite**.

le**í**	le**ímos**
le**íste**	le**ísteis**
le**yó**	le**yeron**

A preparar la fiesta

Escribir Estás preparando una fiesta y un amigo(a) te va a ayudar. Escribe un mensaje para él o ella explicándole lo que necesita hacer. Necesitas ayuda con cinco cosas. *(Hint: Write what to do.)*

modelo

Ana:
Gracias por ayudarme con la fiesta. Éstos son los quehaceres que debes hacer.
   1) Ve de compras.
   2) Compra una tarta para el postre.

■ **MÁS COMUNICACIÓN** p. R18

Miguel says: —¿Y **aprendiste** algo de tus entrevistas?
*And **did you learn** something from your interviews?*

cuatrocientos treinta y nueve
Etapa 3   **439**

Teaching All Students

Extra Help For extra help with affirmative **tú** commands, have students review the explanations on pp. 252 and 322 and redo some of the related activities.

Native Speakers Ask students to name typical wildlife in their home countries. Are any endangered species? Also ask if there is a national bird.

Multiple Intelligences

Naturalist Have students research and present a report on the Galápagos Islands. The report should include the original name of the islands, the types and names of animals found there, the weather, and a brief synopsis of Charles Darwin's work there.

 11 **Objective:** Controlled practice
Affirmative **tú** commands

Answers
1. Ven a casa temprano.
2. Ve a la tienda.
3. Come las verduras.
4. Sé bueno con tu hermano.
5. Lava los platos.
6. Comparte con tu hermano.
7. Di a qué hora vuelves.
8. Ten cuidado.

 12 **Objective:** Transitional practice
Affirmative **tú** commands in conversation

Answers
Answers will vary. Partial sample answers:
1. ¡Lée[lo] mañana!
2. ¡Visíta[lo] mañana!
3. ¡Prepára[lo] mañana!
4. ¡Haz[lo] mañana!
5. ¡Pon[lo] mañana!
6. ¡Ve[lo] mañana!
7. ¡Hábla[le] mañana!
8. *Answers will vary.*

13 **Objective:** Open-ended practice
Affirmative **tú** commands in writing

Answers will vary.

Quick Start Review

 ♻ Preterite

Use OHT 203 or write on the board:
¿Qué hiciste ayer? Escribe 3 oraciones.

Answers
Answers will vary. Answers could include:
Visité a mis abuelos.
Leí una novela.
Preparé la tarea de español.

Teaching Suggestions
Reviewing Regular Preterite

Say a verb infinitive and a subject pronoun. Toss a soft ball to a student who gives the form. If correct, the student tosses the ball back to you. If incorrect, he/she tosses it to another student. Continue with more verbs.

▇ Block Schedule

Retention Check students' retention of the preterite by distributing a worksheet of preterite forms of verbs minus the accent marks. Give students a time limit and have them add the accent marks. (For additional activities, see **Block Scheduling Copymasters**.)

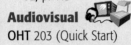
ACTIVIDAD 14 **Objective:** Controlled practice
Regular preterite in reading

Answers

1. me levanté	9. vimos
2. busqué	10. hablaron
3. salí	11. visitó
4. tomamos	12. almorzamos
5. visitamos	13. volvimos
6. saqué	14. compré
7. empecé	15. llegué
8. habló	

ACTIVIDAD 15 **Objective:** Transitional practice
Regular preterite in conversation

Answers will vary.

Juego

Answer: a

ACTIVIDAD 14  Gramática

El viaje

Leer Patricia escribió en su diario sobre su viaje al campo. Completa sus oraciones con uno de los verbos. *(Hint: Complete her diary.)*

1–5	6–10	11–15
buscar	empezar	almorzar
levantarse	hablar	comprar
salir	hablar	llegar
tomar	sacar	visitar
visitar	ver	volver

Esta mañana, yo __1__ a las seis y media. Después de desayunar, __2__ mi grabadora y __3__ de la casa. Miguel y yo __4__ el autobús a las ocho.

Primero, nosotros __5__ el taller de Bárbara. ¡Qué interesante! Yo __6__ fotos y __7__ la entrevista. Bárbara __8__ mucho sobre la vida del campo.

Después, en la granja del tío Julio, Miguel y yo __9__ muchos animales. El tío Julio y Miguel __10__ de la primera vez que Miguel __11__ la granja. ¡Qué cómico! Después de la entrevista nosotros __12__.

Por fin, Miguel y yo __13__ a la ciudad después de ir al mercado en Otavalo. Yo __14__ un regalo allí. Yo __15__ a casa a las seis y media.

■ **MÁS PRÁCTICA** *cuaderno* p. 151
■ **PARA HISPANOHABLANTES** *cuaderno* p. 149

ACTIVIDAD 15

¿Quién lo hizo?

Hablar/Leer Habla con los otros estudiantes para saber quién hizo estas actividades el año pasado. Encuentra tres personas que hicieron cada actividad. Escribe un resumen de las respuestas. *(Hint: Find people who did these activities.)*

modelo

Tú: ¿Sacaste una buena nota el año pasado?

Otro(a) estudiante: Sí, saqué una buena nota en matemáticas.

Resumen: Raúl, Sara y Ana sacaron una buena nota el año pasado.

Actividad	Persona 1	Persona 2	Persona 3
sacar una buena nota	Raúl	Sara	Ana
viajar por una semana			
ver una película de horror			
comer comida mexicana			
escribir una carta			
oír un concierto			

Pronunciación

Si tu mamá te dice «¡Sal para la escuela!», ¿qué vas a necesitar?

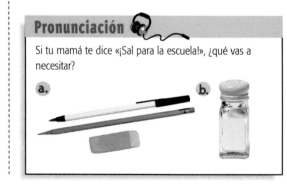

a.   b.

Classroom Community

Paired Activity Have students write a real or imagined diary entry similar to the one in **Actividad 14**. Then have them exchange it with a partner and complete each other's diary.

Game Have students work in pairs. Give each pair 30 index cards, and have students make cards for a memory game. On half the cards they write various subject pronouns. On the other half they write preterite verb forms. Each form must match 1 of the subject pronoun cards. Then students shuffle the cards and spread them out upside down. In turn, each student tries to turn over 2 matching cards.

¿Qué hicieron?

Hablar/Escribir Describe qué hicieron todos. *(Hint: Describe what everyone did.)*

modelo

Patricia visitó una granja el sábado pasado.

Patricia y Miguel yo mi hermano(a) mis padres mi mejor amigo(a) mis amigos y yo ¿?	almorzar comer compartir escribir jugar leer ver visitar	¿?	ayer el sábado pasado anoche anteayer el año pasado el verano pasado la semana pasada

Review: Irregular Preterite

 ¿RECUERDAS? *pp. 395, 419* These are the irregular preterite verbs that you have learned.

dar *to give*

di	dimos
diste	disteis
dio	dieron

decir *to say, to tell*

dije	dijimos
dijiste	dijisteis
dijo	dijeron

estar *to be*

estuve	estuvimos
estuviste	estuvisteis
estuvo	estuvieron

hacer *to make, to do*

hice	hicimos
hiciste	hicisteis
hizo	hicieron

ir *to go* / **ser** *to be*

fui	fuimos
fuiste	fuisteis
fue	fueron

tener *to have*

tuve	tuvimos
tuviste	tuvisteis
tuvo	tuvieron

venir *to come*

vine	vinimos
viniste	vinisteis
vino	vinieron

Patricia might say:

—La entrevista con tu tío Julio fue la mejor porque él me dijo lo que hiciste tú la primera vez que estuviste en la granja.

The interview with your Uncle Julio was the best because he told me what you did the first time you were on the farm.

Teaching All Students

Extra Help For extra help with irregular preterites, have students review the explanations on pp. 395 and 419 and redo some of the related activities.

Multiple Intelligences

Verbal Have students work in small groups and role play a family conversation based on the question, *How was your day?*

Logical/Mathematical Have students pretend that last week they had $100 to spend. Have them explain how they spent it. They must name at least 2 items they bought and 2 activities. The total must be exactly $100.

Objective: Open-ended practice Regular preterite

Answers will vary.

Quick Start Review

♻ Preterite of regular verbs

Use OHT 203 or write on the board: Write 3 past tense sentences using some of the following verbs:

almorzar / sacar / empezar / leer / comer / escribir / buscar / poner

Answers

Answers will vary. Answers could include:
Anoche leí una revista.
La semana pasada mi hermano sacó la basura.
Ayer, la familia comió a las siete.

Teaching Suggestions
Reviewing Irregular Preterites

Call out present tense forms of the verbs with irregular preterites. Students must give the equivalent preterite form. For example: hago / hice.

Block Schedule

FunBreak Have students write their own "mad libs." Each student writes 1–2 paragraphs relating an event that took place in the past. They then rewrite the paragraph(s) and replace various words with blanks. Under the blanks they put the part of speech that is required. Working with a partner, the student asks for words of the appropriate part of speech and writes them in the blanks. Finally, the student rereads the paragraph(s) with the inserted words.

Teaching Resource Options

Print

Más práctica Workbook PE, p. 152

Para hispanohablantes Workbook PE, p. 150

Block Scheduling Copymasters

Unit 6 Resource Book

  Más práctica Workbook TE, p. 110

  Para hispanohablantes Workbook TE, p. 116

  Information Gap Activities, pp. 120–121

  Audioscript, p. 132

  Audioscript *Para hispanohablantes*, p. 132

Audiovisual

Audio Program Cassettes 18A, 18B / CD 18

Audio *Para hispanohablantes* Cassette 18A / CD 18

Technology

Intrigas y aventuras CD-ROM, Disc 1

 ACTIVIDAD 17 Objective: Transitional practice
Listening comprehension/irregular preterite

Answers (See script p. 427B.)

1. El fin de semana pasado, Rosa fue al campo para visitar a sus abuelos.
2. Las gallinas fueron cómicas (e hicieron mucho ruido).
3. Por la tarde, Rosa fue al mercado con su prima.
4. Rosa no compró el saco porque se encontró con una amiga y salió a tomar un refresco.
5. El sábado por la noche, Rosa vio la televisión, leyó una revista y se acostó temprano.

ACTIVIDAD 18 Objective: Transitional practice
Irregular preterite in writing

Answers

Answers will vary.
1. Yo fui...
2. Mis padres dieron...
3. Mis amigos(as) y yo tuvimos...
4. Mi hermano(a) hizo...
5. Mi amigo(a) vino...
6. Mi familia y yo estuvimos...
7. Mis amigos(as) dijeron...

 ACTIVIDAD 19 Objective: Open-ended practice
Preterite in conversation

Answers will vary.

 **ACTIVIDAD 17 Gramática**

Un buen fin de semana

Escuchar Escucha la conversación entre María y Rosa y completa las oraciones. *(Hint: Complete the sentences.)*

1. El fin de semana pasado, Rosa…
2. Las gallinas…
3. Por la tarde, Rosa…
4. Rosa no compró el saco porque…
5. El sábado por la noche, Rosa…

■ **MÁS PRÁCTICA** *cuaderno* p. 152

■ **PARA HISPANOHABLANTES** *cuaderno* p. 150

ACTIVIDAD 18

¿Quién hizo qué?

Escribir Explica lo que todos hicieron. *(Hint: Write what they did.)*

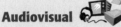 **modelo**

Patricia y Miguel / hacer…

Patricia y Miguel hicieron un viaje.

1. yo / ir…
2. mis padres / dar…
3. mis amigos(as) y yo / tener…
4. mi hermano(a) / hacer…
5. mi amigo(a) / venir…
6. mi familia y yo / estar…
7. mis amigos(as) / decir…

ACTIVIDAD 19

¡Qué noticias!

Hablar/Leer Tú lees un artículo sobre algo que pasó en Quito y tu amigo(a) te pregunta sobre lo que leíste. Contesta las preguntas de tu amigo(a). *(Hint: Answer your friend's questions.)*

¿Cuándo?   ¿Qué?

¿Quién?   ¿Por qué?   ¿Dónde?

Un turista contentísimo

Redacción Puyó

Quito— Ayer, en el centro de Quito, un turista mexicano pasó un día interesante. El turista perdió una bolsa con su pasaporte, su dinero, su tarjeta de crédito… y algo más.

«No sé cómo la perdí», dijo el turista, «pero hablé con un policía y me ayudó de una manera interesante».

El policía mandó al turista a un departamento especial. ¡Allí el turista encontró un perro con su bolsa! Otro policía le explicó todo:

«Salí con mi perro Nacho para hacer nuestra rutina diaria y, al llegar a la esquina, Nacho vio a otro perro con la bolsa. Cuando el perro sacó un sándwich de la bolsa, llegó Nacho y la tomó.

Afortunadamente Nacho sabe hacer bien su trabajo. ¡No hay ningún robo, solamente mucha hambre!»

NOTA CULTURAL

Ecuador is made up of three widely diverse regions: the Pacific coast, the Andes mountains, and the jungles of the Amazon. The variety of habitats makes Ecuador a popular ecotourism destination.

la Amazona

442 cuatrocientos cuarenta y dos
Unidad 6

Classroom Community

Storytelling Have students write their own "believe it or not" story similar to the one in **Actividad 19.** Have volunteers read them to the class. As students are telling their stories, have other students sketch the scenes on the board or dramatize the action.

Group Activity Have students work in groups to debate the most deserving winner of the **Onda Internacional** contest. Each student must name 1 person and give a reason why. Have the group agree on 1 winner and explain their choice to the class.

ACTIVIDAD 20

¡Un año interesante!

Hablar/Escribir ¿Qué hiciste o qué te pasó este año? Preséntale tu historia a la clase. *(Hint: What did you do?)*

Este año en la clase de español
Este año aprendí mucho en la clase de español. Hablé con muchas personas y escribí mucho. Vimos un video interesante sobre unos jóvenes que hablan español. Fuimos a un museo para ver unos artículos de Latinoamérica...

■ **MÁS COMUNICACIÓN** p. R18

ACTIVIDAD 21

Y el ganador es...

Hablar/Escribir Piensa en las personas de los diálogos. ¿Quién va a ganar el concurso? Escoge a una persona y explica por qué esa persona debe ganar. *(Hint: Explain who should win and why.)*

 Francisco
 Isabel
 Ignacio
 Carlos
 Mercedes
 Patricia

modelo

Pienso que Patricia debe ganar el concurso. Ella trabajó mucho...

Pronunciación

Refrán

Pronunciación de la x The letter x is pronounced several different ways. Before a vowel, before the letters **ce** or **ci,** or at the end of a word, x sounds like the English x in the word *taxi*. At the beginning of a word or before a consonant, the x is pronounced like the *s* in *same*. To practice these sounds, pronounce the following.

¡Es un examen excepcional!   **X**ochimilco y Ta**x**co son lugares bonitos.

In Mexico and Central America, the letter x also has the following sounds in words that come from other languages.

j as in **jarra:**   México, Oaxaca, Xalapa
sh as in *shoe:*   Ixtepec, Uxmal
Now try the **refrán** about the taxi.

El taxi gratis no existe.

cuatrocientos cuarenta y tres
Etapa 3   **443**

Teaching All Students

Extra Help Have students review the **Diálogo** on pp. 432–433. They should write down each scene number and any preterite verb forms in that scene. Next to each form, have them write the verb infinitive.

Native Speakers As an alternative to **Actividad 19,** bring in other articles from Spanish-speaking periodicals. Have students work in pairs to ask and answer questions.

Multiple Intelligences

Interpersonal Have 6 students play the roles of the 6 people in **Actividad 21** and sit in chairs at the front of the class. Have the other students come up and interview the contestants, asking questions about their contest submissions and why they hope they will win.

Culture Highlights

● **DIVERSIDAD VEGETAL Y ANIMAL**
Due to its different regions, Ecuador is probably the most biologically diverse country in the world. It has 10% of the world's botanical species in an area that represents only 2% of the world's area. It is also the home of more than a million species of insects.

ACTIVIDAD 20 Objective: Open-ended practice
Describing the school year

Answers will vary.

ACTIVIDAD 21 Objective: Open-ended practice
Choosing the contest winners

Answers will vary.

Teaching Note

You may wish to show the Video Epilogue segment here. See script TE p. 427B. The Epilogue may also be shown during review (see TE p. 448).

Quick Wrap-up

Call on students at random to name 1 thing that happened last year in class or in school.

Dictation

After presenting the **Pronunciación,** have students close their books. Dictate the **refrán** in segments while students write it.

Block Schedule

Research Have students work in pairs to find out more about the 3 diverse regions of Ecuador. One student will be responsible for finding information in books and magazines, while the other researches on the Internet. Have them pool their information and submit a short written report, supported by illustrations. Have pairs present their work to the class. (For additional activities, see **Block Scheduling Copymasters.**)

Teaching Resource Options

Print

Block Scheduling Copymasters
Unit 6 Resource Book
  Audioscript, p. 133
  Audioscript *Para hispanohablantes*,
    p. 133

Audiovisual

OHT 203 (Quick Start)
Audio Program Cassette 18A / CD 18
Audio *Para hispanohablantes*
  Cassette 18A / CD 18
Canciones Cassette / CD

🔔 Quick Start Review

♻ Ecuador

Use OHT 203 or write on the board:
Write 5 statements about Ecuador that
you learned in this unit:

Answers
Answers will vary. Answers could include:
Ecuador queda en América del Sur.
La capital de Ecuador es Quito.
El dinero de Ecuador se llama el sucre.
Unas personas hablan quichua.
El ecuador pasa por Ecuador.

Teaching Suggestions

- **Prereading** Have students imagine
  that they are ready to leave on a bus
  trip around Ecuador. How would they
  be feeling and what would they be
  thinking?

- **Strategy: Reflect on journal
  writing** Discuss the reading strategy
  and have students make a chart on a
  separate sheet of paper. Before
  reading, have them look at the major
  heads of the reading and complete
  the **Lugar** column.

- **Reading** Display a map of Ecuador.
  As students read the journal entries,
  have them trace the route of the
  writer.

- **Post-reading** Ask students to give
  a description of each photo on
  pp. 444–445.

En voces

LECTURA

UN PASEO POR ECUADOR

PARA LEER

STRATEGY: READING

Reflect on journal writing Have you
ever kept a journal or a diary?
How are diaries organized? As you
read this article about a bus trip
through Ecuador, notice the place
and date given for each entry. This
diary-style organization of the
article helps you experience each
day that the writer experiences.
Use the chart to record an
interesting experience you read
from each day.

Fecha	Lugar	Experiencia interesante
17 de abril		
18 de abril		
4 de mayo		
25 de mayo		

Para la mayoría[1] de los ecuatorianos, el autobús es el
transporte más común. Para tener una experiencia muy
ecuatoriana, decidí hacer un viaje en autobús.

GUAYAQUIL, 17 de abril:

Guayaquil es el puerto principal y la ciudad más grande
del país. Para conocer la costa, decidí viajar a Machala.
Compré mi boleto en la terminal moderna. Los buses de
larga distancia tienen cortinas[2] y televisores con
videograbadora. Paseamos por la costa del Pacífico.
Hacía[3] mucho calor y mucha humedad. Vi los cultivos
de arroz, caña de azúcar y plátanos[4]. Por el puerto de
Machala pasan más de un millón de toneladas de
plátanos y camarones[5] por año.

---

[1] majority [2] curtains [3] It was [4] bananas [5] shrimp

Classroom Community

Paired Activity Have students work in pairs to
complete the ¿Comprendiste? and ¿Qué piensas?
questions. Have each student ask his/her partner 1
additional comprehension question for each paragraph
of the reading.

Learning Scenario Divide the class into groups.
One student takes the role of a visitor from outer
space. The visitor wants to understand what a school is,
etc. The other students in the group must answer
questions and describe their school activities.

MACHALA, 18 de abril:

Decidí visitar los pueblitos. Subí a un bus de transporte rural de colores muy alegres con personas muy animadas. El bus llevó todas sus posesiones encima. Fuimos a varios pueblos y plantaciones de café y cacao.

LA SIERRA, 4 de mayo:

Llegué a la sierra de Ecuador, la región central de los Andes. Hacía frío en las montañas. Me levanté a las cinco y subí a un antiguo bus de escuela para ir al mercado indígena de Saquisilí. Viajamos muy lentamente. ¡Qué frío en el bus! Todos los pasajeros llevaron saco o poncho. Algunos se durmieron. Muchas personas llevaron productos al mercado. Vimos los volcanes de Cotopaxi y Tungurahua. Llegamos al Saquisilí y todos bajaron para trabajar o hacer compras.

COCA, 25 de mayo:

La carretera terminó y tuve que seguir en barco por los ríos Napo y Coca, que van al río Amazonas. Vi barcos y canoas con muchos plátanos y pasajeros. En la selva[6] vive poca gente, la mayoría son indígenas. Como ven, ¡se puede conocer mucho viajando en autobús!

---

[6]jungle

¿Comprendiste?
1. ¿Cuál es el transporte más común en Ecuador?
2. ¿En qué región empezó el autor?
3. ¿Qué productos son típicos de la costa?
4. ¿Cómo es el clima de la sierra?
5. ¿Adónde van los ríos Napo y Coca?

¿Qué piensas?
Compara el transporte de cada región. ¿En qué región te gustaría vivir? ¿Por qué?

Hazlo tú
¿Hay regiones como las de Ecuador en Estados Unidos? ¿Cómo son? Describe una de las regiones.

cuatrocientos cuarenta y cinco
Etapa 3 **445**

Cross Cultural Connections
Strategy Have students compare the places in the journal entries with places in the U.S. Can students name an equivalent place in the U.S. for each one in Ecuador? Have them show these places on a map of the U.S. and trace the route they would follow.

Critical Thinking
Have students discuss the advantages and disadvantages of travelling around a new country by bus, by car, or by bicycle. Would one type of transportation be more beneficial in one country than another?

Interdisciplinary Connection
English Work with a teacher from the English department to discuss journal writing. Have the English teacher present a few examples of a good journal entry and have students analyze what makes them interesting.

Culture Highlights
● **GUAYAQUIL** Guayaquil was founded in 1537 as a strategic site along major shipping routes. It has played a major role in Ecuador's economic development. In the 17th century, it was subject to frequent pirate attacks.

¿Comprendiste?
Answers
1. El autobús es el transporte más común.
2. El autor empezó en la costa.
3. Arroz, caña de azúcar y plátanos son típicos de la costa.
4. Hace frío.
5. Van al río Amazonas.

Block Schedule
Variety Divide the class into groups of 3–4. Have each group choose 1 section of the reading and write a dialog that might have taken place between the author and different people on the bus in that region. Have groups present their conversations to the class. (For additional activities, see **Block Scheduling Copymasters**.)

Teaching All Students

Extra Help Check comprehension by asking true/false questions. When the answer is false, students must correct the statement. For example: **Guayaquil queda en las montañas. (Falso. Queda en la costa.) El arroz es un producto típico de la costa. (Cierto.)**

Native Speakers Ask students for a description of bus service in their home countries. Are there different classes of service? Are animals allowed on the bus?

Multiple Intelligences
Visual Have students create topographical maps of Ecuador. They should be sure to include the places mentioned in the **Lectura**.

Teaching Resource Options

Print

Unit 6 Resource Book
 Audioscript, p. 133
 Audioscript *Para hispanohablantes,*
 p. 133

Audiovisual

Audio Program Cassette 18A / CD 18
Audio *Para hispanohablantes*
Cassette 18A / CD 18
OHT 204 (Quick Start)

Quick Start Review

♻ Foods

Use OHT 204 or write on the board:
List at least 2 foods for each of the
following:

• desayuno
• almuerzo
• merienda
• cena

Answers
Answers will vary. Answers could include:
• desayuno: los huevos, el jamón
• almuerzo: la hamburguesa, la sopa
• merienda: las papas fritas, las tapas
• cena: el pescado, el arroz

Teaching Suggestions
Presenting Cultura y comparaciones

• Have students read the Connecting
 Cultures Strategy and write their
 grocery lists. Tell them to talk with a
 grocer some time over the next week
 to find out where the products come
 from and when they are out-of-season
 in the U.S.
• Have students brainstorm a list of
 dishes made with potatoes, tomatoes,
 and corn. Ask if any of the dishes
 have any particular cultural
 association (such as spaghetti or
 tortillas).
• Ask if any students have worked on a
 farm that grows fruits or vegetables,
 or if they have a vegetable garden.
 What does it take for the farm/garden
 to be successful?

En colores

CULTURA Y COMPARACIONES

Cómo las Américas cambiaron la comida europea

PARA CONOCERNOS

STRATEGY:
CONNECTING CULTURES

Identify international foods Make
a grocery list of fresh fruits
and vegetables (4 or 5 items)
that are regularly part of your
family's diet. When is their
growing season in the U.S.?
Where do they come from
when out-of-season? Check
with the produce manager
of your grocery store. Then
decide which foods your
family eats come from other
countries.

Comida	Estación
naranja	marzo-abril

¿**P**uedes imaginarte tu dieta sin papas? Pues, en Europa
no había[1] papas hasta que los conquistadores llegaron a las
Américas. Los europeos comieron la papa por primera vez
en América. La papa, planta nativa de Perú, era[2] la comida
principal de los incas, indígenas de esa zona. La palabra
papa es de origen quechua, la lengua de los incas.

Los españoles empezaron a llevar papas a España.
Comida barata para los marineros[3], así llegó la papa a
Europa. Hoy la papa es una de las comidas principales
de Irlanda, Alemania, Rusia y Polonia.

---
[1] there were no   [2] was   [3] sailors

446 cuatrocientos cuarenta y seis
Unidad 6

Classroom Community

Group Activity Have students read the passage in
groups of 5. Each student is responsible for reading 1
paragraph and being sure that the other group
members understand what they read.

Paired Activity Have each student write 5
true/false or multiple choice questions about the
reading. Then have them exchange papers with a
partner and answer the other person's questions.

El maíz[4] también es de las Américas. El cultivo de maíz empezó en México alrededor del año 3500 a.C.[5] Llegó a Perú alrededor de 3200 a.C., pero no fue tan importante en la dieta de los peruanos como en la dieta de los mexicanos. En México se hicieron las tortillas del maíz.

Otro producto americano que cambió la comida europea es el tomate. No sabemos exactamente cómo y cuándo el tomate llegó a Europa, pero su cultivo era fácil en los países mediterráneos.

Entonces, las papas fritas y la salsa de tomate para los espaguetis son de origen europeo, pero sus ingredientes principales llegaron a Europa de América. ¿Ves? Los viajes de Colón cambiaron muchas cosas, ¡entre ellas la comida europea!

[5] corn   [5] B.C.

¿Comprendiste?

1. ¿De dónde vino la papa?
2. ¿Cómo llegó la papa a Europa?
3. ¿De dónde vino el maíz?
4. El maíz tuvo más importancia en la dieta de qué país, ¿Perú o México?
5. ¿Cómo llegó el tomate a Europa?

¿Qué piensas?

1. En tu opinión, ¿cómo sería la comida europea sin la papa y el tomate? ¿Y la comida norteamericana? ¿Por qué?
2. ¿Cómo crees que llegó la papa de España a otras partes de Europa?

Hazlo tú

Busca una receta con papas, tomates o maíz. Escribe la receta en español. Prepárala y comparte la comida con la clase. ¿Es una receta europea o americana? Explica su origen.

cuatrocientos cuarenta y siete
Etapa 3   **447**

Reading Strategy

Ask students to use the Reading Strategy "Combine strategies," whereby they combine a few reading strategies already practiced. They should first look at the title, photos, and graphics and predict what the reading is about. Then have them skim for the general idea of the content. Next, have them use context clues to guess meanings of new words.

Culture Highlights

● **VARIEDAD DE PAISAJES, VARIEDAD DE PLATOS** Different regions of Ecuador are characterized by different foods. People from the mountain areas tend to like dishes made from corn and potatoes. People from the coastal region tend to favor fish and bananas. One Ecuadorian specialty that is internationally known is **cebiche,** or **ceviche.** This dish consists of raw seafood marinated in lime combined with onions, tomatoes, and spices.

¿Comprendiste?

Answers
1. La papa vino de Perú.
2. Los españoles llevaron la papa a Europa.
3. El maíz vino de México.
4. El maíz tiene más importancia en la dieta de México.
5. No sabemos cómo llegó el tomate a Europa.

Block Schedule

Research Have students go to a market or supermarket to find out the following:
• names of fruits that have been imported from Latin American countries
• names of vegetables that have been imported from Latin American countries
• where potatoes originate from (Do they come from Latin America?)

Teaching All Students

Extra Help Ask students to reread each paragraph, then decide on a title for each one.

Native Speakers Ask students to supply the names of fruits and vegetables that they know of that are not available in the U.S.

Multiple Intelligences

Visual Have students create an advertisement poster for potatoes, tomatoes, and corn. They should show pictures, state prices, and give a sales pitch for each (how good they taste, how healthy they are, etc.).

Teaching Resource Options

Print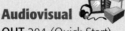

Para hispanohablantes Workbook
  PE, pp. 127–128
Block Scheduling Copymasters
Unit 6 Resource Book
  Para hispanohablantes Workbook
    TE, pp. 117–118
  Videoscript, p. 128
  Information Gap Activities, p. 122
  Family Involvement, pp. 123–124
  Multiple Choice Test Questions,
    pp. 170–178

Audiovisual

OHT 204 (Quick Start)
Audio Program Testing Cassette T2 /
  CD T2
Video Program Videotape 6 /
  Videodisc 3B

Search Chapter 9, Play to 10
Epilogue

Technology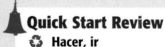

Electronic Teacher Tools/Test
  Generator
Intrigas y aventuras CD-ROM, Disc 1

Teaching Note

You may choose to show the Video Epilogue
segment, which reveals the contest winners.

🔔 Quick Start Review

♻️ **Hacer, ir**

Use OHT 204 or write on the board:
Write 3 sentences each for the verbs
hacer and **ir**. Sentence 1 must be in
the preterite, sentence 2 in the present,
and sentence 3 in the future.

Answers *See p. 427B.*

✓ Teaching Suggestions
What Have Students Learned?

Have students look at the "Now you
can…" notes listed on the left side of
pages 448–449. Remind them to
review the material in the "To review"
notes before doing the activities or
taking the test.

ETAPA 3

Now you can…

• talk about the
  present and future.

To review

• present progressive
  and **ir a** + infinitive,
  see p. 436.

Now you can…

• give instructions to
  someone.

To review

• affirmative **tú**
  commands, see
  p. 438.

En uso
REPASO Y MÁS COMUNICACIÓN

OBJECTIVES
• Talk about the present
  and future
• Give instructions to
  someone
• Discuss the past

ACTIVIDAD 1 ¡Muy ocupados!

Miguel y sus amigos hablan por teléfono de sus actividades.
¿Qué dicen? *(Hint: Tell present and future activities.)*

modelo

yo: estudiar matemáticas / ir al campo

*Ahora **yo** estoy estudiando **matemáticas,** pero más tarde voy a **ir al campo.***

1. Patricia: escribir cartas / hacer unas entrevistas
2. tú: hacer la tarea / alquilar un video
3. mis padres: limpiar la casa / caminar con el perro
4. yo: leer una novela / ir al cine
5. nosotros: ver la televisión / hacer ejercicio en el gimnasio
6. mi hermana: maquillarse / salir con Bernardo
7. ustedes: comer chicharrones / cenar en un restaurante elegante
8. tú: abrir unas cartas / andar en bicicleta

ACTIVIDAD 2 Una cena importante

El arquitecto que Patricia entrevistó viene
a cenar con ella y su familia esta noche. La
madre de Patricia necesita su ayuda. ¿Qué
le dice? *(Hint: Say what Patricia's mother tells her to do.)*

modelo

limpiar el baño

Limpia el baño.

1. lavar los platos
2. barrer el suelo
3. poner la mesa
4. hacer los quehaceres
   cuidadosamente
5. tener cuidado
6. ir al supermercado a comprar
   más refrescos
7. ponerte un vestido
8. servir las bebidas
9. ser simpática durante la cena
10. pasar la aspiradora

448 cuatrocientos cuarenta y ocho
Unidad 6

Classroom Community 🔳

TPR Use **Actividad 2** as a TPR activity. Students must
act out what you tell them to do.

Paired Activity Have students first write 8
sentences about what they did last week: 4 should be
true and 4 should be false. Then, working in pairs,
students read each sentence. The partner must guess if
the statement is true or false.

ACTIVIDAD 3 ¿Qué hiciste?

Patricia habla con una amiga sobre el fin de semana pasado. ¿Qué dice? *(Hint: Tell what happened last weekend.)*

modelo

yo: tomar el autobús al campo   Yo tomé el autobús al campo.

1. yo: visitar una granja en el campo
2. Miguel: decidir acompañarme
3. Miguel y yo: ver muchos animales
4. yo: sacar muchas fotos
5. mi madre: escribir cartas
6. mi padre: leer unas revistas
7. mis hermanos: correr en el parque
8. yo: ver a Ana en el mercado de Otavalo
9. ella: comprar algunas artesanías a muy buen precio
10. yo: llegar a casa muy tarde

ACTIVIDAD 4 Un día especial

Patricia habla con su madre. Completa lo que dicen con el pretérito de los verbos. *(Hint: Complete what they say.)*

Mamá: Patricia, tú __1__ (venir) a casa muy tarde ayer.

Patricia: Sí, mamá. Miguel y yo __2__ (ir) al campo.

Mamá: ¿Y qué __3__ (hacer) ustedes allí?

Patricia: Yo __4__ (hacer) entrevistas con el tío Julio y Bárbara.

Mamá: ¿Ellos te __5__ (decir) algo interesante?

Patricia: Sí. El tío Julio me __6__ (decir) mucho sobre la vida en una granja. La entrevista con Bárbara, la artesana, también __7__ (ser) interesante, y ella me __8__ (dar) este saco.

Mamá: ¡Qué bonito! ¿Ustedes __9__ (ir) a Otavalo por la tarde?

Patricia: Sí, mamá. Nosotros __10__ (estar) en el mercado por tres horas. Allí yo __11__ (tener) la oportunidad de entrevistar a un vendedor. Por eso, yo __12__ (venir) a casa tan tarde. Lo siento.

cuatrocientos cuarenta y nueve
Etapa 3   449

Now you can...
• discuss the past.

To review
• regular preterite verbs, see p. 439.

Now you can...
• discuss the past.

To review
• irregular preterite verbs, see p. 441.

ACTIVIDAD 1 Answers

1. Ahora Patricia está escribiendo cartas, pero más tarde va a hacer unas entrevistas.
2. Ahora tú estás haciendo la tarea, pero más tarde vas a alquilar un video.
3. Ahora mis padres están limpiando la casa, pero más tarde van a caminar con el perro.
4. Ahora yo estoy leyendo una novela, pero más tarde voy a ir al cine.
5. Ahora nosotros estamos viendo la televisión, pero más tarde vamos a hacer ejercicio en el gimnasio.
6. Ahora mi hermana está maquillándose (se está maquillando), pero más tarde va a salir con Bernardo.
7. Ahora ustedes están comiendo chicharrones, pero más tarde van a cenar en un restaurante elegante.
8. Ahora tú estás abriendo unas cartas, pero más tarde vas a andar en bicicleta.

ACTIVIDAD 2 Answers

1. Lava los platos.
2. Barre el suelo.
3. Pon la mesa.
4. Haz los quehaceres cuidadosamente.
5. Ten cuidado.
6. Ve al supermercado a comprar más refrescos.
7. Ponte un vestido.
8. Sirve las bebidas.
9. Sé simpática durante la cena.
10. Pasa la aspiradora.

ACTIVIDAD 3 Answers

1. Yo visité una granja en el campo.
2. Miguel decidió acompañarme.
3. Miguel y yo vimos muchos animales.
4. Yo saqué muchas fotos.
5. Mi madre escribió cartas.
6. Mi padre leyó unas revistas.
7. Mis hermanos corrieron en el parque.
8. Yo vi a Ana en el mercado de Otavalo.
9. Ella compró algunas artesanías a muy buen precio.
10. Yo llegué a casa muy tarde.

ACTIVIDAD 4 Answers

1. viniste	5. dijeron	9. fueron
2. fuimos	6. dijo	10. estuvimos
3. hicieron	7. fue	11. tuve
4. hice	8. dio	12. vine

Teaching All Students

Extra Help Break down the task in **Actividad 1**. Have students first write/say the present progressive part of all items, then all the **ir a** + infinitive parts. Finally, have them read the complete sentences.

Multiple Intelligences

Intrapersonal Have students write 5 commands that they would like to be told.

Block Schedule

Change of Pace Have students create time lines that mark off at least 6 important dates. Next to each date they write what happened or what they did on that date. (For additional activities, see **Block Scheduling Copymasters**.)

Teaching Resource Options

Print

Unit 6 Resource Book
Cooperative Quizzes, pp. 135–136
Etapa Exam, Forms A and B,
    pp. 137–146
Para hispanohablantes Etapa Exam,
    pp. 147–151
Portfolio Assessment, pp. 152–153
Unit 6 Comprehensive Test,
    pp. 154–161
Para hispanohablantes Unit 6
    Comprehensive Test, pp. 162–169
Final Test, pp. 179–186
Multiple Choice Test Questions,
    pp. 170–178

Audiovisual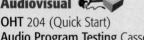

OHT 204 (Quick Start)
Audio Program Testing Cassette T2 /
    CD T2

Technology

Electronic Teacher Tools/Test
    Generator
www.mcdougallittell.com

ACTIVIDAD 5

Rubric: Speaking

Criteria	Scale	
Vocabulary use	1 2 3	A = 8–9 pts.
Sentence structure	1 2 3	B = 6–7 pts.
Ease, fluency	1 2 3	C = 4–5 pts.
		D = 3 pts.
		F = < 3 pts.

ACTIVIDAD 6 *Answers will vary.*

ACTIVIDAD 7 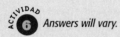 **En tu propia voz**

Rubric: Writing

Criteria	Scale	
Vocabulary use	1 2 3 4 5	A = 14–15 pts.
Accuracy	1 2 3 4 5	B = 12–13 pts.
Creativity, appearance	1 2 3 4 5	C = 10–11 pts.
		D = 8–9 pts.
		F = < 8 pts.

Teaching Note: En tu propia voz

Remind students to review the writing strategy ""Tell who, what, where, when, why, and how" before beginning their vacation paragraphs. A well-written paragraph uses many details to communicate information.

450 Review • UNIDAD 6 Etapa 3

ACTIVIDAD 5  **¿Quién soy yo?**

> ### PARA CONVERSAR
> **STRATEGY: SPEAKING**
> **Rely on the basics** You have practiced many speaking strategies for different contexts. These work in all situations. Keep them in mind as you speak.
>
> 1. Don't be afraid to make mistakes.
> 2. Encourage yourself; think positively.
> 3. Take your time.
> 4. Take risks; improvise.
> 5. Say more, rather than less.
>
> And enjoy speaking… now that you have plenty you can say!

Imagínate que eres una de las personas de este libro. Dile a otro(a) estudiante qué hiciste ayer, qué estás haciendo ahora y qué vas a hacer mañana. Él o ella tiene que adivinar quién eres. *(Hint: Play the role of a character. Your partner must guess who you are.)*

Francisco   Ignacio   Mercedes   Diana
    Alma   Ricardo   Patricia   Luis   Miguel
        Isabel   Carlos   Sofía

ACTIVIDAD 6  **¿Qué hago?**

Vas a uno de estos lugares por primera vez. Los otros estudiantes van a decirte qué debes hacer allí. *(Hint: Select a place; classmates will tell you what to do there.)*

la playa   **el campo**   **un bosque tropical**

una granja   **una ciudad grande**   **¿?**

un mercado mexicano   **las montañas**

modelo
_____
Tú: *Voy a una ciudad grande por primera vez. ¿Qué hago?*
Estudiante 1: *Ve a un concierto.*

ACTIVIDAD 7 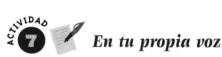 *En tu propia voz*

ESCRITURA Estás pensando en las vacaciones de verano. Escribe un párrafo sobre lo que hiciste el verano pasado y otro párrafo sobre lo que vas a hacer este verano. *(Hint: Write about summer activities.)*

CONEXIONES

La salud You have just read how New World foods changed European cuisine. Select a Spanish-speaking country and write a brief report about what people in that country typically eat. Prepare the food you would most like to taste. Was it difficult or easy to prepare? Is it nutritious?

> ¿Qué desayunan? ¿Almuerzan? ¿Cenan?
> ¿A qué hora almuerzan? ¿Cenan?
> ¿Qué meriendas hay?
> ¿Qué hay de postre?
> ¿Cuál es el plato más famoso de este país?

450 cuatrocientos cincuenta
Unidad 6

Classroom Community

Paired Activity Have students work on the **Conexiones** report and recipe in pairs. You might also invite other staff members to enjoy the dishes and show off your students' accomplishments.

Portfolio Put the final drafts of **Actividad 7** into students' portfolios. The portfolios should be passed on to the Spanish 2 teacher. At the beginning of Spanish 2, students will review this writing to see if their predictions for the summer match what finally happened.

En resumen

YA SABES ♻

TALKING ABOUT THE PRESENT AND FUTURE

Simple Present

Estoy muy feliz.	*I am very happy.*
¡Es un mercado fenomenal!	*It's a phenomenal market!*
La artesanía de Otavalo es excelente.	*The handicrafts from Otavalo are excellent.*

Present Progressive

Miguel y Patricia están caminando y hablando.	*Miguel and Patricia are walking and talking.*

Ir a + *infinitive*

Voy a comprarle un regalo a mi hermana.	*I am going to buy a present for my sister.*
¡Creo que va a salir muy bien y lo quiero ver!	*I think that it is going to come out very well and I want to see it!*

DISCUSSING THE PAST

Regular Preterite

¿Porque te habló de la vida en una granja?	*Because he talked to you about life on a farm?*
¿Y aprendiste algo de tus entrevistas?	*And did you learn something from your interviews?*
Pero aprendí algo mucho más importante también.	*But I learned something much more important too.*
¡Abriste la cerca!	*You opened the fence!*
Trabajé mucho.	*I worked a lot.*

Irregular Preterite

¿Cuál fue la mejor entrevista?	*Which was the best interview?*
No, ¡porque me dijo qué hiciste tú la primera vez que estuviste en la granja!	*No, because he told me what you did the first time that you were at the farm!*
Hice todo lo posible.	*I did everything possible.*

GIVING INSTRUCTIONS TO SOMEONE

Dime.	*Tell me.*
¡Mira, Miguel!	*Look, Miguel!*
Cómprale una bolsa o un artículo de cuero.	*Buy her a handbag or leather goods.*
¡Ven!	*Come on!*
Hazme un favor.	*Do me a favor.*

Juego

1. ¿Qué pasa ahora?
2. ¿Qué pasó antes?
3. ¿Qué va a pasar?

¡El caballo se va a escapar del corral!

La llama está jugando con Rocío.

El ganadero buscó su merienda.

cuatrocientos cincuenta y uno
Etapa 3 **451**

Teaching All Students

Extra Help Help students begin **Actividad 7** by first having them brainstorm a list of details, then a list of sequencing and conjunction words.

Native Speakers For **Actividad 5,** have students share their experiences learning English. Do they agree with the points listed in the Speaking Strategy? Have them give additional advice to their classmates.

Multiple Intelligences

Verbal Tell students to turn to various **Etapa** openers throughout the text. Then have them give a few sentences describing what is happening in each one, using the present progressive.

Interdisciplinary Connections

Health Have students research the nutritional value of foods that are typical of or originated in Latin America, such as potatoes, corn, tomatoes, bananas, etc. They should find out the vitamin content, the fat content, and the caloric content of a typical serving.

🔔 Quick Start Review

♻ Verb tense review

Use OHT 204 or write on the board: For each sentence, write Past, Present, or Future:

1. Hablaron francés en la fiesta.
2. ¿Qué estás comiendo?
3. ¿Quién abrió la puerta?
4. ¿A qué hora van a salir?
5. La clase empieza a las nueve.
6. Fui a Puerto Rico.
7. Voy a trabajar mucho.
8. ¿Qué estás haciendo ahora?

Answers

1.	Past	5.	Present
2.	Present	6.	Past
3.	Past	7.	Future
4.	Future	8.	Present

Teaching Suggestions
Verb Tense Review

Have students sketch a scene showing some kind of action. Then have them exchange papers with a partner. Students must write a past tense sentence, a present tense sentence, and a sentence with **ir a...** that describe their partner's action scene.

Juego

Answers
1. La llama está jugando con Rocío.
2. El ganadero buscó su merienda.
3. ¡El caballo se va a escapar del corral!

■ Block Schedule

FunBreak Have students play one of the games in the **Ampliación** on TE p. 383B.

Teaching Resource Options

Print 📖
Block Scheduling Copymasters

Audiovisual 🎧💻
OHT GO1–GO5; 204 (Quick Start)

Technology 💻
Intrigas y aventuras CD-ROM, Disc 1
www.mcdougallittell.com

🔔 Quick Start Review

♻️ Academic skills

Use OHT 204 or write on the board:
¿Qué hace un buen estudiante?
Escribe 5 oraciones.

Answers
Answers will vary. Answers could include:
Hace todas las tareas.
Estudia mucho para los exámenes.
Siempre trae el libro y el cuaderno a clase.
Escucha al (a la) profesor(a).
Trabaja bien con los otros estudiantes.
Levanta la mano cuando quiere hablar.

Teaching Strategy
Prewriting

• Write students' ideas from the Quick Start on the board. Make another list of what a good student does *not* do.
• Have students talk about which of the behaviors are easy for them and which are difficult.
• Remind students of the **PASS** list at the beginning of the page: **P**urpose, **A**udience, **S**ubject, **S**tructure. This PASS key will help them complete a well-structured assignment.

Post-writing

• Discuss how good school habits translate into good work habits.

Supplementary Vocabulary

hacer lo máximo/ mínimo	to do the maximum/ minimum
manejar el tiempo	to manage time
pasar el tiempo sin obrar	to procrastinate
hacer trampa	to cheat

UNIDAD 6

¡Trabaja para nuestro periódico!

Oportunidades especiales para estudiantes

Escríbenos:
La Prensa
2255 Pacific Avenue
Los Ángeles, CA 90631

En tu propia voz
ESCRITURA

¡Busco trabajo!

A local newspaper is offering paid internships for Spanish students for the summer. Write a formal letter of application in which you emphasize your academic skills.

Purpose:	Apply for employment
Audience:	Potential employer
Subject:	Your qualifications
Structure:	Formal letter of application

PARA ESCRIBIR • STRATEGY: WRITING

Support a general statement with informative details Attract your reader's attention with a strong general statement about your academic skills. Then add details that support your statement.

Modelo del estudiante

> 5 de mayo de 2000
>
> La Prensa
> 2255 Pacific Avenue
> Los Ángeles, CA 90631
>
> Estimado editor:
>
> Me gustaría trabajar para La Prensa este verano. Soy un estudiante muy trabajador y serio. Saco buenas notas en mis clases en M.L. King High School. especialmente en inglés, historia y español. Me gusta estudiar otras culturas y escribir para todas mis clases. El mes pasado recibí un premio de nuestro Departamento de Historia por mi estudio sobre los otavaleños de Ecuador.
>
> Después de mis clases, siempre voy a la biblioteca y hago mi tarea allí. En mi tiempo libre, juego al balconcesto y escribo poesía. Pienso ser escritor o periodista en el futuro. Quiero aprender más de estas profesiones y ahora busco trabajo y experiencia en su periódico. Muchas gracias por su tiempo.
>
> Atentamente,
>
> *Bryan Walter*

The writer makes a **strong general statement** about himself as a serious, skilled student.

Next, the writer adds **evidence** of his academic interests and achievements. He emphasizes writing and Spanish in his letter.

Here he includes **additional information** that he manages his time well.

At the end, the writer adds related **details** about his interest in the writing professions.

Classroom Community

Paired Activity Have students work in pairs outside of class. Ask them to talk to employers in places where teenagers typically work and find out what work habits employers look for. Be sure students call ahead to arrange an appointment and to let the employers know that this is a Spanish assignment. Tell students to be sure to thank the people for their time and information.

Portfolio Have students include this formal letter in their portfolios. Remind them that the letter should look business-like and be free of typos.

Estrategias para escribir

Antes de escribir...

An effective letter requesting employment calls attention to your skills as a student and as a worker. Brainstorm ideas for the following categories: academic skills, interests, work-related experiences, and why you want the internship. Record them on a chart. Write a general statement about your skills. Add supporting evidence. Use the formal openings and closings given in the model.

habilidades académicas	estudio todos los días aprendo rápidamente hablo, leo y escribo en español
intereses	soy buena fotógrafa conferencias para artistas
trabajo, experiencias	periódico de la escuela Photo Finish voluntaria en la liga de fútbol
por qué quiero el trabajo	aprender a trabajar como fotógrafa aprender más del trabajo para un periódico

Revisiones

Share your draft with a partner. Then ask:

- *What makes my general statement impressive?*
- *How well do the details support my general statement?*
- *How appropriate is the information about my skills?*

La versión final

Before you write the final draft, ask yourself these questions:

- *Did I use the preterite correctly?*

Try this: Underline every preterite verb. Identify each as regular or irregular. Refer to pp. 439 and 441 to check the correct endings.

- *Are adverbs formed correctly?*

Try this: Circle all adverbs ending in **-mente.** Be sure the root word is correct and that **-mente** is appropriately placed.

Note the markings used to make a letter small and to capitalize.

 Share your writing on www.mcdougallittell.com

Estimado editor:

Busco trabajo en el departamento de fotografía de su periódico. Soy creativa, inteligente y muy trabajadora. También soy buena fotógrafa. Trabajo cuidadosamente y aprendo rápidamente. El año pasado fui a una conferencia para artistas y recibió un premio por una de mis fotos.

Trabajé como fotógrafa en el periódico de mi escuela...

EDITORIAL MARKS

$\mathcal{A}$ = **lowercase** $\underset{\sim}{a}$ = **capitalize**

Rubric: Writing

Let students know ahead of time which elements of their writing you will be evaluating. A global evaluation is more helpful to students than a correction of every mistake made. Consider the following in scoring compositions:

Sentences	
1	Most are not logical
2	In logical order
3	Flow purposefully

Details	
1	Few details
2	Sufficient basic details
3	Clear and vivid detail

Organization	
1	Not well organized
2	Some organization
3	Strong organization

Accuracy	
1	Errors prevent comprehension
2	Some spelling and agreement errors throughout
3	Very few errors

Criteria	Scale	
Logical sentence order	1 2 3 4 5	A = 14–16 pts.
Clear and vivid detail	1 2 3 4 5	B = 11–13 pts.
Organization	1 2 3 4 5	C = 8–10 pts.
Accuracy	1 2 3 4 5	D = 5–7 pts.
		F = < 5 pts.

Teaching All Students

Extra Help Students may need help brainstorming their skills. Remind them that everyone has valuable skills including listening well, remembering what they are told, persevering, solving problems, thinking creatively, staying cool under pressure, and so on.

Multiple Intelligences

Verbal Have students name skills that one acquires in the following situations that would apply to a job situation: sports team, debating team, drama club, band, chorus, Spanish club, school newspaper.

Block Schedule

Variety Bring in several copies of the Help Wanted section of the newspaper. Have students look for jobs they might be interested in and have the skills for. They should especially look for jobs where their Spanish skills would be helpful. (For additional activities, see **Block Scheduling Copymasters**.)

RECURSOS

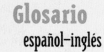

1 Unidad 1 Etapa 1 p. 35
¿Quién es?

Estudiante A The people in the neighborhood are being introduced at a town meeting, but it is hard to hear. Find out from your partner who they are.

modelo

Estudiante A: ¿Quién es el policía?

Estudiante B: Es...

1. el policía...
2. el maestro... Hernán Campos
3. las estudiantes...
4. el doctor... Raúl Guzmán
5. las maestras... Beatriz Simón y Laura Valdez
6. el estudiante...
7. la doctora...
8. los maestros... Patricio Díaz y Esteban Castillo

Estudiante B The people in the neighborhood are being introduced at a town meeting, but it is hard to hear. Find out from your partner who they are.

modelo

Estudiante A: ¿Quién es el policía?

Estudiante B: Es el señor Ruiz.

1. el policía... el señor Ruiz
2. el maestro...
3. las estudiantes... Carolina y Olivia
4. el doctor...
5. las maestras...
6. el estudiante... Felipe
7. la doctora... Ana Colón
8. los maestros...

2 Unidad 1 Etapa 1 p. 39
¿Le gusta…?

Estudiante A Daniela only likes to do the activities pictured. Find out from your partner if Gustavo likes to do the same.

modelo

Estudiante A: ¿Le gusta nadar?

Estudiante B: …

Estudiante B Gustavo only likes to do the activities pictured. Find out from your partner if Daniela likes to do the same.

modelo

Estudiante B: ¿Le gusta correr?

Estudiante A: …

1 Answers

1. A: ¿Quién es el policía?
   B: Es el señor Ruiz.
2. B: ¿Quién es el maestro?
   A: Es Hernán Campos.
3. A: ¿Quiénes son las estudiantes?
   B: Son Carolina y Olivia.
4. B: ¿Quién es el doctor?
   A: Es Raúl Guzmán.
5. B: ¿Quiénes son las maestras?
   A: Son Beatriz Simón y Laura Valdez.
6. A: ¿Quién es el estudiante?
   B: Es Felipe.
7. A: ¿Quién es la doctora?
   B: Es Ana Colón.
8. B: ¿Quiénes son los maestros?
   A: Son Patricio Díaz y Esteban Castillo.

2 Answers

A: ¿Le gusta nadar?
B: No, no le gusta nadar.

B: ¿Le gusta correr?
A: No, no le gusta correr.

A: ¿Le gusta cantar?
B: Sí, le gusta cantar.

B: ¿Le gusta bailar?
A: No, no le gusta bailar.

A: ¿Le gusta patinar?
B: No, no le gusta patinar.

B: ¿Le gusta cantar?
A: Sí, le gusta cantar.

A: ¿Le gusta escribir?
B: No, no le gusta escribir.

B: ¿Le gusta leer?
A: No, no le gusta leer.

3 Answers

Answers will vary.

A: El hombre es bajo, delgado y pelirrojo. Tiene pelo corto. Lleva una camiseta morada, jeans, calcetines blancos y zapatos marrones. Es cómico y divertido. No le gusta trabajar. Es perezoso.

B: La mujer es alta, delgada y rubia. Tiene pelo largo. Es bonita. Lleva zapatos morados, una falda verde, una blusa morada y una chaqueta verde. Es seria y inteligente. Le gusta escribir. Es trabajadora.

4 Answers

Esteban

A: ¿De qué color son los zapatos?
B: Lleva zapatos negros.
A: ¿De qué color son los calcetines?
B: Lleva calcetines blancos.
A: ¿De qué color son los pantalones?
B: Lleva pantalones negros.
A: ¿De qué color es la chaqueta?
B: Lleva una chaqueta roja y blanca.
A: ¿De qué color es la camiseta?
B: Lleva una camiseta azul.

Chela

B: ¿De qué color son los zapatos?
A: Lleva zapatos morados.
B: ¿De qué color son los calcetines?
A: Lleva calcetines blancos.
B: ¿De qué color es la falda?
A: Lleva una falda morada.
B: ¿De qué color es el suéter?
A: Lleva un suéter amarillo.
B: ¿De qué color es la blusa?
A: Lleva una blusa blanca.
B: ¿De qué color es el sombrero?
A: Lleva un sombrero amarillo.

Esteban lleva calcetines blancos y una chaqueta blanca y roja. Chela lleva calcetines blancos y una blusa blanca.

---

3 Unidad 1 Etapa 2 p. 58
¿Cómo es?

Estudiante A Describe the person to your partner. Include what you think his personality might be like. Then draw the person your partner describes to you.

Estudiante B Draw the person your partner describes to you. Then describe your picture to your partner. Include what you think her personality might be like.

---

4 Unidad 1 Etapa 2 p. 61
¿De qué color son?

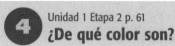

Estudiante A: *¿De qué color son los zapatos?*
Estudiante B: *Lleva zapatos...*

modelo

Estudiante A Ask about the colors of Esteban's clothes. Then describe the colors of Chela's clothing for your partner. Are they wearing anything the same color?

Estudiante B Describe the colors of Esteban's clothing for your partner. Then ask about the colors of Chela's clothes. Are they wearing anything the same color?

modelo

Estudiante A: *¿De qué color son los zapatos?*
Estudiante B: *Lleva zapatos negros.*

5 ¿Cuántos años tiene?
Unidad 1, Etapa 3 p. 77

6 La familia Zavala
Unidad 1, Etapa 3 p. 83

(upside-down, Estudiante A section for activity 5)

Estudiante A Complete the chart with the ages of members of the Zavala family.

modelo

Estudiante A: ¿Cuántos años tiene Josefa?
Estudiante B: Tiene…

Nombre	Edad
1. Josefa	
2. Víctor	65
3. Victoria	38
4. José	
5. Lupita	
6. Eva	4

(upside-down, Estudiante A section for activity 6)

1. hermana / José
2. tío / Eva
3. abuelo / Pepe
4. hermano / Lupita
5. madre / Victoria
6. hijo / Víctor
7. prima / Eva
8. padre / Lupita
9. tía / Pepe
10. hija / Paquita

modelo

Estudiante A: ¿Quién es la hermana de José?
Estudiante B: …

Estudiante A Your partner is looking at the Zavala family tree. Find out the names of various family members.

Estudiante B (activity 5)

Estudiante B Complete the chart with the ages of members of the Zavala family.

modelo

Estudiante A: ¿Cuántos años tiene Josefa?
Estudiante B: Tiene cincuenta y nueve años.

Nombre	Edad
1. Josefa	59
2. Víctor	
3. Victoria	
4. José	33
5. Lupita	15
6. Eva	

Estudiante B (activity 6)

Estudiante B Your partner wants to know the names of members of the Zavala family. Answer his or her questions according to the family tree.

modelo

Estudiante A: ¿Quién es la hermana de José?
Estudiante B: Victoria es la hermana de José.

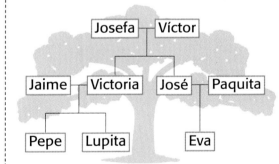

Josefa — Víctor
Jaime — Victoria   José — Paquita
Pepe   Lupita   Eva

5 Answers

1. A: ¿Cuántos años tiene Josefa?
   B: Tiene cincuenta y nueve años.
2. B: ¿Cuántos años tiene Víctor?
   A: Tiene sesenta y cinco años.
3. B: ¿Cuántos años tiene Victoria?
   A: Tiene treinta y ocho años.
4. A: ¿Cuántos años tiene José?
   B: Tiene treinta y tres años.
5. A: ¿Cuántos años tiene Lupita?
   B: Tiene quince años.
6. B: ¿Cuántos años tiene Eva?
   A: Tiene cuatro años.

6 Answers

1. A: ¿Quién es la hermana de José?
   B: Victoria es la hermana de José.
2. A: ¿Quién es el tío de Eva?
   B: Jaime es el tío de Eva.
3. A: ¿Quién es el abuelo de Pepe?
   B: Víctor es el abuelo de Pepe.
4. A: ¿Quién es el hermano de Lupita?
   B: Pepe es el hermano de Lupita.
5. A: ¿Quién es la madre de Victoria?
   B: Josefa es la madre de Victoria.
6. A: ¿Quién es el hijo de Víctor?
   B: José es el hijo de Víctor.
7. A: ¿Quién es la prima de Eva?
   B: Lupita es la prima de Eva.
8. A: ¿Quién es el padre de Lupita?
   B: Jaime es el padre de Lupita.
9. A: ¿Quién es la tía de Pepe?
   B: Paquita es la tía de Pepe.
10. A: ¿Quién es la hija de Paquita?
    B: Eva es la hija de Paquita.

7 Answers

A: ¿Qué clase tiene Rosa?
B: Tiene historia.
A: ¿Qué usa en la clase de historia?
B: Usa un cuaderno.
B: ¿Qué clase tiene César?
A: Tiene inglés.
B: ¿Qué usa en la clase de inglés?
A: Usa una pluma.
A: ¿Qué clase tiene Jesús?
B: Tiene computación.
A: ¿Qué usa en la clase de computación?
B: Usa un ratón.
B: ¿Qué clase tiene Gilberto?
A: Tiene matemáticas.
B: ¿Qué usa en la clase de matemáticas?
A: Usa una calculadora.
B: ¿Qué clase tienes?
A: Tengo...
B: ¿Qué usas en la clase de...?
A: Uso...
A: ¿Qué clase tienes?
B: Tengo...
A: ¿Qué usas en la clase de...?
B: Uso...

8 Answers

1. A: ¿Gabriela tiene que estudiar?
   B: Gabriela tiene que estudiar de vez en cuando. o: De vez en cuando Gabriela tiene que estudiar.
2. A: ¿Gabriela tiene que leer?
   B: Gabriela rara vez tiene que leer.
3. A: ¿Gabriela tiene que llevar uniforme?
   B: Gabriela siempre tiene que llevar uniforme.
4. A: ¿Gabriela tiene que cantar?
   B: Gabriela nunca tiene que cantar.
5. A: ¿Gabriela tiene que correr?
   B: Gabriela tiene que correr todos los días. o: Todos los días Gabriela tiene que correr.
6. A: ¿Gabriela tiene que mirar videos?
   B: Gabriela tiene que mirar videos a veces. o: A veces Gabriela tiene que mirar videos.
7. A: ¿Gabriela tiene que escuchar al profesor?
   B: Gabriela tiene que escuchar mucho al profesor.

7 ¿Qué clase tiene?
Unidad 2 Etapa 1 p. 106

Nombre	Clase	Usa...
Rosa		
César	inglés	pluma
Jesús		
Gilberto	matemáticas	calculadora
yo	¿?	¿?
Estudiante B	¿?	¿?

Estudiante A Find out about the following students' classes by completing the chart with your partner.

modelo

Estudiante A: ¿Qué clase tiene Rosa?
Estudiante B: Tiene...
Estudiante A: ¿Qué usa en la clase de...?
Estudiante B: Usa...

Estudiante B Find out about the following students' classes by completing the chart with your partner.

modelo

Estudiante A: ¿Qué clase tiene Rosa?
Estudiante B: Tiene historia.
Estudiante A: ¿Qué usa en la clase de historia?
Estudiante B: Usa un cuaderno.

Nombre	Clase	Usa...
Rosa	historia	cuaderno
César		
Jesús	computación	ratón
Gilberto		
Estudiante A	¿?	¿?
yo	¿?	¿?

8 ¿Siempre o nunca?
Unidad 2 Etapa 1 p. 111

1. ¿Gabriela tiene que estudiar?
2. ¿leer?
3. ¿llevar uniforme?
4. ¿cantar?
5. ¿correr?
6. ¿mirar videos?
7. ¿escuchar al profesor?

Estudiante B: Gabriela tiene que estudiar...
Estudiante A: ¿Gabriela tiene que estudiar?

modelo

Estudiante A Ask your partner if Gabriela has to do the following activities in her class. Can you guess what class it is?

Estudiante B Answer your partner's questions about Gabriela's class.

modelo

Estudiante A: ¿Gabriela tiene que estudiar?
Estudiante B: Gabriela tiene que estudiar de vez en cuando.

Gabriela: la clase de educación física	
siempre	llevar uniforme
todos los días	correr
mucho	escuchar al profesor
a veces	mirar videos
de vez en cuando	estudiar
rara vez	leer
nunca	cantar

⑨ ¿A qué hora?

(texto de Estudiante A, impreso al revés)

Estudiante A Ask what time your partner will do the following activities. Draw clocks to indicate the times. Then tell your partner what time you will do them.

modelo

Estudiante A: *¿A qué hora vas al doctor?*

Estudiante B: *Voy al doctor a las… ¿Y tú?*

Estudiante A: *Voy al doctor a las nueve y cuarto de la mañana.*

Por la mañana	Por la tarde
1. 9:15 - ir al doctor	**4.** 1:20 - tomar almuerzo
2. 10:50 - tomar una prueba	**5.** 2:45 - ir a casa
3. 12:00 - comprar papel	**6.** 4:30 - visitar a amigos
	7. 5:10 - terminar la tarea
	8. 7:45 - descansar

Estudiante B Tell your partner what time you will do the following activities. Then draw clocks to indicate what time your partner will do them.

modelo

Estudiante A: *¿A qué hora vas al doctor?*

Estudiante B: *Voy al doctor a las nueve menos cuarto de la mañana. ¿Y tú?*

Estudiante A: *Voy al doctor a las…*

Por la mañana

8:45 - ir al doctor

12:00 - tomar almuerzo

Por la tarde

1:05 - tomar una prueba

2:15 - comprar papel

3:50 - ir a casa

4:20 - terminar la tarea

6:30 - visitar a amigos

9:00 - descansar

⑩ ¿Doble visión?

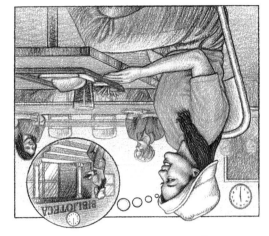

(texto de Estudiante A, impreso al revés)

Estudiante A You and your partner have similar drawings. Ask each other questions to find at least five differences between the two drawings.

Estudiante B You and your partner have similar drawings. Ask each other questions to find at least five differences between the two drawings.

⑨ Answers

1. A: ¿A qué hora vas al doctor?
   B: Voy al doctor a las nueve menos cuarto de la mañana. ¿Y tú?
   A: Voy al doctor a las nueve y cuarto de la mañana.
2. A: ¿A qué hora tomas una prueba?
   B: Tomo una prueba a la una y cinco de la tarde. ¿Y tú?
   A: Tomo una prueba a las once menos diez de la mañana.
3. A: ¿A qué hora compras papel?
   B: Compro papel a las dos y cuarto de la tarde. ¿Y tú?
   A: Compro papel al mediodía.
4. A: ¿A qué hora tomas el almuerzo?
   B: Tomo el almuerzo al mediodía. ¿Y tú?
   A: Tomo el almuerzo a la una y veinte de la tarde.
5. A: ¿A qué hora vas a casa?
   B: Voy a casa a las cuatro menos diez de la tarde. ¿Y tú?
   A: Voy a casa a las tres menos cuarto de la tarde.
6. A: ¿A qué hora visitas a amigos?
   B: Visito a amigos a las seis y media de la tarde. ¿Y tú?
   A: Visito a amigos a las cuatro y media de la tarde.
7. A: ¿A qué hora terminas la tarea?
   B: Termino la tarea a las cuatro y veinte de la tarde. ¿Y tú?
   A: Termino la tarea a las cinco y diez de la tarde.
8. A: ¿A qué hora descansas?
   B: Descanso a las nueve de la noche. ¿Y tú?
   A: Descanso a las ocho menos cuarto de la noche.

⑩ Answers

Questions will vary.

¿De qué color es la camiseta de la chica?
   A: Lleva una camiseta verde.
   B: Lleva una camiseta roja.

¿Cómo es el pelo de la chica?
   A: Tiene pelo largo.
   B: Tiene pelo corto.

¿Qué come la chica?
   A: Come una torta.
   B: Come una hamburguesa.

¿Qué hora es?
   A: Son las once y media.
   B: Son las doce menos cuarto.

¿Adónde va la chica al mediodía?
   A: Va a la biblioteca.
   B: Va a casa.

¿Cómo es el chico?
   A: Es rubio.
   B: Es moreno.

¿Qué lleva el chico?
   A: Lleva una camisa anaranjada.
   B: Lleva una camiseta azul.

¿Cómo es la otra chica?
   A: Es morena.
   B: Es castaña.

¿Quién tiene un vaso de agua?
   A: La otra chica tiene un vaso de agua.
   B: El chico tiene un vaso de agua.

11 Answers

1. A: ¿Marcos va a pasear?
   B: Sí, Marcos va a pasear.
2. A: ¿Marcos va a leer una novela?
   B: Sí, Marcos va a leer una novela.
3. A: ¿Marcos va a ir al supermercado?
   B: No, Marcos no va a ir al supermercado.
4. A: ¿Marcos va a pintar?
   B: Sí, Marcos va a pintar.
5. A: ¿Marcos va a ver la televisión?
   B: Sí, Marcos va a ver la televisión.
6. A: ¿Marcos va a cuidar el pájaro?
   B: No, Marcos no va a cuidar el pájaro.

12 Answers

A: ¿Qué hace primero?
B: Primero, ella lee el periódico. ¿Qué hace después de leer el periódico?
A: Entonces, ella hace ejercicio. ¿Qué hace después de hacer ejercicio?
B: [Luego], ella escucha música. ¿Qué hace después de escuchar música?
A: [Luego], ella va a la biblioteca. ¿Qué hace después de ir a la biblioteca?
B: [Luego], ella come una merienda. ¿Qué hace después de comer una merienda?
A: [Después], ella escribe un poema. ¿Qué hace por fin?
B: Por fin, ella ve la televisión.

---

11 Unidad 2 Etapa 3 p. 151
¿Qué va a hacer?

Estudiante A Find out about Marcos. Ask if he is going to do the following activities.

modelo

Estudiante A: *¿Marcos va a pasear?*

Estudiante B: …

1. pasear
2. leer una novela
3. ir al supermercado
4. pintar
5. ver la televisión
6. cuidar el pájaro

Estudiante B Answer your partner's questions about Marcos according to your drawing.

modelo

Estudiante A: *¿Marcos va a pasear?*

Estudiante B: *Sí, Marcos va a pasear.*

---

12 Unidad 2 Etapa 3 p. 155
¿En qué orden?

	9:00
escribir un poema	8:30
	8:00
ir a la biblioteca	7:30
	7:00
hacer ejercicio	6:30
	6:00

Estudiante A Susana likes to organize her activities, but she left her other calendar at school. Work with your partner to determine the order of her evening activities.

modelo

Estudiante A: *¿Qué hace primero?*

Estudiante B: *Primero, ella... ¿Qué hace después de...?*

Estudiante A: *Entonces, ella hace ejercicio.*

Estudiante B Susana likes to organize her activities, but she left her other calendar at home. Work with your partner to determine the order of her evening activities.

modelo

Estudiante A: *¿Qué hace primero?*

Estudiante B: *Primero, ella lee el periódico. ¿Qué hace después de leer el periódico?*

Estudiante A: *Entonces, ella…*

6:00	leer el periódico
6:30	
7:00	escuchar música
7:30	
8:00	comer una merienda
8:30	
9:00	ver la televisión

13 Unidad 3 Etapa 1 p. 179
Muchas emociones

Estudiante A You and your partner are talking about friends. You know what each person has done and your partner knows how each is feeling. Exchange information.

modelo

Josefina: ayudar a su padre

Estudiante A: *¿Cómo está Josefina?*
Estudiante B: *Está… ¿Qué acaba de hacer?*
Estudiante A: *Acaba de ayudar a su padre.*

1. Milagros: sacar una mala nota
2. Carlos: visitar a su abuelo enfermo
3. Ricardo: tomar un examen
4. Martina: mirar un video

Estudiante B You and your partner are talking about friends. You know how each person is feeling and your partner knows what each has just done. Exchange information.

modelo

Josefina

Estudiante A: *¿Cómo está Josefina?*
Estudiante B: *Está tranquila. ¿Qué acaba de hacer?*
Estudiante A: *Acaba de…*

1. Milagros
2. Carlos
3. Ricardo
4. Martina

14 Unidad 3 Etapa 1 p. 183
Por teléfono

Estudiante A Practice making phone calls. Begin a conversation and then choose logical responses from the list. Your partner will begin the second conversation.

Conversación 1
Soy… ¿Cómo estás?
¿Te gustaría ir al cine por la noche?
Está bien. Hasta luego.
¡Qué lástima!
Buenos días. ¿Puedo hablar con…?

Conversación 2
Muy bien. Adiós.
¿Cuál es tu teléfono?
No está aquí. Regresa más tarde.
¡Claro que sí!

Estudiante B Your partner has just called you on the phone. Choose from the responses to carry on a logical conversation. Then begin a second conversation.

Conversación 1
Gracias, pero no puedo.
¡Muy bien! Voy a patinar por la tarde.
Nos vemos.
Tal vez otro día.
Soy… ¿Quién habla?

Conversación 2
Quiero dejar un mensaje para ella.
253-5652
Buenas tardes. ¿Puedo hablar con Carolina?
Dile que me llame, por favor.
Gracias. Adiós.

---

13 Answers

1. A: ¿Cómo está Milagros?
   B: Está enojada. ¿Qué acaba de hacer?
   A: Acaba de sacar una mala nota.
2. A: ¿Cómo está Carlos?
   B: Está triste. ¿Qué acaba de hacer?
   A: Acaba de visitar a su abuelo enfermo.
3. A: ¿Cómo está Ricardo?
   B: Está preocupado. ¿Qué acaba de hacer?
   A: Acaba de tomar un examen.
4. A: ¿Cómo está Martina?
   B: Está alegre (o contenta). ¿Qué acaba de hacer?
   A: Acaba de mirar un video.

14 Answers

Conversación 1
A: Buenos días. ¿Puedo hablar con…?
B: Soy… ¿Quién habla?
A: Soy… ¿Cómo estás?
B: ¡Muy bien! Voy a patinar por la tarde.
A: ¿Te gustaría ir al cine por la noche?
B: Gracias, pero no puedo.
A: ¡Qué lástima!
B: Tal vez otro día.
A: Está bien. Hasta luego.
B: Nos vemos.

Conversación 2
B: Buenas tardes. ¿Puedo hablar con Carolina?
A: No está aquí. Regresa más tarde.
B: Quiero dejar un mensaje para ella.
A: ¡Claro que sí!
B: Dile que me llame, por favor.
A: ¿Cuál es tu teléfono?
B: 253-5652.
A: Muy bien. Adiós.
B: Gracias. Adiós.

15 Answers

Answers will vary.

A: Óscar juega al baloncesto. ¿Y Aída?
B: No, no juega al baloncesto, pero patina.
A: Óscar anda en patineta. ¿Y Aída?
B: No, no anda en patineta, pero juega al fútbol.
A: Óscar juega al béisbol. ¿Y Aída?
B: No, no juega al béisbol, pero practica el surfing.
A: Óscar juega al fútbol americano. ¿Y Aída?
B: No, no juega al fútbol americano, pero juega al voleibol.
A: Óscar levanta pesas. ¿Y Aída?
B: Sí, levanta pesas.
A: Óscar juega al hockey. ¿Y Aída?
B: Sí, juega al hockey.
A: Óscar juega al tenis. ¿Y Aída?
B: Sí, juega al tenis.

Óscar y Aída levantan pesas, juegan al hockey y juegan al tenis (3 deportes).

16 Answers

1. A: ¿Cómo son la clase de español y la clase de inglés?
   B: La clase de español (no) es tan fácil como la clase de inglés. *o:* La clase de inglés (no) es tan fácil como la clase de español.
2. A: ¿Cómo son tu maestro(a) de educación física y tu maestro(a) de matemáticas?
   B: Mi maestro(a) de educación física es mayor que mi maestro(a) de matemáticas. *o:* Mi maestro(a) de matemáticas es mayor que mi maestro(a) de educación física.
3. A: ¿Cómo son la tarea y una prueba?
   B: La tarea es peor que una prueba. o: Una prueba es peor que la tarea.
4. A: ¿Cómo son la oficina y la biblioteca?
   B: La oficina es menos interesante que la biblioteca. *o:* La biblioteca es menos interesante que la oficina.
5. A: ¿Cómo son la cafetería y el gimnasio?
   B: La cafetería es menos grande que el gimnasio. *o:* El gimnasio es menos grande que la cafetería.
6. A: ¿Cómo son la clase de historia y la clase de arte?
   B: La clase de historia es más divertida que la clase de arte. *o:* La clase de arte es más divertida que la clase de historia.

---

15 Unidad 3 Etapa 2 p. 202
Los deportes

Óscar

modelo

Estudiante A: *Óscar juega al baloncesto. ¿Y Aída?*
Estudiante B: *...*

Estudiante A By looking at Óscar's equipment, you can see which sports he plays. With your partner, determine how many sports he and Aída have in common.

Estudiante B By looking at Aída's equipment, you can see which sports she plays. With your partner, determine how many sports she and Óscar have in common.

modelo

Estudiante A: *Oscar juega al baloncesto. ¿Y Aída?*
Estudiante B: *No, no juega al baloncesto, pero patina.*

Aída

---

16 Unidad 3 Etapa 2 p. 205
En la escuela

6. la clase de historia / la clase de arte
5. la cafetería / el gimnasio
4. la oficina / la biblioteca
3. la tarea / una prueba
2. tu maestro(a) de educación física / tu maestro(a) de matemáticas
1. la clase de español / la clase de inglés

o: *El maestro de español es más simpático que la maestra de historia.*

Estudiante B: *La maestra de historia es más simpática que el maestro de español.*

Estudiante A: *¿Cómo son la maestra de historia y el maestro de español?*

el (la) maestro(a) de historia / el (la) maestro(a) de español

modelo

Estudiante A Ask your partner to compare school experiences.

Estudiante B Answer your partner's questions about school, using the following expressions.

modelo

más simpático(a)

Estudiante A: *¿Cómo son la maestra de historia y el maestro de español?*

Estudiante B: *La maestra de historia es más simpática que el maestro de español.*

   o: *El maestro de español es más simpático que la maestra de historia.*

1. tan fácil como	4. menos interesante
2. mayor	5. menos grande
3. peor	6. más divertida

17 Los dibujos

Unidad 3 Etapa 3 p. 224

Estudiante A Fernando feels differently at 7:30, 1:00, 6:00, and 9:00. Ask about Fernando.

modelo

Estudiante A: *¿Cómo está Fernando a las siete y media?*

Estudiante B: …

1. 7:30
2. 9:00
3. 6:00
4. 1:00

Estudiante B Fernando feels differently at 7:30, 1:00, 6:00, and 9:00. Answer your partner's questions about Fernando, using **tener** expressions.

9:00

7:30

1:00

6:00

18 ¿Lo tiene?

Unidad 3 Etapa 3 p. 227

Estudiante A Catalina is going to the beach. Find out if she has the following items with her. Then tell which items Antonio has for his trip to the mountains.

modelo

Estudiante A: *¿Tiene Catalina los patines?*

Estudiante B: …

los patines

1. las gafas de sol
2. el traje de baño con rayas
3. la merienda
4. los shorts de cuadros
5. el bronceador
6. una revista

Estudiante B Catalina is going to the beach. Answer your partner's questions about Catalina. Then find out if Antonio has the following items for his trip to the mountains.

modelo

los patines

Estudiante A: *¿Tiene Catalina los patines?*

Estudiante B: *No, no los tiene.*

7. el gorro
8. el abrigo
9. el impermeable
10. la bufanda con rayas
11. las gafas de sol
12. el suéter

17 Answers

1. A: ¿Cómo está Fernando a las siete y media?
   B: Tiene sed.
2. A: ¿Cómo está Fernando a las nueve?
   B: Tiene frío.
3. A: ¿Cómo está Fernando a las seis?
   B: Tiene miedo.
4. A: ¿Cómo está Fernando a la una?
   B: Tiene sueño.

18 Answers

1. A: ¿Tiene Catalina las gafas de sol?
   B: Sí, las tiene.
2. A: ¿Tiene Catalina el traje de baño con rayas?
   B: No, no lo tiene. (Tiene el traje de baño, pero no con rayas.)
3. A: ¿Tiene Catalina la merienda?
   B: No, no la tiene.
4. A: ¿Tiene Catalina los shorts de cuadros?
   B: Sí, los tiene.
5. A: ¿Tiene Catalina el bronceador?
   B: Sí, lo tiene.
6. A: ¿Tiene Catalina una revista?
   B: No, no la tiene.
7. B: ¿Tiene Antonio el gorro?
   A: Sí, lo tiene.
8. B: ¿Tiene Antonio el abrigo?
   A: Sí, lo tiene.
9. B: ¿Tiene Antonio el impermeable?
   A: No, no lo tiene.
10. B: ¿Tiene Antonio la bufanda con rayas?
    A: Sí, la tiene.
11. B: ¿Tiene Antonio las gafas de sol?
    A: No, no las tiene.
12. B: ¿Tiene Antonio el suéter?
    A: Sí, lo tiene.

19 Answers

Answers will vary. Students should think of themselves as standing on the sidewalk and looking at the doors of the stores in order to orient themselves.

1. A: ¿Qué está al lado (*o a la derecha*) de la estación de autobuses?
   B: La zapatería está al lado (*o a la derecha*) de la estación de autobuses.
2. A: ¿Qué está al lado (*o a la derecha*) de la zapatería?
   B: La carnicería está al lado (*o a la derecha*) de la zapatería.
3. B: ¿Qué está enfrente de la zapatería y la carnicería?
   A: La pastelería está enfrente de la zapatería y la carnicería.
4. A: ¿Qué está al lado (*o a la izquierda*) de la pastelería?
   B: La papelería está al lado (*o a la izquierda*) de la pastelería.
5. B: ¿Qué está enfrente de la papelería?
   A: La tienda de música y videos está enfrente de la papelería.
6. A: ¿Qué está a la izquierda de la tienda de música y videos?
   B: La farmacia está a la izquierda de la tienda de música y videos.
7. B: ¿Qué está al lado (*o a la izquierda*) de la farmacia?
   A: El banco está al lado (*o a la izquierda*) de la farmacia.
8. A: ¿Qué está enfrente de la farmacia (*o la papelería*)?
   B: La librería está enfrente de la farmacia (*o la papelería*).
9. B: ¿Qué está al lado (*o a la derecha*) de la librería?
   A: El correo está al lado (*o a la derecha*) de la librería.
10. A: ¿Qué está al lado (*o a la derecha*) del correo?
    B: La joyería está al lado (*o a la derecha*) del correo.
11. A: ¿Qué está enfrente de la joyería?
    B: El café está enfrente de la joyería.

20 Answers

1. A: Saca una foto.
   B: [acts out taking a picture]
2. A: Juega al baloncesto.
   B: [acts out playing basketball]
3. A: Come pizza.
   B: No es posible.
4. A: Anda en bicicleta.
   B: No es posible.
5. A: Bebe un refresco.
   B: [acts out drinking a soft drink]
6. A: Escribe tu nombre en un papel.
   B: [acts out writing name on paper]
7. B: Escribe en el pizarrón.
   A: No es posible.
8. B: Usa la computadora.
   A: No es posible.
9. B: Come una hamburguesa.
   A: [acts out eating a hamburger]
10. B: Toca la guitarra.
    A: [acts out playing the guitar]
11. B: Corre en tu lugar.
    A: [acts out running in place]
12. B: Lee un libro.
    A: [acts out reading a book]

---

19 Unidad 4 Etapa 1 p. 251
¿Qué es?

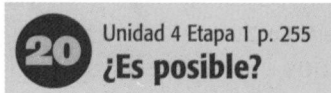

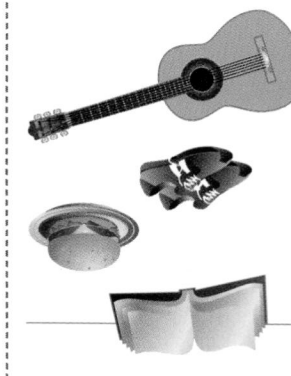

Estudiante A Tú no conoces el centro muy bien. Habla con tu amigo(a) para identificar todos los lugares. (*Hint: Identify the places.*)

modelo

Estudiante A: ¿Qué está enfrente del centro comercial?

Estudiante B: …está enfrente del centro comercial.

Estudiante B Tú no conoces el centro muy bien. Habla con tu amigo(a) para identificar todos los lugares. (*Hint: Identify the places.*)

modelo

Estudiante A: ¿Qué está enfrente del centro comercial?

Estudiante B: La estación de autobuses está enfrente del centro comercial.

---

20 Unidad 4 Etapa 1 p. 255
¿Es posible?

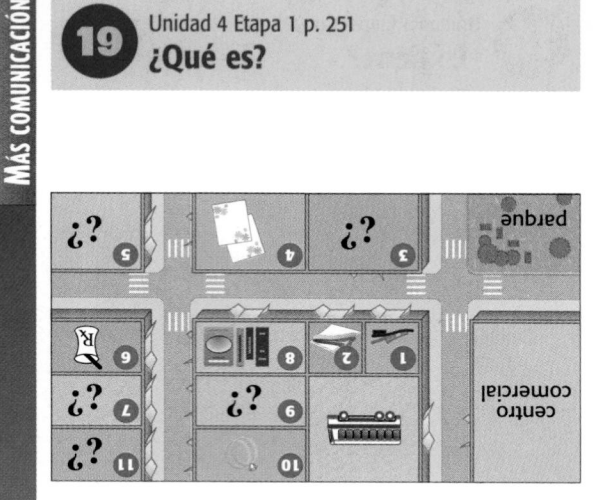

1. sacar una foto
2. jugar al baloncesto
3. comer pizza
4. andar en bicicleta
5. beber un refresco
6. escribir tu nombre en un papel

modelo

tocar el piano

Estudiante A: *Toca el piano.*

Estudiante B: *No es posible.*

Estudiante A Dile a tu amigo(a) qué hacer. Si tiene lo necesario, va a dramatizarla. Si no lo tiene, va a decirte que no es posible. Cambien de papel. (*Hint: Tell your partner what to do. If possible, your partner will act it out.*)

Estudiante B Tu amigo(a) te va a decir qué hacer. Si tienes el objeto necesario, dramatiza la actividad. Si no lo tienes, dile que no es posible. Cambien de papel. (*Hint: Your partner will say what to do. If possible, act it out. If not, say so.*)

modelo

tocar el piano

Estudiante A: *Toca el piano.*

Estudiante B: *No es posible.*

7. escribir en el pizarrón
8. usar la computadora
9. comer una hamburguesa
10. tocar la guitarra
11. correr en tu lugar
12. leer un libro

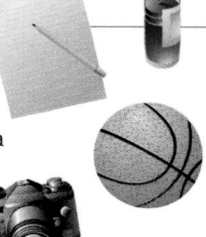

21 ¿Puede hacerlo bien?

Unidad 4 Etapa 2 p. 272

Estudiante A Tu amigo(a) tiene las notas de Emilia. Pregúntale si puede hacer las siguientes actividades bien. *(Hint: Ask if Emilia does these well.)*

modelo

Estudiante A: ¿Puede hacer ejercicio bien?

Estudiante B: …

1. hacer ejercicio
2. hacer un proyecto sobre los pájaros
3. trabajar con números
4. hablar español
5. comprender los mapas

Estudiante B Mira las notas de Emilia y contesta las preguntas de tu amigo(a). *(Hint: Tell if Emilia does these well.)*

modelo

Estudiante A: ¿Puede hacer ejercicio bien?

Estudiante B: Sí, puede hacer ejercicio bien.

Colegio Alta Vista

Emilia Villarreal			
	1	2	3
Español	A		
Matemáticas	B		
Ciencias	D		
Estudios sociales	C–		
Educación física	A+		

22 Los regalos

Unidad 4 Etapa 2 p. 277

Estudiante A Chavela hace una tabla de los regalos que da para la Navidad. Con tu amigo(a), completa la tabla. *(Hint: Complete the chart.)*

modelo

Estudiante A: ¿Qué le da a su madre?

Estudiante B: Le da… a su madre. ¿Cuánto cuesta(n)…?

Estudiante A: Cuesta(n) treinta dólares.

mi madre	$30	carteras
mis hermanos		carteras
mi padre	$25	
mis abuelos		olla
mi prima		casete
mi amiga	$15	

Estudiante B Chavela hace una tabla de los regalos que da para la Navidad. Con tu amigo(a), completa la tabla. *(Hint: Complete the chart.)*

modelo

Estudiante A: ¿Qué le da a su madre?

Estudiante B: Le da unos aretes a su madre. ¿Cuánto cuestan los aretes?

Estudiante A: Cuesta(n)…

mi madre		aretes
mis hermanos	$20	
mi padre		cinturón
mis abuelos	$18	
mi prima	$9	
mi amiga		pulsera

21 Answers

1. A: ¿Puede hacer ejercicio bien?
   B: Sí, puede hacer ejercicio bien.
2. A: ¿Puede hacer un proyecto sobre los pájaros bien?
   B: No, no puede hacer un proyecto sobre los pájaros bien.
3. A: ¿Puede trabajar con números bien?
   B: Sí, puede trabajar con números bien.
4. A: ¿Puede hablar español bien?
   B: Sí, puede hablar español bien.
5. A: ¿Puede comprender los mapas bien?
   B: No, no puede comprender los mapas bien.

22 Answers

A: ¿Qué le da a su madre?
B: Le da unos aretes a su madre. ¿Cuánto cuestan los aretes?
A: Cuestan treinta dólares.
B: ¿Qué les da a sus hermanos?
A: Les da unas carteras. ¿Cuánto cuestan las carteras?
B: Cuestan veinte dólares.
A: ¿Qué le da a su padre?
B: Le da un cinturón. ¿Cuánto cuesta el cinturón?
A: Cuesta veinticinco dólares.
B: ¿Qué les da a sus abuelos?
A: Les da una olla. ¿Cuánto cuesta la olla?
B: Cuesta dieciocho dólares.
B: ¿Qué le da a su prima?
A: Le da un casete. ¿Cuánto cuesta el casete?
B: Cuesta nueve dólares.
A: ¿Qué le da a su amiga?
B: Le da una pulsera. ¿Cuánto cuesta la pulsera?
A: Cuesta quince dólares.

23 Answers

1. A: ¿Te gusta el bistec? ¿A Memo le gusta?
   B: A mí (no) me gusta el bistec. A Memo no le gusta.
2. A: ¿Te gusta la salsa? ¿A Memo le gusta?
   B: A mí (no) me gusta la salsa. A Memo le gusta.
3. A: ¿Te gusta el flan? ¿A Memo le gusta?
   B: A mí (no) me gusta el flan. A Memo le gusta.
4. A: ¿Te gusta la limonada? ¿A Memo le gusta?
   B: A mí (no) me gusta la limonada. A Memo no le gusta.
5. A: ¿Te gustan los frijoles? ¿A Memo le gustan?
   B: A mí (no) me gustan los frijoles. A Memo le gustan.
6. B: ¿Te gustan las enchiladas? ¿A Memo le gustan?
   A: A mí (no) me gustan las enchiladas. A Memo le gustan.
7. B: ¿Te gusta el té? ¿A Memo le gusta?
   A: A mí (no) me gusta el té. A Memo no le gusta.
8. B: ¿Te gustan los postres? ¿A Memo le gustan?
   A: A mí (no) me gustan los postres. A Memo le gustan.
9. B: ¿Te gusta el arroz? ¿A Memo le gusta?
   A: A mí (no) me gusta el arroz. A Memo le gusta.
10. B: ¿Te gusta la ensalada? ¿A Memo le gusta?
    A: A mí (no) me gusta la ensalada. A Memo no le gusta.

24 Answers

1. A: Pide ensalada.
   B: Sí, sirven ensalada.
2. A: Pide flan.
   B: No, no sirven flan.
3. A: Pide sopa.
   B: Sí, sirven sopa.
4. A: Pide pollo.
   B: Sí, sirven pollo.
5. A: Pide pan.
   B: Sí, sirven pan.
6. A: Pide bistec.
   B: No, no sirven bistec.
7. A: Pide una hamburguesa.
   B: Sí, sirven hamburguesas.
8. A: Pide pastel.
   B: Sí, sirven pastel.
9. A: Pide enchiladas.
   B: No, no sirven enchiladas.
10. A: Pide queso.
    B: Sí, sirven queso.
11. A: Pide pan dulce.
    B: No, no sirven pan dulce.
12. A: Pide arroz.
    B: Sí, sirven arroz.

---

23 Unidad 4 Etapa 3 p. 293
¿Riquísimo o no?

Estudiante A Vas a un restaurante con Memo y tu amigo(a). ¿A ellos les gustan estas comidas y bebidas? *(Hint: Do Memo and your partner like these?)*

modelo

Estudiante A: ¿Te gusta el bistec? ¿A Memo le gusta?

Estudiante B: …

	Memo	Mi amigo(a)
las enchiladas	sí	¿?
el té	no	¿?
los postres	sí	¿?
el arroz	sí	¿?
la ensalada	no	¿?

1. el bistec
2. la salsa
3. el flan
4. la limonada
5. los frijoles

Estudiante B Vas a un restaurante con Memo y tu amigo(a). ¿A ellos les gustan estas comidas y bebidas? *(Hint: Do Memo and your partner like these?)*

modelo

Estudiante A: ¿Te gusta el bistec? ¿A Memo le gusta?

Estudiante B: A mí me gusta el bistec. A Memo no le gusta.

6. las enchiladas
7. el té
8. los postres
9. el arroz
10. la ensalada

	Memo	Mi amigo(a)
el bistec	no	¿?
la salsa	sí	¿?
el flan	sí	¿?
la limonada	no	¿?
los frijoles	sí	¿?

---

24 Unidad 4 Etapa 3 p. 299
¿Qué sirven?

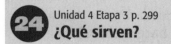

Estudiante A Roberto pide las siguientes comidas. ¿Las sirven en el café Veracruz? *(Hint: Say what Roberto is ordering.)*

modelo

papas fritas

Estudiante A: Pide papas fritas.

Estudiante B: …

1. ensalada
2. flan
3. sopa
4. pollo
5. pan
6. bistec
7. hamburguesa
8. pastel
9. enchiladas
10. queso
11. pan dulce
12. arroz

Estudiante B Dile a tu amigo(a) si sirven las comidas que pide Roberto en el café Veracruz. *(Hint: Tell your partner if these are served.)*

modelo

papas fritas

Estudiante A: Pide papas fritas.

Estudiante B: Sí, sirven papas fritas.

25 ¿Qué hago?
Unidad 5, Etapa 1 p. 323

26 Problemas y soluciones
Unidad 5 Etapa 1 p. 327

Estudiante A No recuerdas qué hacer hoy y tu amigo(a) tiene tu calendario. Adivina las cuatro actividades de la lista. *(Hint: Guess the four activities.)*

modelo

hacer la cama

Estudiante A: *¿Hago la cama hoy?*

Estudiante B: *Sí, haz la cama.*

o: *No, no está en tu calendario.*

1. poner la mesa
2. tocar el piano
3. ir al mercado
4. salir a las 7:30
5. escribir una carta
6. hacer la tarea

Estudiante B Tu amigo(a) no recuerda qué hacer hoy y tú tienes su calendario. Cuando te pregunta, dile que hacer según su calendario. *(Hint: Tell your partner what to do.)*

modelo

hacer la cama

Estudiante A: *¿Hago la cama hoy?*

Estudiante B: *Sí, haz la cama.*

o: *No, no está en tu calendario.*

8   abril

poner la mesa
ir al mercado
salir a las 7:30
hacer la tarea

Estudiante A Tú le dices varios problemas a tu amigo(a) y te dice una solución. Cambien de papel. *(Hint: Tell your partner your problems.)*

modelo

Estudiante A: *No tengo secador de pelo.*

Estudiante B: …

1. Siempre estoy muy cansado(a).
2. Tengo mucho calor.
3. Quiero ver un programa a las diez.
4. No llevo nada en los pies.

no despertarse tan tarde
no ponerse shorts
lavarse los dientes con otra pasta de dientes
peinarse

Estudiante B Tu amigo(a) te dice problemas. Dile una solución con las expresiones de la lista. Cambien de papel. *(Hint: Suggest solutions to your partner.)*

ponerse los zapatos
bañarse en agua fresca
no acostarse tan tarde
secarse el pelo con una toalla
no dormirse antes de las diez

modelo

Estudiante A: *No tengo secador de pelo.*

Estudiante B: *Sécate el pelo con una toalla.*

5. Siempre llego tarde a la escuela.
6. No me gusta la pasta de dientes.
7. No me gusta el pelo hoy.
8. Tengo frío.

---

25 Answers

1. A: ¿Pongo la mesa hoy?
   B: Sí, pon la mesa.
2. A: ¿Toco el piano hoy?
   B: No, no está en tu calendario.
3. A: ¿Voy al mercado hoy?
   B: Sí, ve al mercado.
4. A: ¿Salgo a las siete y media hoy?
   B: Sí, sal a las siete y media.
5. A: ¿Escribo una carta hoy?
   B: No, no está en tu calendario.
6. A: ¿Hago la tarea hoy?
   B: Sí, haz la tarea.

26 Answers

1. A: Siempre estoy muy cansado(a).
   B: No te acuestes tan tarde.
2. A: Tengo mucho calor.
   B: Báñate en agua fresca.
3. A: Quiero ver un programa a las diez.
   B: No te duermas antes de las diez.
4. A: No llevo nada en los pies.
   B: Ponte los zapatos.
5. B: Siempre llego tarde a la escuela.
   A: No te despiertes tan tarde.
6. B: No me gusta la pasta de dientes.
   A: Lávate los dientes con otra pasta de dientes.
7. B: No me gusta el pelo hoy.
   A: Péinate.
8. B: Tengo frío.
   A: No te pongas shorts.

27 Answers

1. A: ¿Dónde están barriendo el suelo?
   B: Están barriéndolo en el baño.
2. A: ¿Dónde están pasando la aspiradora?
   B: Están pasándola en la sala.
3. A: ¿Dónde están planchando la ropa?
   B: Están planchándola en la habitación.
4. A: ¿Dónde están quitando la mesa?
   B: Están quitándola en la cocina.

28 Answers

1. A: ¿Cómo debe pasar la aspiradora?
   B: Debe pasarla lentamente.
2. A: ¿Cómo debe sacar la basura?
   B: Debe sacarla rápidamente.
3. A: ¿Cómo debe barrer el suelo?
   B: Debe barrerlo frecuentemente.
4. A: ¿Cómo debe hacer la tarea?
   B: Debe hacerla pacientemente.
5. A: ¿Cómo debe hacer la cama?
   B: Debe hacerla fácilmente.
6. A: ¿Cómo debe manejar?
   B: Debe manejar tranquilamente.

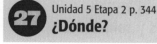

27 Unidad 5 Etapa 2 p. 344
¿Dónde?

Estudiante A Diana y su familia preparan una fiesta. Pregúntale a tu amigo(a) dónde están haciendo los siguientes quehaceres. *(Hint: Ask where they do each chore.)*

modelo

ordenar las flores

Estudiante A: ¿Dónde están ordenando las flores?

Estudiante B: Están ordenándolas en...

1. barrer el suelo
2. pasar la aspiradora
3. planchar la ropa
4. quitar la mesa

Estudiante B Diana y su familia preparan una fiesta. Dile a tu amigo(a) dónde están haciendo los siguientes quehaceres. *(Hint: Tell where they do each chore.)*

modelo

ordenar las flores

Estudiante A: ¿Dónde están ordenando las flores?

Estudiante B: Están ordenándolas en la cocina.

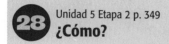

28 Unidad 5 Etapa 2 p. 349
¿Cómo?

Estudiante A ¿Cómo debe hacer Pedro las siguientes actividades? *(Hint: How should Pedro do these?)*

modelo

quitar el polvo

Estudiante A: ¿Cómo debe quitar el polvo?

Estudiante B: Debe quitarlo...

1. pasar la aspiradora
2. sacar la basura
3. barrer el suelo
4. hacer la tarea
5. hacer la cama
6. manejar

Estudiante B ¿Cómo debe hacer Pedro las siguientes actividades? *(Hint: How should Pedro do these?)*

modelo

quitar el polvo: cuidadoso

Estudiante A: ¿Cómo debe quitar el polvo?

Estudiante B: Debe quitarlo cuidadosamente.

a. sacar la basura: rápido
b. hacer la tarea: paciente
c. manejar: tranquilo
d. pasar la aspiradora: lento
e. hacer la cama: fácil
f. barrer el suelo: frecuente

---

29 ¿Quién es?
Unidad 5 Etapa 3 p. 365

Estudiante A Pregúntale a tu amigo(a) sobre tres nuevas estudiantes. *(Hint: Ask about three students.)*

modelo

Estudiante A: ¿Quién es la más alta?

Estudiante B: ... es la más alta.

1. menor
2. pelo más largo
3. más contenta
4. menos alta
5. pelo más corto
6. mayor
7. más cansada

Estudiante B Contesta las preguntas de tu amigo(a) sobre las tres nuevas estudiantes.
(Hint: Answer questions about three students.)

modelo

Estudiante A: ¿Quién es la más alta?

Estudiante B: Olivia es la más alta.

Lina - 17 años   Olivia - 16 años   Inés - 15 años

30 En el supermercado
Unidad 5 Etapa 3 p. 371

2/ 965 ptas   4/ 1.380 ptas   2 kilos/ 250 ptas   2/ 575 ptas

Estudiante A Pregúntale a tu amigo(a) qué compraron las siguientes personas. Cambien de papel. *(Hint: Ask what they bought.)*

modelo

Estudiante A: ¿Qué compró el señor Matute por ochocientas cuarenta pesetas?

Estudiante B: Compró...

el señor Matute / 840 pesetas

1. ustedes / 1.225 pesetas
2. la señora García / 315 pesetas
3. tú / 140 pesetas
4. Alejandra y Cristóbal / 1.425 pesetas

Estudiante B Dile a tu amigo(a) qué compraron. Cambien de papel. *(Hint: Say what they bought.)*

modelo

Estudiante A: ¿Qué compró el señor Matute por ochocientas cuarenta pesetas?

Estudiante B: Compró medio kilo de salchichas.

5. la señora Martínez / 1.380 pesetas
6. tú / 575 pesetas
7. tu amigo / 250 pesetas
8. el señor Aguilera / 965 pesetas

2 litros/ 315 ptas   4/ 1.225 ptas   1 kilo/ 1.425 ptas   12/ 140 ptas   1/2 kilo/ 840 ptas

29 Answers

1. A: ¿Quién es la menor?
   B: Inés es la menor.
2. A: ¿Quién tiene el pelo más largo?
   B: Olivia tiene el pelo más largo.
3. A: ¿Quién es la más contenta?
   B: Lina es la más contenta.
4. A: ¿Quién es la menos alta?
   B: Lina es la menos alta.
5. A: ¿Quién tiene el pelo más corto?
   B: Inés tiene el pelo más corto.
6. A: ¿Quién es la mayor?
   B: Lina es la mayor.
7. A: ¿Quién es la más cansada?
   B: Olivia es la más cansada.

30 Answers

1. A: ¿Qué compraron ustedes por mil doscientas veinticinco pesetas?
   B: Compramos cuatro botellas de zumo.
2. A: ¿Qué compró la señora García por trescientas quince pesetas?
   B: Compró dos litros de leche.
3. A: ¿Qué compraste tú por ciento cuarenta pesetas?
   B: Compré una docena de huevos.
4. A: ¿Qué compraron Alejandra y Cristóbal por mil cuatrocientas veinticinco pesetas?
   B: Compraron un kilo de jamón.
5. B: ¿Qué compró la señora Martínez por mil trescientas ochenta pesetas?
   A: Compró cuatro paquetes de galletas.
6. B: ¿Qué compraste tú por quinientas setenta y cinco pesetas?
   A: Compré dos paquetes de helado.
7. B: ¿Qué compró tu amigo por doscientas cincuenta pesetas?
   A: Compró dos kilos de patatas.
8. B: ¿Qué compró el señor Aguilera por novecientas sesenta y cinco pesetas?
   A: Compró dos latas de aceite.

31 Answers

A: ¿Ángela oyó o leyó algo?
B: Ángela oyó los pájaros.
B: ¿María y Elena oyeron o leyeron algo?
A: María y Elena leyeron una novela.
A: ¿Quique y Alex oyeron o leyeron algo?
B: Quique y Alex leyeron el periódico.
A: ¿Gloria oyó o leyó algo?
B: Gloria oyó el tren.
B: ¿Alfredo y Paco oyeron o leyeron algo?
A: Alfredo y Paco oyeron los aviones.
B: ¿Tavo oyó o leyó algo?
A: Tavo leyó una revista.

32 Answers

Answers will vary.
1. A: Vamos a jugar al baloncesto.
   B: Jugué al baloncesto [el año pasado].
2. A: Vamos a ver la televisión.
   B: Vi la televisión [anoche].
3. B: Vamos a ir al cine.
   A: Fui al cine [la semana pasada].
4. B: Vamos a correr.
   A: Corrí [anteayer].
5. A: Vamos a leer revistas.
   B: Leí revistas [el mes pasado].
6. A: Vamos a ir a una fiesta.
   B: Fui a una fiesta [el sábado pasado].
7. B: Vamos a comer helado.
   A: Comí helado [el verano pasado].
8. B: Vamos a escuchar música.
   A: Escuché música [ayer].

MÁS COMUNICACIÓN

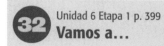

31 Unidad 6 Etapa 1 p. 395
Una noche larga

Estudiante A ¿Qué leyeron u oyeron estas personas en sus camas? Completa la tabla con tu amigo(a). *(Hint: Complete the chart.)*

modelo

Estudiante A: ¿Ángela oyó o leyó algo?
Estudiante B: Ángela...

Ángela	
María y Elena	una novela
Quique y Alex	
Gloria	
Alfredo y Paco	los aviones
Tavo	una revista

Estudiante B ¿Qué leyeron u oyeron estas personas en sus camas? Completa la tabla con tu amigo(a). *(Hint: Complete the chart.)*

modelo

Estudiante A: ¿Ángela oyó o leyó algo?
Estudiante B: Ángela oyó los pájaros.

Ángela	los pájaros
María y Elena	
Quique y Alex	el periódico
Gloria	el tren
Alfredo y Paco	
Tavo	

32 Unidad 6 Etapa 1 p. 399
Vamos a...

Estudiante A Le sugieres a tu amigo(a) a hacer algo. Tu amigo(a) te dice la última vez que lo hizo. Cambien de papel. *(Hint: Suggest you do an activity.)*

la semana pasada   anteayer
anoche   el... pasado   ayer

modelo

Estudiante A: Vamos a estudiar.
Estudiante B: Estudié ayer.

1. jugar al baloncesto
2. ver la televisión
3. ¿?
4. ¿?
5. leer revistas
6. ir a una fiesta
7. ¿?
8. ¿?

Estudiante B Tu amigo(a) te sugiere hacer algo. Dile la última vez que lo hiciste. Cambien de papel. *(Hint: Say the last time you did an activity after you hear the suggestion.)*

la semana pasada   anteayer
anoche   el... pasado   ayer

modelo

Estudiante A: Vamos a estudiar.
Estudiante B: Estudié ayer.

1. ¿?
2. ¿?
3. ir al cine
4. correr
5. ¿?
6. ¿?
7. comer helado
8. escuchar música

R16 RECURSOS
Más comunicación

R16 RECURSOS
Más comunicación

33 Unidad 6 Etapa 2 p. 417
¿Dónde están?

Estudiante A: *Hay un corral en el centro…*

modelo

papel. *(Hint: Describe the farm.)*
amigo(a). Él (Ella) la va a dibujar. Cambien de

Estudiante A Descríbele la granja a tu

Estudiante B Tu amigo(a) te describe una granja. Dibuja lo que oyes. Cambien de papel. *(Hint: Draw the farm described.)*

modelo

Estudiante A: *Hay un corral en el centro…*

---

34 Unidad 6 Etapa 2 p. 421
La carrera

Estudiante B: *La primera es número…*

Estudiante A: *¿Quién es la primera?*

modelo

todos los participantes. *(Hint: Identify all the racers.)*
bien. Trabaja con tu amigo(a) para identificar a

Estudiante A Hay una carrera y no puedes ver

Estudiante B Hay una carrera y no puedes ver bien. Trabaja con tu amigo(a) para identificar a todos los participantes. *(Hint: Identify all the racers.)*

modelo

Estudiante A: *¿Quién es la primera?*

Estudiante B: *La primera es número cincuenta.*

---

33 Answers

Answers will vary.

A: Hay un corral en el centro. El ganadero está dentro del corral con dos cerdos. Está entre los dos cerdos. El ganadero lleva un sombrero. Tiene una bolsa de comida para los cerdos. Les da de comer. Los cerdos son rosados y negros. Un gallo y una gallina están enfrente del corral. El gallo está a la izquierda de la gallina. Hay una cerca detrás del corral. Un caballo marrón está detrás de la cerca. Cuatro pájaros negros están encima de la cerca. Otro pájaro viene.

B: Hay un corral en el centro. Un toro y una vaca están dentro del corral. Son marrones y blancos. Dos gallinas marrones están debajo de la cerca del corral. Hay un caballo blanco detrás del corral. El ganadero está encima del caballo. El ganadero lleva jeans, una camisa roja y un sombrero. Arriba hay un pastor con cuatro llamas.

34 Answers

A: ¿Quién es la primera?
B: La primera es número cincuenta.
B: ¿Quién es el segundo?
A: El segundo es número noventa y ocho.
A: ¿Quién es el tercero?
B: El tercero es número veinticuatro.
A: ¿Quién es la cuarta?
B: La cuarta es número setenta y seis.
B: ¿Quién es el quinto?
A: El quinto es número sesenta y tres.
B: ¿Quién es la sexta?
A: La sexta es número diez.
A: ¿Quién es el séptimo?
B: El séptimo es número cuarenta y dos.
B: ¿Quién es el octavo?
A: El octavo es número ochenta y siete.
A: ¿Quién es la novena?
B: La novena es número treinta y nueve.
B: ¿Quién es la décima?
A: La décima es número setenta y cinco.

35 Answers

1. A: ¿Almuerzo con Angélica hoy?
   B: Sí, almuerza con Angélica hoy.
2. A: ¿Estudio en la biblioteca hoy?
   B: Hoy no.
3. A: ¿Saco la basura hoy?
   B: Sí, saca la basura.
4. A: ¿Mando una carta hoy?
   B: Hoy no.
5. A: ¿Voy al cine hoy?
   B: Sí, ve al cine.
6. A: ¿Estoy en casa a las ocho y media hoy?
   B: Sí, está en casa a las ocho y media.

36 Answers

Answers will vary.
1. B: El hombre se lavó la cara.
2. A: El hombre habló por teléfono.
3. B: El hombre manejó a la ciudad.
4. A: El hombre compró flores.
5. B: El hombre entró en un edificio con las flores.
6. A: El hombre le dio las flores a una mujer.

MÁS COMUNICACIÓN

35 Unidad 6 Etapa 3 p. 439
¿Lo hago?

Estudiante A No recuerdas qué hacer hoy y tu amigo(a) tiene tu calendario. Pregúntale qué haces hoy. *(Hint: Ask what you'll do today.)*

1. almorzar con Angélica
2. estudiar en la biblioteca
3. sacar la basura
4. mandar una carta
5. ir al cine
6. estar en casa a las 8:30

modelo

barrer el suelo

Estudiante A: *¿Barro el suelo hoy?*

Estudiante B: *Sí, barre el suelo hoy.*   **o:** *Hoy no.*

Estudiante B Tu amigo(a) no recuerda qué hacer hoy y tú tienes su calendario. Cuando te pregunta, dile qué hacer según su calendario. *(Hint: Tell your partner what to do according to the calendar.)*

modelo

barrer el suelo

Estudiante A: *¿Barro el suelo hoy?*

Estudiante B: *Sí, barre el suelo hoy.*   **o:** *Hoy no.*

26 junio

almorzar con Angélica
sacar la basura
ir al cine
estar en casa a las 8:30

36 Unidad 6 Etapa 3 p. 443
Parte de la historia

Estudiante A Viste algo en la televisión, pero solamente sabes parte de la historia. Con tu amigo(a), cuenta lo que pasó según los dibujos. Tu amigo(a) empieza. *(Hint: Take turns telling what happened.)*

modelo

Estudiante B: *Un hombre se levantó a las seis de la mañana.*

Estudiante B Viste algo en la televisión, pero solamente sabes parte de la historia. Con tu amigo(a), cuenta lo que pasó según los dibujos. Tú empiezas. *(Hint: Take turns telling what happened.)*

modelo

Estudiante B: *Un hombre se levantó a las seis de la mañana.*

Juegos—respuestas

UNIDAD 1

Etapa 1 **En uso,** p. 45: A Marisol no le gusta hacer las actividades con la letra **c.**

Etapa 2 **En uso,** p. 67: b

Etapa 3 **En acción,** p. 81: El hermano de Marco tiene un año.; **En uso,** p. 91: 1. El abuelo tiene 61 años. 2. Carlos tiene 37 años. 3. Antonio tiene 2 años.

UNIDAD 2

Etapa 1 **En uso,** p. 117: 1. matemáticas, 2. computación, 3. inglés, 4. música

Etapa 2 **En uso,** p. 139: Marco va al auditorio. Maricarmen va a la biblioteca. Josefina va a la oficina.

Etapa 3 **En acción,** p. 148: El perro tiene sed.; **En uso,** p. 163: Adriana camina con el perro. José toca la guitarra. Jorge cuida a sus hermanos.

UNIDAD 3

Etapa 1 **En uso,** p. 189: 1. Miguel va a un concierto. 2. Mariela va al cine. 3. Martina y Martín van de compras (a la tienda).

Etapa 2 **En uso,** p. 211: 1. Ángela: levantar pesas, 2. Memo: surfing, 3. Juanito: fútbol

Etapa 3 **En acción,** p. 226: b; **En uso,** p. 235: c. Chile

UNIDAD 4

Etapa 1 **En uso,** p. 261: Adriana va al aeropuerto. Andrés va a la farmacia. Arturo va al banco.

Etapa 2 **En acción,** p. 274: Lola quiere darle la lila a Lidia.; **En uso,** p. 283: Compras un plato barato por pocos pesos.

Etapa 3 **En uso,** p. 307: Pablo le sirve sopa a Marco, ensalada a Martina y azúcar a Marisol.

UNIDAD 5

Etapa 1 **En acción,** p. 322: Necesita peinarse.; **En uso,** p. 333: 1. un despertador, 2. un secador de pelo, 3. un peine, 4. un espejo

Etapa 2 **En uso,** p. 355: 1. Sofía está en el comedor. 2. Felipe está en la sala. 3. Cristina está en la cocina.

Etapa 3 **En uso,** p. 379: 1. helado: el congelador, 2. platos sucios: el lavaplatos, 3. leche: el frigorífico, 4. carne de res: la estufa

UNIDAD 6

Etapa 1 **En uso,** p. 405: 1. El papá de Adriana es contador. 2. El padre de Susana es fotógrafo. 3. El Sr. Rodríguez es bombero.

Etapa 2 **En uso,** p. 427: El cerdo llegó primero, la llama llegó segunda y la vaca llegó tercera.

Etapa 3 **En acción,** p. 440: a; **En uso,** p. 451: 1. La llama está jugando con Rocío. 2. El ganadero buscó su merienda. 3. ¡El caballo se va a escapar del corral!

Vocabulario adicional

Here are lists of additional vocabulary to supplement the words you know. They include musical instruments, classes, animals, professions, sports, and foods. If you do not find a word here, it may be listed as passive vocabulary in the glossaries.

Los instrumentos

el acordeón	accordion
la armónica	harmonica
el arpa (fem.)	harp
el bajo	bass
el bajón	bassoon
el banjo	banjo
la batería	drum set
el clarinete	clarinet
el corno francés	French horn
el corno inglés	English horn
la flauta	flute
la flauta dulce	recorder
el flautín	piccolo
la mandolina	mandolin
el oboe	oboe
el órgano	organ
la pandereta	tambourine
el saxofón	saxophone
el sintetizador	synthesizer
el tambor	drum
el trombón	trombone
la trompeta	trumpet
la tuba	tuba
la viola	viola
el violín	violin
el violonchelo	cello
el xilófono	xylophone

Más animales

la abeja	bee	el león	lion
el águila (fem.)	eagle	el leopardo	leopard
el alce	moose	el lobo	wolf
la araña	spider	el loro	parrot
la ardilla	squirrel	el mono	monkey
la ballena	whale	el mapache	raccoon
el buey	ox	la mariposa	butterfly
el búho	owl	la mosca	fly
el burro	donkey	el mosquito	mosquito
la cabra	goat	el (la) oso(a)	bear
el cangrejo	crab	la oveja	sheep
el chapulín	grasshopper	la paloma	pigeon, dove
el cisne	swan	la pantera	panther
el conejillo de Indias	guinea pig	el pato	duck
el conejo	rabbit	el pavo	turkey
el coyote	coyote	el pavo real	peacock
el delfín	dolphin	el pingüino	penguin
el elefante	elephant	la rana	frog
el ganso	goose	la rata	rat
el gerbo	gerbil	el ratón	mouse
el grillo	cricket	el sapo	toad
el hámster	hamster	la serpiente	snake
la hormiga	ant	el tiburón	shark
el hurón	ferret	el tigre	tiger
el jaguar	jaguar	la tortuga	turtle
la jirafa	giraffe	el venado	deer
la lagartija	small lizard	el zorro	fox

Más profesiones

el (la) abogado(a)	*lawyer*
el actor	*actor*
la actriz	*actress*
el (la) agente de bolsa	*stockbroker*
el (la) agente de viajes	*travel agent*
el (la) alcalde	*mayor*
el (la) artista	*artist*
el (la) asistente social	*social worker*
el (la) atleta	*athlete*
el (la) auxiliar de vuelo	*flight attendant*
el (la) cantante	*singer*
el (la) carnicero(a)	*butcher*
el (la) carpintero(a)	*carpenter*
el (la) científico(a)	*scientist*
el (la) dentista	*dentist*
el (la) director(a)	*principal, director*
el (la) empleado(a) de banco	*bank clerk*
el (la) enfermero(a)	*nurse*
el (la) farmacéutico(a)	*pharmacist*
el (la) funcionario(a)	*civil servant*
el (la) guía	*guide*
el (la) ingeniero(a)	*engineer*
el (la) jardinero(a)	*gardener*
el (la) joyero(a)	*jeweler*
el (la) mecánico(a)	*mechanic*
el militar	*soldier*
el (la) modelo	*model*
el (la) músico(a)	*musician*
el (la) panadero(a)	*baker*
el (la) peluquero(a)	*hairstylist*
el (la) pescador(a)	*fisher*
el (la) piloto(a)	*pilot*
el (la) plomero(a)	*plumber*
el (la) profesor(a)	*teacher, professor*
el (la) sastre	*tailor*
el (la) vendedor(a)	*salesperson*
el (la) veterinario(a)	*veterinarian*
el (la) zapatero(a)	*shoemaker*

Las clases

el alemán	*German*
la álgebra	*algebra*
la biología	*biology*
el cálculo	*calculus*
la composición	*writing*
la contabilidad	*accounting*
la física	*physics*
el francés	*French*
la geografía	*geography*
la geología	*geology*
la geometría	*geometry*
el italiano	*Italian*
el japonés	*Japanese*
el latín	*Latin*
la química	*chemistry*
el ruso	*Russian*
la salud	*health*
la trigonometría	*trigonometry*

Los deportes

el árbitro	*referee, umpire*
el arquero	*goalie*
el (la) bateador(a)	*batter*
el boxeo	*boxing*
el (la) campeón(ona)	*champion*
el campeonato	*championship*
la carrera	*race*
el cesto	*basket*
el (la) entrenador(a)	*trainer, coach*
el esquí	*ski*
la gimnasia	*gymnastics*
el golf	*golf*
los juegos olímpicos	*Olympics*
el (la) lanzador(a)	*pitcher*
el marcador	*scoreboard*
el palo	*stick, club*
el (la) parador(a)	*catcher*
la pista	*racetrack*
la red	*net*
la tabla hawaiana	*surfboard*
el trofeo	*trophy*
el uniforme	*uniform*

Las frutas y las verduras

el aguacate	*avocado*
la alcachofa	*artichoke*
el apio	*celery*
el arándano	*blueberry*
la banana	*banana*
la berenjena	*eggplant*
el bróculi	*broccoli*
el calabacín	*zucchini*
la calabaza	*squash*
la cereza	*cherry*
la ciruela	*plum*
el coco	*coconut*
la col	*cabbage*
la coliflor	*cauliflower*
el dátil	*date*
el espárrago	*asparagus*
la espinaca	*spinach*
la frambuesa	*raspberry*
la fresa	*strawberry*
la guayaba	*guava*
el kiwi	*kiwi*
el lima	*lime*
el limón	*lemon*
el mango	*mango*
la manzana	*apple*
el melocotón	*peach*
el melón	*melon*
la mora	*blackberry*
la naranja	*orange*
la papaya	*papaya*
el pepino	*cucumber*
la pera	*pear*
el plátano	*banana, plantain*
la sandía	*watermelon*
la toronja	*grapefruit*

Gramática—resumen

Grammar Terms

Adjective (pp. 57–58): a word that describes a noun

Adverb (pp. 107, 347): a word that describes a verb, an adjective, or another adverb

Article (pp. 54–55): a word that identifies the class of a noun (masculine or feminine, singular or plural); English articles are *a, an,* or *the*

Command (p. 252): a verb form used to tell someone to do something

Comparative (p. 202): a phrase that compares two things

Conjugation (pp. 105, 366): a verb form that uses the stem of an infinitive and adds endings that reflect subject and tense

Direct Object (p. 224): the noun, pronoun, or phrase that receives the action of the main verb in a sentence

Gender (p. 57): a property that divides adjectives, nouns, pronouns, and articles into masculine and feminine groups

Indirect Object (p. 273): a noun, pronoun, or phrase that tells to whom/what or for whom/what an action is done

Infinitive (p. 37): the basic form of a verb; it names the action without giving tense, person, or number

Interrogative (p. 131): a word that asks a question

Noun (p. 54): a word that names a thing, person, animal, place, feeling, or situation

Number (p. 58): a property that divides adjectives, nouns, pronouns, articles, and verbs into singular and plural groups

Preposition (p. 78): a word that shows the relationship between its object and another word in the sentence

Pronoun (p. 33): a word that can be used in place of a noun

Reflexive Verb (p. 320): a verb for which the subject and the direct object are the same participant

Subject (p. 33): the noun, pronoun, or phrase in a sentence that performs the action, is the focus of attention

Superlative (p. 364): a phrase that describes which item has the most or least of a quality

Tense (pp. 105, 366): when the action of a verb takes place

Nouns, Articles, and Pronouns

Nouns

Nouns identify things, people, animals, places, feelings, or situations. Spanish nouns are either masculine or feminine. They are also either **singular** or **plural**. **Masculine nouns** usually end in **-o** and **feminine nouns** usually end in **-a**.

To make a noun **plural**, add **-s** to a word ending in a vowel and **-es** to a word ending in a consonant.

Singular Nouns		Plural Nouns	
Masculine	**Feminine**	**Masculine**	**Feminine**
amigo	amiga	amigos	amigas
chico	chica	chicos	chicas
hombre	mujer	hombres	mujeres
suéter	blusa	suéteres	blusas
zapato	falda	zapatos	faldas

Articles

Articles identify the class of a noun: masculine or feminine, singular or plural. **Definite articles** are the equivalent of the English word *the*. **Indefinite articles** are the equivalent of *a*, *an*, or *some*.

Definite Articles	Masculine	Feminine
Singular	**el** amigo	**la** amiga
Plural	**los** amigos	**las** amigas

Indefinite Articles	Masculine	Feminine
Singular	**un** amigo	**una** amiga
Plural	**unos** amigos	**unas** amigas

Pronouns

A **pronoun** can take the place of a noun. The pronoun used is determined by its function or purpose in the sentence.

Subject Pronouns	
yo	nosotros(as)
tú	vosotros(as)
usted	ustedes
él, ella	ellos(as)

Pronouns Used After Prepositions	
de **mí**	de **nosotros(as)**
de **ti**	de **vosotros(as)**
de **usted**	de **ustedes**
de **él**, **ella**	de **ellos(as)**

Direct Object Pronouns	
me	nos
te	os
lo, la	los, las

Indirect Object Pronouns	
me	nos
te	os
le	les

Reflexive Pronouns	
me	nos
te	os
se	se

Demonstrative Pronouns	
éste(a), esto	éstos(as)
ése(a), eso	ésos(as)
aquél(la), aquello	aquéllos(as)

Adjectives

Adjectives describe nouns. In Spanish, adjectives must match the **number** and **gender** of the nouns they describe. When an adjective describes a group with both genders, the masculine form is used. To make an adjective plural, apply the same rules that are used for making a noun plural. Most adjectives are placed after the noun.

Adjectives	Masculine	Feminine
Singular	el chico **guapo**	la chica **guapa**
	el chico **paciente**	la chica **paciente**
	el chico **fenomenal**	la chica **fenomenal**
	el chico **trabajador**	la chica **trabajadora**
Plural	los chicos guapo**s**	las chicas guapa**s**
	los chicos paciente**s**	las chicas paciente**s**
	los chicos fenomenal**es**	las chicas fenomenal**es**
	los chicos trabajador**es**	las chicas trabajadora**s**

Adjectives cont.

Sometimes adjectives are placed before the noun and **shortened**. **Grande** is shortened before any singular noun. Several others are shortened before a masculine singular noun.

Shortened Forms			
alguno	**algún** chico	primero	**primer** chico
bueno	**buen** chico	tercero	**tercer** chico
malo	**mal** chico		
ninguno	**ningún** chico	grande	**gran** chico(a)

Possessive adjectives identify to whom something belongs. They agree in gender and number with the possessed item, not with the person who possesses it.

Possessive Adjectives				
	Masculine		**Feminine**	
Singular	**mi** amigo	**nuestro** amigo	**mi** amiga	**nuestra** amiga
	tu amigo	**vuestro** amigo	**tu** amiga	**vuestra** amiga
	su amigo	**su** amigo	**su** amiga	**su** amiga
Plural	**mis** amigos	**nuestros** amigos	**mis** amigas	**nuestras** amigas
	tus amigos	**vuestros** amigos	**tus** amigas	**vuestras** amigas
	sus amigos	**sus** amigos	**sus** amigas	**sus** amigas

Demonstrative adjectives point out which noun is being referred to. Their English equivalents are *this*, *that*, *these*, and *those*.

Demonstrative Adjectives		
	Masculine	**Feminine**
Singular	**este** amigo	**esta** amiga
	ese amigo	**esa** amiga
	aquel amigo	**aquella** amiga
Plural	**estos** amigos	**estas** amigas
	esos amigos	**esas** amigas
	aquellos amigos	**aquellas** amigas

Interrogatives

Interrogative words are used to ask questions.

Interrogatives		
¿Adónde?	¿Cuándo?	¿Por qué?
¿Cómo?	¿Cuánto(a)? ¿Cuántos(as)?	¿Qué?
¿Cuál(es)?	¿Dónde?	¿Quién(es)?

Comparatives and Superlatives

Comparatives

Comparatives are used when comparing two different things.

Comparatives		
más (+) **más** interesante **que…** Me gusta correr **más que** nadar.	menos (−) **menos** interesante **que…** Me gusta nadar **menos que** correr.	tan(to) (=) **tan** interesante **como…** Me gusta leer **tanto como** escribir.

There are a few irregular comparatives. When talking about the age of people, use **mayor** and **menor**.

Age	Quality
mayor menor	mejor peor

When talking about numbers, **de** is used instead of **que**.

> **más (menos) de** cien…

Superlatives

Superlatives are used to distinguish one item from a group. They describe which item has the most or least of a quality.

The ending **-ísimo(a)** can be added to an adjective to form a superlative.

Superlatives		
	Masculine	**Feminine**
Singular	**el** chico **más** alto **el** chico **menos** alto	**la** chica **más** alta **la** chica **menos** alta
Plural	**los** chicos **más** altos **los** chicos **menos** altos	**las** chicas **más** altas **las** chicas **menos** altas
Singular	mole buen**ísimo**	pasta buen**ísima**
Plural	frijoles buen**ísimos**	enchiladas buen**ísimas**

Affirmative and Negative Words

Affirmative words are used to talk about something or someone, or to say that an event also or always happens. **Negative** words are used to refer to no one or nothing, or to say that events do not happen.

Affirmative	Negative
algo	nada
alguien	nadie
algún (alguna)	ningún (ninguna)
alguno(a)	ninguno(a)
siempre	nunca
también	tampoco

Adverbs

Adverbs modify a verb, an adjective, or another adverb. Many adverbs in Spanish are made by changing an existing adjective.

Adjective	→	Adverb
reciente	→	reciente**mente**
frecuente	→	frecuente**mente**
fácil	→	fácil**mente**
normal	→	normal**mente**
especial	→	especial**mente**
feliz	→	feliz**mente**
cuidadoso(a)	→	cuidadosa**mente**
rápido(a)	→	rápida**mente**
lento(a)	→	lenta**mente**
tranquilo(a)	→	tranquila**mente**

Verbs: Present Tense

Regular Verbs

Regular verbs ending in **-ar**, **-er**, or **-ir** always have regular endings in the present.

-ar Verbs		-er Verbs		-ir Verbs	
habl**o**	habl**amos**	com**o**	com**emos**	viv**o**	viv**imos**
habl**as**	habl**áis**	com**es**	com**éis**	viv**es**	viv**ís**
habl**a**	habl**an**	com**e**	com**en**	viv**e**	viv**en**

Verbs with Irregular yo Forms

Some verbs have regular forms in the present except for their **yo** forms.

Infinitive	→	Yo form
conocer	→	conozco
dar	→	doy
hacer	→	hago
ofrecer	→	ofrezco
poner	→	pongo
saber	→	sé
salir	→	salgo
traer	→	traigo
ver	→	veo

Stem-Changing Verbs

u → ue	
juego	jugamos
juegas	jugáis
juega	juegan

Jugar is the only verb with a **u → ue** stem change.

e → ie	
cierro	cerramos
cierras	cerráis
cierra	cierran

Other **e → ie** verbs: **empezar, entender, merendar, nevar, pensar, perder, preferir, querer.** Reflexive: **despertarse.**

o → ue	
vuelvo	volvemos
vuelves	volvéis
vuelve	vuelven

Other **o → ue** verbs: **almorzar, contar, costar, devolver, dormir, encontrar, llover, mover, poder, recordar.** Reflexive: **acostarse.**

e → i	
pido	pedimos
pides	pedís
pide	piden

Other **e → i** verbs: **repetir, seguir, servir.**

Irregular Verbs

decir	
digo	decimos
dices	decís
dice	dicen

esquiar	
esquío	esquiamos
esquías	esquiáis
esquía	esquían

estar	
estoy	estamos
estás	estáis
está	están

ir	
voy	vamos
vas	vais
va	van

oír	
oigo	oímos
oyes	oís
oye	oyen

ser	
soy	somos
eres	sois
es	son

tener	
tengo	tenemos
tienes	tenéis
tiene	tienen

venir	
vengo	venimos
vienes	venís
viene	vienen

Verbs: Present Participles

Present participles are used to talk about something that is in the process of happening.

Regular Participles		
-ar Verbs	-er Verbs	-ir Verbs
hablando	comiendo	compartiendo
tocando	haciendo	saliendo
usando	perdiendo	viviendo

y Spelling Change	
creer	→ creyendo
leer	→ leyendo
oír	→ oyendo
traer	→ trayendo

Stem Changes	
decir	→ diciendo
dormir	→ durmiendo
pedir	→ pidiendo
servir	→ sirviendo
venir	→ viniendo

Verbs: tú Commands

Affirmative tú Commands

Affirmative tú commands are used to tell a friend or family member to do something. Regular **tú** commands are the same as the third person singular form of the present tense.

Regular Commands		
-ar Verbs	**-er Verbs**	**-ir Verbs**
habla	come	vive
piensa	entiende	pide
almueza	vuelve	sirve

Irregular Commands	
Infinitive → Tú Command	
decir	→ di
hacer	→ haz
ir	→ ve
poner	→ pon
salir	→ sal
ser	→ sé
tener	→ ten
venir	→ ven

Negative tú Commands

Negative tú commands are used to tell a friend or family member **not** to do something.

Regular Commands		
-ar Verbs	**-er Verbs**	**-ir Verbs**
no hables	no comas	no vivas
no mires	no hagas	no oigas
no entres	no vuelvas	no vengas

Commands with Spelling Changes		
-car Verbs	**-gar Verbs**	**-zar Verbs**
no busques	no juegues	no almuerces
no practiques	no llegues	no cruces
no toques	no pagues	no empieces

Irregular Commands	
Infinitive → Tú Command	
dar	→ no des
estar	→ no estés
ir	→ no vayas
ser	→ no seas

GRAMÁTICA—RESUMEN

Verbs: Preterite Tense

Regular Verbs

Regular preterite verbs ending in **-ar**, **-er**, or **-ir** have regular endings.

-ar Verbs		-er Verbs		-ir Verbs	
bailé	bailamos	corrí	corrimos	abrí	abrimos
bailaste	bailasteis	corriste	corristeis	abriste	abristeis
bailó	bailaron	corrió	corrieron	abrió	abrieron

Verbs with Spelling Changes

-car Verbs		-gar Verbs		-zar Verbs	
c → qu		g → gu		z → c	
practiqué	practicamos	pagué	pagamos	crucé	cruzamos
practicaste	practicasteis	pagaste	pagasteis	cruzaste	cruzasteis
practicó	practicaron	pagó	pagaron	cruzó	cruzaron

creer		leer		oír	
i → y		i → y		i → y	
creí	creímos	leí	leímos	oí	oímos
creíste	creísteis	leíste	leísteis	oíste	oísteis
creyó	creyeron	leyó	leyeron	oyó	oyeron

Irregular Verbs

dar		decir		estar		hacer	
di	dimos	dije	dijimos	estuve	estuvimos	hice	hicimos
diste	disteis	dijiste	dijisteis	estuviste	estuvisteis	hiciste	hicisteis
dio	dieron	dijo	dijeron	estuvo	estuvieron	hizo	hicieron

ir		ser		tener		venir	
fui	fuimos	fui	fuimos	tuve	tuvimos	vine	vinimos
fuiste	fuisteis	fuiste	fuisteis	tuviste	tuvisteis	viniste	vinisteis
fue	fueron	fue	fueron	tuvo	tuvieron	vino	vinieron

GLOSARIO
español-inglés

This Spanish-English glossary contains all of the active vocabulary words that appear in the text as well as passive vocabulary from readings, culture sections, and extra vocabulary lists. Most inactive cognates have been omitted. The active words are accompanied by the number of the unit and **etapa** in which they are presented. For example, **a pie** can be found in **4.1** (*Unidad 4, Etapa 1*). **EP** refers to the *Etapa preliminar*. Stem-changing verbs are indicated by the change inside the parentheses—**poder (ue)**, as are irregular **yo** forms.

a to, at
   A la(s)… At…. o'clock. **2.2**
   a la derecha (de) to the right (of) **4.1**
   a la izquierda (de) to the left (of) **4.1**
   a pie on foot **4.1**
   ¿A qué hora es…? (At) What time is…? **2.2**
   a veces sometimes **2.1**
abajo down **6.2**
abierto(a) open **5.2**
el abrigo coat **3.3**
abril April **1.3**
abrir to open **2.3**
la abuela grandmother **1.3**
el abuelo grandfather **1.3**
los abuelos grandparents **1.3**
aburrido(a) boring **1.2**
acá here **4.1**
acabar de… to have just… **3.1**
el aceite oil **5.3**
las aceitunas olives **5.2**
acostarse (ue) to go to bed **5.1**
actualmente nowadays
Adiós. Good-bye. **EP**
adónde (to) where **2.2**
el aeropuerto airport **4.1**
afeitarse to shave oneself **5.1**
agosto August **1.3**
el agua (fem.) water **2.2**

ahora now **1.3**
¡Ahora mismo! Right now! **2.1**
el ajo garlic
al to the **2.2**
   al aire libre outdoors **3.2**
   al lado (de) beside, next to **4.1**
alegre happy **3.1**
el (la) alfarero(a) potter
algo something **4.3**
alguien someone **4.3**
   conocer a alguien to know, to be familiar with someone **2.3**
alguno(a) some **4.3**
allá there **4.1**
allí there **4.1**
almorzar (ue) to eat lunch **4.2**
el almuerzo lunch **2.2**
alquilar un video to rent a video **3.1**
alto(a) tall **1.2**
amarillo(a) yellow **1.2**
el (la) amigo(a) friend **1.1**
anaranjado(a) orange **1.2**
ancho(a) wide **6.1**
andar
   andar en bicicleta to ride a bike **2.3**
   andar en patineta to skateboard **3.2**
el anillo ring **4.2**
el animal animal **2.3**
anoche last night **5.3**
anteayer day before yesterday **5.3**
el antepasado ancestor
antes (de) before **2.3**

antiguo(a) old, ancient **6.1**
el año year **1.3**
   el año pasado last year **5.3**
   ¿Cuántos años tiene…? How old is…? **1.3**
   Tiene… años. He/She is… years old. **1.3**
apagar la luz to turn off the light **5.3**
el apartamento apartment **1.1**
aparte separate
   Es aparte. Separate checks. **4.3**
el apellido last name, surname **EP**
aprender to learn **2.3**
aquel(la) that (over there) **6.2**
aquél(la) that one (over there) **6.2**
aquello that (over there) **6.2**
aquí here **4.1**
el árbol tree **3.3**
el arete earring **4.2**
el armario closet **5.2**
el (la) arquitecto(a) architect **6.1**
la arquitectura architecture **6.1**
arriba up **6.2**
el arroz rice **4.3**
el arte art **2.1**
la artesanía handicraft **4.2**
el (la) artesano(a) artisan **6.2**
los artículos de cuero leather goods **4.2**
asado(a) roasted
el auditorio auditorium **2.2**
el autobús bus **4.1**
la avenida avenue **4.1**
el avión airplane **4.1**

ayer yesterday **5.3**
ayudar (a) to help **2.1**
    ¿Me ayuda a pedir? Could
      you help me order? **4.3**
el azúcar sugar **4.3**
azul blue **1.2**

bailar to dance **1.1**
bajo(a) short (height) **1.2**
el baloncesto basketball **3.2**
el banco bank **4.1**
bañarse to take a bath **5.1**
el baño bathroom **5.2**
barato(a) cheap, inexpensive **4.2**
el barco ship **4.1**
barrer el suelo to sweep the
    floor **5.2**
el barrio district
el barro clay
el bate bat **3.2**
beber to drink **2.3**
    ¿Quieres beber…? Do you
      want to drink…? **2.2**
    Quiero beber… I want to
      drink… **2.2**
la bebida beverage, drink **4.3**
el béisbol baseball **3.2**
la biblioteca library **2.2**
bien well **1.1**
    (No muy) Bien, ¿y tú/usted?
      (Not very) Well, and you? **1.1**
bienvenido(a) welcome **1.1**
el bistec steak **4.3**
blanco(a) white **1.2**
la blusa blouse **1.2**
la boca mouth **5.1**
la bola ball **3.2**
la bolsa bag **1.2;** handbag **4.2**
el bombero firefighter **6.1**
bonito(a) pretty **1.2**
el borrador eraser **2.1**
el bosque forest **3.3**
las botas boots **4.2**
la botella bottle **5.3**
el brazo arm **5.1**
el bronceador suntan lotion **3.3**

bueno(a) good **1.2**
    Buenas noches.
      Good evening. **EP**
    Buenas tardes.
      Good afternoon. **EP**
    Buenos días. Good morning. **EP**
la bufanda scarf **3.3**
buscar to look for, to search **2.1**

el caballo horse **6.2**
la cabeza head **5.1**
    lavarse la cabeza to wash
      one's hair **5.1**
cada each, every **2.3**
el café café **4.1;** coffee **4.3**
la cafetería cafeteria,
    coffee shop **2.2**
los calamares squid **5.2**
el calcetín sock **1.2**
la calculadora calculator **2.1**
la calidad quality **4.2**
caliente hot, warm **4.3**
¡Cállate! Be quiet! **5.3**
la calle street **4.1**
calor
    Hace calor. It is hot. **3.3**
    tener calor to be hot **3.3**
la cama bed **5.1**
    hacer la cama to make
      the bed **5.1**
la cámara camera **6.1**
los camarones shrimp
cambiar to change, to exchange **4.2**
el cambio change, money
    exchange **4.2**
caminar con el perro to walk
    the dog **2.3**
el camino road **4.1**
la camisa shirt **1.2**
la camiseta T-shirt **1.2**
el campo field **3.2;** countryside,
    country **6.2**
la cancha court **3.2**
cansado(a) tired **3.1**
cantar to sing **1.1**
la cara face **5.1**
la carne meat **4.3**
la carne de res beef **5.3**
la carnicería butcher's shop **4.1**

caro(a) expensive **4.2**
    ¡Es muy caro(a)!
      It's very expensive! **4.2**
la carretera highway
el carro car **4.1**
la cartera wallet **4.2**
el (la) cartero(a) mail carrier **6.1**
la casa house **1.1**
el casco helmet **3.2**
el casete cassette **4.2**
castaño(a) brown hair **1.2**
catorce fourteen **1.3**
la cebolla onion **5.3**
la cena supper, dinner **2.3**
cenar to have dinner, supper **2.3**
el centro center, downtown **4.1**
el centro comercial shopping
    center **4.1**
el cepillo (de dientes) brush
    (toothbrush) **5.1**
la cerámica ceramics **4.2**
la cerca fence **6.2**
cerca (de) near (to) **4.1**
el cerdo pig **6.2**
el cereal cereal **5.3**
cero zero **EP**
cerrado(a) closed **5.2**
cerrar (ie) to close **3.2**
el champú shampoo **5.1**
la chaqueta jacket **1.2**
chévere awesome
    ¡Qué chévere!
      How awesome! **1.3**
la chica girl **1.1**
los chicharrones pork rinds **2.3**
el chico boy **1.1**
la chiringa kite
el chorizo sausage **5.2**
cien one hundred **1.3**
las ciencias science **2.1**
cinco five **EP**
cincuenta fifty **1.3**
el cinturón belt **4.2**
la cita appointment **2.2**
la ciudad city **1.3**
¡Claro que sí! Of course! **3.1**
la clase class, classroom **2.1**
la cocina kitchen **5.2**
cocinar to cook **5.3**
el (la) cocinero(a) chef
el colegio school
el collar necklace **4.2**

el color color **1.2**
  ¿De qué color…? What color…? **1.2**
el comedor dining room **5.2**
comer to eat **1.1**
  darle(s) de comer to feed **6.2**
  ¿Quieres comer…? Do you want to eat…? **2.2**
  Quiero comer… I want to eat… **2.2**
cómico(a) funny, comical **1.2**
la comida food, a meal **2.3**
como like, as
cómo how **2.2**
  ¿Cómo es? What is he/she like? **1.2**
  ¿Cómo está usted? How are you? (formal) **1.1**
  ¿Cómo estás? How are you? (familiar) **1.1**
  ¡Cómo no! Of course! **4.1**
  ¿Cómo se llama? What is his/her name? **EP**
  ¿Cómo te llamas? What is your name? **EP**
  Perdona(e), ¿cómo llego a…? Pardon, how do I get to…? **4.1**
la compañía company **6.1**
compartir to share **2.3**
comprar to buy **2.2**
comprender to understand **2.3**
la computación computer science **2.1**
la computadora computer **2.1**
la comunidad community **1.1**
con with **1.3**
  con rayas striped **3.3**
  Con razón. That's why. **2.1**
el concierto concert **3.1**
el concurso contest **1.1**
el congelador freezer **5.3**
conmigo with me **3.1**
conocer (conozco) to know, to be familiar with **2.3**
  conocer a alguien to know, to be familiar with someone **2.3**
el (la) contador(a) accountant **6.1**
la contaminación del aire air pollution **6.1**
contar (ue) to count, to (re)tell **4.2**
contento(a) content, happy, pleased **3.1**
contestar to answer **2.1**

contigo with you **3.1**
el corazón heart **2.3**
corto(a) short (length) **1.2**
el corral corral, pen **6.2**
el correo post office **4.1**
correr to run **1.1**
la cosa thing **4.1**
costar (ue) to cost **4.2**
  ¿Cuánto cuesta(n)…? How much is (are)…? **4.2**
la costumbre custom
creer to think, to believe **3.3**
  Creo que sí/no. I think so. / I don't think so. **3.3**
la crema cream **5.3**
cruzar to cross **4.1**
el cuaderno notebook **2.1**
la cuadra city block **4.1**
cuál(es) which (ones), what **2.2**
  ¿Cuál es la fecha? What is the date? **1.3**
  ¿Cuál es tu teléfono? What is your phone number? **EP**
cuando when, whenever **3.1**
cuándo when **2.2**
cuánto how much **4.2**
  ¿A cuánto está(n)…? How much is (are)…? **5.3**
  ¿Cuánto cuesta(n)…? How much is (are)…? **4.2**
  ¿Cuánto es? How much is it? **4.3**
  ¿Cuánto le doy de propina? How much do I tip? **4.3**
cuántos(as) how many
  ¿Cuántos años tiene…? How old is…? **1.3**
cuarenta forty **1.3**
cuarto(a) quarter **5.3**; fourth **6.2**
cuatro four **EP**
cuatrocientos(as) four hundred **5.3**
la cuchara spoon **4.3**
el cuchillo knife **4.3**
la cuenta bill, check **4.3**
  La cuenta, por favor. The check, please. **4.3**
la cuerda string
el cuero leather
  los artículos de cuero leather goods **4.2**
el cuerpo body **5.1**
cuidadosamente carefully **5.2**
cuidadoso(a) careful **5.2**

cuidar (a) to take care of **2.3**
el cumpleaños birthday **1.3**

dar (doy) to give **4.2**
  darle(s) de comer to feed **6.2**
de of, from **1.1**
  de cuadros plaid, checked **3.3**
  de la mañana in the morning **2.2**
  de la noche at night **2.2**
  de la tarde in the afternoon **2.2**
  De nada. You're welcome. **1.1**
  de vez en cuando once in a while **2.1**
debajo (de) underneath, under **6.2**
deber should, ought to **5.2**
decidir to decide **6.1**
décimo(a) tenth **6.2**
decir to say, to tell **4.1**
dejar to leave (behind)
  dejar un mensaje to leave a message **3.1**
  Deje un mensaje después del tono. Leave a message after the tone. **3.1**
  Le dejo… en… I'll give… to you for… **4.2**
  Quiero dejar un mensaje para… I want to leave a message for… **3.1**
del from the **3.1**
delgado(a) thin **1.2**
delicioso(a) delicious **4.3**
demasiado(a) too much **4.2**
dentro (de) inside (of) **6.2**
el deporte sport
  practicar deportes to play sports **3.1**
deprimido(a) depressed **3.1**
la derecha right
  a la derecha (de) to the right (of) **4.1**
derecho straight ahead **4.1**
el desarrollo development
desayunar to have breakfast **4.3**
el desayuno breakfast **4.3**
descansar to rest **2.2**
desde from **4.1**
el desfile parade

el desierto desert 3.3
el despertador alarm clock 5.1
despertarse (ie) to wake up 5.1
después (de) after, afterward 2.3
detrás (de) behind 4.1
devolver (ue) to return (item) 4.2
el día day EP
    Buenos días. Good morning. EP
    ¿Qué día es hoy? What day
      is today? EP
    todos los días every day 2.1
el diccionario dictionary 2.1
diciembre December 1.3
diecinueve nineteen 1.3
dieciocho eighteen 1.3
dieciséis sixteen 1.3
diecisiete seventeen 1.3
el diente tooth 5.1
    lavarse los dientes to brush
      one's teeth 5.1
diez ten EP
difícil difficult, hard 2.1
el dinero money 4.2
la dirección address, direction 4.1
el disco compacto compact
    disc 4.2
divertido(a) enjoyable, fun 1.2
doblar to turn 4.1
doce twelve 1.3
la docena dozen 5.3
el (la) doctor(a) doctor 1.1
el dólar dollar 4.2
domingo Sunday EP
dónde where 2.2
    ¿De dónde eres? Where are
      you from? EP
    ¿De dónde es? Where is he/
      she from? EP
dormir (ue) to sleep 4.2
dormirse (ue) to fall asleep 5.1
dos two EP
doscientos(as) two hundred 5.3
ducharse to take a shower 5.1
dulce sweet 4.3
durante during 2.2
duro(a) hard, tough 5.1

la edad age 1.3
el edificio building 6.1

el (la) editor(a) editor 6.1
la educación física physical
    education 2.1
el efectivo cash 4.2
él he 1.1
ella she 1.1
ellos(as) they 1.1
emocionado(a) excited 3.1
empezar (ie) to begin 3.2
Encantado(a). Delighted/
    Pleased to meet you. EP
la enchilada enchilada 4.3
en in 1.1
    en vez de instead of
encima (de) on top (of) 6.2
encontrar (ue) to find, to meet 4.2
el encuentro meeting
la encuesta survey
enero January 1.3
enfermo(a) sick 3.1
enfrente (de) in front (of) 4.1
enojado(a) angry 3.1
enorme huge, enormous 6.1
la ensalada salad 4.3
enseñar to teach 2.1
entender (ie) to understand 3.2
entonces then, so 2.3
entrar (a, en) to enter 2.1
entre between 4.1
la entrevista interview 6.1
la época period
el equipo team 3.2
escribir to write 1.1
el (la) escritor(a) writer 6.1
el escritorio desk 2.1
escuchar to listen (to) 2.1
la escuela school 2.1
ese(a) that 6.2
ése(a) that one 6.2
eso that 6.2
el español Spanish 2.1
especial special 5.2
especialmente (e)specially, 5.2
el espejo mirror 5.1
esperar to wait for, to expect 2.1
la esposa wife
el esposo husband
esquiar to ski 3.2
la esquina corner 4.1
la estación de autobuses bus
    station 4.1
las estaciones seasons 3.3
el estadio stadium 3.2

estar to be 2.2
    ¿Está incluido(a)…?
      Is… included? 4.3
    estar de acuerdo to agree 6.1
este(a) this 6.2
éste(a) this one 6.2
esto this 6.2
el estómago stomach 5.1
estrecho(a) narrow 6.1
la estrella star 5.3
el (la) estudiante student 1.1
estudiar to study 2.1
los estudios sociales
    social studies 2.1
la estufa stove 5.3
el examen test 2.1
el éxito success

fácil easy 2.1
fácilmente easily 5.2
la falda skirt 1.2
la familia family 1.1
la farmacia pharmacy,
    drugstore 4.1
favorito(a) favorite 3.2
febrero February 1.3
la fecha date 1.3
    ¿Cuál es la fecha? What is
      the date? 1.3
felicidades congratulations 1.3
feliz happy 1.3
felizmente happily 5.2
feo(a) ugly 1.2
la fiesta party 5.2
el flan caramel custard dessert 4.3
la flor flower 3.3
el folleto brochure
formal formal 6.1
la foto picture
    sacar fotos to take pictures 3.3
el (la) fotógrafo(a) photographer 6.1
frecuente frequent 5.2
frecuentemente often, frequently 5.2
fresco(a) fresh
el frigorífico refrigerator 5.3
los frijoles beans
frío
    Hace frío. It is cold. 3.3
    tener frío to be cold 3.3

la **frontera** border
la **fruta** fruit **2.2**
fuera (de) outside (of) **6.2**
fuerte strong **1.2**
el **fútbol** soccer **3.2**
el **fútbol americano** football **3.2**

las **gafas de sol** sunglasses **3.3**
la **galleta** cookie, cracker **5.3**
la **gallina** hen **6.2**
el **gallo** rooster **6.2**
las **gambas** shrimp
el (la) **ganadero(a)** farmer **6.2**
el (la) **ganador(a)** winner **6.1**
ganar to win **3.2**
el (la) **gato(a)** cat **1.2**
la **gente** people **2.3**
el (la) **gerente** manager **6.1**
el **gimnasio** gymnasium **2.2**
el **gobierno** government
el **gol** goal **3.2**
gordo(a) fat **1.2**
la **gorra** baseball cap **3.2**
el **gorro** cap **3.3**
la **grabadora** tape recorder **6.1**
Gracias. Thank you. **1.1**
   Gracias, pero no puedo.
     Thanks, but I can't. **3.1**
el **grado** degree **3.3**
el **gramo** gram **5.3**
grande big, large **1.2**
la **granja** farm **6.2**
gris gray
el **guante** glove **3.2**
guapo(a) good-looking **1.2**
la **guía telefónica** phone book **3.1**
los **guisantes** green peas
gustar to like
   Le gusta… He/She likes… **1.1**
   Me gusta… I like… **1.1**
   Me gustaría… I'd like… **3.1**
   Te gusta… You like… **1.1**
   ¿Te gustaría…? Would
     you like…? **3.1**
el **gusto** pleasure
   El gusto es mío. The pleasure
     is mine. **EP**
   Mucho gusto. Nice to meet
     you. **EP**

la **habitación** bedroom **5.2**
hablar to talk, to speak **2.1**
   ¿Puedo hablar con…? May I
     speak with…? **3.1**
hacer (hago) to make, to do **2.3**
   Hace buen tiempo. It is nice
     outside. **3.3**
   Hace calor. It is hot. **3.3**
   Hace fresco. It is cool. **3.3**
   Hace frío. It is cold. **3.3**
   Hace mal tiempo. It is bad
     outside. **3.3**
   Hace sol. It is sunny. **3.3**
   Hace viento. It is windy. **3.3**
   hacer ejercicio to exercise **2.3**
   hacer la cama to make the
     bed **5.1**
   hacer volar una chiringa to fly
     a kite
   ¿Qué tiempo hace? What is the
     weather like? **3.3**
la **hamburguesa** hamburger **2.2**
la **harina** flour **5.3**
hasta until, as far as **4.1**
   Hasta luego. See you later. **EP**
   Hasta mañana. See you
     tomorrow. **EP**
hay there is, there are **1.3**
   hay que one has to, must **2.1**
   Hay sol. It's sunny. **3.3**
   Hay viento. It's windy. **3.3**
el **helado** ice cream **5.3**
la **hermana** sister **1.3**
la **hermanastra** stepsister
el **hermanastro** stepbrother
el **hermano** brother **1.3**
los **hermanos** brother(s) and
   sister(s) **1.3**
la **hija** daughter **1.3**
el **hijo** son **1.3**
los **hijos** son(s) and daughter(s),
   children **1.3**
la **historia** history **2.1**
el **hockey** hockey **3.2**
Hola. Hello. **EP**
el **hombre** man **1.1**
el **hombre de negocios**
   businessman **6.1**
el **horario** schedule **2.2**

el **horno** oven **5.3**
el **hotel** hotel **4.1**
hoy today **EP**
   Hoy es… Today is… **EP**
   ¿Qué día es hoy? What day
     is today? **EP**
el **huevo** egg **5.3**

la **iglesia** church **4.1**
Igualmente. Same here. **EP**
el **impermeable** raincoat **3.3**
la **impresora** printer **2.1**
informal informal **6.1**
el **inglés** English **2.1**
inteligente intelligent **1.2**
interesante interesting **1.2**
el **invierno** winter **3.3**
la **invitación** invitation **5.2**
invitar to invite
   Te invito. I'll treat you. I invite
     you. **3.1**
ir to go **2.2**
   ir a… to be going to… **2.3**
   ir al cine to go to a movie
     theater **3.1**
   ir al supermercado to go to
     the supermarket **2.3**
   ir de compras to go shopping
     3.1
   Vamos a… Let's… **6.1**
irse to leave, to go away **5.1**
la **izquierda** left
   a la izquierda (de) to the left
     (of) **4.1**

el **jabón** soap **5.1**
el **jamón** ham **5.2**
el **jardín** garden **5.2**
la **jarra** pitcher **4.2**
los **jeans** jeans **1.2**
el (la) **jefe(a)** boss **6.1**
joven young **1.3**
las **joyas** jewelry **4.2**
la **joyería** jewelry store **4.1**
jueves Thursday **EP**

el (la) jugador(a) player
jugar (ue) to play 3.2
el jugo juice
el juguete toy
julio July 1.3
junio June 1.3
juntos together 4.2

el kilo kilogram 5.3

el lago lake 3.3
la lámpara lamp 5.2
la lana wool 6.2
el lápiz pencil 2.1
largo(a) long 1.2
la lata can 5.3
el lavaplatos dishwasher 5.3
lavar los platos to wash the
    dishes 5.1
lavarse to wash oneself 5.1
    lavarse la cabeza to wash
        one's hair 5.1
    lavarse los dientes to brush
        one's teeth 5.1
la lección lesson 2.1
la leche milk 5.3
la lechuga lettuce 4.3
leer to read 1.1
lejos (de) far (from) 4.1
    ¿Queda lejos? Is it far? 4.1
la lengua language 4.3
lentamente slowly 5.2
lento(a) slow 5.2
levantar pesas to lift
    weights 3.2
levantarse to get up 5.1
la librería bookstore 4.1
el libro book 2.1
la limonada lemonade 4.3
limpiar el cuarto to clean the
    room 5.1
limpio(a) clean 5.1
listo(a) ready 4.3
la literatura literature 2.1
el litro liter 5.3

la llama llama 6.2
la llamada call 3.1
llamar to call 3.1
    Dile/Dígale que me llame.
        Tell him or her to call me. 3.1
la llave key 5.2
llegar to arrive 2.1
    llegar a ser to become
llevar to wear, to carry 2.1; to take
    along 3.3
llover (ue) to rain 3.3
la lluvia rain 3.3
Lo siento… I'm sorry… 4.1
loco(a) crazy 3.2
luego later 2.3
    Hasta luego. See you later. EP
el lugar place 1.1
lujoso(a) luxurious 6.1
lunes Monday EP
la madrastra stepmother
la madre mother 1.3
el (la) maestro(a) teacher 1.1

el maíz corn
malo(a) bad 1.2
mandar una carta to send a
    letter 2.3
manejar to drive 4.1
la mano hand 5.1
la manta blanket 5.1
la mantequilla butter 5.3
mañana tomorrow EP
    Hasta mañana. See you
        tomorrow. EP
    Mañana es… Tomorrow is… EP
la mañana morning 2.2
    de la mañana in the
        morning 2.2
    por la mañana during the
        morning 2.2
el mapa map 4.1
maquillarse to put on makeup 5.1
la máquina contestadora
    answering machine 3.1
el mar sea 3.3
marcar to dial 3.1
marrón brown 1.2
martes Tuesday EP
marzo March 1.3

más more 1.3
    más de more than 3.2
    más… que more… than 3.2
las matemáticas mathematics 2.1
la materia subject 2.1
mayo May 1.3
mayor older 1.3
Me llamo… My name is… EP
la media hermana half-sister
la medianoche midnight 2.2
medio(a) half 5.3
el medio hermano half-brother
el mediodía noon 2.2
mejor better 3.2
menor younger 1.3
menos to, before 2.2; less 3.2
    menos de less than 3.2
    menos… que less… than 3.2
el menú menu 4.3
el mercado market 4.2
merendar (ie) to have a snack 3.2
la merienda snack 2.2
el mes month 1.3
    el mes pasado last month 5.3
la mesa table 5.2
    poner la mesa to set the table 4.3
    quitar la mesa to clear the
        table 5.1
el (la) mesero(a) waiter
    (waitress) 4.3
el metro subway 4.1
la mezcla mixture
mi my 1.3
el microondas microwave 5.3
miércoles Wednesday EP
mil one thousand 5.3
un millón one million 5.3
mirar to watch, to look at 2.1
mismo(a) same 2.1
la mochila backpack 2.1
moderno(a) modern 6.1
el momento moment
    Un momento. One moment. 3.1
la montaña mountain 3.3
morado(a) purple 1.2
moreno(a) dark hair and skin 1.2
la moto(cicleta) motorcycle 4.1
mover (ue) los muebles to move
    the furniture 5.2
la muchacha girl 1.1
el muchacho boy 1.1
mucho often 2.1
mucho(a) much, many 1.1

los **muebles** furniture **5.2**
la **mujer** woman **1.1**
la **mujer de negocios**
   businesswoman **6.1**
el **mundo** world **1.1**
el **museo** museum **2.3**
la **música** music **2.1**
muy very **1.3**

nada nothing **4.3**
nadar to swim **1.1**
nadie no one **4.3**
la **nariz** nose **5.1**
necesitar to need **2.1**
negro(a) black **1.2**
nervioso(a) nervous **3.1**
nevar (ie) to snow **3.3**
la **nieta** granddaughter
el **nieto** grandson
los **nietos** grandchildren
la **nieve** snow **3.3**
ninguno(a) none, not any **4.3**
el **niño** boy
la **niña** girl
no no **EP**; not **1.1**
   ¡No digas eso! Don't say that! **1.2**
   ¡No te preocupes! Don't
      worry! **3.1**
la **noche** night, evening
   Buenas noches.
      Good evening. **EP**
   de la noche at night **2.2**
   por la noche during the
      evening **2.2**
el **nombre** name, first name **EP**
normal normal **5.2**
normalmente normally **5.2**
nosotros(as) we **1.1**
novecientos(as) nine hundred **5.3**
la **novela** novel **2.3**
noveno(a) ninth **6.2**
noventa ninety **1.3**
noviembre November **1.3**
nublado cloudy
   Está nublado. It is cloudy. **3.3**
nuestro(a) our **1.3**
nueve nine **EP**
nuevo(a) new **1.2**
nunca never **2.1**

o or **1.1**
la **obra** work
   la **obra maestra** masterpiece
ochenta eighty **1.3**
ocho eight **EP**
ochocientos(as) eight hundred **5.3**
octavo(a) eighth **6.2**
octubre October **1.3**
ocupado(a) busy **3.1**
la **oficina** office **2.2**
ofrecer (ofrezco) to offer **6.1**
   Le puedo ofrecer… I can offer
      you… **4.2**
oír to hear **2.3**
el **ojo** eye **1.2**
la **ola** wave
la **olla** pot **4.2**
olvidar to forget **5.2**
once eleven **1.3**
el **(la) operador(a)** operator **6.1**
ordenar to arrange **5.2**
ordinario(a) ordinary **6.1**
la **oreja** ear **5.1**
el **oro** gold **4.2**
el **otoño** fall **3.3**
otro(a) other, another **1.2**

paciente patient **1.2**
el **padrastro** stepfather
el **padre** father **1.3**
los **padres** parents **1.3**
pagar to pay **4.2**
el **país** country **1.1**
el **paisaje** landscape
el **pájaro** bird **2.3**
el **pan** bread **4.3**
el **pan dulce** sweet roll **4.3**
la **panadería** bread bakery **4.1**
la **pantalla** screen **2.1**
los **pantalones** pants **1.2**
   los **pantalones cortos** shorts
la **papa** potato
   las **papas fritas** french fries **2.2**
el **papel** paper **2.1**
la **papelería** stationery store **4.1**

el **paquete** package **5.3**
para for, in order to **4.2**
el **paraguas** umbrella **3.3**
la **pared** wall **5.2**
el **parque** park **2.3**
el **partido** game **3.2**
pasar to happen, to pass (by) **2.1**
   pasar la aspiradora
      to vacuum **5.2**
   pasar un rato con los amigos to
      spend time with friends **2.3**
pasear to go for a walk **2.3**
el **paseo** walk
la **pasta** pasta **5.3**
la **pasta de dientes** toothpaste **5.1**
el **pastel** cake **4.3**
la **pastelería** pastry shop **4.1**
el **(la) pastor(a)** shepherd(ess) **6.2**
la **patata** potato **5.3**
patinar to skate **1.1**
los **patines** skates **3.2**
la **patineta** skateboard **3.2**
   andar en patineta
      to skateboard **3.2**
el **pedazo** piece **5.3**
pedir (i) to ask for, to order **4.3**
   ¿Me ayuda a pedir? Could you
      help me order? **4.3**
peinarse to comb one's hair **5.1**
el **peine** comb **5.1**
la **película** movie **3.1**
el **peligro** danger
peligroso(a) dangerous **3.2**
pelirrojo(a) redhead **1.2**
el **pelo** hair **1.2**
la **pelota** baseball **3.2**
pensar (ie) to think, to plan **3.2**
peor worse **3.2**
pequeño(a) small **1.2**
perder (ie) to lose **3.2**
Perdona(e)… Pardon…
   Perdona(e), ¿cómo llego a…?
      Pardon, how do I get to…? **4.1**
perezoso(a) lazy **1.2**
perfecto(a) perfect **4.2**
el **periódico** newspaper **2.3**
el **(la) periodista** journalist **6.1**
pero but **1.1**
el **(la) perro(a)** dog **1.2**
   caminar con el perro to walk
      the dog **2.3**
el **pescado** fish **5.3**
el **pez** fish **2.3**

picante spicy **4.3**
el pie foot **5.1**
   a pie on foot **4.1**
la pierna leg **5.1**
la pimienta pepper **5.3**
pintar to paint **2.3**
la piña pineapple
la piscina swimming pool **3.2**
el pizarrón chalkboard **2.1**
el placer pleasure
   Es un placer. It's a pleasure. **EP**
planchar to iron **5.2**
la planta plant **3.3**
la plata silver **4.2**
el plato plate **4.2**
la playa beach **3.3**
la plaza town square **4.1**
la pluma pen **2.1**
poco a little **2.1**
poder (ue) to be able, can **4.2**
   Gracias, pero no puedo.
     Thanks, but I can't. **3.1**
   Le puedo ofrecer… I can
     offer you… **4.2**
   **¿Puedes (Puede usted) decirme
     dónde queda…?** Could you
     tell me where… is? **4.1**
¿Puedo hablar con…? May I
   speak with…? **3.1**
el poema poem **2.3**
la poesía poetry **2.3**
el (la) policía police officer **1.1**
el pollo chicken **4.3**
poner (pongo) to put **4.3**
   poner la mesa to set the table **4.3**
ponerse (me pongo) to put on **5.1**
   ponerse la ropa to get dressed **5.1**
por for, by, around **4.1**
   por favor please **2.2**
   por fin finally **2.3**
   por la mañana during
     the morning **2.2**
   por la noche during
     the evening **2.2**
   por la tarde during
     the afternoon **2.2**
   por qué why **2.2**
porque because **3.1**
el postre dessert **4.3**
practicar deportes to play sports **3.1**
el precio price **4.2**
preferir (ie) to prefer **3.2**
preocupado(a) worried **3.1**

preparar to prepare **2.1**
presentar to introduce
   Te/Le presento a… Let me
     introduce you to… **1.1**
la primavera spring **3.3**
primero first **2.3**
el primero first of the month **1.3**
primero(a) first **6.2**
el (la) primo(a) cousin **1.3**
el problema problem **2.3**
la profesión profession **6.1**
el programa program
pronto soon **2.1**
la propina tip **4.3**
   ¿Cuánto le doy de propina?
     How much do I tip? **4.3**
la prueba quiz **2.1**
el pueblo town, village **4.3**
el puerco pork **5.3**
la puerta door **5.2**
pues well **1.2**
la pulsera bracelet **4.2**

qué what **2.2**
   ¿A qué hora es…? (At) What
     time is…? **2.2**
   ¡Qué (divertido)! How (fun)! **1.2**
   ¿Qué día es hoy? What day
     is today? **EP**
   ¿Qué hora es? What time is it? **2.2**
   ¡Qué lástima! What a shame! **3.1**
   ¿Qué lleva? What is he/she
     wearing? **1.2**
   ¿Qué tal? How is it going? **1.1**
   ¿Qué tiempo hace? What is the
     weather like? **3.3**
quedar (en) to stay, to be (in a
   specific place), to agree on **4.1**
   **¿Puedes (Puede usted) decirme
     dónde queda…?** Could you
     tell me where… is? **4.1**
   ¿Queda lejos? Is it far? **4.1**
los quehaceres chores **5.1**

querer (ie) to want **3.2**
   ¿Quieres beber…? Do you
     want to drink…? **2.2**
   ¿Quieres comer…? Do you
     want to eat…? **2.2**
   Quiero beber… I want to
     drink… **2.2**
   Quiero comer… I want
     to eat… **2.2**
   **Quiero dejar un mensaje
     para…** I want to leave a
     message for… **3.1**
el queso cheese **4.3**
quién(es) who **2.2**
   ¿De quién es…? Whose is…? **1.3**
   ¿Quién es? Who is it? **1.3**
   ¿Quiénes son? Who are they? **1.3**
quince fifteen **1.3**
quinientos(as) five hundred **5.3**
quinto(a) fifth **6.2**
Quisiera… I would like… **4.3**
quitar
   quitar el polvo to dust **5.2**
   quitar la mesa to clear
     the table **5.1**

el radio radio **4.2**
el radiocasete radio-tape player **4.2**
rápidamente quickly **5.2**
rápido(a) fast, quick **5.2**
la raqueta racket **3.2**
rara vez rarely **2.1**
el ratón mouse **2.1**
la raza race
la razón reason **2.1**
   Con razón. That's why. **2.1**
   tener razón to be right **3.3**
el (la) recepcionista receptionist **6.1**
el receso break **2.2**
la receta recipe
recibir to receive **2.3**
reciente recent **5.2**
recientemente lately, recently **5.2**
recordar (ue) to remember **4.2**
el recuerdo souvenir
el refresco soft drink **2.2**
el regalo gift **4.2**
regatear to bargain **4.2**
la regla rule

regresar to return
  Regresa más tarde. He/She will
    return later. **3.1**
Regular. So-so. **1.1**
el reloj clock, watch **2.2**
el restaurante restaurant **4.3**
el retrato portrait
la revista magazine **2.3**
rico(a) tasty **4.3**; rich
el río river **3.3**
riquísimo(a) very tasty **4.3**
el ritmo rhythm
rojo(a) red **1.2**
la ropa clothing **1.2**
  ponerse la ropa to get dressed **5.1**
rosado(a) pink **1.2**
rubio(a) blond **1.2**

sábado Saturday **EP**
saber (sé) to know **3.2**
el sabor flavor
sabroso(a) tasty **5.3**
sacar
  sacar fotos to take pictures **3.3**
  sacar la basura to take out
    the trash **5.2**
  sacar una buena nota to get
    a good grade **2.1**
la sal salt **5.3**
la sala living room **5.2**
la salchicha sausage **5.3**
salir (salgo) to go out, to leave **4.1**
la salsa salsa **4.3**
la sartén frying pan
Se llama… His/Her name is… **EP**
el secador de pelo hair dryer **5.1**
secarse to dry oneself **5.1**
el (la) secretario(a) secretary **6.1**
segundo(a) second **6.2**
seis six **EP**
seiscientos(as) six hundred **5.3**
la selva jungle
la semana week **EP**
  la semana pasada last week **5.3**
  el semestre semester **2.2**
sencillo(a) simple, plain **6.1**
el señor Mr. **1.1**
la señora Mrs. **1.1**
la señorita Miss **1.1**

septiembre September **1.3**
séptimo(a) seventh **6.2**
ser to be **1.1**
  Es la…/Son las…
    It is… o'clock. **2.2**
  ser de… to be from… **1.1**
serio(a) serious **1.2**
servir (i) to serve **4.3**
sesenta sixty **1.3**
setecientos(as) seven hundred **5.3**
setenta seventy **1.3**
sexto(a) sixth **6.2**
los shorts shorts **3.3**
si if **5.2**
sí yes **EP**
  Sí, me encantaría. Yes, I would
    love to. **3.1**
siempre always **2.1**
siete seven **EP**
el siglo century
la silla chair **5.2**
el sillón armchair **5.2**
simpático(a) nice **1.2**
sin without **4.3**
sobre on, about
  sobre hielo on ice **3.2**
el sofá sofa, couch **5.2**
el sol sun **3.3**
  las gafas de sol sunglasses **3.3**
  Hace sol. It is sunny. **3.3**
  Hay sol. It's sunny. **3.3**
  tomar el sol to sunbathe **3.3**
sólo only **1.3**
solo(a) alone **3.1**
el sombrero hat **1.2**
el sonido sound
la sopa soup **4.3**
sorprender to surprise **5.2**
sorpresa surprise **5.2**
su your (formal), his, her, its,
  their **1.3**
sucio(a) dirty **5.1**
el suelo floor **5.2**
  barrer el suelo to sweep
    the floor **5.2**
el suéter sweater **1.2**
el surfing surfing **3.2**

T

Tal vez otro día. Maybe another
  day. **3.1**
el taller workshop **6.2**
también also, too **1.1**
tampoco neither, either **4.3**
tan… como as… as **3.2**
tanto como as much as **3.2**
las tapas appetizers **5.2**
tarde late **2.1**
la tarde afternoon **2.2**
  Buenas tardes.
    Good afternoon. **EP**
  de la tarde in the afternoon **2.2**
  por la tarde during the
    afternoon **2.2**
la tarea homework **2.1**
la tarjeta de crédito credit card **4.2**
el taxi taxi, cab **4.1**
el (la) taxista taxi driver **6.1**
la taza cup **4.3**
el té tea **4.3**
el teatro theater **2.3**
la tecla key (of an instrument)
el teclado keyboard **2.1**
el tejido textile
el teléfono telephone **3.1**
  ¿Cuál es tu teléfono? What is
    your phone number? **EP**
el televisor television set **5.2**
la temperatura temperature **3.3**
temprano early **3.1**
el tenedor fork **4.3**
tener to have **1.3**
  ¿Cuántos años tiene…? How
    old is…? **1.3**
  tener calor to be hot **3.3**
  tener cuidado to be careful **3.3**
  tener frío to be cold **3.3**
  tener ganas de… to feel like… **3.3**
  tener hambre to be hungry **2.3**
  tener miedo to be afraid **3.3**
  tener prisa to be in a hurry **3.3**
  tener que to have to **2.1**
  tener razón to be right **3.3**
  tener sed to be thirsty **2.3**
  tener sueño to be sleepy **3.3**
  tener suerte to be lucky **3.3**
  Tiene… años. He/She is…
    years old. **1.3**

el tenis tennis **3.2**
tercero(a) third **6.2**
terminar to finish **2.2**
Terrible. Terrible./Awful. **1.1**
la tía aunt **1.3**
el tiempo time **3.1**; weather **3.3**
   Hace buen tiempo. It is nice outside. **3.3**
   Hace mal tiempo. It is bad outside. **3.3**
   ¿Qué tiempo hace? What is the weather like? **3.3**
   el tiempo libre free time **3.1**
la tienda store **2.3**
   la tienda de deportes sporting goods store **3.2**
   la tienda de música y videos music and video store **4.1**
la tierra land
las tijeras scissors **6.2**
el tío uncle **1.3**
los tíos uncle(s) and aunt(s) **1.3**
la tiza chalk **2.1**
la toalla towel **5.1**
tocar to play (an instrument)
   tocar el piano to play the piano **2.3**
   tocar la guitarra to play the guitar **2.3**
todavía still, yet **4.3**
todo(a) all **1.3**
   todos los días every day **2.1**
tomar to take, to eat or drink **2.2**
   tomar el sol to sunbathe **3.3**
el tomate tomato **5.3**
la tormenta storm **3.3**
el toro bull **6.2**
la torta sandwich (sub) **2.2**
la tortilla española potato omelet **5.2**
trabajador(a) hard-working **1.2**
trabajar to work **1.1**
tradicional traditional **6.1**
traer (traigo) to bring **4.3**
   ¿Me trae…? Could you bring me…? **4.3**
el tráfico traffic **6.1**
el traje de baño bathing suit **3.3**
tranquilamente calmly **5.2**
tranquilo(a) calm **3.1**
trece thirteen **1.3**
treinta thirty **1.3**
el tren train **4.1**
tres three **EP**

trescientos(as) three hundred **5.3**
triste sad **3.1**
tu your (familiar) **1.3**
tú you (familiar singular) **1.1**

último(a) last **6.2**
uno one **EP**
usar to use **2.1**
usted you (formal singular) **1.1**
ustedes you (plural) **1.1**
la uva grape

la vaca cow **6.2**
el vaso glass
   el vaso de glass of **2.2**
el (la) vecino(a) neighbor
vegetariano(a) vegetarian **4.3**
veinte twenty **1.3**
vender to sell **2.3**
venir to come **3.1**
la ventana window **5.2**
ver (veo) to see **2.3**
   ¿Me deja ver…? May I see…? **4.2**
   Nos vemos. See you later. **EP**
   ver la televisión to watch television **2.3**
el verano summer **3.3**
la verdad truth **2.2**
   Es verdad. It's true. **1.2**
verde green **1.2**
la verdura vegetable **5.3**
el vestido dress **1.2**
viajar to travel **4.1**
el viaje trip **4.1**
la vida life **2.3**
el video video **4.2**
   alquilar un video to rent a video **3.1**
la videograbadora VCR **4.2**
el videojuego video game **4.2**
viejo(a) old **1.3**
el viento wind **3.3**
   Hace viento. It is windy. **3.3**
   Hay viento. It's windy. **3.3**
viernes Friday **EP**

visitar to visit **2.2**
vivir to live **2.3**
   Vive en… He/She lives in… **1.1**
   Vivo en… I live in… **1.1**
el voleibol volleyball **3.2**
volver (ue) to return, to come back **4.2**
vosotros(as) you (familiar plural) **1.1**
vuestro(a) your (familiar plural) **1.3**

y and **1.1**
   y cuarto quarter past **2.2**
   y media half past **2.2**
ya already, now
ya no no longer **3.1**
yo I **1.1**
el yogur yogurt **5.3**

la zanahoria carrot **5.3**
la zapatería shoe store **4.1**
el zapato shoe **1.2**
el zumo juice **5.3**

GLOSARIO
inglés–español

This English–Spanish glossary contains all of the active words that appear as well as passive ones from readings, culture sections, and extra vocabulary lists. Active words are indicated by the unit and **etapa** number when they appear.

about sobre
accountant el (la) contador(a) **6.1**
address la dirección **4.1**
to be afraid tener miedo **3.3**
after después (de) **2.3**
afternoon la tarde **2.2**
 during the afternoon por la tarde **2.2**
 Good afternoon Buenas tardes. **EP**
 in the afternoon de la tarde **2.2**
afterward después **2.3**
age la edad **1.3**
to agree (on) quedar (en) **4.1**, estar de acuerdo **6.1**
air pollution la contaminación del aire **6.1**
airplane el avión **4.1**
airport el aeropuerto **4.1**
alarm clock el despertador **5.1**
all todo(a) **1.3**
alone solo(a) **3.1**
already ya
also también **1.1**
always siempre **2.1**
ancient antiguo(a) **6.1**
and y **1.1**
angry enojado(a) **3.1**
animal el animal **2.3**
another otro(a) **1.2**
to answer contestar **2.1**
answering machine la máquina contestadora **3.1**
apartment el apartamento **1.1**
appetizers las tapas **5.2**

appointment la cita **2.2**
April abril **1.3**
architect el (la) arquitecto(a) **6.1**
architecture la arquitectura **6.1**
arm el brazo **5.1**
armchair el sillón **5.2**
around por **4.1**
to arrange ordenar **5.2**
to arrive llegar **2.1**
art el arte **2.1**
artisan el (la) artesano(a) **6.2**
as como
 as… as tan… como **3.2**
 as far as hasta **4.1**
 as much as tanto como **3.2**
to ask for pedir (i) **4.3**
at a
 At… o'clock. A la(s)… **2.2**
auditorium el auditorio **2.2**
August agosto **1.3**
aunt la tía **1.3**
avenue la avenida **4.1**
awesome: How awesome! ¡Qué chévere! **1.3**
awful terrible **1.1**

backpack la mochila **2.1**
bad malo(a) **1.2**
 It is bad outside. Hace mal tiempo. **3.3**
bag la bolsa **1.2**
bakery (bread) panadería **4.1**, **(pastry)** pastelería **4.1**
ball la bola **3.2**
bank el banco **4.1**
to bargain regatear **4.2**

baseball (sport) el béisbol **3.2**; **(ball)** la pelota **3.2**
baseball cap la gorra **3.2**
basketball el baloncesto **3.2**
bat el bate **3.2**
bathing suit el traje de baño **3.3**
bathroom el baño **5.2**
to be ser **1.1**; estar **2.2**
 to be (in a specific place) quedar (en) **4.1**
 to be able poder (ue) **4.2**
 to be afraid tener miedo **3.3**
 to be careful tener cuidado **3.3**
 to be cold tener frío **3.3**
 to be familiar with conocer **2.3**
 to be from… ser de… **1.1**
 to be going to… ir a… **2.3**
 to be hot tener calor **3.3**
 to be hungry tener hambre **2.3**
 to be in a hurry tener prisa **3.3**
 to be lucky tener suerte **3.3**
 to be right tener razón **3.3**
 to be sleepy tener sueño **3.3**
 to be thirsty tener sed **2.3**
beach la playa **3.3**
beans los frijoles
because porque **3.1**
to become llegar a ser
bed la cama **5.1**
 to go to bed acostarse (ue) **5.1**
 to make the bed hacer la cama **5.1**
bedroom la habitación **5.2**
beef la carne de res **5.3**
before antes (de) **2.3**
to begin empezar (ie) **3.2**
behind detrás (de) **4.1**
to believe creer **3.3**
belt el cinturón **4.2**

INGLÉS–ESPAÑOL

beside al lado (de) **4.1**
better mejor **3.2**
between entre **4.1**
beverage la bebida **4.3**
big grande **1.2**
bike la bicicleta
    to ride a bike andar en
      bicicleta **2.3**
bill la cuenta **4.3**
bird el pájaro **2.3**
birthday el cumpleaños **1.3**
black negro(a) **1.2**
blanket la manta **5.1**
blond rubio(a) **1.2**
blouse la blusa **1.2**
blue azul **1.2**
body el cuerpo **5.1**
book el libro **2.1**
bookstore la librería **4.1**
boots las botas **4.2**
border la frontera
boring aburrido(a) **1.2**
boss el (la) jefe(a) **6.1**
bottle la botella **5.3**
boy el chico **1.1**, el muchacho **1.1**,
    el niño
bracelet la pulsera **4.2**
bread el pan **4.3**
break el receso **2.2**
breakfast el desayuno **4.3**
to bring traer **4.3**
    Could you bring me…?
      ¿Me trae…? **4.3**
brochure el folleto
brother el hermano **1.3**
brown marrón **1.2**
brown hair castaño(a) **1.2**
brush el cepillo **5.1**
to brush one's teeth lavarse los
    dientes **5.1**
building el edificio **6.1**
bull el toro **6.2**
bus el autobús **4.1**
bus station la estación de
    autobuses **4.1**
businessman el hombre de
    negocios **6.1**
businesswoman la mujer de
    negocios **6.1**
busy ocupado(a) **3.1**
but pero **1.1**
butcher's shop la carnicería **4.1**
butter la mantequilla **5.3**

to buy comprar **2.2**
by por **4.1**

C

cab el taxi **4.1**
café el café **4.1**
cafeteria la cafetería **2.2**
cake el pastel **4.3**
calculator la calculadora **2.1**
call la llamada **3.1**
to call llamar **3.1**
calm tranquilo(a) **3.1**
calmly tranquilamente **5.2**
camera la cámara **6.1**
can la lata **5.3**
can (to be able) poder (ue) **4.2**
    I can offer you… Le puedo
      ofrecer… **4.2**
    Thanks, but I can't. Gracias,
      pero no puedo. **3.1**
cap (knit) el gorro **3.3**, **(baseball)**
    la gorra **3.2**
car el carro **4.1**
careful cuidadoso(a) **5.2**
    to be careful tener cuidado **3.3**
carefully cuidadosamente **5.2**
carrot la zanahoria **5.3**
to carry llevar **2.1**
cash el efectivo **4.2**
cassette el casete **4.2**
cat el (la) gato(a) **1.2**
center el centro **4.1**
century el siglo
ceramics la cerámica **4.2**
cereal el cereal **5.3**
chair la silla **5.2**
chalk la tiza **2.1**
chalkboard el pizarrón **2.1**
change el cambio **4.2**
to change cambiar **4.2**
cheap barato(a) **4.2**
check la cuenta **4.3**
    Separate checks. Es aparte. **4.3**
    The check, please. La cuenta,
      por favor. **4.3**
checked de cuadros **3.3**
cheese el queso **4.3**
chef el (la) cocinero(a)
chicken el pollo **4.3**
chores los quehaceres **5.1**

church la iglesia **4.1**
city la ciudad **1.3**
    city block la cuadra **4.1**
class la clase **2.1**
classroom la clase **2.1**
clay el barro
to clean the room limpiar el
    cuarto **5.1**
clock el reloj **2.2**
to close cerrar (ie) **3.2**
closed cerrado(a) **5.2**
closet el armario **5.2**
clothing la ropa **1.2**
cloudy nublado
    It is cloudy. Está nublado. **3.3**
coat el abrigo **3.3**
coffee el café **4.3**
    coffee shop la cafetería **2.2**
cold
    to be cold tener frío **3.3**
    It is cold. Hace frío. **3.3**
color el color
    What color…?
      ¿De qué color…? **1.2**
comb el peine **5.1**
to comb one's hair peinarse **5.1**
to come venir **3.1**
    to come back volver(ue) **4.2**
comical cómico(a) **1.2**
community la comunidad **1.1**
compact disc el disco
    compacto **4.2**
company la compañía **6.1**
computer la computadora **2.1**
computer science
    la computación **2.1**
concert el concierto **3.1**
congratulations felicidades **1.3**
content contento(a) **3.1**
contest el concurso **1.1**
to cook cocinar **5.3**
cookie la galleta **5.3**
cool: It is cool. Hace fresco. **3.3**
corn el maíz
corner la esquina **4.1**
corral el corral **6.2**
to cost costar (ue) **4.2**
couch el sofá **5.2**
to count contar (ue) **4.2**
country el país **1.1**; el campo **6.2**
countryside el campo **6.2**
court la cancha **3.2**
cousin el (la) primo(a) **1.3**

cow la vaca **6.2**
cracker la galleta **5.3**
crazy loco(a) **3.2**
cream la crema **5.3**
credit card la tarjeta de crédito **4.2**
to cross cruzar **4.1**
cup la taza **4.3**
custom la costumbre

to dance bailar **1.1**
danger el peligro
dangerous peligroso(a) **3.2**
dark hair and skin moreno(a) **1.2**
date la fecha **1.3**
   What is the date? ¿Cuál es la
     fecha? **1.3**
daughter la hija **1.3**
day el día **EP**
   the day before yesterday
     anteayer **5.3**
   What day is today? ¿Qué día
     es hoy? **EP**
December diciembre **1.3**
to decide decidir **6.1**
degree el grado **3.3**
delicious delicioso(a) **4.3**
depressed deprimido(a) **3.1**
desert el desierto **3.3**
desk el escritorio **2.1**
dessert el postre **4.3**
development el desarrollo
to dial marcar **3.1**
dictionary el diccionario **2.1**
difficult difícil **2.1**
dining room el comedor **5.2**
dinner la cena **2.3**
direction la dirección **4.1**
dirty sucio(a) **5.1**
dishwasher el lavaplatos **5.3**
district el barrio
to do hacer **2.3**
doctor el (la) doctor(a) **1.1**
dog el (la) perro(a) **1.2**
   to walk the dog caminar con el
     perro **2.3**
dollar el dólar **4.2**
door la puerta **5.2**
down abajo **6.2**
downtown el centro **4.1**

dozen la docena **5.3**
dress el vestido **1.2**
drink la bebida **4.3**
to drink tomar **2.2**; beber **2.3**
   Do you want to drink…?
     ¿Quieres beber…? **2.2**
   I want to drink… Quiero
     beber… **2.2**
to drive manejar **4.1**
drugstore la farmacia **4.1**
to dry oneself secarse **5.1**
during durante **2.2**
to dust quitar el polvo **5.2**

each cada **2.3**
ear la oreja **5.1**
early temprano **3.1**
earring el arete **4.2**
easily fácilmente **5.2**
easy fácil **2.1**
to eat comer **1.1**, tomar **2.2**
   Do you want to eat…?
     ¿Quieres comer…? **2.2**
   to eat a snack merendar (ie) **3.2**
   to eat breakfast desayunar **4.3**
   to eat dinner cenar **2.3**
   to eat lunch almorzar (ue) **4.2**
   I want to eat… Quiero
     comer… **2.2**
editor el (la) editor(a) **6.1**
egg el huevo **5.3**
eight ocho **EP**
eight hundred ochocientos(as) **5.3**
eighteen dieciocho **1.3**
eighth octavo(a) **6.2**
eighty ochenta **1.3**
eleven once **1.3**
enchilada la enchilada **4.3**
English el inglés **2.1**
enjoyable divertido(a) **1.2**
enormous enorme **6.1**
to enter entrar (a, en) **2.1**
eraser el borrador **2.1**
especially especialmente **5.2**
evening la noche
   during the evening por la
     noche **2.2**
   Good evening. Buenas
     noches. **EP**

every cada **2.3**
   every day todos los días **2.1**
to exchange cambiar **4.2**
excited emocionado(a) **3.1**
to exercise hacer ejercicio **2.3**
to expect esperar **2.1**
expensive caro(a) **4.2**
   It's very expensive! ¡Es muy
     caro(a)! **4.2**
eye el ojo **1.2**

face la cara **5.1**
fall el otoño **3.3**
to fall asleep dormirse (ue) **5.1**
familiar: to be familiar with
   someone conocer a alguien **2.3**
family la familia **1.1**
far (from) lejos (de) **4.1**
   Is it far? ¿Queda lejos? **4.1**
farm la granja **6.2**
farmer el (la) ganadero(a) **6.2**
fast rápido(a) **5.2**
fat gordo(a) **1.2**
father el padre **1.3**
favorite favorito(a) **3.2**
February febrero **1.3**
to feed darle(s) de comer **6.2**
to feel like… tener ganas de… **3.3**
fence la cerca **6.2**
field el campo **3.2**
fifteen quince **1.3**
fifth quinto(a) **6.2**
fifty cincuenta **1.3**
finally por fin **2.3**
to find encontrar (ue) **4.2**
to finish terminar **2.2**
firefighter el bombero **6.1**
first primero **2.3**; primero(a) **6.2**
first name el nombre **EP**
fish el pez **2.3**; el pescado **5.3**
five cinco **EP**
five hundred quinientos(as) **5.3**
flavor el sabor
floor el suelo **5.2**
flour la harina **5.3**
flower la flor **3.3**
to fly a kite hacer volar una
   chiringa
food la comida **2.3**

foot el pie **5.1**
   on foot a pie **4.1**
football el fútbol americano **3.2**
for por **4.1**; para **4.2**
forest el bosque **3.3**
to forget olvidar **5.2**
fork el tenedor **4.3**
formal formal **6.1**
forty cuarenta **1.3**
four cuatro **EP**
four hundred cuatrocientos(as) **5.3**
fourteen catorce **1.3**
fourth cuarto(a) **6.2**
free time el tiempo libre **3.1**
freezer el congelador **5.3**
french fries las papas fritas **2.2**
frequent frecuente **5.2**
frequently frecuentemente **5.2**
fresh fresco(a)
Friday viernes **EP**
friend el (la) amigo(a) **1.1**
   to spend time with friends
      pasar un rato con los
      amigos **2.3**
from de **1.1**; desde **4.1**
fruit la fruta **2.2**
frying pan la sartén
fun divertido(a) **1.2**
funny cómico(a) **1.2**
furniture los muebles **5.2**

game el partido **3.2**
garden el jardín **5.2**
garlic el ajo
to get dressed ponerse la ropa **5.1**
to get up levantarse **5.1**
gift el regalo **4.2**
girl la chica **1.1**, la muchacha **1.1**,
   la niña
to give dar **4.2**
   I'll give… to you for…
      Le dejo… en… **4.2**
glass el vaso **2.2**
glove el guante **3.2**
to go ir **2.2**
   to go away irse **5.1**
   to go for a walk pasear **2.3**
   to go out salir **4.1**
   to go to bed acostarse (ue) **5.1**

goal el gol **3.2**
gold el oro **4.2**
good bueno(a) **1.2**
   Good afternoon.
      Buenas tardes. **EP**
   Good evening.
      Buenas noches. **EP**
   Good morning. Buenos días. **EP**
Good-bye. Adiós. **EP**
good-looking guapo(a) **1.2**
government el gobierno
grade la nota
   to get a good grade sacar una
      buena nota **2.1**
gram el gramo **5.3**
grandchildren los nietos
granddaughter la nieta
grandfather el abuelo **1.3**
grandmother la abuela **1.3**
grandparents los abuelos **1.3**
grandson el nieto
grape la uva
gray gris
green verde **1.2**
guitar la guitarra **2.3**
gymnasium el gimnasio **2.2**

hair el pelo **1.2**
hair dryer el secador de pelo **5.1**
half medio(a) **5.3**
   half past y media **2.2**
half-brother el medio hermano
half-sister la media hermana
ham el jamón **5.2**
hamburger la hamburguesa **2.2**
hand la mano **5.1**
handbag la bolsa **4.2**
handicraft la artesanía **4.2**
to happen pasar **2.1**
happily felizmente **5.2**
happy feliz **1.3**, alegre **3.1**,
   contento(a) **3.1**
hard difícil **2.1**; duro(a) **5.1**
hard-working trabajador(a) **1.2**
hat el sombrero **1.2**
to have tener **1.3**
   to have just… acabar de… **3.1**
   to have to tener que **2.1**
   one has to hay que **2.1**

he él **1.1**
head la cabeza **5.1**
health la salud
to hear oír **2.3**
heart el corazón **2.3**
Hello. Hola. **EP**
helmet el casco **3.2**
to help ayudar (a) **2.1**
   Could you help me order?
      ¿Me ayuda a pedir? **4.3**
hen la gallina **6.2**
her su **1.3**
here acá/aquí **4.1**
highway la carretera
his su **1.3**
history la historia **2.1**
hockey el hockey **3.2**
homework la tarea **2.1**
horse el caballo **6.2**
hot caliente **4.3**
   to be hot tener calor **3.3**
   It is hot. Hace calor. **3.3**
hotel el hotel **4.1**
house la casa **1.1**
how cómo **2.2**
   How (fun)! ¡Qué (divertido)! **1.2**
   How are you? *(familiar)* ¿Cómo
      estás? **1.1** *(formal)* ¿Cómo
      está usted? **1.1**
   How is it going? ¿Qué tal? **1.1**
   How old is…? ¿Cuántos años
      tiene…? **1.3**
   Pardon, how do I get to…?
      Perdona(e), ¿cómo llego
      a…? **4.1**
how much cuánto
   How much do I tip? ¿Cuánto le
      doy de propina? **4.3**
   How much is (are)…? ¿Cuánto
      cuesta(n)…? **4.2**; ¿A cuánto
      está(n)…? **5.3**
   How much is it? ¿Cuánto es? **4.3**
huge enorme **6.1**
to be hungry tener hambre **2.3**
to be in a hurry tener prisa **3.3**
husband el esposo

I yo **1.1**
ice el hielo
  on ice sobre hielo **3.2**
ice cream el helado **5.3**
if si **5.2**
in en **1.1**
  in front (of) enfrente (de) **4.1**
  in order to para **4.2**
included incluido(a)
  Is… included? ¿Está
    incluido(a)…? **4.3**
inexpensive barato(a) **4.2**
informal informal **6.1**
inside (of) dentro (de) **6.2**
instead of en vez de
intelligent inteligente **1.2**
interesting interesante **1.2**
interview la entrevista **6.1**
introduce: Let me introduce you
  (familiar/formal) **to…** Te/Le
    presento a… **1.1**
invitation la invitación **5.2**
to invite invitar
  I invite you. Te invito. **3.1**
to iron planchar **5.2**
its su **1.3**

jacket la chaqueta **1.2**
January enero **1.3**
jeans los jeans **1.2**
jewelry las joyas **4.2**
jewelry store la joyería **4.1**
journalist el (la) periodista **6.1**
juice el zumo **5.3**, el jugo
July julio **1.3**
June junio **1.3**
jungle la selva

key la llave **5.2**; la tecla
keyboard el teclado **2.1**

kilogram el kilo **5.3**
kitchen la cocina **5.2**
kite la chiringa
  to fly a kite hacer volar una
    chiringa
knife el cuchillo **4.3**
to know (a fact) saber **3.2**
  to know someone conocer a
    alguien **2.3**

lake el lago **3.3**
lamp la lámpara **5.2**
land la tierra
landscape el paisaje
language la lengua **4.3**
large grande **1.2**
last último(a) **6.2**
  last month el mes pasado **5.3**
  last name el apellido **EP**
  last night anoche **5.3**
  last week la semana pasada **5.3**
  last year el año pasado **5.3**
late tarde **2.1**
lately recientemente **5.2**
later luego **2.3**
  See you later. Hasta luego. **EP**,
    Nos vemos. **EP**
lazy perezoso(a) **1.2**
to learn aprender **2.3**
leather goods los artículos de
    cuero **4.2**
to leave salir **4.1**, irse **5.1**; **(behind)**
    dejar **3.1**
  I want to leave a message for…
    Quiero dejar un mensaje
    para… **3.1**
  to leave a message dejar un
    mensaje **3.1**
  Leave a message after the tone.
    Deje un mensaje después del
    tono. **3.1**
left la izquierda
  to the left (of) a la izquierda
    (de) **4.1**
leg la pierna **5.1**
lemonade la limonada **4.3**
less menos
  less than menos de **3.2**
  less… than menos… que **3.2**

lesson la lección **2.1**
Let's… Vamos a… **6.1**
letter la carta
  to send a letter mandar una
    carta **2.3**
lettuce la lechuga **4.3**
library la biblioteca **2.2**
life la vida **2.3**
to lift weights levantar pesas **3.2**
like (as) como
to like gustar
  He/She likes… Le gusta… **1.1**
  I like… Me gusta… **1.1**
  I would like…
    Me gustaría… **3.1**
  Would you like…?
    ¿Te gustaría…? **3.1**
  You like… Te gusta… **1.1**
to listen (to) escuchar **2.1**
liter el litro **5.3**
literature la literatura **2.1**
a little poco **2.1**
to live vivir **2.3**
living room la sala **5.2**
llama la llama **6.2**
long largo(a) **1.2**
to look at mirar **2.1**
to look for buscar **2.1**
to lose perder (ie) **3.2**
to be lucky tener suerte **3.3**
lunch el almuerzo **2.2**
  to eat lunch almorzar (ue) **4.2**
luxurious lujoso(a) **6.1**

magazine la revista **2.3**
mail carrier el (la) cartero(a) **6.1**
to make hacer **2.3**
  to make the bed hacer la
    cama **5.1**
man el hombre **1.1**
manager el (la) gerente **6.1**
many mucho(a) **1.1**
map el mapa **4.1**
March marzo **1.3**
market el mercado **4.2**
masterpiece la obra maestra
mathematics las matemáticas **2.1**
May mayo **1.3**

maybe tal vez
  Maybe another day. Tal vez otro día. **3.1**
meal la comida **2.3**
meat la carne **4.3**
to meet encontrar (ue) **4.2**
meeting el encuentro
menu el menú **4.3**
message el mensaje
  I want to leave a message for… Quiero dejar un mensaje para… **3.1**
  to leave a message dejar un mensaje **3.1**
  Leave a message after the tone. Deje un mensaje después del tono. **3.1**
microwave el microondas **5.3**
midnight la medianoche **2.2**
milk la leche **5.3**
million un millón **5.3**
mirror el espejo **5.1**
Miss la señorita **1.1**
mixture la mezcla
modern moderno(a) **6.1**
moment el momento
  One moment. Un momento. **3.1**
Monday lunes **EP**
money el dinero **4.2**
  money exchange el cambio **4.2**
month el mes **1.3**
more más **1.3**
  more than más de **3.2**
  more… than más… que **3.2**
morning la mañana **2.2**
  during the morning por la mañana **2.2**
  Good morning. Buenos días. **EP**
  in the morning de la mañana **2.2**
mother la madre **1.3**
motorcycle la moto(cicleta) **4.1**
mountain la montaña **3.3**
mouse el ratón **2.1**
mouth la boca **5.1**
to move (the furniture) mover (ue) (los muebles) **5.2**
movie la película **3.1**
  to go to a movie theater ir al cine **3.1**
Mr. el señor **1.1**
Mrs. la señora **1.1**
much mucho(a) **1.1**
  as much as tanto como **3.2**

museum el museo **2.3**
music la música **2.1**
  music and video store la tienda de música y videos **4.1**
must: one must hay que **2.1**
my mi **1.3**

name el nombre **EP**
  His/Her name is… Se llama… **EP**
  My name is… Me llamo… **EP**
  What is his/her name? ¿Cómo se llama? **EP**
  What is your name? ¿Cómo te llamas? **EP**
narrow estrecho(a) **6.1**
near (to) cerca (de) **4.1**
necklace el collar **4.2**
to need necesitar **2.1**
neighbor el (la) vecino(a)
neither tampoco **4.3**
nervous nervioso(a) **3.1**
never nunca **2.1**
new nuevo(a) **1.2**
newspaper el periódico **2.3**
next to al lado de **4.1**
nice simpático(a) **1.2**
  It is nice outside. Hace buen tiempo. **3.3**
  Nice to meet you. Mucho gusto. **EP**
night la noche **2.2**
  at night de la noche **2.2**
nine nueve **EP**
nine hundred novecientos(as) **5.3**
nineteen diecinueve **1.3**
ninety noventa **1.3**
ninth noveno(a) **6.2**
no no **EP**
no longer ya no **3.1**
no one nadie **4.3**
none ninguno(a) **4.3**
noon el mediodía **2.2**
normal normal **5.2**
normally normalmente **5.2**
nose la nariz **5.1**
not no **1.1**
notebook el cuaderno **2.1**
nothing nada **4.3**

novel la novela **2.3**
November noviembre **1.3**
now ahora **1.3**
  Right now! ¡Ahora mismo! **2.1**
nowadays actualmente
number el número
  What is your phone number? ¿Cuál es tu teléfono? **EP**

October octubre **1.3**
of de
  Of course! ¡Claro que sí! **3.1**, ¡Cómo no! **4.1**
to offer ofrecer **6.1**
  I can offer you… Le puedo ofrecer… **4.2**
office la oficina **2.2**
often mucho **2.1**, frecuentemente **5.2**
oil el aceite **5.3**
old viejo(a) **1.3**; antiguo(a) **6.1**
  How old is…? ¿Cuántos años tiene…? **1.3**
older mayor **1.3**
olives las aceitunas **5.2**
on en **1.1**, sobre
  on ice sobre hielo **3.2**
  on top (of) encima (de) **6.2**
once in a while de vez en cuando **2.1**
one uno **EP**
one hundred cien **1.3**
onion la cebolla **5.3**
only sólo **1.3**
open abierto(a) **5.2**
to open abrir **2.3**
operator el (la) operador(a) **6.1**
or o **1.1**
orange anaranjado(a) **1.2**
to order pedir (i) **4.3**
  Could you help me order? ¿Me ayuda a pedir? **4.3**
ordinary ordinario(a) **6.1**
other otro(a) **1.2**
ought to deber **5.2**
our nuestro(a) **1.3**
outdoors al aire libre **3.2**
outside (of) fuera (de) **6.2**
oven el horno **5.3**

P

package el paquete **5.3**
to paint pintar **2.3**
pants los pantalones **1.2**
paper el papel **2.1**
parade el desfile
Pardon, how do I get to…?
  Perdona(e), ¿cómo llego
  a…? **4.1**
parents los padres **1.3**
park el parque **2.3**
party la fiesta **5.2**
to pass (by) pasar **2.1**
pasta la pasta **5.3**
pastry shop la pastelería **4.1**
patient paciente **1.2**
to pay pagar **4.2**
peas los guisantes
pen (enclosure) el corral **6.2,**
  (instrument) la pluma **2.1**
pencil el lápiz **2.1**
people la gente **2.3**
pepper la pimienta **5.3**
perfect perfecto(a) **4.2**
period la época
pharmacy la farmacia **4.1**
phone book la guía
  telefónica **3.1**
photographer
  el (la) fotógrafo(a) **6.1**
physical education la educación
  física **2.1**
piano el piano **2.3**
piece el pedazo **5.3**
picture la foto
  to take pictures sacar fotos **3.3**
pig el cerdo **6.2**
pineapple la piña
pink rosado(a) **1.2**
pitcher la jarra **4.2**
place el lugar **1.1**
plaid de cuadros **3.3**
plain sencillo(a) **6.1**
to plan pensar (ie) **3.2**
plant la planta **3.3**
plate el plato **4.2**

to play tocar **2.3;** practicar **3.1,**
  jugar (ue) **3.2**
  to play sports practicar
    deportes **3.1**
  to play (the guitar, piano) tocar
    (la guitarra, el piano) **2.3**
player el (la) jugador(a)
please por favor **2.2**
pleased contento(a) **3.1**
  Pleased to meet you.
    Encantado(a). **EP**
pleasure
  It's a pleasure. Es un placer. **EP**
  The pleasure is mine. El gusto
    es mío. **EP**
poem el poema **2.3**
poetry la poesía **2.3**
police officer el (la) policía **1.1**
pork el puerco **5.3**
pork rinds los chicharrones **2.3**
portrait el retrato
post office el correo **4.1**
pot la olla **4.2**
potato la patata **5.3,** la papa
potter el (la) alfarero(a)
to practice practicar **3.1**
to prefer preferir (ie) **3.2**
to prepare preparar **2.1**
pretty bonito(a) **1.2**
price el precio **4.2**
printer la impresora **2.1**
problem el problema **2.3**
profession la profesión **6.1**
program el programa
purple morado(a) **1.2**
to put poner **4.3**
to put on (clothes) ponerse **5.1**
to put on makeup maquillarse **5.1**

Q

quality la calidad **4.2**
quarter cuarto(a) **5.3**
  quarter past y cuarto **2.2**
quick rápido(a) **5.2**
quickly rápidamente **5.2**
quiet: Be quiet! ¡Cállate! **5.3**
quiz la prueba **2.1**

R

race la carrera; la raza
racket la raqueta **3.2**
radio el radio **4.2**
radio-tape player el radiocasete
  4.2
rain la lluvia **3.3**
to rain llover (ue) **3.3**
raincoat el impermeable **3.3**
rarely rara vez **2.1**
to read leer **1.1**
ready listo(a) **4.3**
reason la razón **2.1**
to receive recibir **2.3**
recent reciente **5.2**
recently recientemente **5.2**
receptionist
  el (la) recepcionista **6.1**
recipe la receta
red rojo(a) **1.2**
redhead pelirrojo(a) **1.2**
refrigerator el frigorífico **5.3**
to remember recordar (ue) **4.2**
to rent a video alquilar un video **3.1**
to rest descansar **2.2**
restaurant el restaurante **4.3**
to retell contar (ue) **4.2**
to return regresar **3.1,** volver (ue)
  4.2; (an item) devolver (ue) **4.2**
  He/She will return later.
    Regresa más tarde. **3.1**
rhythm el ritmo
rice el arroz **4.3**
right
  to be right tener razón **3.3**
  to the right (of) a la derecha
    (de) **4.1**
ring el anillo **4.2**
river el río **3.3**
road el camino **4.1**
roasted asado(a)
room el cuarto **5.1**
rooster el gallo **6.2**
rule la regla
to run correr **1.1**

S

sad triste **3.1**

salad la ensalada **4.3**

salsa la salsa **4.3**

salt la sal **5.3**

same mismo(a) **2.1**

sandwich (sub) la torta **2.2**

Saturday sábado **EP**

sausage el chorizo **5.2,**
la salchicha **5.3**

to say decir **4.1**
Don't say that! ¡No digas
eso! **1.2**

scarf bufanda **3.3**

schedule el horario **2.2**

school la escuela **2.1,** el colegio

science las ciencias **2.1**

scissors las tijeras **6.2**

screen la pantalla **2.1**

sea el mar **3.3**

to search buscar **2.1**

seasons las estaciones **3.3**

second segundo(a) **6.2**

secretary el (la) secretario(a) **6.1**

to see ver **2.3**
May I see…? ¿Me deja
ver…? **4.2**

to sell vender **2.3**

semester el semestre **2.2**

to send a letter mandar una
carta **2.3**

September septiembre **1.3**

serious serio(a) **1.2**

to serve servir (i) **4.3**

to set the table poner la mesa **4.3**

seven siete **EP**

seven hundred setecientos(as) **5.3**

seventeen diecisiete **1.3**

seventh séptimo(a) **6.2**

seventy setenta **1.3**

shame: What a shame! ¡Qué
lástima! **3.1**

shampoo el champú **5.1**

to share compartir **2.3**

to shave afeitarse **5.1**

she ella **1.1**

shepherd(ess) el (la) pastor(a) **6.2**

ship el barco **4.1**

shirt la camisa **1.2**

shoe el zapato **1.2**
shoe store la zapatería **4.1**

shopping
to go shopping ir de compras **3.1**
shopping center el centro
comercial **4.1**

short (height) bajo(a) **1.2;** (length)
corto(a) **1.2**

shorts los shorts **3.3,** los
pantalones cortos

should deber **5.2**

shrimp los camarones, las gambas

sick enfermo(a) **3.1**

silver la plata **4.2**

simple sencillo(a) **6.1**

to sing cantar **1.1**

sister la hermana **1.3**

six seis **EP**

six hundred seiscientos(as) **5.3**

sixteen dieciséis **1.3**

sixth sexto(a) **6.2**

sixty sesenta **1.3**

to skate patinar **1.1**

skateboard la patineta **3.2**

to skateboard andar en
patineta **3.2**

skates los patines **3.2**

to ski esquiar **3.2**

skirt la falda **1.2**

to sleep dormir (ue) **4.2**

to be sleepy tener sueño **3.3**

slow lento(a) **5.2**

slowly lentamente **5.2**

small pequeño(a) **1.2**

snack la merienda **2.2**
to have a snack merendar (ie) **3.2**

snow la nieve **3.3**

to snow nevar (ie) **3.3**

so entonces **2.3**

So-so. Regular. **1.1**

soap el jabón **5.1**

soccer el fútbol **3.2**

social studies los estudios
sociales **2.1**

sock el calcetín **1.2**

sofa el sofá **5.2**

soft drink el refresco **2.2**

some alguno(a) **4.3**

someone alguien **4.3**
to know, to be familiar
with someone conocer a
alguien **2.3**

something algo **4.3**

sometimes a veces **2.1**

son el hijo **1.3**

soon pronto **2.1**

sorry: I'm sorry… Lo siento… **4.1**

sound el sonido

soup la sopa **4.3**

souvenir el recuerdo

Spanish el español **2.1**

to speak hablar **2.1**
May I speak with…? ¿Puedo
hablar con…? **3.1**

special especial **5.2**

specially especialmente **5.2**

spicy picante **4.3**

spoon la cuchara **4.3**

sport el deporte
to play sports practicar
deportes **3.1**

sporting goods store la tienda de
deportes **3.2**

spring la primavera **3.3**

squid los calamares **5.2**

stadium el estadio **3.2**

star la estrella **5.3**

stationery store la papelería **4.1**

to stay quedar (en) **4.1**

steak el bistec **4.3**

stepbrother el hermanastro

stepfather el padrastro

stepmother la madrastra

stepsister la hermanastra

still todavía **4.3**

stomach el estómago **5.1**

store la tienda **2.3**

storm la tormenta **3.3**

stove la estufa **5.3**

straight ahead derecho **4.1**

street la calle **4.1**

string la cuerda

striped con rayas **3.3**

strong fuerte **1.2**

student el (la) estudiante **1.1**

to study estudiar **2.1**

subject la materia **2.1**

subway el metro **4.1**

success el éxito

sugar el azúcar **4.3**

summer el verano **3.3**

sun el sol **3.3**

to sunbathe tomar el sol **3.3**

Sunday domingo **EP**

sunglasses las gafas de sol **3.3**

sunny: It is sunny. Hace sol. **3.3,**
Hay sol. **3.3**
suntan lotion el bronceador **3.3**
supermarket el supermercado
to go to the supermarket ir al
supermercado **2.3**
supper la cena **2.3**
to have supper cenar **2.3**
surfing el surfing **3.2**
surname el apellido **EP**
surprise la sorpresa **5.2**
to surprise sorprender **5.2**
survey la encuesta
sweater el suéter **1.2**
to sweep the floor barrer el
suelo **5.2**
sweet dulce **4.3**
sweet roll el pan dulce **4.3**
to swim nadar **1.1**
swimming pool la piscina **3.2**

T-shirt la camiseta **1.2**
table la mesa **5.2**
to clear the table quitar
la mesa **5.1**
to set the table poner la mesa **4.3**
to take tomar **2.2**
to take a bath bañarse **5.1**
to take a shower ducharse **5.1**
to take along llevar **3.3**
to take care of cuidar (a) **2.3**
to take out the trash sacar la
basura **5.2**
to take pictures sacar fotos **3.3**
to talk hablar **2.1**
tall alto(a) **1.2**
tape recorder la grabadora **6.1**
tasty rico(a) **4.3**, sabroso(a) **5.3**
taxi el taxi **4.1**
taxi driver el (la) taxista **6.1**
tea el té **4.3**
to teach enseñar **2.1**
teacher el (la) maestro(a) **1.1**
team el equipo **3.2**
telephone el teléfono **3.1**
television la televisión
to watch television ver la
televisión **2.3**
television set el televisor **5.2**

to tell decir **4.1**, contar (ue) **4.2**
Tell (*familiar/formal*) **him or her**
to call me. Dile/Dígale que
me llame. **3.1**
temperature la temperatura **3.3**
ten diez **EP**
tennis el tenis **3.2**
tenth décimo(a) **6.2**
terrible terrible **1.1**
test el examen **2.1**
textile el tejido
Thank you. Gracias. **1.1**
that ese(a), eso **6.2**
that (over there) aquel(la) **6.2;**
aquello **6.2**
that one ése(a) **6.2**
that one (over there)
aquél(la) **6.2**
theater el teatro **2.3**
their su **1.3**
then entonces **2.3**
there allá/allí **4.1**
there is, there are hay **1.3**
they ellos(as) **1.1**
thin delgado(a) **1.2**
thing la cosa **4.1**
to think pensar (ie) **3.2;** creer **3.3**
I think so. / I don't think so.
Creo que sí/no. **3.3**
third tercero(a) **6.2**
thirsty: to be thirsty tener sed **2.3**
thirteen trece **1.3**
thirty treinta **1.3**
this este(a) **6.2;** esto **6.2**
this one éste(a) **6.2**
thousand mil **5.3**
three tres **EP**
three hundred trescientos(as) **5.3**
Thursday jueves **EP**
time el tiempo
free time el tiempo libre **3.1**
(At) What time is…? ¿A qué
hora es…? **2.2**
What time is it? ¿Qué hora
es? **2.2**
tip la propina **4.3**
How much do I tip? ¿Cuánto le
doy de propina? **4.3**
tired cansado(a) **3.1**

to a
to the left (of) a la izquierda
(de) **4.1**
to the right (of) a la derecha
(de) **4.1**
today hoy **EP**
Today is… Hoy es… **EP**
What day is today? ¿Qué día es
hoy? **EP**
together juntos **4.2**
tomato el tomate **5.3**
tomorrow mañana **EP**
See you tomorrow. Hasta
mañana. **EP**
Tomorrow is… Mañana es… **EP**
too también **1.1**
too much demasiado(a) **4.2**
tooth el diente **5.1**
toothbrush el cepillo de
dientes **5.1**
toothpaste la pasta de dientes **5.1**
tough duro(a) **5.1**
towel la toalla **5.1**
town el pueblo **4.3**
town square la plaza **4.1**
toy el juguete
traditional tradicional **6.1**
traffic el tráfico **6.1**
train el tren **4.1**
trash la basura **5.2**
to travel viajar **4.1**
to treat: I'll treat you. Te invito. **3.1**
tree el árbol **3.3**
trip el viaje **4.1**
true: It's true. Es verdad. **1.2**
truth la verdad **2.2**
Tuesday martes **EP**
to turn doblar **4.1**
to turn off the light apagar la luz
5.3
twelve doce **1.3**
twenty veinte **1.3**
two dos **EP**
two hundred doscientos(as) **5.3**

ugly feo(a) **1.2**
umbrella el paraguas **3.3**
uncle el tío **1.3**
under debajo (de) **6.2**

INGLÉS–ESPAÑOL

to understand comprender 2.3, entender (ie) 3.2
until hasta 4.1
up arriba 6.2
to use usar 2.1

to vacuum pasar la aspiradora 5.2
vacuum cleaner la aspiradora 5.2
VCR la videograbadora 4.2
vegetable la verdura 5.3
vegetarian vegetariano(a) 4.3
very muy 1.3
video el video 4.2
   to rent a video alquilar un video 3.1
   video game el videojuego 4.2
village el pueblo 4.3
to visit visitar 2.2
volleyball el voleibol 3.2

to wait for esperar 2.1
waiter el mesero 4.3
waitress la mesera 4.3
to wake up despertarse (ie) 5.1
walk el paseo
to walk caminar
   to walk the dog caminar con el perro 2.3
wall la pared 5.2
wallet la cartera 4.2
to want querer (ie) 3.2
warm caliente 4.3
to wash lavar
   to wash one's hair lavarse la cabeza 5.1
   to wash oneself lavarse 5.1
   to wash the dishes lavar los platos 5.1
watch el reloj 2.2
to watch mirar 2.1
   to watch television ver la televisión 2.3
water el agua *(fem.)* 2.2
wave la ola
we nosotros(as) 1.1

to wear llevar 2.1
   What is he/she wearing? ¿Qué lleva? 1.2
weather el tiempo 3.3
   What is the weather like? ¿Qué tiempo hace? 3.3
Wednesday miércoles EP
week la semana EP
weekend el fin de semana
weights: to lift weights levantar pesas 3.2
welcome bienvenido(a) 1.1
   You're welcome. De nada. 1.1
well bien 1.1; pues 1.2
   (Not very) Well, and you *(familiar/formal)*? (No muy) Bien, ¿y tú/usted? 1.1
what cuál(es) 2.2; qué 2.2
   What a shame! ¡Qué lástima! 3.1
   What day is today? ¿Qué día es hoy? EP
   What is he/she like? ¿Cómo es? 1.2
   What is your phone number? ¿Cuál es tu teléfono? EP
when cuándo 2.2; cuando 3.1
where dónde 2.2; (to) where adónde 2.2
   Could you tell me where... is? ¿Puedes (Puede usted) decirme dónde queda...? 4.1
   Where are you from? ¿De dónde eres? EP
   Where is he/she from? ¿De dónde es? EP
which (ones) cuál(es) 2.2
white blanco(a) 1.2
who quién(es) 2.2
   Who are they? ¿Quiénes son? 1.3
   Who is it? ¿Quién es? 1.3
Whose is...? ¿De quién es...? 1.3
why por qué 2.2
   That's why. Con razón. 2.1
wide ancho(a) 6.1
wife la esposa
to win ganar 3.2
wind el viento 3.3
window la ventana 5.2
windy: It is windy. Hace viento. 3.3, Hay viento. 3.3
winner el (la) ganador(a) 6.1

winter el invierno 3.3
with con 1.3
   with me conmigo 3.1
   with you contigo 3.1
without sin 4.3
woman la mujer 1.1
wool la lana 6.2
work la obra
to work trabajar 1.1
workshop el taller 6.2
world el mundo 1.1
worried preocupado(a) 3.1
to worry: Don't worry! ¡No te preocupes! 3.1
worse peor 3.2
to write escribir 1.1
writer el (la) escritor(a) 6.1

year el año 1.3
   He/She is… years old. Tiene… años. 1.3
yellow amarillo(a) 1.2
yes sí EP
   Yes, I would love to. Sí, me encantaría. 3.1
yesterday ayer 5.3
yet todavía 4.3
yogurt el yogur 5.3
you tú *(familiar singular)* 1.1, usted *(formal singular)* 1.1, ustedes *(formal plural)* 1.1, vosotros(as) *(familiar plural)* 1.1
young joven 1.3
younger menor 1.3
your su *(formal)* 1.3, tu *(familiar)* 1.3, vuestro(a) *(plural familiar)* 1.3

zero cero EP

Índice

expressing
   agreement/disagreement, 272, 392
   extremes, 295, 364
   feelings and emotions, 170–171, 176, 189
   frequency, 107, 117, 222, 321
   likes and dislikes, 29, 37, 45, 181, 189, 292
   location, 130, 242–243, 244–245, 250, 408, 409, 414, 416, 427
   obligation, 100, 101, 109, 117
   origin, 35, 40, 41, 45
   possession, 78, 79, 80, 320
   preferences, 199, 202, 211
   sequence of events, 150, 163
extremes, 295, 364

frequency, adverbs of, 107, 117, 222, 321
future, with **ir a +** *infinitive,* 149, 430, 436, 451

-gar verbs, preterite, 368, 439
gender of nouns, 54
grande, 61
greetings, 2, 4, 5, 21, 26–27, 28–29, 32, 45
gustar, present tense, 292
   + *infinitive,* 37, 181

hablar
   negative **tú** commands, 324
   preterite tense, 439
hacer
   commands, 322, 438
   present tense, 153, 201
   preterite, 395, 441
   uses of, 220
hay, 82
   que + *infinitive,* 109
   weather expressions with, 220
i → y spell-changing verb, 154
indefinite
   article, 33, 55
   words, 294
indirect object pronouns, 273, 276, 438
infinitive, defined, 37
interrogatives, 131
intonation, 28, 50, 131, 188
introductions, 4–5, 21, 27, 28–29, 39, 45, 430

invitations, extending and accepting, 170–171, 172–173, 177, 189, 266, 345, 355
ir
   + a + *infinitive,* 149, 398, 430, 436, 451
   commands, 322, 438
   past tense, 292
   present tense, 126
   preterite, 395, 441
-ir verbs
   commands, 252, 322, 324
   present participle, 226
   present tense, 151
   preterite tense, 392
irregular
   commands, 322, 324, 438
   comparatives, 202, 364
   present participles, 342
   present tense, 33, 76, 126, 130, 153, 154, 198, 201, 248, 270, 274, 291, 298
   preterite tense, 394, 395, 419, 441, 451
-ísimo, 295
-ito(a), 175

jugar + a + *sport,* 198

lavarse, present tense, 320
leer
   present progressive, 226, 342, 436
   preterite, 394, 439
llevar, uses of, 56, 225
limpiar, preterite tense, 366, 392
llover, 220
lo, 364
location, describing, 130, 242–243, 244–245, 250, 408, 409, 414, 427

malo, 61
maps
   Caribbean, 167
   Central America, 239
   Ecuador, 383
      Quito, 384
   Mexico, 94–95, 238–239
      Mexico City, 140
      Oaxaca, 240, 254
   Puerto Rico, 166–167
   Spain, 310–311
   Spanish-speaking countries, 6–7
   United States, 22–23

más (…) que, 202
mayor, 202, 364
mejor, 202, 364
menor, 202, 364
menos
   + *minutes,* 128
   … que, 202
-mente adverbs, 347
mí, after **con,** 177

negation, 37, 82, 294
negative
   commands, 324, 325
   words, 294
nevar, 220
ningún/ninguno(a), 294
nouns, 54
numbers
   0–10, 12, 21
   11–100, 77, 91
   200–1,000,000, 369
   ordinal, 418, 427

o → ue stem-changing verbs, 270, 283, 320
object pronouns, 181, 224, 252, 273, 322, 325, 438
ofrecer, preterite, 392
oír
   present progressive, 226, 342, 436
   present tense, 154, 201
   preterite tense, 394
ordinal numbers, 418, 427
origin, expressing, 33, 40, 41, 45

pagar, preterite, 368
para, uses of, 268
past, talking about the, 367, 379, 388–389, 392, 394, 431, 439, 451
pedir
   present progressive, 342
   present tense, 296
pensar, present tense, 199, 270, 296
peor, 202, 364
personal **a,** 153
poner
   commands, 322, 438
   present tense, 291
por, uses of, 246
possession, expressing, 78, 79, 80, 320
possessive adjectives, 80

Créditos

Photography

i Private Collection, Tom Holton/SuperStock; **iv** School Division, Houghton Mifflin Company (t); **vi** Courtesy *¡Que Onda! Magazine* (r); **xii** School Division, Houghton Mifflin Company (b); **xiv** School Division, Houghton Mifflin Company (r); **xxii** School Division, Houghton Mifflin Company (t); **xxiii** School Division, Houghton Mifflin Company; Nancy Sheehan (+); **xxxiii** Patricia A. Eynon (tr); **xxxv** Larry Bussacca/Retna Ltd. (cr); **2** Nancy Sheehan (br); **3** Nancy Sheehan (tl, cl, bl); **4** Nancy Sheehan (tl); Peter Menzel (br); **5** Nancy Sheehan (t, c); **6** Peter Menzel (b); **7** Robert Frerck/Odyssey/Chicago (b); **8** School Division, Houghton Mifflin Company (tl); Nancy Sheehan (tr); **12** School Division, Houghton Mifflin Company (c); **20** Nancy Sheehan; **23** SuperStock (bl); Ken O'Donahue (tr); Larry Busacca/Retna Ltd. (br); **26** Michael Newman/PhotoEdit (tr); **31** Michael Newman/PhotoEdit (bl); **34** Michael Newman/ PhotoEdit (cr); Patricia A. Eynon (br); **36** Dennie Cody **37** Alain Benainous/Liaison International (cr); **42** Jim Whitmer; **43** Alain Banainous/Liaison International (br); Patricia A. Eynon (cl); **53** Richard Hutchings/Photo Researchers, Inc. (br); **56** Bob Daemmrich Photography (c); Courtesy *The Miami Herald* (cr); **62** Bob Daemmrich Photography (cr); Courtesy *¡Que Onda! Magazine* (bl, +); **63** Sygma (t); Courtesy *¡Que Onda! Magazine* (cr); Jak Kilby/Retna (b); **66** Courtesy ¡Que Onda! Magazine; **70** Ken O'Donahue (background); **76** Barney/inStock (b); **78** Michael Newman/PhotoEdit (br); **79** Paul Barton/The Stock Market (tl); Jose L. Pelaez/The Stock Market (tr); Tim Theriault (mid cr); Rob Lewine/The Stock Market (cr); Blaine Harrington III/The Stock Market (br); **84** Patricia A. Eynon (r); Beryl Goldberg (l); **85** Robert Frerck/Odyssey Productions/Chicago (tl); Beryl Goldberg (r); **86** School Division, Houghton Mifflin Company (t); **87** School Division, Houghton Mifflin Company (t); **89** Patricia A. Eynon; **90** Bob Daemmrich Photography (r); **94** *The Flower Seller* by Diego Rivera, oil on masonite, 1942, Christie's Images/The Bridgeman Art Library (br); **95** courtesy, Ballet Folklorico (tr); UPI/Corbis (br); School Division, Houghton Mifflin Company (bc); **109** David Ryan/Photo 20-20 (b); **113** School Division, Houghton Mifflin Company; **128** School Division, Houghton Mifflin Company; **132** Albert Moldvay/National Geographic Society; **134** School Division, Houghton Mifflin Company (cr); **137** School Division, Houghton Mifflin Company; **146** Robert Frerck/Odyssey Productions/Chicago (br); **156** John Boykin/PhotoEdit (r); **157** J. P. Courau/DDB Stock Photo (tr); Susan Kaye (cr); Doug Bryant/DDB Stock Photo (b); **158** Ed Dawson (c); North Wind Picture Archives (b); **159** Ed Dawson (tr); Sean Sprague (c); David Sanger Photography (cr); Beryl Goldberg (bl); **162** Chris Sharp/New England Stock Photo (br); **166** UPI/Corbis-Bettmann (t); Sharon Smith/Photonica (bl); Harold Castro/FPG International & Ken O'Donahue (montage br); **167** Robert Frerck/ Odyssey Productions/Chicago (t, cr); United States Postal Service (cl); Farrell Grehan/Photo Researchers, Inc. (b); **180** Alain Benainous/Liaison International; **184** Bob Daemmrich Photography (l); Ken O'Donahue (r); **185** Bob Daemmrich/Stock Boston (t); Robert Frerck/Odyssey Productions/Chicago (cr); **186** Tony Freeman/PhotoEdit (t); David Simson/Stock Boston (cr); **188** Robert Frerck/Odyssey Productions/Chicago; **189** School Division, Houghton Mifflin Company; Steve Azzara/Liaison International (br); **192** Chris Brown/Unicorn Stock Photography & Dick Young/Unicorn Stock Photography (montage br); **193** Dave Nagel/Liaison International (cr); Scott Liles/Unicorn Stock Photography (br); **197** Randy Wells/Tony Stone Images, Inc./PNI (bl); School Division, Houghton Mifflin Company (cr); **201** Suzanne Murphy/DDB Stock Photography (b); **204** School Division, Houghton Mifflin Company (tl); Randy Wells/Tony Stone Images, Inc./PNI (br); **206** Robert Frerck/Odyssey Productions/Chicago (+); **207** David Seelic/Allsport (c); John Todd/AP Photo (cr); **209** School Division, Houghton Mifflin Company (br); **210** Russell Gordon/Odyssey Productions/Chicago (r); **211** Bob Daemmrich Photography (tr, br); David Simson/Stock Boston (cr); **214** Ken O'Donahue (background); K. Scott Harris (cr); Nik Wheeler (br); **220** K. Scott Harris; **228** Thomas R. Fletcher/Stock Boston (br); Raymond A. Mendez/Animals Animals (+); **229** Jaime Santiago/DDB Stock Photography (tc); School Division, Houghton Mifflin Company (c); **230** Ken O'Donahue (background); **231** Ulrike Welsch (t); Brenda Matthiesen/Unicorn Stock Photography (cl); Thayer Syme/FPG International (cr); **235** Bruno Maso/Photo Researchers, Inc.; **238** Patricia A. Eynon (bl); School Division, Houghton Mifflin Company (t, br); **239** School Division, Houghton Mifflin Company (tl); The Granger Collection (tr); Gayna Hoffman (bl); *Women Reaching for the Moon* by Rufino Tamayo, oil on canvas, 1946, The Cleveland Museum of Art, Gift of the Hanna Fund, 47.69 (br); **243** Dave G. Houser (tc); **246** Patricia A. Eynon (cr); Dave G. Houser (br); **249** Mark Richards/PhotoEdit (tcr); Ed Simpson/Tony Stone Images, Inc. (tr); Robert Fried (bl); Cameramann/The Image Works (bcl); **251** Patricia A. Eynon; **253** Pamela Harper/Harper Horticultural Slide Library; **256** Dave G. Houser (c); Tom Bean/DRK Photo (+); **257** Patricia A. Eynon (t); Rogers/Monkmeyer Press (c, b); **260** Galyn C. Hammond; **274** Robert Frerck/Odyssey/Chicago; **275** School Division, Houghton Mifflin Company; **277** School Division, Houghton Mifflin Company (tr); **281** School Division, Houghton Mifflin Company (tl, tc, bc); **287** Ken O'Donahue (r); **291** Ken O'Donahue (tl, cl, br); PhotoDisc (bl); **297** School Division, Houghton Mifflin Company (cr); Ken O'Donahue (br); **302** Joe Viesti/The Viesti Collection (bl); **305** Felicia Martinez/PhotoEdit; **306** James Schaffer/PhotoEdit (r); **310** The Granger Collection (t); P. G. Sclarinda/Black Star (bl); Tor Eigeland (br); **311** Robert Frerck/Odyssey (tc); A.G.E. FotoStock (br); **320** Bair/Monkmeyer Press (bc); Spencer Grant/PhotoEdit (tr); **326** Courtesy Sony Music Entertainment (Spain); **328** *Self Portrait with Palette,* Pablo Picasso/ARS/Spanish, Private Collection (bl); **329** *Maya with a Doll,* Pablo Picasso/Picasso Museum, Paris, France/Giraudon Paris/Superstock (tl); *Portrait of Jaime Sabartes,* Pablo Picasso/ARS/Giraudon/Art Resource/NY (c); **354** Tony Arruza/Tony Stone Images, Inc. (r); **382** Inga Spence/DDB Stock Photo; **383** Robert Winslow/The Viesti Collection (tl); **395** Joseph F. Viesti/The Viesti Collection (t); **397** Dan McCoy/Rainbow (tl); Richard Palsey/Stock Boston (cr); School Division, Houghton Mifflin Company; **398** Richard Palsey/Stock Boston (cr); **403** Ll'ewellyn/Uniphoto; **404** Tony Freeman/PhotoEdit (r); **405** Michele and Tom Grimm/Tony Stone (tr); Sidney/Monkmeyer Press (br); **409** Mary Altier (cr); Robert Frerck/Odyssey Productions/Chicago (bl); **412** Dietrich C. Gehring/The Viesti Collection (br);

413 Bob Daemmrich/The Image Works (cr); Dorothy Littell Greco/Stock Boston (br); 415 Robert Frerck/Odyssey Productions/Chicago; 422 S. Aitchison/DDB Stock Photo (+); 438 Wolfgang Kaehler (bl); 440 School Division, Houghton Mifflin Company; 442 Robert Frerck/Odyssey Productions/Chicago; 444 Jeff Greenberg/PhotoEdit; 445 School Division, Houghton Mifflin Company (tl); Eric A. Wessman/The Viesti Collection (cr); Wolfgang Kaehler (b); 447 Jan Butchofsky-Houser (background); Robert Pettit/Dembinsky Photo Association (b); Inga Spence/DDB Stock Photo (tr); Robert Frerck/Odyssey Productions/Chicago (cr); 449 Mary Altier;

All other photography: Martha Granger/EDGE Productions

Illustration

Lisa Adams **203**

Gary Antonetti/Ortelius Design **xxvi-xxxi**

Fion Arroyo **83** (b), **155, 205, 227** (b), **307,322, 327, 399, 421** (r); **427, 451, R2**

Susan M. Blubaugh **160, 163, 247** (t), **249, 269, 280, 370**

Roger Chandler, Activity icons

Chris Costello **430** (+)

Naverne Covington **108, 148, 161, 177, 187, 279, 280**

Jim Deigen **353**

Mike Dietz **39, 183**

Elisee Goldstein **142** (+)

Nenad Jakesevic **358** (+)

Catherine Leary **45, 81, 91, 111, 133, 333, 355, 367, 443, R15, R17,** (r)

Jared D. Lee **255, 261, 274, 299, 319** (r)

John Lytle **48** (+), **59** (r), **264** (+)

Patrick O'Brien **330, 414, 446** (+); **R17** (r)

Steve Patricia **26** (+), **242** (+), **243, 415, 417**

Gail Piazza **15, 19, 223, 227** (t), **233, 318, R9** (l)

Matthew Pippin **98** (+), **170, 171, 192, 193, 386** (+)

Rick Powell **65** (b), **88, 200, 323, 344, 421** (l); **R5, R18**

Donna Ruff **31, 67, 83** (t), **120** (+), **377, 424, 425**

School Division, Houghton Mifflin Company **54, 55, 59** (l), **65** (t), **78, 220, 247** (b), **290, 319** (l), **340, 365, 379, R1, R6, R7, R8, R9** (r); **R10, R12, R14**

Stacey Shuitt **314** (+), **332**

Don Stewart **114, 219, 221**

Wood Ronsadille Harlin, Inc. **336** (+), **408** (+)

Rosario Valderamma **218**

Cris Reverdy, Caroline McCarty, Jackie Reeves for Yellow House Studio **10**

Farida Zaman **286** (+)